HARDLY HARMLESS DRUDGERY

Ex coll. Karolyne & Bryan A. Garner

Hardly Harmless Drudgery

A 500-Year Pictorial History of the Lexicographic Geniuses, Sciolists, Plagiarists & Obsessives Who Defined the English Language

Bryan A. Garner
and
Jack Lynch

GODINE

Boston

Published in 2024 by
GODINE
Boston, Massachusetts
godine.com

ISBN: 978-1-56792-807-5 (hardcover)

LIBRARY OF CONGRESS CATALOGING-IN-PUBLICATION DATA

Names: Garner, Bryan A., author. | Lynch, Jack (John T.), author.
Title: Hardly harmless drudgery : a 500-year pictorial history of the lexicographic geniuses, sciolists, plagiarists, & obsessives who defined the English language / Bryan A. Garner and Jack Lynch.
Description: Boston : Godine, 2024. | "This book accompanies the book exhibition 'Hardly Harmless Drudgery,' originally mounted at the Grolier Club in New York City (Spring/Summer 2024)."—Title page verso. | Includes bibliographical references and index.
Identifiers: LCCN 2023052330 (print) | LCCN 2023052331 (ebook) | ISBN 9781567928075 (hardback) | ISBN 9781567928082 (ebook)
Subjects: LCSH: English language—Lexicography. | English language—Lexicography—Pictorial works. | LCGFT: Illustrated works.
Classification: LCC PE1611 .G37 2024 (print) | LCC PE1611 (ebook) | DDC 423.092/2—dc23/eng/20231228
LC record available at https://lccn.loc.gov/2023052330
LC ebook record available at https://lccn.loc.gov/2023052331

Page design by Bryan A. Garner.
Typeset by Ryden McComas Anderson of RosePen Books of Dallas, Texas.

Unless otherwise noted, the books and documents photographed here are part of the Garner Collection.
The book contains 753 photographs.

First Printing, 2024
Printed in Canada

"If the booksellers want a specimen in which a keen critick can spy no faults, they must wait for another generation. Had not the [Accademici della] Crusca faults? Did not the Academicians of France commit many faults? It is enough that a dictionary is better than others of the same kind. A perfect performance of any kind is not to be expected, and certainly not a perfect dictionary."

—Samuel Johnson
20 October 1784, in a letter written less than two months before his death

"Restrictions of space, and the need to bring even huge works like the *Oxford English Dictionary* to a conclusion, inevitably lead to the inclusion of some items and the exclusion of others. The battles along the inclusion/exclusion border, from the beginning, have been almost as ferocious as any territorial border dispute between great powers."

—Robert W. Burchfield
"The Recording of English in Dictionaries and Grammars" (1985)

"Don't you love the *Oxford Dictionary*? When I first read it, I thought it was a really, really long poem about everything."

—David Bowie

Ex coll. Karolyne & Bryan A. Garner

Table of Contents

Comments 449

Introduction

Samuel Johnson—creator not of the first English dictionary, but perhaps of the first great one—wickedly mocked his own trade when he defined *lexicographer* as "a writer of dictionaries; a harmless drudge, that busies himself in tracing the original, and detailing the signification of words." But dictionaries are serious business, and the people who drudge away at them are anything but harmless. This book tells the stories of the most important English-language dictionaries and their makers.

Dictionaries are repositories of erudition, monuments to linguistic authority, and battlefields in cultural and political struggles. They have been announced with almost messianic fervor, decried as evidence of cultural collapse, and relied on in judicial decisions. They are works of almost superhuman endurance, produced by people who devote themselves to years or even decades of wearisome labor. As commodities in a fiercely competitive publishing business, they can keep a company afloat for generations or sink it in a few years. Some are also beautiful objects, products of genuine innovations in typography and book design.

The story of dictionaries is a microcosm of the story of books in general: ancient tablets, then scrolls, then codices, then printed editions, and then digitized formats. But this is the story of *English* dictionaries—itself a microcosm of dictionaries of all types in all languages. With *English* in our subtitle, we palter a bit: we don't quite mean "produced in England," and yet we do, given that we include some multilingual dictionaries made there; nor do we quite confine ourselves to monolingual English-language dictionaries, even though that is our primary focus, including American dictionaries in English. We mean to illustrate the growth of English-language lexicography while not confining ourselves strictly to the one language and certainly not confining ourselves to Shakespeare's scepter'd isle.

Lexicography is perhaps the ultimate illustration of delayed gratification. Imagine working for years, day by day, on the minutest points of language, keeping up a painstaking accuracy without which the entire project will ruin your reputation. Imagine an almost monastic routine that entails a forced seclusion, allowing for minimal interaction with others because conversation, if it becomes at all frequent, fritters away the time of not just one person but at least two. Imagine a quota system by which you must complete a certain number of entries per hour if you're to make the publishing deadline several years hence—and you must do this day by day, without fail. Imagine, too, that you're a solo lexicographer in olden times: you've made a deal that provides for a certain sum of money once you finish a given letter of the alphabet, but you're discovering, through your exhaustive research, that the letter *A* (for starters) contains more than twice as many words as you or anyone else thought. In effect, your hourly wage has been slashed by 60%. That has happened to many a lexicographer.

By the time you reach *C*, the most pullulating letter in the alphabet, you wonder whether you can continue to subsist, much less retain your sanity.

And what, when you look up from the completed entries for *zygote* and *zymurgy*, will the gratification be? Universal adulation? Riches? No. It will be little more than the knowledge of a job well done—a job whose intricacies can be appreciated by almost no human being other than yourself. Certainly nobody else you know. You can't hope for praise, only for escaping reproach. That's how Samuel Johnson put it in 1755.

Johnson's principal definition of *lexicographer* was "a writer of dictionaries." At their best, dictionaries are *written*, not merely compiled. Yet lexicographers are the Rodney Dangerfields of the literary profession. They get little if any respect. Imagine a cocktail party where one of the guests finds herself in conversation with a fascinating person whose speech is laced with witty observations unusually phrased:

"What do you do?"

"I'm a writer."

"Oh, really?—what do you write?"

"I write dictionaries."

That might elicit a scoff. You call yourself a *writer*? You wanted me to believe that you're a novelist, didn't you? That sounds like the most boring job on earth—writing dictionaries.

If you were to insist that it's actually scintillating, you'd sound delusional.

And yet, at its best, lexicography is an enthralling endeavor. You're working with material that belongs to us all: the language. You're analyzing individual words and phrases in an attempt to discover their various meanings. You may discover, for example, that the adjective *any* has seven distinct senses. (Who knew?) Stay with us here: (1) In a conditional, hypothetical, or interrogative sentence, it means "a (no matter which)" or "some" <if you have any salt, I'd like to borrow some> <if any problem arises, call me> <is there any evidence of guilt?>. (2) In a negative assertion, it creates an emphatic negative, meaning "not at all" or "not even one" <it wasn't in any way improper> <she didn't know any member in attendance>. (3) In an affirmative sentence, it means "every" or "all" <any attempt to flout the law will be punished> <you must hand over any items related to the investigation>. (4) In a sentence implying that a selection or discretionary act will follow, it may mean "one or more (unspecified things or people); whichever; whatever" <any student may seek a tutorial> <pick any books you like> <a good buy at any price>. (5) In a declarative sentence or imperative involving a qualitative judgment, it means "of whatever kind" <you'll have to

take any action you consider appropriate>. In this sense, there may be the implication of poor quality <any argument is better than no argument>. (6) In a declarative sentence involving a quantitative judgment, it means "unlimited in amount or extent; to whatever extent necessary" <this computer can process any quantity of numbers simultaneously>. (7) In a related colloquial sense, it may mean "of great size or considerable extent" when following a negative <we won't be able to make any real headway this week>. (Closely paraphrasing Garner 2022a:71.) And then you have to be prepared for some smart aleck to discover still more meanings—meanings that all English speakers know, even if they don't know they know them.

Admittedly, this type of analysis isn't for everyone.

Yet there are people who delight in discovering that a simple word known to everyone can function in these ways. The specifics get worked out over time, and any (sense 3) lexicographer would be foolish to ignore what predecessors have written. In 1755, Samuel Johnson recorded three senses (3, 1, 4, in that order). In 1828, Noah Webster increased the number to four (adding sense 5). Today, the *Oxford English Dictionary* (*OED*) parcels out nine subsenses among four primary senses. In other words, there isn't a single "correct" answer to this kind of question. Semantic "splitters" seek out finer and finer distinctions of meaning, while "lumpers" try to craft definitions broad enough to cover a range of uses. Although some people see their pulses quicken at such realizations, most will instantly tire of thinking about it.

But one of your authors didn't have that option: he was interrogated for five hours in a deposition over the various meanings of *any* because the word was crucial to the interpretation of a patent. Tens of millions of dollars hung on the sense of the word. Side 1 in the lawsuit contended for sense 3; Side 2 wanted sense 1. The sentence at issue said, "Any signals received by the main station will be automatically relayed to a substation." Side 1 wanted that to mean that every signal received would be so relayed; Side 2 wanted it to mean that some signals but not necessarily all would be so relayed. Side 2 was taking the deposition, and the questioning became intense, as dozens of hypothetical sentences containing *any* were put forward for immediate dissection and classification.

The outcome? The lawsuit settled shortly after the deposition. Doubtless both sides claimed a favorable resolution. Life is messy, isn't it?

All of which is to say that these monastic drudges can have a significant impact on the world. If poets deserve the moniker "unacknowledged legislators of the world," lexicographers are the unacknowledged registers of meaning. Not just huge sums of money but even people's lives may depend on a term's interpretation. When judges take the legislature at its word, they want to discover the most plausible meaning.

Courts cite dictionaries more often than any other type of scholarship—even if few lexicographers want to wield that kind of power.

Regardless of what might happen in court, people in general can become irrationally exercised about what dictionaries say. In the 1980s, Robert W. Burchfield, chief editor of the *OED*, received anonymous death threats prompted by the inclusion of a racially charged term—not a word that he used himself, but one whose existence he noted. In 2022, Merriam-Webster had to shut down its offices over emailed death threats incited by the editors' treatment of gender-related terms like *boy* and *girl*: "The moron who created this fake definition," wrote the culprit, "should be hunted down and shot. I am sick and tired of these cultural Marxists denying science and destroying the English Language." The man was found and apprehended. He pleaded guilty to two counts of interstate transmission of threatening communications to commit violence and was sentenced to one year in prison.

Other breathtaking adventures in lexicography might be cited. Sometimes the exploits occur purely within the confines of domesticity. Consider the man who, long before computers or even photocopiers existed, was seven years into his marriage and halfway through his big dictionary. He had labored for more than a decade, and he worked late each night to bring it closer to completion. There was one master copy of his manuscript. His resentful wife had come to view that pile of papers as one enormous symbol of his connubial neglect. And so late one night, after her dictionary-crazed husband had fallen into a slumber, she tossed it into the fire. The nearest contemporary account states: "Well, for all that, the good man had so great a zeale for the advancement of learning, that he began it again, and went through with it to that Perfection that he hath left it to us, a most usefull Worke." (Aubrey 1690:71.) And through it all, he remained with his wife. Any (sense 5) gratification he felt in the end was greatly delayed. (For the full story, see no. 3.)

And so your authors believe that Samuel Johnson, when defining *lexicographer* as "a harmless drudge," meant to be denotatively accurate with *drudge* but self-deprecatingly facetious with *harmless*.

The dictionary as we know it evolved from lists of items carved into tablets, to manuscript scrolls that recorded glosses on other manuscripts, to printed dictionaries after the era of Johannes Gutenberg (1393–1468). The earliest author to use the term *dictionarius* is reputedly John of Garland (1195?–1272?), but it wasn't used widely until Sir Thomas Elyot tried it in 1538. Even then, it was slow to become standard: medieval and early Renaissance wordbooks bore such titles as *abecedarium* ("ABC book"), *alvearie* ("beehive"), *bibliotheca* ("library"), *catholicon* ("a comprehensive collection"), *elementarium* ("for beginners"), *manipulus vocabulorum* ("handful of vocables"), *medulla* ("the quintessence"), *nominale* ("name book"), *ortus vocabulorum* ("garden of words"), and *thesaurus* ("storehouse"). In the late Renaissance, one writer actually tried out *gazophylacium* ("treasury"). As things developed, smaller compilations tended to be called *glossaries*, and those of ancient languages were often called *lexicons*. But there has always been overlap. It wasn't until the 17th century that *dictionary* took on something like its current meaning, as distinct from the other type of alphabetical reference book: the *encyclopedia*, with entries much more discursive and essay-like.

Here we trace the modern history of dictionaries, focusing especially on those of the English language. As you'll see, it was a fitful process—and a fascinating one.

Though intended to stand on its own, this book was prompted by a Grolier Club exhibition in New York City in the second quarter of 2024—also by the name *Hardly Harmless Drudgery*. Hence the item-by-item treatment, with a number assigned to each. Hence, too, the hundreds of photographs. We focus on the books not merely as disembodied texts but as physical objects—often beautiful objects—in which lexicographers and their publishers constantly experimented with typography to make their works easier to use. The exhibition features mostly items from the Garner Collection of dictionaries, which is among the most extensive ever compiled by a private collector. Amounting to more than 4,500 dictionaries, lexicons, and glossaries, it is housed in Dallas, Texas, and was assembled on five continents over 50 years. Within the lexicographic side of the Collection are books, manuscripts, letters, legal documents, broadsides, advertisements, and other ephemera. These account for more than 10% of the entire Garner Collection, which contains some 40,000 items all told.

The photographs throughout this volume are accompanied by small-type attributions recording the permanent location of each item photographed. Some reside not in the Garner Collection but elsewhere: the only known copy of Cawdrey (no. 7), for example, is in the Bodleian Library in Oxford, England. We are grateful for the generosity of Harvard Law Library; the New York Public Library; the Tarlton Law Library at the University of Texas; and Rulon-Miller Books of St. Paul, Minnesota.

Even in a book of this size, we manage to touch on only a tiny portion of the dictionaries that have been published over the years. The British Library alone has more than 10,000 books catalogued under the heading "English language—Dictionaries." Difficult choices had to be made. Omitting Dr. Seuss, for example, seems almost criminal (*The Cat in the Hat Beginner Book Dictionary* [1964]), as does omitting the smallest dictionary ever published, 384 pages but just one inch tall, by the Scotsman David Bryce (*The Smallest English Dictionary in the World* [1893]—but see p. 447).

Nor have we touched on dictionaries of usage, though the sainted H.W. Fowler does get a mention or two for his more usual type of lexicography. We've found no room for learner's dictionaries or collegiate dictionaries. We've pretermitted dictionaries of Australianisms, Canadianisms, and Caribbean English, as well as most types of medical, botanical, scientific, and technical dictionaries. We have included some law, for three reasons: (1) lawyers such as Rastell, Blount, Cowell, Webster, Bouvier, and Black advanced the art significantly, (2) law is a profession whose *only* tool is words, and (3) lawyers (poor lawyers!) have never really gotten their due in the literature on lexicography. Besides, John Cowell is surely the only lexicographer in history whose book was suppressed by sovereign proclamation.

Many readers think of "the dictionary" as if it's a single thing—an objective proclamation of timeless truths about the language. But of course language changes over time, and dictionaries are written by people. The types of people who write (or, at the lower end, assemble) dictionaries are often colorful characters. We offer brief biographical descriptions of the people who labored on these books as a reminder that every dictionary is the product of actual human effort.

So concludes our front matter. Lexicographers often joke, and even more often regret, that nobody reads the front matter of dictionaries. If users did, they'd be more astute in the inferences they'd draw from the text. In any event, what we can usefully suggest about understanding the book is to encourage you to take a few minutes to browse the table of contents (to understand the organization of the book) and to do likewise with the index (to get an inkling of the breadth of coverage). It's a book about English-language dictionaries, and we hope you might find delight when you're least expecting it.

Bryan A. Garner
Jack Lynch

I. Primordial Beginnings

Wordlists have been with us nearly as long as written words themselves. Among the oldest known fragments of a dictionary, a lexical text giving a list of fish, is a Babylonian cuneiform dating from 1600–1500 BCE; in 2012, it sold at a New York City dictionary auction held by Bonhams. Some cuneiform tablets discovered in Syria, with bilingual Sumerian–Akkadian wordlists, are thought to date back even further—to 2300 BCE, the time of the Akkadian Empire.

English lexicography is almost as old as the English language, from its beginnings in the Old English period (roughly 450–1100 CE). Like the language, the lexicography developed slowly—one innovation at a time. But even in the earliest and simplest attempts at cataloguing the language, we can glimpse the origins of the latest high-tech lexicographic developments.

Ex coll. Karolyne & Bryan A. Garner

A selection of pre-1600 foreign-language lexicons and dictionaries not otherwise treated in this book, the earliest (*Vocabularium Iuris*) dating from 1491.

Ex coll. Karolyne & Bryan A. Garner

A Short Prehistory

IN THE POPULAR 2022 DOCUMENTARY *GET BACK*, we see the Beatles trying to work out the words to various well-known songs such as "Let It Be," even as Lennon and McCartney are composing them. In several sequences, as the Beatles experiment with various possible lyrics—right there in view of us all—audience members inevitably shout at their screens something like, "No, Paul, it goes like this!"

A similar feeling besets anyone who looks back over the history of lexicography. "No, it's called a dictionary!" "No, it's supposed to go in alphabetical order!" "No, *strict* alphabetical order!" "No, it contains just definitions, not long essays! Stop that!" "No, please record *all* the words, not just the harder ones!" "Come on, you're supposed to give pronunciations!" And so on.

Those steps alone took a thousand years.

In brief, the story of English lexicography—which goes back to 600 or 700 CE, nearly as far back as the English language itself—goes something like this. It started with marginal glosses of Latin words in manuscripts, providing English (which is to say Old English) equivalents of Latin words for English speakers struggling with a foreign vocabulary. After a time, these glosses were collected into glossaries and Latin–English vocabularies. Then came full-blown English–Latin vocabularies (about which more anon), and then other bilingual dictionaries: English–French, English–Italian, and English–Spanish, all in the year 1599. Although lawyers had an English-only column of a two-language dictionary as early as 1523, it wasn't until 1604 that a broader English-only glossary appeared—with lots of legal terms but also hard words more generally. Hard-word dictionaries abounded for more than a century until, in 1721, Nathan Bailey attempted to include *all* the words, and in 1730 he showed for the first time which syllables were stressed. People then felt the need for a standard dictionary, and in 1755 Samuel Johnson filled that need admirably, discriminating fine shades of meaning and adding illustrative quotations for every sense of every word. Some 36 years later, John Walker for the first time gave extensive pronunciations. In 1828, Noah Webster extended the reach of English-language dictionaries by including North American English; he greatly advanced the art of defining but marred his work with spectacularly outlandish etymologies, prompted by faux scholarship. Then came another American, Joseph Worcester, who bested Webster in many ways, and Webster's posthumous publishers—the Merriam brothers—retained an army of Yale scholars to eliminate Webster's etymological fallacies, clear up the rampant inconsistencies, and defeat Worcester. By now, in the late 19th century, British scholars decided that the English language shouldn't be left entirely to Americans, and so they embarked on a *New English Dictionary*, later to be called the *Oxford English Dictionary*. They bested all their predecessors, assiduously collecting quotations from all periods of English literature and producing the most thorough dictionary ever compiled in any language. It was a great monument to Victorian industriousness and a prodigious feat for the printers. An American team undertook a similar project on a more modest scale, producing the *Century Dictionary* in 1895; excellent though it was, it didn't last more than about 50 years. Meanwhile, Americans produced some superb one-volume dictionaries, both unabridged and abridged, while the British did the same. Someone had to sell enough of these books to pay the bills. Although bad business decisions and unexpected changes in the book market caused several once-thriving enterprises to fail, there was still a great deal of money to be made in dictionary sales. Even when flagship dictionaries lost money, publishers found that the content could be repackaged in different ways for different audiences. College-size dictionaries, seeking the sweet spot between the huge unabridged and the slim pocket dictionaries, became mainstays in schools and offices. In the 1960s, computers were introduced into lexicographic research and production, but the true impact of the computers became clear around the turn of the millennium, when the internet disrupted the entire reference business. Several long-running lexicographic enterprises suspended operations, while others supported their new online editions with advertisements or subscription plans. Yet some dictionaries continue to rack up print sales and appear likely to endure in hard copy.

The earliest English lexicography antedates the printed book. English speakers have always had to communicate in other languages. In speech, that usually meant the major European languages (French, Spanish, Italian). In writing, it meant Latin above all, since Latin was the lingua franca of the church, canon law, and international learning. We can often trace a progression: first readers squeeze English "glosses" (translations or explanations) of difficult words or passages into the margins of Latin manuscripts for their own benefit; then scribes might copy the glosses between the lines of manuscripts for the benefit of future readers; finally, all the glosses from a manuscript would be collected in one place—a glossary—and put into something approximating alphabetical order. (For the early history of alphabetical order, see no. 87.) Relatively few complete copies of reference works have survived the Middle Ages.

Most of the evidence about early manuscript dictionaries is now in the form of individual leaves, or groups of leaves, as opposed to fully intact manuscripts. A good example is the ca. 1430 canon-law wordlist illustrated here:

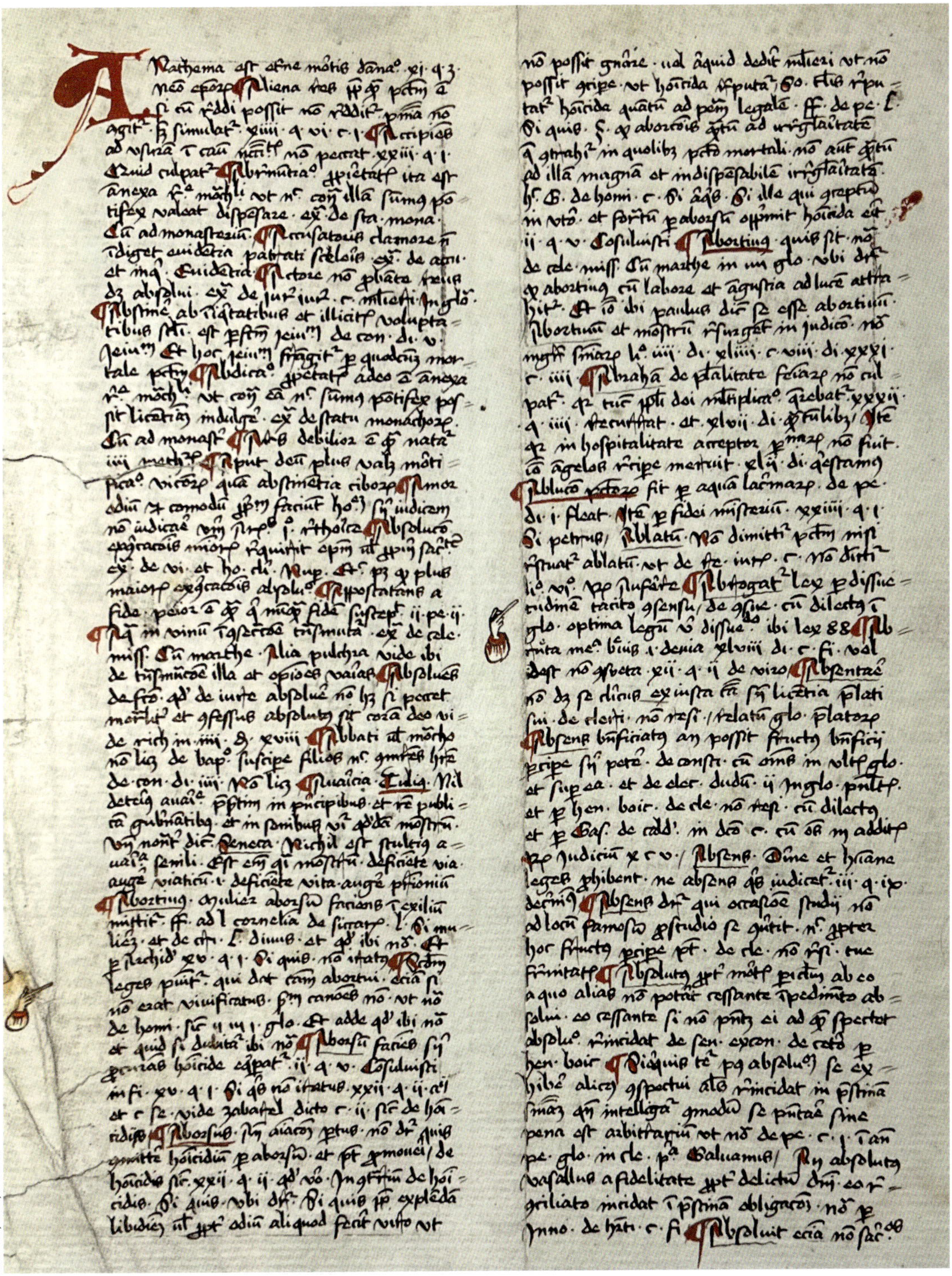

Ex coll. Karolyne & Bryan A. Garner

Leaf from a 15th-century manuscript dictionary. Note the two pointing hands, or manicules, which are characteristic of such early works.

It is a single leaf with double columns of 52 lines in a squat secretarial hand, with important words underlined in red, capitals and paragraphs touched in red, running titles (e.g., "A") at the head of columns on the recto pages, and a calligraphic three-line initial *A* opening the entry *Anathema est eternae mortis damnatio*, meaning "Anathema is the condemnation of eternal death." The page contains several neat manicules (the little pointing hands) and marginalia directing readers to the subject of adjacent readings. Half the entries on these leaves relate to the perennially controversial topic of abortion.

A later example from Italy is a full manuscript (*Eleganze della lingua Latina*) in a single neat hand on all 280 double-column pages. (See p. xxviii.) In the back of the vellum-bound volume are several appendixes: 4.5 pages of *Addita*; 12.5 pages of *Barbara, vel Impura Vocabula Lati: Puritati Reddita*; and 8 pages of *Rectus Verborum Usus*—the last two of these amounting in effect to a usage guide. Also bound as back matter are 27 blank leaves for readers' manuscript additions.

About 1440, an English–Latin dictionary called *Promptorium Parvulorum* appeared in manuscript. Its title translates as "storeroom for young scholars," and it was designed for children studying Latin. It exists in nine 15th-century manuscripts and five early printed editions: an incunable dated 1499 and four later editions through 1528. All these editions are printed in double columns with running headers "Nomina" and "Verba," through the entire alphabet, to distinguish nouns and other parts of speech from verbs.

Scholars have speculated about the compiler's identity, but no conclusive evidence has turned up. He was a friar or anchorite in Lynn, England, and he is often called "the recluse of Lynn." (Starnes 1954:9.) He candidly acknowledged his sources, which was "in refreshing contrast to a tendency, later developed among lexicographers, of concealing the names of the major authors and works upon which they depended." (*Id.* at 11.) Most notable among his sources was Joannes Balbus of Genoa, Italy, whose *Catholicon* dates in manuscript from the 13th century. The *Catholicon* would be printed first in 1460, in Mainz, by Gutenberg; it was the first dictionary to be printed in Europe.

In the 19th century, the scholar Albert Way brought out an edition of *Promptorium* in three volumes (1843, 1853, 1865) for the Camden Society of London. In the preface to volume 3, Way wrote: "Whether we regard the *Promptorium Parvulorum* as an authentic record of the English language in the earlier half of the 15th century, as illustrative of the provincial dialects of East Anglia, or as explanatory of the numerous archaisms of a debased Latinity that pervades early chronicles and documents, its value can scarcely be too highly estimated." (3:xiii.) Way's carefully annotated edition stands as a monument to high-quality Victorian scholarship.

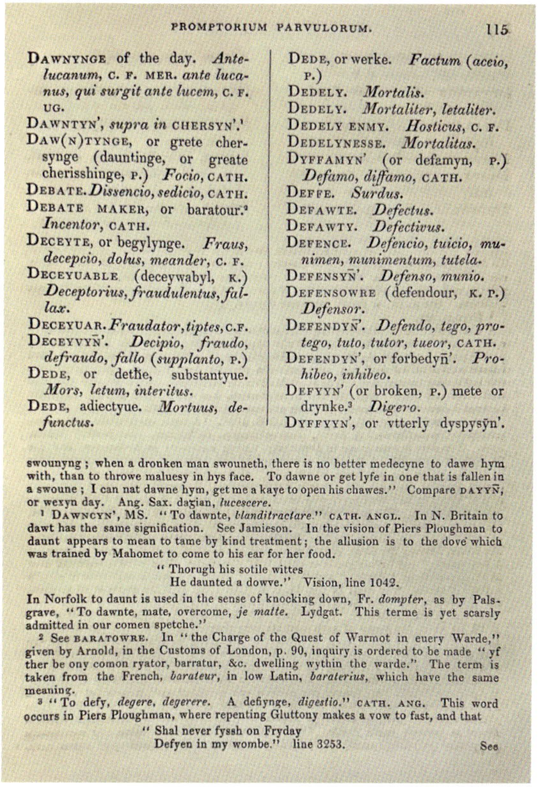

PROMPTORIUM PARVULORUM. 115

DAWNYNGE of the day. *Antelucanum*, C. F. MER. *ante lucanus, qui surgit ante lucem*, C. F. UG.
DAWNTYN', *supra in* CHERSYN'.[1]
DAW(N)TYNGE, or grete chersynge (dauntinge, or greate cherisshinge, P.) *Focio*, CATH.
DEBATE. *Dissencio, sedicio*, CATH.
DEBATE MAKER, or baratour.[2] *Incentor*, CATH.
DECEYTE, or begylynge. *Fraus, decepcio, dolus, meander*, C. F.
DECEYUABLE (deceywabyl, K.) *Deceptorius, fraudulentus, fallax.*
DECEYUAR. *Fraudator, tiptes*, C. F.
DECEYVYN'. *Decipio, fraudo, defraudo, fallo (supplanto*, P.)
DEDE, or dethe, substantyue. *Mors, letum, interitus.*
DEDE, adiectyue. *Mortuus, defunctus.*
DEDE, or werke. *Factum (aceio*, P.)
DEDELY. *Mortalis.*
DEDELY. *Mortaliter, letaliter.*
DEDELY ENMY. *Hosticus*, C. F.
DEDELYNESSE. *Mortalitas.*
DYFFAMYN' (or defamyn, P.) *Defamo, diffamo*, CATH.
DEFFE. *Surdus.*
DEFAWTE. *Defectus.*
DEFAWTY. *Defectivus.*
DEFENCE. *Defencio, tuicio, munimen, munimentum, tutela.*
DEFENSYN'. *Defenso, munio.*
DEFENSOWRE (defendour, K. P.) *Defensor.*
DEFENDYN'. *Defendo, tego, protego, tuto, tutor, tueor*, CATH.
DEFENDYN', or forbedyn'. *Prohibeo, inhibeo.*
DEFYYN' (or broken, P.) mete or drynke.[3] *Digero.*
DYFFYYN', or vtterly dyspysyn'.

swounyng; when a dronken man swouneth, there is no better medecyne to dawe hym with, than to throwe maluesy in hys face. To dawne or get lyfe in one that is fallen in a swoune; I can nat dawne hym, get me a kaye to open his chawes." Compare DAYYN, or wexyn day. Ang. Sax. dagian, *lucescere.*

[1] DAWNCYN', MS. "To dawnte, *blanditractare*." CATH. ANGL. In N. Britain to dawt has the same signification. See Jamieson. In the vision of Piers Ploughman to daunt appears to mean to tame by kind treatment; the allusion is to the dove which was trained by Mahomet to come to his ear for her food.

"Thorugh his sotile wittes
He daunted a dowve." Vision, line 1042.

In Norfolk to daunt is used in the sense of knocking down, Fr. *dompter*, as by Palsgrave, "To dawnte, mate, overcome, *je matte.* Lydgat. This terme is yet scarsly admitted in our comen spetche."

[2] See BARATOWRE. In "the Charge of the Quest of Warmot in euery Warde," given by Arnold, in the Customs of London, p. 90, inquiry is ordered to be made "yf ther be ony comon ryator, barratur, &c. dwelling wythin the warde." The term is taken from the French, *barateur*, in low Latin, *baraterius*, which have the same meaning.

[3] "To defy, *degere, degerere.* A defiynge, *digestio.*" CATH. ANG. This word occurs in Piers Ploughman, where repenting Gluttony makes a vow to fast, and that

"Shal never fyssh on Fryday
Defyen in my wombe." line 3253.

See

A typical page of Way's edition of *Promptorium Parvulorum* (Way 1843 1:115), with annotations in footnotes.

About 1483, the *Monson Catholicon Anglicum* was prepared (it is thought) either in East Riding, Yorkshire, or in Lincoln. Since the late 19th century, this manuscript has been considered one of the most important and oft-cited resources for the study of Middle English. The text represents a crucial milestone in the evolution of the English dictionary, and only one complete manuscript survives.

Substantially larger than earlier Middle English glossaries, it was produced not long after the *Promptorium*. The dictionary has English headwords, which means that it couldn't have been used to translate difficult Latin terms while reading. Instead, its function was almost certainly to aid English speakers in composing Latin. There is no clear preference for any particular field, such as law, medicine, or rhetoric; the words here suggest general educated speech and broad human experience.

There are some 8,000 headwords followed by short explanations of their meanings in Latin, and occasionally Greek. For example:

> an **Almos howse;** *elemosinarium.*
>
> **Angry;** bilosus.
>
> **Bagpype;** *panduca.*
>
> **Belte maker;** *zonarius.*
>
> **Boke;** carta, cartula, codex, codicillus, liber, libellus, volumen, pagina, pagella, sceda.
>
> **Boke bynder or seller;** *bibliopola, bibliator.*
>
> **Brewer;** pandaxator trix, brasiator trix.
>
> a **Farte;** bumbum, bumba, pedicio, trulla.
>
> **Fulharde;** *temerarius.*
>
> **an Hardnes of handis or fete;** callus.
>
> a **Lye;** mendacium, figmentum, commentum (mendaciolulm A.).
>
> **Nakyd;** cinctutus, jnvestis, nudus, nodulus, & cetera.
>
> **Quakynge;** tremens, tremulus, tremulentus.
>
> **Swarme of bees;** examen.
>
> **Tytille of a buke;** titulus, elenchus, ut sequencia sancti evangelij secundum lucam.

Unsurprisingly, many of the words don't survive in Modern English, such as "**Bygirdylle;** marsupium, renale" (a purse).

In 1881, Sidney J.H. Herrtage issued an edition for the Early English Text Society, with a preface by Henry B. Wheatley. Herrtage used the original manuscript, which was then lost for more than 130 years. It resurfaced in a Sotheby's catalogue and was sold in 2013 for $92,500.

In his preface, Wheatley points out that in his notes, Herrtage has made full use of the many 19th-century publications of the Early English Text Society and the Camden Society: they are "quoted on every page," showing that "the labours of late years have already brought forward a rich harvest of illustration, by means of which the difficulties of our beloved tongue are gradually being cleared up." (P. xii.) Further, Wheatley reflects on the rewards of lexicography:

> Those who have not attempted to register words can hardly realise the difficulties in the way of the Dictionary maker. All honour, therefore, to those who have overcome the difficulties, and in this band of honest workers the anonymous compiler of the Catholicon Anglicum occupies a prominent place. The difficulties are truly great, but the lexicographer has his compensation, for

> there is a pleasure in the registration and illustration of words which he only knows who has set his mind to the work with earnestness and enthusiasm. [*Id.*]

The Garner Collection's copy of the 1881 Herrtage edition is noteworthy because it was given in 1885 as a prize to Harold J.R. Murray—the son of James A.H. Murray, the chief editor of the *Oxford English Dictionary*—and was bestowed by the headmaster of the Mill Hill School and the Early English Text Society. Harold Murray had distinguished himself in "Early English," and the award was dated "New Foundation Day" (late September) 1885, just four months after James A.H. Murray had left Mill Hill to live at Sunnyside, Oxford. Soon Harold would work alongside his father on the *OED* and become a significant contributor of illustrative quotations. After leaving Mill Hill, Harold enrolled at Balliol College, Oxford, where Benjamin Jowett was Master. Jowett is said to have remarked to Harold's mother, "Your son Harold is, without exception, the very best undergraduate I have ever known." (Murray 1977:244.)

That degree of erudition and steadiness of temperament would have suited him well in helping his perspicacious father in advancing the work of the *OED*.

But we're getting ahead of ourselves. Let us begin with the cradle of English-only lexicography. But where is that? There is no entirely unambiguous answer.

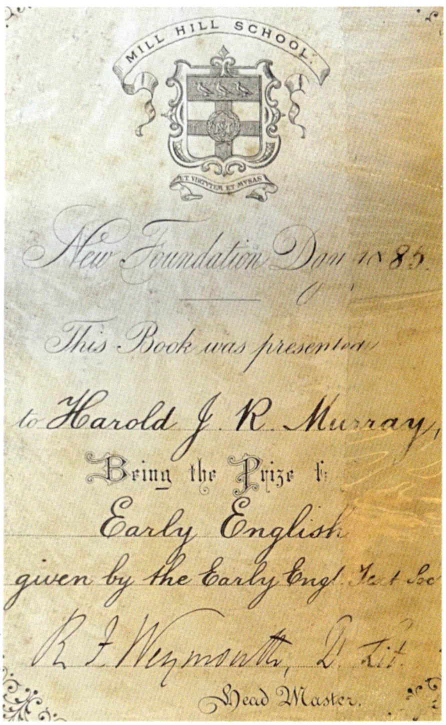

Ex coll. Karolyne & Bryan A. Garner

Bookplate in James A.H. Murray's son's copy of the *Catholicon Anglicum* (Herrtage ed., 1881).

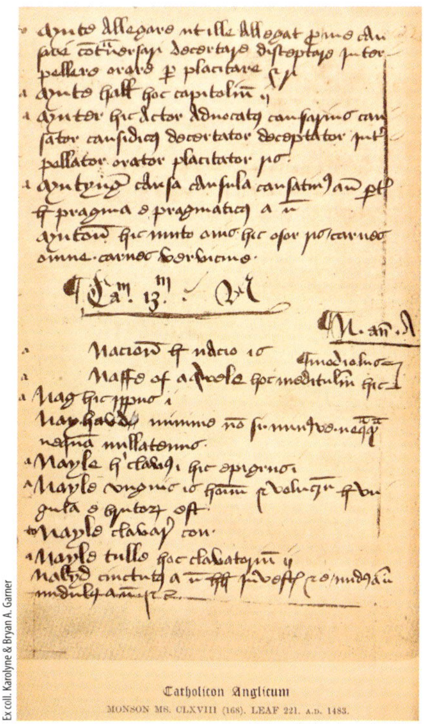

Ex coll. Karolyne & Bryan A. Garner

Leaf from the original *Catholicon Anglicum* (reproduced by Herrtage).

1

ELEGANZE
DELLA LINGUA LATINA
A

A		A	
A bello studio	Consilio Dedita opera	A male, la tua robba è mandata	Fortune tue dissipantur disperduntur. Impetus in tuas fortunas fecit
A bell'agio	Lente	A man salva fidati di lui	Se illi tuto committe, et crede.
A bocca (parlar)	Loqui coram	A mio garbo, o genio	Postquam per ingenium nactus est
A buon ora	Cum primo luce Cum luce.	A modo mio	Qui hunc meo excruciem modo
A canto) starti voglio +	Nullum vestigium abs te discedam Ne latum quidem unquè ab latere tuo discedam	Se farai a modo mio	Si me audies
A cattivo parte [illegible]	Valde laboramus	Mai potei vivere a +	Arbitratu meo vivere nunquam licuit
A che fine dicono tali cose?	Quo hec spectant?	A noi	Omitte ista, atq; ad rem redi
A colpi di pianelle	Utinam tibi commitigari videam sandalio caput	A nessun modo voglio che tu ti metta a contendere	Prorsus te a dimicatione deterreo
A cose alte aver l'animo inteso	Magna molitur	A niente è ridotta	Nullo pacto Respublica nulla est
A Dio piacendo	Approbante Deo	A pari tuo	Tuis similibus viris
(A dirla tra noi)	(Id inter nos liceat dicere)	A passione non giudichi	A certo et vero sensu judicas
A dispetto	In gratiis ut dormiam	A pieno senato	Frequenti senatu
A finchè io non venga forastiere costà	Ne istuc hospes veniam	A posta	Hec arte tractabat virum De industria Consulto Composito factum est
A finche) tiho scritto +	Tibi eo scripsi, ut	A posta per un de' miei t'ho scritto	Tibi rescripsi, hominemque certum misi
A viva forza	Vi	A posta	Ita ne obstinato operam dat? Studio
A forza, a dispetto	Ferietur alio munere		
A guisa Solo in ozio a guisa de vecchi	Ita est quasi facias aliquid Est mi senectutis otium	A poco a poco mi farò suo famigliare	Insinuabo in illius familiaritatem
A gran fatica sostengomi	Vix me sustento	A prender partito) sono cose difficili a +	Sunt res inexplicabiles
A gran rischio) vat di ruinarsi	Maximum ob universo naufragio periculum est	A proposito mio è la solitudine	Mihi adhuc nihil aptius fuit solitudine

A

A 16th- or 17th-century dictionary manuscript created in Italy: *Eleganze della lingua Latina*. The neatness of this handwriting extends through all 280 pages. For more about the contents of this book, see p. xxiv.

II. A Kind of Dawning

Where, precisely, should we begin with modern English lexicography? Much depends on what we mean by "English dictionary," which makes the answer unavoidably murky. As we've seen, glossaries explaining and translating the words of a single text antedate the printed book in Europe, and not long after Gutenberg there are printed books that offer definitions in English. But most of these were bilingual dictionaries—Latin–English, French–English—and when we talk of English dictionaries, we usually mean monoglot dictionaries. But what exactly counts as monoglot? We might call Rastell or Skene the earliest monoglot lexicographers, but as you'll see, there are complications. And in any event, they focused on the language of the law. Perhaps we should look beyond field-specific lexicons.

While we're groping for answers in the shadows of these questions, it seems only right to consider the steps by which English speakers moved from bilingual and trilingual dictionaries—all the way up to hendecaglot (11 languages!)—before settling into monoglot English dictionaries. The progress went in fits and starts, and important contributors such as Sir Thomas Elyot (Latin–English), Thomas Cooper (Latin–English), Thomas Speght (Chaucerian language), and John Minsheu (Spanish–English, as well as the 11-language text) shouldn't be overlooked. Alas, poor Cooper! (See no. 3.)

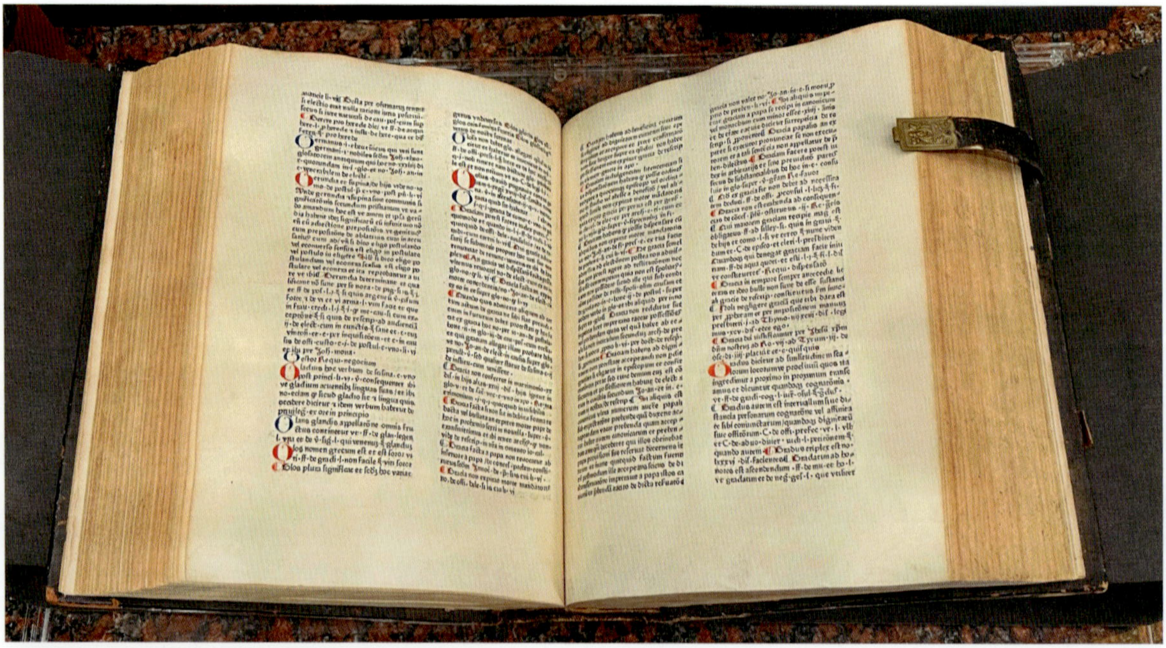

Ex coll. Karolyne & Bryan A. Garner

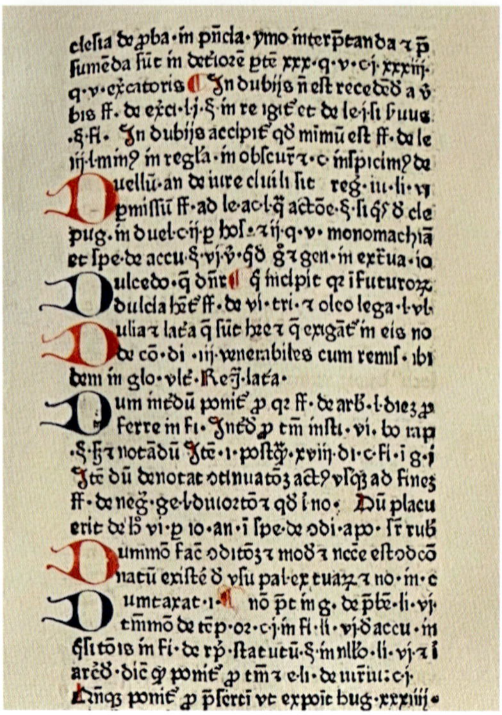

Ex coll. Karolyne & Bryan A. Garner

The oldest print dictionary in the Garner Collection is *Repertorium Iuris*, by Johannes Calderinus (d. 1348). A rubricated incunabulum dated 12 December 1474, it was printed by Michael Wenssler in Basel. Early in its life, it was a chained book: the backboard bears a hole in which the chain was secured to the board. Calderinus, who held a doctorate in canon law, taught in Bologna.

Ex coll. Karolyne & Bryan A. Garner

1

John Rastell

Sir Thomas More's Brother-in-Law

Rastell, John. *Exposiciones Terminoru[m] Legu[m] Angloru[m]*. London: John Rastell, 1523, 1525, 1527, 1530.

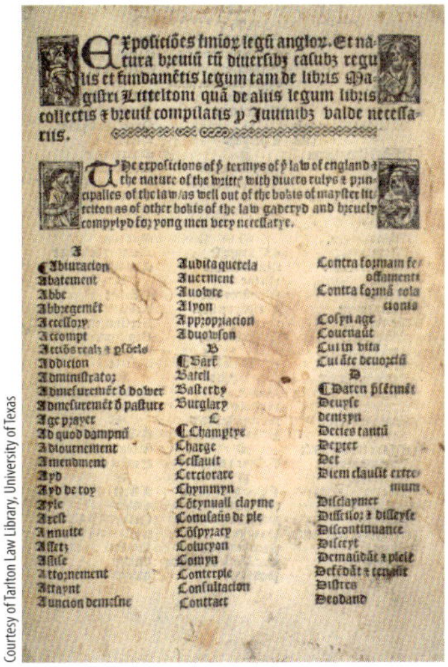

Expositiões tminoꝝ legū angloꝝ. Et natura breuiū cū diuersibꝫ casubꝫ regulis et fundamētis legum tam de libris Magistri Litteltoni quā de aliis legum libris collectis ꝛ breuit compilatis p Iuuinibꝫ valde necessariis.

The exposicions of ẏ termys of ẏ law of england ꝛ the nature of the writtꝭ with diuers rulys ꝛ principalles of the law/as well out of the bokis of mayster littelton as of other bokis of the law gaderyd and breuely compylyd for yong men very necessarye.

A

Abiuracion
Abatement
Abbe
Abbregemēt
Accessory
Accompt
Accions realꝫ ꝛ psōels
Addicion
Administrator
Admesuremēt d dower
Admesuremēt d pasture
Age prayer
Ad quod dampnū
Adiournement
Amendment
Ayd
Ayd de roy
Ayle
Arest
Annuite
Assetz
Assise
Attornement
Attaynt
Auncion demesne
Audita querela
Auerment
Auowre
Alyon
Appropriacion
Aduowson

B

Bark
Batell
Basterdy
Burglary

C

Champtye
Charge
Cessauit
Certiorare
Chymmyn
Cōtynuall clayme
Conusaūs de ple
Cōspyracy
Colucyon
Comyn
Conterple
Consultacion
Contract
Contra formam feoffamenti
Contra formā collacionis
Cosyn age
Couenaūt
Cui in vita
Cui āte deuorciū

D

Darein presentmēt
Deuyse
denizyn
Decies tantū
Depter
Det
Diem clausit extremum
Disclaymer
Disseisor ꝛ disseyse
Discontinuance
Disceyt
Demaūdāt ꝛ pleit
Defēdāt ꝛ tenaūt
Distres
Deodand

Courtesy of Tarlton Law Library, University of Texas

In 1999, the Tarlton Law Library at the University of Texas acquired a copy of Rastell as its one-millionth book. The librarians there soon discovered that it was a "sophisticated" copy, with a 1523 title page (pictured) married to the text of the 1530 edition. (Widener 2003:10.) They might have been put together by John Rastell himself, but the evidence suggests a slightly later date.

A LAWYER BY TRAINING and a printer by trade, John Rastell (ca. 1475–1536) had perhaps the ideal background to become the progenitor of legal lexicography in English. But it took a while for him to find this calling. London-born and Oxford-educated, Rastell first tried his hand at playwriting and worked as a set designer and director for King Henry VIII. Then in 1517, he and two London merchants obtained letters from the king to mount an exploratory expedition to North America. They hoped to establish a base from which to search the Northwest Passage for a rumored route to Asia. After two years, though, the expedition had made it no farther than Ireland, and Rastell returned to London.

Back home, Rastell found greater success in establishing a printing business, producing some 30 books before retiring in 1533. He may have been England's first law publisher, and he was the first to abridge and translate statutes—still written in Latin or French—into English.

This translation work may explain why Rastell's dictionary, *Expositiones Terminorum Legum Angliae* (1523), has a layout with a Law French column alongside an English column. Oddly, the dictionary's authorship would be misattributed to Rastell's son William (1508–1565) by more than a century's worth of scholars, including the prominent English antiquary Anthony à Wood and the incomparable jurist Lord Coke. Perhaps this mistake owes to the fact that William, having followed his father into both the legal and printing professions, issued several later editions under the better-known title *Les Termes de la Ley*. In any event, there is no dispute now over which Rastell was the lexicographer, and his dictionary achieved enduring success, appearing in 29 editions from 1523 to 1819.

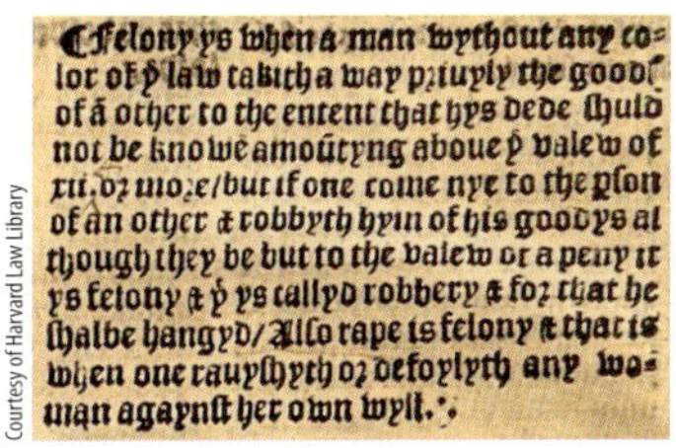

Felony ys when a man wythout any color of ẏ law takith a way priuyly the goodꝭ of ā other to the entent that hys dede shuld not be knowe amoūtyng aboue ẏ valew of xii.d. or more/but if one come nye to the pson of an other ꝛ robbyth hym of his goodys al though they be but to the valew of a peny it ys felony ꝛ ẏ ys callyd robbery ꝛ for that he shalbe hangyd/Also rape is felony ꝛ that is when one rauyshyth or defoylyth any woman agaynst her own wyll.

Courtesy of Harvard Law Library

The 1530 entry for *felony*.

For all his contributions to the English people's understanding of the laws governing them, John Rastell's most popular work during his lifetime was actually *The Pastyme of People: The Cronycles of Dyvers Realmys and Most Specyally of the Realme of Englond* (1529–30), which chronicles English history through the reign of Richard III.

Sometime before Rastell entered the printing trade, he became a close friend of Sir Thomas More—eventually marrying his sister Elizabeth. Initially sympathetic to More's Catholic theology, he zealously joined More's ongoing controversy with Protestant theologian John Frith, publishing *A New Boke of Purgatory* in 1530. Frith responded with *A Disputacion of Purgatorye*, and Rastell shot back with an *Apology against John Frith*. Frith again responded in kind shortly before his execution for heresy in 1533—and this second rebuttal was apparently so forceful that Rastell converted to Protestantism. History is silent about what effect this midlife conversion had on Rastell's marriage.

Courtesy of Harvard Law Library

Harvard Law School's copy of the 1525 edition.

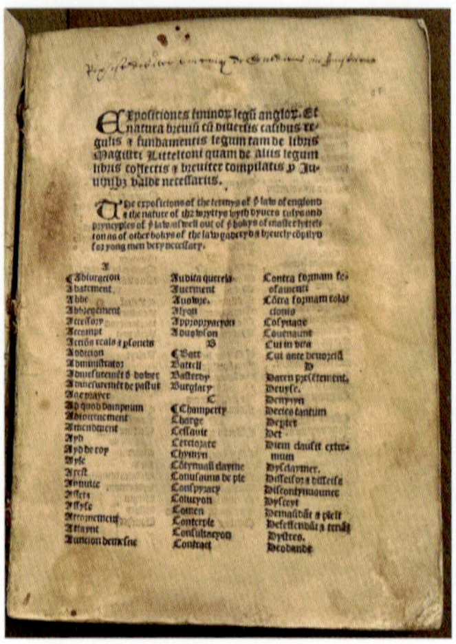

Courtesy of Harvard Law Library

Rastell's end was not a good one: though by all accounts he was a patriot who didn't deserve his fate, he was imprisoned for refusing to pay the tithes legally owed to the Church of England. He died in prison, impoverished, in 1536, a year after King Henry VIII had ordered the execution of his brother-in-law, Sir Thomas More, for treason.

The Garner Collection holds 12 copies of *Termes de la Ley*, ranging from 1579 to 1812. Three of these editions—including the 1579 and 1812—are modern reprints by the Lawbook Exchange. The earliest *original* editions in the collection date from 1592 and 1607, the latter being just three years after what is generally thought to be the first English dictionary: Robert Cawdrey's 1604 book *A Table Alphabeticall* (no. 7), the only copy of which resides in the Bodleian Library in Oxford.

Yet there is a debate about whether Rastell, not Cawdrey, deserves credit for writing the first English dictionary. If the answer is Rastell, then we push back the starting date of English lexicography from 1604 to 1523—and a lawyer gets the credit for being the progenitor of English-language lexicography. If the answer is Cawdrey, then an obscure ex-priest gets the credit.

Again, almost all the editions of *Termes de la Ley* have each page presenting two columns—a Law French column and an English column. Here's an example from the 1525 printing owned by Harvard Law School:

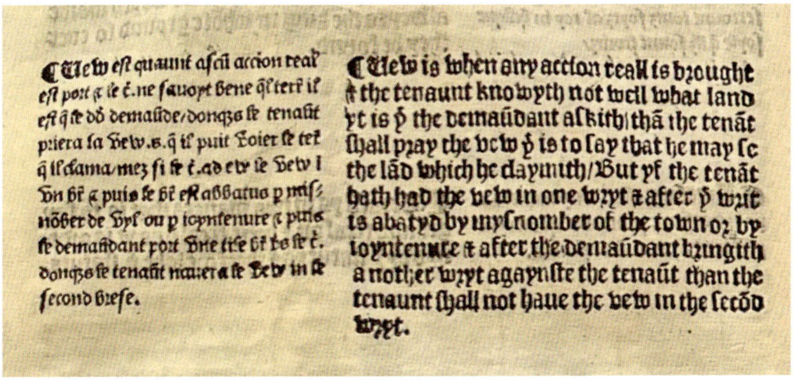

Left column:
"**Vew** est quaunt ascu[n] accion real est port & le t[enant] ne sauoyt bene q[u]il terr il est q[ue] le d[emaundent] demau[n]de / donques le tenau[n]t priera la vew, sc. q[ue] il puit Voier le ter[re] q[u]'il clama / Mez si le t[enant] ad ew le view en un br[iefe] & puis le br[ief] est abbatus p[er] misno[m]ber de le vyl ou q[ue] ioyntenure & puis le demau[n]dant port une tiel b[rief] v[er]s le t[enant] donq[ue]s le tenau[n]t nauera le vew in le second brefe."

Right column:
"**Vew** is when any accion reall is brought & the tenaunt knowyth not well what land yt is y[e] demau[n]dant askith tha[n] the tena[n]t shall pay the vew y[t] is to say that he may se the la[n]d which he claymith / But yf the tena[n]t hath had the vew in one wryt & after y[e] writ is abatyd by mysnomber [misnaming] of the town or by ioyntenure & after the demau[n]dant bringith a nother wryt agaynste the tenau[n]t than the tenaunt shall not haue the vew in the seco[n]d wryt."

The book consists of 169 entries like that—arranged alphabetically. The left-hand side is Law French; the right-hand side is in what modern scholars call Early Modern English (post-1500).

Robert Cawdrey's definition of *view*, by contrast, consists of only seven words: "**viewe**, behold, marke, or consider, or looke uppon." Whereas Rastell defined the noun (the older sense), Cawdrey defined the verb (which came into the language about 200 years later).

Sir John Baker, undoubtedly the greatest living English legal historian—a professor at Cambridge University—argues that Rastell deserves credit for producing the earliest English-language dictionary. He points out that the English-language column in *Termes de la Ley* is itself a stand-alone English-language dictionary. It's certainly not a bilingual dictionary in the usual sense of having a headword in one language and its definition in another. The word *view*, for example, is considered to have entered English in the early 1300s, during the Middle English period. The *Oxford English Dictionary* records the great majority of Rastell's words as having already entered the English language before 1523, when Rastell's book was first printed. If that's so, Rastell gives English headwords and English definitions—and it's therefore an English dictionary.

John Considine, unquestionably the greatest living scholar of historical lexicography—professor emeritus at the University of Alberta—argues for Cawdrey over Rastell. He makes two points against Rastell's *Termes de la Ley* as the first English-language dictionary: (1) it's bilingual; and (2) it doesn't so much define words as explain legal consequences.

Considine argues that the right-hand column doesn't count as a *monolingual* dictionary. We can't pretend, he says, that the left-hand

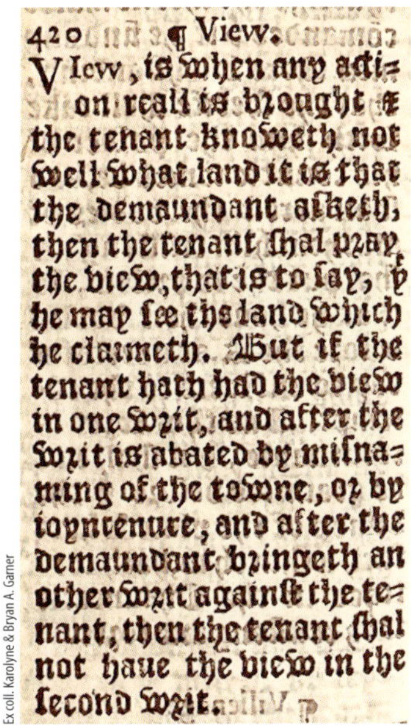

420 ¶ View.
View, is when any action reall is brought & the tenant knoweth not well what land it is that the demaundant asketh, then the tenant shal pray the view, that is to say, y[t] he may see the land which he claimeth. But if the tenant hath had the view in one writ, and after the writ is abated by misnaming of the towne, or by ioyntenure, and after the demaundant bringeth an other writ against the tenant, then the tenant shal not haue the view in the second writ.

Ex coll. Karolyne & Bryan A. Garner

Same entry in 1592 edition, with updated spellings.

Courtesy of Harvard Law Library

From Harvard Law School's 1530 edition.

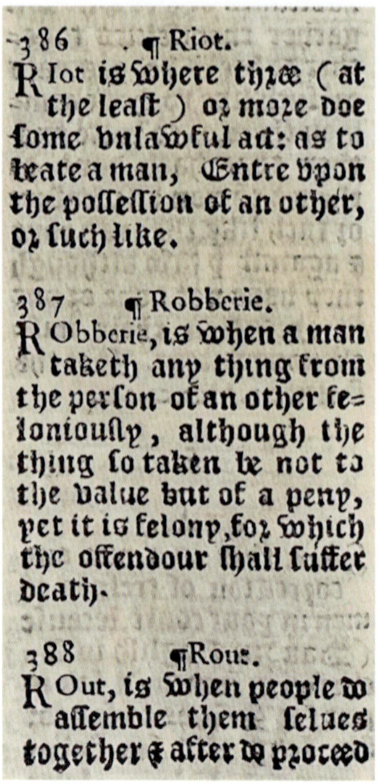

386 ¶ Riot.
Riot is where three (at the leaſt) or more doe ſome unlawful act: as to beate a man, Entre upon the poſſeſſion of an other, or ſuch like.

387 ¶ Robberie.
Robberie, is when a man taketh any thing from the perſon of an other feloniouſly, although the thing ſo taken be not to the value but of a peny, yet it is felony, for which the offendour ſhall ſuffer death.

388 ¶ Rout.
Rout, is when people do aſſemble them ſelves together & after do proceed

Ex coll. Karolyne & Bryan A. Garner

From Paget's 1592 edition. These entries are for French borrowings that were English by the 13th century.

column, in Law French, isn't present. It is. So by definition it's a bilingual work: there are two languages. On this view, the right-hand column is simply a translation of the left. Considine even says that "the headwords were not English." Citing the entry for *estray* as an example, Considine argues that Rastell was "certainly not claiming that *estray* is an English word: it is a Law French word, on which he provides a commentary in French, before repeating the French headword with an English translation of his commentary." This is a linchpin to the argument.

In fact, the *Oxford English Dictionary* doesn't cite *estray* as an English word until 1594. Is that a lexicographic oversight, or instead a clear indication that it really wasn't English until late in the century? On this crucial point, Considine says that the right-hand column just repeats the "French headword with an English translation of his commentary."

Second, Considine argues that Rastell didn't so much define *estray* as explain "how an estray is dealt with by the law." Long before the difference between a dictionary and an encyclopedia would emerge, Rastell began his entry on *estray* with a definition ("Estray is where any beast or cattel is in any lordship and none knows its owner") and continued with 65 words explaining why and how "it shall be seised to the use of the King." Does the extra information disqualify Rastell's work as a dictionary?

Many think not—and conclude that Rastell, the lawyer, should be credited with producing the first English-language dictionary in the 1520s, even if it was a specialist work. After all, lawyers had already adopted the great majority of these French terms into their English contexts. It's a close question whether Rastell deserves priority over Cawdrey, the defrocked priest.

But let's extend the argument—because it's not nearly as close a call whether Rastell's later editions should count as works of English lexicography. The scholarly arguments have traditionally focused on the early Rastell editions from the 1520s. But let's now consider the 1579 and 1592 editions, the former appearing 25 years before Cawdrey. By 1579, the number of total entries had increased from 169 to 282, and in 1592 had soared all the way up to 435. Many of the newly added headwords weren't Law French at all: the book had been supplemented with abundant terms derived from Old English. For the letter *B*, compare the entries from 1525 with those from 1579 and 1592:

Rastell's 1525 *B* Entries	Rastell's 1579 *B* Entries	Rastell's 1592 *B* Entries
Barr	Baile	Baile
Battell	Bailement	Bailement
Basterdy	Bailife	Bailife
Burglary	Bakberinde theefe [OE]	Backberinde theefe [OE]
	Bargaine & sale	Bargaine and sale
	Barre	Barre
	Bastarde	Base fee
	Battaile	Bastarde
	Bigamy	Battaile
	Blodewit [OE]	Bigamy
	Boote [OE]	Bloodwit [OE]
	Brodehalpeny [OE]	Boote [OE]
	Brugbote [OE]	Broodhalpeny [OE]
	Burgbote [OE]	Burgage
	Burghbrech [OE]	Brugbote [OE]
	Burgh English [OE]	Burghbote [OE]
	Burglarie	Burghbrech [OE]
		Burgh English [OE]
		Burglarie

Ex coll. Karolyne & Bryan A. Garner

Ten editions of Rastell in the Garner Collection: 1592, 1607, 1624, 1636, 1642, 1646, 1659, 1685, 1708, and 1721.

By 1579, there had been a more than fourfold increase in *B* entries; by 1592, it was nearly fivefold. The 1579 edition added eight headwords deriving from Old English, and in 1592 two additional headwords (*base fee* and *burgage*), both Latinate terms dating in English from before 1505, joined the wordlist. (For other typical entries, see the photograph at the bottom left on p. 6.) Antedating Cawdrey by a quarter century, isn't this English lexicography?

Who was responsible for it? There are three possibilities: (1) William Rastell (1508–1565), John's son who became a Queen's Bench judge—but he died 14 years before the greatly expanded 1579 edition. (2) An unknown reviser retained by Richard Tottell, the printer of five editions from 1563 to 1579. (3) Thomas Paget, who was responsible for the 1592 and 1598 editions (Cowley 1932:lxxxiii)—the problem being that he wasn't admitted to the bar until 1583, and the first great expansion in headwords had occurred in 1579.

The frustrating answer, then, is that we just don't know. What we do know is that it's entirely legitimate to question the orthodox view that Cawdrey's was the first English-language dictionary. John Rastell might deserve the honor—but if there's serious doubt about that, there should be less doubt about the anonymous reviser of 1579.

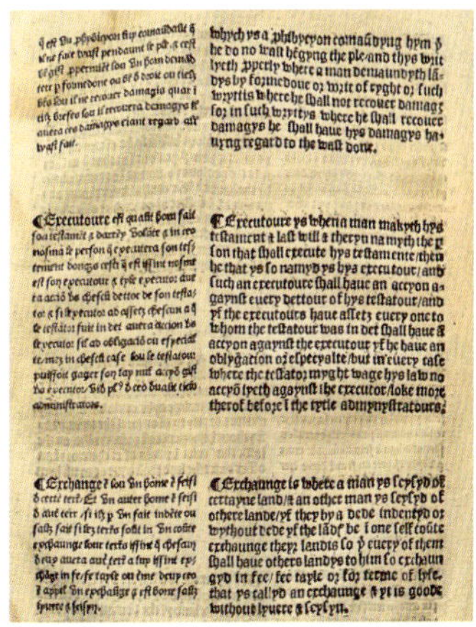

A page from Harvard's 1525 Rastell, in which the right column is exclusively English. The entries are from *estrepement* (dating from 1503 in the *Oxford English Dictionary*), *executor* (ca. 1280), and *exchange* (ca. 1374).

Ex coll. Karolyne & Bryan A. Garner

Sir Thomas and Lady Margaret Elyot as drawn by Hans Holbein the Younger ca. 1532.

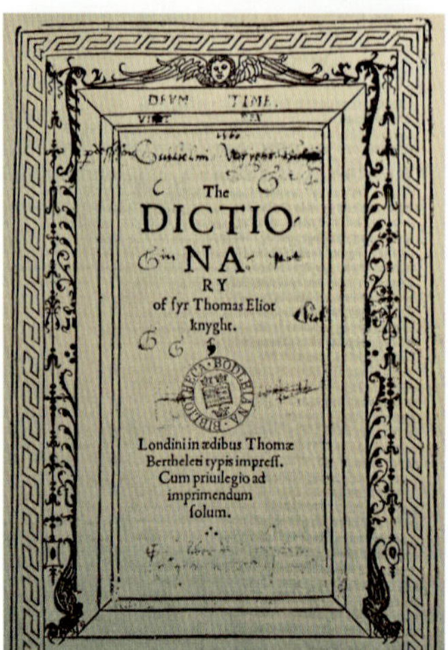

The DICTIONARY of syr Thomas Eliot knyght.

Londini in ædibus Thomæ Bertheleti typis impress. Cum priuilegio ad imprimendum solum.

Courtesy Bodleian Library

Elyot's 1538 title page.

2

Sir Thomas Elyot
Henry VIII's Failed Emissary

Elyot, Thomas. *The Dictionary of Syr Thomas Eliot Knyght.* London: Thomas Berthelet, 1538. 2d ed. 1542. 3d ed. 1548.

Sir Thomas Elyot (1490–1546), humanist and diplomat, was born in Derbyshire just 14 years after William Caxton printed the first book in England. Elyot's father was a judge on the court of common pleas and a justice of assize for the western circuit. Young Thomas was privately tutored at his father's house until the age of 12. Although the evidence isn't conclusive, he may have studied at Oxford and received a BA in 1519 and a degree in civil law in 1524. In any event, he was a justice of the peace in Oxfordshire and Wiltshire from 1515 to 1529, and beginning in 1530 a justice of the peace in Cambridgeshire. In 1531, King Henry VIII sent him on a mission to the Holy Roman Emperor, Charles V, to procure support for an annulment of Henry's marriage to Catherine of Aragon. Failing in that endeavor, Elyot tarried on the Continent, overspent his allowance, and fell out of favor with the king. He then returned to Cambridgeshire and devoted the remainder of his life to humanistic scholarly pursuits.

His most influential book appeared in 1531: *The Boke Named the Governour*, one of the bestselling books of the age. There Elyot explored the English language as a fit subject of education. Concerned about the poverty of the English vocabulary as compared with Latin and Greek, Elyot said that he "intended to augment our Englyshe tongue, wherby men shulde as well expresse more abundantly the thynge that they conceyved in their hertis (wherfore language was ordeyned) havynge wordes apte for the purpose." He had already encountered resistance: "Divers men, rather scornyng my benefite [beneficence] than receyving it thankfully, doo shew them selfes offended (as they say) with my strange termes." To obviate such criticisms, Elyot characteristically glossed his new words with simpler paraphrases, as by writing *animate or gyve courage to*, *education or bringing up of children*, *explicating or unfolding*, *adminiculation or aid*, *obfuscate or hid*, etc. When he wanted to express an idea for which he could think of no adequate English term, he said that he found himself "constrained to usurpe a latine worde, callyng it Maturitie, which word though it be straunge and dark, yet—ones brought in custome, shall be as easye to understande as other wordes late common out of Italy and France, and made denisens among us." Among the 138 words recorded by the *OED* as having their earliest citation in *The Governour* are *accommodate*, *adapt*, *adult*, *agreeableness*, *beneficence*, *bucolic*, *concoction*, *encyclopedia*, *equability*, *excogitate*, *explicate*, *formality*, *fragment*, *frugality*, *hostility*, *modesty*, *refurnish*, *rusticity*, *temperature*, *tractability*, and *venereal*. Elyot was an unabashed neologist who imported and fashioned words wherever he felt the need. The book is therefore lexicographically important.

But his biggest, most language-oriented book was *The Dictionary* of 1538, with its 26,560 entries in a folio volume of 424 double-column pages. His preface proudly announces that his *Dictionary* contains "a thousand mo [sic] Latin words than were in any one Dictionary published in this realm." He established some important lexicographic conventions: (1) the use of *dictionary* in the title as an English word (he was first); (2) alphabetical ordering; (3) distinct typefaces to distinguish headwords from definitions, in this case roman type for Latin headwords and **black letter** for English translations; (4) grammatical categorization; (5) some use of quotations to illustrate meaning and usage; (6) occasional citation of authorities; and (7) a great many "encyclopedic" entries dealing with mythological, biographical, and historical subjects. Elyot marked the beginning not just of true bilingual Latin–English lexicography, but of an approach to English-language lexicography generally. One important commentator has called Elyot's *Dictionary* "the most important event in the entire history of English-language lexicography" (Considine 2022:72)—this despite its being a Latin–English bilingual dictionary.

In his *Dictionary*, Elyot continued his augmentation of the English language. Some 200 terms are recorded in the *OED* as first appearing there, including *askew*, *bawdy house*, *conference*, *gradation*, *investigator*, *perforate*, *replevy* (he was a lawyer!), *saturate*, *tarragon*, *tendril*, *transposition*, *unstitch*, and *wheezing*.

In the second edition of 1542, Elyot demoted the word *Dictionary* from title to subtitle: it was now called *Bibliotheca Eliotæ, Eliotis Librarie, This Dictionarie Now Newly Imprinted.* The third

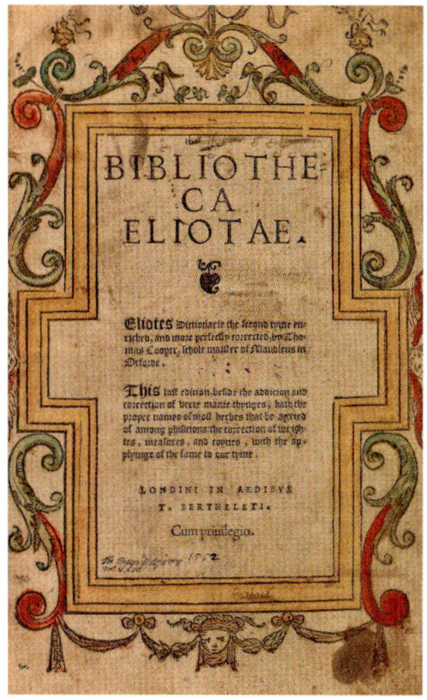
BIBLIOTHECA ELIOTAE.

LONDINI IN AEDIBUS T. BERTHELETI.

Cum privilegio.

The 1548 title page.

"I have also added proper termes belongynge to lawe and phisike, the names of divers herbes knowen among us: also a good number of fishes founden as wel in our ocean, as in our rivers." (From the Dedication to Henry VIII.)

The boke named the Gouernour, deuised by ſ Thomas Elyot knight.

Londini in edibus Tho. Berthelet. An. dñi M.D.xxxi.

Title page of *The Governour* (1531).

The 1548 edition, revised and augmented by Thomas Cooper (see no. 3).

edition of 1548 bore this same title. But by this time, Elyot had been dead for two years. Having no children and believing that his nephews would have no interest in his library, he directed in his will that his books be sold and the proceeds be distributed to impecunious scholars (except he used the word *poor*).

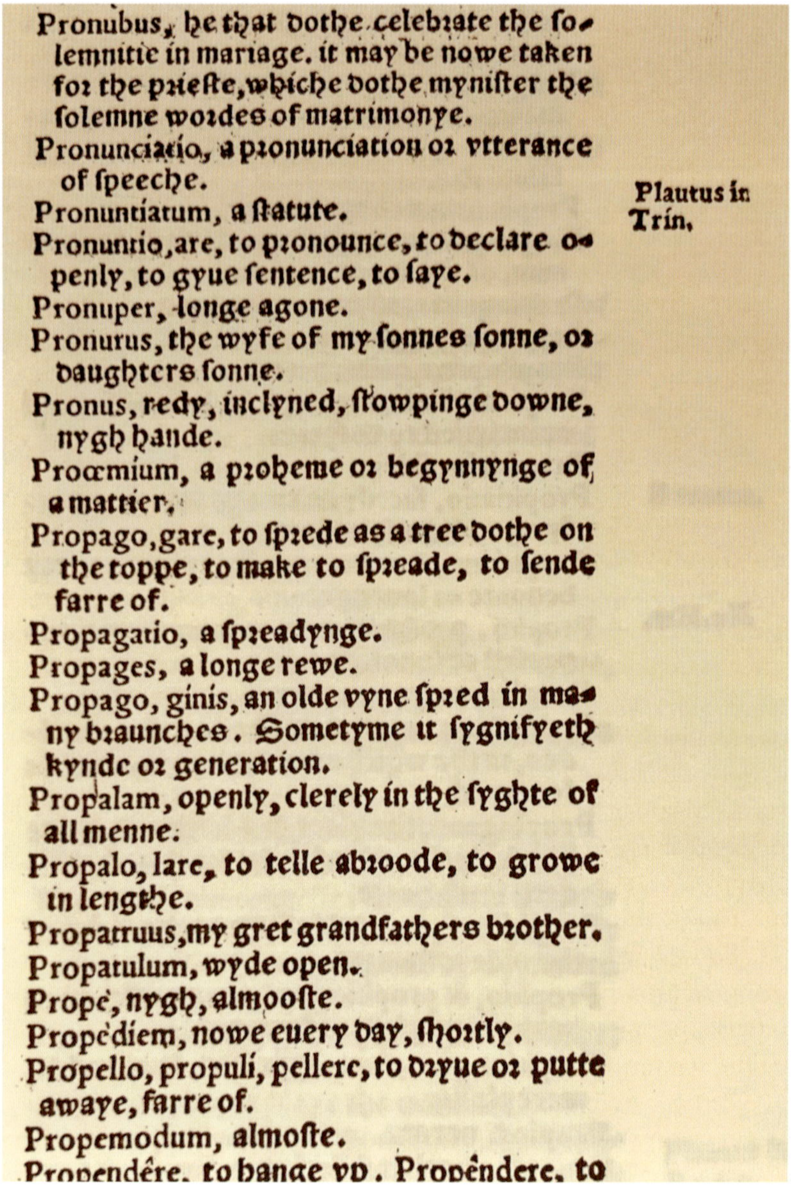
Pronubus, he that dothe celebrate the solemnitie in mariage. it may be nowe taken for the prieſte, whiche dothe myniſter the ſolemne wordes of matrimonye.
Pronunciatio, a pronunciation or vtterance of ſpeeche.
Pronuntiatum, a ſtatute. Plautus in Trin.
Pronuntio, are, to pronounce, to declare openly, to gyue ſentence, to ſaye.
Pronuper, longe agone.
Pronurus, the wyfe of my ſonnes ſonne, or daughters ſonne.
Pronus, redy, inclyned, ſtowpinge downe, nygh hande.
Procœmium, a proheme or begynnynge of a mattier.
Propago, gare, to ſprede as a tree dothe on the toppe, to make to ſpreade, to ſende farre of.
Propagatio, a ſpreadynge.
Propages, a longe rewe.
Propago, ginis, an olde vyne ſpred in many braunches. Sometyme it ſygnifyeth kynde or generation.
Propalam, openly, clerely in the ſyghte of all menne.
Propalo, lare, to telle abroode, to growe in lengthe.
Propatruus, my gret grandfathers brother.
Propatulum, wyde open.
Propé, nygh, almooſte.
Propédiem, nowe euery day, ſhortly.
Propello, propuli, pellere, to dryue or putte awaye, farre of.
Propemodum, almoſte.
Propendêre, to hange vp. Propèndere, to

Entries in the 1538 edition. By 1548, many more had been added.

"Elyot developed a remarkable explanatory dictionary style of his own which in its masterly application was highly user-friendly. This will undoubtedly have contributed to its success as well as to its impact and influence on the next two generations of English lexicographers." (Stein 2014:416.)

3

Thomas Cooper
Calm Under Fire

Cooper, Thomas. *Thesaurus Linguæ Romanæ & Britannicæ*. London: Thomas Berthelet, 1565. Other editions published by Henry Denham in 1573, 1578, 1584 & 1587.

Ex coll. Karolyne & Bryan A. Garner

COOPER (1517?–1594) TAKES THE PRIZE as perhaps history's most stoical lexicographer. When his wife angrily threw his manuscript of this work into the fire—a setback of five years' labor—he tried to restore domestic tranquility and started over again.

He began his lexicographic career working on the 1548 edition of Sir Thomas Elyot's *Bibliotheca Eliotæ*. His name was omitted from the title page because Thomas Berthelet, the publisher, thought that it added no commercial value. Even so, a year after its appearance, Cooper was appointed to the mastership of the Magdalen College School, where he had once been a menial servant.

Meanwhile, in 1546, while he was at work on Elyot's dictionary, Cooper married a woman named Amy, who soon cuckolded her husband with at least two different men. Although she was said to be "utterly profligate" (*DNB*), he habitually forgave her infidelities. The pair soon became the gossip of Oxford. He excused her and refused, against advice, to separate from her. Then Amy threw the only manuscript of his *Thesaurus* into the fire. His response provoked this characterization by a contemporary: "His Life in *Oxford* was very commendable, and in some sort Saint-like; for if it be Saintlike to live unreprovable, to bear a cross patiently, to forgive great injuries freely: this mans example is sampleless in this age." (Harington 1653:62.)

So well respected was he that, after Elizabeth I's accession, he was appointed Bishop of Lincoln and later Bishop of Winchester. Because his episcopal duties prevented him from significantly revising his *Thesaurus*, the later editions were much like the earlier ones.

Perhaps from envy, together with the expected moral immaculacy of clergy, Cooper was often charged with plagiarism. Yet as one commentator has noted, "It is a curious fact . . . that the critics are

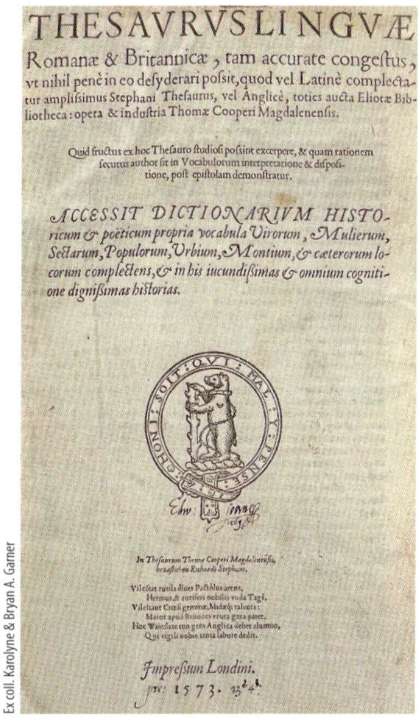
THESAVRVS LINGVÆ
Romanæ & Britannicæ, tam accurate congestus, vt nihil penè in eo desyderari posit, quod vel Latinè complectatur amplissimus Stephani Thesaurus, vel Anglicè, toties aucta Eliotæ Bibliotheca: opera & industria Thomæ Cooperi Magdalenensis.

Quid fructus ex hoc Thesauro studiosi possint excerpere, & quam rationem secutus author sit in Vocabulorum interpretatione & dispositione, post epistolam demonstratur.

ACCESSIT DICTIONARIVM HISTOricum & poëticum propria vocabula Virorum, Mulierum, Sectarum, Populorum, Vrbium, Montium, & cæterorum locorum complectens, & in his iucundissimas & omnium cognitione dignissimas historias.

HONI SOIT QVI MAL Y PENSE

Impressum Londini.
1573.

Ex coll. Karolyne & Bryan A. Garner

The 1573 title page.

not in agreement as to what lexicographers or dictionaries Cooper pilfered, and not one of the critics is entirely correct in his charges." (Starnes 1954:86.)

Modern scholars believe, based on statistical evidence, that William Shakespeare consulted Cooper's *Thesaurus* while composing his plays. (Starnes 1949:47.)

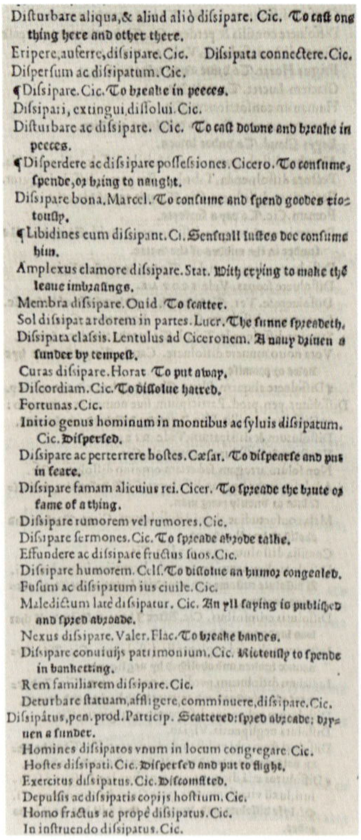

Diſturbare aliqua,& aliud aliò diſsipare. Cic. To caſt one thing here and other there.
Eripere,auferre,diſsipare.Cic. Diſsipata connectere.Cic.
Diſperſum ac diſsipatum.Cic.
¶Diſsipare.Cic.To breake in peeces.
Diſsipari, extingui,diſſolui.Cic.
Diſturbare ac diſsipare. Cic. To caſt downe and breake in peeces.
¶Diſperdere ac diſsipare poſſeſsiones.Cicero.To conſume, ſpende,or bring to naught.
Diſsipare bona.Marcel.To conſume and ſpend goodes rioтously.
¶Libidines eum diſsipant.Ci.Senſuall luſtes doe conſume him.
Amplexus clamore diſsipare.Stat. With crying to make the leaue imbrasings.
Membra diſsipare.Ouid.To ſcatter.
Sol diſsipat ardorem in partes.Lucr.The ſunne ſpreadeth.
Diſsipata claſsis.Lentulus ad Ciceronem. A nauy driuen a ſunder by tempeſt.
Curas diſsipare.Horat To put away.
Diſcordiam.Cic.To diſſolue hatred.
Fortunas.Cic.
Initio genus hominum in montibus ac ſyluis diſsipatum. Cic.Diſperſed.
Diſsipare ac perterrere hoſtes.Cæſar.To diſpearſe and put in feare.
Diſsipare famam alicuius rei.Cicer.To ſpreade the brute or fame of a thing.
Diſsipare rumorem vel rumores.Cic.
Diſsipare ſermones.Cic.To ſpreade abrode talke.
Effundere ac diſsipare fructus ſuos.Cic.
Diſsipare humorem.Celſ.To diſſolue an humor congealed.
Fuſum ac diſsipatum ius ciuile.Cic.
Maledictum latè diſsipatur. Cic. An yll ſaying is publiſhed and ſpred abroade.
Nexus diſsipare.Valer.Flac.To breake bandes.
Diſsipare conuiuijs patrimonium.Cic. Riotouſly to ſpende in banketting.
Rem familiarem diſsipare.Cic.
Deturbare ſtatuam,affligere,comminuere,diſsipare.Cic.
Diſsipâtus,pen.prod.Particip. Scattered:ſpred abroade; dryuen a ſunder.
Homines diſsipatos vnum in locum congregare.Cic.
Hoſtes diſsipati.Cic.Diſperſed and put to flight.
Exercitus diſsipatus.Cic.Diſcomfited.
Depulſis ac diſsipatis copijs hoſtium.Cic.
Homo fractus ac propè diſsipatus.Cic.
In inſtruendo diſsipatus.Cic.

Ex coll. Karolyne & Bryan A. Garner

From the 1573 edition.

"Cooper's elevation in the Church was, after the publication of his dictionary, fairly rapid. He rose successively to be dean of Christ Church (1567), dean of Gloucester (1569), bishop of Lincoln (1570), and bishop of Winchester (1584). It seems probable that his work as a lexicographer was a factor in his preferment in the Church." (Starnes 1954:86.)

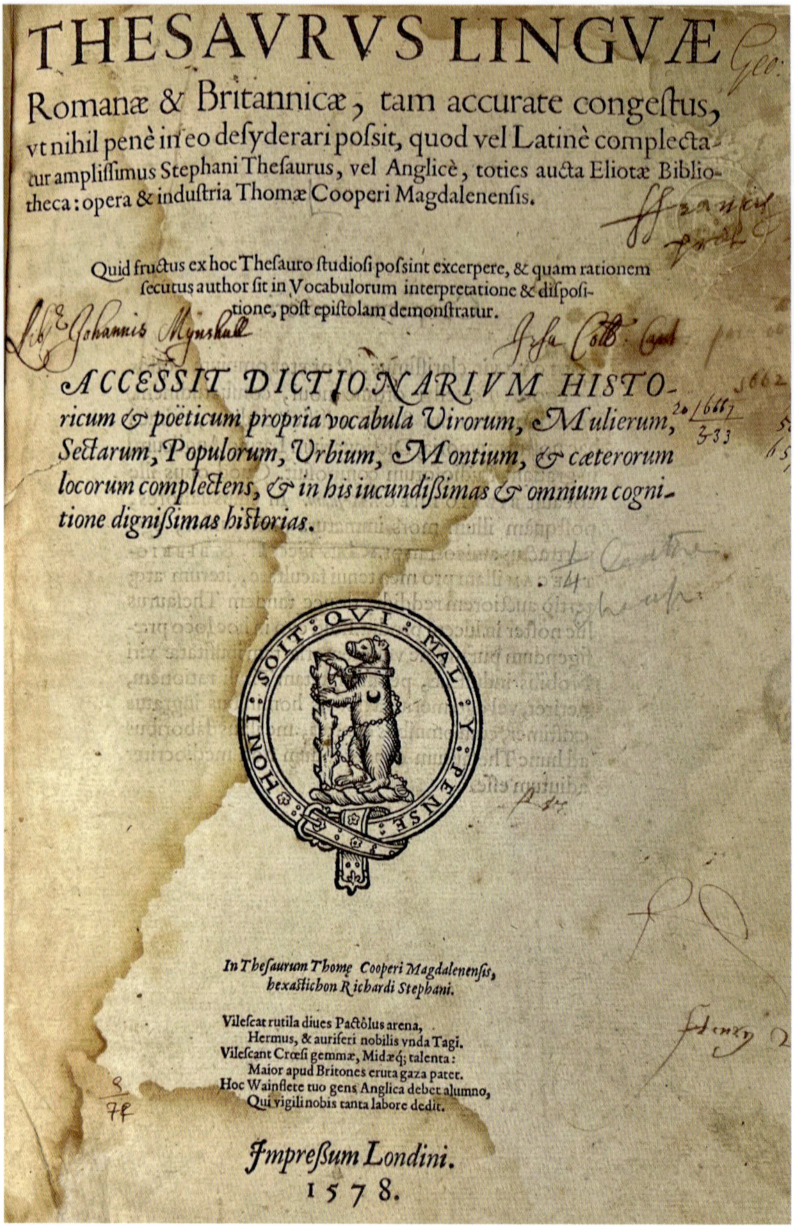

THESAVRVS LINGVÆ Romanæ & Britannicæ, tam accurate congeſtus, vt nihil penè in eo deſyderari poſsit, quod vel Latinè complectatur ampliſſimus Stephani Theſaurus, vel Anglicè, toties aucta Eliotæ Bibliotheca: opera & induſtria Thomæ Cooperi Magdalenenſis.

Quid fructus ex hoc Theſauro ſtudioſi poſsint excerpere, & quam rationem ſecutus author ſit in Vocabulorum interpretatione & diſpoſitione, poſt epiſtolam demonſtratur.

ACCESSIT DICTIONARIVM HISTOricum & poëticum propria vocabula Virorum, Mulierum, Sectarum, Populorum, Vrbium, Montium, & cæterorum locorum complectens, & in his iucundiſsimas & omnium cognitione digniſsimas hiſtorias.

HONI SOIT QVI MAL Y PENSE

In Theſaurum Thomæ Cooperi Magdalenenſis, hexaſtichon Richardi Stephani.

Vileſcat rutila diues Pactolus arena,
Hermus, & auriferi nobilis vnda Tagi.
Vileſcant Crœſi gemmæ, Midæq; talenta:
Maior apud Britones eruta gaza patet.
Hoc Wainflete tuo gens Anglica debet alumno,
Qui vigili nobis tanta labore dedit.

Impreſſum Londini.
1578.

Ex coll. Karolyne & Bryan A. Garner

The title page of John Mynshull's copy of Cooper's *Thesaurus*, with an ownership signature showing that he was at Jesus College, Cambridge. Although this might be thought to be John Minsheu the lexicographer (see nos. 6 & 12)—he spelled his name in various ways—it is more probably a man who became a pensioner at Jesus College, Cambridge, in 1661: one John Minshall.

4

John Skene
Man of the World

Skene, John. ***De Verborum Significatione: The Exposition of the Termes and Difficill Wordes, Conteined in the foure Buikes of Regiam Majestatem, and uthers, in the Actes of Parliament, Infestments, and used in practicque of this Realme, and with diverse rules, and commoun places, or principalles of the Lawes*****. Edinburgh: Robert Waldegrave, 1597.**

Ex coll. Karolyne & Bryan A. Garner

Skene's dictionary is bound toward the back of this volume.

SKENE (1540?–1617), the sixth son of James and Janet Skene of Bandodle, Aberdeenshire, was educated at King's College, Aberdeen, and at St. Mary's College, St. Andrews. He spent seven years in Europe (ca. 1567–1574) studying law and visiting Switzerland, Poland, Scandinavia, and Germany, where he became acquainted with sundry princes. Upon returning to Scotland, Skene was admitted as an advocate in March 1575.

His dictionary resulted from his membership on a commission appointed in 1592 to review and print acts of Parliament and other laws. *De Verborum Significatione* was the first published dictionary of Scots law. Skene was knighted in 1604 and also called in that year to the bar of the Middle Temple (after the Union of the Crowns). He died in March 1617 and is buried in the Greyfriars Kirk, Edinburgh.

This is one of the first two law dictionaries of the Anglo-American world (the other being Rastell's 1523 work [no. 1]). Not well known, it is omitted from John Cowley's *Bibliography of Abridgments, Digests, Dictionaries and Indexes of English Law*. The definitions are a mixture of Law Latin, Law French, and Scots:

- "BASTARDUS, in French Bastard, ane barne unlauchfully gotten outwith the bande of Mariage." Then follows nearly three full pages' worth of disquisition.
- "DISPARAGIUM, like as parage is called equalitie, from the Latine word Paritas. Swa disparagium is called inequalitie in bluid, honour, dignitie, or utherwaies."

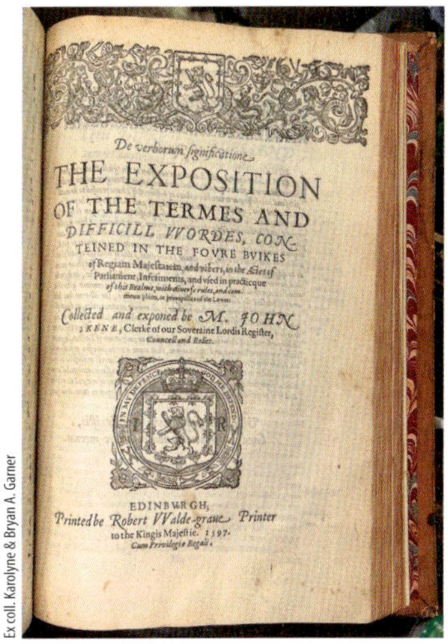

Ex coll. Karolyne & Bryan A. Garner

"In about 1569 [Skene] travelled to Poland. He visited Cracow, where he met many of his countrymen. This surprised him so much that he mentioned them in his famous Scottish legal dictionary, *De Verborum Significatione* (1597)." (Bajer 2012:308n.)

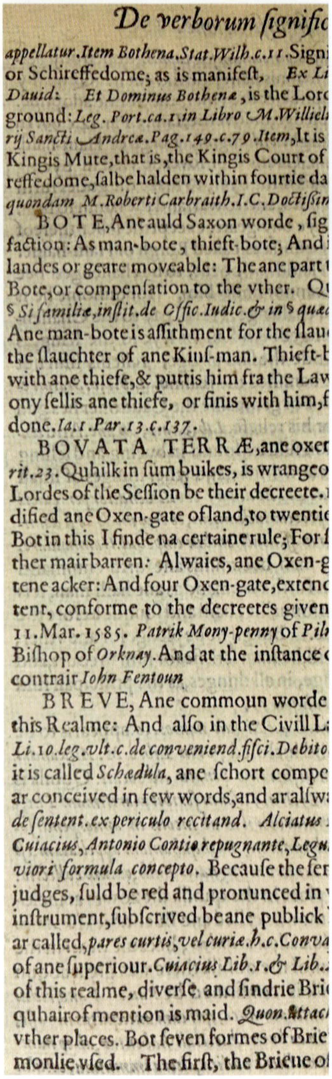

De verborum ſignific
*appellatur.Item Bothena.Stat.Wilh.c.11.*Signi
or Schireffedome; as is manifeſt, *Ex Li*
Dauid: Et Dominus Bothenæ, is the Lorc
ground: *Leg. Port.ca.1.in Libro M.Williel*
rij Sancti Andreæ.Pag.149.c.79.Item, It is
Kingis Mute, that is, the Kingis Court of
reffedome, ſal be halden within fourtie da
quondam M.Roberti Carbraith.I.C.Doctiſsin
BOTE, Ane auld Saxon worde, ſig
faction: As man-bote, thieft-bote; And
landes or geare moveable: The ane part
Bote, or compenſation to the vther. Q
§ *Si familiæ, inſtit.de Offic.Iudic.& in* § *quæ*
Ane man-bote is aſſithment for the ſlau
the ſlauchter of ane Kinſ-man. Thieft-b
with ane thiefe, & puttis him fra the Law
ony ſellis ane thiefe, or finis with him, f
done. *Ia.1.Par.13.c.137.*
BOVATA TERRÆ, ane oxen
rit.23. Quhilk in ſum buikes, is wrangeo
Lordes of the Seſſion be their decreete.
dified ane Oxen-gate of land, to twenti
Bot in this I finde na certaine rule; For
ther mair barren: Alwaies, ane Oxen-g
tene acker: And four Oxen-gate, extenc
tent, conforme to the decreetes given
11.Mar.1585. *Patrik Mony-penny* of *Pil*
Biſhop of *Orknay*. And at the inſtance
contrair *Iohn Fentoun*
BREVE, Ane commoun worde
this Realme: And alſo in the Civill L
Li.10.leg.vlt.c.de conveniend.fiſci.Debito
it is called *Schædula*, ane ſchort compe
ar conceived in few words, and ar alſw
de ſentent.ex periculo recitand. Alciatus
Cuiacius, Antonio Contio repugnante, Legu
viori formula concepto. Becauſe the ſen
judges, ſuld be red and pronunced in
inſtrument, ſubſcrived be ane publick
ar called, *pares curtis, vel curiæ.h.c.Conva*
of ane ſuperiour. *Cuiacius Lib.1.& Lib.*
of this realme, diverſe and ſindrie Bri
quhair of mention is maid. *Quon.Attac*
vther places. Bot ſeven formes of Brie
monlie vſed. The firſt, the Brieue o

Detail from Skene's unpaginated work.

- "TORT, Et non reason, un-reason, wrang, and unlaw. Stat. Rob. Br.cap. Item quod nulla 17. Tort in the French tongue, is wrang or injurie: Unlaw cummis fra On, Privatius particula apud nos & Germanos, eodem modo quo in, apud Latinos, and law, or lauch, id est lex: Quasi sine lege, vel contra legem, vel quod non in re fit. Ius Normand. Lib. 12. c.1. Actiones of wrang and unlaw, appearis to be civill actiones, and are opponed to actiones criminall, touching life and lim. stat. Alex. c. Si quis 9.Cumm seqq. Leg. Mal. Mak. c.4."

A separate part of the book also contains a glossary-like index or abridgment of Scottish statutory law. It is titled *Ane Table of the Principall Maters conteined in this buik, collected and noted be the name of the King, Maker of the Law.* For example: "*Attorney* being ane Gentle man, suld bee send to the Schireffe Courtes be Free-halders, quha may not compeir personnallie, with the seale of their armes, to passe upon serving of inquests, and retoures. James. I. Parliament, 9.c.130. Actornayes in the justice aire, suld be honest and qualified persones. Iam.I. p.3. c.53." Or this: "*Adulterer* persevering in Adulterie, sulde bee denounced rebell, and tinis all his moveable gudes Mar.Par.5.c.20."

De verborum significatione can lay claim to being the second Scottish wordbook, after the bilingual Latin–Scots glossary by Andrew Duncan (*Appendix etymologiae*, 1595). The headwords are unsystematically listed in either Latin or Scots. Some entries are quite long, running for several pages, as with *annexation*, *dissolution*, *feodum*, *homagium*, *maritagium*, *recognition*, *reversion*, and *schiereff*. As in most early law dictionaries, these entries are akin to those in abridgments (legal encyclopedias), explaining much of the law relating to the term. But Skene is unmistakably a lexicographer, given that his entries routinely begin with a definition.

5

Thomas Speght
Chaucerian Standard-Bearer

The workes of our ancient and learned English poet, Geffrey Chaucer, newly printed. To that which was done in the former impression, thus much is now added. . . . The signification of the old and obscure words proved: also caracters shewing from what tongue or dialect they be derived. **Thomas Speght ed. London: Adam Islip, 1598. 2d ed. 1602.**

Ex coll. Karolyne & Bryan A. Garner

When and where Speght (d. 1621) was born is unknown, but he probably grew up in Yorkshire. In 1566, he matriculated at Peterhouse, Cambridge, thanks in part to a scholarship provided by Lady Mildred Cecil.

Cambridge in the mid- to late 1500s was home to many devoted readers of Geoffrey Chaucer, including the soon-to-be-epic poet Edmund Spenser. But while Chaucer continued to attract admirers and enthusiasts, he was rapidly losing readership. Although the number of surviving manuscripts suggests that Chaucer was beloved in the years after his death in 1400, as the decades passed his fame declined. The problem was the language: readers of Early Modern English were having increasing trouble simply making sense of his Middle English text. The vernacular was changing rapidly, and younger generations often found their grandparents' language inaccessible. Near the end of the 16th century, the educator Francis Beaumont lamented how his own age was struggling with England's greatest poet: "Many of [Chaucer's] wordes," he wrote, "are growne too hard and unpleasant." When people of the time spoke of "old words," they generally meant Chaucer's words. (Kerling 1979:7.) And there was little help for them: nobody had yet compiled even a rudimentary glossary of 14th-century English.

Speght was the first to try. After taking his BA from Cambridge in 1570 and his MA three years later, he worked as a schoolmaster and contributed poems to works written by his friends, including one in John Baret's *Alvearie*, an influential multilingual dictionary of 1580.

Ex coll. Karolyne & Bryan A. Garner

The 1602 edition.

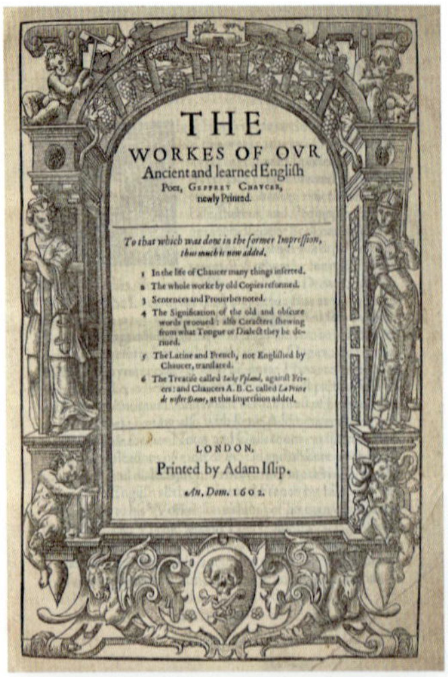

THE
WORKES OF OVR
Ancient and learned Engliſh
Poet, Geffrey Chavcer,
newly Printed.

To that which was done in the former Impreſſion, thus much is now added.

1 In the life of Chaucer many things inserted.
2 The whole worke by old Copies reformed.
3 Sentences and Prouerbes noted.
4 The Signification of the old and obscure words prooued: also Caracters ſhewing from what Tongue or Dialect they be deriued.
5 The Latine and French, not Engliſhed by Chaucer, tranſlated.
6 The Treatiſe called *Iacke Upland*, againſt Friers: and Chaucers A. B. C. called *La Priere de nostre Dame*, at this Impreſſion added.

LONDON,
Printed by Adam Iſlip.
An. Dom. 1602.

Ex coll. Karolyne & Bryan A. Garner

Ex coll. Karolyne & Bryan A. Garner

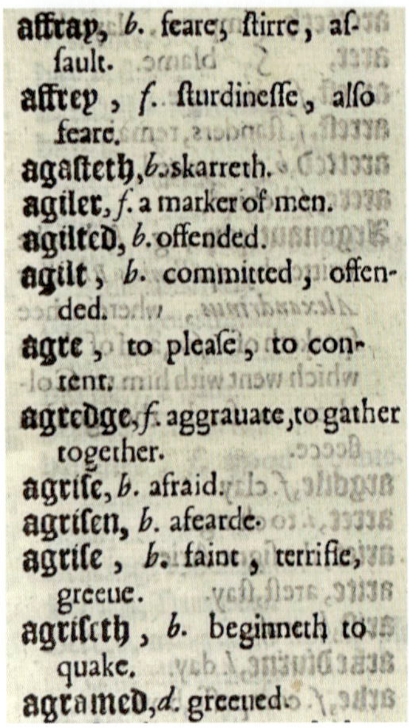

affray, *b.* feare, ſtirre, aſſault.
affrey, *f.* ſturdineſſe, alſo feare.
agaſteth, *b.* skarreth.
agiler, *f.* a marker of men.
agilted, *b.* offended.
agilt, *b.* committed, offended.
agre, to pleaſe, to content.
agredge, *f.* aggrauate, to gather together.
agriſe, *b.* afraid.
agriſen, *b.* afearde.
agriſe, *b.* faint, terrifie, greeue.
agriſeth, *b.* beginneth to quake.
agramed, *d.* greeued.

Ex coll. Karolyne & Bryan A. Garner

But his most important work came when, in the 1590s, he revived his undergraduate enthusiasm for Chaucer and began editing the poet's works. He spent half a decade on *The Workes of Our Ancient and Learned English Poet, Geffrey Chaucer*. It appeared in 1598 with a gracious dedication to Robert Cecil, Elizabeth I's secretary of state and the son of the Lady Mildred Cecil, who "gave mee yearely exhibition all the time of my continuance in Cambridge."

Much of Speght's edition is derivative. He leans heavily on the work of one of his predecessors, John Stow, even taking credit for being the first to publish Chaucerian works that had already appeared in Stow's edition. But while his text was unoriginal, his introductory essays, his notes, his biography of the poet, and especially his glossary of Chaucerian English were genuinely innovative. Speght gave Chaucer the kind of scholarly treatment previously reserved for the Greek and Latin classics, turning the poet of *Troilus and Criseyde* and *The Canterbury Tales* into one of the first English classics.

In his front matter, Speght gives his contemporaries some general advice for reading 14th-century English: "It is his manner . . . by two negatives to cause a greater negation," for instance, and he tended "many times to understand his verbe: as, *I not what men him call*, for, *I know not*, &c." Speght is among the first to suggest that a key to understanding older forms of English lies in the dialects of northern England, where forms long abandoned in London were still circulating. This theme reemerges in the 19th century, as dialect dictionaries are promoted for offering insights into the early history of the language. (See no. 112.)

The most original and lasting part of the book is the section headed "The old and obscure words in Chaucer, explained." Speght doesn't try to define every word in Chaucer, only those that had become unfamiliar in the two centuries since he wrote—words like *thilke* "same," *twifold* "dubble," and *unwist* "unknowne." Some of his glosses are simply guides to navigating outdated spelling, as when he defines *askes* as "ashes," *beest* as "a beast," *bosche* as "a bush," and *chese* as "chuse," and others reflect obsolete rules for forming past tenses, as with *blo* "blew," *bote* "did bite," *clomben* "ascended" (that is, *climbed*), and *ferd* "fared." The definitions are nearly always curt, typically just a synonym: *ally* "kin," *gle* "melody," *gullet* "a throte," *nice* "foolish." On a few occasions, though, he is more expansive—*glose* "flatter: also the exposition of a darke speech," *nadir* "the point opposite to Zenith, or the point under the Horison right under our feet"—and a few entries are long and more encyclopedic than lexical. *Christopher*, for instance, is "a picture of a man: carrying a child on his shoulders over a river," *ecliptike line* is "the circumference of the circle, wherin the Sunne finisheth his yearely motion," and *Pasiphae* is "wife of *Minos* king of Creete, who hauying company with a bull, but rather as *Festus* saith, with a man called *Taurus*, brought foorth *Minotaurus*, who was halfe a man, and half a bull."

A second edition, published in 1602, expanded the first edition's 2,034 glossary entries to 2,607. The revised glossary also provided brief etymological information for all of Chaucer's words, using "*a.*" for words of "Arabicke" origin, "*g.*" for "Greeke," and so on.

Speght died in 1621 with no other books to his credit. A final reprint of his edition appeared in 1687, and while newer editions of Chaucer eventually superseded his work, serious readers of Middle English were still consulting him as late as the 1770s.

Speght's glossary was limited in scope, skimpy in its definitions, and sometimes marred by inaccuracies. But it was a pioneering overview of an earlier stage of the English language, and it helped to introduce obsolete and obsolescent words into the 16th-century "hard word" tradition. It was an essential precursor to A.L. Mayhew and Walter W. Skeat's *Concise Dictionary of Middle English from A.D. 1150 to 1580* (1888) and the great *Middle English Dictionary* conceived in 1925 and completed, 20 volumes later, in 2001 (no. 107). Even the mainstream of English lexicography is indebted to Speght, since his Chaucerian vocabulary was picked over and plagiarized by dictionary writers for more than a century.

The glossaries in the first two editions (1598 & 1602) contained more than 2,000 headwords, and they appeared within a decade of the groundbreaking work of Robert Cawdrey (1604)—whose great innovation, of course, was not merely appending a glossary to a larger text but instead issuing a stand-alone general wordbook.

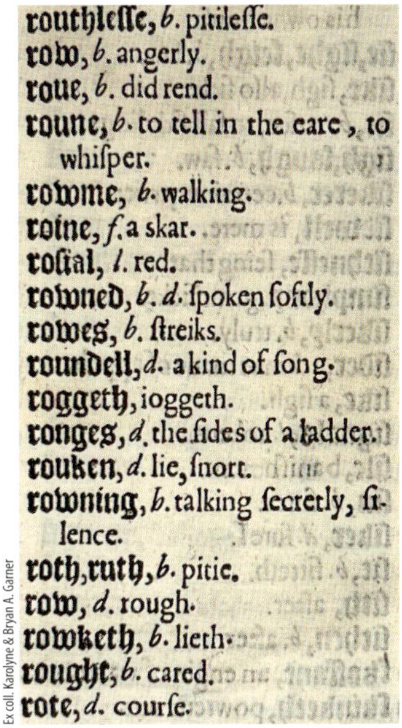
routhlesse, *b.* pitilesse.
row, *b.* angerly.
roue, *b.* did rend.
roune, *b.* to tell in the eare, to whisper.
rowme, *b.* walking.
roine, *f.* a skar.
rosial, *l.* red.
rowned, *b. d.* spoken softly.
rowes, *b.* streiks.
roundell, *d.* a kind of song.
roggeth, ioggeth.
ronges, *d.* the sides of a ladder.
rouken, *d.* lie, snort.
rowning, *b.* talking secretly, silence.
roth, ruth, *b.* pitie.
row, *d.* rough.
rowketh, *b.* lieth.
rought, *b.* cared.
rote, *d.* course.

Ex coll. Karolyne & Bryan A. Garner

"**rubicunde**, *l.* [Latin] redde.
rubifying, *d.* [Dutch] making redde.
rucking, *d.* [Dutch] lying, snorting.
rud, *b.* [British dialect] complexion."

Ex coll. Karolyne & Bryan A. Garner

The sculptor Joseph Durham's 1870 marble bust of Chaucer (25 inches high).

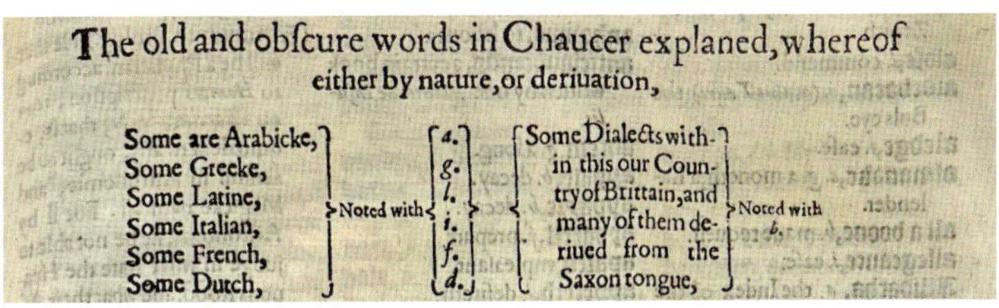
The old and obscure words in Chaucer explaned, whereof either by nature, or deriuation,

Some are Arabicke,	Noted with	*a.*	Some Dialects within this our Countrey of Brittain, and many of them deriued from the Saxon tongue,	Noted with *b.*
Some Greeke,		*g.*		
Some Latine,		*l.*		
Some Italian,		*i.*		
Some French,		*f.*		
Some Dutch,		*d.*		

Ex coll. Karolyne & Bryan A. Garner

Ex coll. Karolyne & Bryan A. Garner

In dedicating the book to four men, Minsheu writes: "If any cavill about the number fower [four]; let him bee advertised, *There be fower elements placed in the world; likewise fower seasons in the yeere: also fower humors that possesse the bodie; and fower vertues that shoulde governe the minde*." (Dedication to Sir John Scot, Sir Henry Bromley, Sir Edward Greuel, and Master William Fortescue.)

6

John Minsheu

Polyglot Extraordinaire

Minsheu, John. *A Dictionarie in Spanish and English, first published into the English tongue by Ric. Percivale Gent. Now enlarged and amplified with many thousand words.* London: Edm. Bollifant, 1599. Bound with *A Spanish Grammar* (1599).

John Minsheu (1560–1627)—variously also known as John Minshull, John Minshon, or Ioannes Minshæs—though of unknown parentage, is thought to have originated in Cheshire, where Minshull was the name of a village. He was educated not formally but through extensive travels, during which he was imprisoned for a time by Spaniards—an adventure that doubtless gained him a knowledge of vernacular Spanish. After returning to England with the help of merchants, he established a language school and compiled his *Dictionarie in Spanish and English* (1599), on the title page of which he styled himself "Professor of Languages in London." He received help from prisoners taken during the defeat of the Spanish Armada. The work was expressly derived from Richard Percyvall's *Bibliotheca Hispanica* (1591), a Spanish–English–Latin vocabulary. Yet on the title page, Minsheu's name is printed much more prominently.

Convinced that Percyvall's work wasn't as useful as it might be, Minsheu reworked it. Three revisions are most significant: he nixed Percyvall's Latin translations; he added "many thousand words," marking his additions with asterisks; and he added an English–Spanish section roughly half the size of the Spanish–English section. In the process, he turned Percyvall's 232-page quarto into *A Dictionarie in Spanish and English*, a closely printed folio of 399 pages.

In the front matter, Minsheu anticipates criticism by suggesting that his readership could be divided into three groups: the good (Bees), the bad (Spiders), and the indifferent (Chameleons). The Bees, who would no doubt praise his work, he esteems highly. The Spiders he holds in "little regard" as "converting all to poyson." The Spider, he writes, "thinketh himselfe graced to have only a grace in backbiting," adding: "Let me aske him this one question, whether he ever published his owne labours in Print?" As for other faultfinders, "let them consider this is my first worke; & as Seneca saith, in every first worke there must be of force some imperfection & error, which if he believe not, I say . . . They that busie themselves in reprehending the faults of other mens writings, their owne are likely never to come to light." After condemning the Spiders for nearly two full pages, he comes to the Chameleons: "these men are not able to judge themselves, or not looking into the matter, harken what another saith of it, and so he affirmeth the same, not weighing whether the other spake of malice or ignorance."

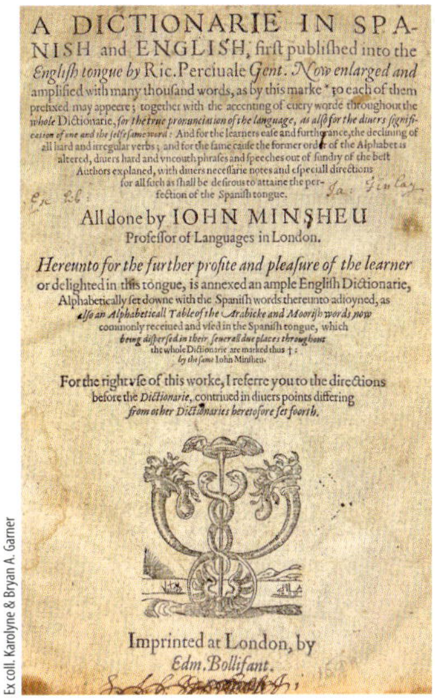
A DICTIONARIE IN SPANISH and ENGLISH, firſt publiſhed into the *Engliſh tongue by* Ric. Perciuale *Gent. Now enlarged and* amplified with many thouſand words, as by this marke * to each of them prefixed may appeere; together with the accenting of euery worde throughout the whole Dictionarie, *for the true pronunciation of the language, as alſo for the diuers ſignification of one and the ſelfe ſame word:* And for the learners eaſe and furtherance, the declining of all hard and irregular verbs; and for the ſame cauſe the former order of the Alphabet is altered, diuers hard and vncouth phraſes and ſpeeches out of ſundry of the beſt Authors explaned, with diuers neceſſarie notes and eſpeciall directions for all ſuch as ſhall be deſirous to attaine the perfection of the Spaniſh tongue.

All done by IOHN MINSHEU Profeſſor of Languages in London.

Hereunto for the further profite and pleaſure of the learner or delighted in this tongue, is annexed an ample Engliſh Dictionarie, Alphabetically ſet downe with the Spaniſh words thereunto adioyned, as *alſo an Alphabeticall Table of the Arabicke and Mooriſh words now* commonly receiued and vſed in the Spaniſh tongue, which *being diſperſed in their ſeverall due places throughout* the whole Dictionarie are marked thus †: *by the ſame* Iohn Minſheu.

For the right vſe of this worke, I referre you to the directions before the *Dictionarie*, contriued in diuers points differing *from other Dictionaries heretofore ſet foorth.*

Imprinted at London, by *Edm. Bollifant.*

Ex coll. Karolyne & Bryan A. Garner

After all this ingratiation of himself to readers, Minsheu takes even further measures to inoculate himself against criticism: "I . . . submit my selfe and doings, to the iudgement of the discreete, learned, and wise, that whatsoever is amisse, being advertised thereof, I promise to labour and with my best endevours to correct and amende." He explains that when the book was being printed, he was "in the country upon necessitie . . . and there remained till it was all done." In lexicography, it is "harde to please fewe, harder to please many, impossible to please all."

"I accent every word in the whole Dictionarie to cause the learner to pronounce it right." ("Directions for the Understanding the Use of this Dictionarie.")

Minsheu demonstrates his practical experience as a teacher: many of his departures from Percyvall were clearly for the convenience of language learners. He indicated the gender of nouns, for instance, and "declined all the Irregular and hardest Verbes thorow this whole Booke . . . in the singular number in two moodes, the Indicative and Subiunctive, and three Tenses." He followed English alphabetization rules, not the Spanish ones that Percyvall had adopted. He added accent marks to "every word in the whole Dictionarie to cause the learner to pronounce it right, otherwise when he speaketh he shall not be understoode of the naturall Spaniard." And he was attentive to spelling variation, "Wherefore I advise the Reader if he finde not the word in B turne to V: if not in V looke to B. . . . So e for i, and i for e. . . . Moreover, when you finde not a word in the single letter, looke in the double; or not in the double, looke in the single." The tips seem to have been welcome to students; the copy in the Garner Collection bears the ownership marks of three 17th-century readers who added their own notes.

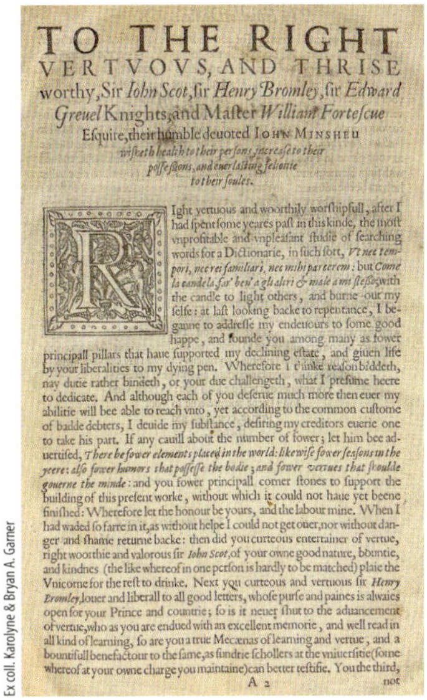
TO THE RIGHT VERTVOVS, AND THRISE worthy, Sir *Iohn Scot*, ſir *Henry Bromley*, ſir *Edward Greuel* Knights, and Maſter *William Forteſcue* Eſquire, their humble deuoted IOHN MINSHEU *wiſheth health to their perſons, increaſe to their poſſeſsions, and euerlaſting felicitie to their ſoules.*

Right vertuous and woorthily worſhipfull, after I had ſpent ſome yeares paſt in this kinde, the moſt vnprofitable and vnpleaſant ſtudie of ſearching words for a Dictionarie, in ſuch ſort, *Vt nec tempori, nec rei familiari, nec mihi parcerem*: but *Come la candela far' ben' a gli altri & male a mi ſteſſo*; with the candle to light others, and burne out my ſelfe: at laſt looking backe to repentance, I beganne to addreſſe my endeuours to ſome good happe, and founde you among many as fower principall pillars that haue ſupported my declining eſtate, and giuen life by your liberalities to my dying pen. Wherefore I thinke reaſon biddeth, nay dutie rather bindeth, or your due challengeth, what I preſume heere to dedicate. And although each of you deſerue much more then euer my abilitie will bee able to reach vnto, yet according to the common cuſtome of badde debters, I deuide my ſubſtance, deſiring my creditors euerie one to take his part. If any cauill about the number of fower; let him bee aduertiſed, *There be fower elements placed in the world: likewiſe fower ſeaſons in the yeere: alſo fower humors that poſſeſſe the bodie; and fower vertues that ſhoulde gouerne the minde*: and you fower principall corner ſtones to ſupport the building of this preſent worke, without which it could not haue yet beene finiſhed: Wherefore let the honour be yours, and the labour mine. When I had waded ſo farre in it, as without helpe I could not get ouer, nor without danger and ſhame returne backe: then did you curteous entertainer of vertue, right woorthie and valorous ſir *Iohn Scot*, of your owne good nature, bountie, and kindnes (the like whereof in one perſon is hardly to be matched) plaie the Vnicorne for the reſt to drinke. Next you curteous and vertuous ſir *Henry Bromley*, louer and liberall to all good letters, whoſe purſe and paines is alwaies open for your Prince and countrie; ſo is it neuer ſhut to the aduancement of vertue, who as you are endued with an excellent memorie, and well read in all kind of learning, ſo are you a true Mecænas of learning and vertue, and a bountifull benefactour to the ſame, as ſundrie ſchollers at the vniuerſitie (ſome whereof at your owne charge you maintaine) can better teſtifie. You the third,

A 2 not

Ex coll. Karolyne & Bryan A. Garner

First page of the two-page dedication.

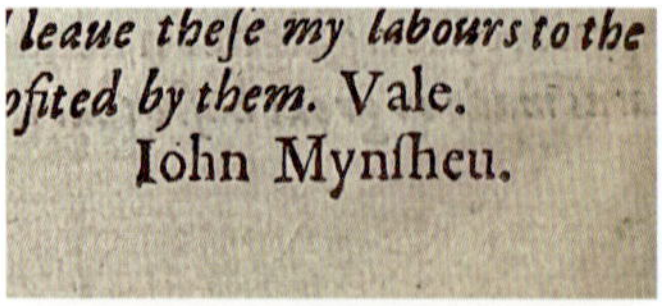
leaue these my labours to the / *ofited by them.* Vale. / Iohn Mynsheu.

Ex coll. Karolyne & Bryan A. Garner

Yours bound and assured / John Minsheu.

Ex coll. Karolyne & Bryan A. Garner

Minsheu was inconsistent in spelling his name even within the space of a few pages.

Minsheu also made some changes suggesting an interest in linguistic matters that went beyond classroom practicalities. He marked nearly a thousand words with daggers—*atún* "a fish called a Tunny," *azúcar* "sugar," and *bellóta* "an acorne"—to indicate the "Arabicke and Moorish words, now commonly received and used in the Spanish tongue" thanks to eight centuries of Islamic rule of the Iberian Peninsula. And he devised an ingenious way to indicate the roots of compound words: "I make the composition [affix] in a smaller letter, and the simple [root] in a greater, thus: *absTenér*, to abstaine, of *Tenér*, to hold, and *abs*, from."

The fuller vocabulary, the marked grammatical gender of nouns, the accented syllables, the indications of compounds, and the Arabic etymologies show the advances Minsheu made on Percyvall, even as he abandoned the Latin:

Percyvall, *Bibliotheca Hispanica* (1591)	Minsheu, *Dictionarie* (1599)
Atañér, **to pertaine**, *Attinere.* Atanor, **a conduit pipe**, *Tubus, fistula.* Atanquia para arrancar pelos, **pincers**, *Vulsella, foreceps.* Atapar, **to stop, to cover**, *Obstruere, operire, tegere.*	Atañér, *to belong to, attaine or pertaine.* † Atanór, m. a conduict pipe, the cocke of a conduict, any trough or pipe that carieth water in the ground. † Atanquía, f. a little paire of pincers to plucke haire off withall, a plaister to take away haire. * aTánto, untill, whilest, even, so farre as. * Atapádo, m. stopped, covered. * Atapadúra, f. a cover, a stoppell, a stopping of any thing. Atapár, to stop, to cover.

"For the giving notice of what I have done without defrauding any thing from the labours of any that have travelled in this kinde, I have made a difference of the words I have merely added by a starre thus *, whereby it may be seene what and how much I have enlarged by my long labour and paines." ("Directions for the Understanding the Use of this Dictionarie.")

Ex coll. Karolyne & Bryan A. Garner

Minsheu's three-column format.

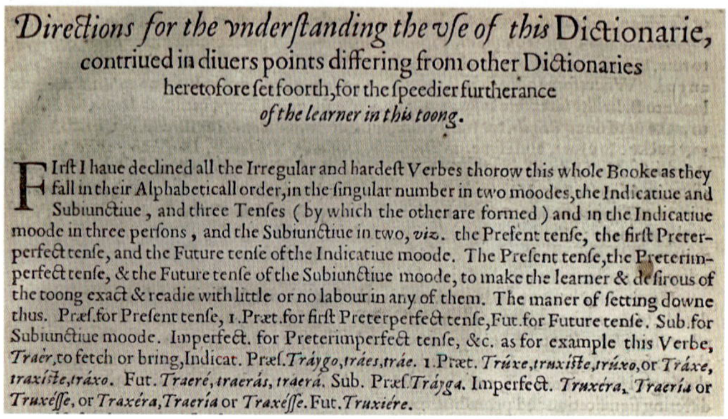
Directions for the vnderstanding the vse of this Dictionarie,
contriued in diuers points differing from other Dictionaries
heretofore set foorth, for the speedier furtherance
of the learner in this toong.

First I haue declined all the Irregular and hardest Verbes thorow this whole Booke as they fall in their Alphabeticall order, in the singular number in two moodes, the Indicatiue and Subiunctiue, and three Tenses (by which the other are formed) and in the Indicatiue moode in three persons, and the Subiunctiue in two, *viz.* the Present tense, the first Preterperfect tense, and the Future tense of the Indicatiue moode. The Present tense, the Preterimperfect tense, & the Future tense of the Subiunctiue moode, to make the learner & desirous of the toong exact & readie with little or no labour in any of them. The maner of setting downe thus. Præs. for Present tense, 1. Præt. for first Preterperfect tense, Fut. for Future tense. Sub. for Subiunctiue moode. Imperfect. for Preterimperfect tense, &c. as for example this Verbe, *Traér*, to fetch or bring, Indicat. Præs. *Tráygo, tráes, tráe.* 1. Præt. *Trúxe, truxíste, trúxo*, or *Tráxe, traxíste, tráxo.* Fut. *Traeré, traerás, traerá.* Sub. Præs. *Tráyga.* Imperfect. *Truxéra, Traería* or *Truxésse*, or *Traxéra, Traería* or *Traxésse.* Fut. *Truxiére.*

Ex coll. Karolyne & Bryan A. Garner

III. The Conventional Start

Tradition holds that Robert Cawdrey's Table Alphabeticall *heads the list of English-only dictionaries, and there is much to be said for the view that 1604 is the terminus a quo (that's now an English phrase, mind you). The next 12 years saw burgeoning efforts from Verstegan (1605), Cowell (1607), Wilson (1612), and Bullokar (1616). Perhaps only the last of these lexicographers was aware of Cawdrey's work. In fact, the only extant copy of Cawdrey's rudimentary dictionary was long ago bound at the back of the Bodleian Library's copy of Bullokar.*

In lexicographic terms, the 17th century was a period of hard-word lists: only the least common terms in the language were considered worthy of inclusion. That was fortunate for the lexicographers of the time, given that unusual words are the easiest to define. Common words pose the real definitional problems, and focusing on "inkhorn terms" made the work much easier. Defining ofclepe *("to call for, summon") is trivial compared to defining the word* of, *and it's far easier to define* takapu *("the Australian gannet") than* take. *Perhaps the 17th-century dictionary-makers instinctively knew as much.*

It was also the period in which skirmishes about plagiarism grew rowdy. Thomas Blount seemed to believe that lexicographers should wait a decent period before plagiarizing their predecessors—not just a year or two after the release of his magnum opus. John Milton's nephew, Edward Phillips, thought otherwise. As a result, some lively hullabaloos erupted.

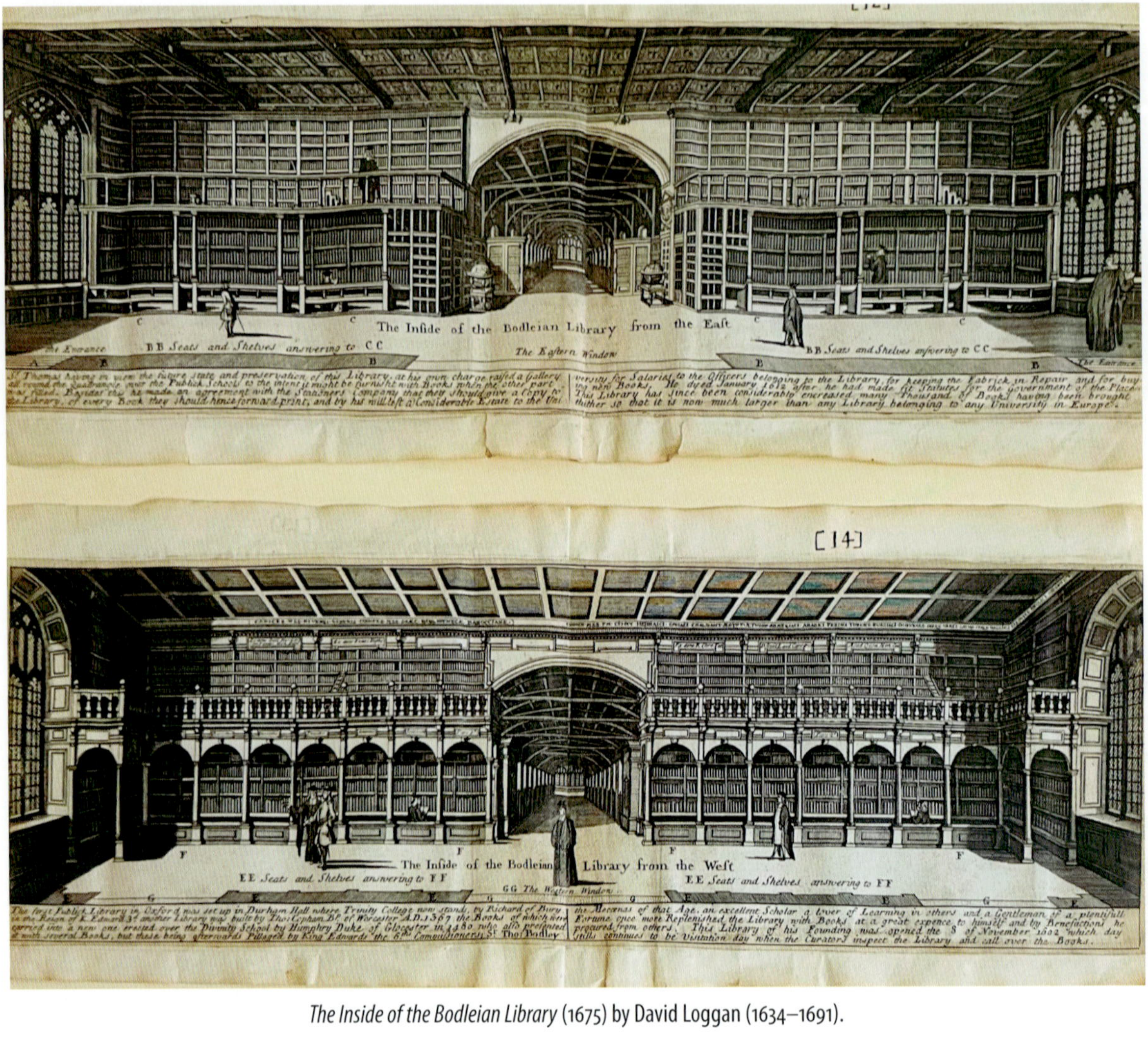

The Inside of the Bodleian Library (1675) by David Loggan (1634–1691).

7

Robert Cawdrey
Enlightening "Ladies and Other Unskilfull Persons"

Cawdrey, Robert. ***A Table Alphabeticall, conteyning and teaching the true writing, and understanding of hard usuall English wordes, borrowed from the Hebrew, Greeke, Latine, or French. &c. With the interpretation thereof by plaine English words, gathered for the benefit & helpe of Ladies, Gentlewomen, or any other unskilfull persons. Whereby they may the more easilie and better understand many hard English wordes, which they shall heare or read in Scriptures, Sermons, or elswhere, and also be made able to use the same aptly themselves.*** **London: Printed by I[ames] R[oberts] for Edmund Weaver, 1604.**

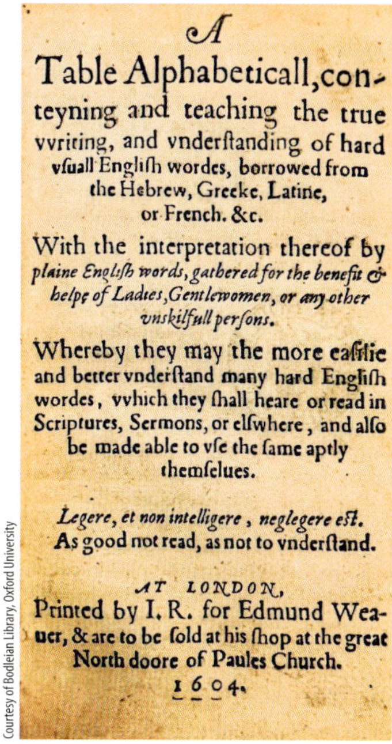
A Table Alphabeticall, conteyning and teaching the true vvriting, and vnderſtanding of hard vſuall Engliſh wordes, borrowed from the Hebrew, Greeke, Latine, or French. &c.

With the interpretation thereof by *plaine Engliſh words, gathered for the benefit & helpe of Ladies, Gentlewomen, or any other vnskilfull perſons.*

Whereby they may the more eaſilie and better vnderſtand many hard Engliſh wordes, vvhich they ſhall heare or read in Scriptures, Sermons, or elſwhere, and alſo be made able to vſe the ſame aptly themſelues.

Legere, et non intelligere, neglegere eſt. As good not read, as not to vnderſtand.

AT LONDON, Printed by I. R. for Edmund Weauer, & are to be ſold at his ſhop at the great North doore of Paules Church. 1604.

Courtesy of Bodleian Library, Oxford University

It's not much to look at: a hastily printed octavo of 130 pages, sloppily typeset and sold by an inexperienced bookseller. But Robert Cawdrey's *Table Alphabeticall* has conventionally been thought to have the best claim to be called the "first English dictionary."

First in what respect? There had been bilingual dictionaries, such as Latin–English and English–Latin. And there had been glossaries devoted to specific professions, especially law. But no earlier work covered words from across the whole language, with both the head-words and the definitions in English.

Cawdrey (1537?–1604?), a sometime schoolteacher, compiled *A Table Alphabeticall* with the assistance of "my sonne *Thomas*, who now is Schoolemaister in London." The title page identifies the book's target audience: "unskilfull persons," including "ladies" and "gentlewomen." He apparently thought his readers would be unskillful indeed, since he devoted a whole paragraph to explaining alphabetical order:

> If thou be desirous (gentle Reader) rightly and readily to understand, and to profit by this Table, . . . then thou must learn the Alphabet, to wit, the order of the Letters as they stand . . . as (b) neere the beginning, (n) about the middest,

"Some men seek so far for outlandish English, that they forget altogether their mothers language, so that if some of their mothers were alive, they were not able to tell, or understand what they say, and yet these fine English Clearks, will say they speak in their mother tongue; but one might well charge them, for counterfeiting the Kings English." (Preface.)

> and (t) towards the end. . . . If thy word beginne with (ca) look in the beginning of the letter (c) but if with (cu) then looke toward the end of that letter. And so of all the rest.

A Table Alphabeticall defines about 2,500 "hard usuall English wordes." Because the attention is on these difficult words, not one of the hundred most common English words (*the*, *is*, *to*, *of*, *and* . . .) earned an entry in Cawdrey. Most of his headwords are derived from French, Latin, or Greek—

> all such words as are derived & drawne from the Greek, are noted with these letter, (g). And the French are marked thus (§) but such words as are derived from the latin, have no marke at all

—and he offers definitions, sometimes no more than a synonym. Roman type—associated with classical learning—is used for learned headwords and Latin usage notes, and **black letter** type—associated with popular print like ballads, jest books, and romances when Cawdrey wrote—is used for the "plain English words":

> science, **knowledge, or skill**
> scripture, **writing**
> scruple, **doubt, difficultie**
> scrutiny, **diligent search, inquiry**
> scrupulous, **full of doubts**
> scurrilitie, **saucie, scoffing**
> seclude, **shutout, or put a part**

His is the first in a long line of 17th-century "hard word" dictionaries, focused on "inkhorn terms"—in the *OED*'s definition, "A term of the literary language, a learned or bookish word."

Cawdrey was accused of plagiarism—a neat trick in a work that's the first of its kind. But while Cawdrey was the first to define English words with English words, he took about half his headwords from a table of difficult words in Edmund Coote's *Englishe Schole-Maister* (1596). Some 40% of his definitions were at least partly cribbed from Thomas Thomas's *Dictionarium linguae latinae et Anglicanae* (1587). Because turnabout has always been fair play among lexicographers, the next significant English dictionary, John Bullokar's *English Expositor* (1616) (no. 11), stole many of Cawdrey's entries. Cawdrey's son stole them right back from Bullokar when he published a revised version of his father's dictionary with the subtitle "The English Expositor."

"Some far iournied gentlemen, at their returne home, like as they love to go in forraine apparell, so they will pouder their talke with over-sea language. He that cometh lately out of France, will talk French English, and never blush at the matter." (Preface.)

Courtesy of Bodleian Library, Oxford University

The 1616 copy of Bullokar (no. 11) in the back of which the only existing copy of Cawdrey's first edition is bound.

"Do we not speak, because we would have other to understand us? or is not the tongue given for this end, that one might know what another meaneth?" (Preface.)

Cawdrey's book went through a few editions but failed to capture the world's attention. It survives in a single copy, now at Oxford's Bodleian Library. Almost nobody seems to have discussed it for a century and a half, and it doesn't appear in the sale catalogues of bibliophiles' estates. But *A Table Alphabeticall* began to attract attention in the late 18th century, as Shakespeare's star was rising and scholars were scrutinizing his language. Before the *Oxford English Dictionary*, there was no systematic attempt to describe the English vocabulary at any moment in time, but a dictionary published in 1604 offered insights into what words meant during Shakespeare's career. Cawdrey covered just a tiny fraction of the vocabulary, and not always competently, but he suggested a way forward to future lexicographers.

"Though *A Table Alphabeticall* went through four editions—1st, 1604, 2nd, date unknown, 3rd, 1613, 4th, 1617—and though the title-page of the 1613 edition employs the phrase 'much inlarged,' the augmentation was negligible. Nor were there any important changes in the edition of 1617, except in the title. This reads, *A Table Alphabeticall, or the English Expositor*. The subtitle was borrowed from a rival publication by Dr. John Bullokar [no. 11], which had been printed in 1616." (Starnes & Noyes 1946:19.)

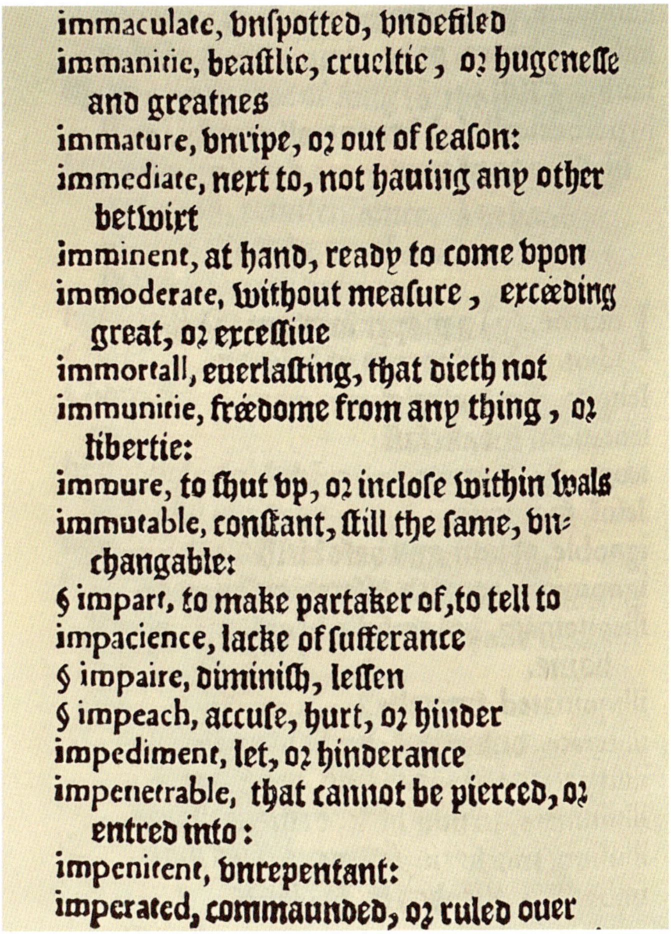
immaculate, vnſpotted, vndefiled
immanitie, beaſtlie, crueltie, or hugeneſſe and greatnes
immature, vnripe, or out of ſeaſon:
immediate, next to, not hauing any other betwixt
imminent, at hand, ready to come vpon
immoderate, without meaſure, exceeding great, or exceſſiue
immortall, euerlaſting, that dieth not
immunitie, freedome from any thing, or libertie:
immure, to ſhut vp, or incloſe within wals
immutable, conſtant, ſtill the ſame, vnchangable:
§ impart, to make partaker of, to tell to
impacience, lacke of ſufferance
§ impaire, diminiſh, leſſen
§ impeach, accuſe, hurt, or hinder
impediment, let, or hinderance
impenetrable, that cannot be pierced, or entred into:
impenitent, vnrepentant:
imperated, commaunded, or ruled ouer

"Cawdrey's dictionary did not, it seems, bring him international fame during his lifetime or in the years following his death. But the appearance in 1604 of a little book containing definitions of some of the 'hard usual' words of the English language marks a turning point in English lexicography and paves the way for some of the most remarkable reference books that have been produced in the English language." (Simpson 2007:29.)

Ex coll. Karolyne & Bryan A. Garner

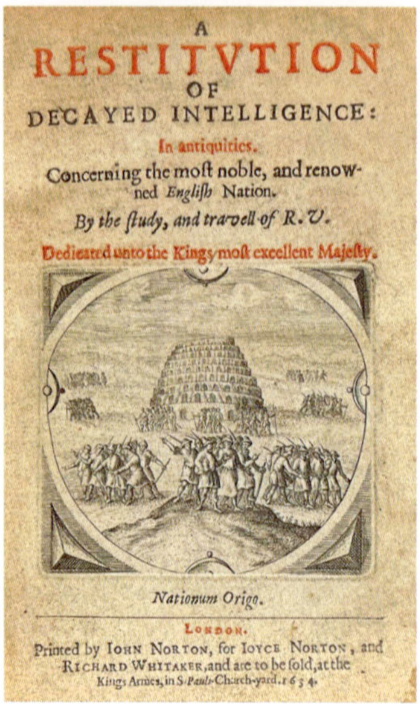

A
RESTITVTION
OF
DECAYED INTELLIGENCE:
In antiquities.
Concerning the moſt noble, and renowned *Engliſh* Nation.
By the ſtudy, and travell of R. V.
Dedicated unto the Kings moſt excellent Majeſty.
Nationum Origo.
LONDON.
Printed by IOHN NORTON, for IOYCE NORTON, and RICHARD WHITAKER, and are to be ſold, at the Kings Armes, in S. *Pauls*-Church-yard. 1654.

Ex coll. Karolyne & Bryan A. Garner

8

Richard Verstegan

Can Intelligence Be Restored?

V[erstegan], R[ichard]. ***A Restitution of Decayed Intelligence: In antiquities. Concerning the most noble and renowned English Nation. By the study and travaille of R.V. Dedicated unto the Kings most excellent Maiestie.*** **Antwerp: Robert Bruney, 1605. Repr. 1608, 1628, 1634, 1653, 1673.**

THOUGH HE CAME a year after Cawdrey and was much reprinted through the years, Richard Verstegan (1550?–1640) is rarely mentioned as an also-ran lexicographer. That's because, although he was compiling an independent glossary, all his words were from the Old English period before ca. 1200. He might also be hampered among lexicographic historians because his glossary appeared not as a standalone book but as a late (though substantial) chapter in a larger work.

He was born Richard Rowland, an Anglicized name that his father (né Verstegan), son of a Gelderland refugee, adopted in England. He studied for a time in Oxford but returned to London without a degree to become a goldsmith. He wrote the first English guidebook to the Continent (*The Post of the World* [1576]) and in the 1580s became a printer there, working in Paris, Rome, Reims, and Antwerp. While in Europe, he revived his ancestral surname. From 1587, he lived in Antwerp. He published religious verse, theological works, and several political tracts. His *Restitution of Decayed Intelligence* (1605) is considered a "seminal work of Anglo-Saxon scholarship." (*ODNB*.)

But was it really an independent glossary? It comes as chapter 7 (pp. 188–240) and is titled "Of the Great Antiquitie of Our Ancient English Toung; and of the proprietie, woorthynes, and amplytude thereof. With an explanation of sundry our moste ancient English woords." So it's part of a larger work. But unlike Speght (no. 5), who a few years earlier wrote a glossary of Chaucer appended to an edition of Chaucer, Verstegan's glossary isn't for the purpose of understanding words earlier in the book. Instead, it's intended to help readers understand the vocabulary of Old English, whatever they might be reading. It's not keyed to the text to which it's attached.

The introduction to the chapter ends:

> And now fearing least wading further heerein I might become offensive where I endevour to please, I wil heer seek to content the curious reader by Alphabetically explaining a number of our moste ancient English woords, some by their moderne ortography, others by shewing, (with the signification of them) what French woords wee have taken in steed of them, as also such as wee have not left of, but still use for choise, though wee have borrowed woords in French to lyke sense. [P. 206.]

"If in some of the Etymologies of our ancient names or words I may appeare to differ from some of the Germanes that have written of the like, it is where I have manifestly found them to have mistaken." (Preface.)

Verstegan was in the Purist camp, opposing the Neologists, who freely imported words from other languages:

> I . . . peradventure have much pleasured some of our English poets, with great choise of our own ancient woords, which as occasion requyred they might, with more reason renew and bring in use again (by som-what facilitating yf need were the ortographie) then to become the borrowers and perpetual debters of such languages as wil not bee beholding to us for somuch as a woord, and when wee have gotten from them as many woords as wee wil, they can never carry a true correspondence unto ours, they beeing of other nature and originall. [Pp. 239–40.]

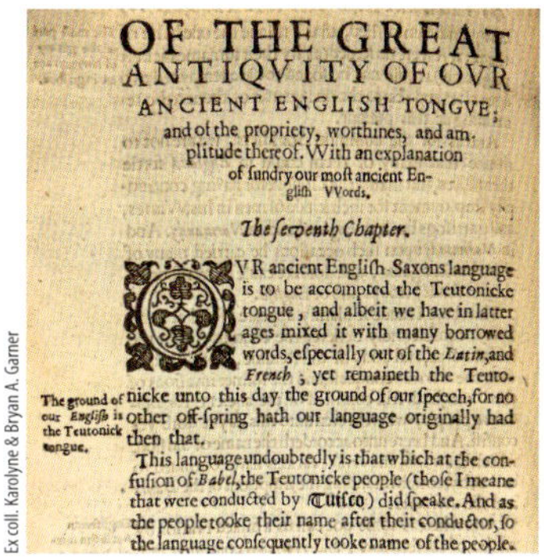
OF THE GREAT ANTIQVITY OF OVR ANCIENT ENGLISH TONGVE; and of the propriety, worthines, and amplitude thereof. With an explanation of ſundry our moſt ancient Engliſh VVords.

The ſeventh Chapter.

OVR ancient Engliſh Saxons language is to be accompted the Teutonicke tongue, and albeit we have in latter ages mixed it with many borrowed words, eſpecially out of the *Latin*, and *French*; yet remaineth the Teutonicke unto this day the ground of our ſpeech, for no other off-ſpring hath our language originally had then that.

The ground of our *Engliſh* is the Teutonick tongue.

This language undoubtedly is that which at the confuſion of *Babel*, the Teutonicke people (thoſe I meane that were conducted by Tuiſco) did ſpeake. And as the people tooke their name after their conductor, ſo the language conſequently tooke name of the people.

Ex coll. Karolyne & Bryan A. Garner

He added: "These our ancient woords heer set downe, I trust wil for this tyme satisfy the reader." (P. 240.)

As for "decayed intelligence," Verstegan was bemoaning the loss in knowledge of Old English. And there can be no doubt that most of the words he was recording, with a few exceptions, were not current in Jacobean English. Both types are evident in these examples, which illustrate Verstegan's ampler definitional treatment than Cawdrey supplied:

"If I may happen to find this my labour so well pleasing and accepted of, as I wish it may be, I shall then be much encouraged (God lending life) to continue my study in the same kind, and in the meane time I take my leave." (Preface.)

- "Aecer, or Acker. A *cornfeild* or *corneland*, wee now use the woord *Aker*, for a certaine space or measure of grownd." (P. 207.)
- "Brydgrome. *The groome of the Bryd*, because on the mariage day he serveth and waiteth on the table of the bryde." (P. 211.)
- "Cunne or kenne. *To descerne*, or to know." (P. 214.)

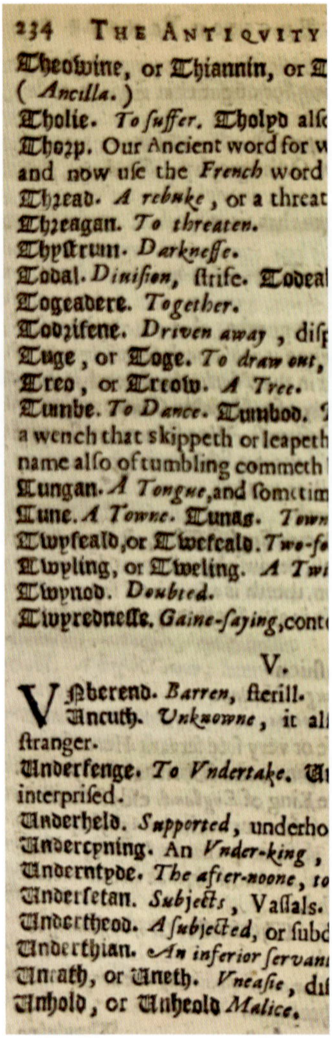
234 THE ANTIQVITY
Theowine, or Thiannin, or T
(*Ancilla.*)
Tholie. *To suffer.* Tholpd als
Thorp. Our Ancient word for w
and now use the *French* word
Thread. *A rebuke*, or a threat
Threagan. *To threaten.*
Thystrun. *Darknesse.*
Todal. *Diuision*, strife. Todeal
Togeadere. *Together.*
Todrifene. *Driven away*, disp
Tuge, or Toge. *To draw out*,
Treo, or Treow. *A Tree.*
Tunbe. *To Dance.* Tumbod.
a wench that skippeth or leapeth
name also of tumbling commeth
Tungan. *A Tongue*, and sometim
Tune. *A Towne.* Tunas. *Town*
Twyfeald, or Twefeald. *Two-fo*
Twyling, or Tweling. *A Twi*
Twynod. *Doubted.*
Twyrednesse. *Gaine-saying*, cont

V.

Vnberend. *Barren*, sterill.
Vncuth. *Unknowne*, it al
stranger.
Vndersenge. *To Vndertake.* V
interprised.
Vnderheld. *Supported*, underho
Vndercyning. An *Vnder-king*,
Vnderntyde. *The after-noone*, to
Vndersetan. *Subiects*, Vassals.
Vndertheod. *A subiected*, or subd
Vnderthian. *An inferior seruant*
Vnrath, or Vneth. *Vneasie*, di
Vnhold, or Vnheold *Malice.*

Ex coll. Karolyne & Bryan A. Garner

Detail from p. 234.

- "**Forscrunken**. *Shrun*[*k*]-*vp*, as members withered or dryed up." (P. 219.)
- "**Freundine** or **Freundina**. A *woman-friend*, a shee-freind by omitting this and other lyke ancient woords, our language is grown defective, as for example. If one say that hee met or spake with a freind of his, it appeereth not whether it were with a man or a woman, where as we might in our language aswel distinguish the masculyne from the feminyne, as others in other languages do." (Pp. 219–20.)
- "**Tale**, *Speech, language, discours*. Wee sometymes strayne the sence, as though a tale were a fable or a ly, because untruthes are told as wel as truthes." (P. 233.)
- "**Unwether**. *A storme*, a tempest." (P. 235.)
- "**Wantrust**. *Distrust*, suspition." (P. 235.)
- "**Were-wulf**. This name remaineth stil known in the Teutonic, & is as much to say as **man-wolf**; the greeks expressing the very like, in *Lycanthropos*." (P. 236.)

Chapter 8, an etymological guide to Saxon names, also touches on linguistic matters such as compounding. Verstegan reflected the orthodoxy of his day when it came to the origins of language:

> Our language . . . consisted in the beginning for the moste parte of woords of monosillable, & each woord beeing of one sillable had [h]is own proper signification put into the myndes of such as first receaved it (at the confusion of *Babel*) by almighty God the author and founder thereof, but by ioyning two woords or more together, that were distinct monosillables before, a new composed woord and therewithal a new sence was at once framed. [P. 242.]

Verstegan's erudition meant that his work had a necessarily limited audience, but the *Restitution* went through further editions in 1628, 1634, 1653, 1655, and 1673. It was an essential reference for other pioneers in the early stages of English, including Franciscus Junius (no. 31), and a full century and a half after its publication, Samuel Johnson (no. 35) was still drawing on it for the etymologies in his *Dictionary*.

One truly extraordinary thing about Verstegan is that, working in Antwerp in 1605, he surely knew nothing about Cawdrey's obscure work the year before in London. In the decade from 1602 to 1612, the English-speaking world seemed suddenly ready for monoglot dictionaries—and if we count Speght's 1602 glossary, five of them appeared in that time.

9

John Cowell
Inciting Bonfires

Cowell, John. *The Interpreter: or Booke Containing the Signification of Words: Wherein is set foorth the true meaning of all, or the most part of such Words and Termes, as are mentioned in the Law Writers, or Statutes of this victorious and renowned Kingdome, requiring any Exposition or Interpretation*. Cambridge: John Legate, 1607.

Ex coll. Karolyne & Bryan A. Garner

Cowell 1607 before and after repairs.

COWELL (1554–1611) is known to history as one of the few lexicographers whose primary work, in a bizarre turn of events, was subjected to book-banning and perhaps even book-burning. After his famous law dictionary, *The Interpreter*, was found to state opinions favoring royal absolutism, King James I—in a move to placate Parliament—summoned Cowell before him in the Privy Council and suppressed the book by proclamation. This move signaled the destruction of Cowell's distinguished career, and he died shortly after in ignominy.

"If I have either omitted any hard word within my circuit, or set it downe not expounded; I give you good leave to impute the one to my negligence, the other to mine ignorance: and so comend these my paines to your best profit, and you unto God." (Preface.)

Born in Devon to unknown parents, Cowell attended Eton and then matriculated at King's College, Cambridge, where he became a fellow in 1573. After receiving his BA in 1575 and his MA in 1578, he devoted himself to the study of civil law. Earning an LLD in 1584, he became a member of Doctors' Commons and practiced for a time before the ecclesiastical and admiralty courts. From 1594 to 1611, he was the regius professor of civil law at Cambridge and master of Trinity Hall. In the first decade of the 17th century, he was the official principal of the archdeacon of Colchester, where he often administered sentences of excommunication. Meanwhile, from 1603 to 1604, he served as vice-chancellor of Cambridge University.

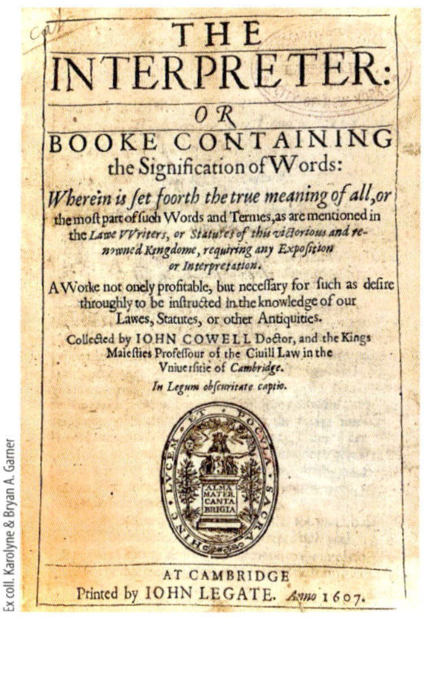

THE INTERPRETER: OR BOOKE CONTAINING the Signification of Words: *Wherein is set foorth the true meaning of all, or* the most part of such Words and Termes, as are mentioned in the *Lawe Writers, or Statutes of this victorious and renowned Kingdome, requiring any Exposition or Interpretation.*

A Worke not onely profitable, but necessary for such as desire throughly to be instructed in the knowledge of our Lawes, Statutes, or other Antiquities.

Collected by IOHN COWELL Doctor, and the Kings Maiesties Professour of the Ciuill Law in the Vniuersitie of *Cambridge*.

In Legum obscuritate captio.

ALMA MATER CANTABRIGIA

AT CAMBRIDGE Printed by IOHN LEGATE. *Anno* 1607.

Ex coll. Karolyne & Bryan A. Garner

Cowell's primary academic pursuit was illustrating similarities between the civil law and the English common law—something that didn't endear him to common-law lawyers. His first book, *Institutiones juris Anglicani* (1605), attempted (in Latin) to give the common law a more organized structure by placing it within the framework of the civil law. Then came *The Interpreter* (1607), which provided both

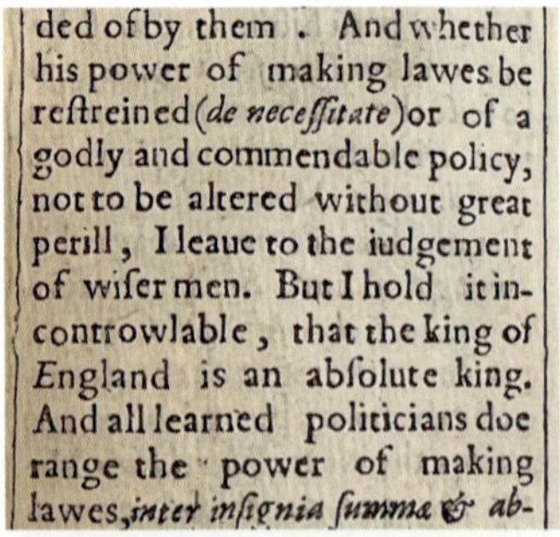
ded of by them . And whether his power of making lawes be reſtreined (*de neceſſitate*) or of a godly and commendable policy, not to be altered without great perill, I leaue to the iudgement of wiſer men. But I hold it incontrowlable, that the king of England is an abſolute king. And all learned politicians doe range the power of making lawes, *inter inſignia ſumma & ab-*

Ex coll. Karolyne & Bryan A. Garner

An excerpt from the objectionable entry on "prerogative."

common-law and civil-law definitions. Just a few definitions were enough to prove incendiary. In the entry for *prerogative*, he asserted that the king had absolute power above the law, with the Parliament merely serving the monarchy: "He is above the Law by his absolute power . . . . The king is above the Parlement, that is the positive lawes of his kingdome, or els that he is not an absolute king." For reasons that may seem obscure today, the common-law lawyers were also angered by Cowell's defense of the jurisdiction of the ecclesiastical and admiralty courts. Sir Edward Coke, chief justice of the common pleas, called him "Dr Cowheel" because he resented slighting comments about his hero, Sir Thomas Littleton, whose 300-year-old work on tenures would soon serve as Coke's main authority for the first volume of his *Institutes of the Lawes of England* (1628). Some believed that Cowell's real project was to demonstrate that the civil law is superior to the common law.

"One thing I have done in this booke, whereof, because it may seeme straunge to some, I thinke to yeld my reasons: and that is the inserting not onely of words belonging to the art of the Lawe, but of any other also, that I thought obscure, of what sort soever; as Fish, Cloth, Spices, Drugs, Furres, and such like. For in this I follow the example of our Civilians, that have thought it their part to expound any thing they could meete with in their walke." (Preface.)

For more than a month, the government was paralyzed as controversy raged over *The Interpreter*. Privately, King James was sympathetic to Cowell and agreed with most of his political ideas. But he realized that the hullabaloo wasn't waning, and the fiscal demands he was then making on Parliament were in jeopardy. So he used his prerogative power to defuse some of the fury and to quell any further debate about the book.

After his Privy Council hearing, Cowell was committed to the custody of an alderman. By some accounts, his *Interpreter* was ordered to be burned by the public hangman on 26 March 1610. (Marke 1965:311–12; Green 1996:190–91.) Others have disputed the burning. (Hicks 1921:44.) Still others have said that copies of the book were merely "recalled." (Cohen 2003:52.) By May 1611, Cowell had resigned his professorship. Two months later he died.

One commentator jocularly suggested that *The Interpreter* "was not allowed to interpret long." (Williams 1890:6.) That isn't really true. According to the most illustrious 20th-century historian of English law, William Holdsworth, that "it long remained the standard Dictionary of English law can be seen from the fact that in 1727 it had passed through some seven editions." (Holdsworth 1972 5:22.)

Ex coll. Karolyne & Bryan A. Garner

Some later editions of Cowell.

Though it appeared only three years after Cawdrey's *Table Alphabeticall*, Cowell's *Interpreter* stands in marked contrast: its entries are maturely developed and fully elaborated, as opposed to the elementary one-line synonyms characteristic of Cawdrey. Cowell gives alternative spellings, citations to authorities, quotations of authorities, distinctions of near-synonyms, and cross-references to related terms.

He is also considerably more encyclopedic in his treatment. Consider two of dozens of possible examples:

Cawdrey (1604)	Cowell (1607)
compromise, **agreement, made by parties chosen on either side.**	*Compromis, (compromissum)* is a mutuall promise of two or more parties at difference, to referre the ending of their controversies, to the arbitrament and equitie of one or more arbitratours. *West* defineth it thus, *parte. 2. Symbol. titulo Compromise. sect. pri.* A compromise or submission (*arbitrium, compromissum, submissio*) is the faculty or power of pronouncing sentence betweene persons at controversie, given to arbitratours by the parties mutuall private consent, without publique authority.
amercement, **fine, or penalty.**	*Amerciament (amerciamentum)* signifieth the pecuniary punishment of an offendor against the King or other Lord in his court, that is found to be (*in misericordia*) i. to have offended, and to stand at the mercie of the King or Lord. There seemeth to be a difference between amerciaments and fines, *Kitchin fol.* 214. And I have heard comon Lawyers say, that fines, as they are taken for punishments, be punishments certaine, which grow expressly from some statute, and that amerciaments be such, as be arbitrably imposed by affeerors. This is in some sort confirmed by *Kitchin fol.* 78. in these words: (*l'amerciament est afire per pares.*) *M. Manwood* in his first part of Forest lawes. *pag.* 166, seemeth to make another difference, as if he would inferre an amerciament to be a more easie, or more mercifull penaltie, and a fine more sharpe and grievous. Take his wordes: If the pledges for such a trespasse (saith he) do appeare by common summons, but not the defendant himself: then the pledges shall be imprisoned, for that default of the defendant: but otherwise it is, if the defendant himself do appeare, and be ready in Court before the Lord Iustice in *eyre*, to receive his iudgment, and to pay his fine. But if such pledges do make default, in that case the pledges shall be amerced, but not fined, &c. The author of the new tearmes of lawe [Rastell], saith, that amerciament is most properly a penalty assessed, by the peeres or equals of the partie amercied for the offence himselfe upon the mercie of the Lord. Who also maketh mention of an amerciament royal, and defineth it to be a pecuniary punishment laid upon a Sheriffe, Coroner, or such like Officer of the kings, amercied by Iustices for his offence. See *Misericordia*.

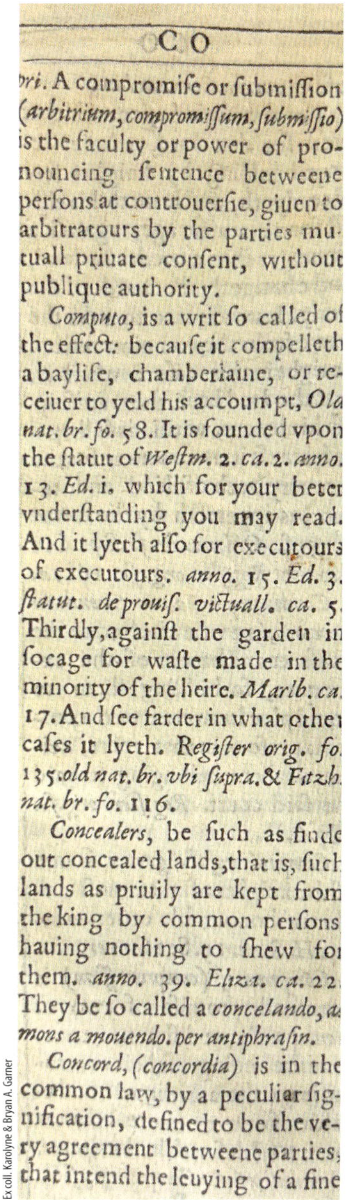

C O

pri. A compromiſe or ſubmiſſion (*arbitrium, compromiſſum, ſubmiſſio*) is the faculty or power of pronouncing ſentence betweene perſons at controuerſie, giuen to arbitratours by the parties mutuall priuate conſent, without publique authority.

Computo, is a writ ſo called of the effect: becauſe it compelleth a baylife, chamberlaine, or receiuer to yeld his accoumpt, *Old nat. br. fo.* 58. It is founded vpon the ſtatut of *Weſtm.* 2. *ca.* 2. *anno.* 13. *Ed.* 1. which for your beter vnderſtanding you may read. And it lyeth alſo for executours of executours. *anno.* 15. *Ed.* 3. *ſtatut. de prouiſ. victuall. ca.* 5. Thirdly, againſt the garden in ſocage for waſte made in the minority of the heire. *Marlb. ca.* 17. And ſee farder in what other caſes it lyeth. *Regiſter orig. fo.* 135. *old nat. br. vbi ſupra.* & *Fitzh. nat. br. fo.* 116.

Concealers, be ſuch as finde out concealed lands, that is, ſuch lands as priuily are kept from the king by common perſons hauing nothing to ſhew for them. *anno.* 39. *Eliza. ca.* 22. They be ſo called *a concelando, as mons a mouendo. per antiphraſin.*

Concord, (concordia) is in the common law, by a peculiar ſignification, defined to be the very agreement betweene parties, that intend the leuying of a fine

This column begins with the latter part of the entry for *compromis*.

In short, Cowell's may have been the second stand-alone English dictionary—if we disqualify Rastell (1523) and Skene (1597)—but it represented an unusual degree of sophistication in comparison with Cawdrey's rudimentary synonymy.

"My time imparted to these studies, being but stolne from mine emploiments of greater necessitie, I cannot make the hast I desire, or perhaps that the discourse may deserve. Wherefore until my leisure may serve to performe that, I intreate you lovingly to accept this." (Preface.)

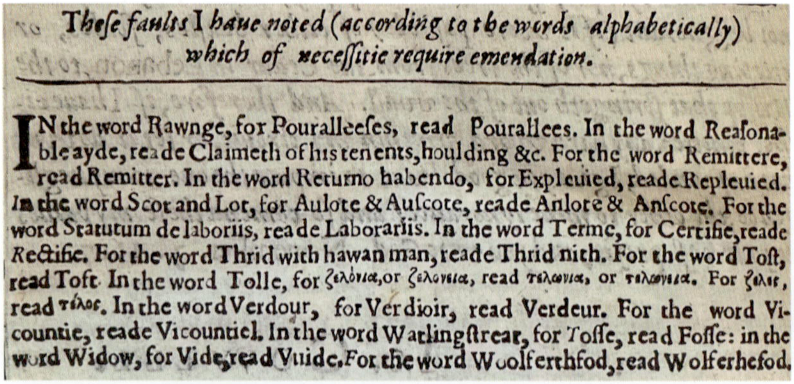

Theſe faults I haue noted (according to the words alphabetically) which of neceſſitie require emendation.

IN the word Rawnge, for Pouralleeſes, read Pourallees. In the word Reaſonable ayde, reade Claimeth of his tenents, houlding &c. For the word Remittere, read Remitter. In the word Returno habendo, for Expleuied, reade Repleuied. In the word Scot and Lot, for Aulote & Auſcote, reade Anlote & Anſcote. For the word Statutum de laboriis, reade Laborariis. In the word Terme, for Certifie, reade Rectifie. For the word Thrid with hawan man, reade Thrid nith. For the word Toſt, read Toft. In the word Tolle, for ζελόνια, or ζελονεια, read τελωνια, or τελωνεια. For ζελος, read τέλος. In the word Verdour, for Verdioir, read Verdeur. For the word Vicountie, reade Vicountiel. In the word Watlingſtreat, for Toſſe, read Foſſe: in the word Widow, for Vide, read Vuide. For the word Woolferthfod, read Wolferhefod.

Ex coll. Karolyne & Bryan A. Garner

The front matter in Cowell's first edition included errata.

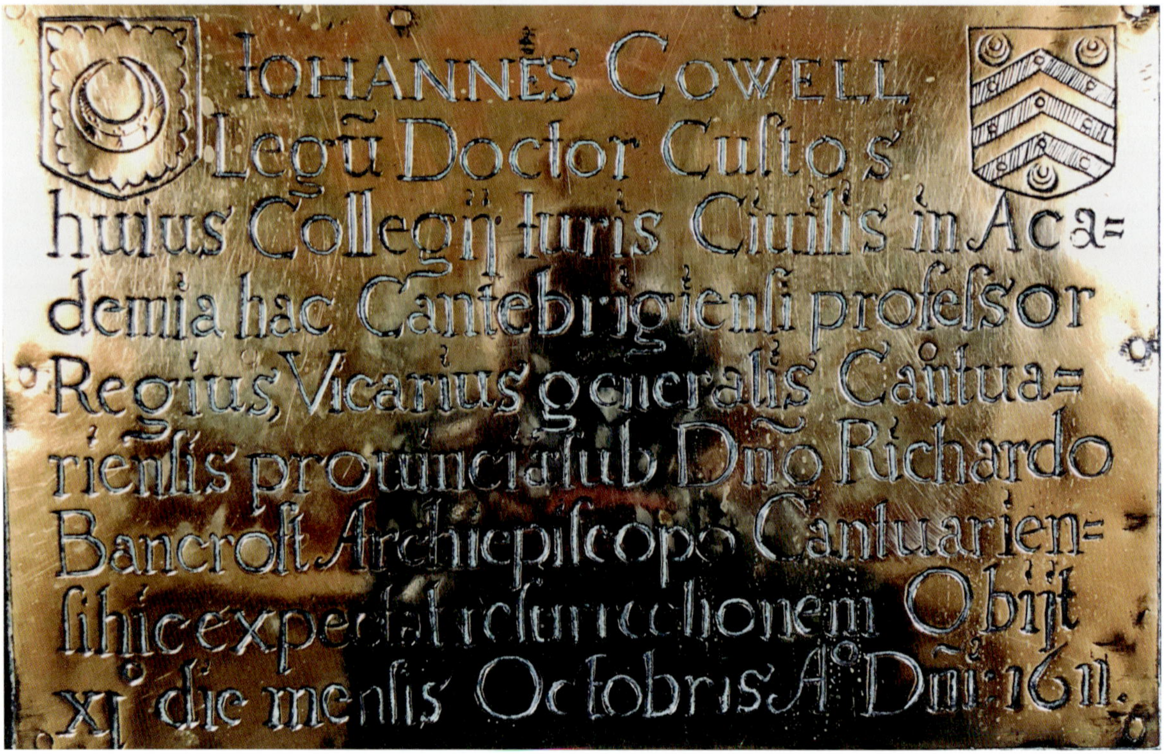

John Cowell's grave marker in the aisle of Trinity Hall Chapel, Cambridge, England.

10

Thomas Wilson

Surprisingly Prescient

Wilson, Thomas. ***A Christian Dictionarie, Opening the signification of the chiefe wordes dispersed generally through Holie Scriptures of the Old and New Testament, tending to increase Christian knowledge.*** **London: W. Iaggard, 1612.**

WILSON (1562/63–1622), born in Durham, entered Queen's College, Oxford, in November 1581 and graduated with his BA in 1584 and his MA in 1586. In the latter year, he became rector of St. George the Martyr in Canterbury. From there he began a literary career, publishing sermons, catechisms, and other theological works. Wilson typically delivered at least three sermons a week, often preaching daily. He had a prodigious memory, retaining what he read and making use of it in his writing.

"If I be longer in the explanation of some words, then [sic] the Nature of a Dictionary wil beare, or do open some wordes, which (to some) may seeme needlesse; impute it eyther unto the waightinesse of the things, which being darke and important, neede opening; or unto the dulnesse of common Capacities, which see little in divine matters; or if ye will, to want of dexterity in my selfe, who have been but of late acquainted with this Trade." (Generall Preface.)

Wilson's big *Christian Dictionarie*, appearing just eight years after Cawdrey's historic work, is the first ecclesiastical dictionary in English. Accustomed as he was to theological apologetics, he likewise engaged in a kind of lexicographic apologetics. The title page promises a dictionary "to increase Christian knowledge": the way to salvation is through the Bible, and the way to the Bible is through the dictionary. It is "a great hinderance to the understanding of things," he explained,

> when words, which betoken and signify things, are not understanded; and a great furtheraunce, when they be understood. Wherefore, as it is necessary in Grammar Schooles, that Children which learne French, Latine, or Greeke, have their Dictionaries and Lexicons allowed them, to enterpret such harde and strange wordes, by knowledge whereof, things to bee learned, become more easie; and their labours, which have composed such Bookes, are much to be commended. [Preface.]

The Generall Preface,
To the Christian Reader.

Ex coll. Karolyne & Bryan A. Garner

"I resolved . . . to publish a great part of this my Christian Dictionarie, which with much and long labour, and not without some fruite (I hope) to the Godly Professors (for whose sake and good, cheefely, I meant it) I am sure, with much gaine of knowledge, and increase of iudgement to my selfe, I have at length (as I could) finished it." (Dedication.)

Ex coll. Karolyne & Bryan A. Garner

Contemporary vellum binding on the 1612 book.

"The end of Teaching, is to cause others to learn; & to learne, is to know things to be, what they are. Now of things to be knowne, words are notes or markes, leading the minde to the comprehension of things." (Generall Preface.)

The result was an unusual combination of purely lexical information and explanations of biblical allusions accompanied by scriptural citations to lead the faithful to the appropriate passages:

Man of death.	sig:	One guilty or worthy of death: 1. *Kinges* 2, 26. *For thou art a man of death.*
Man of Beliall.	sig:	A wicked man. 1. Kings 21, 13. And there came to him wicked men, or men of Beliall.
a Man of renowne.	sig:	A man that is very famous and renowned. *Gen.* 6, 4. *They were men of renowne.*
Manna.	sig: pro	Bread given from heaven, by the ministrie of Angels. *Iohn* 6, 32. *Our Fathers ate Manna.* Psal. 78, 25. *Man did eate the Bred of Angels.* This is corporall and Typicall *Manna.* 2 Christ Iesus. *Revel.* 2, 17. *To him that overcomes, will I give the hidden Manna.* Christ is called Manna, because he is the bread that came downe from heaven, the onely soule-food. And he is called, hidden Manna, because no man can have this bread by Nature; and it is revealed to none but to Gods children.
Manifest.	sig:	Easie to be known, being alwayes open to every mans understanding. *Gal.* 5, 19. *The works of the flesh be manifest.* 2 Declared, and made knowne, being kept secret before in the Counsel of God. 2. *Tim.* 1, 9. *But now is made manifest.* 1. Tim. 3, 16.

No one in 1612 could be ignorant of just how urgent proper interpretations were, both for the individual believer's soul and for the peace of the nation: the Protestant Reformation was still very much a live question. Protestant clerics, unlike most Roman Catholics, trusted lay readers to interpret Scripture themselves without relying on priests to interpret it. But because the burden of proper interpretation had been shifted from the clergy to the faithful, readers needed expert advice in the form of reference books. Wilson promised to be helpful without being partisan. As he explained, "Not onely wordes, which beare difference betweene Protestants and Papists, are written downe and cleared in this Booke, but also there is a taste given, of the oddes and difference it selfe, in most points of Controversie, between us and them."

Like Cowell five years before, Wilson showed a much more bounteous style of defining than the exiguous entries in Cawdrey, who was often content to define a word with a single synonym. Not so Wilson. Consider these entries of identical terms:

Cawdrey (1604)	Wilson (1612)
election, **choise**.	**election** A choosing of some out of many, as if out of a great heape of Flowers or Hearbes, Golde, or precious Stone, or other things, ye would gather the chiefe. Now, where some are chosen, others are refused; and where some be refused, all bee not chosen. 2. The choosing of some, to obtaine salvation by Christ, according to the good pleasure of GOD. 3. The choosing or appointing some unto publicke functions, by voices, or by a common consent. *Acts* 14, 23. *When they had ordained Elders by election in every Church*. Iohn 6, 70. 4. The elect themselves. *Rom.*II, 7. *The Election hath obtained it.*
magistrate, **gouernour**	**magistrate** A person, greater then others, being above others in authority and power. Rom. 13, 3. Magistrates are to be feared. Of Magistrates, some bee cheefe, as the King: Others, be Governors under him, all being sent for the punishment of evil dooers, and for the praise of them that do well. 1. Pet. 2, 14. Unto the chiefe Magistrate, who is called the King, all persons (without exception or exemption) are to submit in all causes. Rom. 13, 1.
testament, **last will**	**testament** That which we commonly call a mans wil, and appointment for the bestowing of his goodes amongst his Children, or Kindred and Friends. Gal. 3, 15. *Though it be but a Mans Testament. Heb.* 9, 16, 17. 2. An appointment or agreement between God and Man, touching free salvation by faith in Christ. Math. 26, 28. *For this is my blood of the New Testament.* This is called a Testament, because it was ratified and confirmed by the death and blood-shed of him, who made the Covenant or agreement with us; to wit, of Christ, and containeth (as it were) his last will written downe.

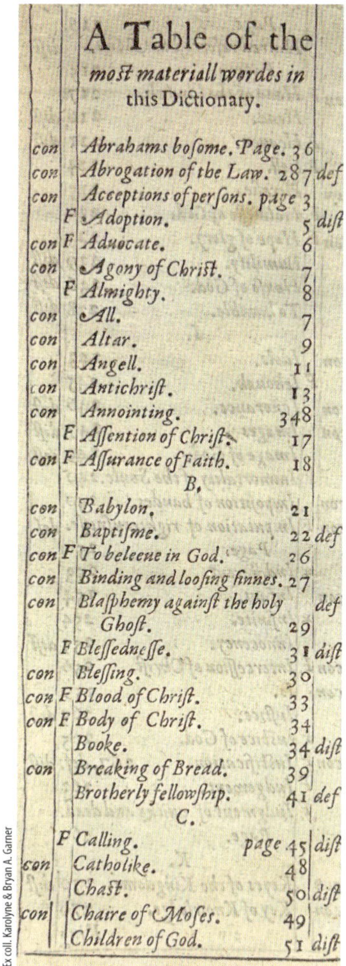
A Table of the

moſt materiall wordes in

this Dictionary.

con		*Abrahams boſome. Page.*	36	
con		*Abrogation of the Law.*	287	*def*
con		*Acceptions of perſons. page*	3	
	F	*Adoption.*	5	*diſt*
con	F	*Aduocate.*	6	
con		*Agony of Chriſt.*	7	
	F	*Almighty.*	8	
con		*All.*	7	
con		*Altar.*	9	
con		*Angell.*	11	
con		*Antichriſt.*	13	
con		*Annointing.*	348	
	F	*Aſſention of Chriſt.*	17	
con	F	*Aſſurance of Faith.*	18	
		B.		
con		*Babylon.*	21	
con		*Baptiſme.*	22	*def*
con	F	*To beleeue in God.*	26	
con		*Binding and looſing ſinnes.*	27	
con		*Blaſphemy againſt the holy Ghoſt.*	29	*def*
	F	*Bleſſedneſſe.*	31	*diſt*
con		*Bleſſing.*	30	
con	F	*Blood of Chriſt.*	33	
con	F	*Body of Chriſt.*	34	
		Booke.	34	*diſt*
con		*Breaking of Bread.*	39	
		Brotherly fellowſhip.	41	*def*
		C.		
	F	*Calling.* page	45	*diſt*
con		*Catholike.*	48	
		Chaſt.	50	*diſt*
con		*Chaire of Moſes.*	49	
		Children of God.	51	*diſt*

Ex coll. Karolyne & Bryan A. Garner

In this unusual table (part of the front matter), *con* = controversial word, *F* = fundamental, *def* = definition, and *dist* = distinctions.

In Wilson, entries then follow for Old Testament and New Testament (in chronological order, not alphabetical!).

"If in the draught . . . of this whole Dictionary, I have failed in any thing (as no doubt but I have, being but a man; and therefore subiect to error, from which no Booke is priviledged, saving the book of Bookes,) I do earnestly entreate thee to cover my slips by love, eyther amending them, or admonishing mee of them: doing unto me, as in the like case thy selfe wouldest bee done unto." (Preface Before the Table.)

These comparative entries illustrate several points. First, they show once again the extremely rudimentary nature of Cawdrey. Second, they show that Wilson often included nonreligious meanings before more specialized religious ones. Third, they mark perhaps the earliest instance of enumerating senses—and Wilson shows himself to be a splitter just eight years after what is putatively the first English dictionary. Fourth, Wilson includes plentiful citations, as well as illustrative quotations. Finally, despite his copiousness, Wilson tends to avoid long, encyclopedic discursiveness; even when he becomes explanatory rather than purely definitional, he sticks to the point and remains relatively succinct.

In all the literature relating to dictionaries, this book is perhaps the most overlooked and underappreciated. Wilson might have been lucky to be overlooked in his time: what he writes under *magistrate*, in the last sentence, might have gotten his book banned and himself imprisoned—like Cowell. He seems to have been fortunate that the temporal authorities paid no attention.

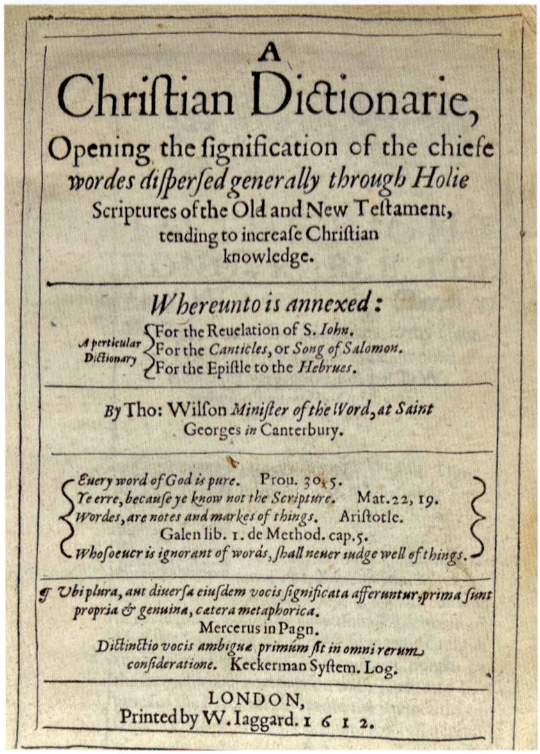

A
Chriſtian Dictionarie,
Opening the ſignification of the chiefe
wordes diſperſed generally through Holie
Scriptures of the Old and New Teſtament,
tending to increaſe Chriſtian
knowledge.

Whereunto is annexed:

A perticular Dictionary For the Reuelation of S. *Iohn*.
For the *Canticles*, or *Song of Salomon*.
For the Epiſtle to the *Hebrues*.

By Tho: Wilſon *Miniſter of the Word, at Saint* Georges *in* Canterbury.

Euery word of God is pure. Prou. 30. 5.
Ye erre, becauſe ye know not the Scripture. Mat. 22. 19.
Wordes, are notes and markes of things. Ariſtotle.
Galen lib. 1. de Method. cap. 5.
Whoſoeuer is ignorant of words, ſhall neuer iudge well of things.

¶ *Vbi plura, aut diuerſa eiuſdem vocis ſignificata afferuntur, prima ſunt propria & genuina, cætera metaphorica.*
Mercerus in Pagn.
Diſtinctio vocis ambiguæ primùm ſit in omni rerum conſideratione. Keckerman Syſtem. Log.

LONDON,
Printed by W. Iaggard. 1612.

Ex coll. Karolyne & Bryan A. Garner

11

John Bullokar
The English Expositor

B., I. [John Bullokar]. ***An English Expositor: Teaching the interpretation of the hardest words used in our Language. With sundry Explications, Descriptions, and Discourses. By I.B. Doctor of Phisicke.*** **London: John Legatt, 1616. 2d ed. 1621. 3d ed. 1641. 4th ed. 1654. 5th ed. 1656.**

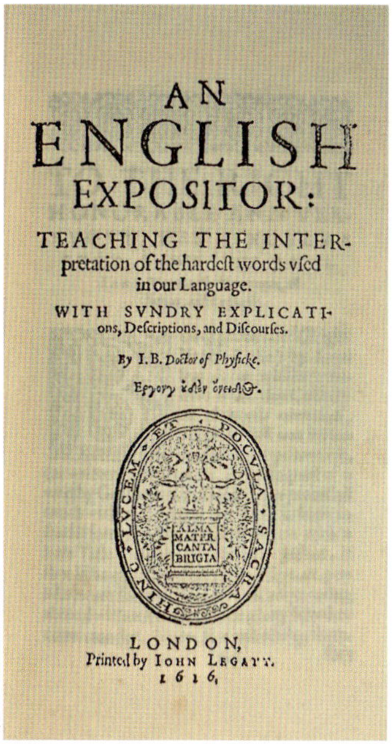
AN ENGLISH EXPOSITOR: TEACHING THE INTERpretation of the hardeſt words vſed in our Language. WITH SVNDRY EXPLICATIons, Deſcriptions, and Diſcourſes. By I.B. Doctor of Phyſicke.

LONDON, Printed by IOHN LEGATT. 1616.

BULLOKAR (BAP. 1574–1627) was born into a Catholic family in Chichester, Sussex, the third child of the grammarian and spelling reformer William Bullokar (ca. 1531–1609) and his wife, Elizabeth (d. 1608). In 1581, his father promised to write a dictionary, but he never did so; William was probably the "worthy gentleman" who urged John to do so. Early in his adult life, he was persecuted for his faith: several times, he and his wife were haled into court for nonattendance at church, and several times were excommunicated from the Church of England. They therefore moved houses within Sussex with some frequency. Bullokar was also subjected to legal proceedings for being an unlicensed schoolmaster. He moved abroad for a time and, in 1612, obtained his MD in Caen, France.

"It is easier (all know) to find faults, then [sic] to mende them, and easier to mend faults in another's worke already written, then to write any new worke free from all fault. If therefore any fault finder, or over curious Criticke (for from the best learned I expect best usage) shall to show his skill grow captious and quarrell at my interpretations, I will desire him to forbeare bitternesse, and temper a while his choler, till having laide this worke aside, hee travell himself in the same or some other new argument." (Preface.)

Meanwhile, though, he had already entered his *English Expositor* in the Stationers' register in 1610. The book was dedicated to Jane, Viscountess Montague, but it wouldn't be published for another six years. Bullokar modestly declared that it was originally intended for private use, that he had barely had the leisure to examine it in the seven years before its publication. Yet it contained innovations: it had much greater depth than Cawdrey, with greater coverage of classically derived technical terminology from various fields, and it was the first dictionary to mark archaisms (with an asterisk). It contained nearly twice as many entries as Cawdrey's, and its definitions were more expansive. It truly established the category of the hard-word dictionary that would dominate the 17th century. Bullokar borrowed from a variety of sources, including Cawdrey's *Table Alphabeticall* and Thomas's Latin–English dictionaries.

"*Expositour*. An expounder or interpreter."

A 1695 edition.

"*Locust*. A great Flye or Grashopper with long legges, breeding in India, and other hot Countries. There are two kindes of them: One with winges, not good to be eaten, and the other without winges, which the inhabitants use for food."

In the end, the *English Expositor* was much more durable than Cawdrey's *Table*. Early in its life it was drawn on by competitors such as Henry Cockeram. New editions continued to appear all the way into the late 18th century: a "19th edition" appeared in Dublin in 1775.

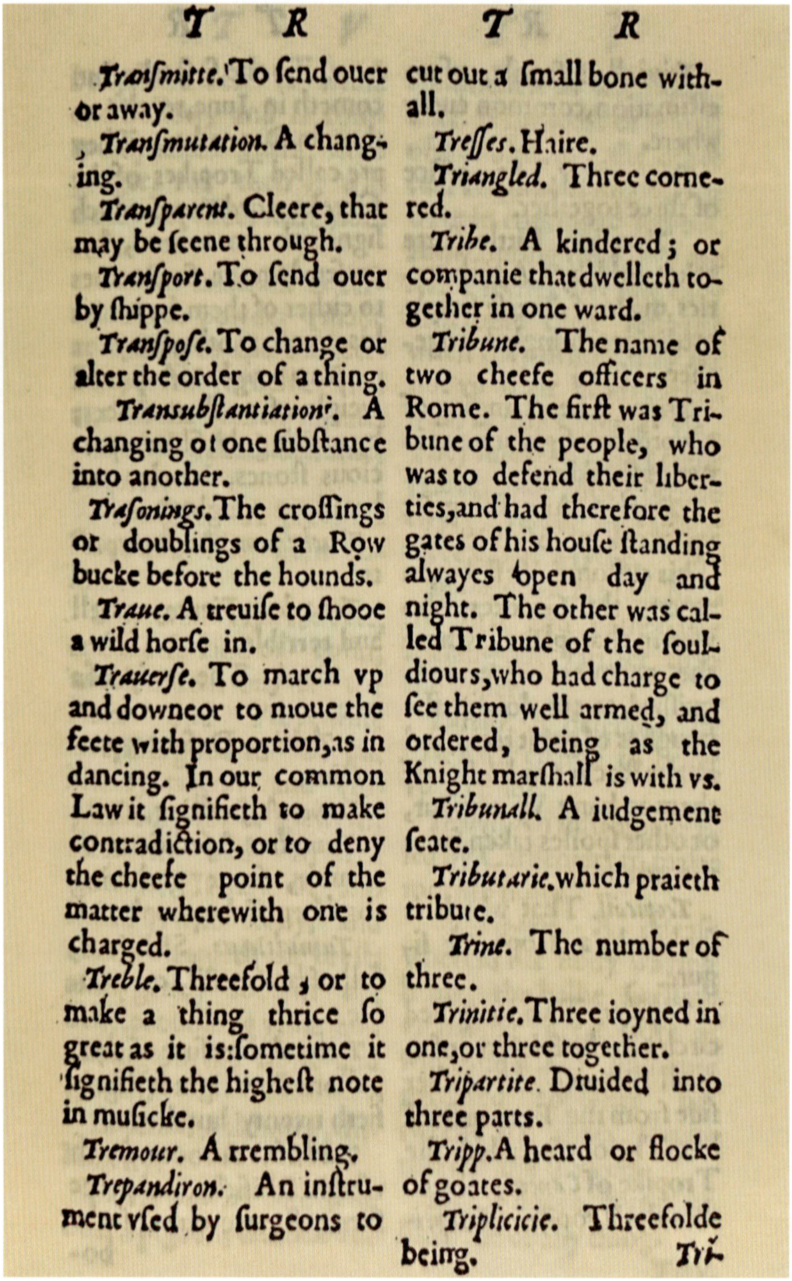

T R T R

Tranſmitte. To ſend ouer or away.

Tranſmutation. A changing.

Tranſparent. Cleere, that may be ſeene through.

Tranſport. To ſend ouer by ſhippe.

Tranſpoſe. To change or alter the order of a thing.

Tranſubſtantiation. A changing of one ſubſtance into another.

Traſonings. The croſſings or doublings of a Row bucke before the hounds.

Traue. A treuiſe to ſhooe a wild horſe in.

Trauerſe. To march vp and downe or to moue the feete with proportion, as in dancing. In our common Law it ſignifieth to make contradiction, or to deny the cheefe point of the matter wherewith one is charged.

Treble. Threefold; or to make a thing thrice ſo great as it is: ſometime it ſignifieth the higheſt note in muſicke.

Tremour. A trembling.

Trepandiron. An inſtrument vſed by ſurgeons to cut out a ſmall bone withall.

Treſſes. Haire.

Triangled. Three cornered.

Tribe. A kindered; or companie that dwelleth together in one ward.

Tribune. The name of two cheefe officers in Rome. The firſt was Tribune of the people, who was to defend their liberties, and had therefore the gates of his houſe ſtanding alwayes open day and night. The other was called Tribune of the ſouldiours, who had charge to ſee them well armed, and ordered, being as the Knight marſhall is with vs.

Tribunall. A iudgement ſeate.

Tributarie. which praieth tribute.

Trine. The number of three.

Trinitie. Three ioyned in one, or three together.

Tripartite. Diuided into three parts.

Tripp. A heard or flocke of goates.

Triplicitie. Threefolde being.

Tri-

From the first edition.

12

John Minsheu
Amplified—Yet Diminished

Minsheu, John. ***ΗΓΕΜΩΝ ΕΙΣ ΤΑΣ ΓΛΩΣΣΑΣ· id est, Ductor in Linguas . . . The Guide into the Tongues. With their agreement and consent one with another, as also their Etymologies, that is, the reasons and Derivations of all or the most part of wordes, in these eleven Languages, viz. 1. English. 2. British or Welsh. 3. Low Dutch. 4. High Dutch. 5. French. 6. Italian. 7. Spanish. 8. Portuguez. 9. Latine. 10. Greeke. 11. Hebrew, &c.*** **London: John Brown, 1617. 2d ed. London: John Haviland, 1625.**

Courtesy of Rulon-Miller Books

The first edition (1617).

MINSHEU'S *GUIDE INTO TONGUES*—the first polyglot dictionary with English headwords—was a monumental undertaking based on an analysis of 11 languages. English headwords are followed by Welsh, Dutch, German, French, Italian, Spanish, Portuguese, Latin, Greek, and Hebrew equivalents, making a large folio of more than 500 pages. To compile the work, Minsheu began in Oxford in 1610, employing native speakers of these languages to read through the "best authors" for material. Senior members of the University endorsed his project, calling it an excellent and rare piece of work worthy of publication. Later that year, he moved to London, where he received the support of William Camden, the historian and topographer, as well as two barristers who gave financial assistance for printing the work. Once the book was published, Minsheu became an itinerant peddler of it in various English towns, using promotional leaflets.

By 1623, Minsheu had disposed of the first edition and embarked on a second, which was published in 1626 and reissued in 1627. By then, he was deaf, "decayed" (as he declared in his last leaflet), and in debt. He died and was buried at All Hallows, London Wall, in April 1627, leaving several young orphans. The Stationers' Company, which had earlier denied Minsheu any support for his publications, now made amends and donated the profits of several publications to Minsheu's eldest son, Edward.

SEX LIN-
GVARVM, LA-
tinæ, Gallicæ, Hispa-
nicæ, Italicæ, Angli-
cæ & Teutonicæ, diluci
dissimũ Dictionarium,
mirum quàm utile, ne di
cam necessarium om-
nibus linguarum
studiosis.

OMNIA (optime Lector)
bona fide recognita casti
gataq; deprehen-
des.

TIGVRI APVD FRO-
schou. M. D. LXVII.

Ex coll. Karolyne & Bryan A. Garner

Antedating Minsheu, this polyglot synonym book appeared in 1567. Minsheu's novelty was placing English first.

Ex coll. Karolyne & Bryan A. Garner

The second edition (1625).

"John Minsheu was the first author to publish a book by subscription, and his *Guide into Tongues*, 1617, was the first book to print a list of subscribers." (Muir 1947:157.)

Called a "false knave" in 1591 and a "rogue" years later by Ben Jonson, Minsheu always had something questionable about him. He plagiarized with abandon, and it is said that "it is unlikely that [he] had much success with his teaching methods." (*ODNB*.) Still, with incessant, grinding labor in the face of unrelenting hardship, he produced a monumental dictionary that was relied on by successors for several generations. Because of its English headwords, it is of great value in the study of 17th-century English.

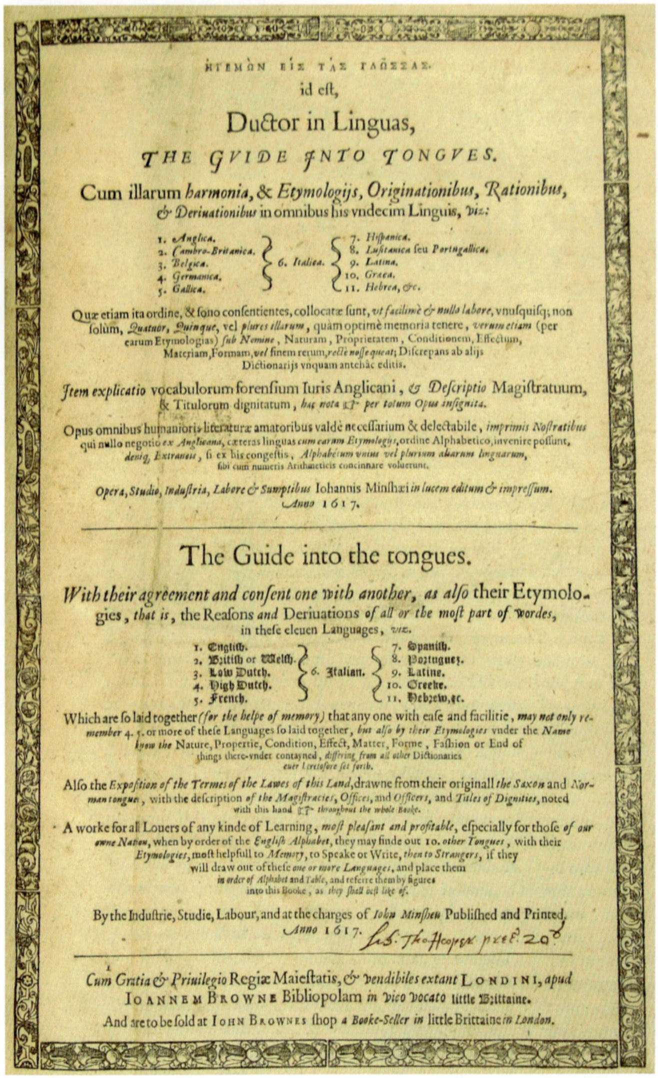

ΗΓΕΜΩΝ ΕΙΣ ΤΑΣ ΓΛΩΣΣΑΣ.
id eſt,
Ductor in Linguas,
THE GVIDE INTO TONGVES.
Cum illarum *harmonia*, & *Etymologijs, Originationibus, Rationibus, & Deriuationibus* in omnibus his vndecim Linguis, *viz:*

1. *Anglica.* 2. *Cambro-Britanica.* 3. *Belgica.* 4. *Germanica.* 5. *Gallica.* 6. *Italica.* 7. *Hiſpanica.* 8. *Luſitanica* ſeu *Portugallica.* 9. *Latina.* 10. *Graeca.* 11. *Hebrea, &c.*

Quæ etiam ita ordine, & ſono conſentientes, collocatæ ſunt, *vt faciliimè & nullo labore*, vnuſquiſq; non ſolùm, *Quatuor, Quinque*, vel *plures illarum*, quàm optimè memoria tenere, *verum etiam* (per earum Etymologias) *ſub Nomine*, Naturam, Proprietatem, Conditionem, Effectum, Materiam, Formam, *vel* finem rerum, *rectè noſſe queat*; Diſcrepans ab alijs Dictionarijs vnquam antehàc editis.

Item explicatio vocabulorum forenſium Iuris Anglicani, & *Deſcriptio* Magiſtratuum, & Titulorum dignitatum, *hac nota* ☞ *per totum Opus inſignita.*

Opus omnibus humanioris literaturæ amatoribus valdè neceſſarium & delectabile, *imprimis Noſtratibus* qui nullo negotio *ex Anglicana*, cæteras linguas *cum earum Etymologijs*, ordine Alphabetico, invenire poſſunt, *deniq, Extraneis*, ſi ex his congeſtis, *Alphabetum vnius vel plurium aliarum linguarum*, ſibi cum numeris Arithmeticis concinnare voluerunt.

Opera, Studio, Induſtria, Labore & Sumptibus Iohannis Minſhæi *in lucem editum & impreſſum.*
Anno 1617.

The Guide into the tongues.

With their agreement and conſent one with another, as alſo their Etymologies, *that is*, the Reaſons *and* Deriuations *of all or the moſt part of wordes*, in theſe eleuen Languages, *viz.*

1. Engliſh. 2. Britiſh or Welſh. 3. Low Dutch. 4. High Dutch. 5. French. 6. Italian. 7. Spaniſh. 8. Portuguez. 9. Latine. 10. Greeke. 11. Hebrew, &c.

Which are ſo laid together *(for the helpe of memory)* that any one with eaſe and facilitie, *may not only remember* 4. 5. or more of theſe Languages ſo laid together, *but alſo by their Etymologies* vnder the *Name know the* Nature, Propertie, Condition, Effect, Matter, Forme, Faſhion or End of things there-vnder contayned, *differing from all other* Dictionaries *euer heretofore ſet forth.*

Alſo the *Expoſition of the Termes of the Lawes of this Land*, drawne from their originall *the Saxon* and *Norman tongue*, with the deſcription *of the Magiſtracies, Offices*, and *Officers*, and *Titles of Dignities*, noted with this hand ☞ *throughout the whole Booke.*

A worke for all Louers of any kinde of Learning, *moſt pleaſant and profitable*, eſpecially for thoſe *of our owne Nation*, when by order of the *Engliſh Alphabet*, they may finde out 10. *other Tongues*, with their *Etymologies*, moſt helpfull to *Memory*, to Speake or Write, *then to Strangers*, if they will draw out of theſe *one or more Languages*, and place them *in order of Alphabet* and *Table*, and referre them by figures into this Booke, as *they ſhall beſt like of.*

By the Induſtrie, Studie, Labour, and at the charges of *Iohn Minſheu* Publiſhed and Printed, *Anno* 1617.

Cum Gratia & Priuilegio Regiæ Maieſtatis, *& vendibiles extant* LONDINI, *apud* IOANNEM BROWNE Bibliopolam *in vico vocato* little Brittaine.

And are to be ſold at IOHN BROWNES ſhop *a Booke-Seller in* little Brittaine *in London.*

Courtesy of Rulon-Miller Books

13

Henry Cockeram

Inveterate Sesquipedalian

C[ockeram], H[enry]. *The English Dictionarie: or, An Interpreter of hard English Words. Enabling as well Ladies and Gentlewomen, young Schollers, Clarkes, Merchants, as also Strangers of any Nation, to the understanding of the more difficult authors already printed in our Language, and the more speedy attaining of an elegant perfection of the English tongue, both in reading, speaking and writing. Being a Collection of the choisest words contained in the Table Alphabeticall and English Expositor, and of some thousands of words never published by any heretofore. By H.C. Gent.* London: Edmund Weaver, 1623. 2d ed. 1626. 3d ed. 1631. 4th ed. 1632. 5th ed. 1637.

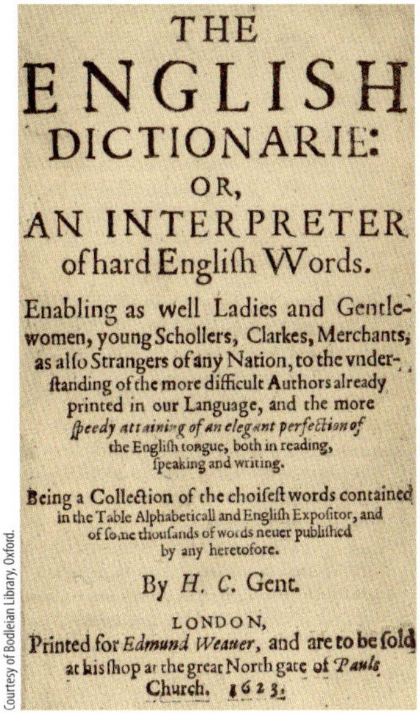

THE
ENGLISH
DICTIONARIE:
OR,
AN INTERPRETER
of hard Engliſh Words.
Enabling as well Ladies and Gentle-women, young Schollers, Clarkes, Merchants, as alſo Strangers of any Nation, to the vnder-ſtanding of the more difficult Authors already printed in our Language, and the more ſpeedy attaining of an elegant perfection of the Engliſh tongue, both in reading, ſpeaking and writing.
Being a Collection of the choiſeſt words contained in the Table Alphabeticall and Engliſh Expoſitor, and of ſome thouſands of words neuer publiſhed by any heretofore.
By H. C. Gent.
LONDON,
Printed for Edmund Weauer, and are to be ſold at his ſhop at the great North gate of Pauls Church. 1623.

Courtesy of Bodleian Library, Oxford.

Cockeram (fl. 1623–1658) of Exeter is known only as the author of this dictionary of English—the first fully English wordbook to use *dictionary* in its title. The first edition, published in the same year as Shakespeare's First Folio, contains six poems serving as blurbs—one of them by John Webster (ca. 1580–1632), the playwright who wrote *The Duchess of Malfi* and many other plays. Webster's stanza ends with this couplet:

> And I will adde this as thy friend, no Poet,
> Thou hast toild to purpose, and the event wil shew it.

If there are two traditions of prefaces in lexicography—the modest and the overweening—Cockeram's falls squarely into the latter category: "What any before me in this kinde have begun, I have not onely fully finished, but throughly perfected." His "method is plaine and easie, being alphabeticall, by which the capacity of the meanest may soone be inlightened."

The small octavo *Dictionarie* is intended for "Ladies and Gentlewomen, young Schollers, Clarkes, Merchants, as also Strangers of any Nation." It is divided into three major sections, listing (1) "the choicest words themselves now in use"; (2) vulgar words with their more

"Cockeram informed the curious that *soporate*, for example, means 'To bring asleepe.' The second half went in the opposite direction, translating 'common sense' into 'choicest words.' Someone who needed to speak about *dung* but blushed at using such a low word could turn to Cockeram and try out *ordure*; someone who feared *drawing near* was too common might find *appropinquation* the better choice. *Mighty* was good, but *armipotent* was better. And *rip, rowe,* and *rub out* were upgraded by Cockeram to *dilorigate, remigate,* and *deterge*." (Lynch 2016:143.)

Ex coll. Karolyne & Bryan A. Garner

The second edition of 1626.

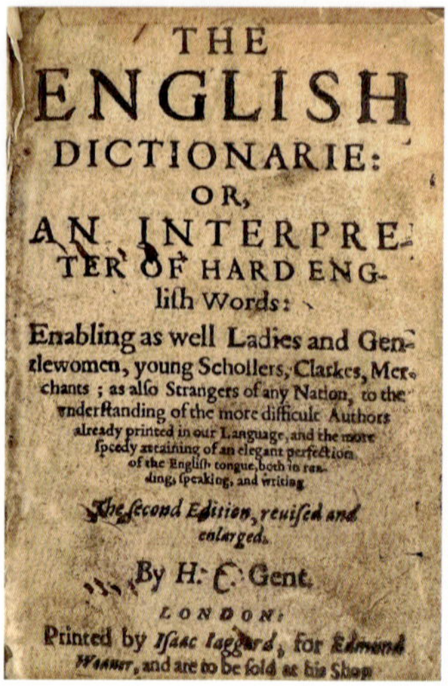

Ex coll. Karolyne & Bryan A. Garner

The second edition of 1626.

refined synonyms; and (3) "Gods and Goddesses, Giants and Devils, Monsters and Serpents, Birds and Beasts, Rivers, Fishes, Herbs, Stones, Trees, and the like." The title page of the first edition alludes to Cawdrey and Bullokar, describing the new book as "a Collection of the choisest words contained in the Table Alphabeticall and English Expositor, and of some thousands of words never published by any heretofore." The next eleven editions, ending in 1670, dropped any mention of these competitors.

Cockeram's claim of presenting unprecedented terminology was certainly true: he seemed to hunt after the recondite and recherché. His pages are full of esoteric "inkhornisms" like these:

- *Adhabitate.* To dwel nigh.
- *Celeripedian.* A swift foot man.
- *Degulate.* To consume in belly cheere.
- *Exosculation.* Kissing or bassing.
- *Inbulbitate.* To befilth one's breech.
- *Leconomancie.* Divination by water in a bason.
- *Obturbation.* A troubling.
- *Phylostorgie.* Parents love towards their children.
- *Rumigerate.* To spread tidings abroad.
- *Ustulate.* To curle or burn.
- *Xenodochie.* Hospitality.

The dictionary's structure is unusual. Most of it consists of two "bookes," each with its own alphabetical sequence, the first running from *abacted* and *abaction* to *zoograph* and *zygote* in 152 pages, followed immediately by the second running from *abate* and *abhominable* to *younger* and *youth* in 106 pages. The first presents the inkhorn terms as headwords and offers everyday words as definitions: "*Læmargie.* Gluttonie," "*Lætable.* Worthy to bee reioyced at," "*Lætificate.* To reioyce," "*Leuigate.* To polish smoothe, to plaine." Book two reverses the order: "Sleepines, *Somnolencie,*" "Slender, *Pergracill,*" "Slenderness, *Exilitie,*" "done by Sleight, *Prestigiously,*" "Slipperie, *Lubrick.*" The form, that is to say, is that of a bilingual dictionary, offering translations from one language to another, but here they're both English. It's an inkhorn–everyday, everyday–inkhorn dictionary. The structure suggests that Cockeram imagined two kinds of readers: one group decoding difficult words into plainer terms, and another seeking to encode their plain terms into something more sonorous.

Like other hard-word dictionaries, Cockeram's must be seen as part of the Renaissance battle between the Neologists, who exulted in enriching the language with new words, and the Purists, who (in the words of Sir John Cheke) wanted the English language "unmix't and unmangled with borrowing of other tunges." Both camps were mostly inhabited by Classicists: the Neologists welcomed foreignisms, and the Purists sought to curb these and to innovate, if at all, from Anglo-Saxon elements.

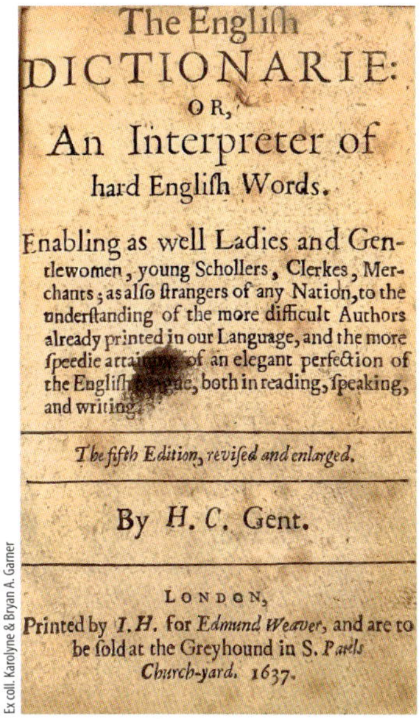

The Engliſh
DICTIONARIE:
OR,
An Interpreter of
hard Engliſh Words.

Enabling as well Ladies and Gentlewomen, young Schollers, Clerkes, Merchants; as alſo ſtrangers of any Nation, to the underſtanding of the more difficult Authors already printed in our Language, and the more ſpeedie atta[illegible] of an elegant perfection of the Engliſh [illegible], both in reading, ſpeaking, and writing.

The fifth Edition, reviſed and enlarged.

By *H. C.* Gent.

LONDON,
Printed by *I. H.* for *Edmund Weaver*, and are to be ſold at the Greyhound in S. *Pauls Church-yard.* 1637.

Ex coll. Karolyne & Bryan A. Garner

The fifth edition of 1637, still during Cockeram's lifetime.

Some have suggested that Cockeram was not just a recorder of words but a Neologist who included his own innovations in his dictionary. After all, the *OED* records 986 words for which the earliest known use is by Cockeram, of which 725 are labeled "rare." Some studies, however, have suggested that Cockeram was often carefully recording strange words that he had, in fact, encountered in literature and other wordbooks. Of the words listed above, for example, the *OED* now includes earlier uses of *exosculation* (1560), *lecanomancy* (so spelled—1610), *phylostorgy* (1607), and *xenodochy* (ca. 1550).

But even if, in retrospect, Cockeram can be seen as guilty of overindulging in linguistic experimentation, the fact remains that many words for which his is the first known use have turned out to be integral parts of the language. Among these (often bearing earlier senses) are *affiliation*, *cowboy*, *defecation*, *emasculation*, *liberate*, *lubricate*, *philanthropy*, *regularize*, *trimester*, and *venerate*. Granted, these are few and far between among the words for which he provides the first known use.

"It is a modern misunderstanding that the Jacobean compilers were searching after the exotic and bizarre, for our stylistic verdicts are pronounced with the benefit of hindsight. From their own vantage point these early dictionary makers were storing potential for enriching the language." (Schäfer 1989 2:2.)

In 1644, the anonymous author of the *Vindex Anglicus* (no. 14) called for the expunging of 49 inelegant inkhorn words from the English language, all of which were drawn from Cockeram's work. Some readers, in other words, were horrified by the outlandish terms they encountered. They may have worried that people might start using them to the detriment of good English style. Their fears proved that whether in the 17th century or the 21st, terms don't generally gain currency just because they're listed in a dictionary.

In the fullness of time, speakers and writers of English—to use some of Cockeram's words—just didn't have an *abarstic* (insatiable) appetite for the *bellitude* (beauty) of Cockeram's logophilic *castaldy* (stewardship). There was no need for Purists to band

Ex coll. Karolyne & Bryan A. Garner

The Huntington Press reprint of 1930.

"Though without sound linguistic knowledge, Cockeram attempts to distinguish among choice words of current usage, vulgar words, and refined and elegant terms. . . . [He] anticipates the idea of a standard of good usage." (Starnes & Noyes 1946:35.)

together to *complore* (bewail) or *crocitate* (croak) in mass *collachrymation* (joint weeping), for *ecasterly* (by my faith) the sesquipedality he was promoting wasn't really *fulcible* (supportable). When it comes to lexiphanicism, the *hesitude* (doubtfulness) of English speakers is *illutible* (incapable of being washed away). People know they might be thought *immorigerous* (rude) or even *inexcult* (socially unpolished) if they constantly use inkhornisms. Their listeners would doubtless *infrendiate* (gnash their teeth) over the *injucundity* (unpleasantness). The *insulsity* (senselessness) of such a *latitation* (concealment) of meaning would prevent any *lubency* (pleasure). *Manducate* (chew) on that awhile. The fact that one lexicographer burns the *mesonoxian* (midnight) oil doesn't mean that others will *nixuriate* (endeavor) to be similarly affected by *noctilucy* (the shining of the moon). Not to *obganiate* (repeat oneself tediously), but people don't *obligure* (feast) on or *obsaturate* (overfill) themselves on difficult words. So the Purists' *obstrigillation* (opposition) seems a matter of needless *obturbation* (bother). Let us *pensitate* (ponder) that we'll all be more *peraffable* (easy to converse with) if we refrain from *pernoctating* (spending whole nights) or *pervigilating* (keeping nightly vigils) for the purpose of memorizing hard words with which to *pupillate* (cry like a peacock). Let's have no *rixation* (quarrel) over that. The simple words of our language *saburrate* it (provide a ballast to it). Overlook this truth to your own *scaevity* (unluckiness). Let us then *sermocinate* (talk) simply, so as to *siderate* (bewilder) nobody. Let's have no *skiamachies* (sham fights) about it. We're not *supparasitating* (flattering) you when we say that we all *succolate* (bear on our shoulders) this responsibility. So let us *tripudiate* (jump for joy) as we all pledge *vetation* (a disallowance) or *vitation* (a shunning) of *vaniloquence* (babbling) and *vaniloquy* (same) suffused with verbal *xenodochy* (entertainment of strangers).

But let's be fair to Cockeram. In his preface, he was perfectly open about his inclusion of ludicrously difficult terminology that would never be encountered in everyday life: "I have also inserted . . . the *mocke-words* which are ridiculously used in our language . . . by . . . many who study rather to bee heard speake, than to understand themselues." (Sig. A4^{v}.) On the one hand, this view is lexicographically absurd if he did indeed *introduce* these words; on the other hand, it is sound to include words that he personally found ridiculous if they were, in fact, attested in literature.

14

Vindex Anglicus

Read and Censure

"Vindex Anglicus; or the Perfections of the English Language." Oxford: H. Hall, 1644. Included in *The Harleian Miscellany* 2:33–37. London: T. Osborne, 1744.

Ex coll. Karolyne & Bryan A. Garner

MANY 16TH- AND 17TH-CENTURY commentators complained that English was a poor medium for expressing thoughts. Latin and Greek, they said, were superior to the debased modern languages—a belief thought to be axiomatic. But English couldn't compete even with French and Italian. It was a mongrel made up of Germanic and Romance words. It lacked grace. It lacked vividness. It changed too rapidly, unlike the classical languages, which they believed, wrongly, had been stable through history. English words were loaded with ugly monosyllables and consonant clusters, especially in the past tense and past participles—not *bridgèd* in two civilized syllables, but *bridg'd* in one barbarous lump. Worst of all, they said, English didn't have nearly enough words to express what needed saying.

Not so the anonymous author of *Vindex Anglicus*, who forcefully advanced the opposite argument—that English is just fine, thank you, and equal if not superior to the world's other languages. Yes, English changes, he acknowledged, but every language changes except *maybe* Hebrew. We can form new words as easily as Latin and Greek can. Our monosyllables and our lack of noun cases make English easier to learn.

As we've seen, many words derived from Latin and Greek entered the English language in the first half of the 17th century, especially in philosophy (*scepticism*, *causation*), science (*electric*, *magnetic*), mathematics (*differential*, *hyperbolic*), and medicine (*diagnostic*, *nutrient*). English speakers felt a lack that could be filled only with classical borrowings. History shows that these words have proved their usefulness. But some 17th-century writers—the "inkhornists"—were agitating for more and more imports. Many of these new words were hardly English at all, just Latin and Greek words with English endings slapped onto them, and early dictionaries were stuffed with them. The *Vindex* author thought they were a disgrace and had no place in the English language:

> Let me afford you a few Examples, and I am deceived if they will not move both your Anger and Laughter; read and censure. *Adpugne, Algale, Adstupiate, Daffe, Defust, Depex, Brochity, Bulbitate, Extorque, Ebriolate, Caprious, Contrast, Catillate, Fraxate, Froyce, Imporcate, Incenabe, Incasse, Gingreate, Glabretall, Halitate, Ligurition, Lurcate, Kemand, Mephitick, Mirminodized, Obsalutate, Orbation, Nixious, Naustible, Plumative, Prodigity, Puellation, Raption, Rerest, Rumatize, Sudate, Solestick, Sracone, Subgrund, Tridiculate, Tristful, Wadshaw, Xantical, Yexate, Vitulate, Undosous, Vambrash, Zoografe.* [2:36.]

"Let us not . . . with a base and busy Avarice, abuse our Language with the Dregs of others, being possessed with the Perfections of them all ready, for by Enfranchising, Refining, and Implanting strange, old, and new Words, it is happily become even the Prince of all the vulgar; from the Dignity of which Nothing hath so much detracted, as our own vain affecting, admiring, and applauding foreign Tongues above Measure: Which makes Strangers judge our own contemptible." (2:36–37.)

Though the anonymous author of the pamphlet never identifies a source of his ugly words, all are taken from Henry Cockeram's *English Dictionarie* (1623). (Graband 2012.)

The author was a Purist who took exception to the Neologists' "thousand . . . unnatural Phrases" that are loathsome to "any curious and judicious Eye." (2:36.) He opposed the "*Moths* and *Cankers*, who, with their shallow Inventions and silly Fancies, must still be engrafting new coined Words in our *English* nursery, without either Art or Judgment." (*Id.*) Their moderating effect was to insist that if "some Pearl or other may be left behind uncheapened," it should be "naturalised here with Judgment and Authority." (*Id.*) "Our Language is copious enough already," he insisted; "we need traffick no more to inrich it." (*Id.*)

Vindex Anglicus was never popular. It appeared in a single edition, and hardly anyone even mentioned it in the century after its publication. But one of its few readers has assured the book a place in lexicographic history.

By the time Edward Harley, 2nd Earl of Oxford and Earl Mortimer, died in 1741, he had built a library of 40,000 volumes. The bookseller Thomas Osborne bought the collection and hired two cataloguers to help him sell it off. One was William Oldys, who had worked for Harley for a few years. The other had little to recommend him other than his learning: a 32-year-old hack writer named Samuel Johnson. (See Kaminski 1981.)

It was not the most productive working relationship. Johnson had no respect for his boss, and as Boswell recounts, it led to a violent confrontation:

> It has been confidently related, with many embellishments, that Johnson one day knocked Osborne down in his shop, with a folio, and put his foot upon his neck. The simple truth I had from Johnson himself. "Sir, he was impertinent to me, and I beat him. But it was not in his shop: it was in my own chamber." [Boswell 1791 1:154.]

But Johnson and Oldys together completed the *Catalogus bibliothecæ Harleianæ* in five volumes (1743–1745), and then selections from some of the collection's rarities as *The Harleian Miscellany; or, A Collection of Scarce, Curious, and Entertaining Pamphlets and Tracts, as Well in Manuscript as in Print, Found in the Late Earl of Oxford's Library* (1744–1746). The *Miscellany* put *Vindex Anglicus* in print for the first time in a century.

The *Vindex* may have helped to shape Johnson's thinking about the sufficiency of the English language, and perhaps contributed to his determination to focus only on words that had demonstrated their utility among English writers. Johnson himself was well known, and often ridiculed, for his Latinate vocabulary. But like the author of the *Vindex*, he believed that English was the equal of any of the languages of Europe, and that lexicographers had no need to run up their word-counts by importing (and inventing) useless neologisms.

Ex coll. Karolyne & Bryan A. Garner

Two sets of the 8-volume *Harleian Miscellany*.

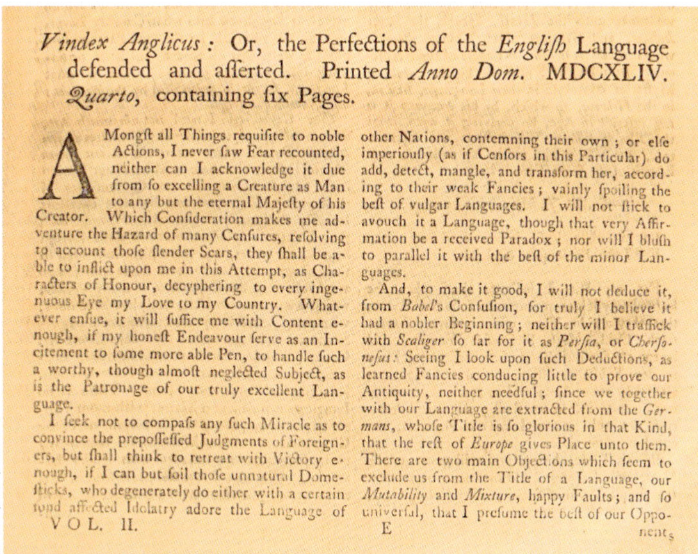

Vindex Anglicus: Or, the Perfections of the *Engliſh* Language defended and aſſerted. Printed *Anno Dom.* MDCXLIV. *Quarto,* containing ſix Pages.

AMongſt all Things requiſite to noble Actions, I never ſaw Fear recounted, neither can I acknowledge it due from ſo excelling a Creature as Man to any but the eternal Majeſty of his Creator. Which Conſideration makes me adventure the Hazard of many Cenſures, reſolving to account thoſe ſlender Scars, they ſhall be able to inflict upon me in this Attempt, as Characters of Honour, decyphering to every ingenuous Eye my Love to my Country. Whatever enſue, it will ſuffice me with Content enough, if my honeſt Endeavour ſerve as an Incitement to ſome more able Pen, to handle ſuch a worthy, though almoſt neglected Subject, as is the Patronage of our truly excellent Language.

I ſeek not to compaſs any ſuch Miracle as to convince the prepoſſeſſed Judgments of Foreigners, but ſhall think to retreat with Victory enough, if I can but foil thoſe unnatural Domeſticks, who degenerately do either with a certain fond affected Idolatry adore the Language of other Nations, contemning their own; or elſe imperiouſly (as if Cenſors in this Particular) do add, detect, mangle, and transform her, according to their weak Fancies; vainly ſpoiling the beſt of vulgar Languages. I will not ſtick to avouch it a Language, though that very Affirmation be a received Paradox; nor will I bluſh to parallel it with the beſt of the minor Languages.

And, to make it good, I will not deduce it, from *Babel's* Confuſion, for truly I believe it had a nobler Beginning; neither will I traffick with *Scaliger* ſo far for it as *Perſia*, or *Cherſoneſus*: Seeing I look upon ſuch Deductions, as learned Fancies conducing little to prove our Antiquity, neither needful; ſince we together with our Language are extracted from the *Germans*, whoſe Title is ſo glorious in that Kind, that the reſt of *Europe* gives Place unto them. There are two main Objections which ſeem to exclude us from the Title of a Language, our *Mutability* and *Mixture*, happy Faults; and ſo univerſal, that I preſume the beſt of our Oppo-

VOL. II. E nents,

Ex coll. Karolyne & Bryan A. Garner

The essay appears in volume 2.

15

John Clayton

Words Not Touched by Former Glossaries

C[layton], J[ohn]. ***Topicks in the Laws of England. Containing Media, apt for Argument, and resolution of Law Cases: also an Exposition of severall words, not touched by former Glossaries.*** **London: Printed for R.L. by William Leake, 1646.**

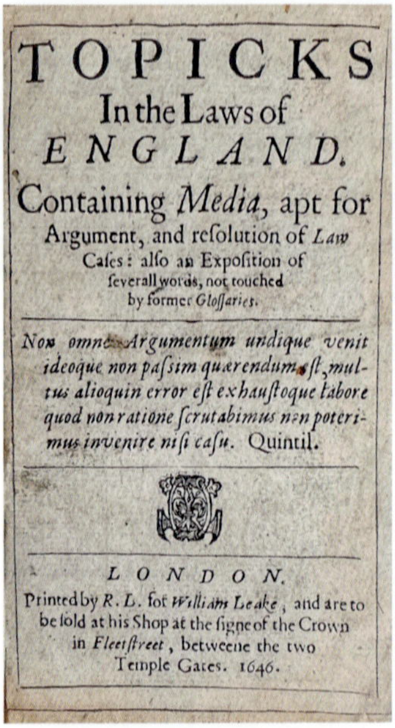

TOPICKS
In the Laws of
ENGLAND.
Containing *Media*, apt for
Argument, and resolution of *Law*
Cases: also an Exposition of
severall words, not touched
by former *Glossaries*.

Non omne Argumentum undique venit ideoque non passim quærendum est, multus alioquin error est exhaustoque labore quod non ratione scrutabimus non poterimus invenire nisi casu. Quintil.

LONDON.
Printed by *R. L.* for *William Leake*, and are to be sold at his Shop at the signe of the Crown in *Fleetstreet*, betweene the two Temple Gates. 1646.

Ex coll. Karolyne & Bryan A. Garner

"Man by his defection from his Maker, lost Truth as well as good, and is fain to gather up the one as well as the other by peecemeale, as a Bee that goes from flower to flower to get any reasonable quantity of honey." (Preface.)

Seven years before Oliver Cromwell (1599–1658) became Lord Protector in 1653, and ten before he sought a comprehensive reform of English law, John Clayton (1620?–1694?) dedicated this book to him. Cromwell was then commander of the New Model Army, besieging English towns in the midst of the English Civil War. Clayton extended good wishes to Cromwell: "It may be a matter of marvell, that any thing of Law should now be heard but to whisper amidst the noyse of lowd Instruments of Warre." And this: "If again it seeme strange to any that I joyne for Patrons of a Lawbooke a Swordman, and one of the long Robe together: let this suffice, that the last is well known to have bin longer time a *Mecœnas* [patron] of Schollers, then a Commander of Souldiers and men are also well perswaded that the points of these swords are bent onely against the adversaries of those Laws which are written upon their hilts." Why didn't Clayton join Cromwell's army instead of writing a book? "With my body I can do little being somewhat in yeers and more unfitted by a sedentary life, besides uncalled upon for such services." (Pp. iii–iv.)

Intended for laymen, this book is an alphabetically arranged explanation of 167 maxims and legal phrases (i.e., "topics"), with full references to various legal authorities supplied in the margin. Why alphabetical order? "The more easie to finde them and make use of them." (P. x.) Clayton seemed to react against the civil-law bent of John Cowell (no. 9): using plain-English terms "brings what we have read in our books quickest to our apprehensions, whereas the turning of those terms into fine Latine, or civill Law expressions, as some of late makes uncouth to the English Lawyer, and far lesse usefull."

The 138-page book opens with a table of contents listing all the entries, some English, some Law French, and some Latin. Clayton rarely translates, though he does explicate: "*Qui tacet consentire videtur*" appears without an English equivalent ("He who is silent is taken to agree"), but he fleshes out the maxim with a practical example: "He which is present at the actuall killing of a man, and puts not debate shall be adjudged assenting." The entries are selective, given that he treats mainly "words not touched by former glossaries." Under *D* appears this: "*Demise* signifies not onely the originall Lease which is made to the Lessee, but the relinquishment, grant or assignement of anything." (Yes, *demise* is an English word, recorded in the *OED* as a verb from 1480 and as a noun from 1509.) And under *M*: "*Meniall* servant. Is hee which is employed in the house for to serve the person of a man." (Pp. 41–42.) And under *S*: "*Sovereigne*, In Law it is no more but the supreme of a house, or a Town, &c. So an Abbot is Sovereigne of the house . . . . Sovereigne of the Town shall pursue fellons, &c. this is the chiefe officer be it Constable, or &c." (P. 48.)

Clayton writes with a sense that every word matters, an attitude surprisingly rare among many of his contemporaries. Where most 17th-century lexicographers were content to gesture vaguely in the direction of a word's meaning, legal lexicographers like Clayton sought precision, given that real outcomes depended on the interpretation of the words used in statutes and other legal instruments. That's why, in a section headed "Expositio verborum" (explanation of words), he tells us "*Puer.* Comprize female as well as *male*" (p. 43)—that is, any reference to a boy includes a girl as well. Where many lexicographers defined words by wantonly tossing out synonyms, Clayton lines up *inhabitant*, *resident*, *commorant*, and *conversant*, and explains: "The genuine sense of these words are [sic] very necessary to be known, by reason they are frequently used in severall statutes." (P. 37.)

Hence Clayton may be the first English lexicographer to explain conjunctions—that *and* often means *or* (the entry is under *et*—p. 34). And he explains why *et cetera* (his headword, though he habitually uses *&c.*) is often legally necessary to make certain legal instruments effective—a plural reference as opposed to a singular. (Pp. 34–35.)

All in all, the book is an early combination of judicial dictionary (courts' holdings on words), maxim book, treatise on interpretation, abridgment of the law, and advocate's prompter. Clayton would surely have agreed that it should be consulted most urgently by someone with a pressing concern, one of his entries in *H* being an English-language maxim no longer known to lawyers: "Hee that needs most let him blow the cole."

Ex coll. Karolyne & Bryan A. Garner

Ex coll. Karolyne & Bryan A. Garner

The first edition (1656) and the second (1661).

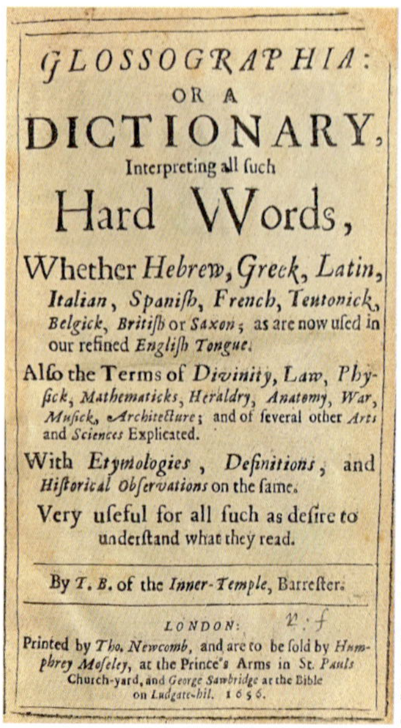

GLOSSOGRAPHIA:
OR A
DICTIONARY,
Interpreting all such
Hard Words,
Whether *Hebrew*, *Greek*, *Latin*, *Italian*, *Spanish*, *French*, *Teutonick*, *Belgick*, *British* or *Saxon*; as are now used in our refined *English Tongue*.
Also the Terms of *Divinity*, *Law*, *Physick*, *Mathematicks*, *Heraldry*, *Anatomy*, *War*, *Musick*, *Architecture*; and of several other *Arts* and *Sciences* Explicated.
With *Etymologies*, *Definitions*, and *Historical Observations* on the same.
Very useful for all such as desire to understand what they read.

By *T. B.* of the *Inner-Temple*, Barrester.

LONDON:
Printed by *Tho. Newcomb*, and are to be sold by *Humphrey Moseley*, at the Prince's Arms in St. *Pauls* Church-yard, and *George Sawbridge* at the Bible on *Ludgate-hill*. 1656.

Ex coll. Karolyne & Bryan A. Garner

16

Thomas Blount

No Peace from Plagiarists

B[lount], T[homas]. ***Glossographia: Or a Dictionary, Interpreting All Such Hard Words, Whether Hebrew, Greek, Latin, Italian, Spanish, French, Teutonick, Belgick, British or Saxon; as are now used in our refined English Tongue.*** **London: Printed by Tho. Newcomb for Humphrey Moseley, 1656. 2d ed. 1661.**

Blount, Thomas. ***NOMO-ΛΕΞΙΚΟΝ [Nomo-Lexicon]: A Law-Dictionary. Interpreting Such Difficult and Obscure Words and Terms, as are found either in Our Common or Statute, Ancient or Modern Lawes.*** **London: Thomas Newcomb for John Martin & Henry Herringman, 1670. 2d ed. 1691. 3d ed. 1717.**

———. ***A World of Errors Discovered in The New World of Words; or, General English Dictionary.*** **London: Printed by T.N. for Abel Roper, John Martin & Henry Herringman, 1673.**

Thomas Blount (1618–1679), born to a Catholic family in Worcestershire, qualified as a barrister at the Inner Temple but was precluded from practicing because of his religion. He made a modest income as a conveyancer, supplemented with two early books: *The Art of Making Devises: Treating of hieroglyphicks, symboles, emblemes, ænigma's, sentences, parables, reverses of medalls, armes, blazons, cimiers, cyphres and rebus* (1646), translated from the French; and *The Academie of Eloquence* (1654), a formbook for letter-writing.

Then he turned to lexicography. His *Glossographia* (1656) was the most scholarly general dictionary to date, and the first to incorporate etymology on any appreciable scale. Blount's was the second dictionary of any kind to cite authorities (Cowell had done so in 1607). Perhaps it's unsurprising that the first two would be lawyers, who rely so much on precedents and cited authorities. *Glossographia*, which saw five editions by 1681, is the classic hard-word dictionary: he listed some words that some commentators regard as his own neologisms, such as *buxiferous*, *diventilate*, *fatiferous*, *nemorivagant*, and *venustate*, none of which have been found in any book before *Glossographia*.

"Few, without the help of a Dictionary, would be able to understand our ordinary English Books. I found nothing considerable in this kinde extant. . . . For these Reasons, and to indulge my own fancy, I began to compile this Work; which has taken me up the vacancy of above Twenty years." (Preface to *Glossographia*.)

Blount was involved in some of the early battles over lexicographic plagiarism. He seemed to believe that it was acceptable to borrow from old books that had fallen into oblivion, but quite wrong to borrow from fresh books that were still enjoying sales. Hence he tacitly borrowed from century-old books by Holyoke and Thomas Thomas—usually refraining from citing them. But when Edward Phillips plagiarized Blount's work just two years after it was published, he became indignant. The first Dictionary Wars ensued.

In 1670, Blount capitalized on his specialized legal knowledge by producing a notable law dictionary: *Nomo-Lexicon*. Here he showed himself to be an antiquarian who delighted in arcana and sometimes ribaldry.

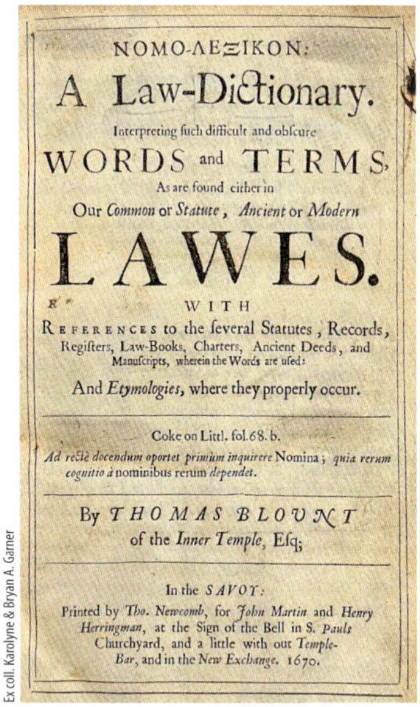
NOMO-ΛΕΞΙΚΟΝ:
A Law-Dictionary.
Interpreting such difficult and obscure
WORDS and TERMS,
As are found either in
Our *Common* or *Statute*, *Ancient* or *Modern*
LAWES.
WITH
References to the several Statutes, Records, Registers, Law-Books, Charters, Ancient Deeds, and Manuscripts, wherein the Words are used:
And *Etymologies*, where they properly occur.

Coke on Littl. fol. 68. b.
Ad recte docendum oportet primum inquirere Nomina; *quia rerum cognitio à* nominibus rerum *dependet.*

By *THOMAS BLOUNT*
of the *Inner Temple*, Esq;

In the *SAVOY*:
Printed by *Tho. Newcomb*, for *John Martin* and *Henry Herringman*, at the Sign of the Bell in S. *Pauls* Churchyard, and a little without *Temple-Bar*, and in the *New Exchange*. 1670.

Ex coll. Karolyne & Bryan A. Garner

Perhaps wiser after his skirmishes with Phillips, Blount was candid about his borrowings. From the first edition of *Nomo-Lexicon*, he gracefully acknowledges: "I have, in this meadow, made little hay with my own fork; but, in the more common words have made use of Cowell, Lambert, Crompton, West, Terms of the law (that is Rastell), etc."

But soon this law dictionary, too, was being pillaged by a competitor. Not long after it appeared, Thomas Manley (1628–1676) was preparing his *ΝΟΜΟΘΕΤΗΣ* [*Nomothetes*] (1671), with both a title and a title page that encouraged confusion with Blount's work. Blount was again frustrated and furious. Somehow he had advance notice of the impending publication, for he wrote to his friend Anthony Wood (1632–1695) that the competing work was "at the presse surreptitiously, being transcribd and mutilated, and disguisd with som new title, and this by a beggarly halfwitted scholar for the purpose." (Bodl. Oxf., MS Wood F.40, fols. 89–90.)

"Though, to gratify the young Student, I have inserted some *Words*, which will seem very common to the more Learned, yet I have rejected divers I found in *Cowel*, as too mean, and indeed not at all deserving an explication; such are *Groome*, *Sluce*, *Copie*, *Revels*, *Toile*, *Wedding*, *Baubels*, &c." (Preface to *Nomo-Lexicon*.)

When Blount's works reached the end of their editions, so did the hard-word tradition in lexicography.

Ex coll. Karolyne & Bryan A. Garner

The fifth edition (1681).

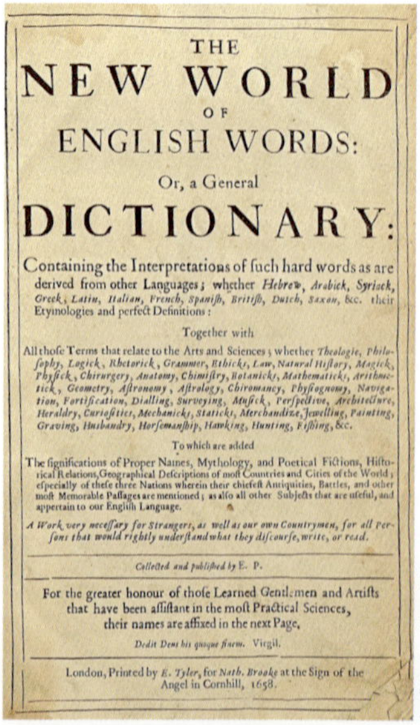

THE
NEW WORLD
OF
ENGLISH WORDS:
Or, a General
DICTIONARY:

Containing the Interpretations of ſuch hard words as are derived from other Languages; whether *Hebrew, Arabick, Syriack, Greek, Latin, Italian, French, Spaniſh, Britiſh, Dutch, Saxon*, &c. their Etymologies and perfect Definitions:

Together with

All thoſe Terms that relate to the Arts and Sciences; whether *Theologie, Philoſophy, Logick, Rhetorick, Grammer, Ethicks, Law, Natural Hiſtory, Magick, Phyſick, Chirurgery, Anatomy, Chimiſtry, Botanicks, Mathematicks, Arithmetick, Geometry, Aſtronomy, Aſtrology, Chiromancy, Phyſiognomy, Navigation, Fortification, Dialling, Surveying, Muſick, Perſpective, Architecture, Heraldry, Curioſities, Mechanicks, Staticks, Merchandize, Jewelling, Painting, Graving, Husbandry, Horſemanſhip, Hawking, Hunting, Fiſhing*, &c.

To which are added

The ſignifications of Proper Names, Mythology, and Poetical Fictions, Hiſtorical Relations, Geographical Deſcriptions of moſt Countries and Cities of the World; eſpecially of theſe three Nations wherein their chiefeſt Antiquities, Battles, and other moſt Memorable Paſſages are mentioned; as alſo all other Subjects that are uſeful, and appertain to our Engliſh Language.

A Work very neceſſary for Strangers, as well as our own Countrymen, for all Perſons that would rightly underſtand what they diſcourſe, write, or read.

Collected and publiſhed by E. P.

For the greater honour of thoſe Learned Gentlemen and Artiſts that have been aſſiſtant in the moſt Practical Sciences, their names are affixed in the next Page.

Dedit Deus his quoque finem. Virgil.

London, Printed by *E. Tyler*, for *Nath. Brooke* at the Sign of the Angel in Cornhill, 1658.

Ex coll. Karolyne & Bryan A. Garner

Title page of the first edition.

"The very sum and comprehension of all Learning in general, is chiefly reducible into those two grand Heads, *Words* and *Things*." (Preface.)

Ex coll. Karolyne & Bryan A. Garner

Engraved frontispiece in the first edition.

17

Edward Phillips

The Pilfering Quick Study

P[hillips], E[dward]. ***The New World of English Words: Or, a General Dictionary: Containing the Interpretations of such hard words as are derived from other Languages; whether Hebrew, Arabick, Syriack, Greek, Latin, Italian, French, Spanish, British, Dutch, Saxon, &c. their Etymologies and perfect Definitions*****. London: Printed by E. Tyler for Nath. Brooke at the Angell in Cornhill, 1658.**

Few people have received a more intense linguistic education than Edward Phillips (1630–1696?), nephew to the poet John Milton. From the ages of nine to nineteen he lived with his uncle, then a schoolmaster, who catechized him and his classmates in divinity, mathematics, astronomy, and languages, including Latin, Greek, Hebrew, Aramaic, Syriac, Italian, and French.

After Phillips left Oxford without a degree, he worked as an amanuensis for his uncle, whose eyesight was failing. He also found work as a hack writer, composing his own poems and editing others', translating fiction, and writing a pickup manual called *The Mysteries of Love and Eloquence; or, The Arts of Wooing and Complimenting*.

Yet Phillips is best known for *The New World of English Words*, defining some 11,000 words in 400 folio pages eccentrically dedicated "To the most illustrious, and impartial sisters, the two universities." He promises a dictionary that will help posterity make sense of "reverend Authours" starting with "*Geffry Chaucer*" and continuing through "our more Modern Poets, as *Spencer*, *Sidny*, *Draiton*, *Daniel*, with our Reformers of the Scene, *Johnson*, *Shakesphear*, *Beaumont*, and *Fletcher*."

Phillips's *New World*, though, wasn't as new as its title page promised. Thomas Blount—whose *Glossographia* (no. 16) had appeared two years earlier and quickly lost market share to Phillips—rebuked him in a pamphlet called *A World of Errors Discovered in the New World of Words*. Phillips, he declared, was a mere "Mercenary" hired "to jumble up another like Book out of this, with some Alterations and

Additions, and give it a new Title." The *New World*, he insisted, had been "extracted almost wholly out of mine." Even Phillips's title—*new world of words*—derives from Blount's well-written preface.

Were the charges justified? Somewhat. Many of Phillips's entries were pretty obviously modeled on Blount's:

Blount, *Glossographia* (1656)	Phillips, *New World* (1658)
Mediocrity (*mediocritas*) a mean, competency, indifferency, temper, moderation.	*Mediocrity*, (lat.) a mean, a middle temper, and indifferency.
Medisance (Fr *mesdisance*) reproach, obloquy, detraction.	*Medisance*, (French) evil speaking, obloquy, or reproach.
Medullar (*medullaris*) pertaining to the marrow, inward.	*Medullar*, (lat.) belonging to the marrow.
Megalopsychie (*megalopsychia*) magnanimity.	*Megalopsychie*, (Greek) Magnanimity, or greatnesse of minde.
Memorial (*memoriale*) that which puts one in mind of, a Remembrancer, a Record, or a book of remembrances.	*Memorial*, (lat.) a remembrancer, or that which puts one in mind of any thing.

But Phillips reworked his source material, trimming, expanding, and altering to improve clarity. He also rejected many of Blount's inkhorn terms (*meliority*, *melitism*, *melliferous*, *mellificate*), using a dagger (†) to identify "Pedantismes," and he defined many words that Blount had skipped (*medication*, *meditation*, *mees*, *memorable*).

Impartial observers, both then and now, agree that Blount had the better case and made the more significant contributions to lexicography. It didn't matter: the market declared Phillips victorious. New and enlarged editions of *The New World of Words* were issued in 1662, 1671, 1678, 1696, 1700, 1706, and 1720, making it the 17th century's most commercially successful dictionary franchise. Blount's scolding about plagiarism had little effect, and Blount's many corrections only helped Phillips improve later editions. In those newly expanded and improved editions, Phillips continued to plagiarize from Blount's dictionary and others' for the rest of his life.

But we don't know about Phillips's end. After Milton's widow gave Phillips her husband's state papers, he published them in 1694, along with a brief biography. Two years later came the fifth edition of his dictionary. After that, Phillips vanishes from the historical record.

Ex coll. Karolyne & Bryan A. Garner

Two first editions (1658), a fourth (1678), and a fifth (1696).

Ex coll. Karolyne & Bryan A. Garner

"Skinner is undoubtedly flawed, but he has one point in his favor. Dr. Johnson used him extensively." (Green 1996:223.)

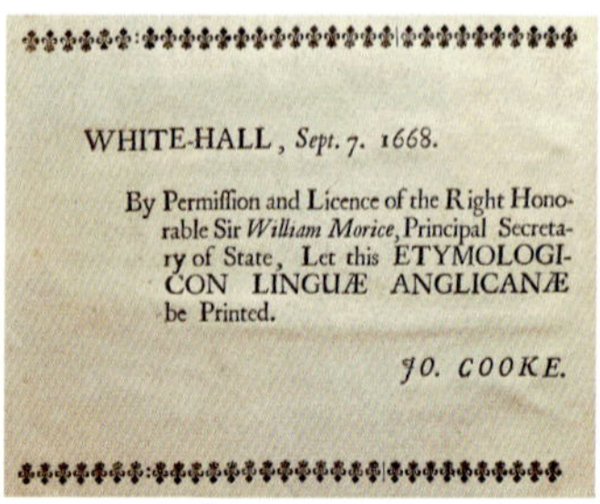

WHITE-HALL, *Sept.* 7. 1668.

By Permiſſion and Licence of the Right Honorable Sir *William Morice*, Principal Secretary of State, Let this ETYMOLOGICON LINGUÆ ANGLICANÆ be Printed.

JO. COOKE.

Ex coll. Karolyne & Bryan A. Garner

18

Stephen Skinner

Often Ignorant, Never Ridiculous

Skinner, Stephen. *Etymologicon Linguæ Anglicanæ, Seu Explicatio vocum Anglicarum Etymologica ex propriis fontibus, scil. ex Linguis duodecim*. London: T. Roycroft, 1671.

Born in London, Skinner (1623–1667) matriculated at Christ Church, Oxford, shortly after his 16th birthday. But the outbreak of the English Civil Wars shortly after drove him "beyond seas." He returned in 1646 to complete his bachelor's and master's degrees, and then traveled to the Continent to study medicine. Heidelberg awarded him an MD in 1654, Oxford followed suit shortly thereafter, and he set up a medical practice in Lincoln. He became so respected as to be elected an honorary fellow of the College of Physicians in 1664. He lived through the Great Plague of 1665, but a "malignant fever" took his life two years later.

At his death, Skinner left abundant philological writing unpublished. Thomas Henshaw, a scientific writer with an Oxford pedigree, gathered these manuscripts, probably supplementing them somewhat with material of his own. The result was *Etymologicon Linguæ Anglicanæ*, the most serious attempt yet to explore the etymologies of English words. Most English dictionaries had made only superficial gestures toward etymology, as by indicating a language of origin: "(*g*)" for Greek, for instance, or "*Teut.*" for "Teutonic" (Germanic). Only John Minsheu's *Guide into Tongues* (1617) provided more, but that was essentially a multilingual dictionary that subordinated etymology.

Skinner, by contrast, lavished scholarly attention on words that had never been seriously studied before, identifying not only their immediate sources but also their deeper history and their cognates in Latin, Greek, Italian, Spanish, Danish, Germanic, "Franco-Gallic," and "Lingua Belgica." In his main alphabetical sequence, he examined just shy of 8,000 words, many of them apparently circulating in speech but never before recorded. He went on to provide separate sequences of about 1,000 plant names (*goats-rue*, *gold-cups*, *golden-apples*, *golden-rod*), 1,300 legal terms (*covenant*, *coverture*, *countenance*, *counterplea*), 3,200 obsolete Middle English words (*eisel*, *eke*, *eld*, *ele*), and 2,000 place names (*Portland*, *Portsmouth*, *Powell*, *Preston*).

Although Skinner's limited knowledge of the history of languages was often erroneous, he understood systematic sound changes better than any of his contemporaries. Samuel Johnson paid to him "the reverence due to instructors and benefactors," observing that "*Skinner* is often ignorant, but never ridiculous." Skinner's essential achievement, though, was recognizing and establishing the fundamental notion that linguistic change is rule-bound. His was an embryonic endeavor to set forth some of the rules.

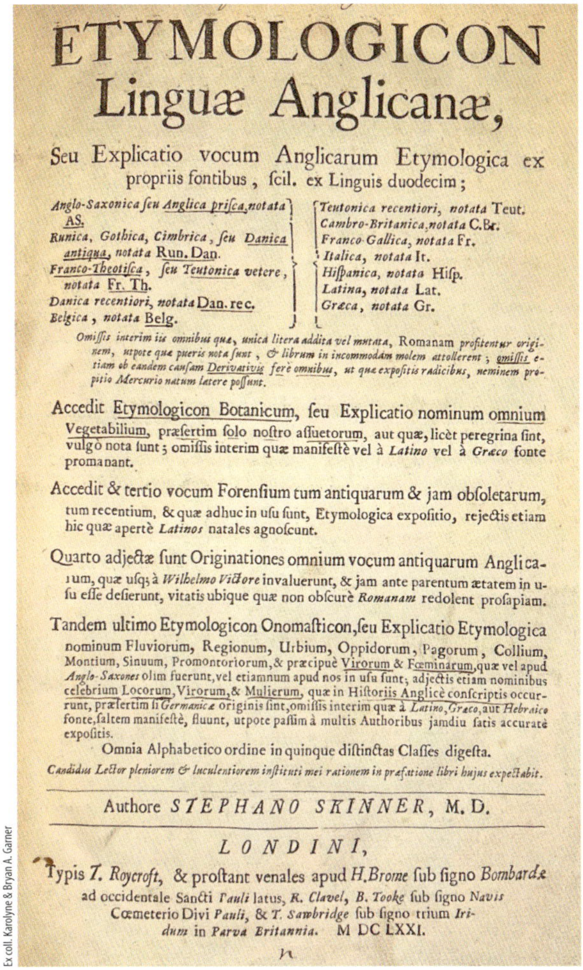

ETYMOLOGICON
Linguæ Anglicanæ,

Seu Explicatio vocum Anglicarum Etymologica ex propriis fontibus, scil. ex Linguis duodecim;

Anglo-Saxonica seu Anglica prisca, notata AS.
Runica, Gothica, Cimbrica, seu Danica antiqua, notata Run. Dan.
Franco-Theotisca, seu Teutonica vetere, notata Fr. Th.
Danica recentiori, notata Dan. rec.
Belgica, notata Belg.
Teutonica recentiori, notata Teut.
Cambro-Britanica, notata C.Br.
Franco-Gallica, notata Fr.
Italica, notata It.
Hispanica, notata Hisp.
Latina, notata Lat.
Græca, notata Gr.

Omissis interim iis omnibus quæ, unica litera addita vel mutata, Romanam *profitentur originem, utpote quæ pueris nota sunt, & librum in incommodam molem attollerent; omissis etiam ob eandem causam Derivativis ferè omnibus, ut quæ expositis radicibus, neminem propitio Mercurio natum latere possunt.*

Accedit Etymologicon Botanicum, seu Explicatio nominum omnium Vegetabilium, præsertim solo nostro assuetorum, aut quæ, licèt peregrina sint, vulgò nota sunt; omissis interim quæ manifestè vel à *Latino* vel à *Græco* fonte promanant.

Accedit & tertio vocum Forensium tum antiquarum & jam obsoletarum, tum recentium, & quæ adhuc in usu sunt, Etymologica expositio, rejectis etiam hic quæ apertè *Latinos* natales agnoscunt.

Quarto adjectæ sunt Originationes omnium vocum antiquarum Anglicarum, quæ usq; à *Wilhelmo Victore* invaluerunt, & jam ante parentum ætatem in usu esse desierunt, vitatis ubique quæ non obscurè *Romanam* redolent prosapiam.

Tandem ultimo Etymologicon Onomasticon, seu Explicatio Etymologica nominum Fluviorum, Regionum, Urbium, Oppidorum, Pagorum, Collium, Montium, Sinuum, Promontoriorum, & præcipuè Virorum & Fœminarum, quæ vel apud *Anglo-Saxones* olim fuerunt, vel etiamnum apud nos in usu sunt; adjectis etiam nominibus celebrium Locorum, Virorum, & Mulierum, quæ in Historiis Anglicè conscriptis occurrunt, præsertim si *Germanicæ* originis sint, omissis interim quæ à *Latino*, *Græco*, aut *Hebraico* fonte, saltem manifestè, fluunt, utpote passim à multis Authoribus jamdiu satis accuratè expositis.

Omnia Alphabetico ordine in quinque distinctas Classes digesta.

Candidus Lector pleniorem & luculentiorem instituti mei rationem in præfatione libri hujus expectabit.

Authore *STEPHANO SKINNER*, M.D.

LONDINI,

Typis *T. Roycroft*, & prostant venales apud *H. Brome* sub signo *Bombardæ* ad occidentale Sancti *Pauli* latus, *R. Clavel*, *B. Tooke* sub signo *Navis* Cœmeterio Divi *Pauli*, & *T. Sawbridge* sub signo trium *Iridum* in *Parva Britannia*. M DC LXXI.

Ex coll. Karolyne & Bryan A. Garner

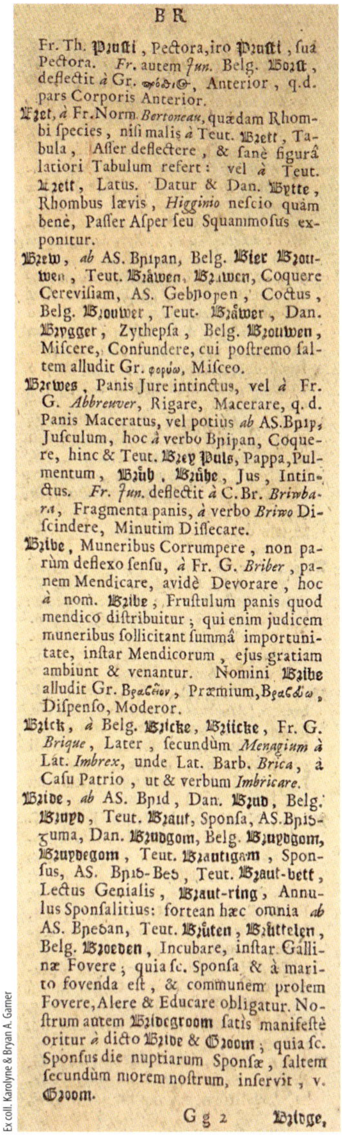

B R

Fr. Th. Prusti, Pectora, iro Prusti, sua Pectora. *Fr.* autem *Jun.* Belg. Borst, deflectit *à* Gr. προσθιος, Anterior, q.d. pars Corporis Anterior.

Bret, *à* Fr. Norm. *Bertoneau*, quædam Rhombi species, nisi malis *à* Teut. Brett, Tabula, Asser deflectere, & sanè figurâ latiori Tabulum refert: vel *à* Teut. Breit, Latus. Datur & Dan. Bytte, Rhombus lævis, *Higginio* nescio quàm benè, Passer Asper seu Squammosus exponitur.

Brew, *ab* AS. Briwan, Belg. Bier Brouwen, Teut. Brawen, Brauwen, Coquere Cerevisiam, AS. Gebrowen, Coctus, Belg. Brouwer, Teut. Brawer, Dan. Brygger, Zythepsa, Belg. Brouwen, Miscere, Confundere, cui postremo saltem alludit Gr. φορύω, Misceo.

Brewes, Panis Jure intinctus, vel *à* Fr. G. *Abbreuver*, Rigare, Macerare, q.d. Panis Maceratus, vel potius *ab* AS. Briw, Jusculum, hoc *à* verbo Briwan, Coquere, hinc & Teut. Brey Puls, Pappa, Pulmentum, Bruh, Brühe, Jus, Intinctus. *Fr. Jun.* deflectit *à* C. Br. *Briwbara*, Fragmenta panis, *à* verbo *Briwo* Discindere, Minutim Dissecare.

Bribe, Muneribus Corrumpere, non parùm deflexo sensu, *à* Fr. G. *Briber*, panem Mendicare, avidè Devorare, hoc *à* nom. Bribe, Frustulum panis quod mendico distribuitur; qui enim judicem muneribus sollicitant summâ importunitate, instar Mendicorum, ejus gratiam ambiunt & venantur. Nomini Bribe alludit Gr. Βραβεῖον, Præmium, Βραβεύω, Dispenso, Moderor.

Brick, *à* Belg. Bricke, Brijcke, Fr. G. *Brique*, Later, secundùm *Menagium à* Lat. *Imbrex*, unde Lat. Barb. *Brica*, à Casu Patrio, ut & verbum *Imbricare*.

Bride, *ab* AS. Brid, Dan. Brud, Belg. Bruyd, Teut. Braut, Sponsa, AS. Brid-guma, Dan. Brudgom, Belg. Bruydgom, Bruydegom, Teut. Brautigam, Sponsus, AS. Brid-Bed, Teut. Braut-bett, Lectus Genialis, Braut-ring, Annulus Sponsalitius: fortean hæc omnia *ab* AS. Bredan, Teut. Brüten, Brütteln, Belg. Broeden, Incubare, instar Gallinæ Fovere; quia sc. Sponsa & à marito fovenda est, & communem prolem Fovere, Alere & Educare obligatur. Nostrum autem Bridegroom satis manifestè oritur *à* dicto Bride & Groom; quia sc. Sponsus die nuptiarum Sponsæ, saltem secundùm morem nostrum, inservit, v. Groom.

Gg 2 Bridge,

Ex coll. Karolyne & Bryan A. Garner

"The bulky folio of Dr. Stephen Skinner . . . is especially noticeable for the number of fictitious Anglo-Saxon words which he invented to stand as etymologies for English words." (Hunter 1895:641.)

Courtesy of Rulon-Miller Books

"I knew not of anything that hath been already done in this kind." (Preface.)

19

John Ray

Birds, Fishes, Metals, and Minerals

Ray, John. ***A Collection of English Words Not Generally Used, with their significations and original, in two alphabetical catalogues, the one of such as are proper to the northern, the other to the southern countries. With an account of the preparing and refining such metals and minerals as are gotten in England.*** **London: H. Bruges for Thomas Burrell, 1674. 2d ed. 1691.**

JOHN WRAY (1627–1705)—so spelled—was born to an Essex blacksmith and attended a grammar school in nearby Braintree. He arrived at Cambridge in 1644, during the English Civil War. He spent a while drifting between two colleges—first Trinity, then St. Catharine's, and then, after his tutor died and the master of the college was expelled for his royalist politics, back to Trinity. There he studied Latin, Greek, and (probably) Hebrew, taking his degree in 1648.

Still he kept drifting. He was elected lecturer in Greek in 1651, then traded that position for one in mathematics two years later, and then switched to humanities two years after that. College fellows were expected to become priests, and though he worried about taking oaths to a revolutionary government he didn't support, he was ordained in 1660, shortly after Charles II was restored to the throne.

Despite studying classics and teaching mathematics, Wray found his passion in the natural sciences, botany above all. In Cambridge, he kept track of all the plants he encountered, and beginning in 1658, he traveled England and Wales, looking for botanical specimens. Later, he broadened his horizons to include Scotland and the Isle of Man. Later still, he expanded his expeditions to take in France, Flanders, the Netherlands, Germany, Italy, Sicily, Malta, and Switzerland, all in one great itinerary that took nearly three years.

A list of 558 species, with both their formal Latin names and their local English ones, went into his first big 1660 botanical publication, the *Catalogus plantarum circa Cantabrigiam nascentium* (Catalogue of plants growing around Cambridge). That was merely a warmup for his monumental *Historia plantarum* in two folio volumes (1686–1688), a thorough description of more than 6,000 plant species. (A third volume, published in 1704, listed some 10,000 more, but without the detail that came from firsthand observation.) Wray was elected a fellow of the Royal Society of London for Improving Natural Knowledge in 1667, just a few years after it was founded, which put him at the center of Britain's scientific establishment. As he began publishing for an increasingly international audience, he changed his name to make it more suitable to Latin title pages. Latin has no *W*, so Wray became Ray and stayed that way.

"I am sensible that this Collection is far from perfect, not conteining perchance more then [sic] one moiety of the Local words used in all the several Counties of *England*. But it is as full as I can at present easily make it, and may give occasion to the curious in each *Countrey* to supply what are wanting, and so make the work compleat." (Preface.)

Most of Ray's work was scientific, but in roaming the world he picked up all sorts of knowledge about linguistic and cultural matters. In collaboration with the ornithologist and ichthyologist Francis Willughby, he published a *Collection of English Proverbs* (1670) and *Observations Topographical, Moral, and Physiological* (1673). Of most interest to lexicologists, though, is *A Collection of English Words Not Generally Used*, first published in 1674. It's a descriptive account of dialect words, and might fairly be reckoned the first book-length work on English dialects.

Early in the history of the English language, there were several distinct dialects, none of which could be called "standard." By the 17th century, though, for most people "English" meant "London English," and departures from it were either ignored or deplored. Yet Ray considered the non-London varieties worthy of study. He had encountered them in various journeys:

> In my travels through several parts of *England* . . . I could not but take notice of the difference of Dialect and variety of local words . . . in divers Counties, by Reason whereof in many places, especially in the North, the Language of the common people is to a stranger very difficult to be understood. [Preface.]

"Whereas I understand that some proverbs admitted in the former edition have given offence to sober and pious persons, as savouring too much of obscenity, being apt to suggest impure fancies to corrupt minds, I have in this omitted all I could suspect for such save only one." (1768 preface to the *Proverbs* book [not naming the one preserved].)

That led him to write to friends: "I desired my friends and acquaintance living in several Countreys to communicate to me what they had observed each of their own Countrey words." (*Id.*)

In justifying his project, Ray was among the first to articulate a belief that would motivate dialect studies for centuries: "I find a great part of these words to be pure Saxon, or manifestly derived thence." (*Id.*) English dialect words, that is to say, especially those from the North of England, preserve older forms of the language and offer

"The words, I now present the *Reader* with, . . . may be of some use to them who shall have some occasion to travel to the Northern Counties." (Preface.)

Ex coll. Karolyne & Bryan A. Garner

Four years before his *Collection of Words* appeared, Ray issued *A Complete Collection of English Proverbs* (1670), which was reissued in expurgated form in 1678 (here shown)—with *A Collection of English Words* appended.

"They [these words] may also afford some diversion to the curious, and give them occasion of making many considerable remarks." (Preface.)

insight into the history of English. To travel north from London was to travel back in time. Ray therefore made extensive use of William Somner's *Dictionarium Saxonico–Latino–Anglicum* (1659) and Skinner's *Etymologicon Linguæ Anglicanæ* (1671, no. 18) to define the language of his contemporaries.

The book is strangely structured. The first section is devoted to "North Country words," from *addle* to *yuck*, in 84 pages: "A *Bannock*, An *Oat-cake* kneaded with water only and baked in the Embers. In Lancashire, and other parts of the North, they make several sorts of Oaten bread"; "A *Barn* or *Bearn:* A Child: it is an ancient Saxon word." Then comes "South and East Countrey Words," *an* to *yaspen*, in 35 pages: "A *Crock:* a Earthen pot to put butter or the like in"; "*Mittens:* Gloves made of linnen or woollen, whether knit or stitched: sometimes also they call so gloves made of leather without fingers." In 1674, though, the linguistic information is followed by "Catalogues of English Birds and Fishes and an Account of the Preparing and Refining Such Metals and Minerals as Are Gotten in England," arranged not alphabetically but by kind: "Rapacious nocturnal Birds," "The Woodpecker kind," "Small Birds with Slender Bills"; "Of the Cetaceous Kind," "Flat-Fishers that swim sideways and lye most part grovelling at the bottome." All these birds, fishes, metals, and minerals take up nearly half the book. The second edition of 1691 drops the birds and fishes but keeps the rest. Even in his linguistic forays, the naturalist remains always a naturalist. Ray also added in 1691 a section called "An Account of Some Errors and Defects in Our English Alphabet, Orthography, and Manner of Spelling."

In all his work, Ray had a scientist's passion for observation. As Rebecca Shapiro puts it, "What makes Ray's book . . . important to the history of lexicography is not so much that he wanted to define hard words, but that he studied and presented the language and culture of the people of England, much as he did its plant life. . . . Ray took a naturalist's view of language." (Shapiro 2017:68.)

His last 18 years were devoted not to etymology but to entomology. He had become lame from the incurable ulcers on his legs, caused, he thought, by an infestation of "invisible insects" making their nests there. His unrelieved discomfort did not end until his death on 17 January 1705; two entomological books (*Methodus* and *Historia*) appeared not long after. But his enduring fame is chiefly attributable to his work in botany.

20

Elisha Coles
No Friend to Tedium

Coles, E[lisha]. ***An English Dictionary: Explaining the difficult Terms that are used in Divinity, Husbandry, Physick, Phylosophy, Law, Navigation, Mathematicks, and other Arts and Sciences.*** **London: Samuel Crouch, 1676. 2d ed. 1677. 3d ed. 1684. 4th ed. 1685.**

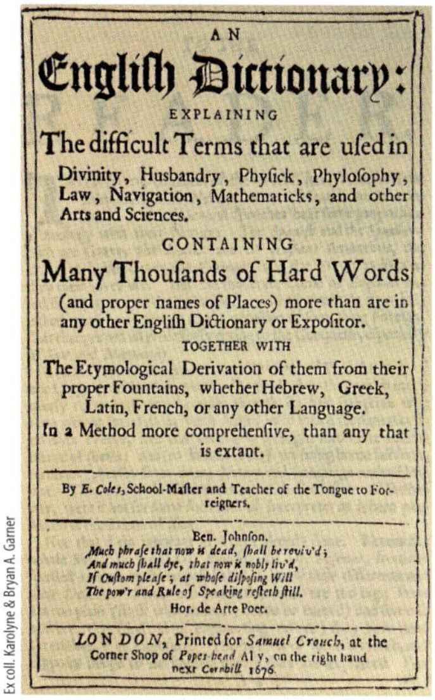
AN
English Dictionary:
EXPLAINING
The difficult Terms that are uſed in
Divinity, Husbandry, Phyſick, Phyloſophy, Law, Navigation, Mathematicks, and other Arts and Sciences.
CONTAINING
Many Thouſands of Hard Words
(and proper names of Places) more than are in any other Engliſh Dictionary or Expoſitor.
TOGETHER WITH
The Etymological Derivation of them from their proper Fountains, whether Hebrew, Greek, Latin, French, or any other Language.
In a Method more comprehenſive, than any that is extant.

By *E. Coles*, School-Maſter and Teacher of the Tongue to Foreigners.

Ben. Johnſon.
Much phraſe that now is dead, ſhall be reviv'd;
And much ſhall dye, that now is nobly liv'd,
If Cuſtom pleaſe; at whoſe diſpoſing Will
The pow'r and Rule of Speaking reſteth ſtill.
Hor. de Arte Poet.

LONDON, Printed for *Samuel Crouch*, at the Corner Shop of *Popes-head* Aly, on the right hand next *Cornhill* 1676.

Ex coll. Karolyne & Bryan A. Garner

"I do not warrant absolute perfection. The pains that are taken in it, will appear at first sight." (Preface.)

THE SON OF A WOLVERHAMPTON SCHOOLMASTER, Elisha Coles (1640?–1680) followed his father into teaching. Although he studied at Magdalen College, Oxford, for three years (1658–1661), he left without a degree. He soon set up a school in Russell Street, London, where he taught Latin to English schoolchildren and English to foreigners. In his mid-30s, he began his career as a prolific author: *The Compleat English Schoolmaster* (1674), *The Newest, Plainest and the Shortest Short-Hand* (1674), *Syncrisis* (1675), and the brilliantly titled *Nolens Volens, or, You Shall Make Latin Whether You Will or No* (1675).

Then, during the last five years of his short life, began the publication of his lexicography, for which he is best known: *An English Dictionary* (1676) and *A Dictionary, English–Latin and Latin–English* (1677). The former saw 13 editions through 1732; the latter, 27 editions through 1772.

Coles's *English Dictionary*, a small octavo printed in three columns per page, contained more entries than any other monolingual dictionary to date—nearly 25,700, including dialect, place names, and technical terms. In his preface ("To the Reader"), he is summarily dismissive of his predecessors:

> Not that I am ignorant of what's already done. I know the whole Succession from Dr. *Bulloker* [sic], to Dr. *Skinner*, from the smallest Volume to the largest Folio. I know their difference and their defects. Some are too little, some are too big; some are so plain (stufft with obscenity not to be named) and some so obscure, that (instead of expounding others) they have need themselves of an Expositor. The method of some is Foolish, and opposes things to be known before they

Ex coll. Karolyne & Bryan A. Garner

The first edition (1676) and the fourth (1685).

> are explained. For then the terms of Art are reduced to their several Heads, you must know (in general) what your word is, before you can possibly tell where to seek it; or else (as they say) you must look a Needle in a bottle of Hay. [Pp. iii–iv.]

Ex coll. Karolyne & Bryan A. Garner

Two copies of the English–Latin dictionary: on both labels, Coles's name is misrendered.

In this self-assured manner, he shows scorn not only for Bullokar and Skinner, but also for Phillips and Blount.

His defense of nonstandard English is practical: "'Tis no disparagement to understand the Canting Terms. It may chance to save your throat from being cut, or (at least) your pocket from being pickt." (Pp. v–vi.)

Coles devised clever ways to keep his dictionary succinct because he was, as he declared, "no friend to vain and tedious repetitions." (P. v.) His etymologies are supplied with abbreviations of one to three characters with which he cited 40 source languages and dialects, ranging from Essex and Wiltshire to Syriac and Turkish. He would sometimes capitalize on successive entries by using the next headword to complete a sentence in the preceding entry, as here:

> *Lupa*, the she-Wolf that nourished *Romulus* in the
> *Lupercal*, a place near *Rome*, where were celebrated the
> *Lupercalia*, Feasts in honour of *Pan*, performed by the
> *Luperci*, Priests of *Pan* . . . .

As shown by that span of entries, the headwords often included items that would today be thought more appropriate in an encyclopedia.

In addition to dialect and cant, Coles focused on hard words. Because he was concerned with comprehensiveness and usability, the entries rarely extend beyond three lines—and most are one or two. For example:

> *Imperious*, Domineering, insulting.
> *Imperforable*, *l.* not to be bored thorow.
> *Imperforation*, a closing up for want of boring or pierceing.
> *Impersonal* [verbs] without the distinction of persons.
> *Impertinence*, a thing not belonging to the matter in hand, a being
> *Impertinent*, nothing to the purpose.
> *Impervestigable*, *l.* impossible to be found or searched out.
> *Impervient*, *l.* which cannot be gone or passed through.
> *Impetiginous*, *l.* full of, or troubled with an
> *Impetigo*, *l.* an Itching scab.

"On the whole, seventeenth-century dictionaries averaged around 8 percent alphabetical errors in the word list, although some, like Blount, cut this back to 4.5 percent, while others, like Coles, reached 11 percent." (Green 1996:58.)

Impetrable, which one may
Impetrate, *l.* obtain by request.
Impetren, *o.* to entreat.
Impetuosity, a being
Impetuous, boisterous, furious, violent.

Note that seven of those entries have etymological notes: *l.* for Latin and *o.* for "Old Word."

One more innovation in the front matter of Coles's dictionary is a two-page chart of homophones and near-homophones (e.g., *lessen* [make less], *lesson* [a lecture]), with brief definitions. Why did he think to include this? "To prevent a vacancy, I thought good here to prefix a Catalogue of the most usual Words, whose sound is the same, but their Sense and Orthography very different." (P. vii.) Here, in a rudimentary way, he was anticipating the usage dictionary. Some of these easily confused words also give us insight into 17th-century English pronunciation: he treats *heard*, *hard*, and *herd* as homophones; he distinguishes "*One*, first number" from "*Own*, proper"; and he does likewise with "*Parson*, of the Parish" and "*Person*, any Man."

"Coles took . . . hundreds of the entries and definitions which he found in *A New World* [no. 17]. That these definitions are from Phillips, not from Bullokar or Blount, a consecutive reading of the dictionaries in question will reveal. Coles and Phillips, for example, have many words in common not in Blount or Bullokar; and, in the case of words running through the series of texts, those in Coles can be shown to be nearer to Phillips than to any other." (Starnes & Noyes 1946:59.)

Dying about age 40, Elisha Coles saw only 2 of the 13 editions of this dictionary. One wonders what literary and lexicographic accomplishments might have followed had his life been longer. What is certain, though, is that even to modern readers of his dictionary, "the pains that are taken in it, will appear at first sight." (P. v.)

Ex coll. Karolyne & Bryan A. Garner

In the early 1970s, the German publisher Georg Olms issued facsimile reprints not only of Coles's *English Dictionary* (bottom here), but also (ascending) of Bullokar (no. 11), Blount (no. 16), Cockeram (no. 13), and others.

"With little substantial change, the *English Dictionary* of Coles went through eleven editions down to 1732. Full of potted encyclopedic information but at times over-ingeniously compact, it can hardly have been in competition with the more expansive Phillips [no. 17]. Coles addressed the needs of less demanding readers who did not mind small print, and would be content with being told simply that *Ajax* was 'A Stout *Grecian*' or that *Hinton* was the name of several small towns." (Osselton 2009:146.)

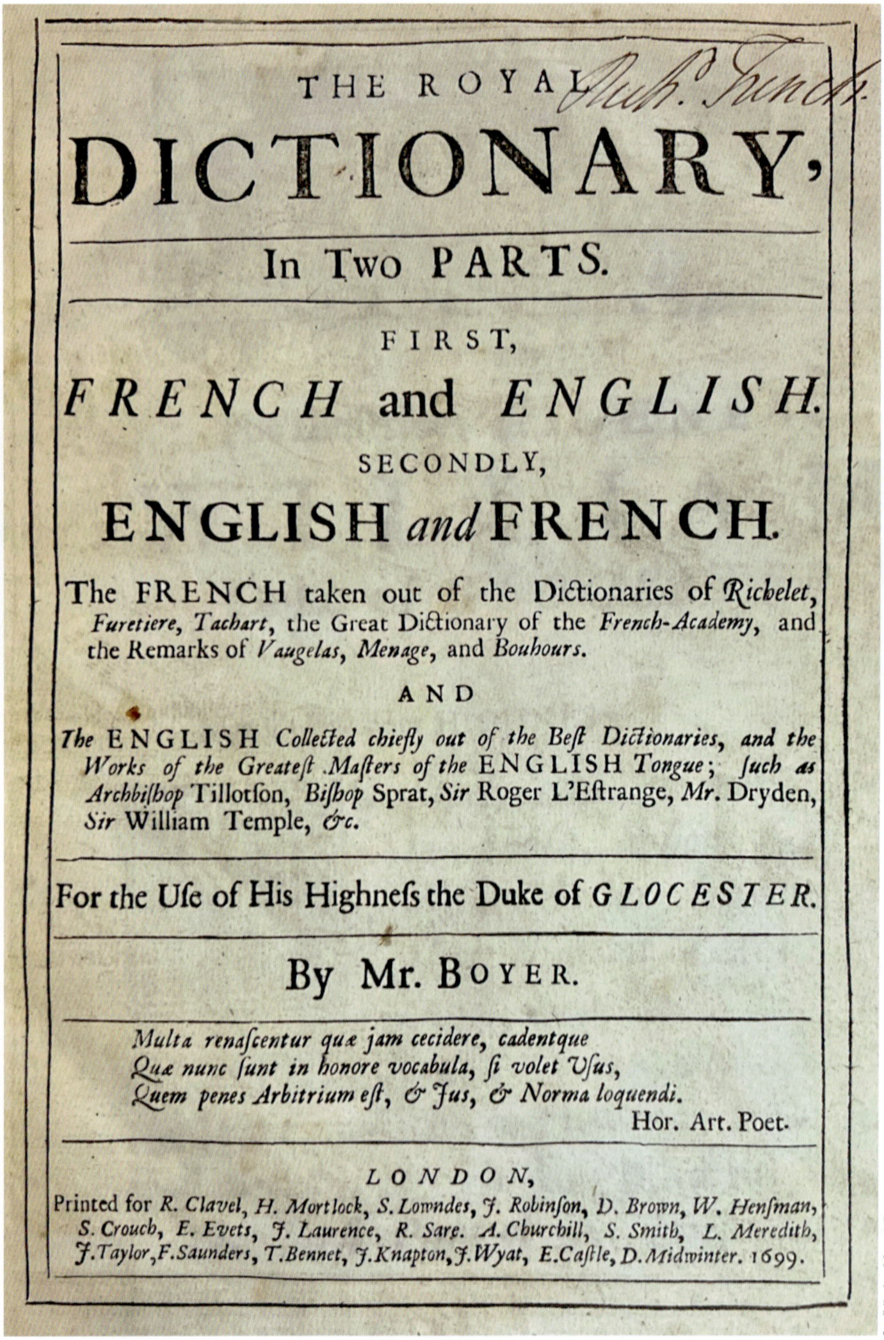
THE ROYAL DICTIONARY,

In Two PARTS.

FIRST,

FRENCH and *ENGLISH.*

SECONDLY,

ENGLISH *and* FRENCH.

The FRENCH taken out of the Dictionaries of *Richelet, Furetiere, Tachart,* the Great Dictionary of the *French-Academy,* and the Remarks of *Vaugelas, Menage,* and *Bouhours.*

AND

The ENGLISH *Collected chiefly out of the Beſt Dictionaries, and the Works of the Greateſt Maſters of the* ENGLISH *Tongue; ſuch as Archbiſhop* Tillotſon, *Biſhop* Sprat, *Sir* Roger L'Eſtrange, *Mr.* Dryden, *Sir* William Temple, *&c.*

For the Uſe of His Highneſs the Duke of *GLOCESTER.*

By Mr. BOYER.

Multa renaſcentur quæ jam cecidere, cadentque
Quæ nunc ſunt in honore vocabula, ſi volet Uſus,
Quem penes Arbitrium eſt, & Jus, & Norma loquendi.
Hor. Art. Poet.

LONDON,

Printed for *R. Clavel, H. Mortlock, S. Lowndes, J. Robinſon, D. Brown, W. Henſman, S. Crouch, E. Evets, J. Laurence, R. Sare. A. Churchill, S. Smith, L. Meredith, J. Taylor, F. Saunders, T. Bennet, J. Knapton, J. Wyat, E. Caſtle, D. Midwinter.* 1699.

The 17th century ended with the publication of Abel Boyer's bilingual *Royal Dictionary* (1699), which supplied many senses to Benjamin Martin (no. 33). This copy bears the ownership signature of Richard Chenevix Trench, "father of the *Oxford English Dictionary*" (see no. 81).

IV. The Early 18th Century

Even today, people commonly say that Samuel Johnson was "the first lexicographer for English." Of course, that's quite untrue. It's even questionable whether he was the first great lexicographer, given the substantial accomplishments of Thomas Blount in the 17th century and Nathan Bailey in the 18th. And for specialists, Johnson could rely on excellent predecessors such as John Quincy in medicine and Giles Jacob in law.

The first half of the 18th century saw the broadening of lexicography from inkhorn terms to some approximation of the entire English vocabulary, as well as the beginnings of a consensus about the differences between a dictionary and an encyclopedia. This is the era in which dictionaries developed many features that we associate with the form now—distinctively printed headwords, numbered senses, cross-references—which is to say that early-18th-century dictionaries are the first ones that look modern to our eyes.

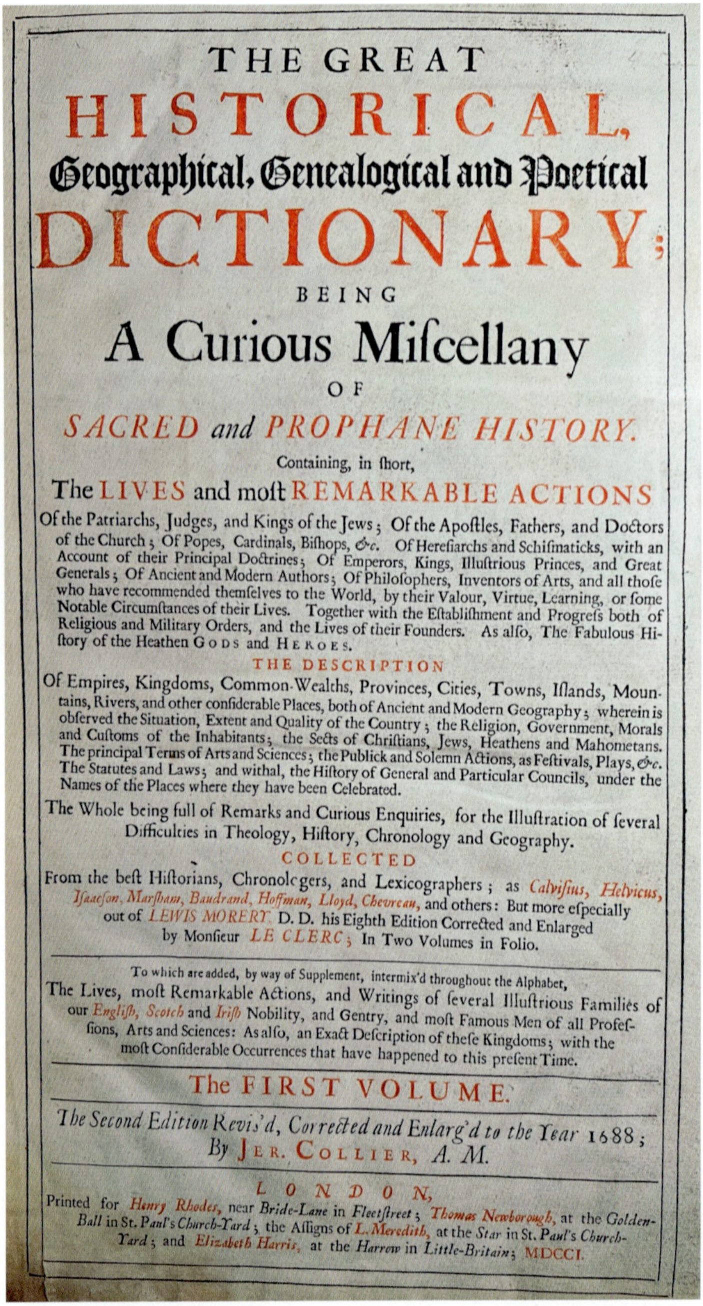

THE GREAT
HISTORICAL,
Geographical, Genealogical and Poetical
DICTIONARY;
BEING
A Curious Miſcellany
OF
SACRED and *PROPHANE HISTORY.*
Containing, in ſhort,
The LIVES and moſt REMARKABLE ACTIONS
Of the Patriarchs, Judges, and Kings of the Jews; Of the Apoſtles, Fathers, and Doctors of the Church; Of Popes, Cardinals, Biſhops, *&c.* Of Hereſiarchs and Schiſmaticks, with an Account of their Principal Doctrines; Of Emperors, Kings, Illuſtrious Princes, and Great Generals; Of Ancient and Modern Authors; Of Philoſophers, Inventors of Arts, and all thoſe who have recommended themſelves to the World, by their Valour, Virtue, Learning, or ſome Notable Circumſtances of their Lives. Together with the Eſtabliſhment and Progreſs both of Religious and Military Orders, and the Lives of their Founders. As alſo, The Fabulous Hiſtory of the Heathen GODS and HEROES.
THE DESCRIPTION
Of Empires, Kingdoms, Common-Wealths, Provinces, Cities, Towns, Iſlands, Mountains, Rivers, and other conſiderable Places, both of Ancient and Modern Geography; wherein is obſerved the Situation, Extent and Quality of the Country; the Religion, Government, Morals and Cuſtoms of the Inhabitants; the Sects of Chriſtians, Jews, Heathens and Mahometans. The principal Terms of Arts and Sciences; the Publick and Solemn Actions, as Feſtivals, Plays, *&c.* The Statutes and Laws; and withal, the Hiſtory of General and Particular Councils, under the Names of the Places where they have been Celebrated.
The Whole being full of Remarks and Curious Enquiries, for the Illuſtration of ſeveral Difficulties in Theology, Hiſtory, Chronology and Geography.
COLLECTED
From the beſt Hiſtorians, Chronologers, and Lexicographers; as *Calviſius, Helvicus, Iſaacſon, Marſham, Baudrand, Hoffman, Lloyd, Chevreau,* and others: But more eſpecially out of *LEWIS MORERY* D. D. his Eighth Edition Corrected and Enlarged by Monſieur *LE CLERC*; In Two Volumes in Folio.

To which are added, by way of Supplement, intermix'd throughout the Alphabet, The Lives, moſt Remarkable Actions, and Writings of ſeveral Illuſtrious Families of our *Engliſh, Scotch* and *Iriſh* Nobility, and Gentry, and moſt Famous Men of all Profeſſions, Arts and Sciences: As alſo, an Exact Deſcription of theſe Kingdoms; with the moſt Conſiderable Occurrences that have happened to this preſent Time.

The FIRST VOLUME.

The Second Edition Reviſ'd, Corrected and Enlarg'd to the Year 1688;
By JER. COLLIER, *A. M.*

LONDON,
Printed for *Henry Rhodes*, near *Bride-Lane* in *Fleetſtreet*; *Thomas Newborough*, at the *Golden-Ball* in St. *Paul's Church-Yard*; the Aſſigns of *L. Meredith*, at the *Star* in St. *Paul's Church-Yard*; and *Elizabeth Harris*, at the *Harrow* in *Little-Britain*; MDCCI.

The 18th century opened with this 1701 three-volume dictionary by Jeremy Collier. By today's standards, it's an encyclopedia much more than a dictionary. Yet the title page is irresistibly worth showing.

Collier (1650–1726).

21

John Kersey

Or So We Think

K., J. *A New English Dictionary: Or, a Compleat Collection of the Most Proper and Significant Words, Commonly Used in the Language; With a Short and Clear Exposition of Difficult Words, and Terms of Art.* London: Printed for Henry Bonwicke and Robert Knaplock, 1702.

Ex coll. Karolyne & Bryan A. Garner

ALTHOUGH THE "J.K." ON THIS TITLE PAGE is probably John Kersey, there's room for doubt. Matters are slightly complicated by the existence of at least one other John Kersey. The one born in 1616, who wrote a popular algebra textbook in 1673, seems to have been the father of our Kersey. If so, ours was probably born around the year 1660, and seems to have entered the dictionary business by way of a job in the publishing trade in the 1680s. The dictionary appeared in 1702 as *A New English Dictionary*—the first new general-purpose monolingual English dictionary since Elisha Coles published *An English Dictionary* in 1676 (no. 20). What we do know is that John Kersey was without question the fully acknowledged lexicographer who in 1708 produced *Dictionarium Anglo-Britannicum*. In fact, this *New English Dictionary* seems to be a warmup for the much grander accomplishment that was to follow, his much more thorough *Dictionarium*.

The preface to J.K.'s 1702 work identifies two precursors: "a little Tract first set forth by *John Bulloker* Doctor of Physick, under the Title of *An English Expositor*, and Mr. *E. Coles*'s *English Dictionary*." Both, he complained, are packed with words "which are scarce ever us'd by any ancient or modern Writer"—monstrosities like *dopaciginous*, *egestuosity*, *elingued*, *horrisonant*, *ignifluous*, *ignipotent*, *impluvious*, *innubilous*, *largifical*, *nidifice*, *odoraminous*, and *umbigiality*. He rejected most of the unused or little-used inkhornisms so typical of 17th-century lexicography. We can see how he turned this into practice by comparing his wordlist to Coles's:

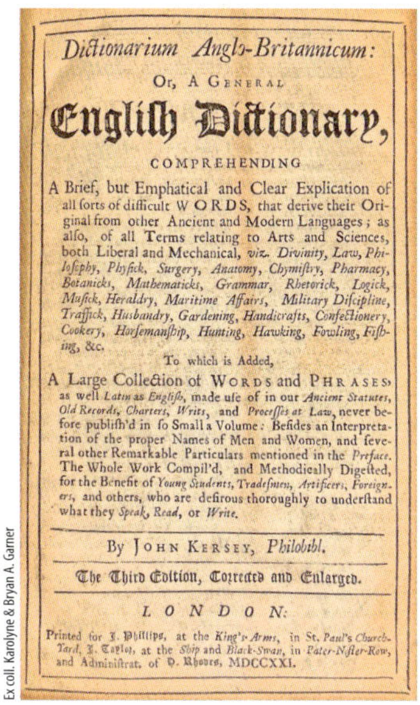
Dictionarium Anglo-Britannicum:

OR, A GENERAL

English Dictionary,

COMPREHENDING

A Brief, but Emphatical and Clear Explication of all sorts of difficult WORDS, that derive their Original from other Ancient and Modern Languages; as also, of all Terms relating to Arts and Sciences, both Liberal and Mechanical, *viz. Divinity, Law, Philosophy, Physick, Surgery, Anatomy, Chymistry, Pharmacy, Botanicks, Mathematicks, Grammar, Rhetorick, Logick, Musick, Heraldry, Maritime Affairs, Military Discipline, Traffick, Husbandry, Gardening, Handicrafts, Confectionery, Cookery, Horsemanship, Hunting, Hawking, Fowling, Fishing,* &c.

To which is Added,

A Large Collection of WORDS and PHRASES, as well *Latin* as *English*, made use of in our *Ancient Statutes, Old Records, Charters, Writs*, and *Processes at Law*, never before publish'd in so Small a Volume: Besides an Interpretation of the proper Names of Men and Women, and several other Remarkable Particulars mentioned in the *Preface*. The Whole Work Compil'd, and Methodically Digested, for the Benefit of *Young Students, Tradesmen, Artificers, Foreigners*, and others, who are desirous thoroughly to understand what they *Speak, Read*, or *Write*.

By JOHN KERSEY, *Philobibl.*

The Third Edition, Corrected and Enlarged.

LONDON:

Printed for J. Phillips, at the *King's-Arms*, in St. *Paul's Church-Yard*, J. Taylor, at the *Ship* and *Black-Swan*, in *Pater-Noster-Row*, and Administrat. of D. Rhodes, MDCCXXI.

Ex coll. Karolyne & Bryan A. Garner

Kersey's later work.

Coles (1676)	**J.K. (1702)**
Græcia, Grææ, graffer, graffically, graie, Graie-Fryer, grains of paradise, graith, grame, gramercy, gramineal, graminous, grammatical, grammar, grammatist, grammaticaster, grammarian, grampus, Grampound, granadil, granado, granary, granate, grand, grandee, Grand Cape, grand-distress, grandezza, grandiloquence, grandiloquent, Grandimomensers, grandinous, Grand Seignior	graff, graft, grafter, grain, grain of paradise, grain-colour, grained, gramercy, grammar, grammarian, grammatical, grample, grampus, granado, granary, grenate, grand, grand-child, grandame, grandee, grandeur, grand-father, Grand Signior

"There is a strong argument to attribute to [Kersey] . . . *A New English Dictionary*, published in 1702 under the initials 'J.K.' It has never been possible to prove completely that John Kersey and 'J.K.' were one and the same—Wheatley is dubious, Starnes and Noyes, although sympathetic, ultimately remain on the fence—whatever the truth, and the evidence must point toward a confirmation of Kersey's role, this dictionary took a new step forward: the Latinized terms that had dominated earlier works were largely discarded, and in their place came the vocabulary of popular, everyday speech, making this, quite literally, an *English* dictionary." (Green 1996:227.)

Kersey ejected most of the encyclopedic entries (*Græcia*, *Grand Cape*) and many of the obscurities (*gramineal*, *granadil*), shifting the focus to ordinary words (*grain*, *grand-child*). In fact, he cribbed much of his wordlist from the English part of bilingual dictionaries, ending up with about 28,000 words in 265 compact duodecimo pages.

He also criticized Coles's definitions, noting that (1) they're sometimes just definitions of Latin words rather than definitions of the English words derived from them, and (2) they often miss important senses. Coles defined *revolution*, for instance, as "a turning round to the first point." J.K. wasn't satisfied: "this Term, which simply denotes a *whirling round*, is us'd in Astronomy, for a certain Course of the Plants, Time, *&c.* and in common acceptation, for some notable change, especially of Government." (Sig. A3[r].)

That's not to say his that own entries are particularly thorough. There are no pronunciations or etymologies; parts of speech are not systematically identified, though "*To*" before verbs and "*A*" or "*An*" before count nouns gesture in that direction. Though he complained about Coles's definitions, his own can be laconic, sometimes merely indicating the existence of a word without giving its meaning. This is a typical run of entries:

> *To* aim at, or *take aim at.*
> *An* aim, or *level.*
> The Air, *an element.*
> *An* Air, in *Musick*, &c.
> *To* air, or dry a thing.
> Airiness.
> Airy.

An Airy, or *young brood of Hawks*, &c.

Aise, or *axweed*, an *herb*.

To ake, as, *my head akes*.

The Head-ake.

The Tooth-ake.

For all his shortcomings, though, J.K. has a place in English lexicographic history: he "established once and for all the practice of including the everyday vocabulary of English alongside 'harder' words." (Osselton 2009:149; Shapiro 2017:105–6.) Inkhorn words never disappeared from dictionaries, and they can be found there still, but after this they were no longer the main attraction of most English dictionaries. Though Kersey's definition of *because*—reading, in its entirety, "because of"—could be better, and though *cat* and *hat* have no definitions at all, the words at least appear in the alphabetical order, alongside even function words like *and*, *the*, *of*, and *from*.

"The importance of this work . . . lies in its introduction into the English dictionary of the bulk of the English language—that is, of the essential words of daily speech, writing, and reading. . . . If J.K. could not at a single step close the gap between the two traditions [hard-word dictionaries and common-word spellers] and produce a modern dictionary with its tolerant inclusiveness and service to all types of people, he at least called attention to the forgotten words and the forgotten class of readers." (Starnes & Noyes 1946:70–71.)

If J.K. is in fact John Kersey, he had several dictionaries ahead of him. A few years later, he revised Edward Phillips's *New World of Words* (no. 17), expanding the 436-page fifth edition into a 712-page "sixth edition, revised, corrected, and improved; with the addition of near twenty thousand words, from the best authors domestic and foreign." Two years after that, he published a *Dictionarium Anglo-Britannicum*, which, though largely derived from Phillips, says on the title page that it is "*By* JOHN KERSEY, *Philobibl.*"—*Philobiblon*, or book lover. Kersey is generally assumed to have been alive in 1721, when a revised edition of his *Dictionarium Anglo-Britannicum* was published, but no good evidence of his latter days has turned up.

Nor, as we've said, is there conclusive evidence that the J.K. on the title page here is in fact John Kersey. Though shared by many, our supposition is disputed by others. For example, the 19th-century scholar Henry B. Wheatley made a contrary inference on a shaky surmise: "These initials [J.K.] are usually supposed to represent John Kersey, but I am inclined to doubt this, because a second edition was published in 1713 with the same initials, and Kersey's Dictionary was published in 1708 with his name." (Wheatley 1854:240.) The answer to this reasoning is that inertia is as inevitable a force with publishers as with others: the easy thing is to carry forward the authorial attribution of the earlier edition. But it's an argument nonetheless.

22

Edward Cocker

What *Is* a Dictionary, After All?

Cocker, Edward. *Cocker's English Dictionary: interpreting the most refined and difficult words in divinity, philosophy, law, physick, mathematicks, husbandry, mechanicks, &c.* John Hawkins ed. London: A. Back & A. Bettesworth, 1704. 2d ed. 1715.

"Our Language may now be said, not only to equal any Modern Tongue spoken in *Europe*, but even the *Greek* and *Latin* itself." (John Hawkins's Preface, 2d ed.)

Cocker (1631–1676), thought to be perhaps from Northamptonshire, was by 1657 teaching writing and arithmetic in St. Paul's Churchyard, London. During his lifetime he compiled some copybooks for schoolchildren, the first of which (*The Pen's Triumph*) is now unknown and untraceable. After he died, his reputation as an author swelled with *Cocker's Decimal Arithmetick* (1685 and five later editions), *Cocker's Accomplish'd Schoolmaster* (1696), and *Cocker's English Dictionary* (1704), all of which may have been sham attempts to capitalize on his name. All three were said to be prepared for publication by John Hawkins, but he had died in 1692, before the latter two appeared from the Back family of publishers. The books' true origin is mysterious and suspect.

In any event, the expanded second and third editions of *Cocker's English Dictionary* (1715, 1724) represent perhaps the height of confusion about what a dictionary is. Although the book is small, it is not principally a wordbook. Instead, it's a gallimaufry of information, with spans of entries such as *Folkston* (a town in Suffolk), *Fons solis* (the fountain of the sun), *Fountainbleau* (the French King's palace), and *fond/fund* (a stock of money or a foundation). Another span of entries, over four three-column pages, has long essays about *James I*; *Jane, Queen of England*; *Jane Grey*; and *Jane Shore*—followed by *Janizaries*.

The compilers, whoever they were, didn't think dictionaries should confine themselves to lexical information—the meanings of words—as opposed to knowledge of all sorts. The nature of lexicography was still unsettled when the third edition appeared in 1724.

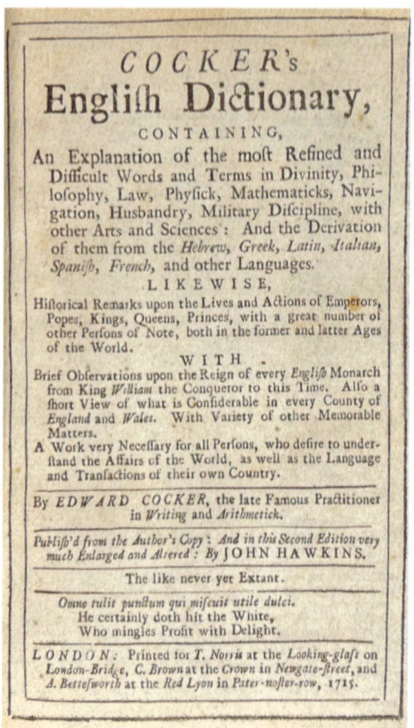

COCKER's
English Dictionary,
CONTAINING,
An Explanation of the moſt Refined and Difficult Words and Terms in Divinity, Philoſophy, Law, Phyſick, Mathematicks, Navigation, Husbandry, Military Diſcipline, with other Arts and Sciences: And the Derivation of them from the *Hebrew*, *Greek*, *Latin*, *Italian*, *Spaniſh*, *French*, and other Languages.
LIKEWISE,
Hiſtorical Remarks upon the Lives and Actions of Emperors, Popes, Kings, Queens, Princes, with a great number of other Perſons of Note, both in the former and latter Ages of the World.
WITH
Brief Obſervations upon the Reign of every *Engliſh* Monarch from King *William* the Conqueror to this Time. Alſo a ſhort View of what is Conſiderable in every County of *England* and *Wales*. With Variety of other Memorable Matters.
A Work very Neceſſary for all Perſons, who deſire to underſtand the Affairs of the World, as well as the Language and Tranſactions of their own Country.

By *EDWARD COCKER*, the late Famous Practitioner in *Writing* and *Arithmetick*.

Publiſh'd from the Author's Copy: And in this Second Edition very much Enlarged and Altered: By JOHN HAWKINS.

The like never yet Extant.

Omne tulit punctum qui miſcuit utile dulci.
He certainly doth hit the White,
Who mingles Profit with Delight.

LONDON: Printed for *T. Norris* at the *Looking-glaſs* on *London-Bridge*, *C. Brown* at the *Crown* in *Newgate-ſtreet*, and *A. Betteſworth* at the *Red Lyon* in *Pater-noſter-row*, 1715.

Ex coll. Karolyne & Bryan A. Garner

Perhaps they were pushing to be more inclusive because of pressures created by the emergence of Bailey (no. 26) in 1721.

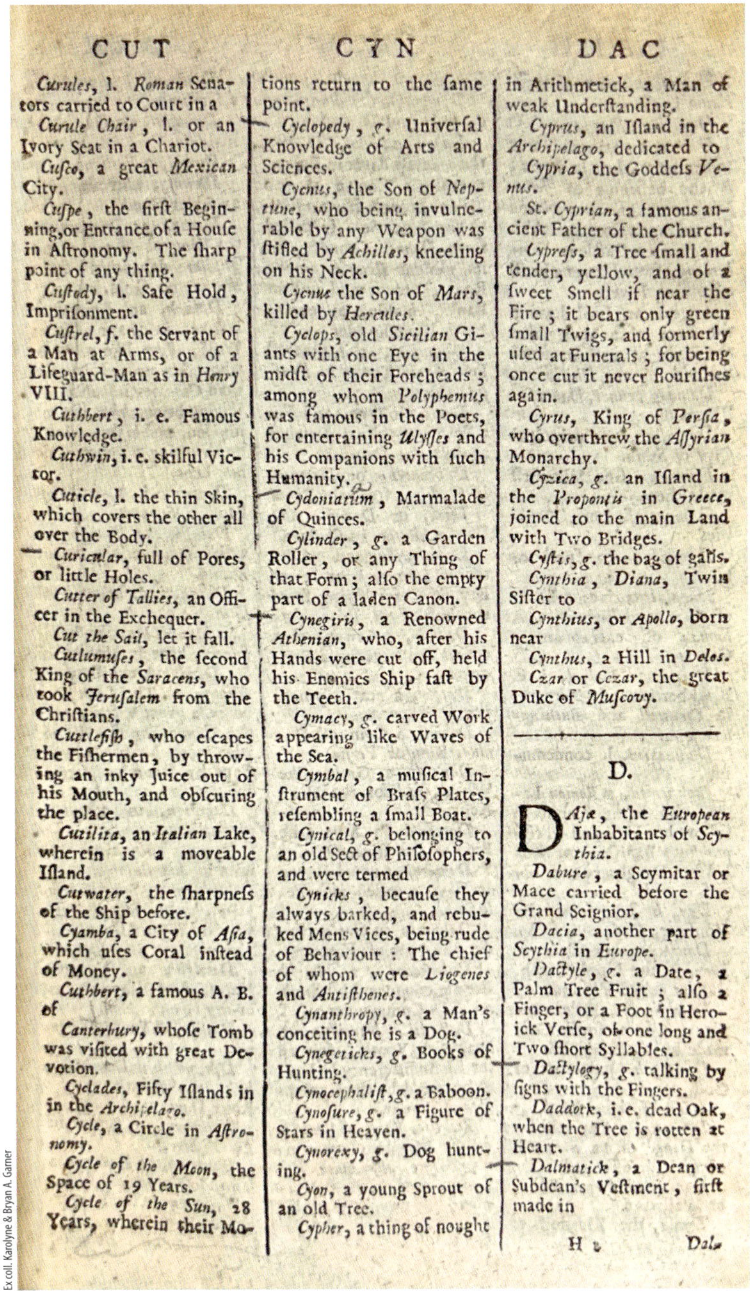

CUT — CYN — DAC

Curules, l. *Roman* Senators carried to Court in a

Curule Chair, l. or an Ivory Seat in a Chariot.

Cuſco, a great *Mexican* City.

Cuſpe, the firſt Beginning, or Entrance of a Houſe in Aſtronomy. The ſharp point of any thing.

Cuſtody, l. Safe Hold, Impriſonment.

Cuſtrel, f. the Servant of a Man at Arms, or of a Lifeguard-Man as in *Henry* VIII.

Cuthbert, i. e. Famous Knowledge.

Cuthwin, i. e. skilful Victor.

Cuticle, l. the thin Skin, which covers the other all over the Body.

Curicular, full of Pores, or little Holes.

Cutter of Tallies, an Officer in the Exchequer.

Cut the Sail, let it fall.

Cutlumuſes, the ſecond King of the *Saracens*, who took *Jeruſalem* from the Chriſtians.

Cuttlefiſh, who eſcapes the Fiſhermen, by throwing an inky Juice out of his Mouth, and obſcuring the place.

Cutilita, an *Italian* Lake, wherein is a moveable Iſland.

Cutwater, the ſharpneſs of the Ship before.

Cyamba, a City of *Aſia*, which uſes Coral inſtead of Money.

Cuthbert, a famous A. B. of

Canterbury, whoſe Tomb was viſited with great Devotion.

Cyclades, Fifty Iſlands in in the *Archipelago*.

Cycle, a Circle in *Aſtronomy*.

Cycle of the Moon, the Space of 19 Years.

Cycle of the Sun, 28 Years, wherein their Motions return to the ſame point.

Cyclopedy, g. Univerſal Knowledge of Arts and Sciences.

Cycnus, the Son of *Neptune*, who being invulnerable by any Weapon was ſtifled by *Achilles*, kneeling on his Neck.

Cycnus the Son of *Mars*, killed by *Hercules*.

Cyclops, old *Sicilian* Giants with one Eye in the midſt of their Foreheads; among whom *Polyphemus* was famous in the Poets, for entertaining *Ulyſſes* and his Companions with ſuch Humanity.

Cydoniatum, Marmalade of Quinces.

Cylinder, g. a Garden Roller, or any Thing of that Form; alſo the empty part of a laden Canon.

Cynegiris, a Renowned *Athenian*, who, after his Hands were cut off, held his Enemics Ship faſt by the Teeth.

Cymacy, g. carved Work appearing like Waves of the Sea.

Cymbal, a muſical Inſtrument of Braſs Plates, reſembling a ſmall Boat.

Cynical, g. belonging to an old Sect of Philoſophers, and were termed

Cynicks, becauſe they always barked, and rebuked Mens Vices, being rude of Behaviour: The chief of whom were *Diogenes* and *Antiſthenes*.

Cynanthropy, g. a Man's conceiting he is a Dog.

Cynegeticks, g. Books of Hunting.

Cynocephaliſt, g. a Baboon.

Cynoſure, g. a Figure of Stars in Heaven.

Cynorexy, g. Dog hunting.

Cyon, a young Sprout of an old Tree.

Cypher, a thing of nought in Arithmetick, a Man of weak Underſtanding.

Cyprus, an Iſland in the *Archipelago*, dedicated to

Cypria, the Goddeſs *Venus*.

St. *Cyprian*, a famous ancient Father of the Church.

Cypreſs, a Tree ſmall and tender, yellow, and of a ſweet Smell if near the Fire; it bears only green ſmall Twigs, and formerly uſed at Funerals; for being once cut it never flouriſhes again.

Cyrus, King of *Perſia*, who overthrew the *Aſſyrian* Monarchy.

Cyzica, g. an Iſland in the *Propontis* in *Greece*, joined to the main Land with Two Bridges.

Cyſtis, g. the bag of galls.

Cynthia, *Diana*, Twin Siſter to

Cynthius, or *Apollo*, born near

Cynthus, a Hill in *Delos*.

Czar or *Cezar*, the great Duke of *Muſcovy*.

D.

D*Ajæ*, the *European* Inhabitants of *Scythia*.

Dabure, a Scymitar or Mace carried before the Grand Seignior.

Dacia, another part of *Scythia* in *Europe*.

Dactyle, g. a Date, a Palm Tree Fruit; alſo a Finger, or a Foot in Heroick Verſe, of one long and Two ſhort Syllables.

Dactylogy, g. talking by ſigns with the Fingers.

Daddock, i. e. dead Oak, when the Tree is rotten at Heart.

Dalmatick, a Dean or Subdean's Veſtment, firſt made in

H 2 Dal-

Ex coll. Karolyne & Bryan A. Garner

From the 1715 edition.

Ex coll. Karolyne & Bryan A. Garner

Ex coll. Karolyne & Bryan A. Garner

23

John Harris

Encyclopedic Polymath

Harris, John. *Lexicon Technicum: or, An Universal English Dictionary of Arts and Sciences: Explaining not only the Terms of Art, but the Arts Themselves*. London: Printed for Dan. Brown et al., 1704. 2d ed. 2 vols. 1708–1710.

HARRIS (1666?–1719) studied at Trinity College, Oxford, graduating with a BA in 1686. He was a cleric—variously a chaplain, curate, prebendary, and rector. Naturally interested in theology (he wrote a tract against atheism), Harris was also drawn to mathematics and the sciences, especially astronomy and microscopy.

In 1704, he produced a lexicon that came to be regarded as the prototype of Enlightenment dictionaries and encyclopedias. In it he promoted the foundational importance of Newtonian physics. Some have called it the first encyclopedia of science and technology.

"That which I have aimied at, is to make it a Dictionary not only of bare *Words* but *Things*. . . . I found much less help from Dictionaries already published, then [sic] one might have expected from their *Titles*." (Preface.)

But is Harris's work really more encyclopedia than dictionary? The categories had yet to be worked out. Today we think of encyclopedias as consisting of long, discursive essays and dictionaries as containing short entries consisting primarily of definitions with illustrations. We also know, in retrospect, that American dictionaries have tended to contain more encyclopedic information than British ones. It is a question of degree.

In the *Lexicon Technicum*, the average quarto page contains more than 20 short entries. But some entries—as for *interest* (the kind you calculate), *microscope*, and *sound*—extend over several pages. At left is a typical span of entries.

GLANS, the ſame with *Balenus* and *Suppoſitorium*.
GLANDULUM *Corpus*, the ſame with *Proſtata*.
GLANDULOSA *Tunica Inteſtinorum*. See *Papillæ Inteſtinorum*.
GLASS *of Antimony*. See *Regulus of Antimony*.
GLASSY *Humour* of the Eye. See *Vitrous Humour*.
GLASSY *Tunicle*. See *Vitreous Tunicle*.
GLAUCOMA, is a fault in the Eye, or a Tranſmutation of the Chryſtalline Humour, into a Gray or Sky-colour.
GLAUCOSIS, the ſame with *Glaucoma*.
GLEBE-LAND, *Church-Land*, is moſt commonly taken for Land belonging to a Pariſh Church beſide the Tythe.
GLENE, the ſame with *Pupilla*: Alſo the Cavity of a Bone which receives another within it.
GLENOIDES, are two Cavities in the lower part of the firſt Vertebre of the Neck.

Ex coll. Karolyne & Bryan A. Garner

That is followed by 13 full columns on *globe*, with many definitions and "problems" set forth. So the book really is something of a hybrid between a dictionary and an encyclopedia. The book is typographically advanced: there are print illustrations and tables throughout, including several foldouts.

In his preface, Harris blasted many predecessors. Étienne Chauvin's *Lexicon Rationale* "is too much filled with School Terms, to be usefully instructive; and is as defective in the Modern Improvements of Mathematical and Physical Learning, as it abounds with a Cant which was once mistaken for *Science*." The Académie française's *Grand Dictionnaire des Art & des Sciences* "is only a bare Explication of Terms of Art; and it seems rather to have been design'd to improve and propagate the *French Language*, than to inform and instruct the Humane Mind in general." Harris prized technical terminology and disdained the *Grand Dictionnaire*'s tendency to be "filled every where with *Simple Terms*, so that you are told what a Dog, a Cat, a Horse and a Sheep is . . . yet how the bare Names of Animals and Vegetables, of Metals and Minerals, can be reckoned as *Terms of Art* . . . I confess I cannot see." As for Phillips's *New World of Words* (no. 17), "the Compiler had the *Ill Luck* to Collect many *Foreign* Faults, and to understand little or nothing of the *Arts* and *Sciences* himself."

Why this long condemnation of precursors? "I Write not this only to disparage the Performances of others, or to build my self a Reputation on their Ruines: But I think my self obliged to Acquaint the Reader with the plain truth of Things, without Favour or Affection."

For his extensive inclusion of legal terminology, Harris engaged an outside consultant: "I did my self actually consult the best [law] Books and Dictionaries I could get recommended to me; and from thence I transcribed abridgedly all that seem'd necessary to be inserted here; and since that I have had it carefully examined and corrected by a Gentleman of known Ability in that Profession."

He ended by exhorting readers to be gentle with him, given that corrections were sure to come: "by no means be prejudicial to the first impression."

Ex coll. Karolyne & Bryan A. Garner

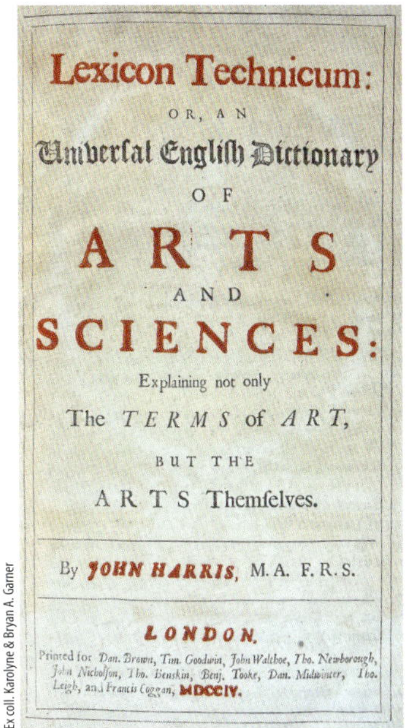

Lexicon Technicum:
OR, AN
Universal English Dictionary
OF
ARTS
AND
SCIENCES:
Explaining not only
The *TERMS* of *ART*,
BUT THE
ARTS Themselves.

By *JOHN HARRIS*, M.A. F.R.S.

LONDON,
Printed for *Dan. Brown, Tim. Goodwin, John Walthoe, Tho. Newborough, John Nicholson, Tho. Benskin, Benj. Tooke, Dan. Midwinter, Tho. Leigh,* and *Francis Coggan*, MDCCIV.

Ex coll. Karolyne & Bryan A. Garner

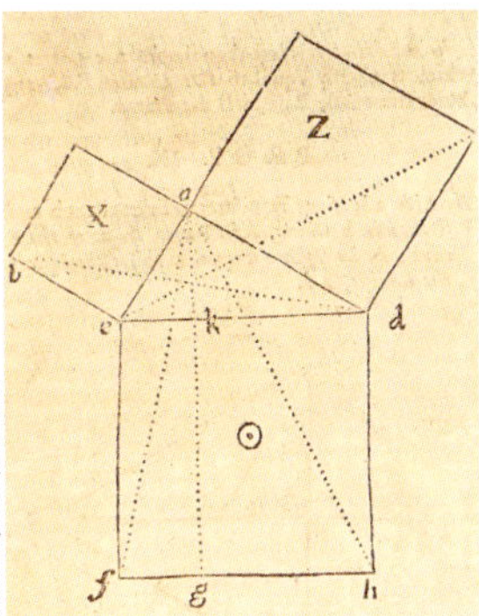

Ex coll. Karolyne & Bryan A. Garner

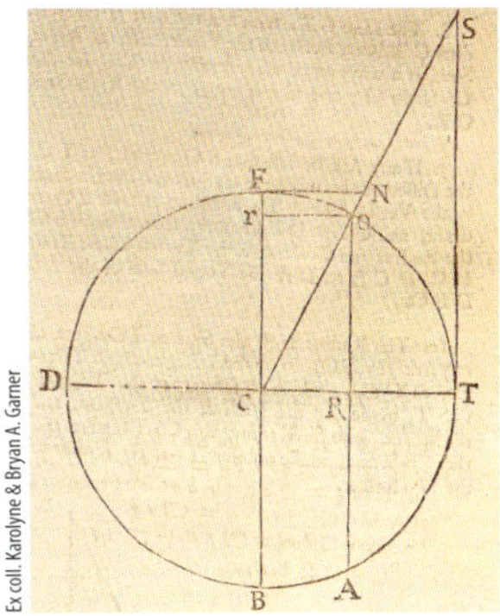

Ex coll. Karolyne & Bryan A. Garner

Even in the first edition of 1704, Harris's book contained hundreds of diagrams. These are 2 of the 59 appearing in the entry for *triangle*.

Ex coll. Karolyne & Bryan A. Garner

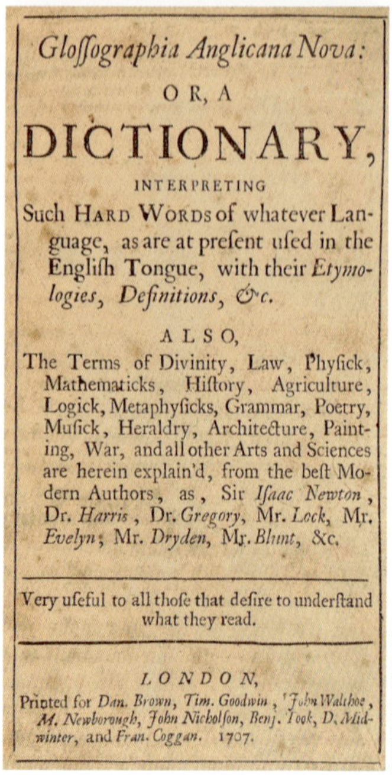

Gloſſographia Anglicana Nova:
OR, A
DICTIONARY,
INTERPRETING
Such HARD WORDS of whatever Language, as are at preſent uſed in the Engliſh Tongue, with their *Etymologies, Definitions, &c.*

ALSO,
The Terms of Divinity, Law, Phyſick, Mathematicks, Hiſtory, Agriculture, Logick, Metaphyſicks, Grammar, Poetry, Muſick, Heraldry, Architecture, Painting, War, and all other Arts and Sciences are herein explain'd, from the beſt Modern Authors, as, Sir *Iſaac Newton*, Dr. *Harris*, Dr. *Gregory*, Mr. *Lock*, Mr. *Evelyn*, Mr. *Dryden*, Mr. *Blunt*, &c.

Very uſeful to all thoſe that deſire to underſtand what they read.

LONDON,
Printed for *Dan. Brown, Tim. Goodwin*, *John Walthoe*, *M. Newborough, John Nicholſon, Benj. Took, D. Midwinter*, and *Fran. Coggan*. 1707.

Ex coll. Karolyne & Bryan A. Garner

24

Anonymous

Not Your Father's *Glossographia*

***Glossographia Anglicana Nova: or, A Dictionary, Interpreting Such Hard Words of whatever Language, as are at present used in the English Tongue, with their Etymologies, Definitions, &c.* London: Dan. Brown et al., 1707.**

ALTHOUGH THE TITLE INVITES CONFUSION with Thomas Blount's *Glossographia* of 1656 (no. 16), this is a wholly different book. In fact, we know nothing about the author's identity, though he seems to have been unusually scientifically literate. The great strength of this work is its treatment of the technical vocabulary, which is carefully defined. The entries for words such as *calcination*, *fluxion*, and *force* show conversance with the latest discoveries in mathematics, physics, and chemistry. The anonymous lexicographer made extensive use of John Harris's *Lexicon Technicum* (no. 23), but this was promotion rather than plagiarism: the books shared a publisher, and this *Glossographia* encourages users to consult Harris. The ample borrowings from other dictionaries are less defensible.

The book is especially devoted to words used in the learned professions—the church, the law, and medicine, as well as the university. Their characteristic "hard words," as the title page promises, abound on every page: *liquidescency*, *lispound*, *litation*, *lithontripicks*, and so on. But the inclusion of familiar words—*listless*, *litany*, *literate*, *litigation*—shows that the dictionary isn't exclusively concerned with inkhornisms. Occasional citations of "the best Modern Authors," including Isaac Newton, John Locke, and John Dryden, serve as evidence that words are actually in use.

Though much about this work is derivative—the compiler admits as much—it's important in being among the first properly illustrated English dictionaries, with dozens of woodcuts showing mostly heraldic escutcheons. They are probably attributable to the efforts of the printer, Daniel Brown, who three years before had issued Harris's heavily illustrated work.

25

John Quincy
The Defining Apothecary/Physician

Quincy, John. ***Lexicon Physico-Medicum: or, A New Physical Dictionary, Explaining the Difficult Terms used in the several Branches of the Profession, and in such Parts of Philosophy as are introductory thereunto.*** **London, 1719. 2d ed. 1722. 5th ed. 1737. 6th ed. 1743.**

John Quincy (1683?–1723) arrived at university at a time of intellectual excitement in what we would call the natural sciences. Physics and biology were in the midst of revolutions, and at least as important, some schools and universities were beginning to teach the new science rather than medieval orthodoxy. Against this background, Quincy earned his medical degree in 1712 at the University of Edinburgh, which was rapidly becoming an international center for medical education.

After an apprenticeship, Quincy set up in London as both an apothecary and a physician, two roles that were often combined in the 18th century. He published several books on medicine, including a translation of Nathaniel Hodges's *Loimologia*, an influential work on the bubonic plague written by a physician who lived through the Great Plague of London.

Quincy's most enduring work is the *Lexicon Physico-Medicum*. The book leaned heavily on the *Lexicon Medicum* (1598) of Bartolomeo Castelli of Messina, which glossed medical terms in Greek, Latin, Arabic, Hebrew, French, and Italian. But while Quincy called Castelli's dictionary "a Work of Exactness and Labour," it was far behind the times—based on "the Ancients, and (if I may so call them) the Fathers in Medicine"—and it needed updating:

> Since the Introduction of Mathematical Reasoning, and the Application of Mechanical Laws to a Study, indeed not otherwise knowable, the Books of Physicians abound with Terms very unmanageable, and which are not explained in any one Work extant; for Want of which Recourse, those

Ex coll. Karolyne & Bryan A. Garner

The first edition (1719).

Ex coll. Karolyne & Bryan A. Garner

The sixth edition label (1743).

> Books are, to many Readers, who at first are not aware of the Change, as difficult and unintelligible, as if wrote in Languages altogether unknown. [Pp. x–xi.]

"Insomuch that the Terms of Philosophical Writers have been transplanted into the Discourses of Physicians, . . . it [has been] frequently necessary to explain such new Terms for the use of those who have not Liesure [sic] or Opportunity to go the same Compass." (P. x.)

The dictionary mixes short definitions ("*Cardialgia*, the Heart-burn, a Pain supposed to be felt in the Heart, but more properly in the Stomach, and sometimes rises all along from thence up to the *Oesophagus*"; "*Inflammation*, is when the Blood is obstructed so as to croud in a greater Quantity into any particular Part, and give it a greater Colour and Heat than usual") with long essays, including five pages on *plant*, seven on *narcoticks*, and eight on *laws of nature*, a wide-ranging survey of Newtonian physics.

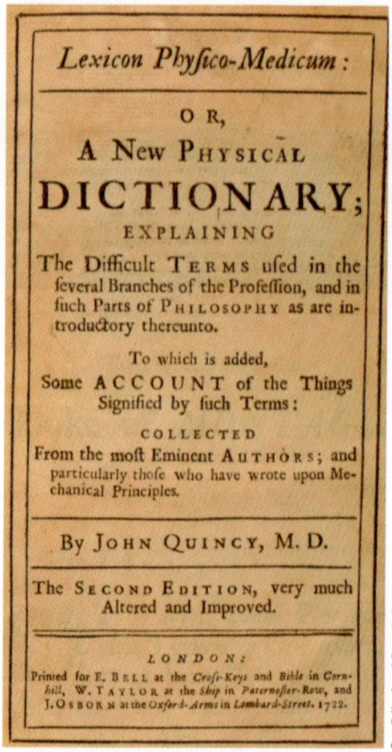

Lexicon Phyſico-Medicum:

OR,

A New PHYSICAL

DICTIONARY;

EXPLAINING

The Difficult TERMS uſed in the ſeveral Branches of the Profeſſion, and in ſuch Parts of PHILOSOPHY as are introductory thereunto.

To which is added,

Some ACCOUNT of the Things Signified by ſuch Terms:

COLLECTED

From the moſt Eminent AUTHORS; and particularly thoſe who have wrote upon Mechanical Principles.

By JOHN QUINCY, M. D.

The SECOND EDITION, very much Altered and Improved.

LONDON:

Printed for E. BELL at the *Croſs-Keys* and *Bible* in *Cornhill*, W. TAYLOR at the *Ship* in *Paternoſter-Row*, and J. OSBORN at the *Oxford-Arms* in *Lombard-Street*. 1722.

Ex coll. Karolyne & Bryan A. Garner

The second edition title page.

Sir Norman Moore, the medical historian responsible for Quincy's entry in the *Dictionary of National Biography* in 1896, was unforgiving of his old-fashioned medical knowledge: his *Medico-Physical Essays* "show that his main skill was as an apothecary," and "He considered dried millipedes good for tuberculous lymphatic glands." But it's unfair to judge an early-18th-century physician by late-19th-century standards. Quincy summed up his age's medical knowledge well, he wrote clearly, and he steered clear of medical controversy.

Quincy died three years after the first edition appeared. Updated editions continued to appear after his death—at least 11 more in the 18th century and many more in the 19th—and they reflect advances in the world's medical knowledge. Among the most important changes is *inoculation*, defined in the first edition as "the grafting of one Tree upon another; which is often so contrived as to have many different Fruits proceed from the same Stock, by grafting different Slips into its several Branches." In 1722, though, after Lady Mary Wortley Montagu brought a practice back from Istanbul to her native England, the entry grew longer:

"The Books of Physicians abound with Terms very unmanageable, and which are not explained in any one Work extant." (P. x.)

> This Term of late hath been also much used in a very different Manner, for the Practice now introduced of transplanting the Small-Pox, by Infusion of the Matter from ripened Pustules, into the Veins of the uninfected, in the hopes of procuring a milder Sort than what frequently comes by Infection.

A sixth edition, "with new improvements from the latest chymical and mechanical authors," appeared in 1743.

Although the *Lexicon Physico-Medicum* was an important dictionary in its own right, it had an even more important lexicographic legacy: most of the medical entries in Johnson's *Dictionary* (no. 35) depend on Quincy. He is cited more than 300 times, including under *alcohol*, *anorexy*, *aorta*, *asthma*, *capillary*, *carcinoma*, *cataract*, *dose*, *dropsy*, *elixir*, *epilepsy*, *glaucoma*, *inflammation*, *jaundice*, *kidney*, *narcotick*, *pathology*, and *vertigo*, and probably appears nearly as often without citation.

"On my present Behalf I desire it to be believed, that a sincere Willingness, and desire to communicate to others what I think to have been of use to my self, is the real Motive of the Publication hereof. Opportunities of Information are not alike afforded to all; and Assistances easiest to come at, may be very welcome to those who cannot procure others. I remember the Time, when such a Work as this would have been very acceptable to my self; it therefore may be allow'd me very naturally to suppose it agreeable to others in the same Course of Study." (1st ed., p. xvi.)

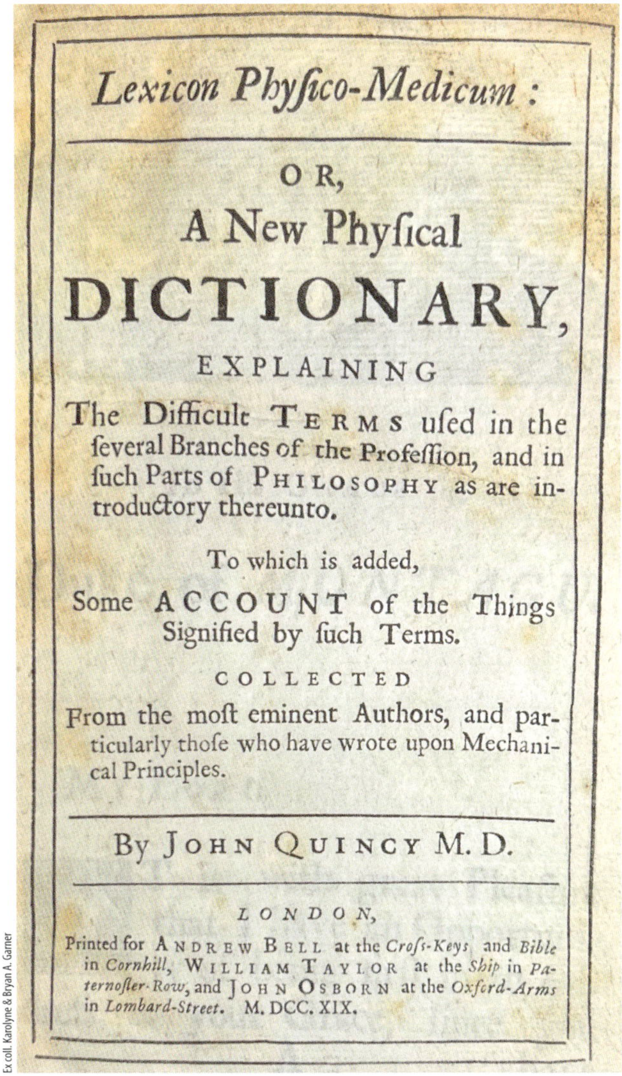

Lexicon Phyſico-Medicum:

OR,

A New Phyſical

DICTIONARY,

EXPLAINING

The Difficult TERMS uſed in the ſeveral Branches of the Profeſſion, and in ſuch Parts of PHILOSOPHY as are introductory thereunto.

To which is added,

Some ACCOUNT of the Things Signified by ſuch Terms.

COLLECTED

From the moſt eminent Authors, and particularly thoſe who have wrote upon Mechanical Principles.

By JOHN QUINCY M. D.

LONDON,

Printed for ANDREW BELL at the *Croſs-Keys* and *Bible* in *Cornhill*, WILLIAM TAYLOR at the *Ship* in *Paternoſter-Row*, and JOHN OSBORN at the *Oxford-Arms* in *Lombard-Street*. M. DCC. XIX.

Ex coll. Karolyne & Bryan A. Garner

The first edition title page.

"Quincy's dictionary . . . includes a number of terms which we would not normally associate with medicine, including *congruity, form, levity, light, musick, moment, regular body,* and *tide*. His view is that unless these things are properly understood, medicine will remain in a state of confusion." (McConchie 2018:153.)

Ex coll. Karolyne & Bryan A. Garner

26

Nathan Bailey

Prolific Philologos

Bailey, N[athan]. ***An Universal Etymological English Dictionary: Comprehending the Derivations of the Generality of Words in the English Tongue, either Antient or Modern, from the Antient British, Saxon, Danish, Norman and Modern French, Teutonic, Dutch, Spanish, Italian, as also from the Latin, Greek, and Hebrew Languages, each in their Proper Characters.*** **London: E. Bell et al., 1721.**

———. ***The Universal Etymological English Dictionary: In Two Parts.*** **[Supplementary volume.] London: T. Cox, 1727.**

———. ***Dictionarium Britannicum: Or, A more Compleat Universal Etymological English Dictionary Than any Extant*** **[*etc.*]. Folio. London: T. Cox, 1730. Also: 2d ed. 1736.**

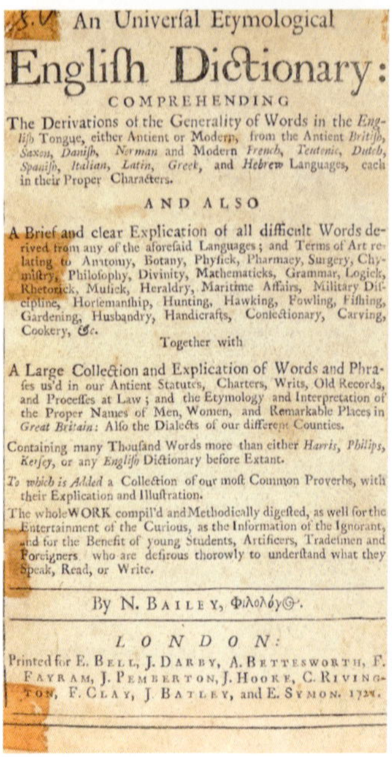

An Univerſal Etymological

English Dictionary:

COMPREHENDING

The Derivations of the Generality of Words in the *Engliſh* Tongue, either Antient or Modern, from the Antient *Britiſh*, *Saxon*, *Daniſh*, *Norman* and Modern *French*, *Teutonic*, *Dutch*, *Spaniſh*, *Italian*, *Latin*, *Greek*, and *Hebrew* Languages, each in their Proper Characters.

AND ALSO

A Brief and clear Explication of all difficult Words derived from any of the aforeſaid Languages; and Terms of Art relating to Anatomy, Botany, Phyſick, Pharmacy, Surgery, Chymiſtry, Philoſophy, Divinity, Mathematicks, Grammar, Logick, Rhetorick, Muſick, Heraldry, Maritime Affairs, Military Diſcipline, Horſemanſhip, Hunting, Hawking, Fowling, Fiſhing, Gardening, Husbandry, Handicrafts, Confectionary, Carving, Cookery, *&c.*

Together with

A Large Collection and Explication of Words and Phraſes us'd in our Antient Statutes, Charters, Writs, Old Records, and Proceſſes at Law; and the Etymology and Interpretation of the Proper Names of Men, Women, and Remarkable Places in *Great Britain*: Alſo the Dialects of our different Counties.

Containing many Thouſand Words more than either *Harris*, *Philips*, *Kerſey*, or any *Engliſh* Dictionary before Extant.

To which is Added a Collection of our moſt Common Proverbs, with their Explication and Illuſtration.

The whole WORK compil'd and Methodically digeſted, as well for the Entertainment of the Curious, as the Information of the Ignorant, and for the Benefit of young Students, Artificers, Tradeſmen and Foreigners who are deſirous thorowly to underſtand what they Speak, Read, or Write.

By N. BAILEY, Φιλολόγος.

LONDON:

Printed for E. BELL, J. DARBY, A. BETTESWORTH, F. FAYRAM, J. PEMBERTON, J. HOOKE, C. RIVINGTON, F. CLAY, J. BATLEY, and E. SYMON. 1721.

Ex coll. Karolyne & Bryan A. Garner

The 1721 octavo.

NATHAN BAILEY (1679?–1742), baptized in 1691, was old enough in 1692 to sign a church document. (He belonged to a Seventh-Day Baptist congregation that didn't believe in infant baptism.) There has been some confusion over whether his first name was Nathan or Nathaniel. Most of the authorial attributions are to "N. Bailey" or "Nat. Bailey." But the dedication in the 1730 text (second state) gives the unabbreviated name "Nathan," which has led many scholars to conclude that the shorter name is correct.

By the 1720s, he was working as a schoolmaster in Stepney, and his early publications grew out of that teaching experience, starting with a Latin textbook, *English and Latin Exercises for Schoolboys* (1706). It was popular enough to go through 22 authorized editions, along with a few piracies, and was in print well into the next century.

Bailey wrote not one but two important English dictionaries. The *Universal Etymological English Dictionary*, an octavo volume of nearly a thousand pages, appeared in 1721, attributed to "N. Bailey, Φιλόλογος"—*philologos*, word-lover. The book leans heavily on Kersey's *Dictionarium Anglo-Britannicum* (no. 21), adopting its wordlist and many of its definitions with only minimal changes. And while the title advertises etymology as its main selling point, most of Bailey's word histories are borrowed from a few familiar sources. Despite its shortcomings, it was the most extensive English dictionary published to that point, and it covered more of the English vocabulary than any of its predecessors. It also introduced a few innovations into English lexicography: headwords are set in FULL CAPS, making it easier for users to scan a column of type to find where the entries begin.

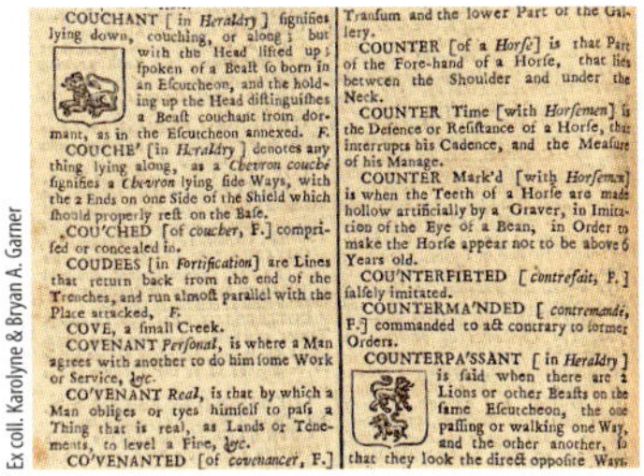

COUCHANT [in *Heraldry*] signifies lying down, couching, or along; but with the Head lifted up; spoken of a Beast so born in an Escutcheon, and the holding up the Head distinguishes a Beast couchant from dormant, as in the Escutcheon annexed. *F.*

COUCHE' [in *Heraldry*] denotes any thing lying along, as a *Chevron couché* signifies a *Chevron* lying side Ways, with the 2 Ends on one Side of the Shield which should properly rest on the Base.

COU'CHED [of *coucher*, F.] comprised or concealed in.

COUDEES [in *Fortification*] are Lines that return back from the end of the Trenches, and run almost parallel with the Place attacked, *F.*

COVE, a small Creek.

COVENANT *Personal*, is where a Man agrees with another to do him some Work or Service, &c.

CO'VENANT *Real*, is that by which a Man obliges or tyes himself to pass a Thing that is real, as Lands or Tenements, to level a Fine, &c.

CO'VENANTED [of *covenancer*, F.]

Transum and the lower Part of the Gallery.

COUNTER [of a *Horse*] is that Part of the Fore-hand of a Horse, that lies between the Shoulder and under the Neck.

COUNTER Time [with *Horsemen*] is the Defence or Resistance of a Horse, that interrupts his Cadence, and the Measure of his Manage.

COUNTER Mark'd [with *Horsemen*] is when the Teeth of a Horse are made hollow artificially by a Graver, in Imitation of the Eye of a Bean, in Order to make the Horse appear not to be above 6 Years old.

COU'NTERFIETED [*contrefait*, F.] falsely imitated.

COUNTERMA'NDED [*contremandé*, F.] commanded to act contrary to former Orders.

COUNTERPA'SSANT [in *Heraldry*] is said when there are 2 Lions or other Beasts on the same Escutcheon, the one passing or walking one Way, and the other another, so that they look the direct opposite Ways.

Ex coll. Karolyne & Bryan A. Garner

Two small woodcuts in the 1727 edition.

In 1727, Bailey issued a strangely miscellaneous "Volume II," with its own alphabetical sequence. The title page promises "thousands of Words not in the former Volume," "a considerable Number of Terms of art in Anatomy, Botany, Heraldry, Logick . . . ," "proper Names of Persons and Places in *Great Britain*," the "Theogony, Theology, and Mythology of the *Egyptians*, *Greeks*, *Romans*, &c.," plus a separate alphabetical sequence for "An orthographical dictionary, shewing both the orthography and the orthoepia of the English tongue." It deserves attention for being among the first English dictionaries to make extensive use of woodcut illustrations, and it's the first general English dictionary to indicate stressed syllables with an accent mark: A'BACUS, ABA'DDIR, ABA'GION . . . .

Nathan Bailey.

Three years later, Bailey combined the two volumes, added a few thousand more words, and rewrote many of his entries. FULL CAPS in headwords are replaced by Mixed Caps and small caps. (Luna 2005:187.) The new book got a new title, *Dictionarium Britannicum: or A more Compleat Universal Etymological English Dictionary Than any Extant*, now in one folio volume of more than 800 pages. It's a significant advance over its predecessor. The definitions are still perfunctory—*crow*, "a bird well known"; *happy*, "prosperous, felicitous, blessed"—and sometimes more encyclopedic than lexicographic: his entire entry for *tabacco* reads "[takes its Name from the Island *Tabago*, in the *West-Indies*] being from thence brought into *England* by Sir *Francis Drake*, in the Year 1585." Bailey pays no attention to the most difficult polysemous words in the language, dispensing with the definitions for *take*, for instance, in just one line: "to lay hold on, to seize; also to receive from another." Still, Bailey took dictionaries far beyond the hard-word tradition, including "several 1000 *English* Words and Phrases, in no *English* Dictionary before extant," and giving unprecedented attention to common words, scientific and technical terms, dialect terms—even some vulgarisms and obscenities ("To Swive . . .

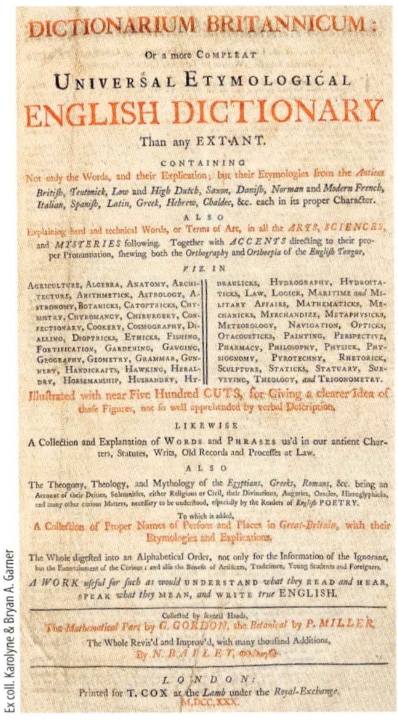

DICTIONARIUM BRITANNICUM:

Or a more COMPLEAT

UNIVERSAL ETYMOLOGICAL

ENGLISH DICTIONARY

Than any EXTANT.

CONTAINING

Not only the Words, and their Explication; but their Etymologies from the *Antient British*, *Teutonick*, *Low* and *High Dutch*, *Saxon*, *Danish*, *Norman* and *Modern French*, *Italian*, *Spanish*, *Latin*, *Greek*, *Hebrew*, *Chaldee*, &c. each in its proper Character.

ALSO

Explaining hard and technical Words, or Terms of Art, in all the *ARTS*, *SCIENCES*, and *MYSTERIES* following. Together with *ACCENTS* directing to their proper Pronuntiation, shewing both the *Orthography* and *Orthoepia* of the *English Tongue*,

VIZ. IN

AGRICULTURE, ALGEBRA, ANATOMY, ARCHITECTURE, ARITHMETICK, ASTROLOGY, ASTRONOMY, BOTANICKS, CATOPTRICKS, CHYMISTRY, CHYROMANCY, CHIRURGERY, CONFECTIONARY, COOKERY, COSMOGRAPHY, DIALLING, DIOPTRICKS, ETHICKS, FISHING, FORTIFICATION, GARDENING, GAUGING, GEOGRAPHY, GEOMETRY, GRAMMAR, GUNNERY, HANDICRAFTS, HAWKING, HERALDRY, HORSEMANSHIP, HUSBANDRY, HYDRAULICKS, HYDROGRAPHY, HYDROSTATICKS, LAW, LOGICK, MARITIME *and* MILITARY AFFAIRS, MATHEMATICKS, MECHANICKS, MERCHANDIZE, METAPHYSICKS, METEOROLOGY, NAVIGATION, OPTICKS, OTACOUSTICKS, PAINTING, PERSPECTIVE, PHARMACY, PHILOSOPHY, PHYSICK, PHYSIOGNOMY, PYROTECHNY, RHETORICK, SCULPTURE, STATICKS, STATUARY, SURVEYING, THEOLOGY, *and* TRIGONOMETRY.

Illustrated with near Five Hundred CUTS, for Giving a clearer Idea of those Figures, not so well apprehended by verbal Description.

LIKEWISE

A Collection and Explanation of WORDS and PHRASES us'd in our antient Charters, Statutes, Writs, Old Records and Processes at Law.

ALSO

The Theogony, Theology, and Mythology of the *Egyptians*, *Greeks*, *Romans*, &c. being an Account of their Deities, Solemnities, either Religious or Civil, their Divinations, Auguries, Oracles, Hieroglyphicks, and many other curious Matters, necessary to be understood, especially by the Readers of *English* POETRY.

To which is added,

A Collection of Proper Names of Persons and Places in *Great-Britain*, with their Etymologies and Explications.

The Whole digested into an Alphabetical Order, not only for the Information of the Ignorant, but the Entertainment of the Curious; and also the Benefit of Artificers, Tradesmen, Young Students and Foreigners.

A WORK useful for such as would UNDERSTAND *what they* READ *and* HEAR, SPEAK *what they* MEAN, *and* WRITE *true* ENGLISH.

Collected by several Hands,

The Mathematical Part by G. GORDON, *the Botanical by* P. MILLER.

The Whole Revis'd and Improv'd, with many thousand Additions,

By N. BAILEY,

LONDON:

Printed for T. COX at the *Lamb* under the *Royal-Exchange*.

M.DCC.XXX.

Ex coll. Karolyne & Bryan A. Garner

The 1730 folio.

Ex coll. Karolyne & Bryan A. Garner

The 1730 folio, *Dictionarium Britannicum*.

to copulate with a Woman"; "A Turd . . . Ordure, Dung"). He included entries for the *F*-word, the *C*-word, and the *S*-word—none of which appear in Johnson.

Bailey published an expanded edition of the *Dictionarium Britannicum* in 1736. Its coverage of 60,000 words made it the most extensive English dictionary, a title that it would hold for decades—even Johnson didn't match it. One of Johnson's early biographers, in fact, says that he used an "interleaved" copy of Bailey's 1736 dictionary as a starting point for his own. Scholars disagree over the plausibility of the account (see Hawkins 2009:108 and note), but Bailey's work certainly informed Johnson's, and he kept it close as he made his way through the alphabet.

Bailey died in 1742, and he disappears from most histories of lexicography after he was eclipsed by Johnson in 1755. But posthumous editions of Bailey competed with Johnson in the marketplace through century's end. Bailey found admirers in William Pitt the Elder (1708–1778) and, a century later, young Abraham Lincoln (1809–1865). The *Universal Etymological English Dictionary* has been called "the most popular and representative dictionary of the eighteenth century." (Starnes & Noyes 1946:107.) Among the fictional devotees of Bailey's *Universal Etymological English Dictionary* are the inexperienced but confident Mrs. Western in Henry Fielding's *Tom Jones* (1749) and the ten-year-old Lydgate in George Eliot's *Middlemarch* (1871–1872).

For the important 1755 revision of Bailey, see no. 36.

Ex coll. Karolyne & Bryan A. Garner

Arrayed here are 30 of the 41 octavo editions of Bailey. Well, okay, there are admittedly a couple of duplicates.

27

Giles Jacob
Blunderbuss of Law

Jacob, Giles. *A New Law-Dictionary*. London: W. Strahan & W. Woodfall, 1729.

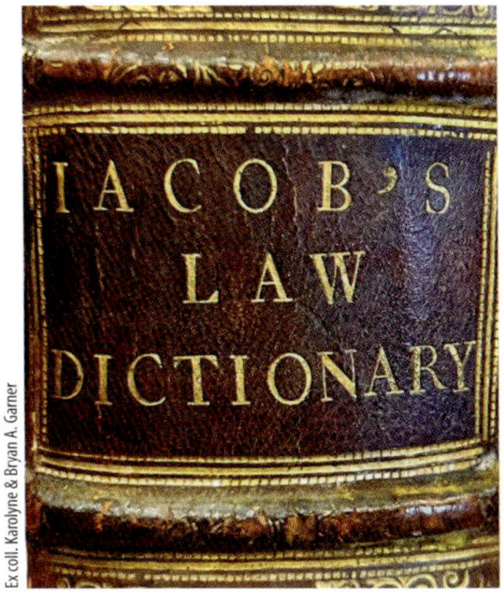

Ex coll. Karolyne & Bryan A. Garner

THE LEADING LEGAL WRITER of his day, Giles Jacob (1686–1744) is best remembered for his *New Law-Dictionary*, which is thought to have been consulted by many of America's founders. It went through eleven 18th-century editions and remained the most popular book of its kind for over a century.

Trained in litigation, Jacob began his writing career with *The Compleat Court-Keeper* (1713), which detailed how to administer estate matters. He also wrote a treatise, *Tractatus de Hermaphroditus* (1718), examining the legal status of intersex people. Like Rastell before him, he turned his attention for a time to the literary, writing a series of farcical poems and plays, including an unproduced play called *Love in a Wood; or, The Country Squire* (1714) and a satire of Alexander Pope's *Rape of the Lock* entitled *The Rape of the Smock* (1717). Jacob admired Pope, and the two had become friendly enough that when Jacob was compiling his *Poetical Register* (1719–1720), a collection of biographies of contemporary and earlier authors, he submitted Pope's own biographical entry to Pope for his review.

"I may with great Truth and Justice affirm, that considerably above two Thirds of my Work, with some Hundreds of very material Words, are entirely New in a Performance of this Kind; and the Other Part is greatly Improv'd, although Abridg'd as to Quantity by omitting a great Deal of Obsolete Matter." (Preface.)

Unfortunately for Jacob, this same publication would ultimately prove the friendship's undoing and earn him the poet's everlasting scorn. In the *Poetical Register*, Jacob criticized as obscene the play *Three Hours after Marriage* (1717), probably unaware that Pope had coauthored it anonymously. Contemporary critical consensus seems to have agreed with Jacob's evaluation, but Pope—who knew as well as anyone how to hold a grudge—never forgave him, describing Jacob in *The Dunciad* (published nearly a decade later) as "the Scourge of Grammar," continuing, "mark with awe, / Nor less revere him, Blunderbuss of Law."

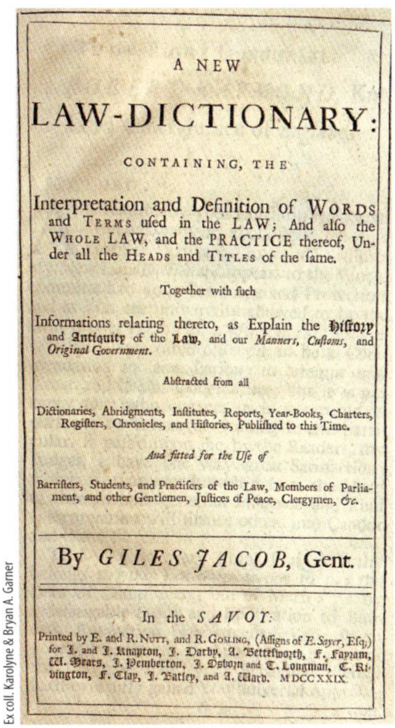
A NEW
LAW-DICTIONARY:
CONTAINING, THE
Interpretation and Definition of WORDS and TERMS used in the LAW; And also the WHOLE LAW, and the PRACTICE thereof, Under all the HEADS and TITLES of the same.
Together with such
Informations relating thereto, as Explain the History and Antiquity of the Law, and our *Manners, Customs*, and *Original Government*.
Abstracted from all
Dictionaries, Abridgments, Institutes, Reports, Year-Books, Charters, Registers, Chronicles, and Histories, Published to this Time.
And fitted for the Use of
Barristers, Students, and Practisers of the Law, Members of Parliament, and other Gentlemen, Justices of Peace, Clergymen, *&c.*
By *GILES JACOB*, Gent.
In the *SAVOY*:
Printed by E. and R. Nutt, and R. Gosling, (Assigns of *E. Sayer*, Esq;) for J. and J. Knapton, J. Darby, A. Bettesworth, F. Fayram, W. Mears, J. Pemberton, J. Osborn and T. Longman, C. Rivington, F. Clay, J. Batley, and A. Ward. MDCCXXIX.

Ex coll. Karolyne & Bryan A. Garner

The same year when the first volume of the *Poetical Register* appeared (1719), Jacob also published a very successful legal volume,

"As to the other Dictionaries, let who will for the Future Enlarge them, it must be always confess'd, that it was I who first attempted a Body of the Law, and the Practise of it, in any Law-Dictionary." (Preface.)

"Jacob's innovation in legal dictionaries was to enlarge the focus to include much more material under most entries. Beyond the usual definition with references to sources, Jacob would offer almost encyclopedic treatment of the terms." (Cohen 2003:57.)

Lex Constitutionis, a compendium of statute, common, and criminal law. He followed this in 1725 with *The Student's Companion; or, The Reason of the Laws of England*, Jacob's favorite among his own publications.

Finally, in 1729 Jacob published the first edition of *A New Law-Dictionary*, an innovation nine years in the making. It combined a legal dictionary with an abridgment of statute law—and was the first such guide in English to do so. It was in its fifth edition when Jacob died in 1744, and it remains his most famous work. (But his best-selling, and final, publication was *Every Man His Own Lawyer* [1736], a guide to legal practice for lay citizens who might become involved in litigation.) The dictionary would reach its tenth edition in 1782, and then it was taken over by Thomas Edlyne Tomlins, who produced an 11th edition in 1797 and another in 1809. In the latter edition, Tomlins's name supplanted Jacob's as the author.

All in all, Jacob's literary output was extraordinary: 31 separate titles in just about as many years. Understandably, he has been dubbed "Mr. Grub Street at the Bar."

Ex coll. Karolyne & Bryan A. Garner

The folio editions of Jacob's *New Law Dictionary* published from 1729 to 1782.

28

John Barrow

Methodical Digeſter

[Barrow, John]. ***Dictionarium Polygraphicum: Or, The Whole Body of Arts Regularly Digeſted, Containing [ten categories follow]*. 2 vols. London: C. Hitch & C. Davis, and S. Auſten, 1735.**

Ex coll. Karolyne & Bryan A. Garner

All we know of Barrow is what we can glean from the books he published. There we find nothing about the dates of his birth or death, but they do tell us that he was a teacher of mathematics, and that he served as a schoolmaster for the "young gentlemen"—boys, really—on ships of the Royal Navy.

"We hope our endeavours to . . . render [the arts treated here] intelligible even to a moderate capacity, will not be thought an unnecessary undertaking." (Preface, 1:i.)

His first book, the *Dictionarium Polygraphicum*, appeared in two volumes in 1735. This treatise on the visual arts probably isn't a dictionary by any strict definition, but Barrow says he "cast this work into the form of a Dictionary, because we judged such a disposition the most methodical of any." (1:i.) He is refreshingly honest that his erudition is secondhand: "Our observations have been carefully collected from the most celebrated authors, and digested into . . . an easy and regular series of instructions." (1:ii.)

Barrow retired from shipboard teaching to concentrate on his writing. He returned to the "methodical" lexicographic format in his *Dictionarium Medicum Universale* (1745; 2d ed. 1754), a *New and Universal Dictionary of Arts and Sciences* (1751; 2d ed. 1756) in a thousand folio pages, and a *New Geographical Dictionary* (1759–60; 2d ed. 1762–63). He also published an influential *Navigatio Britannica; or, A Complete System of Navigation in All Its Branches, Both with Regard to Theory and Practice* (1750), a four-volume *Naval History of Great Britain* in 1758 (2d ed. 1776), a *New and Impartial History of England* in ten pocket-sized volumes (1763), and a three-volume *Collection of Authentic, Useful, and Entertaining Voyages and Discoveries* in 1765. He several times disavows original research, describing his method instead as synthesis and abridgment.

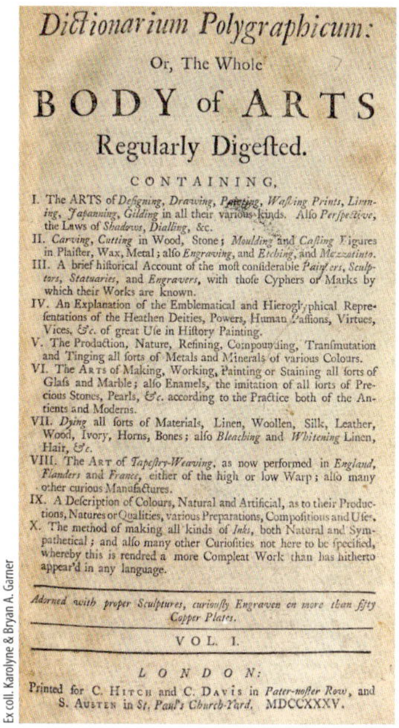

Dictionarium Polygraphicum:

Or, The Whole

BODY of ARTS

Regularly Digeſted.

CONTAINING,

I. The ARTS of *Deſigning*, *Drawing*, *Painting*, *Waſhing Prints*, *Limning*, *Japanning*, *Gilding* in all their various kinds. Alſo *Perſpective*, the Laws of *Shadows*, *Dialling*, &c.

II. *Carving*, *Cutting* in Wood, Stone; *Moulding* and *Caſting* Figures in Plaiſter, Wax, Metal; alſo *Engraving*, and *Etching*, and *Mezzotinto*.

III. A brief hiſtorical Account of the moſt conſiderable *Painters*, *Sculptors*, *Statuaries*, and *Engravers*, with thoſe Cyphers or Marks by which their Works are known.

IV. An Explanation of the Emblematical and Hieroglyphical Repreſentations of the Heathen Deities, Powers, Human Paſſions, Virtues, Vices, *&c.* of great Uſe in Hiſtory Painting.

V. The Production, Nature, Refining, Compounding, Tranſmutation and Tinging all ſorts of Metals and Minerals of various Colours.

VI. The Arts of Making, Working, Painting or Staining all ſorts of Glaſs and Marble; alſo Enamels, the imitation of all ſorts of Precious Stones, Pearls, *&c.* according to the Practice both of the Antients and Moderns.

VII. *Dying* all ſorts of Materials, Linen, Woollen, Silk, Leather, Wood, Ivory, Horns, Bones; alſo *Bleaching* and *Whitening* Linen, Hair, *&c.*

VIII. The Art of *Tapeſtry-Weaving*, as now performed in *England*, *Flanders* and *France*, either of the high or low Warp; alſo many other curious Manufactures.

IX. A Deſcription of Colours, Natural and Artificial, as to their Productions, Natures or Qualities, various Preparations, Compoſitions and Uſes.

X. The method of making all kinds of *Inks*, both Natural and Sympathetical; and alſo many other Curioſities not here to be ſpecified, whereby this is rendred a more Compleat Work than has hitherto appear'd in any language.

Adorned with proper Sculptures, curiouſly Engraven on more than fifty Copper Plates.

VOL. I.

LONDON:

Printed for C. Hitch and C. Davis in *Pater-noſter Row*, and S. Austen in *St. Paul's Church-Yard*. MDCCXXXV.

Ex coll. Karolyne & Bryan A. Garner

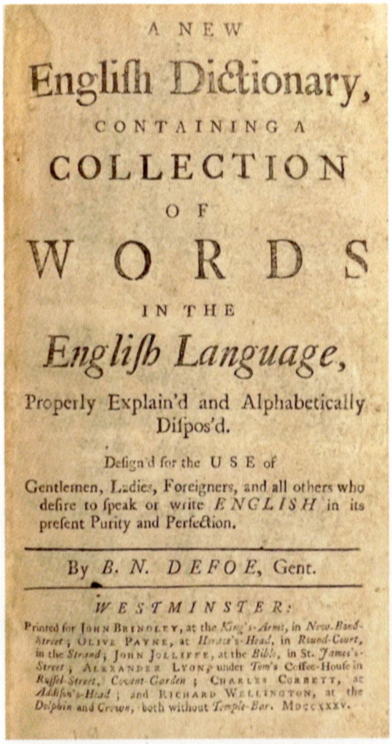

A NEW
English Dictionary,
CONTAINING A
COLLECTION
OF
WORDS
IN THE
English Language,
Properly Explain'd and Alphabetically Dispos'd.

Design'd for the USE of
Gentlemen, Ladies, Foreigners, and all others who desire to speak or write *ENGLISH* in its present Purity and Perfection.

By *B. N. DEFOE*, Gent.

WESTMINSTER:
Printed for JOHN BRINDLEY, at the *King's-Arms*, in *New-Bond-Street*; OLIVE PAYNE, at *Horace's-Head*, in *Round-Court*, in the *Strand*; JOHN JOLLIFFE, at the *Bible*, in St. *James's-Street*; ALEXANDER LYON, under *Tom's* Coffee-House in *Russel-Street*, *Covent-Garden*; CHARLES CORBETT, at *Addison's-Head*; and RICHARD WELLINGTON, at the *Dolphin and Crown*, both without *Temple-Bar*. MDCCXXXV.

Ex coll. Karolyne & Bryan A. Garner

The first edition, attributed to Defoe.

Ex coll. Karolyne & Bryan A. Garner

The first edition (1735).

29

Benjamin Norton Defoe
An Acorn Falls Far from the Tree

Defoe, B[enjamin] N[orton]. ***A New English Dictionary, Containing a Collection of Words in the English Language, Properly Explain'd and Alphabetically Dispos'd.*** **London: John Brindley, Olive Payne, et al., 1735. Also: 1737, 1739 [attributed to J. Sparrow], and 1741 [attributed to James Manlove].**

THE CELEBRATED WRITER Daniel Defoe (1660?–1731) was plagued with disappointments toward the end of his life. He was sued for an age-old debt and lost in the Court of Exchequer, as a result of which he faced jail time if he couldn't pay a large judgment. In the final year of his life, he moved several times to evade creditors. In his last letter, he described himself as "sinking under the weight" of "insupportable sorrows." (*ODNB*.) One of these was that his son Benjamin Norton Defoe (1690–1770), from whom he had become estranged, had abandoned law studies to become a hack writer who had been imprisoned for seditious writing.

Four years after his father's death, Benjamin, being true to his hackdom, produced this dictionary, which had all the hallmarks of Grub Street: an inane preface, a secondhand vocabulary, and nothing original in the definitions. It was a distinctly "mediocre compilation, and it lacked even the benefit of such shaping of the prefatory apparatus and such advertising as a progressive bookseller could have given it." (Starnes & Noyes 1946:142.) It was essentially an abridgment of the 1733 edition of Bailey (no. 26), omitting two-thirds of the vocabulary; omitting also everything relating to etymology, grammar, pronunciation, and usage; but reproducing verbatim Bailey's definitions.

So undistinguished and unsuccessful was the book that within six years, various London publishers issued the selfsame book with various authorial attributions: B.N. Defoe (1735), Anonymous (1737), J. Sparrow (1739), and James Manlove (1741). The name Defoe didn't seem to help sales. Nor did the association with the publisher Olive (or Oliver) Payne, who was on each of the first three printings. Shortly after Payne's final edition (1739), under the spurious authorship of "J. Sparrow," Payne went bankrupt. His publishing of the dictionary was marked by "inexperience and desperation." (Starnes & Noyes 1946:141.)

Such is the history of one of the most obscure dictionaries of the 18th century.

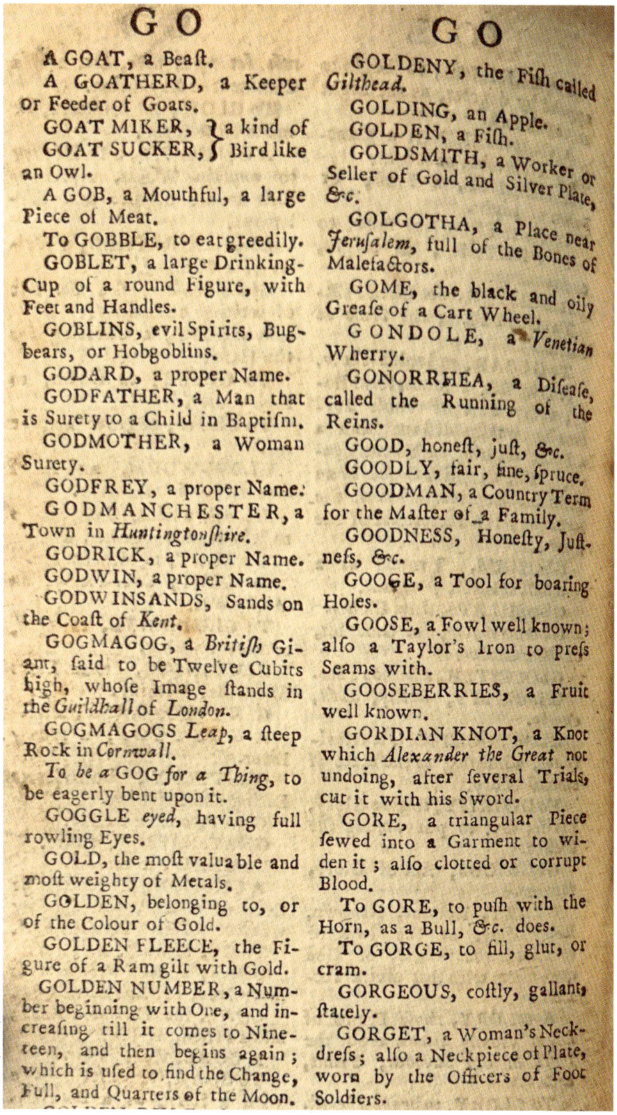

GO

A GOAT, a Beaſt.
A GOATHERD, a Keeper or Feeder of Goats.
GOAT MIKER, } a kind of
GOAT SUCKER, } Bird like an Owl.
A GOB, a Mouthful, a large Piece of Meat.
To GOBBLE, to eat greedily.
GOBLET, a large Drinking-Cup of a round Figure, with Feet and Handles.
GOBLINS, evil Spirits, Bugbears, or Hobgoblins.
GODARD, a proper Name.
GODFATHER, a Man that is Surety to a Child in Baptiſm.
GODMOTHER, a Woman Surety.
GODFREY, a proper Name.
GODMANCHESTER, a Town in *Huntingtonſhire.*
GODRICK, a proper Name.
GODWIN, a proper Name.
GODWINSANDS, Sands on the Coaſt of *Kent.*
GOGMAGOG, a *Britiſh* Giant, ſaid to be Twelve Cubits high, whoſe Image ſtands in the *Guildhall* of *London.*
GOGMAGOGS *Leap*, a ſteep Rock in *Cornwall.*
To be a GOG *for a Thing*, to be eagerly bent upon it.
GOGGLE *eyed*, having full rowling Eyes.
GOLD, the moſt valuable and moſt weighty of Metals.
GOLDEN, belonging to, or of the Colour of Gold.
GOLDEN FLEECE, the Figure of a Ram gilt with Gold.
GOLDEN NUMBER, a Number beginning with One, and increaſing till it comes to Nineteen, and then begins again; which is uſed to find the Change, Full, and Quarters of the Moon.

GO

GOLDENY, the Fiſh called *Gilthead.*
GOLDING, an Apple.
GOLDEN, a Fiſh.
GOLDSMITH, a Worker or Seller of Gold and Silver Plate, &c.
GOLGOTHA, a Place near *Jeruſalem*, full of the Bones of Malefactors.
GOME, the black and oily Greaſe of a Cart Wheel.
GONDOLE, a *Venetian* Wherry.
GONORRHEA, a Diſeaſe, called the Running of the Reins.
GOOD, honeſt, juſt, &c.
GOODLY, fair, fine, ſpruce.
GOODMAN, a Country Term for the Maſter of a Family.
GOODNESS, Honeſty, Juſtneſs, &c.
GOOGE, a Tool for boaring Holes.
GOOSE, a Fowl well known; alſo a Taylor's Iron to preſs Seams with.
GOOSEBERRIES, a Fruit well known.
GORDIAN KNOT, a Knot which *Alexander the Great* not undoing, after ſeveral Trials, cut it with his Sword.
GORE, a triangular Piece ſewed into a Garment to widen it; alſo clotted or corrupt Blood.
To GORE, to puſh with the Horn, as a Bull, &c. does.
To GORGE, to fill, glut, or cram.
GORGEOUS, coſtly, gallant, ſtately.
GORGET, a Woman's Neckdreſs; alſo a Neckpiece of Plate, worn by the Officers of Foot Soldiers.

Ex coll. Karolyne & Bryan A. Garner

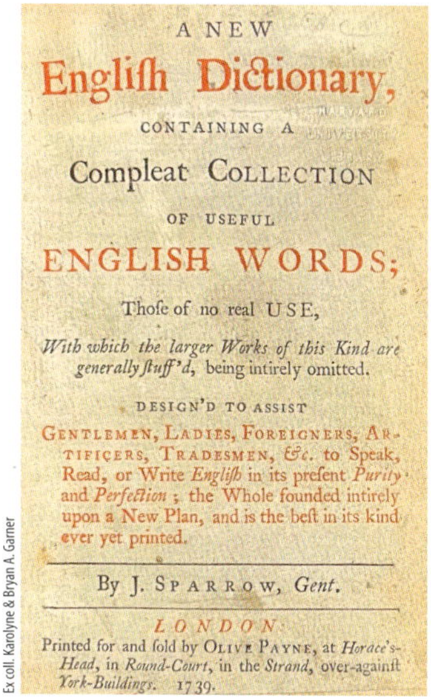

A NEW
English Dictionary,
CONTAINING A
Compleat COLLECTION
OF USEFUL
ENGLISH WORDS;
Thoſe of no real USE,
With which the larger Works of this Kind are generally ſtuff'd, being intirely omitted.
DESIGN'D TO ASSIST
GENTLEMEN, LADIES, FOREIGNERS, ARTIFICERS, TRADESMEN, &c. to Speak, Read, or Write *Engliſh* in its preſent *Purity* and *Perfection*; the Whole founded intirely upon a New Plan, and is the beſt in its kind ever yet printed.
By J. SPARROW, *Gent.*
LONDON:
Printed for and ſold by OLIVE PAYNE, at *Horace's-Head*, in *Round-Court*, in the *Strand*, over-againſt *York-Buildings*. 1739.

Ex coll. Karolyne & Bryan A. Garner

The third edition, attributed to Sparrow.

"DICTIONARY, a Collection of all the Words of a Language explained in alphabetical Order."

Ex coll. Karolyne & Bryan A. Garner

Until recently, this Sparrow volume (1739) belonged to Harvard University.

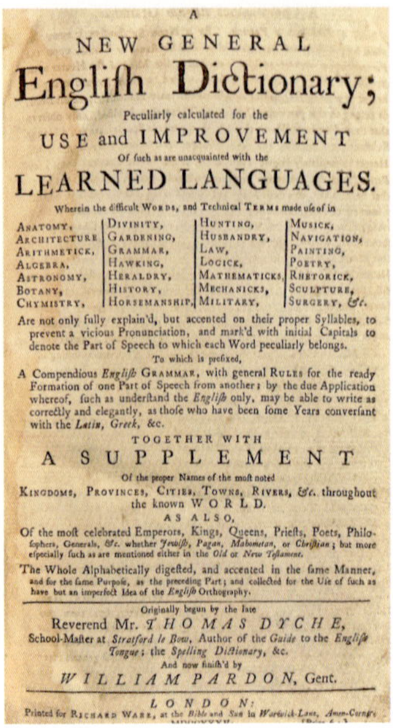

A

NEW GENERAL

Engliſh Dictionary;

Peculiarly calculated for the

USE and IMPROVEMENT

Of ſuch as are unacquainted with the

LEARNED LANGUAGES.

Wherein the difficult WORDS, and Technical TERMS made uſe of in

ANATOMY,	DIVINITY,	HUNTING,	MUSICK,
ARCHITECTURE	GARDENING,	HUSBANDRY,	NAVIGATION,
ARITHMETICK,	GRAMMAR,	LAW,	PAINTING,
ALGEBRA,	HAWKING,	LOGICK,	POETRY,
ASTRONOMY,	HERALDRY,	MATHEMATICKS,	RHETORICK,
BOTANY,	HISTORY,	MECHANICKS,	SCULPTURE,
CHYMISTRY,	HORSEMANSHIP,	MILITARY,	SURGERY, &c.

Are not only fully explain'd, but accented on their proper Syllables, to prevent a vicious Pronunciation, and mark'd with initial Capitals to denote the Part of Speech to which each Word peculiarly belongs.

To which is prefixed,

A Compendious *Engliſh* GRAMMAR, with general RULES for the ready Formation of one Part of Speech from another; by the due Application whereof, ſuch as underſtand the *Engliſh* only, may be able to write as correctly and elegantly, as thoſe who have been ſome Years converſant with the *Latin*, *Greek*, &c.

TOGETHER WITH

A SUPPLEMENT

Of the proper Names of the moſt noted

KINGDOMS, PROVINCES, CITIES, TOWNS, RIVERS, &c. throughout the known WORLD.

AS ALSO,

Of the moſt celebrated Emperors, Kings, Queens, Prieſts, Poets, Philoſophers, Generals, &c. whether *Jewiſh*, *Pagan*, *Mahometan*, or *Chriſtian*; but more eſpecially ſuch as are mentioned either in the *Old* or *New Teſtament*.

The Whole Alphabetically digeſted, and accented in the ſame Manner, and for the ſame Purpoſe, as the preceding Part; and collected for the Uſe of ſuch as have but an imperfect Idea of the *Engliſh* Orthography.

Originally begun by the late

Reverend Mr. *THOMAS DYCHE*,

School-Maſter at *Stratford le Bow*, Author of the *Guide* to the *Engliſh Tongue*; the *Spelling Dictionary*, &c.

And now finiſh'd by

WILLIAM PARDON, Gent.

LONDON:

Printed for RICHARD WARE, at the *Bible* and *Sun* in *Warwick-Lane*, *Amen-Corner*

Ex coll. Karolyne & Bryan A. Garner

30

Thomas Dyche & William Pardon

Conspicuously Downmarket?

Dyche, Thomas; and William Pardon. ***A New General English Dictionary; Peculiarly calculated for the Use and Improvement Of such as are unacquainted with the Learned Languages.*** **London: Richard Ware, 1735. 2d ed. 1737.**

Dyche (d. 1727?) was a schoolmaster who, educated in Derbyshire, had moved to London, and by 1708 was keeping a school in Dean Street, Fetter Lane. Two years later, he became master of the free school at Stratford le Bow. His early publications included a Latin–English vocabulary—*Vocabularium Latiale, or, A Latin Vocabulary* (1707); a pronunciation book and grammar—*A Guide to the English Tongue* (1707); and a spelling book—*A Dictionary of All the Words Commonly Us'd in the English Language* (1723).

Dyche's 823-page dictionary, *A New General English Dictionary*, was unfinished at his death and had to be completed over the next eight years by William Pardon, of whom little is known except that he also wrote *A New and Compendious System of Practical Arithmetick* (1738). Dyche & Pardon's *New General English Dictionary* was the first to include an English grammar in the front matter (ten pages' worth), an innovation that would soon become a staple in 18th-century dictionaries. With around 20,000 entries, the dictionary contains about half the number of headwords found in Bailey's first edition (1721). Dyche and Pardon's entries consistently give the headword's part of speech followed by a plain-language definition. Perhaps because Dyche had already focused on pronunciation elsewhere, this element is omitted from his dictionary.

It has been said that Dyche & Pardon's effort was "largely derivative from Bailey's dictionaries" (Collison 1971:191) and "consciously downmarket" (Green 1996:238). But if we test these assertions against examples of definitions, these assessments seem decidedly unfair:

Bailey (1730)	Dyche & Pardon (1735)
ATTRA´CTION [in *Mechanicks*] the Act of a moving Power, whereby a Moveable is brought nearer to the Mover. The Power opposite to *Attraction* is called *Repulsion*.	ATTRA´CTION (S.) in *natural Philosophy*, is that Power or property whereby one Body or Thing acts upon another of a different Sort, and by such acting brings or draws the Body acted upon nearer to itself. This is sometimes called Suction, and sometimes Gravitation; and so in the *Newtonian* Philosophy, it is that Power or Principle whereby all Bodies mutually tend to each other.
To GRUNT, [*grunnire*, L. Grynter, *Dan.*] to make a noise like a Hog.	GRUNT (V.) to make a disagreeable Noise like a Hog.
[No entry.]	LOW-TI´DE (S.) spoken of the Water of a River when it has ebbed to its lowest Mark; also when a man has little or no Money in his Pockets.
MEDA´LLION, a Medal of an extraordinary large Size, such as Princes used to present to some particular Persons, as a token of their esteem.	MEDA´LLION (S.) Medals of a very large Size struck upon extraordinary Occasions, and presented by Princes to their Generals or other great men as a Mark of their Favour and Esteem, for being the Instrument of performing uncommon Exploits, and were never used as Coin, as the lesser-sized Medals frequently were.
REDEE´MER [*redemptor*, L.] a Ransomer, a Deliverer, a Saviour.	REDEE´MER (S.) a Deliverer, Saviour, Purchaser, or Setter at Liberty, &c., this Name is given, by way of Eminence, to *Jesus Christ*, the Redeemer and Saviour of the whole World; but in *Moses's Law*, it was also given to him who had the Right of Redemption in any Inheritance, or even the Person of a near Kinsman, that may redeem it out of the Hands of a Stranger, or of any other *Jew*, that had bought it without waiting for the Sabbatical Year, when it returned of itself to the Family that originally owned it.
To RE-INFO´RCE [of *re* again, and *enforcer*, F.] to add new Force or Strength, to recruit.	REINFO´RCE (V.) to recruit, or add new Strength, Power, or Force to a Person, Army, or Cause.
TULIP [*tulipa*, Ital. *tulipe*, F.] a Flower.	TU´LIP (S.) a Flower much noted for its great Variety of Stripes and Colours.

Ex coll. Karolyne & Bryan A. Garner

"*A New General English Dictionary* by Thomas Dyche and William Pardon, first published in 1735, was mentioned by Denis Diderot in the 1750 *Prospectus* of the *Encyclopédie* as a dictionary to which the latter work was indebted; as a matter of fact, in the 1750s, French editions of Dyche and Pardon's dictionary were published in Avignon, Paris, and Amsterdam." (Iamartino 2020:73–74.)

Ex coll. Karolyne & Bryan A. Garner

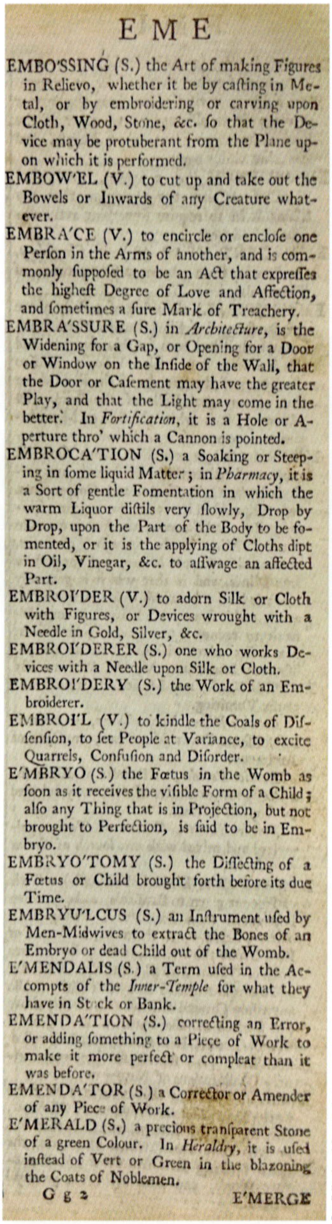

EME

EMBO'SSING (S.) the Art of making Figures in Relievo, whether it be by caſting in Metal, or by embroidering or carving upon Cloth, Wood, Stone, &c. ſo that the Device may be protuberant from the Plane upon which it is performed.

EMBOW'EL (V.) to cut up and take out the Bowels or Inwards of any Creature whatever.

EMBRA'CE (V.) to encircle or encloſe one Perſon in the Arms of another, and is commonly ſuppoſed to be an Act that expreſſes the higheſt Degree of Love and Affection, and ſometimes a ſure Mark of Treachery.

EMBRA'SSURE (S.) in *Architecture*, is the Widening for a Gap, or Opening for a Door or Window on the Inſide of the Wall, that the Door or Caſement may have the greater Play, and that the Light may come in the better. In *Fortification*, it is a Hole or Aperture thro' which a Cannon is pointed.

EMBROCA'TION (S.) a Soaking or Steeping in ſome liquid Matter; in *Pharmacy*, it is a Sort of gentle Fomentation in which the warm Liquor diſtils very ſlowly, Drop by Drop, upon the Part of the Body to be fomented, or it is the applying of Cloths dipt in Oil, Vinegar, &c. to aſſwage an affected Part.

EMBROI'DER (V.) to adorn Silk or Cloth with Figures, or Devices wrought with a Needle in Gold, Silver, &c.

EMBROI'DERER (S.) one who works Devices with a Needle upon Silk or Cloth.

EMBROI'DERY (S.) the Work of an Embroiderer.

EMBROI'L (V.) to kindle the Coals of Diſſenſion, to ſet People at Variance, to excite Quarrels, Confuſion and Diſorder.

E'MBRYO (S.) the Fœtus in the Womb as ſoon as it receives the viſible Form of a Child; alſo any Thing that is in Projection, but not brought to Perfection, is ſaid to be in Embryo.

EMBRYO'TOMY (S.) the Diſſecting of a Fœtus or Child brought forth before its due Time.

EMBRYU'LCUS (S.) an Inſtrument uſed by Men-Midwives to extract the Bones of an Embryo or dead Child out of the Womb.

E'MENDALIS (S.) a Term uſed in the Accompts of the *Inner-Temple* for what they have in Stock or Bank.

EMENDA'TION (S.) correcting an Error, or adding ſomething to a Piece of Work to make it more perfect or compleat than it was before.

EMENDA'TOR (S.) a Corrector or Amender of any Piece of Work.

E'MERALD (S.) a precious tranſparent Stone of a green Colour. In *Heraldry*, it is uſed inſtead of Vert or Green in the blazoning the Coats of Noblemen.

Gg 2 E'MERGE

A full column from Dyche & Pardon (2d ed. 1737).

In this random sample, the definitions in Dyche & Pardon are mostly superior. Take, for example, *attraction*. In Bailey, the genus-word is *act*—as if attraction were invariably a species of act. But in Dyche & Pardon, *attraction* is more aptly defined as a *power* or *property*. Modern dictionaries tend to use all three words in defining *attraction*: "an act, power, or property." The point, though, is that the Dyche & Pardon definition shows originality and acuity of analysis. By contrast, John Harris's *Lexicon Technicum* (1704) defined *attraction* as "the drawing of one thing to another."

Other points merit mention. In the entry for *low-tide*, Dyche & Pardon impressively record a second, metaphorical sense. Their entry for *medallion* distinguishes medallions from coins: they are struck not routinely but on special occasions, and they never circulate as money. *Redeemer* deals explicitly with both secular and sacred meanings. For *tulip*, Bailey provides only a genus; Dyche & Pardon note the distinctive pattern and coloring.

The Dyche & Pardon dictionary has been criticized as wordy, containing too much encyclopedic information: "Its basic weakness lay in its failure to recognize and remain within the confines of the dictionary, and an equally grave fault was the general verbosity and occasional triviality of the definitions." (Starnes & Noyes 1946:138.) That is fair when you consider an entry such as *medal*, which occupies almost a full page of discursus, ending with: "the *Dutch* have been very particular in relating every remarkable Transaction of theirs by Medals, ever since their Revolt from the *Spanish* Yoke."

And yet in the more usual entries of five to ten lines, the definitions are somewhat more informative than those in dictionaries of comparable size. The focus was on what the lexicographers took to be the practical needs of users: sound information delivered quickly—or "bounded within a narrow Compass," as they explained in their introduction. They also said there that one reason for abjuring etymology was a sensible skepticism about accuracy: "Derivations and Etymologies, are entirely left out . . . Because of their Uncertainty, in a very large Number of Instances."

Over the course of the 18th century, the Dyche & Pardon dictionary showed how the distinction between dictionaries and encyclopedias evolved. Consider what happened to the entry for *labyrinth* by the final edition of 1794 (labeled the 17th but actually the 18th), prepared posthumously and anonymously:

Dyche & Pardon (1735)	Dyche & Pardon (1794)
LA'BYRINTH (S.) a Term for the regular disposing of Buildings, Trees, or Walks, with so many Windings and Turnings that it is difficult to find the Way out of it; antient History furnishes us with four very famous ones, the first built by *Dedalus* in the Isle of *Crete*, to secure the Minotaur; the second, that built by the Command of *Psamneticus* King of *Egypt*, in the Isle of *Meroe*, said to consist of 3000 Edifices, among which are 12 Palaces; the third, that of *Lemnos*, famed for its sumptuous Pillars; the fourth, that of *Italy*, which *Porsenna* King of *Hetruria* designed for a Sepulcre for himself and Successors; it is now a common Thing in a large Garden to have a Labyrinth in one Part of it; in *common Speech*, it signifies any Difficulty that a Person knows not how to extricate himself from; among the *Anatomists*, the second Cavity of the internal Ear, which is hollowed out of the *Os Petrosum*, is so called.	*La'byrinth* (S.) a maze, a place formed with so many intricate windings that it is difficult to find the way out; in *Anatomy*, the second cavity of the internal ear, which is hollowed with several windings.

Ex coll. Karolyne & Bryan A. Garner

"I doubt not but the Teachers will soon find the Benefit from the Improvement their Scholars will insensibly make, not only in Orthograghy [sic], or true Spelling, but in writing coherently and correctly, the Want whereof is universally complained of among the Fair Sex." (Introduction to 1737 2d ed.)

Ex coll. Karolyne & Bryan A. Garner

The idea that this dictionary is "downmarket" or geared to "a lower level" (Starnes & Noyes 1946:128) is an inference derived not from the choice of headwords or the nature of the definitions, but rather from three questionable premises: (1) the omission of etymology; (2) the statement on the title page that the English grammar is intended for "such as understand *English* only"; and (3) a self-deprecating statement at the end of the introduction: "The Whole is intended for the Information of the Unlearned, and particularly recommended to those Boarding Schools, where English only is taught, as is the Case commonly among the Ladies." But such modesty is a familiar conventional pose, and identifying the "unlearned" as a target audience seems to have made good business sense going back at least to Cawdrey. And even if the inference is correct—if their book was marketed to less sophisticated readers—Dyche & Pardon should be credited with significantly improving the art of defining.

Detail from frontispiece.

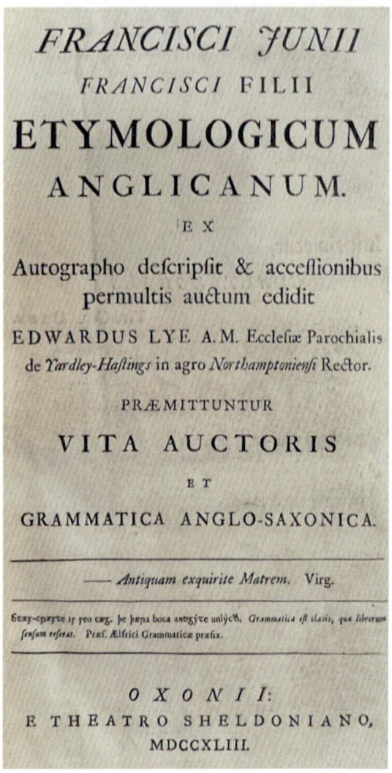

FRANCISCI JUNII

FRANCISCI FILII

ETYMOLOGICUM

ANGLICANUM.

EX

Autographo deſcripſit & acceſſionibus permultis auctum edidit

EDWARDUS LYE A.M. Eccleſiæ Parochialis de *Yardley-Haſtings* in agro *Northamptonienſi* Rector.

PRÆMITTUNTUR

VITA AUCTORIS

ET

GRAMMATICA ANGLO-SAXONICA.

—— *Antiquam exquirite Matrem.* Virg.

Stæf-cræfte is seo cæg, þe þæra boca andgyte unlycð. *Grammatica eſt clavis, quæ librorum ſenſum reſerat.* Præf. Ælfrici Grammaticæ præfix.

OXONII:

E THEATRO SHELDONIANO,

MDCCXLIII.

Ex coll. Karolyne & Bryan A. Garner

31

Franciscus Junius

Bibliophilic Comparativist

Junius, Franciscus. *Etymologicum Anglicanum ex Autographo descripsit & accessionibus permultis auctum editit.* Oxford's Sheldonian Theater: Edward Lye, 1743.

François du Jon (1591–1677), son of a French father and a Flemish mother, was born in Germany, raised in the Netherlands, and employed first in France, then in England. It's fitting that such a cosmopolite is known by the Latin form of his name, the one used by the international scholarly community: Franciscus Junius.

Junius studied philology and theology at the University of Leiden, one of Europe's great intellectual centers. He spent just two years in the ministry because of the political and theological upheavals of the early 17th century. In May 1621, he moved to England to serve as a kind of senior aide to Thomas Howard, Earl of Arundel—tutor to his children, overseer of his private library, and adviser on his art collection. Art was his passion. Junius, a personal friend of Anthony Van Dyck and Peter Paul Rubens, wrote extensively on the visual arts, including a widely translated work on art theory and a posthumously published encyclopedia of classical art.

After more than 20 years in England, he returned to the Netherlands and turned his attention from the visual arts to the languages of northern Europe. This made him stand out among early modern philologists. Most educated men in 17th-century Europe knew Latin, and many knew Greek. Early English dictionaries therefore tend to be strong in their etymologies of words that come from these classical languages. But the core of the English vocabulary belongs not to the Italic family, like Latin, nor to the Hellenic, like Greek, but to the Germanic family, and experts in the Germanic languages were badly underrepresented.

Junius was a pioneer in using comparative methods to describe the whole Germanic language family, including not only English and German but Dutch, Scots, Danish, Swedish, Icelandic, and others more obscure. The lack of scholarship on most of these languages forced him to be an autodidact, and he took the responsibility seriously. He was said to rise every morning at four; he worked on his manuscripts until one, took a two-hour break for exercise, and then went back to work until eight at night. He collected books and manuscripts, corresponded with other savants throughout Europe, and even developed his own types and punches for Saxon, Gothic, Danish, Icelandic, and the Runic languages, which were so little known that no fonts existed to print them.

Junius was a pioneer in Old English, the form of the language prevalent before roughly 1100, which had been almost entirely forgotten—Richard Verstegan (no. 8) was one of very few who had taken the subject seriously. Junius studied manuscripts from the library of Sir Robert Bruce Cotton. (Cotton's collection, which included the only manuscript of *Beowulf*, later became one of the "foundation collections" of the British Museum, and eventually of the British Library.) Junius was the first to edit the poems attributed to Cædmon, said to be the first poet to write in English, and he compiled a pathbreaking Latin–Old English glossary. He was similarly proficient in Middle English, producing a glossary of Chaucer's language and a learned edition of the important Middle English text known as the *Ormulum*. He even bought the sole manuscript of the *Ormulum* and donated it to Oxford's library, where it remains today under the shelfmark Bodleian Library MS Junius 1.

He made advances in historical linguistics through a comparative study of the whole Germanic language family, including many of its little-known members. He spent time in Friesland, for instance, a community on the North Sea, to learn Frisian, the English language's closest relative. (Today there are still about half a million Frisian speakers in Germany and the Netherlands.) His expertise extended as far as Gothic, an extinct language known only thanks to a single book, the *Codex Argenteus*, copied in the sixth century from a fourth-century translation of the Christian Gospels. Junius published these Gothic Gospels accompanied by a *Gothicum Glossarium, quo Argentei Codicis Vocabula explicantur* in 1664. There were few areas in Germanic historical linguistics where he did not make a mark.

Junius's most important contribution to English lexicography, the *Etymologicum Anglicanum*, appeared in 1743, almost 70 years after his death. Edward Lye, another Germanic authority, published it

Ex coll. Karolyne & Bryan A. Garner

Ex coll. Karolyne & Bryan A. Garner

In 1970, the Los Angeles firm of Sherwin & Freutel issued a facsimile edition of Junius.

using the same fonts that Junius had developed and then bequeathed to Oxford University Press. Junius's dictionary spends little time on definitions—he rarely gives more than a single Latin synonym for each word—but his etymologies are exceptionally detailed in their treatment of Germanic languages, including Old English (he labels it "A.S." for "Anglo-Saxon"), Dutch, Danish, Swedish, German, Alemannic, the ancient Belgian language, Cimbrian, and Gothic, as well as Celtic languages including Welsh, Gaulish, and Irish and Scottish Gaelic. Yet his understanding of the relations among these languages was still limited. A proper understanding of the historical development of the Germanic languages—a family tree containing the North Germanic languages of Scandinavia, the sole attested East Germanic language, Gothic, and the West Germanic languages including German, Dutch, and English—would come only in the 19th century, particularly after Jacob Grimm (of the famous Brothers Grimm) and Karl Verner explained the systematic sound changes by which these languages had evolved. But Junius's labors of compilation were essential steps.

Although Junius's daunting erudition meant that he could never hope for a large audience, the right people knew his work. Samuel Johnson, for instance, leaned heavily on Junius, and the 19th-century rediscovery of Old English literature would have been impossible without his efforts.

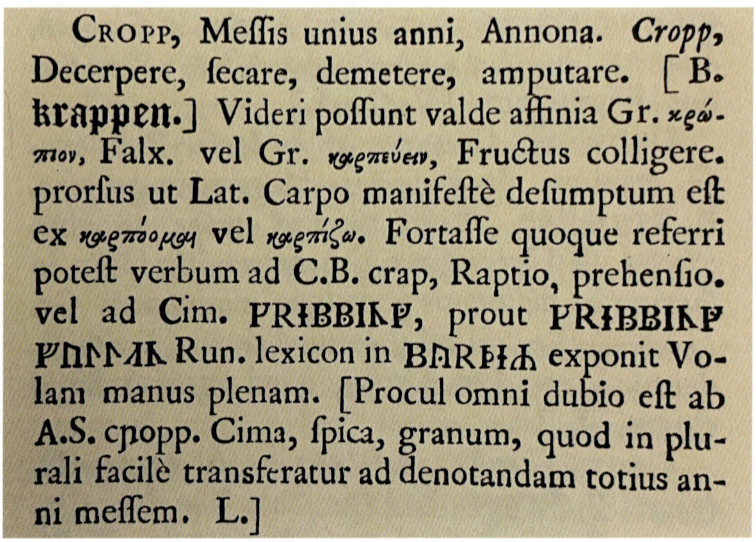
CROPP, Meſſis unius anni, Annona. *Cropp*, Decerpere, ſecare, demetere, amputare. [B. **krappen**.] Videri poſſunt valde affinia Gr. κρώπιον, Falx. vel Gr. καρπεύειν, Fructus colligere. prorſus ut Lat. Carpo manifeſtè deſumptum eſt ex καρπόομαι vel καρπίζω. Fortaſſe quoque referri poteſt verbum ad C.B. crap, Raptio, prehenſio. vel ad Cim. PRIBBIKP, prout PRIBBIKP PNNMK Run. lexicon in BARPIA exponit Volam manus plenam. [Procul omni dubio eſt ab A.S. cꞃopp. Cima, ſpica, granum, quod in plurali facilè transferatur ad denotandam totius anni meſſem. L.]

Ex coll. Jack Lynch

A typical entry in Junius, showing the typefaces he cut.

32

Samuel Johnson
Beating the Alphabet with Sluggish Resolution

Johnson, Samuel. *The Plan of a Dictionary of the English Language; Addressed to the Right Honourable Philip Dormer, Earl of Chesterfield; One of His Majesty's Principal Secretaries of State*. London: Printed for J. & P. Knapton, T. Longman and T. Shewell, C. Hitch, A. Millar, and R. Dodsley, 1747.

In early 1746, a group of booksellers drew up plans for a new dictionary—a huge folio covering the entire vocabulary, grounded in the works of the best English authors. It was to be a monument to the British nation and its literature, a document to rival the *Vocabolario* of the Accademia della Crusca (1612) and the *Dictionnaire* of the Académie française (1694).

"It is not enough that a dictionary delights the critic, unless at the same time it instructs the learner." (*Plan*, p. 5.)

Why the booksellers thought Samuel Johnson (1709–1784) should be in charge remains something of a mystery. He had accomplished little by the middle of the 1740s. However they arrived at the decision, though, they chose wisely. Nobody would have been better qualified for the job. In April 1746, Johnson drafted "A Short Scheme for compiling a new Dictionary of the English Language." The booksellers approved, and the contract was signed on 18 June 1746.

But how was he to support himself while he worked? The booksellers advanced £1,575—a generous amount, the equivalent of a six-figure payment today. But it would not be enough to support Johnson and his assistants through years of work.

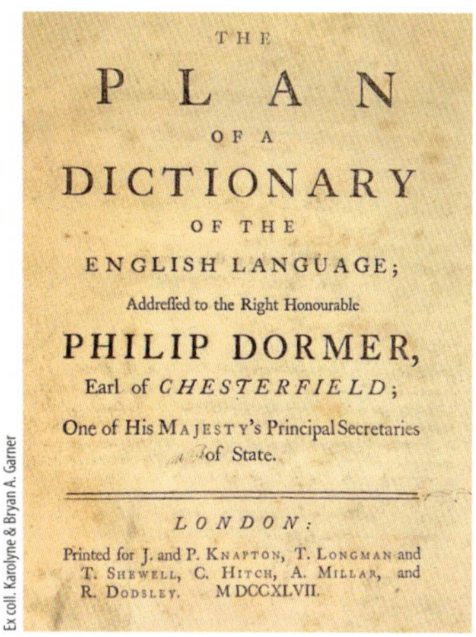

THE

PLAN

OF A

DICTIONARY

OF THE

ENGLISH LANGUAGE;

Addreffed to the Right Honourable

PHILIP DORMER,

Earl of *CHESTERFIELD*;

One of His Majesty's Principal Secretaries of State.

LONDON:

Printed for J. and P. Knapton, T. Longman and T. Shewell, C. Hitch, A. Millar, and R. Dodsley. M DCCXLVII.

Ex coll. Karolyne & Bryan A. Garner

The modern system of royalties, to say nothing of advances on royalties, had not yet come into being. In those days, most large-scale publishing projects depended on the patronage of wealthy benefactors, usually nobles. The understanding was that the patron would fund the author while the work was being written; in return, the author would begin the book with a flattering dedication, informing the world that Lord So-and-So is a friend of learning, a man whose nobility is rivaled only by his charity, an unrivaled paragon of virtue in a depraved world . . . Sometimes the over-the-top praise can seem

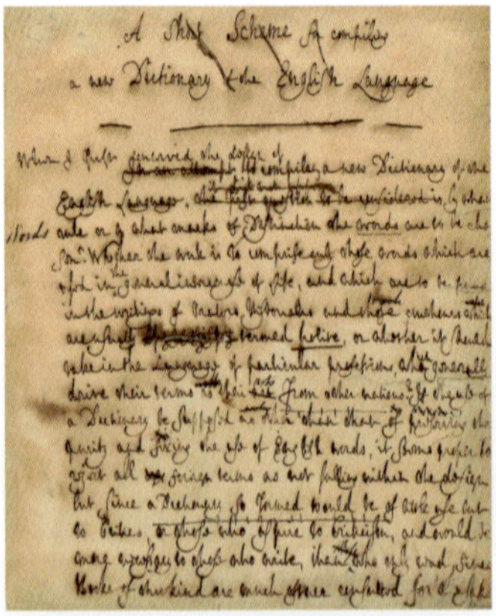
A Short Scheme for compiling a new Dictionary of the English Language

Courtesy of Hyde Collection, Houghton Library, Harvard University

Johnson's manuscript "A Short Scheme for Compiling a New Dictionary," now in Harvard's Hyde Collection, became the *Plan* published in 1747.

sarcastic to modern readers. But everyone understood how the game was played.

This type of literary fawning didn't come easily to Johnson, who was fiercely proud and despised the thought of accepting outside help. It had always been so. When he was a young child, his schoolmistress worried that his severe nearsightedness might put him in danger on his walk home. She followed him at a distance to ensure that he remained safe. But the boy spotted her, and regarding "her careful attention as an insult to his manliness," he "ran back to her in a rage, and beat her, as well as his strength would permit." (Boswell 1791 1:39.) When Johnson was an impoverished first-year student at Oxford and a fellow student quietly and anonymously left him a new pair of shoes to replace his tattered old ones, "he threw them away with indignation." (*Id.* at 77.) He couldn't abide charity.

But with no other way to support himself while writing the *Dictionary*, he did what he had to do. In 1747, he revised his "Scheme" into *The Plan of a Dictionary of the English Language*, addressed "To the Right Honourable PHILIP DORMER, Earl of *CHESTERFIELD*; One of His Majesty's Principal Secretaries of State." Chesterfield was interested in the project—some speculate that he had read the "Scheme," and he certainly read the fair copy of the *Plan* before it was published.

"They that take a dictionary into their hands have been accustomed to expect from it a solution of almost every difficulty." (*Plan*, p. 5.)

Although the publication's immediate purpose was to request patronage, the *Plan* is the first systematic statement of lexicographic principles published in English. Johnson showed that, even at the very beginning of his labors, he grasped many of the knottiest problems that lexicographers face. He understood better than anyone else the challenges posed by extremely polysemous words, especially phrasal verbs. He saw that the boundary between lexical and encyclopedic information is hard to maintain. He commented on the difficulty of deciding when foreign words are naturalized into English, and he recognized that logic was not always able to overcome long-established norms. He first spelled out his policy for definitions: starting with root meanings, moving on to extended senses, and finally to metaphorical ones. He noted that words often had connotations that made them appropriate in some linguistic registers but not in others. He also understood that the hardest words to define are the most common—"*horse*, *dog*, *cat*, *willow*, *alder*, *dasy*, *rose*, and a thousand others, of which it will be hard to give an explanation not more obscure than

Ex coll. Karolyne & Bryan A. Garner

the word itself." Every working lexicographer today recognizes these challenges.

What may be most interesting about the *Plan*, though, is just how much of it Johnson rejected when he actually came to write the *Dictionary*. The *Plan* is explicitly prescriptive in its aims, as when he explains his mission to Chesterfield:

> When I survey the plan which I have laid before you . . . I am frighted at its extent, and, like the soldiers of Cæsar, look on Britain as a new world, which it is almost madness to invade. But I hope . . . I shall at least discover the coast, civilize part of the inhabitants, and make it easy for some other adventurer to proceed farther, to reduce them wholly to subjection, and settle them under laws.

Johnson's imagery is explicitly military and colonialist—a strange choice from one of the century's most emphatic critics of colonial conquest. In the Preface to the *Dictionary*, written after he had done all the work, he no longer spoke of invasions and control. Instead, he described the language's many inconsistencies, which are "not to be imputed to me, who do not form, but register the language; who do not teach men how they should think, but relate how they have hitherto expressed their thoughts."

In the first year of publication, the *Plan* was issued in several different forms. The first edition first state is the so-called Chesterfield issue, which has five lines explicitly addressed to the Earl of Chesterfield: "To the Right Honourable / PHILIP DORMER, / Earl of *CHESTERFIELD*; / One of His Majesty's Principal Secretaries of State. My Lord, ..." These lines were mysteriously removed in the first edition second state, called the "non-Chesterfield issue," leaving an empty space around the salutation "My Lord." (Had Johnson been slighted by Chesterfield in the interim?) A second edition, in a somewhat smaller octavo format, also appeared in 1747, likewise being a "non-Chesterfield issue."

"I expect that sometimes the desire of accuracy, will urge me to superfluities, and sometimes the fear of prolixity between me to omissions; that in the extent of such variety I shall be often bewildred [sic], and in the mazes of such intricacy, be frequently entangled; that in one part refinement will be subtilized beyond exactness, and evidence dilated in another beyond perspicuity." (*Plan*, pp. 33–34.)

Ex coll. Karolyne & Bryan A. Garner

Three 1747 imprints of the *Plan*: two first editions (bottom) and one second (top).

Ex coll. Karolyne & Bryan A. Garner

"The [subject] of *English Dictionaries* especially has been so far from any thing of a Progressive Improvement, that it is manifestly retrograde, and sinks from its low Apex; from bad, to very bad indeed." (1754 ed., p. iii.)

Ex coll. Karolyne & Bryan A. Garner

The 1737 precursor.

33

Benjamin Martin

Self-Taught Omnivore

Martin, Benjamin. *Lingua Britannica Reformata; or, A New English Dictionary*. London: J. Hodges et al., 1749. 2d ed. 1754.

WE KNOW ALMOST NOTHING about the early life of Benjamin Martin (1705–1782), but any son of a farmer who went on to publish books on philology, mathematics, optics, and mechanics must have been a serious autodidact. In the 1730s, he established his own school in Sussex and published the first in a long line of books: *The Philosophical Grammar* (1735), *Bibliotheca Technologica* (1737), and *Institutions of Language* (1748). His most important work on the language, *Lingua Britannia Reformata*, a 16-shilling octavo, was published in 1749.

Martin was an inventor with an inventor's temperament: he sought out problems and systematically set about solving them. He built a portable microscope of his own design, developed a system of cartography to account for the earth's spheroidal shape, designed a new clock mechanism, and tried unsuccessfully to sell to the Royal Navy a bilge pump he invented.

He brought that same tinkerer's spirit to lexicography: after enumerating "the proper Requisites of a Genuine English Dictionary," he surveyed the English dictionaries published to date, noted where they failed to meet his standard, and worked efficiently and systematically to address them. *Lingua Britannica Reformata* is a model of planning and organization.

Among Martin's lexicographic "requisites" is the comprehensive coverage of all the common words in use in the language. He therefore included many words and senses that earlier dictionaries had missed: his dictionary comes in just under 25,000 entries, more than Kersey's or Dyche and Pardon's. He came well shy of Bailey's 40,000 headwords, though this was by choice: he excluded encyclopedic information, obsolete words, and obscure words that nobody actually used. Other dictionaries swelled their pages with thousands of recondite terms, many of them barely English at all. Martin refused to play that game, and produced a kind of anti-inkhorn dictionary. Bailey's *Dictionarium Britannicum* (no. 26), for instance, has the run of entries *hyæna*, *hyaloides*, *hypernagium*, *hybernal*, *hybistrica*, *hyboma*, *hybrida*, *hydatides*, *hydatoides*, *hydatis*, *hydatoscopia*, *hyde-gild*, and *hydra*. Martin goes straight from *hyæna* to *hydra* with none of the intervening hard words. He also resolved to give up-to-date spellings "according to the current Usage of the most approved and polite Writers of the Age," trading old-fashioned forms like *logick* and *phrensy* for the more modern *logic* and *frenzy*.

Martin's most important innovation was numbered senses, an idea he may have borrowed from Johnson's *Plan of a Dictionary* (no. 32). He certainly benefited from bilingual dictionaries, which had to break out a word's senses to ensure that the words in one language mapped neatly onto those of another. Where Bailey's definitions, for instance, wantonly pile up undiscriminated synonyms—*riot* "a Company of People, a Mob, or Rabble; a Combustion, Noise, Trouble, or Disturbance"—Martin breaks those meanings out, usually one a line:

1 a multitude, a throng of people.
2 going forcibly to commit a riot.
3 a squabble, or noise.
4 the way which solders are to march.
5 defeat, or discomfiture.

There's a logic to the order: in keeping with Johnson's *Plan*, he begins with the original sense of the etymon and then traces each word through its looser and more metaphorical meanings, wrapping up each entry with compounds and idioms.

Although the typography of Martin's book isn't particularly attractive, it is innovative. He was thinking seriously about how the physical form of the book could convey lexicographic content. Headwords that had not yet been entirely naturalized into English appeared in italics, another idea he may have adapted from Johnson's *Plan*: *ASTROITES*, *ATONIA*. He used his own novel system of single and double accent marks to indicate stressed syllables, and some headwords are followed by a superscript number: "Where I have observed the Number of Syllables in a Word to be any ways doubtful or uncertain to the Unlearned, I have shewn the Number by a

Ex coll. Karolyne & Bryan A. Garner

Benjamin Martin.

"The immediate precursor of Johnson's dictionary was compiled by the mathematician and instrument-maker Benjamin Martin. . . . Its issue may have been influenced and accelerated by the publication of Johnson's *Plan of a Dictionary of the English Language* (1747), for it carefully differentiated between the different meanings of individual words, setting them out logically and providing them with definitions of a far higher standard than had previously been achieved. The preface to this work is of particular importance since it takes pains to explain the principles on which the dictionary was compiled. Though fewer than 25,000 words were defined (including many scientific terms, and a number of foreign words which were italicized), this dictionary was outstanding for its time, and the fact that it ran only to a second edition (1754) must be attributed rather to the overwhelming triumph of Johnson's still greater work, than to any imperfections of its own." (Collison 1971:193.)

Figure at the End of the Word. Thus in the Word *Antipodes*[4], the Figure (4) shews there are *four* Syllables." (P. vii.) He combined Bailey's CAPITAL headwords with Kersey's hanging indention to facilitate skimming, and he applied the hanging indention to the numbered senses as well:

> FI´LLET, 1 a hair lace.
> 2 a band of cloth.
> 3 the fleshy part of a leg of veal.
> 4 a book-binder's ornament on a book.
> FI´LLY, a young mare.
> FILM, 1 a thin skin, within the body, dividing the flesh, or any near member one from another.
> 2 a skin, or scum upon the surface of mineral waters.
> 3 a woody skin, that separates the seeds in the pods of plants.
> FILOSE´LLA (of *filoselle*, F.) a sort of coarse silk.

"Though upon the Whole, I presume this Dictionary is by much the most perfect of its Kind; yet I am not so vain as to think it without Faults and Imperfections." (1754 ed., p. xii.)

As a result, it's easier to find an entry or a sense in Martin's dictionary text than in nearly anything that came before. That sort of hanging indention has been a standard feature of dictionaries ever since.

Martin's misfortune was to publish his dictionary in 1749. Bailey's dictionaries provided the most serious competition for the first few years, but Martin's book sold well enough to warrant, in 1754, a "second edition, greatly improved and augmented." When Johnson's *Dictionary* appeared in April 1755, though, Martin was driven out of the lexicography business for good. He continued publishing books, mostly on scientific topics (*An Essay on Visual Glasses*, *The Theory of Comets*, *The Nature and Construction of a Solar Eclipse Explained*), and many of them went through multiple editions. His main source of income for the rest of his life, though, was selling scientific instruments—but not enough to save him from dying bankrupt in 1782.

Ex coll. Karolyne & Bryan A. Garner

Ex coll. Karolyne & Bryan A. Garner

Ex coll. Karolyne & Bryan A. Garner

Three printer's devices from the 1740 edition of Martin's *Bibliotheca Technologica*.

V. The Age of Authority

During the 18th century, people increasingly demanded rigor, expertise, and empirically grounded confidence. For the English-speaking world, none provided these desiderata more effectively than Samuel Johnson. With the promise of support from a patron, he embarked on a grand dictionary on a new design; when the promised support never materialized, he completed the work in straitened circumstances—only to be offered patronly support as he crossed the finish line. By now, Johnson's name could lend luster to the patron because Johnson had performed the admirable task in a startlingly admirable way: he defined not just English terminology but 18th-century England itself. Everything changed in 1755.

There followed the inevitable epigones, abridgers, and plagiaries, along with a few who worked to fill the gaps Johnson had left, primarily in pronunciation. One of Johnson's friends, John Walker, seemed assured of not offending Johnson by doing a "backward dictionary," alphabetized according to word terminations—a rhyming dictionary that focused on how words are pronounced. Only seven years after Johnson's death did he attempt a more conventional dictionary in normal alphabetical order. Johnson's good friend Hester Piozzi—well, his good friend as long as her last name was Thrale—came out with a synonym book (1794) ten years after Johnson's death. She took issue with him when she could.

But nobody of the time, not even the ludicrously contentious William Kenrick, could compose a dictionary except in the shadow of Samuel Johnson.

Ex coll. Jack Lynch

In this Victorian imagining of the scene, Johnson waits in Lord Chesterfield's anteroom—and is ultimately rebuffed.
Etching after Edward Matthew Ward, *Doctor Johnson in the Ante-Room of the Lord Chesterfield Waiting for an Audience, 1748*.

34

Samuel Johnson

Disclaiming a Patron

7 February 1755 letter from Samuel Johnson to Lord Cheſterfield. James Boswell's transcription from Johnson's dictation.

Ex coll. Karolyne & Bryan A. Garner

A LEXICOGRAPHIC QUARREL produced one of the most effective and memorable comeuppance letters ever sent.

Johnson, knowing that the booksellers' payment of £1,575 would not be enough to support him and his staff over several years, did what many other 18th-century authors did: he approached a patron and requested financial support in return for a flattering dedication. One of the booksellers, Robert Dodsley, recommended Philip Dormer Stanhope, 4th Earl of Chesterfield (1694–1773), a highly regarded man of letters and patron of the arts. He seemed a natural choice.

It did not go well. Chesterfield blew him off.

To be fair, he didn't neglect him entirely. We have evidence of one payment of £10, and there may have been others. But it wasn't close to what Johnson needed. More to the point, the commoner Johnson had the audacity to believe that the noble Chesterfield refused to pay him the respect he deserved. Without his lordship's financial backing, Johnson was forced to go it alone. Over the nine years he worked on his dictionary he had to support himself with other writing projects, including his greatest poem, *The Vanity of Human Wishes* (1749), and the periodical essay series *The Rambler* (1750–1752).

"As it is unavoidable to wish, it is natural likewise to hope, that your Lordship's patronage may not be wholly lost." (1747 *Plan*, p. 32.)

As the *Dictionary*'s publication date grew closer, though, literary London was abuzz: this was going to be a major work of scholarship, a monumental dictionary to rival the works of the Italian and French academies. Chesterfield decided that he wanted a piece of it. Remembering the lexicographer who had awkwardly approached him in 1747, Chesterfield worked to charm him. It was a bizarre reversal of the usual order, with one of Britain's most distinguished men of letters—a peer of the realm, no less—striving to impress a mere literary hireling.

Lord Chesterfield.

"Johnson's rejection of Chesterfield did not endear him to the booksellers who had underwritten the *Dictionary*. Dodsley pointed out that he 'had a property' in it 'to which his Lordship's patronage might have been of consequence.' For 'might' we can read 'would'; Dodsley is trying not to inflame Johnson any further, yet is also trying to palliate his own sense of commercial disadvantage." (Hitchings 2005:185.)

Ex coll. Karolyne & Bryan A. Garner

In November and December 1754, Chesterfield published a highly flattering two-part review—properly a preview, since the book had not yet been published—in a magazine called *The World*. The timing was just right to allow a grateful Johnson to write a fawning dedication for the *Dictionary*, letting the public know that he, Chesterfield, deserved some of the credit for the new work.

"I think the public in general," Chesterfield wrote, "and the republic of letters in particular, greatly obliged to Mr. Johnson, for having undertaken and executed so great and desirable a work." The English language, he insisted, was in "a state of anarchy," and needed an authority figure to beat it into shape. "Toleration, adoption and naturalization have run their lengths. Good order and authority are now necessary." That authority would come from the new dictionary, which would tell the English how to speak and write.

Chesterfield's rhetoric got only more extreme from there:

> I hereby declare that I make a total surrender of all my rights and privileges in the English language, as a free-born British subject, to the said Mr. Johnson, during the term of his dictatorship. Nay more; I will not only obey him, like an old Roman, as my dictator, but, like a modern Roman, I will implicitly believe him as my pope, and hold him to be infallible while in the chair.

Anyone else might have been thrilled to receive such a declaration from such a distinguished man of letters, but Johnson read it with contempt. "This courtly device failed of its effect," Boswell wrote. "Johnson, who thought that 'all was false and hollow,' despised the honeyed words, and was even indignant that Lord Chesterfield should, for a moment, imagine, that he could be the dupe of such an artifice." (Boswell 1791 1:259.)

And even though Johnson had expressed some authoritarian impulses in the *Plan* he addressed to Chesterfield in 1747—"Barbarous or impure words and expressions . . . are carefully to be eradicated wherever they are found"—by the time he finished his *Dictionary*, he knew that the language was too rich and complex to be constrained. He was no longer interested in being anyone's dictator, and certainly not in being anyone's pope.

Johnson complained about Chesterfield's ploy to his friend David Garrick: "I have sailed a long and painful voyage round the world of the English language; and does he now send out two cock-boats to tow me into the harbour?" On 7 February 1755, he wrote this letter to Chesterfield, a masterpiece of insolence born of wounded pride:

> My Lord
>
> I have been told that two papers in the World in which I and my labours are recommended to the Publick were written by your Lordship. To be so distinguished is an honour which being very little accustomed to favours from the Great, I know not well how to receive, or in what terms to acknowledge.
>
> When upon some slight invitation I first visited your Lordship I was overpowered like the rest of Mankind by the enchantment of your address, and could not forbear to wish that I might be le *Vainqueur du Vainqueur* de la terre ["the conqueror of the conqueror of the world"], that I might obtain that regard for which I saw the world contending. But after a short time I found my attendance so little regarded that neither Pride nor modesty would suffer me to continue it. When I had once addressed your Lordship in publick I had exhausted all the art of pleasing that a retired and uncourtly Scholar can possess. I had done all that I could and no man is well pleased to have his all neglected, be it ever so little.
>
> Seven years My Lord are now passed since I waited in your anterooms or was repulsed from your door in which time I have carried on my work through difficulties of which it is useless to complain and brought it at last to the verge of publication, without one word of encouragement one act of assistance or one smile of favour. Such treatment I did not expect, for I never had a Patron before. The Shepherd in Virgil grew at last acquainted with love, and found him a native of the rocks.
>
> Is not a Patron My Lord one who looks with unconcern on a Man struggling for life in the water, and when he has reached ground, encumbers him with help? The regard now shewn me by your Lordship had it been early had been kind. But it has been delayed till I am indifferent and cannot enjoy it, till I am solitary and cannot impart it, till I am known and do not want it.
>
> I hope it is no very cynical asperity not to confess obligation where no benefit has been received or to be unwilling that the World should consider me as owing that to a Patron which Providence has enabled me to do for myself.

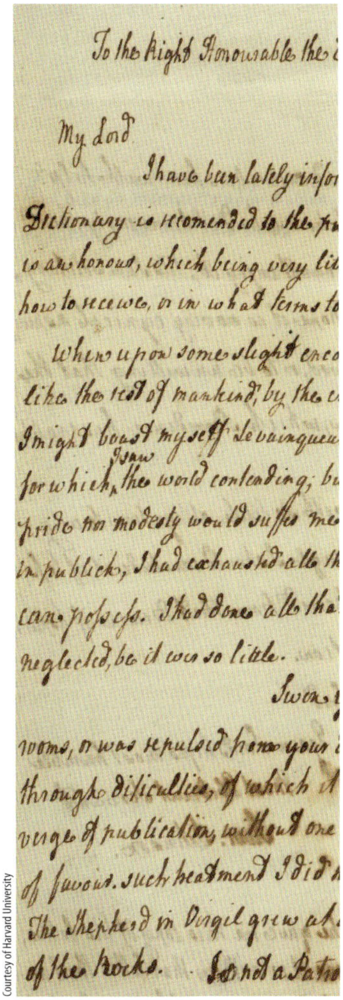
To the Right Honourable the
My Lord
I have been lately infor
Dictionary is recomended to the pu
is an honour, which being very lit
how to receive, or in what terms to
When upon some slight enco
like the rest of mankind, by the
I might boast myself Le vainqueu
for which I saw the world contending; bu
pride nor modesty would suffer me
in publick, I had exhausted all th
can possess. I had done all tha
neglected, be it ever so little.
Seven
rooms, or was repulsed from your
through difficulties, of which
verge of publication, without one
of favour. such treatment I did
The Shepherd in Virgil grew at
of the rocks. Is not a Patro

An early copy of the letter (detail).

"The message that Johnson sent in February 1755 has long been recognized as one of the great letters of all time. Packed into six fairly short paragraphs are all the exasperations and pain of years of frustration and disdain. The satirical touches are keen and to the point. No one could ever be uncertain just what he meant." (Clifford 1979:135–36.)

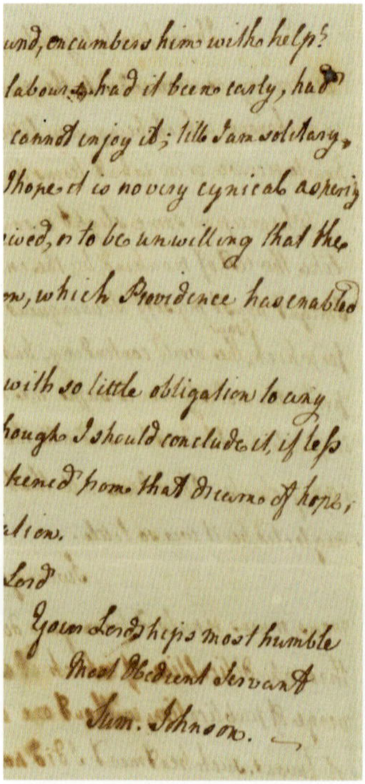
und, encumbers him with help?
labours had it been early, had
cannot enjoy it; till I am solitary,
I hope it is no very cynical asperity
ceived, or to be unwilling that the
on, which Providence has enabled
with so little obligation to any
though I should conclude it, if less
kened from that dream of hope,
tion.
Lord
Your Lordship's most humble
Most Obedient Servant
Sam. Johnson.

Courtesy of Harvard University

End of the letter (detail).

> Having carried on my work thus far with so little help from any favourer of learning I shall not be surprised though I should conclude it, if less be possible, with less; for I have been long awakened from that dream of hope in which I once boasted myself with so much exultation My Lord
>
> Your Lordship's most humble
> Most Obedient Servant
> Sam. Johnson.

The scholar Alvin Kernan calls this letter "the Magna Carta of the modern author, the public announcement that the days of courtly letters were at last ended." Others have called it a "declaration of independence," the end of the patronage system. Of course, history doesn't happen like that; patronage had been declining, and still had years to go. But if we want to find one moment that marks the birth of the modern author—proud, self-sufficient, dependent on market forces rather than the good graces of the rich and powerful—7 February 1755 is as good as any, and it's noteworthy that the genre that killed the patronage system was the dictionary. Johnson would never again approach a patron. In the body of the *Dictionary*, he managed to get in one more jab at Chesterfield. He defined *patron* as "One who countenances, supports or protects," and then added, "Commonly a wretch who supports with insolence, and is paid with flattery."

"Johnson's noble letter to Lord Chesterfield has long been seen as an instrument or a marker of the emergence of the profession of writing from its dependence upon patronage." (Tankard 2022:111.)

Though the letter became known at once to the literati of London, it wasn't published until Boswell issued it in pamphlet form in 1790. It sold for half a guinea.

Chesterfield, who died in 1773, kept the original for years on his table so that he might occasionally see it. Although he must have felt Johnson's vitriol, he conceded that "this man has great powers." The original is now lost. The copy transcribed here and partially shown, the property of Harvard University, is one of two made under Johnson's own supervision; it was transcribed by James Boswell from Johnson's dictation. The transcription differs slightly from most published versions, which come from a different lifetime copy.

35

Samuel Johnson
Beating 40 Frenchmen

Johnson, Samuel. *A Dictionary of the English Language . . . to which are prefixed, a history of the language, and an English grammar.* 2 vols. London: Printed by W. Strahan for J. & P. Knapton et al., 1755.

Ex coll. Karolyne & Bryan A. Garner

Scarce first edition with untrimmed pages.

"Elegance and Propriety of Stile have been very much neglected among us," complained the philosopher David Hume in 1741. "We have no dictionary of our Language." (Hume 1741:179.) A few years later, the clergyman and man of letters William Warburton agreed: "We have neither Grammar nor Dictionary, neither Chart nor Compass, to guide us through this wide sea of Words." (Warburton 1747 1:xxv.)

"Among those unhappy mortals ['who toil at the lower employments of life'] is the writer of dictionaries; whom mankind have considered, not as the pupil, but the slave of science, the pionier [sic] of literature, doomed only to remove rubbish and clear obstructions from the paths through which Learning and Genius press forward to conquest and glory, without bestowing a smile on the humble drudge that facilitates their progress." (Preface.)

No dictionary as late as the 1740s?—how, then, to account for the dozens of dictionaries we've already seen?

What they meant was that English had no *standard* dictionary, no *authoritative* dictionary, no dictionary to rival the great national dictionaries of Continental Europe, the *Dictionnaire de l'Académie française* above all.

Why no *Dictionary of the British Academy*? Britons have long had different attitudes toward linguistic authority from those in Continental Europe, where officially appointed academies took the lead on codifying their languages. But while Britain occasionally mused on an institution modeled on the Académie française, no Anglophone country has ever had a government-sponsored academy to take responsibility for the language.

Ex coll. Jack Lynch

In 2005, the Royal Mint issued this 50p coin to commemorate the 250th anniversary of Johnson's *Dictionary*.

Johnson's *Dictionary* was what the 18th century called a "booksellers' project," one initiated not by an academy, nor even by an author, but by a few publishers (called "booksellers" at the time, since there was no clear line between publishing and retailing). In this case, it was a syndicate of booksellers, known as a "conger," who pooled their resources to share both the risks and the profits of expensive projects. In 1746, they approached Samuel Johnson (1709–1784) to ask him to write a dictionary.

Johnson was a curious choice. At the time, he was little more than a hack writer, an overeducated but undercredentialed 36-year-old with no university degree. He had published one significant poem (*London*, in 1738), an obscure political satire (*Marmor Norfolciense*, in 1739), a few short biographies, and a reasonable amount of pedestrian magazine journalism. Nothing in his record suggested that he was the person to survey the entire English language. Yet the choice, however unexpected, was inspired. Johnson had the breadth of learning, the sensitivity to usage, and the sheer endurance that it would take to compile a dictionary.

"When first I engaged in this work, I resolved to leave neither words nor things unexamined, and pleased myself with the prospect of hours which I should revel away in feasts of literature, with the obscure recesses of northern learning, which I should enter and ransack. . . . But these were the dreams of a poet doomed at last to wake a lexicographer." (Preface.)

Ex coll. Karolyne & Bryan A. Garner

Still, this would be on a scale that Johnson had never attempted before—a scale that no English lexicographer had attempted before. The booksellers wanted a dictionary to rival the *Vocabolario degli Accademici della Crusca* (1612) and the *Dictionnaire de l'Académie française* (1694). These huge projects had occupied large teams of academics for many years. The French Académie, with its 40 "immortels," spent 40 years on their *Dictionnaire*. Johnson said he'd do it unaided in three years. Although friends scoffed, he was undaunted. "Let me see," he said. "Forty times forty is sixteen hundred. As three to sixteen hundred, so is the proportion of an Englishman to a Frenchman." (Boswell 1791 1:186.) The hyperbolic humor is a reminder that dictionaries are often bound up with national identity.

While we can only speculate about how Cockeram, Blount, and Bailey wrote their dictionaries, we have firsthand accounts of Johnson's working methods. These accounts differ on some minor points, but the broad outlines of his methods are clear, and they give us our earliest insight into how dictionaries have been compiled. (For details, see Reddick 1996 and Reddick 2005.)

"A large work is difficult because it is large, even though all its parts might singly be performed with facility; where there are many things to be done, each must be allowed its share of time and labour, in the proportion only which it bears to the whole; nor can it be expected, that the stones which form the dome of a temple, should be squared and polished like the diamond of a ring." (Preface.)

Let's begin with the quotations, Johnson's most important innovation in English lexicography. Lexicons of Greek and Latin often included quotations from classical authors, and a smattering of quotations had appeared in earlier English dictionaries, but no English dictionary had done anything like what Johnson proposed. He did not merely deploy quotations to illustrate words; he built his *Dictionary* around them. The quotations told him which words to include, they told him what words meant, and they told him in what situations they were used. They were the foundation of everything that followed.

The work began with a reading program. Johnson made his way through hundreds of books, looking for examples of words in use. There was no such thing as a lexicographic corpus in the 1740s, so he was forced to assemble his own. He focused especially on great literature in English: Shakespeare above all, but Milton, Spenser, Sidney, Dryden, and Pope all contributed thousands of quotations. Scottish, Welsh, and Irish writers were represented as well as English. Johnson read philosophers (John Locke, Joseph Glanvill), physicians (John Quincy, John Arbuthnot), scientists (Isaac Newton, Richard Boyle), jurists (John Ayliffe, John Cowell), statesmen (Francis Bacon, Sir Walter Raleigh), clergymen (Richard Allestree, Henry Hammond), and historians (Richard Knolles, the Earl of Clarendon). The King James Version of the Bible is the most-quoted book in the *Dictionary*. Most of Johnson's sources flourished between the late 16th century and the late 17th, but sometimes he looked back as far as Chaucer, and though he vowed not to draw from living authors, he sometimes included quotations from his friends. Most of the authors were male, though he included a few women writers as well. In a few places, he slyly quoted his own publications. Sometimes he may have relied on his remarkable memory, but most of the quotations come directly from printed sources. Boswell insisted that he "quoted no authour whose writings had a tendency to hurt sound religion and morality." (Boswell 1791 1:189; see DeMaria 1986.)

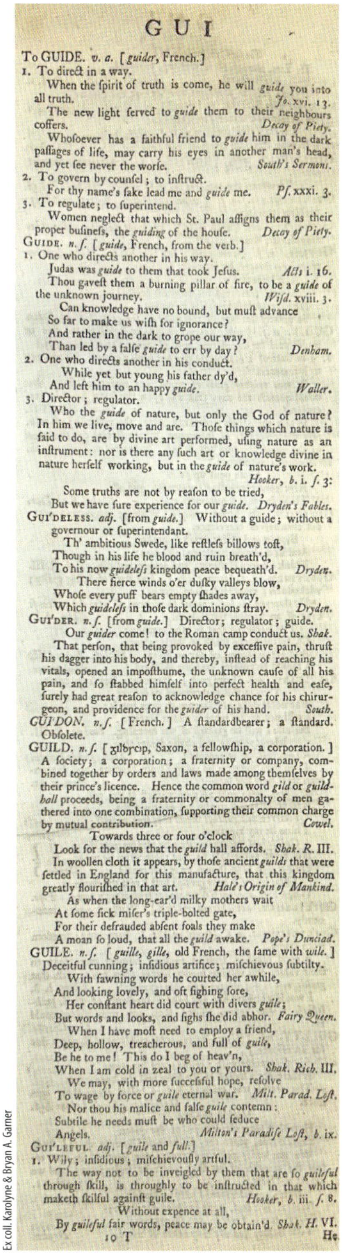
GUI

To GUIDE. *v. a.* [*guider*, French.]
1. To direct in a way.
When the ſpirit of truth is come, he will *guide* you into all truth. *Jo.* xvi. 13.
The new light ſerved to *guide* them to their neighbours coffers. *Decay of Piety.*
Whoſoever has a faithful friend to *guide* him in the dark paſſages of life, may carry his eyes in another man's head, and yet ſee never the worſe. *South's Sermons.*
2. To govern by counſel; to inſtruct.
For thy name's ſake lead me and *guide* me. *Pſ.* xxxi. 3.
3. To regulate; to ſuperintend.
Women neglect that which St. Paul aſſigns them as their proper buſineſs, the *guiding* of the houſe. *Decay of Piety.*
GUIDE. *n. ſ.* [*guide*, French, from the verb.]
1. One who directs another in his way.
Judas was *guide* to them that took Jeſus. *Acts* i. 16.
Thou gaveſt them a burning pillar of fire, to be a *guide* of the unknown journey. *Wiſd.* xviii. 3.
Can knowledge have no bound, but muſt advance
So far to make us wiſh for ignorance?
And rather in the dark to grope our way,
Than led by a falſe *guide* to err by day? *Denham.*
2. One who directs another in his conduct.
While yet but young his father dy'd,
And left him to an happy *guide*. *Waller.*
3. Director; regulator.
Who the *guide* of nature, but only the God of nature? In him we live, move and are. Thoſe things which nature is ſaid to do, are by divine art performed, uſing nature as an inſtrument: nor is there any ſuch art or knowledge divine in nature herſelf working, but in the *guide* of nature's work. *Hooker, b.* i. *ſ.* 3:
Some truths are not by reaſon to be tried,
But we have ſure experience for our *guide*. *Dryden's Fables.*
GUI'DELESS. *adj.* [from *guide.*] Without a guide; without a governour or ſuperintendant.
Th' ambitious Swede, like reſtleſs billows toſt,
Though in his life he blood and ruin breath'd,
To his now *guideleſs* kingdom peace bequeath'd. *Dryden.*
There fierce winds o'er duſky valleys blow,
Whoſe every puff bears empty ſhades away,
Which *guideleſs* in thoſe dark dominions ſtray. *Dryden.*
GUI'DER. *n. ſ.* [from *guide.*] Director; regulator; guide.
Our *guider* come! to the Roman camp conduct us. *Shak.*
That perſon, that being provoked by exceſſive pain, thruſt his dagger into his body, and thereby, inſtead of reaching his vitals, opened an impoſthume, the unknown cauſe of all his pain, and ſo ſtabbed himſelf into perfect health and eaſe, ſurely had great reaſon to acknowledge chance for his chirurgeon, and providence for the *guider* of his hand. *South.*
GUI'DON. n. ſ. [French.] A ſtandardbearer; a ſtandard. Obſolete.
GUILD. *n. ſ.* [ᵹilꝺꞅcip, Saxon, a fellowſhip, a corporation.] A ſociety; a corporation; a fraternity or company, combined together by orders and laws made among themſelves by their prince's licence. Hence the common word *gild* or *guildhall* proceeds, being a fraternity or commonalty of men gathered into one combination, ſupporting their common charge by mutual contribution. *Cowel.*
Towards three or four o'clock
Look for the news that the *guild* hall affords. *Shak. R.* III.
In woollen cloth it appears, by thoſe ancient *guilds* that were ſettled in England for this manufacture, that this kingdom greatly flouriſhed in that art. *Hale's Origin of Mankind.*
As when the long-ear'd milky mothers wait
At ſome ſick miſer's triple-bolted gate,
For their defrauded abſent foals they make
A moan ſo loud, that all the *guild* awake. *Pope's Dunciad.*
GUILE. *n. ſ.* [*guille*, *gille*, old French, the ſame with *wile.*] Deceitful cunning; inſidious artifice; miſchievous ſubtilty.
With fawning words he courted her awhile,
And looking lovely, and oft ſighing ſore,
Her conſtant heart did court with divers *guile*;
But words and looks, and ſighs ſhe did abhor. *Fairy Queen.*
When I have moſt need to employ a friend,
Deep, hollow, treacherous, and full of *guile*,
Be he to me! This do I beg of heav'n,
When I am cold in zeal to you or yours. *Shak. Rich.* III.
We may, with more ſucceſsful hope, reſolve
To wage by force or *guile* eternal war. *Milt. Parad. Loſt.*
Nor thou his malice and falſe *guile* contemn:
Subtile he needs muſt be who could ſeduce
Angels. *Milton's Paradiſe Loſt, b.* ix.
GUI'LEFUL. *adj.* [*guile* and *full.*]
1. Wily; inſidious; miſchievouſly artful.
The way not to be inveigled by them that are ſo *guileful* through ſkill, is throughly to be inſtructed in that which maketh ſkilful againſt guile. *Hooker, b.* iii. *ſ.* 8.
Without expence at all,
By *guileful* fair words, peace may be obtain'd. *Shak. H.* VI.
10 T He

Ex coll. Karolyne & Bryan A. Garner

From the first edition (1755).

A few of the books he marked survive today, so we can see exactly how he worked. When he saw a passage he wanted to include, he used a lead pencil to make vertical lines, one at the beginning and one at the end of the passage. He then underlined the word he wanted to illustrate and wrote its first letter in the margin. As he finished reading each book, he handed it off to his assistants, who copied the quotations and brief citations onto slips of paper.

These quotation slips became the raw material of the *Dictionary*. Johnson used them to assemble the list of words that would get entries. His wordlist consisted of roughly 43,000 headwords. Earlier lexicographers could boast higher counts, but Johnson consciously chose to omit things that other dictionaries included: proper nouns, proverbs, figures from classical mythology, village market days, and so on. Most important, he was determined to include only words that were actually in use. Though the main narrative strand in the story of English lexicography is the progression from hard-word dictionaries to coverage of the entire language, inkhorn terms still abounded in dictionaries. Johnson wanted to keep only those that could be found in literature, but he was hesitant to cut too hastily. "Of such I have omitted many, because I had never read them," he wrote; "and many I have inserted, because they may perhaps exist, though they have escaped my notice." He warned, though, that they are "to be yet considered as resting only upon the credit of former dictionaries," and always attributed them to earlier dictionaries, either by compiler's name or with a generic "Dict."

"Most men think indistinctly, and therefore cannot speak with exactness." (Preface.)

For each word, Johnson drafted an etymology. We have to admit that these are a mixed bag. Johnson was prodigiously learned, and his treatment of words derived from Greek and Latin is sound. Like all his contemporaries, he was on shakier ground when he treated Germanic words, though he made good use of Franciscus Junius's *Etymologicum Anglicanum* (1743) (no. 31), the most thorough guide to Germanic etymologies available. Still, he was sometimes embarrassingly wrong. He ventures a guess on the origin of *spider*: "May not *spider* be *spy dor*, the insect that watches the *dor*?" (We now know that it comes from Old English *spinnan* "to spin.") At least he was refreshingly willing to confess ignorance when he lacked good evidence. Of *dickens* he says, "I know not whence derived," and of *pun* he writes, "I know not whence this word is to be deduced."

Ex coll. Karolyne & Bryan A. Garner

Boswell and Johnson in Fleet Street.

Then it was time to sort the quotation slips into senses, and to draft a definition (he said "explanation") for each sense. He confessed that this was the "part of my work on which I expect malignity most frequently to fasten." But working lexicographers today agree that Johnson was an excellent definer, and no lexicographer had ever thought harder about what went into defining words.

The most obvious innovation in Johnson's definitions is his use of numbered senses to capture polysemous words. Though he wasn't the first to use numbered senses—Benjamin Martin beat him to the punch, barely, perhaps having been prompted by Johnson's *Plan*—he used them far more extensively than any predecessor. His definitions are correspondingly richer and more precise than any that came before him.

"Dr Johnson made an often-quoted reply to a lady who congratulated him on having excluded improper words from his dictionary: 'You have evidently been looking for them, madam.'" (Brook 1981:88–89.)

Most important, Johnson was the first dictionary writer to give phrasal verbs serious attention. We'd describe them as verbs paired with either prepositions or adverbs, where the meaning of the compound cannot be divined from the components: think of *run down*, *run into*, *run off*, *run over*, or *take in*, *take off*, *take on*, *take over*, *take up*. The resulting meanings, Johnson wrote, are "so far distant from the sense of the simple words, that no sagacity will be able to trace the steps by which they arrived at the present use."

A few definitions achieved renown for their wit. Johnson relished opportunities to tweak Scots, so he wickedly defined *oats* as "a grain, which in England is generally given to horses, but in Scotland supports the people." *Lexicographer* is famously "a writer of dictionaries; a harmless drudge, that busies himself in tracing the original, and detailing the signification of words." (Hardly!) He inserted a sly tribute to his hometown, Lichfield, by defining *lich* with a mention of the "city in Staffordshire," adding: "*Salve magna parens*"—an uncited quotation from Virgil, meaning "Hail, great parent." His political sentiments slipped out in his definition of *excise*: "A hateful tax levied upon commodities, and adjudged not by the common judges of property, but wretches hired by those to whom excise is paid." Given his fondness for his cat Hodge, it's unsurprising that his definition of the verb *worm*, in the veterinary sense, suggests no partiality to dogs: "To deprive a dog of something, nobody knows what, under his tongue, which is said to prevent him, nobody knows why, from running mad."

These famous entries have led some to think of the *Dictionary* as a collection of quirky pseudo-definitions, a precursor to Ambrose Bierce's *Devil's Dictionary* (no. 115). But there are only a few examples of this levity scattered throughout the book. Much more important is the unprecedented attention he gave to offering precise definitions of all words in widespread circulation.

He now had all the material he needed for the body of the dictionary. He gathered the organized slips with the quotations, etymologies, and definitions, and passed them back to the amanuenses, who copied everything onto sheets that the printer would use in typesetting. Perhaps because he was still an inexperienced writer he had "a large portion" of the *Dictionary* copied onto both sides of a sheet of paper—this wasn't how things were done in 18th-century print shops, and it cost him £20 to have it recopied on one side. (Boswell 1791 1:189.)

17 Gough Square, London, where Johnson wrote the *Dictionary*.

"The qualities [Johnson] inserted, and they are of immeasurable value, are those that only a man of letters of the highest repute could bring to bear. The central body of his illustrative quotations was drawn from the greatest literary, philosophical, and scientific works of the period from Sidney to the Restoration, that is from the 1580s to 1660. And they were drawn from these works by a writer who knew the originals well, and was not merely setting down context-free sentences in order to fit inherited definitions. The illustrative examples form a kind of concordance to the most memorable utterances of his day." (Burchfield 1985:86.)

In his *Plan* (1747), Johnson considered several ideas for the physical display of information on the page:

> The words appropriated to poetry will be differentiated by some mark prefixed. . . . Antiquated or obsolete words . . . will be likewise pointed out by some note of exclusion, but not of disgrace. . . . Words used in burlesque and familiar compositions . . . will be diligently characterised by marks of distinction. [Johnson 2005:52–53]

None of these came to pass. Still, Johnson remains typographically innovative: "if we look at how the *Dictionary*'s typography articulates its underlying structure, we can see that Johnson's page . . . set the standard for English dictionaries for a century." (Luna 2005:175.) The pages make good use of white space, with hanging indention making it easy to find headwords and sense numbers. In headwords, the primary stress is marked by an acute accent after the vowel. Bailey introduced capital letters for headwords in 1721, and then switched to mixed caps and small caps in 1730. Johnson uses both: root words are in CAPS, derived forms in MIXED CAPS, giving us MI´NISTER for the noun, To MI´NISTER for the verb, MINISTE´RIAL, MI´NISTERY, and MI´NISTRAL. In quotations, the first line is indented, the headwords are in italic, and the citations are italic and flush-right:

> Th' offence is holy that she hath committed,
> And this deceit loses the name of craft,
> Of *disobedience*, or unduteous title. *Shak. M. W. of Winds.*
>
> Of man's first *disobedience*, and the fruit
> Of that forbidden tree, sing heav'nly muse. *Milton.*
>
> Murder, adultery, or *disobedience* to parents, have a general notion antecedently to laws. *Stillingfleet.*

The design takes advantage of the printed book's physical form to convey lexical information and to ensure that readers can find the information they need quickly.

The last things to be written were the preliminaries, consisting of a preface, a grammar, and a history of the English language. The grammar and the history have attracted few proponents, but the preface is a remarkable document, the first serious and systematic attempt by an English lexicographer to reckon with the challenges of capturing the language in a dictionary. He had already explored some

"In the beginning, skilful advertising helped the *Dictionary* establish its dominance over numerous and persistent competitors. Throughout the eighteenth century and well into the nineteenth, this dominance was maintained, and even when the *Dictionary* no longer came so close to giving complete satisfaction as it once had done, the attempt was made merely to supplement it or to keep its essential virtues unchanged in revised and extended editions. Advertising, supplements, and editions revised by Johnson and by others must be considered in the attempt to state the avenues and extent of Johnson's influence in lexicography." (Sledd & Kolb 1955:205.)

"In the whole tradition of English language and literature the *only* dictionary compiled by a writer of the first rank is that of Dr Johnson. The muses spared him a while from his main literary work before letting him return to his poems, his essays, and his tracts. If Dryden in the seventeenth century, Macaulay in the nineteenth, and T.S. Eliot in the twentieth had found it possible to withdraw from their main pursuits for a similar interval, and diverted their own 'intolerable wrestle with words' to the realm of lexicography, the result would very likely have been as beguiling, and as influential." (Burchfield 1979:n.p.)

of these ideas in his *Plan of an English Dictionary* (no. 32), published shortly after he agreed with the booksellers, but years of experience changed his mind on several important matters. Whereas the *Plan* envisions the lexicographer as an invader seeking to civilize a savage nation, the completed *Dictionary* rejects any proposal for an official academy and says that the lexicographer's job is not to form the language, but to register it. His experience wrestling with the language had made him more descriptive than he had been at the beginning of the project.

Ex coll. Karolyne & Bryan A. Garner

In the 1930s, this Johnson first edition (at right) belonged to a Merriam executive who had it rebound in the Merriam-style buckram of *Webster's Second* (at left—no. 100).

"I am not yet so lost in lexicography, as to forget that *words are the daughters of earth, and that things are the sons of heaven*. Language is only the instrument of science, and words are but the signs of ideas: I wish, however, that the instrument might be less apt to decay, and that signs might be permanent, like the things which they denote." (Johnson 2005:79.)

Although Johnson promised the *Dictionary* in three years, the work took longer than expected. He discovered what countless lexicographers before and after him have learned: that dictionaries are almost invariably delivered late. And because he never got the patronage he hoped for, he was forced to write for money to support himself through this period. It became one of the most productive of his life. In 1748 he published *The Vision of Theodore*; the next year saw the publication of his most important poem, *The Vanity of Human Wishes*, and the stage debut of his only play, *Irene*. From 1750 to 1752, he published his essay series *The Rambler*, considered by many his greatest work, and in 1753, he contributed to *The Adventurer*.

It was a productive time but also a melancholy one. In 1752, his wife, Elizabeth ("Tetty"), 20 years older than he, died suddenly. Those close to Johnson couldn't fathom what Johnson saw in his wife, who seemed vulgar to them, but Johnson was devastated by her death. That's probably what led to his gloomy conclusion in the final sentence of his preface:

> I have protracted my work till most of those whom I wished to please, have sunk into the grave, and success and miscarriage are empty sounds: I therefore dismiss it with frigid tranquillity, having little to fear or hope from censure or from praise.

The *Dictionary* was published on 15 April 1755. The English vocabulary from *A* to *zootomy* was covered in two folio volumes containing 2,300 pages and weighing 12 pounds. Roughly 43,000 headwords are supported with some 115,000 quotations. The entire text runs to roughly 3.5 million words. Two thousand copies were printed, and the book sold for £4 10*s*.

Ex coll. Karolyne & Bryan A. Garner

The folio editions of Johnson's *Dictionary* (1755–1785).

Ex coll. Karolyne & Bryan A. Garner

One of three first editions in the Garner Collection.

"Such is its merit, that our language does not possess a more copious, learned, and valuable work." (James Harris as quoted in Boswell 1791 3:115.)

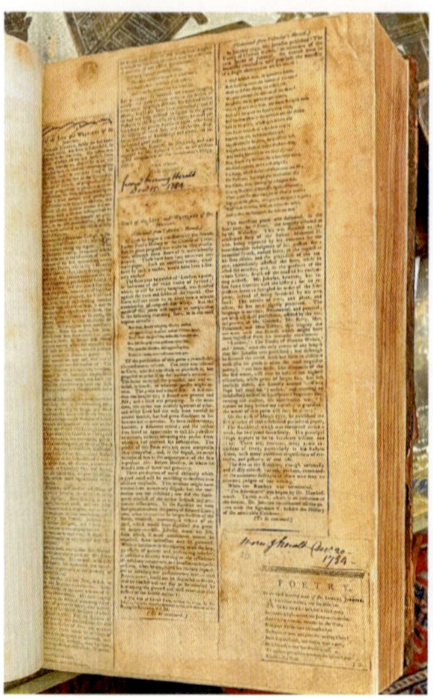

Ex coll. Karolyne & Bryan A. Garner

The first edition above contains several contemporary newspaper obituaries and tributes pasted in to free endpapers.

There were critics from the beginning, including the distinguished economist Adam Smith, who in the year of the book's publication published an unsigned review in the *Edinburgh Review*. Like so many others, he recognized the *Dictionary* as a masterpiece: "When we compare this book with other dictionaries, the merit of its author appears very extraordinary." (Quoted in Boulton 1971:115.) Yet he found fault in a way that presaged those who faulted *Webster's Third* (no. 102)—in a way that continues to provoke debate: "But we cannot help wishing, that the author had trusted less to the judgment of those who may consult him, and had oftener passed his own censure upon those words which are not of approved use." (*Id.*)

With the appearance of Johnson's *Dictionary*, it was no longer possible to lament the lack of an English dictionary: the book could proudly assume its place alongside the Italian *Vocabolario* and the French *Dictionnaire*. Johnson's name was synonymous with dictionaries for generations, and his book was not superseded until the publication of the *Oxford English Dictionary*, completed a century and three-quarters after his *Dictionary*.

The work occupied nine years from the agreement with the booksellers to publication day. And the ratio 1600 to 9 is nearly as impressive as 1600 to 3. His friend David Garrick celebrated his achievement in a stirring little patriotic poem:

> Talk of war with a Briton, he'll boldly advance,
> That one English soldier will beat ten of France;
> Would we alter the boast from the sword to the pen,
> Our odds are still greater, still greater our men:
> In the deep mines of science though Frenchmen may toil,
> Can their strength be compar'd to Locke, Newton, and
> Boyle?
> Let them rally their heroes, send forth all their pow'rs,
> Their verse-men and prose-men, then match them with
> ours!
> First Shakspeare and Milton, like gods in the fight,
> Have put their whole drama and epick to flight;
> In satires, epistles, and odes, would they cope,
> Their numbers retreat before Dryden and Pope;
> And Johnson, well arm'd like a hero of yore,
> Has beat forty French, and will beat forty more!
>
> [Boswell 1791 1:300–1]

36

Joseph Nicol Scott

Defining Physician

Bailey, Nathan. *An Universal Etymological English Dictionary* [etc.]. Joseph Nicol Scott ed. 16th ed. London: R. Ware et al., 1755.

The year 1755 might not have been the most propitious for the appearance of the big folio edition of Bailey's *Universal Etymological Dictionary*, which Joseph Nicol Scott (1702/3–1769), a physician, expanded from previous editions. After all, the appearance of Johnson's celebrated *Dictionary* made for formidable commercial competition. But Scott included 60,000 entries as compared with Johnson's 43,000 or so. (Earlier editions of Bailey also contained about 60,000.) Because Scott included few illustrative quotations, he was able to include an average of more than 60 entries per page; because Johnson included copious quotations throughout his entries, he averaged only about 20 per page. It turns out that 1755 was Scott's year *because* his big folio was intended to compete with Johnson.

Ex coll. Karolyne & Bryan A. Garner

Scott's 1755 folio (right) alongside the 15th octavo edition of 1753.

"Dr. Scott . . . carried into all companies a disputatious turn of mind . . . which had the unhappy effect of rendering his company and manners less pleasing and acceptable, and was a bar to success in his professional work." (*Monthly Magazine* 14:512 [1803].)

But does this really deserve to be called a new dictionary, and does Scott really deserve credit for it? Two respected lexicographic scholars have suggested that the book was only nominally his: "Both the circumstances of publication and the make-up of the work indicate . . . that this dictionary was designed as a booksellers' measure to hold the market against that redoubtable newcomer in lexicography, Samuel Johnson." (Starnes & Noyes 1946:179.) Scott is said to have done little apart from writing the preface, correcting some etymologies, and revising some medical and religious items.

To test the quality of Scott's contributions, we might compare eight medical entries in the octavo *Universal Etymological English Dictionary* (6th ed. 1733) against Scott's 1755 folio and against Johnson's 1755 first edition. The following chart omits all but headwords

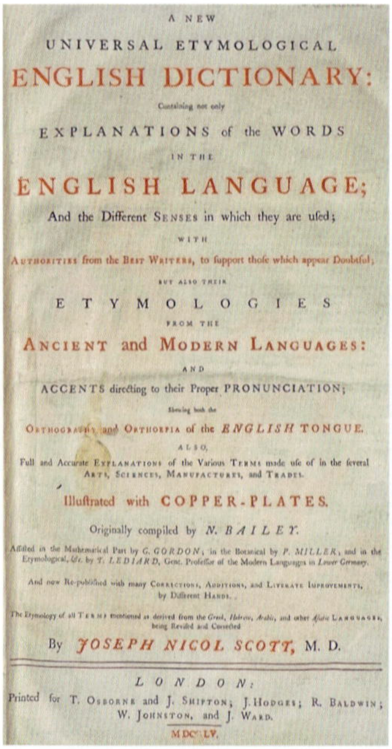
A NEW
UNIVERSAL ETYMOLOGICAL
ENGLISH DICTIONARY:
Containing not only
EXPLANATIONS of the WORDS
IN THE
ENGLISH LANGUAGE;
And the Different SENSES in which they are used;
WITH
AUTHORITIES from the BEST WRITERS, to support those which appear Doubtful;
BUT ALSO THEIR
ETYMOLOGIES
FROM THE
ANCIENT and MODERN LANGUAGES:
AND
ACCENTS directing to their Proper PRONUNCIATION;
Shewing both the
ORTHOGRAPHY and ORTHOEPIA of the *ENGLISH* TONGUE.
ALSO,
Full and Accurate EXPLANATIONS of the Various TERMS made use of in the several ARTS, SCIENCES, MANUFACTURES, and TRADES.
Illustrated with COPPER-PLATES.
Originally compiled by *N. BAILEY.*
Assisted in the Mathematical Part by *G. GORDON*; in the Botanical by *P. MILLER*, and in the Etymological, *&c.* by *T. LEDIARD*, Gent. Professor of the Modern Languages in *Lower Germany*.
And now Re-published with many CORRECTIONS, ADDITIONS, and LITERATE IMPROVEMENTS, by Different HANDS.
The Etymology of all TERMS mentioned as derived from the *Greek*, *Hebrew*, *Arabic*, and other *Asiatic* LANGUAGES, being Revised and Corrected
By *JOSEPH NICOL SCOTT*, M. D.
LONDON:
Printed for T. OSBORNE and J. SHIPTON; J. HODGES; R. BALDWIN; W. JOHNSTON, and J. WARD.
MDCCLV.

Ex coll. Karolyne & Bryan A. Garner

Title page of Scott's Bailey (1755).

and the definitions—the idea being to focus on the quality of the definitions alone.

Bailey (6th ed. 1733)	Scott's Bailey (1755)	Johnson (1755)
ABSCESS an Ulceration arising in any Part of the Body, and tending to Suppuration; the same with Imposthume.	ABSCESS a preternatural tumor (or morbid cavity) in the body, in which the collected matter degenerates into pus or sanies.	ABSCESS A morbid cavity in the body; a tumour filled with matter; a term of chirurgery.
BILE a thick, yellow, bitter Liquor, separated in the Liver, collected in the Gall-bladder, and discharged into the lower end of the *Duodenum* or beginning of the *Jejunum*, by the common Duct.	BILE the gall or choler; an humour of the body, partly saline, of a yellow colour, which is separated from the blood of animals in the liver, and is received into two vessels, *viz.* the gall-bladder, and the porus biliarius, and thence discharged by the common duct into the duodenum. Its use is to sheathe or blunt the acids of the chyle, because they, being entangled with its sulphurs, thicken it so, that it cannot be sufficiently diluted by the pancreatic juice to enter the lacteals.	BILE A thick, yellow, bitter liquour, separated in the liver, collected in the gall-bladder, and discharged into the lower end of the duodenum, or beginning of the jejunum, by the common duct. Its use is to sheathe or blunt the acids of the chyle; because they, being entangled with its sulphurs, thicken it so, that it cannot be sufficiently diluted by the succus pancreaticus, to enter the lacteal vessels. *Quincy.* [This entry comes verbatim from John Quincy's *Lexicon Physico-Medicum*.]

Bailey (6th ed. 1733)	Scott's Bailey (1755)	Johnson (1755)
CONSUMPTION is a Defect of Nourishment, or the consuming, decaying, and wasting of the Body, and particularly of the Muscular Flesh; also a consuming of Provisions, Commodities, &c.	CONSUMPTION 1. The act of consuming or wasting, especially of provisions, commodities, &c. 2. The state of wasting or perishing. 3. [With physicians] the wasting or decay of the body; frequently attended with a fever, and distinguished into several kinds, according to its various causes, parts, and effects, &c. Stoppages of womens courses set them into a consumption.	CONSUMPTION 1. The act of consuming; waste; destruction. 2. The state of wasting or perishing. 3. [In physick.] A waste of muscular flesh. It is frequently attended with a hectick fever, and is divided by physicians into several kinds, according to the variety of its causes. *Quincy*. [This entry, too, quotes Quincy nearly verbatim.]
FIBULA [in *Anatomy*] the lesser Bone of the Shank.	FIBULA [with anatomists] the lesser and outer bone of the leg; the focile minus much smaller than the tibia, it lies on the outside of the leg. Hippocrates uses the word for that part only of the bone that forms the outer ancle, perhaps because they used to buckle their shoes in that place.	FIBULA The outer and lesser bone of the leg, much smaller than the tibia: it lies on the outside of the leg; and its upper end, which is not so high as the knee, receives the lateral knob of the upper end of the tibia into a small sinus, which it has in its inner side. Its lower end is received into the small sinus of the tibia, and then it extends into a large process, which forms the outer ankle. *Quincy*. [Also taken nearly word for word.]

"As to our style, we have chosen the plain and unadorned; as best suiting Works of this Nature; and indeed the *florid* Diction is an artifice too often used to cover a *poverty* of Thought, and to screen a set of Sentiments, which, if strip'd of this false Colouring, would scarce bear a close Inspection. . . . Our chief Ambition has been to advance the Truth; and not to amuse our Readers with *historic Romance*, and *scholastic Jargon*." (Scott's preface, p. iv.)

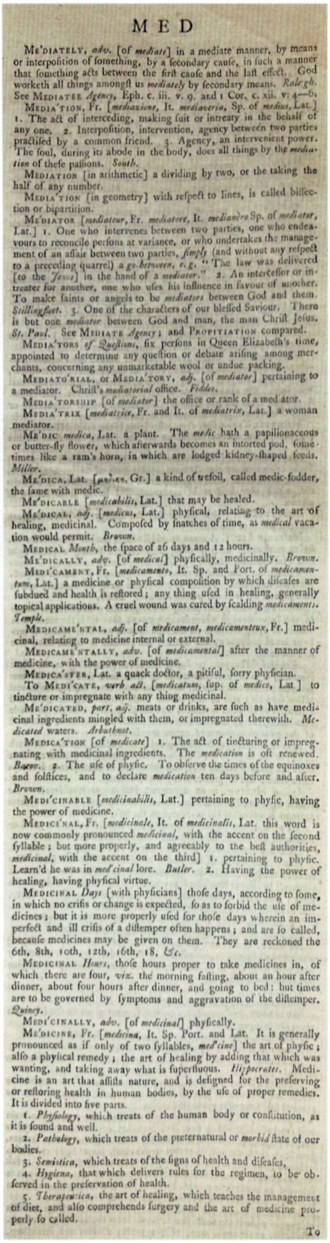

MED

ME'DIATELY, *adv.* [of *mediate*] in a mediate manner, by means or interpoſition of ſomething, by a ſecondary cauſe, in ſuch a manner that ſomething acts between the firſt cauſe and the laſt effect. God worketh all things amongſt us *mediately* by ſecondary means. *Raleigh.* See MEDIATEE *Agency*, Eph. c. iii. v. 9. and 1 Cor. c. xii. v: 4—6.

MEDIA'TION, Fr. [*mediazione*, It. *medianeria*, Sp. of *medius*, Lat.] 1. The act of interceding, making ſuit or intreaty in the behalf of any one. 2. Interpoſition, intervention, agency between two parties practiſed by a common friend. 3. Agency, an intervenient power. The ſoul, during its abode in the body, does all things by the *mediation* of theſe paſſions. *South.*

MEDIATION [in arithmetic] a dividing by two, or the taking the half of any number.

MEDIA'TION [in geometry] with reſpect to lines, is called biſſection or bipartition.

ME'DIATOR [*mediateur*, Fr. *mediatore*, It. *medianero* Sp. of *mediator*, Lat.] 1. One who intervenes between two parties, one who endeavours to reconcile perſons at variance, or who undertakes the management of an affair between two parties, *ſimply* (and without any reſpect to a preceding quarrel) a *go-between*, *e.g.* "The law was delivered [to the *Jews*] in the hand of a *mediator*." 2. An interceſſor or intreater for another, one who uſes his influence in favour of another. To make ſaints or angels to be *mediators* between God and them. *Stillingfleet.* 3. One of the characters of our bleſſed Saviour. There is but one *mediator* between God and man, the man Chriſt Jeſus. *St. Paul.* See MEDIATE *Agency*; and PROPITIATION compared.

MEDIA'TORS *of Queſtions*, ſix perſons in Queen Elizabeth's time, appointed to determine any queſtion or debate ariſing among merchants, concerning any unmarketable wool or undue packing.

MEDIATO'RIAL, or MEDIA'TORY, *adj.* [of *mediator*] pertaining to a mediator. Chriſt's *mediatorial* office. *Fiddes.*

MEDIA'TORSHIP [of *mediator*] the office or rank of a mediator.

MEDIA'TRIX [*mediatrice*, Fr. and It. of *mediatrix*, Lat.] a woman mediator.

ME'DIC *medica*, Lat. a plant. The *medic* hath a papilionaceous or butter-fly flower, which afterwards becomes an intorted pod, ſometimes like a ram's horn, in which are lodged kidney-ſhaped ſeeds. *Miller.*

ME'DICA, Lat. [μηδικη, Gr.] a kind of trefoil, called medic-fodder, the ſame with medic.

ME'DICABLE [*medicabilis*, Lat.] that may be healed.

ME'DICAL, *adj.* [*medicus*, Lat.] phyſical, relating to the art of healing, medicinal. Compoſed by ſnatches of time, as *medical* vacation would permit. *Brown.*

MEDICAL *Month*, the ſpace of 26 days and 12 hours.

ME'DICALLY, *adv.* [of *medical*] phyſically, medicinally. *Brown.*

MEDI'CAMENT, Fr. [*medicamento*, It. Sp. and Port. of *medicamentum*, Lat.] a medicine or phyſical compoſition by which diſeaſes are ſubdued and health is reſtored; any thing uſed in healing, generally topical applications. A cruel wound was cured by ſcalding *medicaments*. *Temple.*

MEDICAME'NTAL, *adj.* [of *medicament*, *medicamenteux*, Fr.] medicinal, relating to medicine internal or external.

MEDICAME'NTALLY, *adv.* [of *medicamental*] after the manner of medicine, with the power of medicine.

MEDICA'STER, Lat. a quack doctor, a pitiful, ſorry phyſician.

To MEDI'CATE, *verb act.* [*medicatum*, ſup. of *medico*, Lat.] to tincture or impregnate with any thing medicinal.

ME'DICATED, *part. adj.* meats or drinks, are ſuch as have medicinal ingredients mingled with them, or impregnated therewith. *Medicated* waters. *Arbuthnot.*

MEDICA'TION [of *medicate*] 1. The act of tincturing or impregnating with medicinal ingredients. The *medication* is oft renewed. *Bacon.* 2. The uſe of phyſic. To obſerve the times of the equinoxes and ſolſtices, and to declare *medication* ten days before and after. *Brown.*

MEDI'CINABLE [*medicinabilis*, Lat.] pertaining to phyſic, having the power of medicine.

MEDICI'NAL, Fr. [*medicinale*, It. of *medicinalis*, Lat. this word is now commonly pronounced *medicinal*, with the accent on the ſecond ſyllable; but more properly, and agreeably to the beſt authorities, *medicinal*, with the accent on the third] 1. pertaining to phyſic. Learn'd he was in *med'cinal* lore. *Butler.* 2. Having the power of healing, having phyſical virtue.

MEDICINAL *Days* [with phyſicians] thoſe days, according to ſome, in which no criſis or change is expected, ſo as to forbid the uſe of medicines; but it is more properly uſed for thoſe days wherein an imperfect and ill criſis of a diſtemper often happens; and are ſo called, becauſe medicines may be given on them. They are reckoned the 6th, 8th, 10th, 12th, 16th, 18, &c.

MEDICINAL *Hours*, thoſe hours proper to take medicines in, of which there are four, *viz.* the morning faſting, about an hour after dinner, about four hours after dinner, and going to bed: but times are to be governed by ſymptoms and aggravation of the diſtemper. *Quincy.*

MEDI'CINALLY, *adv.* [of *medicinal*] phyſically.

ME'DICINE, Fr. [*medicina*, It. Sp. Port. and Lat. It is generally pronounced as if only of two ſyllables, *med'cine*] the art of phyſic; alſo a phyſical remedy; the art of healing by adding that which was wanting, and taking away what is ſuperfluous. *Hippocrates.* Medicine is an art that aſſiſts nature, and is deſigned for the preſerving or reſtoring health in human bodies, by the uſe of proper remedies. It is divided into five parts.

1. *Phyſiology*, which treats of the human body or conſtitution, as it is found and well.

2. *Pathology*, which treats of the preternatural or *morbid* ſtate of our bodies.

3. *Semiotica*, which treats of the ſigns of health and diſeaſes,

4. *Hygiena*, that which delivers rules for the regimen, to be obſerved in the preſervation of health.

5. *Therapeutica*, the art of healing, which teaches the management of diet, and alſo comprehends ſurgery and the art of medicine properly ſo called.

To

Bailey (6th ed. 1733)	Scott's Bailey (1755)	Johnson (1755)
MEDICINE the Art of Physick; also a physical Remedy.	MEDICINE the art of physic; also a physical remedy; the art of healing by adding that which was wanting, and taking away what is superfluous. *Hippocrates.* Medicine is an art that assists nature, and is designed for the preserving or restoring health in human bodies, by the use of proper remedies. It is divided into five parts. *Physiology*, which treats of the human body or constitution, as it is found and well. *Pathology*, which treats of the preternatural or *morbid* state of our bodies. *Semiotica*, which treats of the signs of health and diseases. *Hygiena*, that which delivers rules for the regimen, to be observed in the preservation of health. *Therapeutica*, the art of healing, which teaches the management of diet, and also comprehends surgery and the art of medicine properly so called. [These names of these five divisions also appear in Quincy, without explanation, in the entry for *medicine*.]	MEDICINE Physick; any remedy administered by a physician.

Bailey (6th ed. 1733)	Scott's Bailey (1755)	Johnson (1755)
[No entry.]	PROGNOSIS 1. A knowing before, fore-knowledge, fore-boding. 2. [In physic] the seeing *something future*, relative to disease.	[No entry.]
PROGNOSTICK a boding Sign or Token of something to come.	PROGNOSTIC 1. A sign or token that indicates something about to happen, a token forerunning. 2. The skill of foretelling diseases or their events. 3. A prediction.	PROGNOSTICK 1. The skill of foretelling diseases or the event of diseases. 2. A prediction. 3. A forerunning.
TIBIA [*Anatomy*] that Part of Leg between the Knee and the Ankle; the Bone of the Leg, called also *Focile Majus*.	TIBIA [with anatomists] the bone between the knee and the ankle; called also *focile majus*.	[No entry, even though Johnson uses the word *tibia* three times in quoting Quincy for *fibula*. Quincy's long, encyclopedic entry begins: "*Tibia*, is the inner and bigger Bone of the Leg, called also *Focile Majus*."]

"Languages, like all other human Acquisitions, are formed, augmented, and attain their Perfection; and, after a Series of Years, again degenerate, and even often sink into Oblivion." (Scott's "Historical Account of the English Language," p. v.)

All in all, Scott's work is creditable—an improvement on the 1733 edition of Bailey and, for these entries on medical topics, superior to the treatments found in Johnson. That is perhaps unsurprising, coming from a physician, but worth noting nevertheless.

But one astonishing fact should provoke wonderment. How did both Johnson and Scott come to have the same definition for *network*? How, in their dictionaries published the same year, did they both come up with the famously opaque wording attributed to Johnson: "any thing reticulated or decussated at equal distances, with interstices between the intersections"? There were no overlapping publishers between the books. No precedent for this exact wording has been found, and the wordings are identical in Johnson and in Scott. The answer to the riddle: in the months after Johnson published in mid-April 1755, Scott or his amanuenses scoured Johnson's *Dictionary* to swell Scott's work, lifting the fresh entries from Johnson. They just copied them out time and again, so as to leave plenty of intersections but no interstices.

Ex coll. Karolyne & Bryan A. Garner

Another copy of Scott's 1755 tome.

Ex coll. Karolyne & Bryan A. Garner

37

Samuel Johnson's Folio Severely Abstracted

Johnson, Samuel. ***A Dictionary of the English Language: In Which The Words are deduced from their Originals, Explained in their Different Meanings, and Authorized by the Names of the Writers in whose Works they are found. Abstracted from the Folio Edition, By Samuel Johnson, A.M.*** **2 vols. London: J. Knapton et al., 1756.**

Samuel Johnson's big *Dictionary* was immediately recognized as a scholarly triumph—a tribute to English writers and to the English language. Commercially, though, it was a flop. Men of letters and learned academicians celebrated it, but hardly anyone bought it.

The problem was the cost. The first edition sold for £4 10*s*—at a time when, by Johnson's own estimation, someone could live frugally in London on just £30 a year. The *Dictionary*, in other words, sold for something like 15% of a family's annual wages. Small wonder that sales were anemic.

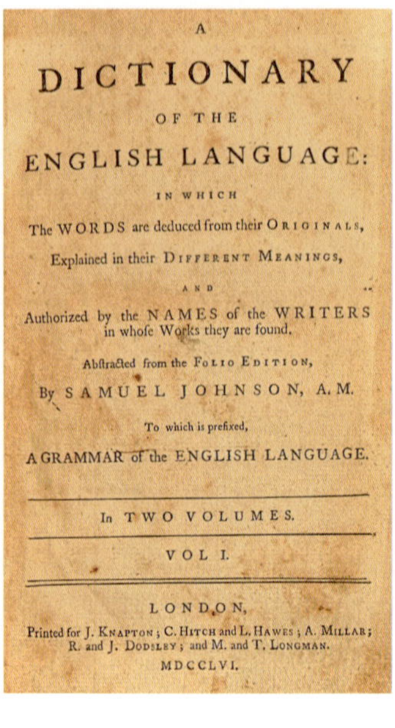
A
DICTIONARY
OF THE
ENGLISH LANGUAGE:
IN WHICH
The WORDS are deduced from their ORIGINALS,
Explained in their DIFFERENT MEANINGS,
AND
Authorized by the NAMES of the WRITERS
in whofe Works they are found.
Abftracted from the FOLIO EDITION,
By SAMUEL JOHNSON, A.M.
To which is prefixed,
A GRAMMAR of the ENGLISH LANGUAGE.
In TWO VOLUMES.
VOL I.
LONDON,
Printed for J. KNAPTON; C. HITCH and L. HAWES; A. MILLAR; R. and J. DODSLEY; and M. and T. LONGMAN.
MDCCLVI.

Ex coll. Karolyne & Bryan A. Garner

The publishers thought they might have better luck with serial publication. A second edition, a page-by-page reprint of the first, was divided into 165 weekly numbers, which sold for sixpence each. (The total cost—6*d.* per number × 165 weeks = £4 2*s.* 6*d.*—was a modest discount on the price of the first edition.) But this version sold even worse than the first. The early numbers were printed in 2,300 copies, but as demand slumped, the publishers cut their losses by reducing the print run. Just 768 copies of the pages from volume 2 were printed. The scheme was another failure.

The publishers had invested too much in Johnson's *Dictionary* to abandon it, but it was unavoidably expensive. The materials and the labor that went into 2,300 closely printed folio pages in two columns of small pica made it impossible to lower the price.

But if it was impossible to sell a big book at a modest price, perhaps they could turn that big book into a small book? They tried an experiment in marketing: abridging, or "abstracting," the two huge folios into two compact octavos. No substantive changes were made to the definitions, but the quotations were jettisoned. Here, for instance, is the first edition's complete entry for *memory*:

> MEMORY. *n.s.* [*memoire*, Fr. *memoria*, Latin.]
>
> 1. The power of retaining or recollecting things past; retention; reminiscence; recollection.
>
> *Memory* is the power to revive again in our minds those ideas which after imprinting have disappeared, or have been laid aside out of sight. *Locke.*
>
> The *memory* is perpetually looking back, when we have nothing present to entertain us: it is like those repositories in animals that are filled with stores of food, on which they may ruminate, when their present pasture fails. *Addison's Spectator.*
>
> 2. Exemption from oblivion.
>
> That ever-living man of *memory*,
Henry the Fifth! *Shakesp. Henry VI.*
>
> 3. Time of knowledge.
>
> Thy request think now fulfill'd, that ask'd
How first this world, and face of things, began,
And what, before thy *memory*, was done. *Milton.*
>
> 4. Memorial; monumental record.
>
> Be better suited;
These weeds are *memories* of those worser hours:
I pr'ythee put them off. *Shakesp. King Lear.*
>
> A swan in *memory* of Cycnus shines;
The mourning sisters weep in wat'ry signs. *Addison.*
>
> 5. Reflection; attention. Not in use.
>
> When Duncan is asleep, his two chamberlains
Will I with wine and wassel so convince,
That *memory*, the warder of the brain,
Shall be a fume. *Shakespeare's Macbeth.*

And here's what remains in the "abstracted" version:

> MEMORY. *s.* [*memoria*, Latin.]
>
> 1. The power of retaining or recollecting things past; retention; reminiscence; recollection. *Locke.*
> 2. Exemption from oblivion. *Shakesp.*
> 3. Time of knowledge. *Milton.*
> 4. Memorial; monumental record. *Addison.*
> 5. Reflection; attention. Not in use. *Shakespeare.*

"A small dictionary appeared yet to be wanting to common readers: and, as I may without arrogance claim to myself a longer acquaintance with the lexicography of our language than any other writer has had, I shall hope to be considered as having more experience at least than most of my predecessors, and as more likely to accommodate the nation with a vocabulary of life." (Preface, p. iii.)

Ex coll. Karolyne & Bryan A. Garner

The 1756 abridgment (at right) looks positively Lilliputian alongside the folio edition. Without quotations, it was a more compact and affordable book.

"The words of this dictionary, as opposed to others, are more diligently collected, more accurately spelled, more faithfully explained, and more authentically ascertained. Of an abstract it is not necessary to say more; and I hope, it will not be found that truth requires me to say less." (Preface, p. iv.)

In William Thackeray's *Vanity Fair*, Becky Sharp, delighted to be freed from school, hurls Johnson's octavo "dixonary" from the window of her carriage.

"Johnson's bald statements about the virtues of his work [in this abridgment] and the failures of others' are similar to the protestations of other lexicographers of this period and later, many of them rivals of Johnson. . . . And the preface, like its octavo format, is very well suited for this task: its brevity, assurance, clarity, and matter-of-factness match precisely what Johnson and the booksellers wanted the abridgment itself to be. If Johnson appears to be condescending towards and impatient with the intended audience, this is perhaps part of the intended persona of the learned master of language, the embodiment of an English academy, condescending to 'epitomize' his great work for the common reader." (Reddick 1996:87.)

Gone is all the evidence of how words have been used. We lose John Locke's philosophical explication of how memory works and the resonant lines from *King Lear* and *Paradise Lost*. Instead, we have just a few authors' names, serving to "authorize" meanings.

In early January 1756, the booksellers offered this "abstracted" dictionary for 10 shillings—a discount of nearly 90% on the folio—and it finally paid off. This time, 5,000 copies sold in short order, followed by a pirated Dublin edition in 1758 (discounted to 7*s.*), a second London edition of another 5,000 copies in 1760, a third in 1766. Johnson's bibliographer, J.D. Fleeman, counted nearly 100 editions of this abridgment through 1881, along with another 300-some "miniature" editions between 1786 and 1893. Although one might question whether the last names alone really serve any discernible purpose, the best answer is probably this: users might be gratified to know that Shakespeare, Milton, Addison, or some other famous writer used a given term in the very sense in which they now intend to use it.

Multivolume unabridged editions—first in folio, later in quarto—continued to appear in the 18th and 19th centuries. By 1816, an imposing two-volume "eleventh edition" of the original *Dictionary* had been published; if we count the piracies and hidden editions, it was really the 18th. But these enormous works were far outnumbered by the abridgments. It's a curious paradox. Johnson's most distinctive contribution to English lexicography was his systematic use of illustrative quotations, an innovation he introduced from classical and Continental lexicography. But his book flourished in the marketplace only when those quotations were excised. When we think of "Johnson's *Dictionary*," we think of the monumental two-volume folios. The 18th- and 19th-century public, though, thought of the abridgments. Unless she had an exceptionally strong arm, Becky Sharp must have thrown one of these smaller versions from the carriage in Thackeray's *Vanity Fair*.

Johnson's booksellers were the first English publishers to learn a lesson that many have had to learn since: flagship dictionaries are rarely profitable. The only way to recover on an investment is to produce smaller works that can be sold at less expense in great numbers. Even today, huge projects like the *Oxford English Dictionary* and *Webster's Third New International* impress the scholars and earn the prestige, but spinoffs like *The Concise Oxford Dictionary* and *Merriam-Webster's Collegiate Dictionary* keep the lights on.

38

James Buchanan
The Lumping Enumerator

Buchanan, James. *Linguæ Britannicæ Vera Pronunciatio: or, A New English Dictionary*. London: A. Millar, 1757.

Ex coll. Karolyne & Bryan A. Garner

BUCHANAN (FL. 1753–1773) produced several literacy books, including *The Complete English Scholar* (1753), *A New Pocket Book for Young Gentlemen and Ladies; or, A Spelling Dictionary of the English Language* (1757), *The British Grammar* (1762), *Essay Towards Establishing a Standard and Uniform Pronunciation of the English Language* (1766), *A Regular English Syntax* (1767), and *A Plan of an English Grammar School Education* (1770). But nothing except what is deducible from these titles—that he was heavily involved in pedagogy—is known of his life.

The innovation in Buchanan's *Linguæ Britannicæ* was to supply not just accented syllables but full pronunciations by marking vowels as long or short. And he did this in the headwords themselves:

Lȳnx, (S.) A wild beaſt of the wolf kind, ſpotted, and remarkable for the quickneſs of its ſight. *L.*
Lȳ'ra, (S.) The lyre, a northern conſtellation of 13 ſtars. *L.*
Lȳre, (S.) A ſtringed muſical inſtrument.
Lȳric, (A.) Belonging to the lyre.
Lȳric Verſes, Such as were ſung to that inſtrument.
Ly'riſt, (S.) One that plays on the lyre.
Machĭnā'tion, (S.) 1. A contriving or plotting. 2. A plot.
Machĭnā'tor, (S.) A plotter.
Machī'ne, (S.) An engine to raiſe or ſtop the motion of bodies. *L.*
Machī'nery, (S.) 1. The ſcenes and other decorations of the ſtage. 2. In an epic poem, the deſcent of gods, goddeſſes, and the other foreign ornaments with which the poet raiſes and embelliſhes his ſubject.
Mā'ckărel, (S.) A ſea fiſh.

Ex coll. Karolyne & Bryan A. Garner

In this way, Buchanan laid the groundwork for later pronouncing dictionaries such as those by John Walker (no. 47) and Thomas Sheridan (no. 50).

Buchanan sought to fill a void with a pocket-sized dictionary—smaller than Bailey and the abridged (two-volume) Johnson and "portable for the use of schools, and as a *vade mecum* for grown persons . . . to which they may always have immediate recourse, either for

"Since . . . upon a right apprehension of words, depends the rectitude of our notions, and in order to form our judgment right, they must be understood in their proper meaning, used in their true sense either in writing or speaking, would it not be very unhappy for the generality of people, if they could acquire a proper knowledge of the significations of the words of their own tongue no sooner, nor no other way, than by a study of ten or eleven years in the Latin and Greek languages?" (Preface, p. ii.)

the orthography, signification, accent, just quantities of the syllables, or proper pronunciation of a word." (P. iv.) He had clear ideas about what belonged in a dictionary and what didn't. He took pains to enumerate meanings but didn't believe that every metaphorical meaning deserved its own sense. He laid out his principles with admirable lucidity:

> As a misinterpretation of the significations of words, must have a pernicious influence upon those who depend upon a dictionary for their expositor; an accurate enumeration and distinction of the several significations of each respective word, has been my chiefest care. And accordingly have distinguished the various acceptations of words by figures, 1, 2, 3, 4, 5, 6, &c. placing them first which are directly the same as in the original tongues; after which follow the general and popular significations. But I have often suppressed the figurative and metaphorical uses of words, as too apt to mislead and perplex youth, who have not arrived to a sufficient strength of judgment rightly to apply them. I have likewise rejected all obsolete, bad, low, and despicable words, to make room for those that are new, and a great number of technical terms, which are so explained, as to convey a clear, just, and scientific notion of them even to those who are unacquainted with the arts to which they belong. [P. v.]

Ex coll. Karolyne & Bryan A. Garner

A few Buchanan titles on grammar.

The "bad, low, and despicable words," in Buchanan's view, didn't include the word *fart*, which he defined as "An eruption of wind backwards," or *piss*, curtly glossed as "Urine." But *adventuresome*, *bang*, and *cudden*, all opprobriated by Johnson as "low words," are excluded.

Buchanan's enumeration of senses followed closely upon Johnson's practice from two years before—or, with Johnson's abridgment, from the year before. How does Buchanan compare to Johnson's abridgment? A few entries will illustrate:

Johnson's Abridgment (1756)	**Buchanan (1757)**
A´PPETITE. *s.* [*appetitus*, Lat.] The natural desire of good. *Hooker.* The desire of sensual pleasure. *Dryden.* Violent longing. *Clarendon.* Keenness of stomach; hunger. *Bacon.*	*A´ppĕtīte*, (S.) 1. A relish for eating and drinking. 2. All the bodily sensations are collectively called the appetites. *L.*

Johnson's Abridgment (1756)	Buchanan (1757)
FE´LLOWSHIP. *s.* [from *fellow.*] Companionship; consort; society. *Calamy.* Association; confederacy; combination. *Knolles.* Equality. Partnership; joint interest. *Dryden.* Company; state of being together. *Shakespeare.* Frequency of intercourse; social pleasure. *Bacon.* Fitness and fondness for festal entertainments. *Clarendon.* An establishment in the college with share in its revenue. *Swift.* [In arithmetic.] That rule of plural proportion whereby we balance accompts, depending between divers persons, having put together a general stock. *Cocker.*	*Fĕ´llowshĭp,* (S.) 1. Company, society. 2. Partnership. 3. The place of a member of a college. 4. In arithmetic, a rule that teaches how, by having given the several stocks of persons who are partners in trade, to proportion to every one of them his due share of loss and gain.
To RENOU´NCE. *v. a.* [*renoncer*, Fr. *renuncio*, Latin.] To disown; to abnegate. *Dryden.* To RENOU´NCE. *v. n.* To declare renunciation. *Dryden.*	*Renou´nce,* (V.) 1. To forsake or abandon. 2. To disown. 3. To revoke at cards. *L.*
WORK. *s.* [*weorc*, Saxon; *werk*, Dutch.] Toil; labour; employment. *Eccles.* A state of labour. *Temple.* Bungling attempt. *Stillingfleet.* Flowers or embroidery of the needle. *Spenser. Shakespeare.* Any fabric or compages of art. *Pope.* Action; feat; deed. *Hammond.* Any thing made. *Donne.* Management; treatment. *Shakespeare.* *To set on* WORK. To employ; to engage. *Hooker.*	*Work*, (S.) 1. All sorts of labour, whether mechanically, as some trade, &c. or studiously in languages, arts, sciences, &c. 2. The produce of such labour. 3. Any thing done, as a book written, a house built, &c. 4. Deed or action.

"It is certain, that the best English dictionaries hitherto published are too bulky and unhandy to be used in, or carried to and from school by youth. There was therefore still wanting one more portable for the use of schools, and as a *vade mecum* for grown persons, formed upon a different but more advantageous plan than any before extant: and to which they may always have immediate recourse." (Preface, p. iv.)

From these examples, we might conclude that Johnson was more of a splitter in defining (proliferating senses), Buchanan more of a lumper (consolidating senses). With *appetite*, Johnson's senses 1–3 could all be grouped together as desires, longings, or cravings; Buchanan's sense 2 would have been improved by replacing *sensations* with *desires*. With *fellowship*, Johnson's splitting into nine senses is probably unhelpful for a small dictionary; also, Johnson's sense 8 is less clear than Buchanan's sense 3 (as in *the faculty elected him a fellow, with the fellowship to begin in September*). With *renounce*, Buchanan's sense 1 uses two helpful synonyms omitted by Johnson, and Buchanan's sense 3 was missed by Johnson. Also, Johnson's second entry is entirely circular, given that he defines *renunciation* (both in the big dictionary and in the abridgment) as "the act of renouncing." With *work*, Buchanan's senses 2 and 3 are more clearly expressed than Johnson's sense 7 (as in *works of art*), but then there is the question whether Buchanan's senses 2 and 3 are really separate at all.

In sum, a fastidious dictionary buyer in the 1750s, in need of a smallish dictionary, wouldn't have been wise to assume that Johnson's abridgment was plainly superior to all its competitors. Buchanan had genuine merit, and his entries were often superior to the slightly larger Bailey dictionaries then in print.

"If some should think me animated with a more than ordinary Zeal in the Cause of an English Education, its important Consequences will very well justify my aspiring to so glorious a Prize. I hope I have kept within the Rules of strict Decorum, my Aim being to serve my Country, without offending any." (Buchanan's *Complete English Scholar* [1753], p. xvii.)

"An 1841 notice in the *Common School Journal*, seemingly reviewing Buchanan's *Regular English Syntax*, calls the book 'a most egregious plagiarism' (vol. 3, no. 15, p. 231), adding: 'More than half the volume is copied, verbatim,' from the *British Grammar*. In fact, though, that work has often been published anonymously, without Buchanan's name on the title page. So Buchanan has simply 'plagiarized' himself—and the accuser is mistaken." (Garner 2021a:15.)

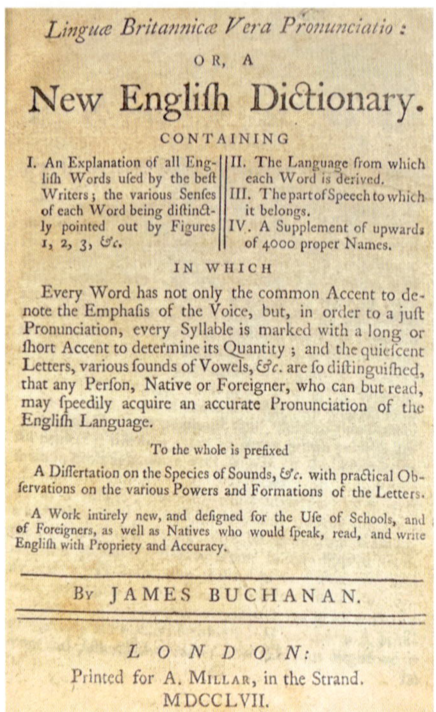
Linguæ Britannicæ Vera Pronunciatio: OR, A

New Engliſh Dictionary.

CONTAINING

I. An Explanation of all Engliſh Words uſed by the beſt Writers; the various Senſes of each Word being diſtinctly pointed out by Figures 1, 2, 3, &c.

II. The Language from which each Word is derived.

III. The part of Speech to which it belongs.

IV. A Supplement of upwards of 4000 proper Names.

IN WHICH

Every Word has not only the common Accent to denote the Emphaſis of the Voice, but, in order to a juſt Pronunciation, every Syllable is marked with a long or ſhort Accent to determine its Quantity; and the quieſcent Letters, various ſounds of Vowels, &c. are ſo diſtinguiſhed, that any Perſon, Native or Foreigner, who can but read, may ſpeedily acquire an accurate Pronunciation of the Engliſh Language.

To the whole is prefixed

A Diſſertation on the Species of Sounds, &c. with practical Obſervations on the various Powers and Formations of the Letters.

A Work intirely new, and deſigned for the Uſe of Schools, and of Foreigners, as well as Natives who would ſpeak, read, and write Engliſh with Propriety and Accuracy.

By JAMES BUCHANAN.

LONDON:
Printed for A. MILLAR, in the Strand.
MDCCLVII.

Ex coll. Karolyne & Bryan A. Garner

39

Daniel Fenning
Good Definer, Shaky Grammarian

Fenning, D[aniel]. *The Royal English Dictionary: or, A Treasury of the English Language*. London: S. Crowder, 1761. 2d ed. 1763. 3d ed. 1778.

FENNING (1714/15–1767), whose parentage and childhood are unknown, married in July 1735 and lived in Bures, where he taught. In the late 1740s, he moved to London, gave up teaching, and began to work for the Royal Exchange Assurance Company, to whose governors and directors he dedicated *The Young Algebraist's Companion* (1750), the earliest of his 14 books.

His *Royal English Dictionary*, dedicated to King George III, is often dated 1741 (as in Kennedy 1927), but in fact, it appeared in 1761. The discrepancy derives from a printing error that occurred in many copies on the title page: the date appears as MDCCXLI, but only because the printer transposed the *X* and the *L*.

Given that this octavo dictionary appeared six years after Johnson's big book and five years after the two-volume abridgment, Fenning tried to differentiate his own by steering a middle course and making it one volume. Without mentioning Johnson, he declares that the public shouldn't wonder at the variety of dictionaries available, but "should rather wonder that their variety is not greater." (P. v.) Almost all of them, he says, are worthwhile:

> As most lexicographers have had a different point in view, their labours have all proved, in some degree, of general use; and none, unless the mere copier of a precedent work, can be said to be useless. Yet, while the different branches of lexicography were kept distinct, the public seemed to have been defrauded of the profit that might have been acquired from their cultivation. Neither time, nor curiosity, nor wealth, have put it in the power of every one to be master of the various *Dictionaries* which have been published in the different branches of science. To unite these scattered rays, as it were, into one focus, has been the intention of the author

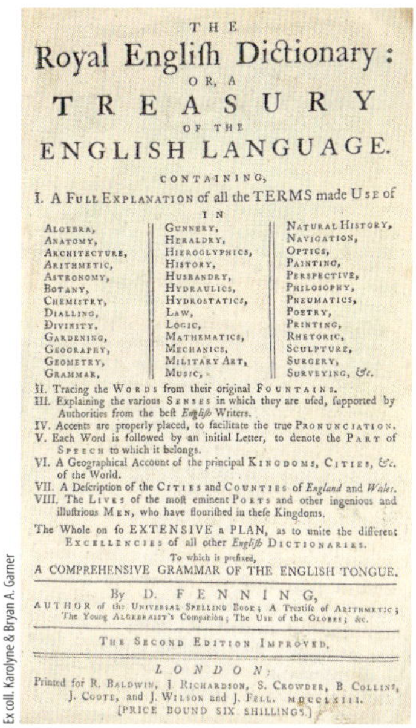

THE
Royal English Dictionary:
OR, A
TREASURY
OF THE
ENGLISH LANGUAGE.

CONTAINING,

I. A FULL EXPLANATION of all the TERMS made USE of IN

ALGEBRA,	GUNNERY,	NATURAL HISTORY,
ANATOMY,	HERALDRY,	NAVIGATION,
ARCHITECTURE,	HIEROGLYPHICS,	OPTICS,
ARITHMETIC,	HISTORY,	PAINTING,
ASTRONOMY,	HUSBANDRY,	PERSPECTIVE,
BOTANY,	HYDRAULICS,	PHILOSOPHY,
CHEMISTRY,	HYDROSTATICS,	PNEUMATICS,
DIALLING,	LAW,	POETRY,
DIVINITY,	LOGIC,	PRINTING,
GARDENING,	MATHEMATICS,	RHETORIC,
GEOGRAPHY,	MECHANICS,	SCULPTURE,
GEOMETRY,	MILITARY ART,	SURGERY,
GRAMMAR,	MUSIC,	SURVEYING, *&c.*

II. Tracing the WORDS from their original FOUNTAINS.
III. Explaining the various SENSES in which they are uſed, ſupported by Authorities from the beſt *Engliſh* Writers.
IV. Accents are properly placed, to facilitate the true PRONUNCIATION.
V. Each Word is followed by an initial Letter, to denote the PART of SPEECH to which it belongs.
VI. A Geographical Account of the principal KINGDOMS, CITIES, *&c.* of the World.
VII. A Deſcription of the CITIES and COUNTIES of *England* and *Wales*.
VIII. The LIVES of the moſt eminent POETS and other ingenious and illuſtrious MEN, who have flouriſhed in theſe Kingdoms.

The Whole on ſo EXTENSIVE a PLAN, as to unite the different EXCELLENCIES of all other *Engliſh* DICTIONARIES.

To which is prefixed,
A COMPREHENSIVE GRAMMAR OF THE ENGLISH TONGUE.

By D. FENNING,
AUTHOR of the UNIVERSAL SPELLING BOOK; A Treatiſe of ARITHMETIC; The Young ALGEBRAIST'S Companion; The USE of the GLOBES; &c.

THE SECOND EDITION IMPROVED.

LONDON:
Printed for R. BALDWIN, J. RICHARDSON, S. CROWDER, B. COLLINS, J. COOTE, and J. WILSON and J. FELL. MDCCLXIII.
[PRICE BOUND SIX SHILLINGS.]

Ex coll. Karolyne & Bryan A. Garner

"The knowledge of our own language should be the first object of our thoughts, and the chief employment of our leisure hours." (Preface, p. vii.)

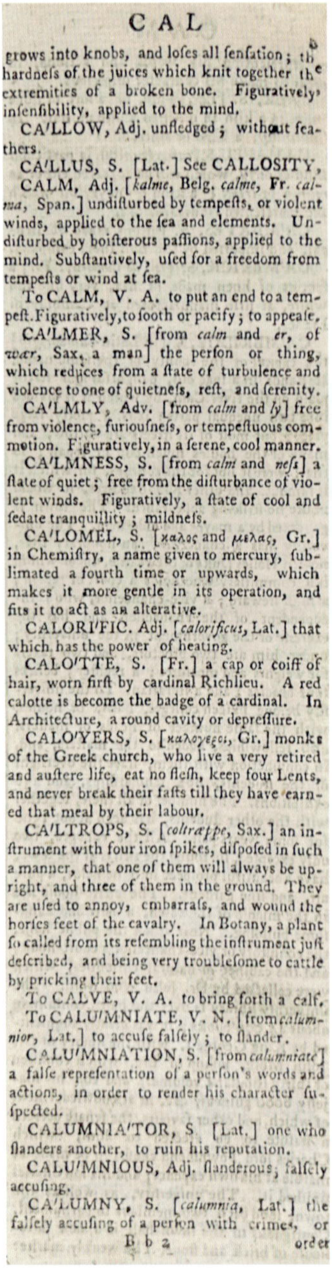

CAL

grows into knobs, and loſes all ſenſation; the hardneſs of the juices which knit together the extremities of a broken bone. Figuratively, inſenſibility, applied to the mind.

CA'LLOW, Adj. unfledged; without feathers.

CA'LLUS, S. [Lat.] See CALLOSITY,

CALM, Adj. [*kalme*, Belg. *calme*, Fr. *calma*, Span.] undiſturbed by tempeſts, or violent winds, applied to the ſea and elements. Undiſturbed by boiſterous paſſions, applied to the mind. Subſtantively, uſed for a freedom from tempeſts or wind at ſea.

To CALM, V. A. to put an end to a tempeſt. Figuratively, to ſooth or pacify; to appeaſe.

CA'LMER, S. [from *calm* and *er*, of *wær*, Sax. a man] the perſon or thing, which reduces from a ſtate of turbulence and violence to one of quietneſs, reſt, and ſerenity.

CA'LMLY, Adv. [from *calm* and *ly*] free from violence, furiouſneſs, or tempeſtuous commotion. Figuratively, in a ſerene, cool manner.

CA'LMNESS, S. [from *calm* and *neſs*] a ſtate of quiet; free from the diſturbance of violent winds. Figuratively, a ſtate of cool and ſedate tranquillity; mildneſs.

CA'LOMEL, S. [καλος and μελας, Gr.] in Chemiſtry, a name given to mercury, ſublimated a fourth time or upwards, which makes it more gentle in its operation, and fits it to act as an alterative.

CALORI'FIC. Adj. [*calorificus*, Lat.] that which has the power of heating.

CALO'TTE, S. [Fr.] a cap or coiff of hair, worn firſt by cardinal Richlieu. A red calotte is become the badge of a cardinal. In Architecture, a round cavity or depreſſure.

CALO'YERS, S. [καλογεροι, Gr.] monks of the Greek church, who live a very retired and auſtere life, eat no fleſh, keep four Lents, and never break their faſts till they have earned that meal by their labour.

CA'LTROPS, S. [*coltræppe*, Sax.] an inſtrument with four iron ſpikes, diſpoſed in ſuch a manner, that one of them will always be upright, and three of them in the ground. They are uſed to annoy, embarraſs, and wound the horſes feet of the cavalry. In Botany, a plant ſo called from its reſembling the inſtrument juſt deſcribed, and being very troubleſome to cattle by pricking their feet.

To CALVE, V. A. to bring forth a calf.

To CALU'MNIATE, V. N. [from *calumnior*, Lat.] to accuſe falſely; to ſlander.

CALU'MNIATION, S. [from *calumniate*] a falſe repreſentation of a perſon's words and actions, in order to render his character ſuſpected.

CALUMNIA'TOR, S [Lat.] one who ſlanders another, to ruin his reputation.

CALU'MNIOUS, Adj. ſlanderous; falſely accuſing.

CA'LUMNY, S. [*calumnia*, Lat.] the falſely accuſing of a perſon with crimes, or

B b 2 order

Ex coll. Karolyne & Bryan A. Garner

A sample of Fenning's work.

of this work; who is so far from depreciating the labours of
his predecessors, as to own, that, were it not owing to them,
this work would have been wanting in many of its perfections.
[*Id.*]

Up to that last word, Fenning sounds attractively modest. With that reference to his *perfections*, he suddenly begins touting his work as "a dictionary on a more extensive plan than any that have already been published." (P. iv.) Everything is "delivered in a succinct manner." (*Id.*) The grammar that opens the book "is plainer (if not more comprehensive) than any that have yet appeared." (*Id.*) And yet Fenning's own grammar is shaky. In the midst of this self-praise, he proclaims: "Every word made use of in the common occurrences of life, or in the several arts and sciences necessary for the subsistence or improvement of our being are [read *is*] explained." (*Id.*)

Still, for *plainness* of definitions, Fenning had a point. Consider these entries from the Johnson abridgment and from Fenning:

Johnson Abridgment (1756)	**Fenning (1761)**
A'DAGE. *s.* [*adagium*, Lat.] A maxim; a proverb. *Glanville.*	ADA'GE. S. [*adagium*, Lat.] a maxim or principle received as self-evident. A proverbial saying.
FENCE. *s.* [from *defence.*] 1. Guard; security; outwork; defence. *Decay of Piety.* 2. Inclosure; mound; hedge. *Dryden.* 3. The art of fencing; defence. *Shakesp.* 4. Skill in defence. *Shakespeare.*	FENCE, S. [a contraction of *defence*] any thing or means made use of to guard from danger. "There is no *fence* against inundations." *L'Estrange.* An enclosure, hedge, or paling, serving to keep persons from entering any spot of ground.
NE'TWORK. *s.* [*net* and *work.*] Any thing reticulated or decussated, At equal distances. *Spenser*	NE'TWORK, S. the work with which a net is made; any thing made with interstices resembling the meshes of a net.
TIGHT, *a.* [*dicht*, Dutch.] 1. Tense; close; not loose. *Moxon. Swift.* 2. Free from fluttering rags; less than neat. *Gay. Swift.*	TIGHT, Adj. [*dicht*, Belg.] close, or stretched hard, opposed to loose. Cleanly dressed; something less than neat. Not leaky, applied to casks or vessels.

In the first of those entries, Fenning has the advantage in providing definitional phrases, as opposed to mere synonyms. In the second, the same advantage mostly applies, though Johnson (as is typical of his excellent innovation) supplies numbered senses. In the third, Johnson is opaque where Fenning is comprehensible. In the fourth, Fenning usefully supplies the defining phrases "stretched hard" and "cleanly dressed," and he also includes a sense missing from Johnson: "not leaky." Despite the great advantage conferred by Johnson's numbered senses, one may wonder whether the authorial names, in the absence of the quotations supplied in his big folio edition, really serve any practical value (apart from the semblance of authoritativeness).

Fenning, then, undeniably had his merits. His dictionary appeared in five editions through 1775, the last three being posthumous.

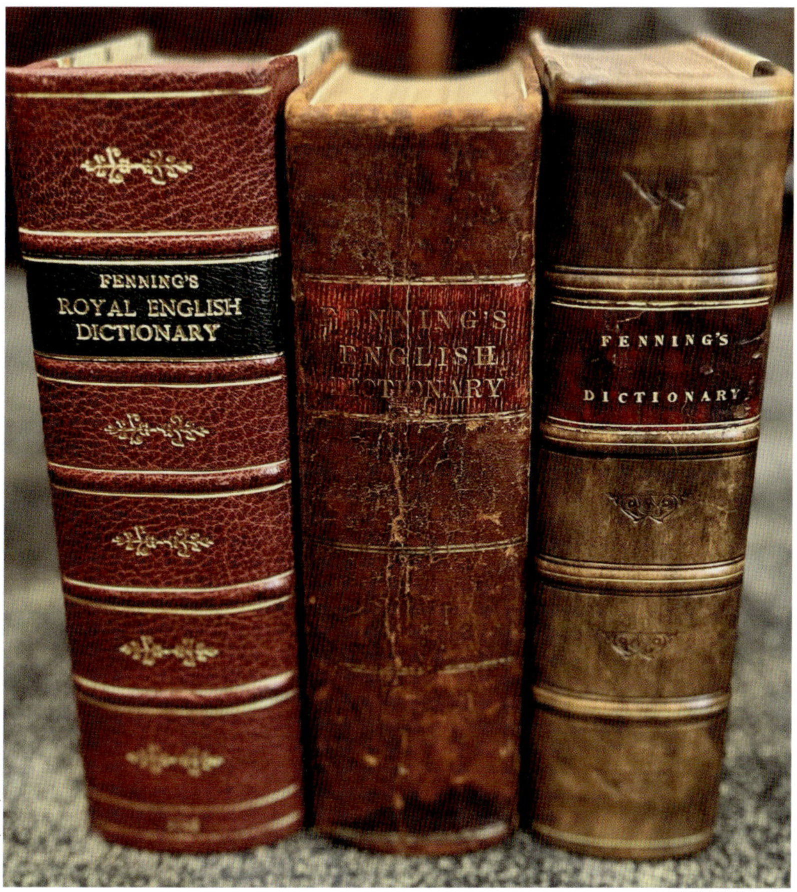

Ex coll. Karolyne & Bryan A. Garner

"We shall find a strong obligation to make the language of our country the subject of our meditations. Without this application, we must be strangers to propriety, and blind to the beauties, which the pages of our learned countrymen display to our minds." (Preface, p. vii.)

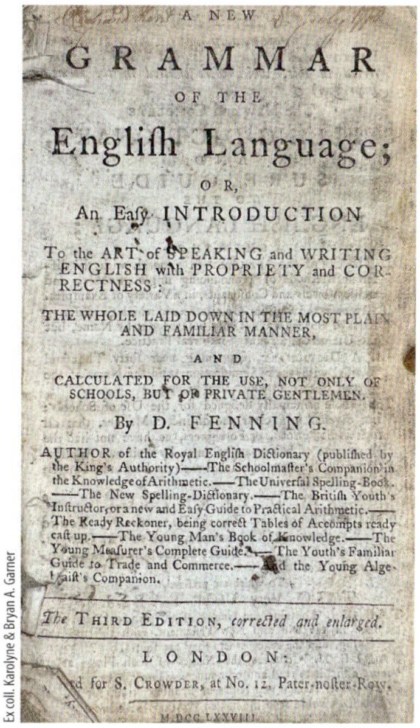

A NEW
GRAMMAR
OF THE
Engliſh Language;
OR,
An Eaſy INTRODUCTION
To the ART of SPEAKING and WRITING ENGLISH with PROPRIETY and CORRECTNESS:
THE WHOLE LAID DOWN IN THE MOST PLAIN AND FAMILIAR MANNER,
AND
CALCULATED FOR THE USE, NOT ONLY OF SCHOOLS, BUT OF PRIVATE GENTLEMEN.
By D. FENNING.
AUTHOR of the Royal Engliſh Dictionary (publiſhed by the King's Authority)——The Schoolmaſter's Companion in the Knowledge of Arithmetic.——The Univerſal Spelling-Book.——The New Spelling-Dictionary.——The Britiſh Youth's Inſtructor, or a new and Eaſy Guide to Practical Arithmetic.——The Ready Reckoner, being correct Tables of Accompts ready caſt up.——The Young Man's Book of Knowledge.——The Young Meaſurer's Complete Guide.——The Youth's Familiar Guide to Trade and Commerce.——And the Young Algebraiſt's Companion.
The THIRD EDITION, *corrected and enlarged.*
LONDON:
[illegible]d for S. CROWDER, at No. 12, Pater-noſter-Row.
M.DCC.LXXVIII.

Ex coll. Karolyne & Bryan A. Garner

From the start, Fenning's *Royal English Dictionary* included a 16-page grammar in the front matter. By 1771, he had expanded this into a stand-alone grammar of 167 pages. The title page above is from the third edition of 1778.

"In his own day Fenning was probably best-known for his *Universal Spelling Book*. It was reprinted in about 100 editions up to 1860, and was used extensively in America. Many of Fenning's other textbooks also continued to be printed and revised well into the nineteenth century." (*ODNB*.)

"Without vanity it can be affirmed, That this small volume exceeds all other Dictionaries for the use of those who would write and pronounce the English tongue accurately and with ease and propriety." (Preface, p. x.)

Ex coll. Karolyne & Bryan A. Garner

40

John Entick

Victim of Unreasonable Search and Seizure

Entick, John. *The New Spelling Dictionary, Teaching to Write and Pronounce the English Tongue with Ease and Propriety*. London: Edward & Charles Dilly, 1765. 2d ed. 1766. 3d ed. 1767. 4th ed. 1769. 5th ed. 1770. Etc. 40th ed. Wilmington: Peter Brynberg, 1800.

Entick (1703–1773), who lived in East London, is known in legal circles for a 1765 lawsuit in which he was the plaintiff. Writing for the antigovernment periodical *The Monitor* in 1762, he had fulminated against the administration in a series of seven editorials, as a result of which Lord Halifax issued a general warrant to have Entick's papers seized. In a four-hour ransacking, the King's messengers broke locks and doors and seized 100 charts and 100 pamphlets. Entick then sued the authorities for trespass and illegal seizure and won a judgment for £300 in damages. The case became a landmark for privacy in English law and established the principle that the state may do only what is expressly authorized by law, while the individual may do everything that isn't prohibited by law. The case also became a guide for the Founding Fathers who wrote the Fourth Amendment to the U.S. Constitution.

Two years after the disastrous pillaging, Entick's *New Spelling Dictionary* was published. Many earlier lexicographers, Entick wrote in the preface, had suffered from either "unnecessary prolixity" or "abstruse brevity." (P. iii.) His plan was to include on a single line the word, its part of speech, and its various meanings—"so that, except in a very few cases, where it could not be avoided, the eye takes i[n] at once every thing necessary for *understanding*, *pronouncing* and *spelling*." (P. iv.) In that respect, the book was a genuine tour de force, and Entick recognized as much: "I think it may without vanity be affirmed, That this small volume, in point of usefulness, correctness, elegance and cheapness, greatly exceeds all other Dictionaries of the English language, which have been hitherto published." (*Id.*)

Noah Webster apparently agreed: an early American printing of Entick's work (probably the 1800 edition) provided the basis for Webster's 1806 *Compendious Dictionary* (no. 57), which had similarly brief entries.

The tireless bibliographer Alston noted that he could find evidence of only one copy of the 1770 London edition—the one here illustrated—and that, in the 1920s, it had been located in Tokyo and later destroyed by fire. The copy in the Garner Collection—with the title page shown below—may be the only extant copy.

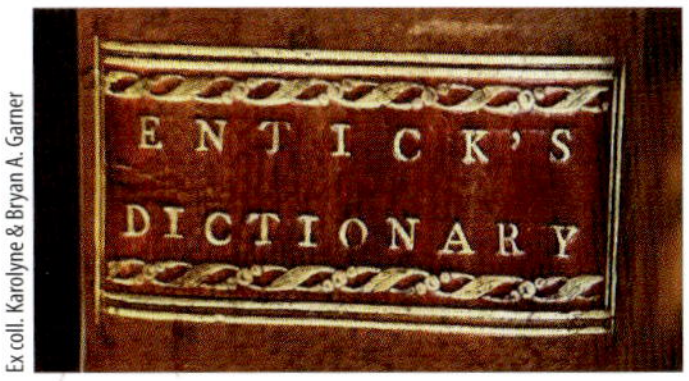

Ex coll. Karolyne & Bryan A. Garner

"Entick's Dictionary of the English Language has acquired so great a degree of celebrity, in its extensive circulation, that any attempt to demonstrate its usefulness and intrinsic value, would be completely superfluous." (Advertisement in 1810 London ed.)

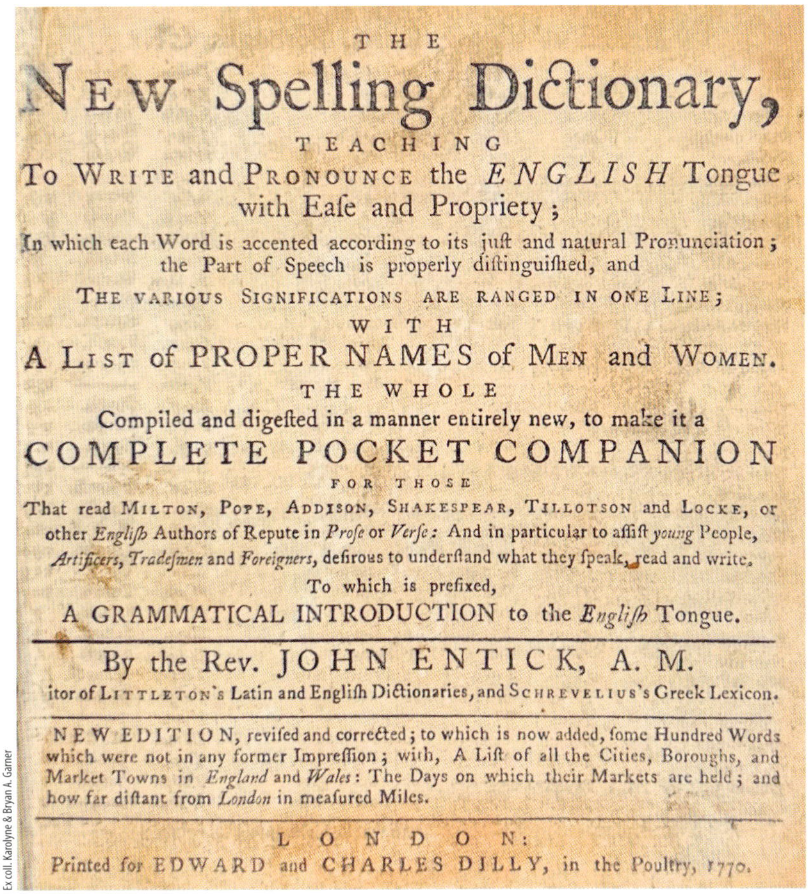

THE

NEW Spelling Dictionary,

TEACHING

To WRITE and PRONOUNCE the *ENGLISH* Tongue with Eafe and Propriety;

In which each Word is accented according to its juft and natural Pronunciation; the Part of Speech is properly diftinguifhed, and

THE VARIOUS SIGNIFICATIONS ARE RANGED IN ONE LINE;

WITH

A LIST of PROPER NAMES of MEN and WOMEN.

THE WHOLE

Compiled and digefted in a manner entirely new, to make it a

COMPLETE POCKET COMPANION

FOR THOSE

That read MILTON, POPE, ADDISON, SHAKESPEAR, TILLOTSON and LOCKE, or other *Englifh* Authors of Repute in *Profe* or *Verfe*: And in particular to affift *young* People, *Artificers*, *Tradefmen* and *Foreigners*, defirous to underftand what they fpeak, read and write.

To which is prefixed,

A GRAMMATICAL INTRODUCTION to the *Englifh* Tongue.

By the Rev. JOHN ENTICK, A. M.

itor of LITTLETON's Latin and Englifh Dictionaries, and SCHREVELIUS's Greek Lexicon.

NEW EDITION, revifed and corrected; to which is now added, fome Hundred Words which were not in any former Impreffion; with, A Lift of all the Cities, Boroughs, and Market Towns in *England* and *Wales*: The Days on which their Markets are held; and how far diftant from *London* in meafured Miles.

LONDON:

Printed for EDWARD and CHARLES DILLY, in the Poultry, 1770.

Ex coll. Karolyne & Bryan A. Garner

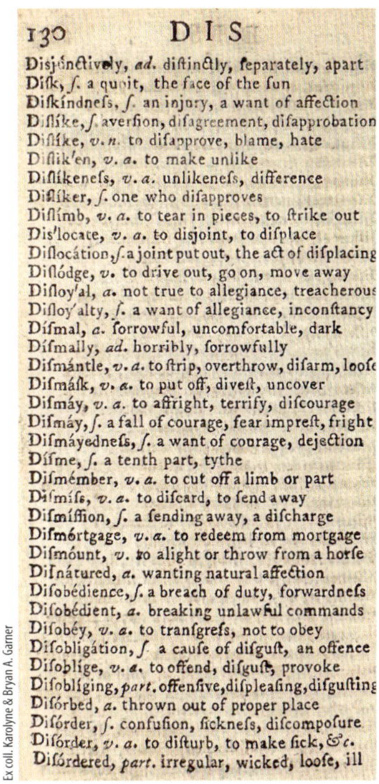

130 DIS

Disjúnctively, *ad.* diftinctly, feparately, apart
Difk, *f.* a quoit, the face of the fun
Difkíndnefs, *f.* an injury, a want of affection
Diflíke, *f.* averfion, difagreement, difapprobation
Diflíke, *v. n.* to difapprove, blame, hate
Diflik'en, *v. a.* to make unlike
Diflíkenefs, *v. a.* unlikenefs, difference
Diflíker, *f.* one who difapproves
Diflímb, *v. a.* to tear in pieces, to ftrike out
Dis'locate, *v. a.* to disjoint, to difplace
Diflocátion, *f.* a joint put out, the act of difplacing
Diflódge, *v.* to drive out, go on, move away
Difloy'al, *a.* not true to allegiance, treacherous
Difloy'alty, *f.* a want of allegiance, inconftancy
Dífmal, *a.* forrowful, uncomfortable, dark
Dífmally, *ad.* horribly, forrowfully
Difmántle, *v. a.* to ftrip, overthrow, difarm, loofe
Difmáfk, *v. a.* to put off, diveft, uncover
Difmáy, *v. a.* to affright, terrify, difcourage
Difmáy, *f.* a fall of courage, fear impreft, fright
Difmáyednefs, *f.* a want of courage, dejection
Dífme, *f.* a tenth part, tythe
Difmémber, *v. a.* to cut off a limb or part
Difmífs, *v. a.* to difcard, to fend away
Difmíffion, *f.* a fending away, a difcharge
Difmórtgage, *v. a.* to redeem from mortgage
Difmóunt, *v.* to alight or throw from a horfe
Difnátured, *a.* wanting natural affection
Difobédience, *f.* a breach of duty, forwardnefs
Difobédient, *a.* breaking unlawful commands
Difobéy, *v. a.* to tranfgrefs, not to obey
Difobligátion, *f.* a caufe of difguft, an offence
Difoblíge, *v. a.* to offend, difguft, provoke
Difoblíging, *part.* offenfive, difpleafing, difgufting
Diforbed, *a.* thrown out of proper place
Diforder, *f.* confufion, ficknefs, difcompofure
Diforder, *v. a.* to difturb, to make fick, &c.
Difordered, *part.* irregular, wicked, loofe, ill

Ex coll. Karolyne & Bryan A. Garner

41

Ann Fisher

England's First Female Lexicographer

Fisher, Ann. *An Accurate New Spelling Dictionary, and Expositor of the English Language*. 2d ed. London: Printed for the author and sold by Hawes, Clarke & Collins, and G. Robinson, 1773.

Ex coll. Karolyne & Bryan A. Garner

"That the English Language is as copious, significant, and harmonious as any in the World, none pretend to dispute." (Fisher's *Practical New Grammar*, 1762 ed., p. iv.)

Born in Cumberland, Ann Fisher (1719–1778) at age 32 married the Newcastle printer Thomas Slack. For many years, the two of them published the *Newcastle Chronicle*, which remained a family enterprise for several more generations. A mother of nine, Fisher wrote several educational texts, including a grammar. Her *Practical New Grammar with Exercises of Bad English*, putatively published in 1745, is thought to be no longer extant in its first edition. Likewise, this *New Spelling Dictionary*, thought to have been printed first in 1771, could not be located at all by the bibliographer Alston. This copy of the 1773 edition is thought to be the earliest extant.

Just as Fisher was the earliest female grammarian of modern English (see Garner 2021a:19), she was—by virtue of this book—the earliest female English lexicographer. Her other books, apart from her *Practical New Grammar*, included *The Pleasing Instructor, or Entertaining Moralist* (1756), *The New English Tutor* (1774), and *The Instructor; or, Young Man's Best Companion* (1779). Her books typically have her name printed "A. Fisher," perhaps disguising to a biased readership that she was a woman.

She was strikingly innovative in her work, here as elsewhere. Her preface, for example, shows an original mind at work: "Certainly no man, but from the pitiful pride of authorship, or the envy of another's success, would sit down to write or compile a book upon any subject, which had been as well or better treated of by his predecessors." (P. i.) She understands the realities of lexicography: "Though Dictionaries are but vocabularies, or catalogues of the unconnected words of our common language, to which we all have an equal right, and must all class in the same alphabetical order; yet as no man living, perhaps, is capacitated merely from the promptness of human memory (without the help of any other dictionary) to recollect or write down even an hundred words in alphabetical order, without omitting many, very many of the most useful ones; so consequently no book of this kind, for that very reason, should be considered as an original work." (Pp. i–ii.) She also understands the extent of her contributions: "Without censuring the performances of others, I shall only point out the originality of my own." (P. ii.)

Ex coll. Karolyne & Bryan A. Garner

Fisher's innovations are fivefold: (1) she includes "more modern, primitive, or original conversation words, than any other large Dictionary whatever"; (2) in alphabetizing words, she treats *I* and *J* as separate letters, and *U* and *V*, reacting against her predecessors who "have ever blended and confounded" them; (3) she denotes the parts of speech "by English terms, *viz.*, names, qualities, relative-names, &c. as in the best practical English Grammars"; (4) she has "greatly enhance[d] the value of the book" with encyclopedic information by adding "an entire new Dictionary of the Heathen Gods and Goddesses, and of the most illustrious heroes treated of by Homer, Virgil, Ovid, and other eminent authors"; and (5) "the Abstract of Etymology and Syntax is plain, concise, and more practicable to learners, than more tedious treatises, and is compiled from FISHER'S ENGLISH GRAMMAR, the first that exhibited an Etymology on the plan and system of Syntax rules peculiarly adapted to the genius and idioms of the English language, independent of any other tongue." (Pp. iii–iv.) She was confident: "I have . . . the pleasure to believe, that all the best English schoolmasters in the kingdom look upon me for the quickest and most effectual modes of inculcating the knowledge of the English language." (P. iv.)

"To know any science, is one thing,—to communicate it to the conceptions of others, is quite another; requiring the additional knowledge of the human mind, which too few school authors are endowed with; not distinguishing what is proper to be inculcated, from what is impracticable; insomuch that we have abstracters of abstracts in the Dictionary way, (aiming at the quantity rather than the quality of Words, and not distinguishing in their respective patrons the words in present use from the history of progressive language through successive centuries) swelling a Spelling-Dictionary to the thickness of a school Bible." (P. iv.)

Fisher also excluded all obsolete words so that the "young scholar, not conversant in alphabetical order," would not have to "hunt for a modern word, as he would for a needle in a bottle of hay." (P. v.) She was sure, therefore, that she had created "one of the most elegant, and most expressive vocabularies of our language in its present state." Yet she submitted it "humbly . . . to the more impartial judgement of the public." (*Id.*)

AN ACCURATE NEW
Spelling Dictionary, and Expofitor
OF THE
ENGLISH LANGUAGE.
A much larger COLLECTION of Modern WORDS than any Book of the Kind and Price extant:
And fhewing how the fame are to be written correctly, and pronounced properly; with the different Meanings or Significations of each Word.
An entire New DICTIONARY of all the
Heathen Gods and Goddeffes:
And, alfo of the moft illuftrious HEROES treated of by HOMER, VIRGIL, OVID, and other antient Poets: With a fummary Account of their Origin, Defcent, Exploits, &c.
TO THE WHOLE IS PREFIXED,
A compendious, practical *Grammar* of the *Englifh Language.*
By A. FISHER,
Author of the Practical New Englifh Grammar, with Exercifes of Bad Englifh; The New Englifh Tutor, calculated for the New Method of Teaching, &c.
The SECOND EDITION, much improved.
LONDON: Printed for the AUTHOR, and fold by Hawes, Clarke, and Collins, and G. Robinfon, in Pater-nofter Row; E. Stevens, in Stationers' Court; and T. Slack, in Newcaftle. M.DCC.LXXIII.

Ex coll. Karolyne & Bryan A. Garner

Like Entick before her (no. 40), Fisher keeps almost all her entries to a single line. To the modern eye, her entries feel much more modern: for example, it's more usual now to encounter "Disorder, n." than it is "Disorder, *ſ*." (with the old-fashioned long *s*)—even if Fisher meant *name* as opposed to *noun*; Entick's *ſ* meant *substantive*.

Ex coll. Karolyne & Bryan A. Garner

Fisher's grammar (1762 edition of *A Practical New Grammar*, at left), her book on pedagogy (two editions of *The Pleasing Instructor* 1777 & 1785), and her book of self-instruction (1794 edition of her *Young Man's Best Companion*).

Some of Fisher's one-liners are almost necessarily circular. For example, she defines *paganism* as "heathenism." Then, under *heathenism*, she doesn't merely use the single-word equivalent. Instead, she takes two lines for the definition: "Heathenism, *n.* paganism, denial of the true God, a worshiper of idols." It would have been a better definition if she had replaced *worshiper* with *worship*, given that *heathenism* isn't an agent noun. In any event, Entick's earlier entries were identical, except that his entry for *heathenism* didn't include "a worshiper of idols." Otherwise, the two sets of definitions are verbatim.

Which leads us back to her preface, in which she candidly states that "no book of this kind . . . should be considered as an original work, divested of all modes and improvements peculiar to itself." (P. ii.) Once we admit that, Fisher asserts, "the number of original dictionaries must be very few." (*Id.*)

In reading her prefaces, here and in other books, one is struck by Fisher's self-assured tone and her resistance to closely paraphrasing all the usual bromides that other lexicographers of the era were stating. With "A. Fisher," whoever that might seem to be to readers of the time, one was in good hands.

"[The principles of] Fisher's English Grammar . . . most grammarians have . . . pirated, or *humbly* imitated, without improving upon, or even allowing me the originality of them." (P. iv.)

The first edition of this book, like that of her grammar (see Garner 2021a:19), is thought to be no longer extant. In fact, there is no other copy known of the edition here displayed. All editions are scarce. Although Alston notes Newcastle editions of 1774 and 1781, he says of them: "no copy located." And in his corrected supplement, he has crossed out both entries. Later editions are now known to exist only at the universities of Cambridge, Newcastle, and William & Mary.

The inability to locate or verify first editions of her two most important books—the grammar and the dictionary—isn't the only mystery surrounding Ann Fisher. There is the curious connection between her and the grammarian Isaac Hodgson, who proclaimed in the preface to his grammar that he was "hurt" by unfair criticisms of Fisher's work. Both books use a curious print-cursive signature at the end of the preface—in the same font. Said to be a Southampton headmaster, Hodgson is otherwise untraceable. (See Garner 2021a:38.)

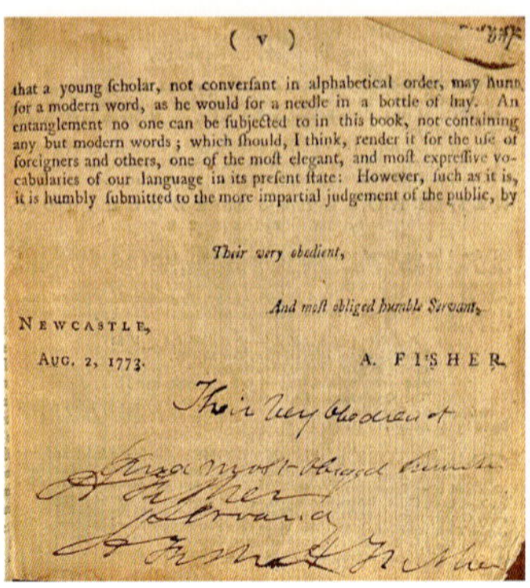
(v)

that a young scholar, not conversant in alphabetical order, may hunt for a modern word, as he would for a needle in a bottle of hay. An entanglement no one can be subjected to in this book, not containing any but modern words; which should, I think, render it for the use of foreigners and others, one of the most elegant, and most expressive vocabularies of our language in its present state: However, such as it is, it is humbly submitted to the more impartial judgement of the public, by

Their very obedient,

And most obliged humble Servant,

NEWCASTLE, AUG. 2, 1773. A. FISHER.

Ex coll. Karolyne & Bryan A. Garner

Fisher inscribed the end of her preface.

Why would one author claim to be "hurt" by criticism of another? She was in Newcastle, and he was 331 miles away, in Southampton. Perhaps *Hodgson* was a pseudonym. Fisher might have been defending herself under a nom de plume (or nom de guerre—see no. 86).

The mystery deepens. Fisher's eldest daughter, Sarah Slack, married one Solomon Hodgson. At the time, Sarah's parents, Thomas and

Ann, were publishers of the *Newcastle Chronicle*. Ann Fisher died in 1778, and her husband six years later. Solomon Hodgson then took over as the newspaper's editor and publisher until his death in 1800. Sarah Hodgson, his wife, assumed the role from 1800 until her death in 1822, and then her son Thomas Hodgson took over until his death in 1848.

Sarah and Solomon were both born about 1760, meaning that they were only about 17 years old when the 1777 edition of the "Isaac Hodgson" grammar appeared. But the same passage about Hodgson's being "hurt" about the criticisms of Ann Fisher appeared in the earlier 1770 edition. Sarah and Solomon, the future spouses, were then 10 years old. Barring an arranged marriage of some kind, Ann Fisher could hardly have known that Solomon would one day join the family.

Sarah and Solomon are buried beside Thomas and Ann in the St. John's Church cemetery at Newcastle. Maybe it's all just a coincidence. The mystery remains: who was Isaac Hodgson, and why was he "hurt" by criticisms of Ann Fisher?

And another question remains: is her name *Ann* or *Anne*? Modern scholars spell it both ways, and they're about equally divided. In the Garner Collection are two autographs: one says "A. Fisher," and the other spells out the name fully, but the handwriting is ambiguous on the point. On balance, our instincts have us going with *Ann*.

Finally, did the last sentence of the first paragraph in this entry, together with the first sentence of the second paragraph, register itself in your mind? The copy of the book here showcased is the *oldest existing dictionary by an English woman*—and seemingly unique. It therefore has great importance in the history of lexicography.

Fisher's dual fame—first female English lexicographer and first female English grammarian of Modern English—is surrounded by enigma. Like the first edition of her dictionary (1771), the first edition of her grammar (thought to date from 1745) doesn't survive. Why might that be? Let us venture a speculative answer. Her husband, Thomas Slack, printed most editions of the grammar, and one might think that the two of them would surely have made a good supply. The bibliographer Alston notes that in the 1750 second edition, "the pagination is erratic." (Alston 1965 1:25.) Yet in all her work, Fisher seems to have been a perfectionist. She never let the grammar be printed outside Newcastle until the seventh (London) edition of 1762. Might it be that she herself destroyed early copies that she thought didn't meet her high standards? The same might be true of her dictionary.

"I, for my Part, have the Satisfaction to be assured, by Experience, that any Person of a tolerable Capacity may, in a short Time, be taught to write English independent of the Knowledge of any other Tongue, and that as properly and correctly as if for the Press." (Fisher's *Practical New Grammar*, 1762 ed., p. vii.)

Ex coll. Karolyne & Bryan A. Garner

The 1773 *Spelling Dictionary*.

42

Frederick Barlow

The Compleat Plagiariſt

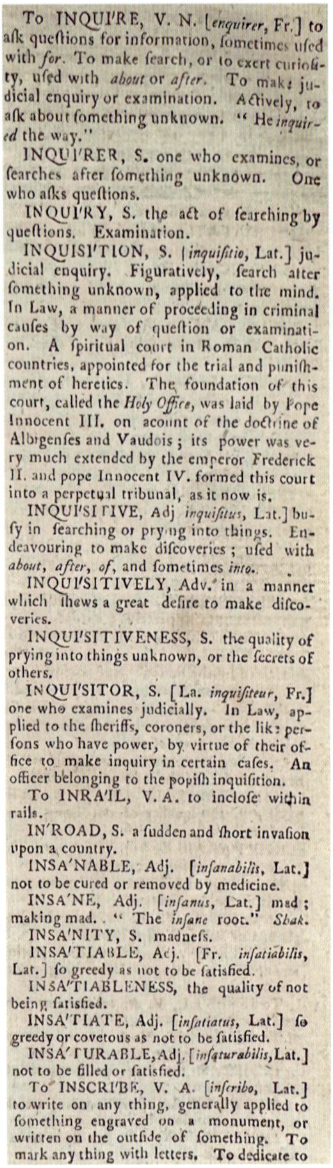

To INQUI'RE, V. N. [*enquirer*, Fr.] to aſk queſtions for information, ſometimes uſed with *for*. To make ſearch, or to exert curioſity, uſed with *about* or *after*. To make judicial enquiry or examination. Actively, to aſk about ſomething unknown. "He *inquired* the way."

INQUI'RER, S. one who examines, or ſearches after ſomething unknown. One who aſks queſtions.

INQUI'RY, S. the act of ſearching by queſtions. Examination.

INQUISI'TION, S. [*inquiſitio*, Lat.] judicial enquiry. Figuratively, ſearch after ſomething unknown, applied to the mind. In Law, a manner of proceeding in criminal cauſes by way of queſtion or examination. A ſpiritual court in Roman Catholic countries, appointed for the trial and puniſhment of heretics. The foundation of this court, called the *Holy Office*, was laid by Pope Innocent III. on acount of the doctrine of Albigenſes and Vaudois; its power was very much extended by the emperor Frederick II. and pope Innocent IV. formed this court into a perpetual tribunal, as it now is.

INQUI'SITIVE, Adj *inquiſitus*, Lat.] buſy in ſearching or prying into things. Endeavouring to make diſcoveries; uſed with *about*, *after*, *of*, and ſometimes *into*.

INQUI'SITIVELY, Adv. in a manner which ſhews a great deſire to make diſcoveries.

INQUI'SITIVENESS, S. the quality of prying into things unknown, or the ſecrets of others.

INQUI'SITOR, S. [La. *inquiſiteur*, Fr.] one who examines judicially. In Law, applied to the ſheriffs, coroners, or the like perſons who have power, by virtue of their office to make inquiry in certain caſes. An officer belonging to the popiſh inquiſition.

To INRA'IL, V. A. to incloſe within rails.

IN'ROAD, S. a ſudden and ſhort invaſion upon a country.

INSA'NABLE, Adj. [*inſanabilis*, Lat.] not to be cured or removed by medicine.

INSA'NE, Adj. [*inſanus*, Lat.] mad; making mad. "The *inſane* root." *Shak.*

INSA'NITY, S. madneſs.

INSA'TIABLE, Adj. [Fr. *inſatiabilis*, Lat.] ſo greedy as not to be ſatisfied.

INSA'TIABLENESS, the quality of not being ſatisfied.

INSA'TIATE, Adj. [*inſatiatus*, Lat.] ſo greedy or covetous as not to be ſatisfied.

INSA'TURABLE, Adj. [*inſaturabilis*, Lat.] not to be filled or ſatisfied.

To INSCRI'BE, V. A. [*inſcribo*, Lat.] to write on any thing, generally applied to ſomething engraved on a monument, or written on the outſide of ſomething. To mark any thing with letters. To dedicate to

Ex coll. Karolyne & Bryan A. Garner

Barlow, Frederick. *The Complete English Dictionary: or, General Repository of the English Language. Containing a Copious Explanation of All the Words in the English Language; Together with Their Different Significations . . . By the Rev. Frederick Barlow, M.A. Vicar of Burton. Assisted by several other gentlemen*. 2 vols. London: For the author, [1772–1773].

WE KNOW NEXT TO NOTHING about Frederick Barlow beyond what he tells us on his title page—that he was the vicar of Burton, a market town about 15 miles from Samuel Johnson's birthplace of Lichfield. He has left virtually no other trace in the historical record, and we know nothing of his birth, death, or education. He has two publications to his credit, *The Complete English Dictionary* in 1772 and *The Complete English Peerage* in 1775. Everything else is a blank.

The Complete English Dictionary was first announced to the world in a proposal "To the Public" in 1772, which appeared in several versions in newspapers starting in February 1772. There Barlow explained his motivation for giving the world a new dictionary. Britain had several excellent large-scale dictionaries, he admitted, but "the Purchase of those voluminous Works, which have already been published on this Subject, is too expensive for those who stand in the greatest Need of Information in this Branch of Literature." There were, on the other hand, cheaper options, but "Bailey's, Dyche's, Fenning's, and other Dictionaries are confined to the Limits of one Volume in Octavo," too short to be useful. Barlow therefore applied the Goldilocks principle: "As the former, therefore, is too prolix, and the latter too concise, being a mere Abridgement, we imagined that a Medium between the two Extremes would, at once, contribute to the Improvement and Oeconomy of the Purchasers." The plan was for two octavo volumes running to a total of about a thousand pages, twice the size of most abridged dictionaries but much smaller than the folios. It would include extensive encyclopedic information, making it the only reference book a family would need.

The newspaper advertisements made it sound appealing:

> AN ENTIRE NEW WORK.
>
> To be comprised in only Twenty-Four Numbers, Price Sixpence each Number, making Two large Volumes in Octavo. . . . Elegantly printed on a new Type and fine Paper, embellished with a beautiful Frontispiece, (the Whole to be illustrated with Variety of Copper-Plates, adapted to the Work)

With 24 numbers sold at sixpence each, the complete dictionary would cost 12 shillings, just 15% of the cost of Johnson's folio *Dictionary* of 1755—but still 20% more expensive than Johnson's abridged edition of 1756.

And what did readers get for their sixpence a week? Perhaps the best way to understand the character of Barlow's *Complete English Dictionary* is to read a run of entries side by side with the corresponding entries in William Rider's *New Universal English Dictionary*, published more than a decade earlier:

Rider (1759)	Barlow (1772–1773)
PLA´CID, *adj.* (*placidus*, Lat.) gentle, quiet: Kind, mild.	PLA´CID, Adj. [*placidus*, Lat.] gentle, quiet; kind, soft, mild, not turbulent.
PLA´CIDLY, *adv.* in a gentle, kind, or mild manner.	PLA´CIDLY, Adv. in a gentle, kind, quiet, or mild manner.
PLA´CIT, S. (*placitum*, Lat.) a decree.	PLA´CIT, S. [*placitum*, Latin.] a decree. A determination.
PLA´CKET, or PLA´QUET, S. a petticoat.	PLA´CKET, or PLA´QUET, S. a petticoat.
PLA´GIARISM, S. (from *plagiary*) theft, or the act of stealing the thoughts of, or works of an author, without owning it.	PLA´GIARISM, S. theft; literary theft, or the act of stealing the thoughts of, or works of an author, without owning it.

Barlow's promise of "AN ENTIRE NEW WORK," it turns out, was not perfectly accurate. In fact, it's a challenge to find a sentence in Barlow's book that's not plagiarized. Nearly all the strictly lexical content comes from Rider, though Rider's name appears nowhere in the book. The plagiarisms are usually verbatim but sometimes modestly tweaked (one function of a *barometer* is "to discover the heights

Courtesy of Rulon-Miller Books

"Philology, or the Definition of Words, is a Study as necessary to the Native as the Foreigner. It is for the Honour of this Nation, that this Branch of Learning is more cultivated at present in our own Island than in any other Part of the Globe." (Preface, p. iii.)

"That every Person may have an Opportunity of judging the Execution of this Work, the First Number may be perused gratis, and returned if not approved." (Postscript to the preface, p. iii.)

of mountains" in Rider, but "to discover the height of hills, &c." in Barlow). More specialized dictionaries, encyclopedias, and gazetteers supplied what could not be found in Rider.

The dictionary never saw a second edition, but it did have a perversely appropriate afterlife. Other lexicographers plagiarized the work that Barlow himself had plagiarized and thereby kept his work in circulation well into the 19th century.

Ex coll. Karolyne & Bryan A. Garner

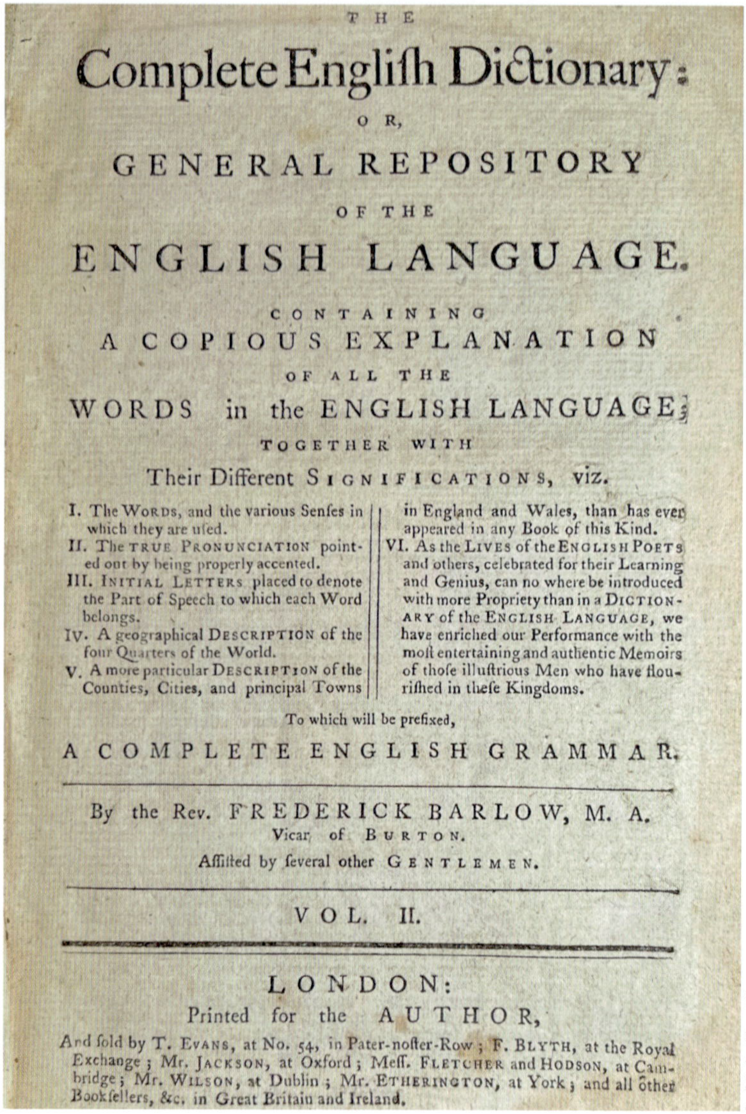

THE

Complete Engliſh Dictionary:

OR,

GENERAL REPOSITORY

OF THE

ENGLISH LANGUAGE.

CONTAINING

A COPIOUS EXPLANATION

OF ALL THE

WORDS in the ENGLISH LANGUAGE;

TOGETHER WITH

Their Different SIGNIFICATIONS, viz.

I. The WORDS, and the various Senſes in which they are uſed.
II. The TRUE PRONUNCIATION pointed out by being properly accented.
III. INITIAL LETTERS placed to denote the Part of Speech to which each Word belongs.
IV. A geographical DESCRIPTION of the four Quarters of the World.
V. A more particular DESCRIPTION of the Counties, Cities, and principal Towns in England and Wales, than has ever appeared in any Book of this Kind.
VI. As the LIVES of the ENGLISH POETS and others, celebrated for their Learning and Genius, can no where be introduced with more Propriety than in a DICTIONARY of the ENGLISH LANGUAGE, we have enriched our Performance with the moſt entertaining and authentic Memoirs of thoſe illuſtrious Men who have flouriſhed in theſe Kingdoms.

To which will be prefixed,

A COMPLETE ENGLISH GRAMMAR.

By the Rev. FREDERICK BARLOW, M. A.
Vicar of BURTON.
Aſſiſted by ſeveral other GENTLEMEN.

VOL. II.

LONDON:
Printed for the AUTHOR,
And ſold by T. EVANS, at No. 54, in Pater-noſter-Row; F. BLYTH, at the Royal Exchange; Mr. JACKSON, at Oxford; Meſſ. FLETCHER and HODSON, at Cambridge; Mr. WILSON, at Dublin; Mr. ETHERINGTON, at York; and all other Bookſellers, &c. in Great Britain and Ireland.

Ex coll. Karolyne & Bryan A. Garner

43

William Kenrick

Brandy Always at the Ready

Kenrick, William. *A New Dictionary of the English Language*. London: John & Francis Rivington et al., 1773.

In the same year as Johnson came out with the fourth and best edition of his magnum opus, the notorious William Kenrick (1725?–1779) came out with the only edition of his dictionary. Kenrick—"one of London's most despised, drunken, and morally degenerate hack writers" (Fussell 1951:539)—had been publishing satires, poems, panegyrics, French translations, plays, and criticism for a quarter-century. He had become a Grub Street hack known especially for berating writers who, like Oliver Goldsmith and Samuel Johnson, enjoyed more success than he did. Kenrick never wanted for literary enemies. Though not without talents, he had little idea how best to use them, and he grossly overestimated his own abilities. The first edition of the *DNB* states that Kenrick "had a strong love of notoriety, a jealous and perverse temper, and was often drunk and violent." He "seldom wrote without a bottle of brandy at his elbow," and "even his more serious works seldom occupied him more than two days."

The second edition, known as the *ODNB*, asserts that Kenrick's *New Dictionary* "drew almost entirely on Johnson's efforts and must have further galled the great lexicographer." Kenrick confesses the pervasive borrowing, with uncharacteristic praise: "With respect to the etymology, explanation of words, and illustration of idiom and phraseology, the reader will find that I have generally followed the celebrated dictionary of the learned Dr. Johnson." (P. viii.) The primary purpose of the book was to improve pronunciation, and his prefatory "rhetorical grammar" is indeed exclusively devoted to orthoepy and articulation. Hence throughout the dictionary he prints each headword a second time with a number (1–16) over each syllable "to determine the exact quality of sound to be given to it."

"There will be noticed a little singularity in the mode of spelling some words ending in *c* or *ck*; as *lunatic* and *lunatick* which, for distinction sake merely, I spell with a *c* when they are adjectives, and with *ck* when they are substantives." (Introduction, p. viii.)

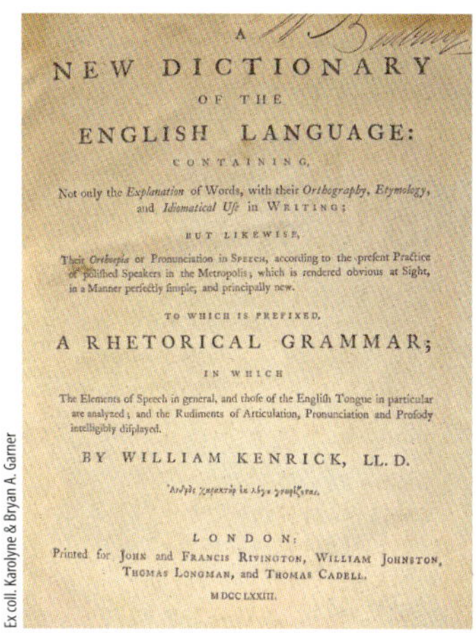

A NEW DICTIONARY OF THE ENGLISH LANGUAGE: CONTAINING, Not only the *Explanation* of Words, with their *Orthography*, *Etymology*, and *Idiomatical Use* in WRITING; BUT LIKEWISE, Their *Orthoepia* or Pronunciation in SPEECH, according to the present Practice of polished Speakers in the Metropolis; which is rendered obvious at Sight, in a Manner perfectly simple, and principally new.

TO WHICH IS PREFIXED, A RHETORICAL GRAMMAR; IN WHICH The Elements of Speech in general, and those of the English Tongue in particular are analyzed; and the Rudiments of Articulation, Pronunciation and Prosody intelligibly displayed.

BY WILLIAM KENRICK, LL.D.

LONDON: Printed for JOHN and FRANCIS RIVINGTON, WILLIAM JOHNSTON, THOMAS LONGMAN, and THOMAS CADELL. MDCCLXXIII.

Ex coll. Karolyne & Bryan A. Garner

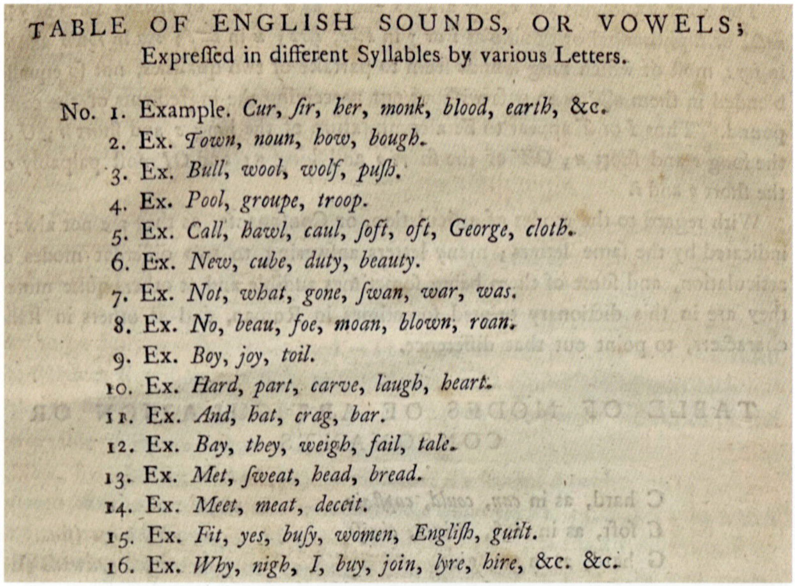

TABLE OF ENGLISH SOUNDS, OR VOWELS;
Expreſſed in different Syllables by various Letters.

No. 1. Example. *Cur, ſir, her, monk, blood, earth,* &c.
2. Ex. *Town, noun, how, bough.*
3. Ex. *Bull, wool, wolf, puſh.*
4. Ex. *Pool, groupe, troop.*
5. Ex. *Call, bawl, caul, ſoft, oft, George, cloth.*
6. Ex. *New, cube, duty, beauty.*
7. Ex. *Not, what, gone, ſwan, war, was.*
8. Ex. *No, beau, foe, moan, blown, roan.*
9. Ex. *Boy, joy, toil.*
10. Ex. *Hard, part, carve, laugh, heart.*
11. Ex. *And, hat, crag, bar.*
12. Ex. *Bay, they, weigh, fail, tale.*
13. Ex. *Met, ſweat, head, bread.*
14. Ex. *Meet, meat, deceit.*
15. Ex. *Fit, yes, buſy, women, Engliſh, guilt.*
16. Ex. *Why, nigh, I, buy, join, lyre, hire,* &c. &c.

Ex coll. Karolyne & Bryan A. Garner

The entries in Kenrick's dictionary amount to stripped-down versions of Johnson, word for word in the definitions. All he has done is to provide the double headword, the second version having superscript numerals. Supplying these would have been an easily delegable task—a printer's assistant could do it—so conceivably this project might indeed have occupied him little more than two days.

Kenrick's life was one of frustrated striving. He had four partners—three wives and another woman, Elizabeth (d. 1818), with whom he had three children. Toward the end of his union with Elizabeth (lasting from 1770 to 1775), and two years after the publication of his *New Dictionary*, he founded *The London Review of English and Foreign Literature*. The following year, in 1776, he abandoned Elizabeth and married Frances Gymer. Then a warehouse fire consumed most of a full print run of the *London Review*, as a result of which Kenrick defaulted on financial obligations and spent most of 1777 and half of 1778 in Fleet Prison for debt. A year after his release from prison, he died and was buried in Chelsea Old Church. Because the church was substantially altered in the 19th century, no memorial remains.

When he is remembered at all in literary history, it is mostly in this way: "Dr. Kenrick was really a man of talents, and deficient only in the knowledge of making a proper use of them." (Chalmers 1815 19:324.)

Ex coll. Karolyne & Bryan A. Garner

44

James Barclay
Cribbed Distinctions Between Synonyms

Barclay, James. *Complete and Universal English Dictionary on a New Plan* [etc.]. London: Richardson & Urquhart et al., 1774. 2d ed. 1782. 3d ed. 1792.

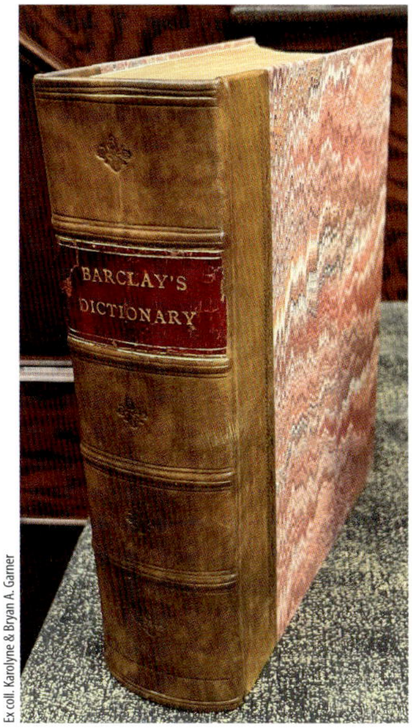

Ex coll. Karolyne & Bryan A. Garner

JAMES BARCLAY (CA. 1720–1778) first entered the documentary record in 1763, when a sermon he wrote—*What Is Meant by Coming unto Christ, and the Reasons of Men's Refusing to Come, Briefly Considered*—was published as a 44-page sixpenny pamphlet. It identified him as "Mr. James Barclay, Master of the Academy at Tottenham High-Cross." Not long after, he was a curate at nearby All Saints Church in Edmonton, an 18th-century rural village in the county of Middlesex, now part of Greater London.

His most important work was his *Complete and Universal English Dictionary* (1774). It was an ambitious project. While Johnson had excluded most encyclopedic information, Barclay boasted of the range of his coverage in an everything-but-the-kitchen-sink title page:

> Complete and Universal English Dictionary on a New Plan: Including Not Only I. A Full Explanation of Difficult Words and Technical Terms in all Faculties and Professions, whether in Algebra, Anatomy, Architecture, Arithmetic, Astronomy, Botany, Chemistry, Dialling, Divinity, Gardening, Geography, Geometry, Grammar, Heraldry, History, Husbandry, Hydrostatics, Law, Mathematics, Mechanics, Military Art, Music, Natural History, Navigation, Optics, Painting, Perspective, Philosophy, Pneumatics, Poetry, Rhetoric, Sculpture, Surveying, &c. But II. A Pronouncing Dictionary: in which the Proper Sounds of English Words are given in a Manner so plain and simple, that both Natives and Foreigners may Correct an Improper, or acquire a right Pronunciation of the English Language. III. The Origin of each Word; its different Meanings or Applications explained; and Illustrated by Authorities, and properly Accented; as also followed by Initial Letters, denoting the Part of Speech to which it is appropriated. IV. The Difference between

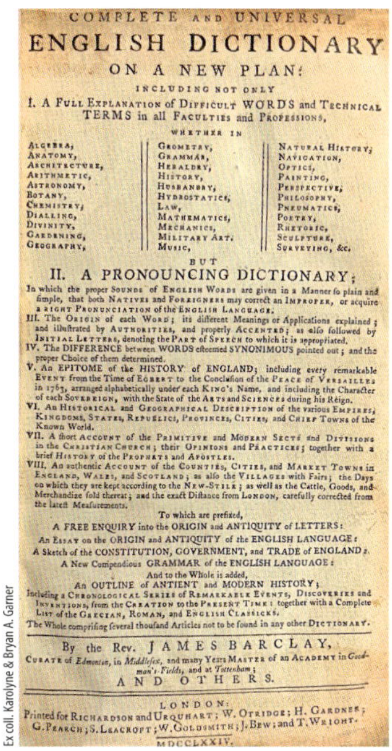

COMPLETE AND UNIVERSAL
ENGLISH DICTIONARY
ON A NEW PLAN:
INCLUDING NOT ONLY
I. A FULL EXPLANATION of DIFFICULT WORDS and TECHNICAL TERMS in all FACULTIES and PROFESSIONS,
WHETHER IN

ALGEBRA,	GEOMETRY,	NATURAL HISTORY,
ANATOMY,	GRAMMAR,	NAVIGATION,
ARCHITECTURE,	HERALDRY,	OPTICS,
ARITHMETIC,	HISTORY,	PAINTING,
ASTRONOMY,	HUSBANDRY,	PERSPECTIVE,
BOTANY,	HYDROSTATICS,	PHILOSOPHY,
CHEMISTRY,	LAW,	PNEUMATICS,
DIALLING,	MATHEMATICS,	POETRY,
DIVINITY,	MECHANICS,	RHETORIC,
GARDENING,	MILITARY ART,	SCULPTURE,
GEOGRAPHY,	MUSIC,	SURVEYING, &c.

BUT
II. A PRONOUNCING DICTIONARY;
In which the proper SOUNDS of ENGLISH WORDS are given in a Manner ſo plain and ſimple, that both NATIVES and FOREIGNERS may correct an IMPROPER, or acquire a RIGHT PRONUNCIATION of the ENGLISH LANGUAGE.
III. The ORIGIN of each WORD; its different Meanings or Applications explained; and illuſtrated by AUTHORITIES, and properly ACCENTED; as alſo followed by INITIAL LETTERS, denoting the PART of SPEECH to which it is appropriated.
IV. The DIFFERENCE between WORDS eſteemed SYNONIMOUS pointed out; and the proper Choice of them determined.
V. An EPITOME of the HISTORY of ENGLAND; including every remarkable EVENT from the Time of EGBERT to the Concluſion of the PEACE of VERSAILLES in 1763, arranged alphabetically under each KING's Name, and including the Character of each SOVEREIGN, with the State of the ARTS and SCIENCES during his Reign.
VI. An HISTORICAL and GEOGRAPHICAL DESCRIPTION of the various EMPIRES, KINGDOMS, STATES, REPUBLICS, PROVINCES, CITIES, and CHIEF TOWNS of the Known World.
VII. A ſhort ACCOUNT of the PRIMITIVE and MODERN SECTS and DIVISIONS in the CHRISTIAN CHURCH; their OPINIONS and PRACTICES; together with a brief HISTORY of the PROPHETS and APOSTLES.
VIII. An authentic ACCOUNT of the COUNTIES, CITIES, and MARKET TOWNS in ENGLAND, WALES, and SCOTLAND; as alſo the VILLAGES with Fairs; the Days on which they are kept according to the NEW-STILE; as well as the Cattle, Goods, and Merchandize ſold thereat; and the exact Diſtance from LONDON, carefully corrected from the lateſt Meaſurements.
To which are prefixed,
A FREE ENQUIRY into the ORIGIN and ANTIQUITY of LETTERS:
An ESSAY on the ORIGIN and ANTIQUITY of the ENGLISH LANGUAGE:
A Sketch of the CONSTITUTION, GOVERNMENT, and TRADE of ENGLAND:
A New Compendious GRAMMAR of the ENGLISH LANGUAGE:
And to the Whole is added,
An OUTLINE of ANTIENT and MODERN HISTORY;
Including a CHRONOLOGICAL SERIES of REMARKABLE EVENTS, DISCOVERIES and INVENTIONS, from the CREATION to the PRESENT TIME: together with a Complete LIST of the GRECIAN, ROMAN, and ENGLISH CLASSICKS.
The Whole compriſing ſeveral thouſand Articles not to be found in any other DICTIONARY.

By the Rev. JAMES BARCLAY,
CURATE of *Edmonton*, in *Middleſex*, and many Years MASTER of an ACADEMY in *Goodman's-Fields*, and at *Tottenham*;
AND OTHERS.

LONDON:
Printed for RICHARDSON and URQUHART; W. OTRIDGE; H. GARDNER; G. PEARCH; S. LEACROFT; W. GOLDSMITH; J. BEW; and T. WRIGHT.
MDCCLXXIV.

Ex coll. Karolyne & Bryan A. Garner

words esteemed Synonimous pointed out; and the proper Choice of them determined. V. An Epitome of the History of England . . . . VI. An Historical and Geographical Description of the various Empires, Kingdoms, States, Republics, Provinces, Cities, and Chief Towns of the Known World. VII. A short Account of the Primitive and Modern Sects and Divisions in the Christian Church . . . . VIII. An authentic Account of the Counties, Cities, and Market Towns in England, Wales, and Scotland . . . . To which are prefixed, A Free Enquiry into the Origin and Antiquity of Letters: An Essay on the Origin and Antiquity of the English Language: A Sketch of the Constitution, Government, and Trade of England: A New Compendious Grammar of the English Language: And to the Whole is added, an Outline of Antient and Modern History; . . . The Whole comprising several thousand Articles not to be found in any other Dictionary.

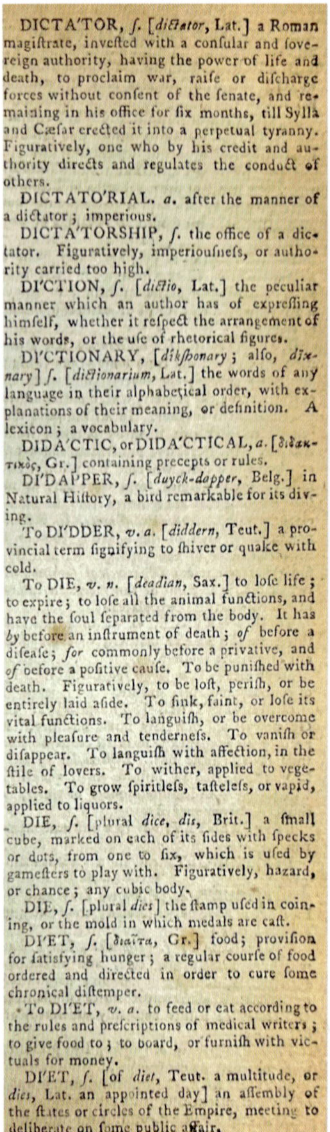

DICTA'TOR, *ſ.* [*dictator*, Lat.] a Roman magiſtrate, inveſted with a conſular and ſovereign authority, having the power of life and death, to proclaim war, raiſe or diſcharge forces without conſent of the ſenate, and remaining in his office for ſix months, till Sylla and Cæſar erected it into a perpetual tyranny. Figuratively, one who by his credit and authority directs and regulates the conduct of others.

DICTATO'RIAL. *a.* after the manner of a dictator; imperious.

DICTA'TORSHIP, *ſ.* the office of a dictator. Figuratively, imperiouſneſs, or authority carried too high.

DI'CTION, *ſ.* [*dictio*, Lat.] the peculiar manner which an author has of expreſſing himſelf, whether it reſpect the arrangement of his words, or the uſe of rhetorical figures.

DI'CTIONARY, [*dikſhonary*; alſo, *dixnary*] *ſ.* [*dictionarium*, Lat.] the words of any language in their alphabetical order, with explanations of their meaning, or definition. A lexicon; a vocabulary.

DIDA'CTIC, or DIDA'CTICAL, *a.* [διδακτικὸς, Gr.] containing precepts or rules.

DI'DAPPER, *ſ.* [*duyck-dapper*, Belg.] in Natural Hiſtory, a bird remarkable for its diving.

To DI'DDER, *v. a.* [*diddern*, Teut.] a provincial term ſignifying to ſhiver or quake with cold.

To DIE, *v. n.* [*deadian*, Sax.] to loſe life; to expire; to loſe all the animal functions, and have the ſoul ſeparated from the body. It has *by* before an inſtrument of death; *of* before a diſeaſe; *for* commonly before a privative, and *of* before a poſitive cauſe. To be puniſhed with death. Figuratively, to be loſt, periſh, or be entirely laid aſide. To ſink, faint, or loſe its vital functions. To languiſh, or be overcome with pleaſure and tenderneſs. To vaniſh or diſappear. To languiſh with affection, in the ſtile of lovers. To wither, applied to vegetables. To grow ſpiritleſs, taſteleſs, or vapid, applied to liquors.

DIE, *ſ.* [plural *dice*, *dis*, Brit.] a ſmall cube, marked on each of its ſides with ſpecks or dots, from one to ſix, which is uſed by gameſters to play with. Figuratively, hazard, or chance; any cubic body.

DIE, *ſ.* [plural *dies*] the ſtamp uſed in coining, or the mold in which medals are caſt.

DI'ET, *ſ.* [διαῖτα, Gr.] food; proviſion for ſatisfying hunger; a regular courſe of food ordered and directed in order to cure ſome chronical diſtemper.

To DI'ET, *v. a.* to feed or eat according to the rules and preſcriptions of medical writers; to give food to; to board, or furniſh with victuals for money.

DI'ET, *ſ.* [of *diet*, Teut. a multitude, or *dies*, Lat. an appointed day] an aſſembly of the ſtates or circles of the Empire, meeting to deliberate on ſome public affair.

A a 4 DI'ET-

From the second edition of 1782.

The encyclopedic entries are some of the longest in the book: Charles I gets nearly 5 double-columned pages, George I gets 3, and George II gets a remarkable 16—some of it lifted from Oliver Goldsmith's *History of England.* (George III, the sitting monarch, gets just a single page, but he was still young.)

And where Johnson strove to restrict his wordlist to words actually in use, Barclay reveled in obscurity. Though he did not exclude common words, admitting words like *have* and *from*, it's easy to see that his heart was in the inkhorn terms that got so much attention in the 17th century. We see runs of words like *hyacinthine*, *hyads*, *hyaline*, *hybridous*, *hydatides*, *hydra*, *hydragogues*, and *rubican*, *rubicund*, *rubied*, *rubific*, *rubiform*, *rubify*, *rubiginous*, *rubious*.

Barclay marks the primary stress on each polysyllabic word and gives a very simple etymology. Definitions are reminiscent of pre-Johnson dictionaries, with multiple senses listed one after another, rather than broken out under numbered senses:

> CROSS, *s.* [*croix*, Fr.] an instrument made of two pieces of wood, cutting or crossing each other at right angles, on which malefactors were executed among the Romans. The sign made by the priest on the forehead of a person when baptized, by drawing two marks, which cross each other, with his fingers dipped in water; one line drawn athwart another. Figuratively, the Christian religion; or the doctrine of a crucified Savior; the manner in which Christ died; any thing which is contrary to a person's wishes, and is a trial of his patience. Also money so called, being marked with a cross.

Though he didn't give phrasal verbs the kind of attention that Johnson gave, he did treat some of the more common ones, as when the entry for *get* includes examples of *get off*, *get in*, *get drunk*, *get over*, and *get up*.

Barclay deserves credit for being the first English lexicographer to try to discriminate synonyms in a systematic way. He advertised the subject's importance in his front matter, declaring, "The *Synonimous* [sic] part of our Dictionary we modestly assert to be entirely new; the use of which, both in speaking and writing, must at first view appear to every intelligent Reader." (P. viii.) About 300 entries include a section "SYNON," with a short discussion of related words. "*Glory*," for example, "expresses something more singular than *honour*: the one makes us undertake voluntarily the most difficult things; the other leads us willingly to the execution of the most rigorous exactions. An indifference to *glory* may pass unnoticed, but not with respect to *honour*." Nearly all his synonym differences have been cribbed from John Trusler's *Difference, between Words, Esteemed Synonymous, in the English Language* (1766). (Noyes 1951:965.)

"The pronunciation of our language is too often arbitrary (so much, indeed, that the inhabitants of one county can scarce understand those of another)." (Preface, p. vii.)

Ex coll. Karolyne & Bryan A. Garner

First among the "improvements peculiar to the Dictionary," according to the preface, was the pronunciation system. Barclay was one of many lexicographers who saw pronunciation as the gaping hole left by Johnson. Buchanan (no. 38), Fenning (no. 39), Entick (no. 40), Kenrick (no. 43), and soon Perry (no. 46) and Walker (no. 47) were all vying for commercial advantage by devising an appealing system of pronunciation. "We have taken," wrote Barclay, "all possible care to adopt the best, most plain and useful modes of speaking, without perplexing or puzzling the Reader with the almost endless and unintelligible niceties of what are pedantically called Orthoepical Rules, or rules for right pronunciation." (P. vii.) In a footnote on the first page of his preface, he instructs readers on how to pronounce the word *pronunciation* and other words with the same suffix: "Under this article of *Pronunciation*, the Reader will be pleased to observe, that . . . the final *tion*, with very few exceptions, is always pronounced *shon*."

One commentator observes of this book that it "won immediate acceptance from the public, especially the lower classes, for whom it acted, until well into the Victorian age, as an important means of self-education." (*DNB*.) The *Complete and Universal English Dictionary* went through at least two dozen editions over a century.

Ex coll. Karolyne & Bryan A. Garner

45

John Ash
An Unforgettable Curmudgeon

Ash, John. *The New and Complete Dictionary of the English Language*. 2 vols. London: Edward & Charles Dilly, 1775. 2d ed. 1795.

Ash (1724–1779), a grammarian as well as a lexicographer, was born in Devon, was baptized in Loughwood, and became a Baptist minister in Pershore, Worcestershire. When he was 36, he wrote an English grammar "to oblige a few" of his friends, but two years later, in 1762, another grammar was published, and it was much more popular: Robert Lowth's *Short Introduction to English Grammar*. So the next year, in 1763, he gave a new subtitle to his work: *An Easy Introduction to Dr Lowth's English Grammar*, which was kept through the next 40 editions. This suggests, of course, that he was both opportunistic and derivative.

In his *New and Complete Dictionary*, Ash ambitiously announced, at the outset of the "advertisement" serving as a preface, that his work was unprecedented: "The plan of this Work is extensive beyond any thing that has yet been attempted of the kind in the English Language." (P. iii.) He understood a dictionary to be not a mere wordbook but something more comprehensive. To drive up his headword count, he included "not only all the appellatives or common words, whether names of men and women, heathen gods and goddesses, heroes, princes, poets, historians, wise men and philosophers of special note, whether ancient or modern: Of all the principal kingdoms, cities, towns, seas and rivers in the known world, more especially in Great Britain and Ireland: Of beasts, birds, fishes and insects: Of trees, plants, herbs, minerals and fossils." (*Id.*) Because the book went to press "before the manuscript copy was quite completed," he added a supplement—assuring readers that he "has introduced . . . all the words he could find or remember." (P. iv.)

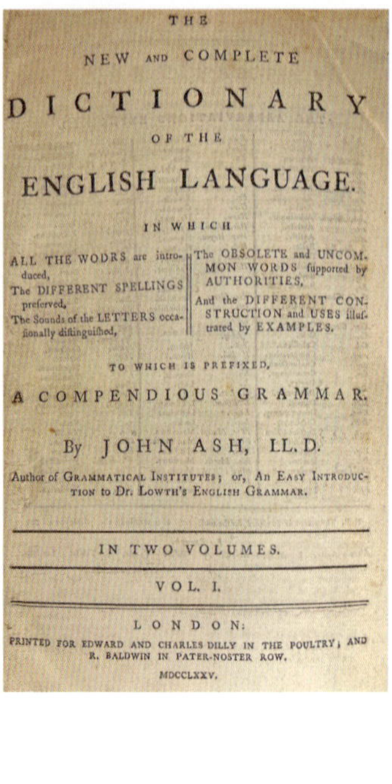
THE
NEW AND COMPLETE
DICTIONARY
OF THE
ENGLISH LANGUAGE.
IN WHICH
ALL THE WORDS are introduced,
The DIFFERENT SPELLINGS preserved,
The Sounds of the LETTERS occasionally distinguished,
The OBSOLETE and UNCOMMON WORDS supported by AUTHORITIES,
And the DIFFERENT CONSTRUCTION and USES illustrated by EXAMPLES.
TO WHICH IS PREFIXED,
A COMPENDIOUS GRAMMAR.
By JOHN ASH, LL.D.
Author of GRAMMATICAL INSTITUTES; or, An EASY INTRODUCTION to Dr. LOWTH'S ENGLISH GRAMMAR.
IN TWO VOLUMES.
VOL. I.
LONDON:
PRINTED FOR EDWARD AND CHARLES DILLY IN THE POULTRY; AND R. BALDWIN IN PATER-NOSTER ROW.
MDCCLXXV.

Ex coll. Karolyne & Bryan A. Garner

Four folio editions of Johnson's *Dictionary* had appeared, the most recent in 1773, and yet Ash mentions neither Johnson nor any other lexicographic predecessor. He included a few illustrative quotations, but often cited "authorities" in the form of writers' names alongside definitions whenever he considered, "any thing appeared to be uncommon or doubtful." (P. iii.) The most frequently cited names are Chaucer, Dryden, and Bailey (that is, Scott's Bailey [no. 36]).

"The author has . . . introduced all the words he could find or remember. But the copiousness of the English Language, as might well be expected, leaves him short of that perfection which the plan seems to require." (Postscript to Advertisement, p. 2.)

To convey a sense of his coverage, it may be useful to compare an alphabetical span of headwords in Ash to the same spans in near-contemporaries:

Johnson (4th ed. 1773)	**Bailey (Scott ed. 1755)**	**Kenrick (1773)**	**Ash (1st ed. 1775)**
Hippish	Hippelaphus	Hippish	Hippace
Hippocentaur	Hippeus	Hippocrass	Hipparchus
Hippocrass	Hippia		Hipped
	Hippiades		Hipped
	Hippiatrice		Hippelaphus
	Hip, or Hippo		Hippeus
	Hipping-Hold		Hippeus
	Hippocamelus		Hippia
	Hippocampa		Hippiades
	Hippocentaur		Hippiatics
	Hippocourius		Hippiatric
	Hippocras		Hippice
			Hippicon
			Hipping
			Hippinghand
			Hippish
			Hippishness
			Hippius
			Hippo
			Hippo
			Hippobosca
			Hippocamelus
			Hippocampa
			Hippocampa
			Hippocastanum
			Hippocentaur
			Hippocourius
			HIPPOCRAS

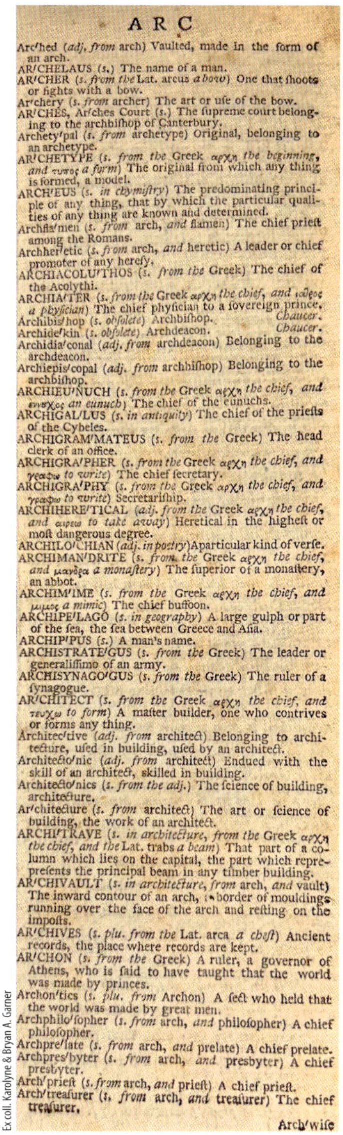
ARC

Arc'hed (*adj. from* arch) Vaulted, made in the form of an arch.
AR'CHELAUS (*s.*) The name of a man.
AR'CHER (*s. from the* Lat. arcus *a bow*) One that ſhoots or fights with a bow.
Ar'chery (*s. from* archer) The art or uſe of the bow.
AR'CHES, Ar'ches Court (*s.*) The ſupreme court belonging to the archbiſhop of Canterbury.
Archety'pal (*s. from* archetype) Original, belonging to an archetype.
AR'CHETYPE (*s. from the* Greek αρχη *the beginning, and* τυπος *a form*) The original from which any thing is formed, a model.
ARCH'EUS (*s. in chymiſtry*) The predominating principle of any thing, that by which the particular qualities of any thing are known and determined.
Archfla'men (*s. from* arch, *and* flamen) The chief prieſt among the Romans.
Archher'etic (*s. from* arch, *and* heretic) A leader or chief promoter of any hereſy.
ARCHIACOLU'THOS (*s. from the* Greek) The chief of the Acolythi.
ARCHIA'TER (*s. from the* Greek αρχη *the chief, and* ιατρος *a phyſician*) The chief phyſician to a ſovereign prince.
Archibis'hop (*s. obſolete*) Archbiſhop. *Chaucer.*
Archide'kin (*s. obſolete*) Archdeacon. *Chaucer.*
Archidia'conal (*adj. from* archdeacon) Belonging to the archdeacon.
Archiepis'copal (*adj. from* archbiſhop) Belonging to the archbiſhop.
ARCHIEU'NUCH (*s. from the* Greek αρχη *the chief, and* ευνουχος *an eunuch*) The chief of the eunuchs.
ARCHIGAL'LUS (*s. in antiquity*) The chief of the prieſts of the Cybeles.
ARCHIGRAM'MATEUS (*s. from the* Greek) The head clerk of an office.
ARCHIGRA'PHER (*s. from the* Greek αρχη *the chief, and* γραφω *to write*) The chief ſecretary.
ARCHIGRA'PHY (*s. from the* Greek αρχη *the chief, and* γραφω *to write*) Secretariſhip.
ARCHIHERE'TICAL (*adj. from the* Greek αρχη *the chief, and* αιρεω *to take away*) Heretical in the higheſt or moſt dangerous degree.
ARCHILO'CHIAN (*adj. in poetry*) A particular kind of verſe.
ARCHIMAN'DRITE (*s. from the* Greek αρχη *the chief, and* μανδρα *a monaſtery*) The ſuperior of a monaſtery, an abbot.
ARCHIM'IME (*s. from the* Greek αρχη *the chief, and* μιμος *a mimic*) The chief buffoon.
ARCHIPE'LAGO (*s. in geography*) A large gulph or part of the ſea, the ſea between Greece and Aſia.
ARCHIP'PUS (*s.*) A man's name.
ARCHISTRATE'GUS (*s. from the* Greek) The leader or generaliſſimo of an army.
ARCHISYNAGO'GUS (*s. from the* Greek) The ruler of a ſynagogue.
AR'CHITECT (*s. from the* Greek αρχη *the chief, and* τευχω *to form*) A maſter builder, one who contrives or forms any thing.
Architec'tive (*adj. from* architect) Belonging to architecture, uſed in building, uſed by an architect.
Architecto'nic (*adj. from* architect) Endued with the skill of an architect, skilled in building.
Architecto'nics (*s. from the adj.*) The ſcience of building, architecture.
Ar'chitecture (*s. from* architect) The art or ſcience of building, the work of an architect.
ARCHI'TRAVE (*s. in architecture, from the* Greek αρχη *the chief, and the* Lat. trabs *a beam*) That part of a column which lies on the capital, the part which repreſents the principal beam in any timber building.
AR'CHIVAULT (*s. in architecture, from* arch, *and* vault) The inward contour of an arch, a border of mouldings running over the face of the arch and reſting on the impoſts.
AR'CHIVES (*s. plu. from the* Lat. arca *a cheſt*) Ancient records, the place where records are kept.
AR'CHON (*s. from the* Greek) A ruler, a governor of Athens, who is ſaid to have taught that the world was made by princes.
Archon'tics (*s. plu. from* Archon) A ſect who held that the world was made by great men.
Archphilo'ſopher (*s. from* arch, *and* philoſopher) A chief philoſopher.
Archpre'late (*s. from* arch, *and* prelate) A chief prelate.
Archpres'byter (*s. from* arch, *and* presbyter) A chief presbyter.
Arch'prieſt (*s. from* arch, *and* prieſt) A chief prieſt.
Arch'treaſurer (*s. from* arch, *and* treaſurer) The chief treaſurer.
Arch'wife

Ex coll. Karolyne & Bryan A. Garner

With Ash's doubly recorded headwords, he intended to document separate words. Hence *hippo*$_{I}$ is "the hip, a lower species of melancholy" and *hippo*$_{2}$ is "a species of serpents." These strange senses of *hippo* are unrecorded in the *Oxford English Dictionary*. The serpent

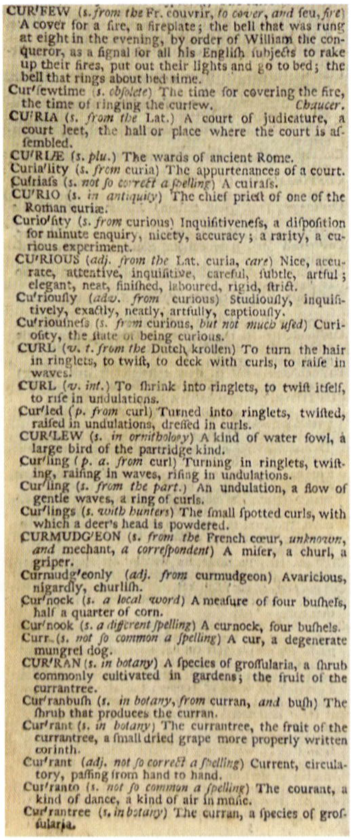

CUR'FEW (*s. from the* Fr. couvrir, *to cover, and* feu, *fire*) A cover for a fire, a fireplate; the bell that was rung at eight in the evening, by order of William the conqueror, as a fignal for all his Englifh fubjects to rake up their fires, put out their lights and go to bed; the bell that rings about bed time.
Cur'fewtime (*s. obfolete*) The time for covering the fire, the time of ringing the curfew. *Chaucer.*
CU'RIA (*s. from the* Lat.) A court of judicature, a court leet, the hall or place where the court is affembled.
CU'RIÆ (*s. plu.*) The wards of ancient Rome.
Curia'lity (*s. from* curia) The appurtenances of a court.
Cu'riafs (*s. not fo correct a fpelling*) A cuirafs.
CU'RIO (*s. in antiquity*) The chief prieft of one of the Roman curiæ.
Curio'fity (*s. from* curious) Inquifitivenefs, a difpofition for minute enquiry, nicety, accuracy; a rarity, a curious experiment.
CU'RIOUS (*adj. from the* Lat. curia, *care*) Nice, accurate, attentive, inquifitive, careful, fubtle, artful; elegant, neat, finifhed, laboured, rigid, ftrict.
Cu'rioufly (*adv. from* curious) Studioufly, inquifitively, exactly, neatly, artfully, captioufly.
Cu'rioufnefs (*s. from* curious, *but not much ufed*) Curiofity, the ftate of being curious.
CURL (*v. t. from the* Dutch krollen) To turn the hair in ringlets, to twift, to deck with curls, to raife in waves.
CURL (*v. int.*) To fhrink into ringlets, to twift itfelf, to rife in undulations.
Cur'led (*p. from* curl) Turned into ringlets, twifted, raifed in undulations, dreffed in curls.
CUR'LEW (*s. in ornithology*) A kind of water fowl, a large bird of the partridge kind.
Cur'ling (*p. a. from* curl) Turning in ringlets, twifting, raifing in waves, rifing in undulations.
Cur'ling (*s. from the part.*) An undulation, a flow of gentle waves, a ring of curls.
Cur'lings (*s. with hunters*) The fmall fpotted curls, with which a deer's head is powdered.
CURMUDG'EON (*s. from the* French cœur, *unknown, and* mechant, *a correfpondent*) A mifer, a churl, a griper.
Curmudg'eonly (*adj. from* curmudgeon) Avaricious, nigardly, churlifh.
Cur'nock (*s. a local word*) A meafure of four bufhels, half a quarter of corn.
Cur'nook (*s. a different fpelling*) A curnock, four bufhels.
Curr (*s. not fo common a fpelling*) A cur, a degenerate mungrel dog.
CUR'RAN (*s. in botany*) A fpecies of groffularia, a fhrub commonly cultivated in gardens; the fruit of the currantree.
Cur'ranbufh (*s. in botany, from* curran, *and* bufh) The fhrub that produces the curran.
Cur'rant (*s. in botany*) The currantree, the fruit of the currantree, a fmall dried grape more properly written corinth.
Cur'rant (*adj. not fo correct a fpelling*) Current, circulatory, paffing from hand to hand.
Cur'ranto (*s. not fo common a fpelling*) The courant, a kind of dance, a kind of air in mufic.
Cur'rantree (*s. in botany*) The curran, a fpecies of groffularia.

Ex coll. Karolyne & Bryan A. Garner

sense remains a mystery. The melancholy sense derives from Scott's edition of Bailey: "Hip, or Hippo . . . a disease called *hypochondriacus affectus*, a lower species of melancholy." Yet Bailey isn't cited there.

If the goal was to accumulate sheer numbers of headwords, Ash did indeed excel his predecessors. (His unexplained habit of using all capitals for some but not all headwords is a matter of speculation: it might appear that the more technical terms are capitalized, but if that was the plan, the execution was haphazard.) Ash preferred boosting his headword count with technical terms and proper nouns, not with slang: he thought it neither "necessary [n]or expedient to rake into the mere cant of any profession, much less of gamesters, highwaymen, pickpockets and gipsies." (P. iii.)

In lexicographic posterity, Ash suffered the misfortune of an infamous blunder he made in copying Samuel Johnson's (incorrect) etymology of *curmudgeon*. In 1755, Johnson wrote: "curmudgeon . . . is a vitious manner of pronouncing *cœur mechant*, Fr. an unknown correspondent." Johnson had received this information from an anonymous letter-writer. Shaky in his knowledge of Romance languages and misled by Johnson's punctuation, Ash misunderstood the abbreviation "Fr." as relating to what followed instead of what preceded: "curmudgeon (s. *from the* French cœur, *unknown, and* mechant, *a correspondent*)." Johnson meant to record *cœur* [heart] *méchant* [wicked] as denoting a wicked or worthless heart; Ash, embarrassingly, corrupted the etymology with false French.

"Ash's dictionary was partially an attempt to introduce more readers to his views on teaching grammar, for it contains a treatise on the subject. He was hardly alone in his efforts." (Shapiro 2017:307.)

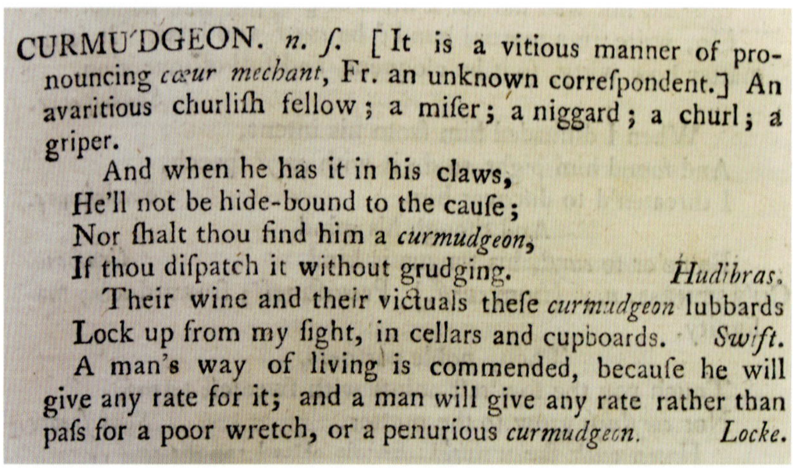

CURMU'DGEON. *n. f.* [It is a vitious manner of pronouncing *cœur mechant*, Fr. an unknown correfpondent.] An avaritious churlifh fellow; a mifer; a niggard; a churl; a griper.

And when he has it in his claws,
He'll not be hide-bound to the caufe;
Nor fhalt thou find him a *curmudgeon*,
If thou difpatch it without grudging. *Hudibras.*

Their wine and their victuals thefe *curmudgeon* lubbards
Lock up from my fight, in cellars and cupboards. *Swift.*

A man's way of living is commended, becaufe he will give any rate for it; and a man will give any rate rather than pafs for a poor wretch, or a penurious *curmudgeon*. *Locke.*

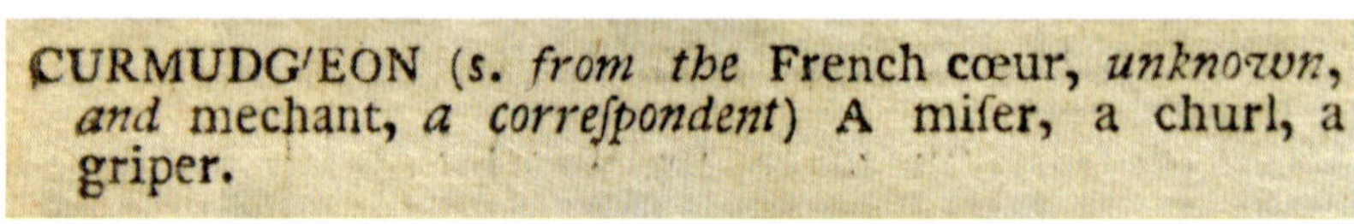

CURMUDG'EON (*s. from the* French cœur, *unknown, and* mechant, *a correfpondent*) A mifer, a churl, a griper.

Johnson above, Ash below. Ash's spectacular bungle with the word *curmudgeon* doesn't appear to have been pointed out during his lifetime. When he died at 55, four years after the dictionary's appearance, he probably didn't realize what he had done here.

Ex coll. Karolyne & Bryan A. Garner

46

William Perry

The Lexicographer Who Wanted to Be Read

Perry, W[illiam]. ***The Royal Standard English Dictionary.*** **Edinburgh: David Willison for the author, 1775. [No second or third eds. known.] 4th ed. 1786. 1st Am. ed. 1788.**

Ex coll. Karolyne & Bryan A. Garner

William Perry (1747–1808) has the distinction of having produced the first dictionary ever printed on American soil. The work itself is a one-line-per-entry simple vocabulary of 427 octavo pages in the main text in the first edition, which grew to 559 pages in the fourth, and 596 in the first American. It was the distinguished and prolific printer Isaiah Thomas of Worcester, Massachusetts, who brought out five American editions through 1800. By 1804, American editions were being printed by Ebenezer Merriam (see photo p. 244)—whose apprentices were his nephews George and Charles (see p. 243). These editions of Perry marked the beginning of the Merriam family's dictionary-publishing empire.

"Few subjects have of late years more employed the pens of every class of critics, than the improvement of the English language. The greatest abilities in the nation have been exerted in cultivating and reforming it." (1791 preface, p. iii.)

The book was intended as an aid in spelling and pronunciation for those ambitious to acquire full literacy. In his preface, Perry told users how to benefit from the book: "As to adult persons, those who wish to make the English pronunciation familiar to them, without the assistance of a teacher, must repeat six or eight pages of the following *Dictionary* daily, according to the pronunciation there pointed out; and when they shall have gone through the whole, to begin again, and thus continue till the end aimed at be accomplished." (P. xii.) Hence Perry saw this work not so much as a reference book in which words could be looked up, but instead as an exercise book for boosting vocabulary and mastering pronunciation. One imagines late 18th-century users reciting by candlelight sequences like these: *deplorer*, *deplumation*, *deplume*, *depone*, *deponent*, *depopulate*, *depopulation*, *depopulator*, *deport*, *deportment*, *depose*, *deposite* [sic], *deposition*, *depository*, *depravation*, *deprave*, *depravedness*, *depraver*, *depravity* . . . This was a dictionary not to be consulted, but to be recited.

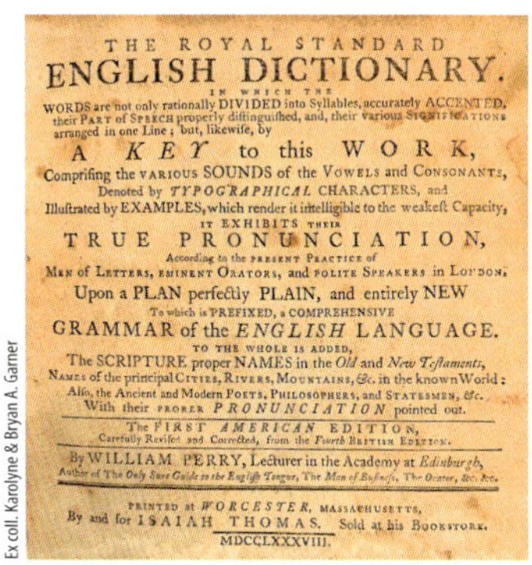

THE ROYAL STANDARD
ENGLISH DICTIONARY.
IN WHICH THE
WORDS are not only rationally DIVIDED into Syllables, accurately ACCENTED, their PART of SPEECH properly diſtinguiſhed, and, their various SIGNIFICATIONS arranged in one Line; but, likewiſe, by
A *KEY* to this WORK,
Compriſing the VARIOUS SOUNDS of the VOWELS and CONSONANTS, Denoted by *TYPOGRAPHICAL* CHARACTERS, and Illuſtrated by EXAMPLES, which render it intelligible to the weakeſt Capacity,
IT EXHIBITS THEIR
TRUE PRONUNCIATION,
According to the PRESENT PRACTICE of
MEN of LETTERS, EMINENT ORATORS, and POLITE SPEAKERS in LONDON;
Upon a PLAN perfectly PLAIN, and entirely NEW
To which is PREFIXED, a COMPREHENSIVE
GRAMMAR of the *ENGLISH* LANGUAGE.
TO THE WHOLE IS ADDED,
The SCRIPTURE proper NAMES in the *Old* and *New Teſtaments*, NAMES of the principal CITIES, RIVERS, MOUNTAINS, &c. in the known World: Alſo, the Ancient and Modern POETS, PHILOSOPHERS, and STATESMEN, &c. With their PROPER *PRONUNCIATION* pointed out.

The FIRST *AMERICAN* EDITION,
Carefully Reviſed and Corrected, from the *Fourth* BRITISH EDITION.

By WILLIAM PERRY, Lecturer in the Academy at *Edinburgh*, Author of *The Only Sure Guide to the Engliſh Tongue*, *The Man of Buſineſs*, *The Orator*, &c. &c.

PRINTED at *WORCESTER*, MASSACHUSETTS,
By and for ISAIAH THOMAS. Sold at his BOOKSTORE.
MDCCLXXXVIII.

Ex coll. Karolyne & Bryan A. Garner

The first American edition (1788) was dedicated to the American Academy of Arts & Sciences.

Ex coll. Karolyne & Bryan A. Garner

The two dictionaries: 1775 (left) and 1791 (right).

47

John Walker

The Great Pronouncer

Walker, J[ohn]. ***A Dictionary of the English Language, Answering at once the Purposes of Rhyming, Spelling, and Pronouncing. On a Plan not hitherto attempted.*** **London: T. Becket, 1775.**

Walker, John. ***A Critical Pronouncing Dictionary and Expositor of the English Language.*** **London: Sold by G.G.J. & J. Robinson and T. Cadell, 1791.**

THE TITLE PAGE of *A Dictionary of the English Language*, by John Walker (1732–1807), promises "a plan not hitherto attempted." And what was that? "As in other dictionaries words follow each other in an alphabetical order according to the letters they *begin* with, in this they follow each other according to the letters they *end* with. All words therefore that *end* with *a* are placed first in this Dictionary . . . . Those that *end* with *b* are placed next, and so of the rest."

Why would anyone do such a thing? Walker was setting out to describe not meanings or usage but *sounds*. The spoken word fascinated the man, who began life as an actor. He had a reasonably successful career in Dublin and on London's Covent Garden stage, but he fell far short of theatrical greatness. An obituary notice summed up the opinion of "the remaining few who remember him on the stage," which was that "his gesture was ungraceful, and . . . his enunciation was monotonous."

In 1769, therefore, he left the stage to open a school and, after a few years, to tutor adults in elocution. He must by this time have shaken his monotony because his tutorials became hugely popular, and soon he numbered among his clients Members of Parliament, the children of the nobility, and even the son of the Russian prime minister. His circle of friends included Samuel Johnson (to whom he dedicated two of his books), the actor David Garrick, and the philosopher and politician Edmund Burke, who praised him for his mastery of "the harmonies, cadences, and proprieties of our language."

Entries in *A Dictionary of the English Language* are alphabetized from back to front, and every word gets a few curt definitions, clear syllabification, an accent to show primary stress, and a part of speech (here *s.* for *substantive*, *v.a.* for *verb active*):

Com-pa'tri-ot	One of the same country, s.
Lot	Fortune; portion; quota; chance, s.
Zeal'ot	A person full of zeal, s.
Es-cha-lot'	A kind of small onion; shallot, s.
To blot	To blur; efface; disgrace; darken, v.a.
Blot	A blur; spot; crime, s.
Clot	Any thing clotted or curdled, s.

The one-line definitions are sometimes cribbed from his friend Johnson: *to blot*, for instance, simply squeezes together Johnson's numbered senses: "1. To obliterate . . . 2. To efface; to erase . . . 3. To make black spots on a paper; to blur . . . 4. To disgrace; to disfigure . . . 5. To darken."

Walker's eccentric method shines new light on two aspects of the language that had been neglected in earlier dictionaries. The first is morphology, the way in which words are made from smaller units. Whereas once individual speakers had almost unlimited freedom to form words—the adjective *hardy* might form nouns *hardiesse*, *hardihood*, *hardiment*, or *hardiness*—the 18th century looked for standardization. Walker allowed curious readers to answer questions that couldn't even have been asked of other dictionaries—show me, for instance, all the words that are formed with *-ify* (*ramify*, *exemplify*, *amplify*, *dignify* . . .) or *-liness* (*earthliness*, *sickliness*, *unseemliness*, *cleanliness* . . .).

Walker's other important innovation was his attention to the spoken as opposed to the written language. Johnson had explicitly disavowed any attempt to record speech; for him, the language was a written phenomenon above all. Walker, though, was concerned with sounds. He was, in fact, a little embarrassed to be producing "a mere rhyming dictionary," which he knew had a reputation "either as a bauble for school-boys, or a resource for poetasters." And yet he knew that such a book would be useful, even if not entirely respectable, and grouping words by their endings was one way to highlight rhymes.

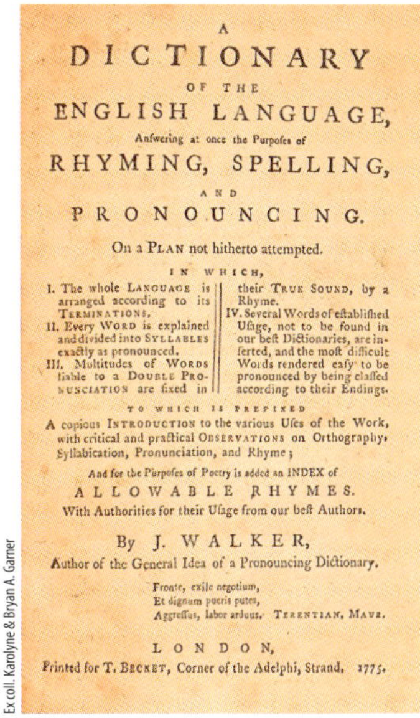

A

DICTIONARY

OF THE

ENGLISH LANGUAGE,

Anſwering at once the Purpoſes of

RHYMING, SPELLING,

AND

PRONOUNCING.

On a PLAN not hitherto attempted.

IN WHICH,

I. The whole LANGUAGE is arranged according to its TERMINATIONS.
II. Every WORD is explained and divided into SYLLABLES exactly as pronounced.
III. Multitudes of WORDS liable to a DOUBLE PRONUNCIATION are fixed in their TRUE SOUND, by a Rhyme.
IV. Several Words of eſtabliſhed Uſage, not to be found in our beſt Dictionaries, are inſerted, and the moſt difficult Words rendered eaſy to be pronounced by being claſſed according to their Endings.

TO WHICH IS PREFIXED

A copious INTRODUCTION to the various Uſes of the Work, with critical and practical OBSERVATIONS on Orthography, Syllabication, Pronunciation, and Rhyme;

And for the Purpoſes of Poetry is added an INDEX of

ALLOWABLE RHYMES.

With Authorities for their Uſage from our beſt Authors.

By J. WALKER,

Author of the General Idea of a Pronouncing Dictionary.

Fronte, exile negotium,
Et dignum pueris putes,
Aggreſſus, labor arduus. TERENTIAN. MAUR.

LONDON,

Printed for T. BECKET, Corner of the Adelphi, Strand, 1775.

Ex coll. Karolyne & Bryan A. Garner

The 1775 title page.

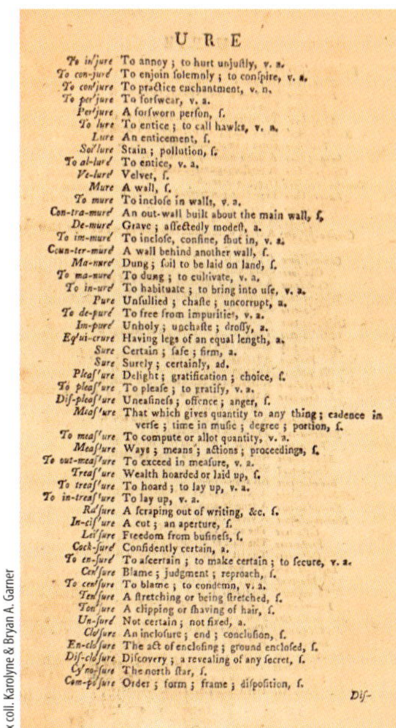

URE

To in'jure	To annoy; to hurt unjuſtly, v. a.
To con-jure'	To enjoin ſolemnly; to conſpire, v. a.
To con'jure	To practice enchantment, v. n.
To per'jure	To forſwear, v. a.
Per'jure	A forſworn perſon, ſ.
To lure	To entice; to call hawks, v. a.
Lure	An enticement, ſ.
Soi'lure	Stain; pollution, ſ.
To al-lure'	To entice, v. a.
Ve-lure'	Velvet, ſ.
Mure	A wall, ſ.
To mure	To incloſe in walls, v. a.
Con-tra-mure'	An out-wall built about the main wall, ſ.
De-mure'	Grave; affectedly modeſt, a.
To im-mure'	To incloſe, confine, ſhut in, v. a.
Coun-ter-mure'	A wall behind another wall, ſ.
Ma-nure'	Dung; ſoil to be laid on land, ſ.
To ma-nure'	To dung; to cultivate, v. a.
To in-ure'	To habituate; to bring into uſe, v. a.
Pure	Unſullied; chaſte; uncorrupt, a.
To de-pure'	To free from impurities, v. a.
Im-pure'	Unholy; unchaſte; droſſy, a.
Eq'ui-crure	Having legs of an equal length, a.
Sure	Certain; ſafe; firm, a.
Sure	Surely; certainly, ad.
Pleaſ'ure	Delight; gratification; choice, ſ.
To pleaſ'ure	To pleaſe; to gratify, v. a.
Diſ-pleaſ'ure	Uneaſineſs; offence; anger, ſ.
Meaſ'ure	That which gives quantity to any thing; cadence in verſe; time in muſic; degree; portion, ſ.
To meaſ'ure	To compute or allot quantity, v. a.
Meaſ'ure	Ways; means; actions; proceedings, ſ.
To out-meaſ'ure	To exceed in meaſure, v. a.
Treaſ'ure	Wealth hoarded or laid up, ſ.
To treaſ'ure	To hoard; to lay up, v. a.
To in-treaſ'ure	To lay up, v. a.
Ra'ſure	A ſcraping out of writing, &c. ſ.
In-ciſ'ure	A cut; an aperture, ſ.
Lei'ſure	Freedom from buſineſs, ſ.
Cock-ſure'	Confidently certain, a.
To en-ſure'	To aſcertain; to make certain; to ſecure, v. a.
Cen'ſure	Blame; judgment; reproach, ſ.
To cen'ſure	To blame; to condemn, v. a.
Ten'ſure	A ſtretching or being ſtretched, ſ.
Ton'ſure	A clipping or ſhaving of hair, ſ.
Un-ſure'	Not certain; not fixed, a.
Clo'ſure	An incloſure; end; concluſion, ſ.
En-clo'ſure	The act of encloſing; ground encloſed, ſ.
Diſ-clo'ſure	Diſcovery; a revealing of any ſecret, ſ.
Cy'no-ſure	The north ſtar, ſ.
Com-po'ſure	Order; form; frame; diſpoſition, ſ.

Diſ-

Ex coll. Karolyne & Bryan A. Garner

Note the unusual method for ordering entries according to terminal letters.

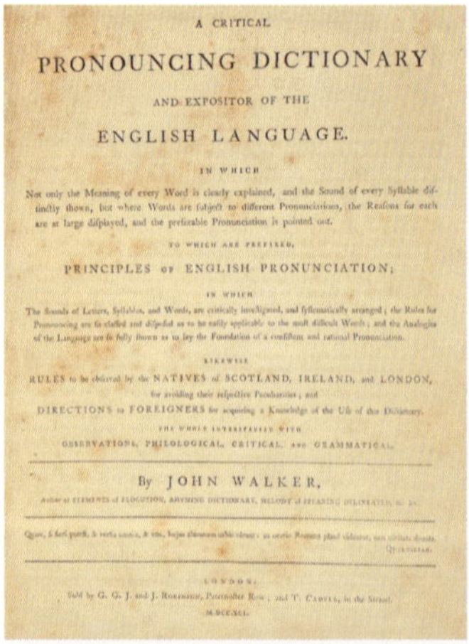
A CRITICAL
PRONOUNCING DICTIONARY
AND EXPOSITOR OF THE
ENGLISH LANGUAGE.
IN WHICH
Not only the Meaning of every Word is clearly explained, and the Sound of every Syllable distinctly shewn, but where Words are subject to different Pronunciations, the Reasons for each are at large displayed, and the preferable Pronunciation is pointed out.
TO WHICH ARE PREFIXED,
PRINCIPLES OF ENGLISH PRONUNCIATION;
IN WHICH
The Sounds of Letters, Syllables, and Words, are critically investigated, and systematically arranged; the Rules for Pronouncing are so classed and disposed as to be easily applicable to the most difficult Words; and the Analogies of the Language are so fully shewn as to lay the Foundation of a consistent and rational Pronunciation.
LIKEWISE
RULES to be observed by the NATIVES of SCOTLAND, IRELAND, and LONDON, for avoiding their respective Peculiarities; and
DIRECTIONS to FOREIGNERS for acquiring a Knowledge of the Use of this Dictionary.
THE WHOLE INTERSPERSED WITH
OBSERVATIONS, PHILOLOGICAL, CRITICAL, AND GRAMMATICAL.
By JOHN WALKER,
LONDON:
Sold by G. G. J. and J. Robinson, Paternoster Row; and T. Cadell, in the Strand.
M.DCC.XCI.

Ex coll. Karolyne & Bryan A. Garner

The 1791 title page.

Ex coll. Karolyne & Bryan A. Garner

An 1824 edition in painted vellum.

Of course, words with the same endings do not always rhyme—*tortoise*, *turquoise*, *despise*, for instance, or *busybody*, *melody*, *psalmody*, *threnody*—and rhyming words do not always share endings—*size*, *guise*, *buys*, *tries*, *sighs*. To solve these problems, Walker added a 45-page "Index of Perfect and Allowable Rhymes." This section is in (forward) alphabetical order by rhyming syllable—*eg*, *eld*, *elf*, *elk*, *ell*—with lists of rhyming words under each. The heading *ole*, for example, leads readers to *hole*, *pole*, *sole*, but also *coal*, *bowl*, and *droll*, described as "perfect rhymes," with near-misses—*gull*, *bull*, *doll*, *fool*—listed as "allowable rhymes." (Who decides what's "allowable"? Walker quotes prominent English poets, Alexander Pope above all, as authority for off-rhymes like *bourne/return* and *throne/begun*.) The index also provides cross-references for the inflectional endings that might appear at the ends of words, so that under *oise* we are directed to "the plurals of nouns and third persons singular present tense of verbs in *oy*, as *boys*, *cloys*, &c."

Walker was convinced that his reverse alphabetical order was "perfectly simple" and that even the least sophisticated reader would, after "two or three trials," find it "as intelligible as the common order." (P. xxiv.) Readers have disagreed. The running heads on successive pages reading *edy*, *udy*, *rey*, *ify*, *rfy*, *ogy*, *rgy*, and *phy* suggest just how disorienting reverse alphabetical order can be. But the *Dictionary of the English Language* and its descendants, often published under the title *Rhyming Dictionary*, proved phenomenally successful.

In 1791, Walker's *Critical Pronouncing Dictionary* (1791)—the more famous book that spawned many successor dictionaries in Britain and America—appeared. It had no peers in 18th-century lexicography for its treatment of the spoken word. Here reverting to common order, Walker undertook to show both the sound of every syllable and preferable pronunciations where two or more pronunciations were in current use. In the front matter, he laid out "rules to be observed by the natives" of Scotland and Ireland for avoiding their respective peculiarities. One innovation was a running header containing a key to understanding the vowel notations in the text. Walker was strongly prescriptive: "The accent of cultured London is 'undoubtedly the best.' Everyone else mispronounces, especially those who are 'at a considerable distance from the capital'—namely the Scots and Irish. Cockney, however, is 'a thousand times more offensive and disgusting' as these." (Crystal 2010:52.) One study has shown that when Walker conflicted with Sheridan (no. 50) on the pronunciation of a word, 80% of the time Walker's preference became "the modern pronunciation required by American dictionaries and taught in American schools." (Friend 1967:30.)

It was precisely Walker's clear-cut right/wrong treatment of pronunciation that made him so successful and influential. He was sometimes said to have settled all doubts about pronunciation. One writer, in *The Athenaeum*, called this dictionary "the statute book of English orthoepy." (*ODNB*.)

That's not to say that he had no detractors. One mid-19th-century pronunciation expert called Walker one of "those word-peddlars, those letter-drivers, those stiff-necked pedantic philosophical, miserably informed, and therefore supremely certain, self-confident and self-conceited orthographers." (Ellis 1869 1:155.)

Nevertheless, his later dictionary went through dozens of editions and was in print even in the early 20th century—not counting the many anonymous dictionaries that stole or adapted Walker's definitions without acknowledgment. Perhaps because of Lyman Cobb's adaptations of Walker in the United States (see no. 64), Noah Webster came to see Walker's success as a great evil being perpetrated on the American people. (See p. 234.) As influential as Webster could be, nobody much listened to him on this point.

"The work I have to offer on the subject . . . not only exhibits the principles of pronunciation, as others have done, divides the words into syllables, and marks the sounds of the vowels . . . , but where words are subject to different pronunciations, it shows the reasons from analogy for each; produces authorities for one side and the other, and points out the pronunciation which is preferable." (1791 preface, p. iv.)

Ex coll. Karolyne & Bryan A. Garner

Some later editions of Walker's *Critical Pronouncing Dictionary*.

Ex coll. Karolyne & Bryan A. Garner

Many editions were issued as "Johnson & Walker" dictionaries—like this 1830 Boston imprint.

Ex coll. Karolyne & Bryan A. Garner

"Besides the produce of our own attention and assiduity, we shall avail ourselves of the labours of others. Many ingenious and interesting articles are disseminated in the variety of Dictionaries already extant; with all these performances we shall endeavour to enrich this Work." (Preface.)

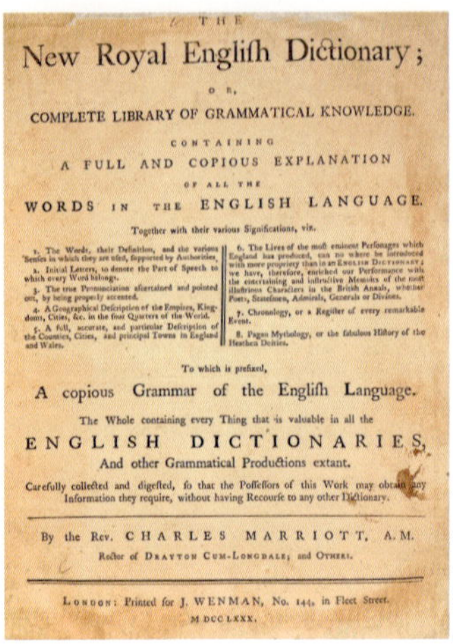
THE

New Royal Englifh Dictionary;

OR,

COMPLETE LIBRARY OF GRAMMATICAL KNOWLEDGE.

CONTAINING

A FULL AND COPIOUS EXPLANATION

OF ALL THE

WORDS IN THE ENGLISH LANGUAGE.

Together with their various Significations, viz.

1. The Words, their Definition, and the various Senfes in which they are ufed, fupported by Authorities.
2. Initial Letters, to denote the Part of Speech to which every Word belongs.
3. The true Pronunciation afcertained and pointed out, by being properly accented.
4. A Geographical Defcription of the Empires, Kingdoms, Cities, &c. in the four Quarters of the World.
5. A full, accurate, and particular Defcription of the Counties, Cities, and principal Towns in England and Wales.
6. The Lives of the moft eminent Perfonages which England has produced, can no where be introduced with more propriety than in an ENGLISH DICTIONARY; we have, therefore, enriched our Performance with the entertaining and inftructive Memoirs of the moft illuftrious Characters in the British Annals, whether Poets, Statefmen, Admirals, Generals or Divines.
7. Chronology, or a Regifter of every remarkable Event.
8. Pagan Mythology, or the fabulous Hiftory of the Heathen Deities.

To which is prefixed,

A copious Grammar of the Englifh Language.

The Whole containing every Thing that is valuable in all the

ENGLISH DICTIONARIES,

And other Grammatical Productions extant.

Carefully collected and digefted, fo that the Poffeffors of this Work may obtain any Information they require, without having Recourfe to any other Dictionary.

By the Rev. CHARLES MARRIOTT, A.M.

Rector of DRAYTON CUM-LONGDALE; and OTHERS.

LONDON: Printed for J. WENMAN, No. 144, in Fleet Street.

MDCCLXXX.

Ex coll. Karolyne & Bryan A. Garner

48

Charles Marriott

Palliating Readers' Ignorance

Marriott, Charles. *The New Royal English Dictionary; or, Complete Library of Grammatical Knowledge Containing a Full and Copious Explanation of All the Words in the English Language*. 2 vols. London: J. Wenman, 1780.

The Reverend Charles Marriott, MA, was rector of Drayton Cum-Longdale, in Norfolk, when this big two-volume dictionary was published. Little else is known about the lexicographer except what he disclosed in his preface, which begins by asserting his bias against those lacking grammatical knowledge: "To be ignorant of our mother tongue is not only a misfortune, but a disgrace; especially as Grammar is a branch of learning now more cultivated in England than in any other part of the globe; those persons, therefore, who speak or write with impropriety, are even without an excuse to palliate their ignorance."

In the second paragraph, he praises Johnson without naming him: "To one eminent writer we are much indebted, for the ingenious and laborious task he has undertaken and performed, for the benefit of the natives of his kingdom, and foreigners of all denominations." But then he immediately faults the existing Johnson dictionaries: "His folio Dictionary is a very valuable performance; but Four Pounds Ten Shillings (the price of that book) cannot be afforded by every one; and his abridgment in octavo, is too much an abridgment to be satisfactory, and of general use."

The same deficiencies, he says, infect "every Dictionary hitherto published" because each one "is either a large folio which costs several pounds, or a small volume in octavo, of the price of six or twelve shillings." Since folios are too big and octavos too small, *The New Royal English Dictionary* is a pair of quartos. For their day, the entries had some genuine merits. This *New Royal English Dictionary* is an adaptation of Barlow's *Complete English Dictionary* (no. 42), but whereas Barlow copied most of his definitions verbatim, Marriott often revises them for clarity and accuracy. Consider the verb *attire*, which Johnson defined as "to dress; to habit; to array." Marriott's definition is "to adorn with cloaths or dress. Figuratively, to embellish or adorn." Marriott's is the superior entry. The same is true with the noun *attire*, at least with the main definition. Johnson: "clothes; dress; habit." Marriott: "cloaths or dress to adorn or embellish a person." But whereas Johnson helpfully has three separately numbered senses (clothing, hunting, and botany), Marriott combines the meanings (in the same order) without separating the senses—just using separate sentences. Yet he corrects a mistaken form in Johnson, who erroneously uses the term **semiform attire*, which should be *seminiform attire* (referring to seed-bearing parts of a plant). This error occurred in all the editions that appeared in Johnson's lifetime and long after. Worse yet, Johnson had no entry for *semiform* or *seminiform*. Then again, neither did Marriott.

"This work will be extensive and copious; and, though less expensive than the folios on the same subject, it will contain five times the quantity of any octavo Dictionary in one volume." (Preface.)

But much to his credit, Marriott elaborated his own definition and corrected a technical term incorrectly rendered in Johnson. Marriott was no servile copyist—as can be seen throughout his *New Royal English Dictionary*.

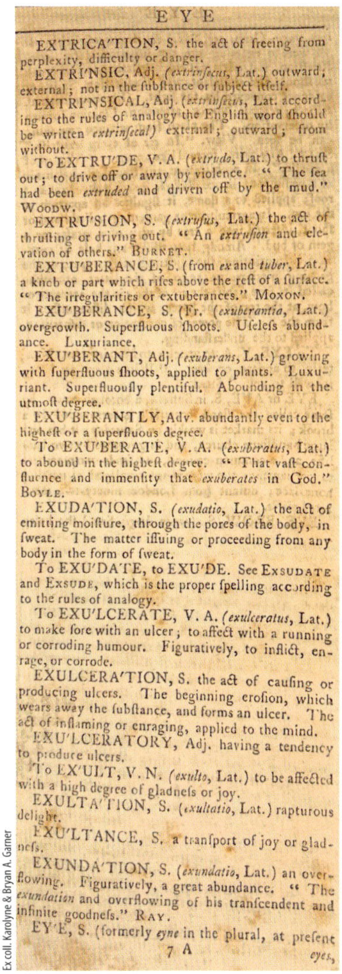

E Y E

EXTRICA'TION, S. the act of freeing from perplexity, difficulty or danger.

EXTRI'NSIC, Adj. (*extrinfecus*, Lat.) outward; external; not in the fubftance or fubject itfelf.

EXTRI'NSICAL, Adj. (*extrinfecus*, Lat. according to the rules of analogy the Englifh word fhould be written *extrinfecal)* external; outward; from without.

To EXTRU'DE, V. A. (*extrudo*, Lat.) to thruft out; to drive off or away by violence. "The fea had been *extruded* and driven off by the mud." Woodw.

EXTRU'SION, S. (*extrufus*, Lat.) the act of thrufting or driving out. "An *extrufion* and elevation of others." Burnet.

EXTU'BERANCE, S. (from *ex* and *tuber*, Lat.) a knob or part which rifes above the reft of a furface. "The irregularities or extuberances." Moxon.

EXU'BERANCE, S. (Fr. (*exuberantia*, Lat.) overgrowth. Superfluous fhoots. Ufelefs abundance. Luxuriance.

EXU'BERANT, Adj. (*exuberans*, Lat.) growing with fuperfluous fhoots, applied to plants. Luxuriant. Superfluoufly plentiful. Abounding in the utmoft degree.

EXU'BERANTLY, Adv. abundantly even to the higheft or a fuperfluous degree.

To EXU'BERATE, V. A. (*exuberatus*, Lat.) to abound in the higheft degree. "That vaft confluence and immenfity that *exuberates* in God." Boyle.

EXUDA'TION, S. (*exudatio*, Lat.) the act of emitting moifture, through the pores of the body, in fweat. The matter iffuing or proceeding from any body in the form of fweat.

To EXU'DATE, to EXU'DE. See Exsudate and Exsude, which is the proper fpelling according to the rules of analogy.

To EXU'LCERATE, V. A. (*exulceratus*, Lat.) to make fore with an ulcer; to affect with a running or corroding humour. Figuratively, to inflict, enrage, or corrode.

EXULCERA'TION, S. the act of caufing or producing ulcers. The beginning erofion, which wears away the fubftance, and forms an ulcer. The act of inflaming or enraging, applied to the mind.

EXU'LCERATORY, Adj. having a tendency to produce ulcers.

To EX'ULT, V. N. (*exulto*, Lat.) to be affected with a high degree of gladnefs or joy.

EXULTA'TION, S. (*exultatio*, Lat.) rapturous delight.

EXU'LTANCE, S. a tranfport of joy or gladnefs.

EXUNDA'TION, S. (*exundatio*, Lat.) an overflowing. Figuratively, a great abundance. "The *exundation* and overflowing of his tranfcendent and infinite goodnefs." Ray.

EY'E, S. (formerly *eyne* in the plural, at prefent

7 A *eyes*,

One weakness in Marriott suggests that his work is a throwback to Cocker (no. 22) and other quasi-encyclopedists: he included many elements that were extraneous to his word definitions. Just as the world was coming to understand a fundamental difference between dictionaries and encyclopedias, he tried to make his dictionary do much more than define words and phrases. His explanation for this practice suggests the extent of his overinclusiveness: "This work will also comprehend the Biography, or lives of the most celebrated persons who have flourished in these kingdoms; and a geographical description of the world; including a particular account of the counties, cities, and principal towns of England and Wales." Yet he didn't stop there. He combined these discussions with a "chronology of the world, or a complete register of every remarkable event; and the whole of heathen mythology." Interspersing these elements was doubtless a misjudgment, especially given the length accorded to them. If he had spent more time just on vocabulary, his strong suit, he might have found a much more receptive readership.

Instead, the book's genuine merits went unrecognized, and the book never saw a second edition. Marriott didn't really discover the commercial lacuna he had hoped to fill, and he himself never achieved enough fame to earn a biographical note in any of the usual places.

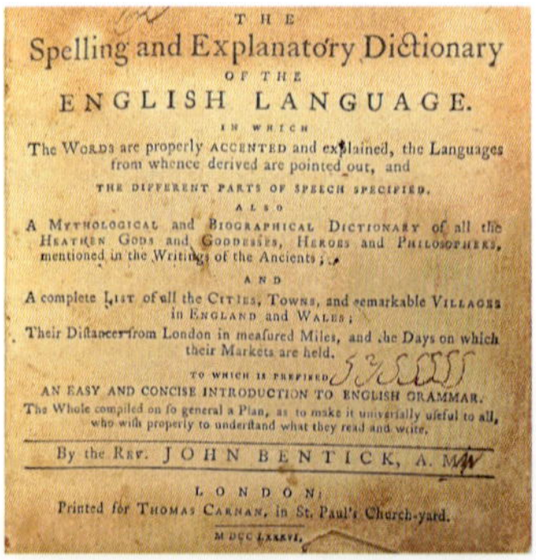
THE
Spelling and Explanatory Dictionary
OF THE
ENGLISH LANGUAGE.
IN WHICH
The WORDS are properly ACCENTED and explained, the Languages from whence derived are pointed out, and
THE DIFFERENT PARTS OF SPEECH SPECIFIED.
ALSO
A MYTHOLOGICAL and BIOGRAPHICAL DICTIONARY of all the HEATHEN GODS and GODDESSES, HEROES and PHILOSOPHERS, mentioned in the Writings of the Ancients;
AND
A complete LIST of all the CITIES, TOWNS, and remarkable VILLAGES in ENGLAND and WALES;
Their Distances from London in measured Miles, and the Days on which their Markets are held.
TO WHICH IS PREFIXED,
AN EASY AND CONCISE INTRODUCTION TO ENGLISH GRAMMAR.
The Whole compiled on so general a Plan, as to make it universally useful to all, who wish properly to understand what they read and write.
By the REV. JOHN BENTICK, A. M.
LONDON:
Printed for THOMAS CARNAN, in St. Paul's Church-yard.
MDCCLXXXVI.

Ex coll. Karolyne & Bryan A. Garner

Ex coll. Karolyne & Bryan A. Garner

Ex coll. Karolyne & Bryan A. Garner

Inscription by future King of England.

49

John Bentick
An Apparition?

Bentick, John. *The Spelling and Explanatory Dictionary of the English Language*. London: Printed for Thomas Carnan, 1786.

WAS THE REV. JOHN BENTICK a real person, or was he the fictitious invention of his publisher, John Newbery's stepson named Thomas Carnan, who was canny in publishing and marketing small dictionaries? Perhaps Carnan hoped to confuse the public with a book having the look and feel of John Entick's *New Spelling Dictionary*. We might never know. Despite the close similarities, Bentick's typesetting is distinct, the definitions are even more truncated, and the grammar in the front matter is different. The only hint in Alston's bibliography questioning authorial authenticity occurs in the index: "BENTICK, John. [Fictitious?]"

The preface strongly echoes Entick in declaring that existing dictionaries tended to be either overlong or laconic: "I have had many Opportunities of observing, from actual Practice, wherein consisted the Defects of those Dictionaries, which were professedly compiled for the Use of Schools and young People in general. Some of them were too concise, and very defective in their Explanations of Words; while others rested their principal Merit on the Number of Pages they contained, though a great Part of them consisted in obsolete and useless words." (P. iii.)

Neither Carnan nor Bentick, if he existed, could have been overjoyed with sales: the book saw only the one edition. The print run was probably small, given how few copies are known to exist today.

In the Garner Collection copy of Bentick, the front pastedown is inscribed by the future King William IV: "G.M. Ragland from H.R.H. the Duke of Clarence [on] board the *Valiant* 1790." He had been made Duke of Clarence in 1789, and in 1790 he was put in command of the Valiant, a warship with 74 guns. William would become king in 1830. A few letters in the inscription are obscured by traces of sealing wax.

50

Thomas Sheridan
The Playwright's Father

Sheridan, Thomas. *A General Dictionary of the English Language*. 2 vols. London: J. Dodsley et al., 1780. 2d ed. 1784. 3d ed. 1789.

Thomas Sheridan (1719?–1788) came from an eminently lettered Irish family. His father, also Thomas, was a cleric, a grammarian, and one of Jonathan Swift's close friends; his wife, Frances, was a successful novelist and playwright; his son, Richard Brinsley Sheridan, was late-18th-century Britain's greatest playwright.

He began studying at London's Westminster School starting in 1733, but the family's financial troubles brought him back to Ireland. With the aid of a scholarship, he went on to Trinity College, Dublin, in 1735. After he completed his MA, he followed his passion to the stage, debuting as Richard III at Dublin's Smock Alley Theatre in 1743 and eventually becoming a manager of the Theatre Royal. He quickly became the most popular actor on the Irish stage, and he took that fame with him when he began performing in London.

"While the ingenious natives of other countries in Europe, particularly the Italians, French, and Spaniards, in proportion to their progress in civilization and politeness, have, for more than a century, been employed, with utmost industry, in cultivating and regulating their speech; we still remain in the state of all barbarous countries in that respect, having left our's [sic] wholly to chance." (Preface.)

He supplemented the theatrical income with two other kinds of employment. One was as a teacher of elocution, teaching "proper" pronunciation to people whose accents marked them as outsiders. Sheridan, an Irishman, was himself an outsider, and yet he guided his fellow Irishmen, Scots, the Welsh, and those from the English provinces toward a perfect English accent. Among his protégés in the early 1760s was James Boswell, a Scot eager to appear to advantage in English society.

Sheridan's other employment was as a writer on education. In 1756, he published *British Education*, and he followed it with *A Dissertation on the Causes of the Difficulties Which Occur in Learning the English Tongue* (1761), *A Course of Lectures on Elocution* (1762), *A Plan of Education for the Young Nobility and Gentry of Great Britain* (1769), and *Lectures on the Art of Reading* (1775). His *General Dictionary* marks

Ex coll. Karolyne & Bryan A. Garner

The first edition spine label (1780).

a culmination of his labors, both as an educator and as an authority on the language.

We may think definitions are the essential business of most dictionaries, but Sheridan seems to have given them almost no thought: he simply lifted nearly all of them from Johnson. Sheridan, for instance, defines *sack* as "A bag, a pouch, commonly a large bag; the measure of three bushels; a woman's loose robe." Compare Johnson's definitions for *sack*:

> 1. A bag; a pouch; commonly a large bag.
> 2. The measure of three bushels.
> 3. A woman's loose robe.

As Sheridan acknowledged, "In the explanatory part he has chiefly followed Dr. Johnson; only sometimes making use of plainer words."

There's no evidence that Johnson was offended. The two men were once close. Boswell tells us that Sheridan raved about "Johnson's extraordinary knowledge, talents, and virtues," and "boast[ed] of his being his guest sometimes till two or three in the morning." He worked to secure Johnson a government pension in 1762. By the end of that year, though, when both men were on the pension list, "an irreconcileable difference had taken place" between them. Johnson, who "thought slightingly of Sheridan's art," ungenerously quipped in company: "What! have they given *him* a pension? Then it is time for me to give up mine." (He followed it by saying, "However, I am glad that Mr. Sheridan has a pension, for he is a very good man.") The sarcasm, but not the takeback, reached Sheridan, who "could never forgive this hasty contemptuous expression." Johnson made no effort to patch things up, saying, "Why, Sir, Sherry is dull, naturally dull; but it must have taken him a great deal of pains to become what we now see him. Such an excess of stupidity, Sir, is not in Nature." (Boswell 1791 1:385–87, 453; 2:258.) Despite the falling-out, though, Sheridan recognized the superiority of Johnson's definitions.

Sheridan's passion was not definition but pronunciation, and he made much of orthoepy—proper pronunciation. This is an especially tricky matter in English-language lexicography because the connections between our spellings and our pronunciations are notoriously oblique. Anyone familiar with the alphabet can pronounce nearly every Italian or Spanish word correctly, but English is famously counterintuitive, partly because it has adopted words from many sources,

"When a foreigner arrives in London, and, as the first necessary point, enquires for a master to teach him the language, to his utter astonishment he is told, that there are none to be found." (Preface.)

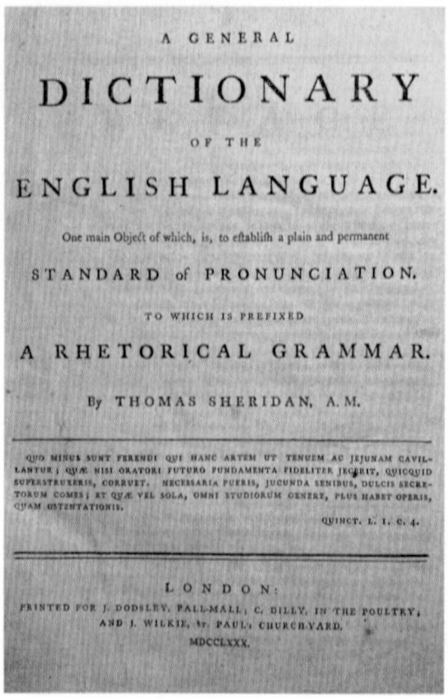

A GENERAL

DICTIONARY

OF THE

ENGLISH LANGUAGE.

One main Object of which, is, to establish a plain and permanent

STANDARD of PRONUNCIATION.

TO WHICH IS PREFIXED

A RHETORICAL GRAMMAR.

By THOMAS SHERIDAN, A.M.

QUO MINUS SUNT FERENDI QUI HANC ARTEM UT TENUEM AC JEJUNAM CAVILLANTUR; QUÆ NISI ORATORI FUTURO FUNDAMENTA FIDELITER JECERIT, QUICQUID SUPERSTRUXERIS, CORRUET. NECESSARIA PUERIS, JUCUNDA SENIBUS, DULCIS SECRETORUM COMES; ET QUÆ VEL SOLA, OMNI STUDIORUM GENERE, PLUS HABET OPERIS, QUAM OSTENTATIONIS.

QUINCT. L. I. C. 4.

LONDON:

PRINTED FOR J. DODSLEY, PALL-MALL; C. DILLY, IN THE POULTRY, AND J. WILKIE, ST. PAUL'S CHURCH-YARD.

MDCCLXXX.

Ex coll. Karolyne & Bryan A. Garner

"Out of our numerous army of authors, very few can be selected who write with accuracy." (Preface.)

each with its own rules (the *ch* in the Germanic *cheese* has a different sound from the *ch* in the French *chivalry*, which is in turn different from the *ch* in the Greek *chaos*), and partly because English spelling began to settle down while the sound system was still changing rapidly in the 15th century. Learners are confronted by a riot of doubled letters, silent letters, single letters standing for several sounds, and single sounds represented by several letters. What is a newcomer to the language to make of *though*, *tough*, and *through*, or *laughter* and *slaughter*, or *meat* and *great*, or *bead* and *dead*?—to say nothing of words like *colonel*, *Wednesday*, *indict*, and *yacht*.

In his dictionary, Sheridan acknowledged, "Of all the languages known in the world, the English is supposed to be the most difficult; and foreigners in general look upon it as impracticable to arrive at any degree of perfection." But he was convinced that the simplicity of its grammar—and some English writers went so far as to say that English has no grammar at all—should make it "the most easy of attainment of any other." (Sig. a1^{r}.) The key was to devise a system that would make proper pronunciations visible to everyone.

That raises several questions, starting with: *whose* pronunciation? Accents vary with geography and social class, and who's to say which one is proper? Sheridan decided that he was the one. For him, the best accent was that of the royal court in and around London, "the source of fashions of all kinds. All other dialects, are sure marks, either of provincial, rustic, pedantic, or mechanic education; and therefore have some degree of disgrace annexed to them." (Sheridan 1762:30.) He wasn't always successful. As Noah Webster pointed out in 1828, Sheridan "gives to *s* the sound of *sh*, in *sudorific*, *superb*, and other words where *s* is followed by *u* long. These he pronounces *shooderific*, *shooperb*, *shooperfluity*, &c. This pronunciation of *s* corresponding to the Shemitic ש, he probably learnt in Ireland." But upper-class London English was the goal.

Even within any given accent, there is always room for variation. In his *Plan of a Dictionary* (no. 32), Johnson wrote, "Some words have two sounds, which may be equally admitted, as being equally defensible by authority." In the 18th century, for example, *contrary* could be accented on the first syllable or the second; *great* could rhyme with either *hate* or *seat*, and *leisure* could rhyme with either *pleasure* or *seizure*. But Sheridan tolerated no variety: each word got one and only one pronunciation.

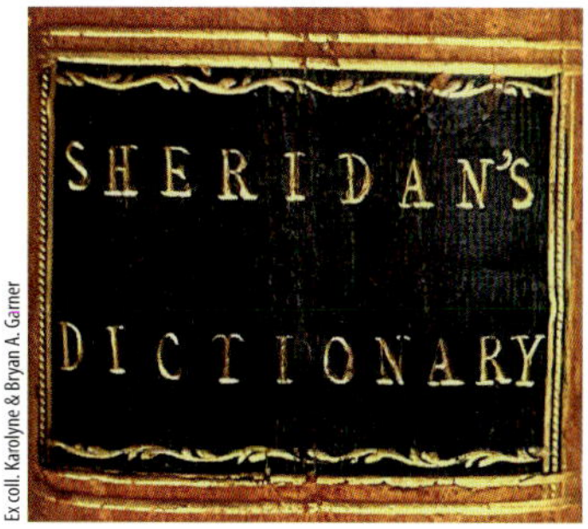

Ex coll. Karolyne & Bryan A. Garner

The second edition spine label (1784).

"Low as the state of the written language is, that of the spoken is infinitely worse; with regard to which, nothing has been done, even to render a right pronunciation of words attainable. And with respect to every other point, we are so far from having any way opened for teaching a just and graceful delivery, that even from our learning the first elements of speech, we are so wholly perverted by false rules, and afterwards corrupted by bad habits, that there is scarce a possibility of arriving at any degree of perfection in the most useful and pleasing art that can adorn and dignify human nature." (Preface.)

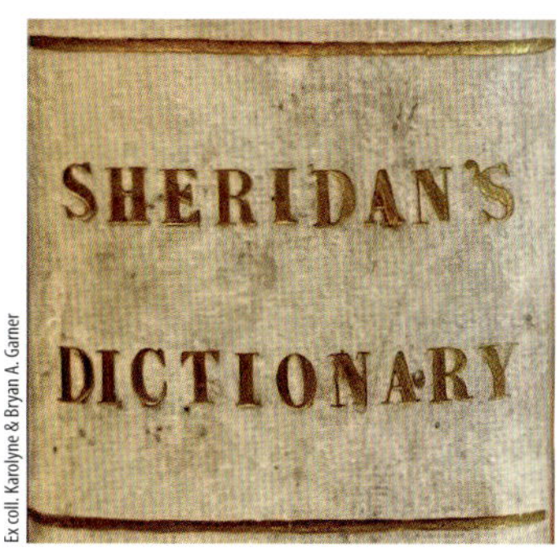

Ex coll. Karolyne & Bryan A. Garner

The third edition spine label (1789).

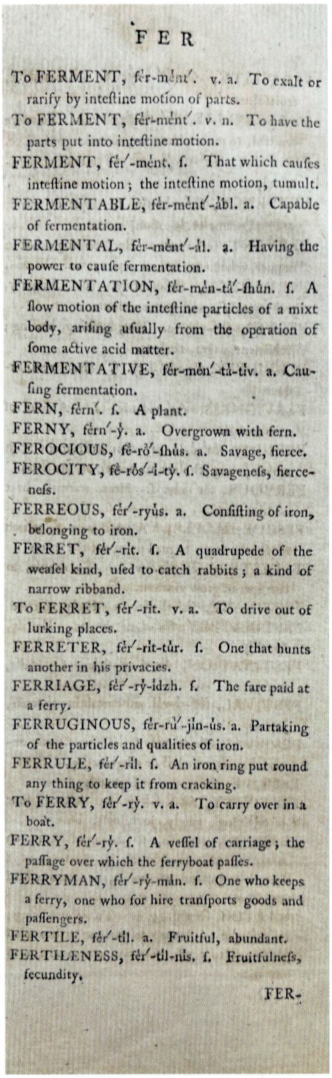

FER

To FERMENT, fer-ment′. v. a. To exalt or rarify by inteſtine motion of parts.

To FERMENT, fer-ment′. v. n. To have the parts put into inteſtine motion.

FERMENT, fer′-ment. ſ. That which cauſes inteſtine motion; the inteſtine motion, tumult.

FERMENTABLE, fer-ment′-abl. a. Capable of fermentation.

FERMENTAL, fer-ment′-al. a. Having the power to cauſe fermentation.

FERMENTATION, fer-men-ta′-ſhun. ſ. A ſlow motion of the inteſtine particles of a mixt body, ariſing uſually from the operation of ſome active acid matter.

FERMENTATIVE, fer-men′-ta-tiv. a. Cauſing fermentation.

FERN, fern′. ſ. A plant.

FERNY, fern′-y. a. Overgrown with fern.

FEROCIOUS, fe-ro′-ſhus. a. Savage, fierce.

FEROCITY, fe-ros′-i-ty. ſ. Savageneſs, fierceneſs.

FERREOUS, fer′-ryus. a. Conſiſting of iron, belonging to iron.

FERRET, fer′-rit. ſ. A quadrupede of the weaſel kind, uſed to catch rabbits; a kind of narrow ribband.

To FERRET, fer′-rit. v. a. To drive out of lurking places.

FERRETER, fer′-rit-tur. ſ. One that hunts another in his privacies.

FERRIAGE, fer′-ry-idzh. ſ. The fare paid at a ferry.

FERRUGINOUS, fer-ru′-jin-us. a. Partaking of the particles and qualities of iron.

FERRULE, fer′-ril. ſ. An iron ring put round any thing to keep it from cracking.

To FERRY, fer′-ry. v. a. To carry over in a boat.

FERRY, fer′-ry. ſ. A veſſel of carriage; the paſſage over which the ferryboat paſſes.

FERRYMAN, fer′-ry-man. ſ. One who keeps a ferry, one who for hire tranſports goods and paſſengers.

FERTILE, fer′-til. a. Fruitful, abundant.

FERTILENESS, fer′-til-nis. ſ. Fruitfulneſs, fecundity.

FER-

Ex coll. Karolyne & Bryan A. Garner

That leads to a second urgent question: how to capture the spoken word on the page. The International Phonetic Alphabet didn't appear until the end of the 19th century. Earlier writers had tried to record pronunciations, but the first to have any significant success was Thomas Dyche, a schoolmaster who used an acute mark (´) to indicate the primary stress in polysyllabic words. (Sheldon 1946; Pouillon 2018.) Nathan Bailey adopted this system in a general-purpose dictionary in the second volume of his *Orthographical Dictionary* (1727)—MOMENTA´NEOUS, MO´MENTARY, MO´NARCH, MONA´RCHICAL—and employed it throughout the 1730 edition of the *Dictionarium Britannicum*. That set the standard for orthoepic information in dictionaries for a generation: uppercase headwords, with an acute accent after the vowel in the stressed syllable.

Sheridan introduced some changes to this system. He put the information about pronunciation not in the headword but immediately after it, which allowed him to address instances in which spelling and pronunciation had diverged more than usual: ("HONOUR, on´-nur"; "PHTHISICK, tiz´-zik"; "CHIRURGEON, sur´-jun"). He extended the Dyche–Bailey system by indicating both primary and secondary stresses in long words: *overrate* is o´-vur-ra″t. He also placed the accent at the end of the relevant syllable, not immediately after the vowel. With his help, we can see that some words have shifted their stressed syllables over the centuries: *balcony* was bal-ko´-ny, *incognito* was in-kog´-ny-to, and *lamentable* was lam´-men-tabl.

English pronunciation is more than just accented syllables, and so Sheridan developed a system for indicating vowel quality. He recognized three different sounds for each vowel, and assigned them numbers from 1 to 3:

Scheme of the Vowels.

	First.	Second.	Third.
a	h$\overset{1}{a}$t	h$\overset{2}{a}$te	h$\overset{3}{a}$ll
e	b$\overset{1}{e}$t	b$\overset{2}{e}$ar	b$\overset{3}{e}$er
i	f$\overset{1}{i}$t	f$\overset{2}{i}$ght	f$\overset{3}{i}$eld
o	n$\overset{1}{o}$t	n$\overset{2}{o}$te	n$\overset{3}{o}$ose
u	b$\overset{1}{u}$t	b$\overset{2}{u}$sh	bl$\overset{3}{u}$e
y	love-l$\overset{1}{y}$	l$\overset{2}{y}$e.	

Each vowel was then printed in the pronunciations with the appropriate number in superscript above the vowel: $\overset{1}{\text{a}}$ for the phoneme that linguists now identify as /æ/, $\overset{3}{\text{e}}$ for /i/. It's not a complete set of English vowel sounds, but no lexicographer had done better.

Sheridan also thought about the consonants. He recognized that some English letters correspond to multiple phonemes and can change their character depending on whether they are voiced or voiceless, so he usually renders English *x* as either *ks* ("EXCEPT, ek-sept´") or *gz* ("EXACT, egz-akt´"). He recognized that the digraph *ch* (as in *chap*) was not a single phoneme but /tʃ/, which he transcribed as *tsh*, and English *j* is usually transcribed as *dzh*. He did not, however, create any new symbols for consonants, which left some ambiguity in the system. He used *th*, for instance, to represent both the voiced and unvoiced sounds, as in "THEY, the´" and "THICK, thik´." He used the digraph *sh* for the single phoneme /ʃ/.

Sheridan's late years were melancholy. He had few friends. He had never been particularly kind or supportive to his children, and by this time his relationship with his famous son had soured. Having taken over as manager of Drury Lane Theatre, Richard Brinsley Sheridan made it clear that he did not invite his father's involvement, despite his years of experience. Worse still, when at last Richard relented and invited him to work as manager, it was on condition (as Thomas wrote to his other son) that he wouldn't appear as a performer. To complicate matters, Thomas's health was declining. In 1788, his daughter Elizabeth set out with him on a trip from Dublin to Portugal to help him regain his health, but he died en route. (Realizing that the end was near, Richard traveled to be with his father in his final hours.) Because money was tight, he left instructions that he was to be buried "in as private and cheap a manner as possible."

His dictionary outlived him, but not by much. It went through several editions in London, Dublin, and Philadelphia, but its afterlife was not long. That's because it was an essential influence on the next major orthoepist-cum-lexicographer, John Walker, whose *Critical Pronouncing Dictionary* (no. 47) effectively rendered Sheridan's work obsolete. But as the first English lexicographer to take pronunciation seriously, he deserves a place in the history of English dictionaries.

"It must be obvious, that in order to spread abroad the English language as a living tongue, and to facilitate the attainment of its speech, it is necessary in the first place that a standard of pronunciation should be established." (Preface.)

Ex coll. Karolyne & Bryan A. Garner

Thomas's son, Richard Brinsley Sheridan (1751–1816), the celebrated playwright.

"Dr. Johnson's spelling has been implicitly followed in the present Dictionary. It scarce deviates from that used by the writers in Queen Anne's reign; as he has judiciously rejected several innovations attempted since that time by vain and pragmatical writers, who, from an affectation of singularity, have attempted to introduce changes, upon principles which will by no means stand the test of examination." (Preface.)

Ex coll. Karolyne & Bryan A. Garner

51

Heſter Piozzi
Supplying a Need Left by Her Late Friend

Piozzi, Heſter Lynch. *British Synonymy; or, An Attempt at Regulating the Choice of Words in Familiar Conversation.* 2 vols. London: G.G. & J. Robinson, 1794.

THOUGH SHE WAS BORN Hester Lynch Salisbury and published as Hester Piozzi, she is best known to history as Hester Thrale (1741–1821), probably Samuel Johnson's closest friend. Her proximity to one of the great men of English letters has been both a help and a hindrance to Piozzi's reputation. It has guaranteed a steady stream of readers for more than two centuries, but it has also relegated her to a supporting role, interesting only for the light she sheds on her more famous friend. But while she never completed anything with the impact of Johnson's *Dictionary* (who else besides Noah Webster did?), she was a lexicographic pioneer in her own right.

Piozzi's *British Synonymy* responded to a real need. Commentators in the 1590s worried that the English language lacked the richness of vocabulary that marked Greek, Latin, and the languages of modern Europe. They publicly fretted that English wasn't ready to assume its place in the republic of letters. By the 1790s, though, the attitude had changed: now the challenge was dealing with the sheer abundance of the English vocabulary.

English, for instance, has *freedom*, *liberty*, *independence*, and *unrestraint*—how was one to choose among them? Are *malice*, *maliciousness*, and *malignity* interchangeable? What about *elect*, *select*, and *choose*? A few English works had addressed questions like these before, including John Trusler's *Difference, between Words, Esteemed Synonymous, in the English Language* (1766), but none was really satisfactory.

In spring 1792, therefore, Piozzi recorded in her diary that she was at work on "a two Volume Book of *Synonymes* in English, like what the Abbé Girard has done in French"—that is, Abbé Gabriel Girard's *Justesse de la langue françoise* (1718). Her English work, she joked, would be useful for "Foreigners, and other Children of six feet high," because she knew that nonnative speakers of English had the greatest difficulty in distinguishing the subtle differences among words. Piozzi was exceptionally attentive to their needs, especially after her marriage to an Italian music master, Gabriel Piozzi, in 1784.

British Synonymy is not a long list in the mode of the usual thesaurus. Instead, Piozzi gives a series of mini-essays, each a few pages long, exploring the shades of meaning in clusters of similar words. English, for instance, has *loud*, *noisy*, *clamorous*, *turbulent*, *stormy*, *vehement*, and *blustering*, all of which share meanings. She explains, therefore, that "Natives of England know instinctively, but foreigners must be informed, that these attributives have most effect being appropriated some to things and some to persons: we cannot for example call the weather CLAMOROUS, let tempests rage never so high . . . ." (1:385.) Elsewhere we learn that *defy* and *challenge* "are synonyms when applied to a single combat . . . but the first verb is vastly more comprehensive than the second." A man might be "PERTINACIOUS in attack, OBSTINATE in defence of his argument; and . . . FIXED in belief." In another section she sorted through her age's vocabulary for mental illness: "I think LUNACY seems to be the legal term, INSANITY, and sometimes MELANCHOLY, the medical ones; while PHRENZY, MADNESS and DISTRACTION are the poetical expressions of what we call MENTAL DERANGEMENT."

Naturally, Piozzi made good use of Johnson, whose name she mentioned more than four dozen times, but she seemed more concerned with keeping her distance from her friend's work. She often cited Johnson's definitions only to disagree with them, qualify them, or show how they might be clearer, thereby declaring her independence from the lexicographer who had been her close companion for decades. And when the book reviews maliciously hinted that she was secretly recycling materials left unpublished by Johnson, she was badly stung. Those reviewers, she wrote to her daughter, "do me much wrong in supposing I had any Fragments of his upon Synonymy to consult—the Public has been denied nothing written by him which I possess'd, & I never had a Moment's Talk with him on the Subject."

Piozzi does not offer Johnson's comprehensive survey of the English language (no. 35), Crabb's systematic rigor (no. 60), or Roget's vast taxonomy of the English vocabulary (no. 76). But whereas Johnson reels off multiple meanings for most words and Roget dumps a list of synonyms on readers and leaves them to pick one without

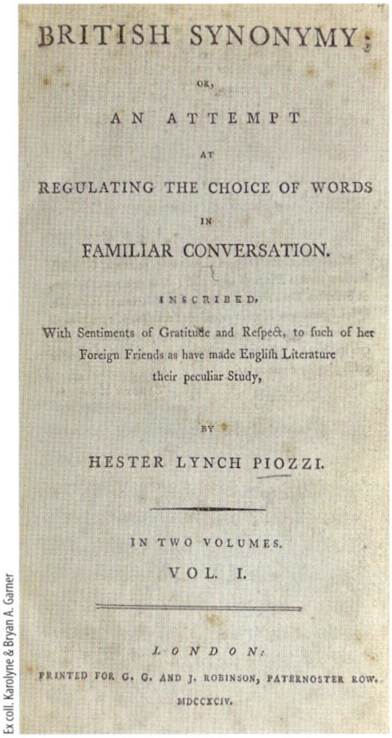

BRITISH SYNONYMY;
OR,
AN ATTEMPT
AT
REGULATING THE CHOICE OF WORDS
IN
FAMILIAR CONVERSATION.
INSCRIBED,
With Sentiments of Gratitude and Respect, to such of her Foreign Friends as have made English Literature their peculiar Study,
BY
HESTER LYNCH PIOZZI.
IN TWO VOLUMES.
VOL. I.
LONDON:
PRINTED FOR G. G. AND J. ROBINSON, PATERNOSTER ROW.
MDCCXCIV.

Ex coll. Karolyne & Bryan A. Garner

Ex coll. Karolyne & Bryan A. Garner

Ex coll. Loren & Frances Rothschild

"While men teach to write with propriety, a woman may at worst be qualified—through long practice—to direct the choice of phrases in familiar talk." (Preface.)

guidance, Piozzi patiently explicates exactly how words were or should be (in her view) used in conversation. Sometimes she notes that one word is used of a person and another of a situation; sometimes she advises readers that one word is formal and another casual; sometimes she suggests that near-synonyms differ in degree, or that one is a subset of another. The book is therefore valuable for the sociolinguistic insights it gives us, and her explanations of usage are far more detailed than anything that had appeared in conventional dictionaries.

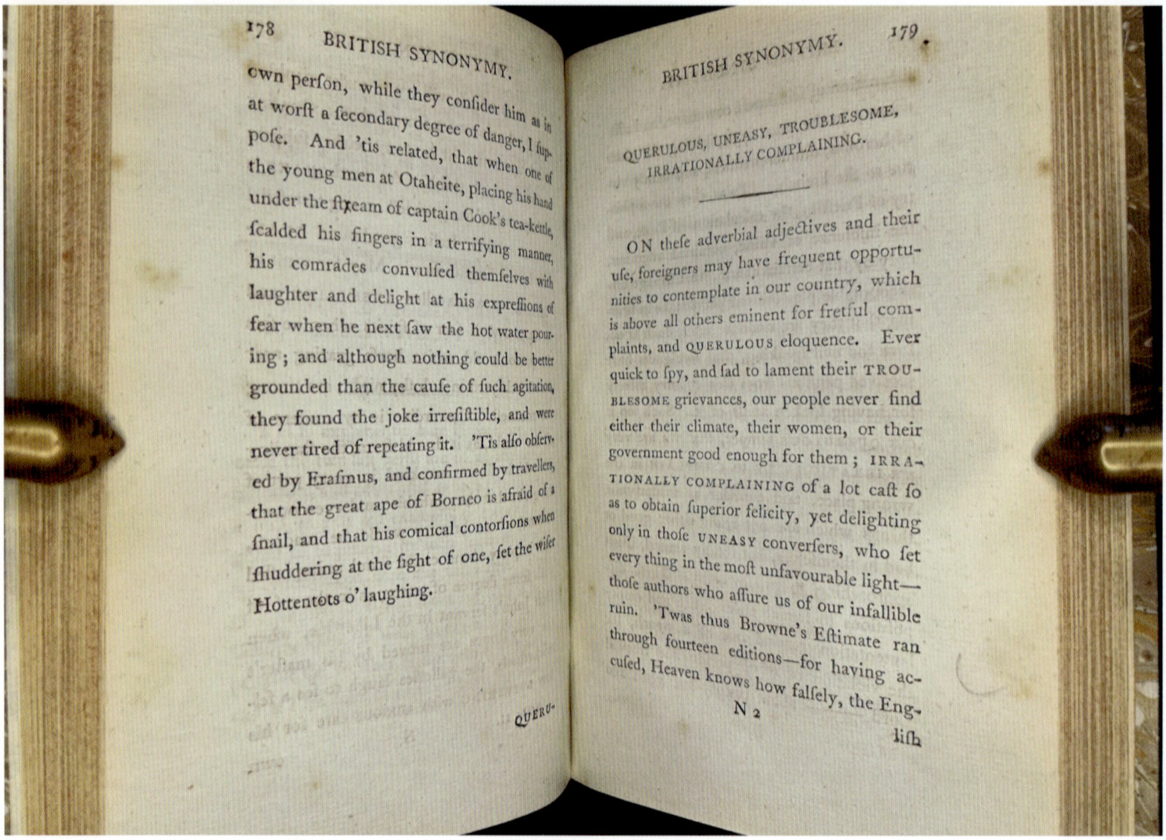

178 BRITISH SYNONYMY.

own perſon, while they conſider him as in at worſt a ſecondary degree of danger, I ſuppoſe. And 'tis related, that when one of the young men at Otaheite, placing his hand under the ſtream of captain Cook's tea-kettle, ſcalded his fingers in a terrifying manner, his comrades convulſed themſelves with laughter and delight at his expreſſions of fear when he next ſaw the hot water pouring; and although nothing could be better grounded than the cauſe of ſuch agitation, they found the joke irreſiſtible, and were never tired of repeating it. 'Tis alſo obſerved by Eraſmus, and confirmed by travellers, that the great ape of Borneo is afraid of a ſnail, and that his comical contorſions when ſhuddering at the ſight of one, ſet the wiſer Hottentots o' laughing.

QUERU-

BRITISH SYNONYMY. 179

QUERULOUS, UNEASY, TROUBLESOME, IRRATIONALLY COMPLAINING.

ON theſe adverbial adjectives and their uſe, foreigners may have frequent opportunities to contemplate in our country, which is above all others eminent for fretful complaints, and QUERULOUS eloquence. Ever quick to ſpy, and ſad to lament their TROUBLESOME grievances, our people never find either their climate, their women, or their government good enough for them; IRRATIONALLY COMPLAINING of a lot caſt ſo as to obtain ſuperior felicity, yet delighting only in thoſe UNEASY converſers, who ſet every thing in the moſt unfavourable light—thoſe authors who aſſure us of our infallible ruin. 'Twas thus Browne's Eſtimate ran through fourteen editions—for having accuſed, Heaven knows how falſely, the Eng-

N 2

liſh

Ex coll. Karolyne & Bryan A. Garner

From volume 2.

52

Johnson Redivivus

The Year 1818

Johnson, Samuel. *A Dictionary of the English Language*. 5 vols. Henry J. Todd ed. 1st issue. London: Longman, Hurst, Rees, Orme & Brown et al., 1818.

———. *A Dictionary of the English Language*. 1st American ed. from the 11th London ed. 2 vols. Philadelphia: Moses Thomas, 1818.

Ex coll. Karolyne & Bryan A. Garner

The 1818 Philadelphia quarto.

Up to 1818, Johnson's *Dictionary* was widely reprinted in all kinds of formats, large and small, but it remained almost entirely unrevised. The first major reworking, apart from Johnson's own revision in 1773, was by Henry J. Todd (bap. 1763–d. 1845), a cleric who had been educated at Magdalen College, Oxford, and whose most significant literary work had been an edition of Milton's poetry (which remained the standard for 50 years). Among other things, Todd was a librarian, antiquary, and book collector. He was an exacting scholar and, in religious matters, famously disputatious.

"That there may soon be new makers of an English dictionary, it is warrantable to conjecture, knowing, as I do, that other gentlemen have bestowed attention upon the subject." (H.J. Todd, Introduction, p. vi.)

Todd might have worked on his edition of Johnson for seven years, perhaps beginning in 1812. The advertisement printed at the beginning of the five-volume quarto text is dated 1 August 1814, and it suggests that the editor has been working amain for some time. Although he begins by proclaiming that Johnson's *Dictionary* "has been rightly pronounced a wonderful achievement," his justification for undertaking the revision—as if any were needed after 60 years—is that "Dr. Johnson admitted that . . . he had not satisfied his own expectations." And so he proposed chiefly to supply words that had been omitted, to rectify etymologies, and to supply illustrative quotations where they were missing.

Ex coll. Karolyne & Bryan A. Garner

The 1818 Todd edition of Johnson (Lindley Murray's copy).

As might be expected of a conscientious librarian, Todd was well aware of the literature: Ash's exhaustive vocabulary (no. 45), George Mason's *Supplement to Johnson's English Dictionary* (1803) (Todd deprecated Mason's "perpetually insulting the memory of Johnson"),

"For the paucity of curious or satisfactory information, which my additions and alterations exhibit; and for the abundance of inaccuracies and faults which have escaped my care; I may not, I hope, solicit the pardon of the candid reader in vain." (H.J. Todd, Introduction, p. vii.)

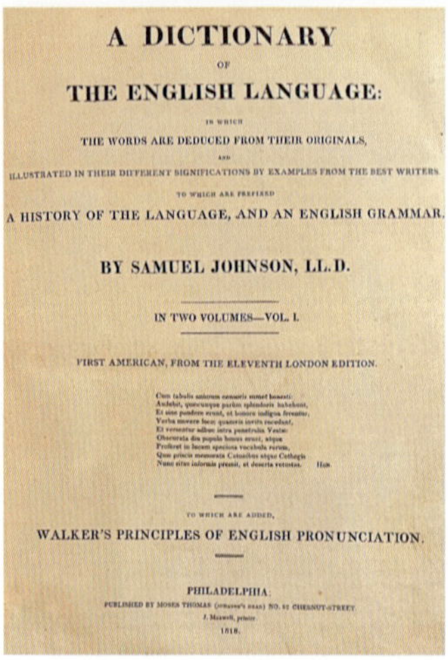

A DICTIONARY
OF
THE ENGLISH LANGUAGE:
IN WHICH
THE WORDS ARE DEDUCED FROM THEIR ORIGINALS,
AND
ILLUSTRATED IN THEIR DIFFERENT SIGNIFICATIONS BY EXAMPLES FROM THE BEST WRITERS.
TO WHICH ARE PREFIXED
A HISTORY OF THE LANGUAGE, AND AN ENGLISH GRAMMAR.

BY SAMUEL JOHNSON, LL.D.

IN TWO VOLUMES—VOL. I.

FIRST AMERICAN, FROM THE ELEVENTH LONDON EDITION.

Cum tabulis animum censoris sumet honesti:
Audebit, quæcunque parum splendoris habebunt,
Et sine pondere erunt, et honore indigna ferentur,
Verba movere loco; quamvis invita recedant,
Et versentur adhuc intra penetralia Vestæ:
Obscurata diu populo bonus eruet, atque
Proferet in lucem speciosa vocabula rerum,
Quæ priscis memorata Catonibus atque Cethegis
Nunc situs informis premit, et deserta vetustas. Hor.

TO WHICH ARE ADDED,
WALKER'S PRINCIPLES OF ENGLISH PRONUNCIATION.

PHILADELPHIA:
PUBLISHED BY MOSES THOMAS ([illegible]) NO. [illegible] CHESNUT-STREET.
J. Maxwell, printer.
1818.

Ex coll. Karolyne & Bryan A. Garner

and Jonathan Boucher's abortive *Supplement to Dr. Johnson's Dictionary* (1807) (Todd thought Boucher showed "how much remains to be done, in order to have a perfect view of the English language"). Meanwhile Todd had allies, including James Boswell of the Middle Temple, son of Johnson's biographer, who supplied him with Edmond Malone's copy of Johnson's *Dictionary*—a copy with Malone's copious additions interleaved (some 1,052 of them!). Other annotated copies, with Thomas Bagshaw's 600 or so additional references and Samuel Henshall's marginalia, were also consulted. Of the latter, to which Todd devotes a paragraph, he concludes: "I am not aware of having derived advantage from this favour." (P. iv.)

Todd likewise consulted a collection of Horne Tooke's books, with profuse annotations—one of them "abounding with his notes of haughtiest mood"—and had the good sense generally to recognize that "the manuscript remarks afforded no intelligence of consequence." (P. v.) If only Noah Webster had made a similar conclusion! (See no. 58.)

All in all, the Todd revision is a sympathetic one of which Johnson might have approved. Most of Johnson's definitions, especially the famous ones, remained unchanged. Todd rejected many low words and included "expressions of dignity." In his sign-off, he sought to inoculate the book against "any of the animadversions which will be made on my attempt." And he announced to the world that he was "now relinquish[ing] altogether the labours of lexicography," which indeed he seems to have done. (P. viii.)

Meanwhile, 1818 saw the publication of the first big American edition of Johnson's *Dictionary*. The Philadelphia publisher, Moses Thomas, used the printer James Maxwell, who reissued his own version of the edition, with a new title page, the following year. Why might that have happened? It appears that Moses Thomas became insolvent as a result of the book's poor sales, which, in the words of the principal Johnson bibliographer, "was the last straw in Moses Thomas's financial downfall." (Fleeman 2000 1:463.)

VI. Linguistic Independence & Its Sequelae

Noah Webster is treated as a "Founding Father" because of what he did for the American language. He was eager to liberate Americans from their bondage to Samuel Johnson. At first, when creating a simple spelling book (1783), he rather revered Johnson; soon he understood Johnson to be a competitor with faults, not a sage to be followed; and by the time he began compiling his own dictionary (1806), he was reviling Johnson. By 1816, he was hypocritically declaring that the world would be better off had Johnson's Dictionary *never been written. Webster was a strange mix of qualities; he was a superb definer but a delusional etymologist, an untiring worker but a disastrous businessman. He would spend a decade composing useless and imaginary word histories in the egregiously misguided belief that many English terms couldn't be rightly understood without resort to the Ethiopian and Chaldean languages, and then his poor judgment would guarantee that he'd lose money on the result.*

Webster desperately wanted to be linguistically influential, but most of his early efforts were relatively ineffective. He chafed for a very long time alongside others who worked still within Johnson's long shadow.

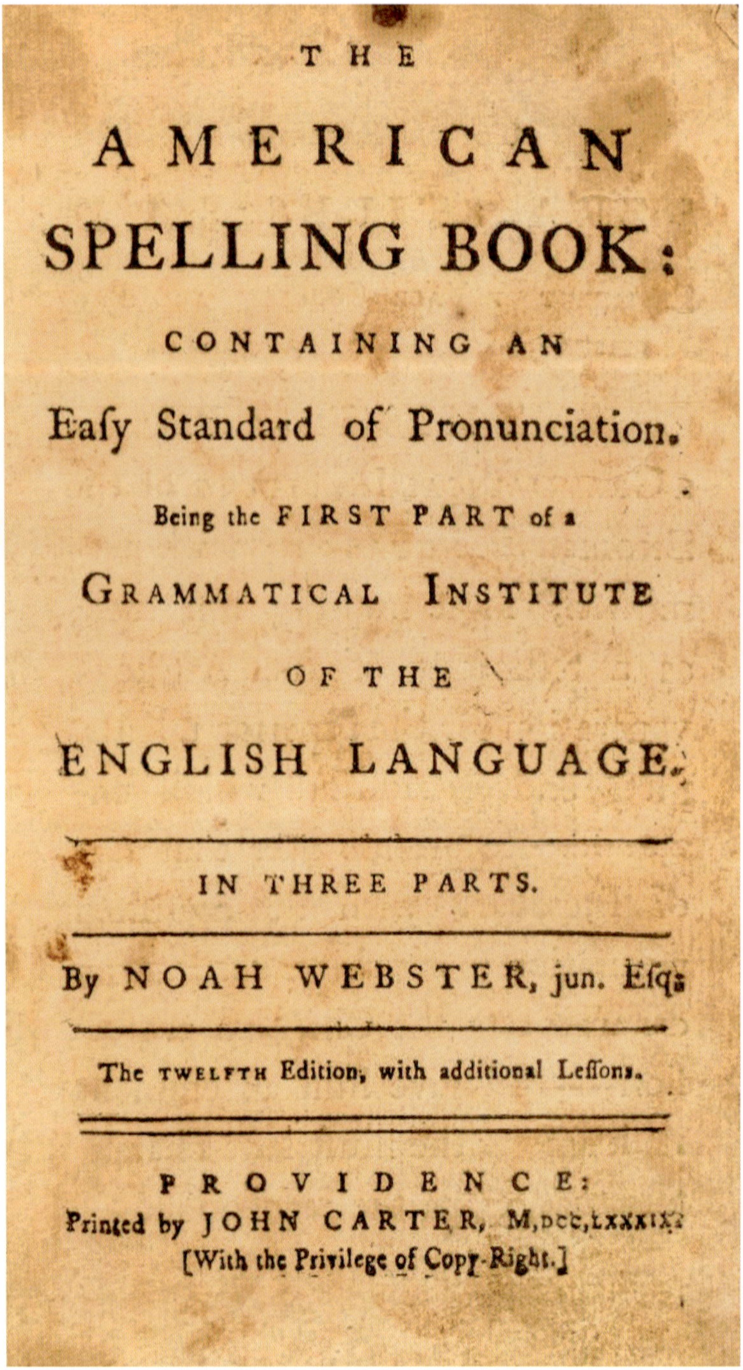

THE

AMERICAN

SPELLING BOOK:

CONTAINING AN

Eaſy Standard of Pronunciation.

Being the FIRST PART of a

GRAMMATICAL INSTITUTE

OF THE

ENGLISH LANGUAGE.

IN THREE PARTS.

By NOAH WEBSTER, jun. Eſq.

The TWELFTH Edition, with additional Leſſons.

PROVIDENCE:
Printed by JOHN CARTER, M,DCC,LXXXIX.
[With the Privilege of Copy-Right.]

Ex coll. Karolyne & Bryan A. Garner

Ex coll. Karolyne & Bryan A. Garner

The Garner Collection holds the only complete copy of this 1789 imprint of Webster's speller (renamed *The American Spelling Book* in 1787). The other known copy, at the American Antiquarian Society, has some pages described as mutilated and others missing altogether.

53

Noah Webster
He Can Spell

Webster, Noah. *A Grammatical Institute of the English Language, comprising, an easy, concise, and systematic method of education, . . . Part I. Containing, a new and accurate standard of pronunciation. . . .* Hartford: Hudson & Goodwin, for the Author, 1783.

Photo by Bryan A. Garner

Statue of Noah Webster in front of West Hartford City Hall. Sculptor: Korczak Ziolkowski. Erected 1932.

BORN IN WEST HARTFORD, Connecticut, Noah Webster (1758–1843) came of age during the American Revolution. After graduating from Yale in 1778, he was apprenticed in law studies to Oliver Ellsworth, a Constitution drafter and the third Chief Justice of the United States. Webster largely failed in law practice and moved in 1782 to Goshen, New York, to open the first of several grammar schools he founded. These were also unsuccessful.

Webster composed his three-part *Grammatical Institute* in three successive years: a speller (1783), a grammar (1784), and a reader (1785). Confusingly, all three books bear the same main title—a bad idea suggested to Webster by Ezra Stiles, president of Yale. Volume 1 can be seen as Webster's first venture into lexicography.

"The author feels the danger to which he exposes himself by this publication: He foresees that some will find fault with it, because they think it has merit; others, because they think it has none: Some will condemn it from motives of prejudice, some from ignorance, some perhaps from worse motives." (Introduction, p. 13.)

The three-part speller–grammar–reader format mimicked earlier series in single volumes—by the British writers Thomas Dilworth (*A New Guide to the English Tongue*, 1740) and James Buchanan (*The Complete English Scholar in Three Parts*, 1753). In volume 1, the speller—which is Webster's first alphabetically arranged wordbook—he was most closely following Dilworth, but he explicitly sought to differentiate himself from this famous predecessor in five ways: (1) he changed the method for syllabification, so that not every syllable had to begin with a consonant; (2) he made the suffixes *-sion* and *-tion* represent a single syllable (not *na ti on* but *na tion*); (3) he criticized Dilworth's idea that a letter such as *b* in *subtle* is actually pronounced like *t*, as opposed to being merely silent; (4) he argued that Dilworth's listing English towns was useless to Americans; and (5) he faulted Dilworth's grammar. (Monaghan 1983:36–37.)

Ex coll. Karolyne & Bryan A. Garner

Various 18th-century editions of Webster's *Grammatical Institute*.

"The principal part of instructors are illiterate people, and require some easy guide to the *standard* of pronunciation." (Introduction, p. 6.)

In newspapers in June 1784, Webster was nevertheless attacked for plagiarism by "Dilworth's Ghost." He was accused of "transcribing" authors in a "laughable affair," resulting in "an 'Institute' very badly copied" and "greatly defective." Webster was said to lack "the Modesty of some of the Authours whom [he had] copied and abused." He might be subject to a lawsuit "for Plagiarism." These allegations, which probably related to both his first two volumes, must have stung. They probably had a long-term effect on Webster, since he spent much of the rest of his career accusing others of plagiarism.

Ex coll. Karolyne & Bryan A. Garner

The famous "porcupine portrait" of Webster, which first appeared on the 1786 edition of Webster's reader.

The print run for Webster's speller was 5,000 copies, and by 1785 Webster was claiming that 12,000 were in print. Yet few exist today. During the 20th century, the bibliographers Skeel and Alston located relatively few pre-1800 copies. In 1968, the Noah Webster House issued a facsimile of the first edition created by reprinting parts of two copies—one belonging to Trinity College and the other to the Connecticut State Library.

By the 19th century, this book had evolved into a rip-roaring bestseller known as the "blueback speller." The other two parts of the *Grammatical Institute* were never nearly as popular. The reason is that spelling books were seen as gateways to learning how to read. Hence children everywhere were thought to need them to achieve literacy.

At this point in Webster's career, he was unsympathetic to spelling reform. He derided the idea of omitting the *u* from such words as *favour*, *honour*, and *labour*, and he scorned omitting the medial *e* from words such as *abridgement* and *judgement*. Hence he retained the old-fashioned spellings for the time being, until Benjamin Franklin emboldened him to embark on radically simplified spellings.

"The pronunciation of our language, tho' the most important and difficult part of grammar, is *left* to parents and nurses—to ignorance and caprice." (Introduction, p. 5.)

This book became the first in a series of Webster releases that Lyman Cobb would use to show the extreme inconsistencies in Webster's spelling (see no. 64). Here Webster followed Johnson's example for showing stress and syllabification. Later, he would turn on Johnson to the point of excoriating him.

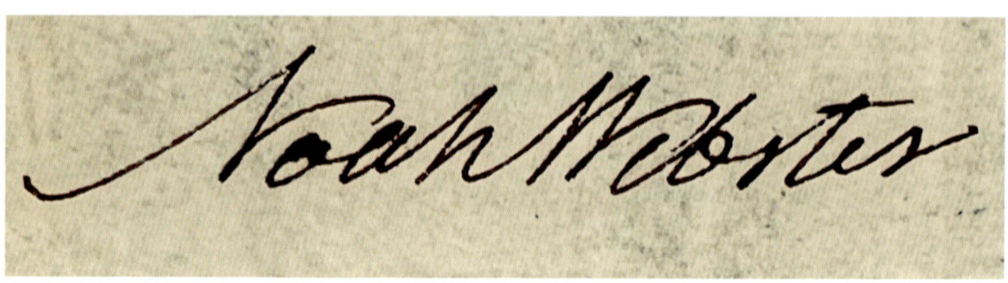

Ex coll. Karolyne & Bryan A. Garner

54

Samuel Johnson Jr.
Not Who You Think

Johnson, Samuel, Jr. ***A School Dictionary, Being a Compendium of the Latest and most Improved Dictionaries. Comprising an Easy and Concise Method of teaching Children the true meaning and pronunciation of the most useful words in the English Language, Not attainable by common School Books: In which the parts of Speech are distinguished and explained, and a general rule is given for spelling derivative, and compound words.*** **New Haven: Printed and sold by Edward O'Brien, [1797–1798].**

Elliott, John; and Samuel Johnson. ***A selected, pronouncing and accented Dictionary: Comprising a Selection of the choicest Words found in the best English Authors.*** **2d ed. [of preceding work]. Suffield, Conn.: Edward Gray for Oliver D. & I. Cook, 1800.**

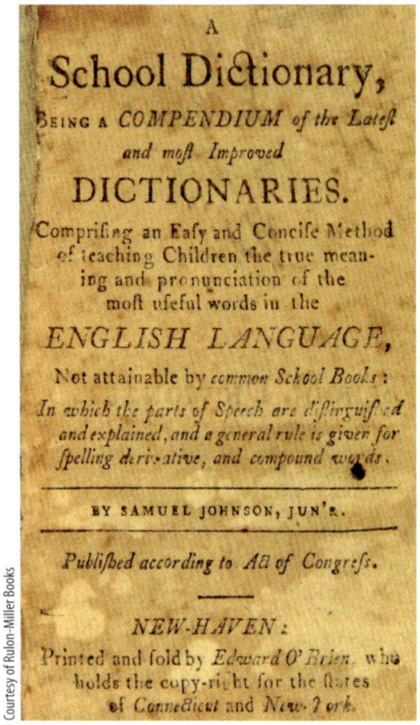
A
School Dictionary,
Being a COMPENDIUM of the Lateſt and moſt Improved
DICTIONARIES.
Compriſing an Eaſy and Conciſe Method of teaching Children the true meaning and pronunciation of the moſt uſeful words in the
ENGLISH LANGUAGE,
Not attainable by common School Books:
In which the parts of Speech are diſtinguiſhed and explained, and a general rule is given for ſpelling derivative, and compound words.
BY SAMUEL JOHNSON, JUN'R.
Publiſhed according to Act of Congreſs.
NEW-HAVEN:
Printed and ſold by Edward O'Brien, who holds the copy-right for the ſtates of Connecticut and New-York.

Courtesy of Rulon-Miller Books

The first edition (1797–1798).

"WHATEVER opinion may be formed of the merit of this work, we shall enjoy the satisfaction of contributing our mite in attempting to disseminate the seeds of literature among the youth of our country, and also of being first in an undertaking of this kind, on which ground we beg the favourable notice of an impartial public." (1800 preface, p. 6.)

IT *HAS* TO BE A PSEUDONYM, doesn't it? Samuel Johnson—"the" Samuel Johnson, the man whose name was virtually synonymous with "dictionary"—had no children. So if a dictionary appears by "Samuel Johnson, Jun'r," surely it must be an allusion to the great lexicographer.

But it isn't. Samuel Johnson Jr. was, in fact, Samuel Johnson Jr. (1757–1836), a little-known teacher unrelated to his famous namesake. He was the son (or grandnephew, as some accounts have it) of yet a different Samuel Johnson (1696–1772), the first president of King's College, which would later become Columbia University. Samuel Jr. was born in Guilford, Connecticut, two years after Johnson's *Dictionary* was published, and he became a schoolteacher there.

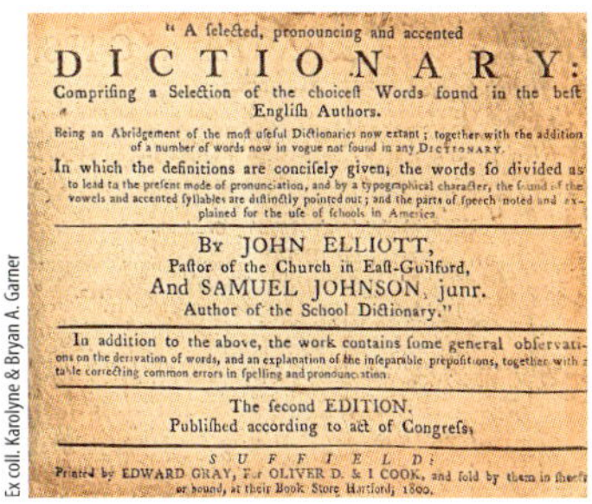
" A ſelected, pronouncing and accented
DICTIONARY:
Compriſing a Selection of the choiceſt Words found in the beſt English Authors.
Being an Abridgement of the moſt uſeful Dictionaries now extant; together with the addition of a number of words now in vogue not found in any DICTIONARY.
In which the definitions are conciſely given; the words ſo divided as to lead to the preſent mode of pronunciation, and by a typographical character, the ſound of the vowels and accented ſyllables are diſtinctly pointed out; and the parts of ſpeech noted and explained for the uſe of ſchools in America.
BY JOHN ELLIOTT,
Paſtor of the Church in Eaſt-Guilford,
And SAMUEL JOHNSON, junr.
Author of the School Dictionary."
In addition to the above, the work contains ſome general obſervations on the derivation of words, and an explanation of the inſeparable prepoſitions, together with a table correcting common errors in ſpelling and pronunciation.
The ſecond EDITION.
Publiſhed according to act of Congreſs,
SUFFIELD:
Printed by EDWARD GRAY, For OLIVER D. & I COOK, and ſold by them in ſheets or bound, at their Book Store Hartford; 1800.

Ex coll. Karolyne & Bryan A. Garner

The second edition (1800).

His *School Dictionary* is a small, cheaply printed duodecimo of fewer than 200 pages covering around 4,100 words, and is hard to distinguish from many similar dictionaries of the same vintage. But it has one claim on our attention: it's the first English-language dictionary

Courtesy of Rulon-Miller Books

The first edition (1797–1798).

"Having seen in manuscript, the small Dictionary compiled by the Rev'd John Elliott and Mr. Samuel Johnson, we are of opinion, that the plan and execution are such as will justify the hope, that it will be of extensive utility as a school book." (Recommendation printed in front matter of 1800 edition and subscribed by Chauncey Goodrich [the elder], Elizur Goodrich [who prompted Noah Webster to undertake his *Compendious*, no. 57], Theodore Dwight [the journalist], et al.)

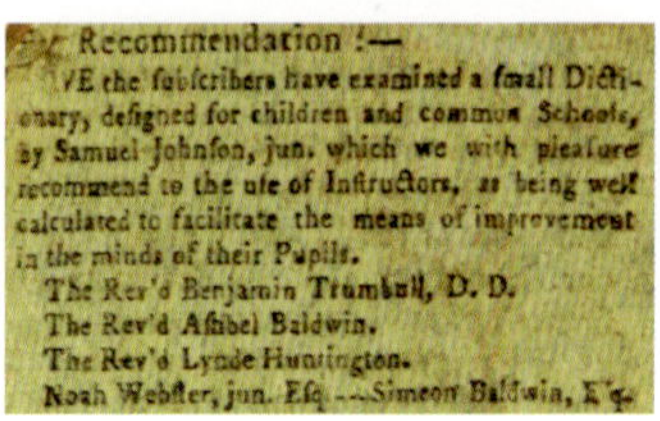

Recommendation :—

WE the fubfcribers have examined a fmall Dictionary, defigned for children and common Schools, by Samuel Johnfon, jun. which we with pleafure recommend to the ufe of Inftructors, as being well calculated to facilitate the means of improvement in the minds of their Pupils.

The Rev'd Benjamin Trumbull, D. D.
The Rev'd Afhbel Baldwin.
The Rev'd Lynde Huntington.
Noah Webfter, jun. Efq.—Simeon Baldwin, Efq.

Ex coll. Karolyne & Bryan A. Garner

Note the last recommender here listed.

to be compiled by an American. No date appears on the title page, but scholars have reliably dated it to 1797 or 1798. Although Noah Webster's monumental labors (and his energetic self-promotion) have made him the Founding Father of American lexicography, Samuel Johnson Jr. got there first.

As the title promises, Johnson wrote with students in mind. He omits both very common and very obscure words, focusing instead on those that students might need to look up. The entries are concise:

> *G*ĕn u ine, *a.* not counterfit
>
> *G*ē og ra phy, *s.* knowledge of the earth
>
> *G*ē o man cer, *s.* a fortune teller
>
> *G*ē o măn cy, *s.* act of foretelling by figures
>
> *G*ē om e try, *s.* the science of quality, extension or magnitude abstractly considered, art of measuring the earth
>
> *G*es ture, *s.* motion in speaking; action: *v.a.* to accompany with
>
> Gew gaw, *s.* a showy trifle; a bauble, a toy, splendid plaything, *a.* trifling
>
> G*h*ast ly, *a.* like a ghost, pale, horrible
>
> G*h*er kin, *s.* a pickled cucumber

A lot of information is packed into a little space: not only spellings and definitions, but also the quality of (many) vowels, syllable breaks, and parts of speech (*s.* for *substantive*, *a.* for *adjective*, *v.a.* for *verb active*). Italics indicate "soft" *g*'s and silent *h*'s.

Johnson's rapid-fire definitions, most of which fit on a single line, are usually accurate, and were probably useful to his schoolboy readers. He did make his defining task easier by skipping over the most difficult words. In this selection, for instance, he goes from *gesture* to *gewgaw* without stopping at the notoriously polysemous *get*, presumably because it is too familiar to need a definition. He addresses technical terms, though his definitions are not particularly precise or useful: *gravitation* is just "a tendency to the centre," *electricity* "spring or force in bodies," and *barometer* "a weather glass."

Originality is not among Johnson's virtues. "Candour compels him to acknowledge," he confessed in his preface, "that the principal part of this little compendium is a collection from preceding Authors of established reputation." (P. 3.) In fact, most of the definitions are plagiarized. His definition of *geomancy* is lifted verbatim from *A General Dictionary of the English Language* (1768), *geometry* from Entick's *New Spelling Dictionary* (1788), both *gesture* and *gewgaw* from William Perry's *Royal Standard English Dictionary* (1775), and *ghastly* from an anonymous *General and Complete Dictionary* (1785). To be fair, any of these might have been plagiarized from earlier dictionaries, and later lexicographers would go on to plagiarize them yet again.

Noah Webster, one year younger than Johnson Jr. but already much more accomplished in the 1790s, was one of several signatories to an advertisement declaring *A School Dictionary* "well calculated to facilitate the means of improvement" in students. Just a few years later, though, Webster changed from supporter to competitor: once Webster's *Compendious Dictionary* appeared in 1806, the two lexicographers were commercial rivals. There is no question about who won: Johnson's *Dictionary* spawned two revised editions in 1800, but Webster's dictionaries are legion, and they continue to be published to this day.

"Mr. Elliot [sic], I have not time to examine every sheet of your manuscript, but have read many sheets in different parts of it: your general plan and execution I approve of, and sincerely wish you success in your labors." (Extract from a Noah Webster letter printed as a recommendation in front matter of 1800 edition.)

In what is called a second edition of 1800, with a very different title intended to appeal to adults, Johnson's coauthor, John Elliott (1768–1824), is given priority both on the title page and at the end of the preface. For many years before and after its publication, Elliott was a pastor in East Guilford, and he must have contributed many new terms: it had more than twice as many headwords as Johnson's earlier solo effort. Elliott's definitions, though, could be startlingly sectarian and tendentious. *Anti-christ*, for example, is defined as "one who opposes Christ, the pope." *Popery* is defined as "the Romish religion." Yet *pontiff* is treated more equably: "the pope, a priest, bishop of Rome."

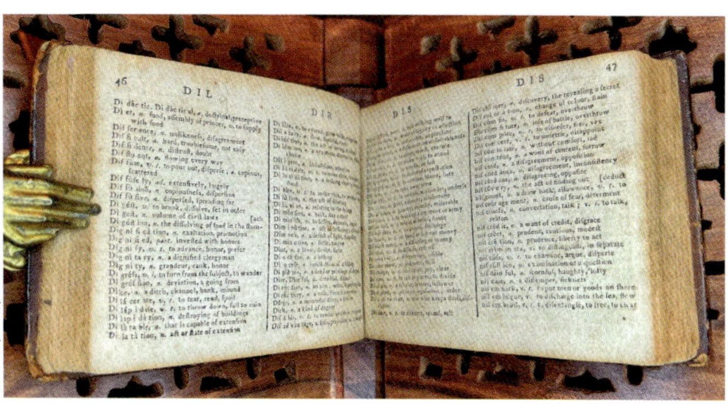

Ex coll. Karolyne & Bryan A. Garner

The second edition (1800) has an unusual trim size: 4 × 4½ inches.

John Horne Tooke, Esqr.

"The mystery is at last unravelled. I shall no more wonder now that you engross his company at Purley, whilst his other friends can scarce get a sight of him. This, you say, was President Bradshaw's feat." (The obscure opening words of the introduction, 1:1.)

Ex coll. Karolyne & Bryan A. Garner

The second edition of volume 1 (1798) and first of volume 2 (1805)—in original boards.

55

John Horne Tooke
Philological Cult Leader

Tooke, John Horne. *'Επεα πτεροεντα; or, The Diversions of Purley*. 2d ed. 2 vols. London: For the author. Vol. 1, 1786; vol. 2, 1805.

PHILOLOGISTS ARE NOT TYPICALLY KNOWN for adventurous lives, but John Horne Tooke (1736–1812) was not a typical philologist. He led a surprisingly eventful life and became one of the most influential writers on language for half a century. He was also profoundly wrong in pretty much everything he wrote.

John Horne was named after his father, a successful dealer in poultry who lived in a rich part of town, with Frederick, Prince of Wales, as a neighbor. Horne was uncommonly serious when young. A woman who knew him in his early days later told his biographer that "he never was a boy; with him there was no interval between childhood and age." (Stephens 1813 1:22.) He was educated at Westminster School and Eton, and it was not always easy for a prosperous but middle-class boy to navigate the world of aristocrats. His academic performance was merely adequate. He couldn't be bothered with the required readings, and he sometimes hired other boys to do his schoolwork for him. Still, he was a voracious reader, especially of Shakespeare and Milton.

In January 1754, he matriculated at St. John's College, Cambridge, where he was once again made uncomfortably aware of his middle-class origins. He enrolled as a sizar, a student who earned part of his tuition by doing chores for richer students—a constant reminder of his place in the class hierarchy. He graduated with an honors degree in mathematics in 1758.

The clerical life that his parents had chosen for him held no appeal; he wanted to be a lawyer. Though he briefly ran away to enroll in the Inner Temple, in the end his parents' wishes prevailed. In 1759 he was ordained deacon, and in 1760 priest. He was remembered as a capable but uninspiring preacher.

After a tour of Continental Europe, where he learned languages and met Enlightenment giants like Jean le Rond d'Alembert, David Hume, Voltaire, and Adam Smith, he returned to England and became involved in radical political causes. As a democratic critic of the monarchy, he got involved in revolutionary societies and surrounded himself with prominent radicals, including the politician John Wilkes and a friend named William Tooke.

"By his general expression of—*what is commonly called Learning*—I can pretty well guess what he thinks of grammatical learning in particular." (1:4.)

Political tension was rising in the 1770s, as the American Colonies rebelled and troublemakers like the pseudonymous "Junius" highlighted government corruption. Horne sided with the Americans against the Crown and raised money for American causes, which he personally delivered to Benjamin Franklin. Some of this rabble-rousing resulted in legal action against him, and he was forced to pay fines. But when he placed a notice in the papers that he was raising funds for "our beloved American fellow-subjects" who had been "inhumanly murdered by the King's troops," the legal situation became more serious. He was found guilty of libel, fined £200, and sentenced to a year in the King's Bench prison.

Ex coll. Jack Lynch

This "conder token"—a privately minted coin—was struck to celebrate Horne Tooke's 1794 legal triumph. The obverse reads "TRIED FOR HIGH TREASON"; the reverse reads "ACQUITTED BY HIS JURY COUNSEL."

It was not a particularly cruel imprisonment, because Horne was allowed to rent a room outside as long as he stayed near the prison. The man jailed for radicalism met weekly with other radicals at a tavern. Still, the ordeal was bad for his health, and he complained of contracting a "jail-distemper, which uniformly abated with the use of claret"—a bottle a day. (He later blamed the wine for giving him gout.)

In this period, he wrote his first significant work on language. *A Letter to Mr Dunning* (1778), a 71-page work on English "particles" (conjunctions and prepositions), was later incorporated into *Diversions of Purley*. Samuel Johnson, whom Horne pilloried on both linguistic and political grounds, still admired the pamphlet. Boswell tells us that Johnson admitted, "Were I to make a new edition of my *Dictionary*, I would adopt several of Mr. Horne's etymologies; I hope they do not put the dog in the pillory for his libel; he has too much literature for that." (Boswell 1791 3:354.)

"I think Grammar difficult, but I am very far from looking upon it as foolish: indeed so far, that I consider it as absolutely necessary in the search after philosophical truth." (1:5.)

Upon his release from prison, Horne resumed his legal studies. When he applied for admission to the bar in 1779, though, he was rejected: as a clergyman, he was not eligible to be called to the bar. Exceptions to this policy were often made for others, but not for Horne. Another application in 1782 was rejected just as quickly, and a third try, a dozen years later, also went nowhere. Horne stewed about the rejections, and it's not hard to sympathize with someone who was denied the career he wanted because he had been forced, however briefly, into a career he didn't want.

"Truth, in my opinion, has been improperly imagined at the bottom of a well: it lies much nearer to the surface; though buried indeed at present under mountains of learned rubbish." (1:10–11.)

In this period Horne grew ever closer to William Tooke, a benefactor who strongly hinted that Horne would be his heir. The two spent time together at Tooke's house in Purley, then a village outside London, since absorbed into Greater London. In 1782, Horne added Tooke's name to his own.

Ex coll. Karolyne & Bryan A. Garner

Horne Tooke, as he is usually known from this time on, devoted much of his considerable energy to his philological interests, and in 1786 he published the first volume of *The Diversions of Purley*. But he remained a political gadfly, attacking the government for financial corruption in the war with the Colonies and calling for parliamentary reform, and he continued to cultivate literary and political friends at a number of clubs and societies. When the French Revolution broke out in 1789, the stakes of political radicalism grew enormously. The mob had just deposed and would soon execute the king of France. The British government, determined to avoid that fate at home, cracked down on politically suspicious people, clubs, and publishers. Horne Tooke, who publicly congratulated the French National Assembly, which helped publish Thomas Paine's radical *Rights of Man*, and wich ran a doomed parliamentary campaign against Charles James Fox, gave the government plenty of reasons to be suspicious.

"There are two sorts of things: 1. *Res quæ permanent*. 2. *Res quæ fluunt*. There must therefore be *two* sorts of words or *parts of speech*: viz. 1. *Notæ rerum quæ permanent*. 2. *Notæ rerum quæ fluunt*." (1:19.)

The authorities began searching his mail and surrounding him with spies. In May 1794, on the basis of one of his letters, he was arrested for promoting an insurrection. Horne Tooke maintained that they had misread the plain meaning of his letter, but to no avail: he was taken to the Tower of London to face charges.

This confinement was infinitely more serious than his previous experience. Then he was being held for libel; now he was facing charges of high treason. There was no dashing off to the pub, and a guilty verdict would likely mean death. Still, he was undaunted, and through five months in the Tower he inspired his fellow prisoners with acts of defiance. After a six-day trial in October 1794, the jury retired for only a few minutes, and returned to acquit him. Britain's radicals rejoiced, and the London Corresponding Society struck a commemorative medal to honor the occasion.

Horne Tooke left prison a celebrity, and was warmly welcomed home by his supporters. He hosted weekly dinners for British radicals, attracting philosophers including William Godwin and Jeremy Bentham and poets including Samuel Taylor Coleridge and Anna Barbauld. He launched another campaign for a seat in Parliament in 1796—again unsuccessful—and continued calling for prison reform and other progressive causes.

"In English, and in all Languages, there are only *two* sorts of words which are *necessary* for the communication of our thoughts . . . 1. Noun, and 2. Verb." (1:65.)

In 1801, he finally made it to Parliament by a curious path, especially for a campaigner for democracy. A powerful friend urged him to stand for Parliament representing the "rotten borough" of Old Sarum in the southwest of England, notorious for having almost no residents but still electing two members to Parliament. It had long been a symbol of political corruption, and now Horne Tooke was to benefit by it. He won—no surprise; the uncontested seat was essentially a gift from the landowners who controlled it—and served until Parliament was dissolved a year and a half later. (The Old Sarum constituency was finally absorbed into another borough in 1832.)

Ex coll. Karolyne & Bryan A. Garner

An 1840 edition.

Horne Tooke's story might have significantly changed in 1802 when William Tooke died. But this friend, namesake, and putative benefactor left Horne Tooke just £500. That would be a generous bequest in most circumstances, but Horne Tooke had been led to expect much more. Legal wrangling with the actual heirs dragged on for ten years and went against him. He was not poor, but any thoughts of a wealthy retirement evaporated.

The last decade of his life was marked by slowly but steadily declining health, including episodes of gout, rheumatism, kidney stones, and, at the very end, gangrene in the legs. He found the strength to write a second volume of the *Diversions*, but destroyed an in-progress volume 3. He knew that death was approaching, and had his own tomb built in his garden. John Horne Tooke died in March 1812.

"The fears of my printer (which I cannot call unfounded, in the present degraded state of the press) do not permit me to expose (as ought to be done) the circumstances producing, preceding, accompanying, and following my strange trial of six days for High Treason." (2:sig. $A2^{r}$.)

This political hell-raiser never wrote a dictionary, but his presence hung over lexicography for decades. Linguists and lexicographers remember him for this book with an odd title: *Ἔπεα πτεροεντα; or, The Diversions of Purley*. The first half is in a forbiddingly untranslated classical language, while the second promises something genial and entertaining. The *ἔπεα* (*epea* "words") is the root of *epic*, and the *πτερ-* (*pter* "wing") shows up in English *helicopter* and *pterodactyl*: *winged words*. It was an attempt at "philosophical grammar"—observations on the nature of language generally, rather than of any particular language—and it was conducted in the form of a dialogue between two characters, one of whom, "H.," spoke for Horne Tooke himself.

Written in a curiously numinous style, the book was grounded on two addled principles: first, that every word has only one meaning; second, that there are only two parts of speech, nouns and verbs.

What about *into*, *but*, *easily*, and *yellow*?—are they "really" nouns or verbs? Well, neither, Horne Tooke was obliged to admit, though they were once, and deep down they remain so. They're merely what remains after the true words were subjected to abbreviation. They concealed long processes of condensing nouns and verbs to speed up communication. But a conjunction like *if* is "really" *give*, with the suggestion that it is a fact being offered for consideration: "The truth of the matter is, that IF is merely a *Verb*. It is merely the imperative of the Gothic and Anglo-saxon verb [*gifan*]. . . . And accordingly our corrupted IF has always the signification of the English Imperative *Give*; and no other." (1:141.)

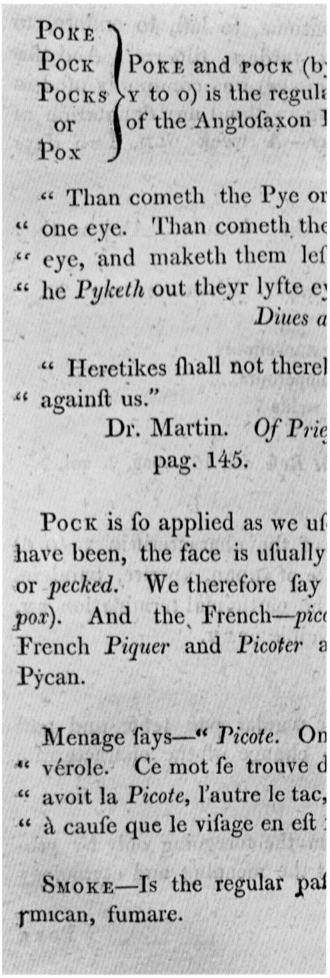

POKE
POCK
POCKS
or
POX
POKE and POCK (b
Y to O) is the regul
of the Anglofaxon

" Than cometh the Pye or
" one eye. Than cometh the
" eye, and maketh them lef
" he *Pyketh* out theyr lyfte e
Diues a

" Heretikes fhall not therel
" againft us."
Dr. Martin. *Of Prie*
pag. 145.

POCK is fo applied as we uf
have been, the face is ufually
or *pecked*. We therefore fay
pox). And the French—*pic*
French *Piquer* and *Picoter* a
Pýcan.

Menage fays—" *Picote*. On
" vérole. Ce mot fe trouve d
" avoit la *Picote*, l'autre le tac,
" à caufe que le vifage en eft

SMOKE—Is the regular pa
ꝩmican, fumare.

Detail from volume 2.

That declaration that it has "no other" meaning accounts for much of the oddity of his argument. Where Johnson—English lexicography's first great splitter—patiently identified subtle shades of meaning, sometimes dozens for a single word, Tooke, the ultimate lumper, denied any distinctions. When a character in *The Diversions* points out that Johnson "has numbered up *twenty* different meanings of this Preposition FROM," Tooke replies that "in all his instances . . . FROM continues to retain invariably one and the same single meaning." (1:378, 380–81.) And if a word had two meanings that he was unable to reconcile, he would just declare that it was *actually* two separate words, which "corruption" had turned into one.

We might forgive the perverse arguments if he demonstrated great skill with etymologies, but they're no better. Modern linguists know that etymologies are established by patiently tracking the sound changes that make sense within the phonological system of the language. Horne Tooke, on the other hand, etymologized on a whim. When he wrote, for instance, "The difference between a T and a D is so very small, that . . . in the derivation of words it is scarce worth regarding," he authorized himself to ignore any evidence that didn't fit his theory. (1:395–96.) (Linguists know that /d/ can, under certain conditions, evolve into /t/—Grimm's Law explains how Latin *decem* and Greek δέκα (*déka*) correspond to English *ten* and Dutch *tien*—but this isn't to say that the distinction can simply be ignored.) If you squint just so, Tooke seems to suggest, you can make *this* word look a bit like *that* one—maybe *through* looks a little bit like *door*—and your problem is solved. Any superficial similarity between words is good enough to explain one by the other. It amounted to permission to ignore complexity.

Unsurprisingly, many of the etymologies he discovered by this "method" went badly astray. He insisted that *stern* comes from Old English *styrnan* "move," and "is the same word and has the same meaning, whether we say—a STERN countenance, i. e. a *moved* countenance, moved by some passion; or the STERN of a ship, i. e. The *moved* part of a ship, or that part by which the ship is *moved*" (2:73)—but we now know that the words are unrelated. "BOLD—is the past participle of the verb *To Build*." (2:128.) No, it isn't. While we're at it, *odd* has nothing to do with *owed*, nor *bread* to *brayed*.

Worse, even when his etymologies were correct (and they often were), he insisted on the "etymological fallacy"—that words "really" mean what their roots meant. Once he notes that *decree*, *discreet*, and *secret* all come from the same root, or *rogue*, *rock*, *rocket*, *rug*, *ruck*, *array*, *rail*, *rig*, and *ray* (2:225), he convinces himself that nothing more need be said about them—their meanings and usage should be obvious to everyone. But the fact that *wrong* is related to *wring* (2:89) doesn't help us understand what either word means or how it's used. For Tooke, these are trivial details, unworthy of the attention of philosophers.

Why did he put so much energy into such a perverse project? *The Diversions of Purley* was an attempt to democratize language. Etymology had a moral urgency. He titled a chapter "The Rights of Man," asking, "What do you mean by the words RIGHT and WRONG?" (2:3), and the question is as political as it is linguistic. Politics and language are ultimately the same thing. Abstract nouns, he insisted, are almost entirely past participles, and the price of not knowing this is catastrophic: "These words, these Participles and Adjectives, not understood as such, have caused a metaphysical jargon and a false morality, which can only be dissipated by etymology." (2:18.) Philology shall set you free. In his *Life of Milton*, Samuel Johnson observed, "No man forgets his original trade: the rights of nations and of kings sink into questions of grammar, if grammarians discuss them." This is true of Tooke: when the grammarian found himself obliged to fight

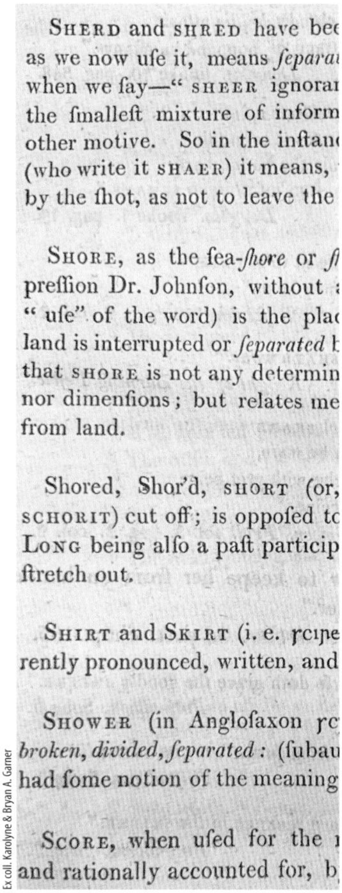
SHERD and SHRED have bee
as we now uſe it, means *ſeparat*
when we ſay—" SHEER ignorar
the ſmalleſt mixture of inform
other motive. So in the inſtan
(who write it SHAER) it means,
by the ſhot, as not to leave the

SHORE, as the ſea-*ſhore* or *ſ*
preſſion Dr. Johnſon, without
" uſe" of the word) is the plac
land is interrupted or *ſeparated* b
that SHORE is not any determin
nor dimenſions; but relates me
from land.

Shored, Shor'd, SHORT (or,
SCHORIT) cut off; is oppoſed tc
LONG being alſo a paſt particip
ſtretch out.

SHIRT and SKIRT (i. e. ſcyre
rently pronounced, written, and

SHOWER (in Anglofaxon ſc
broken, divided, ſeparated: (ſubau
had ſome notion of the meaning

SCORE, when uſed for the
and rationally accounted for, b

Ex coll. Karolyne & Bryan A. Garner

Detail from volume 2.

John Horne Tooke.

for his life in the courts, he imagined it in linguistic terms. It was a misread letter that nearly led to his execution, and he noted that he was "made the miserable victim of—*Two Prepositions and a Conjunction.*" (1:102.)

Horne Tooke was erudite, creative, impassioned, eloquent—and very, very *wrong*. He immodestly announced that "all future etymologists, and perhaps some philosophers, will acknowledge their obligation to me." (1:191.) This is, sad to say, largely true—if not for all future etymologists, then at least for those who worked in the next half-century. The radical grammarians William Cobbett and William Hazlitt admired both the linguistics and the politics. Leigh Hunt called him "perhaps the first philologist of his nation." (Hunt 1962:135.) His fingerprints are all over the dictionaries of Noah Webster (who quotes him approvingly) and Charles Richardson (who published a whole book elaborating Horne Tooke's principles). (Shoemaker 1936:118–19; Murray 1977:134.) *The Diversions of Purley* sold well, paying between £4,000 and £5,000 in royalties.

But the influence was unfortunate. Jonathon Green says that we can't ignore Horne Tooke's "gloriously specious system of etymology" (Green 1996:353), and two historians of dictionaries describe him as "one of the most systematically frantic etymologists who ever lived." (Sledd & Kolb 1955:183.)

"Odd—Is the participle *Owed, Ow'd.* Thus, when we are counting by couples or by pairs; we say—One pair, two pairs, &c. and one *Owed, Ow'd,* to make up another pair. It has the same meaning when we say—An odd man, or an odd action: it still relates to *pairing.*" (2:33.)

Ex coll. Karolyne & Bryan A. Garner

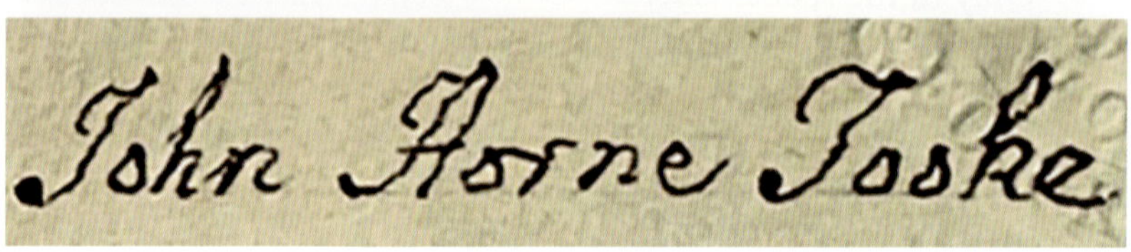

Ex coll. Karolyne & Bryan A. Garner

56

Lindley Murray
The One Realm in Which He Couldn't Best Webster

Murray, Lindley. *An English Spelling-book*. York: Longman, Hurst, Rees & Orme, 1804. 2d ed. 1804. 3d ed. [1805?]. 4th ed. 1805.

Ex coll. Karolyne & Bryan A. Garner

KNOWN AS A GRAMMARIAN, not a lexicographer, Lindley Murray (1745–1826) is nevertheless important in the history of lexicography. The success of his 1795 *English Grammar* caused Noah Webster to understand, to some degree, that he couldn't effectively compete in the field of grammar. Webster had issued a trio of literacy books—a speller (1783), a grammar (1784), and a reader (1785)—to form a three-part *Grammatical Institute*, as originally titled.

In 1794, Webster leased a New York storefront from Murray in lower Manhattan, with an option to purchase. By then, the Pennsylvania-born Murray had been in York, England, for a decade, essentially exiled from the United States after opposing the Revolutionary War. The deal was concluded through Murray's brother John, a prominent New York businessman, who doubtless informed Lindley about the identity of his lessee/buyer. (Garner 2020a:475–79.)

Was it a mere coincidence that Murray soon issued a grammar (1795), a reader (1799), and a speller (1804)—the very trio of works for which his lessee/buyer was known? Perhaps. But if so, it's surely one of the greatest real-estate-related coincidences in literary history. And shortly after Noah Webster breached his lease and forfeited his bond in 1798, with his finances in utter disarray, he was thoroughly eclipsed by Murray in two categories: the grammar and the reader. Those two books made Murray the bestselling literacy-book author of the 19th century, and he became known as "the Father of English Grammar."

Only in the speller category did Webster triumph. Indeed, sales of his speller sustained him financially through the 1828 publication of his *American Dictionary*—and after, since the *Dictionary* did nothing positive for his income.

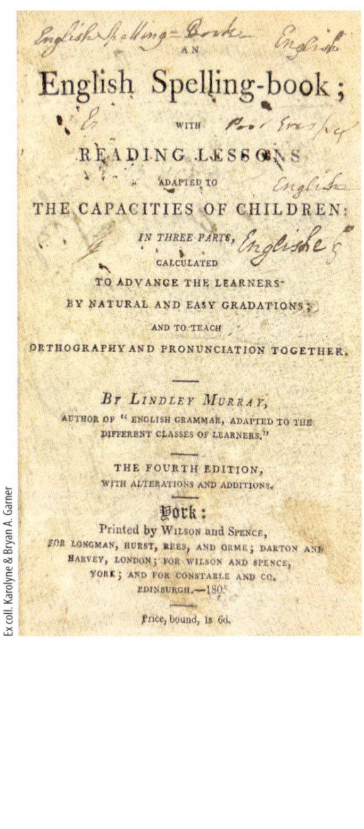
AN
English Spelling-book;
WITH
READING LESSONS
ADAPTED TO
THE CAPACITIES OF CHILDREN:
IN THREE PARTS,
CALCULATED
TO ADVANCE THE LEARNERS
BY NATURAL AND EASY GRADATIONS;
AND TO TEACH
ORTHOGRAPHY AND PRONUNCIATION TOGETHER.

BY LINDLEY MURRAY,
AUTHOR OF "ENGLISH GRAMMAR, ADAPTED TO THE DIFFERENT CLASSES OF LEARNERS."

THE FOURTH EDITION,
WITH ALTERATIONS AND ADDITIONS.

York:
Printed by WILSON and SPENCE,
FOR LONGMAN, HURST, REES, AND ORME; DARTON AND HARVEY, LONDON; FOR WILSON AND SPENCE, YORK; AND FOR CONSTABLE AND CO. EDINBURGH.—180[illegible]

Price, bound, 1s 6d.

Ex coll. Karolyne & Bryan A. Garner

Murray's speller, meanwhile, his only real wordbook, was his worst-selling book. Although it was already in a fourth printing

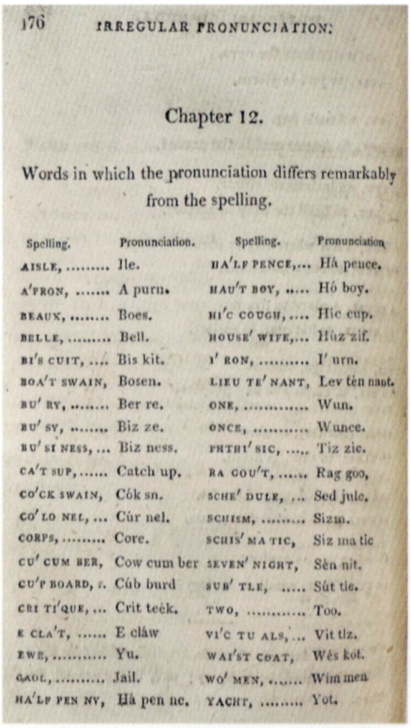

176 IRREGULAR PRONUNCIATION:

Chapter 12.

Words in which the pronunciation differs remarkably from the spelling.

Spelling.	Pronunciation.	Spelling.	Pronunciation.
AISLE, ...	Ile.	HA'LF PENCE,...	Há pence.
A'PRON, ...	A purn.	HAU'T BOY, ...	Hó boy.
BEAUX, ...	Boes.	HI'C COUGH, ...	Hic cup.
BELLE, ...	Bell.	HOUSE' WIFE,...	Húz zif.
BI'S CUIT, ...	Bis kit.	I' RON, ...	I' urn.
BOA'T SWAIN,	Bosen.	LIEU TE' NANT,	Lev tén nant.
BU' RY, ...	Ber re.	ONE, ...	Wun.
BU' SY, ...	Biz ze.	ONCE, ...	Wunce.
BU' SI NESS, ...	Biz ness.	PHTHI' SIC, ...	Tiz zic.
CA'T SUP, ...	Catch up.	RA GOU'T, ...	Rag goo,
CO'CK SWAIN,	Cók sn.	SCHE' DULE, ...	Sed jule.
CO' LO NEL, ...	Cúr nel.	SCHISM, ...	Sizm.
CORPS, ...	Core.	SCHIS' MA TIC,	Siz ma tic
CU' CUM BER,	Cow cum ber	SEVEN' NIGHT,	Sèn nit.
CU'P BOARD, r.	Cúb burd	SUB' TLE, ...	Sút tle.
CRI TI'QUE, ...	Crit teék.	TWO, ...	Too.
E CLA'T, ...	E cláw	VI'C TU ALS, ...	Vit tlz.
EWE, ...	Yu.	WAI'ST COAT,	Wés kot.
GAOL, ...	Jail.	WO' MEN, ...	Wim men
HA'LF PEN NY,	Há pen ne.	YACHT, ...	Yot.

Ex coll. Karolyne & Bryan A. Garner

Ex coll. Karolyne & Bryan A. Garner

Lindley Murray's house in York, England.

by 1805 and went through 45 editions or printings by 1854, it never became well known. Unlike Murray's other literacy books, which are perennially in plentiful supply among booksellers, copies of the speller are scarce in the book trade. And there is hardly a mention of the speller in the copious literature discussing Murray. Further, the planned sequel advertised in the back matter (*An English Vocabulary; or, A Sequel to Murray's English Spelling Book*) never materialized. These facts suggest small print runs.

The book recommended all the standard British English spellings: *behaviour*, *centre*, *travelled*, and so on. There was nothing reformist about it: "The orthography of Johnson, and the pronunciation of Walker, have been, almost universally, adopted in this work. They are authorities which few persons will be inclined to dispute." (Pp. vii–viii.)

Murray was characteristically didactic here, with lessons in morals and manners interspersed throughout his examples. He was sensitive to his audience: "The infant capacity (as Quinctilian justly observes) may be compared to a narrow-necked vessel, into which the liquor enters only by drops; and runs over, when either the quantity, or the quality, is not adapted to entrance. Though a gradual rise in these lessons has been carefully observed, they will, it is presumed, be found to possess a considerable degree of simplicity throughout the book." (P. vi.)

For Lindley Murray's own copy of the 1818 edition of Johnson's *Dictionary*, see p. 159. Tucked inside is Murray's holographic will disposing of his most important books, the first listed being the Johnson. And for the improbable story of how this book was acquired, by the merest chance, on Charing Cross Road in the 1990s, see Garner 2021a:240–42.

Ex coll. Karolyne & Bryan A. Garner

Ex coll. Karolyne & Bryan A. Garner

Ex coll. Karolyne & Bryan A. Garner

57

Noah Webster at His Most Compendious

Webster, Noah. ***A Compendious Dictionary of the English Language. In which five thousand Words are added to the number found in the best English compends; The Orthography is, in some instances, corrected; The Pronunciation marked by an Accent or other suitable Direction; and the Definitions of many Words amended and improved.*** **New Haven: Sidney's Press, 1806.**

Noah Webster's 1806 Copyright Certificate for the *Compendious Dictionary*, issued by William Thornton of the U.S. Patent Office.

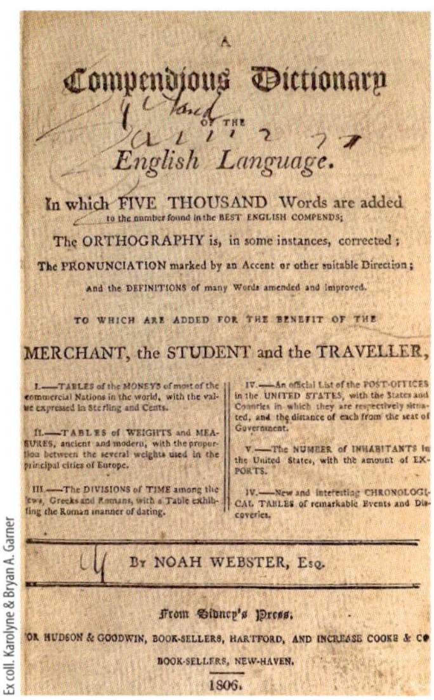

Ex coll. Karolyne & Bryan A. Garner

NOAH WEBSTER (1758–1843) is known as the Father of the American Dictionary, as the Father of American Copyright Law, and sometimes even as the Father of Epidemiology. (Yes, he surveyed and tracked instances of yellow fever and scarlet fever as they were sweeping the East Coast.) In the popular mind, of course, his closest association is with dictionaries.

Webster's first wordbook, a "speller" dated 1783, simply listed words so that their spellings could be memorized by rote. (See no. 53.) A friend, Elizur Goodrich, suggested that he should undertake a full-fledged dictionary, but Webster rejected the idea. By 1790, he had moved from Connecticut to New York to become a journalist, saying he had forsworn linguistic studies.

But he couldn't stay away. When the newspaper business failed, he moved back to Connecticut and reverted to lexicography and grammar. And on 4 June 1800, he placed an announcement in the New Haven newspapers:

> Mr. Webster of this city . . . has in hand a Dictionary of the American Language. . . . The plan contemplated extends to a small Dictionary for schools, one for the counting-house, and a large one for men of science. The first is nearly ready for the

Ex coll. Karolyne & Bryan A. Garner

press—the second and third will require the labor of some years. [Leavitt 1947:23.]

Webster was staking his claim on America's vocabulary, urging consumers not to buy other dictionaries until his was complete and warning potential rivals away.

"Nearly ready for the press" was, to be generous, a bit optimistic. It took until 1806 for him to produce his *Compendious Dictionary of the English Language*. The book isn't particularly attractive. It's small: by *compendious* Webster meant, in his own definition, "short, brief, concise, summary." The type is also small, and the two-column page layout is extremely dense. Webster acknowledged his debt to John Entick's *Spelling Dictionary* (no. 40), which strove to pack information into the smallest possible compass.

The wordlist contained around 40,000 words, most of them drawn from Entick, but with many distinctively American additions. (Martin 2019:48.) Webster, already known for his blueback speller, introduced some of his spelling reforms in the dictionary: here we see such American spellings as *defense* (not *defence*), *offense* (not *offence*), *favor* (not *favour*), and *honor* (not *honour*). (Landau 2009a:184.) The book opens with a thoughtful preface that takes some shots at Samuel Johnson, and it ends with 50 pages of miscellaneous encyclopedic information: "Number of inhabitants in the several states," "Proportion of the weights of the chief cities of Europe to that of Amsterdam," "A Table of the moneys of the principal commercial countries in the world," "List of the Post-Offices in the United States."

Ex coll. Karolyne & Bryan A. Garner

Most of the book, though—355 pages—is concerned strictly with lexical matters. A typical run of entries:

Force, *n.* violence, strength, armed power, fate
Force, *v.* to oblige, overpower, storm, ravish, cut
Fórcedly, *ad.* with or by force, violently
Fórceful, *a.* violent, hot, vehemently, strong
For´ceps, n. nippers to extract any thing
Fórcible, *a.* violent, strong, powerful, binding
Fórcibleness, *n.* force, violence, strength
Fórcibly, *ad.* by force, strongly, powerfully, fully
For´cipate, *a.* formed like pinchers

Webster managed to keep entries to a single line by ignoring etymology—later to become one of his particular passions—and by incorporating pronunciation information into the headwords. Silent letters appeared in italics, as in "Tho*ugh*." He explained: "When a vowel has the accent over it, its sound is long . . . . When the accent is placed after a consonant, the preceding vowel is short." (P. xiv.) He sometimes explained phonetic matters with bracketed notes like "Gew´gaw, [g hard]" (which *g*?—both?) or "Rough, [ruff]." But he did nothing to tell readers that *friend* has an [ɛ] sound or *from* an [ə], or whether *forcedly* is two syllables or three. More important, Webster conserved space with extremely curt definitions—usually just an indiscriminate spray of synonyms. There's no attempt to distinguish senses, and certainly no attempt to wrestle with the complexities of polysemous verbs: *get* is just "to procure, gain, win, learn, arrive, induce"; *take* is "to receive, seize, trap, suppose, hire, please." Both these problems are traceable verbatim to Entick. But Webster's entries are sometimes marred by errors not in Entick: the adjective *forceful* shouldn't be defined by the adverb *vehemently*.

Had this been Webster's only dictionary, he would not be remembered as a lexicographer. But the preface to the *Compendious* promised "a dictionary which shall exhibit a far more correct state of the language than any work of this kind." (P. xxiii.) This recalled that advertisement from 1800, which promised another work for "men of science"—he meant learning generally—that would be the "labor of some years." "Some" turned out to be 28, and the *American Dictionary* is the work that gave Noah Webster his reputation. It's rewarding to put entries from the *Compendious* next to those in the *American* to see how far Webster came in the intervening years. Compare, for instance, the definition of *tell* in the *Compendious*—"to relate, utter, inform, report, count, reckon"—with the *American Dictionary* in 1828:

> 1. To utter; to express in words; to communicate to others. . . . 2. To relate; to narrate; to rehearse particulars; as, to *tell* a story. . . . 3. To teach; to inform; to make known; to show by words. . . . 4. To discover; to disclose; to betray. . . . 5. To count; to number. . . . 6. To relate in confession; to confess or acknowledge. . . . 7. To publish. . . . 8. To unfold; to interpret; to explain. . . . 9. To make excuses. . . . 10. To make known. . . . 11. To discover; to find; to discern. . . . *Tell*, though equivalent in some respects to *speak* and *say*, has not always the same application. We say, to *tell* this, that or what, to *tell* a story, to *tell* a word, to *tell* truth or falsehood, to *tell* a number, to *tell* the reasons, to *tell* something or nothing; but we never

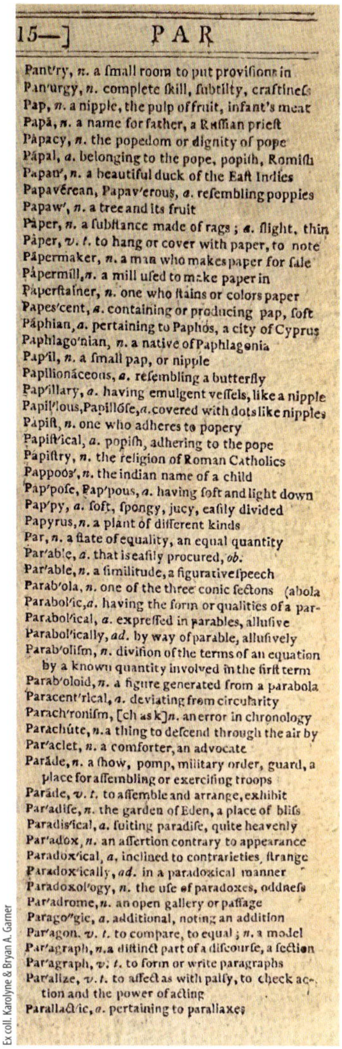
15—] PAR

Pant'ry, *n.* a ſmall room to put proviſions in
Pan'urgy, *n.* complete ſkill, ſubtilty, craftineſs
Pap, *n.* a nipple, the pulp of fruit, infant's meat
Papá, *n.* a name for father, a Ruſſian prieſt
Pápacy, *n.* the popedom or dignity of pope
Pápal, *a.* belonging to the pope, popiſh, Romiſh
Papaw', *n.* a beautiful duck of the Eaſt Indies
Papavérean, Papav'erous, *a.* reſembling poppies
Papaw', *n.* a tree and its fruit
Páper, *n.* a ſubſtance made of rags; *a.* ſlight, thin
Páper, *v. t.* to hang or cover with paper, to note
Pápermaker, *n.* a man who makes paper for ſale
Pápermill, *n.* a mill uſed to make paper in
Páperſtainer, *n.* one who ſtains or colors paper
Papes'cent, *a.* containing or producing pap, ſoft
Páphian, *a.* pertaining to Paphos, a city of Cyprus
Paphlago'nian, *n.* a native of Paphlagonia
Pap'il, *n.* a ſmall pap, or nipple
Papilionáceous, *a.* reſembling a butterfly
Pap'illary, *a.* having emulgent veſſels, like a nipple
Papil'lous, Papillóſe, *a.* covered with dots like nipples
Pápiſt, *n.* one who adheres to popery
Papiſt'ical, *a.* popiſh, adhering to the pope
Pápiſtry, *n.* the religion of Roman Catholics
Pappoos', *n.* the indian name of a child
Pap'poſe, Pap'pous, *a.* having ſoft and light down
Pap'py, *a.* ſoft, ſpongy, jucy, eaſily divided
Papyrus, *n.* a plant of different kinds
Par, *n.* a ſtate of equality, an equal quantity
Par'able, *a.* that is eaſily procured, *ob.*
Par'able, *n.* a ſimilitude, a figurative ſpeech
Parab'ola, *n.* one of the three conic ſections (abola
Parabol'ic, *a.* having the form or qualities of a par-
Parabol'ical, *a.* expreſſed in parables, alluſive
Parabol'ically, *ad.* by way of parable, alluſively
Parab'oliſm, *n.* diviſion of the terms of an equation by a known quantity involved in the firſt term
Parab'oloid, *n.* a figure generated from a parabola
Paracent'rical, *a.* deviating from circularity
Parach'roniſm, [ch as k] *n.* an error in chronology
Parachúte, *n.* a thing to deſcend through the air by
Par'aclet, *n.* a comforter, an advocate
Paráde, *n.* a ſhow, pomp, military order, guard, a place for aſſembling or exerciſing troops
Paráde, *v. t.* to aſſemble and arrange, exhibit
Par'adiſe, *n.* the garden of Eden, a place of bliſs
Paradis'ical, *a.* ſuiting paradiſe, quite heavenly
Par'adox, *n.* an aſſertion contrary to appearance
Paradox'ical, *a.* inclined to contrarieties, ſtrange
Paradox'ically, *ad.* in a paradoxical manner
Paradoxol'ogy, *n.* the uſe of paradoxes, oddneſs
Par'adrome, *n.* an open gallery or paſſage
Parago'gic, *a.* additional, noting an addition
Par'agon, *v. t.* to compare, to equal; *n.* a model
Par'agraph, *n.* a diſtinct part of a diſcourſe, a ſection
Par'agraph, *v. t.* to form or write paragraphs
Par'alize, *v. t.* to affect as with palſy, to check action and the power of acting
Parallac'tic, *a.* pertaining to parallaxes

Ex coll. Karolyne & Bryan A. Garner

say, to *tell* a speech, discourse or oration, or to *tell* an argument or a lesson. It is much used in commands. *Tell* me the whole story; *tell* me all you know, or all that was said. *Tell* has frequently the sense of *narrate*; which *speak* and *say* have not.

The *Compendious* wasn't the very first American dictionary—that had appeared in 1798—and it wasn't even a particularly impressive dictionary by the standards of its day. Because of its place in the career of America's first great lexicographer, though, it is recognized as the first important American dictionary.

On 6 March 1806, the U.S. State Department issued to the Father of American Copyright Law (Webster) a copyright certificate signed by William Thornton (1759–1828), Superintendent of the Patent Office and Architect of the Capitol. This historic certificate, acquired by the Garner Collection in 2021 as part of a group of documents that once belonged to Noah Webster, reads as follows:

> Department of State
> Patent Office 6th March 1806—
>
> I certify that Noah Webster Esquire hath deposited in the Office of this Department, agreeably to an Act of Congress for encouraging the progress of Learning &c.—his Work entitled "A Compendious Dictionary of the English Language . . . ." &c. &c.
>
> William Thornton

Ex coll. Karolyne & Bryan A. Garner

In 1970, Bounty Books published this facsimile of the *Compendious*, with an introduction by Philip B. Gove.

"The publication of *A Compendious Dictionary* . . . stirred great opposition in the *Monthly Anthology*, a magazine conducted by a group of liberals in theology who were conservative in politics, literature, and language. When Webster announced his acceptance of Calvinistic tenets of religion, the hostility of the Bostonians increased. They devoted more space to a minute dissection of Webster's books than to those of any other writer." (Warfel 1953:xxxix.)

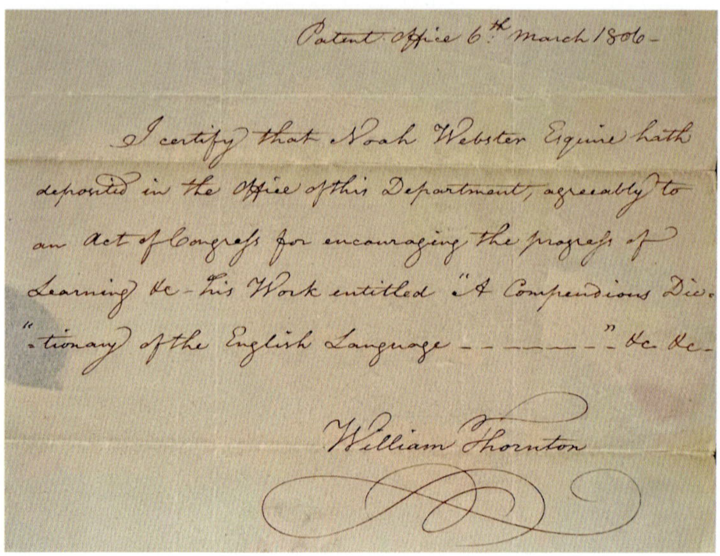

Patent Office 6th March 1806 –

I certify that Noah Webster Esquire hath deposited in the Office of this Department, agreeably to an Act of Congress for encouraging the progress of Learning &c.—his Work entitled "A Compendious Dic-"tionary of the English Language — — — — —" &c. &c.

William Thornton

Ex coll. Karolyne & Bryan A. Garner

Webster's 1806 copyright certificate.

58

Two Important Webster Documents

June 1809 ALS from Noah Webster to Samuel M. Hopkins of New York, discussing his plans for a specimen sheet of his proposed massive dictionary.

July 1812 mortgage deed dated 13 July 1812 by which Noah Webster, then living in New Haven, mortgaged real estate in Amherst to Oliver Dickinson of Hadley, Massachusetts.

Ex coll. Karolyne & Bryan A. Garner

NOT ALL WEBSTER DOCUMENTS in the Garner Collection relate to lexicography, but the first of these does: just three years after publication of his *Compendious Dictionary*, Webster has had specimen entries typeset for the purpose of gaining support for his unabridged dictionary.

New Haven June 14, 1809

Dear Sir,

I have sent to Dr Mason a specimen of my proposed Dictionary, with a few preceding observations which I request you to get a sight of—It occurred to me that the issuing of the half sheet in some such form, might aid me in my designs, & a specimen of the works was mentioned by Dr Mason.

What measures my friends will think it best to take, I know not. Perhaps they may sign a recommendation of my design, & of the school books whose sales must supply me with the means of prosecuting it, & consent that I should publish it with the specimen.

They will take time & decide. If any thing is done, I wish it may be within 4 or 5 weeks, as I purpose to go eastward about that time.

I saw Dr Miller & Dr Hosack of the physicians & Dr Bruch [?] of the Episcopal Church, who expressed the utmost readiness to cooperate with other Gentlemen in this design. To the other gentlemen, I wish Dr Romeyer [?] & some others of the clergy, lawyers & physicians may be added.

Since I was in New York, I have been examining the Ethiopic language, & have got about half through the Lexicon. I find this a branch of the great Assyrian stock; about one third of the language being Hebrew

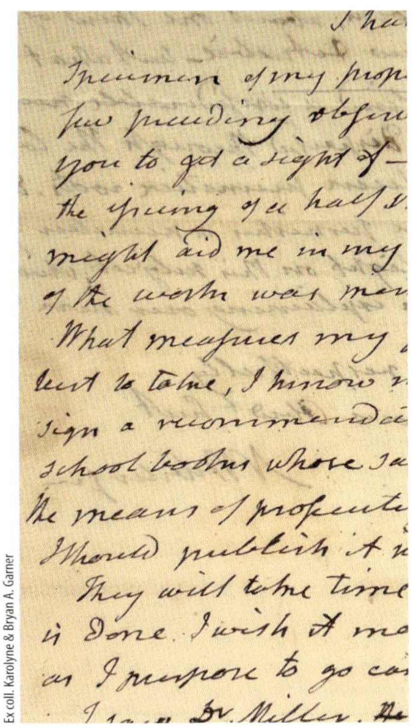

Ex coll. Karolyne & Bryan A. Garner

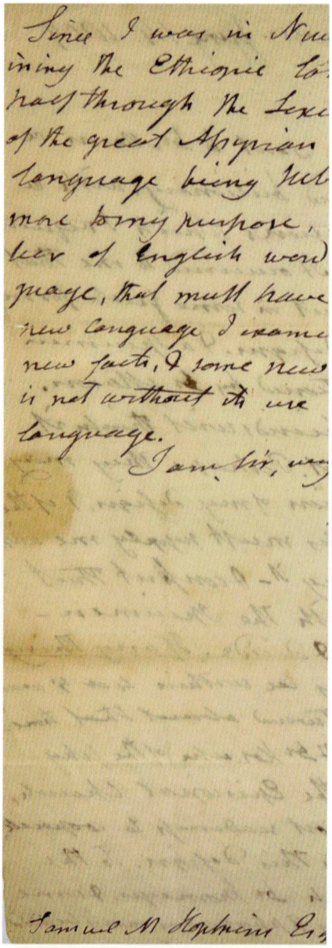

Since I was in New
ining the Ethiopic lo
nas through the Lexi
of the great Assyrian
language being Heb
more to my purpose,
ber of English word
guage, that must have
new language I examine
new facts, & some new
is not without its use
language.
I am Sir, ver

Samuel M Hopkins Esq

Ex coll. Karolyne & Bryan A. Garner

Detail from the 1809 letter.

"[Johnson's] *Dictionary*, the accuracy of which must depend on minute distinctions or laborious researches into unentertaining books, . . . [is] extremely imperfect and full of error. . . . The confidence now reposed in its accuracy is the *greatest injury to philology* that now exists." (Noah Webster in an 1807 letter [Boulton 1971:127, 139].)

& Arabic—but what is more to my purpose, I find a considerable number of English words dispersed through the language, that must have been primitive roots. Every new language I examine furnishes a number of new facts, & some new light on this subject, which is not without its use in explaining our own language.

I am, Sir, very respectfully

your obed^{t} serv^{t}

N Webster jun.

Samuel M Hopkins Esq

No such specimen sheet has ever been recorded. Skeel records a broadside of 1807 (Skeel 1958:581) and notes a "subscription blank, headed with an appeal for support in the project," printed as Appendix XXVII in Emily Field's *Notes on the Life of Noah Webster*. Two articles by Webster (in the *Panoplist* of February 1810 and in the *Monthly Anthology* of March 1810) appeared about this time, also asking for support. Skeel records a "specimen of the lexicography of Webster's dictionary; but not of the type" appearing putatively in 1826, consisting of "a caption title and sample words from the dictionary, taken from A through G, mostly from C." (Skeel 1958:232–33.) But perhaps this is misdated, and it's really from as early as 1809. That may be the reality. After all, the letter here uses the term *specimen*, and the broadside has the heading: "The following is a specimen of the lexicography of Webster's dictionary; but not of the type . . . ."

A "prospectus" appearing in 1826 was published as an advertisement in the *Connecticut Herald* (2 May 1826), with 14 recommendations from prominent men—but no specimen has ever emerged, despite the evidence in this 1809 letter that one had been produced. Hence this is an important letter from the early period of Webster's struggles to produce his large *Dictionary*.

In the final paragraph, we see that Webster is already engaged in the time-wasting exercise of "examining the Ethiopic language," etc., looking for semblances of English words and therefore purporting to discover "primitive roots." Strangely, as one biographer puts it, "the search for truth would lead this brilliant polymath to build an alternative universe entirely out of gibberish." (Kendall 2010:276.)

The second document here relates to the place where Webster created this alternative universe. In 1812, having nearly reached 50, Webster found himself once again in financial straits. He had been trying to sell his New Haven home (Arnold House), and he finally succeeded. On July 13, he purchased a half-finished double house in Amherst, his purpose being to economize for the sake of his family. At this point, he had seven children and plenty of furniture, including his circular table on which he toiled on his dictionary. Not everyone in his family was pleased with the move: two of his daughters were leaving behind their beaus. One was William Ellsworth, who had become engaged to 22-year-old Emily. The other was Chauncey Goodrich, who had become connected with 19-year-old Julia.

This deed essentially constituted a mortgage on Webster's new house in Amherst. He simultaneously borrowed $3,000 from Oliver Dickinson, the uncle of Emily Dickinson, and agreed to repay that amount with interest within four years—in default of which the house would become Dickinson's. Secured by two notes payable to Dickinson, this deed would become void if Webster kept his end of the bargain. Ultimately, Webster seems to have needed additional time to make the payments: he took six years. But he didn't default, as he had done in the 1790s on a real-estate deal with Lindley Murray. (Garner 2020a:479–80.)

The deed is a printed form with blanks filled in, and it contains rather exuberant legalese:

> I, Noah Webster of Newhaven [sic] in the State of Connecticut Esquire / For and in consideration of the sum of three thousand Dollars current money in the Commonwealth aforesaid, to me in hand paid, before the ensealing hereof, by Oliver Dickinson of Hadley in the County of Hampshire & Commonwealth of Massachusetts yeoman / the receipt whereof I do hereby acknowledge and am fully satisfied, contented, and paid, HAVE given, granted, bargained, sold, aliened, released, conveyed and confirmed, and by these Presents, do freely, clearly and absolutely give, grant, bargain, sell, alien, release, convey and confirm, unto him—the said Oliver, his Heirs and Assigns forever . . . .

Soon Webster would be at home in Amherst, employing the Horne Tooke method of etymology he adopted: scurrying around his circular desk to find superficial resemblances in dictionaries of various languages, and then recording them as cognate terms without further investigation. Webster's false, fanciful etymologizing set him back at least a decade in completing the big dictionary. By the 1860s, Webster dictionaries would have all this etymological nonsense removed.

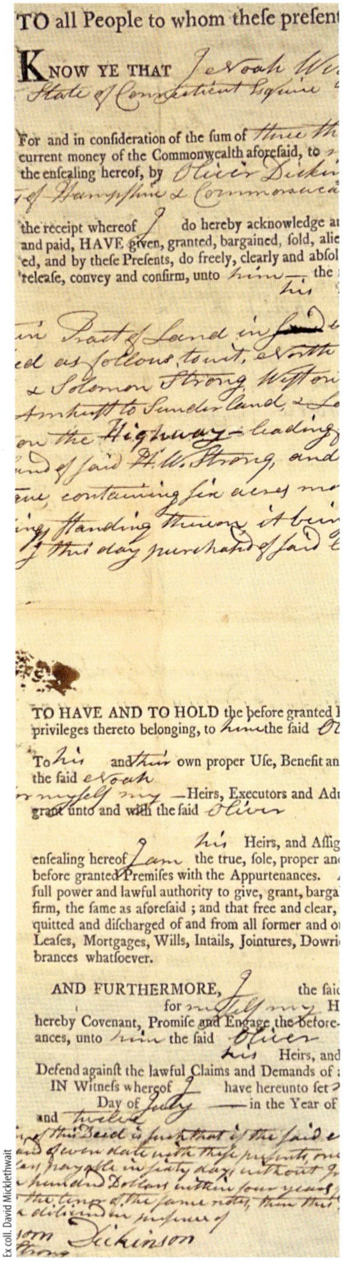
TO all People to whom thefe prefen
KNOW YE THAT
For and in confideration of the fum of
current money of the Commonwealth aforefaid, to
the enfealing hereof, by
the receipt whereof do hereby acknowledge a
and paid, HAVE given, granted, bargained, fold, ali
ed, and by thefe Prefents, do freely, clearly and abfol
releafe, convey and confirm, unto the
TO HAVE AND TO HOLD the before granted
privileges thereto belonging, to the faid
To and own proper Ufe, Benefit an
the faid
—Heirs, Executors and Adı
grant unto and with the faid
Heirs, and Affig
enfealing hereof the true, fole, proper an
before granted Premifes with the Appurtenances.
full power and lawful authority to give, grant, barga
firm, the fame as aforefaid ; and that free and clear,
quitted and difcharged of and from all former and o
Leafes, Mortgages, Wills, Intails, Jointures, Dowri
brances whatfoever.
AND FURTHERMORE, the fai
for
hereby Covenant, Promife and Engage the before-
ances, unto the faid
Heirs, and
Defend againft the lawful Claims and Demands of
IN Witnefs whereof have hereunto fet
Day of —in the Year of
and

Ex coll. David Micklethwait

Detail from the 1812 deed.

Ex coll. Karolyne & Bryan A. Garner

59

William Taylor

Sifting Through Our Double Nomenclature

Taylor, W[illiam], Jr. *English Synonyms Discriminated.* London: W. Pople, 1813.

William Taylor (1765–1836) was born to a middle-class merchant family in Norwich, about 110 miles northeast of London. When he was seven, his Unitarian parents sent him to the nearby Palgrave Academy, a "dissenting academy." Because those who didn't adhere to the Church of England were excluded from the universities, such academies offered them a parallel educational track. The one chosen by Taylor's parents in 1774 had no reputation to speak of at the time, but it was to become one of the most important educational establishments of the century. It was led by Anna Letitia Barbauld (1743–1825), one of the great poets and intellects of the age, and her husband, Rochemont (1749–1808). Palgrave was perhaps the best, and certainly the most intellectually exciting, place where he might have studied. (See McCarthy 1997.) Taylor would later call Anna Letitia Barbauld "the mother of my mind." (McCarthy 2008:448.)

Starting in 1779, Taylor made several trips to the Continent, on one of which he developed the interest in German literature that stayed with him the rest of his life. Soon he began publishing translations of contemporary German literature, including Johann Wolfgang von Goethe's *Iphigenie auf Tauris* (1789), Gotthold Ephraim Lessing's *Nathan der Weise* (1790), and Gottfried August Bürger's *Lenore* (1790)—the last a favorite of Barbauld and her brother, John Aikin.

"Those things are called *synonymous*, which describe the same things by other names: to *synonymize* is to express one thought in different phrases: *synonymy* is the use, a *synonymist* the user of synonyms, and *synonimicon* describes a dictionary of them." (Introduction, p. v.)

In the 1790s Taylor was an extraordinarily energetic writer. He wrote philosophical-cum-political dialogues to promote his radical political ideas, his biblical scholarship drew on the "higher criticism" fashionable in Germany, and he turned out a prodigious number of book reviews—one critic counts 1,754 reviews and articles in his name (*DNB*). As his biographer, David Chandler, observes, "He should almost certainly be considered the outstanding British reviewer of the 1790s." (*ODNB*.)

But Taylor lost momentum in the new century. He became convinced that he was no longer writing his best work, and his finances grew feeble. In 1811, his family was forced to move to a smaller house. Perhaps in response to the decline in his fortunes, he published *Synonyms Discriminated* in 1813. Others—John Trusler in *The Difference, between Words, Esteemed Synonymous* (1766) and Hester Piozzi in *British Synonymy* (1794)—had done similar things (Taylor mentions Piozzi only to dismiss her). But the *Monthly Review* noted that Taylor's knowledge of Germany made him perfectly suited to the task: he "found, in an acquaintance with German literature, the means of essentially facilitating the task of discriminating English words of kindred signification." (Anon. 1815:314.)

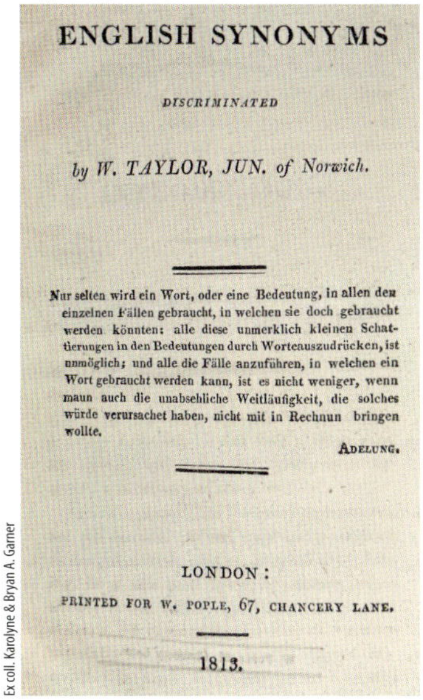
ENGLISH SYNONYMS

DISCRIMINATED

by W. TAYLOR, JUN. of Norwich.

Nur selten wird ein Wort, oder eine Bedeutung, in allen den einzelnen Fällen gebraucht, in welchen sie doch gebraucht werden könnten: alle diese unmerklich kleinen Schattierungen in den Bedeutungen durch Worteauszudrücken, ist unmöglich; und alle die Fälle anzuführen, in welchen ein Wort gebraucht werden kann, ist es nicht weniger, wenn maun auch die unabsehliche Weitläufigkeit, die solches würde verursachet haben, nicht mit in Rechnun bringen wollte.

ADELUNG.

LONDON:

PRINTED FOR W. POPLE, 67, CHANCERY LANE.

1813.

Ex coll. Karolyne & Bryan A. Garner

Taylor explained the need for his work by sketching a grand history of vocabulary growth. "Rude ages," he said, suffered from a poverty of words: "Thus in Hebrew *ruakh* spirit, stands for *breath*, for *temper*, for *soul*, and for *ghost*"—not enough words. Linguistic poverty leads to imports, "which enrich but encumber the national vocabulary." That then leads to an overabundance of synonyms—too many words. Only a properly mature culture has just the right number of words. "The english language," he announced, "has not yet completed this last spire of the progress. Our double nomenclature is still too numerous." (Pp. vii–viii.) His mission, therefore, was to ensure that we use our words with proper economy.

"Our tongue abounds especially with duplicates, one of which is borrowed from some gothic, the other from some roman, dialect. *Freedom, happiness,* are saxon, *liberty, felicity,* are latin, terms, which are not merely similar, but identical, in meaning: so are the adjectives *friendly, amical;* and the verbs *to lessen, to diminish*." (Introduction, p. vi.)

The book consists of short articles that consider two or more words—one entry has as many as twelve—and explains their proper application: *die* and *expire*, for instance, or *little* and *small*, or the trio *talent*, *genius*, and *intellect*. (There is no discernible order to the articles, but an alphabetical index at the back directs readers to the appropriate part of the book.) The result is something of a gallimaufry. Sometimes the entries are admirably pithy, as when he discriminates *untruth*, *lie*, and *falsehood*: "An untruth is an involuntary, a lie is a voluntary falsehood." (P. 2.) Others give us insights into cultural attitudes in Regency England, as in the entry on *public-house*, *hotel*, *tavern*, *inn*, and *ale-house*: "A gentleman may not frequent an ale-house; a lady may not frequent a tavern. The master of an hotel disdains, the master of an inn dislikes, to hear his place of entertainment called a public-house: this word is falling in respectability." (P. 109.)

Taylor was proud of his etymologies—prouder than he had any reason to be. They were, he was convinced, the key to words' true meanings, and the *Critical Review* agreed: "Etymology, if it be not the polar-star, is at least the compass of synonymy. [Taylor] is the first writer who has been fully sensible of this truth." (Anon. 1816:583.) But they often enticed him into insisting on distinctions that had no basis in usage. He provided a decent discussion of what *village*, *hamlet*, and *town* mean, for instance, but then felt obliged to insist on what they *should* mean: "town being derived from *tunan*, to shut, ought to mean a village walled in: hamlet being a diminutive, and village a collective, they ought rather to differ in size than in kind." (P. 69.) Worse still, he sometimes combined factitious distinctions with erroneous etymologies, as with *ay* and *yes*: "Both these words derive from the french imperative *ayez* have it so!" (They don't.) "*Ay* being the first syllable suspends the sense after uttering as it were the *have*, and *yes* being the concluding syllable completes the assent and subjoins the *so*. Ay therefore should be a weaker and less entire assentation than yes: indeed it is often merely suspensive, and not at all affirmative." (P. 192.)

Though the reviews were generally positive ("a very useful manual for those who aim at speaking and writing their own language with accuracy": Anon. 1815:314), at least part of the book's reception must have been awkward for Taylor. Lexicographers are accustomed to being stolen from, but he must have been stung by plagiarism from someone he had counted a friend for decades. George Crabb (1778–1851) had known and liked Taylor since his childhood in Palgrave. But his *English Synonymes Explained, in Alphabetical Order* (1816) owed a significant debt to his old friend. As the *Critical Review* noted when it reviewed the two together, "Mr. T. has great reason to complain of the treatment he has received from Mr. C. . . . Mr. T.'s book, it is apparent to us, could never have been out of Mr. C.'s hands." To be fair to Crabb, though, his borrowings usually improve Taylor's original: as the *Critical Review* noted, his "frequent practice is to amplify and preach upon the text Mr. T. has furnished him with." (Anon. 1816:582, 590–91.)

Taylor's career-topping work, *Historic Survey of German Poetry, Interspersed with Various Translations*, 3 vols. (1828–1830), brought together much of what he had written since the 1780s. It was a disappointment. Thomas Carlyle acknowledged Taylor's eminence in

Warm. Hot.

Warm is a mild and welcome, hot a strong and unwelcome, degree of heat. Milk is warm as it comes from the cow, hot as it boils on the fire. Warm is opposed to cool, and hot to cold.

Sleepy. Drowsy.

He is sleepy, who tends to fall asleep any where; he is drowsy, who tends to fall asleep while he is sitting up. To be sleepy is often welcome; to be drowsy is always indecorous.

"Our English books of synonymy would perhaps admit of some amendment by an approximation to foreign models. I have thought fit at least to make the experiment, and to write anew several definitions of the terms, which are most commonly examined and compared in the circulating catalogues of synonyms. This task has proved an agreeable relaxation to me during the intervals of severer but less popular studies." (Introduction, pp. xvii–xviii.)

Vocabulary. Dictionary. Lexicon. Glossary.

Vocabulary describes any word-book; but dictionaries, lexicons, and glossaries are word-books alphabetically arranged. In vocabularies for spelling, the words are often classed according to the number of syllables. A dictionary may be confined to the words and phrases of a language; or it may be set apart for mythology, science, biography. Lexicon, being a word derived from the greek, is more commonly used of a dictionary for the greek, or some other dead language. A glossary is a collection of obsolete or unusual expressions, a supplement to the dictionary of current and living speech, intended to facilitate the perusal of antiquated or provincial or technical writings.

German studies, but concluded that "this *Historic Survey* has not any thing historical in it; but is a mere aggregate of Dissertations, Translations, Notices and Notes, bound together indeed by the circumstance that they are all about German Poetry." (Carlyle 1831:156, 164.) Taylor had outlived his moment. His health declined slowly through the 1830s, and he died in 1836.

"If invited by the public patronage, I shall occasionally continue this task of definition, and may probably accumulate, during the ensuing year, materials for another such volume." (Introduction, pp. xviii–xix.)

Ex coll. Karolyne & Bryan A. Garner

60

George Crabb

Synonymist

Crabb, George. *English Synonymes Explained, in Alphabetical Order*. London: Baldwin, Cradock & Joy, 1816.

Ex coll. Karolyne & Bryan A. Garner

"For the sentiments scattered through this work I offer no apology." (1816 preface.)

THERE WERE TWO literary contemporaries with identically pronounced names: George Crabbe (1754–1832), the poet and clergyman; and George Crabb (1778–1851), the barrister and failed clergyman. It is the latter man with whom we are here concerned. He studied medicine but couldn't tolerate the sight of blood without fainting; studied for the ministry but was forced to leave when he had a sudden change of religious views; lived in Germany for six years while teaching English; and finally, in his mid-30s, entered Oxford, where he graduated seven years later with a BA in 1821 with high honors in mathematics. Soon he wrote two encyclopedias: *The Universal Technological Dictionary* (1823) and *The Universal Historical Dictionary* (1825). In 1829, at the age of 51, he was called to the bar, where he had an office practice because he was shy, retiring, and bookish. He wrote various legal treatises, such as a *History of English Law* (1829), *The Conveyancer's Assistant* (1835), and *The Law of Real Property* (1846).

Today he is primarily remembered as the synonymist who curiously used the French spelling *synonyme*. In one form or another, the book that came to be known as *Crabb's English Synonyms* (or sometimes Crabb's original spelling *Synonymes*) would stay in print for 160 years, through the 1970s.

In the preface to his first edition, Crabb called the study of synonyms a major chasm in English literature: "not a single writer . . . has treated it in a scientific manner adequate to its importance." (P. iii.) That he makes no mention of John Trusler's *Difference, between Words, Esteemed Synonymous* (1766), Hester Piozzi's *British Synonymy* (1794), or even his friend William Taylor's *English Synonyms Discriminated* (1813) suggests that he believes they were failures—impressionistic, roundabout, and belletristic.

People today are apt to think of synonym books as collections of words with closely related or overlapping senses, such as we find in a *Roget's Thesaurus* (no. 76)—simple lists, supported by no analysis or discussion. We're told that *anxious* belongs to the class containing *worried* and *uneasy*, but it's our job to determine whether *bothered*, *jittery*, *unquiet*, and *apprehensive* are appropriate in context. Crabb's book, though, like Taylor's and Piozzi's, belongs to a genre more closely aligned with the usage dictionary. It takes a small group of synonyms and, in the space of a paragraph or two, elucidates their shades of meaning, differentiating one from the next by sense, by idiom, or by suitability in a given context. The term we often use to describe the creation of a reference book is *compiled*, which suggests a simple mechanical process of bringing things together. Yet a book like Crabb's is truly *written*, not compiled, and is written for a serious reader. It is replete with reasoning and analysis. And though some book reviewers accused Crabb of plagiarizing from William Taylor's recently published synonymy (no. 59), most of his borrowings are acknowledged, and—no offense to Taylor—Crabb almost always improved the material as he reworked it.

Crabb's book, in 772 double-columned quarto pages, required extreme authorial care. We can see his exacting nature in the book's structure. Crabb follows Piozzi in putting the book in alphabetical order by the first of each cluster of synonyms—an entry on *perception, idea, conception, notion* is followed by *perish, die, decay*, then *perpetrate, commit*, and then *pillar, column*. But since only one word in each cluster can determine alphabetical positioning, copious cross-references lead from synonyms to the main articles in which they are discussed: "DISORDERLY, *v. Irregular* . . . TO DISOWN, *v. To deny*. . . . TO DISOWN, *v. To disclaim*." Neither Piozzi nor Taylor provided users with this essential help. To make the book more usable still, Crabb's edition of 1826 opens with a 58-page alphabetical index, allowing readers to locate every word discussed within seconds. To find a discussion of *stupid* in Piozzi, you'd have to know to look under *dull* on page 176 of volume 1. You might well give up the search. In Crabb, you can find it in a trice.

For that very entry, let us compare the approach of the two synonymists (Taylor has no corresponding entry):

"Although a work of this description does not afford much scope for system and arrangement, yet I laid down to myself the plan of arranging the words according to the extent or universality of their acceptation, placing those first which had the most general sense and application." (1816 preface.)

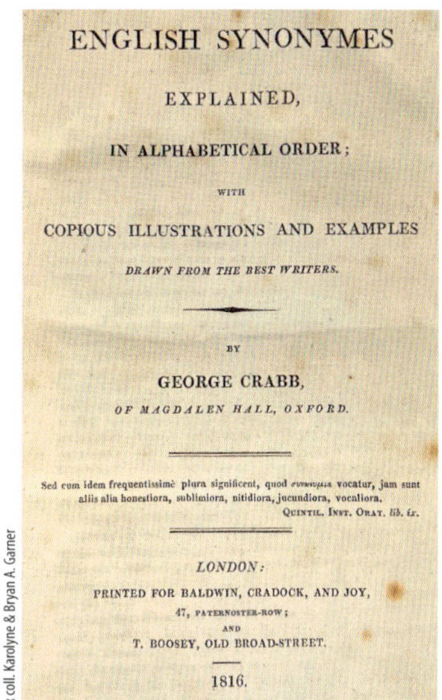
ENGLISH SYNONYMES

EXPLAINED,

IN ALPHABETICAL ORDER;

WITH

COPIOUS ILLUSTRATIONS AND EXAMPLES

DRAWN FROM THE BEST WRITERS.

BY

GEORGE CRABB,

OF MAGDALEN HALL, OXFORD.

Sed cum idem frequentissimè plura significent, quod συνωνυμια vocatur, jam sunt aliis alia honestiora, sublimiora, nitidiora, jucundiora, vocaliora.

QUINTIL. INST. ORAT. *lib. ix.*

LONDON:

PRINTED FOR BALDWIN, CRADOCK, AND JOY,

47, PATERNOSTER-ROW;

AND

T. BOOSEY, OLD BROAD-STREET.

1816.

Ex coll. Karolyne & Bryan A. Garner

"Notwithstanding all my care . . . , I was compelled to curtail much of what I had written, for fear of increasing the volume to an inconvenient extent." (1816 preface.)

"It may seem surprising that the English, who have employed their talents successfully in every branch of literature, and in none more than in that of philology, should yet have fallen below other nations in the study of their synonymes." (1816 preface.)

Piozzi (1794)	Crabb (1816)
DULL, STUPID, HEAVY Of the first upon this flat and insipid list Mr. Pope has greatly enlarged the signification, and taught us to call every thing DULL that was not immediately and positively witty. This is too much, surely; and indeed one finds it received so only in the Dunciad or Essay upon Criticism. Information may be HEAVY sometimes without being STUPID or DULL, I think; its own weight of matter may render it so; and he who conveys useful knowledge should neither be mocked nor slighted because he happens to be unskilled in the art of levigating his learning to hit the strength or rather feebleness of moderns to endure it. There is however a kind of talk that is merely HEAVY, and in no sense important. Such conversation has been lately called a *bore*, from the idea that it gave some old sportsman originally I believe of a horse that hangs upon his rider's hand with a weight of STUPID impulse, as if he would *bore* the very ground through with his nose; tiring the man upon his back most cruelly. The cant phrase used at those public schools, where they call a boy who is not quick-witted, and cannot be made a scholar, a *blunt*, is so good, that I sigh for its removal into social life, where blunts are exceedingly frequent, and we have no word for them. Dullard is out of use; we find it now only in Shakespeare. [Pp. 176–77.]	STUPID, DULL. STUPID, in Latin *stupidus* from *stupeo* to be amazed or bewildered, expresses an amazement which is equivalent to a deprivation of understanding. DULL, through the medium of the German *toll* and Swedish *stollig*, comes from the Latin *stultus* simple or foolish, denotes a simple deficiency; *stupidity* in its proper sense is natural to a man; although a particular circumstance may have a similar effect upon the understanding. He who is questioned in the presence of others may appear very *stupid* in that which is otherwise very familiar to him: *dull* is an incidental quality, arising principally from the state of the animal spirits; a writer may sometimes be *dull* who is otherwise vivacious and pointed. A person may be *dull* in a large circle while he is very lively in private intercourse. A *stupid* butt is only fit for the conversation of ordinary people. Addison. It is the great advantage of a trading nation that there are very few in it so *dull* and heavy who may not be placed in stations of life which may give them an opportunity of making their fortunes. Addison. [P. 740.]

Ex coll. Karolyne & Bryan A. Garner

"I write not to please or displease any description of person; but I trust that what I have written according to the dictates of my mind will meet the approbation of those whose good opinion I am most solicitous to obtain. . . . I throw myself on the indulgence of the public, with the assurance that, having used every endeavor to deserve their approbation, I shall not make an appeal to their candor in vain." (1816 preface.)

This short example reveals the differences in approach: where Piozzi is rambling, Crabb is systematic—beginning with etymology, amplifying the distinctions, and then illustrating with quotations. Crabb's preface explains that he found all his quotations not by looking in Johnson's *Dictionary*, but through his own reading of the original authors (probably a slight aimed at Piozzi). How sound are

Crabb's etymologies? Not bad: his treatment of *stupid* accords with what is today found in the *OED*; his treatment of *dull* rightly connects the word to the German *toll*, though he is extravagant in connecting it also to the Latin *stultus* and perhaps even to the Swedish *stollig*.

We might further compare these treatments against the best of the 20th-century books within the genre: *Webster's Dictionary of Synonyms* (1942). Notice how much closer Crabb comes to this modern discussion than Piozzi, whose treatment lacks this rigor:

> **Stupid, dull, dense, crass, dumb** agree in meaning conspicuously lacking in intelligence or power to absorb ideas or impressions, or exhibiting such a lack. **Stupid** implies a benumbed or dazed state of mind that is either congenital or the result of intoxication, a shock, illness, or the like; although it seldom is applied to the insane or the imbecile, it often also suggests senselessness; as, "*stupid* with age" (*Shak.*); *stupid* with drink; "he could not stand *stupid* people, especially those who are made *stupid* by education" (*Wilde*). "What force, what fury drove us into saying the *stupid*, intolerant, denunciatory things we said . . . ?" (*L.P. Smith*). **Dull** (see also dull, 2) suggests slowness or sluggishness of mind that may be constitutional, or the result of lack of mental exercise, or of overwork, or of a physical condition. A person or thing that is *stupid* reveals a deadness or a deadening of the mental powers; a person or thing that is *dull* manifests a lack of mental quickness or alertness or heavy, labored mental processes; thus, constitutionally *dull* pupils progress slowly until they are awakened by good teaching; constitutionally *stupid* pupils are usually subnormal physically or mentally; a *dull* book is so lacking in brightness, liveliness, or other signs of a stimulated mind, that it bores the reader; a *stupid* book exasperates the reader by its fatuousness, inanity, or other signs of mental ineptness; so, all work and no play makes Jack a *dull* boy; "Compared with her, other women were heavy and *dull*" (*Cather*). . . . [P. 798.]

The modern treatment places much less stock in etymology: *current meaning* is the thing. What is striking about this genre, though—a genre pioneered by Trusler, loosely contemplated by Piozzi, developed by Taylor, greatly perfected by Crabb, and reaching its apotheosis (so far) in Merriam-Webster's little-used book—is the unrelenting acuteness of mind required to discern the minute differences between semantically related terms.

"If synonyms were words which had always exactly the same meaning, there would be no need for such a book. It is the differences, unseen by the undiscerning, the ignorant, or the careless, between words that are of similar import, that gave Crabb his meticulous labor and a life beyond his years." (Finley 1917:v.)

Ex coll. Karolyne & Bryan A. Garner

"Inestimable bad is done not only by putting good words to a purposely bad use, but by using good words with a good purpose inaccurately, whether from ignorance, chronic slovenliness, or occasional carelessness. So I am constrained [wrong word?] to join in this celebration of Crabb's centennial . . . because of what he has done to help keep from debasement our old English coin as medium of intellectual exchange." (Finley 1917:vi–vii.)

John Pickering.

"The preservation of the *English language* in its purity throughout the United States is an object deserving the attention of every American who is a friend to the literature and science of his country." (Prefatory Essay, p. 9.)

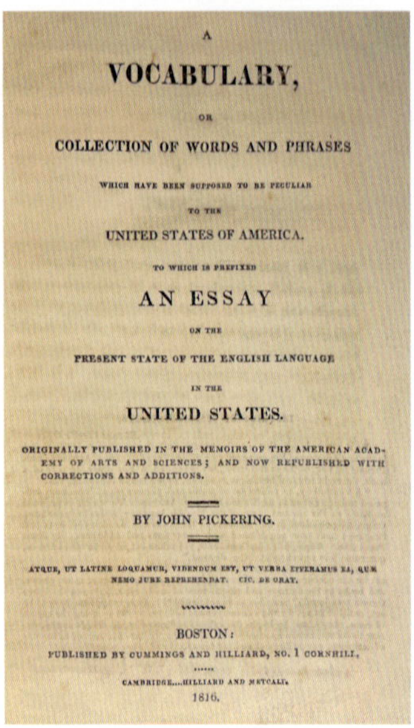

A
VOCABULARY,
OR
COLLECTION OF WORDS AND PHRASES
WHICH HAVE BEEN SUPPOSED TO BE PECULIAR
TO THE
UNITED STATES OF AMERICA.
TO WHICH IS PREFIXED
AN ESSAY
ON THE
PRESENT STATE OF THE ENGLISH LANGUAGE
IN THE
UNITED STATES.
ORIGINALLY PUBLISHED IN THE MEMOIRS OF THE AMERICAN ACADEMY OF ARTS AND SCIENCES; AND NOW REPUBLISHED WITH CORRECTIONS AND ADDITIONS.
BY JOHN PICKERING.
ATQUE, UT LATINE LOQUAMUR, VIDENDUM EST, UT VERBA EFFERAMUS EA, QUÆ NEMO JURE REPREHENDAT. CIC. DE ORAT.
BOSTON:
PUBLISHED BY CUMMINGS AND HILLIARD, NO. 1 CORNHILL.
CAMBRIDGE....HILLIARD AND METCALF.
1816.

Ex coll. Karolyne & Bryan A. Garner

61

John Pickering's Americanisms and Noah Webster's Galling Answer

Pickering, John. ***A Vocabulary, or Collection of Words and Phrases which have been supposed to be peculiar to the United States of America. To which is prefixed an essay on the present state of the English language in the United States.*** **Boston: Cummings & Hilliard, 1816.**

Webster, Noah. ***A Letter to the Honorable John Pickering, on the subject of his Vocabulary; or, Collection of Words and Phrases, supposed to be peculiar to the United States of America.*** **Boston: West & Richardson, 1817. [Reprinted in Warfel 1953:341–94.]**

Pickering (1777–1846) was born in Salem, Massachusetts, one of the ten children of Timothy and Rebecca White Pickering. His father was a revolutionary, a militant Federalist, and a conservative gadfly who was a failed U.S. Secretary of State and an undistinguished member of the U.S. Senate and House of Representatives. John Pickering graduated from Harvard University in 1796, became a practicing lawyer in 1804, and spent much of the rest of his life declining prestigious academic posts so that he could pursue his philological interests. From 1839 to 1846, he served as president of the American Academy of Arts and Sciences.

Pickering's *Vocabulary* was the first attempt to collect peculiar Americanisms into a glossary of provincialisms. In 1814, he presented it orally to the American Academy of Arts and Sciences, and it was reprinted as a stand-alone book in 1816. In his preface, he expressed his conviction that most readers wouldn't understand the effort that necessarily goes into lexicography, even if it's for a partial glossary:

> The present volume is the result of [my] labour; for labour it may truly be called. To those persons indeed, who have never undertaken to make such a collection, and to investigate, compare and cite the numerous authorities, which a work of this nature demands, the present volume will, perhaps,

> appear not to have been a very arduous task. But when the reader shall have examined it, and have observed the various citations, and the continual references to dictionaries and glossaries, he will be able to form some judgment of the time and pains it must have cost me. [P. iv.]

Meanwhile, Pickering was conscious of the criticism he would inevitably receive from ultracrepidarians who might object to "mere vulgarisms":

> It should . . . be recollected, that I was not making a *dictionary* of our language, but a *glossary of provincialisms*; that many words would be admitted into such a work (as they are in fact by the English glossarists) which would be rejected from a dictionary; and, that it seemed to be useful . . . to insert *all* words, *the legitimacy of which had been questioned*; in order that their claim to a place in the language might be discussed and settled. . . . In this country, as is the case in England, we have thirsty reformers and presumptuous sciolists, who would unsettle the whole of our admirable language for the purpose of making it conform to their whimsical notions of propriety. Some of our corruptions have originated with such people. [Pp. v–vi.]

For the benefit of general lexicographers, Pickering supplied a 206-page book filled with useful information. Pickering carefully assessed what had been said in philological literature about each term; it was painstaking work. The words that Pickering listed were mostly either American neologisms or new American senses for old words. Many were also regionalisms. The entries for *B* are *back and forth*, *backwoodsmen*, *balance* (= remainder), *banditti* as a plural, *bank-bill*, *barbecue*, *base* (= to found or build upon), *be* (as in *Be you ready?*), *beaker*, *belittle*, *bestowment*, *betterments*, *bluff* (= a cliff), *boatable* (= navigable), *boating* (= transporting by boat), *book-store* (as opposed to *bookseller*), *bottom* (= to base), *bottom-lands* (= the rich flat land on the bank of a river), *brack* (= a breach or flaw in a piece of cloth), *brash* (= brittle), *breachy* (= [of oxen] so unruly as to be likely to break through an enclosure), *bread-stuff* (= bread-corn, meal), *bridge* (= [of a bumpy road] to raise with logs), *brief* (= prevalent, common, rife), and *brush* (= *brushwood*).

Although one might have expected Noah Webster to be grateful for this effort, given that he was at work on his unabridged dictionary, instead he seems to have felt threatened. Pickering was asserting

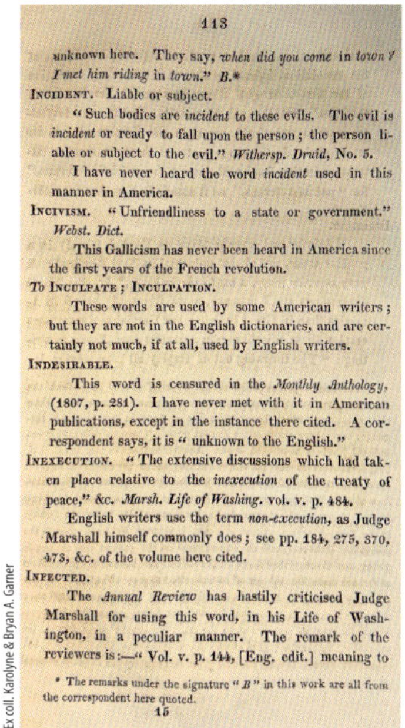

113

unknown here. They say, *when did you come in town? I met him riding in town.*" B.*

INCIDENT. Liable or subject.

"Such bodies are *incident* to these evils. The evil is *incident* or ready to fall upon the person; the person liable or subject to the evil." *Withersp. Druid*, No. 5.

I have never heard the word *incident* used in this manner in America.

INCIVISM. "Unfriendliness to a state or government." *Webst. Dict.*

This Gallicism has never been heard in America since the first years of the French revolution.

To INCULPATE; INCULPATION.

These words are used by some American writers; but they are not in the English dictionaries, and are certainly not much, if at all, used by English writers.

INDESIRABLE.

This word is censured in the *Monthly Anthology*, (1807, p. 281). I have never met with it in American publications, except in the instance there cited. A correspondent says, it is "unknown to the English."

INEXECUTION. "The extensive discussions which had taken place relative to the *inexecution* of the treaty of peace," &c. *Marsh. Life of Washing.* vol. v. p. 484.

English writers use the term *non-execution*, as Judge Marshall himself commonly does; see pp. 184, 275, 370, 473, &c. of the volume here cited.

INFECTED.

The *Annual Review* has hastily criticised Judge Marshall for using this word, in his Life of Washington, in a peculiar manner. The remark of the reviewers is:—"Vol. v. p. 144, [Eng. edit.] meaning to

* The remarks under the signature "B" in this work are all from the correspondent here quoted.

15

Ex coll. Karolyne & Bryan A. Garner

"Webster took his revenge . . . in *A Letter to the Honorable John Pickering*—not a private letter to Pickering but a published pamphlet of no fewer than sixty-four pages. He challenges Pickering word-by-word, indignantly assailing the resistance that Pickering had thrown into his path toward becoming America's great language reformer." (Martin 2019:60.)

Ex coll. Karolyne & Bryan A. Garner

himself as a philological authority, after all, and America had room, Webster seemed to think, for only one such person. And he concluded that it was *he*, after all, that Pickering was calling a "presumptuous sciolist." Webster wrote: "Whether you number me with the thirsty reformers and presumptuous sciolists is a fact which I shall take no pains to discover, nor if known would the fact give me the smallest concern. . . . As I have pushed my [linguistic] inquiries probably much farther than any other man, I am satisfied that the evidence I can lay before the public will convince you that there is a rich mine of knowledge to be opened on this subject that your English friends have never yet discovered." (P. 372.) Yet Webster had been mining etymological pyrite, not gold.

A born controversialist with an ever-quarrelsome spirit, Webster issued a rambling 64-page pamphlet attacking Pickering on every conceivable point, often digressing into complaints about Lindley Murray and others against whom he held grudges (even, over several pages, judges who had ruled against him on copyright issues). He couldn't help himself: "When I first read your *Vocabulary* . . . , I found in it many things which appeared to deserve animadversion and thought it incumbent on me, whose Dictionary you have often cited, to publish some remarks . . . and to correct what I apprehend to be erroneous opinions on the subject." (Pp. 341–42.) In fact, all Pickering had done was to point out many words that appeared in Webster's 1806 *Compendious Dictionary* but not elsewhere. They weren't overt criticisms, and Webster might have taken these citations as praise. Instead, he interpreted them as affronts.

Webster kindly recorded the evolution of his emotional reactions upon reading the *Vocabulary*: "I hesitated whether it would be expedient to trouble you or the public with my explanations and strictures." (P. 342.) But a pile of grievances soon overtook the hesitation: "The unfriendly dispositions manifested towards me by men of high standing in the republic of letters, and particularly in this commonwealth, and the virulence with which every effort to detect errors in long received opinions has hitherto been assailed . . . [afford] little ground to expect that any remarks of mine would have a salutary influence upon public opinion." (*Id.*) Webster was a peace-loving man: "To a man who seeks his own tranquillity and whose sole object is to enlighten and benefit his fellow citizens, controversy, even when conducted with liberality, is extremely irksome." (*Id.*) Webster would

"As an etymologist Webster was something less than adequate. . . . He chose to ignore (perhaps because of an inability to read German, one of those twenty-three languages he is reported to have 'mastered') the really significant work which had been done in linguistics in his day, preferring the tower of Babel explanation of the origin of individual tongues to the scientific methods of the Indo-Europeanists. . . . Webster's ignorance of Old English was deplorable as compared with what was well known by British scholars in his day. In the light of such facts, it is difficult not to question his proficiency in some of the other languages which he 'mastered' in the course of a myriad half-circuits around his famous desk." (Pyles 1952:167, 171–72.)

Ex coll. Karolyne & Bryan A. Garner

A Webster figurine.

prefer quiet serenity: "I would spend the small portion of life that remains to me in the humble walks of obscurity. In controversy with my fellow citizens, on any subject, I will *not* be engaged." (*Id.*) Yet his friends had overborne him with solicitations to answer Pickering.

If Webster were to respond accurately to Pickering, he said, his erudition would naturally result in a long treatise: "It is not my intention to animadvert upon every word in your collection. This would require a book larger than yours, and far exceed the limits I must prescribe to myself." (*Id.*)

Webster's extended diatribe abounds with absurd statements:

- *There are no true neologisms:* "'We [Americans] have formed some new words.' You cannot by this expression, mean words radically new or from new roots: for this, I am confident, is not true. And let me remark, Sir, that in this sense, probably, no new words have been introduced either into the English or into any other language since the dispersion of men." (P. 343.)
- *Americans aren't neologists:* "The charge against the people of this country of introducing new words is to a great degree unfounded. . . . I question whether ten words can be found among men of reputable character in the United States which are not authorized by English usage." (P. 346.)
- *All words were at first concrete:* "All the words in any language which express abstract ideas were first applied to sensible objects." (*Id.*)
- *Neologisms should be restricted:* "New words should not be introduced into a copious language without reason nor contrary to its analogies." (P. 368.)
- Island *is a repellent solecism:* "Another instance [of barbarism], Sir, occurs in the word *island*, than which a more barbarous word does not exist. This word does not belong to the English language." (P. 371.) (It's a strange beef to have with a word that had been used in English for more than a millennium. He made the same case in his *American Dictionary*: "There is no such legitimate word in English, and it is found only in books.")
- *English grammar is hopelessly flawed:* "The truth is, the grammar of our language is in a very imperfect state—full of error and confusion. To disembarrass it from this confusion is a work of no small labor." (P. 376.)

Ex coll. Karolyne & Bryan A. Garner

"In Webster, America produced what might have been expected from the New World, the preeminent cracker-barrel lexicographer, who knew all the answers. More a hack of all intellectual trades than a scholar, he was passably schooled but not learned, not even in the subject for which he is now best known. He was intelligent, but he had neither wit nor profundity, and he probably never felt the lack of either quality. He was alert, devout, industrious, patriotic, persistent, public-spirited, conceited, and perverse. Ignorance never dampened his fire, nor did a sense of humor temper his finality." (Laird 1970:263.)

"Etymology is an abstruse and difficult subject, and in no branch of literature have the imaginations of men wantoned with more licentiousness, than in tracing words to their originals." (Noah Webster 1839:19.)

- *The word* if *is a verb:* "When Lowth and Johnson, for example, call *if* a conjunction, and I discover that it is a verb with no connective use any more than *go* and *come*, I will not call it a conjunction." (*Id.*) This comes straight from Horne Tooke (no. 55).
- *The books of all Webster's predecessors aren't needed:* "So numerous are the errors, inaccuracies, and defects of the books on philology, which are received as authorities, as Vossius, Junius, Skinner, Lowth, Johnson, Harris, Walker, Murray, etc., that if our students could be entirely freed from the influence of their opinions and their minds left perfectly unbiassed, it would be a benefit to philological learning if all their writings on this subject could become extinct." (Pp. 378–79.)
- *Many English words have their origins in the Ethiopian language:* "I can assert that a great many Ethiopic words are in European languages; indeed, there are words in English which can hardly be understood without the aid of the Ethiopic." (P. 382.)

And so on. Before assuring Pickering of his "friendly disposition" and his "personal respect which is sincerely entertained," Webster expressed great optimism for his own beneficial influence over posterity: "I have contributed in a small degree to the instruction of at least four millions of the rising generation; and it is not unreasonable to expect that a few seeds of improvement planted by my hand may germinate and grow and ripen into valuable fruit when my remains shall be mingled with the dust." (P. 394.)

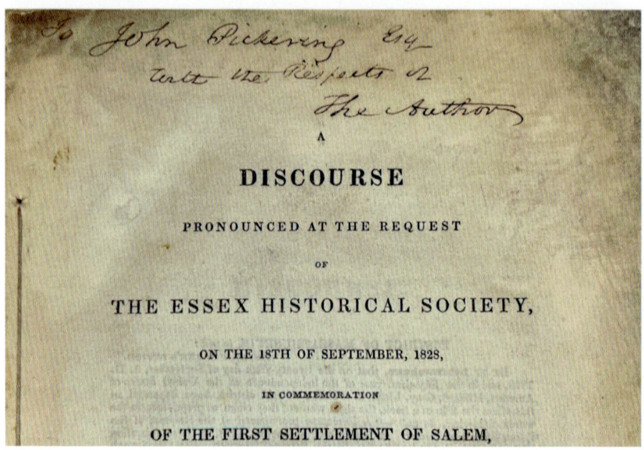
To John Pickering Esq
with the Respects of
The Author

A

DISCOURSE

PRONOUNCED AT THE REQUEST

OF

THE ESSEX HISTORICAL SOCIETY,

ON THE 18TH OF SEPTEMBER, 1828,

IN COMMEMORATION

OF THE FIRST SETTLEMENT OF SALEM,

Ex coll. Karolyne & Bryan A. Garner

The Garner Collection's copy of Justice Joseph Story's 1828 pamphlet inscribed to John Pickering.

VII. Lexical Warfare

At last in 1828, Noah Webster's magnum opus appeared: the two-volume American Dictionary of the English Language. *The impressive quarto offered the best definitions that had yet appeared. But his book was deeply flawed, as both allies and competitors would soon discover. Exhausted, Webster delegated the authority for an abridgment to his son-in-law Chauncey Goodrich, together with his publisher Sherman Converse. Together they hired Joseph Worcester, who interrupted work on his own dictionary to abridge (and clean up) Webster. Then Worcester resumed his own project, completing an astonishing three abridged dictionaries in just three years. Viewing Worcester's own book as insider competition, the infuriated Webster disowned Converse, railed against Worcester, and tried to distance himself from his own abridgment by assigning it to Goodrich, who soon became wealthy from the smaller dictionary. (He cut Goodrich and his wife, Webster's daughter Julia, from his will.) Meanwhile, Webster's big version didn't sell.*

Enter Lyman Cobb, who attacked Webster for spelling inconsistencies while promoting an Americanized version of John Walker's dictionary. Cobb damaged Webster and had much success with his books. The stakes were high: there was big money in dictionaries.

After Webster died virtually penniless, the rights in his dictionaries ignited strife among his heirs—including the disinherited Goodriches. After brothers George and Charles Merriam acquired the rights in Webster dictionaries, they decided to work with Goodrich, causing even more rancor. Meanwhile, the Merriams assailed the now-serious competitor Worcester on various fronts, and Worcester shot back. To make matters worse, a British publisher issued a version of Webster's dictionary called "Webster's & Worcester's Dictionary" on the spine. The accusations grew increasingly acrimonious.

After Worcester issued his magnum opus in 1860—the same year that Chauncey Goodrich died—the Merriams engaged Noah Porter of Yale to overhaul the Webster line of dictionaries. He excised what was left of Noah Webster's sermonizing and hired a German specialist, Mahn, to eliminate all the whimsical etymologies. Only then did the Merriam-Webster brand gain decisive ascendancy.

Others entered the lexicographic fray. In tranquiler Great Britain, William Cobbett issued three dictionaries in three consecutive years, signing prefaces from the room where Samuel Johnson once lived. Charles Richardson tried an experimental dictionary almost without definitions. Peter Mark Roget, a compulsive list-maker, published his groundbreaking thesaurus—the most popular of all time. We were entering a lexicographic heyday.

Ex coll. David Mickelthwait

Lyman Cobb's well-worn copy of Webster's big 1828 dictionary. For a sample of Cobb's marginalia in the volumes, see p. 213.

62

Noah Webster's Deeply Flawed Magnum Opus

Webster, Noah. *An American Dictionary of the English Language*. 2 vols. New York: Sherman Converse, 1828.

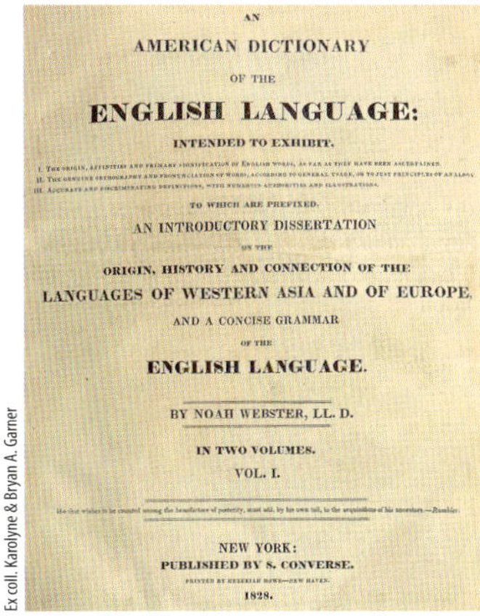
AN
AMERICAN DICTIONARY
OF THE
ENGLISH LANGUAGE:
INTENDED TO EXHIBIT,
TO WHICH ARE PREFIXED,
AN INTRODUCTORY DISSERTATION
ON THE
ORIGIN, HISTORY AND CONNECTION OF THE
LANGUAGES OF WESTERN ASIA AND OF EUROPE,
AND A CONCISE GRAMMAR
OF THE
ENGLISH LANGUAGE.
BY NOAH WEBSTER, LL. D.
IN TWO VOLUMES.
VOL. I.
NEW YORK:
PUBLISHED BY S. CONVERSE.
1828.

Ex coll. Karolyne & Bryan A. Garner

ALTHOUGH NOAH WEBSTER produced his compact one-volume *Compendious Dictionary* in 1806, this big two-volume work earned him the title Father of the American Dictionary. Released in November 1828, it was an important declaration of American identity, heralding the nation's linguistic independence from Great Britain. It marked the biggest milestone in English lexicography between Johnson's *Dictionary* (1755) and the *OED* (1928).

But even with a modest print run of 2,500 copies, retailing for $20 apiece, it failed to sell out over the next 13 years. The price was too high for most potential customers.

"If any man, whatever may be his abilities in other respects, should attempt to compile a new Dictionary, or amend Johnson's, without a profound knowledge of etymology, he will unquestionably do as much harm as good." (Noah Webster in an 1807 letter [Boulton 1971:139].)

Webster's achievement was remarkable in several respects. His wordlist, for instance, was much more comprehensive than that of earlier dictionaries. If we take the span of entries from *la* to *laird*, Webster provides 141 entries as compared to Johnson's 84. Some 17% of his headwords—12,000 of the total of 70,000—hadn't appeared in earlier dictionaries. He had mined the resources of American English to include such words as *caucus*, *electioneer*, *parachute*, *revolutionize*, *safety-valve*, *skunk*, *tomahawk*, and *wampum*. He developed his own system of recording pronunciations, which required him to have a new typeface cut to distinguish the "hard" and "soft" sounds of *C* and *G*.

Webster's definitions, too, were generally superior to those of his predecessors. Like Johnson, he was a splitter, identifying multiple meanings of most words and breaking them out with numbered senses. His definitions were also admirably clear. Consider the entry for *mortgage*. Johnson had defined it as "a dead pledge; a thing put into the hands of a creditor." For most readers, that's wholly unenlightening. Webster provides an etymology, "Fr. *mort*, dead, and *gage*, pledge," and continues, "Literally, a dead pledge; the grant of an estate

Ex coll. Karolyne & Bryan A. Garner

One of the copies in the Garner Collection.

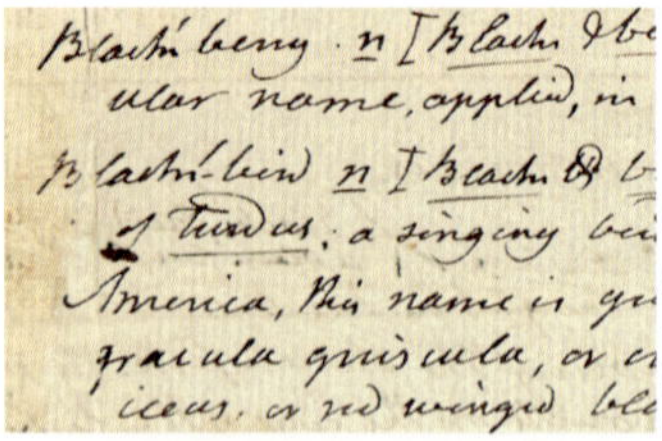

Ex coll. Karolyne & Bryan A. Garner

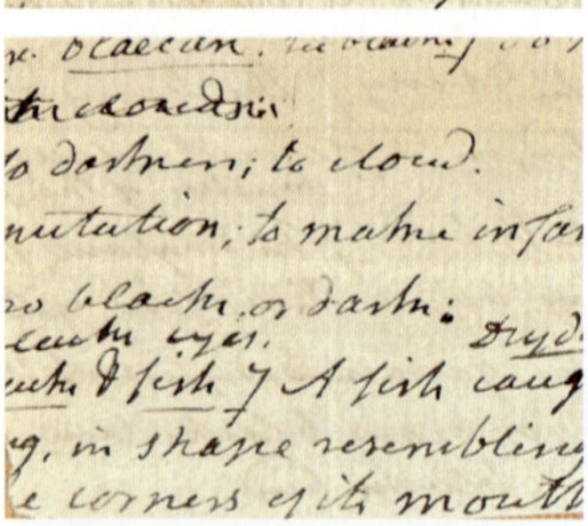

Ex coll. Karolyne & Bryan A. Garner

Detail from two fragments of Webster's 1828 manuscript sent by his daughter Eliza Steele Wheeler Jones (1803–1888) to William C. Roberson. In response to Roberson's request, Jones wrote: "I can only give you a scrap."

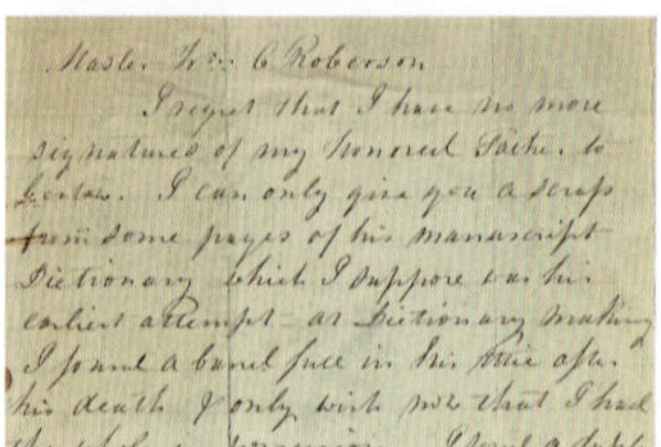

Ex coll. Karolyne & Bryan A. Garner

Ex coll. Jack Lynch

In 1958, the U.S. Postal Service issued a 4¢ stamp to honor Noah Webster.

in fee as security for the payment of money, and on the condition that if the money shall be paid according to the contract, the grant shall be void, and the mortgagee shall re-convey the estate to the mortgager." The entry then continues with a long quotation from Blackstone, but rather characteristically for Webster, it's impossible to tell where the Blackstone quotation begins—even if we can tell where it ends. The scholarship was hardly punctilious by modern standards.

Not everything in the *American Dictionary*, though, met the high standard of the definitions. Webster was completely ignorant of—or maybe uninterested in—the philological revolution that was changing our understanding of the Indo-European languages, and as a result, many of his etymologies were outlandish: over and over, he erroneously attempted to tie English words to Ethiopic (Ge'ez) and Chaldee (Aramaic), languages entirely unrelated to English.

Webster was also passionate about orthography—perhaps too passionate. He is more responsible than anyone else for most of the spellings labeled "chiefly American" today: American *color* for British *colour*, *center* for *centre*, *gray* for *grey*, *defense* for *defence*, *labeled* for *labelled*, all of which he convincingly argued were more logical than their traditional counterparts. (None were original with Webster, though he did much to promote their currency in the U.S.) But some of his quirkier thoughts about orthography had led him to try bizarre experiments in reformed spelling. And even in his *Dictionary* of 1828, he perversely held on to a few of his idiosyncratic positions (*chimist* rather than *chemist*, *porpess* rather than *porpoise*). He also dogmatically editorialized about "incorrect spellings" (*heinous* should be *hainous*, *island* should be *ieland*, *tongue* should be *tung*), and he introduced some weird new spellings (*bild*, *bridegoom*, *furlow*, *nighmar*, *parsnep*, *ribin*, *selvedge*, and *turnep*). What's worse, in hundreds of entries Webster would use one spelling in a headword and another throughout the sprawling two-volume text.

Even if you could overlook the false etymologies and the orthographic eccentricity, Webster's entries themselves were replete with digressive verbosity, prudishness, and a New Englander's provincialism. For example, sense 1 of *sauce* is given as "a mixture or composition to be eaten with food for improving its relish." Then comes sense 2: "In New England, culinary vegetables and roots eaten with flesh. This application of the word falls in nearly with the definition." The meaning of the second sentence is obscure; is it referring to sense 1? There follows an illustrative quotation from Robert Beverly's *History of Virginia* (1705). And then comes what appears to be Noah Webster's own editorial remark (still in sense 2): "*Sauce* consisting of stewed apples, is a great article in some parts of New England; but cranberries make the most delicious *sauce*."

Examples of this type appear throughout the two volumes. Take the entry for *cattle*. It begins with more than 13 lines of etymological speculation in brackets—typical of Webster's etymologies—mentioning words from the languages Armoric (the native tongue of the Gauls of Armorica), Portuguese, Syriac, and the biblical Chaldee—none of which, we now know, had any influence on the English word. Then comes sense 1, with 20 lines of type that begin: "Beasts or quadrupeds in general, serving for tillage, or other labor, and for food to man." There follow 18 lines of encyclopedic information about what is and isn't included in this "primary sense," but suddenly Webster reverts again to etymology: "But whether from a word originally signifying a beast, for in early ages beasts constitute the chief part of a man's property, or from a root signifying to *get* or possess, Gr. κταομαι, It. *cattare*, or from *capitalia*, it is not easy to determine." Then, still within sense 1, comes a hedging differentiation between British English and American English: "This word is restricted to domestic beasts; but in England it includes horses, which it ordinarily does not, in the United States, at least not in New-England."

Then comes sense 2, spread over 18 lines and duplicating much of what has already been said. From the beginning, it reads: "In the United States, cattle, in common usage, signifies only beasts of the bovine genus, oxen, bulls, cows and their young. In the laws respecting domestic beasts, horses, sheep, asses, mules and swine are distinguished from *cattle* . . . ." But then, still in reference to American usage, Webster delivers a legal opinion that undercuts what he has said in sense 1 and just above in the redundant sense 2: "It is probable that a law giving damages for a trespass committed by *cattle* breaking into an inclosure, would be adjudged to include horses."

The prose within this entry roams as aimlessly as cattle might.

It took a few years for Webster's eccentric etymologizing—which cumulatively delayed the dictionary by more than a decade—to be brought to light. But by the mid-19th century, some commentators were calling it out. For example, an 1860 review of Joseph Worcester's

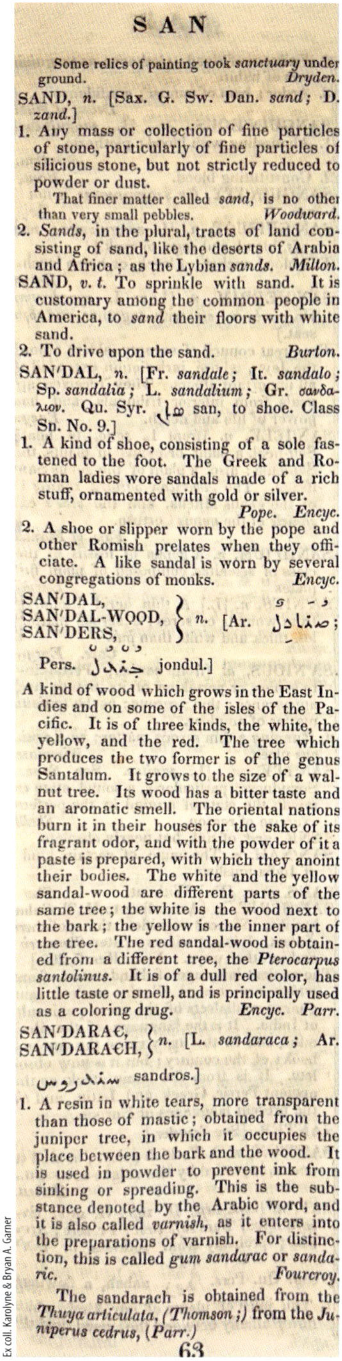

SAN

Some relics of painting took *sanctuary* under ground. *Dryden.*

SAND, *n.* [Sax. G. Sw. Dan. *sand;* D. *zand.*]

1. Any mass or collection of fine particles of stone, particularly of fine particles of silicious stone, but not strictly reduced to powder or dust.

That finer matter called *sand*, is no other than very small pebbles. *Woodward.*

2. *Sands*, in the plural, tracts of land consisting of sand, like the deserts of Arabia and Africa; as the Lybian *sands*. *Milton.*

SAND, *v. t.* To sprinkle with sand. It is customary among the common people in America, to *sand* their floors with white sand.

2. To drive upon the sand. *Burton.*

SAN'DAL, *n.* [Fr. *sandale;* It. *sandalo;* Sp. *sandalia;* L. *sandalium;* Gr. σανδαλιον. Qu. Syr. ܣܐܢ san, to shoe. Class Sn. No. 9.]

1. A kind of shoe, consisting of a sole fastened to the foot. The Greek and Roman ladies wore sandals made of a rich stuff, ornamented with gold or silver. *Pope. Encyc.*

2. A shoe or slipper worn by the pope and other Romish prelates when they officiate. A like sandal is worn by several congregations of monks. *Encyc.*

SAN'DAL, SAN'DAL-WOOD, SAN'DERS, *n.* [Ar. صندل; Pers. جندل jondul.]

A kind of wood which grows in the East Indies and on some of the isles of the Pacific. It is of three kinds, the white, the yellow, and the red. The tree which produces the two former is of the genus Santalum. It grows to the size of a walnut tree. Its wood has a bitter taste and an aromatic smell. The oriental nations burn it in their houses for the sake of its fragrant odor, and with the powder of it a paste is prepared, with which they anoint their bodies. The white and the yellow sandal-wood are different parts of the same tree; the white is the wood next to the bark; the yellow is the inner part of the tree. The red sandal-wood is obtained from a different tree, the *Pterocarpus santolinus.* It is of a dull red color, has little taste or smell, and is principally used as a coloring drug. *Encyc. Parr.*

SAN'DARAC, SAN'DARACH, *n.* [L. *sandaraca;* Ar. سندروس sandros.]

1. A resin in white tears, more transparent than those of mastic; obtained from the juniper tree, in which it occupies the place between the bark and the wood. It is used in powder to prevent ink from sinking or spreading. This is the substance denoted by the Arabic word, and it is also called *varnish*, as it enters into the preparations of varnish. For distinction, this is called *gum sandarac* or *sandaric.* *Fourcroy.*

The sandarach is obtained from the *Thuya articulata*, (*Thomson;*) from the *Juniperus cedrus*, (*Parr.*)

63

Note the Arabic, Persian, and Syriac etymologies.

dictionary accurately described the problems that Webster had pervasively introduced:

> The whole Websterian system of linguistic comparison is so vicious that no surgery can save it, and his theory of language is enough to take away one's breath to read it. In the making of his Dictionary, he seems to have begun by providing himself with a stock in trade of twenty vocabularies. Furnished with these crude and uncriticized lists of words—prominent among them Chaldaic, Syriac, and Chinese—he set himself to hunt in these likely sources the radicals of English words. One trembles at the possible result, and well one may; for in the whole history of linguistic lucubrations (and there have been very monstrous ones) there is none so monstrous as that engendered by the great American lexicographer. [Anon. 1860:1.]

During the 22 years when he was compiling the big work, Webster supported his family mostly from the profits of his spelling book. Understandably, he began wearing spectacles about the time of starting. As he flitted around his famous circular desk, checking various earlier dictionaries, both monolingual and bilingual, he found the work exhilarating: "While engaged in composing my *Dictionary*, I was often so much excited by discoveries I made, that my pulse, whose ordinary action is scarcely 60 beats to the minute, was accelerated to 80 or 85." (Letter to Dr. Thomas Miner, 21 Nov. 1836, in 1 *The New Englander* 567 [1843].) As any experienced lexicographer can attest, it is indeed exciting to record what no predecessor has noticed. (Of course, it's even better when the excitement isn't based, as in Webster's case, on the etymological position that all languages descended from the speech of Adam—and that the story about the Tower of Babel is literally true.) He finished the first complete draft in England, where he had been staying with his son William for the express purpose of bringing the work to a close: "When I finished my copy I was sitting at my table in Cambridge, England, January, 1825. When I arrived at the last word, I was seized with a tremor that made it difficult to proceed. I, however, summoned up strength to finish the work, and then walking about the room I soon recovered." (*Id.* at 568.)

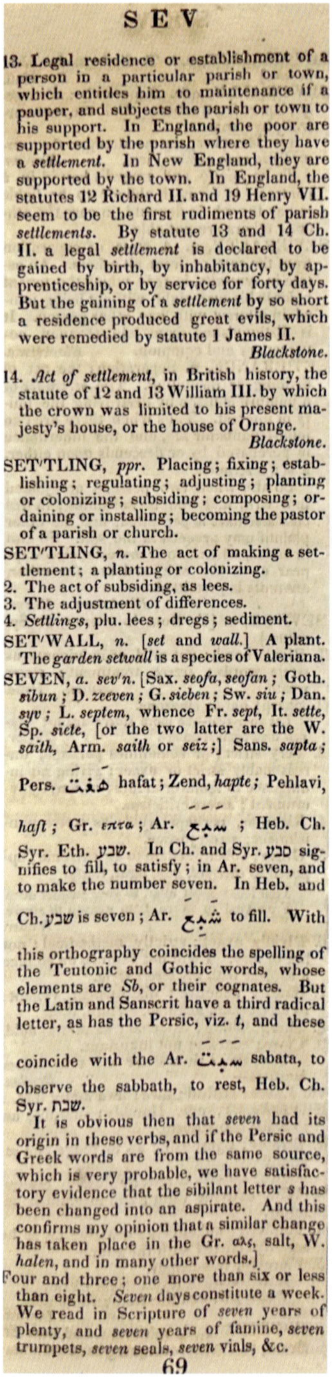

S E V

13. Legal residence or establishment of a person in a particular parish or town, which entitles him to maintenance if a pauper, and subjects the parish or town to his support. In England, the poor are supported by the parish where they have a *settlement*. In New England, they are supported by the town. In England, the statutes 12 Richard II. and 19 Henry VII. seem to be the first rudiments of parish *settlements*. By statute 13 and 14 Ch. II. a legal *settlement* is declared to be gained by birth, by inhabitancy, by apprenticeship, or by service for forty days. But the gaining of a *settlement* by so short a residence produced great evils, which were remedied by statute 1 James II. *Blackstone.*

14. *Act of settlement*, in British history, the statute of 12 and 13 William III. by which the crown was limited to his present majesty's house, or the house of Orange. *Blackstone.*

SET'TLING, *ppr.* Placing; fixing; establishing; regulating; adjusting; planting or colonizing; subsiding; composing; ordaining or installing; becoming the pastor of a parish or church.

SET'TLING, *n.* The act of making a settlement; a planting or colonizing.
2. The act of subsiding, as lees.
3. The adjustment of differences.
4. *Settlings*, plu. lees; dregs; sediment.

SET'WALL, *n.* [*set* and *wall.*] A plant. The *garden setwall* is a species of Valeriana.

SEVEN, *a.* sev'n. [Sax. *seofa, seofan*; Goth. *sibun*; D. *zeeven*; G. *sieben*; Sw. *siu*; Dan. *syv*; L. *septem*, whence Fr. *sept*, It. *sette*, Sp. *siete*, [or the two latter are the W. *saith*, Arm. *saith* or *seiz*;] Sans. *sapta*; Pers. هفت hafat; Zend, *hapte*; Pehlavi, *haft*; Gr. επτα; Ar. سبع; Heb. Ch. Syr. Eth. שבע. In Ch. and Syr. סבע signifies to fill, to satisfy; in Ar. seven, and to make the number seven. In Heb. and Ch. שבע is seven; Ar. شبع to fill. With this orthography coincides the spelling of the Teutonic and Gothic words, whose elements are *Sb*, or their cognates. But the Latin and Sanscrit have a third radical letter, as has the Persic, viz. *t*, and these coincide with the Ar. سبت sabata, to observe the sabbath, to rest, Heb. Ch. Syr. שבת.

It is obvious then that *seven* had its origin in these verbs, and if the Persic and Greek words are from the same source, which is very probable, we have satisfactory evidence that the sibilant letter *s* has been changed into an aspirate. And this confirms my opinion that a similar change has taken place in the Gr. αλς, salt, W. *halen*, and in many other words.]

Four and three; one more than six or less than eight. *Seven* days constitute a week. We read in Scripture of *seven* years of plenty, and *seven* years of famine, *seven* trumpets, *seven* seals, *seven* vials, &c.

69

Note the Chaldee, Ethiopic, Persian, and Syriac etymologies. Cf. p. 259.

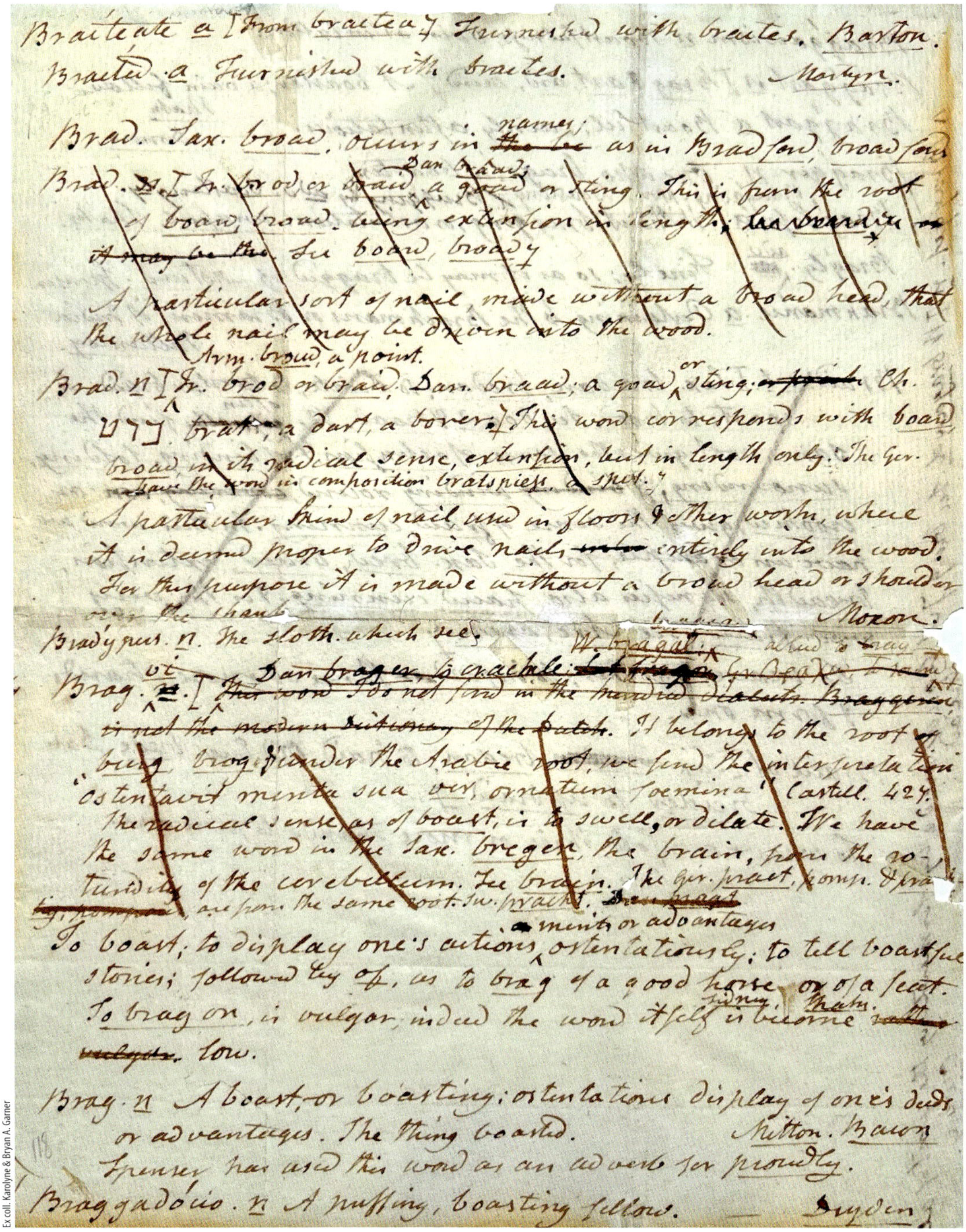

Bracteate a [From bractea] Furnished with bractes. Barton.
Bracted a Furnished with bractes. Martyn.

Brad. Sax. broad. occurs in names; as in Bradford, broad ford

Brad. n. [Ir. brod or braid, Dan braad; a goad or sting. This is from the root of board, broad, being extension in length. See board, broad]
A particular sort of nail, made without a broad head, that the whole nail may be driven into the wood.
Arm. broud, a point.

Brad. n [Ir. brod or braid, Dan. braad; a goad or sting; Ch. ברד brad, a dart, a borer.] This word corresponds with board, broad in its radical sense, extension, but in length only. The Ger. have the word in composition bratspiess, a spit.]
A particular kind of nail used in floors & other work, where it is deemed proper to drive nails entirely into the wood. For this purpose it is made without a broad head or shoulder over the shank. Moxon.

Bradypus. n. The sloth. which see.

Brag. v.i. [Dan bragen, to crackle [illegible] It belongs to the root of brag. [illegible] Under the Arabic root, we find the interpretation "ostentavit merita sua vir, ornatum foemina" Castell. 427. The radical sense, as of boast, is to swell, or dilate. We have the same word in the Sax. bregen, the brain, from the rotundity of the cerebellum. See brain. The Ger. pracht, pomp. & [illegible] are from the same root. Sw. pracht.
To boast; to display one's actions, merits or advantages ostentatiously; to tell boastful stories; followed by of, as to brag of a good horse or of a feat. To brag on, is vulgar; indeed the word itself is become low.

Brag. n A boast, or boasting; ostentatious display of one's deeds or advantages. The thing boasted. Milton. Bacon
Spenser has used this word as an adverb for proudly.

Braggadocio. n A puffing, boasting fellow. Dryden

A near-final manuscript leaf of Webster's 1828 *American Dictionary*, in his own hand. Before publication, he would supplement this with entries for the botanical terms *bracteole* and *bracteolate*, as well as a second noun *brag* ("a game at cards"). He would also cut the etymology erroneously tying the verb *brag* to Arabic and to the Saxon word meaning "brain" or "cerebellum." But in the published version, he retained the false etymological ties of the noun *brad* to Armoric and Chaldee.

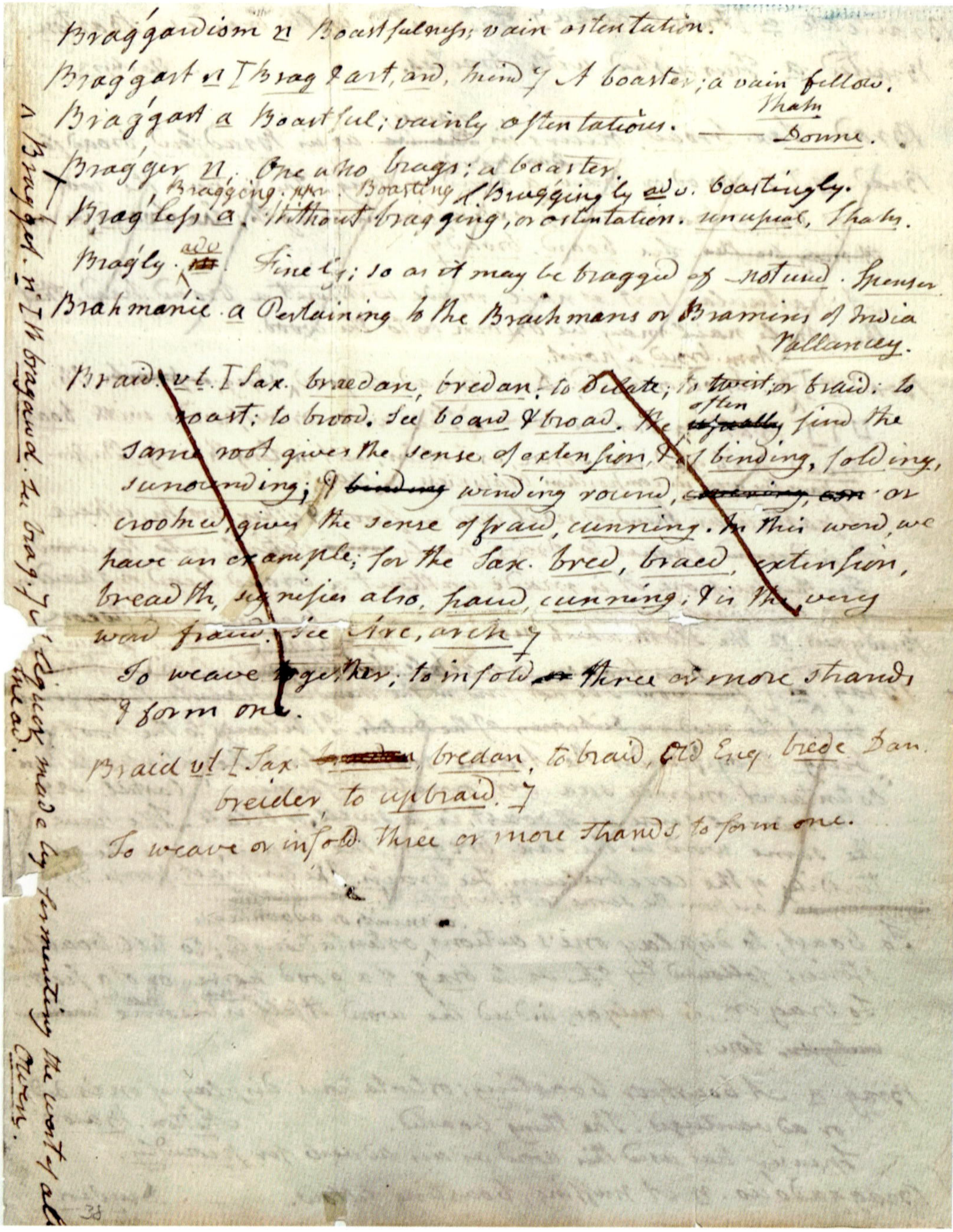
Braggardism n. Boastfulness; vain ostentation.
Braggart n. [Brag & art, ard, mind] A boaster; a vain fellow. Shaks.
Braggart a. Boastful; vainly ostentatious. — Donne.
Bragger n. One who brags; a boaster.
Bragging ppr. Boasting. Braggingly adv. Boastingly.
Bragless a. Without bragging, or ostentation. unusual. Shaks.
Bragly adv. Finely; so as it may be bragged of. not used. Spenser
Brahmanic a. Pertaining to the Brachmans or Bramins of India. Vallancey.
Braid v.t. [Sax. brædan, bredan, to dilate; to twist, or braid; to boast; to brood. See board & broad. We often find the same root gives the sense of extension, & of binding, folding, surrounding; & winding round, or crooked, gives the sense of fraud, cunning. In this word, we have an example; for the Sax. bred, braed, extension, breadth, signifies also, fraud, cunning; & is the very word fraud. See Arc, arch.]
To weave together; to infold three or more strands & form one.
Braid v.t. [Sax. bredan, to braid, Old Eng. brede. Dan. breider, to upbraid.]
To weave or infold three or more strands to form one.
Bragget n. [W. bragawd. See Brag.] Liquor made by fermenting the worts of ale and mead.
38

Ex coll. Karolyne & Bryan A. Garner

This is the reverse of the manuscript leaf shown on the preceding page. As with that page, Webster would later make several alterations. The most notable point here is Webster's wise excision of the false etymology tying the verb *braid* to notions of fraud and cunning. (Yet his marginal attribution of the drink known as *bragget* to the Welsh etymon *bragawd* is correct!) On this page and the preceding one, Webster's attributions (in order) to Moxon, Milton, Bacon, Dryden, Donne, Shakespeare, and Spenser all derive from Samuel Johnson's *Dictionary*.

63

Joseph Worcester
Three Frenetic Years

Ex coll. Karolyne & Bryan A. Garner

Johnson's English Dictionary, as improved by Todd, and abridged by Chalmers; with Walker's Pronouncing Dictionary, combined. Joseph Worcester ed. Boston: Charles Ewer & T. Harrington Carter, 1828.

An American Dictionary of the English Language; exhibiting the origin, orthography, pronunciation, and definitions of words: By Noah Webster, LL.D. Joseph Worcester ed. New York: Sherman Converse, 1829.

Worcester, Joseph. _A Comprehensive Pronouncing and Explanatory Dictionary of the English Language, with Pronouncing Vocabularies of Classical and Scripture Proper Names._ By Joseph Worcester. New York: Collins & Hannay. Boston: Hilliard, Gray, Little & Wilkins, 1830.

THREE YEARS—1828 TO 1830—saw what must be the greatest output ever by a single lexicographer: an industrious Bostonian named Joseph E. Worcester (1784–1865). First came his one-volume abridgment of Samuel Johnson's *Dictionary* for an American audience. In the preface, he wrote: "With what fidelity the Editor of this volume has performed his task, the public will judge. Entire accuracy, in such a work, is not to be attained; yet he hopes, that, in this respect, this work will bear a favourable comparison with most others of the kind." (P. xvi.)

Immediately Worcester set to work on his own dictionary, only to be implored to pause that work to abridge the Noah Webster's big two-volume dictionary, then newly published. The requests came from Webster's publisher, Sherman Converse, and Webster's son-in-law Chauncey Goodrich. (Webster himself, exhausted, had delegated responsibility for the abridgment.) Worcester demurred again and again, but Converse and Goodrich were dauntless both in their insistence and in their financial blandishments. They offered a $2,000 fee,

Ex coll. Karolyne & Bryan A. Garner

Worcester's three-year yield.

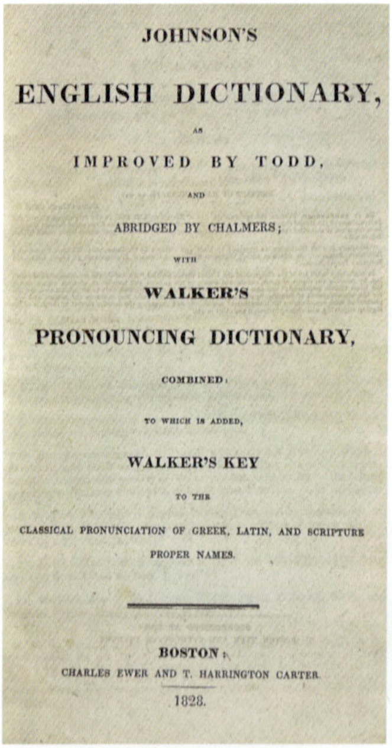

JOHNSON'S

ENGLISH DICTIONARY,

AS

IMPROVED BY TODD,

AND

ABRIDGED BY CHALMERS;

WITH

WALKER'S

PRONOUNCING DICTIONARY,

COMBINED:

TO WHICH IS ADDED,

WALKER'S KEY

TO THE

CLASSICAL PRONUNCIATION OF GREEK, LATIN, AND SCRIPTURE PROPER NAMES.

BOSTON:

CHARLES EWER AND T. HARRINGTON CARTER.

1828.

Ex coll. Karolyne & Bryan A. Garner

Title page of Worcester's Johnson.

equivalent to nearly $80,000 today. After weeks of resisting, Worcester relented and set to work, producing the abridged Webster's in 1829.

The preface, ostensibly written by Webster, acknowledged Worcester's central role: "The author of the American Dictionary of the English Language has been prevented, by the state of his health, from attending, in person, to its abridgment into the octavo form. The work has, therefore, been committed, for this purpose, to Mr. J.E. Worcester, of *Cambridge, Massachusetts*, who has strictly adhered to the general principles laid down for his direction by the author." (P. iii.) In fact, Worcester had made innumerable corrections in Webster's work, and Webster, when he saw Worcester's handiwork, was horrified. Why? According to one account, the abridgment made Webster look "like someone who had written a first draft of a book with inconsistent and half-baked ideas, requiring experts to come in, clean up the mess, and make it fit for publication. . . . The more he thought about it, the angrier he became." (Martin 2019:105.)

Worcester then returned to his own dictionary, *A Comprehensive Pronouncing and Explanatory Dictionary of the English Language*. It was much smaller, but publishing it in 1830—so soon after the other two dictionaries—was still an extraordinary achievement. He began his preface with this statement:

> The Compiler of this Dictionary, some time since, performed the task of editing "Johnson's Dictionary" . . . and while executing that labor, he formed the plan of this work. . . . But he delayed the execution of his design, in consequence of undertaking to abridge Dr. Webster's "American Dictionary of the English Language," a work of vast learning and research, containing far the most complete vocabulary of the language that has yet appeared. . . . In preparing this work, much use was made of Jameson's Dictionary; but the two works which may be properly considered as forming the basis of it, are the two dictionaries of Johnson and Walker, of which Jameson's professes to be chiefly a combination. . . . The words which Jameson selected from Todd, and the others which he added, are here retained, together with many more derived from . . . Dr. Webster's Dictionary, and other miscellaneous sources.

Sherman Converse (1790–1873), who soon became insolvent (see no. 65).

Noah Webster was enraged, and his publishers would also declare their indignation over the next several decades. Worcester spent the rest of his life defending himself against charges of plagiarism—scandalous charges that were levied not so much because of the realities as because of appearances. By all accounts, he was an honorable man. But he had undoubtedly shown bad judgment—or at least extreme ingenuousness—in thinking that he could, with impunity, produce three competing dictionaries for different publishers in three consecutive years.

The distinctive entries for *judgment* are representative of the kinds of differences to be found throughout the dictionaries:

Ex coll. Karolyne & Bryan A. Garner

Worcester's Johnson (1828):

JUDGEMENT, judje´mĕnt, *n. s.* [*jugement,* Fr.] The power of discerning the relations between one term or one proposition and another. *Locke.* Doom; the right or power of passing judgement. *Shak.* The act of exercising judicature. 2 *Kings,* xxv. Determination; decision. *Glanville.* The quality of distinguishing propriety and impropriety; criticism. *Dennis.* Opinion; notion. *Shak.* Sentence against a criminal. *Milton.* Condemnation. This is a theological use. *Rom.* v. Punishment inflicted by Providence, with reference to some particular crime. *Addison.* Distribution of justice. *Acts,* xviii. Judiciary law; statute. *Deut.* vii. The last doom. *Shakspeare.*

Worcester's Webster (1829):

JUDG´MENT, *n.* [Fr. *jugement.*] 1. The act of judging; the act or process of the mind in comparing its ideas, to find their agreement or disagreement, and to ascertain truth. 2. The faculty of the mind by which man is enabled to compare ideas and ascertain the relations of terms and propositions. 3. The determination of the mind, formed from comparing the relations of ideas, or the comparison of facts and arguments.—4. In *law,* the sentence or doom pronounced in any cause, civil or criminal, by the judge or court by which it is tried. 5. The right or power of passing sentence. 6. Determination; decision. 7. Opinion; notion.—8. In *Scripture,* the spirit of wisdom and prudence, enabling a person to discern right and wrong, good and evil. 9. A remarkable punishment; an extraordinary calamity inflicted by God on sinners. 10. The spiritual government of the world. 11. The righteous statutes and commandments of God are called his *judgements.* 12. The doctrines of the gospel, or God's word. 13. Justice and equity. *Luke* xi. *Is.* i. 14. The decrees and purposes of God concerning nations. *Rom.* xi.

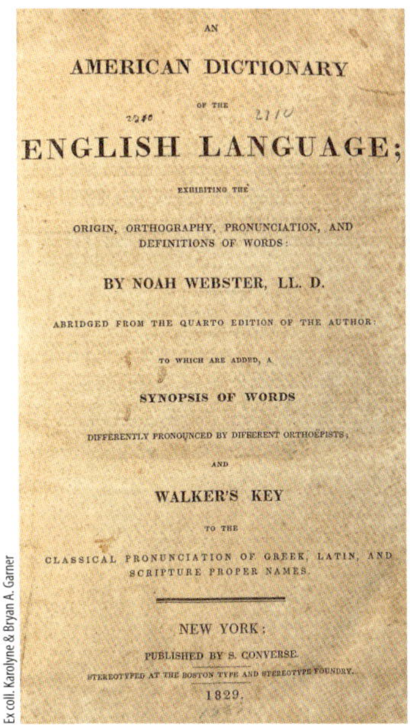
AN
AMERICAN DICTIONARY
OF THE
ENGLISH LANGUAGE;
EXHIBITING THE
ORIGIN, ORTHOGRAPHY, PRONUNCIATION, AND DEFINITIONS OF WORDS:
BY NOAH WEBSTER, LL. D.
ABRIDGED FROM THE QUARTO EDITION OF THE AUTHOR:
TO WHICH ARE ADDED, A
SYNOPSIS OF WORDS
DIFFERENTLY PRONOUNCED BY DIFFERENT ORTHOEPISTS;
AND
WALKER'S KEY
TO THE
CLASSICAL PRONUNCIATION OF GREEK, LATIN, AND SCRIPTURE PROPER NAMES.
NEW YORK:
PUBLISHED BY S. CONVERSE.
STEREOTYPED AT THE BOSTON TYPE AND STEREOTYPE FOUNDRY.
1829.

Ex coll. Karolyne & Bryan A. Garner

Title page of Worcester's Webster.

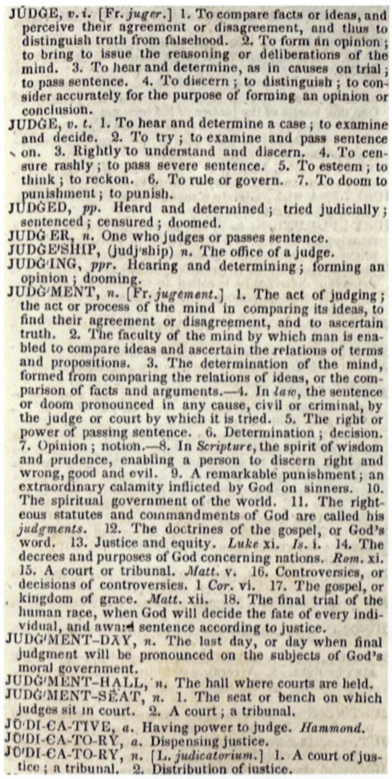

JŪDĠE, *v. i.* [Fr. *juger.*] 1. To compare facts or ideas, and perceive their agreement or disagreement, and thus to distinguish truth from falsehood. 2. To form an opinion; to bring to issue the reasoning or deliberations of the mind. 3. To hear and determine, as in causes on trial; to pass sentence. 4. To discern; to distinguish; to consider accurately for the purpose of forming an opinion or conclusion.
JUDĠE, *v. t.* 1. To hear and determine a case; to examine and decide. 2. To try; to examine and pass sentence on. 3. Rightly to understand and discern. 4. To censure rashly; to pass severe sentence. 5. To esteem; to think; to reckon. 6. To rule or govern. 7. To doom to punishment; to punish.
JUDĠED, *pp.* Heard and determined; tried judicially; sentenced; censured; doomed.
JUDĠ'ER, *n.* One who judges or passes sentence.
JUDĠE'SHIP, (judj'ship) *n.* The office of a judge.
JUDĠ'ING, *ppr.* Hearing and determining; forming an opinion; dooming.
JUDĠ'MENT, *n.* [Fr. *jugement.*] 1. The act of judging; the act or process of the mind in comparing its ideas, to find their agreement or disagreement, and to ascertain truth. 2. The faculty of the mind by which man is enabled to compare ideas and ascertain the relations of terms and propositions. 3. The determination of the mind, formed from comparing the relations of ideas, or the comparison of facts and arguments.—4. In *law*, the sentence or doom pronounced in any cause, civil or criminal, by the judge or court by which it is tried. 5. The right or power of passing sentence. 6. Determination; decision. 7. Opinion; notion.—8. In *Scripture*, the spirit of wisdom and prudence, enabling a person to discern right and wrong, good and evil. 9. A remarkable punishment; an extraordinary calamity inflicted by God on sinners. 10. The spiritual government of the world. 11. The righteous statutes and commandments of God are called his *judgments*. 12. The doctrines of the gospel, or God's word. 13. Justice and equity. *Luke* xi. *Is.* i. 14. The decrees and purposes of God concerning nations. *Rom.* xi. 15. A court or tribunal. *Matt.* v. 16. Controversies, or decisions of controversies. 1 *Cor.* vi. 17. The gospel, or kingdom of grace. *Matt.* xii. 18. The final trial of the human race, when God will decide the fate of every individual, and award sentence according to justice.
JUDĠ'MENT-DĀY, *n.* The last day, or day when final judgment will be pronounced on the subjects of God's moral government.
JUDĠ'MENT-HALL, *n.* The hall where courts are held.
JUDĠ'MENT-SĒAT, *n.* 1. The seat or bench on which judges sit in court. 2. A court; a tribunal.
JŪ'DI-CA-TĪVE, *a.* Having power to judge. *Hammond.*
JŪ'DI-CA-TO-RY, *a.* Dispensing justice.
JŪ'DI-CA-TO-RY, *n.* [L. *judicatorium.*] 1. A court of justice; a tribunal. 2. Distribution of justice.

Ex coll. Karolyne & Bryan A. Garner

A snippet from Worcester's Webster.

15. A court or tribunal. *Matt. v.* 16. Controversies, or decisions of controversies. 1 *Cor.* vi. 17. The gospel, or kingdom of grace. *Matt.* xii. 18. The final trial of the human race, when God will decide the fate of every individual, and award sentence according to justice.

Worcester's *Comprehensive* (1830):

Judgment, *n.* the act of judging; a determination; decision; sentence; discernment; criticism; opinion; punishment; doom.

In his own work, Worcester was scrupulous in not being a mere copyist. He genuinely abridged the first two works and then created his own. But it was the *appearance* of possible impropriety—leading to public charges against him—that led to his PR difficulties.

Worcester would go on to produce distinguished successor editions to his own work. But for the rest of his life, he was dogged by the ill-considered decision to relent to the 1828 entreaties of Goodrich and Converse.

For Worcester's big unabridged dictionary of 1860, see no. 79.

In late 2023, the Garner Collection acquired an archive of Sherman Converse's letters written mostly during the last decade of his life, after he had left publishing. They deal mostly with the politics of the Civil War. He was a broken man. In the earliest of the letters, from October 1860, Converse wrote to a close friend: "I look back on my useless life with daily regret." (See no. 65.)

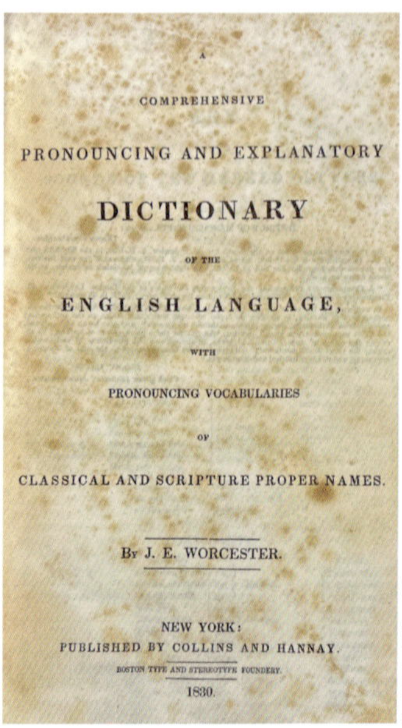

A

COMPREHENSIVE

PRONOUNCING AND EXPLANATORY

DICTIONARY

OF THE

ENGLISH LANGUAGE,

WITH

PRONOUNCING VOCABULARIES

OF

CLASSICAL AND SCRIPTURE PROPER NAMES.

BY J. E. WORCESTER.

NEW YORK:
PUBLISHED BY COLLINS AND HANNAY.
BOSTON TYPE AND STEREOTYPE FOUNDERY.
1830.

Ex coll. Karolyne & Bryan A. Garner

Title page of Worcester's *Comprehensive*.

Ex coll. Karolyne & Bryan A. Garner

Some other works by Worcester, including (at left) his two-volume *Geographical Dictionary, or Universal Gazetteer* (1817).

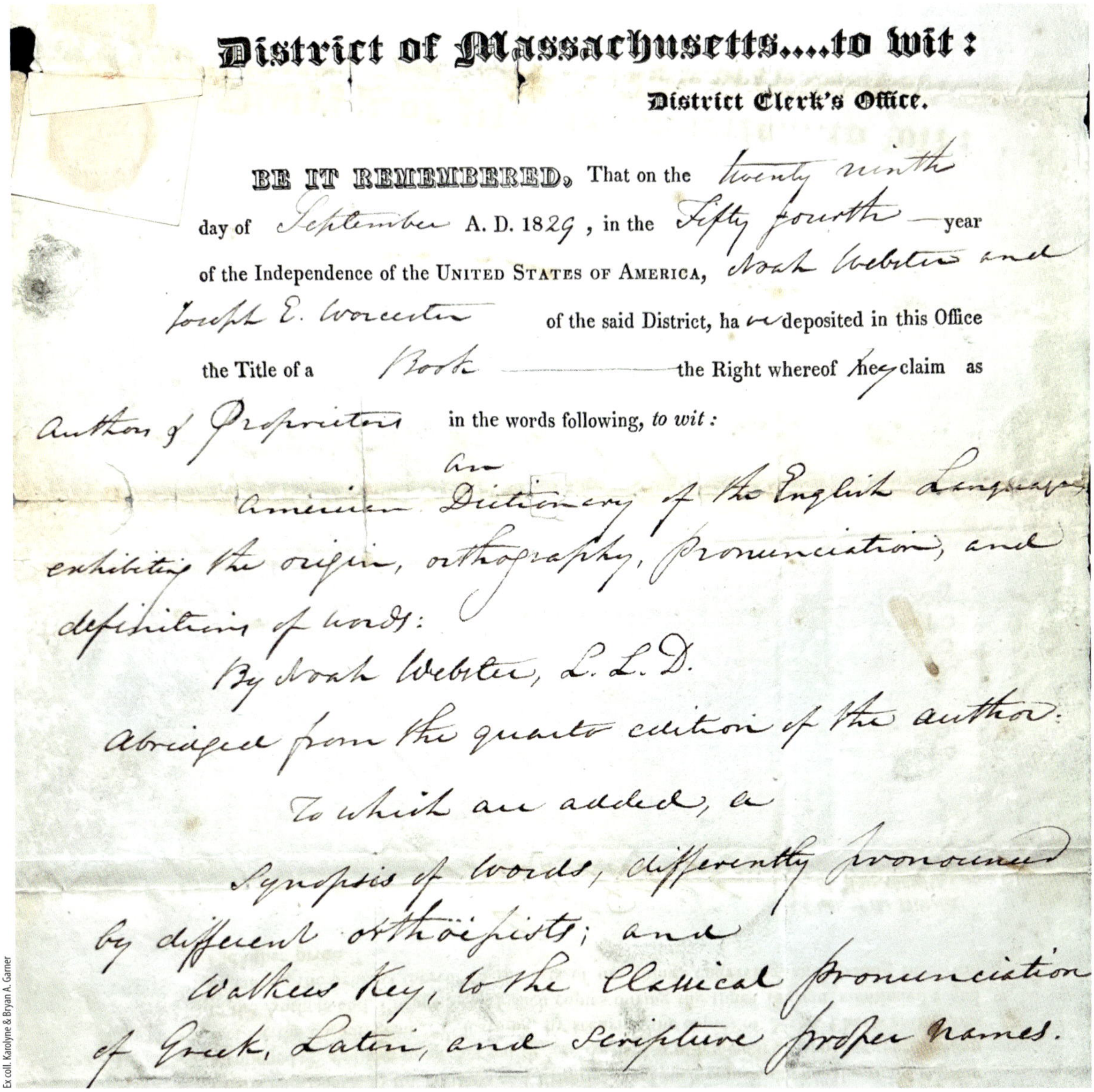

District of Massachusetts....to wit:

District Clerk's Office.

BE IT REMEMBERED, That on the twenty ninth day of September A. D. 1829, in the Fifty fourth year of the Independence of the UNITED STATES OF AMERICA, Noah Webster and Joseph E. Worcester of the said District, have deposited in this Office the Title of a Book the Right whereof they claim as authors & Proprietors in the words following, *to wit:*

An American Dictionary of the English Language exhibiting the origin, orthography, pronunciation, and definitions of words:

By Noah Webster, L.L.D.

Abridged from the quarto edition of the author:

To which are added, a

Synopsis of words, differently pronounced by different orthoëpists; and

Walker's Key, to the Classical pronunciation of Greek, Latin, and Scripture proper names.

Ex coll. Karolyne & Bryan A. Garner

From Noah Webster's personal archive, this is the certificate recording the copyright in the 1829 abridgment of Webster's *American Dictionary of the English Language*, deposited with the clerk of the District of Massachusetts. The handwriting is that of Chauncey A. Goodrich, Webster's son-in-law. Notably, Goodrich applied in the names of Webster and Joseph Worcester as coauthors and coproprietors—doubtless because Worcester was the compiler of the "Synopsis of Words" and of "Walker's Key." The inclusion of Worcester's name as coauthor and his additions infuriated Webster: "When Webster saw the completed work in print he was horrified. How could he have let this happen? . . . The more he thought about it, the angrier he became." (Martin 2019:105.) Goodrich soon acquired from Worcester a disclaimer of any interest in the copyright, and then he extracted from Webster an assignment of all his "right & interest in the premium for copyright of said book." (Quoted at Martin 2019:109.) The result was a small fortune for Goodrich.

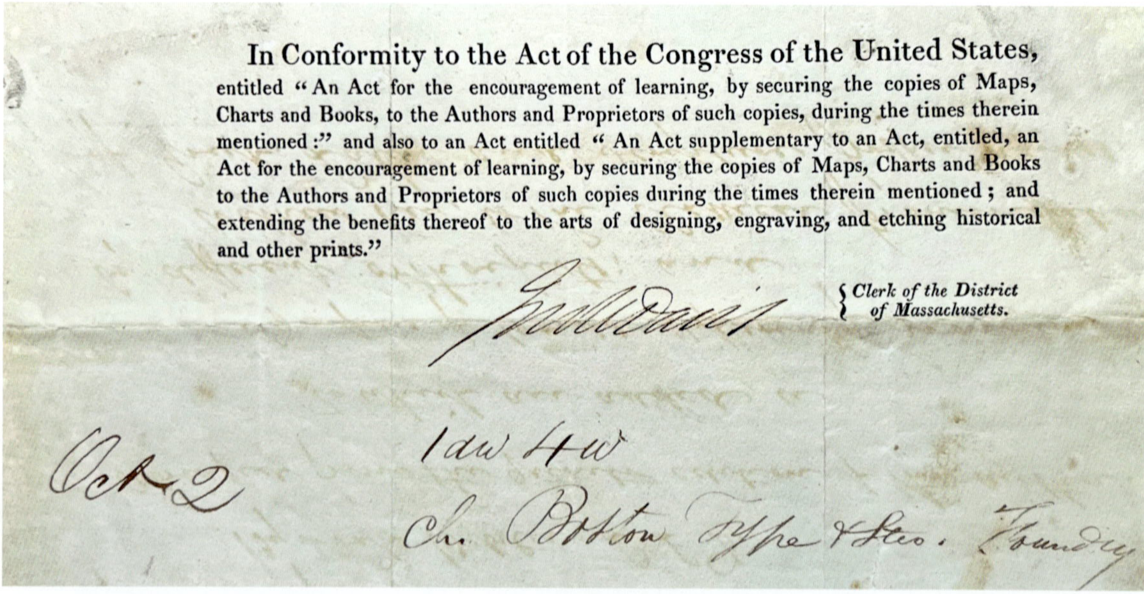

In Conformity to the Act of the Congress of the United States,
entitled "An Act for the encouragement of learning, by securing the copies of Maps, Charts and Books, to the Authors and Proprietors of such copies, during the times therein mentioned:" and also to an Act entitled "An Act supplementary to an Act, entitled, an Act for the encouragement of learning, by securing the copies of Maps, Charts and Books to the Authors and Proprietors of such copies during the times therein mentioned; and extending the benefits thereof to the arts of designing, engraving, and etching historical and other prints."

Clerk of the District of Massachusetts.

Oct 2

1dw 4w

Ch. Boston Type & Stereo. Foundry

Ex coll. Karolyne & Bryan A. Garner

As required by the federal Copyright Act of 1790, the application was made (on 29 September 1829) to the Clerk of the District of Massachusetts. Why Massachusetts, when Webster lived in Connecticut? The answer is that one application was made in Connecticut and another in Massachusetts because of Worcester's residency there. Both are reproduced on the copyright page of the 1829 book, except that the Massachusetts version there bears a copyright date two and a half months earlier (12 July 1829). Why the discrepancy in dates? The only substantive difference, apart from small disparities in capitalization and punctuation, is the inclusion, in the handwritten part here, of the words *authors and* in the phrase *authors and proprietors* (see p. 209)—more accurately tracking the statutory language. This later, superseding version appears to be a corrected one made from abundant caution.

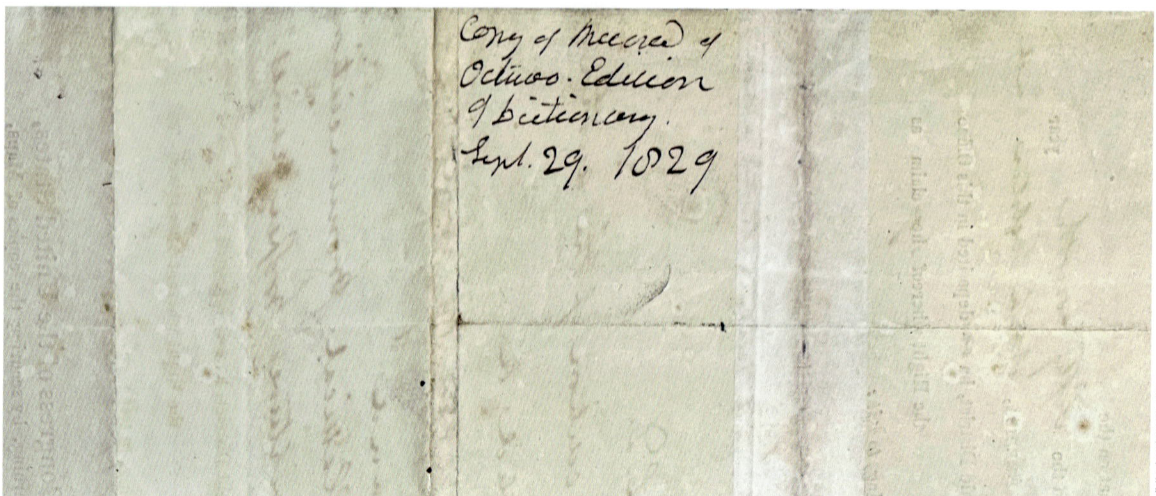

Copy of Record of Octavo. Edition of Dictionary. Sept. 29. 1829

Ex coll. Karolyne & Bryan A. Garner

This filing notation on the outer part of the document is in Webster's own hand: "Copy of Record of Octavo Edition of Dictionary. Sept. 29, 1829." Note Webster's characteristically idiosyncratic capital *R* beginning the third word. Two years after this copyright recordation, Webster would play a pivotal role in the enactment of the Copyright Act of 1831, extending the original term of copyright protection from 14 to 28 years. By then he had already assigned the copyright in this particular book—the biggest money-maker—to Chauncey Goodrich (see pp. 227, 230–31).

64

Lyman Cobb

Walker's Promoter, Webster's Tormentor

Cobb, Lyman. ***Cobb's Abridgment of J. Walker's Critical Pronouncing Dictionary, and Expositor of the English Language*. Ithaca, N.Y.: Mack & Andrus, 1828.**

———. *A Critical Review of the Orthography of Dr. Webster's Series of Books for Systematick Instruction in the English Language; including his former spelling-book and the Elementary Spelling-Book, compiled by Aaron Ely, and published under the name of Noah Webster, LL.D.* New York: Collins & Hannay, 1831.

———. *The Reticule and Pocket Companion; or, A Miniature Lexicon of the English Language*. New York: Harper & Bros., 1834.

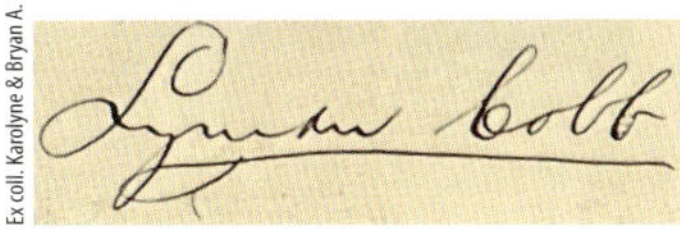

Ex coll. Karolyne & Bryan A. Garner

Born in Lenox, Massachusetts, Lyman Cobb (1800–1864) lacked a formal education beyond what he received in a log-cabin school in rural New York. At 16, he was teaching in such a school. Somehow he became fixated on English spelling—an obsession that, despite his other passions such as abolishing corporal punishment, would become paramount in his life.

At the age of 21 he issued a spelling book: *A Just Standard for Pronouncing the English Language Containing the Rudiments of the English Language*, published in Ithaca. He more aptly renamed the 1825 edition *Spelling Book, Being a Just Standard for Pronouncing the English Language*. He rejected Webster's spelling reforms and championed the Scotsman John Walker's spellings and pronunciations, insisting on *publick*, *honour*, and so on. He had been disgusted with the rampant disorder in Webster's spellings since the 1780s.

Ex coll. Karolyne & Bryan A. Garner

In the 18th century, American English was orthographically indistinguishable from that of Britain. In his first book, therefore, the "speller" of 1783 (no. 53), Webster generally followed the spellings in Johnson's dictionaries. As an American patriot, though, Webster was

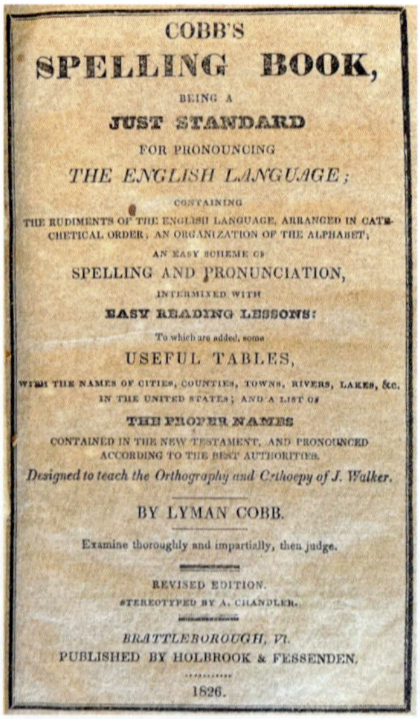

COBB'S
SPELLING BOOK,
BEING A
JUST STANDARD
FOR PRONOUNCING
THE ENGLISH LANGUAGE;
CONTAINING
THE RUDIMENTS OF THE ENGLISH LANGUAGE, ARRANGED IN CATECHETICAL ORDER; AN ORGANIZATION OF THE ALPHABET;
AN EASY SCHEME OF
SPELLING AND PRONUNCIATION,
INTERMIXED WITH
EASY READING LESSONS:
To which are added, some
USEFUL TABLES,
WITH THE NAMES OF CITIES, COUNTIES, TOWNS, RIVERS, LAKES, &c. IN THE UNITED STATES; AND A LIST OF
THE PROPER NAMES
CONTAINED IN THE NEW TESTAMENT, AND PRONOUNCED ACCORDING TO THE BEST AUTHORITIES.
Designed to teach the Orthography and Orthoepy of J. Walker.

BY LYMAN COBB.

Examine thoroughly and impartially, then judge.

REVISED EDITION.
STEREOTYPED BY A. CHANDLER.

BRATTLEBOROUGH, Vt.
PUBLISHED BY HOLBROOK & FESSENDEN.
1826.

Ex coll. Karolyne & Bryan A. Garner

"We may with propriety expect an author to be consistent with himself; and as Mr. Webster's Dictionary and Spelling-Book differ from each other in the spelling of seventy or eighty words, we certainly shall be justifiable in refusing to adopt his system." (*Cobb's Spelling Book*, 1831 ed., p. 3.)

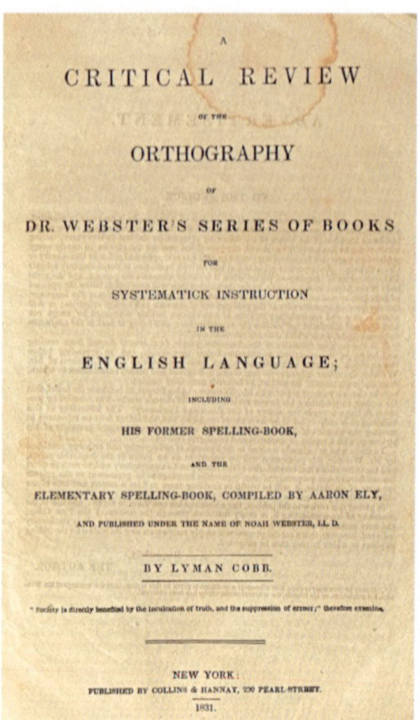

A
CRITICAL REVIEW
OF THE
ORTHOGRAPHY
OF
DR. WEBSTER'S SERIES OF BOOKS
FOR
SYSTEMATICK INSTRUCTION
IN THE
ENGLISH LANGUAGE;
INCLUDING
HIS FORMER SPELLING-BOOK,
AND THE
ELEMENTARY SPELLING-BOOK, COMPILED BY AARON ELY,
AND PUBLISHED UNDER THE NAME OF NOAH WEBSTER, LL. D.

BY LYMAN COBB.

"Society is directly benefited by the inculcation of truth, and the suppression of error;" therefore examine.

NEW YORK:
PUBLISHED BY COLLINS & HANNAY, 230 PEARL-STREET.
1831.

Ex coll. Karolyne & Bryan A. Garner

eager for American spelling to diverge from the British—he thought that it would be a marker of national identity. In his 1787 reissue of the book, therefore, under the title *The American Spelling Book*, Webster included many spelling reforms. (They came too late to influence the U.S. Constitution, which uses such traditional spellings as *behaviour*, *chuse*, *controul*, *encrease*, *labour*, and *offence*.) Webster followed it a few years later with an essay collection replete with entirely novel spellings like *az*, *breefly*, *cleer*, *dezerv*, *geografy*, *haz*, *hiz*, *tru*, *valu*, and thousands of others:

> In the essays, ritten within the last year, a considerable change of spelling iz introduced by way of experiment. . . . There iz no alternativ. Every possible reezon that could ever be offered for altering the spelling of wurds, stil exists in full force. [Webster 1790:xi.]

The orthographic radicalism drew stinging criticism. The journalist Ebenezer Hazard derided this "new mode of spelling recommended and exemplified in the *fugitiv Essays ov No-ur Webster eskwier junier*, critick and coxcomb general of the United States." (Skeel 1912 1:297.) Duly chastened by a chorus of scorn, Webster mostly stifled his reformative impulse when issuing spelling books and dictionaries. But it didn't stop him from constant orthographic fiddling.

Webster's changes of mind, combined with the tens of thousands of copies of his earlier editions still in circulation, with new ones with the older spellings still being produced by various printers to whom Webster had given a license, produced only confusion. His constant tinkering from the 1780s to the 1820s led to a profusion of inconsistencies between books, and even within single books.

Lyman Cobb, preoccupied with spelling, noticed Webster's wild irregularities. In his 1806 *Compendious Dictionary* (no. 57), Webster advocated spellings such as *determin*, *melasses*, and *tung*. By 1828, he was promoting additional reforms such as *bronz*, *chimical*, *entransing*, *granit*, *heartach*, etc. And by that time, literally millions of his earlier books were in circulation, favoring other spellings for those and similar words.

Cobb was successful enough that his own competing books—a speller and Walker's abridged dictionary—were becoming bestsellers. Cobb's speller alone sold an astonishing 4 million copies at a time when the entire population of the United States was around

13 million. He promoted his own work mainly by trashing Webster as hopelessly unreliable. Referring to Webster's "multitudinous errours," Cobb wrote: "It must be conceded, that either the works of his meridian thought [i.e., at the height of his powers], or those of his dotage, are not entitled to confidence." (P. vi.)

Relentlessly feisty in promoting the superiority of his books, Cobb launched 17 different attacks on Webster in various newspapers. These were collected in 1831 in a 56-page pamphlet called *A Critical Review of the Orthography of Dr. Webster's Series of Books*. The last ten pages consisted of a seven-column display of all Webster's many discrepancies through the years. For example, in 1806 and 1817, Webster recorded the proper spelling as *bridegroom*; in 1828, he recorded it as *bridegoom*, without the second *r*, in keeping with its Old English etymology of *brydguma*; and in 1831, two different Webster books collided by listing the word under the competing spellings. What were people to follow?

Cobb pointed to other anomalies. From 1783 to 1831, Webster consistently recommended the spelling *dime*, but in 1831 another Webster book came out recommending *disme*. There were hundreds if not thousands of similar examples. To compound the problem, Webster's dictionaries often recommended one spelling but then used another in his own definitions of other words (for example, recording the headword as *wagon* but using *waggon* in various definitions). This occurred throughout the alphabet.

Through Webster's "mischievous influence of innovation," Cobb said, he had "done more to introduce irregularity in orthography than all of the other works published in this country within fifty years." Usually Cobb was on the right side of linguistic history. If we take just Webster's 1828 spellings, we see that Cobb, not Webster, usually ended up the victor in American English. Consider Webster's *holyday* against Cobb's *holiday*, Webster's *learnt* against Cobb's *learned*, Webster's *turkies* against Cobb's *turkeys*, and Webster's *woodchuk* against Cobb's *woodchuck*. And Cobb was consistent throughout his writings.

When the abridgment of Webster's big dictionary came out in 1829—a work commissioned by Chauncey Goodrich and completed by Joseph Worcester—many of Webster's departures from mainstream spelling were rejected. That meant further contradictory spellings within the Webster oeuvre, providing even more fodder for Cobb's literary assaults.

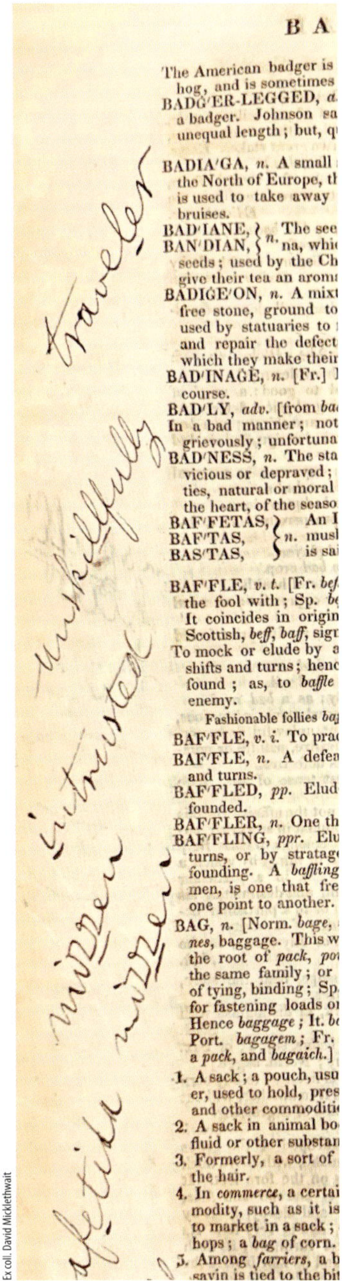
B A
The American badger is
hog, and is sometimes
BADG'ER-LEGGED, *a.*
a badger. Johnson sa
unequal length; but, q
BADIA'GA, *n.* A small
the North of Europe, th
is used to take away
bruises.
BAD'IANE, } *n.* The see
BAN'DIAN, } na, whi
seeds; used by the Ch
give their tea an arom
BADIGE'ON, *n.* A mixt
free stone, ground to
used by statuaries to
and repair the defect
which they make their
BAD'INAGE, *n.* [Fr.]
course.
BAD'LY, *adv.* [from *ba*
In a bad manner; not
grievously; unfortuna
BAD'NESS, *n.* The sta
vicious or depraved;
ties, natural or moral
the heart, of the seaso
BAF'FETAS, } An I
BAF'TAS, } *n.* musl
BAS'TAS, } is sai
BAF'FLE, *v. t.* [Fr. *bef*
the fool with; Sp. *b*
It coincides in origin
Scottish, *beff, baff,* sign
To mock or elude by a
shifts and turns; henc
found; as, to *baffle*
enemy.
Fashionable follies *baf*
BAF'FLE, *v. i.* To pra
BAF'FLE, *n.* A defea
and turns.
BAF'FLED, *pp.* Elud
founded.
BAF'FLER, *n.* One th
BAF'FLING, *ppr.* Elu
turns, or by stratag
founding. A *baffling*
men, is one that fre
one point to another.
BAG, *n.* [Norm. *bage,*
nes, baggage. This w
the root of *pack, po*
the same family; or
of tying, binding; Sp
for fastening loads o
Hence *baggage*; It. *b*
Port. *bagagem*; Fr.
a *pack,* and *bagaich.*]
1. A sack; a pouch, usu
er, used to hold, pres
and other commoditi
2. A sack in animal bo
fluid or other substan
3. Formerly, a sort of
the hair.
4. In *commerce,* a certai
modity, such as it is
to market in a sack;
hops; a *bag* of corn.
5. Among *farriers,* a b
savin is tied to the bit

Ex coll. David Micklethwait

In his copy of Webster's 1828 *Dictionary*, Cobb sedulously marked every spelling on which he differed with Webster, as well as every spelling on which Webster was inconsistent. Almost every page has notes like these in the margins.

Ex coll. Karolyne & Bryan A. Garner

The tiny *Reticule* ($3\frac{3}{8} \times 2\frac{1}{8}$ inches).

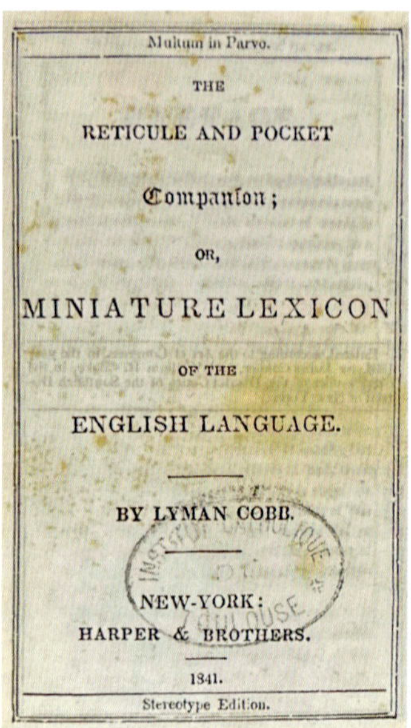
Multum in Parvo.

THE

RETICULE AND POCKET

Companion;

OR,

MINIATURE LEXICON

OF THE

ENGLISH LANGUAGE.

BY LYMAN COBB.

NEW-YORK:

HARPER & BROTHERS.

1841.

Stereotype Edition.

Ex coll. Karolyne & Bryan A. Garner

In the last two decades of Webster's life—he died in 1843—the spellings in his books lay in plethoric disarray. Although Webster urged people to pay attention only to his latest pronouncements, Cobb urged looking at them all. Meanwhile, publishers to which Webster had long before given licenses were continuing to issue what he considered superseded volumes. He called this "a most infamous trespass" on his reputation.

At one point, Webster slightingly called Cobb "a schoolmaster in one of our western villages, who had the misfortune to compile a Spelling-Book and small Dictionary," adding a reference to Cobb's "persevering malevolence rarely exhibited even in this world of evil." Webster's tone was imperious: "The weakness of the man must be equal to his malevolence, if he supposes that twenty wagon [one *g*!] loads of [his] pamphlets distributed by mail would do me any harm or himself any good." (Webster 1831.) But given the onslaught represented by Cobb on the one hand and Joseph Worcester's own dictionaries on the other, Webster felt seriously embattled. (For more Webster attacks on Cobb, see pp. 233–34.)

Meanwhile, Cobb succeeded in promoting and selling his books. In 1834, he published his miniature dictionary titled *The Reticule and Pocket Companion*, which was based on his earlier abridgment of Walker's work. This tiny book—with a text block measuring just $3\frac{1}{2}$ by 2 inches—saw many editions, including one under the name *The Ladies' Reticule Companion* (1844). In all its editions, Cobb used an innovation never repeated in the annals of lexicography: each page is surrounded, at the margins, by maxims, proverbs, and occasional grammatical exercises. For example, on the final page of the preface (p. 4) appear the following. Top: "Secrecy is the soul of all great designs." Right: "It is dangerous to take liberties with great men." Bottom: "Ignorance is the mother of superstition." Left: "In most quarrels there is a fault on both sides." (Note that two of these, about quarrels and great men, might bear on Cobb's campaigns against Webster!) Cobb must have believed that these sayings would encourage some users to look at his dictionary simply to discover the multifarious sayings. But he was ever alert to faultfinders, given that the preface states: "A misunderstanding having occurred between the editor and the foreman of the stereotype office, in relation to the alphabetical arrangement of the maxims, some repetitions may appear in the different parts of the work." (*Id.*) Might this foreman have been

Abel Chandler, who stereotyped several of Cobb's works from 1826 to 1834—and also worked with Noah Webster? (See no. 67.)

In 1860, Cobb moved to Westchester County, New York, where he spent much of the remainder of his life with his son, an Episcopal priest named Lyman Cobb Jr., who in his youth had helped on his father's various books. In the end, Cobb Sr. died in Colesburg, Pennsylvania, utterly impecunious—a word not included in his *Reticule*.

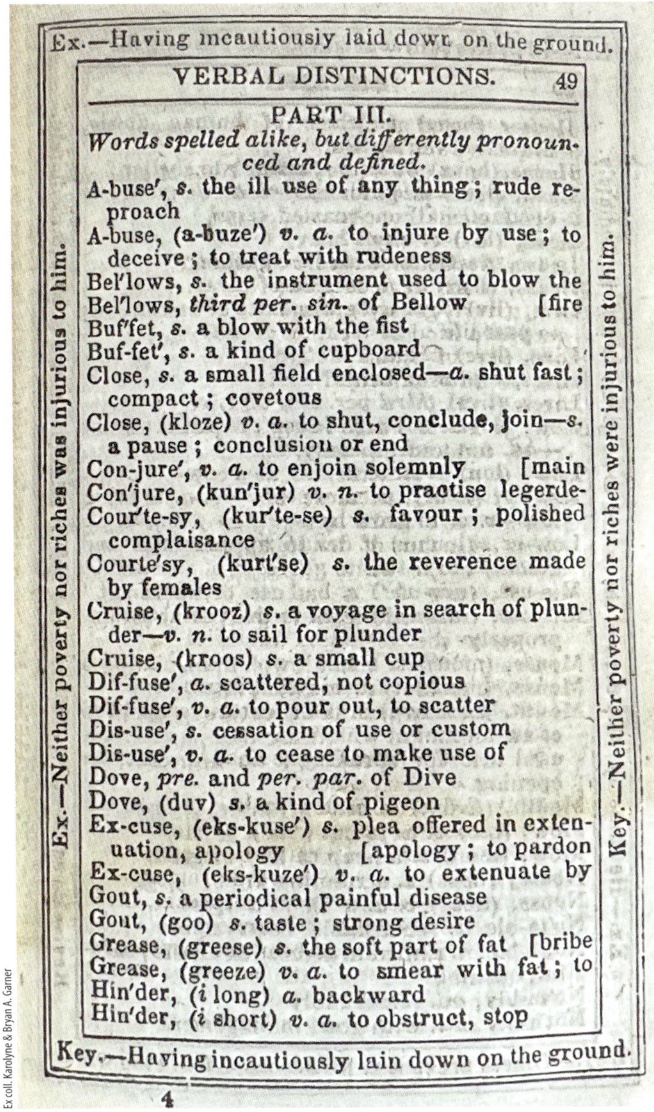
Ex.—Having incautiously laid down on the ground.

VERBAL DISTINCTIONS. 49

PART III.

Words spelled alike, but differently pronounced and defined.

A-buse′, *s.* the ill use of any thing; rude reproach
A-buse, (a-buze′) *v. a.* to injure by use; to deceive; to treat with rudeness
Bel′lows, *s.* the instrument used to blow the [fire
Bel′lows, *third per. sin.* of Bellow
Buf′fet, *s.* a blow with the fist
Buf-fet′, *s.* a kind of cupboard
Close, *s.* a small field enclosed—*a.* shut fast; compact; covetous
Close, (kloze) *v. a.* to shut, conclude, join—*s.* a pause; conclusion or end
Con-jure′, *v. a.* to enjoin solemnly [main
Con′jure, (kun′jur) *v. n.* to practise legerde-
Cour′te-sy, (kur′te-se) *s.* favour; polished complaisance
Courte′sy, (kurt′se) *s.* the reverence made by females
Cruise, (krooz) *s.* a voyage in search of plunder—*v. n.* to sail for plunder
Cruise, (kroos) *s.* a small cup
Dif-fuse′, *a.* scattered, not copious
Dif-fuse′, *v. a.* to pour out, to scatter
Dis-use′, *s.* cessation of use or custom
Dis-use′, *v. a.* to cease to make use of
Dove, *pre.* and *per. par.* of Dive
Dove, (duv) *s.* a kind of pigeon
Ex-cuse, (eks-kuse′) *s.* plea offered in extenuation, apology [apology; to pardon
Ex-cuse, (eks-kuze′) *v. a.* to extenuate by
Gout, *s.* a periodical painful disease
Gout, (goo) *s.* taste; strong desire
Grease, (greese) *s.* the soft part of fat [bribe
Grease, (greeze) *v. a.* to smear with fat; to
Hin′der, (*i* long) *a.* backward
Hin′der, (*i* short) *v. a.* to obstruct, stop

Ex.—Neither poverty nor riches was injurious to him.

Key.—Neither poverty nor riches were injurious to him.

Key.—Having incautiously lain down on the ground.

4

Ex coll. Karolyne & Bryan A. Garner

From the *Reticule*: Note the grammatical choices presented in the margins as exercises.

"That the selection of words is the best that could have been made, or that the definitions are the most explicit that could possibly have been given, the editor is not prepared to assert; but that great pains have been taken in both these particulars, he is enabled confidently to state." (Preface to the *Reticule*.)

65

Webster's British Foray

Webster, Noah. *A Dictionary of the English Language*. 1st British ed. 2 vols. London: Black, Young & Young, 1831.

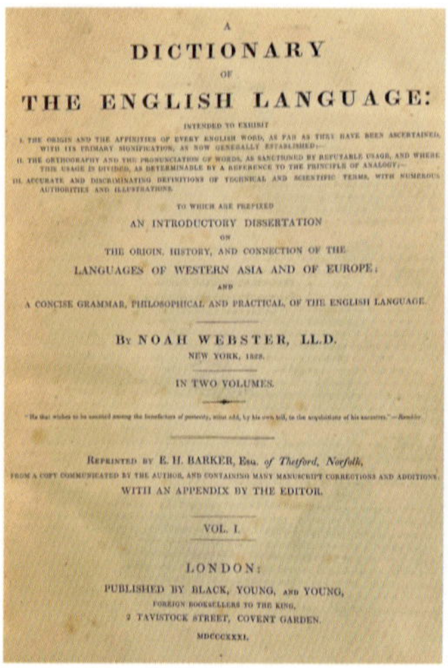
A
DICTIONARY
OF
THE ENGLISH LANGUAGE:
INTENDED TO EXHIBIT
I. THE ORIGIN AND THE AFFINITIES OF EVERY ENGLISH WORD, AS FAR AS THEY HAVE BEEN ASCERTAINED, WITH ITS PRIMARY SIGNIFICATION, AS NOW GENERALLY ESTABLISHED;—
II. THE ORTHOGRAPHY AND THE PRONUNCIATION OF WORDS, AS SANCTIONED BY REPUTABLE USAGE, AND WHERE THIS USAGE IS DIVIDED, AS DETERMINABLE BY A REFERENCE TO THE PRINCIPLE OF ANALOGY;—
III. ACCURATE AND DISCRIMINATING DEFINITIONS OF TECHNICAL AND SCIENTIFIC TERMS, WITH NUMEROUS AUTHORITIES AND ILLUSTRATIONS.
TO WHICH ARE PREFIXED
AN INTRODUCTORY DISSERTATION
ON
THE ORIGIN, HISTORY, AND CONNECTION OF THE
LANGUAGES OF WESTERN ASIA AND OF EUROPE;
AND
A CONCISE GRAMMAR, PHILOSOPHICAL AND PRACTICAL, OF THE ENGLISH LANGUAGE.
BY NOAH WEBSTER, LL.D.
NEW YORK, 1828.
IN TWO VOLUMES.
REPRINTED BY E. H. BARKER, ESQ. *of Thetford, Norfolk,*
FROM A COPY COMMUNICATED BY THE AUTHOR, AND CONTAINING MANY MANUSCRIPT CORRECTIONS AND ADDITIONS.
WITH AN APPENDIX BY THE EDITOR.
VOL. I.
LONDON:
PUBLISHED BY BLACK, YOUNG, AND YOUNG,
FOREIGN BOOKSELLERS TO THE KING,
2 TAVISTOCK STREET, COVENT GARDEN.
MDCCCXXXI.

Ex coll. Karolyne & Bryan A. Garner

"In the gradual progress of language, many words acquire new meanings, while the old ones become obsolete. . . . So numerous are such instances, that between *thirty and forty thousand* definitions are contained in this work, which are not known to exist in any other." (Advertisement, p. iv.)

THE PRINTER/PUBLISHER of Noah Webster's 1828 *American Dictionary*, Sherman Converse of New Haven, had had a relationship with Webster for six years before that book appeared. In 1822, Converse published Webster's *Philosophical and Practical Grammar* (not a bestseller), and a year later he printed (for another bookseller) Webster's *Letters to a Young Gentleman Commencing His Education* (again, not a bestseller). These publishing experiences seem not to have made Webster fond of Converse: when Webster returned from England in 1825, Converse was not among the first several printers he approached to print his big two-volume work. None of the others, however, were willing to risk the investment. In the end, Converse agreed and saved the enterprise. Rather than being grateful, though, Webster thought it was Converse who should be grateful to play a role in what Webster believed to be a major work in American literary history.

By the time the book appeared, the two men had already experienced the beginnings of a rupture in their relationship. Although the 1828 edition shows a copyright notice of 14 April 1828, three months earlier—in mid-January—Webster had written a characteristically crabby letter, telling Converse that contrary to his own thinking, he (1) had no right to produce a British edition, and (2) had no right to produce an abridged edition. Webster's tone might be considered condescending: "Your exertions for the [work] I consider as very meritorious, & highly deserving of ample reward. If you make money by your exertions, I shall very much rejoice, & the more you make by our contract, the more rejoiced I shall be. But surely, Sir, the labour of two or three years bears a small proportion to that of 20 years!"

In the end, Webster relented on the abridgment (see no. 63) but not on the British edition. The abridged version, as we saw, enraged Webster, and soon the two men weren't speaking to each other. When Webster's son-in-law Chauncey Goodrich traveled to Washington with Converse in December 1830 to promote copyright legislation in

Congress, Webster wrote to his daughter: "I have not seen him & I hope I shall not." (Martin 2019:109–10.) The two men were incurably estranged. Within three years, Converse would be bankrupt. He soon lost his health in addition to his money, and he never really recovered.

And so Webster negotiated his own British contract with the London firm of Black, Young & Young. That firm removed *American* from the title, had an English editor (E.H. Barker of Thetford, Norfolk) rework the text a little (but *labor* wasn't changed to *labour*), and printed 3,000 copies. Despite the enmity that had developed between Noah Webster and Joseph Worcester, the latter's "Synopsis of Words Differently Pronounced by Different Orthoepists" was included in the front matter—with full attribution to Worcester and his "American edition of 1829." The book sold briskly enough in Great Britain that another edition was printed in 1832—even while copies of the 1828 American edition lay unsold and unbound in a warehouse.

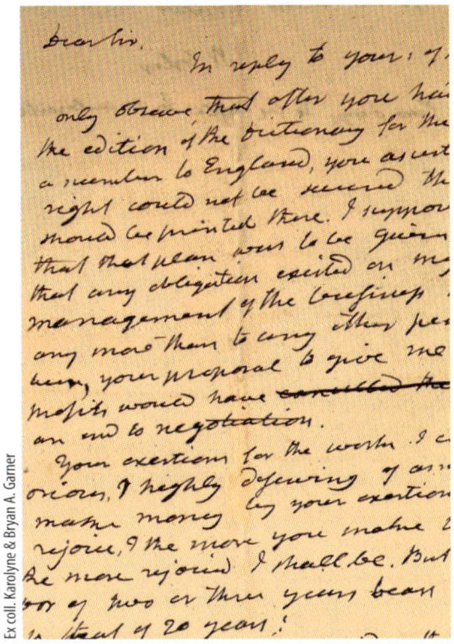

Ex coll. Karolyne & Bryan A. Garner

The beginning of Webster's letter to Sherman Converse dated 20 January 1828 (detail).

Ex coll. Karolyne & Bryan A. Garner

First British edition (1831).

"In numerous instances, JOHNSON has mistaken the precise sense of legal terms, confounding *house-breaking*, for example, with *burglary*, *theft* with *robbery*, *murder* with the simple killing of a man unlawfully. In the present work, legal terms are defined, it is believed, with technical precision." (Advertisement in front matter.)

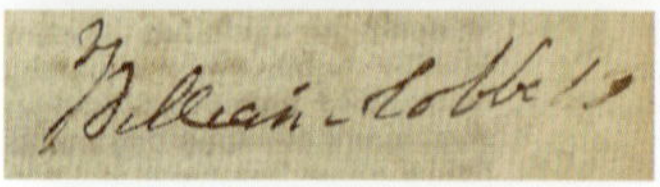

Ex coll. Karolyne & Bryan A. Garner

Ex coll. Karolyne & Bryan A. Garner

The three books here discussed—speller in the middle.

66

William Cobbett

Forever a Firebrand

Cobbett, William. ***A Spelling-Book, with appropriate lessons in reading, and with a stepping-stone to English grammar.*** **London: Mills, Jowett & Mills, 1831.**

———. ***A Geographical Dictionary of England and Wales.*** **London: Wm. Cobbett, 1832.**

———. ***A New French and English Dictionary.*** **London: Mills, Jowett & Mills, 1833.**

Toward the end of his storied life, the political writer and controversialist Cobbett (1763–1835) became fascinated by lexicography. Immediately after Joseph Worcester produced three dictionaries in three consecutive years, Cobbett did much the same, though in his case they were different types of books: a speller, a geographical dictionary, and a French–English dictionary. Years before, during his second exile in the United States, he had produced his famous *Grammar of the English Language* (1818).

Cobbett undoubtedly led the most eventful life of all lexicographers and grammarians. He was a highly original thinker who had been home-schooled, often calling himself a "self-taught ploughboy"; became a populist pamphleteer, the most incendiary writer of his day; fled to France in 1792 and then America to avoid prosecution for treason; fled from the United States in 1800 to avoid a libel prosecution, returning to England; became the first compiler of the parliamentary proceedings now known as *Hansard*; was imprisoned in Newgate from 1810 to 1812 for condemning the flogging of militiamen at Ely; to avoid another prosecution, fled again to the United States in 1817, where on Long Island he wrote his *Grammar* in the form of letters to his son (along the way criticizing the grammar of major British figures such as King George III); secretly exhumed the bones of Thomas Paine and returned to England, hoping somehow that the skeleton would fuel Britons' eagerness for political reform (but instead attracting ridicule and derision); publicly sided with Queen Caroline in her notorious adultery trial; farmed 80 acres south of the Thames in the late 1820s; was tried for treason in 1831 for fomenting rebellion among rural workers, flamboyantly conducting his own defense and being acquitted; became a Member of Parliament representing Oldham in the early 1830s, while engaged in lexicography; wrote more than 20 other books; died bankrupt; and became the subject of more than a dozen biographies.

Cobbett's speller served as a companion to his *Grammar* and helped solidify the British standards of spelling. How was his speller distinctive? "All the other 'SPELLING BOOKS,' that I have ever seen, contain more or less about RELIGION, and about ARITHMETIC, GEOGRAPHY, ASTRONOMY, and perhaps about a dozen other things. Religion, to be *real*, must be implanted in the *heart*; nothing can make that plantation but the *convictions of the mind*; and these are to be produced by *reasoning*, and not by parrot-like tutoring, comprised in spelling-book prayers." (P. iii.) And so he renounced the practice, instead giving everyday lessons, step by step. How did he write this book while farming and defending himself against treason charges? "The greater part of it was written *before six o'clock in the morning*, previous to the commencement of the business of the day." (P. iv.)

The *Geographical Dictionary* is something of a gazetteer of England, through which Cobbett had traveled extensively. "If it prove tiresome to [readers]," Cobbett wrote in his preface, "I beseech them to think of what it must have been to its author! . . . It has at last taught me, at the end of three-score years of labour, that there is *something that can fatigue*." (P. viii.) He ended the preface with a factually inaccurate statement: "It is a truly curious fact that I am putting this on paper in the VERY ROOM in which Dr. Johnson wrote his plaintive preface to the prodigious production of his patient toil. Wm. Cobbett. No. 11, Bold-court, 28 June, 1832." (*Id.*) Why inaccurate? Johnson wrote his 1755 preface at 17 Gough Square; he moved to Bolt Court more than twenty years later.

For his *French and English Dictionary*, Cobbett seemed to have an unlimited audience: "There are two descriptions of persons who stand in need of a Dictionary; namely, those who have *learned grammar thoroughly*; and those *who have not*." (P. iv.) It's an extensive work: part I (*Français–Anglais*) consists of 418 double-column pages; part II

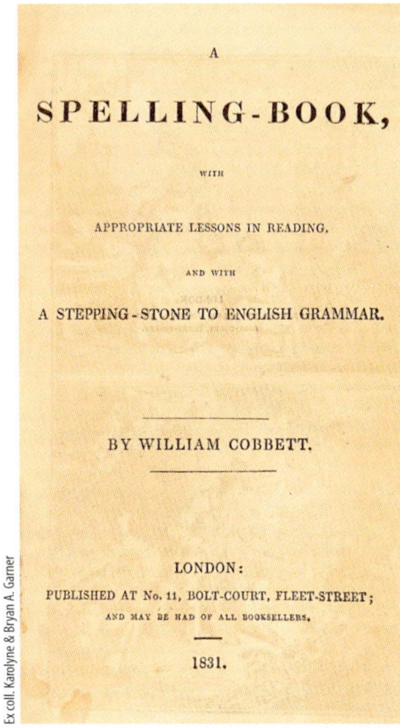
A

SPELLING-BOOK,

WITH

APPROPRIATE LESSONS IN READING,

AND WITH

A STEPPING-STONE TO ENGLISH GRAMMAR.

BY WILLIAM COBBETT.

LONDON:

PUBLISHED AT No. 11, BOLT-COURT, FLEET-STREET;

AND MAY BE HAD OF ALL BOOKSELLERS.

1831.

Ex coll. Karolyne & Bryan A. Garner

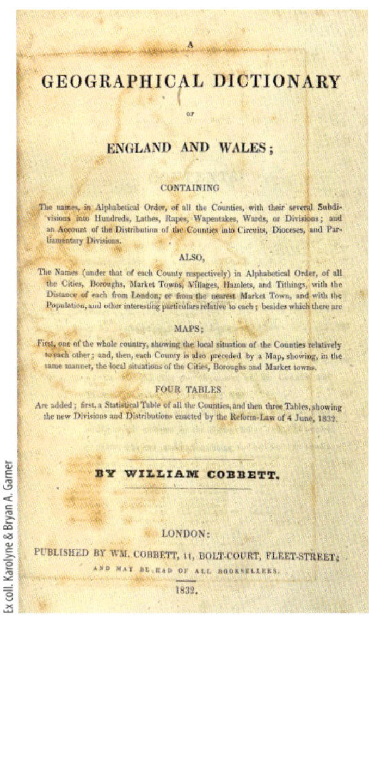
A

GEOGRAPHICAL DICTIONARY

OF

ENGLAND AND WALES;

CONTAINING

The names, in Alphabetical Order, of all the Counties, with their several Subdivisions into Hundreds, Lathes, Rapes, Wapentakes, Wards, or Divisions; and an Account of the Distribution of the Counties into Circuits, Dioceses, and Parliamentary Divisions.

ALSO,

The Names (under that of each County respectively) in Alphabetical Order, of all the Cities, Boroughs, Market Towns, Villages, Hamlets, and Tithings, with the Distance of each from London, or from the nearest Market Town, and with the Population, and other interesting particulars relative to each; besides which there are

MAPS;

First, one of the whole country, showing the local situation of the Counties relatively to each other; and, then, each County is also preceded by a Map, showing, in the same manner, the local situations of the Cities, Boroughs and Market towns.

FOUR TABLES

Are added; first, a Statistical Table of all the Counties, and then three Tables, showing the new Divisions and Distributions enacted by the Reform-Law of 4 June, 1832.

BY WILLIAM COBBETT.

LONDON:

PUBLISHED BY WM. COBBETT, 11, BOLT-COURT, FLEET-STREET;

AND MAY BE HAD OF ALL BOOKSELLERS.

1832.

Ex coll. Karolyne & Bryan A. Garner

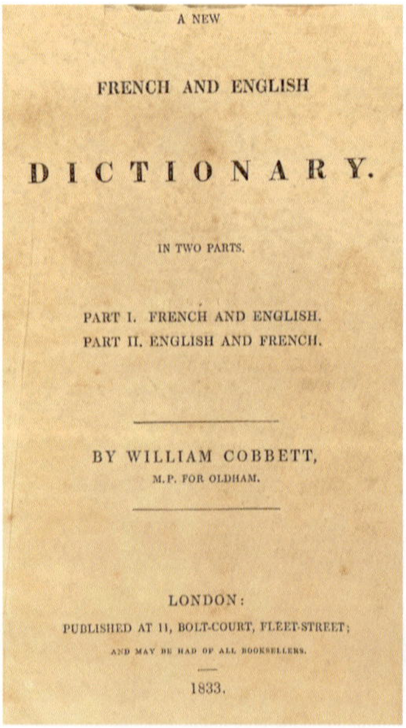

A NEW

FRENCH AND ENGLISH

DICTIONARY.

IN TWO PARTS.

PART I. FRENCH AND ENGLISH.
PART II. ENGLISH AND FRENCH.

BY WILLIAM COBBETT,
M.P. FOR OLDHAM.

LONDON:
PUBLISHED AT 11, BOLT-COURT, FLEET-STREET;
AND MAY BE HAD OF ALL BOOKSELLERS.

1833.

Ex coll. Karolyne & Bryan A. Garner

(English–French) consists of another 438. He recommended to "young English people" that they should "recollect that every hour of labour which they now bestow will be productive of fruit to be enjoyed to the last hour of their lives; to bear in mind, that, if they once acquire the habit of labour now, that habit will stick by them; and, above all things, to bear in mind, that, if they let slip this season for labour, it will never return." (Pp. vi–vii.) Once again he channeled Dr. Johnson, though a little mistakenly: "With this advice to those who are to use the book, I send the book itself to the press out of that very room in which Dr. Johnson compiled his dictionary." (P. vii.) It was a nice thought.

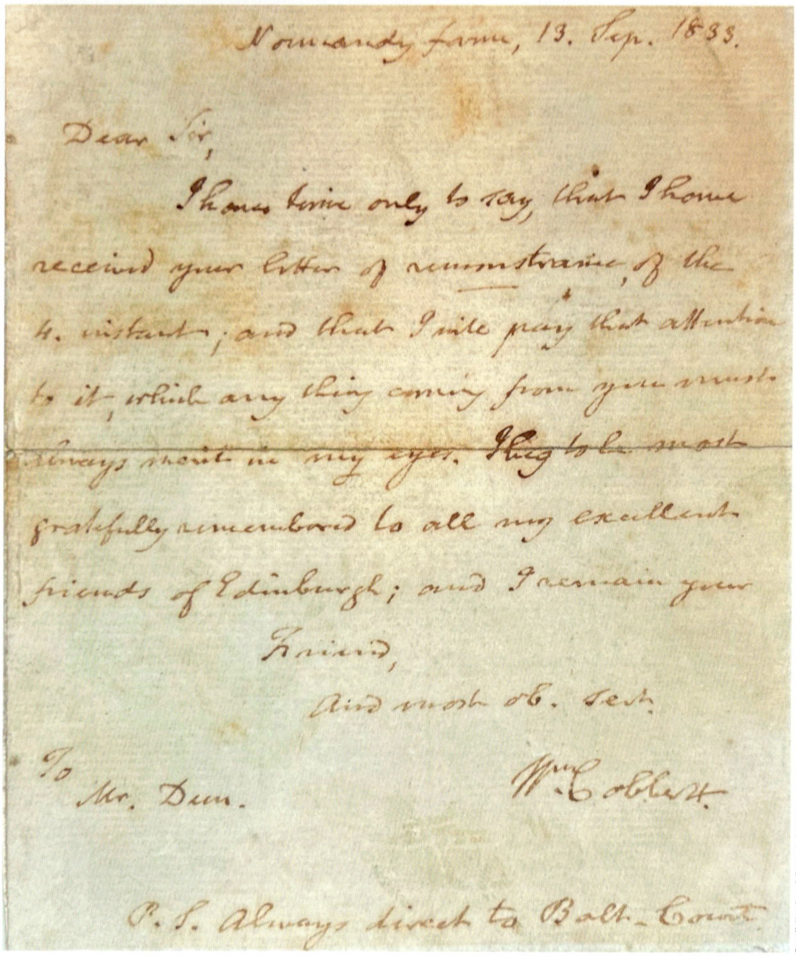

Normandy farm, 13. Sep. 1833.

Dear Sir,

I have time only to say, that I have received your letter of remonstrance of the 4. instant; and that I will pay that attention to it, which any thing coming from you must always merit in my eyes. Beg to be most gratefully remembered to all my excellent friends of Edinburgh; and I remain your Friend,

And most ob. Sert

To Mr. Dun.

Wm Cobbett

P.S. Always direct to Bolt-Court

Ex coll. Karolyne & Bryan A. Garner

An 1833 letter to an Edinburgh teacher named B.F. Dun, of whom Cobbett wrote generously in *Cobbett's Tour in Scotland* (1833), pp. 115–17. The letter probably related to that book, and not to one of Cobbett's recently published dictionaries. But we can only speculate.

67

Webster Solicits Technical Terms

Nov. 1834 Letter from Noah Webster to his printer, Abel Chandler of Concord, Massachusetts, inquiring about technical terminology.

IN 1832, ABEL CHANDLER received a patent on his stereotyping blocks used in printing. A year later, he stereotyped Noah Webster's *Primary School Dictionary*, for which he was responsible during its printings of the 1830s. We don't know how well Noah Webster knew Chandler—this seems to be the only known letter between them—but the letter illustrates a lexicographer's attempt to enlist an ally.

In that way, it is an archetypal letter: lexicographers habitually call on their friends and acquaintances to help collect out-of-the-way words—teenagers for the newest slang, for example, and specialists for technical terms. What is surprising is Webster's suggestion that he might receive a deluge of letters with a public announcement. More likely, it seems to us, he feared alerting competitors to his methods of word-gathering.

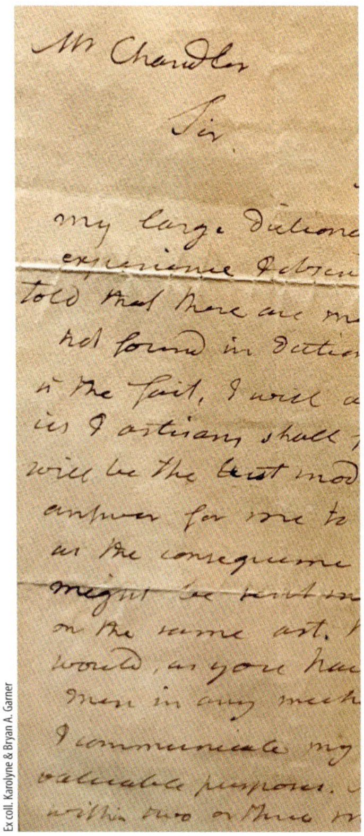

Ex coll. Karolyne & Bryan A. Garner

Detail from the letter.

New Haven Novr 25 1834

Mr. Chandler

Sir

I intend this winter to revise my large dictionary & add such improvements as experience & observations have suggested. I am told that there are many words used in the arts which are not found in dictionaries, English or American. If this is the fact, I will add any such as respectable mechanics & artisans shall furnish me with. I know not what will be the best mode of obtaining them. It would not answer for me to make a request in the public proper, as the consequence might be that multitudes of letters might be sent me from various quarters, & many on the same art. But if you & Mr. E White or others would, as you have opportunity, speak to such leading men in any mechanical employments as you know, & communicate my wishes, this would answer all valuable purposes. Any communications made to me within two or three months, would be very acceptable.

I am, Sir,

your obed^{t} serv^{t}

N Webster

68

Charles Richardson

A Dictionary Without Definitions?

Richardson, Charles. *A New Dictionary of the English Language*. 2 vols. London: William Pickering, 1836–1837. Also 1838, 1839, 1844, 1851, 1855, etc.

Ex coll. Karolyne & Bryan A. Garner

"The great first principle upon which I have proceeded, in the department of the Dictionary which embraces the explanation, is that so clearly evolved, and so incontrovertibly demonstrated in the 'Diversions of Purley'; namely, that a word has one meaning, and one only." (Preface, p. 41.)

BORN JUST OUTSIDE LONDON and educated in South Yorkshire, Richardson (1775–1865) defied his family's wish that he pursue the law, choosing instead to become a schoolteacher. By the time he was in his mid-30s, he was the master of his own school in Surrey.

While running the school, he came across the works of the cranky polymath John Horne Tooke (1736–1812), who recorded his eccentric linguistic theories in *Ἔπεα πτερόεντα*, better known as *The Diversions of Purley* (1786–1805, no. 55). A cultural and political radical, Tooke had a particular dislike for the greatest lexicographic authority of his day, the conservative Samuel Johnson, calling his *Dictionary* "the most imperfect and faulty, and the least valuable of any of his productions," insisting that its author "possessed not one single requisite for the undertaking." Tooke never wrote a dictionary, but Richardson leapt at the chance to put his hero's principles into practice. His *New Dictionary* was conceived as part of the vast *Encyclopædia Metropolitana* planned by Samuel Taylor Coleridge.

Richardson attacked Johnson on many fronts—"No man," he wrote, "can possibly succeed in compiling a truly valuable Dictionary of the English language, unless he entirely desert the steps of Johnson"—but it was Johnson's definitions that got him most worked up. One of Johnson's great achievements was the minute discrimination of meanings: 65 numbered senses for *go*, 75 for *run*, 134 for *take*. In lexicological terms, Johnson was a committed splitter, always looking to distinguish subtle shades of meaning. Richardson, like his spiritual mentor Horne Tooke, was a committed lumper. He famously insisted, "Each one word has one meaning, and one only; that from it all usages must spring and be derived."

Since, as Tooke taught him, "intrinsic meanings" are to be found in etymologies, a dictionary should offer a deep dive into a word's origins, after which all its many applications—Richardson refused to call them "meanings," just "uses" or "applications"—would be obvious. He told readers, for instance, that *flag* comes from *fly*, which explains "*Flag* (of a ship, &c.)—because it *flies* in the wind." *Flagging energy* makes sense when we think of the same flag when the wind doesn't blow. With this "intrinsic meaning" in hand, he assumed, any reasonable reader could intuit all the word's applications in English.

But is that enough to understand the meaning of, for instance, *flagship*, *keep the flag flying*, *honor the flag*, *flag on the play*, or *flagged for your attention*?

Again, once Richardson the devotee explained that *head* means "That part . . . which is *heav'd*, raised, or lifted up, above the rest," he thought *head of the class*, *head of the bed*, *head of a nail*, *head of the queue*, *head waiter*, *head gasket*, *head of cattle*, *out of one's head*, *off the top of one's head*, *put our heads together*, and *on your own head be it* were all straightforward. Derived forms got similarly brusque treatment. Johnson devoted separate headwords for *abstract* noun, *abstract* verb transitive, *abstract* verb intransitive, *abstracted*, *abstractedly*, *abstraction*, *abstractive*, and *abstractly*, but Richardson found this "needless and burdensome," and simply grouped them all together with one definition of the root, leaving readers to figure out what the derived forms meant. Even more distantly related words got lumped under a single heading. Richardson's general definition of *civil* is your only guide to *civilian*, *civilization*, and *civility*. Once you know the innate meaning of *month*, he assumed, then *monthly*, *month's-mind*, *moon*, *moon-calf*, *moonet*, *moonish*, *moonless*, *moonlight*, *moonling*, *moonshine*, *moonshiny*, and *moony* should be evident.

Richardson's approach might still have been defensible were it not for one problem: his etymologies are terrible. Tooke gave him bad ideas about the relations among languages, and—like Noah Webster, who was also under Tooke's spell—Richardson was too often seduced by superficial similarities between words that share no history. *Flag* has nothing to do with *fly* other than the coincidence of two letters, *head* does not come from *heave*, and so on through thousands of entries built on shaky foundations. Webster, who was sympathetic with the one-word-one-meaning view, nevertheless accused Richardson of failing "in most cases . . . to find that meaning."

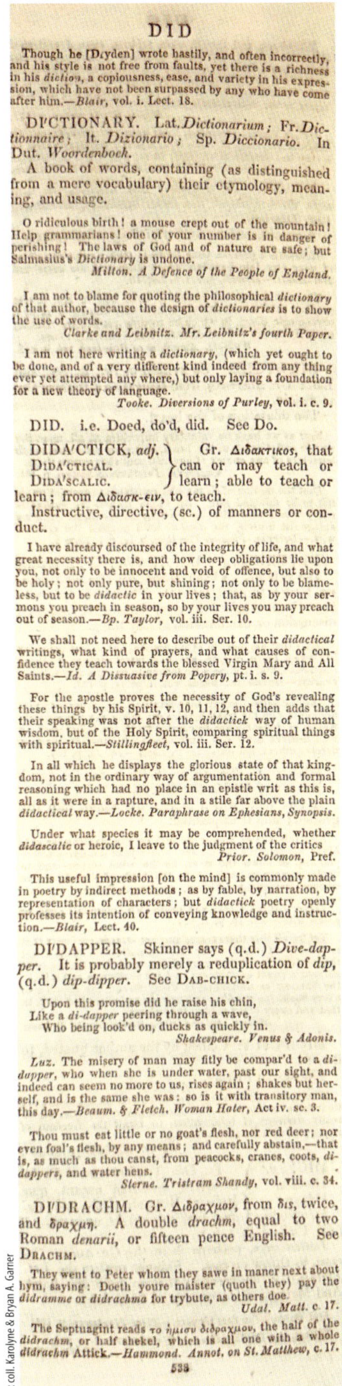

DID

Though he [Dryden] wrote hastily, and often incorrectly, and his style is not free from faults, yet there is a richness in his *diction*, a copiousness, ease, and variety in his expression, which have not been surpassed by any who have come after him.—*Blair*, vol. i. Lect. 18.

DI'CTIONARY. Lat. *Dictionarium;* Fr. *Dictionnaire;* It. *Dizionario;* Sp. *Diccionario.* In Dut. *Woordenboek.*

A book of words, containing (as distinguished from a mere vocabulary) their etymology, meaning, and usage.

O ridiculous birth! a mouse crept out of the mountain! Help grammarians! one of your number is in danger of perishing! The laws of God and of nature are safe; but Salmasius's *Dictionary* is undone.
Milton. A Defence of the People of England.

I am not to blame for quoting the philosophical *dictionary* of that author, because the design of *dictionaries* is to show the use of words.
Clarke and Leibnitz. Mr. Leibnitz's fourth Paper.

I am not here writing a *dictionary*, (which yet ought to be done, and of a very different kind indeed from any thing ever yet attempted any where,) but only laying a foundation for a new theory of language.
Tooke. Diversions of Purley, vol. i. c. 9.

DID. i.e. Doed, do'd, did. See Do.

DIDA'CTICK, *adj.* / DIDA'CTICAL. / DIDA'SCALIC. } Gr. Διδακτικος, that can or may teach or learn; able to teach or learn; from Διδασκ-ειν, to teach.

Instructive, directive, (sc.) of manners or conduct.

I have already discoursed of the integrity of life, and what great necessity there is, and how deep obligations lie upon you, not only to be innocent and void of offence, but also to be holy; not only pure, but shining; not only to be blameless, but to be *didactic* in your lives; that, as by your sermons you preach in season, so by your lives you may preach out of season.—*Bp. Taylor*, vol. iii. Ser. 10.

We shall not need here to describe out of their *didactical* writings, what kind of prayers, and what causes of confidence they teach towards the blessed Virgin Mary and All Saints.—*Id. A Dissuasive from Popery*, pt. i. s. 9.

For the apostle proves the necessity of God's revealing these things by his Spirit, v. 10, 11, 12, and then adds that their speaking was not after the *didactick* way of human wisdom, but of the Holy Spirit, comparing spiritual things with spiritual.—*Stillingfleet*, vol. iii. Ser. 12.

In all which he displays the glorious state of that kingdom, not in the ordinary way of argumentation and formal reasoning which had no place in an epistle writ as this is, all as it were in a rapture, and in a stile far above the plain *didactical* way.—*Locke. Paraphrase on Ephesians, Synopsis.*

Under what species it may be comprehended, whether *didascalic* or heroic, I leave to the judgment of the critics
Prior. Solomon, Pref.

This useful impression [on the mind] is commonly made in poetry by indirect methods; as by fable, by narration, by representation of characters; but *didactick* poetry openly professes its intention of conveying knowledge and instruction.—*Blair*, Lect. 40.

DI'DAPPER. Skinner says (q.d.) *Dive-dapper.* It is probably merely a reduplication of *dip*, (q.d.) *dip-dipper.* See DAB-CHICK.

Upon this promise did he raise his chin,
Like a *di-dapper* peering through a wave,
Who being look'd on, ducks as quickly in.
Shakespeare. Venus & Adonis.

Luz. The misery of man may fitly be compar'd to a *didapper*, who when she is under water, past our sight, and indeed can seem no more to us, rises again; shakes but herself, and is the same she was: so is it with transitory man, this day.—*Beaum. & Fletch. Woman Hater*, Act iv. sc. 3.

Thou must eat little or no goat's flesh, nor red deer; nor even foal's flesh, by any means; and carefully abstain,—that is, as much as thou canst, from peacocks, cranes, coots, *didappers*, and water hens.
Sterne. Tristram Shandy, vol. viii. c. 34.

DI'DRACHM. Gr. Διδραχμον, from δις, twice, and δραχμη. A double *drachm*, equal to two Roman *denarii*, or fifteen pence English. See DRACHM.

They went to Peter whom they sawe in maner next about hym, saying: Doeth youre maister (quoth they) pay the *didramme* or *didrachma* for trybute, as others doe.
Udal. Matt. c. 17.

The Septuagint reads το ἡμισυ διδραχμον, the half of the *didrachm*, or half shekel, which is all one with a whole *didrachm* Attick.—*Hammond. Annot. on St. Matthew*, c. 17.

538

Ex coll. Karolyne & Bryan A. Garner

Although Sir James Murray called *A New Dictionary* "a dictionary without definitions" (Murray 1900:44), that goes too far. Richardson provided definitions, just vague ones, and only for what he considered root words. His dictionary enjoyed some esteem for a while, and at the beginning of the work on the *Oxford English Dictionary* the editor, Herbert Coleridge, thought it "an excellent model for such a work as that which we proposed." (Gilliver 2016:15.) But its popularity was limited to those who already had extensive background in philology. It was nearly useless to those who didn't already know what all the words meant, and only minimally useful to those who did.

"I may myself be suffered to avow a peculiar gratification in the plan upon which this Dictionary has been composed. It is a copious and careful record of the Language from its earliest state; it contains the choicest sentiments of English wisdom, poetry, and eloquence; it may be deemed a supplial of many books; and as such merely it may be estimated at higher worth in foreign climes than on its native shores. At the very moment, when I am concluding this final page, I have reason to believe that the early portions of these volumes have found a resting place upon the tables of an English Settler on the banks of La Plata; I am assured that they are admitted to relieve the languor of military inaction at the Mess of Abednuggar; and that they have already found employment for the acuteness of nearly a century of critics in the United States of North America." (Preface, p. 61.)

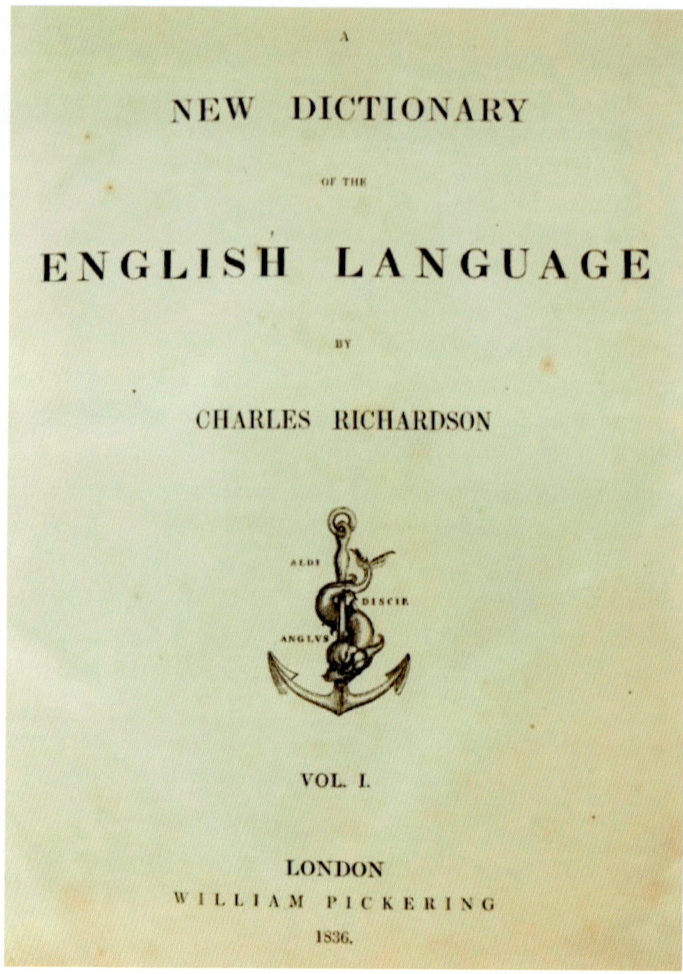

A

NEW DICTIONARY

OF THE

ENGLISH LANGUAGE

BY

CHARLES RICHARDSON

VOL. I.

LONDON

WILLIAM PICKERING

1836.

Ex coll. Karolyne & Bryan A. Garner

69

John Bouvier
America's First Legal Lexicographer

Bouvier, John. *A Law Dictionary*. 2 vols. Philadelphia: T. & J.W. Johnson, 1839. 2d ed. 1843. 3d ed. 1848. 4th ed. 1852. 5th ed. 1854. 6th ed. 1856.

Ex coll. Karolyne & Bryan A. Garner

THOUGH FRENCH BY BIRTH, John Bouvier (1787–1851) created the first truly American law dictionary; he is the Noah Webster of legal lexicography. Born in Codognan, France, Bouvier emigrated with his family, when he was 15, to Philadelphia. Like Rastell, father of the English law dictionary, he began his career as a printer. After apprenticing with a printer and bookseller, Bouvier opened his own printing business in 1812 (becoming a U.S. citizen the same year), and in 1814, he published the first issue of the *American Telegraph*, a weekly newspaper.

Bouvier also began studying law during this period, and in 1818 he was admitted to the Pennsylvania bar. Four years later, he was admitted as an attorney to the Supreme Court of Pennsylvania. In 1836, he was appointed Recorder of the City of Philadelphia by the governor, who two years later appointed him as an associate judge of the Court of Criminal Sessions.

As Bouvier rose in the legal profession, he became increasingly aware of the need for an American law dictionary. The English law dictionaries that he and other lawyers used in training and practice were insufficient for the needs of the new nation's legal system because they were based on foreign jurisprudence and incorporated vestiges of feudal law, which was already mostly obsolete even in England. "What," Bouvier asked, "have we to do with those laws of Great Britain which relate to the person of their king, their nobility, their clergy, their navy, their army; with their game laws; their local statutes . . . ?" American lawyers and judges needed a practical reference work based on their own legal system. So in 1839, after many years' labor, Bouvier published his two-volume solution to this deficiency: *A Law Dictionary, adapted to the Constitution and Laws of the United States of*

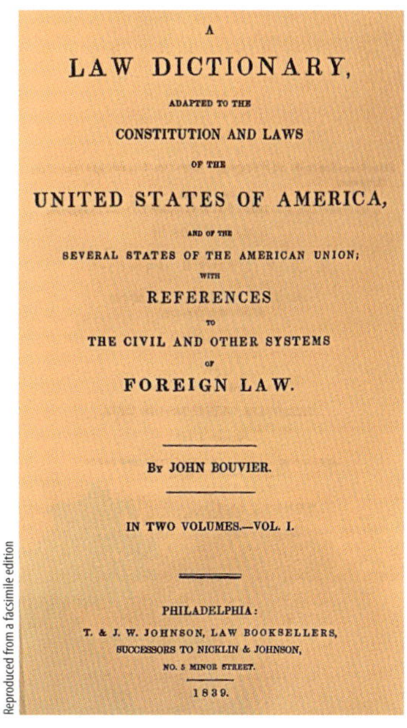
A
LAW DICTIONARY,
ADAPTED TO THE
CONSTITUTION AND LAWS
OF THE
UNITED STATES OF AMERICA,
AND OF THE
SEVERAL STATES OF THE AMERICAN UNION;
WITH
REFERENCES
TO
THE CIVIL AND OTHER SYSTEMS
OF
FOREIGN LAW.

BY JOHN BOUVIER.

IN TWO VOLUMES.—VOL. I.

PHILADELPHIA:
T. & J. W. JOHNSON, LAW BOOKSELLERS,
SUCCESSORS TO NICKLIN & JOHNSON,
NO. 5 MINOR STREET.
1839.

Reproduced from a facsimile edition

America, and of the several States of the American Union. It is believed to be the first dictionary based on American law, and it was an overnight success, praised by such eminent contemporary jurists as James Kent, Chancellor of New York, and Justice Joseph Story of the U.S. Supreme Court.

Ex coll. Karolyne & Bryan A. Garner

Bouvier continued working tirelessly to improve American legal literature, publishing two further editions of his dictionary within his lifetime and publishing the four-volume *Institutes of American Law* shortly before his death in 1851. He died at 64, a week after being found "stricken with apoplexy" while working in his office. It was believed that his death was a result of his unwavering commitment to his work. Even if it shortened his life, Bouvier's contribution to American law endures after his death: a year later, his dictionary entered its fourth edition.

In successive editions of 1914, 1926, and 1934, the editors transformed the book from a dictionary into an encyclopedia, replete with essays, restatements of the law, and copious citations, as a result of which the book became quickly dated, and *much* harder to revise. For example, Bouvier's 1839 entry for the word *constitution* consisted of 127 words, followed by a short entry for *constitutional*; in Francis Rawle's third revision of 1914 (pictured below at bottom right), the entry consisted of 1,246 words, followed by a 14,000-word entry on *Constitution of the United States of America*. That entry is nothing but a period piece today, and its case-specific discussions proved impossible to keep up to date.

"To those who are aware of the difficulties of the task, the author deems it unnecessary to make any apology for the imperfections which may be found in the work. His object has been to be useful; if that has been accomplished in any degree, he will be amply rewarded for his labor; and he relies upon the generous liberality of the members of the profession to overlook the errors which may have been committed in his endeavors to serve them." (Preface, p. xi.)

Ex coll. Karolyne & Bryan A. Garner

70

Noah Webster's Disappointing Finale

Webster, Noah. *An American Dictionary of the English Language; first edition in octavo, containing the whole vocabulary of the quarto, with corrections, improvements and several thousand additional words*. 2 vols. New Haven: Published by the author. Printed by B.L. Hamlen, 1841.

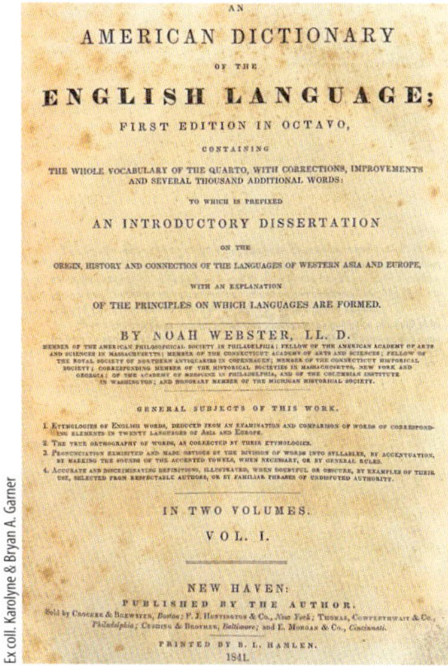
AN
AMERICAN DICTIONARY
OF THE
ENGLISH LANGUAGE;
FIRST EDITION IN OCTAVO,
CONTAINING
THE WHOLE VOCABULARY OF THE QUARTO, WITH CORRECTIONS, IMPROVEMENTS AND SEVERAL THOUSAND ADDITIONAL WORDS:
TO WHICH IS PREFIXED
AN INTRODUCTORY DISSERTATION
ON THE
ORIGIN, HISTORY AND CONNECTION OF THE LANGUAGES OF WESTERN ASIA AND EUROPE,
WITH AN EXPLANATION
OF THE PRINCIPLES ON WHICH LANGUAGES ARE FORMED.

BY NOAH WEBSTER, LL. D.
MEMBER OF THE AMERICAN PHILOSOPHICAL SOCIETY IN PHILADELPHIA; FELLOW OF THE AMERICAN ACADEMY OF ARTS AND SCIENCES IN MASSACHUSETTS; MEMBER OF THE CONNECTICUT ACADEMY OF ARTS AND SCIENCES; FELLOW OF THE ROYAL SOCIETY OF NORTHERN ANTIQUARIES IN COPENHAGEN; MEMBER OF THE CONNECTICUT HISTORICAL SOCIETY; CORRESPONDING MEMBER OF THE HISTORICAL SOCIETIES IN MASSACHUSETTS, NEW YORK AND GEORGIA; OF THE ACADEMY OF MEDICINE IN PHILADELPHIA, AND OF THE COLUMBIAN INSTITUTE IN WASHINGTON; AND HONORARY MEMBER OF THE MICHIGAN HISTORICAL SOCIETY.

GENERAL SUBJECTS OF THIS WORK.
1. ETYMOLOGIES OF ENGLISH WORDS, DEDUCED FROM AN EXAMINATION AND COMPARISON OF WORDS OF CORRESPONDING ELEMENTS IN TWENTY LANGUAGES OF ASIA AND EUROPE.
2. THE TRUE ORTHOGRAPHY OF WORDS, AS CORRECTED BY THEIR ETYMOLOGIES.
3. PRONUNCIATION EXHIBITED AND MADE OBVIOUS BY THE DIVISION OF WORDS INTO SYLLABLES, BY ACCENTUATION, BY MARKING THE SOUNDS OF THE ACCENTED VOWELS, WHEN NECESSARY, OR BY GENERAL RULES.
4. ACCURATE AND DISCRIMINATING DEFINITIONS, ILLUSTRATED, WHEN DOUBTFUL OR OBSCURE, BY EXAMPLES OF THEIR USE, SELECTED FROM RESPECTABLE AUTHORS, OR BY FAMILIAR PHRASES OF UNDISPUTED AUTHORITY.

IN TWO VOLUMES.
VOL. I.

NEW HAVEN:
PUBLISHED BY THE AUTHOR.
Sold by CROCKER & BREWSTER, *Boston*; F. J. HUNTINGTON & CO., *New York*; THOMAS, COWPERTHWAIT & CO., *Philadelphia*; CUSHING & BROTHER, *Baltimore*; and E. MORGAN & CO., *Cincinnati*.
PRINTED BY B. L. HAMLEN.
1841.

Ex coll. Karolyne & Bryan A. Garner

Note "published by the author."

WHEN NOAH WEBSTER announced to his family in 1839 that he would mortgage his house to raise enough money to self-publish the next big edition of his *American Dictionary*—after all, the publishers were making a great deal of money on the one-volume abridgment that he had assigned to his son-in-law Chauncey Goodrich—the family was horrified. Every self-publishing venture in which he had dabbled, from his journalistic years in New York to more recent failed undertakings, had been financially disastrous. But with Sherman Converse out of the picture for nearly a decade and other publishers wary of the big two-volume work that had never sold swiftly, Webster was intent on issuing his magnum opus himself.

"The genuine English idiom is as well preserved by the unmixed English of this country, as it is by the best *English* writers. . . . It is true, that many of our writers have neglected to cultivate taste, and the embellishments of style; but even these have written the language in its genuine *idiom*." (Preface, p. vii.)

Originally, Webster proposed to publish as many as 5,000 copies; in the end, he reduced the number to 3,000, given the bad economic times. To that extent, he mitigated the publishing blunder: in the two years left of his life, less than half the full print run sold. At his death, some 1,420 copies were still on hand in unbound sheets.

Ex coll. Karolyne & Bryan A. Garner

Webster had deluded himself into thinking that etymology—his greatest weakness—was his greatest strength. He tried to tie *cost* and *cough* to Persian words (printed in Persian characters); *crush* to Arabic, Ethiopian, Hebrew, and Chaldee; and *crystal* to Arabic and Chaldee. Multiply those instances by several thousand. All this nonsense was entirely the product of his flawed method of looking into foreign dictionaries and trying to find words that superficially resembled English words in some way, while knowing nothing about the actual processes by which languages evolve over time. In an advertisement for this 1841 dictionary, Webster wrote: "To trace words to their origin, and show their primary or radical signification; to ascertain the origin of a great number of English words derived from other languages . . . : *hic labor, hoc opus est*. In this department of etymology, all European books which I have seen are most miserably deficient." (Laird 1970:283.) He had become the ultimate lexicographic ultracrepidarian: he denounced all etymologists who were more circumspect and factual.

Webster promoted the book. One inscribed copy, now in the Harlan Crow Library, was sent as a gift to President William Henry Harrison on his inauguration day. The inscription reads, in Webster's hand: "Presented to President Harrison, March 4 1841, with the authors [sic] respects & with cordial wishes for the prosperity of the United States, under his administration. / Noah Webster / New Haven, Connecticut / February 24, 1841." The President wouldn't have had much time to consult the book. On the fateful day of his Inaugural, in chilly weather, Harrison gave the longest inaugural address in history (nearly two hours long), rode on horseback in a parade, stood in a three-hour receiving line at the White House, and attended three balls. He caught pneumonia on that overextended day, never really recovered, and died on 4 April.

"If the language can be improved in regularity, so as to be more easily acquired by our own citizens, and by foreigners, and thus be rendered a more useful instrument for the propagation of science, arts, civilization and Christianity;—if it can be rescued from the mischievous influence of sciolists, and that dabbling spirit of innovation, which is perpetually disturbing its settled usages and filling it with anomalies;—if, in short, our vernacular language can be redeemed from corruptions, and our philology and literature from degradation; it would be a source of great satisfaction to me to be one among the instruments of promoting these valuable objects. If this object can not be effected, and my wishes and hopes are to be frustrated, my labor will be lost, and this work must sink into oblivion." (Preface, p. viii.)

In short, the hope of having President Harrison as an "influencer" for the work probably came to naught. Webster doubtless sent out dozens of such gratis copies for promotional purposes.

Webster knew the importance of marketing and sales. So he retained a young relative, J.W. Webster of Waterbury, Connecticut, as an itinerant peddler on a commission basis. The young Webster, out of work at the time, asked for a small advance to start out with in April 1841. At the end of the month, working door to door in Northampton, Massachusetts, the young Webster had sold only two copies. Apparently, another sales agent had preceded him there, so he proposed to go up the river to Providence, Rhode Island, where he might have a fair chance.

Once there, he placed a commendation-filled advertisement in the local newspaper at a cost of $5. Then, in mid-May, he wrote to his uncle. His previously fine handwriting showed signs of distress, with pained ink stains that told their own story: "Thus far I have not been able to dispose of a *single copy*, & I have seen 60, or 70, Gentlemen who were thought to be most literary." Wanting to return home, he wrote: "I am entirely disheartened from my continuation of ill luck." But he had a hotel bill to pay, and he couldn't leave town, as he explained to his uncle: "Please write me immediately for my expences [sic] are accumulating rapidly, board being very high at the Hotels in the City—." (Monaghan 1983:179–80.)

The record tells us nothing about how J.W. Webster was extricated from his predicament, but we do know that Noah Webster didn't engage him further.

"It satisfies my mind that I have done all that my health, my talents and my pecuniary means would enable me to accomplish. I present it to my fellow citizens, not with frigid indifference, but with my ardent wishes for their improvement and happiness; and for the continued increase of the wealth, the learning, the moral and religious elevation of character, and the glory of my country." (Preface, p. viii.)

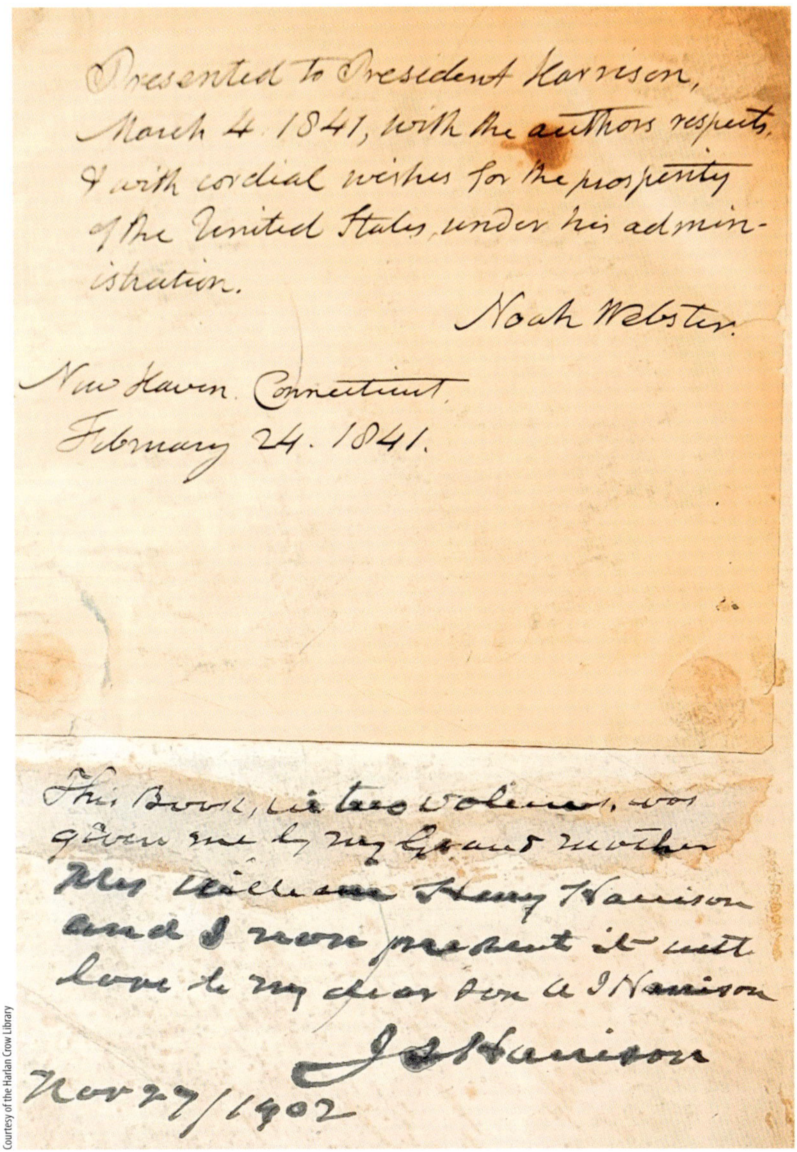
Presented to President Harrison, March 4. 1841, with the authors respects, & with cordial wishes for the prosperity of the United States, under his administration.

Noah Webster.

New Haven. Connecticut, February 24. 1841.

This Book, in two volumes, was given me by my Grand mother Mrs William Henry Harrison and I now present it with love to my dear son W I Harrison

J S Harrison

Nov 27/1902

Webster's inscription for President William Henry Harrison, who died 39 days after receiving this gift (if indeed he received the gift on the date of inscription). The book descended to President Harrison's grandson, John Scott Harrison Jr. (1844–1926).

71

Webster's Tetchiest Letters

Unpublished letters from the Garner Collection (1787–1842).

In Webster's defense, we might say that the man felt perpetually aggrieved. Upon the publication of his first book, a speller, he was publicly (and probably justly) ridiculed as a plagiarist; for the rest of his life, he berated others for plagiarism. With the publication of his second book, a grammar, he sought to become America's grammarian; soon he realized that he was being vastly outsold, even in the United States, by an expatriate American living in England (Lindley Murray)—his former landlord, in a manner of speaking, who never entered the field until becoming Webster's landlord. After the publication of his third book, a reader, he discovered that the reading public on both sides of the Atlantic preferred an anthology by none other than this same man: Lindley Murray. And when Webster published his first Americanized dictionary in 1806, based on an English dictionary by William Entick, his hometown publisher in New Haven continued printing the original Entick, which seemed to sell better.

Endowed with monumentally poor business judgment, Webster was perpetually on the verge of insolvency, except when his rich brother-in-law, the fraudster James Greenleaf, bailed him out in the 1780s and 1790s. The notorious Greenleaf would ultimately come to ruin, losing his money, going to jail, and shaming Webster by familial association.

Meanwhile, the financially comfortable Lindley Murray was soon allowing American printers to issue his books free of any obligation to pay royalties, which meant that Webster—who was dependent on royalties for his living—was thereby guaranteed reduced revenues. And people preferred the organization and literary style of Murray's reference books anyway.

When Webster's big *American Dictionary* appeared in 1828, it was abridged by a man, Joseph Worcester (no. 63), who would soon compete against Webster in the dictionary market. That was galling. And Webster's son-in-law Chauncey A. Goodrich, who was largely responsible for Worcester's involvement, allowed Worcester to alter

Ex coll. Karolyne & Bryan A. Garner

Folders containing some of the 30 or so original Webster documents in the Garner Collection.

the spellings that Webster cared about so deeply. Infuriated, Webster distanced himself from the abridgment by assigning the rights to it to Goodrich, as a result of which Goodrich soon became wealthy: the abridgment was the only Webster dictionary that sold well at the time. (This was partly due to Worcester's improvements of it.) Goodrich made as much as $6,000 annually in royalties—more than three times his professorial salary at Yale. Meanwhile, Webster himself was storing hundreds of unsold, unbound copies of his two-volume magnum opus, which people didn't want and couldn't afford.

In 1833, Webster even rewrote the Bible—*The Holy Bible, Containing the Old and New Testaments, in the Common Version: With Amendments of the Language*, by Noah Webster, LL.D.—substituting modern words for the KJV's archaisms and toning down indelicacies like *whoremonger* and *piss*. But that book didn't sell well.

In 1841, he financed his big dictionary (no. 70) by taking out a mortgage on his house. That venture failed, as so many others had before, and the book didn't sell. All the while, Webster was being relentlessly assailed by Lyman Cobb (no. 64), a rival spelling expert, who was issuing anti-Webster pamphlets and distributing them throughout New England and the Midwest. One basis of Cobb's criticisms was the divergences in spelling between Webster's other recent books and the Worcester abridgment, which bore Webster's name.

Hence grievance was a major part of Webster's mental makeup, and this affected all his relationships. One of his biographers writes that Webster went out of his way to alienate just about everybody he ever knew. (Kendall 2010:268.)

Within the Garner Collection are 21 previously unpublished autograph letters amply showing this unpleasant aspect of Webster's personality. Three of them were written during the final year of his life. These extracts, beginning in 1787, are a fair sampling:

- "I consider this delay, evasion or refusal, by whatever name it ought to be called, as a repetition of incivilities or rather injuries which I have before experienced in Philadelphia; & as a continuation of that want of attention & politeness for which the citizens are distinguished." (*10 Dec. 1787 ALS from Noah Webster to Tench Coxe of Philadelphia.*)
- "I wrote to you some weeks ago relative to procuring me a sum of money, & have rec'd no answer. I wish to know what you have done or can do, as soon as possible." (*10 Apr. 1791 ALS from Noah Webster to Josiah Blakeley, a businessman who,*

"[Webster] was above all else a scholar, a man of intellect, whose single-minded pursuit of high goals rendered him incapable of overlooking an error in others or tolerating one in himself. His high principles found expression in a long, unblemished life. His letters reflect an ardent desire to make truth prevail: truth in religion, truth in politics, and truth in language. It is fitting that he should still stand beside us, silently holding his Dictionary, to guide the expression of our thoughts." (Warfel 1953:xliv.)

"All of Webster's criticisms [of spellers] had the same thrust. Where the other spelling books had any merit, it was because they were—depending on his frame of mind at the time of writing—inspired by, modeled upon, copied from, or frank plagiarisms of his own work. Where they were deficient, it was because they were pursuing orthography and pronunciation that differed from his own." (Monaghan 1983:185.)

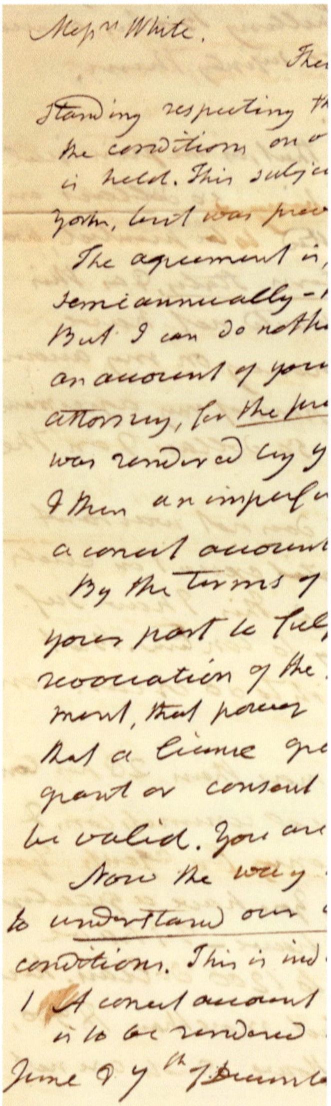
Messrs White.
The
standing respecting th
the conditions on
is held. This subje
York, but was prev
The agreement is,
semiannually –
But I can do nothi
an account of you
attorney, for the pre
was rendered by y
then an imperfe
a correct account
By the terms of
your part to fulf
revocation of the
ment, that power
that a license gra
grant or consent
be valid. You are
Now the way
to understand our
conditions. This is ind
1 A correct account
is to be rendered
June & 7th Decemb

Ex coll. Karolyne & Bryan A. Garner

The 1832 letter to White Gallagher & White (detail).

from 1785 to 1793, frequently dined with Webster. [*See Webster 1989:362.*])

- "Sir, I received from you last summer, by your Brother, 15 dol^{rs} on acc^{t} of the Dictionaries. I understand you sent some of them—I believe 50—to Mr Seward of Utica. If so, you retain, if I recollect right, 150 copies—or 250. I wish for a settlement—if the books are sold—you deducting expenses & your commission. At any rate I wish for an amount of sales—& any balance in your hands. I sold the books at 42 cents—42 dollars the hundred—at the time of publication—as I have waited so long, if any profit has accrued, I ought to receive it." (*6 Jan. 1812 ALS from Noah Webster to Albany bookseller Daniel Steele, requesting his share of the income from sales of his* Compendious Dictionary [*no. 57*].)
- "I had no idea that any obligation existed on my part to give the management of the business in England to you any more than to any other person. And if there had been, your proposal to give me *one third* of the profits would have [brought? meant?] an end to negotiation. . . . Where you obtained the idea that I had thoughts of giving my manuscripts to Yale College Library, I cannot conceive. I have no recollection that that idea ever entered my mind, & I am confident it never did." (*20 Jan. 1828 ALS from Noah Webster to Sherman Converse, the publisher of Webster's unabridged 1828* Dictionary. *For more on the misfortunes of Converse, see nos. 63 & 65.*)
- "I can do nothing towards the adjustment, till I receive an amount of your transactions under the power of attorney, for *the preceding* [*nine?*] *months*. No such account was rendered by you in June last; nor until September, & then an imperfect & incorrect one; & I did not obtain a correct account, till I was in New York in Nov^{r}.

  By the terms of our agreement, a failure on your part to fulfill the covenants operates as a revocation of the power of attorney; & at this moment, that power is, in strictness, null & void; so that a license granted now, without a further grant or consent on my part, would probably not be valid. You are probably not aware of this.

  Now the way to a harmonious intercourse, is, to *understand our agreement*, & to comply with its conditions. This is indispensable in the present case.

  1. A correct account of the transactions under your agency is to be rendered to me regularly on the 7th of June & 7th December.
  2. You are to purchase of my son or the company with which he is connected, 30,000 Spelling Books annually

if he or they request it & will supply them. These articles are essential." (*10 Dec. 1832 ALS from Noah Webster to White Gallagher & White, publishers of Webster's spelling book.*)

- "I see Lyman Cobb is sending his books into Tennessee, as he is into other quarters. He is an extraordinary man. His history is shortly this. He was a poor boy in Lenox, Mass^{t}. Mr Hamlin the printer here was in school with him. He afterwards lived with a Mr Bosworth [sic] of Albany, as a menial, but I am told he was addicted to lying for which he was flogged. He then ran away & the first thing Boswell [sic] heard from him was, he had made a Spelling Book. It seems he went westward & kept school, then in Walker's dictionary adopted his plan of spelling & pronunciation. After he published his sp book he attacked *mine*, marked every thing in which I differ from Walker, published a long series of papers ag^{t} me first in the Albany paper, then in a pamphlet which he sent by mail into all quarters. When my dictionary appeared, he again wrote ag^{t} me in a New York paper, finding fault with my discrepancies of orthography, published a pamphlet which you have doubtless seen. There were discrepancies in my books, for I attend my old orthography in many words, in order to reduce the spelling to uniformity. Cobb superintended Alexander's dictionary, published by Connor, altering the English orthography, & adding *k* after c, as in *monicker*, & inserting *u* in *errour*, *inferiour*. In this book are many plagiarisms from my dictionary, as there are in his little reticule." (*26 Oct. 1836 ALS from Noah Webster to Henry Henrick, a newspaper editor in Knoxville.*)
- "M^{r}. Boswell. I wish the foregoing to be inserted in both of your papers, under the Hartford Head, as a *communication*, rather than as an *advertisement*. Please to accept the inclosed bill of 3 dollars, & send me two or three copies of your daily papers in which the notice is inserted." (*24 Mar. 1841 ALS from Noah Webster to John L. Boswell, editor of the* Hartford Courant*—seeking to have an ad disguised as a news item. The ad as published concluded with these words, presumably written by Webster: "It is remarkable that the novelty and accuracy of definitions in the American Dictionary have induced some persons to read the two volumes from beginning to end in course."*)
- "I see Cobb's New sp. book is highly praised in the New York Sun. I have not yet seen it. We have a great many such books & all are the best." (*31 Mar. 1842 ALS from Noah Webster to Samuel Parker, the husband of Webster's niece in Ithaca, New York.*)

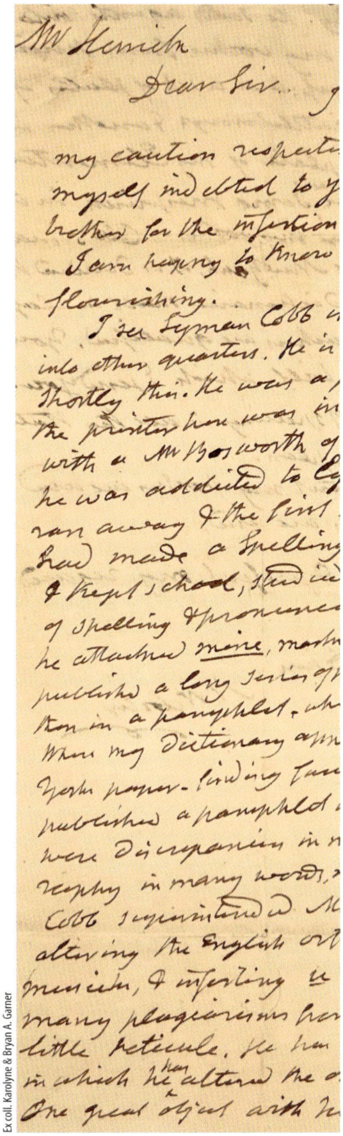

Ex coll. Karolyne & Bryan A. Garner

Webster's 1836 letter to Henry Henrick (detail).

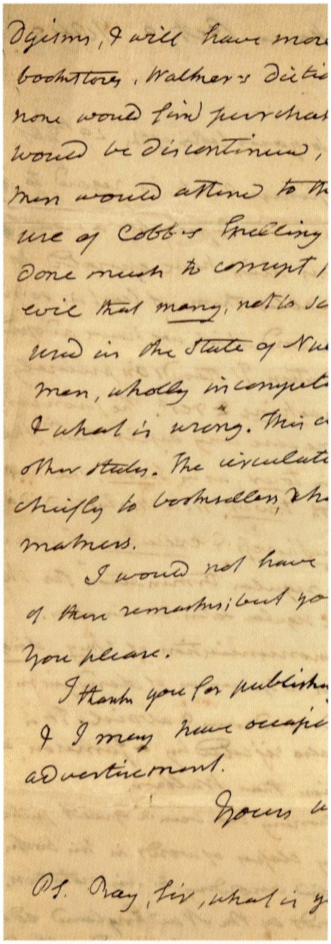
ogism, & will have more
bookstores, Walker's dicti
none would find purchas
would be discontinued,
men would attend to th
use of Cobb's Spelling
done much to corrupt
evil that many, not to sa
used in the State of New
men, wholly incompete
& what is wrong. This e
other states. The circulati
chiefly to booksellers, wh
makers.
I would not have
of these remarks; but yo
you please.
I thank you for publishi
& I may have occasi
advertisement.
Yours w
P.S. Pray, Sir, what is y

Ex coll. Karolyne & Bryan A. Garner

Oct. 1842 letter to O.A. Bowie (detail).

Photo ex coll. Karolyne & Bryan A. Garner

- "In most of our New England bookstores, Walker's dictionary is not kept for sale, for none would find purchasers. The use of it in the other states would be discontinued, if the teachers of schools & literary men would attend to the rules in my dictionary. The use of Cobb's Spelling Books, in some towns, has done much to corrupt pronunciation. It is a great evil that *many*, not to say *most* of the school books used in the State of New York are compiled by illiterate men, wholly incompetent to determine what is right & what is wrong. This evil, to some extent, exists in other states. The circulation and use of such books are owing chiefly to booksellers, who are as ignorant as the bookmakers. I would not have my name used in the publication of these remarks; but you may use them yourself, if you please. I thank you for publishing articles favorable to my designs; & I may have occasion soon to send you an advertisement." (*3 Oct. 1842 ALS from Noah Webster to O.A. Bowie, editor of the* Hartford Journal. *Webster has tried to induce the editor to adopt Webster's words as his own—disguising their true source. He also suggests that he is willing, if pleased by Bowie's actions, to pay for advertisements in the future—which might be read as a petty bribe.*)

The 1841 letter is particularly enlightening. Webster has asked the editor of the *Hartford Courant* to place what is essentially an advertisement as a news item. On 26 March 1841, just two days after Webster's letter, the ad ran. It included eight snippets from British reviews. The first, by a clergyman in the *Liverpool Mercury*, said of Webster: "By far the best English Dictionary, indeed the only one to which appeal can now be made as an authority." From the *Aberdeen Observer*: "This publication will go far to remove the unjust prejudices which prevail in this country against the literature of Americans." Two others state that Webster has wholly eclipsed Johnson. The British recommendations culminate with the claim that Webster's dictionary is "the nearest approximation to a perfect dictionary of the language which we have ever seen."

Few might have suspected that Webster himself had placed the piece. But what is truly extraordinary is that no evidence can now be found that any such British reviews ever actually appeared in print outside Webster's own ads. They seem, in short, to have been fabricated. Perhaps Webster wagered that the fabrications would be just as undetectable as his illusory etymologies were. It certainly took time: the falsified blurbs have never before been exposed.

72

President John Quincy Adams on Webster's Legacy

Sept. 1843 ALS of John Quincy Adams (1767–1848), the former President, to William G. Webster supporting the purchase of Noah Webster's synopsis of his *Dictionary* for the Library of Congress.

After his father's death in May 1843, William Greenleaf Webster (1801–1869) began working to ensure his father's legacy—and perhaps to ensure his own livelihood by doing so. After all, two sons-in-law had become lexicographers: Chauncey A. Goodrich was making a small fortune from his abridged edition of Webster, and William C. Fowler had started work on his own abridgment. Meanwhile, William G. Webster had been adjudicated bankrupt in 1842; he was trying to find a footing, and it seemed that lexicography was becoming a cottage industry among family members. By 1846, the name William G. would begin appearing on the title pages of various "pocket editions" of Webster dictionaries. There was money in the name Webster, and William G. alone could claim the cognomen.

But the enterprising son thought of another way to acquire income, perhaps at the same time securing the memory of his late father. Soon after his father's death, William G. wrote to former President John Quincy Adams to suggest that Congress purchase the "synopsis" of his father's *Dictionary*. What did this mean, exactly?

There are two possibilities, the first of which is the less likely. The only "synopsis" published in Webster dictionaries is the "Synopsis of Words Differently Pronounced by Different Orthoëpists," which first appeared in Worcester's abridgment of Webster's dictionary (no. 63). It was, in fact, prepared by Joseph Worcester, its purpose being "to exhibit, at one view, the manner in which words of doubtful, disputed, or various pronunciation, are pronounced by the most eminent English orthoepists." In 17 printed pages, it compares the work of Webster (no. 62), Sheridan (no. 50), Walker (no. 47), Perry (no. 46), and three others. Webster is known to have detested this synopsis

President John Quincy Adams.

"Mr. Webster . . . is prosecuting his plan of a large English dictionary, and although my sentiments on such subjects do not agree entirely with him, I wish that his industry may meet with its rewards, and his ingenuity with encouragement. He published . . . some censures upon Johnson's *Dictionary*, and some criticisms on other writers, which I thought incorrect. In one of my lectures I . . . contested several of [his] criticisms." (Letter of John Quincy Adams to Abigail Adams, 9 Aug. 1809.)

Shortly after writing this letter, Adams became embroiled in an unsuccessful effort to prevent the annexation of Texas into the Union.

William G. Webster Esq[r] New York
Quincy 11 Sept[r]. 1843
Dear Sir
It would give me pleasure were it in my power to encourage the expectation that the Congress of the United States would be disposed to manifest their veneration for the memory of your father and to patronize the liberal arts and literature, by purchasing the synopsis of his great work and causing it to be deposited in their library. Nor would I in any manner *dis*courage the proposal. On the contrary, should you conclude to prepare a memorial presenting the obvious considerations in favour of that measure, and will do me the honour of entrusting it to me, I will very cheerfully present it to the House, and will give it such a direction as may be most promotive of its success.
I am very respectfully,
Sir, your obed[t] serv[t]
John Quincy Adams

because it elevated other pronunciation experts to his plane, and it suggested that his view on any given word was only one among many. Nevertheless, his son-in-law Chauncey Goodrich retained the synopsis in all the abridged editions, and it became a major selling point for the dictionary. In fact, it was even included in the two-volume British unabridged edition (no. 65) despite its omission—at Webster's insistence—from the later analogous American edition (no. 70).

The other possibility is more likely. By November 1821, Webster had completed his "Synopsis of the Principal Words in Twenty Languages," which was intended as an etymological appendix to his dictionary. Yet it would never be published, and today it lies in the archives of the New York Public Library. (It was acquired by that great institution with the rest of William's archive.) This synopsis is generally unknown to the world of scholarship, which might be just as well given the fallacious means by which Webster approached the subject of etymology (see pp. 182–83, 196, 200–2).

All of which is to say that Congress never acted on William G. Webster's proposal to sell the document. Congress never even debated whether to appropriate the money that William sought. Yet President John Quincy Adams's enthusiastic response, in his own elegant handwriting, survives in the Garner Collection. Although Adams sanguinely hinted at a happy outcome, that was never to be.

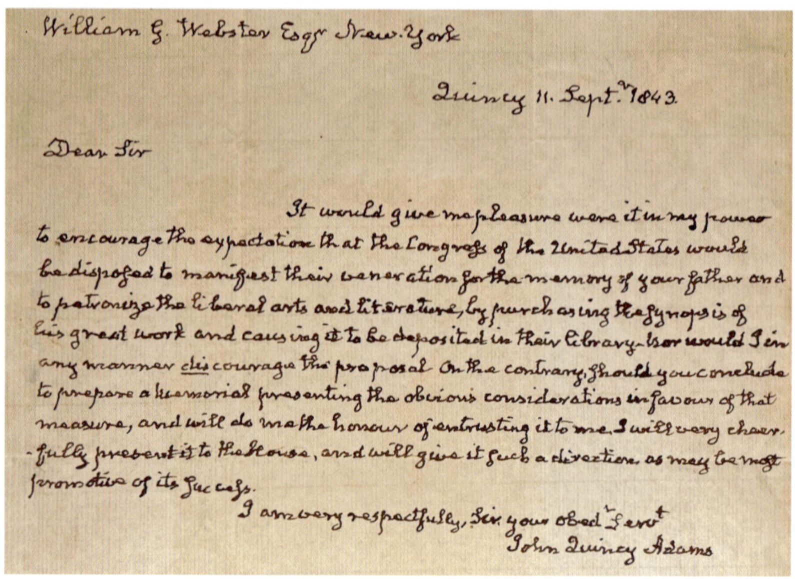

William G. Webster Esq[r] New York
Quincy 11. Sept[r]. 1843.
Dear Sir
It would give me pleasure were it in my power to encourage the expectation that the Congress of the United States would be disposed to manifest their veneration for the memory of your father and to patronize the liberal arts and literature, by purchasing the synopsis of his great work and causing it to be deposited in their library. Nor would I in any manner discourage the proposal. On the contrary, should you conclude to prepare a memorial presenting the obvious considerations in favour of that measure, and will do me the honour of entrusting it to me, I will very cheerfully present it to the House, and will give it such a direction as may be most promotive of its success.
I am very respectfully, Sir, your obed[t] Serv[t]
John Quincy Adams

Ex coll. Karolyne & Bryan A. Garner

73

The Goodrich–Fowler Wrangling
Family Rift over Spelling

After Noah Webster's death, the seething correspondence between Noah Webster's sons-in-law, Chauncey A. Goodrich (1790–1860) and William Chauncey Fowler (1793–1881), addressed mostly Goodrich's work on the abridgment of Webster's famous dictionary. Goodrich, a Yale professor, and Fowler, an Amherst professor, each believed that he had the high moral ground. The letters received by Goodrich are held at Yale University in the Goodrich Family Papers; the letters received by William G. Webster, Noah's son, are in the New York Public Library; the letters received by Fowler are held in the Garner Collection.

Goodrich oversaw the revisions of Webster's dictionary for George Merriam and Charles Merriam, who bought the rights in 1844. A newly printed edition appeared in September 1847 (no. 74), in the midst of family strife. This fascinating correspondence reveals the family frictions that left the two men and their families not speaking to each other for many years. Fowler saw Goodrich's changes in the patriarch's orthography as a betrayal of the great lexicographer's memory, and he was trying to turn the rest of the family against Goodrich. By the end of the correspondence, Fowler's wife, Harriet (1797–1844), Noah's daughter, had been dead nearly a decade. Goodrich's wife, Noah's daughter Frances Julianna (1793–1869), outlived Harriet by 25 years and wanted peace within the family, favoring (naturally) her husband.

But this correspondence is about much more than family turmoil. It relates to a turning point in English-language lexicography—at the peripety of which it would finally be decided either how words would be spelled in American English, or else how words would be spelled in Webster dictionaries. If Webster dictionaries had retained Noah Webster's idiosyncrasies, then competitors such as Joseph Worcester (no. 63) and Lyman Cobb (no. 64) might have gained a competitive advantage. Goodrich knew that Webster was out of step with what the public would find acceptable, and he was trying to align Webster dictionaries with what might be (and was proving to be) a salable

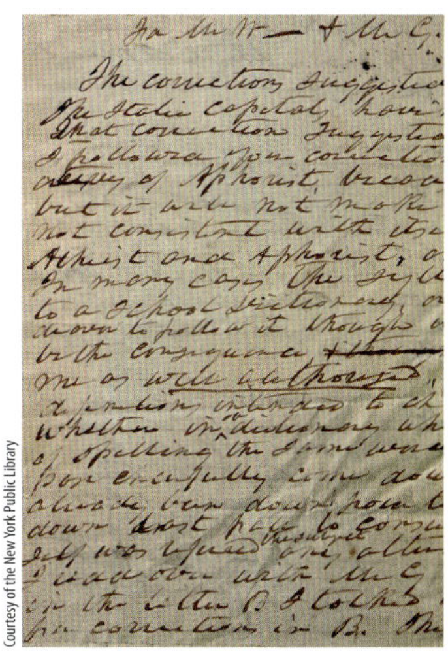

Courtesy of the New York Public Library

Detail from a letter by William C. Fowler to William G. Webster and Chauncey A. Goodrich (8 Mar. 1845).

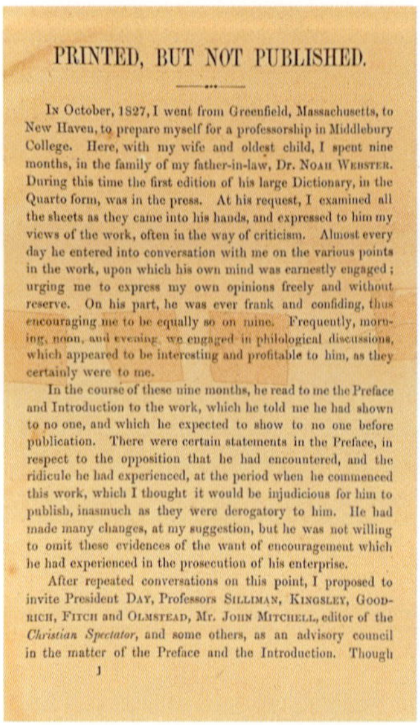

PRINTED, BUT NOT PUBLISHED.

In October, 1827, I went from Greenfield, Massachusetts, to New Haven, to prepare myself for a professorship in Middlebury College. Here, with my wife and oldest child, I spent nine months, in the family of my father-in-law, Dr. Noah Webster. During this time the first edition of his large Dictionary, in the Quarto form, was in the press. At his request, I examined all the sheets as they came into his hands, and expressed to him my views of the work, often in the way of criticism. Almost every day he entered into conversation with me on the various points in the work, upon which his own mind was earnestly engaged; urging me to express my own opinions freely and without reserve. On his part, he was ever frank and confiding, thus encouraging me to be equally so on mine. Frequently, morning, noon, and evening, we engaged in philological discussions, which appeared to be interesting and profitable to him, as they certainly were to me.

In the course of these nine months, he read to me the Preface and Introduction to the work, which he told me he had shown to no one, and which he expected to show to no one before publication. There were certain statements in the Preface, in respect to the opposition that he had encountered, and the ridicule he had experienced, at the period when he commenced this work, which I thought it would be injudicious for him to publish, inasmuch as they were derogatory to him. He had made many changes, at my suggestion, but he was not willing to omit these evidences of the want of encouragement which he had experienced in the prosecution of his enterprise.

After repeated conversations on this point, I proposed to invite President Day, Professors Silliman, Kingsley, Goodrich, Fitch and Olmstead, Mr. John Mitchell, editor of the *Christian Spectator*, and some others, as an advisory council in the matter of the Preface and the Introduction. Though

1

Ex coll. Karolyne & Bryan A. Garner

This copy of *Printed, but Not Published* comes from William C. Fowler's archive. It was once ripped in half—all 32 pages. At some point, a Fowler descendant taped it back together, page by page.

set of conventions. By the time of his death in 1860, Goodrich had retained Noah Porter of Yale to take over the editing of Webster's works. Meanwhile, the Merriam brothers were insistent on achieving salability for commercial reasons. So Fowler's hidebound doggedness in wanting to follow Noah Webster's odd spellings must have seemed quixotic to everyone else involved.

Amid these letters are handwritten charts that Goodrich made to compare various spelling schemes, as well as draft entries that he was putting forward.

A climactic point was reached in 1849 or so, when Fowler issued a 32-page pamphlet titled *Printed, but Not Published*. It was written in 1846 and read to former Governor William W. Ellsworth and his wife, Emily Webster Ellsworth, "with the declared intention of printing it when motives and purposes should become interpreted by facts and events." (P. 32.) Fowler intended it to counter whatever negative things Goodrich was saying about him: "These pages are not intended for the public, but for the family of Dr. Webster, and such others as Mr. Goodrich has conversed with on the subject matter." (*Id.*) The piece is essentially a long attack on Goodrich and his "unauthorized" changes to Webster dictionaries. Fowler protested against Goodrich's less drastic and prescriptive treatment of orthography and pronunciation than Webster's. Fowler resented the fact that he, Webster's most trusted literary executor, had somehow been sidelined. Fowler transparently resented Goodrich's financial success with the abridgment, and he even issued a rival abridgment—which failed to reach a second printing. Fowler asserted that Goodrich's "shrewdness and skill" had enabled him to achieve a "sharp bargain" with Webster. When Fowler had entreated Goodrich to share royalties, Goodrich responded that he had given Yale College $5,000 as an endowment toward a new divinity professorship. Goodrich said that he was using the royalties for "holy purposes" at Yale. In fact, though, Goodrich himself was the incumbent of the professorship!

So disturbed was Goodrich by the pamphlet that he composed a prayer about it in his diary:

> I cannot doubt that I needed exactly this trial to humble and purify my soul. It is impossible to penetrate the depth of self-complacency. . . . Here was the tenderest place in which to touch me. I hope before God I can say . . . 1) That I have never prayed more fervently for any one than for the author

> of this attack. My heart warm[ed] toward him in prayer. . . .
> 2) I feel much more dead to worldly things, especially to public estimation. This is what I needed.
>
> [Quoted in Martin 2019:172–73.]

The deterioration in familial relations began during Webster's lifetime and ended with a complete cessation of contact for seven years after 1847, when Fowler questioned William G. Webster whether the division of property after the death of Rebecca Webster (Noah's wife) had been fair. By demanding a copy of her will and an inventory of items distributed, he affronted William. On 25 February 1847, Governor Ellsworth wrote to William G. Webster: "After some letters between Mr. Fowler & myself, I utterly despair of all cordial intercourse or friendly cooperation on his part, for the future, however clear may be, even his *interest* in such cooperation. He is the most extraordinary man I ever met with." (Quoted in Micklethwait 2000:262 & Martin 2019:177.) Two weeks later, Ellsworth wrote to William: "Brother William, he will not assent to *anything*; tis his very principle of action. His late letters to me have been little better than an insult." (*Id.*) Micklethwait gives an admirably thorough account of the affair from every vantage except Goodrich's—a vantage now supplied by the Goodrich letters to Fowler recently acquired by the Garner Collection.

One letter in that archive is particularly noteworthy. In December 1853, Fowler wrote to ask Goodrich for his "views of the relations between us in respect to Webster's dictionaries" because they "might modify" his own. Goodrich responded with a pointed 16-page "statement of *facts*," dated 16 January 1854, in which he recounted, in searching detail, his own fair-minded efforts at settling the question of spellings in the Merriam versions of Webster dictionaries: "The Messrs. Merriam informed me, from the first, that they had no hope of succeeding in the new Edition unless important alterations could be made in the Orthography."

Goodrich explained his reasons for resisting Fowler's January 1845 demand to be made coeditor with Goodrich: "The supervision of a *single* responsible Editor was indispensable to the success of such an undertaking." But he assured Fowler that "no disrespect, or unkindness, was intended." If the two had become equal coeditors, "we should spend half our time in discussing the alterations proposed; so that the Revision could never be completed within the period for which

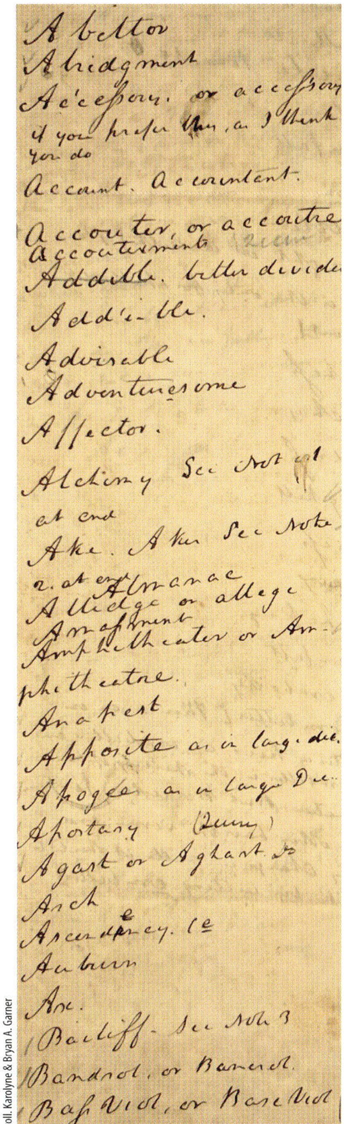
Abettor
Abridgment
Accessory, or accessary
if you prefer them, as I think you do
Account. Accountant.
Accouter, or accoutre
Accouterments
Addible. better divide
Addible.
Advisable
Adventuresome
Affector.
Alchimy See Note at end
Ake. Aker See Note a. at end
Almanac
Allege or allege
Amphitheater or Amphitheatre.
Anapest
Apposite as in larg. dic.
Apogee as in large Dic.
Apostasy (query)
Agast or Aghast do
Arch
Ascendency. ce
Auburn
Axe.
Bailiff - See Note 3
Bandrol, or Banerol.
Bass Viol, or Base Viol
See Note 4.

Detail from Chauncey Goodrich's list of spellings that he and William G. Webster, Noah's son, had agreed on. They submitted these to William C. Fowler in hopes of consensus.

I had contracted with the Merriams." In a compromise of February 1845, brokered by Governor Ellsworth (their fellow brother-in-law), Goodrich agreed to an extraordinary compromise: when Goodrich was ready to print, he would submit all his alterations to the inspection of the entire Webster family, "so that any of them might have an opportunity to object." Then, "if objections were brought forward," Governor Ellsworth and Henry White—the two executors of Noah Webster's will—"were to examine and decide whether the alterations should nor should not be made." But the executors essentially allowed Goodrich to have full discretion in these matters.

According to Goodrich's 1853 letter, the cause of all this mid-1840s friction was Lyman Cobb (no. 64), whose "violent attacks" on Webster's orthography were so successful that Webster dictionaries had been "voted out of all the public schools in Boston." In the *New York Observer*, Webster's spellings had been treated "with the utmost contempt." There was a concerted effort, Goodrich explained, "to forestall public opinion as to the forthcoming editions of Webster's Dictionaries." The Merriam brothers were bombarding Goodrich with "papers containing such attacks, & insisted that further alterations of the Orthography *must be made.*" When the Merriams put the question to Governor Ellsworth, he declared that Cobb had been so successful in his onslaught against "Dr. Webster's vulnerable points" that Goodrich should have full sanction to make any modifications he wanted, "untrammeled and uncontrolled by anyone."

It was an emergency.

But Fowler demanded an early look at all proof sheets as they came from the printer, to be sent to him at Amherst, even though the compromise had provided that the proof sheets would be available in Governor Ellsworth's office in Hartford—with ten days' notice of an examination period for all family members before a family meeting might be held to lodge objections. When Fowler's demand was refused, he wrote to Goodrich, on 16 February 1846: "Earnestly and formally do I hereby enter my protest against your course in this affair, as a *violation* of my rights and a *breach of faith.*" Yet Goodrich assured Fowler that he had not expected "to print without consulting you and the rest of the family as to the proposed alterations."

The whole brouhaha may well be the only time in history that questions of spelling have resulted in a long-term familial meltdown. Goodrich accused Fowler of using "language which one gentleman

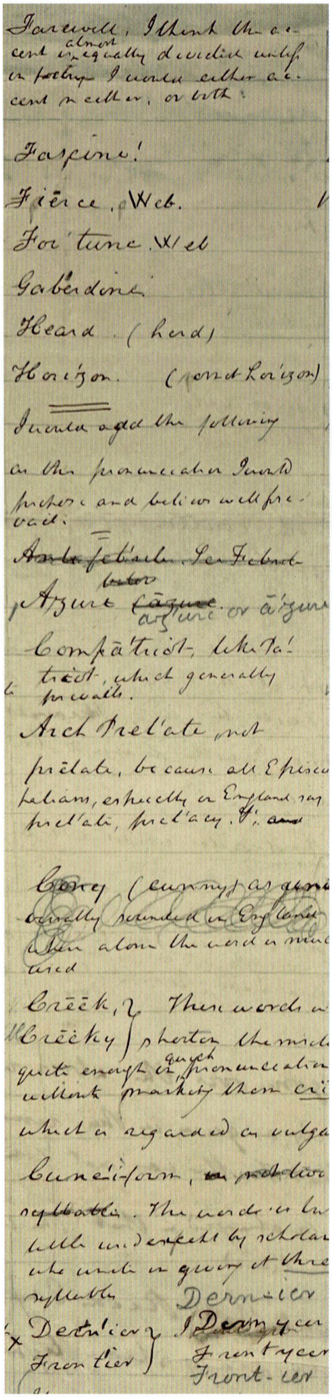

Detail from a list of pronunciations that Goodrich submitted to Fowler.

never applies to another, except with the deliberate intention to render all further intercourse *impossible*." Goodrich therefore sought the advice of a respected judge and the sitting Connecticut governor (Roger Sherman Baldwin) about how to proceed with Fowler. In their view, the executors (led by Governor Ellsworth) "had the right to improve [the literary property] to the best advantage, under the sanction of a majority of the legatees; and that this was especially true of a Dictionary, which *must* be revised from time to time, to keep pace with the progress of the language, if it is to be a permanent advantage either to the family or the public."

Goodrich, meanwhile, sought absolution: "After the Revision was concluded, Mr. Ellsworth and the other members of the family gave me written statements, exonerating me from all blame, in respect to all transactions between you and me, in which they were concerned or of which they had any knowledge."

Both men—Goodrich and Fowler—were theologians. They were also concerned with having the upper hand spiritually. Goodrich wrote: "If I know my own heart (and I wish, at this serious moment, to speak as under the eye of Him who searches the hearts of all) I never cherished unkind or resentful feelings toward you; and I have never ceased, as in earlier days, to wish and to pray for the happiness and prosperity of yourself and children. . . . For some years past, I have thought but rarely upon what once gave me so much pain, and I am ready to have it pass from this time into final oblivion." And then his Parthian shot: "Such are the facts touching 'the relations between us in respect to Webster's Dictionaries,' as I believe they will appear in that day when we shall both of us render an account of all the deeds done in the body."

It appears that Goodrich and Fowler reached some sort of arbitrated settlement of their disputes. An 1855 contract appended to U.S. Supreme Court briefs in 1912 recited that the Goodriches, the Ellsworths, Henry and Eliza Jones, and William G. Webster, together with Louisa Webster, had "endeavored to obtain, and suppose[d] they ha[d] obtained all the rights and interests of William C. Fowler and Henry Trowbridge and his wife, from and after the aforesaid 14th day of April 1856 in the matter added by Dr. Webster to said American Dictionary in the year 1840, and also in the Abridgements of said Dictionary formerly published by Francis J. Huntington," etc. In other words, it appears that in 1855, consideration was paid to Fowler

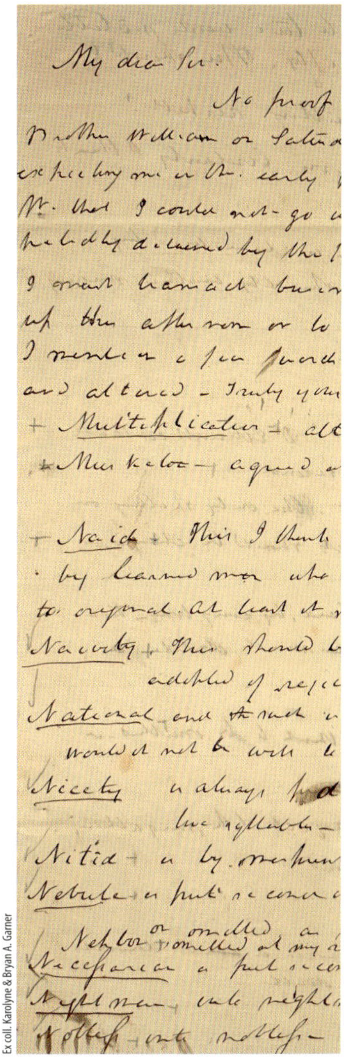

Ex coll. Karolyne & Bryan A. Garner

In late 1845, attempts at consensus were nearing an end. (Detail from letter by Goodrich to Fowler.)

to be effective beginning 14 April 1856 for the assignment of all rights in these lexicographic materials.

But even this 1855 settlement was a year in the making. The skittish Fowler had been expected to sign a year earlier. How do we know? In the final known letter from Goodrich to Fowler, dated 15 August 1854, Goodrich asked Fowler to call at Mr. [Henry] White's house to sign "the contract . . . with the Power of Attorney. . . . The contract will be in his hands very soon after nine o'clock, and it would be a convenience to him if you would call early at his *house*." Henry White, remember, was coexecutor of Noah Webster's estate. The contract referred to seems to be a settlement of the dispute between Goodrich and Fowler. After this communication, no further letters are known to have passed between the men.

"Fowler continued to live in a fool's paradise regarding his influence on the Merriam edition. . . . He had been banished from editorial roles, and with the death of his wife, Harriet, in 1844 he was no longer even an heir and therefore no longer legally eligible to receive income from Webster's books—although the family relented, including him anyway following a good deal of soul-searching on their part." (Martin 2019:177.)

All in all, the letters show that Fowler "stood ready to fight back at every turn against Goodrich's anticipated corrections, deletions, and additions." (Martin 2019:273.) He was meddlesome, impertinent, and feckless. If he had succeeded in blocking Goodrich's changes in spelling, Webster dictionaries might not have succeeded as they did in the marketplace. In this alternative reality, it's possible that we would now associate the name Worcester or even Cobb, not Webster, with American dictionaries. Imagine that.

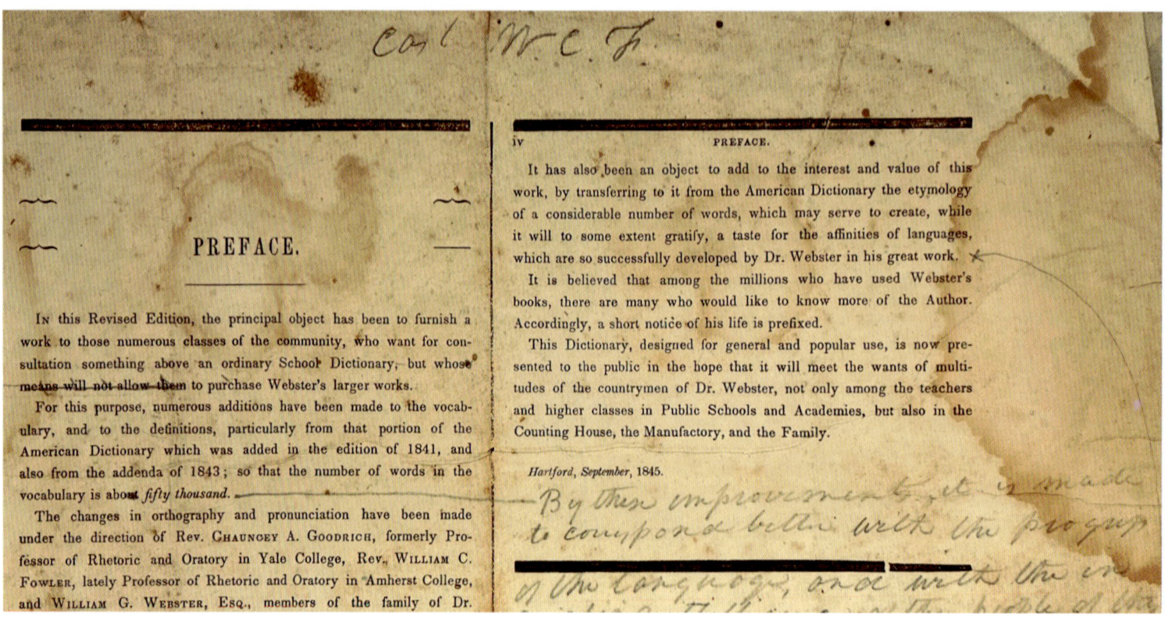

PREFACE.

In this Revised Edition, the principal object has been to furnish a work to those numerous classes of the community, who want for consultation something above an ordinary School Dictionary, but whose means will not allow them to purchase Webster's larger works.

For this purpose, numerous additions have been made to the vocabulary, and to the definitions, particularly from that portion of the American Dictionary which was added in the edition of 1841, and also from the addenda of 1843; so that the number of words in the vocabulary is about *fifty thousand*.

The changes in orthography and pronunciation have been made under the direction of Rev. Chauncey A. Goodrich, formerly Professor of Rhetoric and Oratory in Yale College, Rev. William C. Fowler, lately Professor of Rhetoric and Oratory in Amherst College, and William G. Webster, Esq., members of the family of Dr.

iv PREFACE.

It has also been an object to add to the interest and value of this work, by transferring to it from the American Dictionary the etymology of a considerable number of words, which may serve to create, while it will to some extent gratify, a taste for the affinities of languages, which are so successfully developed by Dr. Webster in his great work.

It is believed that among the millions who have used Webster's books, there are many who would like to know more of the Author. Accordingly, a short notice of his life is prefixed.

This Dictionary, designed for general and popular use, is now presented to the public in the hope that it will meet the wants of multitudes of the countrymen of Dr. Webster, not only among the teachers and higher classes in Public Schools and Academies, but also in the Counting House, the Manufactory, and the Family.

Hartford, September, 1845.

Ex coll. Karolyne & Bryan A. Garner

William C. Fowler's penciled corrections to the preface of his 1845 "University Edition" of *Webster's Dictionary of the English Language*, published by Huntington & Savage. Fowler mistakenly believed that his edition would settle Webster spellings once and for all. Note his initials at the top.

74

Enter the Merriams

Webster, Noah. *An American Dictionary of the English Language*. Springfield: George & Charles Merriam, 1847 (copyright date) or 1848 (title page).

Noah Webster worked almost entirely alone; his was the sole intelligence behind the *American Dictionary* of 1828, and the dictionary was *his* in the way that almost no modern dictionary is the work of one person. But while Webster had seemingly boundless energy for writing and promoting his books, he never had a mind for business. His story could easily have been similar to that of the dozens of others in this book who created a major dictionary, saw it through a few editions, and then faded from the scene. Webster, however, has been the name most associated with "dictionary" for almost two centuries. And that's owing to the efforts of two brothers, George and Charles Merriam, who enter the story of dictionaries in the 1840s.

Ex coll. Karolyne & Bryan A. Garner

After Noah Webster's death in 1843, the booksellers J.S. & C. Adams of Amherst bought the unsold copies of the 1841 edition of Webster's *American Dictionary* (no. 70). More than 1,400 of the print run of 3,000 remained unsold. But the Adamses had no more luck in selling it than Webster did. The problem, familiar to so many dictionary publishers before and since, was that projects on this scale were prohibitively expensive. Webster had asked $20 for his dictionary in the 1820s, worth around $800 in today's money, so it's unsurprising that he didn't sell many. The Adamses dropped the price to $15—still around $600 in modern currency—but sales, all too predictably, remained minimal. The Adamses prudently decided to withdraw.

That's when the Merriam brothers came on the scene. Even as the quarrel between the Webster clan and Worcester raged, the G. &. C. Merriam Company bought the copyright to Webster's *American Dictionary*, and hired Webster's son-in-law Chauncey A. Goodrich of Yale College to revise it for future editions. They recognized that, despite the financial failures, Webster's name had cachet, especially if they combined it with that of a Yale professor, and they believed that a series of big and small "Webster's" dictionaries could be profitable.

Charles Merriam.

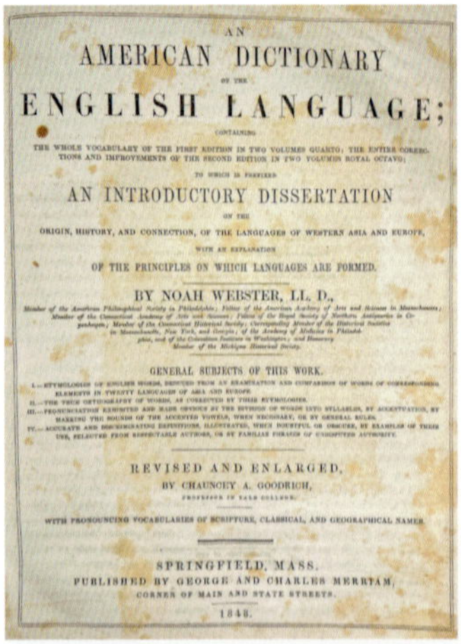

AN
AMERICAN DICTIONARY
OF THE
ENGLISH LANGUAGE;
CONTAINING
THE WHOLE VOCABULARY OF THE FIRST EDITION IN TWO VOLUMES QUARTO; THE ENTIRE CORRECTIONS AND IMPROVEMENTS OF THE SECOND EDITION IN TWO VOLUMES ROYAL OCTAVO;
TO WHICH IS PREFIXED
AN INTRODUCTORY DISSERTATION
ON THE
ORIGIN, HISTORY, AND CONNECTION, OF THE LANGUAGES OF WESTERN ASIA AND EUROPE,
WITH AN EXPLANATION
OF THE PRINCIPLES ON WHICH LANGUAGES ARE FORMED.
BY NOAH WEBSTER, LL. D.,
GENERAL SUBJECTS OF THIS WORK.
REVISED AND ENLARGED,
BY CHAUNCEY A. GOODRICH,
PROFESSOR IN YALE COLLEGE.
WITH PRONOUNCING VOCABULARIES OF SCRIPTURE, CLASSICAL, AND GEOGRAPHICAL NAMES.
SPRINGFIELD, MASS.
PUBLISHED BY GEORGE AND CHARLES MERRIAM,
CORNER OF MAIN AND STATE STREETS.
1848.

Ex coll. Karolyne & Bryan A. Garner

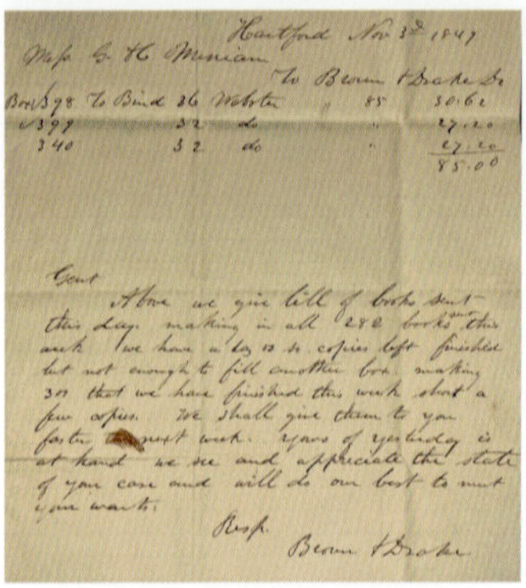

Ex coll. Karolyne & Bryan A. Garner

This 1849 invoice sent to G. & C. Merriam shows that Brown & Drake bindery was binding nearly 300 dictionaries a week at a cost of 85 cents per book.

The first dictionary with both "Merriam" and "Webster" on the title page appeared in 1845, though it's not, strictly speaking, a Merriam-Webster production: the Merriams had bought the unsold sheets of an earlier edition and simply reissued them with a new title page. But a genuinely new edition of the *American Dictionary*, overseen by Goodrich, was copyrighted in 1847 (with 1848 on the title page). It was hardly an extensive revision; there was no wholesale rewriting of definitions or etymologies. Goodrich's main project was taking the material that Webster had included as an appendix in 1840 and incorporating it into the main *A–Z* sequence, and he altered some of Webster's quirkier spellings to reflect widespread American practice. In the new edition, two volumes became one, and 2,000 pages became 1,367. But they managed to lose none of the content by printing a quarto rather than an octavo and using more compact typography. And remarkably, they managed to sell it for just $6.

The spine of the standard binding introduced a new word into discussions of dictionaries: *unabridged.* The term *unabridged dictionary* is now so familiar that it's easy to miss how odd it is. It advertises the dictionary not in positive terms, focusing on what's in it, but on the fact that it has *not* been cut. It's as if to say, "Don't worry, we haven't removed anything." The Merriams wanted to reassure potential customers that they were getting the full dictionary—and, just as important, that it was more than they'd get from Worcester.

It worked. For the first time, thanks to the low price and the Merriams' energetic promotion, a Webster's dictionary managed to turn a profit. (Sokolowski 2020:172–73.) The Webster family even earned some royalties. The war with Worcester wasn't over, and there were crises to come. But the G. & C. Merriam Co. ensured that Webster's name would remain famous generations after his death.

The offices of G. & C. Merriam in Springfield in 1847.

The Merriam family had a history of dictionary publishing. George and Charles's uncle, Ebenezer Merriam, published editions of Perry's dictionary (no. 46) during the first decade of the 19th century. The nephews learned their trade as apprentices to their uncle.

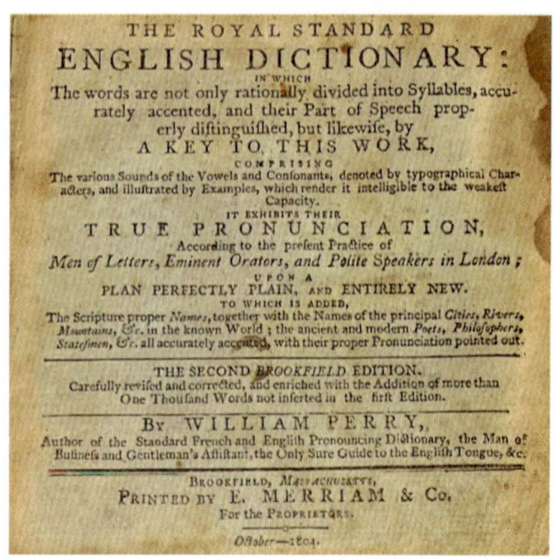

THE ROYAL STANDARD
ENGLISH DICTIONARY:
IN WHICH
The words are not only rationally divided into Syllables, accurately accented, and their Part of Speech properly diſtinguiſhed, but likewiſe, by
A KEY TO THIS WORK,
COMPRISING
The various Sounds of the Vowels and Conſonants, denoted by typographical Characters, and illuſtrated by Examples, which render it intelligible to the weakeſt Capacity.
IT EXHIBITS THEIR
TRUE PRONUNCIATION,
According to the preſent Practice of
Men of Letters, Eminent Orators, and Polite Speakers in London;
UPON A
PLAN PERFECTLY PLAIN, AND ENTIRELY NEW.
TO WHICH IS ADDED,
The Scripture proper *Names*, together with the Names of the principal *Cities, Rivers, Mountains, &c.* in the known World; the ancient and modern *Poets, Philoſophers, Stateſmen, &c.* all accurately accented, with their proper Pronunciation pointed out.
THE SECOND *BROOKFIELD* EDITION.
Carefully reviſed and corrected, and enriched with the Addition of more than One Thouſand Words not inſerted in the firſt Edition.
BY WILLIAM PERRY,
Author of the Standard French and Engliſh Pronouncing Dictionary, the Man of Buſineſs and Gentleman's Aſſiſtant, the Only Sure Guide to the Engliſh Tongue, &c.
BROOKFIELD, *MASSACHUSETTS*,
PRINTED BY E. MERRIAM & Co.
For the PROPRIETORS.
October—1804.

Ex coll. Karolyne & Bryan A. Garner

75

John Russell Bartlett
The Man Who Preserved but Didn't Perpetuate Slang

Bartlett, John Russell. *Dictionary of Americanisms: A Glossary of Words and Phrases, Usually Regarded as Peculiar to the United States.* New York: Bartlett & Welford, 1848.

Ex coll. Karolyne & Bryan A. Garner

Ex coll. Karolyne & Bryan A. Garner

WE'VE ALREADY HAD TO DEAL with two 18th-century lexicographers named Samuel Johnson, and we've had to keep one early-19th-century George Crabb distinct from another early-19th-century George Crabbe. It seems that we also have to worry about two contemporaneous American lexicographers named John Bartlett, both of whom worked in bookshops. John Russell Bartlett (1805–1886) of Providence, Rhode Island, was principally an ethnologist and topographer; John Bartlett (1820–1905) of Cambridge, Massachusetts, was principally a compiler of Shakespeare concordances and of his famous quotation book (*Familiar Quotations*). The former wrote *Dictionary of Americanisms* (1848), and the latter wrote *A Collection of College Words and Customs* (1851).

Here we're concerned with the *Dictionary of Americanisms*, which went into four editions by 1877—each later one significantly expanded over its predecessor. In a way, the book is an exercise in ethnology and a study in frozen culture, since Bartlett was fascinated by what he recognized as New England terminology that reflected earlier English usage: "It may be said, without exaggeration, that nine-tenths of the colloquial peculiarities of New England are derived directly from Great Britain; and that they are now provincial in those parts from which the early colonists emigrated, or are to be found in the writings of well-accredited authors of the period when that emigration took place." (P. iv.) A bit of American insecurity and defensiveness creeps in: "It is obvious that we have the best authority for the use of the words referred to. . . . The idiom of New England is as pure English, taken as a whole, as was spoken in England at the period when these colonies were settled." (*Id.*)

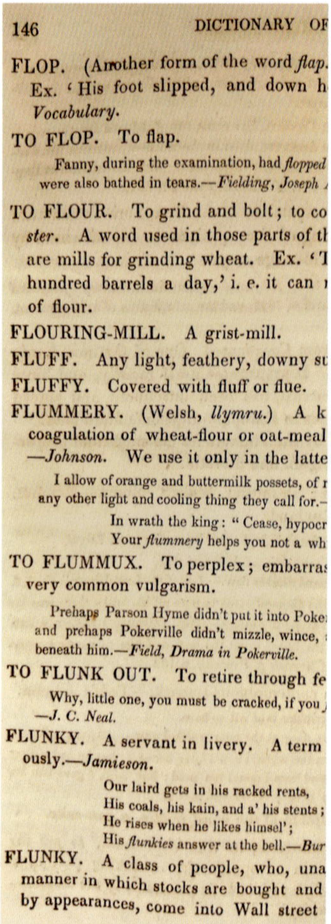
146 DICTIONARY OF

FLOP. (Another form of the word *flap*. Ex. 'His foot slipped, and down h *Vocabulary*.

TO FLOP. To flap.

Fanny, during the examination, had *flopped* were also bathed in tears.—*Fielding*, *Joseph*

TO FLOUR. To grind and bolt; to co *ster*. A word used in those parts of tl are mills for grinding wheat. Ex. 'T hundred barrels a day,' i. e. it can of flour.

FLOURING-MILL. A grist-mill.

FLUFF. Any light, feathery, downy su

FLUFFY. Covered with fluff or flue.

FLUMMERY. (Welsh, *llymru*.) A k coagulation of wheat-flour or oat-meal —*Johnson*. We use it only in the latte

I allow of orange and buttermilk possets, of r any other light and cooling thing they call for.—

In wrath the king: "Cease, hypocr
Your *flummery* helps you not a wh

TO FLUMMUX. To perplex; embarras very common vulgarism.

Prehaps Parson Hyme didn't put it into Poke and prehaps Pokerville didn't mizzle, wince, beneath him.—*Field*, *Drama in Pokerville*.

TO FLUNK OUT. To retire through fe

Why, little one, you must be cracked, if you —*J. C. Neal*.

FLUNKY. A servant in livery. A term ously.—*Jamieson*.

Our laird gets in his racked rents,
His coals, his kain, and a' his stents;
He rises when he likes himsel';
His *flunkies* answer at the bell.—*Bur*

FLUNKY. A class of people, who, una manner in which stocks are bought and by appearances, come into Wall street

Detail from p. 146.

Bartlett's method was to list all the words that seemed to him to be Americanisms, without necessarily knowing whether they had a British precedent. Then he consulted British dialect dictionaries, which were beginning to abound. (See no. 112.) He erred on the side of inclusiveness: "It is very difficult to draw the line between what should be admitted and what excluded; and I have thought it better to err on the side of copiousness, than by too rigid a system of selection to run into the opposite extreme." (*Id.* at vii.) He had three broad categories: (1) words recorded by Johnson and Webster but noted as being "low or vulgar, or only to be heard in familiar conversation"; (2) words found only in provincial British glossaries but noticed by Bartlett in American speech; and (3) slang terms never yet recorded in any known dictionary.

Although his methods were more sophisticated than those of Pickering (no. 61), he very much reflected the linguistic views of the time: "I do not take as a standard the nasal twang, the drawing enunciation, or those perversions of language which the ignorant and uneducated adopt. Nor would I acknowledge the abuse of many of our most useful words." (P. iv.) And he insisted that the United States was not unique in having these qualities: "For these perversions I make no other defence or apology but that they occur in all countries and in every language." (*Id.*)

By the time of his fourth edition (1877), Bartlett found it necessary to defend himself against the charge that he shouldn't have included slang: "Objections have been made to the incorporation of slang terms . . . on the ground that it tends to preserve them and perpetuate their use." (P. iv.) If only dictionary users consulted reference books so compulsively and faithfully! "It is true that it does preserve them, but it does not perpetuate their use; for they often disappear as suddenly as they come into existence." (*Id.*) Bartlett understood linguistic utilitarianism: "Slang terms will remain in use only so long as they may be useful in colloquial language." (*Id.*)

76

Roget's Thesaurus
An Astonishingly Creative Treasury

Roget, Peter Mark. *Thesaurus of English Words and Phrases, classified and arranged so as to facilitate the expression of ideas and assist in literary composition*. London: Longman, Brown et al., 1852. 2d ed. 1853.

Roget ca. 1815.

"It is now nearly fifty years since I first projected a system of verbal classification similar to that on which the present Work is founded. Conceiving that such a compilation might help to supply my own deficiencies, I had, in the year 1805, completed a classed catalogue of words on a small scale, but on the same principle, and nearly in the same form, as the Thesaurus now published." (1852 Preface.)

ROGET (1779–1869), a physician and philologist, was born in London, but his family moved to Edinburgh when he was 14, six years after it was noticed that the boy was compulsively making lists of various kinds. He would never abandon the habit. At 14, he entered the University of Edinburgh to study medicine. Before long, the polymath qualified for the practice of medicine, and began publishing dozens of papers on medical as well as nonmedical subjects. He even tried to invent a calculating machine.

Early in his career, long before he became the Fuller Professor of Physiology at the Royal Institution in London, he dreamed of creating a thesaurus. The word comes from Greek and means "storehouse" or "treasury." Thanks to its suggestions of limitless riches, it had long been used as the title of wordbooks, including the hugely influential Latin dictionary the *Thesaurus linguae latinae* (1531) of Robert Estienne (also known as Robertus Stephanus) and Thomas Cooper's Latin–English *Thesaurus linguae Romanæ & Britannicæ* (1565). It was Roget's innovation to apply the term *thesaurus* to what had earlier been known as a *synonymy*. After retiring from his medical practice in 1840, he devoted himself to this task, which was nearly half a century in the making. At the age of 70, he began working full time on the project, and he completed it at age 73.

Roget ca. 1865.

The book was an immediate success. The first printing of 1,000 copies, on 17 January 1852, sold quickly, and the book went through more than 25 printings by the time of Roget's death in 1869. Roget had been working on an enlarged edition, and his lawyer son, John Lewis Roget, brought out that edition ten years later and continued work on the book until his death in 1908. Roget's engineer grandson, Samuel Romilly Roget, edited new editions until his death

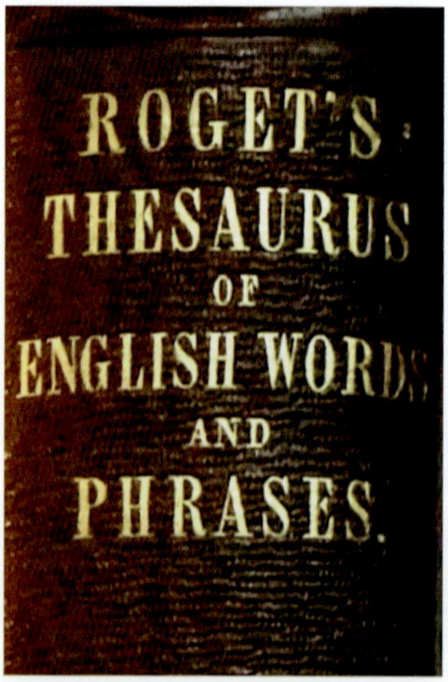

Ex coll. Karolyne & Bryan A. Garner

The first edition spine label (1852).

"Roget's Thesaurus is probably, at the present time, more extensively used than any similar book, and deservedly so, on account of its completeness. But, to our thinking, the arrangement of Roget's work is too complex for speedy reference." (*American Literary Gazette* 42 [15 May 1871].)

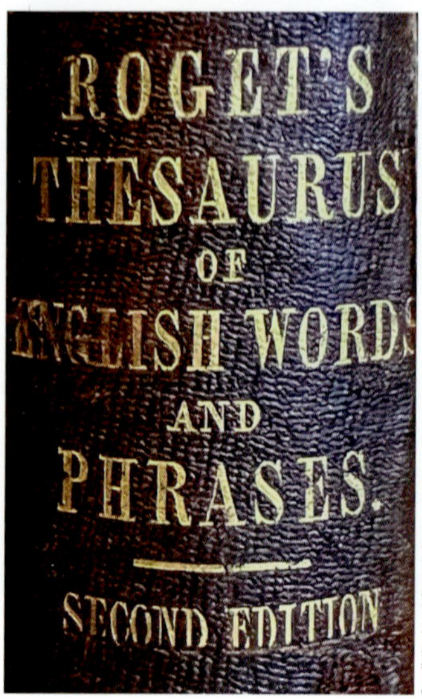

Ex coll. Karolyne & Bryan A. Garner

Second edition spine label (1853).

in 1952. *Roget's Thesaurus* has been continuously in print since its first appearance. The mid-20th-century craze for crossword puzzles fueled ever-greater sales of the book.

What makes this particular synonym book so appealing? It's Roget's extraordinarily thorough classification of almost every conceivable thought, as arranged through English vocables. The 1000 sections of the book are distributed among six major divisions: Abstract Relations, Space, Matter, Intellect, Volition, and Affections. The division for Abstract Relations consists of terms relating to (1) existence, (2) relation, (3) quantity, (4) order, (5) number, (6) time, (7) change, and (8) causation. The first degree of no. 7 (change) is "simple change," in these sections (nos. 140–48): (140) difference at different times, (141) absence of change, (142) change from absence to rest, (143) continuance in action, (144) gradual change to something different, (145) reversion, (146) sudden or violent change, (147) change of one thing for another, and (148) double or mutual change. Here, for example, is an early version of section 144:

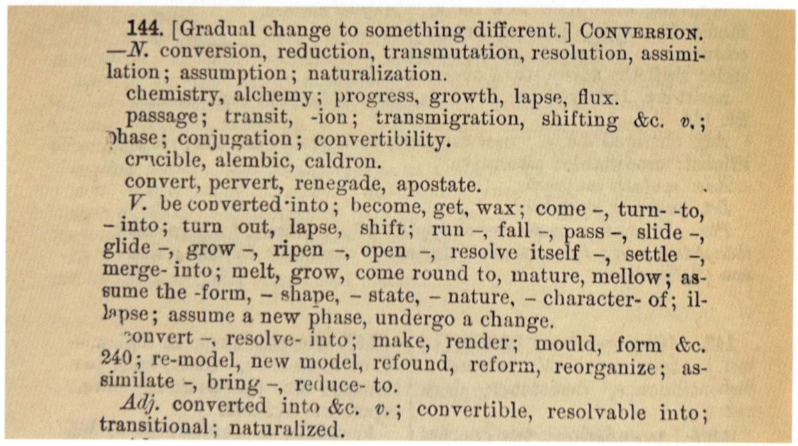

144. [Gradual change to something different.] CONVERSION. —*N.* conversion, reduction, transmutation, resolution, assimilation; assumption; naturalization.

chemistry, alchemy; progress, growth, lapse, flux.

passage; transit, -ion; transmigration, shifting &c. *v.*; phase; conjugation; convertibility.

crucible, alembic, caldron.

convert, pervert, renegade, apostate.

V. be converted into; become, get, wax; come –, turn- -to, - into; turn out, lapse, shift; run –, fall –, pass –, slide –, glide –, grow –, ripen –, open –, resolve itself –, settle –, merge- into; melt, grow, come round to, mature, mellow; assume the -form, - shape, - state, - nature, - character- of; illapse; assume a new phase, undergo a change.

convert –, resolve- into; make, render; mould, form &c. 240; re-model, new model, refound, reform, reorganize; assimilate –, bring –, reduce- to.

Adj. converted into &c. *v.*; convertible, resolvable into; transitional; naturalized.

Ex coll. Karolyne & Bryan A. Garner

That's a microcosm of the whole, which is highly structured and intricate.

Unlike the synonym books of Piozzi (no. 51), Taylor (no. 59), and Crabb (no. 60), Roget's doesn't explain the words in any way. There are no distinctions, no definitions. The words are simply listed, one after the other. It's for the user to figure out what word might best fit into a given context, either by drawing on personal knowledge or by further consulting a dictionary. The book is a vocabulary "prompter" for those who question whether they're calling up just the right word.

In his 1852 preface, Roget modestly professed knowledge of "its numerous deficiencies and imperfections, and of its falling far short of the degree of excellence that might be attained." (P. v.) He moderated his ambitions, he tells his readers, and "trust[ed] to the indulgence of those for whose benefit it is intended, and to the candor of critics, who, while they find it easy to detect faults, can at the same time duly appreciate difficulties." (*Id.*) In fact, though, there were few critics—just an appreciative book-buying public.

Ex coll. Karolyne & Bryan A. Garner

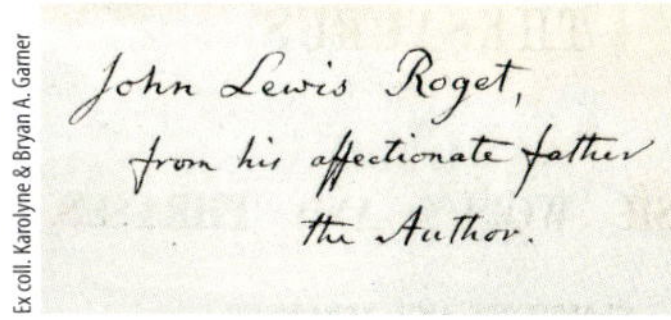

Roget's inscription of the copy given to his son and ultimately passed to his grandson.

In 1879, his son John wrote a much more extensive preface that showed him to be fully up to the task of revising the work and understanding the nuances and intricacies of his father's invention. He wrote: "Any attempt at a philosophical arrangement, under categories, of the words of our language, must reveal the fact that it is impossible to separate and circumscribe the several groups by absolutely distinct boundary lines." (P. vii.) Inevitably, he asserted, there will be "found to exist, between the words in one group and those in another, a variety of mutual affinities, corresponding with similar relations among the ideas expressed." (*Id.*) Of course, he was writing with the benefit of his late father's notes.

"I should be ungrateful were I not to acknowledge the assistance derived, both by my father and myself, from various suggestions made by well-wishers to the work, some of whom have been personally unknown to either of us." (John L. Roget's 1879 Preface.)

When the grandson, Samuel Romilly Roget, took over in 1908, he carried on in the same spirit, "making such additions that have seemed suitable from time to time." (1925 ed., p. viii.) He corrected "a few hitherto unnoticed errors" and added "some hundreds of new words and phrases . . . throughout the book, some of which have only recently become a part of the language as the result of progress in the various arts of peace and the unfortunate necessities of war." (*Id.*) But he didn't vary from the original 1,000 sections.

In the Garner Collection is an 1853 second edition inscribed by Roget to his son, John L. Roget, and bearing the bookplate of the grandson Samuel Romilly Roget. In short, this copy once belonged to the author of the book and then to each of the subsequent two editors. It contains annotations in a minuscule hand, probably that of Roget himself but possibly of the son who inherited his mantle. Under *wealth*, for example, a note says: "'Almighty Dollar' term 1st used in W. Irving's 'Creole Village' [1837]. See 'Wolfert's Roost & Tales'." The latter collection was first published in 1855. Given that Peter Mark Roget didn't die until 1869, the note might well be his. And given that the *Oxford English Dictionary* didn't yet exist, it's extraordinary that Roget accurately traced the earliest use of *almighty dollar* to Irving: the *OED* today cites uses from Irving in 1836 (*New-York Mirror*) and

Ex coll. Karolyne & Bryan A. Garner

A 1909 edition.

Charles Dickens in 1842. The annotations are therefore remarkable. In any event, the inscribed copy uniquely joins a familial with an editorial provenance.

Roget's Thesaurus and its originator have spawned a series of biographies, the primary ones being these:

- Joshua Kendall, *The Man Who Made Lists: Love, Death, Madness, and the Creation of Roget's Thesaurus* (2008).
- Nick Rennison, *Peter Mark Roget: The Man Who Became a Book* (2007).
- D.L. Emblen, *Peter Mark Roget: The Word and the Man* (1970).

There is even a children's book: Jen Bryant & Melissa Sweet, *The Right Word: Roget and His Thesaurus* (2014). And there is a scholarly biography of the book itself: Werner Hüllen, *A History of Roget's Thesaurus: Origins, Development, and Design* (2004).

Meanwhile, the name *Roget* became so synonymous with "synonym-book" that all manner of publishers have taken to using it, including many that have nothing to do with the original. That is, they don't use Roget's 1,000 categories and his typology of ideas. Instead, they simply use alphabetical ordering of words and typically announce that they're in "dictionary format." An example is *Roget's II: The New Thesaurus—Expanded Edition* (1988), by the editors of the *American Heritage Dictionary* (no. 104). Nowhere is the name Peter Mark Roget mentioned in the front matter; it's nowhere but in the title of the book. Another example is the highly improbable *Bartlett's Roget's Thesaurus*, published in 1996 by Little, Brown. Originally a British project developed by Bloomsbury Publishing, it attempted to unite the legacy of Roget with that of John Bartlett's *Familiar Quotations*: "two reference giants are joined at last in another landmark work." But apart from the name, it had no relation to either man.

Ex coll. Karolyne & Bryan A. Garner

Assorted 20th-century editions of books called "Roget"—even if many had little to do with Roget's original book.

Today there are more than a dozen publishers—many of them major houses—that issue a so-called *Roget's Thesaurus*. But on the whole, the future of the genre doesn't look bright: lists of synonyms are freely available online. A click of the computer mouse will prompt you to dozens of synonyms and near-synonyms. And so this publishing category, in dictionary format, seems moribund, defunct, in decline, on the wane, in extremis, and not long for this world.

And yet writers of all sorts continue to marvel at Peter Mark Roget's analytical method of divvying up everything under the sun into 1,000 categories.

77

Dictionary-War Munitions

Worcester, Joseph E. *A Gross Literary Fraud Exposed: Relating to the Publication of Worcester's Dictionary in London*. Boston: Jenks, Hickling, and Swan, 1853.

A Summary Summing of the Charges, with Their Refutations, in Attacks upon Noah Webster, LL.D., His Dictionaries, or His Publishers, Made by Mr. Joseph Worcester, Mr. Sherman Converse, Messrs. Jenks, Hickling, and Swan. Springfield: G. & C. Merriam Co., 1854.

"A Gross Literary Fraud Exposed; Relating to the Publication of Worcester's Dictionary in London," as Webster's Dictionary. Springfield: G. & C. Merriam Co., 1854.

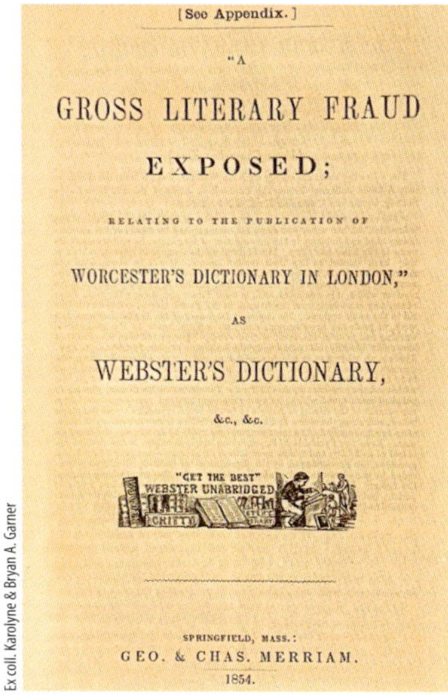
[See Appendix.]

"A

GROSS LITERARY FRAUD

EXPOSED;

RELATING TO THE PUBLICATION OF

WORCESTER'S DICTIONARY IN LONDON,"

AS

WEBSTER'S DICTIONARY,

&c., &c.

"GET THE BEST" WEBSTER UNABRIDGED

SPRINGFIELD, MASS.:

GEO. & CHAS. MERRIAM.

1854.

Ex coll. Karolyne & Bryan A. Garner

[Gould, Edward]. *A Reply to Messrs. G. and C. Merriam's Attack upon the Character of Dr. Worcester and His Dictionaries*. Boston: Jenks, Hickling & Swan, 1854.

Have We a National Standard of English Lexicography? Or Some Comparisons of the Claims of Webster's Dictionaries and Worcester's Dictionaries. Springfield: G. & C. Merriam Co., 1855.

Sargent, Epes. *The Critic Criticised: A Reply to a Review of Webster's System in the Democratic Review for March, 1856. From the Democratic Review for June, 1856*. Springfield: G. & C. Merriam Co., 1856.

Dictionaries in the Boston Mercantile Library and Boston Atheneum. Springfield: G. & C. Merriam Co., 1856.

Andrews, I.W. *Webster's Dictionaries*. Springfield: G. & C. Merriam Co., 1856.

Philorthos. [Poole, William Frederick.] *The Orthographical Hobgoblin*. Springfield: G. & C. Merriam Co., 1859.

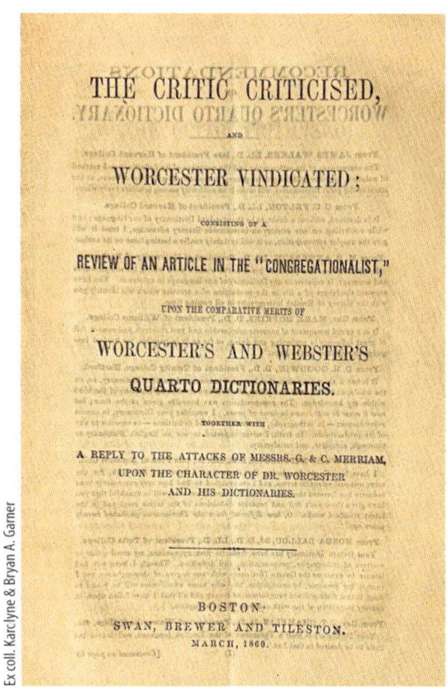
THE CRITIC CRITICISED,

AND

WORCESTER VINDICATED;

CONSISTING OF A

REVIEW OF AN ARTICLE IN THE "CONGREGATIONALIST,"

UPON THE COMPARATIVE MERITS OF

WORCESTER'S AND WEBSTER'S

QUARTO DICTIONARIES.

TOGETHER WITH

A REPLY TO THE ATTACKS OF MESSRS. G. & C. MERRIAM,

UPON THE CHARACTER OF DR. WORCESTER

AND HIS DICTIONARIES.

BOSTON:

SWAN, BREWER AND TILESTON.

MARCH, 1860.

Ex coll. Karclyne & Bryan A. Garner

Swan, William D. ***A Critic Criticized: And Worcester Vindicated. Consisting of a Review of an Article in the "Congregationalist" upon the Comparative Merits of Worcester's and Webster's Quarto Dictionaries.*** **Boston: Swan Brewer, 1860.**

"Equal Justice": The Two Dictionaries or the Reviewer Reviewed. A Reply to a Correspondent of the New York World. **Springfield: G. & C. Merriam Co., 1860.**

"If in what we have felt constrained to say in our own vindication, aught has been uttered which shall have wounded the feelings of Dr. Worcester, that, in itself, is cause to us of sincere regret. Should wrongful assaults be made upon us in the future, we shall repel them as best we may." (George & Charles Merriam, *A Gross Literary Fraud Exposed* [1854], p. 12.)

THE 1850S WERE A CRUCIAL DECADE in the commercial battles between Webster and Worcester dictionaries. Who would prevail in the American dictionary market?

Oddly enough, the opening salvo came from England—by someone not directly involved. In the 1850s, a London publisher of questionable scruples, Henry G. Bohn, acquired the British rights to publish Worcester's 1846 *Universal and Critical Dictionary*, in the preface to which Worcester carefully explained that he had in no way used Webster's work. Without altering that statement, Bohn reworked the title to say that the dictionary had been *Compiled from the Materials of Noah Webster, LL.D. by Joseph E. Worcester*. This calumny infuriated both Worcester and the Merriams, and like the assassination of Archduke Ferdinand in 1914, it sparked a world war.

Worcester attacked Bohn, and the Merriams attacked Worcester—repeatedly. Ten pamphlets were issued between the warring publishers, and the Merriams achieved an advantage by putting out seven, probably in far greater numbers so as to overwhelm the market. The Merriams were clever about this. After Worcester issued his original defense (*A Gross Literary Fraud Exposed*), arguing that he'd been grossly libeled by Bohn, the Merriams quickly published two pamphlets, one with Worcester's own title turned against him. That is, the Merriams also used *A Gross Literary Fraud Exposed* but added three words to the end of Worcester's 14-word title (*as Webster's Dictionary*). "Have you read *A Gross Literary Fraud Exposed*?" someone might ask. "You must get it!" The plentiful copies of the Merriams' propagandizing pamphlet ensured that *their* version of the story, replete with outright charges against Worcester and quasi-defamatory innuendos woven throughout, would be the one more likely encountered.

Ex coll. Karolyne & Bryan A. Garner

The misleading spine of a Bohn publication.

It was a sordid affair. Although the cognoscenti tended to be sympathetic with Worcester, public opinion understandably swayed toward Webster. The best play-by-play account of the brouhaha is found at pp. 197–222 of Peter Martin's book *The Dictionary Wars* (2019).

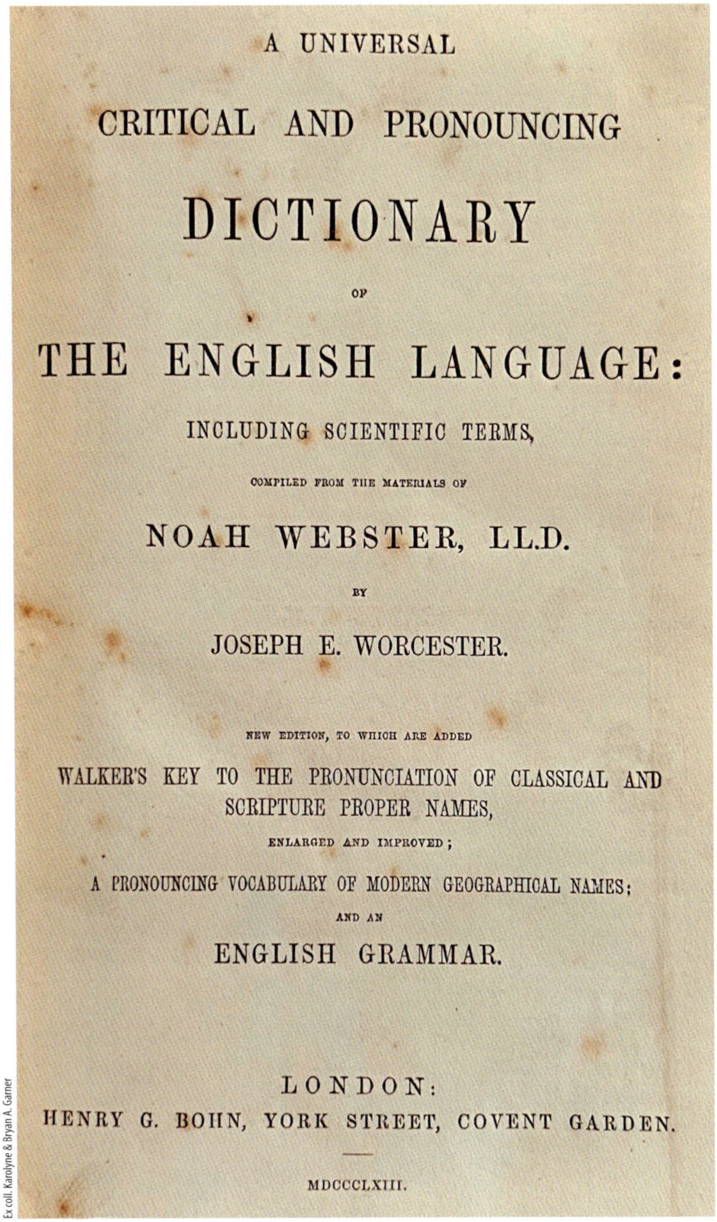

A UNIVERSAL

CRITICAL AND PRONOUNCING

DICTIONARY

OF

THE ENGLISH LANGUAGE:

INCLUDING SCIENTIFIC TERMS,

COMPILED FROM THE MATERIALS OF

NOAH WEBSTER, LL.D.

BY

JOSEPH E. WORCESTER.

NEW EDITION, TO WHICH ARE ADDED

WALKER'S KEY TO THE PRONUNCIATION OF CLASSICAL AND SCRIPTURE PROPER NAMES,

ENLARGED AND IMPROVED;

A PRONOUNCING VOCABULARY OF MODERN GEOGRAPHICAL NAMES;

AND AN

ENGLISH GRAMMAR.

LONDON:

HENRY G. BOHN, YORK STREET, COVENT GARDEN.

MDCCCLXIII.

Ex coll. Karolyne & Bryan A. Garner

Bohn's offending title page.

"If Webster is not the standard of orthography in America, there is no standard. Worcester's orthography is neither American nor English, but is a mongrel, vacillating compilation, without purpose or system other than assumed *usage*." (*Orthographical Hobgoblin* [1859], p. 5.)

"The truth is, that Noah Webster possessed no extraordinary natural ability, and not sufficiently profound philological learning to qualify him for preeminence as an accurate and natural etymologist. . . . His labors, though long and patiently protracted, were to a great extent barren of any satisfactory results. He had not and, with his mind and the state of his learning, could not have had, the right view of the subject. . . . His etymologies are to a great extent merely fanciful or conjectural, and many of those which are really valuable are taken from preceding philologists without the proper credit being given." (*The Critic Criticized* [1860], p. 41.)

"There was serious money to be made, and the dictionary war showed a cutthroat ruthlessness that rarely reflected the products over which it was being fought. It was a verbal war, as was fitting, but it was still remarkably vicious." (Green 1996:331.)

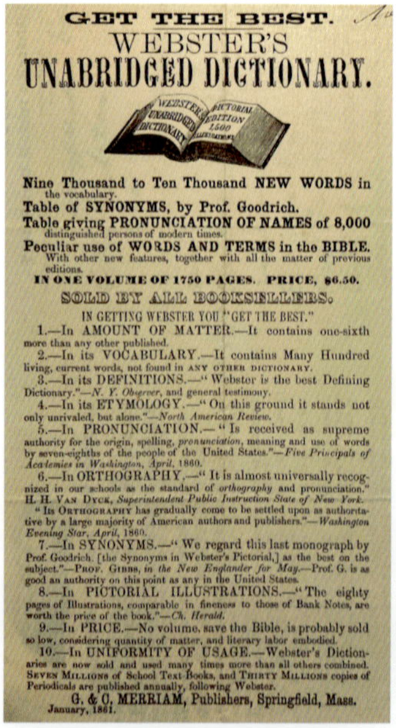

GET THE BEST.

WEBSTER'S

UNABRIDGED DICTIONARY.

Nine Thousand to Ten Thousand NEW WORDS in the vocabulary.

Table of SYNONYMS, by Prof. Goodrich.

Table giving PRONUNCIATION OF NAMES of 8,000 distinguished persons of modern times.

Peculiar use of WORDS AND TERMS in the BIBLE. With other new features, together with all the matter of previous editions.

IN ONE VOLUME OF 1750 PAGES. PRICE, $6.50.

SOLD BY ALL BOOKSELLERS.

IN GETTING WEBSTER YOU "GET THE BEST."

1.—In AMOUNT OF MATTER.—It contains one-sixth more than any other published.

2.—In its VOCABULARY.—It contains Many Hundred living, current words, not found in ANY OTHER DICTIONARY.

3.—In its DEFINITIONS.—"Webster is the best Defining Dictionary."—*N. Y. Observer*, and general testimony.

4.—In its ETYMOLOGY.—"On this ground it stands not only unrivaled, but alone."—*North American Review.*

5.—In PRONUNCIATION.—"Is received as supreme authority for the origin, spelling, *pronunciation*, meaning and use of words by seven-eighths of the people of the United States."—*Five Principals of Academies in Washington, April*, 1860.

6.—In ORTHOGRAPHY.—"It is almost universally recognized in our schools as the standard of *orthography* and pronunciation." H. H. Van Dyck, *Superintendent Public Instruction State of New York.*
"Its Orthography has gradually come to be settled upon as authoritative by a large majority of American authors and publishers."—*Washington Evening Star, April*, 1860.

7.—In SYNONYMS.—"We regard this last monograph by Prof. Goodrich. [the Synonyms in Webster's Pictorial,] as the best on the subject."—Prof. Gibbs, *in the New Englander for May.*—Prof. G. is as good an authority on this point as any in the United States.

8.—In PICTORIAL ILLUSTRATIONS.—"The eighty pages of Illustrations, comparable in fineness to those of Bank Notes, are worth the price of the book."—*Ch. Herald.*

9.—In PRICE.—No volume, save the Bible, is probably sold so low, considering quantity of matter, and literary labor embodied.

10.—In UNIFORMITY OF USAGE.—Webster's Dictionaries are now sold and used many times more than all others combined. Seven Millions of School Text-Books, and Thirty Millions copies of Periodicals are published annually, following Webster.

G. & C. MERRIAM, Publishers, Springfield, Mass.
January, 1861.

Ex coll. Karolyne & Bryan A. Garner

An advertisement for the 1859 edition boasted of illustrations "comparable in fineness to those of Bank Notes."

78

Webster's Unsporting Pictorial Dictionary

Webster, Noah. *An American Dictionary of the English Language*. Chauncey A. Goodrich ed. Springfield: George & Charles Merriam, 1859.

The *American Dictionary* of 1859 constitutes a milestone in English-language lexicography—America's first illustrated dictionary—but only by chance.

The Merriam brothers kept the Webster–Worcester quarrel going long after Webster's death in 1843. Both teams were working on major new editions, and they knew that the results would determine the fortune of both enterprises.

Late in the 1850s the Merriams learned that Worcester was about to beat them to press with his two-volume *Dictionary of the English Language* (no. 79)—a potential disaster. They learned, even worse, that Worcester's dictionary would be the first illustrated dictionary in American history. It would include several hundred woodcuts, each an inch or two high, providing graphic information to supplement the textual definitions.

The Merriams resolved to beat Worcester to the punch—but how? Their revised text would not be ready for a few years, so they'd have to reissue the previous edition with illustrations. But doing it properly would require them to set the type of the entire dictionary anew, the work of many months—months that they didn't have. They therefore took the plates of the 1847 edition and scrambled, "by prodigies of purchase and persuasion," to find 1,500 woodcuts. Instead of placing them next to the relevant entries, they packed them all into an 81-page section at the beginning of the book. The result was advertised as the "Pictorial Edition," and proudly declared itself the first illustrated American dictionary. This was "true enough," as R.K. Leavitt admitted, "if dubious in its sportsmanship." (Leavitt 1947:58; see also Sokolowski 2020:173–74.)

Ex coll. Karolyne & Bryan A. Garner

Worcester's *Dictionary* followed not long after, with a freshly revised text and illustrations in the right places, but it didn't help: the public believed that Webster's was first. As Charles Merriam noted, "Worcester after that fell comparatively harmless to the ground." The Pictorial Edition sold so well that a second printing followed in 1860. When the fully revised and illustrated version appeared in 1864, "upwards of three thousand engravings" were properly placed. Such line drawings have been a standard part of school dictionaries ever since.

Ex coll. Karolyne & Bryan A. Garner

TRE WEBSTER'S UNABRIDGED DICTIONARY. WIT

TREES—Continued.

SAGUERUS.

Gomuti-palm (Saguerus saccharifer).

A genus of plants, nat. order Palmaceæ. *S. saccharifer* the gomuti-palm, inhabits tropical Asia. It yields a saccharine fluid abundantly, and also sago. It is likewise a great source of palm-wine.

SHADDOCK, p. 1016.

Shaddock Tree (Citrus decumana).

It is a native of China and Japan, and was brought to the West Indies by a Captain Shaddock, hence the name. The pulp is white, of a sweet taste mingled with acidity.

SPRUCE, p. 1070.

The name given to several species of trees of the genus Abies. The Norway spruce fir is the *A. excelsa*, or *Pinus abies*, Linn., which yields the valuable timber known under the name of white or Christiana deal.

Norway Spruce (Abies excelsa).

TREES—Continued.

SHITTIM, p. 1023.

Shittim wood (Acacia vera).

It is of the size of a large mulberry tree.

STAR-APPLE, p. 1077.

Chrysophyllum Cainito is the most important species. It is a native of the West Indies. The fruit resembles a large apple, which in the inside is divided into ten cells, each containing a black seed, surrounded by a gelatinous pulp. It is eaten in the warm climates of America by way of dessert.

Star-Apple (Chrysophyllum Cainito).

TEAK, p. 1132.

It grows to an immense size, and is remarkable for its very large leaves, which are from 12 to 24 inches long, and from 8 to 16 broad. Teak timber is found to be excellent for ship-building, and has been called the oak of the East.

Teak (Tectona grandis).

WAX-PALM, p. 1253.

The *C. andicola*, unlike most other palms, avoids the heat of tropical plains, and thrives best where the temperature of the air is lowered by the proximity of perpetual snow. It is called *Palma de cera* by the Spaniards, and grows to the height of 180 ft. The trunk is marked by rings, caused by the falling off of the leaves, which are eighteen to twenty feet long, and is covered with a thick secretion, consisting of two thirds resin and one third wax.

Wax-Palm (Ceroxylon andicola).

TRUNK-HOSE, p. 1180.

A kind of short wide breeches gathered in above the knees, or immediately under them, and distinguished according to their peculiar cut as French, Gallic, or Venetian. This garment prevailed during the reign of Henry VIII., Elizabeth, and James I.

Costume, time of Queen Elizabeth. Doublet and Trunk-hose.

V.

VASE, p. 1227, def. 1.

Grecian Vases.

Ancient vases of metal, stone, and clay, and of all varieties of shape, have come down to our time. The most numerous class are those of painted, dried or baked, clay, which have been discovered by thousands in tombs and catacombs in Etruria, Southern Italy, Sicily, Greece, and some of the Grecian islands.

VELOCIPEDE, p. 1229.

A carriage for one person, having two wheels placed one before the other, in the same line, and connected by a beam, on which the person sits astride, and propels the vehicle, by striking the tips of his toes against the earth.

clxiii

Ex coll. Karolyne & Bryan A. Garner

"Another distinguishing peculiarity (and, it is believed, excellence) here introduced, is that the illustrations in a given department are grouped and presented by themselves. . . . The advantages of this arrangement are obvious, as are those of having the Illustrations together." ("Introduction to the Illustrations.")

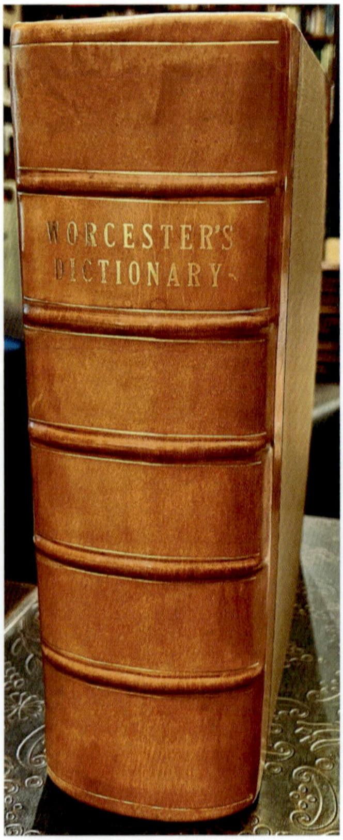

Ex coll. Karolyne & Bryan A. Garner

The first edition (1860).

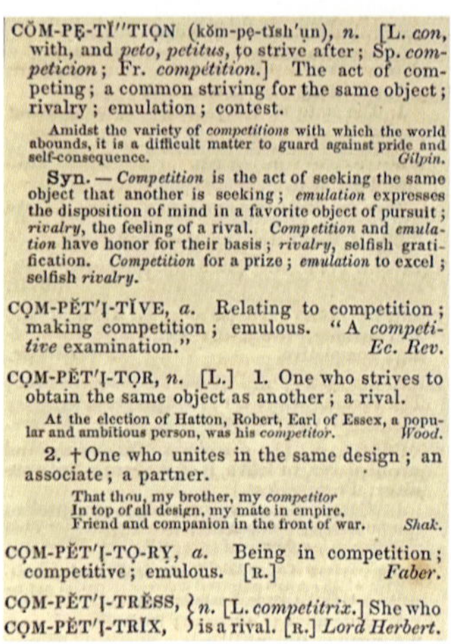

CŎM-PĘ-TĬ''TIỌN (kŏm-pẹ-tĭsh'ụn), *n.* [L. *con,* with, and *peto, petitus,* to strive after; Sp. *competicion*; Fr. *compétition.*] The act of competing; a common striving for the same object; rivalry; emulation; contest.

Amidst the variety of *competitions* with which the world abounds, it is a difficult matter to guard against pride and self-consequence. *Gilpin.*

Syn. — *Competition* is the act of seeking the same object that another is seeking; *emulation* expresses the disposition of mind in a favorite object of pursuit; *rivalry,* the feeling of a rival. *Competition* and *emulation* have honor for their basis; *rivalry,* selfish gratification. *Competition* for a prize; *emulation* to excel; selfish *rivalry.*

CỌM-PĔT'Ị-TĬVE, *a.* Relating to competition; making competition; emulous. "A *competitive* examination." *Ec. Rev.*

CỌM-PĔT'Ị-TỌR, *n.* [L.] 1. One who strives to obtain the same object as another; a rival.

At the election of Hatton, Robert, Earl of Essex, a popular and ambitious person, was his *competitor.* *Wood.*

2. †One who unites in the same design; an associate; a partner.

That thou, my brother, my *competitor*
In top of all design, my mate in empire,
Friend and companion in the front of war. *Shak.*

CỌM-PĔT'Ị-TỌ-RỴ, *a.* Being in competition; competitive; emulous. [R.] *Faber.*

CỌM-PĔT'Ị-TRĔSS, } *n.* [L. *competitrix.*] She who
CỌM-PĔT'Ị-TRĬX, } is a rival. [R.] *Lord Herbert.*

Ex coll. Karolyne & Bryan A. Garner

Worcester included notes distinguishing near-synonyms.

79

Joseph Worcester's Doomed Magnum Opus

Worcester, Joseph. *A Dictionary of the English Language.* Boston: Hickling, Swan & Brewer, 1860.

IN 1846, IN THE MIDST of the Dictionary Wars, Joseph Worcester issued his *Universal and Critical Dictionary of the English Language*, his first big dictionary to compete with Webster. Here Worcester greatly increased his coverage of the English vocabulary. This book simply sparked another outbreak in the Wars. Then Worcester began working toward the performance of a lifetime: *A Dictionary of the English Language.*

In the prefatory matter, Worcester shows himself to be a magnanimous rival of Webster. The final paragraph of his history of English lexicography reads in full:

> In 1828, the first edition of the "American Dictionary of the English Language," by Noah Webster, LL.D. was published,—a work of great labor and learning, comprising a much more full vocabulary than Johnson's Dictionary, and containing many and great improvements with respect both to the etymology and definitions of words. This dictionary has been much enlarged and greatly improved in succeeding editions, by the Rev. Chauncey A. Goodrich, D.D., and it has received numerous and high commendations, and has met with great success. [P. lvii.]

There isn't one word of remonstrance or animadversion despite all the accusations leveled at Worcester by the Merriam brothers.

Just as Chauncey Goodrich was building a team of allies to improve Webster's dictionaries, Worcester had built his own team: his father-in-law, a Harvard faculty member, had suggested words and helped enlist Harvard colleagues to do the same. Worcester had this advantage: while Goodrich had inherited his dictionary and felt constrained by some degree of filial piety (as well as the watchful eye of cautious family members), Worcester had created his own work and could do whatever he pleased.

A review in the *New Englander* in May 1860 praised the book highly: "The publication of an original, comprehensive Dictionary of the English language, is no ordinary event. . . . The enormous labor of adjusting the almost endless details of orthography, etymology, orthoepy, definition, illustration, etc., demands a lifetime, or at least no small portion of a lifetime, for even a tolerable performance of the task." (P. 412.) The reviewer directly compared the rival works, old Webster vs. new Worcester, and his judgment comes as something of a surprise: "The man is well enough off, perhaps, who possesses either; and he is to be congratulated who is able to own both. But if a man can have but one, in our judgment Webster's is the one for him to choose. For on the whole, we are forced to conclude that great as are the merits of Worcester, they by no means eclipse those of Webster, but, on the contrary, themselves suffer eclipse." (P. 428.)

But that view was hardly universal. Many believed that Worcester had, in fact, displaced Webster—a fact that only caused the Merriam brothers to redouble their efforts.

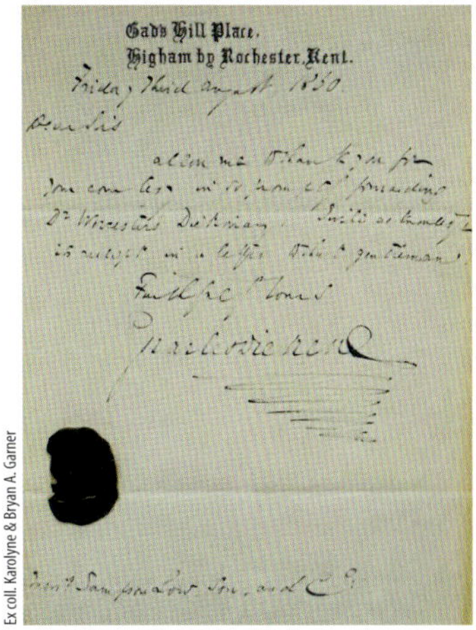
Gads Hill Place,
Higham by Rochester, Kent.

Ex coll. Karolyne & Bryan A. Garner

Charles Dickens acknowledges receipt of Worcester's 1860 edition.

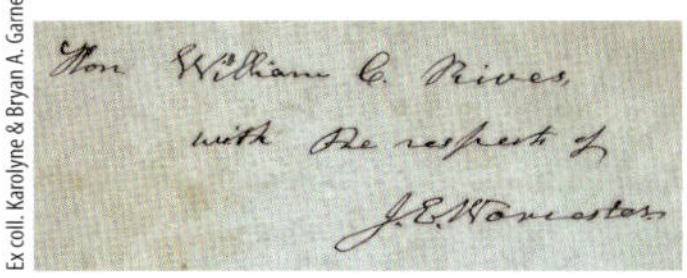
Hon William C. Rives
with the respects of
J.E. Worcester

Ex coll. Karolyne & Bryan A. Garner

The copy shown on p. 256 was inscribed to William C. Rives, a former U.S. senator from Virginia. By 1861, he was a member of the Confederate Congress. The book was later owned by the linguist T.R. Lounsbury and Yale University before coming into the Garner Collection.

Ex coll. Karolyne & Bryan A. Garner

Ex coll. Karolyne & Bryan A. Garner

Various post-1860 editions of Worcester.

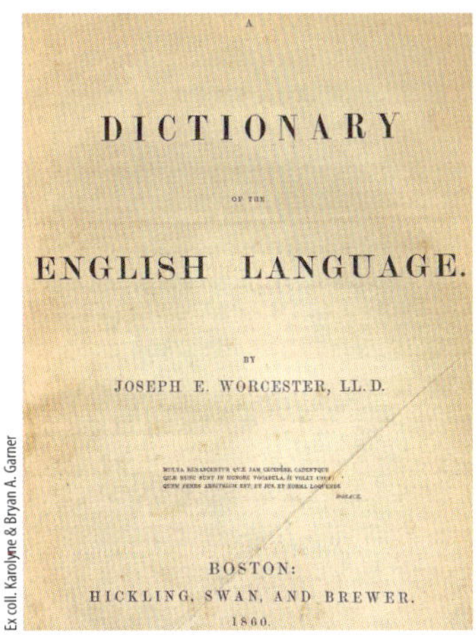
A

DICTIONARY

OF THE

ENGLISH LANGUAGE.

BY

JOSEPH E. WORCESTER, LL.D.

BOSTON:
HICKLING, SWAN, AND BREWER.
1860.

Ex coll. Karolyne & Bryan A. Garner

Title page of the 1860 edition.

80

The Webster-Mahn Can . . .

An American Dictionary of the English Language. Chauncey A. Goodrich & Noah Porter eds. Royal quarto ed. Springfield: G. & C. Merriam Co., 1864.

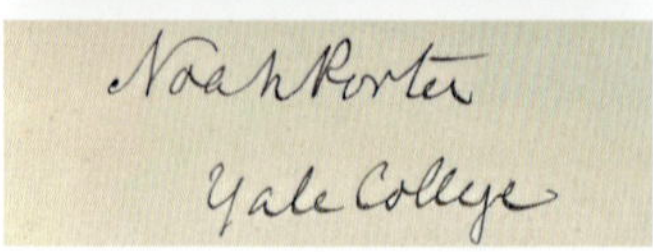

Ex coll. Karolyne & Bryan A. Garner

"In preparing for the present revision, the attention of both the Editor and the Publishers was first directed to the Etymology. They were aware that, however admirable the industry and valuable the contributions of Dr. Webster in this department, the science of comparative Philology was by no means perfect in his time, if indeed it could be said to exist at all." (Noah Porter's preface, p. iii—and please overlook the misrelated participle at the outset of the quotation.)

This dictionary, known to scholars as *Webster-Mahn*, was in its day among the best ever produced. It marked the jettisoning of almost everything that had been characteristic of Noah Webster himself, and it signaled a decisive move by the Merriam-Webster dynasty to gain advantage over Joseph Worcester, who, at 80, was now in the last year of his life.

But why *Webster-Mahn* as a moniker, when Chauncey Goodrich and Noah Porter were listed as the chief editors? Goodrich had died four years before its appearance, and Noah Porter had headed the project. The name Mahn came from the German philologist Dr. C.A.F. Mahn (1802–1887) of Berlin, whom Porter had engaged to write etymologies from scratch. Although there were improvements in every aspect of the lexicography—made possible by Porter's enlisting the help of dozens of Yale faculty members—it was in the etymology department that the book was most thoroughly upgraded. During a trip through Germany in 1854, Noah Porter had met with Mahn, who spoke with astuteness about the shortcomings of American dictionaries. Porter warned the Merriams that these deficiencies, if widely known, would inevitably result in ruin for the Webster brand. And so Mahn was engaged to remedy the pervasive etymological flaws that Noah Webster had introduced. During a decade of work, Mahn established a systematic, streamlined method for presenting etymologies—one that is recognizably modern.

Take the example of the noun and verb *ooze*. We might assess the two 19th-century performances (Noah Webster vs. C.A.F. Mahn) against what modern etymologists say. The *OED* says that the word is "inherited from Germanic," adding: "Cognate with Middle Low German *wōs*, *wōse* foam, scum, Old Swedish *ōs*, Old Danish *ōs* (Danish regional *os*) juice from a plant; further etymology uncertain and disputed. (Probably not related to Old Icelandic *vás* wetness, toil, fatigue from storm, etc.)" In its verb entry for *ooze*, the *OED* mentions the 18th-century dialectal form *weeze*.

Now let's see how Noah Webster and C.A.F. Mahn stack up.

In his 1841 two-volume quarto, Noah Webster confessed that "the origin of this word is not easily ascertained," but then he proceeded to give the Ethiopian word meaning "to flow," the Amharic word meaning "to sweat," and then another Ethiopian word for "to go out," followed by the "nearly allied" Hebrew word meaning "to go out," and the Saxon and German words meaning "water." He seems to have mentioned the Ethiopian words only because the first character resembles a large phi (Φ), which is suggestive of an *O*.

In his 1864 revisions, C.A.F. Mahn replaced all this outlandish conjecture, reducing five lines to half a line for the etymology of the noun *ooze*: "Prov. Eng. *weeze*." For the verb *ooze*, Mahn wrote this: "Cf. Prov. Eng. *ouse*, the liquor in a tanner's vat, A.S. *wós*, juice, ooze, broth, *wase*, dirt, mire, mud, *wósig*, oozy, juicy, moist, O. Fries. & D. *wase*, mud, Icel. *veisa*, sewer, ditch, pool." In short, Mahn is much closer to what the *OED* tells us today—not identical, true, but similar.

Multiply that instance by 5,000, and you'll have an idea of what Mann achieved. If you flip through Noah Webster's 1828 dictionary or his 1841 revision, you'll see entry after entry containing strange-looking characters representing non-Indo-European languages that have nothing to do with the English words with which Webster made false associations. All this etymological rubbish was removed in 1864.

Noah Porter gingerly explained the replacements this way: "However admirable the industry and valuable the contributions of Dr. Webster in [etymology], the science of comparative Philology was by no means perfect in his time, if indeed it could be said to exist at all." (Preface, p. iii.) What a change 20 years had wrought! "It is only within a very few years that the true principles on which this science rests have been suggested and confirmed, and the methods have been determined by which future investigations may be successfully prosecuted." (*Id.*) Mahn's work was put forward as a "valuable contribution to the stores of linguistic knowledge," with the thought that it would be "acknowledged by scholars as one of marked superiority." Indeed it was.

Meanwhile, the religious language with which Noah Webster had imbued his definitions was removed. Porter instructed his staff to condense and contract the definitions, and they did. The task fell to two scholars in their mid-30s: William D. Whitney, who would later take the helm of the *Century Dictionary* (no. 88), and Daniel

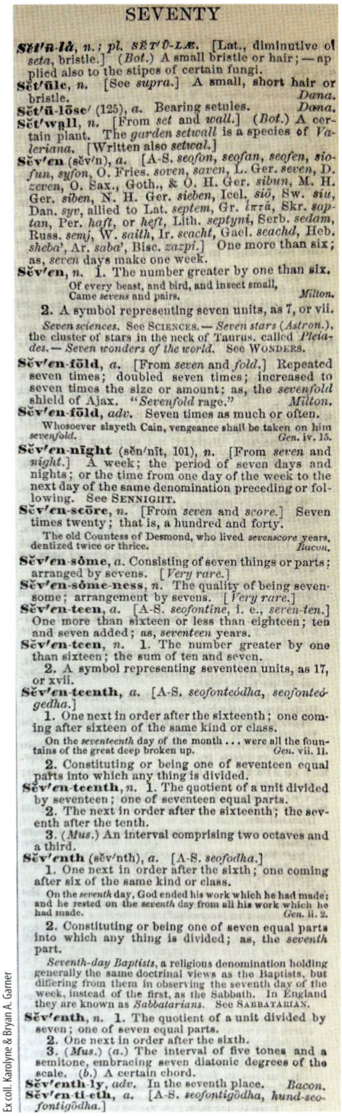

SEVENTY

Sĕt′ū-lă, *n.*; *pl.* SĔT′Ū-LÆ. [Lat., diminutive of *seta*, bristle.] (*Bot.*) A small bristle or hair;—applied also to the stipes of certain fungi.

Sĕt′ūle, *n.* [See *supra.*] A small, short hair or bristle. *Dana.*

Sĕt′ū-lōse′ (125), *a.* Bearing setules. *Dana.*

Sĕt′wall, *n.* [From *set* and *wall.*] (*Bot.*) A certain plant. The *garden setwall* is a species of *Valeriana.* [Written also *setwal.*]

Sĕv′en (sĕv′n), *a.* [A-S. *seofon*, *seofan*, *seofen*, *siofun*, *syfon*, O. Fries. *soven*, *saven*, L. Ger. *seven*, D. *zeven*, O. Sax., Goth., & O. H. Ger. *sibun*, M. H. Ger. *siben*, N. H. Ger. *sieben*, Icel. *siö*, Sw. *siu*, Dan. *syv*, allied to Lat. *septem*, Gr. ἑπτά, Skr. *saptan*, Per. *haft*, or *heft*, Lith. *septyni*, Serb. *sedam*, Russ. *semj*, W. *saith*, Ir. *seacht*, Gael. *seachd*, Heb. *sheba'*, Ar. *saba'*, Bisc. *zazpi.*] One more than six; as, *seven* days make one week.

Sĕv′en, *n.* 1. The number greater by one than six.

Of every beast, and bird, and insect small,
Came *sevens* and pairs. *Milton.*

2. A symbol representing seven units, as 7, or vii.

Seven sciences. See SCIENCES.—*Seven stars* (*Astron.*), the cluster of stars in the neck of Taurus, called *Pleiades.*—*Seven wonders of the world.* See WONDERS.

Sĕv′en-fōld, *a.* [From *seven* and *fold.*] Repeated seven times; doubled seven times; increased to seven times the size or amount; as, the *sevenfold* shield of Ajax. "*Sevenfold* rage." *Milton.*

Sĕv′en-fōld, *adv.* Seven times as much or often.

Whosoever slayeth Cain, vengeance shall be taken on him *sevenfold.* *Gen.* iv. 15.

Sĕv′en-nīght (sĕn′nīt, 101), *n.* [From *seven* and *night.*] A week; the period of seven days and nights; or the time from one day of the week to the next day of the same denomination preceding or following. See SENNIGHT.

Sĕv′en-scōre, *n.* [From *seven* and *score.*] Seven times twenty; that is, a hundred and forty.

The old Countess of Desmond, who lived *sevenscore* years, dentized twice or thrice. *Bacon.*

Sĕv′en-sŏme, *a.* Consisting of seven things or parts; arranged by sevens. [*Very rare.*]

Sĕv′en-sŏme-ness, *n.* The quality of being sevensome; arrangement by sevens. [*Very rare.*]

Sĕv′en-teen, *a.* [A-S. *seofontine*, i. e., *seven-ten.*] One more than sixteen or less than eighteen; ten and seven added; as, *seventeen* years.

Sĕv′en-teen, *n.* 1. The number greater by one than sixteen; the sum of ten and seven.

2. A symbol representing seventeen units, as 17, or xvii.

Sĕv′en-teenth, *a.* [A-S. *seofonteódha*, *seofonteógedha.*]

1. One next in order after the sixteenth; one coming after sixteen of the same kind or class.

On the *seventeenth* day of the month . . . were all the fountains of the great deep broken up. *Gen.* vii. 11.

2. Constituting or being one of seventeen equal parts into which any thing is divided.

Sĕv′en-teenth, *n.* 1. The quotient of a unit divided by seventeen; one of seventeen equal parts.

2. The next in order after the sixteenth; the seventh after the tenth.

3. (*Mus.*) An interval comprising two octaves and a third.

Sĕv′enth (sĕv′nth), *a.* [A-S. *seofodha.*]

1. One next in order after the sixth; one coming after six of the same kind or class.

On the *seventh* day, God ended his work which he had made; and he rested on the *seventh* day from all his work which he had made. *Gen.* ii. 2.

2. Constituting or being one of seven equal parts into which any thing is divided; as, the *seventh* part.

Seventh-day Baptists, a religious denomination holding generally the same doctrinal views as the Baptists, but differing from them in observing the seventh day of the week, instead of the first, as the Sabbath. In England they are known as *Sabbatarians.* See SABBATARIAN.

Sĕv′enth, *n.* 1. The quotient of a unit divided by seven; one of seven equal parts.

2. One next in order after the sixth.

3. (*Mus.*) (*a.*) The interval of five tones and a semitone, embracing seven diatonic degrees of the scale. (*b.*) A certain chord.

Sĕv′enth-ly, *adv.* In the seventh place. *Bacon.*

Sĕv′en-ti-eth, *a.* [A-S. *seofontigōdha*, *hund-seofontigōdha.*]

Ex coll. Karolyne & Bryan A. Garner

Compare C.A.F. Mahn's etymology for *seven* with that of Noah Webster (see p. 202). Gone are the whimsical musings about word histories.

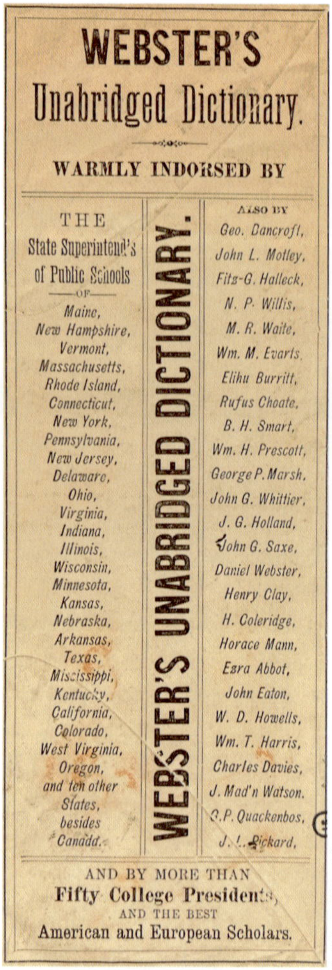

Ex coll. Karolyne & Bryan A. Garner

Like many other 19th-century businesses, the Merriams used every square centimeter of space on envelopes to promote their products. This 1887 envelope promoted the 1884 reissue of *Webster-Mahn*.

C. Gilman, who would later become president successively of Johns Hopkins University and the University of California, Berkeley. They performed their commission admirably.

Though not the very first, this was still among the earliest English dictionaries to take advantage of a typographical novelty: in the 1830s, type foundries began developing typeface families that included **boldface letters**. In the 1860s these new letters started being used in dictionaries to indicate headwords—the first real innovation in the presentation of headwords since Nathan Bailey introduced capitals to facilitate skimming in 1721. Pronunciation was another strength. The editors removed some of the earlier editions' eccentricities and brought pronunciation more closely in line with prevailing practices. In his preface, Porter asserted that "a more thoroughly practical and satisfactory treatment of the subject cannot be found in the language." (Preface, p. viii.)

Noah Porter, in short, had led an extensive team in remaking the dictionary. At the time, he was a professor of moral philosophy at Yale. For years he had been a staunch opponent of slavery. But his leadership on the dictionary hadn't been easy for the Merriam brothers to obtain. Porter had worked on the 1854 edition of Ogilvie's *Comprehensive English Dictionary*, so he knew a good deal about lexicography even before beginning to help his Yale colleague Chauncey Goodrich on various dictionary tasks in the late 1850s. When Goodrich, shortly before his death, invited Porter to undertake the chief editorship, Porter declined, citing his professorial duties. But after Goodrich died, the Merriams and the Webster family successfully prevailed on him. The Merriams assured him that they expected "two or three hours a day." They wrote to him: "We should like to make you a pecuniary proposition . . . , if you will entertain it on such a basis, to cover say two years." (Merriam 1893:117–19.)

Porter relented, and soon his duties expanded beyond the original commitment—probably as the result of his own conscientiousness. "He was too valuable to be used sparingly," as the Merriam company would write a few years later. "His fund of general information, his intelligence as to the sources of knowledge, his wise judgment of the fitness of men for various branches of the work, his mental acuteness trained by metaphysics and serviceable for the niceties of language, his swiftness in decision—and, not least, his equal appreciation of literary and business conditions, qualifying him to mediate between the publisher's necessities of time and space and the scholar's fastidiousness and slowness of execution,—these qualities brought him into constant requisition." (*Id.* at 118–19.) It was also said that every page "passed under his critical eye, page by page and line by line," and that he read through the entire set of proofs when they were ready.

In a sense, then, it could be called an injustice that this edition came to be known as *Webster-Mahn*. With even greater justification, it might have been called *Webster-Porter.* Seven years after its completion, Porter became president of Yale College. His skillful leadership on the dictionary undoubtedly contributed to his elevation.

This 1864 Webster ended the Dictionary Wars for good: never again would the Merriams have such a serious rival. According to John Morse, president and publisher of Merriam-Webster as the 20th century turned into the 21st, it also marked the dawn of an era. He remarked: "*Webster's Unabridged* of 1864 moved dictionary-making from the herculean but idiosyncratic effort of one individual to a disciplined and methodical effort of a well-organized group." (Sokolowski 2020:182.) And it provided a model for another well-organized group: the nascent *Oxford English Dictionary* looked to Webster's 1864 dictionary as the state of the art in lexicography. In devising the "Webster ratio," they worked to tie their own page count to a manageable multiple of Webster's. (*Id.* at 186.)

Although Porter's decision to replace Webster's etymologies with Mahn's was a decisive step forward for Merriam's dictionaries, it would induce competitors to claim disingenuously, many decades later, that the newly improved dictionaries weren't the authentic work of Noah Webster. (See p. 362.)

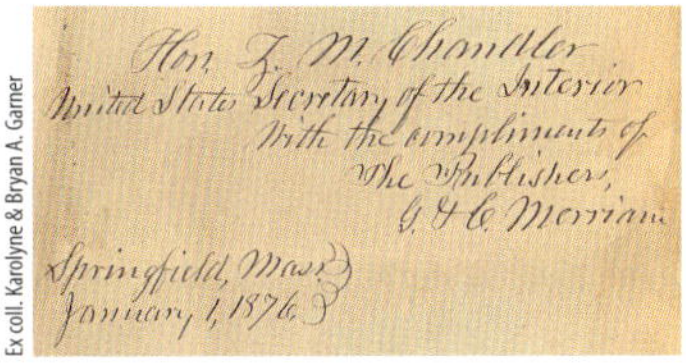
Hon. Z. M. Chandler
United States Secretary of the Interior
With the compliments of
The Publishers,
G. & C. Merriam
Springfield, Mass
January 1, 1876

Ex coll. Karolyne & Bryan A. Garner

In marketing *Webster-Mahn*, the Merriam brothers sent copies to high officials such as the U.S. Secretary of Interior Zachariah Chandler. A friend of Lincoln's, he was appointed by President Ulysses S. Grant.

"Dr. Webster . . . had not emancipated himself entirely from the influence of Johnson's example in accumulating definitions that are really the same, though at first sight they may appear to be different. Dr. Webster insists, also, with earnestness, that it is the duty of the lexicographer to give first the primitive signification of every word, and to develop and arrange the dependent meanings in the order in which they were derived. But his theory in respect to these and other points was better than his practice." (Noah Porter's preface, p. iii.)

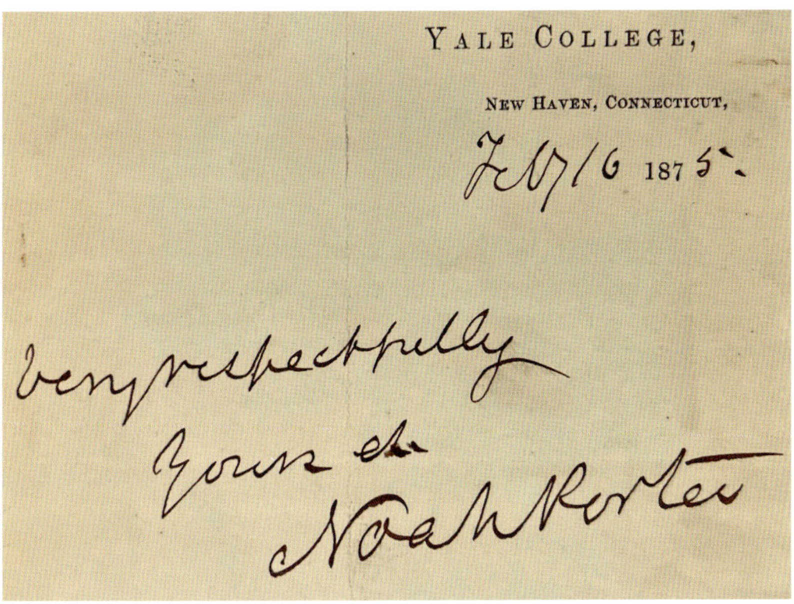
YALE COLLEGE,
NEW HAVEN, CONNECTICUT,
Feb/16 1875.
Very respectfully
Yours &c.
Noah Porter

Ex coll. Karolyne & Bryan A. Garner

Ex coll. Karolyne & Bryan A. Garner

Chandler's fancily bound copy.

Ex coll. Karolyne & Bryan A. Garner

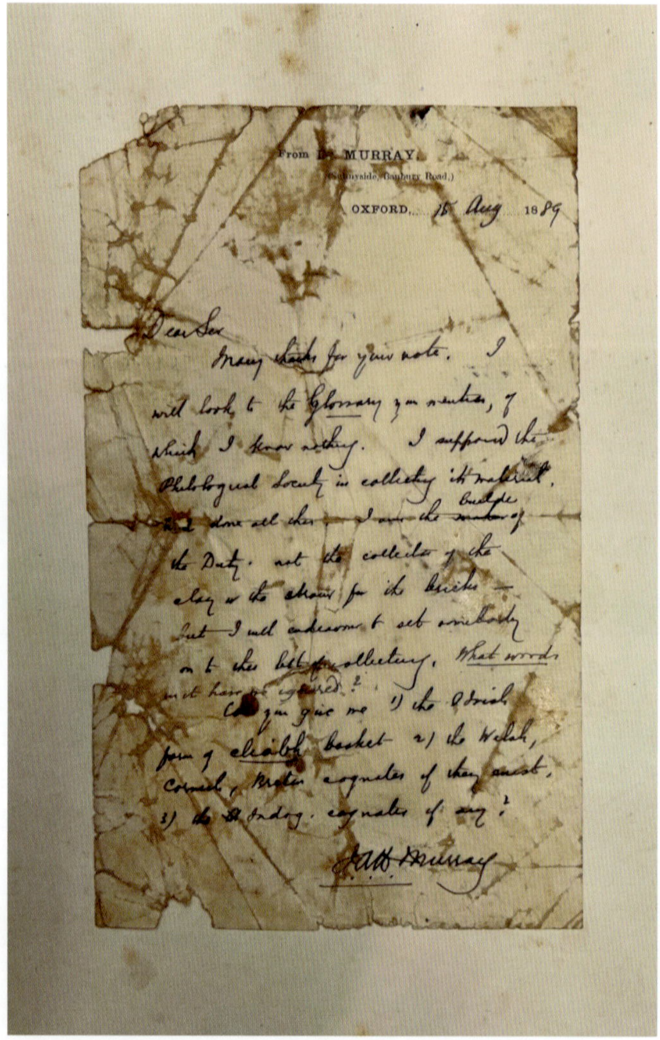
From Dr. MURRAY,
(Sunnyside, Banbury Road,)
OXFORD, 15 Aug 1889

Dear Sir

Many thanks for your note. I will look to the Glossary you mention, of which I know nothing. I supposed the Philological Society in collecting its material had done all that — I am the builder of the Dictionary, not the collector of the clay or the straw for the bricks — but I will endeavour to set somebody on to this bit of collecting. What words [illegible]?

Can you give me 1) the O.Irish form of cliabh basket 2) the Welsh, Cornish, Breton cognates if they exist, 3) the Indog. cognates if any?

J.A.H. Murray

Ex coll. Karolyne & Bryan A. Garner

The spines on this leatherbound copy of the first edition of the *OED* bear the imprint *Murray's English Dictionary*. Inside volume 1 is a pasted-in letter from one of Murray's correspondents. You might think that *Murray's English Dictionary* is a mark of respect or affection, but it may indeed be the opposite: it may signal the view that it's just Murray's idiosyncratic work. That is, the original owner seems to have been R.O. Williams, who one year after receiving Murray's letter published a book suggesting that the *OED* would "lower the standard for such work." (Williams 1890:44.) Claiming to be a major contributor to Noah Porter's editions of Webster dictionaries, Williams (after receiving Murray's letter above) applied unsuccessfully for work on the *OED*. In an earlier letter, Williams had challenged Murray's method of collecting evidence, in response to which Murray writes here: "I am the builder of the Dictionary, not the collector of the clay or the straw for the bricks." Murray then issues a challenge to Williams: "Can you give me 1) the O. Irish form of *cliabh* basket 2) the Welsh, Cornish, Breton cognates if they exist 3) the Indog. [Indo-Germanic] cognates if any? J.A.H. Murray." Instead of following through, Williams wrote a book called *Our Dictionaries and Other Language Topics*, in which he blasted the *OED* in an eight-page diatribe.

VIII. The *OED* Era

It had been more than a century since Samuel Johnson first published his revolutionary Dictionary. *His work had been modestly revised and updated from time to time, but it was eventually eclipsed by Webster and Worcester—both of which enjoyed rapid British sales. Meanwhile, it became something of a rage in the U.K. to compile dictionaries of regional English.*

Richard Chenevix Trench, a philologically oriented clergyman, delivered a lecture in which he called for a new type of dictionary: one that would (1) cover the entire English language, (2) show the history of every meaning of every word, and (3) back it all up with illustrative quotations to support every single sense. That lecture is the conventional start of the story of what became the Oxford English Dictionary, *the greatest dictionary of the language ever attempted. After some false starts, the work began in earnest in the 1870s, and soon James A.H. Murray took over as chief editor. He oversaw most of the 12-volume dictionary before his death in 1915; after that, the work was completed by Henry Bradley, William Craigie, and C.T. Onions, who enlisted the help of the remarkably talented J.R.R. Tolkien.*

Several other vast dictionaries were undertaken around the same time. In the multivolume realm, Robert Hunter in the U.K. and William Dwight Whitney in the U.S. completed major dictionary projects. In the big one-volume realm, the Merriam brothers completed an international dictionary that went through several major revisions. Isaac K. Funk started the Funk & Wagnalls line. Henry Cecil Kennedy Wyld, an Oxford linguist, completed a massive one-volume dictionary just one year before Oxford University Press issued the Shorter Oxford *in two volumes. And the year after that, the Merriam company came out with the most impressive Webster dictionary to date—with little of Noah left in it.*

W.W. Skeat explored the etymological front in the light of modern thinking about historical linguistics, as did poor Ernest Weekley, who was so busy with words that he didn't notice that his wife had begun a relationship with one of his students, D.H. Lawrence. They eloped, leaving Weekley bereft.

Specialist dictionaries came along: Black's Law Dictionary, *Craigie's* Dictionary of American English, *and Craigie's erstwhile (and disaffected) employee Mathews's* Dictionary of Americanisms. *And everyone was eyeing the work of Eric Partridge, but his work must await a later chapter.*

Ex coll. Karolyne & Bryan A. Garner

The Right Hon. and Most Reverend Richard Chenevix Trench, D.D., Lord Archbishop Designate of Dublin. From *The Illustrated London News*, 21 Nov. 1863, p. 513.

81

Richard Chenevix Trench

Poet–Theologian with Big Ideas

Trench, Richard Chenevix. *On Some Deficiencies in Our English Dictionaries*. London: J.W. Parker & Son, 1857. 2d ed. 1860.

Ex coll. Karolyne & Bryan A. Garner

Ex coll. Karolyne & Bryan A. Garner

A Dubliner by birth, Richard Chenevix Trench (1807–1886) spent most of his childhood near Southampton, attending Harrow School and then Trinity College, Cambridge (BA 1829, MA 1833, BD 1850). Although he was a poet and theologian, his career entailed one ecclesiastical post after another throughout England until he became the Archbishop of Dublin in 1863.

In the 1850s, when his philological pursuits peaked, he was professor of divinity at King's College, London, and dean of Westminster (among other things). First came *On the Study of Words* (1851), in which he described language as "the amber in which a thousand precious and subtle thoughts have been safely embedded and preserved." (P. 33.) Then came *English Past and Present* (1855), which opens with a long anonymous epigraph that says in part: "A history of the language in which all . . . such words as have become obsolete should be followed down to their final extinction, in which all the most remarkable words should be traced through their successive phases of meaning, . . . would throw more light on the development of the human mind than all the brainspun systems of metaphysics that ever were written." (P. 10.) The third in his popular trilogy was *A Select Glossary of English Words Used Formerly in Senses Different from Their Present* (1859), in which he modestly acknowledged that he had "had some share, though a small one, in the suggestion of a new English Dictionary to be published by the Philological Society." (P. xi.)

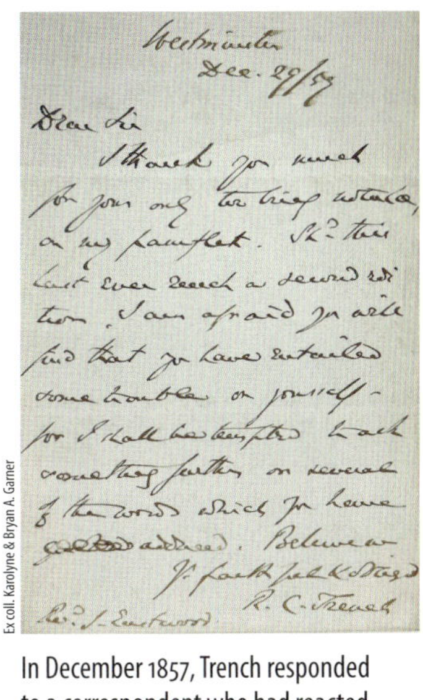

Westminster
Dec. 29/57

Dear Sir

I thank you much for your only too kind notice on my pamphlet. Sh^d this last ever reach a second edition, I am afraid you will find that you have entailed some trouble on yourself—for I shall be tempted to ask something further on several of the words which you have adduced. Believe me

Y^r faithfully & obliged
R. C. Trench

Rev. J. Eastwood

Ex coll. Karolyne & Bryan A. Garner

In December 1857, Trench responded to a correspondent who had reacted to his piece on deficiencies in dictionaries: "I shall be tempted to ask something further on several of the words which you have adduced."

What was his role in the *OED*? He provided the impetus: in 1857, he wrote the influential but—unlike his other books—hard-to-find work explaining prevalent lexicographic deficiencies. *On Some Deficiencies in Our English Dictionaries*, originally delivered before the Philological Society in London, isolated six shortcomings in existing dictionaries: (1) they weren't based on a comprehensive survey of English writings; (2) they failed to include obsolete terms by any consistent method; (3) they failed to discriminate between synonyms; (4) they were missing illustrative quotations; (5) they were cluttered with irrelevant and redundant information; and (6) they were inconsistent in their coverage of families and groups of words. Trench wanted "an entirely new Dictionary"—"no patch upon old garments, but a new garment throughout." (P. 1.)

"[Trench] wanted a new English dictionary to be prepared which would, with certain exceptions, contain all words previously unregistered as well as those already present in Victorian dictionaries, and would exhibit each word and each meaning in a historical manner, that is with the senses arranged in chronological order, and with illustrative quotations from verified printed sources as the main confirmatory and elucidatory apparatus." (Burchfield 1985:88–89.)

Trench looked to the major dictionaries being developed in Europe, Germany above all, and wanted to see the same sort of historically informed lexicography applied to English. He delivered a clear, forceful statement that the dictionary must be "an inventory of the language," and that the lexicographer must be the historian of a language, not a prudish critic: "the business which [the lexicographer] has undertaken is to collect and arrange all words . . . whether they do or do not commend themselves to his judgement." (Pp. 69–70.) Given his role as prime mover, it isn't at all extravagant to call Trench "the first father of the *OED*." (Brewer 2007b:109.)

Ex coll. Karolyne & Bryan A. Garner

A selection of Trench's books.
For a copy of an early dictionary owned by Trench, see p. 62.

82

The Philological Society's No-Word-Left-Behind Policy

***Proposal for the Publication of a New English Dictionary of the Philological Society*. London: Trübner & Co., 1859.**

After Richard Chenevix Trench pointed out the shortcomings of current English dictionaries, the Philological Society formed an Unregistered Words Committee charged with preparing a supplement to the latest edition of either Johnson or Richardson. The committee consisted of a philological triumvirate: Trench, along with two lawyers-turned-litterateurs, Frederick J. Furnivall and Herbert Coleridge. They soon concluded what Trench had already explicitly stated: a supplement would not be enough—they would have to start from scratch.

The *Proposal for the Publication of a New English Dictionary* spells out "the main outlines of the plan upon which the New Dictionary will be constructed," and is therefore the first public glimpse of what would eventually become the *Oxford English Dictionary*. Though countless details would change in the planning process, the *Proposal* contains a forceful statement of a principle that has guided the *OED* from the very beginning:

> the first requirement of every lexicon is, that it should contain *every word occurring in the literature of the language it professes to illustrate*. We entirely repudiate the theory, which converts the lexicographer into an arbiter of style, and leaves it in his discretion to accept or reject words according to his private notions of their comparative elegance or inelegance.

This was to be a scientific dictionary on scientific principles, and this meant that it was to be both comprehensive and descriptive. Squeamishness had no place.

That's not to say that there would be no limits. "We admit as authorities all English books," the *Proposal* explained, "except such as are devoted to purely scientific subjects." (P. 3.) The scientific vocabulary, the Society decided, was too vast and too subject to change

Ex coll. Karolyne & Bryan A. Garner

The *Proposal* was generally bound with Herbert Coleridge's monograph *A Glossarial Index to the Printed English Literature of the Thirteenth Century* (Trübner, 1859).

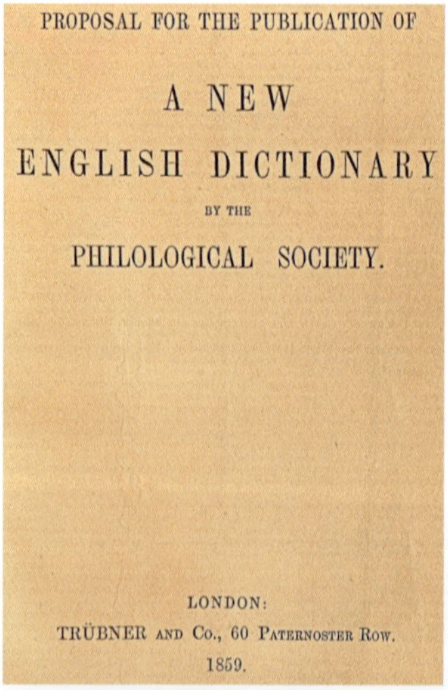
PROPOSAL FOR THE PUBLICATION OF

A NEW

ENGLISH DICTIONARY

BY THE

PHILOLOGICAL SOCIETY.

LONDON:

TRÜBNER AND Co., 60 PATERNOSTER ROW.

1859.

Ex coll. Karolyne & Bryan A. Garner

Ex coll. Karolyne & Bryan A. Garner

The crucial years in which the *OED* was envisioned.

to be included in any general-purpose dictionary. They also "decided to commence with the commencement of English," which for them meant the Middle English period, around the year 1250—"that definite appearance of an English type of language, distinct from the preceding semi-Saxon." (*Id.*) That *terminus a quo* would later be pushed back to 1150.

The *Proposal* also called on the public for "such further help in the reading and noting of books as will enable the plan to be carried out satisfactorily." Amateur enthusiasts would scrutinize thousands of books and pass their materials on to the philologists. The other great historical dictionary of a modern language would provide the model. "We do but follow the example of the Grimms"—the brothers Jacob and Wilhelm, whose monumental *Deutsches Wörterbuch* had begun in 1838—"when we call upon Englishmen to come forward and write their own Dictionary for themselves." (P. 8) Fearing that they might be overwhelmed with quotations from a few too-familiar authors, they warned volunteers off the obvious sources: readers focusing on "the period 1526–Milton," for instance, should collect "words, senses of words, and phrases, not in the Bible or Shakspere." (Pp. 6–7.)

With the request that "each word or phrase should be written out with its quotation and reference on a separate half-sheet of note-paper, *lengthwise, and on one side of the paper only*," the *OED*'s reading program—the largest lexicographic crowdsourcing project in history—was officially underway. To this day, amateur volunteers continue to send materials to Oxford University Press, though digital forms have taken the place of half-sheets of notepaper.

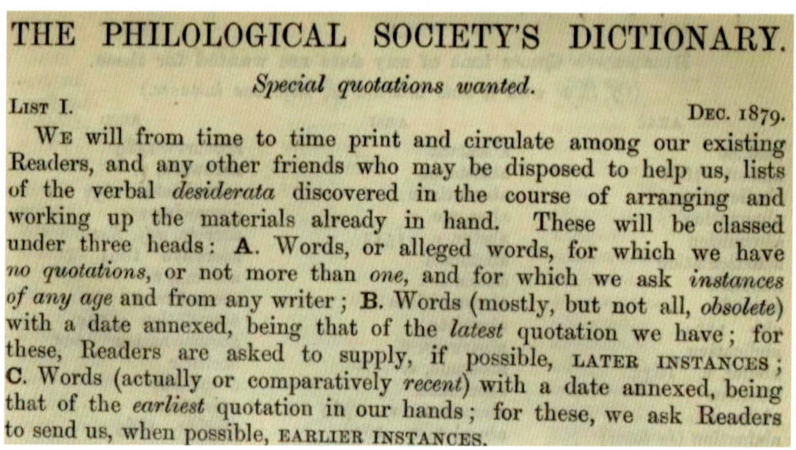
THE PHILOLOGICAL SOCIETY'S DICTIONARY.

Special quotations wanted.

LIST I. DEC. 1879.

WE will from time to time print and circulate among our existing Readers, and any other friends who may be disposed to help us, lists of the verbal *desiderata* discovered in the course of arranging and working up the materials already in hand. These will be classed under three heads: **A.** Words, or alleged words, for which we have *no quotations*, or not more than *one*, and for which we ask *instances of any age* and from any writer; **B.** Words (mostly, but not all, *obsolete*) with a date annexed, being that of the *latest* quotation we have; for these, Readers are asked to supply, if possible, LATER INSTANCES; **C.** Words (actually or comparatively *recent*) with a date annexed, being that of the *earliest* quotation in our hands; for these, we ask Readers to send us, when possible, EARLIER INSTANCES.

Ex coll. Karolyne & Bryan A. Garner

1879 Instructions for Readers.

83

Walter William Skeat
Etymologizing Father of Ghoſt-Words

Skeat, W[alter] W[illiam]. ***A Mœso-Gothic Glossary.*** **London: Asher & Co., 1868.**

———. ***An Etymological Dictionary of the English Language, arranged on an hiſtorical basis.*** **Oxford: Clarendon Press, 1879–1882. 2d ed. 1884. 3d ed. 1897. 4th ed. 1910.**

———. ***A Concise Etymological Dictionary of the English Language.*** **Oxford: Clarendon Press, 1882. 2d ed. 1885. 3d ed. 1887. 4th ed. 1890.**

Walter William Skeat (1835–1912), the child of an architect, was born in a fashionable part of London. At King's College School, he studied under Thomas Oswald Cockayne, who would go on to publish an important edition of Old English medical texts. At 18, Skeat matriculated at Christ's College, Cambridge, to study theology and mathematics.

Degree in hand, Skeat became a deacon and then a curate, first at East Dereham in Norfolk, and then at Godalming in Surrey. Because his clerical career was cut short by a malady of the throat, he found a lectureship in mathematics at his old college. (Did lecturing involve less declaiming?) Though he taught mathematics, Skeat's passion was language. The young philologist caught the eye of Frederick James Furnivall, founder of the Early English Text Society, who encouraged him to put his learning to use by preparing a volume for the series. Skeat quickly and capably edited *The Romans of Lancelot of the Laik* (1865), a late-15th-century Scottish poem of around 3,500 lines, making it just the sixth publication of the Early English Text Society. It was the first of Skeat's many EETS contributions: in rapid succession, he published selections from *Piers Plowman* and the *Romans of Partenay or of Lusignen* in 1866, a complete version of the so-called "A text" of Langland's *Piers Plowman* and *Pierce the Ploughman's Crede* in 1867, the "B text" in 1869, and so on—nearly two dozen book-length

Ex coll. Karolyne & Bryan A. Garner

"It would be a far less error to look upon Mœso-Gothic as an older form of Anglo-Saxon than of High-German; and we may certainly go as far as to say this—that to study Mœso-Gothic is, practically, more the business of Englishmen than of any one else. . . ." (P. vii.)

Ex coll. Karolyne & Bryan A. Garner

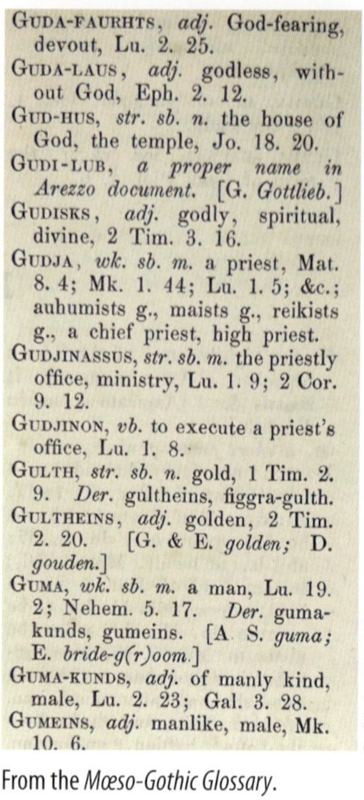

GUDA-FAURHTS, *adj.* God-fearing, devout, Lu. 2. 25.
GUDA-LAUS, *adj.* godless, without God, Eph. 2. 12.
GUD-HUS, *str. sb. n.* the house of God, the temple, Jo. 18. 20.
GUDI-LUB, *a proper name in Arezzo document.* [G. *Gottlieb.*]
GUDISKS, *adj.* godly, spiritual, divine, 2 Tim. 3. 16.
GUDJA, *wk. sb. m.* a priest, Mat. 8. 4; Mk. 1. 44; Lu. 1. 5; &c.; auhumists g., maists g., reikists g., a chief priest, high priest.
GUDJINASSUS, *str. sb. m.* the priestly office, ministry, Lu. 1. 9; 2 Cor. 9. 12.
GUDJINON, *vb.* to execute a priest's office, Lu. 1. 8.
GULTH, *str. sb. n.* gold, 1 Tim. 2. 9. *Der.* gultheins, figgra-gulth.
GULTHEINS, *adj.* golden, 2 Tim. 2. 20. [G. & E. *golden;* D. *gouden.*]
GUMA, *wk. sb. m.* a man, Lu. 19. 2; Nehem. 5. 17. *Der.* gumakunds, gumeins. [A. S. *guma;* E. *bride-g(r)oom.*]
GUMA-KUNDS, *adj.* of manly kind, male, Lu. 2. 23; Gal. 3. 28.
GUMEINS, *adj.* manlike, male, Mk. 10. 6.

Ex coll. Karolyne & Bryan A. Garner

From the *Mœso-Gothic Glossary.*

contributions to the series from 1865 to 1900. He also edited both Old and Middle English texts for other publishers, including a four-volume edition of the Old English Gospels (Cambridge University Press, 1871–1887) and a seven-volume Chaucer (Clarendon Press, 1894–1897). Any one of these projects would be a career-defining achievement for most scholars, but Skeat turned them out year after year. The secret to his productivity? He wouldn't dally. "In very difficult cases," he explained, "my usual rule has been not to spend more than three hours over one word. During that time, I made the best I could of it, and then let it go." (P. xi.) It worked for him, and the books he prepared were impeccably edited. Many remained the standard editions for decades.

By the 1870s it was clear that his philological interests were too serious to be a mathematician's side-hustle. He therefore gave up the lectureship and in 1878 was elected the first Elrington and Bosworth Professor of Anglo-Saxon at Cambridge. This placed him at the center of the British philological scene, and he became active in the greatest lexicographic program in the history of the English language: the *OED*.

Two of his many books warrant discussion here. The first is his dictionary of "Mœso-Gothic." Gothic is a dead language, the only attested member of the East Germanic language family, spoken in the fourth century in the Balkan region known as Moesia. Only a tiny amount of writing in the Gothic language survives, nearly all of it from an incomplete manuscript of a Gothic translation of the Christian Gospels. Because it represents an otherwise unknown branch of the Germanic language family—which includes English as well as German, Dutch, and the Scandinavian languages—Gothic plays an important role in comparative philology. Although there were already a few dictionaries of Gothic, Skeat was convinced a new one was called for. Franciscus Junius and Stephen Skinner, he said, had been deservedly praised—they were "men who did good work in their day"—but it was no longer their day, and all their "statements require careful verification in the 19th century." (P. viii.)

As a sound historical lexicographer, Skeat understood the importance of illustrative quotations. But because the canon of surviving Gothic literature is so small, he saw no need for full quotations—anyone able to make sense of the dictionary would have an edition of the

Gothic Gospels on hand. Nothing was needed beyond brief citations of Bible passages:

> GA-MOTJAN, *vb.* to meet, Mk. 5. 2; 14. 13; Lu. 14. 31; 17. 12. *Der.* withra-gamotjan.
>
> GA-MUNAN, *vb.* to mind, to remember, Mk. 8. 18; Lu. 17. 32; Jo. 15. 20; &c. *From* minan.
>
> GA-MUNDS, *str. sb. f.* remembrance, Mk. 14. 9; 1 Cor. 11. 24; Eph. 1. 16. *From* minan.
>
> GA-NAGLJAN, *vb.* to nail, Col. 2. 14. [G. *nageln*; E. *nail.*]

Here we see how Skeat signaled his etymologies ("*From*"), derived forms ("*Der.*"), and cognates in other Germanic languages, in this case German and English. He also used an asterisk to mark "*supposed root-words*," hypothetical forms that "must have existed" (p. xxi) but for which no direct evidence survives.

As a definer, Skeat was a patient splitter. The entry for *than*, adv. gets a series of meanings and idioms: "(1) then, thereupon . . . (2) when, whenever, as long as . . . (3) but, and, however, therefore, for, for also, although;—jah-than, for also, however, although;—ei-than, therefore;—mith-than, meanwhile, now;—mith-thanei, whilst; —nauh-than, still however;—-ni nauh-than, not any longer, never . . . ." Some entries come with grammatical guidance: *u* is "*an enclitic used in asking a question, as in* skuld-u ist, is it lawful," and *uf* is "*prep. with dat. and acc.*"—that is, a preposition used with the dative and accusative cases. Usually he sticks to what he can demonstrate conclusively, but sometimes he makes informed speculation, as when he offers his thoughts on pronunciation: the letter *u*, he says, "is probably equivalent to *oo* in *cool*; or, if unaccented, to *oo* in *foot*."

Once his Gothic dictionary had shown that Skeat could manage serious lexicographic projects, he was ready for a vastly larger project: not just the 4,000 or so words used in the Gothic Gospels, but a much broader swath of the English language, nearly 14,000 words. Skeat insisted that English had no solid etymological dictionary. But what, we might ask, about Charles Richardson (no. 68)?—his *New Dictionary* (1836–1837) was still fairly recent, and it was obsessed with etymology, to the point at which it nearly crowded the definitions out. Skeat diplomatically praised Richardson's *Dictionary* as "an admirable store-house of quotations illustrating such words as are of no great antiquity in the language." His etymologies, though, were worse than

"The present work was undertaken with the intention of furnishing students with materials for a more scientific study of English etymology than is commonly found in previous works upon the subject." (*Etymological Dictionary* [pictured below], p. v.)

Ex coll. Karolyne & Bryan A. Garner

"When real words are cited [in various works], they are wrongly explained. Thus, in Todd's Johnson [no. 52], we find a derivation of *bond* from A.S. '*bond*, bound.' Now *bond* is not strictly Anglo-Saxon, but an Early English form, signifying 'a band,' and is not a past participle at all; the A.S. for 'bound' being *gebunden*. The error is easily traced." (P. viii.)

Ex coll. Karolyne & Bryan A. Garner

"The science of philology is comparatively modern, so that our earlier writers had no means of ascertaining principles that are now well established, and, instead of proceeding by rule, had to go blindly by guesswork, thus sowing crops of errors which have sprung up and multiplied till it requires very careful investigation to enable a modern writer to avoid all the pitfalls prepared for him by the false suggestions which he meets with at every turn." (P. viii.)

Ex coll. Karolyne & Bryan A. Garner

A 1912 volume.

useless, and Skeat didn't beat around the bush: "it would probably be difficult to find a worse philologist than Richardson." (*Etymological Dictionary*, p. v.) All the work had to be done again, in keeping with the best principles of historical lexicography.

Fortunately, Skeat had access to archives of the Philological Society. He used the material that had been collected for the *OED*, and he apprised Murray and his team of his findings while they were still compiling the dictionary. Skeat's *Etymological Dictionary of the English Language* (1879–1882), created in a symbiotic relationship with the *OED*, remains useful today. Because it was too big for student use, Skeat also prepared a *Concise* version. By reducing the book's trim size, the density of the typography, and the number of pages, and letting symbols and abbreviations take the place of some of the discursive etymologies, he managed to whittle it to about 60% of its original size.

The *Dictionary* is jam-packed with erudition, as in this typical entry:

> **Mother** (1) a female parent. (E.) M.E. *moder*. A.S. *móder*, *módor*, a mother; the change from *d* to *th* seems due to Scand. influence. †Du. *moeder*, Icel. *móðir*, Dan. Swed. *moder*, G. *mutter*, Irish and Gael. *mathair*, Russ. *mate*, Lithuan. *moté*, L. *mater*, G. μήτηρ, Skt. *mátá*, *mátri*. β. All formed with Aryan suffix *-tar* (of the agent) from √MA, orig. to measure; cf. Skt. *má*, to measure. Orig. sense uncertain; prob. 'manager' of the household.

Much is going on here. "E." tells us that the word's history is to be found within English, rather than being a recent borrowing from another language, with "M.E." and "A.S." indicating the Middle English and "Anglo-Saxon" (Old English) phases. The dagger or obelus (†) indicates cognate words, those that share ancestry with English words without being in the same line of descent—linguistic aunts, uncles, and cousins rather than parents or children. Here we're told that languages as diverse as Dutch, Icelandic, Danish, Swedish, Irish, Russian, Lithuanian, Latin, Greek, and Sanskrit have related forms. He then dives deep into the "Aryan" prehistory—we'd say Proto-Indo-European—tracing *mother* to the root (√) *ma* "to measure" combined with the suffix *-tar*, giving us something like "measurer." (Not all of Skeat's speculations have held up in the light of subsequent research. It's now believed that *mother* comes from "the baby-talk form *ma*" with the "kinship term suffix" *-ter*.)

Skeat knew Latin, Greek, and the usual modern European languages expected of the Victorian learned class, and specialized in the Germanic languages. Still, he was able to track down English words with very different origins. He includes *soy* from Japanese, *tea* from Chinese, *messiah* from Hebrew, *myrrh* from Arabic, *caftan* from Turkish, *ghoul* from Persian, *pariah* from Tamil, *bamboo* from Malay, *pundit* from Sanskrit, and *moose* from Algonquian.

Skeat gets the credit for coining a particularly colorful bit of lexicographic jargon. He began a paper he delivered to the Philological Society in May 1886 by citing Noah Webster's *American Dictionary* (1828) under *abacot*, defined as "The cap of State, formerly used by English Kings, wrought into the figure of two crowns." The word was found in a 16th-century text, and for generations it had been copied from one dictionary to another. It turns out, though, that the word was a 16th-century typo, a lapsus calami that was meant to be *bycoket* "a cap." *Abacot* never existed. "As it is convenient to have a short name for words of this character," Skeat told the Philological Society, "I shall take leave to call them 'ghost-words.' Like ghosts, we may seem to see them, or may fancy that they exist; but they have no real entity. We cannot grasp them; when we would do so, they disappear." (Skeat 1887:352.) In his lecture, Skeat identified dozens of these ghosts, most of which had begun life either as typos or as a typesetter's misreading of someone's handwriting. He saw the ghost-word *kime* where it should read *knife*, *reuk* where it should read *renk*, *punniten* where it should read *permuten*, *couuen* where it should read *connen*, *rentfull* where it should read *reufull*. All had appeared in dictionaries and, once something makes its way into a dictionary, it can be copied by one lexicographer after another until the crack of doom. Skeat did what he could to lay these ghosts to rest. (For two more-recent instances of ghost-words, see pp. 296 and 374.)

Upon Skeat's death in 1912, one obituarist noted that "all through his life he devoted himself to the public, particularly to their philological knowledge, and in him we miss a scholar and a ready reference at all times on that and other subjects." (*Miscellanea Genealogica et Heraldica* 5:185 [1914].) Another called him "the most famous English scholar of his generation," adding: "It is good to think that he lived to see the fruit of his labours, and that he died in the midst of them." (*Notes and Queries* [11th ser.] 6:299–300 [1912].)

Ex coll. Karolyne & Bryan A. Garner

A 1901 volume.

"It is many years since a new and comprehensive dictionary was first planned by the Philological Society, and we have now good hope that, under the able editorship of Dr. Murray, some portion of this great work may ere long see the light." (P. vi.)

Ex coll. Karolyne & Bryan A. Garner

84

James A.H. Murray

Compulsive Correspondent

IN 2022, A PILOT EDITION of the correspondence of James Augustus Henry Murray (1837–1915) was published as a website called "The Murray Scriptorium" (murrayscriptorium.org). It contains an edited selection of letters from the vast holdings in the Murray Papers of the Bodleian Library, in the Archives of Oxford University Press, and in several collections beyond Oxford, including the Garner Collection. All relate to the creation of the *Oxford English Dictionary* and to the professional and personal life of its principal editor. The Murray Scriptorium publishes open-access, fully edited copies of Murray's correspondence (and when relevant his other papers) to enable researchers, educators, and readers beyond academia to explore the foundations of the *Oxford English Dictionary*.

Murray estimated that he received 30 to 40 letters a day at the beginning of his editorship, when he was at Mill Hill School, declining within three years to about 60 a week when he was at Sunnyside (78 Banbury Road), his home in Oxford. After the move to Oxford in January 1885, Murray was sending so many letters that the Post Office, for Murray's convenience, installed a pillar box just outside Sunnyside. It's still in service.

"It is worth remembering that all of [Murray's] correspondence had to be written by hand; and that the letters had, what is more, to be written twice.... Murray... preferred the tribulations of simply writing everything out once again, of making a fair copy." (Winchester 2003:147.)

Decades later, in a lecture to the London Institution in 1910, Murray described his range of correspondents:

> I write to the Director of the Royal Botanic Gardens at Kew about the first record of the name of an exotic plant; to a quay-side merchant at Newcastle about the *keels* on the Tyne; to a Jesuit father on a point of Roman Catholic Divinity; to the Secretary of the Astronomical Society about the primum mobile or the solar constant; to the India Office about a letter of the year 1620 containing the first mention of *Punch*; to a Wesleyan minister about the itineracy; to Lord Tennyson to ask where he got the word *balm-cricket* and what he meant by it.... In fact a lexicographer if he wants to be accurate, has to be a universal enquirer about everything under the Sun, and over it. [Gilliver 2016:268.]

Murray's actual Scriptorium (white structure at right), in the backyard of Sunnyside.

One of Murray's regular correspondents was his immediate predecessor, Frederick J. Furnivall. In an 1894 letter now in the Garner Collection, Murray demonstrated the detailed exactitude that he expected for his lexicography, as well as reflecting on staffing issues and the challenges of keeping up the momentum:

> 27 Nov. 1894
>
> Dear D[r]. Furnivall,
>
> The foot-note here appears to indicate that the phrase can be carried back to 1662. Could you get us the quot. of that date. I do not know what the *Rump* Collection means. *Devil* proves a most formidable article, the phrases being so many.
>
> I have got no one in Mr. Mitchell's place yet; and the struggle to keep the work going is very desperate.
>
> I have tried to get one of the Ladies who took a first class in English and Philology here, in which case I should also get a girl as junior clerkly assistant—but have been unsuccessful for the present, I regret to say.
>
> Yours very truly,
>
> J.A.H. Murray

The phrase discussed in the first paragraph is *when the devil is blind*, meaning "at a date infinitely remote." The illustrative quotation derives from an 1874 reprint of *Rump Songs* (1662), and its appearance in the *OED* suggests that Furnivall dutifully supplied the missing information: "**1662** *Rump Songs* (1874) I.9 But when this comes to passe, say the Devil is blind." (*OED1* 3:286.)

Another letter in the Garner Collection illustrates the irascible tone that occasionally could be found in the great lexicographer's correspondence. It was written in April 1901 to an American newspaper editor, perhaps at the *Baltimore Sun*. The year before, one James Brady wrote to that newspaper to challenge the conventional wisdom about ethnic identity, a favorite subject in turn-of-the-century American newspapers. He focused on "the name Anglo-Saxon, meaning a pure race of people," which was increasingly being used to describe Americans. Brady emphatically insisted that Americans could not be considered pure Anglo-Saxon—there is "one of English to 10 of other nationalities" in the country, which makes the term "sublimely ridiculous." Americans—he meant white Americans—are not predominantly English but "the descendants of the Celts, who, in all ages and at all times, know their rights as freemen and dare maintain

Ex coll. Karolyne & Bryan A. Garner

"Of the quotations actually used in *Dictionary* entries, only a small proportion (perhaps as low as 10 percent) were from the material collected by readers working under Coleridge's or Furnivall's direction—so that the declaration which appeared, at Furnivall's insistence, on the *Dictionary*'s title page, that it was 'founded mainly on the materials collected by the Philological Society' arguably overstates the part played by the Society." (Gilliver 2016:262.)

their rights." For that matter, even the English themselves could not claim pure Anglo-Saxon ancestry; they were "descended from Britons, Romans, Belgæ, Danes, Normans, etc."—they had lost whatever "racial purity" they might ever have possessed.

"Pen in hand, the words flowed easily, and one cannot doubt that he really enjoyed letter writing. One suspects that he must often have used attention to the pile of letters as an excuse for not beginning the grind of proof correcting and that it gave him satisfaction to feel he had achieved something positive. At least he had posted a dozen letters and had not to record at the end of the day that he had done absolutely nothing but wrestle unsuccessfully with an elusive definition." (Murray 1977:182.)

Murray was reluctantly drawn into the discussion by the newspaper editor. At the time, Murray was toiling through the entries from *H* to *K* in the *New English Dictionary*. Being a Celtic Scot himself, Murray was deeply learned in what was then known as Anglo-Saxon, and now usually called Old English. Amateur etymologists have long been the plague of serious lexicographers, and he responded testily to Brady in his response: "I am afraid I could not tell you whether 'the "idea" was before suggested,' unless I were to inquire at all the Lunatic Asylums of the world. And if we did find out that some other lunatic, in or out of some asylum, had on some occasion suggested 'the idea,' what would it matter?" These words take on an additional resonance when we remember that Murray had already befriended a "madman" confined to a "lunatic asylum"—he first met the prodigious *OED* contributor but troubled soul William Minor at Broadmoor Hospital in 1891. (Winchester 1998:176.)

Quarrels over *Anglo-Saxon* continue even today. The term's history is complex. Although variations on the term were used in the eighth to tenth centuries, it did not become widespread until a millennium later, when "race science" sought to identify the various groups in the human taxonomy. *Anglo-Saxon* became a favorite name for the "superior" strain of humanity. Those unsavory associations have intensified in recent years as white-supremacist hate groups have indulged in fantasies about descent from a "pure" race in the Middle Ages. Many professional students of the Middle Ages are appalled by this appropriation of their subject. The International Society of Anglo-Saxonists, a learned society of more than 500 members devoted to "the languages, literatures, arts, history, and material culture of the period," regretted that the term was being "used outside the field to describe those holding repugnant and racist views." They therefore took up the question whether it was worth preserving the name of their society. The debate grew heated, leading to angry exchanges and high-profile resignations. In September 2019, the membership voted to abandon "Anglo-Saxon," and the society was reborn as the International Society for the Study of Early Medieval England.

"He could not resist teaching: rather than throw a stupid letter in the wastepaper basket, he must show the writer why it was foolish. In 1880 a Mrs Pott sent him lengthy lists of words which she imagined were peculiar to the works of Francis Bacon, asking which other authors first used them. James wrote out a draft and then a fair copy of his reply, running to five octavo pages. He explained that it would take him three weeks to look for her words among the still only partly sorted dictionary slips, 'and with 15 years' work before me, 3 hours is more than I *ought* to spend on it.'" (Murray 1977:181.)

This turmoil was perhaps presaged in Murray's 1901 letter—as was the title of Winchester's book (and film) about Murray, *The Professor and the Madman*.

For more information on the nature and content of Murray's correspondence as a whole, see Brewer & Turton 2021.

"Murray was often regarded as a kind of public linguistic oracle to be consulted at will on matters of semantic nicety or phonetic indecision. Few, it seemed, were prepared to wait for the publication of the relevant fascicle for the answers to their questions. Instead they wrote directly to Murray, requesting conclusive opinions." (Mugglestone 2005:144.)

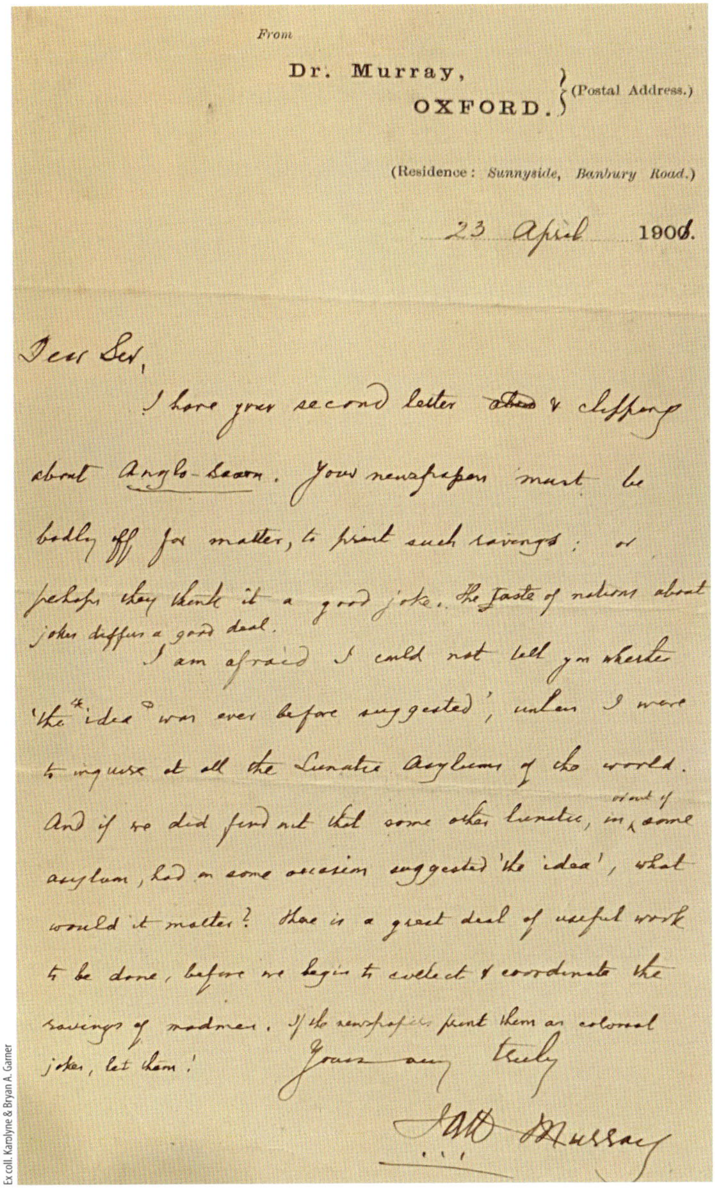

From

Dr. Murray, OXFORD. (Postal Address.)

(Residence: *Sunnyside, Banbury Road.*)

23 April 1901.

Dear Sir,

I have your second letter & clipping about Anglo-Saxon. Your newspaper must be badly off for matter, to print such ravings; or perhaps they think it a good joke. The taste of nations about jokes differs a good deal.

I am afraid I could not tell you whether 'the idea' was ever before suggested; unless I were to inquire at all the Lunatic Asylums of the world. And if we did find out that some other lunatic, in (out of) some asylum, had on some occasion suggested 'the idea', what would it matter? There is a great deal of useful work to be done, before we begin to collect & coordinate the ravings of madmen. If the newspapers print them as colossal jokes, let them!

Yours very truly

JAH Murray

Ex coll. Karolyne & Bryan A. Garner

The letter about *Anglo-Saxon*.

The mailbox installed on Banbury Road just outside James A.H. Murray's house.

"As [Murray] said, he could write to various specialists—as a geologist to Archibald Geikie, as a botanist to Thistleton Dyer, as an anatomist to Burdon Sanderson, as a chemist to Roscoe and Thorpe, and 'not as the man in the street merely.' . . . For proof, one need only look at the many letters, preserved in the archives of the Oxford University Press, from distinguished scientists writing to Murray in response to the various enquiries he had sent them." (Hoare & Salmon 2000:160.)

Ex coll. Karolyne & Bryan A. Garner

The New Revised (1897).

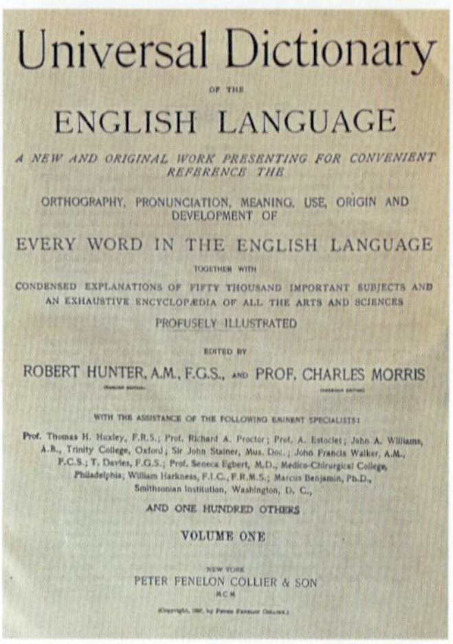

Universal Dictionary

OF THE

ENGLISH LANGUAGE

A NEW AND ORIGINAL WORK PRESENTING FOR CONVENIENT REFERENCE THE

ORTHOGRAPHY, PRONUNCIATION, MEANING, USE, ORIGIN AND DEVELOPMENT OF

EVERY WORD IN THE ENGLISH LANGUAGE

TOGETHER WITH

CONDENSED EXPLANATIONS OF FIFTY THOUSAND IMPORTANT SUBJECTS AND AN EXHAUSTIVE ENCYCLOPÆDIA OF ALL THE ARTS AND SCIENCES

PROFUSELY ILLUSTRATED

EDITED BY

ROBERT HUNTER, A.M., F.G.S., AND PROF. CHARLES MORRIS

WITH THE ASSISTANCE OF THE FOLLOWING EMINENT SPECIALISTS:

Prof. Thomas H. Huxley, F.R.S.; Prof. Richard A. Proctor; Prof. A. Estoclet; John A. Williams, A.B., Trinity College, Oxford; Sir John Stainer, Mus. Doc.; John Francis Walker, A.M., F.C.S.; T. Davies, F.G.S.; Prof. Seneca Egbert, M.D., Medico-Chirurgical College, Philadelphia; William Harkness, F.I.C., F.R.M.S.; Marcus Benjamin, Ph.D., Smithsonian Institution, Washington, D. C.,

AND ONE HUNDRED OTHERS

VOLUME ONE

NEW YORK

PETER FENELON COLLIER & SON

MCM

Ex coll. Karolyne & Bryan A. Garner

Ex coll. Karolyne & Bryan A. Garner

The Universal (1900).

85

Robert Hunter

Dictionary in Search of a Name

***The Encyclopædic Dictionary: A New and Original Work of Reference to All the Words in the English Language*. Robert Hunter ed. 7 vols. in 14 parts. London: Cassell & Co., 1879–1888. Various titles through 1911.**

ROBERT HUNTER (1823–1897) was born in Newburgh, Fife, and educated in Aberdeen at Marischal College, where he graduated with his MA in 1845. He became a Free Church missionary teacher in Bermuda and then India; in both places, he developed a fascination with natural history, geology, and paleontology. He left the Free Church in the mid-1860s—he couldn't take the required oath, with what he considered an objectionable statement about the creation—to became a Presbyterian minister. His earliest books were *The History of India* (1863) and *History of the Missions of the Free Church of Scotland in India and Africa* (1873).

Then, in his later years, he became a lexicographer. With the help of "scores of specialists," he produced the most exhaustive British dictionary before the *Oxford English Dictionary*, which was underway at the time. It first appeared in fascicles issued from 1879 to 1888. But over the next 23 years, in what might reflect difficulties in marketing on both sides of the Atlantic, the multivolume work came out under all sorts of titles, among them these:

- *Lloyd's Encyclopædic Dictionary: A New and Original Work of Reference to the Words in the English Language*. 7 vols. London: Edward Lloyd Ltd., 1895.
- *New Revised Encyclopædic Dictionary*. 4 vols. Boston: Newspaper Syndicate, 1897.
- *The American Dictionary and Cyclopedia*. 10 vols. New York: Dictionary & Cyclopedia Co., 1899.
- *Universal Dictionary of the English Language*. 4 vols. New York: Peter Fenelon Collier & Son, 1900.

- *The International Encyclopaedic Dictionary.* 6 vols. Akron, Ohio: D.H. McBride & Co., 1900.
- *The Modern Eclectic Dictionary of the English Language.* 6 vols. New York: P.F. Collier & Son, 1904.
- *The New American Encyclopedic Dictionary.* 10 vols. Chicago: Riverside Publishing Co., 1911.

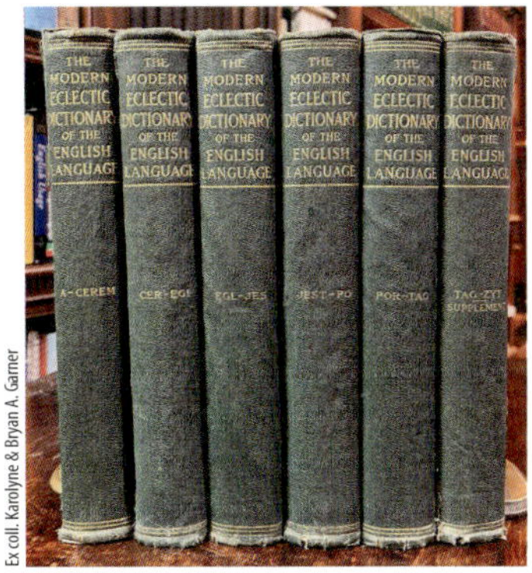

Ex coll. Karolyne & Bryan A. Garner

The Modern Eclectic (1904).

The contractual arrangements for these editions are unknown, and some may have been unauthorized.

Hunter's wordlist is vast—he included not only the common stock of vocabulary but many scientific and technical terms (*pimilepterina*, *pimelic*, *pimelite*, *pimeolodus* . . .) and, as the title promises, much encyclopedic information, as under *Pythagorism*:

> *Philos.*, *Astron.*, *&c.*: The system of belief attributed to Pythagoras, born in Samos about 540 B.C., his mother being a Samian and his father, it is believed, a Phœnician. After travelling in Egypt, Persia, &c., in question of knowledge, he settled in Croton . . . .

"In many respects the Encyclopædic Dictionary differs from its predecessors. In the first place, as its title implies, it is not an ordinary dictionary, in the sense of being a mere alphabetical list of the words composing our language, but it partakes also to a great extent of the character of an Encyclopædia. In fact it is professedly at the same time a dictionary and an encyclopædia." (*Lloyd's Encyclopædic Dictionary*, vol. 1, p. v.)

In his lexicography Hunter was an enthusiastic splitter, highlighting even illusory distinctions for subsenses. This sometimes took him into distinction-without-a-difference territory. Does anyone benefit, for instance, from all these distinct senses for the noun *hand*?

> (1) Performance, handiwork, workmanship. . . . (2) Power or capability of performance; skill. . . . (3) An act, a deed, that which is done. . . . (4) Action, labour; act of the hand; exertion. . . . (5) Manner of proceeding or action. . . . (6) Agency; part or share in acting or performing. . . . (7) Agency, medium. . . . (8) Side, direction, part. . . . (9) Part, quarter, side. . . . (10) Possession, power, control, management, superintendence. . . . (11) Advantage, gain, superiority. . . . (12) Influence, power, control. . . .

How is "An act, a deed" different from "Action, labour"? Is there really a difference between "Side, direction, part" and "Part, quarter, side"? Is "Possession, power, control" somehow separate from "Influence, power, control"? Critics noticed, as when a contemporary commentator wrote of his work: "Its definitions are too minutely divided. There is sometimes no difference at all in the senses distinguished." (Williams 1890:34.)

Ex coll. Karolyne & Bryan A. Garner

The American Encyclopedic (1911).

And yet the wordlist was the most comprehensive yet to appear in any English dictionary: *crenellation*, *crenelle*, *crenelled*, *crenelles*,

crengle, crenic, crenic acid, crenilabrus, crenulate, creole, creolian, creophilus, creosol, creosote, crepance, crepidoder, crepidula . . . . The mere existence of this book—with its 5,300 triple-columned pages—aided all the supersized rivals that were underway: the *Oxford English Dictionary* (no. 96), the *Century Dictionary* (no. 88), and *Webster's International Dictionary* (no. 89).

Despite their radically different titles and formats, the five dictionaries shown in this entry are essentially the same work by Hunter. What's in a name? Or . . .

Ex coll. Karolyne & Bryan A. Garner

Lloyd's Encyclopædic (1895).

86

Mark Twain

What's in a Nom de Plume?

April 1883 ALS from Mark Twain to John Bellows, a lexicographer living in Gloucester, England. Three-page letter.

If you use a pseudonym and are drawn to Gallicisms, how do you know whether to call your fictitious name a *nom de plume* or a *nom de guerre*? Both terms are in the dictionaries—even English dictionaries. If you're Mark Twain (1835–1910), you might find the opportunity when the publisher of a bilingual French–English dictionary sends you a promotional copy. That's exactly what happened in 1883, thereby occasioning both a hilarious Twain letter and a funny Twain short story. Here's the letter, which was acquired by the Garner Collection at a 2004 Sotheby's auction:

> Hartford, Conn., Apl. 11/83
>
> Dear Mr. Bellows—
>
> Through my publisher on this side & yours on the other, I have received your note recently written to the latter; & in reply I hasten to shout that I shall be very glad indeed to receive a copy of your book, for Mrs. Clemens will not allow me to keep hers in my study, & somebody long ago stole my own copy—our pastor, I think, who was probably beguiled by its pious aspect. And when you send it, I wish you would write on the fly-leaf why it is that you & the other authorities ignore "*nom de plume*." Is it a vulgarism? is it slang? I suspect it. And is *nom de guerre* the correct thing? But wait—you ignore that, also. That is, I *think* you do—can't go to the bedroom to look, because then I should have to explain why I am sitting up enjoying myself so late to-night; & I would rather tell seven lies than make one explanation.
>
> Faithfully Yours,
>
> Mark Twain
>
> née S.L. Clemens.

Yes, he wrote *née*—not *né*.

Ex coll. Karolyne & Bryan A. Garner

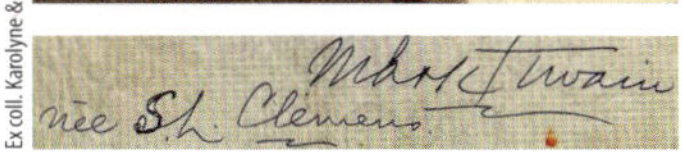

Ex coll. Karolyne & Bryan A. Garner

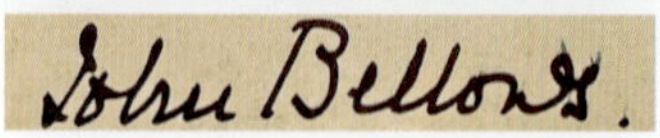

Ex coll. Karolyne & Bryan A. Garner

In later editions of his dictionary, Bellows noted *nom de guerre* as meaning "pseudonym: fictitious." Then: "*Nom de plume* is rarely used in French." Yet Bellows and his family seem not to have been fond of Twain's reference to his "pious aspect": in *John Bellows: Letters and Memoir* (Elizabeth Bellows ed.; London: Headley Bros., 1905), Twain is nowhere mentioned.

Yet Twain wrote about Bellows in a passage just barely "crowded out" of his 1880 book *A Tramp Abroad*, but included in a less-well-known 1896 collection: "When the minister gets up to preach, he finds his house full of devout foreigners, each ready and waiting, with his little book in his hand—a morocco-bound Testament, apparently. But only apparently; it is Mr. Bellows's admirable and exhaustive little French-English dictionary, which in look and binding and size is just like a Testament and those people are there to study French. The building has been nicknamed 'The Church of the Gratis French Lesson.'" (Twain, "Paris Notes," in *Tom Sawyer Abroad, Tom Sawyer, Detective, and Other Stories* [New York: Harper & Bros., 1896], pp. 348–49.) Hence the letter bears a literary connection to one of Twain's minor short stories. Which is to say that the strategy of Bellows's having his publisher send a copy of his dictionary to Twain paid off, if only obscurely.

Ex coll. Karolyne & Bryan A. Garner

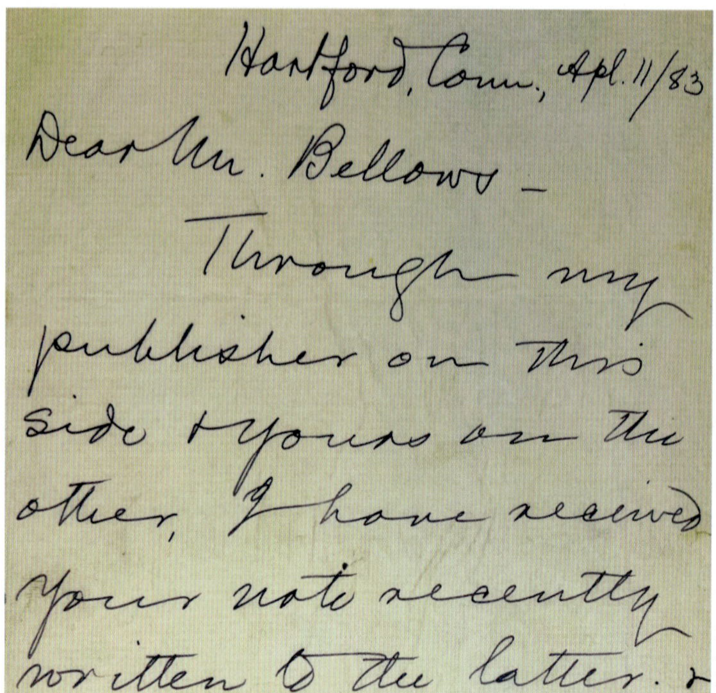

Hartford, Conn., Apl. 11/83

Dear Mr. Bellows—

Through my publisher on this side & yours on the other, I have received your note recently written to the latter; &

Ex coll. Karolyne & Bryan A. Garner

87

Henry Sweet

Touches of Henry Higgins

***The Epinal Glossary, Latin and Old-English of the Eighth Century*. Henry Sweet ed., with W. Griggs. London: Trübner & Co., 1883.**

HENRY SWEET (1845–1912) described himself as "of mixed West-of-England and Frisian parentage on father's side, of mixed Lowland Scotch and Scotch Highland parentage on mother's side." Despite terrible eyesight from youth, Sweet was a passionate reader, and he taught himself Old English and Old Icelandic.

Sweet was destined to become a philologist, and since many of the best philologists in Europe were trained in Germany, he enrolled at the University of Heidelberg in 1863. But he stayed only briefly, returning to London to work for a few years in his uncle's London law firm.

It was odd that someone so learned should have no university degree, so Sweet matriculated at Balliol College in Oxford in 1869, where he studied classics under Benjamin Jowett. Although his academic performance was disappointing—he received only fourth-class honors, a category not even recognized as honors at Oxford today—he was already making a name for himself as one of the great scholars of the Germanic languages. While still an undergraduate he published an edition of an Old English text, the *Liber Regulae Pastoralis*, written by Pope Gregory around 590 and translated by King Alfred the Great in the late ninth century.

Sweet developed connections to the larger philological scholarly world. On three occasions he read papers before the Philological Society, and he would go on to serve as the society's president, in which role he provided guidance on what became the *Oxford English Dictionary*. He was active, too, in the Early English Text Society, founded in 1864, producing annotated scholarly editions of Old and Middle English works. Without the EETS, there would be no *OED*.

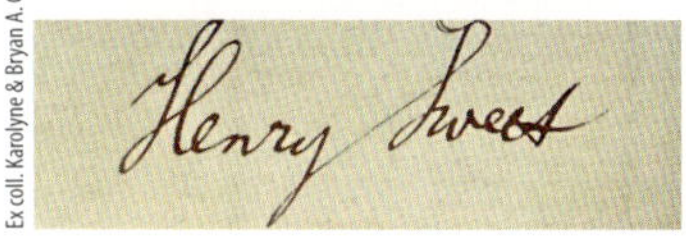

Ex coll. Karolyne & Bryan A. Garner

Ex coll. Karolyne & Bryan A. Garner

With a trim size of 17 x 13½ inches, *The Epinal Glossary* easily had the largest format of Sweet's many books. The large pages made facsimile pages possible, so that readers could examine reproductions of the original manuscripts.

"The fundamental distinction between a dictionary and a cyclopedia is, that the dictionary has to explain *words*, the cyclopedia has to explain *things*." (Sweet 1900:142.)

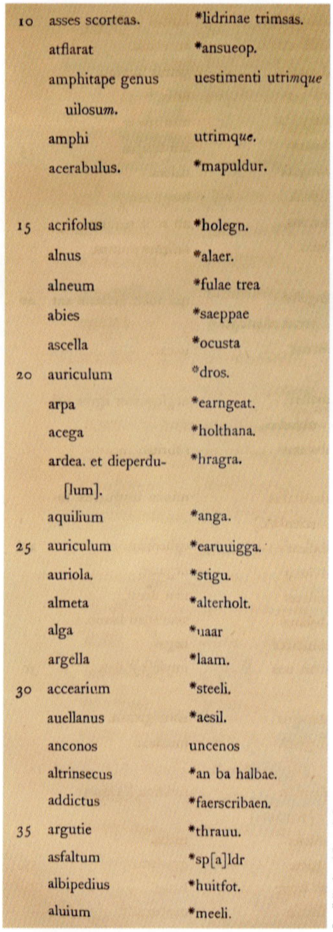

asses scorteas.	*lidrinae trimsas.
atflarat	*ansueop.
amphitape genus uilosum.	uestimenti utrimque
amphi	utrimque.
acerabulus.	*mapuldur.
acrifolus	*holegn.
alnus	*alaer.
alneum	*fulae trea
abies	*saeppae
ascella	*ocusta
auriculum	*dros.
arpa	*earngeat.
acega	*holthana.
ardea. et dieperdu-[lum].	*hragra.
aquilium	*anga.
auriculum	*earuuigga.
auriola.	*stigu.
almeta	*alterholt.
alga	*uaar
argella	*laam.
accearium	*steeli.
auellanus	*aesil.
anconos	uncenos
altrinsecus	*an ba halbae.
addictus	*faerscribaen.
argutie	*thrauu.
asfaltum	*sp[a]ldr
albipedius	*huitfot.
aluium	*meeli.

Ex coll. Karolyne & Bryan A. Garner

Detail from Sweet's p. 2.

"The first business of a dictionary is to give the meanings of the words in plain, simple, unambiguous language." (Sweet 1900:148.)

The Epinal Glossary is one of these EETS titles, and one with particular importance in the history of dictionaries. Sometimes called the *Glossaire d'Épinal* or the *Épinal-Erfurt Glossary*, it was written around the year 700, making it one of the earliest surviving Old English texts of any sort. After being forgotten for most of a millennium, the language was being rediscovered in the early 19th century. Sweet arranged to borrow the manuscript in 1879 and, at the request of James A.H. Murray, then president of the Philological Society, raised money to secure a photolithographic reproduction, still an expensive proposition. His mission was simply "to give a correct text of this precious linguistic document." (P. iii) Sweet's text remained the standard edition until 1988, when a team of scholars—Bernhard Bischoff, Mildred Budny, Geoffrey Harlow, M.B. Parkes, and J.D. Pfeifer—gave it much more thorough treatment as volume 22 of *Early English Manuscripts in Facsimile* ("The Épinal, Erfurt, Werden, and Corpus Glossaries").

Written nearly 750 years before Gutenberg, *The Epinal Glossary* is a reminder that English-language lexicography is much older than the printed book in the West. As an aid for English speakers struggling with Latin vocabulary, the glossary pairs Latin words with English translations. Latin *anser* "goose," for instance, is glossed by English *goos*, Latin *boreus* "northeast wind" by English *eastnorþwind*, Latin *cartilaga* "cartilage" by English *naesgristlae* (literally "nose-gristle"), Latin *capsis* "trunk" by English *cest* (the origin of "chest"), Latin *cerus* "stag" by English *elch* (the origin of *elk*), and so on.

Sweet carefully described the Epinal manuscript and its relation to five other Old English manuscript glossaries. He hypothesized that the glossary's ultimate source "must be sought in interlinear and marginal glosses in Latin books" (p. vi)—that is, someone added English words between the lines or in the margins of Latin manuscripts, and later copied them in one place.

Incidentally, *The Epinal Glossary* captures an important phase in the history of alphabetical order. Though the alphabet has had an order at least since biblical times, hardly anyone made use of it to organize information until surprisingly late. But *The Epinal Glossary* uses what's known as *a*-order alphabetization. As Sweet explained: "It consists in simply throwing the words together under their initial letter, without further alphabetical arrangement" (p. vi): *am-* comes before *ax-*, which comes before *ar-*, which comes before *an-*. The

Latin words are subjected to this *a*-order alphabetization, so in a typical stretch of entries we see *mustacia*, *manticum*, *mascus*, *modernos*, *mergulus*, *marsopicus*. Other manuscripts derived from the same Old English source introduce *ab*-order, paying attention to the first two letters of each word, though, as Sweet observed, "None of them has got so far as the strict *abc*- order of our modern dictionaries." (P. vi.)

"The main function of a dictionary is to give the meanings of separate words. Some dictionaries confine themselves strictly to this function. But a dictionary which does not sacrifice everything to giving as large a vocabulary as possible in the shortest space ought to give a good deal more than this." (Sweet 1900:140.)

For years, Sweet remained in Oxford, supporting himself with a bit of family money and the revenue from writing and taking on the occasional private student. Finally, at the age of 56, he was appointed to an Oxford readership in phonetics.

Those who knew Sweet described his grouchy demeanor and noted that he had, or at least kept, few friends. The phonetician M.K.C. MacMahon described him as "a solitary and fairly lonely man." (*ODNB*.) But he had a playful side, as described in his 1905 *Who's Who* entry, which listed his recreations:

> climbing, gardening, chemistry, alphabets in boyhood; swimming, skating, European languages and literatures in youth; riding, fishing, cycling, literary controversy, spelling and university reform, oriental languages and literatures in middle age; sociology, spiritualism, music, literary composition in old age—looks forward to flying.

By "flying," as Sweet would later clarify, he meant airplanes, not hot-air balloons.

Ex coll. Karolyne & Bryan A. Garner

Some other Sweet titles.

Strange as it sounds for an uncharismatic expert in English phonology to achieve celebrity, Sweet was sufficiently well known to inspire one of the most enduring literary characters of the early 20th century, *Pygmalion*'s Henry Higgins. "Higgins is not a portrait of Sweet," George Bernard Shaw clarified in his preface; "still, as will be seen, there are touches of Sweet in the play."

"The greatest drawback to the use of a dictionary is bulkiness. The mere physical labour of pulling volume after volume of a big dictionary off the shelf and then replacing them is alone enough to deter the student from the attempt to utilize the material stored up in them." (Sweet 1900:146.)

Sweet died in 1912. A year later his student Henry Cecil Kennedy Wyld (see no. 98) published 23 of Sweet's "best and most original" short works, including one he wrote before he even began his undergraduate degree. (Sweet 1913.) His *Student's Dictionary of Anglo-Saxon* (1897) remained in print well into the late 20th century, and his *Anglo-Saxon Reader in Prose and Verse* (1876) was published in a new edition as recently as 2016. He remains a living presence in Old English studies. The Henry Sweet Society for the History of Linguistic Ideas, founded in 1984, is a thriving organization with its home at the Dublin Institute for Advanced Studies.

Ex coll. Karolyne & Bryan A. Garner

88

William Dwight Whitney
Lexicographic Centurion

***The Century Dictionary and Encyclopedic Lexicon of the English Language*. William Dwight Whitney chief ed. 6 vols. in 24. New York: Century Co., 1889–1891.**

In 1882, the Century Company of New York published the four-volume *Imperial Dictionary* of the Scotsman John Ogilvie (1797–1867)—a work that had been revised by Noah Porter in the early 1850s. By this time, Porter had moved on to become chief editor of Merriam's Webster dictionaries (no. 80). In any event, in both the American market and the British market, Ogilvie's work had little cachet.

So the corporate leaders at the Century Company—including, as of 1890, Noah Webster's grandson William Webster Ellsworth—decided to embark on a major American dictionary, using the *Imperial* as its starting point. The project was the brainchild of William Dwight Whitney (1827–1894), the linguist and Sanskrit scholar at Yale University, who led the project. At Noah Porter's instance, Whitney had already contributed to *Webster-Mahn* (no. 80). And he had already written *Language and the Study of Language* (1867), *Oriental and Linguistic Studies* (1874), *The Life and Growth of Language* (1875), and *Sanskrit Grammar* (1879).

To help on the project, Whitney recruited his two brothers, Josiah D. Whitney, a geologist of Harvard University, and Henry M. Whitney, an English professor of Beloit College. He also enlisted the celebrated linguist Thomas R. Lounsbury of Yale University to work on entries with a Middle English component. With a managing editor (Benjamin E. Smith), 7 editorial assistants, and 30 subject specialists, the staff was somewhat more modest than its contemporary G. & C. Merriam's staff. Yet the results were equally impressive, and maybe more so.

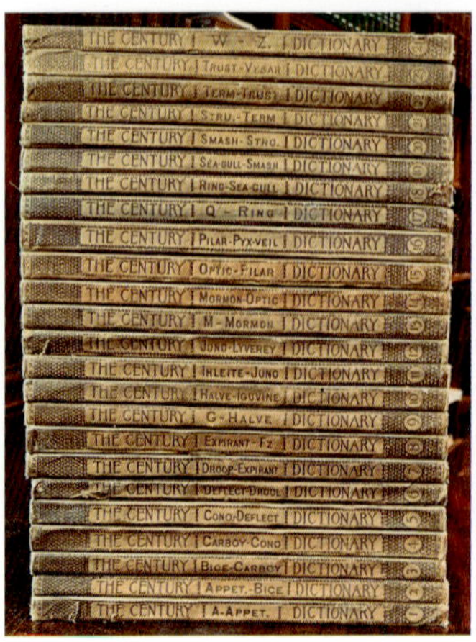

Ex coll. Karolyne & Bryan A. Garner

The 24 fascicles in which the first edition was released.

In the 11-page preface, Whitney explained that the plan of the work was threefold: (1) to construct a general dictionary of the English language that will be "serviceable for every literary and practical use"; (2) to collect more completely the technical terms of the various sciences, arts, trades, and professions than has yet been attempted; and (3) to add to the definitions proper enough encyclopedic matter, including pictorial illustrations, that will make a convenient book of general reference. Along the way, Whitney made some astute observations about lexicography:

- "The first duty of a comprehensive dictionary is collection, not selection. When a full account of the language is sought, every omission of a genuine English form, even when practically necessary, is so far a defect; and it is therefore better to err on the side of broad inclusiveness than of narrow exclusiveness." (P. v.)
- "Even slang must be noticed by the lexicographer who desires to portray the language in its natural and full outlines, and these phases of English have therefore been treated with liberality." (P. vi.)
- "No English dictionary, however, can well include every word or every form of a word. . . . Words and forms discoverable in the literature of all periods of the language, in the various dialects, and in colloquial use . . . have no practical claim upon the notice of the lexicographer." (*Id.*)
- "There are . . . two distinct groups of forms in the etymologies: those in the line of derivation or direct descent, and those in the lines of cognation or collateral descent. A Greek word, for example, may occur not only in Anglo-Saxon (and English), but also in . . . other tongues, and the full account of the English form requires the mention of the most important of these other forms as 'parallel with' or 'equal to' the Anglo-Saxon and English." (P. viii.)
- "Of the great body of words constituting the familiar language the spelling is determined by well-established usage, and . . . it is not the office of a dictionary like this to propose improvements, or to adopt those which have been proposed." (*Id.*)
- "Still greater than the variation in the orthography, even the accepted orthography, of English words, is the variation in the pronunciation. And here the same general principles must govern the usage of the dictionary. No attempt is made to record all the varieties of popular, or even of

Ex coll. Karolyne & Bryan A. Garner

The 1897 edition, with two "new volumes"—the top two here—which were issued in 1909.

Ex coll. Karolyne & Bryan A. Garner

The 1911 edition.

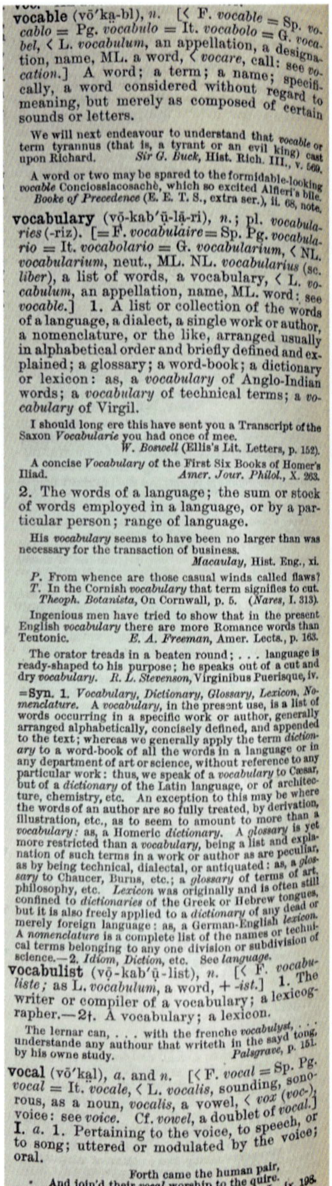

vocable (vō'ka-bl), *n.* [< F. *vocable* = Sp. *vocablo* = Pg. *vocabulo* = It. *vocabolo* = G. *vocabel*, < L. *vocabulum*, an appellation, a designation, name, ML. a word, < *vocare*, call: see *vocation*.] A word; a term; a name; specifically, a word considered without regard to meaning, but merely as composed of certain sounds or letters.

We will next endeavour to understand that *vocable* or term tyrannus (that is, a tyrant or an evil king) cast upon Richard. *Sir G. Buck*, Hist. Rich. III., v. 569.

A word or two may be spared to the formidable-looking *vocable* Conciossiacosachè, which so excited Alfieri's bile. *Booke of Precedence* (E. E. T. S., extra ser.), ii. 68, note.

vocabulary (vō-kab'ū-lā-ri), *n.*; pl. *vocabularies* (-riz). [= F. *vocabulaire* = Sp. Pg. *vocabulario* = It. *vocabolario* = G. *vocabularium*, < NL. *vocabularium*, neut., ML. NL. *vocabularius* (sc. *liber*), a list of words, a vocabulary, < L. *vocabulum*, an appellation, name, ML. word: see *vocable*.] 1. A list or collection of the words of a language, a dialect, a single work or author, a nomenclature, or the like, arranged usually in alphabetical order and briefly defined and explained; a glossary; a word-book; a dictionary or lexicon: as, a *vocabulary* of Anglo-Indian words; a *vocabulary* of technical terms; a *vocabulary* of Virgil.

I should long ere this have sent you a Transcript of the Saxon *Vocabularie* you had once of mee. *W. Boswell* (Ellis's Lit. Letters, p. 152).

A concise *Vocabulary* of the First Six Books of Homer's Iliad. *Amer. Jour. Philol.*, X. 263.

2. The words of a language; the sum or stock of words employed in a language, or by a particular person; range of language.

His *vocabulary* seems to have been no larger than was necessary for the transaction of business. *Macaulay*, Hist. Eng., xi.

P. From whence are those casual winds called flaws? *T.* In the Cornish *vocabulary* that term signifies to cut. *Theoph. Botanista*, On Cornwall, p. 5. (*Nares*, I. 313).

Ingenious men have tried to show that in the present English *vocabulary* there are more Romance words than Teutonic. *E. A. Freeman*, Amer. Lects., p. 163.

The orator treads in a beaten round; . . . language is ready-shaped to his purpose; he speaks out of a cut and dry *vocabulary*. *R. L. Stevenson*, Virginibus Puerisque, iv.

=**Syn.** 1. *Vocabulary, Dictionary, Glossary, Lexicon, Nomenclature.* A *vocabulary*, in the present use, is a list of words occurring in a specific work or author, generally arranged alphabetically, concisely defined, and appended to the text; whereas we generally apply the term *dictionary* to a word-book of all the words in a language or in any department of art or science, without reference to any particular work: thus, we speak of a *vocabulary* to Cæsar, but of a *dictionary* of the Latin language, or of architecture, chemistry, etc. An exception to this may be where the words of an author are so fully treated, by derivation, illustration, etc., as to seem to amount to more than a *vocabulary*: as, a Homeric *dictionary*. A *glossary* is yet more restricted than a *vocabulary*, being a list and explanation of such terms in a work or author as are peculiar, as by being technical, dialectal, or antiquated: as, a *glossary* to Chaucer, Burns, etc.; a *glossary* of terms of art, philosophy, etc. *Lexicon* was originally and is often still confined to *dictionaries* of the Greek or Hebrew tongues, but it is also freely applied to a *dictionary* of any dead or merely foreign language: as, a German-English *lexicon*. A *nomenclature* is a complete list of the names or technical terms belonging to any one division or subdivision of science.—2. *Idiom, Diction*, etc. See *language*.

vocabulist (vō-kab'ū-list), *n.* [< F. *vocabuliste*; as L. *vocabulum*, a word, + *-ist*.] 1. The writer or compiler of a vocabulary; a lexicographer.—2†. A vocabulary; a lexicon.

The lernar can, . . . with the frenche *vocabulyst*, . . . understande any authour that writeth in the sayd tong, by his owne study. *Palsgrave*, p. 151.

vocal (vō'kal), *a.* and *n.* [< F. *vocal* = Sp. Pg. *vocal* = It. *vocale*, < L. *vocalis*, sounding, sonorous, as a noun, *vocalis*, a vowel, < *vox* (*voc-*), voice: see *voice*. Cf. *vowel*, a doublet of *vocal*.] I. *a.* 1. Pertaining to the voice, to speech, or to song; uttered or modulated by the voice; oral.

Forth came the human pair,
And join'd their *vocal* worship to the quire.
Milton, P. L., ix. 198.

Ex coll. Karolyne & Bryan A. Garner

educated, utterance, or to report the determinations made by different recognized authorities. It has been necessary, rather, to make a selection of words to which alternative pronunciations should be accorded, and to give preference among these according to the circumstances of each particular case." (P. ix.)

- "The attempt has been made to portray the language as it actually is, separating more or less sharply those senses of each word which are really distinct, but avoiding that over-refinement of analysis which tends rather to confusion than to clearness." (P. xi.)
- "Many thousands of words have . . . been gathered which have never before been recorded in a general dictionary, or even in special glossaries. Their definitions are intended to be so precise as to be of service to the specialist, and, also, to be simple and 'popular' enough to be intelligible to the layman." (P. xii.)

In something of a break from recent lexicographic tradition, the *Century*'s treatment of terms was unapologetically encyclopedic: "Not only have many technical matters been treated with unusual fullness, but much practical information of a kind which dictionaries have hitherto excluded has been added. The result is that *The Century Dictionary* covers to a great extent the field of the ordinary encyclopedia." (P. xv.) But there was a principal difference: "The information given is for the most part distributed under the individual words and phrases with which it is connected, instead of [as in an encyclopedia] being collected under a few general topics." (*Id.*) On a single page there are long encyclopedic entries for *mortar*[1] ("The chief use of mortars now is in the preparation of drugs. Mortars are made of hard and heavy wood . . ."), *mortar*[2] ("The use of mortar dates back to the earliest recorded history, but various materials were employed for that purpose. 'Bitumen' (asphaltum and maltha) or bituminous mixtures . . ."), and *mortgage* ("mortgages ceased to be regarded in most jurisdictions as a transfer of the title, and are now generally held to create a mere lien").

The definitions are detailed and often minutely discriminated; the polysemous verb *put* gets seven columns to cover 13 main meanings and dozens of subsenses and phrases. Illustrative quotations—drawn from English and American sources from the 14th century to the late 19th, but leaning heavily on the same 17th- and 18th-century British authors that Johnson used in 1755—show the words in use. Whitney believed that his team had assembled a storehouse of quotations second only to that of the *OED*. The etymologies were thorough—often extravagant—but generally sound, in keeping with the best thinking on language change at the end of the 19th century:

> **five** (fīv), *a.* and *n.* [< ME. *five*, earlier *fif*, < A.S. *fīf*, rarely with pl. term. *fīfe* = OS. OFries. *fīf* = MLG. *vīf*, LG *fīf* = D. *fijf* = OHG. *finf*, *fimf*, *funf*, MHG. *vunf*, *vünf*, G. *fünf* = Icel. *fimm* = Sw. Dan. *fem* = Goth. *fimf* = L. *quinque* (for **pinque*) (> It. *cinque* = Sp. Pg. *cinco* = Pr. *cinc* = F. *cinq*) = Oscan *pomtis* = W. *pump* = OIr *cōic*, mod. Ir. *cūig* = Gael *cōig*, *cūig* = Gr. πεντε, dial. πεμπε = Lith. *penki* = Lett. *peezi* = OBulg. *peⁿtĭ* = Slov. *peti* = Bohem. *paty* = Serv. *peti* = Pol. *piaty* = Russ. *pyati* = Skt. *pancha*, five (whence ult. E. *punch*[4], q. v.). Hence *fifth*, *fifty*, etc.]

Ex coll. Karolyne & Bryan A. Garner

Two copies of the enormous single-volume *Century* (1914) bound in corduroy. The 3 x 5 catalogue card gives an indication of its size.

The *Century* was first issued in 24 fascicles that were to make up six full volumes. Because the work was completed in 1891, while the *OED* was still working on the letter *C*, it proved a tremendous boon to James A.H. Murray and his fellow editors, who could consult the *Century* as they progressed through the alphabet.

In 1901—seven years after Whitney's death—an advertisement for the work proclaimed: "Over 155,000 sets of *The Century Dictionary & Cyclopedia & Atlas* have been sold thus far, and it is safe to say that these volumes, which, in most cases, are at the disposal of whole families, or schools, or offices—are consulted A MILLION TIMES A DAY!" The ad writers insisted that those who purchased the dictionary had gained admission to an institution of higher learning: "The Great College of America is this College in the Home. It has a larger membership than the sum of all the English-speaking universities, for it is composed of 'Century' Students, and the Class of 1902 is now forming."

Ex coll. Karolyne & Bryan A. Garner

Front cover of 34-page brochure advertising the one-volume *Century Dictionary*. Notice the folding spine.

In 1914, a special one-volume version was produced on ultra-thin India paper, with corduroy covers. It was made to lie flat, with a highly flexible spine that would form itself into an upside-down *U*. It was undoubtedly the thickest one-volume dictionary ever produced.

The *Century* suffered a slow demise. It was revived in the early 1950s as a two-volume abridgment, and later in the decade as a loose-leaf dictionary. But by then, it had been commercially eclipsed. The historical materials had been superseded by the *OED*, and the abridged materials had been bested by Merriam-Webster. The dictionary market no longer had a place for the *Century*. Yet it was the greatest historical dictionary ever produced by Americans, and its early incarnations were a marvel not only of classic dictionary elements (etymologies, definitions, illustrations) but also of typography.

Ex coll. Karolyne & Bryan A. Garner

The 1895 edition.

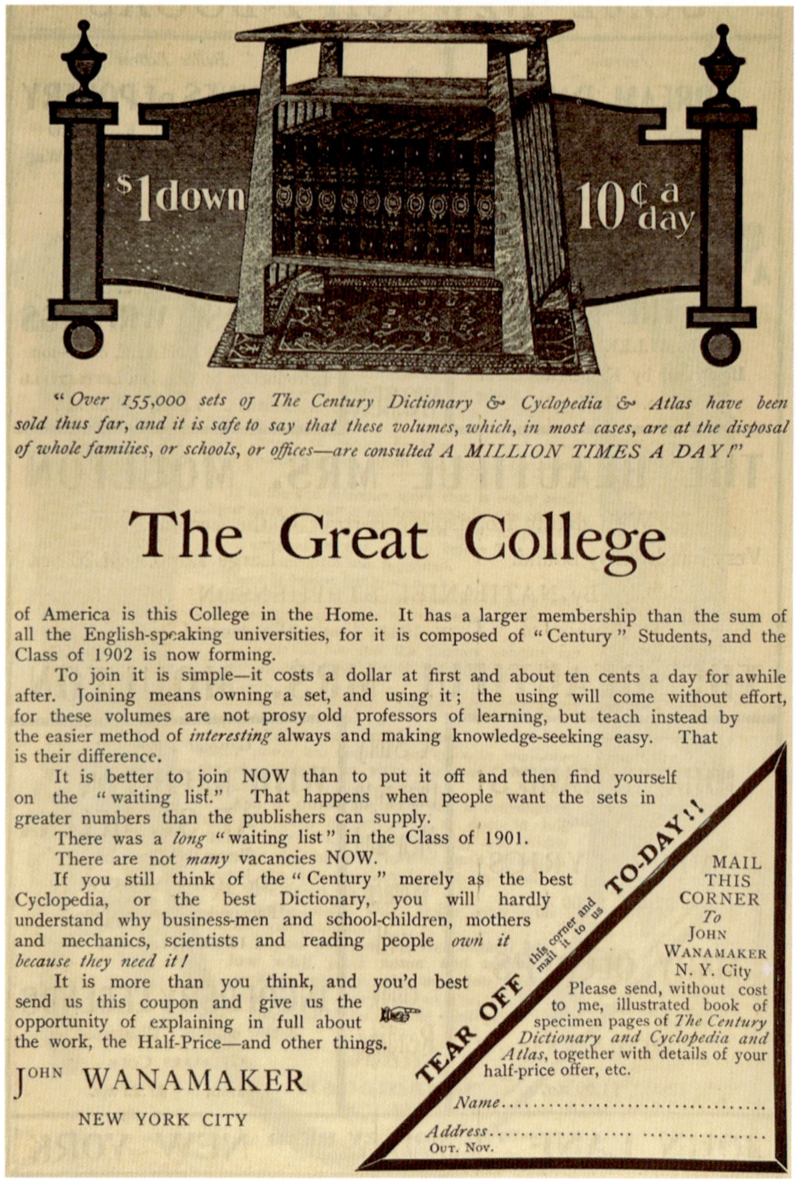

Ex coll. Karolyne & Bryan A. Garner

A 1901 ad in *The Outlook*.

89

Webster Goes International

Webster's International Dictionary of the English Language: Being the authentic edition of Webster's Unabridged Dictionary comprising the issues of 1864, 1879, and 1884. **Noah Porter ed. Springfield: G. & C. Merriam Co.; London: George Bell & Sons, 1890.**

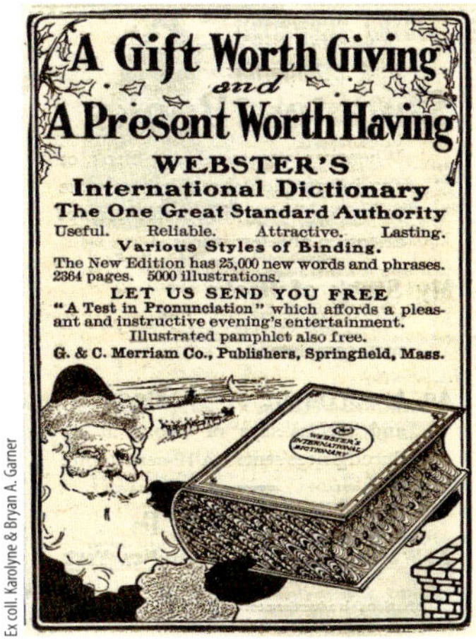

Ex coll. Karolyne & Bryan A. Garner

FOR GENERATIONS, "WEBSTER'S" had been synonymous with "American." As early as the blueback speller in 1783—published the same year that the Treaty of Paris officially ended the War of American Independence—Noah Webster was agitating for the American cause. He wanted distinctive American spellings, his wordlist reflected distinctively American institutions, and he used American linguistic authorities alongside Shakespeare and Milton. His most important predecessor, Samuel Johnson, was as English as English could be, and had said, "I am willing to love all mankind, *except an American* . . . Rascals—Robbers—Pirates." (Boswell 1791 3:290.) We can think of the title of Webster's greatest accomplishment, *An American Dictionary of the English Language* (1828), as a response to the notorious Tory: he took Johnson's *Dictionary of the English Language* and ostentatiously inserted the word *American* into it.

"The revision now given to the public is the fruit of over ten years of labor by a large editorial staff, in which publishers and editors have spared neither expense nor pains to produce a comprehensive, accurate, and symmetrical work." (Noah Porter's preface, p. iv.)

At the end of the 19th century, though, the Merriams felt that the American focus meant that they were not reaching a huge potential market. They therefore decided to market themselves in a new way: no longer *An American Dictionary of the English Language*, their flagship product was to be *Webster's International Dictionary of the English Language*. "The present substitution of 'International' for 'American,'" an appendix explained, "marks an accomplished change in the relations of the English speaking peoples. It is not their separation, but their community, which is now emphasized by the best thought and feeling in every department of life and literature."

Ex coll. Karolyne & Bryan A. Garner

Noah Porter (1811–1892) is listed as the editor of the *International*, as he had been for several other Merriam dictionaries. In 1864, he had become chief editor of the distinguished edition of *Webster's* known as *Webster-Mahn* (no. 80). Seven years later, he became president of Yale

"It would seem on the one hand that the revision and emendation of a work so satisfactory as the edition of 1864 would be the least expensive of time and labor. And yet it has been proved on the other hand by our experience that no work may be made so expensive of both time and labor as that involved in careful verification, condensation, and adjustment." (Noah Porter's preface, p. iii.)

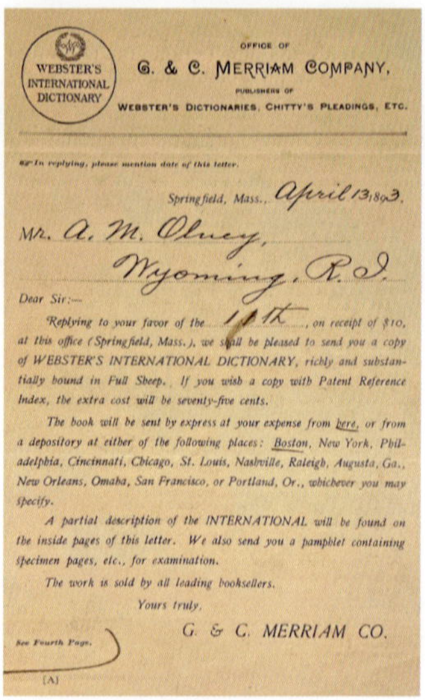

WEBSTER'S INTERNATIONAL DICTIONARY

OFFICE OF
G. & C. MERRIAM COMPANY,
PUBLISHERS OF
WEBSTER'S DICTIONARIES, CHITTY'S PLEADINGS, ETC.

In replying, please mention date of this letter.

Springfield, Mass., April 13, 1893.

Mr. A. M. Olney,
Wyoming, R. I.

Dear Sir:—

Replying to your favor of the 11th, on receipt of $10, at this office (Springfield, Mass.), we shall be pleased to send you a copy of WEBSTER'S INTERNATIONAL DICTIONARY, richly and substantially bound in Full Sheep. If you wish a copy with Patent Reference Index, the extra cost will be seventy-five cents.

The book will be sent by express at your expense from here, or from a depository at either of the following places: Boston, New York, Philadelphia, Cincinnati, Chicago, St. Louis, Nashville, Raleigh, Augusta, Ga., New Orleans, Omaha, San Francisco, or Portland, Or., whichever you may specify.

A partial description of the INTERNATIONAL will be found on the inside pages of this letter. We also send you a pamphlet containing specimen pages, etc., for examination.

The work is sold by all leading booksellers.

Yours truly,

G. & C. MERRIAM CO.

See Fourth Page.

[A]

Ex coll. Karolyne & Bryan A. Garner

An 1893 invoice for *Webster's International* sent to A.M. Olney, a teacher in Wyoming, Rhode Island.

"The condensation which becomes imperative from the increase of human knowledge may often seem to shrivel and contract the product in which the reader looks for amplitude of statement, proof, and illustration, and yet even an Unabridged Dictionary has its limits." (Noah Porter's preface, p. iii.)

College. He was a respected philosopher and theologian. In these roles, especially with respect to theology, he was very much in line with the man who had selected him—Chauncey Goodrich. He was the intellectual descendant of Noah Webster, though he well understood the need to clear Websterian detritus from the big dictionary. By 1880, when the *International* was begun in earnest, Porter was somewhat removed from the editorial process: he no longer exercised the kind of close personal oversight that he had given in the 1860s. Yet he remained the "general umpire upon delicate points of detail." (Merriam 1893:120.) And until his death in March 1892, he was "the official and salaried editor of Webster's Dictionary." (*Id.* at 119.)

The result is a giant: 1,681 triple-columned pages of definitions, plus 98 pages of front matter and over 300 pages of back matter. The physical form of the dictionary overwhelms readers with a sense of *monumentality*. In Sidney Landau's words, "The bulk and size of the book . . . immediately calls to mind the appearance of later unabridged dictionaries that would remain the gold standard of American lexicography into the 1960s." (Landau 2009a:201.) It may be the first dictionary to feature a "thumb index," cuts into the fore-edge of the book to allow for easy opening to specific passages—an innovation suggested by a man who would later become chief editor (see no. 93).

The *International* contains about 175,000 entries, more than 50,000 above the count in *Webster-Mahn* in 1864, and a supplement published in 1900 added another 25,000 terms. The focus was now on the scientific vocabulary. The preface even acknowledged that some critics were upset "that so much space is given to explanations and illustrations that are purely technical rather than literary," but that's what the modern world demanded. (Landau 2009a:201.) An increasingly technological modernity needed an increasingly technological dictionary.

As in other big Merriam dictionaries since the 1850s, this one was illustrated with line drawings—here scattered throughout the book and gathered into an 84-page section at the end. The editors continued their project of bringing the etymologies in line with modern scholarship; now Edward S. Sheldon, a Harvard professor of Romance philology, was in charge. Pronunciation, too, got new attention. Though Merriam retained the phonetic system used in its earlier works rather than the brand-new International Phonetic Alphabet, the company explained the phonology behind the symbols in more detail than had been done in a mass-market dictionary before. Noah Webster had done much to promote distinctively American spellings in his *American Dictionary*; now, in the *International*, American and British spellings would coexist—though American spellings came first. Quotations, or at least citations, appeared in many definitions, and at the end of many entries was a list of synonyms, sometimes with advice on distinguishing among them.

The *International* can be seen as a kind of turning point in lexicographic history. On the one hand, it points back to the past: many of its quotations, now less provincially American, were still eminently literary and could have appeared in Johnson's 1755 *Dictionary*. On the other hand, it points to the future: the big-money editorial project helped establish the form of an unabridged dictionary, with up-to-date scientific and technical vocabulary, informed by cutting-edge scholarship and drawing on a team of specialists in many fields.

Its descendants—*Webster's New International Dictionary* in 1909 (no. 93), *Webster's Second New International Dictionary* in 1934 (no. 100), and *Webster's Third New International Dictionary* in 1961 (no. 102)—have been the flagships of the Merriam fleet ever since. Merriam's smaller dictionaries, including the *Collegiate* line, have always been drawn from the latest *International*.

"The prominence given to the definitions and illustrations of scientific, technological and zoological terms will attract the attention of every reader and perhaps elicit the displeasure of many critics. While we sympathize with their regret that so much space is given to explanations and illustrations that are purely technical rather than literary, we find ourselves compelled to yield to the necessity which in these days requires that the dictionary which is ever at hand should carefully define the terms that record the discoveries of Science, the triumphs of Invention, and the revelations of Life." (Noah Porter's preface, p. iii.)

Ex coll. Karolyne & Bryan A. Garner

"*Webster's International Dictionary* is an old friend with a new title, and to some extent a new face. Though it is undoubtedly more complete than the *Complete Dictionary* of 1880, it has been well advised to drop the title *Complete*, seeing that no dictionary can ever fairly claim it." (*The Athenæum* No. 3351:80 [16 Jan. 1892].)

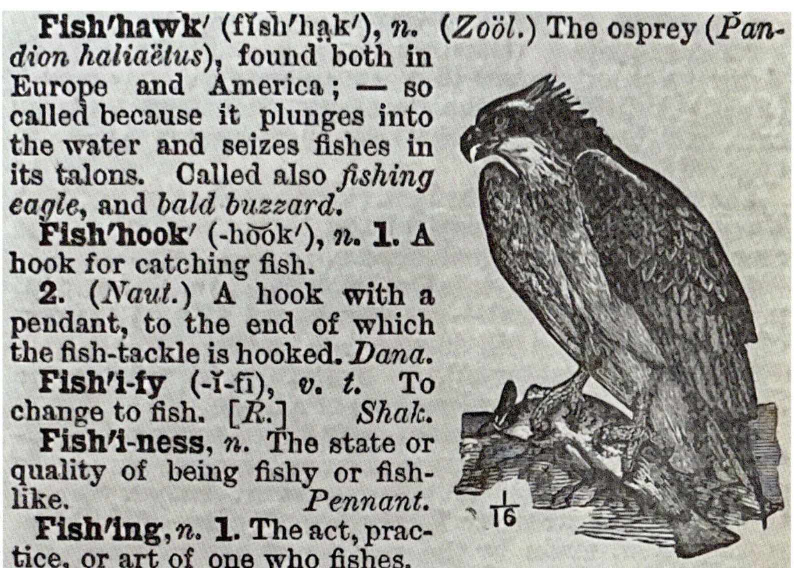

Fish′hawk′ (fĭsh′hạk′), *n.* (*Zoöl.*) The osprey (*Pandion haliaëtus*), found both in Europe and America; — so called because it plunges into the water and seizes fishes in its talons. Called also *fishing eagle*, and *bald buzzard*.

Fish′hook′ (-ho͝ok′), *n.* **1.** A hook for catching fish.

2. (*Naut.*) A hook with a pendant, to the end of which the fish-tackle is hooked. *Dana.*

Fish′i-fy (-ĭ-fī), *v. t.* To change to fish. [*R.*] *Shak.*

Fish′i-ness, *n.* The state or quality of being fishy or fish-like. *Pennant.*

Fish′ing, *n.* **1.** The act, practice, or art of one who fishes.

2. A fishery. *Spenser.*

1/16

Fishhawk.

Ex coll. Karolyne & Bryan A. Garner

Drawing by John P. Schmelzer. © 2008 by Bryan A. Garner

90

Henry Campbell Black
Stay-at-Home Scholar

Black, Henry Campbell. ***A Dictionary of Law containing definitions of the terms and phrases of American and English Jurisprudence, Ancient and Modern.*** **St. Paul: West Pub. Co., 1891. 2d ed. 1910. 3d ed. 1933.**

ALTHOUGH *BLACK'S LAW DICTIONARY* MAY BE the best-known book in American law today, the lexicographer for whom it is named is considerably less well documented. Henry Campbell Black (1860–1927) was a prolific scholar: aside from the first two editions of the now-eponymous law dictionary, he published numerous legal treatises in his lifetime, along with over 1,000 scholarly articles on legal topics and political issues. Yet there is no entry for him in the 24-volume *American National Biography*, nor in the *Oxford International Encyclopedia of Legal History*, nor even in *West's Encyclopedia of American Law*. Perhaps that's because, unlike his lexicographic forebears, he seemed to garner little interest from biographers or historians during his lifetime or in the years afterward. What we know of Black's life comes largely from passing mentions in local newspaper announcements, census records, and other genealogical ephemera. He seems to have typified the "harmless drudge," leading a quiet life of scholarly endeavor.

Born in Ossining, New York, in 1860, Black received bachelor's and master's degrees from Trinity College in Hartford, Connecticut. He studied law in Pennsylvania and in 1883 was admitted to the bar there. But evidently this career didn't suit Black: frustrated with the demands of law practice, he left the profession—and Pennsylvania—after only five years. In 1888, Black and his parents moved to Washington, D.C., where he would remain for the rest of his life.

This move would mark the beginning of a prodigious scholarly career. Just a few years later, at age 31, Black published *A Dictionary of Law* (1891), the seminal edition of what the world now knows as *Black's Law Dictionary*. Ten years later, the dictionary received its

Ex coll. Karolyne & Bryan A. Garner

The first edition (1891).

first U.S. Supreme Court citation—in *Western Union Telegraph Co. v. Call Publishing Co.*, for its definition of *common law*—and so began a successful career of its own. Today *Black's Law Dictionary* is the most-cited book in Supreme Court cases, having been cited in over 385 opinions since 1901. (*Webster's Third*, by comparison, has been cited in 266 Supreme Court opinions.)

Black's staggering body of work—and the absence of biographical details about his life—may have a common cause: from what we can tell, Black was the archetypal homebody. He lived with his parents for the first 50 years of his life and was married only a year before his mother's death, when he was 49. He had met his wife, presumably, in his home: she was a lodger who had lived with the Black family for over a decade. The two were married there as well, on April 26, 1910.

One can imagine that all the time Black spent in his home afforded him ample time to write. And write he did. Ceaselessly. Among his treatises are these:

- *Essay on the Constitutional Prohibitions Against Legislation Impairing the Obligation of Contracts* (1887).
- *A Treatise on the Law of Tax Titles* (1888; 2d ed. 1893).
- *A Treatise on the Law of Judgments* (1891; 2d ed. 1902).
- *A Treatise on the Laws Regulating the Manufacture and Sale of Intoxicating Liquors* (1892).
- *Handbook of American Constitutional Law* (1895; 2d ed. 1897; 3d ed. 1909; 4th ed. 1926).
- *Handbook on the Construction and Interpretation of the Laws* (1896; 2d ed. 1911).
- *Handbook on the Law of Judicial Precedents or the Science of Case Law* (1912).
- *A Treatise on the Law of Income Taxation Under Federal and State Laws* (1913).
- *A Treatise on the Law and Practice of Bankruptcy* (1914).
- *The Relation of the Executive Power to Legislation* (1919).

The same year that he married, 1910, Black published the second edition of *A Law Dictionary* (note the slight change in title). Meanwhile, of course, he wrote countless articles for legal journals, magazines, and encyclopedias. In 1916 he received an honorary Doctor of Laws from his alma mater, and in 1917 he became editor of *The Constitutional Review*, a position he would hold until his death a

Ex coll. Karolyne & Bryar A. Garner

From third edition dustjacket (1933).

Ex coll. Karolyne & Bryan A. Garner

The 11 editions of *Black's Law Dictionary* (1891–2019). A 12th edition is due to be released in 2024.

Ex coll. Karolyne & Bryan A. Garner

An editor's copy of the 1933 third edition of *Black's Law Dictionary* with suggestions about desirable additions. Flags are affixed with pins.

"It is chiefly required in a dictionary that it should be comprehensive. Its value is impaired if any single word that may reasonably be sought between its covers is not found there. But this comprehensiveness is possible (within the compass of a single volume) only on condition that whatever is foreign to the true function of a lexicon be rigidly excluded. The work must therefore contain nothing but the legitimate matter of a dictionary, or else it cannot include all the necessary terms." (Preface, p. iii.)

decade later. According to newspaper obituaries, Black died at home on 19 March 1927, "after a long illness."

Black's Law Dictionary has gone through 11 editions. It has sold into the millions of copies, and the print edition continues to sell. But today it is most often accessed online, where the editions within copyright protection are available only through the subscription service Westlaw.

Interestingly, a ghost-word inhabited the pages of *Black's Law Dictionary* for 89 years—from the second edition through the sixth. In the first edition of 1891, Black included the headword *vitilitigate*, meaning "to litigate vexatiously." The term is attested in the *OED* with a single 17th-century citation, from the 1670 third edition of Thomas Blount's *Glossographia* (no. 16). Somehow, the typesetter for the second edition, which was prepared by Black himself, dropped a syllable, so that the headword became *vitiligate*. No such word is known in legal literature, except in the second (1910), third (1933), fourth (1948), fifth (1980), and sixth (1990) editions of *Black's*. Not until the seventh edition of 1999 was the entry corrected. Even though there was plenty of vexatious litigation during that 89-year period (see, e.g., no. 108), the ghost-word seems never to have found its way into print.

Ex coll. Karolyne & Bryan A. Garner

A sampling of Henry Campbell Black's nonlexicographic books.

91

Look *That* Up in Your Funk & Wagnalls

A Standard Dictionary of the English Language. Isaac Kauffman Funk ed. 2 vols. London & Toronto: Funk & Wagnalls, 1894–1895.

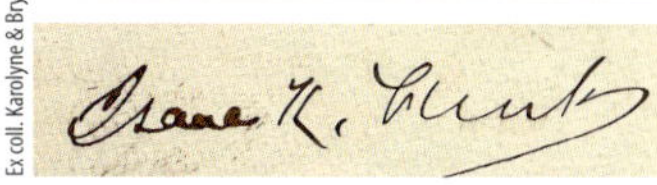

Ex coll. Karolyne & Bryan A. Garner

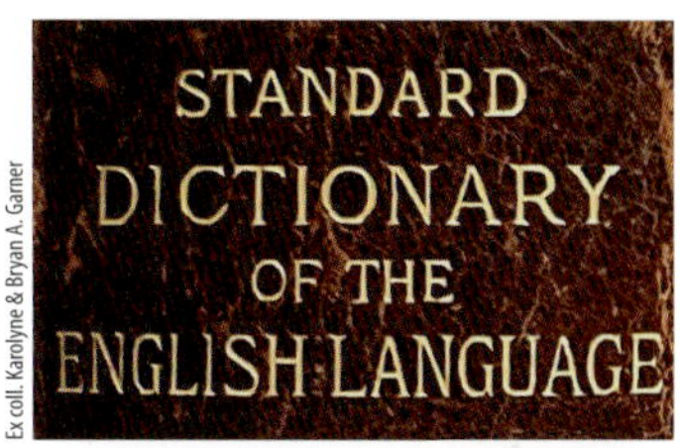

Ex coll. Karolyne & Bryan A. Garner

Isaac K. Funk at work (ca. 1910).

THE SON OF OHIO FARMERS, Isaac Kauffman Funk (1839–1912) attended Wittenberg College in Springfield, Ohio, and then became a Lutheran pastor and an entrepreneurial religious publisher. In the late 19th century, his most famous publications were the *Christian Radical* and the *Homiletic Review*. In the late 1870s, he took a lawyer-partner named Adam Willis Wagnalls, and together they incorporated as Funk & Wagnalls Company and began general publishing, specializing in low-cost books such as a "Standard Library" that cost an advance payment of $4 for 26 volumes published over the course of a year. In the era before international copyright, Funk often engaged in literary piracy, for which he was occasionally pilloried.

In 1890, Funk undertook to produce *A Standard Dictionary of the English Language*, for which he would serve as chief editor. It was an original work rather than a revision of an earlier dictionary. His staff of several hundred definers labored for more than three years to produce the behemoth work of more than 2,300 triple-columned pages of small print. It was also the first dictionary to include color pages.

Funk was a practical and innovative self-made lexicographer who was convinced that people consult dictionaries not for word histories but for prevalent current meanings. He realized that many, perhaps most, readers skip over etymologies, and so he moved them from the beginning of entries to the end. He arranged his definitions not from literal to figurative, as some dictionaries had done, nor in chronological order of their appearance, as historical dictionaries did, but simply from the commonest to the least common meanings of words. Consider *character*, adapted from the Greek *χαρακτήρ*, "instrument for marking or graving." Johnson started his entry for *character* with the most literal and etymological meaning, "1. A mark; a stamp; a representation," and only then progressed through "2. A letter used in writing or printing. . . . 3. The hand or manner of writing," reaching "A representation of any man as to his personal qualities" only

Ex coll. Karolyne & Bryan A. Garner

Ex coll. Karolyne & Bryan A. Garner

with sense 4. Webster in 1828 was similar: "1. A mark made by cutting or engraving . . . . 2. A mark or figure made by stamp or impression, as on coins. . . . 3. The manner of writing . . . 4. The peculiar qualities, impressed by nature or habit on a person, which distinguish him from others; these constitute *real character*." The *OED* did the same, only at greater length, starting with "1. A distinctive mark impressed, engraved, or otherwise formed" and not getting to "The sum of the moral and mental qualities which distinguish an individual" until the 16th definition. Not so Funk. He started with the meaning that was most common in the 1890s: "1. The combination of qualities distinguishing any person." The "figure engraved or indented" meaning is there, but postponed until sense 11.

Funk's initial cost was reputedly $1.1 million (more than $36 million in today's money); he invested another $425,000 (more than $14 million today) to produce the revised and enlarged edition of 1903. Frank H. Vizetelly (1864–1938), a talented lexicographer, wrote of Funk's "foresight, genius, and fearless initiative," as well as his "indefatigable energy and practical scholarship." (Vizetelly 1915:18.)

Vizetelly explained the working protocol. Individual words were copied onto blank cards, which were bundled and passed to orthoepists for a simplified phonetic rendering. Each packet would then go to a definer, who would consult seven dictionaries while crafting a new definition "that did not infringe the rights of any one of the books." This job "gave steady employment to forty definers." (*Id.* at 24–25.) There were multiple rounds of revision and correction.

The first edition of 1894–1895 included 304,000 entries, outstripping the competitor *Webster's International*, published just three years earlier. After Merriam-Webster issued its *New International* in 1909 with more than 400,000 entries, Funk & Wagnalls answered in 1913 by issuing its *New Standard* with more than 450,000 entries. The advertising for this book was as hyperbolic as any that has ever appeared for any dictionary: "All human knowledge since the world began is concentrated in one amazing book." It was called "the world's greatest single volume, the Bible alone excepted." It was called "the most expensive book ever published."

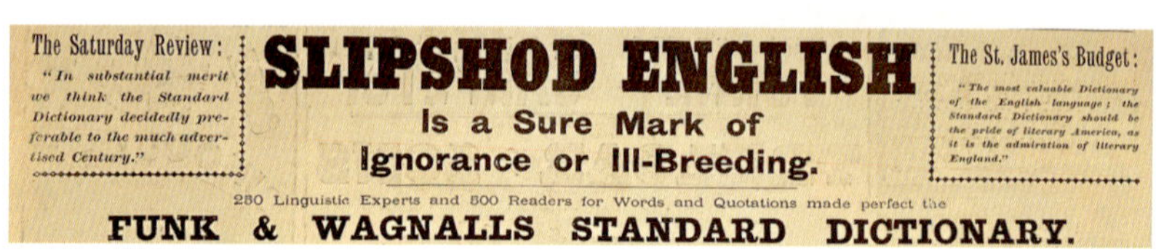

Ex coll. Karolyne & Bryan A. Garner

Finally, in 1934, Merriam-Webster came out with its *Second New International* boasting 552,000 entries—a colossal effort that was undoubtedly spurred on by the competition with Funk & Wagnalls.

By the 1920s and 1930s, Funk & Wagnalls had no real staff: Isaac Kauffman Funk had died and Frank Vizetelly was growing old. Isaac Funk's nephew Charles Earle Funk supervised the preparation of Vizetelly's *College Standard Dictionary* (1922) and then of the company's *New Practical Standard Dictionary* (1946), but by now the company wasn't competing in ongoing lexicographic efforts; rather, it relied on the residual goodwill of its name and its past glories.

For a few years after 1968, Funk & Wagnalls became part of a punning catchphrase after the television show *Rowan & Martin's Laugh-In* featured the exclamation *Look that up in your Funk & Wagnalls!* The NBC network, which broadcast the show, became concerned that the name of the dictionary should be carefully pronounced, but the cast had great fun playing with the suggestion that if anybody didn't understand anything, they should look that up in their "F-F-F-F-Funk and Wagnalls."

Ex coll. Karolyne & Bryan A. Garner

Senior staff in 1913: all white men except for the pioneering feminist educator Ella Flagg Young, a suffragist and the first female head of the National Education Association.

Vizetelly 1915:19

The general editorial room in 1915.

Vizetelly 1915:19

The managers' editorial room in 1915.

Ex coll. Karolyne & Bryan A. Garner

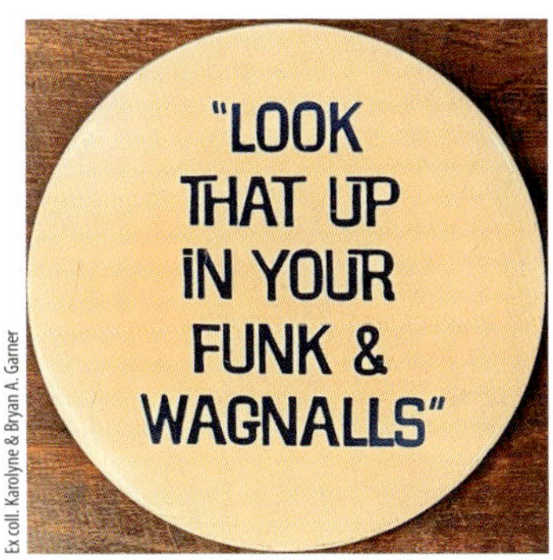

Ex coll. Karolyne & Bryan A. Garner

Ex coll. Karolyne & Bryan A. Garner

92

James A.H. Murray
A Darwinian Approach to His Craft

Murray, James A.H. *The Evolution of English Lexicography*. Oxford: Clarendon Press, 1900.

Ex coll. Karolyne & Bryan A. Garner

"Although . . . James [was given] . . . the honour of being invited to give the Romanes Lecture in Oxford in 1900 on *The Evolution of English Lexicography*, the old grievance that the University had found no appointment for him and had not given him an honorary doctorate, continued to rankle." (Murray 1977:290.)

During the 1890s, James A.H. Murray traveled around England to give talks promoting the *OED*. Usually he repeated the same lecture, with only small changes. But when asked to give the Romanes Lecture in Oxford in the year 1900, he became anxious. He thought he must do something new and better—"something really good," as he put it, "for I have a name to keep up, and that means work." (Quoted in Murray 1977:290.)

Unsurprisingly, he shows himself here to be a thoroughgoing scholar of lexicographic history. He documents the stages by which, over centuries, alphabetical order was canonized. The first stage was first-letter order (600–700 CE); the second was second-letter order (ca. 720 CE); then we arrived at third-letter order (ca. 950 CE). The glossaries were becoming more advanced, and they were becoming more *English*. The glosses gradually, through the 11th century, became exclusively English. He shows such familiarity with the manuscript material that the piece seems to be the product of personally working with the original materials.

Murray concedes that alphabetical ordering has its disadvantages: "Experience has shown that . . . an alphabetical order makes the matter of a dictionary very disjointed, scattering the terminology of a particular art, science, or subject, all over the book, and even when related words come together, often putting the unimportant derivative in front of the important primitive word." That's quite a concession. But as Murray argues, it's still better than the alternatives because only by alphabetizing can "a word or heading . . . be found with least trouble and exercise of thought." One might have expected a lexicographer to take alphabetizing for granted, but Murray didn't. He painstakingly examined his own first principles.

Murray had a good sense of proportion. Robert Cawdrey's contributions to English lexicography, in his *Table Alphabeticall* (no. 7), are dealt with in a single sentence of 59 words. Samuel Johnson's contributions are dealt with in several paragraphs amounting to more than 1,800 words.

In the long passage on Johnson, Murray asserted that he had "raised English lexicography altogether to a higher level," adding: "In his hands it became a department of literature. . . . From the first quarter of the nineteenth century, the lexicographical supremacy of Johnson's Dictionary was undisputed, and eminent students of language busied themselves in trying, not to supersede it, but to supplement and perfect it." (Pp. 42–43.)

"It is never possible to forecast the needs and notions of those who shall come after us; but with our present knowledge it is not easy to conceive what new feature can now be added to English Lexicography." (P. 49.)

Soon Murray reached the necessity of discussing his own work, the *OED*, which was still then called either the *NED* (or *New English Dictionary*) or the *Oxford Dictionary*. (He used both terms.) He wasn't an immodest man, but nor was he modest here: "In the Oxford Dictionary, permeated as it is through and through with the scientific method of the century, Lexicography has for the present reached its supreme development." (P. 49.) But he was understandably defensive about his failure to meet the initially projected deadlines: "All the great dictionaries of the modern languages have taken a long time to make." (P. 48.) Immediately after that statement came perhaps the most obscure one in his talk: "But the speed with which the New English Dictionary has now advanced nearly to its half-way point can advantageously claim comparison with the progress of any other great dictionary, even when this falls far behind in historical and inductive character." (Pp. 48–49.) In a footnote to this assertion, Murray cited German, Dutch, and Italian dictionaries whose progress was hopelessly slow.

Perhaps the most surprising conclusion in the piece is that the story of English-language lexicography is most strongly and decisively mirrored by—even caused by—women's liberation. The first four general English-only dictionaries (Cawdrey [no. 7], Bullokar [no. 11], Cockeram [no. 13], and Blount [no. 16]) were all specifically compiled for the advancement of women. Jump forward two centuries, to Murray's time: "But for the movement to let women share in the advantages of a university education, it is doubtful whether the nineteenth century would have witnessed the establishment of a School of English Language and Literature at Oxford." Hence English lexicography and English studies are, in Murray's words, "intimately interwoven with the advances which have been made . . . in the higher education of women." (P. 30.)

"At the 'Dictionary Dinner' held in 1897, at Queen's College, Henry Bradley declared that it would have been a national calamity if anyone but Murray had been appointed Editor of the Dictionary." (Murray 1977:28.)

Ex coll. Karolyne & Bryan A. Garner

93

William Torrey Harris
Webster Refurbished

***Webster's New International Dictionary*. William Torrey Harris ed. Springfield: G. & C. Merriam Co., 1909.**

While serving as superintendent of St. Louis schools in 1878, William Torrey Harris (1835–1909) reviewed a Merriam-Webster dictionary. He suggested there that the publishers introduce thumbcuts to mark the beginnings of new letters in the alphabet. By 1900, he had moved to Concord, Massachusetts, and become the chief editor of the *New International*. At the time, he was also the U.S. Commissioner of Education—a position he held until 1906. As to his lexicography, his primary biographer states (a little hyperbolically) that "though based on the editions of 1890 and 1900, [Webster's] had become practically a new book under his editorship, with 2700 pages and 400,000 title words in the vocabulary." (Leidecker 1946:600.)

Harris also innovated the "divided page," which put uncommon or obsolete words at the foot of the page, making it "possible to incorporate in the dictionary an amount of words which otherwise would have encumbered the handiness of the volume, or made a second volume necessary, or else would have precluded the feasibility of including words which nevertheless belong in a dictionary." (*Id.* at 604.) When the book first appeared in this form in 1909, "the divided page was hailed immediately as a stroke of genius." (*Id.*) It would be kept in *Webster's Second* but scrapped in *Webster's Third*.

Upon Harris's death in 1909, the Merriam-Webster officials passed a resolution that said in part: "Succeeding to a line of illustrious lexicographers—Webster, Goodrich, and Porter—his name will always be associated with the crowning of their work by the *New International Dictionary*." (*Id.*)

Harris's contributions to philosophy are memorialized in Edward L. Schaub, *William Torrey Harris 1835–1935* (1936), a book that omits any mention of Harris's lexicography. But it does quote much

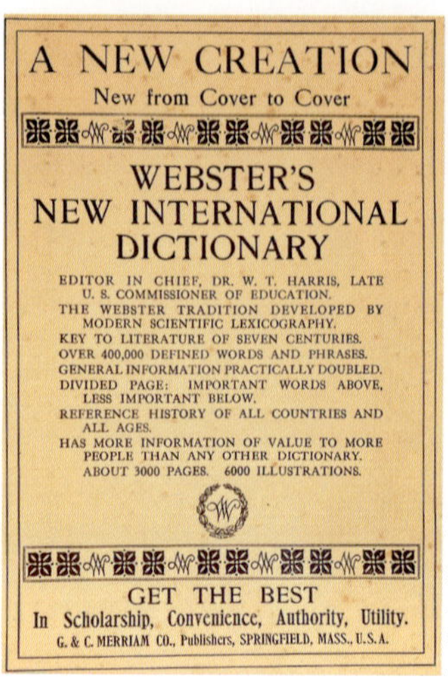
A NEW CREATION
New from Cover to Cover

WEBSTER'S
NEW INTERNATIONAL
DICTIONARY

EDITOR IN CHIEF, DR. W. T. HARRIS, LATE U. S. COMMISSIONER OF EDUCATION.
THE WEBSTER TRADITION DEVELOPED BY MODERN SCIENTIFIC LEXICOGRAPHY.
KEY TO LITERATURE OF SEVEN CENTURIES.
OVER 400,000 DEFINED WORDS AND PHRASES.
GENERAL INFORMATION PRACTICALLY DOUBLED.
DIVIDED PAGE: IMPORTANT WORDS ABOVE, LESS IMPORTANT BELOW.
REFERENCE HISTORY OF ALL COUNTRIES AND ALL AGES.
HAS MORE INFORMATION OF VALUE TO MORE PEOPLE THAN ANY OTHER DICTIONARY.
ABOUT 3000 PAGES. 6000 ILLUSTRATIONS.

GET THE BEST
In Scholarship, Convenience, Authority, Utility.
G. & C. MERRIAM CO., Publishers, SPRINGFIELD, MASS., U.S.A.

Ex coll. Karolyne & Bryan A. Garner

A four-page brochure announcing the 1909 edition: "a reference library in one volume."

of his philosophical writing, which is replete with numinous passages like this: "A spiritual first principle makes mind the source of the universe and the explanation of nature and history. Mind is consciousness, personality, will, intellect, love. In the absolute personality, intellect and will and love are one, because each in its perfection is all." (*Id.* at 9.) Today it is said that "by and large his philosophy of education has been recognized for its importance to its time and place but has had no lasting influence on U.S. educational policy." (*ANB.*)

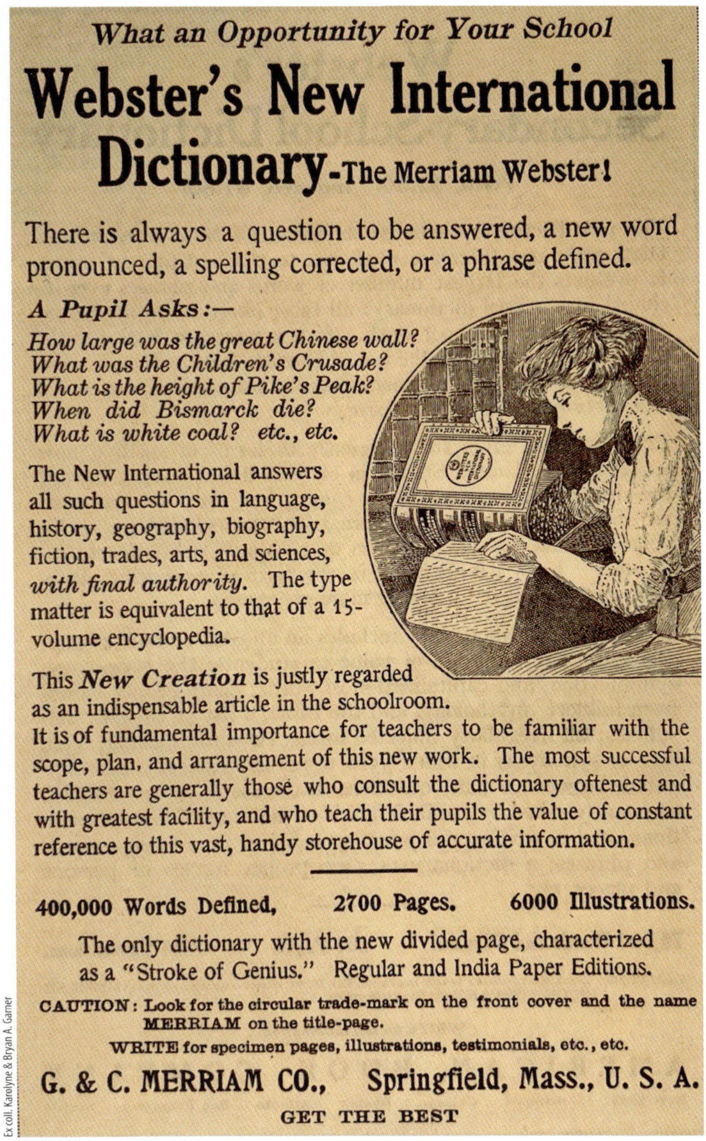

Ex coll. Karolyne & Bryan A. Garner

Advertisement in a teacher's journal.

Ex coll. Karolyne & Bryan A. Garner

Apparently, this 1918 promotional pamphlet appealed to people in ways that it wouldn't today.

Ex coll. Karolyne & Bryan A. Garner

Ex coll. Karolyne & Bryan A. Garner

94

J.R.R. Tolkien

Imaginative Philologist

Tolkien, J.R.R. *A Middle English Vocabulary. Designed for Use with Sisam's Fourteenth Century Verse & Prose.* Oxford: Clarendon Press, 1922. Also: 1929.

J.R.R. Tolkien (1892–1973) is undoubtedly the most popular writer ever to have engaged in serious lexicography. He was born in South Africa, where his father was a branch manager of the Bank of Africa. After losing his father at age 4 and his mother at 12, he became a ward of Father Francis Morgan, a Catholic priest in Birmingham, England. When at age 16 Tolkien fell in love with a fellow lodger in Birmingham, Edith Bratt (1889–1971), who was three years older, Father Morgan separated them and forbade any further communication between them until Tolkien came of age (21). Tolkien honored his promise not to communicate with her. In December 1910, he won a spot at Oxford, where he read classics; in 1913, he achieved only a second-class degree because he spent much time on extracurricular studies in Germanic languages. He then shifted to English studies, where he studied with the three great philologists Kenneth Sisam (1887–1971), Joseph Wright (1855–1930), and William Craigie (1867–1957). In 1915, he achieved a first in his finals. And just after midnight on his 21st birthday in 1913, he had written to his beloved Edith Bratt. They were soon engaged, and married in March 1916.

During World War I, he served in the Lancashire Fusiliers, fighting in the battle of the Somme. He contracted trench fever in October 1916 and was returned to England. Shortly after the Armistice, he returned to Oxford and worked under Henry Bradley on the *Oxford English Dictionary*. In 1920, he was appointed reader in English language at the University of Leeds.

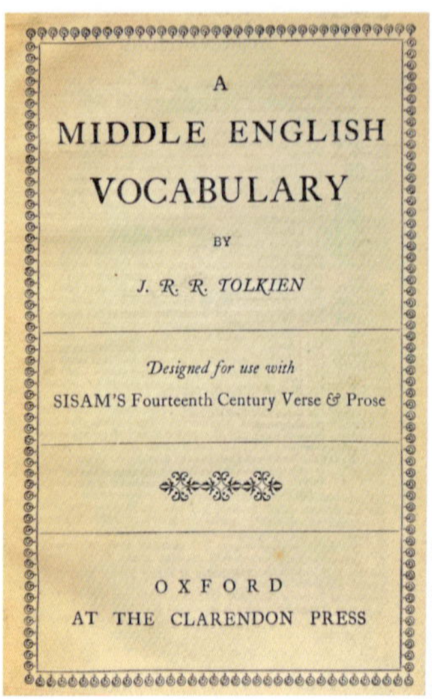

A
MIDDLE ENGLISH
VOCABULARY
BY
J. R. R. TOLKIEN
Designed for use with
SISAM'S Fourteenth Century Verse & Prose
OXFORD
AT THE CLARENDON PRESS

Ex coll. Karolyne & Bryan A. Garner

His work on the *OED* began in 1918, when he was hired by Craigie but joined the team of Henry Bradley, working on the ground floor of the Old Ashmolean Building, in what was known as the "Dictionary Room." Tolkien was brought in primarily for his expertise in Old and Middle English. He was put to work on words beginning with *W*, where Bradley's team was then at work. He worked on *warm*, *wash*, *wasp*, *water*, *wick*, and *winter*. Most of the manuscript etymology of *warm* is in Tolkien's hand. (Gilliver et al. 2006:9.)

Tolkien's *Middle English Vocabulary* began as a glossary to accompany Sisam's book *Fourteenth Century Verse and Prose*, first published in 1921 with copious notes but no glossary. Sisam had pulled Tolkien off the *OED* staff to complete the glossary. Tolkien wrote to OUP that "this mole-hill glossary . . . [had] grown into a mountain by accumulated domestic distractions." (Gilliver et al. 2006:33.) While working on the glossary, Tolkien encountered many terms that predated their first use recorded in the *OED*. In the margins of Bradley's office copy, he wrote in the details of several dozens of these terms.

Tolkien's glossary contains more than 4,500 entries and nearly 6,800 definitions. The work is exceedingly fastidious: each definition is keyed to a textual passage, and there are nearly 15,000 of these citations, all of which had to be individually identified and selected. The book also has 1,900 cross-references, often to account for linguistic variants. Apart from the utility of the work for *OED* editors, the book proved useful for students of English literature: it went into a second printing in 1929.

Tolkien never lost interest in the *OED*. While serving as Merton Chair in the English language and literature in the late 1940s, one of his star students was the Rhodes Scholar Robert W. Burchfield, who would become chief editor of the *Supplement to the OED* (no. 105). They stayed in touch with each other for the rest of Tolkien's life. In the Garner Collection is a 1972 letter from Tolkien to Burchfield:

> Merton College
> June 11 1972
>
> My dear Burchfield
>
> In unpacking my books from store I discovered this book [*Kentish Place-Names*] which belongs to you. You lent it me a long while ago—but as I was in hospital at the time of my removal from Oxford, I was not guilty of removing it to Poole, though guilty (with more excuse) for not returning it later. Forgive me.
>
> Yours ever,
> J.R.R. Tolkien

Tolkien died 15 months later, already lionized for the way in which he imbued his extremely popular fantasy works with a surprising dose of traditional philology.

Ex coll. Karolyne & Bryan A. Garner

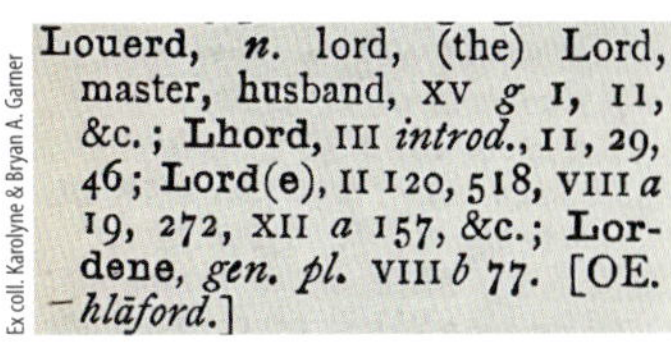

Louerd, *n.* lord, (the) Lord, master, husband, XV *g* 1, 11, &c.; **Lhord,** III *introd.*, 11, 29, 46; **Lord(e),** II 120, 518, VIII *a* 19, 272, XII *a* 157, &c.; **Lordene,** *gen. pl.* VIII *b* 77. [OE. *hlāford.*]

Ex coll. Karolyne & Bryan A. Garner

Ex coll. Karolyne & Bryan A. Garner

Bust by Stephen Paterson (b. 1967).

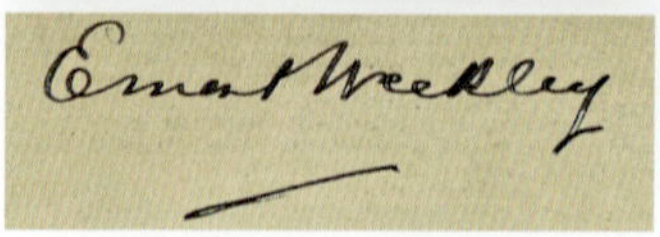

Ex coll. Karolyne & Bryan A. Garner

"When they returned from their honeymoon, Weekley informed his parents-in-law: 'I am married to an earthquake.'" (Wilson 2021:80.)

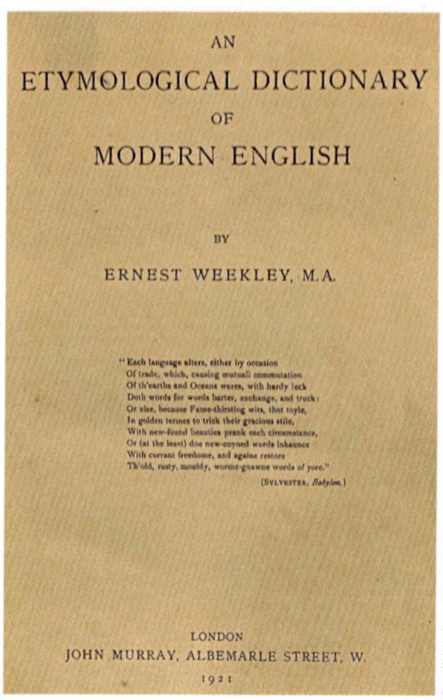

AN
ETYMOLOGICAL DICTIONARY
OF
MODERN ENGLISH

BY

ERNEST WEEKLEY, M.A.

"Each language alters, either by occasion
Of trade, which, causing mutuall commutation
Of th'earths and Oceans wares, with hardy luck
Doth words for words barter, exchange, and truck:
Or else, because Fame-thirsting wits, that toyle,
In golden termes to trick their gracious stile,
With new-found beauties prank each circumstance,
Or (at the least) doe new-coyned words inhaunce
With currant freedome, and againe restore
Th'old, rusty, mouldy, worme-gnawne words of yore."
(SYLVESTER, *Babylon*.)

LONDON
JOHN MURRAY, ALBEMARLE STREET, W.
1921

Ex coll. Karolyne & Bryan A. Garner

95

Ernest Weekley

Frieda Lawrence's First

Weekley, Ernest. *An Etymological Dictionary of Modern English*. London: J. Murray, 1921.

———. *A Concise Etymological Dictionary of Modern English*. London: John Murray, 1924.

Born in London, Weekley (1865–1954) was the second of nine children. He began his education at Dane Hill House, Margate, Kent, and at 17 was schoolmastering at Colchester and then Dane Hill. In 1891, he studied at the University of Bern, where he became fluent in German. In 1893, he studied at Trinity College, Cambridge, soon securing a major scholarship there and in 1896 earning a brilliant first-class degree, with special distinctions in French and German. He then studied at the Sorbonne and later at Freiburg under the German etymologist Friedrich Kluge (1856–1926). In Freiburg, he met and fell in love with Emma Maria Frieda Johanna, Baroness von Richthofen (1879–1956), and they were married there in 1899. They had three children.

As Weekley was preoccupied with writing his first popular book on etymology, *The Romance of Words* (1912), Frieda met one of his French-language students, the budding novelist D.H. Lawrence (1885–1930). Lawrence had come to the Weekleys' house to discuss a possible lectureship in Germany, and soon he and Frieda had begun a torrid affair. Weekley was obliviously buried in his philological endeavors. Eight weeks after the affair began, Frieda and D.H. eloped to Frieda's parents' house in Metz, eastern France. A devastated Weekley hired detectives to trace their movements through Europe, but he couldn't persuade her to return. He petitioned for divorce on grounds of adultery, and the decree was entered in April 1914. In July of that year, Frieda and D.H. were married in London. Over the next year or so, Frieda negotiated with Weekley and his solicitor about whether and how she could see her children; Weekley finally relented, but only on condition that Lawrence not be present.

Ex coll. Karolyne & Bryan A. Garner

Weekley's regular home was that of his parents until 1938, when the house was demolished to construct a new road to the airport. He rented a house in Richmond, Surrey, but it was bombed in the autumn of 1940. He spent the rest of the war years at Cricieth, Caernarvonshire, renting a flat there. After the war, he moved to 446 Upper Richmond, Putney, where he lived with his eldest daughter, Elsa, her husband, Teddy, and their two children. In 1952, Frieda made a final trip to England to visit her children, but she could not be invited to Elsa's home because of Weekley's presence there. Teddy drove her past the house, where Frieda spotted the back of Ernest's head through the window of his study, where he sat peering at a book. He was now almost blind. She proposed a meeting with him, if the children would allow it, but they refused.

At the age of 90, at home in Putney, Weekley died of lung cancer. At least two fictional characters are based on him: the Rev. Arthur Saywell, a country parson in Lawrence's *The Virgin and the Gypsy* (1930); and John Beavis, a sarcastic sociologist in Aldous Huxley's *Eyeless in Gaza* (1936).

But what of Weekley's lexicography? It was good, but not so fascinating as some of the poignant stories of his life. The Garner Collection holds a small archive of correspondence that Weekley had toward the end of his life with John Clark, a Minnesota English professor who collaborated with Eric Partridge on a book about punctuation. Clark also contributed a chapter to Weekley's last book, *The English Language* (1952). Less than a year before Weekley's death, he wrote a wide-ranging letter to Clark dealing with etymology, Bastille Day, *Webster's New World Dictionary*, and his dictionary collection destroyed by Hitler's bombs. It succinctly captures his profound humanity:

> 14.vii.53
>
> Dear Confrère,
>
> Many thanks for your friendly letter of Independence Day! Today is the great French anniversary (taking of the Bastille) and tomorrow is Saint Swithin's day, which, if wet, will mean 40 days of rain! I agree with you as to the general excellence of Webster's N.W.D. Its definitions seem generally good, though I am quite unqualified to deal with

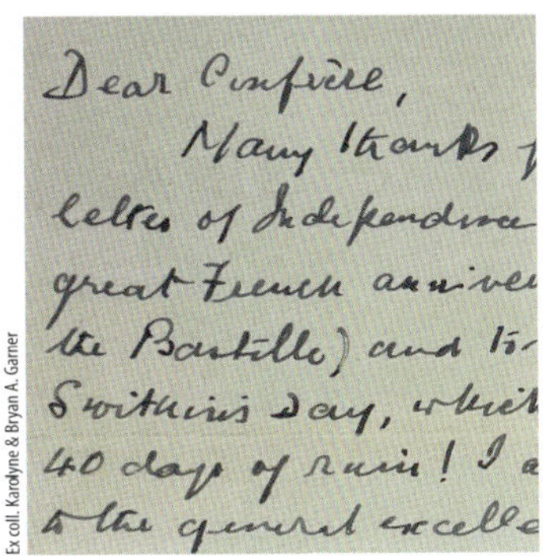

Ex coll. Karolyne & Bryan A. Garner

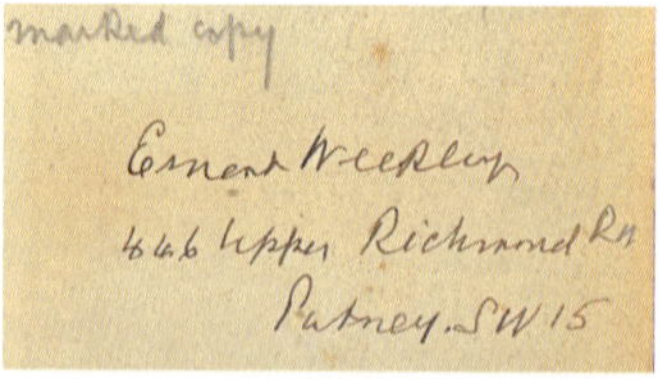

Ex coll. Karolyne & Bryan A. Garner

Weekley's signature in his own corrected copy, with a sample of his emendations.

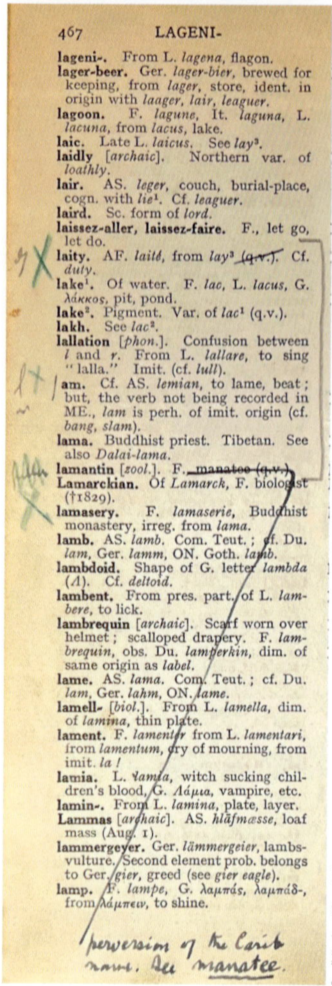

467 LAGENI-

lageni-. From L. *lagena*, flagon.
lager-beer. Ger. *lager-bier*, brewed for keeping, from *lager*, store, ident. in origin with *laager, lair, leaguer.*
lagoon. F. *lagune*, It. *laguna*, L. *lacuna*, from *lacus*, lake.
laic. Late L. *laicus*. See *lay*³.
laidly [*archaic*]. Northern var. of *loathly*.
lair. AS. *leger*, couch, burial-place, cogn. with *lie*¹. Cf. *leaguer*.
laird. Sc. form of *lord*.
laissez-aller, laissez-faire. F., let go, let do.
laity. AF. *laité*, from *lay*³ ~~(q.v.)~~. Cf. *duty*.
lake¹. Of water. F. *lac*, L. *lacus*, G. λάκκος, pit, pond.
lake². Pigment. Var. of *lac*¹ (q.v.).
lakh. See *lac*².
lallation [*phon.*]. Confusion between *l* and *r*. From L. *lallare*, to sing "lalla." Imit. (cf. *lull*).
lam. Cf. AS. *lemian*, to lame, beat; but, the verb not being recorded in ME., *lam* is perh. of imit. origin (cf. *bang, slam*).
lama. Buddhist priest. Tibetan. See also *Dalai-lama*.
lamantin [*zool.*]. F. ~~manatee (q.v.)~~
Lamarckian. Of *Lamarck*, F. biologist (†1829).
lamasery. F. *lamaserie*, Buddhist monastery, irreg. from *lama*.
lamb. AS. *lamb*. Com. Teut.; cf. Du. *lam*, Ger. *lamm*, ON. Goth. *lamb*.
lambdoid. Shape of G. letter *lambda* (Λ). Cf. *deltoid*.
lambent. From pres. part. of L. *lambere*, to lick.
lambrequin [*archaic*]. Scarf worn over helmet; scalloped drapery. F. *lambrequin*, obs. Du. *lamperkin*, dim. of same origin as *label*.
lame. AS. *lama*. Com. Teut.; cf. Du. *lam*, Ger. *lahm*, ON. *lame*.
lamell- [*biol.*]. From L. *lamella*, dim. of *lamina*, thin plate.
lament. F. *lamenter* from L. *lamentari*, from *lamentum*, cry of mourning, from imit. *la!*
lamia. L. *lamia*, witch sucking children's blood, G. Λάμια, vampire, etc.
lamin-. From L. *lamina*, plate, layer.
Lammas [*archaic*]. AS. *hlāfmæsse*, loaf mass (Aug. 1).
lammergeyer. Ger. *lämmergeier*, lambs-vulture. Second element prob. belongs to Ger. *gier*, greed (see *gier eagle*).
lamp. F. *lampe*, G. λαμπάς, λαμπάδ-, from λάμπειν, to shine.

perversion of the Carib name. See manatee.

Ex coll. Karolyne & Bryan A. Garner

the scientific vocabulary, and the general arrangement is excellent. The editors seem to have made a good deal of use of my modest contributions to etymology (*anlace, burgee, jackanapes, plat*, etc.), but, as you say, they have kept too many of the old traditional fictions. It always seems to me that those who busy themselves with etymology should be real linguists, e.g. the WNWD has an absurd etymology for the name Guy. While anybody who knows French thinks at once of the danse de Saint-Guy and thus arrives at Vitus. Many current etymologies start from the present instead of going back to earliest recorded meanings, e.g. pump, a dancing shoe, assigned to pompe. This data from Skeat, who was no linguist. But the pumps that Robinson Crusoe and still earlier mariners wore were light slippers popular in far Eastern waters. So also fail (fencing). Excuse all this shop!

Yes, I have seen the "new" etymology for caprice and think it frankly idiotic! I expect you have noticed how almost impossible it is to catch up and destroy the crazy etymologies that were once accepted. I recently asked a very well-read and intelligent old lady if she knew the origin of beef-eater and was told at once that it is French and means a servant at the side-board. Interrogation of a distinguished university graduate produced the same answer. After all, correct etymology is not vital to the welfare of mankind!

It is very kind of you to send me one more dictionary, but please don't, for I feel that you have done too much for me already. The number of dictionaries ancient and modern is amazing. Before the late unlamented Mr. Hitler bombed my house in Richmond I had a very valuable collection, especially my antiques, and including a complete set of Lat. English dicts. from the 16th and 17th centuries, most useful to establishing early meanings, but quite neglected by [lay?] word-hunters. I hope you do not find my script too illegible. I have never learnt to type and I write on my knee in a most capacious and comfortable armchair, a gift from my old students.

Once more, many thanks for your appreciative (too appreciative!) and welcome letters and all good wishes from

Yours very sincerely,

Ernest Weekley

96

The Oxford English Dictionary
Lexicon totius Anglicitatis

The Oxford English Dictionary. A New Dictionary on Historical Principles, founded mainly on the materials collected by the Philological Society. **James A.H. Murray, Henry Bradley, W.A. Craigie & C.T. Onions eds. 10 vols. in 12. 1st ed. Oxford: Clarendon Press, 1888–1928.**

THE *OXFORD ENGLISH DICTIONARY*—universally known as the *OED*, and universally recognized as the greatest achievement in the history of English lexicography—was conceived in 1857, when Richard Chenevix Trench delivered a paper before the Philological Society, *On Some Deficiencies in Our English Dictionaries* (no. 81). He called for an English dictionary that could rival what was happening in Germany, especially Franz Ludwig Carl Friedrich Passow's *Handwörterbuch der griechischen Sprache* (Concise Dictionary of the Greek Language, 1819–1824) and the *Deutsches Wörterbuch* begun by the Brothers Grimm in 1838 (and completed only in 1961).

The Philological Society briefly wondered whether a revision of Johnson's *Dictionary*—now more than a century old—could do what Trench called for, then quickly realized that it could be done only from scratch. They sketched out their goals. The coverage would be more comprehensive than that of any other English dictionary. They resolved to include every word that had been in general circulation since the end of the Old English period, roughly 1150 CE. (Words that originated before that date but survived later would be included and their histories traced back as far as the evidence allowed, but those that were born and died in the Old English period would be left for a separate Old English dictionary.) The coverage would be strictly lexical, not encyclopedic, so proper nouns would be admitted only when they had a more general application. They chose to omit most dialect, most professional jargon, and many words from other languages that weren't yet entirely naturalized in English.

Beyond that, though, they would be as comprehensive as possible. The scope was to be international, wherever English has been

The young Herbert Coleridge.

"Early editors were extraordinarily optimistic about how quickly they expected the dictionary to be finished, as their correspondence shows. Coleridge presumed that the first part of the dictionary would be published in two years . . . . However, within two years of his editorship, Coleridge died of consumption at the age of thirty, and the dictionary was left without an editor." (Ogilvie 2013:31.)

Ex coll. Karolyne & Bryan A. Garner

A few of the many books spawned by the *OED*.

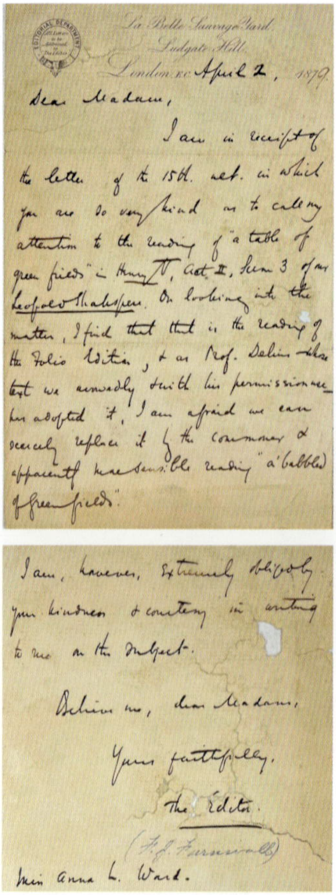

La Belle Sauvage Yard,
Ludgate Hill,
London, E.C. April 2, 1879.

Dear Madam,

I am in receipt of the letter of the 15th ult. in which you are so very kind as to call my attention to the reading of "a table of green fields" in Henry V, Act II, Scene 3 of my Leopold Shakspere. On looking into the matter, I find that that is the reading of the Folio Edition, & as Prof. Delius' text we avowedly with his permission have adopted it, I am afraid we can scarcely replace it by the common & apparently more sensible reading "a' babbled of green fields".

I am, however, extremely obliged by your kindness & courtesy in writing to me on the subject.

Believe me, dear Madam,

Yours faithfully,

The Editor.

(F.J. Furnivall)

Miss Anna L. Ward.

Ex coll. Karolyne & Bryan A. Garner

Though superseded as editor on 1 March 1879, Furnivall nevertheless signed this letter, a month later, as "The Editor." His correspondent was Anna L. Ward, the editor of quotation books. She was urging a variant reading of a line in Shakespeare's *Henry V*.

Ex coll. Karolyne & Bryan A. Garner

A 1911 tribute volume.

spoken. The treatment was to be purely descriptive, cataloguing words with no regard for whether they were "proper." They would record words and meanings condemned as improper, vulgar, illiterate, and offensive. (Only two words in the entire language were omitted on grounds of indecency. The words that we euphemize as *the F-word* and *the C-word* did not appear in the *OED* until the 1970s: see Gilliver 2016:297, 467–68.) The dictionary would tell the complete story of every one of these words, from their first entry into the language to the present.

Such a monumental task would require an exceptionally able editor in chief. The Philological Society's first choice was Herbert Coleridge, the poet's grandson. Still in his twenties when he was tapped, Coleridge wrote: "I confidently expect, unless any unforeseen accident should occur to paralyse our efforts, that in about two years we shall be able to give our first number to the world." (Coleridge 1860:77.) But the unforeseen accident struck: a few months later, Coleridge, having just turned 30, was dead of tuberculosis.

The next choice was Frederick Furnivall (1825–1910), founder of the Early English Text Society, the Chaucer Society, the Ballad Society, the New Shakspere Society, the Browning Society, the Wyclif Society, and the Shelley Society. But his temperament was all wrong: he had no patience for slow, meticulous scholarship. After a short time, he wisely chose to step aside.

The 1870s saw two major developments: first, the Philological Society reached an agreement with Oxford University Press to be their publisher; second, they at last found their editor. James A.H. Murray (1837–1915) was a 38-year-old Scottish schoolmaster with an interest in Scottish dialect. He had no degree and only a few scholarly accomplishments to his credit, but the polymathic polyglot had exactly the combination of skills and temperament to oversee the Anglophone world's grandest lexicographic project.

Every *OED* entry would be based on words as they had actually been used by English writers. By contrast, the *Dictionnaire de l'Académie française* (1694) included some samples of French words in use, but many of the sentences were invented for the occasion. Because it was grounded in usage, the *OED* would require an almost unimaginable amount of reading. Johnson and Webster could read their sources more or less unaided, but the scale of the new dictionary meant that no editor could hope to do all the requisite reading in a lifetime. Even the full membership of the Philological Society couldn't possibly read everything necessary. The project called for crowdsourcing more than a century before the word *crowdsourcing* was coined. In 1879, therefore, Murray published an "Appeal to the English-Speaking and English-Reading Public," encouraging volunteers to read widely and compile evidence that would inform the dictionary. He offered guidance: "Make a quotation for *every* word that strikes you as rare, obsolete, old-fashioned, new, peculiar, or used in a peculiar way," but be sure to include everyday words as well. Volunteers were to write their quotations in original spelling on half-sheets of notepaper, providing precise citations.

These slips, eventually numbering 5 million, were the raw material out of which the dictionary was constructed. Murray's job was to sort them, to divide them into senses, to arrange the evidence chronologically under each sense, and to write the etymologies and definitions. Sound etymologies were particularly needed because English lacked a dictionary informed by philological advances since William Jones had hypothesized the existence of an Indo-European language family. Although Webster and Richardson wrote after Jones's discovery, they were too much under the spell of John Horne Tooke (no. 55) to produce sound etymologies. Murray, on the other hand, "considered himself and his circle to be pioneers of a systematic and rigorous approach to etymology." (Ogilvie 2020c:61.)

Etymologies told the stories of words before they entered the English language; their stories after their appearance in English were traced in the quotations, which take up a large majority of the dictionary's pages. Every sense of every word is illustrated by a series of quotations, starting with the earliest example that the readers had turned up, and then including at least one additional quotation for each century in which each sense is known to have been used.

It's tempting to treat these earliest citations as the moments that the words were coined, but that's probably rarely the case—not least because words typically circulate orally long before they're written down. And words can be found only where they're sought: one reason why Shakespeare has a reputation for coining so many words is that the *OED*'s volunteer readers spent more time reading his works than those of his less interesting contemporaries. But these first citations are the best evidence we have for when words entered circulation.

The scope of the dictionary was (and remains!) overwhelming, and the coverage remarkable. Though it's an excellent source of charming obscurities—*anatiferous* "producing ducks or geese,"

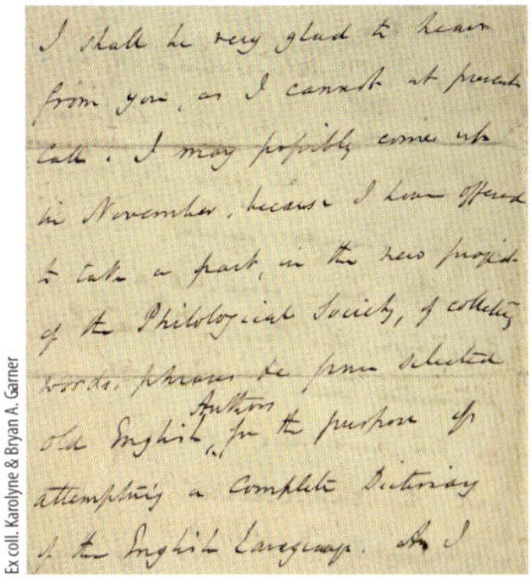
I shall be very glad to hear from you, as I cannot at present tell. I may possibly come up in November, because I have offered to take a part in the new project of the Philological Society, of collecting words, phrases &c from selected old English Authors, for the purpose of attempting a Complete Dictionary of the English Language. As I

Ex coll. Karolyne & Bryan A. Garner

Detail from an 1857 letter showing that Trench's call to action was being answered. In September of that year, Samuel Prince (d. 1865) wrote to George Cruikshank (1792–1878), the illustrator, that he was beginning to collect illustrative quotations for the project.

Ex coll. Karolyne & Bryan A. Garner

Murray's carte de visite.

haematophagous "feeding upon, or living in, blood," *obnubilate* "to darken, dim, cover, or hide with or as with a cloud"—the *OED*'s real strength is its treatment of the everyday vocabulary. Johnson was the first to work systematically to distinguish the senses of polysemous words, and the *OED* is the logical conclusion of this process. The meanings for *set*, both noun and verb, with all their quotations, fill 24 triple-columned pages of small print—the length of a short novel. Polysemous verbs like *get*, *give*, *go*, *have*, *run*, and *take* are comparable. Murray and his team did a remarkable job of defining difficult words like *time*, *game*, *yellow*, *money*, *justice*, and *water*.

All this detail took up both a great deal of space and a great deal of time, which also meant a great deal of money—money that the Press had hoped to hold on to. The history of the dictionary is a largely a history of a struggle between the editorial staff and the publishers. Early plans called for a four-volume dictionary that would appear in six years, and the Press expected something on that scale. But the work kept growing, and the Delegates of Oxford University Press kept urging the lexicographers to keep their work within reasonable bounds and to deliver it promptly.

Murray's early plans called for a dictionary three times the size of Chauncey A. Goodrich & Noah Porter's edition of Webster's *American Dictionary* (1864)—the "Webster-Mahn edition" (no. 80)—though the "Webster ratio" kept sliding. Oxford acknowledged that it was willing to publish a dictionary 4.5 times the size of Webster, but soon that grew to 6 times the size, and then to 10. The Delegates repeatedly urged the lexicographers to cut unnecessary entries and unnecessary quotations within entries, but the lexicographers couldn't agree about what was unnecessary. It's remarkable that the project was ever completed. Kenneth Sisam (1887–1971), who from 1922 oversaw the completion of the first edition, complained of the "natural dilatoriness of lexicographers," adding: "It is the exception for any huge dictionary to be finished." (Brewer 2007b:18.)

Toward the outset in the early 1860s, the publication was projected to be completed in about ten years. Yet the first installment didn't appear until February 1884, a fascicle covering *A* through *ant* (appropriately enough!) and published under the title *A New English Dictionary on Historical Principles: Founded Mainly on the Materials Collected by the Philological Society*. Four years later, when they had reached the end of *B*, the first few fascicles reappeared in volume

"We think of the *OED* as a radical dictionary because of its size, its scholarship, and its methods, and it was radical *for English*. But if you compare it with other languages, there was nothing about its creation in the mid-nineteenth century that had not been done before in Europe. . . . The English editors were able to pick and choose the best methods from different European dictionaries." (Ogilvie & Safran 2023:58.)

Ex coll. Karolyne & Bryan A. Garner

In 1893, Sir William Rothenstein drew portraits of 24 Oxonians—James A.H. Murray among them. They were published as lithographs in 1896. The full sheet is 11½ × 17½ inches.

"Sir James Murray and his colleagues established a model for all time. . . . By one practical test or another the *OED* emerges as the most ambitious and the most successful treatment of a national language ever undertaken." (Burchfield 1991:168.)

form. The volume for *C* followed five years later, then *D* and *E* in 1897, *F* and *G* in 1900 . . . Progress was slow, but at last it was steady.

Murray didn't live to see the finished dictionary: he died in 1915, when his team had reached *shyster*. To the right is a poignant photograph of him sitting in his "Scriptorium," the 30′ × 17′ corrugated-iron shed in his garden that he used as a workshop, surrounded by much of his staff, including daughters Elsie and Rosfrith, just two weeks before he died. It was his last day there.

A succession of editors—Henry Bradley, William Craigie, and Charles Talbut Onions—brought the project to full fruition on 19 April 1928, when the final fascicle, *wise–wyzen*, appeared (*x–zyxt* had appeared out of order in 1921). The event was marked by an exhibition at Oxford's Bodleian Library, formal presentations of the dictionary to King George V in London and to President Calvin Coolidge in Washington, and a grand banquet for 150 men—women were excluded—in Goldsmith's Hall, London. An article in the *Times* declared 1928 "the Year of the Dictionary." (Gilliver 2016:386.)

But work didn't stop in 1928. By then the *A*'s were more than 40 years old, and much of the research for the whole dictionary had been conducted in the 1870s and '80s. The lag meant that some important words had been excluded: *appendicitis*, an obscure technical term when *A* appeared, had grown familiar by the 1920s, and readers noticed its absence. (Gilliver 2016:289–90.) In 1902, William Craigie drafted an entry for the newly discovered element *radium*, but Murray warned that it "may turn out to be a regrettable blunder" if the science didn't hold up, and so the entry was nixed. (Gilliver 2016:302–3.) The Wright Brothers were children when *A* was published, but in 1927 Charles Lindbergh flew across the Atlantic—and a host of fashionable *aero-* words were nowhere to be found. The team therefore published a thirteenth volume in 1933, identified as a *Supplement*, containing words from across the entire alphabet. It filled gaps in the main series and corrected some oversights.

The completion of the *Supplement* provided an occasion to reissue the whole work. The full text—headwords, etymologies, usage notes, definitions, quotations, the lot—ran to roughly 37 million words, about fifty times the length of the King James Bible. The original pages were reorganized from ten volumes into twelve, and the work got a new title: no longer *A New English Dictionary*, it was now officially *The Oxford English Dictionary*.

"I wish from my heart that people would accept my work at the Dictionary as my simple effort to do my duty, and leave me quietly to do it, giving me wherewith to do it well, & without the pecuniary struggle that it has so often been, since I undertook it. Yet this too is no doubt also the divine plan for me, and will one day also be seen to have been all for the best." (James A.H. Murray in 1903 [as quoted in Murray 1977:21]).

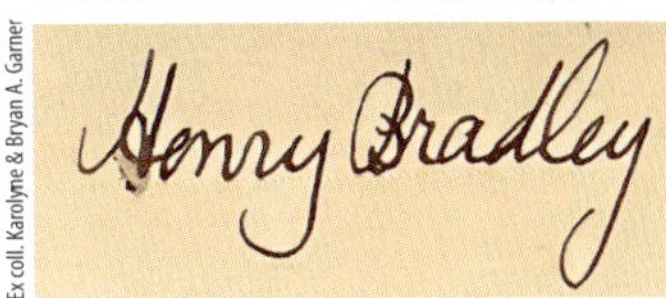

Ex coll. Karolyne & Bryan A. Garner

97

Rescued *OED* Printing Plates

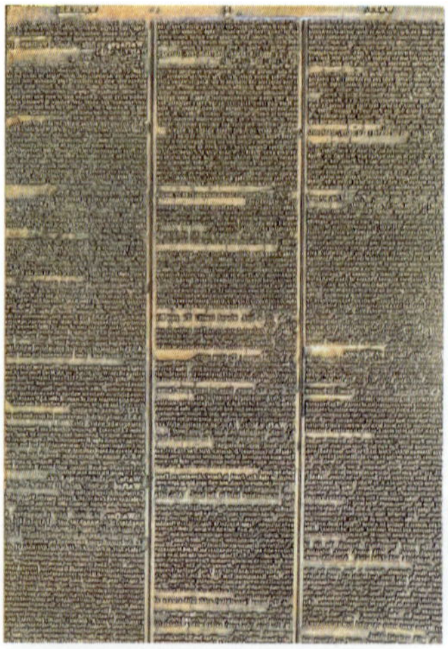

Ex coll. Karolyne & Bryan A. Garner

WAFT to WAFTER.

"All the steel-and-antinomy printing plates that served the *OED* for decades past were dumped, eventually to be tossed away. A few still survive: I still have, mounted in a frame, the plate for page 452 of volume V, which encompasses the words *Humoral* to *Humour*. . . . I would like to think that it might have been made in perhaps June 1899 and used to print sheets for the following 70 years." (Winchester 2003:246.)

THE PRINTING OF THE FIRST EDITION of the *OED* must have been a sight to behold: in the words of the lexicographer who became chief editor in the late 1980s, "the enormous printing machines stood two storeys tall, like the massive machines you see in old clips of newspaper offices, rattling out sheet after sheet of text for binding and then publication." (Simpson 2016:142.) The electro copper printing plates, measuring 9.7 inches by 7.4 inches and weighing 3.5 pounds apiece, had been painstakingly prepared in the late 19th and early 20th centuries. Then state-of-the-art, this technology would be swept away in the late 1980s by computerized typesetting.

Once the decision had been made to integrate Robert Burchfield's *OED Supplement* into the *OED* to create a second edition—an operation that Burchfield had declared "impossible" throughout the 1970s—the thousands of printing plates for the first edition became worthless. Their total weight was over 20 tons, and they were slated to be recycled as scrap.

Meanwhile, with the advent of computer-generated type, the executives at Oxford University Press decided to convert part of the printing works to offices for various other publishing divisions at the Press. So workers there began loading large quantities of the printing plates onto skips so that they could be transported elsewhere for melting down. When the IT Director at the Press, Ewen Fletcher, noticed this commotion, he alerted Richard Charkin (head of the Academic Division), Edmund Weiner and John Simpson (coeditors of the second edition), and Timothy Benbow (the newly appointed director of the *OED* project), who went down to the printing works to investigate what was happening. It was a part of the Press that the coeditors had never seen.

They tried to think of alternative uses for these plates, which could no longer be used for their original purposes. They decided to try selling them as souvenirs at the OUP bookshop on High Street; over quite some period, only a few of them sold. Everyone involved in OUP lexicography was allowed to take what they wanted: Edmund Weiner took two, John Simpson took ten, and Timothy Benbow took

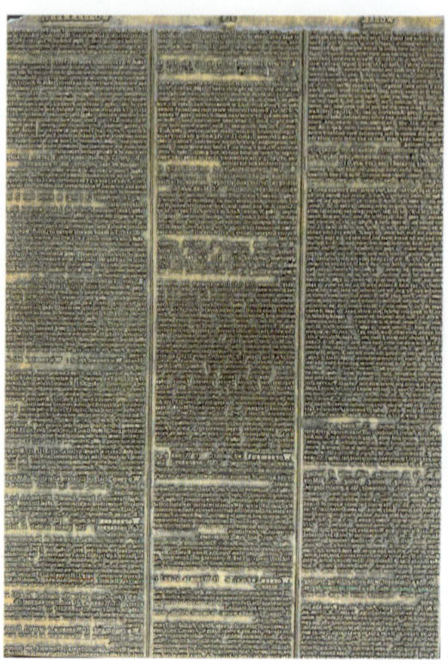

Ex coll. Karolyne & Bryan A. Garner

WORSE to WORSENMENT.

one (the first page of *Z*). Somewhere between 100 and 300 plates were spared.

The Garner Collection in Dallas has 18 of them, acquired from the late dictionary collector Tom Rodgers, who said that he had been allowed to take all he wanted from the printworks. He must have been visiting OUP at just the right time in the early to mid-1980s, before the decision had been made to sell them on High Street. Each plate is accompanied by a page printed from it:

Vol. 2, p. 1302: **cylinder** to **cymar**
Vol. 5, sig. 1, p. 87: **hard and fast** to **hard fern**
Vol. 5, p. 316: **herewithal** to **heritably**
Vol. 7, sig. 69, p. 1101: **pomegranate-tree** to **pommage**
Vol. 12 sig. 9, p. 136: **vermin** to **vermivorousness**
Vol. 12, sig. 22, p. 8: **waft** to **wafter**
Vol. 12, sig. 39, p. 278: **welky** to **well**
Vol. 12, sig. 46, p. 60: **whirl** to **whirligig**
Vol. 12, sig. 62, p. 316: **worse** to **worse**
Vol. 12, sig. 62, p. 318: **worse** to **worsenment**
Vol. 12, sig. 62, p. 319: **worser** to **worship**
Vol. 12, sig. 62, p. 320: **worship** to **worship**
Vol. 12, sig. 63, p. 328: **worth** to **worth**
1st Supplement (1933), p. 305: **vampish** to **verge**
1st Supplement (1933), p. 306: **verge** to **vimana**
1st Supplement (1933), p. 307: **vimful** to **voice**
1st Supplement (1933), p. 317: **whizzing** to **willow-ware**
1st Supplement (1933), p. 320: **woodbine** to **wow**

Most people who see and hold the plates are stunned by their intricacy and their weight. When you consider that there were 15,487 pages in the first edition and the 1933 supplement, and therefore that many plates had to be stored and periodically placed into the presses, the scale of the old-fashioned book production boggles the mind.

Ex coll. Karolyne & Bryan A. Garner

"In the past, huge storerooms had been stocked with these old copper printing plates. Over time the plates grew worn and were no longer of any use. Eventually they were recycled by being melted down and reused. . . . [Edmund Weiner] and I were horrified by what seemed to be the wilful destruction of the dictionary's history." (Simpson 2016:143.)

Ex coll. Karolyne & Bryan A. Garner

Seven printing plates displayed in front of a first edition.

Ex coll. Karolyne & Bryan A. Garner

Ex coll. Karolyne & Bryan A. Garner

Three Wyld classics.

98

Henry Cecil Kennedy Wyld

Lexicographic Cul-de-Sac

Wyld, Henry Cecil. ***The Universal Dictionary of the English Language: A new and original compilation giving all pronunciations in simplified and in standard phonetic notations, extensive etymologies, definitions, the latest accepted words in scientific, technical and general use, with copious illustrative phrases and colloquialisms.*** **London: Amalgamated Press, 1932.**

Wyld (1870–1945), the grandson of Scots, was the son of a commander in the service of the East India Company. He was educated privately at Lausanne and then enrolled successively at the universities of Bonn and Heidelberg, and then at Corpus Christi College, Oxford, where he studied linguistics and philology under Henry Sweet (see no. 87), earning his BA in 1899. With the help of Sweet's recommendation, he was appointed lecturer at University College, Liverpool, where he began an impressive record of linguistics-related publications: *The Historical Study of the Mother Tongue* (1906), *The Growth of English* (1907), *The Collected Papers of Henry Sweet* (1913; Sweet had died the year before), *A Short History of English* (1914), *A History of Modern Colloquial English* (1920), and *Studies in English Rhymes from Surrey to Pope* (1923). Most of these books went into several editions. In 1920, he was elected professor of English language and literature at Merton College, Oxford, where he remained for the rest of his life.

Wyld's big one-volume book *The Universal Dictionary of the English Language* appeared in 1932, focusing on contemporary usage, both literary and colloquial. Given his own eminence and the dictionary's ambitious scope, many contemporaries began thinking of him as a *Johnson redivivus*. Wyld's preface—"The Charm of Word Study"—was alluring. For example:

> If we reflect upon the subject at all, we shall soon realize that even our own English language which we know so well, and use so readily, though familiar is yet mysterious. Many

> persons who have but little time for special studies, though they may read and think about many things outside their daily routine of cares and duties, so far as their leisure may permit, have been unable to devote much attention to the study of words of their native tongue. They can speak it and read it and write it; they can say all, or nearly all, they want to say in it—and this is no mean accomplishment—and yet there are whole aspects of English of which, from the circumstances of their lives, they are totally unaware. English speech plays an enormous part in the lives of all of us, and yet when we come to think, we find that we know next to nothing about it. [P. i.]

Wyld's undertaking was a curious one: here he was in Merton College, Oxford, working away on a one-volume dictionary that clearly benefited from the great *Oxford English Dictionary.* Meanwhile, work had begun on the *Shorter Oxford English Dictionary* (*SOED*), which would appear just months later, in February 1933, with an impressive print run of 10,000 copies. Yet Wyld of Merton was racing to publish a competing work with the Amalgamated Press of London. He had always published in London, never with Oxford University Press; he presumably saw no conflict of interest, whereas some at the University might have viewed his work as being antithetical to the interests of the Press and therefore of the University. In any event, he persevered.

Wyld's book would be big—more than 1,400 pages—but it came nowhere near the size of the *OED* or the *Century.* Wyld understood that his competition was other stout one-volume works. He sought to surpass all similarly sized works in three categories: etymology (a strong suit for him), clarity of definitions, and informative illustrative uses (mostly of his own devising). Wyld meant to open new worlds of thought: "The extent to which our Dictionary will succeed in enabling readers to whom this aspect of the subject is quite unfamiliar to enter . . . new worlds . . . must depend largely upon themselves." (P. i.) In the following example, 89% of Wyld's entry consists of etymological notes (including the historical sense 1 of the *SOED* entry), at the end of which he has a fine seven-word definition; by comparison, only 12% of the corresponding *SOED* entry consists of etymological notes.

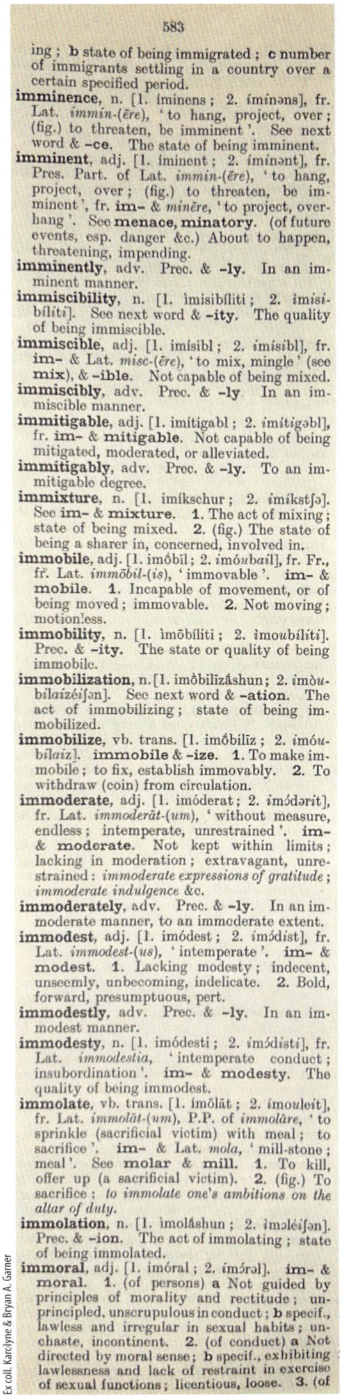

583

ing ; **b** state of being immigrated ; **c** number of immigrants settling in a country over a certain specified period.

imminence, n. [1. íminens ; 2. íminəns], fr. Lat. *immin-(ēre)*, 'to hang, project, over ; (fig.) to threaten, be imminent'. See next word & **-ce.** The state of being imminent.

imminent, adj. [1. íminent ; 2. íminənt], fr. Pres. Part. of Lat. *immin-(ēre)*, 'to hang, project, over ; (fig.) to threaten, be imminent', fr. **im-** & *minēre*, 'to project, overhang'. See **menace, minatory.** (of future events, esp. danger &c.) About to happen, threatening, impending.

imminently, adv. Prec. & **-ly.** In an imminent manner.

immiscibility, n. [1. ìmisibíliti ; 2. ìmisibíliti]. See next word & **-ity.** The quality of being immiscible.

immiscible, adj. [1. imísibl ; 2. imísibl], fr. **im-** & Lat. *misc-(ēre)*, 'to mix, mingle' (see **mix**), & **-ible.** Not capable of being mixed.

immiscibly, adv. Prec. & **-ly** In an immiscible manner.

immitigable, adj. [1. imítigabl ; 2. imítigəbl], fr. **im-** & **mitigable.** Not capable of being mitigated, moderated, or alleviated.

immitigably, adv. Prec. & **-ly.** To an immitigable degree.

immixture, n. [1. imíkschur ; 2. imíkstʃə]. See **im-** & **mixture. 1.** The act of mixing; state of being mixed. **2.** (fig.) The state of being a sharer in, concerned, involved in.

immobile, adj. [1. imóbīl ; 2. imóubail], fr. Fr., fr. Lat. *immōbil-(is)*, 'immovable'. **im-** & **mobile. 1.** Incapable of movement, or of being moved ; immovable. **2.** Not moving ; motionless.

immobility, n. [1. ìmōbíliti ; 2. ìmoubíliti]. Prec. & **-ity.** The state or quality of being immobile.

immobilization, n. [1. imòbilīzáshun ; 2. imòubilaizéiʃən]. See next word & **-ation.** The act of immobilizing ; state of being immobilized.

immobilize, vb. trans. [1. imóbilīz ; 2. imóubilaiz]. **immobile** & **-ize. 1.** To make immobile ; to fix, establish immovably. **2.** To withdraw (coin) from circulation.

immoderate, adj. [1. imóderat ; 2. imɔ́dərit], fr. Lat. *immoderāt-(um)*, 'without measure, endless ; intemperate, unrestrained'. **im-** & **moderate.** Not kept within limits ; lacking in moderation ; extravagant, unrestrained : *immoderate expressions of gratitude* ; *immoderate indulgence* &c.

immoderately, adv. Prec. & **-ly.** In an immoderate manner, to an immoderate extent.

immodest, adj. [1. imódest ; 2. imɔ́dist], fr. Lat. *immodest-(us)*, 'intemperate'. **im-** & **modest. 1.** Lacking modesty ; indecent, unseemly, unbecoming, indelicate. **2.** Bold, forward, presumptuous, pert.

immodestly, adv. Prec. & **-ly.** In an immodest manner.

immodesty, n. [1. imódesti ; 2. imɔ́disti], fr. Lat. *immodestia*, 'intemperate conduct ; insubordination'. **im-** & **modesty.** The quality of being immodest.

immolate, vb. trans. [1. ímōlāt ; 2. ímouleit], fr. Lat. *immolāt-(um)*, P.P. of *immolāre*, 'to sprinkle (sacrificial victim) with meal ; to sacrifice'. **im-** & Lat. *mola*, 'mill-stone ; meal'. See **molar** & **mill. 1.** To kill, offer up (a sacrificial victim). **2.** (fig.) To sacrifice : *to immolate one's ambitions on the altar of duty.*

immolation, n. [1. ìmoláshun ; 2. ìmɔléiʃən]. Prec. & **-ion.** The act of immolating ; state of being immolated.

immoral, adj. [1. imóral ; 2. imɔ́rəl]. **im-** & **moral. 1.** (of persons) **a** Not guided by principles of morality and rectitude ; unprincipled, unscrupulous in conduct ; **b** specif., lawless and irregular in sexual habits ; unchaste, incontinent. **2.** (of conduct) **a** Not directed by moral sense ; **b** specif., exhibiting lawlessness and lack of restraint in exercise of sexual functions ; licentious, loose. **3.** (of

Ex coll. Karclyne & Bryan A. Garner

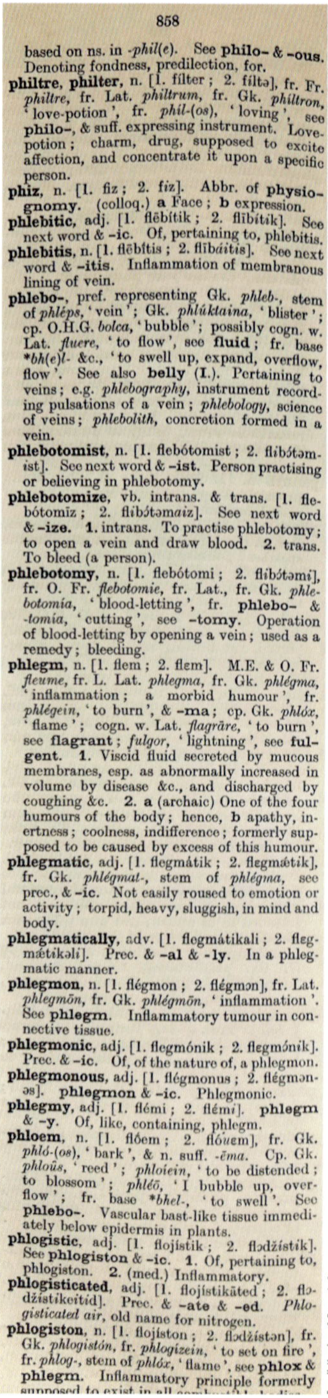

858

based on ns. in *-phil(e)*. See **philo-** & **-ous.** Denoting fondness, predilection, for.

philtre, philter, n. [1. fílter ; 2. fíltə], fr. Fr. *philtre*, fr. Lat. *philtrum*, fr. Gk. *phíltron*, 'love-potion', fr. *phíl-(os)*, 'loving', see **philo-**, & suff. expressing instrument. Love-potion ; charm, drug, supposed to excite affection, and concentrate it upon a specific person.

phiz, n. [1. fiz ; 2. fiz]. Abbr. of **physiognomy.** (colloq.) **a** Face ; **b** expression.

phlebitic, adj. [1. flēbítik ; 2. flībítik]. See next word & **-ic.** Of, pertaining to, phlebitis.

phlebitis, n. [1. flēbítis ; 2. flībáitis]. See next word & **-itis.** Inflammation of membranous lining of vein.

phlebo-, pref. representing Gk. *phleb-*, stem of *phléps*, 'vein'; Gk. *phlúktaina*, 'blister'; cp. O.H.G. *bolca*, 'bubble'; possibly cogn. w. Lat. *fluere*, 'to flow', see **fluid** ; fr. base **bh(e)l-* &c., 'to swell up, expand, overflow, flow'. See also **belly** (**I.**). Pertaining to veins ; e.g. *phlebography*, instrument recording pulsations of a vein ; *phlebology*, science of veins ; *phlebolith*, concretion formed in a vein.

phlebotomist, n. [1. flebótomist ; 2. flibɔ́təmist]. See next word & **-ist.** Person practising or believing in phlebotomy.

phlebotomize, vb. intrans. & trans. [1. flebótomīz ; 2. flibɔ́təmaiz]. See next word & **-ize. 1.** intrans. To practise phlebotomy ; to open a vein and draw blood. **2.** trans. To bleed (a person).

phlebotomy, n. [1. flebótomi ; 2. flibɔ́təmi], fr. O. Fr. *flebotomie*, fr. Lat., fr. Gk. *phlebotomía*, 'blood-letting', fr. **phlebo-** & *-tomía*, 'cutting', see **-tomy.** Operation of blood-letting by opening a vein ; used as a remedy ; bleeding.

phlegm, n. [1. flem ; 2. flɛm]. M.E. & O. Fr. *fleume*, fr. L. Lat. *phlegma*, fr. Gk. *phlégma*, 'inflammation ; a morbid humour', fr. *phlégein*, 'to burn', & **-ma** ; cp. Gk. *phlóx*, 'flame'; cogn. w. Lat. *flagrāre*, 'to burn', see **flagrant** ; *fulgor*, 'lightning', see **fulgent. 1.** Viscid fluid secreted by mucous membranes, esp. as abnormally increased in volume by disease &c., and discharged by coughing &c. **2. a** (archaic) One of the four humours of the body ; hence, **b** apathy, inertness ; coolness, indifference ; formerly supposed to be caused by excess of this humour.

phlegmatic, adj. [1. flegmátik ; 2. flɛgmǽtik], fr. Gk. *phlégmat-*, stem of *phlégma*, see prec., & **-ic.** Not easily roused to emotion or activity ; torpid, heavy, sluggish, in mind and body.

phlegmatically, adv. [1. flegmátikali ; 2. flɛgmǽtikəli]. Prec. & **-al** & **-ly.** In a phlegmatic manner.

phlegmon, n. [1. flégmon ; 2. flégmən], fr. Lat. *phlegmōn*, fr. Gk. *phlégmōn*, 'inflammation'. See **phlegm.** Inflammatory tumour in connective tissue.

phlegmonic, adj. [1. flegmónik ; 2. flɛgmɔ́nik]. Prec. & **-ic.** Of, of the nature of, a phlegmon.

phlegmonous, adj. [1. flégmonus ; 2. flégmənəs]. **phlegmon** & **-ic.** Phlegmonic.

phlegmy, adj. [1. flémi ; 2. flémi]. **phlegm** & **-y.** Of, like, containing, phlegm.

phloem, n. [1. flóem ; 2. flóuɛm], fr. Gk. *phló-(os)*, 'bark', & n. suff. *-ēma*. Cp. Gk. *phloûs*, 'reed'; *phloíein*, 'to be distended ; to blossom'; *phléō*, 'I bubble up, overflow'; fr. base **bhel-*, 'to swell'. See **phlebo-.** Vascular bast-like tissue immediately below epidermis in plants.

phlogistic, adj. [1. flojístik ; 2. flɔdžístik]. See **phlogiston** & **-ic. 1.** Of, pertaining to, phlogiston. **2.** (med.) Inflammatory.

phlogisticated, adj. [1. flojístikāted ; 2. flɔdžístikeitid]. Prec. & **-ate** & **-ed.** *Phlogisticated air*, old name for nitrogen.

phlogiston, n. [1. flojíston ; 2. flɔdžístən], fr. Gk. *phlogistón*, fr. *phlogízein*, 'to set on fire', fr. *phlog-*, stem of *phlóx*, 'flame', see **phlox** & **phlegm.** Inflammatory principle formerly

Ex coll. Karolyne & Bryan A. Garner

Wyld (1932)	*SOED* (1933)
augur (**I.**), n. [1. áwger; 2. ɔ́gə] Lat., member of the college of priests in ancient Rome who foretold the future, esp. by observing flight or notes of birds; the word is for **avi-ger*, the first element of wh. is *avis*, 'bird', see **aviary,** & the second prob. fr. Lat. *gerere*, wh. has many & various meanings, e.g. 'bear, conduct, direct, manage' (see **gerent**); the view that *gur* is fr. an old vb. meaning 'look at, consider', & cogn. w. O. Slav. *zǐrěti*, 'see, glance at' &c., is now thought less probable. One who predicts events; fortune-teller, soothsayer.	**Augur,** sb. [ǭ·gəɹ] 1549. [a. L.; perh. f. *avis* + *gar*, conn. w. *garrire*; or f. *augere* (Fick).] **1.** *Rom. Hist.* A religious official, who interpreted omens derived from the flight, singing, and feeding of birds, the appearance of the entrails of sacrificial victims, etc., and advised upon the course of public business in accordance with them. **2.** Hence: A soothsayer, diviner, or prophet generally 1593. **1.** Augures, that by observation of the birds of the air . . . made men believe they knew things to come HOOPER. **2.** A. accursed! denouncing mischief still POPE. vars. †**Augurer,** †**Augurist.** Hence **Augurate, Augurship,** the office, or term of office, of an a. **Augurous** *a.* presaging (*rare*).

Wyld omitted the cognates listed in the *SOED*.

In other entries, such as for the adjective *international*, you can readily see genuine merit in the ground covered by Wyld as opposed to the *SOED*:

Wyld (1932)	*SOED* (1933)
international (**I.**), adj. [1. ìnternáshunal; 2. ìntənǽʃənəl] **inter** & **national.** Existing between, carried on between, relating to, representing, different nations; *international peace, trade*; *an international code, conference*; *international games* &c.; *international law*, the law of nations, the body of rules regarded by the nations of the world as binding on them in their relations with each other, in peace and war; styled *public*, in distinction from *private, international law*, which deals with the rights and obligations of private citizens in a foreign country or with the conflict of laws of different countries.	**International** [intəɹnæ·ʃənăl]. 1780. [INTER II.2.] *adj.* **A.** Existing, constituted, or carried on between different nations; pertaining to the relations between nations. **b.** (with capital *I.*) Belonging to the International Working Men's Association, a society of working-men founded in London in 1864 (and dissolved in 1874), the objects of which were identified with those of the socialism of Marx. The great science of i. law, the determining authority in questions of right between independent states HALLAM An I. Exhibition 1861, yacht race 1888.

Here Wyld's entry is palpably superior: the *SOED*, after all, devoted 7 of its 11 lines to a London society that existed for barely a decade in the 19th century. Wyld, by contrast, gives six current collocations and aptly elucidates not just *international law* (also termed *public international law*) but also *private international* law. And he accomplished this using only 88 words in the entry, as opposed to the *SOED*'s 82.

In short, Wyld's lexicographic style had significant merit even if his product was short-lived. Through the 1930s, Wyld secured an impressive number of copublishing deals with George Routledge, Herbert Joseph, and the Selfridge department-store chain in England, E.P. Dutton in New York, Standard American Corporation in Chicago, Maskew Miller in Cape Town, and even Maruzen in Tokyo, ensuring that his dictionary remained in print into the 1980s. But no one took the trouble to do a serious revision of the original dictionary, meaning that it ultimately proved a dead end.

"One of the charms of etymology is that it reveals the human mind at work, forever striving to express new ideas and shades of meaning, adapting and readapting material which is as old as man himself, so that it shall reflect the modes of thought, the needs and hopes, the occupations and habits, of every age and of every manner of life." (Preface, p. iv.)

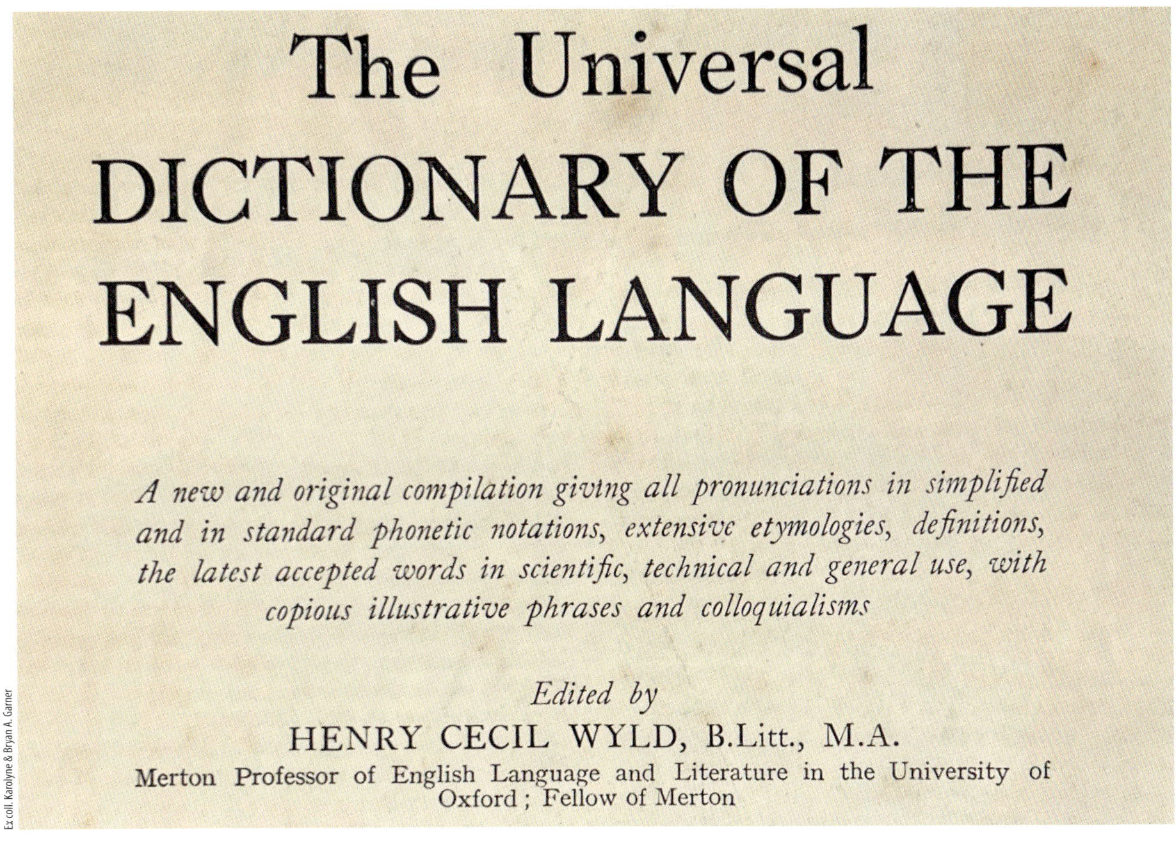
The Universal
DICTIONARY OF THE
ENGLISH LANGUAGE

A new and original compilation giving all pronunciations in simplified and in standard phonetic notations, extensive etymologies, definitions, the latest accepted words in scientific, technical and general use, with copious illustrative phrases and colloquialisms

Edited by
HENRY CECIL WYLD, B.Litt., M.A.
Merton Professor of English Language and Literature in the University of Oxford; Fellow of Merton

Ex coll. Karolyne & Bryan A. Garner

Ex coll. Karolyne & Bryan A. Garner

The first edition of 1933.

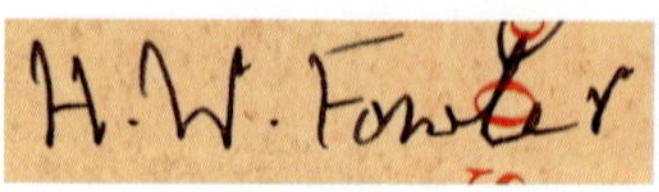

Ex coll. Karolyne & Bryan A. Garner

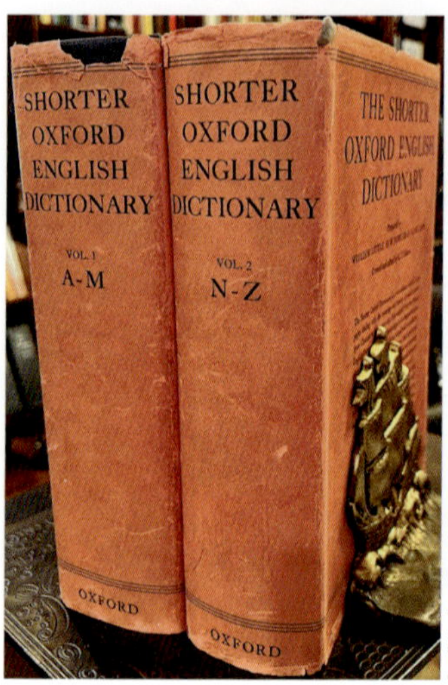

Ex coll. Karolyne & Bryan A. Garner

The second edition of 1936.

99

Short, Shorter, and Shortest Oxford Dictionaries

***The Concise Oxford Dictionary of Current English*. H.W. Fowler & F.G. Fowler eds. Oxford: Clarendon Press, 1911.**

***The Pocket Oxford Dictionary of Current English*. H.W. Fowler & F.G. Fowler eds. Oxford: Clarendon Press, 1924.**

***The Little Oxford Dictionary of Current English*. George Ostler & Jessie Coulson eds. Oxford: Clarendon Press, 1930.**

***The Shorter Oxford English Dictionary on Historical Principles*. William Little, H.W. Fowler, J. Coulson & C.T. Onions eds. 2 vols. Oxford: Clarendon Press, 1933. 2d ed. 1936. 3d ed. 1955. 4th ed. 1993. 5th ed. 2002. 6th ed. 2007.**

***The Compact Edition of the Oxford English Dictionary: Complete Text Reproduced Micrographically*. 2 vols. Oxford: Clarendon Press, 1971.**

***The New Oxford Dictionary of English*. Oxford: Clarendon Press, 1998. Subsequent editions titled *The Oxford Dictionary of English*.**

The great virtue of the *Oxford English Dictionary* has always been its size: no other English dictionary can compete with its historical coverage. But the great vice of the *Oxford English Dictionary* has always been its size: it occupies a bookcase and has been priced accordingly. Almost from the earliest days, there was constant negotiation over how big the dictionary should be, and a belief that, if it proved to be too big (whatever that meant), then it should be complemented by a shorter version (whatever that meant).

When in 1879 the Philological Society entered into the original indenture with Oxford University Press, the subject of an abridgment was explicitly dealt with: at their discretion, "the Delegates [of the Press] may (if and whenever they think fit) prepare and publish any

Dictionaries compiled or abridged from the principal Dictionary, and in such form as they may think fit."

It's a perennial problem in all large-scale reference publishing: the monumental multivolume works generate the intellectual excitement, but they rarely sell enough copies to recover their costs. In 1911, for instance, Oxford University Press tallied up the expenses and revenues associated with the *OED*: they had spent £150,000 on a book that had brought in just £60,000. (Gilliver 2016:318.) To avoid financial catastrophe, they'd need to sell smaller dictionaries in large numbers.

In 1911 Humphrey Milford (1877–1952), head of the Press, was musing on a whole range of dictionaries, ranging from a 1-shilling "elementary" version to a 30-shilling "abridged." (Gilliver 2016:318.) Though he didn't get exactly what he asked for, Milford's vision largely came to pass: OUP produced a wide array of smaller dictionaries based on the *OED*. The first to market was *The Concise Oxford Dictionary of Current English*, published on 16 June 1911. The title page says that the contents are "adapted . . . from The Oxford Dictionary." It was the work of two brothers, known then, and even better known now, for their writing on the language: Henry Watson Fowler (1858–1933) and Francis George Fowler (1871–1918).

How to abridge the *OED*? What's expendable? We get our first hint on the title page: the dictionary focuses on *current* English, meaning the words that a reader was likely to encounter in 1911. The *OED*, by contrast, has entries on words not spoken in almost a millennium. Very few readers will ever encounter words like *moderable*, *moderacy*, *moderance*, *moderant*, *moderantism*, and *moderantist*, so the Fowlers skipped them; *moderate*, on the other hand, both adjective and verb, is still in use, so it remains. The historical information is jettisoned, along with nearly all the quotations. The Fowlers did, however, give extensive attention to the common words that prove so challenging to lexicographers: the prepositions (what does *of* mean?) and the polysemous nouns (*heart*, *time*) and verbs (*show up*, *show off*, *show yourself*, *show mercy*, *show it to be false*).

Information is packed tightly. The type is small and the margins are smaller; there's very little white space to relieve the eye. The Fowlers exercised "the severest economy of expression—amounting to the adoption of telegraphese—that readers can be expected to put up with." (P. iv.) Exceedingly curt etymologies appear at the end, rather

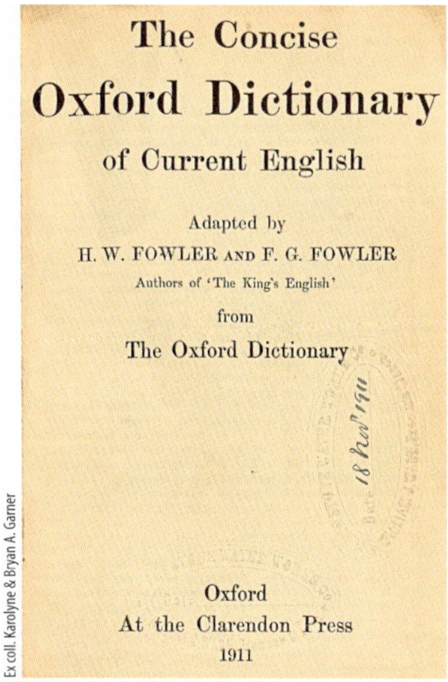
The Concise
Oxford Dictionary
of Current English
Adapted by
H. W. FOWLER AND F. G. FOWLER
Authors of 'The King's English'
from
The Oxford Dictionary
Oxford
At the Clarendon Press
1911

Ex coll. Karolyne & Bryan A. Garner

The first edition of 1911.

Ex coll. Karolyne & Bryan A. Garner

The fourth edition of 1951.

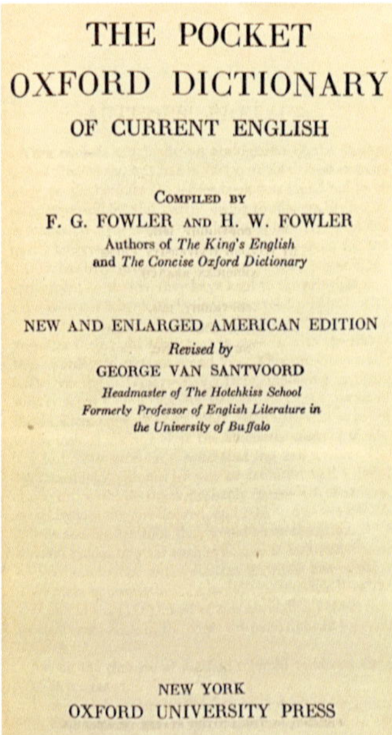

THE POCKET
OXFORD DICTIONARY
OF CURRENT ENGLISH

COMPILED BY
F. G. FOWLER AND H. W. FOWLER
Authors of *The King's English*
and *The Concise Oxford Dictionary*

NEW AND ENLARGED AMERICAN EDITION
Revised by
GEORGE VAN SANTVOORD
Headmaster of The Hotchkiss School
Formerly Professor of English Literature in
the University of Buffalo

NEW YORK
OXFORD UNIVERSITY PRESS

Ex coll. Karolyne & Bryan A. Garner

The 1935 American edition of the *Pocket*.

Ex coll. Karolyne & Bryan A. Garner

than beginning, of each entry: *review* is "f. F *reveue* (now *-vue*) orig. fem. p.p. of *revoir* f. L RE- 9 (*vidēre* see)," *mask* is "f. F. *masque* Sp. *máscara*, or f. med.L *mascus*, etym. dub." Most pronunciations were omitted "on the assumption that the reader is already familiar with the normal values of some letters and combinations," though they made exceptions for very irregular pronunciations—"**cough**[I] (kawf, kŏf)"—and occasionally they editorialized: "**often** (aw′fn, ŏ′fn; *vulg.* -ten)."

There's a curious fact about this abridgment: it appeared before parts of the work it was abridging. In 1911, the *OED* had published only through the end of *P*, though *R* was nearly finished. After that, nothing was ready to be seen. The Fowlers' job was to condense the *OED*, not to produce a new dictionary, but from *S* to *Z* there was nothing to condense. For these words, they depended on other dictionaries and their own abilities.

Selling for three shillings sixpence, the book proved immediately successful. Not only were the reviews strong, but the book sold 40,000 copies in less than a year. (Gilliver 2016:318.) The line remains strong today. The current *Concise*, the 12th edition (2011), edited by Angus Stevenson and Maurice Waite, contains close to a quarter-million entries—a gloriously loose idea of "concise"—and is the preferred authority for spellings at the United Nations and NATO.

The *OED* begat the *Concise*, and the *Concise* begat the *Pocket*—that is, the *Pocket Oxford Dictionary of Current English*. This, too, was the work of the Fowler brothers, though F.G. Fowler's death in 1918 left H.W. to complete the work alone. The trim size is even smaller than the already-small *Concise*, just 7 inches tall. In the space of two sentences, a publisher's notice calls the work both a "modest compendium" and a "triumph of condensation," and despite the apparent contradiction, it probably deserves both titles. "The great Oxford Dictionary," the publisher announces, "is the ultimate source of most of the information . . . . It is thus possible to claim for the little book unique authority among books of its size and price." (P. v.)

There are some departures from the policies of the *Concise*. H.W. Fowler admitted that he had abandoned "the C.O.D. assumption that pronunciation might be dispensed with for most words." Etymologies, on the other hand, "have been cut down to little more than bare statements of ultimate origin" because "the function of etymology in a small dictionary is taken to be the merely negative one of saving the reader from imagining a connexion between words that are in fact independent." (P. iv.)

But OUP still hadn't finished repackaging *OED* content. In 1930 appeared *The Little Oxford Dictionary of Current English*, "based on the Pocket Oxford Dictionary." The chief editor was George Ostler, but his death in 1929 left Jessie Senior (1903–1987) to complete the work. Senior, "who contrived to fit in her wedding" while she was working on the *Little*, became Jessie Coulson, and went on "to become a prolific Oxford lexicographer." (Gilliver 2016:400n.) The title is apt: this is a very little book. It's smaller than even the *Pocket*, only about five inches high, and thinner, with just 626 pages. Like its predecessors, it was marketed for combining the convenience of a small book with the authority of a very big one.

"Since the publication of the Pocket Dictionary the publishers have to deplore the loss of H.W. FOWLER, a lexicographer of rare genius. They have been fortunate in securing, for this edition, the services of his friend and collaborator, H.G. Le Mesurier." (Prefatory note to the 2d ed. of the *Pocket Oxford*, p. i.)

All these reduced versions claimed the cultural authority of the *OED*, but they also removed the historical information that was the *OED*'s defining feature. One adaptation of the *OED*, though, preserves the historical character of its model. In 1903, William Little (1848–1922) of Corpus Christi College signed a contract to produce *The Shorter Oxford English Dictionary on Historical Principles*; after his death in 1922, H.W. Fowler and Jessie Coulson brought it across the finish line.

Ex coll. Karolyne & Bryan A. Garner

Limited-edition pewter binding on the 1990 printing of the *Little Oxford Dictionary* (6th ed.).

Overseeing the entire affair was C.T. Onions, who explained that the 15,000 large quarto pages of the *OED* had been compressed into 2,500 regular quarto pages. Onions was characteristically straightforward:

> The aim of this Dictionary is to present in miniature all the features of the principal work. It is designed to embrace not only the literary and colloquial English of the present day together with such technical and scientific terms as are most frequently met with or are likely to be the subject of inquiry, but also a considerable proportion of obsolete, archaic, and dialectal words and uses.

"*The Shorter Oxford English Dictionary* . . . is thoroughly up to date by having included in it new words, and new meanings of words, arising from such causes as the development of science and industrial invention, and the increased influence of American thought and speech." (1933 preface, p. iv.)

The *Shorter* used different principles to abridge its model. Though it did not follow the lead of the Fowlers in limiting their survey to "current English," they did narrow the historical range. The full *OED* strives to include words that have circulated since the year 1150. The *SOED* pushes the date later, covering words in circulation since 1700, along with words that appear in selected works from before that date (Shakespeare's plays, the King James Bible, and so

Courtesy of Oxford University Press

Charles Talbut Onions.

on). Quotations make up the bulk of the very bulky *OED*; they've been severely trimmed and often omitted from the *SOED*. The *OED* strives for precision in its historical information: it dates *mutic* to 1777, *mutiny* to 1567, and *mutism* to 1824. Since its fourth edition, the *SOED* has dated these to L18, M16, and E19—late 18th, mid-16th, and early 19th century, respectively.

Onions continually revised and augmented the *Shorter* through three editions, and he produced addenda as late as 1959. A fourth edition finally appeared in 1993 under the distinguished editorship of Lesley Brown, who took 13 years to make a thorough revision. A fifth edition came in 2002, and a sixth in 2007. This latest version contains 600,000 words, phrases, and definitions, and about one-third of the coverage of the full *OED*. Though it is also available as a smartphone app, it remains the largest print version of an English dictionary that is still maintained by Oxford University Press.

"Almost every member of the lexicographical team took part in the first round of editing. Proofs of the results were sent out to advisers for criticisms and suggestions, and many individual entries were also submitted to subject specialists. Comments from both these sources were then fed into a revision of the whole text by senior lexicographers. But for the requirement of publication, this revision could continue forever." (Preface to the 4th ed. of the *Shorter*, p. viii.)

One other condensed version of the *OED* demands our attention: the *Compact*. With this we need not ask what was omitted, because it's all there—just very, *very* small.

The plan for the *Compact* came from OUP's New York office in 1968, when a new micrographic technique suggested that they might be able to issue the full text of the *OED* in miniature. With an investment of just over £100,000 (nearly £1.5 million today), the Press reproduced the entire 12-volume *OED* in 2 volumes, with four pages of the original appearing on each page as four blocks of tiny print, arranged 2 × 2. Only young eyes can read the *Compact* without the accompanying magnifying glass, but for the first time the whole *OED*—followed soon by a third volume containing the four-volume *Supplement*, and then a second edition of the *Compact* that reproduced *nine* pages of *OED2* on each page, arranged 3 × 3—could be owned by "thousands of individuals who could never have afforded the full-size version." (Gilliver 2016:489.) And once the Book of the Month Club chose to promote it, sales took off—around 25,000 copies in the first year alone.

Ex coll. Karolyne & Bryan A. Garner

Lesley Brown's fourth edition.

Also claiming a place among *OED* adaptations is *The New Oxford Dictionary of English*, first published in 1998. This project shared much of its research, and occasionally some staff, with the *OED*. But it was not an abridgment or even a repackaging of the *OED*. It was a new dictionary, built on its own foundations. It was noteworthy for applying new principles for defining "to account for the dynamism, imaginativeness, and flexibility of ordinary usage." As the preface explained, the focus was on "identifying what is 'central and typical,' as distinct from the time-honoured search for 'necessary conditions' of meaning. . . . Past attempts to cover the meaning of all possible uses of a word have tended to lead to a blurred, unfocused result, in which the core of the meaning is obscured by many minor uses. . . . The result is fewer meanings, with sharper, crisper definitions." The editors took advantage of digital tools to analyze the British National Corpus, a database of tens of millions of words of text—the digital age's equivalent of Johnson's trawl through English literature or the *OED*'s vast reading program.

As is often the case when practical lexicography imports ideas from academic linguistics, some traditionalists balked. And in the second edition the title *New Oxford Dictionary of English* was abandoned for *The Oxford Dictionary of English*, a move that has produced confusion: the *OED* and the *ODE* are interchangeable in too many journalists' minds. But as Gilliver notes, "It was a critical and commercial success, and went on to become a key member of OUP's family of English dictionaries, and a version of the text eventually formed the heart of the Oxford Dictionaries website." (Gilliver 2016:565n.)

Ex coll. Karolyne & Bryan A. Garner

The 1971 *Compact OED1*, with four printed pages reduced to one by microprinting. Patented by Albert Boni (1892–1981), this new printing method put the full text of the *OED* into the hands of thousands of readers.

CHILL

Childbed (tʃəi·ldbed). ME. [f. CHILD *sb.* + BED *sb.*] **1.** The bed in which a child is born 1594. **2.** The state of a woman in labour ME. **3.** The womb. Now *dial.* 1535. Also *attrib.*

Child-birth (tʃəi·ldbɜ̄ɹþ). 1549. [f. as prec. + BIRTH.] The bearing or birth of a child.

Childe; see CHILD *sb.* I. 5.

Childermas (tʃi·ldəɹmæ̆s). *arch.* [Repr. an OE. wd., f. *cildra* gen. pl. + *mæsse.*] The festival of the Holy Innocents (the 28th of December), commemorating the slaughter of the children by Herod (*Matt.* ii. 16). Usually *c.-day, -tide.*

Childhood (tʃəi·ldhud). [OE. *cildhád*; see -HEAD.] **1.** The state or stage of life of a child; the time during which one is a child; the time from birth to puberty. Also *fig.* **2.** *concr.* This state or age personified 1605. †**3.** Childishness -ME. †**4.** = *childship* -1626. Also *attrib.*

1. *fig.* The C. of our ioy *Rom. & Jul.* III. iii. 95. 2. The well-governed c. of this realm SCOTT. 4. *Lear* II. iv. 181. Phr. *Second c.*: the state of childishness incident to extreme old age.

Childish (tʃəi·ldiʃ), *a.* [OE. *cildisc*; see -ISH[1].] **1.** Of, belonging, or proper to a child or to childhood. **2.** Not befitting mature age; puerile, silly ME.

1. C. trebble *A. Y. L.* II. vii. 162. 2. What cannot be auoided, 'Twere c. weaknesse to lament *3 Hen. VI,* v. iv. 38. Hence **Chi·ldish·ly** *adv.*, **-ness.**

Childlike, child-like (tʃəi·ldləik), *a.* 1586. [f. CHILD *sb.*] **1.** Belonging to or becoming a child; filial. **2.** Like a child; (of qualities, etc.) like those of a child. (Usu. in a good sense, as opp. to *childish.*) 1738. Also as *adv.*

1. Her child-like dutie *Two Gent.* III. i. 75. 2. The c. heart WESLEY. Hence **Chi·ldlikeness.**

†**Childre, children,** pl. of CHILD.

Childwife, child-wife. †**1.** (tʃəi·ld,wəif), A woman in, or just out of, childbed -1636. **2.** (tʃəi·ld,wəi:f), A wife who is a child. (Always with hyphen.) 1852.

†**Childwite** (tʃəi·ldwəit). ME. [f. OE. *cild* + *wite* penalty.] *Old Law.* A fine paid to the lord for getting his bondwoman with child -1607.

Chile, chili, vars. of CHILLI.

Chiliad (ki·liăd). 1598. [ad. L. *chilias, -ad-,* a. Gr.] **1.** A group of 1,000 (things); a thousand. **2.** A period of 1,000 years 1653; *esp.* the millennium (*Rev.* xx. 1–5) 1702.

2. After some. . Centuries, or even Chiliads HARTLEY.

Chiliagon (ki·liăgǫ̆n). 1692. [f. Gr. χίλιοι + γωνία.] A plane figure with a thousand angles.

Chiliahedron (ki:liăhī·drǫ̆n). *rare.* 1690. [f. Gr. χίλιοι + ἕδρα.] A plane figure having a thousand sides.

Chiliarch (ki·li,aɹk). 1656. [ad. L., a. Gr. χιλιάρχης, -ος, f. χίλιοι + ἀρχός.] The commander of a thousand men. So **Chi·liarchy,** †a body of a thousand men; the post of c.

Chiliasm (ki·li,æ̆z'm). 1610. [ad. Gr. χιλιασμός, f. χιλιάς.] The doctrine of the millennium; the opinion that Christ will reign in bodily presence on earth for a thousand years. So **Chi·liast,** an adherent of c. **Chilia·stic,** †**-al** *a.*, **-ally** *adv.*

†**Chili·ndre.** ME. [ad. med.L. *chilindrus,* for L. *cylindrus,* a. Gr.] A portable sun-dial of cylindrical form used in early times -1530.

Chilio-; see KILO-.

Chill (tʃil), *sb.* [OE. *cęle, cięle* :—OTeut. type *kaliz,* f. *kalan* to be COLD. App. obs. by 1400, but revived since *c* 1600.]

†**I.** In OE. and ME. (*chile, chele, cheele.*) Replaced by mod. COLD.

II. [f. the vb. or adj.] (*chill.*) **1.** An unnaturally lowered bodily temperature marked by shivering, etc.; the cold fit of an ague; now *esp.* a sudden affection of physical cold, which is often a first stage or symptom of illness 1601. **2.** A coldness of the air, water, etc., which makes one shiver; a cold which has a depressing effect on the body 1788. Also in *pl.* **3.** *fig.* A depressing influence upon the feelings; depressing coldness of manner 1821. **4.** *techn.* An iron mould, or a piece of iron in a sand mould, for making chilled castings; cf. CHILL *v.* 1874.

Ex coll. Karolyne & Bryan A. Garner

From the 1933 *Shorter*.

Photo courtesy of Acme Photo

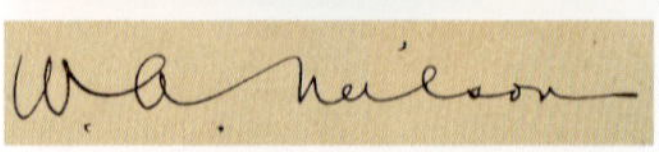

Ex coll. Karolyne & Bryan A. Garner

Announcing

The Publication of

WEBSTER'S

NEW INTERNATIONAL

DICTIONARY

Second Edition

HOTEL KIMBALL

Springfield, Massachusetts

MONDAY EVENING

JUNE 25 · 1934

Ex coll. Karolyne & Bryan A. Garner

A 42-page commemorative pamphlet was issued after the 1934 dinner celebrating the publication of *W2*, which was hailed as "the interpreter of both past and contemporary civilization."

100

William Allan Neilson

Refurbishing Webster Again

***Webster's New International Dictionary*. William Allan Neilson ed. 2d ed. Springfield: G. & C. Merriam Co., 1934.**

WITH A STAFF OF MORE THAN 300 and an investment of some $25 million (in today's money), "Webster's Second"—or *W2*, as it's known to initiates—was the most ambitious dictionary project that Merriam-Webster had ever undertaken. It was led by William Allan Neilson (1869–1946), president of Smith College, a literary scholar who was born in Perthshire, Scotland; was educated at the University of Edinburgh; and then took his PhD in English literature from Harvard University, where he joined the faculty. He was a Shakespeare scholar and an expert in poetics. In 1917, he became the president of Smith College, where he spent the rest of his teaching career. In 1924, he was invited to become the chief editor of *W2*—and he accepted, saying of the dictionary, "There is probably no book that has been written in a hundred years that has done so much . . . for the country at large as [this] Dictionary." (Thorp 1956:326.) Retaining Neilson for this work was in keeping with the idea of having respected academics—close to what we now call "public intellectuals"—hold the post, as Noah Porter did from 1864 and William Torrey Harris (no. 93) from 1900.

Neilson managed both personnel decisions and, to a great extent, editorial decisions. Almost without fail during his tenure, he traveled every Tuesday one hour from Smith to be in the Springfield offices. He presided over weekly meetings with Merriam's president (Asa S. Baker), the general editor (Thomas Knott), and the managing editor (Paul Carhart), who brought forward whatever contentious issues emerged. And Neilson made astute hiring decisions, capitalizing on his experience in hiring faculty members. For example, at one point the well-known litterateur Logan Pearsall Smith, who was living in the United States, was suggested for a position. Neilson was pragmatically wary, writing to Baker: "I have thought of him as a somewhat elegant gentleman of leisure who would prefer to live in England and write little essays. I gather, however, that his book on words and idioms has a good deal of learning in it with some tendency to be arbitrary." He continued: "I should think it very unlikely that he would be willing to work in harness even if he turned out to be properly equipped. . . . He has never held any academic or business position, and I suspect that he is too much of a kid-glove person for our purposes." (Thorp 1956:328.)

These were astute managerial observations. Despite what many people think, dictionary editors don't work in leisurely fashion, pursuing abstruse etymologies in a relaxed way. When a lexicographic project is underway, a certain number of entries must be completed each hour or each day—almost by quota. It's the only way that schedules can be met. The subeditors are indeed working "under harness." There is no time for the many high-maintenance dilettantes who inevitably apply for lexicographic positions. They must be spurned.

W2 kept very much to the *New International* editorial protocols, including the divided page introduced by William Torrey Harris in the first decade of the 20th century. Like Harris, Neilson used his connections to locate specialist reviewers such as Joseph Sweetman Ames of Johns Hopkins University on physics; John Samuel Kenyon of Hiram College on phonetics; George Lyman Kittredge of Harvard University on synonyms; Reginald Edgar Lyons of Warner Brothers and Metro-Goldwyn-Mayer for film; Douglas Clyde MacIntosh of Yale University on theology; Sydney P. Noe of the American Numismatic Society on coins; Roscoe Pound, dean of Harvard Law, on legal terms; Alfred Dwight Sheffield of Wellesley College on grammar—and two Harvard experts on reptiles and paleontology. There were dozens of others. Neilson himself acted as the expert on Scotticisms and British universities.

Page by page, the editors benefited from the recently completed *OED*. They doubtless also reviewed the entries in the *Century Dictionary* and *Funk & Wagnalls*—just as the editors of all three of those works had benefited from earlier dictionaries published by Merriam. The key was to compose entries that were different enough to seem entirely independent.

The Merriam Co. engaged as proofreader a man whose father had served that role for the *Century Dictionary* in the early 1890s, the Funk & Wagnalls *Standard Dictionary* later in that decade, and

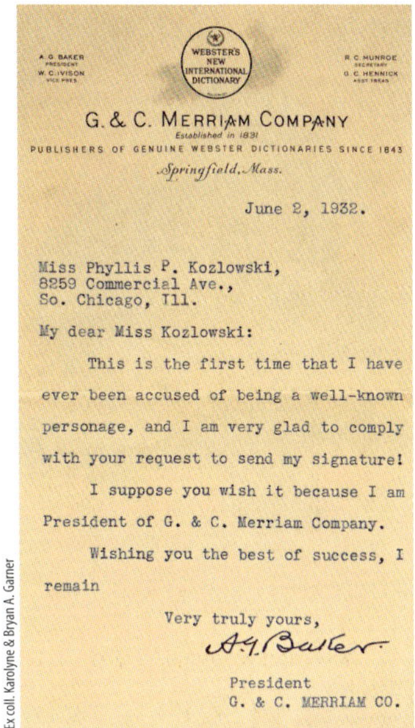
WEBSTER'S NEW INTERNATIONAL DICTIONARY

G. & C. MERRIAM COMPANY
Established in 1831
PUBLISHERS OF GENUINE WEBSTER DICTIONARIES SINCE 1843
Springfield, Mass.

June 2, 1932.

Miss Phyllis P. Kozlowski,
8259 Commercial Ave.,
So. Chicago, Ill.

My dear Miss Kozlowski:

This is the first time that I have ever been accused of being a well-known personage, and I am very glad to comply with your request to send my signature!

I suppose you wish it because I am President of G. & C. Merriam Company.

Wishing you the best of success, I remain

Very truly yours,

A. G. Baker

President
G. & C. MERRIAM CO.

Ex coll. Karolyne & Bryan A. Garner

Even while *W2* was in preparation, at least one autograph seeker considered the president of Merriam (Asa Baker) a celebrity.

"The present work . . . is the result of a complete and detailed scrutiny of every feature: choice of vocabulary, etymologies, pronunciations, definitions, typography, pictorial illustrations, and arrangement." (Neilson's preface, p. v.)

The Editorial Department at work on *W2* in 1933.

Webster's New International in the early 1900s. As was his father's, his name was Edward N. Teall. Here's what he wrote in 1940:

> As the grandson of one dictionary man and the son of another, and myself somewhat experienced in the making of dictionaries, I know that the dictionary is about as human as anything can be, and a product of hard work rather than of inspiration. As a boy, I heard my father and grandfather talk dictionary. They discussed the problems of their work with the same enthusiasm that baseball fans display in arguing the merits of one club and another. They were together on the Century; then my father went through the making of the Standard and an edition of Webster. I think he must have read every word in the three books, and read them all critically. [Teall 1940:88–89.]

His message to the mid-20th-century dictionary user was emphatic: "I verily believe that a dictionary, to be bought for a few dollars, can be made the equivalent of a college education costing thousands. *Can* be; but how few of us ever delve for its riches!" (*Id.* at 93.) He then explained what is involved in this delving: "We lose much of what the dictionary offers because we are too lazy to follow up the cross-references. The dictionary has to economize on space—and how!—and it likes to present a fact only once. The cross-references are not merely important, they are vital." (*Id.*)

With 600,000 entries, the big *W2* dominated the marketplace throughout the mid-20th century. In fact, well into the 21st century it remained a favorite of Supreme Court justices such as Antonin Scalia. (Garner 2018:14–15, 38–39.)

"Editorship by college presidents was part of the Merriam-Webster tradition." (Thorp 1956:327.)

Ex coll. Karolyme & Bryan A. Garner

Ex coll. Karolyme & Bryan A. Garner

Publisher-supplied blotter paper sent to bookstores for marketing purposes.

101

William Craigie & Mitford Mathews
American Style

Craigie, William A., and J.R. Hulbert. *A Dictionary of American English on Historical Principles*. 20 fascicles in green wraps as originally issued. Chicago: Univ. of Chicago Press, 1936–1944. Also: 4 red-cloth vols. as usually issued, 1944.

Collection of 378 dictionary slips containing illustrative quotations for use in Craigie's *Dictionary*. (Part of the Garner Collection.)

Mathews, Mitford M. *A Dictionary of Americanisms on Historical Principles*. 2 vols. Chicago: Univ. of Chicago Press, 1951.

Ex coll. Karolyne & Bryan A. Garner

The distinguished lexicographer sorts through quotation slips.

"It is only by close comparison with the English record that it is possible to decide how much is really new in the American vocabulary." (Prefatory Note, 1:xi.)

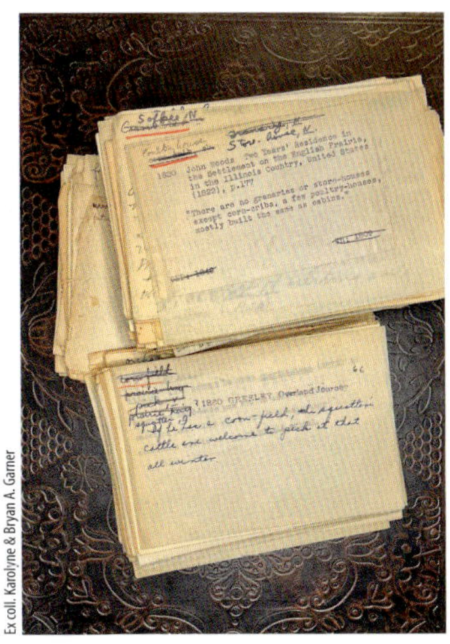

Ex coll. Karolyne & Bryan A. Garner

Slips used in compiling the *DAE*.

THE SCOTSMAN WILLIAM CRAIGIE (1867–1957), a graduate of St. Andrews University, joined the editorial staff of the *Oxford English Dictionary* in 1897. Four years later, he was appointed coeditor of the great work, alongside James A.H. Murray and Henry Bradley, and he began with the letter *Q*. By 1928, when the *OED* was completed, Craigie had edited about 20% of the entire work. He was also responsible for one-third of the 1933 *Supplement*. In 1916, he was appointed professor of Anglo-Saxon at Oxford University, and in 1925 accepted a position at the University of Chicago, where he undertook his *Dictionary of American English on Historical Principles* (*DAE*). For eight years, then, he worked on the *OED* from Chicago while simultaneously making progress on the *DAE*. According to the *ODNB*, "Craigie was the ablest and most productive lexicographer of his time, and was universally recognized as the supreme master of the art and techniques of dictionary making."

How did a Scotsman become the editor of an American dictionary? William A. Craigie gave us an unusually precise recollection of how this came to be. "One day in the summer of 1924," he recorded, "I was reading some proofs of the *Oxford English Dictionary*"—as one of the coeditors, he was responsible for *N*, *Q*, *R*, *U*, *V*, and much of *S* and *W*—and he noticed an unusual number of American authors among the citations for words beginning with *un-*. "It would be interesting," he mused, "to know how far back the words could be traced in American use." But alas, "we had no means of ascertaining this point." (Craigie 1926:14.)

"It has been found necessary to collect and present a mass of evidence far surpassing in quantity what anyone would naturally anticipate." (Preface, 1:v.)

There were already dictionaries of "Americanisms," of course—words used only, or primarily, in America—including, most thoroughly and recently, Richard H. Thornton's *American Glossary* (2 vols., 1912; supplement 1931). But Craigie wanted not a collection of uniquely American words, or not *just* such a collection. "If we are to have a real history of the English of this country," he wrote, "every word which can legitimately be considered a part of the language must have its place in the record." (Craigie 1931:16.) And so he set out to create the definitive dictionary of the English language in America.

Ex coll. Karolyne & Bryan A. Garner

Craigie convinced the University of Chicago to support the project financially, along with the General Education Board and the American Council of Learned Societies. The Delegates of Oxford University Press granted him access to their materials, including the vast collection of quotations assembled by the *OED*'s reading program.

Given that the mission was to cover "words and phrases which are clearly or apparently of American origin, or have greater currency here than elsewhere," along with "every word denoting something which has a real connection with the development of the country and the history of its people" (1:v), it's curious that Craigie never defines "American." Since Canada is nowhere mentioned in the preliminaries, he seems to mean the United States and the territory that eventually became the United States. But many questions are left unanswered. What about British-born Americans (John Smith, Thomas Paine, Andrew Carnegie) or American-born Britons (John Singleton Copley, Henry James, T.S. Eliot)? Craigie gives no hints about what makes American English American.

"Full use has naturally been made of the successive collections of Americanisms by Pickering [no. 61], Bartlett [no. 75], Schele de Vere, Farmer [no. 114], Clapin, and Thornton, as well as of the special works by Mr. Mencken and Professor Krapp." (Preface, 1:vi.)

The dictionary's format is predictably similar to the *OED*: each word gets a series of definitions, each supported by quotations arranged in chronological order, with an attempt to identify the earliest written example in American sources. The biggest departure from *OED* policies was the omission of pronunciations and etymologies, since those were usually covered elsewhere and did not need to be repeated. A few symbols help users understand the relationship of these American words to the main stock of English vocabulary. An asterisk before a headword or a sense number "indicates that the word or sense is found in English before 1600"—that is, one with a history that predates European settlement in North America—while a "+" in the same place "indicates that the word or sense clearly or to all appearance originated within the present limits of the United States." (1:xv.) It's possible for both to appear in a single entry: *middling*, for example, gets an asterisk for being a very old word, but several of its senses ("Tobacco of an intermediate grade," "Cotton which in quality comes up to the standard or basic") get the cross for being distinctively American.

"The great majority of the words included here are of such a nature that their normal pronunciation is familiar to every educated person, and special comment is required only in rare instances." (Preface, 1:vi.)

He and his team found American words by reading "Prose and verse literature by American writers of repute"—someone clearly had an American writer of repute in mind in drafting the very first entry, the letter *A*, with its use as a badge of shame for adulterers—"Prose and verse by minor writers," "Local histories, letters, journals, memoirs, newspapers, and records," "Books of travel," "Early school and college textbooks," and, for the modern period especially, American newspapers and magazines. (Barns 1927:625.) They paid particular attention to the contributions from Spanish, French, Dutch, and various Native American languages.

Ex coll. Karolyne & Bryan A. Garner

The four volumes issued in 1944.

The question that Craigie received most often was whether his dictionary would cover American slang. "To this I reply," he wrote, "that there is a place for all things, and that the proper place for slang, as such, is either on the tongue of those who like to use it or in the pages of a slang dictionary"—but he was not writing a slang dictionary. Still, he realized that some of "the slang of one generation will be part of the usual speech of the next, and will in the end become a natural part of the written language," and that must be covered. (Craigie 1926:22.)

"For a large proportion of the words, also, the ultimate etymology has only a remote interest, and has been indicated only when the word has come directly into American use or without having clearly passed through English before its adoption here." (Preface, 1:vi.)

The book was widely reviewed. Some complained that the decision to consider only words that had entered the language before the 20th century omitted too many good candidates. Some thought that the absence of pronunciations was a bad decision, given the many differences between American and English speech. Most, though, agreed with the distinguished American medievalist Kemp Malone, who, despite some significant reservations, concluded on the appearance of the first volume: "The dictionary upon its completion will take

Ex coll. Karolyne & Bryan A. Garner

The one-volume edition.

"The study of a people's language throws light upon every aspect of that people's culture." (Mathews, p. v.)

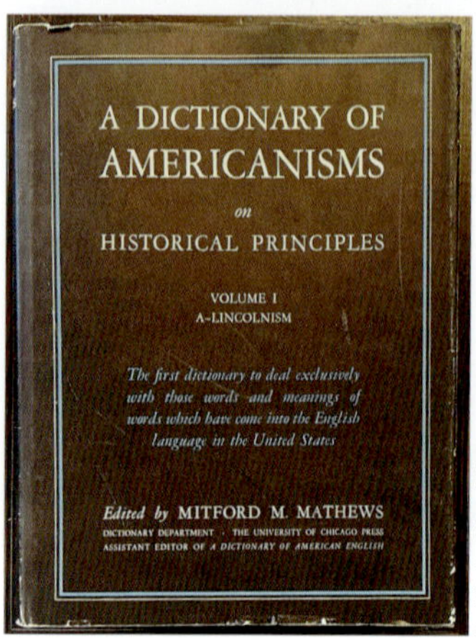

Ex coll. Karolyne & Bryan A. Garner

The two-volume edition.

its place among the fundamental works on the history of our culture, indeed (so the philologist is tempted to say) as the chief of these." (Malone 1937:376.)

Just as the *DAE* was beginning to be printed in fascicles in 1936, Craigie resigned his chair at Chicago and moved back to Oxfordshire, where he had a place in the charming hamlet of Christmas Common, Watlington. From there, he approved the final work on the *DAE* while simultaneously working on his *Dictionary of the Older Scottish Tongue*, which he carried through the letter *I* by 1955.

Aided by a staff of seven, including the young Mitford M. Mathews, Craigie oversaw the preparation of the *DAE* over a nine-year period. The dictionary totaled 2,527 pages in four volumes, with some 150,000 illustrative quotations supporting 35,000 main entries. The bibliography numbers over 2,500 titles, and the preface lists the names of 400 excerptors.

Some of their original work slips have been preserved. The Garner Collection possesses some 378 of them, many but not all of which contain information that appears in the *DAE*. An 1836 quotation from William Gilmore Simms's novel *Mellichampe* is the second illustration of *corn meal* ("meal made from maize"): "He brought forth from the recess which had supplied him with his evening repast a small sack of corn-meal." The 4 × 6-inch slips are mostly handwritten, and most of them bear stamps giving the year, the last name of the author, and the title of the work; volume numbers and page numbers were typically handwritten by the excerptor, as were the quotations themselves (a few were typed). They derive from a great variety of unidentified hands. A few slips are book pages cut down to fit on the slips, with a few words underlined. In the upper left corner of each slip is a list of terms to be potentially illustrated; those that were selected for use were crossed out in pencil.

Despite the painstakingly methodical nature of the work, the *DAE* was not fully adequate. Craigie had proposed a timeline for completion, and he was intent on meeting it. And so he accounted for American English only through the year 1900, and he excluded most slang. All in all, the treatment of the American vocabulary was, by *OED* standards, comparatively meager.

Almost immediately upon completion of the *DAE*, Mitford M. Mathews undertook *A Dictionary of Americanisms on Historical Principles* (1951), as if to supersede Craigie's work. He had grievances:

although he had learned lexicography from Craigie, Mathews often found his mentor's work arbitrary and his manner imperious. Mathews restored many American coinages that, in his view, Craigie had stubbornly and imprudently excluded from the *DAE*. Mathews's two-volume work, also published by the University of Chicago, contained exclusively Americanisms and a somewhat higher ratio of quotations (100,000) to main entries (14,000). But if you count subentries, Mathews's number of entries climbs to 50,000.

In comparison with Craigie, Mathews more sharply differentiated American from British English: while the *DAE* included all English words that might be applied to American culture, Mathews's work recorded only terms that had originated in the United States. Among these are *almighty dollar*, *appendicitis*, *automobile*, *bifocals*, *department store*, *electrocute*, *escalator*, *ferris wheel*, *flunk*, *ivory tower*, *locomotive*, *pony express*, *sideburns*, *stampede*, *vamoose*, *widow's walk*, and *wisteria*. In a 1953 interview by the *Chicago Tribune*, Mathews said: "As long as Americans think and work creatively, they will be adding new words to the language. Take the term *Ivy League*, which has been cropping up everywhere. It didn't get into the first edition of the dictionary, but it's sure to be included in the next." Alas, there was no second edition.

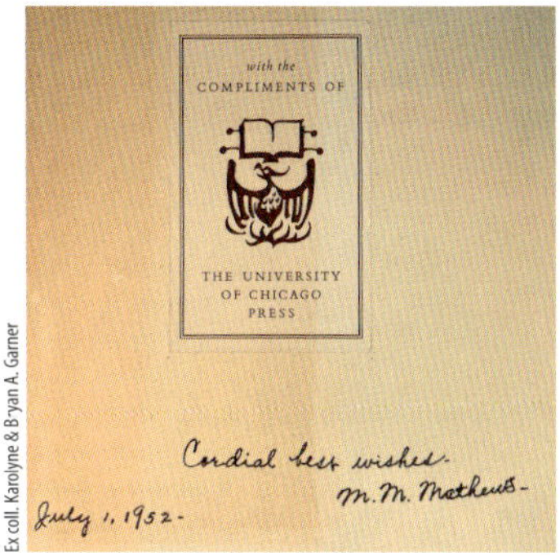

Ex coll. Karolyne & Bryan A. Garner

Mathews's inscription in a first edition of his book.

"If the work helps to stimulate increasingly competent study of the field to which it is devoted and if in its offerings and methodology it facilitates the efforts of those who will in time improve upon it, I shall be greatly pleased." (Mathews, p. xiv.)

Ex coll. Karolyne & Bryan A. Garner

The 20 fascicles in which the *DAE* was originally released.

"Look what just arrived!"

Ex coll. Karolyne & Bryan A. Garner

Ex coll. Karolyne & Bryan A. Garner

About a century ago, this box containing *Webster's New International Dictionary* arrived at the home of Mr. and Mrs. Harry L. Krotzer of Throop, Pennsylvania, where Mr. Krotzer was a schoolteacher. Note the label on the side of the box (at right).

IX. What's a Guardian to Do?

The general public had come to believe that "the dictionary" was a literary monolith delivered, like the laws of Moses, from on high. The popular mind didn't associate a lexicographer with being a "writer of dictionaries," as Johnson defined the term; it probably didn't even know the word lexicographer. *The literati, meanwhile, tended to think that lexicographers should uphold standards and defend a language under assault.*

But lexicographers themselves tended to think—in a tradition begun by Johnson, supported by Webster, and confirmed by the OED*—that lexicographers should dispassionately register the language, not reshape it. Philip B. Gove caught the world by surprise when he brought these principles to bear on the flagship Merriam dictionary, which had for decades been advertised as the "supreme" and "unquestioned" authority. The result,* Webster's Third, *disavowed any such authority. Gove eliminated such censorious labels as "colloquial" and "dialect," replacing the latter with "nonstandard." (The former simply disappeared as a category.)* Webster's Second *had called* ain't *"dialectal or illiterate"; Gove removed the warning label because some educated people said it. Upon the publication of his big book in 1961, it was as if a bomb had exploded in literary America. It was an early salvo in what we now call the culture wars.*

Random House and American Heritage came on the scene, hoping to benefit from Merriam-Webster's self-inflicted wounds. Soon realizing how difficult it was to sell dictionaries in America without the mighty name of Webster, Random House renamed its book The Random House Webster's Dictionary. *Thus began the last in a series of battles to preserve Webster (on a red cover) as a protected trademark of the G. & C. Merriam Co. The entire saga, beginning with the Merriams' taking over Webster dictionaries in the first place, is told here for the first time in print.*

The OED *tried to keep pace by concluding its long project of compiling a* Supplement, *which, begun in 1957, was finally completed in four volumes in 1986, at last bringing recent words into a dictionary that had begun publishing a full century earlier. The* Supplement's *editor, Robert W. Burchfield, declared that his work could never be merged into the main* OED, *but this was accomplished just three years later, in 1989—so that his* Supplement *effectively had a short shelf life as a stand-alone book. It has now been woven into the fabric of the* OED.

To little or no fanfare, the Middle English Dictionary *was completed in 2001. Chaucerians everywhere rejoiced.*

Ex coll. Karolyne & Bryan A. Garner

102

Webster's Third

For Many, It Wasn't a Charm

***Webster's Third New International Dictionary*. Philip Babcock Gove ed. 2 vols. Springfield: G. & C. Merriam Co., 1961.**

LONG SINCE HAVING ACHIEVED commercial dominance in the field of dictionaries, Merriam-Webster began in the 1940s preparing the next big edition of its unabridged dictionary. Shortly after the death of William Allan Neilson in 1946, Philip Babcock Gove (1902–1972) was named chief editor, and his staff began studying various problems of language behavior—learning what they could from structural linguistics. The editors studied functional shift, objects of transitive verbs, logico-historical ordering of senses, cardinal and ordinal numbers, interjections, attributive nouns, phrasal verbs, reflexive verbs, and affixes of all types. They gathered linguistic variants, noticing, for example, that *basketful* and *cupful* have not only the standard plurals *basketfuls* and *cupfuls* but also the nonstandard forms *basketsful* and *cupsful*. The pronunciation editor, Edward Artin, went into the field to record speech so as to account for every variation he could, as opposed to the "general American" pronunciations that had come to be regarded as standard. There was a move away from the notions of "correct" and "incorrect." The idea that some words were "colloquialisms" would be scrapped.

Was this the best and highest use of the staff's time? Arguably yes. They were bringing the big book in line with the prevailing thought of language specialists and making lexicography objective, scientific, *modern*.

But arguably no. Many users wanted things from a dictionary that *Webster's Third* did not offer—refused to offer—and they weren't satisfied when the language specialists insisted that they wanted the wrong thing. A more conventional approach might have left intact the normative aspects of *Webster's Second* (1934) while devoting tens of thousands of worker hours into marshaling and defining more terminology from more specialties, such as astronomy, computing, cookery,

Ex coll. Karolyn & Bryan A. Garner

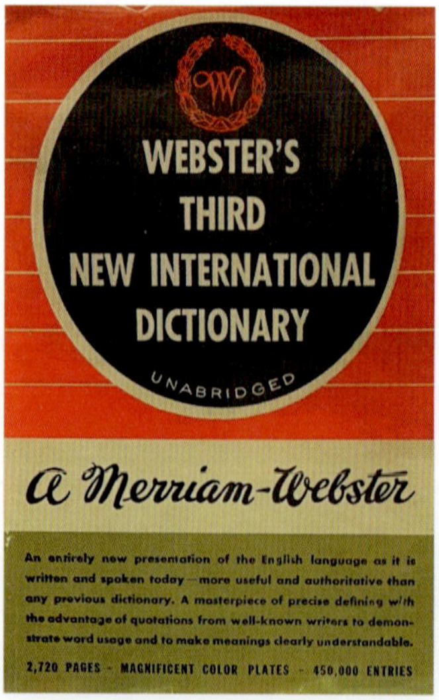

Ex coll. Karolyne & Bryan A. Garner

Ex coll. Karolyne & Bryan A. Garner

The three-volume format.

law, medicine, musicology, psychiatry, telecommunications, and zoology. The fields could be multiplied many times over.

For every dictionary staff undertaking a new edition, the question arises: Given finite resources—and resources are always finite, even when digital publication frees us from paper costs—where should we direct them for the newly improved work? This probably depends on an allied question: What do the users of our dictionary want from us? And that in turn depends on an underlying question: Who is our audience?

Consider pronunciations. Webster's dictionaries have never used the International Phonetic Alphabet, preferring their own notational systems. *W3* made some innovations that confused readers. Whereas *W2* recorded the pronunciation of *mercurial* as (mûr·kū′rĭ·ăl), *W3* recorded \¦mər¦kyrēəl, ˌmə(r)ˈk-, (ˈ)m¦k-, (ˈ)məik-\. Does it matter whether ordinary dictionary users would struggle to understand what the phonetic notations mean? And do users want one pronunciation of *mercurial*, or would they rather have four variations for its first syllable? A vast amount of editorial energy was spent setting forth phonetic variations for *W3*'s 450,000 entries. The cognate entry *mercury* went from a single pronunciation in *W2* to five in *W3*.

Meanwhile, the semantic content of definitions was significantly reconfigured. *Jurisprudence*, which had four main senses in *W2*, had just two in *W3*: what had been split into separate meanings were now lumped. (By contrast, *Black's Law Dictionary* today records seven discrete senses.) Many words deemed obsolete were deleted to make room for new words. For example, Ben Jonson's *merdurinous* ("consisting of excrement and urine"), recorded in *W2*, was omitted from *W3*. At the same time, rare derivatives were often elevated to main entries: whereas *W2* tended to subordinate derivatives either at the end of an entry or at the foot of the divided page, *W3* often gave them greater prominence as main entries. The unusual adverb *melancholily*, for example, was taken from the fine print at the bottom of the page up to the main text and given its own entry occupying three lines. This upgrading of adverbs occurred consistently: *loweringly*, listed in *W2* as a mere derivative of the adjective *lowering* ("frowning")—in a third of a line—takes up two lines of print in *W3*.

Again, any single instance seems trivial, but consider the effort involved in doing this kind of thing tens of thousands of times. Is it a useful endeavor, or is it makework? That depends on the user, and even a given user's needs might change from moment to moment.

One aspect of *W3* that should have been universally applauded was the enhanced coverage of everyday expressions. Reviewers drew attention to *astronaut*, *automation*, *bazooka*, *big wheel*, *blast-off*, *boo-boo*, *brainwashing*, *countdown*, *den mother*, *desegregation*, *drag race*, *drip-dry*, *fall-out*, *footsie*, *hard sell*, *hot rod*, *jeep*, *jerk*, *mccarthyism*, *megaton*, *no-show*, *nuclear*, *radioactive*, *red-baiting*, *rock 'n' roll*, *schlemiel*, *sit-in*, *space station*, *wage dividend*, and *zip gun*. Traditionalists complained about the "permissiveness" of admitting informal terms like *ants in one's pants*, *palooka*, and *schlemiel*, but surely it's better to include them than to leave curious readers baffled about their meaning.

The style of the definitions was also new to users, and occasionally produced baffling entries. Informed by the latest thinking in semantics, Gove instituted a policy of "single-statement definitions": all definitions were to consist of a single phrase, beginning with a category (known as the *genus*) and followed by the features (the *differentiae*) that distinguish a thing from other members of the genus. A *casement*, for instance, is a kind of window sash, and it's distinguished from other window sashes because it "opens on hinges fastened to the upright side of the frame": genus and differentiae. Gove decreed there was to be as little punctuation as possible. And definitions were almost always, except in the case of function words, to be substitutable with the word being defined: that is, the part of speech in the definition must be such that, if you were to replace a word with its *W3* definition, the result would be grammatically coherent (though probably inelegant). Definitions also used certain formulas consistently through the dictionary: readers could be sure that "usu[ally]," "esp[ecially]," and "of or relating to" were being used precisely and consistently, and that all the *-able* and *-ible* words, whether in the *A*'s or the *Z*'s, were defined in the same way.

Many of the definitions generated by this policy are admirably clear. A *sister* is "a female human being [the genus, with the part of speech matching the noun being defined] related to another person by having the same parents [the things that distinguish sisters from other female human beings]." (Subsequent senses cover animal siblings, nuns, and people who share common interests or passions.) The verb *murder* is "to kill [the genus, with the part of speech matching the verb being defined] (a human being) unlawfully and with premeditated

Courtesy of Merriam-Webster Inc.

"*Webster's Third New International Dictionary* is a completely new work, redesigned, restyled, and reset. Every line of it is new. . . . G. & C. Merriam Company now offers [this book] as a prime linguistic aid to interpreting the culture and civilization of today." (Gove's preface, p. 4a.)

Photo by Fabian Bachrach, courtesy of Merriam-Webster Inc.

Philip Babcock Gove.

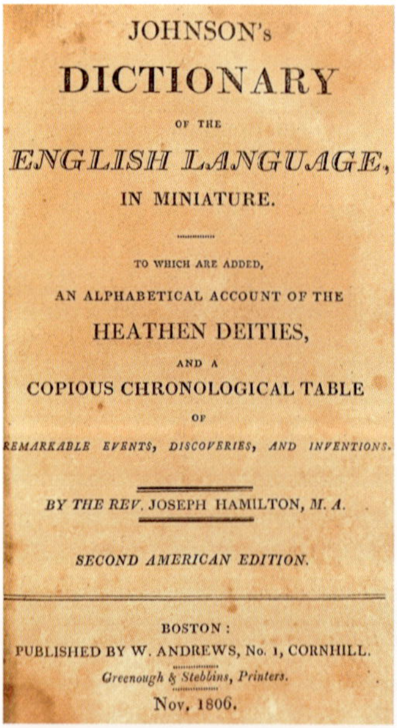

JOHNSON's
DICTIONARY
OF THE
ENGLISH LANGUAGE,
IN MINIATURE.

TO WHICH ARE ADDED,
AN ALPHABETICAL ACCOUNT OF THE
HEATHEN DEITIES,
AND A
COPIOUS CHRONOLOGICAL TABLE
OF
REMARKABLE EVENTS, DISCOVERIES, AND INVENTIONS.

BY THE REV. JOSEPH HAMILTON, *M. A.*

SECOND AMERICAN EDITION.

BOSTON:
PUBLISHED BY W. ANDREWS, No. 1, CORNHILL.
Greenough & Stebbins, Printers.
Nov. 1806.

Ex coll. Karolyne & Bryan A. Garner

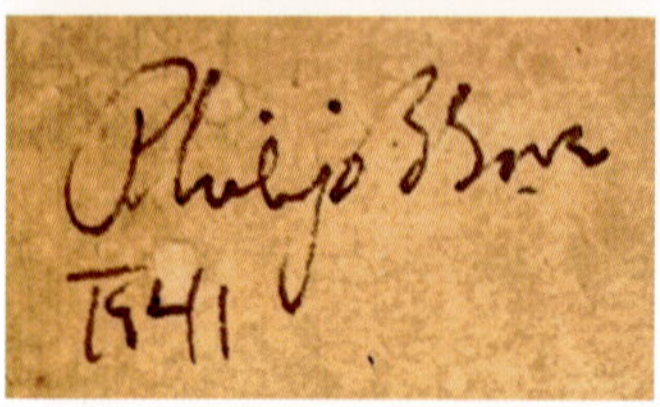

Ex coll. Karolyne & Bryan A. Garner

As early as 1941, Gove owned an American edition of *Johnson's Dictionary*.

"This new Merriam-Webster unabridged is the record of this language as it is written and spoken. It is offered with confidence that it will supply in full measure that information on the general language which is required for accurate, clear, and comprehensive understanding of the vocabulary of today's society." (Gove's preface, p. 5a.)

malice or willfully, deliberately, and unlawfully [the things that distinguish murdering from other kinds of killing]." The adjective *lateral* gets several definitions, the first of which is "of or relating to the side: situated on, directed toward, or coming from the side."

Single-statement definitions are especially good at pinning down the precise meaning of things we encounter every day. Native English speakers know what a *quilt* is, but if asked to define it, most of us would stumble and resort to vague hand gestures before rambling through a list of miscellaneous things we know about quilts. Not Gove's team: a *quilt* is "a bed coverlet made of two layers of cloth of which the top one is usu. pieced or appliquéd and having a filling of wool, cotton, or down held in place by stitched designs or tufts worked through all thicknesses." A Martian who had never encountered a quilt before would, after reading that definition, be able to identify quilts.

And yet any formula, applied too rigorously, can produce monstrosities. Consider the primary definition of *hotel* in *W2*:

> **hotel** . . . A house providing lodging and usually meals for the public, esp. for transients; an inn, esp. one of the better class.

Here is the revised entry in *W3*:

> **hotel** . . . a building of many rooms chiefly for overnight accommodation of transients and several floors served by elevators, usu. with a large open street-level lobby containing easy chairs, with a variety of compartments for eating, drinking, dancing, exhibitions, and group meetings (as of salesmen or convention attendants), with shops having both inside and street-side entrances and offering for sale items (as clothes, gifts, candy, theater tickets, travel tickets) of particular interest to a traveler, or providing personal services (as hairdressing, shoe shining), and with telephone booths, writing tables, and washrooms freely available.

Did the single-statement style bring us any closer to the essence of a hotel?

But there are further problems with both entries just cited. Neither one mentions that the lodging is available *for a fee*. That is, a hotel is place of business. Further, both dictionaries assume that a hotel is merely a physical structure. They ignore the idea that the word often denotes the business itself, not merely the building (*Did the hotel give you your money back?*). In short, there should be one definition for the building and another for the business that operates there. The staffers might have concentrated on *this* type of issue instead of on whether washrooms are "freely available."

Ultimately the story of *W3* is the story of two different conceptions of lexicographic authority. It helps to think about two broad classes of dictionary users: those who encounter a word and want to know its meaning, and those who want to say something of their own and seek guidance on how to say it effectively. In practice, every dictionary user is both these things, but different needs can dominate at different times—sometimes we want impartial facts; sometimes we want helpful advice. It's notoriously difficult to serve the needs of both audiences in one book. And in 1961, Merriam caught many of its customers unawares by abruptly changing the needs it was serving. Many readers expected Merriam-Webster dictionaries to pass judgments on good and bad usage. This wasn't an unreasonable expectation: for decades, Merriam had advertised its dictionaries with slogans like THE SUPREME AUTHORITY or even UNQUESTIONED AUTHORITY (see p. 328). But Gove and his team disavowed *any* authority about what's good or bad. They were trying to report what they regarded as facts, not judgments.

"The arrangement of senses in *Webster's Third* for most words is strikingly and admirably fresh. The editor and his staff systematically reconsidered the facts, no doubt with a weather eye on the *OED*, but mostly with a view to arranging them in a way that reflected their quotational material. Their filed-away citations—some thirteen million of them—are numerically richer than those held by any other dictionary house." (Burchfield 1991:156.)

The criticisms they attracted must have stung. In the *Detroit News*, a local minister asserted that "the greatest of all American dictionaries has been corrupted at center," adding: "The greatest language on earth has lost a guardian. When the editors 'concretized' their philosophy and 'finalized' their policy, 'irregardless' was blessed. When it comes to a standardless dictionary, include me out." (Emrich 1962:129.) That's just one example in what must have seemed like an onslaught. In defending himself and his colleagues, Gove was necessarily less rhetorically flamboyant: "The responsibility of a dictionary is to record the language, not set its style. For us to attempt to prescribe the language would be like Life reporting the news as its editors would prefer it to happen." (Gove 1961:92.)

"No man should let another choose his language for him; for speech and reason make us human. The choice is never easy, partly because no linguistic form is good in itself, absolutely and for all purposes, partly because the determinants of choice are various—the character of the speaker (or writer), the nature of his audience, the relation between them, the situation, the subject, the speaker's intent, and so on. We are not likely to choose well unless we know what we have to choose from. That is one reason why we need a descriptively accurate dictionary. The constructive critic of the *Third International* will be the man who shows how its descriptions can be improved." (Sledd 1962:272.)

And now we get to a point that we've so far overlooked: *W3* instantly became the most controversial dictionary ever published. The literati were as furious as the professional linguists were satisfied. Cultural conservatives were outraged; cultural progressives were energized. In retrospect, we can see the culture wars of the 1960s coming into being: traditionalists called *W3* a "beatnik" dictionary and likened *Webster's Third New International* to the Third International of Soviet Communist Party. By 1962, a year after its publication, there had been

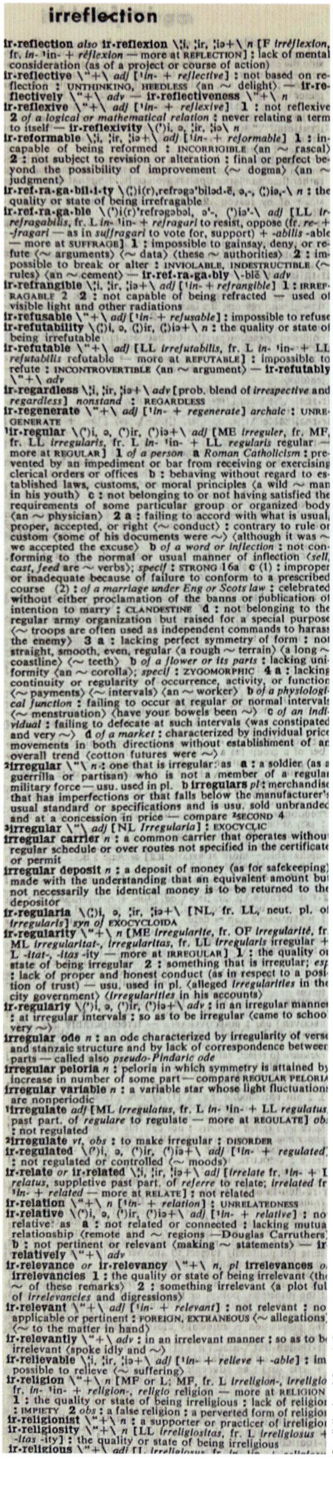

irreflection

ir·reflection *also* **ir·reflexion** \ˌi, ˌir, ˌiə+\ *n* [F *irréflexion*, fr. *in-* ¹in- + *réflexion* — more at REFLECTION] **:** lack of mental consideration (as of a project or course of action)

ir·reflective \"+\ *adj* [¹*in-* + *reflective*] **:** not based on reflection **:** UNTHINKING, HEEDLESS ⟨an ~ delight⟩ — **ir·reflectively** \"+\ *adv* — **ir·reflectiveness** \"+\ *n*

ir·reflexive \"+\ *adj* [¹*in-* + *reflexive*] **1 :** not reflexive **2** *of a logical or mathematical relation* **:** never relating a term to itself — **ir·reflexivity** \(ˈ)i, ə, ˌir, ˌiə\ *n*

ir·reformable \ˌi, ˌir, ˌiə+\ *adj* [¹*in-* + *reformable*] **1 :** incapable of being reformed **:** INCORRIGIBLE ⟨an ~ rascal⟩ **2 :** not subject to revision or alteration **:** final or perfect beyond the possibility of improvement ⟨~ dogma⟩ ⟨an ~ judgment⟩

ir·ref·ra·ga·bil·i·ty \(ˌ)i(r)ˌrefrəgəˈbiləd-ē, ə,-, (ˌ)iə,-\ *n* **:** the quality or state of being irrefragable

ir·ref·ra·ga·ble \(ˈ)i(r)ˈrefrəgəbəl, əˈ-, (ˈ)iəˈ-\ *adj* [LL *irrefragabilis*, fr. L *in-* ¹in- + *refragari* to resist, oppose (fr. *re-* + *-fragari* — as in *suffragari* to vote for, support) + *-abilis* -able — more at SUFFRAGE] **1 :** impossible to gainsay, deny, or refute ⟨~ arguments⟩ ⟨~ data⟩ ⟨these ~ authorities⟩ **2 :** impossible to break or alter **:** INVIOLABLE, INDESTRUCTIBLE ⟨~ rules⟩ ⟨an ~ cement⟩ — **ir·ref·ra·ga·bly** \-blē\ *adv*

ir·refrangible \ˌi, ˌir, ˌiə+\ *adj* [¹*in-* + *refrangible*] **1 :** IRREFRAGABLE 2 **2 :** not capable of being refracted — used of visible light and other radiations

ir·refusable \"+\ *adj* [¹*in-* + *refusable*] **:** impossible to refuse

ir·refutability \(ˌ)i, ə, (ˌ)ir, (ˌ)iə+\ *n* **:** the quality or state of being irrefutable

ir·refutable \"+\ *adj* [LL *irrefutabilis*, fr. L *in-* ¹in- + LL *refutabilis* refutable — more at REFUTABLE] **:** impossible to refute **:** INCONTROVERTIBLE ⟨an ~ argument⟩ — **ir·refutably** \"+\ *adv*

ir·regardless \ˌi, ˌir, ˌiə+\ *adv* [prob. blend of *irrespective* and *regardless*] *nonstand* **:** REGARDLESS

ir·regenerate \"+\ *adj* [¹*in-* + *regenerate*] *archaic* **:** UNREGENERATE

¹**ir·regular** \(ˈ)i, ə, (ˈ)ir, (ˈ)iə+\ *adj* [ME *irreguler*, fr. MF, fr. LL *irregularis*, fr. L *in-* ¹in- + LL *regularis* regular — more at REGULAR] **1** *of a person* **a** *Roman Catholicism* **:** prevented by an impediment or bar from receiving or exercising clerical orders or offices **b :** behaving without regard to established laws, customs, or moral principles ⟨a wild ~ man in his youth⟩ **c :** not belonging to or not having satisfied the requirements of some particular group or organized body ⟨an ~ physician⟩ **2 a :** failing to accord with what is usual, proper, accepted, or right ⟨~ conduct⟩ **:** contrary to rule or custom ⟨some of his documents were ~⟩ ⟨although it was ~ we accepted the excuse⟩ **b** *of a word or inflection* **:** not conforming to the normal or usual manner of inflection ⟨*sell*, *cast*, *feed* are ~ verbs⟩; *specif* **:** STRONG 16a **c (1) :** improper or inadequate because of failure to conform to a prescribed course **(2) :** *of a marriage under Eng or Scots law* **:** celebrated without either proclamation of the banns or publication of intention to marry **:** CLANDESTINE **d :** not belonging to the regular army organization but raised for a special purpose ⟨~ troops are often used as independent commands to harass the enemy⟩ **3 a :** lacking perfect symmetry of form **:** not straight, smooth, even, regular ⟨a rough ~ terrain⟩ ⟨a long ~ coastline⟩ ⟨~ teeth⟩ **b** *of a flower or its parts* **:** lacking uniformity ⟨an ~ corolla⟩; *specif* **:** ZYGOMORPHIC **4 a :** lacking continuity or regularity of occurrence, activity, or function ⟨~ payments⟩ ⟨~ intervals⟩ ⟨an ~ worker⟩ **b** *of a physiological function* **:** failing to occur at regular or normal intervals ⟨~ menstruation⟩ ⟨have your bowels been ~⟩ **c** *of an individual* **:** failing to defecate at such intervals ⟨was constipated and very ~⟩ **d** *of a market* **:** characterized by individual price movements in both directions without establishment of an overall trend ⟨cotton futures were ~⟩

²**irregular** \"\ *n* **:** one that is irregular: as **a :** a soldier (as a guerrilla or partisan) who is not a member of a regular military force — usu. used in pl. **b irregulars** *pl* **:** merchandise that has imperfections or that falls below the manufacturer's usual standard or specifications and is usu. sold unbranded and at a concession in price — compare ²SECOND 4

³**irregular** \"\ *adj* [NL *Irregularia*] **:** EXOCYCLIC

irregular carrier *n* **:** a common carrier that operates without regular schedule or over routes not specified in the certificate or permit

irregular deposit *n* **:** a deposit of money (as for safekeeping) made with the understanding that an equivalent amount but not necessarily the identical money is to be returned to the depositor

ir·regularia \(ˌ)i, ə, ˌir, ˌiə+\ [NL, fr. LL, neut. pl. of *irregularis*] *syn of* EXOCYCLOIDA

ir·regularity \"+\ *n* [ME *irregularite*, fr. OF *irregularité*, fr. ML *irregularitat-*, *irregularitas*, fr. LL *irregularis* irregular + L *-itat-*, *-itas* -ity — more at IRREGULAR] **1 :** the quality or state of being irregular **2 :** something that is irregular; *esp* **:** lack of proper and honest conduct (as in respect to a position of trust) — usu. used in pl. ⟨alleged *irregularities* in the city government⟩ ⟨*irregularities* in his accounts⟩

ir·regularly \(ˈ)i, ə, (ˈ)ir, (ˈ)iə+\ *adv* **:** in an irregular manner **:** at irregular intervals **:** so as to be irregular ⟨came to school very ~⟩

irregular ode *n* **:** an ode characterized by irregularity of verse and stanzaic structure and by lack of correspondence between parts — called also *pseudo-Pindaric ode*

irregular peloria *n* **:** peloria in which symmetry is attained by increase in number of some part — compare REGULAR PELORIA

irregular variable *n* **:** a variable star whose light fluctuations are nonperiodic

¹**irregulate** *adj* [ML *irregulatus*, fr. L *in-* ¹in- + LL *regulatus*, past part. of *regulare* to regulate — more at REGULATE] *obs* **:** not regulated

²**irregulate** *vt*, *obs* **:** to make irregular **:** DISORDER

ir·regulated \(ˈ)i, ə, (ˈ)ir, (ˈ)iə+\ *adj* [¹*in-* + *regulated*] **:** not regulated or controlled ⟨~ moods⟩

ir·relate *or* **ir·related** \ˌi, ˌir, ˌiə+\ *adj* [*irrelate* fr. ¹*in-* + L *relatus*, suppletive past part. of *referre* to relate; *irrelated* fr. ¹*in-* + *related* — more at RELATE] **:** not related

ir·relation \"+\ *n* [¹*in-* + *relation*] **:** UNRELATEDNESS

ir·relative \(ˈ)i, ə, (ˈ)ir, (ˈ)iə+\ *adj* [¹*in-* + *relative*] **:** not relative: as **a :** not related or connected **:** lacking mutual relationship ⟨remote and ~ regions —Douglas Carruthers⟩ **b :** not pertinent or relevant ⟨making ~ statements⟩ — **ir·relatively** \"+\ *adv*

ir·relevance *or* **ir·relevancy** \"+\ *n*, *pl* **irrelevances** *or* **irrelevancies** **1 :** the quality or state of being irrelevant ⟨the ~ of these remarks⟩ **2 :** something irrelevant ⟨a plot full of *irrelevancies* and digressions⟩

ir·relevant \"+\ *adj* [¹*in-* + *relevant*] **:** not relevant **:** not applicable or pertinent **:** FOREIGN, EXTRANEOUS ⟨~ allegations⟩ ⟨~ to the matter in hand⟩

ir·relevantly \"+\ *adv* **:** in an irrelevant manner **:** so as to be irrelevant ⟨spoke idly and ~⟩

ir·relievable \ˌi, ˌir, ˌiə+\ *adj* [¹*in-* + *relieve* + *-able*] **:** impossible to relieve ⟨~ suffering⟩

ir·religion \"+\ *n* [MF or L; MF, fr. L *irreligion-*, *irreligio*, fr. *in-* ¹in- + *religion-*, *religio* religion — more at RELIGION] **1 :** the quality or state of being irreligious **:** lack of religion **:** IMPIETY **2** *obs* **:** a false religion **:** a perverted form of religion

ir·religionist \"+\ *n* **:** a supporter or practicer of irreligion

ir·religiosity \"+\ *n* [LL *irreligiositas*, fr. L *irreligiosus* + *-itas* -ity] **:** the quality or state of being irreligious

ir·religious \"+\ *adj* [L *irreligiosus*, fr. *in-* ...

Ex coll. Karolyne & Bryan A. Garner

a firestorm of negative reviews (literati) together with rearguard defenses (linguists), and together they gave the impression that the fate of the world hung in the balance. James Sledd and Wilma R. Ebbitt collected more than 70 of these reviews and articles into an anthology: *Dictionaries and* That *Dictionary: A Casebook on the Aims of Lexicographers and the Targets of Reviewers* (1962). It makes for fascinating reading on both linguistic and political grounds.

A few years after the conflagration, Gove sighed over the critics' condemnation of "the dictionary, the science, structural linguists, and [himself] all in the same vituperative breath." (Gove 1972:157.) For a balanced account of the affair and its history, mostly sympathetic to Gove, see Herbert C. Morton, *The Story of Webster's Third: Philip Gove's Controversial Dictionary and Its Critics* (1994). For another engaging account, see David Skinner, *The Story of Ain't: America, Its Language, and the Most Controversial Dictionary Ever Published* (2012).

The Merriam-Webster *International* series of unabridged dictionaries appeared, for a time, at fairly regular intervals: the *International* (1890), the *New International* (1909), *Webster's Second New International* (*W2*) (1934), and then *W3* (1961). Starting with *Webster's Seventh New Collegiate Dictionary* in 1963, the expensive *W3* became the basis of the more affordable college editions, and today it's the basis of the online *Merriam-Webster Unabridged*. So far, though, we are without a *W4*.

Photo courtesy of Peter Sokolowski

The Merriam-Webster quotation files as they look today.

103

Random House
A Computing First

The *Random House Dictionary of the English Language*. Jess Stein & Laurence Urdang eds. New York: Random House, 1966.

THE GENEALOGY OF THIS DICTIONARY, begun in the 1950s, is fascinating. What began in 1895 as the *Century Dictionary* (no. 88) was abridged and issued in 1927 as the *New Century Dictionary*, in two volumes. That became the basis for Clarence Barnhart's (1900–1993) one-volume *American College Dictionary* (1947), which set a high standard for plain, accurate, clear definitions. Barnhart's work was then expanded into the unabridged work here discussed. It was heavily revised in the 1980s, under the editorship of the slang expert Stuart Berg Flexner (1928–1990), and came out in a second edition of 1987.

The timing of the 1966 release was propitious: the controversy surrounding *Webster's Third* had led many to yearn for a big dictionary that reflected a more traditional balance between descriptivism and prescriptivism. *Random House* filled this need with entries that were likely to be first consulted by those who wanted a litmus test—like the entry for *ain't* to the right.

The first word in both definitions is *nonstandard*. Some users of a prescriptive bent might have preferred *substandard*, but the less judgmental word *nonstandard* would do just fine as compared to the explicit statement in *Webster's Third* that the word, "though disapproved by many and more common in less educated speech, [is] used orally in most parts of the U.S. by many cultivated speakers." A potential dictionary buyer who consulted this one entry in *Random House* would probably be gratified.

Meanwhile, *Random House* was marketed as the first dictionary in history to rely on computers for parts of its editing and production. In the words of a contemporary commentator, "This could not fail to persuade the average reader in this technological age that the end product would be more accurate than something turned out by mere humans, and it also disarmed beforehand those nonaverage readers

THE RANDOM HOUSE DICTIONARY of the ENGLISH LANGUAGE
JESS STEIN
Editor in Chief
LAURENCE URDANG
Managing Editor
RANDOM HOUSE / NEW YORK

Ex coll. Karolyne & Bryan A. Garner

Title page.

"It is an entirely new dictionary, written in midcentury for twentieth-century users." (Preface, p. v.)

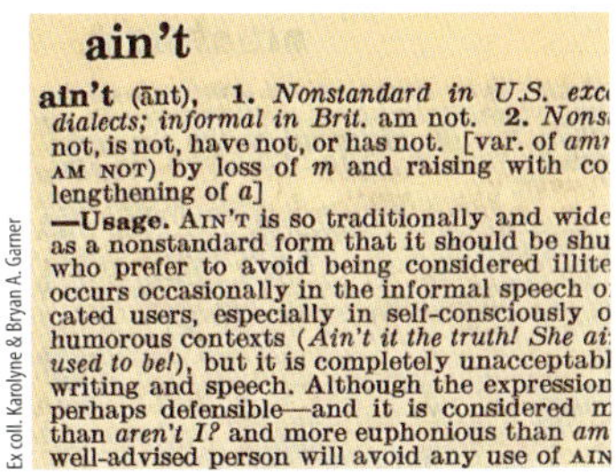
ain't

ain't (ānt), 1. *Nonstandard in U.S. exc… dialects; informal in Brit.* am not. 2. *Nons…* not, is not, have not, or has not. [var. of *am…* AM NOT) by loss of *m* and raising with co… lengthening of *a*]
—**Usage.** AIN'T is so traditionally and wide… as a nonstandard form that it should be shu… who prefer to avoid being considered illite… occurs occasionally in the informal speech o… cated users, especially in self-consciously o… humorous contexts (*Ain't it the truth! She ai… used to be!*), but it is completely unacceptabl… writing and speech. Although the expression… perhaps defensible—and it is considered m… than *aren't I?* and more euphonious than *am…* well-advised person will avoid any use of AIN…

Ex coll. Karolyne & Bryan A. Garner

Detail from the *ain't* entry.

"In the planning and preparation of this dictionary, we have endeavored to preserve all that is worthy in the great lexicographic traditions of Samuel Johnson, Noah Webster, James A.H. Murray, William Craigie, William Dwight Whitney, and others. We have resisted the temptation to introduce novelty in the guise of innovation." (Preface, p. v.)

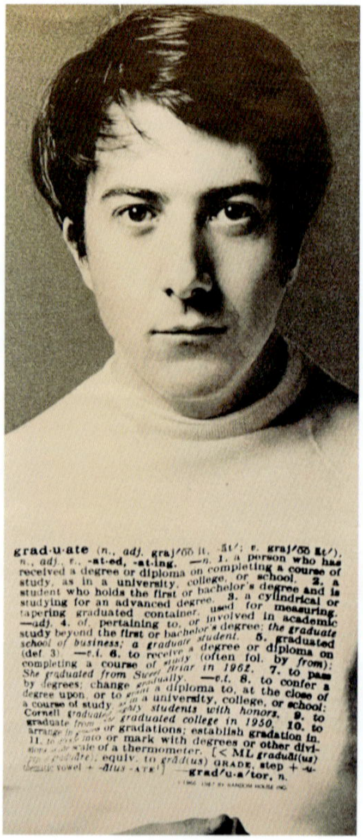

In 1968, the year after release of the film *The Graduate*, Random House widely advertised the Random House Sweatshirt of the English Language.

Ex coll. Karolyne & Bryan A. Garner

Compare the photo on p. 369.

who hold that the facts about any language can be ascertained only by 'scientific' study." (Reed 1967:62.) We had entered a brave new lexicographic world—even if the computing, by today's standards, was extremely crude and rudimentary.

Although it contains only 260,000 entries in its nearly 2,100 pages—190,000 fewer entries than *Webster's Third—Random House* includes many "encyclopedic" entries in the main text, listing place names, famous people, and organizational names. The dictionary is heavily illustrated, often with two or three images per page. In the back matter are four elementary bilingual glossaries (French, Spanish, Italian, and German), a full-color 64-page atlas of the world, names and dates of historical events, a directory of colleges and universities, biblical names, famous proverbs and mottoes, and a roster of presidents and vice presidents of the United States.

The big book was quickly abridged down to a college-size dictionary to compete with Merriam-Webster's *Collegiate Dictionary* and the similar *Webster's New World* published by the World Publishing Company. But the college market for easy-to-handle desktop dictionaries was fiercely competitive.

Meanwhile, somebody at Random House realized that the name *Webster* had been declared legally generic years before. Merriam-Webster had no trademark on *Webster*, and dozens of publishers other than Merriam-Webster had issued so-called Webster dictionaries. Struggling to compete more effectively, Random House in 1991 reissued its abridgment as *The Random House Webster's College Dictionary*, keeping the red binding and the bright-red dustjacket that all three of the main college dictionaries used.

This move attracted a 1991 lawsuit by Merriam-Webster. For the rest of that story, see pp. 369–71.

In the end, Random House extricated itself from the dictionary business. It's part of a disconcerting pattern in recent decades: in living memory we have lost the *Funk & Wagnalls Standard Dictionary*, the *American Heritage Dictionary*, the *Cassell Dictionary*, the *Penguin English Dictionary*, *Webster's New World Dictionary*, the *World Book Dictionary*, the *Microsoft Encarta Dictionary*, and, most recently, the *Macmillan Dictionary*—some have shut down the projects completely; others maintain them as zombie brands with no staff and no plans for future editions. Random House, at least, managed the transition better than most: its information found an afterlife at Dictionary.com (no. 129), which continues to develop it.

104

American Heritage
E.B. White Likes Vichyssoise

***The American Heritage Dictionary of the English Language.* William Morris ed. Boston & New York: American Heritage Pub. & Houghton Mifflin Co., 1969.**

In 1954, James Parton (1912–1988) founded the *American Heritage* magazine on an investment of $60,000. At the time, he had decades of experience working for *Time* magazine and *The New York Herald Tribune*. The magazine was a quick success, appearing every other month in hardcover with lavish color illustrations—and no advertising. Five years later, he tried unsuccessfully to buy Merriam-Webster.

The idea of reference books appealed to him, though, and soon he hired William Morris, who had once been a salesman for Merriam-Webster, to produce a dictionary for the American Heritage Publishing Company. It was planned to step into the prescriptive role that Merriam-Webster had so controversially disavowed. Because *Webster's Third* (no. 102) had been perceived as recklessly permissive, the *American Heritage Dictionary* would prescribe copiously, backed by the authority of a usage panel of distinguished writers. The book would be replete with usage notes and word-history notes.

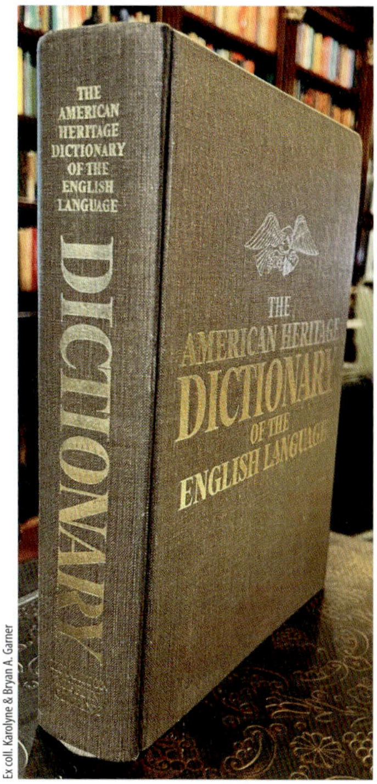

Ex coll. Karolyne & Bryan A. Garner

"We have undertaken to eliminate 'dictionary shorthand'—the frustrating signs, symbols, and abbreviations that are commonplace in other dictionaries." (Introduction, p. vii.)

When it appeared, the dictionary appealed to many—and the usage panel became a small army of literary supporters who boosted the book. Over its five print editions, as Gove's vision of the dictionary became more accepted, it gradually became much less prescriptive and more like *Webster's Third*. Meanwhile, Merriam-Webster, after the appearance of this new competitor, began incorporating usage notes and word-history notes. As it had done a century before with Worcester, Merriam-Webster co-opted the best features of its leading competitors. It was a converging lexicographic evolution.

The last print edition of the *American Heritage*, the 5th, appeared in 2011. In 2018, the company dissolved its usage panel, explaining that market conditions made it difficult to sell print dictionaries. Not long after, the editorial team was also laid off. Though the dictionary remains available in print and electronic form, there are no plans for further editions.

A funny thing happened in the marketing of the first edition. In October 1969, the editors sent the noted writer E.B. White a copy, perhaps hoping that he would write a review or lend an endorsement. He responded this way:

Ex coll. Karolyne & Bryan A. Garner

The MacLeish portrait. (P. 781.)

> North Brooklin, Me
> October 8, 1969
>
> Dear Mr. Jensen:
>
> Thank you for the gift of the Dictionary of the English language. It is my favorite language.
>
> I have used the book many times since receiving it. I was prepared for the picture of the sea-horse—all dictionaries, I have discovered, show the sea horse. [He writes the word inconsistently.] I was ready and willing for Greta Garbo, the times being what they are. But I was fit to be tied when I came on MacLeish. I'm not as pretty as Garbo, but by God I'm just as pretty as MacLeish.
>
> Sincerely,
>
> EB White

Keen to market the book more vigorously, the editors pressed further for an endorsement:

Ex coll. Karolyne & Bryan A. Garner

From the beginning, *American Heritage* ads emphasized the prescriptive bent, here by featuring Edwin Newman, the author of *Strictly Speaking* (1974).

> January 16, 1970
>
> Dear Mr. White,
>
> Your amusing letter thanking me for the American Heritage Dictionary has given a few people around here much pleasure, and now I discover that the people at Houghton Mifflin would like to quote it in some kind of promotion for the Dictionary, although I don't know exactly when. Would you have any objection to our letting them do it? I am sure you would be in good company. In case you forget the letter, I am attaching a xerox of it herewith. But if you don't let people quote you, as a matter of policy, I'm sure no one will be offended.
>
> I had a lot to do with the Dictionary, but I disclaim all responsibility for the peculiar selection we seem to have made in pictures of writers. I can't find any rhyme or reason in it, and propose to make considerable alteration when we come to a revised edition. Would you care to share the cover with MacLeish?

We have a great deal of fun here with your charming stepdaughter-in-law Carol Angell. And I would be obliged if you would give my best wishes to your wife.

Sincerely,

Oliver Jensen

White's next letter caused momentary puzzlement:

January 22, 1970

Dear Mr. Jensen:

I think I'd rather not have that letter of mine used for promotion of the Dictionary by Houghton Mifflin. It was all right in its place, which was on your desk, but I don't want it published.

I must return to the kitchen now and continue with my preparation of vichyssoise.

Yrs,

EB White

Only after some checking did the editors realize that, in their headword for *vichyssoise*, they had misspelled the word, transposing the positions of the *s* and the *ss*. The error was corrected, naturally, in the second printing.

Photo by Jill Krementz

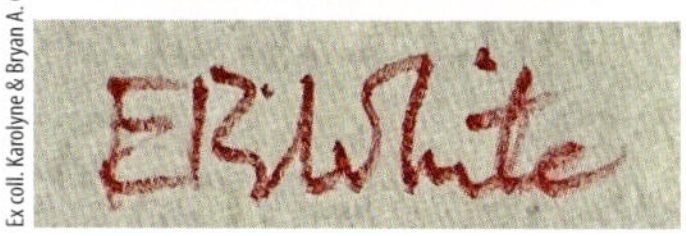

Ex coll. Karolyne & Bryan A. Garner

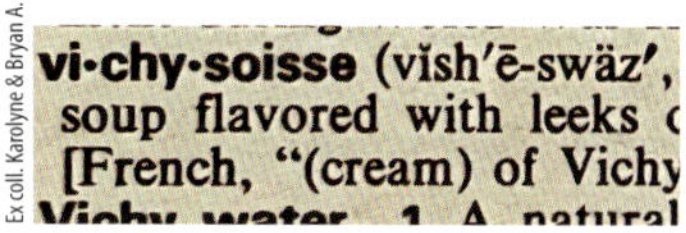

vi·chy·soisse (vĭsh′ē-swäz′,
soup flavored with leeks
[French, "(cream) of Vichy

Ex coll. Karolyne & Bryan A. Garner

Detail from entry with misspelled headword.

"What a dictionary ought to be is a treasury of information about every aspect of words, our most essential tools of communication. It should be an agreeable companion. By knowledgeable use of the dictionary we should learn where a word has come from, precisely what its various shades of meaning are today, and its social status." (Introduction, p. vi.)

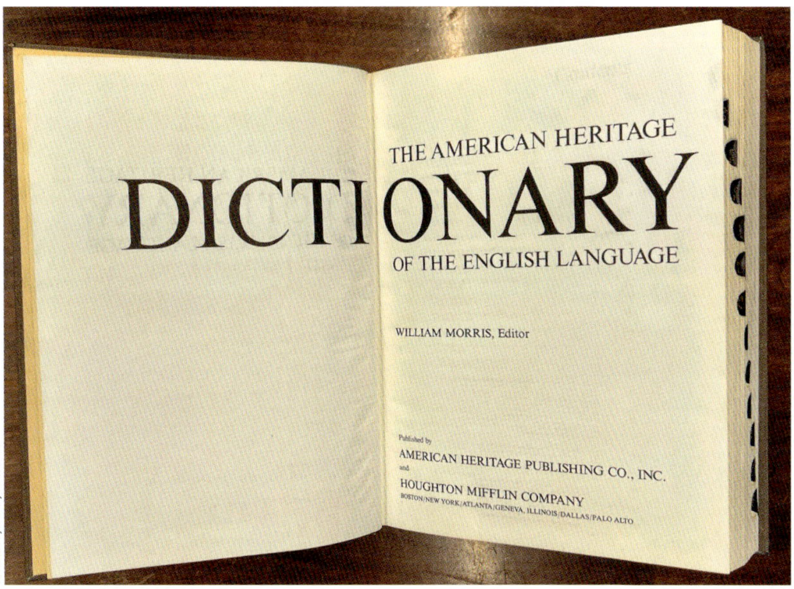

Ex coll. Karolyne & Bryan A. Garner

Photo by Terence Spencer, Camera Press London

Ex coll. Karolyne & Bryan A. Garner

"In the supplementary volumes to the *OED* I had little choice but to adopt Murray's main principles. He was, as it were, my Homer and my Virgil. Nouns are nouns (or rather substantives) in the *Supplement* as they were in the *OED*—they are never described as count nouns or mass nouns, and there are no plurals described as zero plurals. The way in which such words operate is made plain, of course, but in a Murrayan manner." (Burchfield 1991:174–75.)

Ex coll. Karolyne & Bryan A. Garner

The four volumes of Burchfield's *Supplement* (1972–1986).

105

Robert Burchfield

Dashing His Frame

***A Supplement to the Oxford English Dictionary*. R.W. Burchfield ed. 4 vols. Oxford: Clarendon Press, 1972–1986.**

A GALA NINE-COURSE DINNER marked the completion of the *Oxford English Dictionary* (no. 96) in 1928: the English language, from *A* to *zyxt*, was now recorded for the ages. Three-quarters of a century's labor had transformed Richard Chenevix Trench's vision into a set of monumental volumes. The work was *finished*.

. . . or, not *quite*. As those volumes had appeared over several decades, the lexicographers kept notes of their errors and omissions. And so a supplemental volume appeared, to much less fanfare, in 1933, correcting errors in the original. *Now* the work was finished.

. . . or, once again, not quite. A half-century had passed since *aardvark* and *abacus* were typeset, and in that time the language refused to stand still. Technological developments, wars, and a teetering British Empire all caused the English vocabulary to grow rapidly in the early 20th century. The current version of the *OED* records more than 10,000 new words that entered the language in the 25 years after the publication of the one-volume *Supplement* in 1933—*transistor*, *TV*, *carry-out*, *market share*, *pedestrianize*, *privatization*, *ecosystem*, *radar*, and *steroid*—and another 30,000 older words that acquired new senses. Was it time to start over? No one had the energy to do all that work again, but the *OED*, just completed, was already embarrassingly out of date. The Press grudgingly decided that a supplement was needed to keep the dictionary current.

Finding an editor proved a chore. The editors of the final volumes of the original *OED*, worn out after years of labor, weren't interested. An experienced lexicographer accepted the job but was immediately hired away to another position. Finally the Delegates of Oxford University Press settled on a young New Zealander, Robert Burchfield (1923–2004), who took up the post in July 1957.

Burchfield had no lexicographic experience—"I had never defined a word in my life," he confessed—and he arrived in Oxford to find just one experienced assistant. He was forced to teach himself how dictionaries are made and managed. The first step, he decided, was to read every word on all 15,487 pages of the thirteen-volume *OED*. He also systematically sorted through the notes left by the previous lexicographers, and then revived the reading program that allowed volunteers to identify words and senses omitted from the earlier volumes.

The plan called for a one-volume replacement for the 1933 *Supplement*, to be completed in seven years. But eight years of work resulted in no published volume, just the realization that the job was too big for a single volume. Instead, it would have to be three. (Or four, as they eventually realized.) Burchfield discovered that he "had seriously underestimated the task of collecting modern English vocabulary," especially after *Webster's Third New International* was published in 1961 with its exceptionally thorough coverage of new words and senses. Merriam editor Philip B. Gove wrote to Burchfield, offering cooperation, to which Burchfield agreed both gratefully and eagerly. Because the Oxford offices had not been diligent about keeping their citation files current after the first *Supplement* appeared in 1931, Burchfield often turned to Merriam for information—and, by one estimate, in about a third of the cases Springfield supplied an earlier citation than Oxford had. Though the G. & C. Merriam Co. and Oxford University Press were commercial rivals, the editorial teams collegially shared resources for nearly a decade—until the relationship degenerated into accusations of plagiarism and libel. (Burchfield 1984b, Urdang 1984.)

"I must confess that the journey has been a rough one—as it clearly was for my revered predecessor James Murray—and that it has always been discouraging to see the waves of new words lapping in behind as one dashed one's frame against the main flood." (Burchfield 1991:176.)

The first volume of the *Supplement* was published in 1972, fifteen years into Burchfield's tenure. A second volume followed in 1976, a third in 1982, and the fourth and final in 1986. The new work contained more than 69,000 entries, backed up by more than a half-million quotations. Many of its words were new—*database*, *dopamine*, *laser*, *multicultural*—but it also contained older words and senses that had been omitted from the original *OED*, as well as ante- and postdatings for many words and senses. Nearly 130 years after Trench's lecture, the dictionary—now in 16 volumes—was finally *finished*.

"I completed the editing of the final volume of the *Supplement to the Oxford English Dictionary* on 25 March 1985, and when the last proofs of the volume have been dealt with I shall bid farewell to the 'oars and coat and badge' of lexicography." (Burchfield 1991:188–89.)

. . . or, not *quite*. In 1984, even before the final volume of the *Supplement* was issued, the *New Oxford English Dictionary* (*NOED*) project was initiated, which would produce a second edition of the whole *OED* and set the stage for a third. Burchfield knew as well as anyone else that the language is always a moving target.

106

Simpson & Weiner

What Was Once Thought Impossible

***The Oxford English Dictionary*. 2d ed. 20 vols. John Simpson & E.S.C. Weiner eds. Oxford: Clarendon Press, 1989.**

Ex coll. Karolyne & Bryan A. Garner; courtesy of Oxford University Press

"The keyboarding [began] on 1 November 1984. . . . It is a noble plan, and it is a stroke of luck that the work of many scholars and men of letters of the last hundred years has provided a suitable foundation on which scholars of the future can build with their capacious computers." (Burchfield 1991:175.)

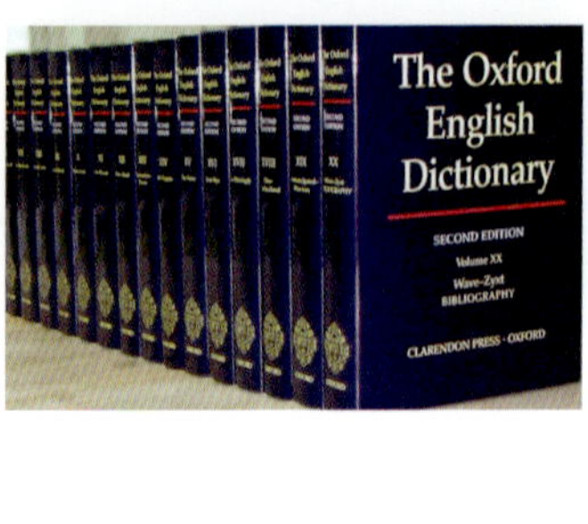

IN 1979, ROBERT BURCHFIELD was asked when the *OED* would be combined with his *Supplement*. "Never," he replied. "It can't be done." But in the mid-1980s, when his four-volume *Supplement* was nearing completion, Oxford University Press decided to overcome the many obstacles and merge it into the main text of the *OED*. The work would finally be an up-to-date dictionary, with entries for *micro-processor* and *pixel*, *disco* and *psychedelic*, *New Left* and *Third World*, *LSD* and *UFO*.

Up through the mid-1980s, the *OED* was a nuisance to use. Looking up a word meant looking first in the main alphabetical sequence in the 12-volume *OED* published from 1884 to 1928, and then in the 4-volume *Supplement* of 1972–1986. Either or both might contain relevant information, and there was no way to be sure without consulting them.

And so the editorial team turned their thoughts to merging the main sequence together with the *Supplement* to produce a single, fully integrated dictionary. The vision was spelled out in a brochure called *A Future for the OED*, released in March 1983.

Who would be in charge? Burchfield had been on the job since the 1950s, and it was time to pass the lexicographic torch. Two of his senior editors, John Simpson (b. 1953) and Edmund Weiner (b. 1950), took over the editorship, and Tim Benbow became project director. The New OED Project, as it was known, would require more than the small team of lexicographers who had been working on the project through the years. The *OED* has always been a huge enterprise, but late-20th-century enterprises were inherently more complex than mid-Victorian enterprises. The dictionary could no longer be managed by a group of gentleman amateurs; lexicography on this scale required multiple partnerships with international vendors, computer manufacturers, software companies, academic institutions, and government agencies. To support the project, the United Kingdom's Department of Trade offered a subvention of £288,750 (worth nearly a million pounds today), and IBM provided cutting-edge equipment.

The main *OED* editors had long focused intently on the *Supplement*, refusing to get sidetracked by rethinking what had already been finished. As editor John Simpson put it, "we planned simply to republish what had already been published in thc past, but in a new format." (Simpson 2016:135.) But the staff of the *New Shorter Oxford English Dictionary* had been revising and correcting their dictionary, and Burchfield, Simpson, and Weiner borrowed some of their expertise. Since they would have to review the entire dictionary, they could take the opportunity to make a very few improvements. They added about 5,000 words that the *Supplement* had missed, corrected a few errors, modified the way in which parts of speech appeared, and replaced Murray's idiosyncratic respelling system for presenting pronunciations with the International Phonetic Alphabet.

It's difficult even to conceive of the scale of this task. It took 18 months—120 person-years—to type the third of a billion characters that made up the *OED* and *Supplement*; proofreading the result took another 60 person-years. Then they had to merge the three separate sequences into one. The task sounds like something that could easily be automated, but it was vastly more complex. A later volume might add to, delete from, or alter the text of an earlier volume, and all those changes had to be checked. All the cross-references had to be reconsidered as new numbered senses were added to the mix. It was "the biggest scissors and paste job in history." (Gilliver 2016:519.)

Remarkably, they kept to their schedule and made the promised deadline of March 1989—a rare achievement in dictionary publishing and, in the words of Howard Jackson, "the first time that any part of the OED had appeared on time." (Jackson 2002:58.) What had been 16 volumes—the first edition plus the supplements—was now one 20-volume dictionary, as up to date as any print dictionary of that size could be.

"Although the *raison d'être* of this new edition is the integration of the two texts, and adherence to the instructions of the *Supplement*, whether explicitly stated or contextually implied, is the guiding principle of the work, the material brought over from the *Supplement* is by no means the only feature that differentiates the second edition from the first. New vocabulary has been added, certain important general revisions, and numerous local corrections, have been made, and the whole text has been given an entirely new typographical format." (*OED2*, 1:xi.)

"I joined the staff of the *Oxford English Dictionary* as an editorial assistant in 1976, and I remained with the dictionary for thirty-seven years, until my retirement in 2013. For the last twenty of those years, I was chief editor. From my first days at the *OED*, I found myself fascinated by the work of creating a dictionary. What captivated me was the English language and its history: how it arose in obscurity 1,500 years ago, and how it grew to define the nations that spoke it." (Simpson 2016:xi.)

107

It's Yclept the *Middle English Dictionary*

Middle English Dictionary. Hans Kurath, Sherman M. Kuhn & Robert E. Lewis eds. 13 vols. Ann Arbor: Univ. of Michigan Press, 1952–2001.

Hans Kurath (1891–1992).

"Our basic principle in determining meaning is not to claim more knowledge than we can glean from the quotations themselves and from their context." (1:14.)

THERE HAD BEEN Middle English dictionaries before, including a late-Victorian one edited by Francis Henry Stratmann and a *Concise Dictionary of Middle English from A.D. 1150 to 1580* by A.L. Mayhew and W.W. Skeat. Given that the *OED* sought to include every word that has been current since 1150, it contained, at least in principle, the entire Middle English vocabulary: something on the order of 8% of the *OED* is devoted to Middle English. (The current online *OED* includes 47,799 words with a first citation from 1150 to 1500, words as fundamental to our language as *a*, *not*, and *or*, and as obscure as *stingis-dint* "a fine for an assault with a stick," *lorthew* "a teacher," and *umquhile* "sometimes.") In the words of editor Robert E. Lewis, "the *OED* was intended primarily as a dictionary of Modern English, and Middle English usage, though systematically and quite adequately presented as background for later usage, is not treated from the point of view of the Middle Ages." (Lewis 2007:3.)

Middle English poses special challenges to lexicographers. English underwent upheavals between roughly 1100 and 1500. The Norman Invasion put French speakers in positions of authority in England, and over the next few centuries more and more French words mingled with our Germanic ones. In the beginning of this period, English was the language of a conquered people. Over time, it regained its place as the language of politics, diplomacy, and the arts, but only as remade with thousands of French lexical imports. Grammar itself was changing. Inflections—alterations to words' forms that indicate grammatical role—were very common in Old English; most of them died out over the next few centuries. In the later Middle English period came the mysterious Great Vowel Shift, which radically altered English phonology. Print arrived in England only at the very end of the era, meaning that most Middle English texts existed only in manuscript: a work written in Chester some time between 1280 and 1320 might survive in only two copies, one in London (1360) and one in York (1420), with hundreds of variants between them. How to record that? How to date it? Different spellings were found in different parts of the country, and words sometimes included letters that have since fallen out of use. The ancestor of our word *wrath*, to take but one example among thousands, might appear in Middle English as *wratthe*, *wrat*, *wraugth*, *wræþdæ*, *wræððe*, and *wrettis*, among other possibilities—a lexicographic headache. So varied is Middle English, both chronologically and regionally, that only a large dictionary might do it justice. (Lewis 2007:5.)

The project was conceived in 1919. Like the *OED*, it emerged from a paper read before the Philological Society of London, as it happens by the *OED*'s then editor, William Craigie. He called for a series of period-specific dictionaries to expand on the *OED*'s coverage. In 1925, the Modern Language Association assumed control of the project. Things moved slowly in the early days, and several times the project was nearly shuttered. (Adams 2009a:335–37.) But when it found a home at the University of Michigan in 1930, the foundations were more stable, and the donation of all the relevant quotation slips from the *OED*'s collection was a magnificent boon. It took nearly 30 years for the first installment, the "Plan and Bibliography" by Hans Kurath (1891–1992) and Sherman Kuhn (1907–1991), to appear. But once publication began, 128-page fascicles came out through the rest of the century—a total of 115 of them. Newly published Middle English texts meant that the canon of literature was growing as the dictionary proceeded. Early estimates called for a dictionary of about 8,000 pages. When publication finally wrapped up in 2001, the complete dictionary was 14,939 pages.

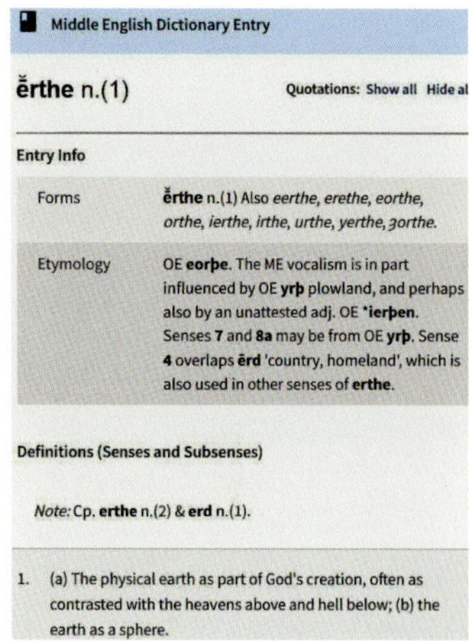
Middle English Dictionary Entry

ĕrthe n.(1) Quotations: Show all Hide al

Entry Info

Forms **ĕrthe** n.(1) Also *eerthe, erethe, eorthe, orthe, ierthe, irthe, urthe, yerthe, ȝorthe.*

Etymology OE **eorþe**. The ME vocalism is in part influenced by OE **yrþ** plowland, and perhaps also by an unattested adj. OE ***ierþen**. Senses **7** and **8a** may be from OE **yrþ**. Sense **4** overlaps **ērd** 'country, homeland', which is also used in other senses of **erthe**.

Definitions (Senses and Subsenses)

Note: Cp. **erthe** n.(2) & **erd** n.(1).

1. (a) The physical earth as part of God's creation, often as contrasted with the heavens above and hell below; (b) the earth as a sphere.

In 2007, the *MED* got an afterlife. First, the original "Plan and Bibliography" appeared in a much-revised and expanded second edition, reflecting all the ways in which the work had changed since the 1950s. Michael Adams calls this "an indispensable guide to the complex and unexpectedly unstable text of the *MED*." (Adams 2008:66.) Second, the whole thing was made freely available and searchable online in an electronic edition by Frances McSparran. It remains an essential tool for the study of English in the Middle Ages.

Ex coll. Karolyne & Bryan A. Garner

Assorted Merriam dictionaries from 1844 (top) to 1895 (bottom).

108

The Slow Death of "Webster" as a Trademark

A Shaggy-Dog Story

As Noah Webster was coming to be known as the Father of the American Dictionary, his name took on a life of its own. In the United States, *Webster* came to be synonymous with "the dictionary." The name began losing the distinctiveness that allowed it to serve as a trademark; it is now available to anyone who might create or publish a dictionary of any kind or quality. How did this happen?

A full account of the legal maneuvers has never before been given. Yet it's a story worth telling—a lexicographic version of *Jarndyce v. Jarndyce*. The saga played out over 150 years, from 1844 to 1994. It involved some of the most famous judges in the United States, including (twice) the U.S. Supreme Court.

Although Noah Webster lived a long and storied life, this particular narrative unfolded after his death in 1843. The next year, G. & C. Merriam Co. acquired from Noah Webster's estate the rights to his 1841 magnum opus, *An American Dictionary of the English Language*, commonly called *Webster's Dictionary*. Merriam also secured the right to create revised editions of this work. But throughout the 1840s and 1850s, New York publishers such as Harper & Row and Huntington & Savage were publishing shorter Webster dictionaries.

Merriam published its first new edition of *Webster's Dictionary* in 1847 (no. 74), and then 17 years later came out with its new unabridged version of *Webster's Dictionary* (known as the *Webster-Mahn* edition [no. 80]). Thanks to the success of that dictionary—together with the 1865 death of Merriam's primary competitor, Joseph Worcester—Merriam had almost 30 years of serene success. Although the success might last, the serenity wouldn't.

In the 19th century, copyright and trademark law played a crucial role in Merriam's legal battles. Merriam purchased the rights from Noah Webster's estate while the Copyright Act of 1831 was in effect. It was a statute that Noah Webster himself had fought to get enacted—as a result of which he also acquired the moniker "the

Father of American Copyright Law." How strange that this statute played a role in both promoting his posthumous fame and detracting from the rights of his legal successors.

The 1831 Act allowed for an initial protected period of 28 years, with a renewal period of 14 years. Once the copyright expired, all aspects of the protected work—including its title—entered the public domain. So the copyright for Merriam's 1847 revision of *Webster's Dictionary*, after the one allowed renewal, was set to expire in 1889. All its content would enter the public domain.

Meanwhile, in that year of expiration, the then-current trademark statute was the Trademark Act of 1881. Although it offered some protections, the 1881 Act didn't allow an applicant to obtain a trademark on an ordinary name. So nobody could acquire a statutory right by registering such a name.

By 1889, Merriam was selling successor editions, including its 1864 edition of *Webster-Mahn*, as revised and supplemented in 1879 and 1884. The title was emblazoned across the front cover: *An American Dictionary of the English Language*. On the back appeared the words *Webster's Dictionary, Unabridged*. Meanwhile, other publishers had begun printing and selling almost identical copies of Merriam's newly unprotected 1847 revision under the name *Webster's Dictionary* or *Webster's Unabridged Dictionary*. Naturally, these publishers used the name *Webster's* in advertisements.

Merriam's first attempt to retain exclusivity came in an 1890 federal lawsuit in Missouri against Holloway Publishing, which had reprinted the 1847 *Webster's Dictionary* and copied Merriam's customary picture of an open book in its advertisements.[1] Merriam claimed that Holloway had infringed its trademark in three ways: (1) using Merriam's open-book device in ads, (2) using the title *Webster's Dictionary* or *Webster's Unabridged Dictionary* on its copied dictionaries, and (3) replicating the text of the 1847 *Webster's Dictionary*.

On the first two claims, the court sided with Merriam. Even though the open-book device hadn't been trademarked, the court found it necessary to determine whether Holloway's use of Merriam's open-book device in advertisements was intended to—and actually did—deceive consumers. The court also said that by using *Webster's*

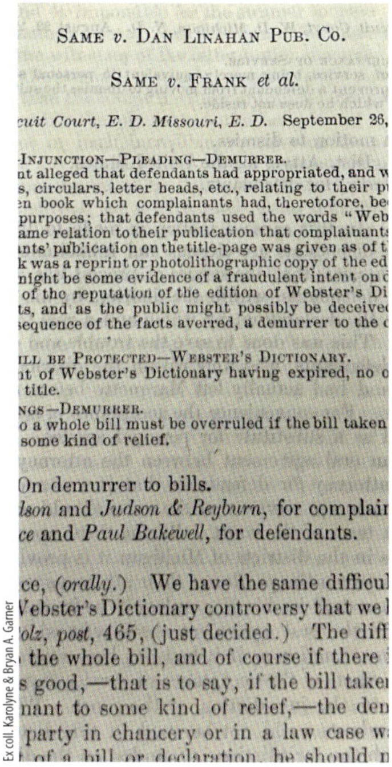

SAME *v.* DAN LINAHAN PUB. CO.

SAME *v.* FRANK *et al.*

cuit Court, E. D. Missouri, E. D. September 26,

INJUNCTION—PLEADING—DEMURRER.
nt alleged that defendants had appropriated, and w
s, circulars, letter heads, etc., relating to their p
n book which complainants had, theretofore, be
purposes; that defendants used the words "Web
ame relation to their publication that complainant
nts' publication on the title-page was given as of t
k was a reprint or photolithographic copy of the ed
night be some evidence of a fraudulent intent on c
of the reputation of the edition of Webster's Di
ts, and as the public might possibly be deceive
sequence of the facts averred, a demurrer to the c

ILL BE PROTECTED—WEBSTER'S DICTIONARY.
it of Webster's Dictionary having expired, no c
title.
NGS—DEMURRER.
o a whole bill must be overruled if the bill taken
some kind of relief.

On demurrer to bills.
lson and *Judson & Reyburn*, for complai
ce and *Paul Bakewell*, for defendants.

ce, (*orally*.) We have the same difficu
Vebster's Dictionary controversy that we
olz, post, 465, (just decided.) The diff
the whole bill, and of course if there
s good,—that is to say, if the bill take
nant to some kind of relief,—the de
party in chancery or in a law case w

Ex coll. Karolyne & Bryan A. Garner

Detail from the case.

Ex coll. Karolyne & Bryan A. Garner

About 1889, Holloway Publishing issued this small eight-page pamphlet without ever disclosing itself as publisher of *Webster's Unabridged*.

---

1 *Merriam v. Holloway Pub. Co.*, 43 F. 450, 450 (C.C.E.D. Mo. 1890).

Dictionary in its title, Holloway might have had some fraudulent intent to capitalize on Merriam's reputation.

Yet the court rejected Merriam's third claim—that the 1847 *Webster's* was "their book"—as "nonsense."[2] The court decided that Merriam was attempting to extend its copyright of *Webster's Dictionary* indefinitely "under the pretense that it is protected by trademark law."[3] The court reasoned that the 1847 dictionary was "Merriam's book" only in the same way that all consumers could claim that a purchased copy would be "their book." Because the copyright had expired, the law no longer protected *Webster's* or *Webster's Dictionary*. Both were "unrestricted public property."[4]

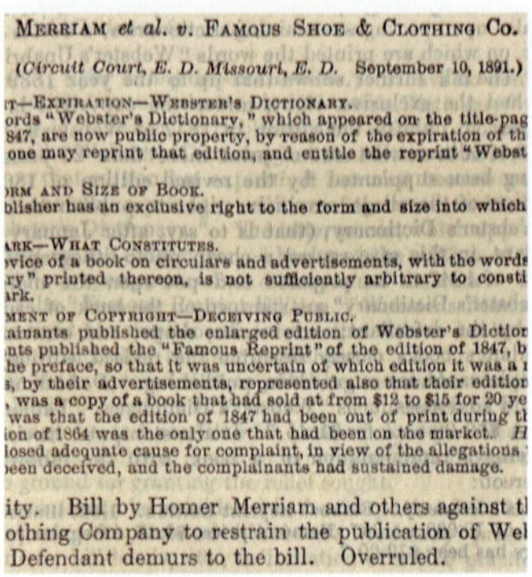
MERRIAM *et al.* *v.* FAMOUS SHOE & CLOTHING CO.

(*Circuit Court, E. D. Missouri, E. D.* September 10, 1891.)

T—EXPIRATION—WEBSTER'S DICTIONARY.
ords "Webster's Dictionary," which appeared on the title-pag
847, are now public property, by reason of the expiration of th
one may reprint that edition, and entitle the reprint "Webst

RM AND SIZE OF BOOK.
blisher has an exclusive right to the form and size into which

ARK—WHAT CONSTITUTES.
vice of a book on circulars and advertisements, with the words
ry" printed thereon, is not sufficiently arbitrary to consti
ark.

MENT OF COPYRIGHT—DECEIVING PUBLIC.
ainants published the enlarged edition of Webster's Dictior
nts published the "Famous Reprint" of the edition of 1847, b
he preface, so that it was uncertain of which edition it was a
, by their advertisements, represented also that their editior
, was a copy of a book that had sold at from $12 to $15 for 20 ye
was that the edition of 1847 had been out of print during tl
ion of 1864 was the only one that had been on the market. *H*
losed adequate cause for complaint, in view of the allegations
een deceived, and the complainants had sustained damage.

ity. Bill by Homer Merriam and others against tl
othing Company to restrain the publication of Wel
Defendant demurs to the bill. Overruled.

Ex coll. Karolyne & Bryan A. Garner

Detail from the 1891 case.

A year later, in 1891, Merriam returned to the same court, seeking to enjoin Famous Shoe & Clothing Co. from republishing the 1847 *Webster's Dictionary*.[5] Here Merriam studiously avoided copyright claims. Instead, it was now suing for (1) trademark infringement over Famous's use of *Webster's Dictionary* in the title, (2) trademark infringement, given that Famous's reprints were of the same size and shape as Merriam's current dictionary, (3) trademark infringement for Famous's use of the open-book device with the words *Webster's Dictionary* in ads, and (4) unfair competition, meaning that the competitor was engaging in a deceitful misappropriation akin to counterfeiting.

Siding with Famous on the three trademark claims, the court found the open-book device insufficiently arbitrary to be a trademark. It also reiterated that the 1847 *Webster's Dictionary* was public property, adding that Famous's right to use the words *Webster's Dictionary* on the 1847 version was just as clear as Merriam's right to use those words. Likewise, "no publisher can claim an exclusive right to make a book of a certain form or size."[6] So Merriam had no right to relief based on trademark law.

Yet the court sided with Merriam on its unfair-competition claim, holding that Merriam was entitled to a final hearing on

---

2 *Id.* at 452.

3 *Id.* at 451.

4 *Id.*

5 *Merriam v. Famous Shoe & Clothing Co.*, 47 F. 411, 413 (C.C.E.D. Mo. 1891).

6 *Id.* at 412–13.

whether relief was justified.[7] Famous had removed from its reprint all information—such as the title page's acknowledgment of Chauncey A. Goodrich, a preface giving a history of that edition, and the copyright date—that would have signaled that Famous was publishing an out-of-copyright work. Hence a final hearing was needed to determine Merriam's relief because, without the omitted information, a consumer would be hard pressed to differentiate between Merriam's then-current dictionary and Famous's reprint of the old 1847 edition.[8] Merriam's victory was only to win the right to further hearings—in short, more litigation, of which there is no record. The lawsuit probably settled.

The 19th-century magazine logo.

Merriam was becoming litigious. In the following year came another legal contest. Undeterred by setbacks in the first two cases, Merriam sought to enjoin Texas Siftings Publishing Co., which produced a weekly humor magazine (*Texas Siftings*), from reselling cheap reprints of the 1847 edition.[9] But the complaint this time was not based on any supposed trademark rights in the name *Webster's Dictionary*. Merriam was instead claiming unfair competition because Texas Siftings represented through advertisements that its 1847 reprints were copies of Merriam's "latest dictionaries."

Texas Siftings was offering new magazine subscribers a bargain price on the dictionary. The publisher of these reprints was Ogilvie & Co., run by one George W. Ogilvie, who would bedevil Merriam well into the 20th century.

In the *Texas Siftings* case, the court noted with approval the previous Merriam cases, reiterating that the 1847 edition's copyright had expired and that the name *Webster's Dictionary* "is not a trademark."[10] Yet the court did enjoin Texas Siftings from continuing its ads in their current form because they "made free and ingenious use of misrepresentations, which were intended and calculated to mislead the public into a belief that the book was the one which had long been produced and sold by [Merriam]."[11] This was another success based on the law of unfair competition.

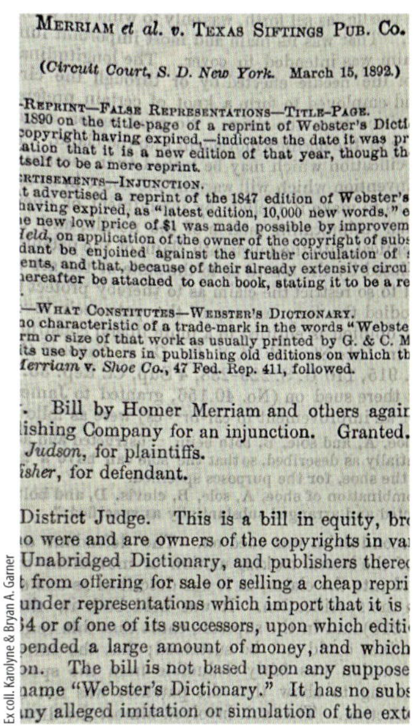

MERRIAM *et al.* v. TEXAS SIFTINGS PUB. CO.

(*Circuit Court, S. D. New York.* March 15, 1892.)

-REPRINT—FALSE REPRESENTATIONS—TITLE-PAGE.
1890 on the title-page of a reprint of Webster's Dicti
copyright having expired,—indicates the date it was pr
ation that it is a new edition of that year, though th
tself to be a mere reprint.

RTISEMENTS—INJUNCTION.
t advertised a reprint of the 1847 edition of Webster's
having expired, as "latest edition, 10,000 new words," e
e new low price of $1 was made possible by improvem
ield, on application of the owner of the copyright of subs
dant be enjoined against the further circulation of
ents, and that, because of their already extensive circu
hereafter be attached to each book, stating it to be a re

—WHAT CONSTITUTES—WEBSTER'S DICTIONARY.
no characteristic of a trade-mark in the words "Webste
rm or size of that work as usually printed by G. & C. M
its use by others in publishing old editions on which th
Merriam v. *Shoe Co.*, 47 Fed. Rep. 411, followed.

. Bill by Homer Merriam and others agai
lishing Company for an injunction. Granted.
Judson, for plaintiffs.
isher, for defendant.

District Judge. This is a bill in equity, br
o were and are owners of the copyrights in va
Unabridged Dictionary, and publishers there
t from offering for sale or selling a cheap repri
under representations which import that it is
64 or of one of its successors, upon which editi
pended a large amount of money, and which
on. The bill is not based upon any suppose
name "Webster's Dictionary." It has no subs
any alleged imitation or simulation of the ext

Ex coll. Karolyne & Bryan A. Garner

Detail from the 1892 case.

7 *Id.* at 414–15.

8 *Id.* at 412, 414.

9 *Merriam v. Texas Siftings Pub. Co.*, 49 F. 944, 944 (C.C.S.D.N.Y. 1892).

10 *Id.* at 942–48.

11 *Id.* at 948.

Ex coll. Karolyne & Bryan A. Garner

The volume containing the fateful *Singer* opinion.

The trio of cases from 1890 to 1892 concerned only reprints of Noah Webster's or Merriam's previous works. Although the copyright law of the time so implied, no court had expressly declared *Webster's* or the phrase *Webster's Dictionary* to be utterly generic and available to any dictionary. Yet the legal landscape was changing.

In 1896, a sewing-machine case in the U.S. Supreme Court provided the basis for declaring *Webster's* generic.[12] Famous for its patented sewing machines, Singer Manufacturing Co. had registered a trademark using the word, but the company never registered the term *Singer* itself. After Singer's patent expired, competitors began making identical machines. One even called its machine an "improved Singer."[13] Singer sued for an injunction, which was denied. On appeal to the Supreme Court, Singer raised specific questions: Had *Singer* become a generic designation for a sewing machine? Or did it exclusively identify the manufacturer?

The Court answered right up front: *Singer* was a "generically descriptive" name for the company's machines.[14] The Court reasoned that during the patented period, Singer became a generic name for a sewing machine while also alerting the public to the machine's manufacturer. But the company had failed to place the name Singer on all its machines, even if they were described in ads as Singer machines. Likewise, Singer didn't use the word to reflect the origin of manufacture until after the copyright had expired.[15] Singer had abandoned any right to the name through generic use.

Crucially, the *Singer* Court cited the earlier Merriam cases—a signal that should have alerted Merriam that it had no exclusive right to *Webster's*. Its own death knell approached.

Then came George W. Ogilvie's full-on guerrilla war against Merriam. After being the behind-the-scenes instigator in the *Texas Siftings* case, Ogilvie reemerged with new ploys intended to topple Merriam. It took vigilance and stamina to defend against his business and legal stratagems.

---

12 *Singer Mfg. Co. v. June Mfg. Co.*, 163 U.S. 169, 16 S. Ct. 1002, 41 L. Ed. 118 (1896).

13 *Singer Mfg. Co. v. June Mfg. Co.*, 41 F. 208, 209–11 (N.D. Ill. 1889), *rev'd on other grounds*, 163 U.S. 169, 16 S. Ct. 1002, 41 L. Ed. 118 (1896).

14 163 U.S. at 180.

15 *Id.* at 181–83.

Before exploring the fresh lawsuits, we might look into this pertinacious, mysterious man George W. Ogilvie. Born in New York in 1860, he was the son of Scottish immigrants. He established his publishing business in Chicago at the age of 24, with a New York branch two years later and a London branch five years after that. He published Bibles and many other works. In 1896, the poet James Whitcomb Riley publicly claimed to have won a judgment in a Chicago federal court against Ogilvie for "publishing unauthorized collections of his poems." It was said that the court ruled in Riley's favor "upon every point in contention, including an order confiscating all books, sheets and plates of the unauthorized edition and a permanent injunction."[16] There was no official report of the lawsuit.

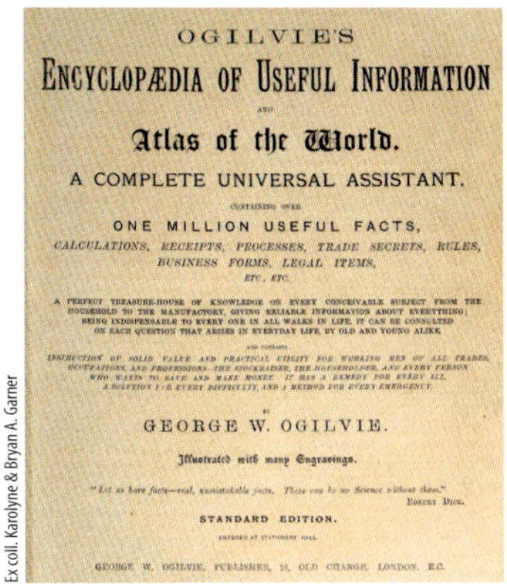
OGILVIE'S
ENCYCLOPÆDIA OF USEFUL INFORMATION
AND
Atlas of the World.
A COMPLETE UNIVERSAL ASSISTANT.
CONTAINING OVER
ONE MILLION USEFUL FACTS,
CALCULATIONS, RECEIPTS, PROCESSES, TRADE SECRETS, RULES, BUSINESS FORMS, LEGAL ITEMS, ETC., ETC.
A PERFECT TREASURE-HOUSE OF KNOWLEDGE ON EVERY CONCEIVABLE SUBJECT FROM THE HOUSEHOLD TO THE MANUFACTORY, GIVING RELIABLE INFORMATION ABOUT EVERYTHING; BEING INDISPENSABLE TO EVERY ONE IN ALL WALKS IN LIFE. IT CAN BE CONSULTED ON EACH QUESTION THAT ARISES IN EVERYDAY LIFE, BY OLD AND YOUNG ALIKE.
BY
GEORGE W. OGILVIE.
Illustrated with many Engravings.
STANDARD EDITION.
GEORGE W. OGILVIE, PUBLISHER, 16, OLD CHANGE, LONDON, E.C.

Ex coll. Karolyne & Bryan A. Garner

In 1896, Ogilvie's London branch published this big reference book, listing him as the author.

According to a 1905 publication, Ogilvie devoted the years 1897 to 1904 readying for publication "the first complete Webster's dictionary of the English language ever edited and published west of Massachusetts."[17] Under the pseudonym George W. Conklin, he reportedly wrote and sold 8 million copies of various reference books.[18] He was never afraid of a controversy: in 1902, he walked into a Brooklyn church and announced that prayers were needed for the soul of his brother, the rival publisher J.S. Ogilvie (a member of that church). George publicly wagered $10,000 that he could prove that these prayers were needed, asserting: "I invite him to a contest. . . . Let him place $10,000 in the hands of some trust committee. I will do likewise. Let an unprejudiced committee decide upon the question as to whether he needs the saving-grace of prayer." The principal charge was that J.S. Ogilvie had misappropriated an inheritance from their grandfather in Scotland. It concerned some Scottish property that allegedly descended jointly to George and J.S. from their grandfather through their father.[19] Nothing seems to have come of the flamboyant

---

16 "Infringed Copyright: James Whitcomb Riley Secures Judgment Against Chicago Publishers," *Sidney Daily News*, 16 Mar. 1896, at 1.

17 *The Book of Chicagoans: A Biographical Dictionary of Leading Men of the City of Chicago* 438 (John W. Leonard ed., 1905).

18 *Id.*

19 "Will Bet Prayer Is Needed: G.W. Ogilvie Makes a Peculiar Offer Concerning His Brother, J.S. Ogilvie," *Brooklyn Daily Eagle*, 26 Jan. 1902, at 10. *See also* "Asks Prayers for Brother He Quarreled With," *Chicago Trib.*, 23 Jan. 1902, at 4 (adding

Ex coll. Karolyne & Bryan A. Garner

Justice Oliver Wendell Holmes.

wager, but George succeeded in causing great chagrin to his brother—and not just about this alleged wrongdoing.

About a month after the prayer incident, George accused J.S. of smuggling pornography with the intent to publish it. George somehow managed to steal from J.S.'s publishing house the plates of a mildly salacious novel, *Madame du Barry* (a sort of 19th-century *Fifty Shades of Grey*). He handed them off to an anti-vice organization headed by Anthony Comstock, the infamous censor. George's intent was to expose and humiliate J.S. for the un-Christian scheme to publish the book, and it became quite a scandal. Pretending innocence of any involvement in the strange delivery of J.S.'s property to Comstock's vice squad,[20] George pledged to reporters that he would "continue to make it uncomfortable for his brother until he had adjusted matters."[21]

Deprived of any Scottish inheritance and thoroughly alienated from his brother, George W. Ogilvie turned to American law to gain every possible advantage in his publishing business. After all, he claimed to have devoted seven full years to lexicography, and he had dictionaries to sell.

In 1905, Congress dramatically changed trademark law by amending the 1881 Trademark Act.[22] You could now trademark a proper name if it had been in use for ten years under conditions named in the statute. The legislative amendments also made the circuit courts the final courts of appeal—with no further appeals to the U.S. Supreme Court. Copyright law, meanwhile, remained unchanged: all aspects of a protected work entered the public domain after a copyright expired.

Against this backdrop, Ogilvie conjured two new schemes in 1904–1905. The first involved acquiring a copy of *Webster's Brief International Dictionary*, published in London by George Bell & Sons under license from Merriam. The dictionary was almost identical to Merriam's *Webster's High School Dictionary*. Ogilvie's copying was an especially brazen move, given that the Bell firm acted as Merriam's

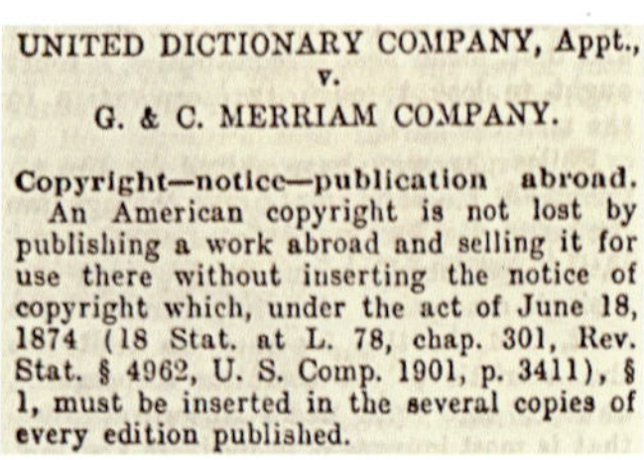

UNITED DICTIONARY COMPANY, Appt.,
v.
G. & C. MERRIAM COMPANY.

Copyright—notice—publication abroad. An American copyright is not lost by publishing a work abroad and selling it for use there without inserting the notice of copyright which, under the act of June 18, 1874 (18 Stat. at L. 78, chap. 301, Rev. Stat. § 4962, U. S. Comp. 1901, p. 3411), § 1, must be inserted in the several copies of every edition published.

Ex coll. Karolyne & Bryan A. Garner

Front matter for the U.S. Supreme Court opinion affirming the Seventh Circuit's judgment against Ogilvie's company.

that J.S. had bought out George's business some years before, engendering bad blood).

20 *See* "Ogilvie Gives Up Controversial Book," *Leavenworth Times* (Kan.), 22 Feb. 1902, at 7.

21 *Id.*

22 33 Stat. at L. 724, chap. 592, Comp. Stat. 1913, § 9485.

London agent.[23] After retypesetting the dictionary and trying to publish it stateside, Ogilvie claimed that because the London-published *Webster's Brief International Dictionary* didn't have the copyright notice required by U.S. law, it was unprotected in the United States.[24] Merriam promptly sued, and the case wound its way through the courts. Unsurprisingly, the Seventh Circuit was not amused by Ogilvie's scheme, holding that U.S. copyright law could not require the copyright notice abroad because the law did not have an extraterritorial effect.[25] In 1908, the U.S. Supreme Court affirmed with an opinion by Justice Oliver Wendell Holmes.

Ogilvie's other scheme was reminiscent of those from the 1890s. Ogilvie had begun advertising his *Webster's Imperial Dictionary*, which was merely an enlarged and revised version of Merriam's 1847 book.[26] Ogilvie's ads called it the latest "complete authentic" Webster's Dictionary. Merriam responded by sending threatening letters to the trade, claiming that Merriam had the exclusive right to *Webster's* in dictionary titles. Ogilvie sued Merriam, asking the court to enjoin Merriam from sending the threatening letters. Merriam cross-claimed, asserting that Ogilvie's use of *Webster's* in books and in advertising infringed on Merriam's latest dictionary, *Webster's International Dictionary*.

The district court granted Ogilvie's injunction against Merriam, holding that if Merriam indeed had the exclusive right to use *Webster's* even after the 1889 expiration of copyright, it would be perpetuating "the monopoly secured by copyright."[27] But in a small victory for Merriam, the court enjoined Ogilvie from sending out his circulars if they copied Merriam's ads for its *International Dictionary*. The court also expanded the order to require Ogilvie's company to signal unmistakably its status as the publisher of its dictionaries.[28]

Ex coll. Karolyne & Bryan A. Garner

In the "Authorised Edition" of the London-published *Webster's Brief International Dictionary* (1894), the only authorized spelling of *authorize* is *authorize*.

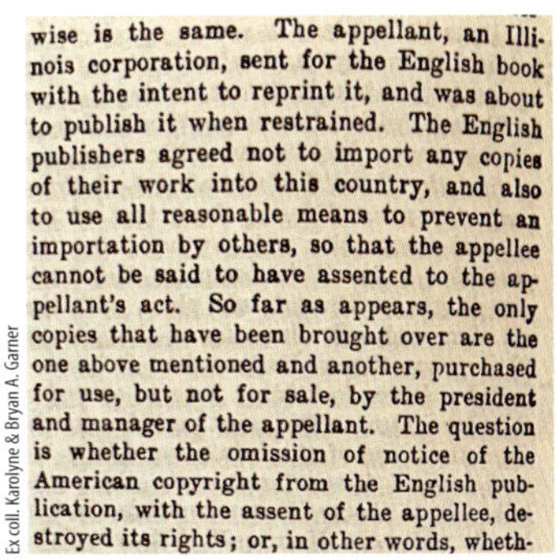

wise is the same. The appellant, an Illinois corporation, sent for the English book with the intent to reprint it, and was about to publish it when restrained. The English publishers agreed not to import any copies of their work into this country, and also to use all reasonable means to prevent an importation by others, so that the appellee cannot be said to have assented to the appellant's act. So far as appears, the only copies that have been brought over are the one above mentioned and another, purchased for use, but not for sale, by the president and manager of the appellant. The question is whether the omission of notice of the American copyright from the English publication, with the assent of the appellee, destroyed its rights; or, in other words, wheth-

Ex coll. Karolyne & Bryan A. Garner

Excerpt from the Holmes opinion: "the president and manager of the appellant" refers to Ogilvie.

23 *G. & C. Merriam Co. v. United Dictionary Co.*, 146 F. 354, 355 (7th Cir. 1906), *aff'd sub nom. United Dictionary Co. v. G & C Merriam Co.*, 208 U.S. 260, 28 S. Ct. 290, 52 L. Ed. 478 (1908) (United Dictionary Co. being another of Ogilvie's companies).

24 *Id.* at 356–57.

25 *Id.* at 358–59.

26 *Ogilvie v. G. & C. Merriam Co.*, 149 F. 858, 860 (C.C.D. Mass. 1907), *aff'd as modified*, 159 F. 638 (1st Cir. 1908).

27 *Id.* at 860.

28 *Id.* at 861, 863–64.

More important, the district court was the first to identify the twofold significance of *Webster's*, which at first signaled a generic name for a dictionary—one now in the public domain. But it also now suggested to the public a dictionary published and sold by Merriam.[29] If the first point alone had been true, publishing works from the public domain would be a free-for-all. Yet when the first significance accompanies the second, those re-creating the work must alert the public that they aren't the work's "original" publishers.

The First Circuit agreed with the lower court's reasoning, upholding the injunction against Merriam.[30] In denying Merriam's appeal, the court followed the Supreme Court's reasoning in *Singer*, explaining that there was an explicit right to re-create works in the public domain. But this right was subject to the prohibition against seeking to deceive potential purchasers into believing that they were buying the original publisher's work.

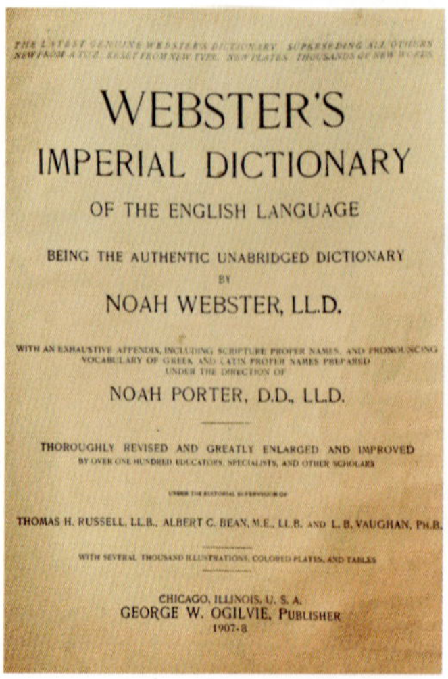

THE LATEST GENUINE WEBSTER'S DICTIONARY SUPERSEDING ALL OTHERS
NEW FROM A TO Z. RESET FROM NEW TYPE. NEW PLATES. THOUSANDS OF NEW WORDS

WEBSTER'S
IMPERIAL DICTIONARY
OF THE ENGLISH LANGUAGE

BEING THE AUTHENTIC UNABRIDGED DICTIONARY
BY
NOAH WEBSTER, LL.D.

WITH AN EXHAUSTIVE APPENDIX, INCLUDING SCRIPTURE PROPER NAMES, AND PRONOUNCING VOCABULARY OF GREEK AND LATIN PROPER NAMES PREPARED UNDER THE DIRECTION OF
NOAH PORTER, D.D., LL.D.

THOROUGHLY REVISED AND GREATLY ENLARGED AND IMPROVED
BY OVER ONE HUNDRED EDUCATORS, SPECIALISTS, AND OTHER SCHOLARS

THOMAS H. RUSSELL, LL.B., ALBERT C. BEAN, M.E., LL.B. AND L. B. VAUGHAN, PH.B.

WITH SEVERAL THOUSAND ILLUSTRATIONS, COLORED PLATES, AND TABLES

CHICAGO, ILLINOIS, U. S. A.
GEORGE W. OGILVIE, PUBLISHER
1907-8

Ex coll. Karolyne & Bryan A. Garner

Neither the district court nor the First Circuit declared *Webster's* or *Webster's Dictionary* to be a generic term available for *all* dictionaries. Those names were only generic terms for Merriam's old dictionaries now *in the public domain*: namely, the 1847 edition. So *Webster's* and *Webster's Dictionary* were not yet fully generic terms, and Merriam—for the time being—still had exclusive right to call new dictionaries *Webster's*.

Meanwhile, throughout this litigation, George W. Ogilvie engaged in lexicographic muckraking. In the February 1907 journal *School Education*, for example, he wrote an article blasting G. & C. Merriam Co. for publishing dictionaries that were inauthentic: they didn't even resemble what had come from the pen of Noah Webster. In many lawsuits against publishers of more genuine Webster dictionaries, Ogilvie asserted, "the Merriam Company were whipped, unqualifiedly and absolutely."[31] Ogilvie quoted various letters in support of his *Webster's Imperial*, including a minister who said he was so pleased with it that he had discarded his copy of Merriam's 1890 *Webster's International*. Ogilvie then called the Merriam work

29 *Id.* at 860.

30 *G. & C. Merriam Co. v. Ogilvie*, 159 F. 638, 643 (1st Cir. 1908) (Ogilvie did not appeal).

31 George W. Ogilvie, "Interesting Facts About Webster Dictionaries," *School Educator* 26:37 (1907).

"an obsolescent, if not wholly obsolete, dictionary."[32] Pointing out one supposed error in the big Merriam dictionary as representative of "hundreds that we know of," Ogilvie asserted: "If you want a *dictionary* and not a 'joke book,' get Webster's Imperial Dictionary."[33]

Invited to respond, Merriam issued this statement: "We have no wish to enter into a newspaper controversy, preferring to leave the matter for the Courts to decide."[34] Perhaps the editors were heeding the modern proverb, sometimes wrongly attributed to George Bernard Shaw: Never wrestle with a pig; you will both get dirty, and the pig likes it.

Yet as we've seen, the litigation didn't go well for Merriam.

Soon George W. Ogilvie reemerged with yet two more anti-Merriam maneuvers, one in Ohio and the other in New York. In the Ohio case, Merriam sued Saalfield Publishing Co., which had acquired part of Ogilvie's publishing enterprises after he had supposedly exited the publishing business.[35] But this was something of a sham. Although the exact nature of the contract wasn't revealed, Saalfield had begun selling copies of the English *Twentieth Century Dictionary*, mostly under the title *Webster's Intercollegiate Dictionary*, with the same marketing methods that Ogilvie had used.[36] (Saalfield was also publishing *Webster's Imperial Dictionary* [1908–1909] and *Webster's Sterling Dictionary of the English Language* [1908].) Merriam sued, complaining that the name *Intercollegiate* was confusingly close

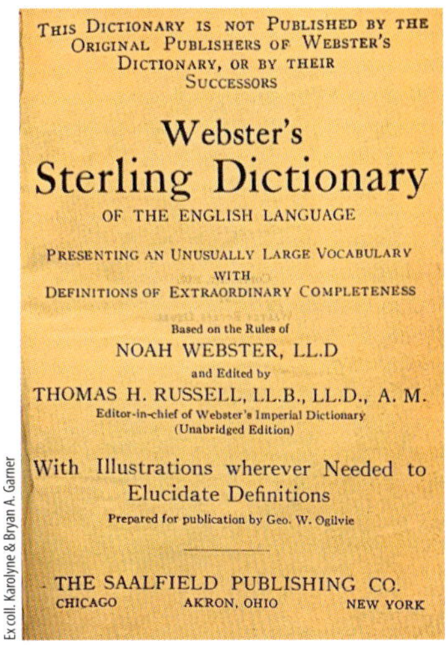
THIS DICTIONARY IS NOT PUBLISHED BY THE ORIGINAL PUBLISHERS OF WEBSTER'S DICTIONARY, OR BY THEIR SUCCESSORS

Webster's
Sterling Dictionary
OF THE ENGLISH LANGUAGE

PRESENTING AN UNUSUALLY LARGE VOCABULARY WITH DEFINITIONS OF EXTRAORDINARY COMPLETENESS

Based on the Rules of
NOAH WEBSTER, LL.D
and Edited by
THOMAS H. RUSSELL, LL.B., LL.D., A. M.
Editor-in-chief of Webster's Imperial Dictionary (Unabridged Edition)

With Illustrations wherever Needed to Elucidate Definitions
Prepared for publication by Geo. W. Ogilvie

THE SAALFIELD PUBLISHING CO.
CHICAGO AKRON, OHIO NEW YORK

Ex coll. Karolyne & Bryan A. Garner

32 *Id.* at 38.

33 *Id.*

34 *Id.*

35 *G. & C. Merriam Co. v. Saalfield*, 190 F. 927, 932 (6th Cir. 1911). *See* "George W. Ogilvie Bought Out by Saalfield Publishing Company and Thousands of Bibles and Dictionaries Will Be Made Here," *Akron Beacon J.*, 21 May 1908, at 1 (announcing that [1] "the enormous publishing business of one of Chicago's greatest publishing firms, the George W. Ogilvie & Co.," would be brought to Akron, [2] "the largest part of the purchase . . . is that of the Webster Imperial dictionary, which was prepared by over 100 educators, specialists and scholars under the supervision of Thomas H. Russell, editor-in-chief," and [3] "Mr. Saalfield becomes owner and publisher of three other dictionaries known as Webster's Intercollegiate dictionary, Webster's Adequate dictionary, and Webster's Sterling dictionary"). It's true: in 1907, George W. Ogilvie published a book titled *Webster's Adequate Dictionary.*

36 *Saalfield*, 190 F. at 933–34.

Ex coll. Karolyne & Bryan A. Garner

One of many Webster-styled imprints issued by Ogilvie's Syndicate Publishing Co. of New York.

to Merriam's *Webster's Collegiate Dictionary* (1898). As it turned out, Saalfield was found to be a proxy for Ogilvie, who secretly directed and paid for Saalfield's legal defense. Ogilvie was trying to avoid the injunction issued against him by the First Circuit. The Sixth Circuit saw through the ruse and held that Saalfield was subject to the same injunction that had been issued against Ogilvie years earlier.[37]

Ogilvie found more success in New York. He sought to publish an English dictionary—the *British Empire Dictionary*—under a new name, *Webster's Crown Dictionary*. After suing Ogilvie's new company, Syndicate Publishing Co., Merriam adopted another argument: how could Ogilvie call his dictionary a *Webster's* when the base material—the *British Empire Dictionary*—was not a *Webster's* at all?[38] The answer, unfortunately, eroded Merriam's position even further.

In the most influential decision discussed here, the celebrated Judge Learned Hand examined what it means when the public sees the word *Webster's*. Merriam advocated an analysis that would align with past decisions: *Webster's* signaled to the public a dictionary published by Merriam. Judge Hand was unconvinced. *Webster's*, he said, "at least denotes what I should call literary descent from Webster's original books . . . and that this succession goes back without break to some work by Webster himself."[39]

Ex coll. Karolyne & Bryan A. Garner

Note the name at the base of the spine.

If Merriam succeeded in its argument that *Webster's* signaled both literary descent from Noah Webster and a work published by Merriam, Judge Hand wrote, it would be "foisting upon the public a spurious work" because Merriam's current dictionary (the 1909 edition) had "almost totally different literary contents from any book with which Noah Webster had anything to do."[40] As a result, the "constant iteration" that Merriam, and only Merriam, had the exclusive right to use the term *Webster's* in a dictionary title was "merely a childish extravagance."[41] So the question became whether Ogilvie's *Webster's Crown Dictionary* could trace its lineage back to Noah Webster.

37 *Id. See also G. & C. Merriam Co. v. Saalfield*, 238 F. 1, 14 (6th Cir. 1917).

38 *G. & C. Merriam Co. v. Syndicate Pub. Co.*, 207 F. 515, 515, 517 (2d Cir. 1913).

39 *Id.* at 516.

40 *Id.* at 516–17.

41 *Id.* at 517.

Luckily for Ogilvie, it could. About 70% of *Webster's Crown Dictionary* was based on the *British Empire Dictionary*—a revised version of the British *Imperial Dictionary* (1855), whose title page announced that it was made "on the basis of Webster's English Dictionary." (The *Imperial*, believe it or not, was by a Scotsman named John Ogilvie, LLD, who may have been distantly related to George.) So the publishing world learned a valuable lesson. If any dictionary could somehow trace its ancestry back to Noah Webster, it could call itself a *Webster's* as long as it included the following disclaimer:

> This dictionary is not published by the original publishers of Webster's Dictionary or by their successors.[42]

Oddly, this statement, which was soon attached to many mediocre dictionaries, had almost the opposite of its intended effect. It essentially enhanced the dictionaries on whose title pages it appeared, as if the publishers were purposely boasting about distancing themselves from old-fashioned "original publishers."

Equally important, the publishers no longer had to revise the much-out-of-date 1841 *Webster's*. They could now update and revise more recent works descended from Noah Webster.

The Second Circuit affirmed Judge Hand's decision, commenting only to say that it didn't agree with Merriam's proposition that the phrase *Webster's Dictionary* had the distinctive meaning suggesting a Merriam publication.[43]

Merriam appealed to the U.S. Supreme Court, which dismissed the appeal because the 1905 amendment to the Trademark Act had made decisions of the intermediate federal appellate courts final in the absence of a claim based on a federal statute or the Constitution—neither of which Merriam had established.[44] The Court commented: "After the expiration of a copyright . . . , it is well settled that the further use of the name by which the publication was known and sold under the copyright cannot be acquired by registration as a trademark; for the name has become public property, and is not subject

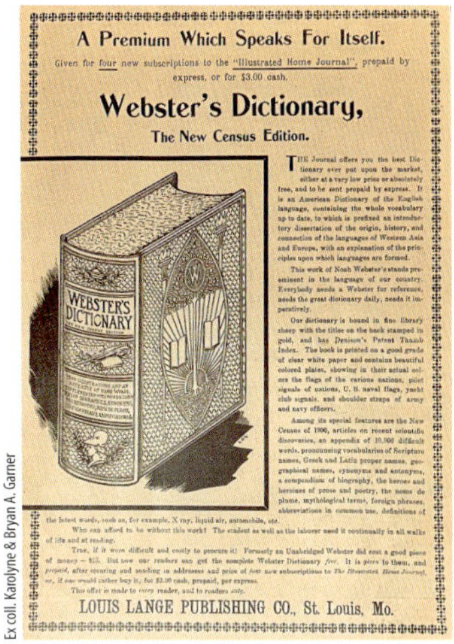

Ex coll. Karolyne & Bryan A. Garner

This 1903 advertisement is for a *Webster's Dictionary* (the "New Census Edition"!) published in St. Louis by the Louis Lange Publishing Co.

Judge Learned Hand of the Southern District of New York.

42 *G. & C. Merriam v. Ogilvie*, 170 F. 167, 168 (1st Cir. 1909); *accord G. & C. Merriam v. Saalfield*, 198 F. 369, 378 (6th Cir. 1912).

43 *Syndicate Pub. Co.*, 207 F. at 520.

44 *G. & C. Merriam Co. v. Syndicate Pub. Co.*, 237 U.S. 618, 621, 624 (1915) (citing Act Feb. 20, 1905, 33 Stat. 724, chap. 592).

Arkansas Congressman William A. Oldfield (1874–1928)

to . . . appropriation."[45] It further noted that in the *Singer* case, it had approved the reasoning of the early Merriam cases. Because *Webster's* and *Webster's Dictionary* were common names for literary descendants of Noah Webster's work, they were now altogether generic terms. Merriam therefore had no exclusive right to them.

Meanwhile, there was some behind-the-scenes sleaze at play. An Arkansas congressman, William A. Oldfield, who was chair of the House Committee on Patents, was accused by two congressional staffers of trying to "sell" legislation on the Webster question. Oldfield's erstwhile private secretary (C.E. Kay), together with his erstwhile stenographer and typist (Elsie Hunt), swore out affidavits that Oldfield had sought, in December 1914, to extract $10,000 from either Ogilvie or Merriam for passing or defeating legislation that would allow anyone to publish Webster dictionaries with impunity.[46] (These affidavits were made public in March 1916 by Oldfield's political opponent, Tom W. Campbell.) Applying to Congress, Ogilvie was seeking an explicit amendment to the Copyright Act. Because the House Committee was evenly divided, Oldfield told Kay, within Hunt's hearing, that he could "pick up some easy money" from one side or the other in this bitter fight.[47] C.E. Kay wrote a letter to President Woodrow Wilson, alerting him to Oldfield's corruption. Nothing seems to have come from these allegations—no ethics reprimand, much less removal from office—and Oldfield served several more terms in Congress until his death in 1928. Nor did the Webster-related legislation progress to enactment.

George W. Ogilvie also died in 1928,[48] but his ghost would continue to torment Merriam for many years. The successor to his publishing enterprise, Alfred H. Cahen's burgeoning World

Ex coll. Karolyne & Bryan A. Garner

By the 1930s, Merriam was aggressively warning people to avoid competitors called Webster.

45 *Id.* at 622.

46 These are reproduced in *Judsonia Weekly Advance* (Ark.), 22 Mar. 1916, at 1, 6.

47 *Id.* at 1.

48 "Woman's Kindness Brings Her $5000," *Asbury Park Evening News* (N.J.), 27 Jan. 1928, at 1 (describing contents of Ogilvie's will, including a trust for older brother David P. Ogilvie [d. 1940], a $2,500 gift to "sister" [estranged wife] Jennie Ogilvie, and appointment of Central Trust [later Hanover Trust] as trust of the residuary estate). *See also* Library of Congress, Copyright Office, *Catalogue of Copyright Entries* 1964 (1934) (noting Hanover Trust as one of the "executors of George W. Ogilvie, the proprietor," under *Munro*).

Syndicate Publishing Company in Cleveland, had taken over Ogilvie's books. For example, World Syndicate published *The New Age Webster Dictionary Self-Pronouncing* in 1933 and, three years later, *Webster's Universal Dictionary*—both with the mandatory disclaimer on the title page. (It also issued several editions of George W. Conklin's *Words as They Look: A Quick-Reference Speller*. Remember that Conklin was George W. Ogilvie's pseudonym.) In the end, World Syndicate would give rise to the *Webster's New World Dictionaries*.

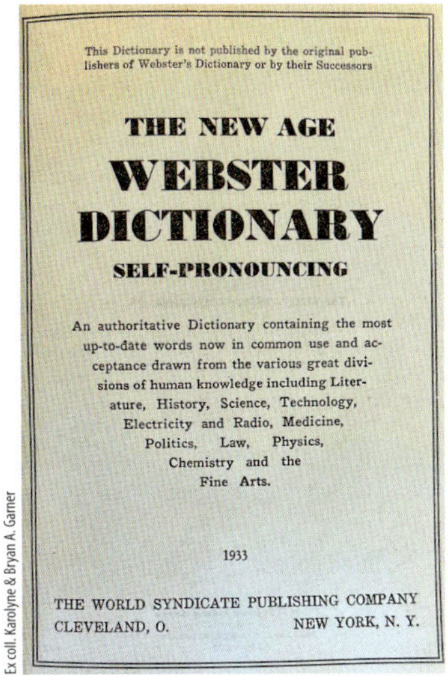
This Dictionary is not published by the original publishers of Webster's Dictionary or by their Successors

THE NEW AGE
WEBSTER
DICTIONARY
SELF-PRONOUNCING

An authoritative Dictionary containing the most up-to-date words now in common use and acceptance drawn from the various great divisions of human knowledge including Literature, History, Science, Technology, Electricity and Radio, Medicine, Politics, Law, Physics, Chemistry and the Fine Arts.

1933

THE WORLD SYNDICATE PUBLISHING COMPANY
CLEVELAND, O. NEW YORK, N. Y.

Ex coll. Karolyne & Bryan A. Garner

A 1933 World imprint.

About 1940, Merriam decided to institute proceedings against World Syndicate and a few other publishers before the Federal Trade Commission (FTC), which Congress had created in 1914. The statute that gave birth to the agency prohibited unfair methods of competition and unfair acts or practices that affect commerce. It empowered the FTC to prosecute violators before administrative tribunals.[49] Merriam charged World Syndicate and other dictionary publishers of engaging in unfair competition and false advertising.[50] The next year, shortly before the attack on Pearl Harbor, the FTC filed a formal complaint against World Syndicate, two other publishers, and three individuals, beginning an investigation and adjudicative proceeding that would last through the end of the decade. The FTC complaint borrowed heavily from Merriam's original filing and its amicus curiae brief. The first three paragraphs dryly and laconically recited the facts that the respondents had been in the business of publishing and selling dictionaries throughout the United States, and that many of their competitors used *Webster* or *Webster's* in the titles of their publications. The respondents were accused of sometimes failing to include or make conspicuous the disclaimer, "This dictionary is not published by the original publishers of Webster's Dictionary or by their successors." The competitors also claimed, probably falsely, that experts had updated the contents.

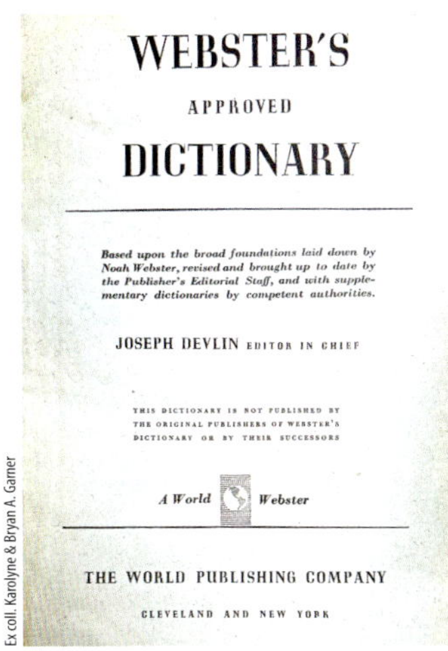
WEBSTER'S
APPROVED
DICTIONARY

Based upon the broad foundations laid down by Noah Webster, revised and brought up to date by the Publisher's Editorial Staff, and with supplementary dictionaries by competent authorities.

JOSEPH DEVLIN EDITOR IN CHIEF

THIS DICTIONARY IS NOT PUBLISHED BY THE ORIGINAL PUBLISHERS OF WEBSTER'S DICTIONARY OR BY THEIR SUCCESSORS

A World Webster

THE WORLD PUBLISHING COMPANY
CLEVELAND AND NEW YORK

Ex coll. Karolyne & Bryan A. Garner

A 1943 World imprint.

Merriam's allegations contained many factual and legal errors. It was asserted that Merriam (1) had acquired "all of the publisher's rights to the 1828 dictionary,"[51] when in fact it was the 1841 edition; (2) had been assigned the "right, title, and interest" in the "tradename

49 15 U.S.C. § 45.

50 *In re World Syndicate Publishing*, 46 F.T.C. 223, 224 (1942).

51 *Id.* at 226.

Ex coll. Karolyne & Bryan A. Garner

Webster's Collegiate Dictionary was first published by Merriam in 1898. Pictured here is a 1912 thin-paper deluxe edition.

Webster's Dictionary,"[52] when in fact it had never been registered as a tradename; and (3) had been the sole publisher "of a dictionary known as *Webster* or *Webster's* until 1904,"[53] overlooking all the litigation of the 1890s. These allegations were followed by claims that *Webster* and *Webster's* signaled completeness, comprehensiveness, and accuracy,[54] and that the public generally associated the name Noah Webster with excellence and with Merriam.

The FTC adjudicators found that the respondents had indeed engaged in unfair competition and misrepresented their products in specific ways. In its final order, the FTC ordered World Syndicate and the other respondents to stop claiming that their dictionaries published up to that time (1) were compiled or published by Noah Webster or his successors; (2) had been "edited or revised by a staff of eminent authorities in philology or lexicography" or by certain individuals when neither was true; and (3) contained newer or better content than dictionaries published by others when the dictionaries were wholly or substantially identical to older dictionaries and had only different titles, covers, bindings, jackets, or prefaces.[55]

But these were Pyrrhic victories. The FTC tribunal also pointed out the many erroneous claims in Merriam's complaint. The company had never acquired the publishing rights to Noah Webster's 1828 dictionary or an "exclusive right to publish Webster's Dictionaries," and it had not purchased "Webster's Dictionary" as a tradename.[56] An unnamed witness for World Syndicate Publishing who had personally been publishing dictionaries since 1887—someone who had almost certainly worked with George W. Ogilvie—testified that every dictionary his firm sold from 1889 to 1904 had the name *Webster's* in its title, without any agreement or arrangement with Merriam. The firm had sold more than 15 million copies. At least 11 other companies were found to be selling *Webster's* dictionaries before 1904. (Several of these companies likley belonged to George W. Ogilvie.) Since then, even more companies (many owned by Ogilvie) had published and sold dictionaries with that name. Although the FTC acknowledged

52 *Id.*

53 *Id.*

54 *Id.* at 227.

55 *Id.* at 243.

56 *Id.* at 223.

that Merriam's dictionaries were "most superior" in the opinions of erudite people, the evidence didn't establish that the general public understood or believed that any dictionary titled *Webster* or *Webster's Dictionary* must be a Merriam publication. Of the 40 members of the public who testified in the adjudicative proceeding, more than 30 didn't assume that Merriam published all *Webster* or *Webster's* dictionaries. The others were vague and indefinite in their understanding. Most of those witnesses didn't even connect the name *Webster* with Noah Webster and didn't know whether the lexicographer was Noah or Daniel. Professors and librarians testified that the general public didn't pay attention to publishers. The FTC concluded: "To the public, the word *Webster* simply means a dictionary."[57]

The year was 1947. Shortly after the conclusion of the FTC proceedings, the World Publishing Company issued a four-page pamphlet—an "interim statement . . . on the right to use the name of Noah Webster in the title of dictionaries." (World Publishing Company 1947.) In restrained prose, this little-known document, of which few copies must have been printed, quotes voluminously from the FTC trial examiner's opinion. It was nothing like the rodomontade that George Ogilvie, who had died 19 years before, might have produced, but it would have gladdened Ogilvie: it signaled a posthumous victory. "It is regarded as of interest," Ogilvie's successors staidly declared, "that once more the G. and C. Merriam Company's claims of exclusivity are rejected, and that the name of Noah Webster, lexicographer and founder of the American tradition in dictionary making, has once more been held to belong to the American people and not to a private corporation." (*Id.* at 4.)

Ex coll. Karolyne & Bryan A. Garner

The books litigated in the 1990s.

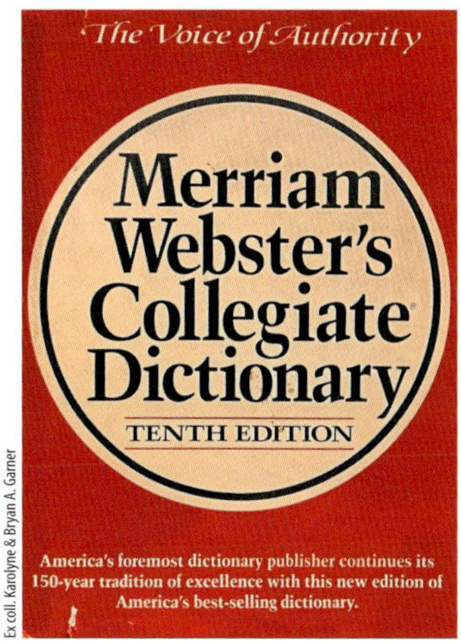

Ex coll. Karolyne & Bryan A. Garner

Merriam didn't file another lawsuit about the term *Webster's* until the 1990s. This last stand was against Random House.

In 1982, Merriam had changed its name to Merriam-Webster, doubtless trying to help the public differentiate between itself and other dictionary publishers. But competition was still raging, and in 1991 Random House made a move on Merriam-Webster's lucrative college-dictionary line. Random House had apparently concluded, like others before it, that any English-language dictionary not called *Webster's* was at a disadvantage in the American market. So Random House retitled its collegiate-size dictionary as *The Random House*

57 *Id.*

Ex coll. Karolyne & Bryan A. Garner

"Sorry: Which one did you ask for?"

"Merriam has pursued aggressively copycats and alleged infringers. . . . At issue in a lawsuit against a California software company, settled by a consent judgment in July 1984, was the 'bull's eye' that encircles the dictionary name on Merriam-Webster covers. Defendant Cornucopia Software had sold a spell-check software program in packaging sporting a bull's eye that encircled the words 'Electric Webster.' Cornucopia agreed to pay $10,000 and to stop using the design." (DeBenedictis 1984:25.)

Ex coll. Karolyne & Bryan A. Garner

A 1988 Houghton Mifflin dictionary that had nothing to do with Merriam-Webster.

Webster's College Dictionary. Among its entries was one for *Webster's* as "a dictionary of the English language." Merriam-Webster sued for infringement of both trademark and trade dress, on grounds that Random House's combined use of *Webster's* and *College*, coupled with the red cover, created a likelihood of confusion.[58]

The dictionaries certainly looked similar. Merriam-Webster's collegiate dictionary had a red dustjacket, with the title in large letters across the front. Random House's dictionary had an almost identical crimson—maybe a shade different—with the Random House logo perched atop the large *Webster's* to command the eye's attention. But despite its similarity, "Random House" appeared four times on the jacket.

Random House was not the only publisher using *Webster's* in similar-looking dictionary titles. Houghton Mifflin had introduced a *Webster's University Dictionary* in 1984. Simon & Schuster had introduced *Webster's New World Dictionary* in 1988. Both dictionaries were marketed with red dustjackets and titles with white lettering.

Before the monthlong trial, the federal district court denied Merriam-Webster's request for an injunction, stating that consumers were unlikely to be confused after looking at the book's cover because Random House's name was printed unmistakably there.[59] The court reasoned that *Webster's* is a descriptive term for dictionaries but also stated that *Webster's* had no secondary (distinctive) meaning.[60]

The jury awarded Merriam-Webster more than $2 million in lost profits and punitive damages.[61] The jury also found *Webster's Collegiate* to be a valid trademark—even though Merriam-Webster had never registered the phrase. It found that Random House had intentionally adopted Merriam-Webster's trade dress and had diluted the distinctiveness of Merriam-Webster's trademark *Webster's Collegiate* in violation of New York law.[62] Even so, the jury found that the word *Webster's*, as applied to dictionaries, was generic.

58 *Merriam-Webster, Inc. v. Random House, Inc.*, 35 F.3d 65, 68 (2d Cir. 1994).

59 *Merriam-Webster, Inc. v. Random House, Inc.*, 1991 WL 50951, at *6 (S.D.N.Y. 4 Apr. 1991).

60 *Id.* at *3.

61 *Merriam-Webster, Inc.*, 35 F.3d at 68–69.

62 *Random House, Inc.*, 815 F. Supp. 691, 695 (S.D.N.Y. 1993).

After posttrial motions, the trial court doubled the damages to $4 million. (Isn't litigation fun?) It was a major victory for Merriam-Webster. Three years later, on appeal, the Second Circuit Court of Appeals reversed, nullifying all the damages. (Again, isn't litigation fun?) The appellate court held that under New York law, Random House hadn't diluted Merriam's trademarks or trade dress on two grounds: (1) there wasn't a likelihood of confusion between dustjackets, and (2) *Webster's* was utterly generic.[63]

With the reversal on appeal, the parties were left essentially in the same positions they had occupied before this litigation began—if you disregard their huge legal fees and the years of frazzled nerves while the business folks awaited each of the dozens of rulings that inched toward the ultimate resolution.

Merriam-Webster hasn't sued anyone over the use of *Webster's* since the 1990s.

If *Webster's* is worthless as a trademark or signal of distinctiveness, why do publishers still attach *Webster's* to so many American dictionaries? The answer is that although it may be worthless in law, it isn't worthless in business. For generations, Merriam and its successors promoted *Webster's* so successfully that people came to trust the name as authoritative. As George W. Ogilvie well understood, Americans have been conditioned to believe—no matter how illogically—that the name itself signals high-quality content.

Few names have achieved fame comparable to *Webster's*. But fame comes at a price: in this case, the price of what intellectual-property lawyers call "genericide"—the loss of a trademark that becomes a mere household name as opposed to a brand name.[64] Today Merriam-Webster boasts what it reasonably can: "Other publishers may use the name Webster, but only Merriam-Webster products are backed by over 150 years of accumulated knowledge and experience."[65] True enough.

Today, the copyrighted material of Merriam-Webster's competitors has migrated into various channels. Random House's content has been integrated into Dictionary.com (no. 129). The *Webster's New*

Ex coll. Karolyne & Bryan A. Garner

A 1953 book by Eric Partridge, in which the lexicographer argues that "the 'shaggy dog' story does indeed represent the acme of the storyteller's art, for it demands a wittily unexpected and sudden ending, all the more unexpected in that the 'lead-in' and the 'lead-up' have to be deceptively leisurely and almost diffuse. . . . However absurd it may be, a 'shaggy dog' must never be silly." (Partridge 1953:52.)

63 *Merriam-Webster, Inc.*, 35 F.3d at 67, 72.

64 *See Black's Law Dictionary* 838 (Bryan A. Garner ed., 11th ed. 2019).

65 Merriam-Webster, About Us, FAQ (2022) https://www.merriam-webster.com/about-us/faq.

World line, deriving from George W. Ogilvie, became a distinguished desk reference under the transformative editorship of David B. Guralnik in the 1950s and 1960s. World Publishing (Ogilvie's successor in interest) was acquired by Times Mirror in 1963, then by William Collins Sons in 1974, then by Simon & Schuster in 1980, then by John Wiley & Sons in the 1990s, then by Houghton Mifflin before 2014, and then by Collins Reference before 2020. Since the 1970s, *Webster's New World*—a fine piece of work under any imprint—has become the official dictionary of American journalistic outlets, including the Associated Press, *The New York Times*, *The Wall Street Journal*, and United Press International. Its front matter contains no disclaimers about not being affiliated with Merriam-Webster: there's no legal requirement, after all.

Ex coll. Karolyne & Bryan A. Garner

The back of Partridge's 1953 dustjacket.

And so this shaggy-dog story comes to an end. But *shaggy-dog* in which sense?

> ***Merriam-Webster's Collegiate Dictionary*** (11th ed. 2011): **shaggy-dog** . . . *adj* (1946): of, relating to, or being a long-drawn-out circumstantial story concerning an inconsequential happening that impresses the teller as humorous or interesting but the hearer as boring and pointless.
>
> ***Webster's New World College Dictionary*** (5th ed. 2014): **shaggy dog (story)** [as if from such an anecdote involving a *shaggy dog*] a long, rambling joke or anecdote involving strange or absurd incidents and regarded as ultimately pointless.
>
> ***Dictionary.com*** (accessed 10 July 2023): **shaggy-dog story** a funny story, traditionally about a talking dog, that, after an often long and involved narration of unimportant incidents, has an absurd or irrelevant punch line.

The only definitional points from which we dissent are Merriam-Webster's use of the words *boring* and *inconsequential* and its omission of any reference to a punchline. This story certainly wasn't boring or inconsequential to Merriam-Webster as it was unfolding! So maybe Merriam-Webster would argue that, by definition, this hasn't been a shaggy-dog story at all. But it certainly qualifies as long, it involves strange and even absurd incidents, and the narrative is highly involved. Oh, and let us add this final line: over a long period of pugilistic publishing, George W. Ogilvie landed plenty of below-the-belt punches.

X. Offbeat English

"Slang" isn't quite broad enough to cover all the varieties of nonstandard, nonliterary, or informal English: a 20th-century lexicographer made it "slang and unconventional English," which seems suitably expansive for the racy and raucous language of those who care little about primness and propriety.

Some of the works in this section are practical dictionaries, while others are pranks or manifestos in alphabetical order. Slang, dialect, argot, taboo words, and various other types of convention-flouting language—as everyone knows—can be fun. The anonymous B.E. knew this in the 17th century, and interest since his time has only intensified. But the language of marginalized groups can also give us disconcerting glimpses of worlds that we rarely see into, and the compilers of these collections are often driven by a determination to change the world. This chapter details some of the highlights in the story of nonstandard-English lexicography.

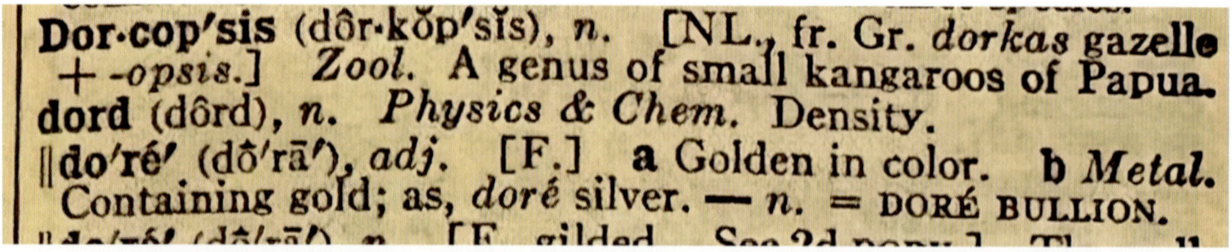

Dor·cop′sis (dôr·kŏp′sĭs), *n.* [NL., fr. Gr. *dorkas* gazelle + *-opsis.*] *Zool.* A genus of small kangaroos of Papua.
dord (dôrd), *n.* *Physics & Chem.* Density.
‖**do′ré′** (dō′rā′), *adj.* [F.] **a** Golden in color. **b** *Metal.* Containing gold; as, *doré* silver. — *n.* = DORÉ BULLION.

Ex coll. Karolyne & Bryan A. Garner

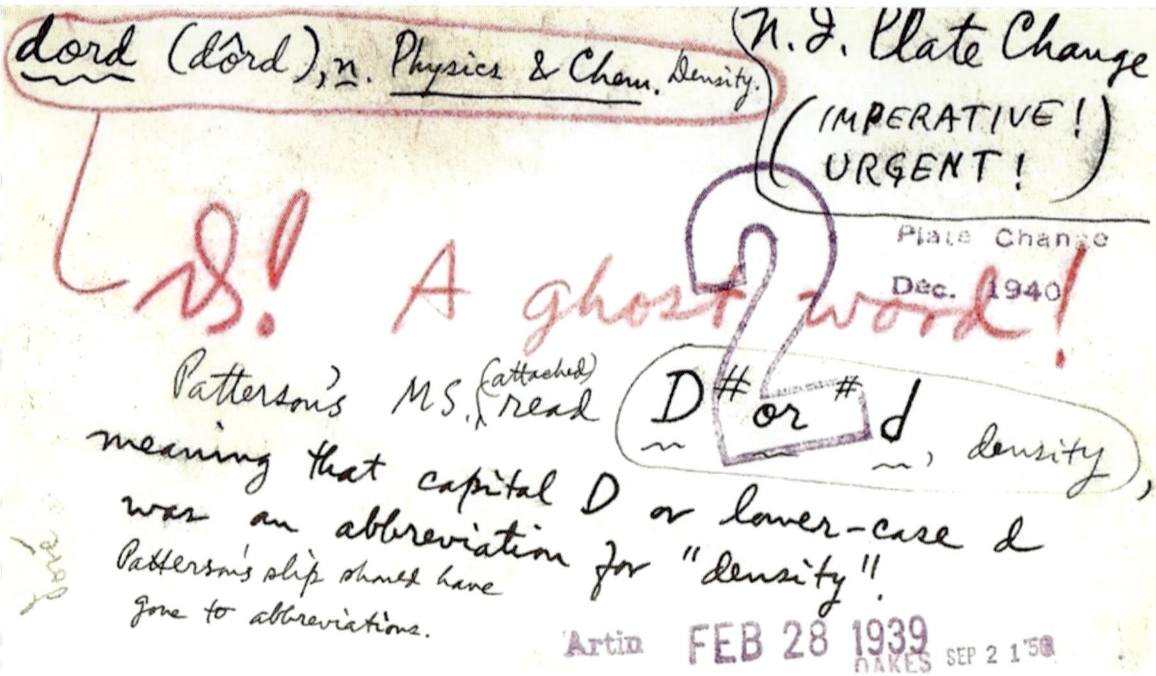

dord (dôrd), n. Physics & Chem. Density.
N. J. Plate Change
(IMPERATIVE! URGENT!)
Plate Change
Dec. 1940
2
D! A ghost word!
Patterson's MS. (attached) read (D or d, density), meaning that capital D or lower-case d was an abbreviation for "density"!
Patterson's slip should have gone to abbreviations.
Artin FEB 28 1939
OAKES SEP 2 1'58

Courtesy of Merriam-Webster, Inc.

An especially peculiar type of "offbeat English": in 1934, the *Webster's Second* editors noted that "density" might be abbreviated with an upper- or lowercase *d*—that is, "*D* or *d*"—and in the process inadvertently created the ghost-word *dord*. Two editors, one wielding a black pen and the other a red pencil, were aghast. The printing plates weren't corrected until late 1940. For more on ghost-words, see p. 273.

109

B.E.

The Bigotries of Lowlifes

E., B. *A New Dictionary of the Terms Ancient and Modern of the Canting Crew, In its Several Tribes, of Gypsies, Beggers, Thieves, Cheats, &c.* London: Printed for W. Hawes et al., [ca. 1699].

ALL WE KNOW ABOUT THE AUTHOR is what he tells us on his title page—"*B.E.* Gent."—and we can't even take for granted that the initials are real. Nobody has offered a convincing argument about B.E.'s identity. Nor do we know when the book was published, though scholarly detective work has convincingly narrowed it to around 1698–1699.

The title identifies the dictionary's subject as "cant," a word not much used today. Lexicologist Julie Coleman offers a useful definition: "Cant is the secret language of marginalized groups: beggars, prostitutes, drug-takers, and criminals of all kinds." (Coleman 2009a:212–22.) It shares features with jargon (the technical language of a profession) and with slang (an informal language, often of marginalized groups). Because it is not always possible to differentiate between them, cant and slang dictionaries are often treated together in histories of dictionaries.

This was not wholly new territory when B.E. got to it. Thomas Harman included a brief cant glossary in *A Caveat for Commen Cursetors Vulgarely Called Vagabones* (1567), a pioneering work of "rogue literature," and about a century later, Richard Head (1637?–1686?) offered a larger examination of cant in *The English Rogue Described, in the Life of Meriton Latroon, a Witty Extravagant* (1666). But nobody had done it at book length, and most historians now consider B.E.'s work the "first autonomous dictionary of non-standard English." (*Id.* at 317.)

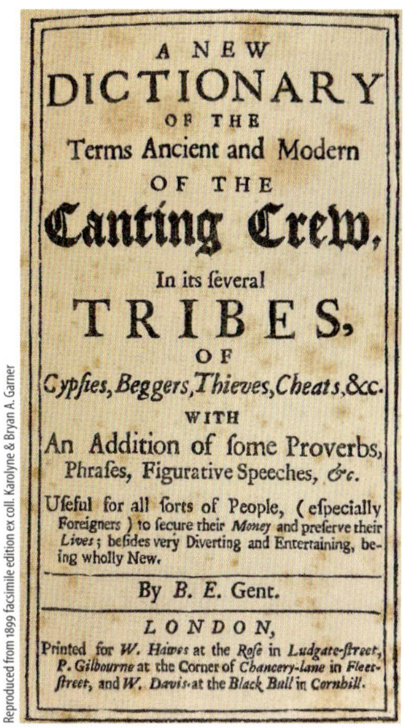
A NEW
DICTIONARY
OF THE
Terms Ancient and Modern
OF THE
Canting Crew,
In its ſeveral
TRIBES,
OF
Gypſies, Beggers, Thieves, Cheats, &c.
WITH
An Addition of ſome Proverbs, Phraſes, Figurative Speeches, *&c.*
Uſeful for all ſorts of People, (eſpecially Foreigners) to ſecure their *Money* and preſerve their *Lives*; beſides very Diverting and Entertaining, being wholly New.
By *B. E.* Gent.
LONDON,
Printed for *W. Hawes* at the *Roſe* in *Ludgate-ſtreet*, *P. Gilbourne* at the Corner of *Chancery-lane* in *Fleet-ſtreet*, and *W. Davis* at the *Black Bull* in *Cornhill*.

"From B.E. forward, slang lexicography assumes that readers want etymologies, analysis of polysemy, labeling, etc., and that any adequate explanation of English vocabulary—cant and slang included—depends on such explanatory features." (Adams 2020a:77.)

B.E. covers about 3,200 words and phrases in 176 pages of definitions. This is a typical run:

> *Minks*, a proud Flirt.
>
> *Mint*, c. Gold; also a late Sanctuary (in *Southewark*) for such as broke either out of Necessity, or in Design to bring their Creditors the more easily to a Composition. Hence *Minters*, the Inhabitants.
>
> *Miquelets*, Mountaneers, (in Spain) or Spanish Rapparies.
>
> *Miscreant*, a lewd, wicked Fellow.
>
> *Mish*, c. a Shirt or Smock.
>
> *Mish-topper*, c. a Coat or Petticoat.

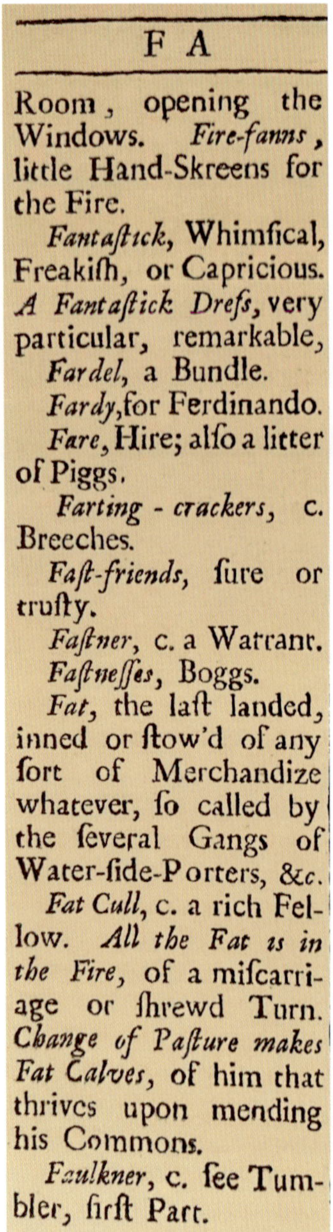

F A

Room, opening the Windows. *Fire-fanns*, little Hand-Skreens for the Fire.

Fantaſtick, Whimſical, Freakiſh, or Capricious. *A Fantaſtick Dreſs*, very particular, remarkable,

Fardel, a Bundle.

Fardy, for Ferdinando.

Fare, Hire; alſo a litter of Piggs.

Farting - crackers, c. Breeches.

Faſt-friends, ſure or truſty.

Faſtner, c. a Warrant.

Faſtneſſes, Boggs.

Fat, the laſt landed, inned or ſtow'd of any ſort of Merchandize whatever, ſo called by the ſeveral Gangs of Water-ſide-Porters, &c.

Fat Cull, c. a rich Fellow. *All the Fat is in the Fire*, of a miſcarriage or ſhrewd Turn. *Change of Paſture makes Fat Calves*, of him that thrives upon mending his Commons.

Faulkner, c. ſee Tumbler, firſt Part.

The book has no notes on pronunciation and only a handful of etymologies. In the absence of useful front matter, we are left to guess that the "c." after some headwords stands for "cant." Definitions are terse, often mere synonyms, and are sometimes unhelpfully circular: *ding-dong*, for instance, is defined as "Helter-skelter"; *helter-skelter* is defined as "Pell-mell"; and *pel-mel* is defined as "helter-skelter."

A few areas of the lexicon are well represented here, as in most other slang dictionaries: terms related to crime (*bravo* "a Mercenary Murderer, that will Kill any Body," *bung-nipper* "a Cutpurse, or Pick-pocket"), drink (*mawdlin* "weepingly Drunk," *we bows'd it about* "we Drank damn'd hard"), and sex (*baggage* "a Whore or Slut," *school of Venus* "a Bawdy-house"). But we also get sweet glimpses into 17th-century domestic life: "*Nug*, a Word of Love, as, *my Dear Nug*, my Dear Love." At their best, these cant terms achieve a kind of poetry of the streets: a foolish man can be a *booberkin*, a *dulpickle*, or a *jobbernoll*; *rustygutts* is a delightful term for "an old blunt Fellow"; a whim is *tringum-trangum*; and what's not to love about *fizzle* "a little or low-sounding Fart"?

But there's also a lot of ugliness—misogyny and racism above all. Maybe it's lighthearted ribbing to call Wales *Itch-land*, Scotland *Louse-land*, and Ireland *Teague-land*, but the Dutch probably objected to being called *Frog-landers*. Worse still, *Jew* is "any over-reaching Dealer, or hard, sharp Fellow" and *Turk* "any cruel hard-hearted man." Worst of all is the treatment of "gypsies"—sometimes, it seems, used for the Romani people, but often for any vagabonds—who are mentioned on the title page as one of the main sources of cant. Here is B.E.'s venomous definition:

> *Gypsies*, a Counterfeit Brood of wandering Rogues and Wenches, herding together, and Living promiscuously, or in common, under Hedges and in Barns, Disguising themselves with Blacking their Faces and Bodies, and wearing an Antick Dress, as well as Devising a particular *Cant*, Strolling up and down, and under colour of Fortune-telling, Palmestry Physiognomy, and the Cure of Diseases; impose allwaies upon the unthinking Vulgar, and often Steal from them, whatever is not too Hot for their Fingers, or too Heavy to carry off.

The preface is even worse, comparing the migration of the Romani to the spread of syphilis throughout Europe.

The audience for books like this is presumably those who are not gypsies, beggars, thieves, and cheats, but reasonably well-off, respectable members of society who are curious about a form of speech generally inaccessible to them. Publishers of slang and cant dictionaries promote their wares with sensationalism, as when B.E. or his publisher described the book as "Useful for all sorts of People, (especially Foreigners) to secure their *Money* and preserve their *Lives*." Pay up, it says, because understanding what these lowlifes are saying could literally save you from a violent death.

B.E.'s work had a long afterlife. It was revised, repackaged, and plagiarized throughout the 18th century. It was appropriated both in *Bacchus and Venus; or, A Select Collection of 200 of the Most Witty and Diverting Songs and Catches in Love and Gallantry* (1737) and in *The Scoundrel's Dictionary; or, An Explanation of the Cant Words Used by Thieves, House-Breakers, Street-Robbers and Pick-Pockets about Town* (1754). Since few collectors thought them worth preserving, many publications like these have disappeared without a trace. But B.E.'s book did influence one of the most influential slang dictionaries, Francis Grose's 1785 *Classical Dictionary of the Vulgar Tongue* (no. 110). Perhaps more important, its entries made their way into standard dictionaries too: starting with Nathan Bailey in 1721, mainstream lexicographers began incorporating slang and cant into their wordlists (Starnes & Noyes 1946:221), and Johnson carried on the tradition. Today the *OED* quotes B.E.'s definitions more than 1,200 times, including 120 entries for which the *New Dictionary of . . . the Canting Crew* is the earliest known citation.

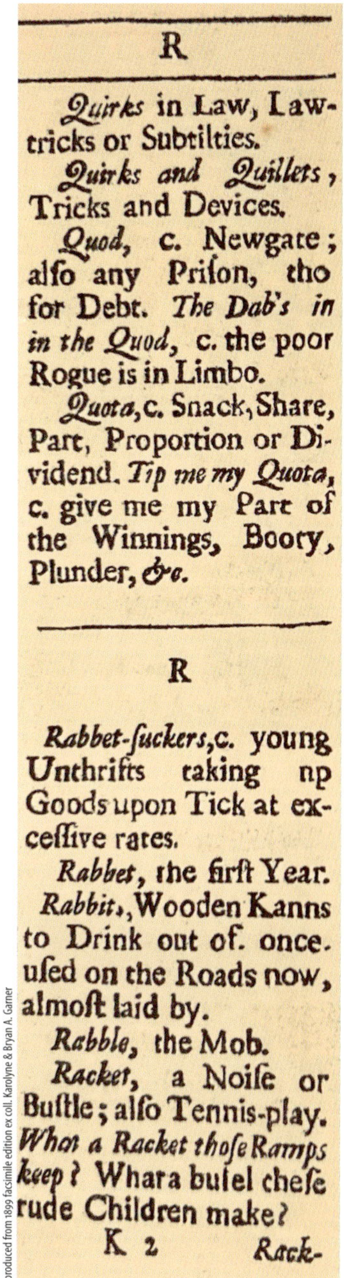

R

Quirks in Law, Law-tricks or Subtilties.

Quirks and Quillets, Tricks and Devices.

Quod, c. Newgate; alſo any Priſon, tho for Debt. *The Dab's in in the Quod*, c. the poor Rogue is in Limbo.

Quota, c. Snack, Share, Part, Proportion or Dividend. *Tip me my Quota*, c. give me my Part of the Winnings, Booty, Plunder, &c.

R

Rabbet-ſuckers, c. young Unthrifts taking np Goods upon Tick at exceſſive rates.

Rabbet, the firſt Year.

Rabbit, Wooden Kanns to Drink out of. once. uſed on the Roads now, almoſt laid by.

Rabble, the Mob.

Racket, a Noiſe or Buſtle; alſo Tennis-play. *What a Racket thoſe Ramps keep? Whata buſel theſe rude Children make?*

K 2 *Rack-*

Reproduced from 1899 facsimile edition ex coll. Karolyne & Bryan A. Garner

110

Francis Grose

The Antiquarian Falstaff

[Grose, Francis]. *A Classical Dictionary of the Vulgar Tongue*. London: S. Hooper, 1785.

Ex coll. Karolyne & Bryan A. Garner

"The freedom of thought and speech, arising from, and privileged by our constitution, gives a force and poignancy to the expressions of our common people, not to be found under arbitrary governments, where the ebullitions of vulgar wit are checked by the fear of the bastinado, or of a lodging during pleasure in some goal or castle." (Preface, p. i.)

By the late 18th century Britain was well served by general-purpose dictionaries: Johnson's above all, but Bailey, Ash, Walker, Perry, and others continued to be read. And yet, as Francis Grose put it, the curious reader "might hunt through all the ordinary Dictionaries, from Alpha to Omega, in search of the words, 'black legs, lame duck, a plumb, malingeror, nip cheese, darbies, and the new drop,' although these are all terms of well-known import, at New-market, Exchange-alley, the City, the Parade, Wapping, and Newgate." (P. ii.) What to do?

Enter Francis Grose (bap. 1731–1791), one of the more colorful characters in the annals of lexicography—larger than life in more ways than one. The child of a Swiss jeweler, a militia captain first in Hampshire, then in Surrey, and a Fellow of the Society of Antiquaries, he was described in the *DNB* as "a sort of antiquarian Falstaff," and his friend Robert Burns called him "a fine, fat, fodgel wight [fat creature] / O' stature short, but genius bright." He was widely known for his humor and love of food and drink. He was sometimes ridiculed for it, but was always happy to join in the good-humored laughing.

His *Classical Dictionary* is slightly smaller than B.E.'s *New Dictionary of the Canting Crew* (1699), with 3,893 entries. (Coleman 2004b:19.) But while B.E.'s interest was "cant," with only incidental treatment of other nonstandard terms, Grose's purview was wider, taking in the "vulgar"—that is, common—speech in all its variety. He looked in the usual places—English authors, including Shakespeare and Swift—but he supplemented it with actual fieldwork, making "nocturnal sallies" into London neighborhoods to collect the living language.

Virtually all dictionaries are the product of some degree of plagiarism, but theft is especially prominent in slang lexicography. More than 1,900 of Grose's entries are borrowings from B.E., most of them unacknowledged. But B.E.'s ghost had no grounds to complain, since many of *his* entries had been stolen from Richard Head's *Canting Vocabulary* (1673). And Grose was better than most in this respect: as Julie Coleman puts it, "Unlike many of his predecessors in canting lexicography, Grose gives credit to his sources. Instead of claiming originality, he parades his scholarly credentials." (Coleman 2004b:18.) He includes a smattering of etymologies, usage labels, and illustrative quotations—things rarely seen in explorations of slang and cant.

"Captain Grose," as he billed himself, went on to write *A Provincial Glossary, with a Collection of Local Proverbs, and Popular Superstitions* (1787), and both these explorations of nonstandard English went through multiple editions well into the 19th century. He died of an "apoplectic fit" in Dublin in 1791, while collecting materials for a book on Irish antiquities.

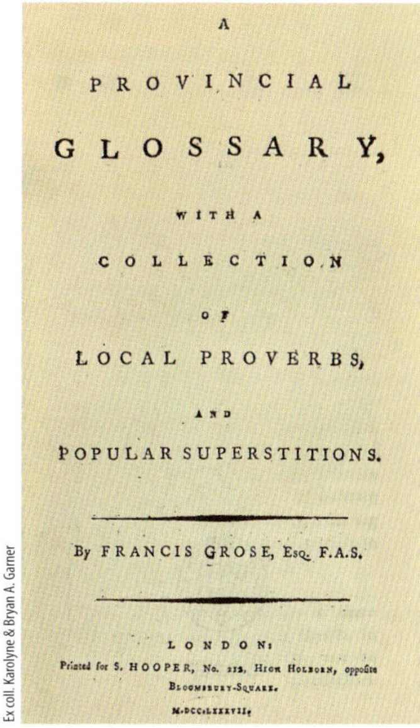
A
PROVINCIAL
GLOSSARY,
WITH A
COLLECTION
OF
LOCAL PROVERBS,
AND
POPULAR SUPERSTITIONS.

By FRANCIS GROSE, Esq. F.A.S.

LONDON:
Printed for S. HOOPER, No. 212, High Holborn, opposite Bloomsbury-Square.
M.DCC.LXXXVII.

Ex coll. Karolyne & Bryan A. Garner

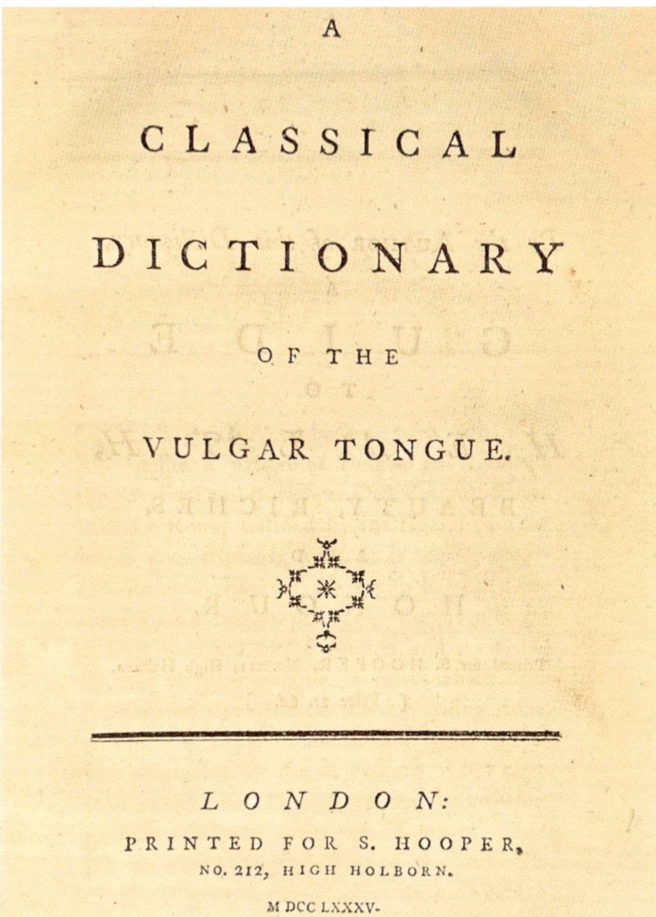
A
CLASSICAL
DICTIONARY
OF THE
VULGAR TONGUE.

LONDON:
PRINTED FOR S. HOOPER,
NO. 212, HIGH HOLBORN.
M DCC LXXXV.

Ex coll. Karolyne & Bryan A. Garner

Ex coll. Karolyne & Bryan A. Garner

111

Charles Pigott

Lexicographic Cynic

Pigott, Charles. *A Political Dictionary: Explaining the True Meaning of Words. Illustrated and Exemplified in the Lives, Morals, Character and Conduct of the Following Most Illustrious Personages, Among Many Others. The King, Queen, Prince of Wales, Duke of York, Pope Pius VI. Emperor, King of Prussia . . . .* New York: Printed for Thomas Greenleaf, 1795.

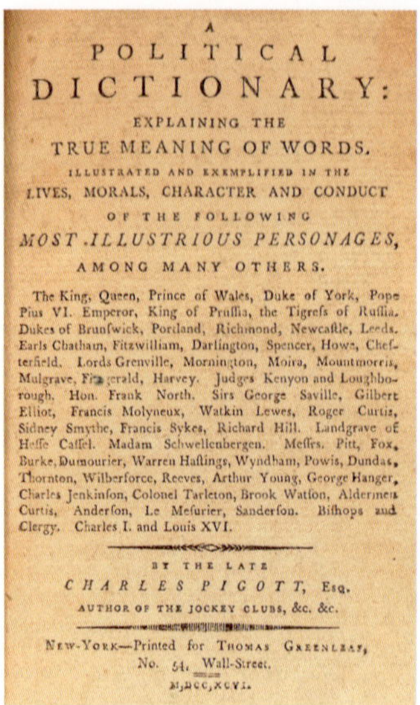

A
POLITICAL
DICTIONARY:
EXPLAINING THE
TRUE MEANING OF WORDS.
ILLUSTRATED AND EXEMPLIFIED IN THE
LIVES, MORALS, CHARACTER AND CONDUCT
OF THE FOLLOWING
MOST ILLUSTRIOUS PERSONAGES,
AMONG MANY OTHERS.

The King, Queen, Prince of Wales, Duke of York, Pope Pius VI. Emperor, King of Pruſſia, the Tigreſs of Ruſſia. Dukes of Brunſwick, Portland, Richmond, Newcaſtle, Leeds. Earls Chatham, Fitzwilliam, Darlington, Spencer, Howe, Cheſterfield. Lords Grenville, Mornington, Moira, Mountmorris, Mulgrave, Fitzgerald, Harvey. Judges Kenyon and Loughborough. Hon. Frank North. Sirs George Saville, Gilbert Elliot, Francis Molyneux, Watkin Lewes, Roger Curtis, Sidney Smythe, Francis Sykes, Richard Hill. Landgrave of Heſſe Caſſel. Madam Schwellenbergen. Meſſrs. Pitt, Fox, Burke, Dumourier, Warren Haſtings, Wyndham, Powis, Dundas, Thornton, Wilberforce, Reeves, Arthur Young, George Hanger, Charles Jenkinſon, Colonel Tarleton, Brook Watſon, Aldermen Curtis, Anderſon, Le Meſurier, Sanderſon. Biſhops and Clergy. Charles I. and Louis XVI.

BY THE LATE
CHARLES PIGOTT, Esq.
AUTHOR OF THE JOCKEY CLUBS, &c. &c.

NEW-YORK—Printed for THOMAS GREENLEAF,
No. 54, Wall-Street.
M,DCC,XCVI.

Ex coll. Karolyne & Bryan A. Garner

"Mankind will continue to be tyrannized over, and to be miserable, till they . . . get rid at once of all those barbarous prejudices and preposterous customs, that have so long poisoned their existence." (P. 66.)

For such a prolific author—with books on the British Constitution, games, manners, politics, the rights of kings, the rights of nobles, the rights of priests, and war, among other topics—Charles Pigott (d. 1794) is remarkably obscure and elusive. We know that he was American, and we can deduce that he had a wickedly sardonic sense of humor. That is clear from his definitions, which are notable precursors to the wit of Ambrose Bierce:

- "*Cruelty.* Lord Hood commanding a man of war filled with helpless prisoners to be sunk; the horrors perpetrated on men and women in La Vendee by rebels fighting against the liberties of their native country; criminal laws that inflict capital punishment for trivial offences; the Slave Trade." (P. 12.)
- "*Faith.* Credulity, superstition. An article loudly extolled and vehemently insisted on, in all ages, by priests and kings. Success has crowned their exertions. Mankind, on every occasion, have *opened a gullet* wide enough to swallow the absurdist paradoxes, the most glaring impossibilities." (Pp. 28–29.)
- "*Grateful.* Obsolete. It is at present used for *great fool.*" (P. 60.)
- "*Malcontents.* The greater part of this nation; consisting of the laborious poor, from whom the earnings of impoverished industry are squeezed and torn, for the support of our happy Constitution, the pride of the world! the envy of surrounding nations! &c. &c." (P. 86.)

- "*Qualification*. Implies frequently, the quantum of money necessary for a representative in Parliament to possess, before he shall be supposed to have sufficient knowledge to give his aye or no upon the weighty affairs of the nation." (P. 125.)
- "*Religion*. A superstition invented by the archbishop of hell, and propagated by his faithful diocesans the clergy, to keep the people in ignorance and darkness, that they may not see the work of iniquity that is going on." (P. 132.)
- "*Robbers*. East and West India plunderers, Prime Ministers, Judges, and Bishops." (P. 137.)
- "*Trinity*. The incomprehensible union of three persons into one Godhead. Whosoever will not believe this will be damned. *Therefore*, whosoever does not believe what is incomprehensible will be damned. Q.E.D." (P. 179.)
- "*Tyrant*. For examples look into history, no matter of what country!" (P. 181.)
- "*University*. A place where ignorance is *taught*. This is absolutely the case at Oxford and Cambridge, where you may see monks, sensual, beastly, hoggish monks, wrapped up in all the ignorance, as well as the superstitious garb, of the 9th century!" (P. 184.)
- "*War*. Of all things in this world, it seems to me most strange, that men, large parties of men, perfectly indifferent to, and ignorant of the merits of the dispute, should voluntarily enter into the service of a sanguinary tyrant, and, as far as in them lay, to massacre and destroy their fellow-creatures who are opposed to them, and who are as innocent and as ignorant as they, of the whole subject and occasion of the quarrel." (P. 190.)

"If half that wide lapse of time, which at once consumes itself and the health of the body in excesses were spent in the improvement of the mind, what a wonderful change, what a revolution would be produced: kings would not then tyrannize over their subjects, and be idolized for it; nor would priests plunge the bulk of mankind in darkness and ignorance, and be revered for it!" (P. 198.)

Ex coll. Karolyne & Bryan A. Garner

Not all his entries were so playful. Pigott was a passionate republican, supporting both the American cause and the French Revolution. His entry for *monarch* begins, "A word which in a few years is likely to be obsolete. It signifies a man, who is begotten by another man, to rule over millions of his fellow-creatures; to trample upon their necks, and to build his own aggrandisement on the misery and degradation of his subjects." The entry for *fame* is motivated by the same zeal for change: "Tremble, ye cruel Potentates, who plunge your subjects in misery and tears, who desolate nations, and convert the fruitful earth into a sterile burying ground. Tremble for your impending fate! It requires not the spirit of prophecy to foretel your d–f–l is at hand."

Yet Pigott didn't live long enough to find out whether his vision came true: he died in 1794, leaving others to publish his *Political Dictionary* posthumously.

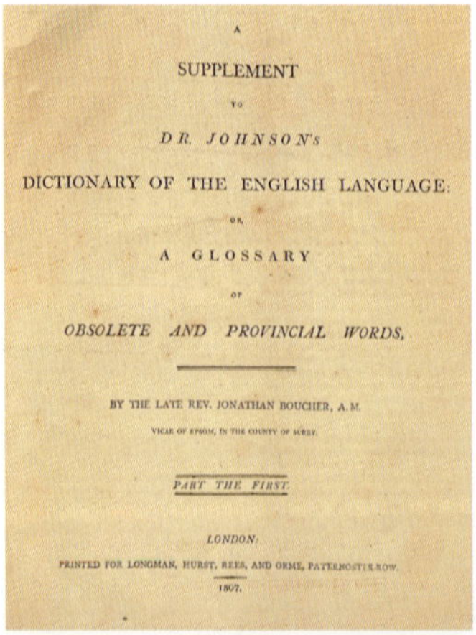
A
SUPPLEMENT
TO
DR. JOHNSON'S
DICTIONARY OF THE ENGLISH LANGUAGE:
OR,
A GLOSSARY
OF
OBSOLETE AND PROVINCIAL WORDS.
BY THE LATE REV. JONATHAN BOUCHER, A.M.
VICAR OF EPSOM, IN THE COUNTY OF SURREY.
PART THE FIRST.
LONDON:
PRINTED FOR LONGMAN, HURST, REES, AND ORME, PATERNOSTER-ROW.
1807.

Ex coll. Karolyne & Bryan A. Garner

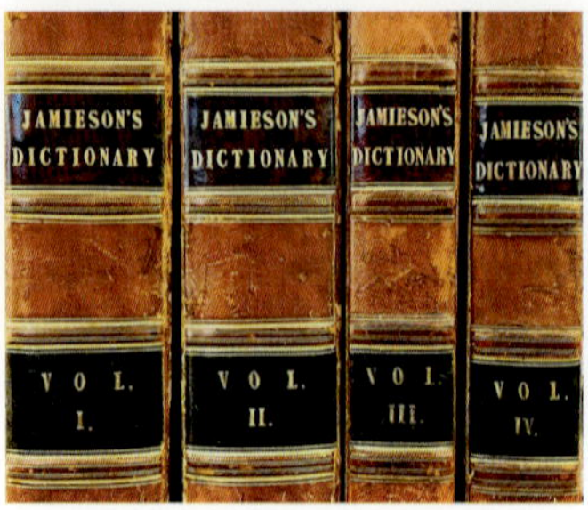

Ex coll. Karolyne & Bryan A. Garner

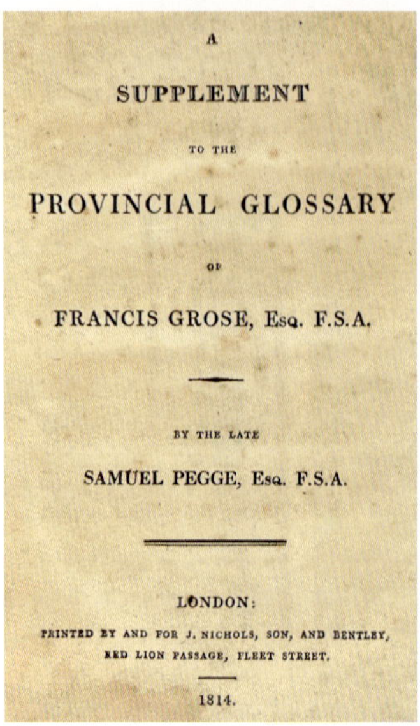
A
SUPPLEMENT
TO THE
PROVINCIAL GLOSSARY
OF
FRANCIS GROSE, Esq. F.S.A.
BY THE LATE
SAMUEL PEGGE, Esq. F.S.A.
LONDON:
PRINTED BY AND FOR J. NICHOLS, SON, AND BENTLEY,
RED LION PASSAGE, FLEET STREET.
1814.

Ex coll. Karolyne & Bryan A. Garner

112

19th-Century Provincial British Wordbooks

Boucher, Jonathan. ***A Supplement to Dr. Johnson's Dictionary of the English Language: or, A Glossary of Obsolete and Provincial Words.*** **1st ed. London: Longman, Hurst, Rees & Orme, 1807.**

Jamieson, John. ***An Etymological Dictionary of the Scottish Language.*** **2 vols. Edinburgh: W. Creech, 1808. Plus two-vol. supplement, 1825.**

Pegge, Samuel. ***A Supplement to the Provincial Glossary of Francis Grose.*** **London: J. Nichols, 1814.**

Kennet, White. ***A Glossary to Explain the Original, the Acceptation, and Obsoleteness of Words and Phrases [in Oxfordshire].*** **London: R. & A. Taylor, 1816.**

[Picken, Ebenezer]. ***A Dictionary of the Scottish Language.*** **Edinburgh: J. Sawers, 1818.**

Wilbraham, Roger. ***An Attempt at a Glossary of Some Words Used in Cheshire.*** **London: W. Bulmer & W. Nicol, 1820.**

Moor, Edward. ***Suffolk Words and Phrases.*** **Woodbridge: J. Loder, 1823.**

Hunter, Joseph. ***The Hallamshire Glossary.*** **London: W. Pickering, 1829.**

Cooper, William Durrant. ***A Glossary of Provincialisms in Use in the County of Sussex.*** **Brighton: W. Fleet, 1836.**

Holloway, William. ***A General Dictionary of Provincialisms, written with a view to rescue from oblivion the fast fading relics of by-gone days.*** **Lewes: Sussex Press & Baxter and Son, 1839.**

[Lewis, G.C.]. *A Glossary of Provincial Words Used in Herefordshire and Some of the Adjoining Counties*. London: J. Murray, 1839.

Akerman, John Y. *A Glossary of Provincial Words and Phrases Used in Wiltshire*. London: J.R. Smith, 1842.

Brown, Thomas. *A Dictionary of the Scottish Language*. London: Simpkin & Marshall, 1845.

Halliwell, James Orchard. *A Dictionary of Archaic and Provincial Words: Obsolete Phrases, Proverbs, and Ancient Customs, from the 14th Century*. London: J.R. Smith, 1847.

Evans, Arthur B. *Leicestershire Words, Phrases and Proverbs*. London: W. Pickering, 1848.

[Dinsdale, F.T.]. *A Glossary of Provincial Words Used in Teesdale in the County of Durham*. London: J.R. Smith, 1849.

Anon. *A Glossary of Provincial Words Used in the County of Cumberland*. London: J.G. Bell, 1851.

Anon. *A Glossary of Provincial Words Used in the County of Dorset*. London: J.G. Bell, 1851.

Anon. *A Glossary of Provincial Words Used in the County of Gloucestershire*. London: J.G. Bell, 1851.

Baker, Anne Elizabeth. *Glossary of Northamptonshire Words and Phrases*. 2 vols. London: John Russell Smith, 1854.

[Robinson, Francis K.]. *A Glossary of Yorkshire Words and Phrases Collected in Whitby and the Neighborhood*. London: J.R. Smith, 1855.

Wright, Thomas. *Dictionary of Obsolete and Provincial English, containing words from the English writers previous to the nineteenth century which are no longer in use or are not used in the same sense*. 2 vols. London: H.G. Bohn, 1857.

Cleishbotham the Younger. *A Handbook of the Scottish Language: A Compendious Dictionary*. London: J.L. Smith, 1858.

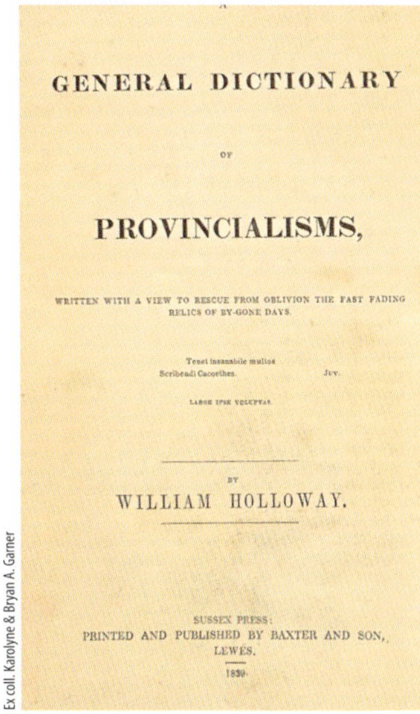

GENERAL DICTIONARY

OF

PROVINCIALISMS,

WRITTEN WITH A VIEW TO RESCUE FROM OBLIVION THE FAST FADING RELICS OF BY-GONE DAYS.

BY

WILLIAM HOLLOWAY.

SUSSEX PRESS:
PRINTED AND PUBLISHED BY BAXTER AND SON,
LEWES.

Ex coll. Karolyne & Bryan A. Garner

Ex coll. Karolyne & Bryan A. Garner

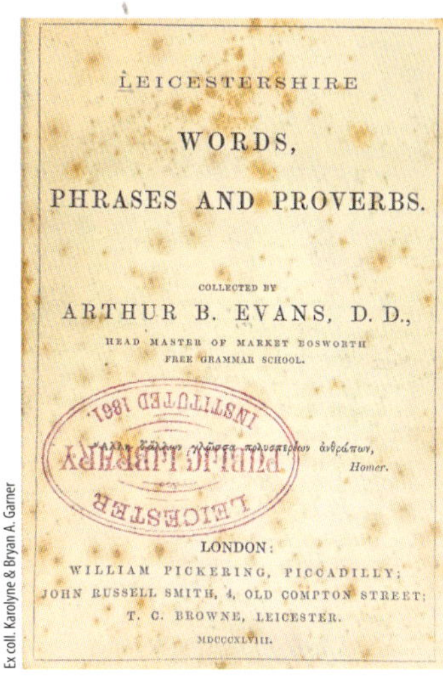

LEICESTERSHIRE

WORDS,

PHRASES AND PROVERBS.

COLLECTED BY

ARTHUR B. EVANS, D. D.,

HEAD MASTER OF MARKET BOSWORTH FREE GRAMMAR SCHOOL.

Homer.

LONDON:
WILLIAM PICKERING, PICCADILLY;
JOHN RUSSELL SMITH, 4, OLD COMPTON STREET;
T. C. BROWNE, LEICESTER.
MDCCCXLVIII.

Ex coll. Karolyne & Bryan A. Garner

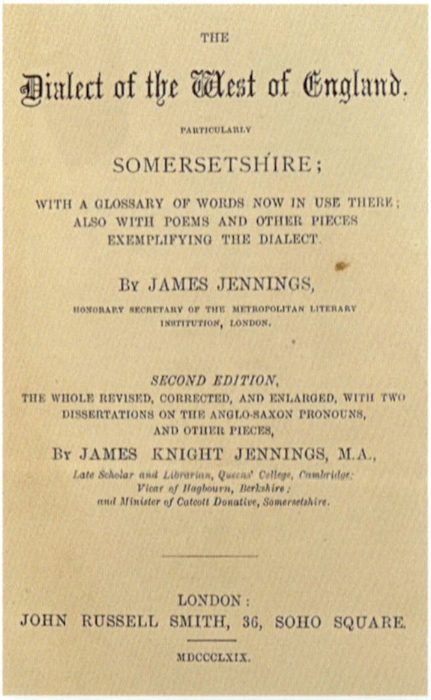
THE

Dialect of the West of England.

PARTICULARLY

SOMERSETSHIRE;

WITH A GLOSSARY OF WORDS NOW IN USE THERE;
ALSO WITH POEMS AND OTHER PIECES
EXEMPLIFYING THE DIALECT.

BY JAMES JENNINGS,

HONORARY SECRETARY OF THE METROPOLITAN LITERARY
INSTITUTION, LONDON.

SECOND EDITION,
THE WHOLE REVISED, CORRECTED, AND ENLARGED, WITH TWO
DISSERTATIONS ON THE ANGLO-SAXON PRONOUNS,
AND OTHER PIECES,

BY JAMES KNIGHT JENNINGS, M.A.,

Late Scholar and Librarian, Queens' College, Cambridge;
Vicar of Hagbourn, Berkshire;
and Minister of Catcott Donative, Somersetshire.

LONDON:
JOHN RUSSELL SMITH, 36, SOHO SQUARE.

MDCCCLXIX.

Ex coll. Karolyne & Bryan A. Garner

Ex coll. Karolyne & Bryan A. Garner

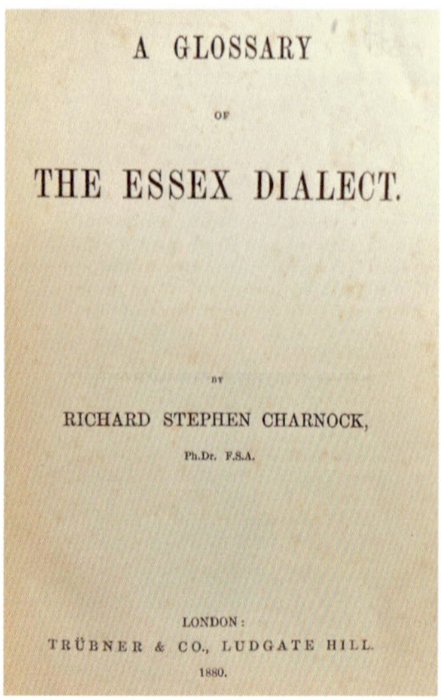
A GLOSSARY

OF

THE ESSEX DIALECT.

BY

RICHARD STEPHEN CHARNOCK,

Ph.Dr. F.S.A.

LONDON:
TRÜBNER & CO., LUDGATE HILL.
1880.

Ex coll. Karolyne & Bryan A. Garner

Dickinson, William. *A Glossary of the Words and Phrases of Cumberland*. Whitehaven: Callander & Dixon, 1859.

Linton, E. Lynn. *Provincialisms of the Lake District*. London: Smith, Elder & Co., 1864.

Brogden, John Ellet. *Provincial Words and Expressions in Lincolnshire*. London: Robert Hardwicke, 1866.

Edmonston, Thomas. *An Etymological Glossary of the Shetland and Orkney Dialect*. Edinburgh: A. & C. Black, 1866.

Huntley, Richard W. *A Glossary of the Cotswold (Gloucestershire) Dialect*. London: J.R. Smith, 1868.

Jennings, James. *The Dialect of the West of England, Particularly Somersetshire*. London: John Russell Smith, 1869.

Morris, J.P. *A Glossary of the Words and Phrases of Furness*. London: J. Russell Smith, 1869.

Williams, Wadham P.; and William A. Jones. *A Glossary of Provincial Words and Phrases in Use in Somersetshire*. London: Longmans, Green et al., 1873.

Parrish, William Douglas. *A Dictionary of the Sussex Dialect and Collection of Provincialisms in Use in the County of Sussex*. 2d ed. Lewes: Farncombe & Co, 1875.

Porson, A. *Notes of Quaint Words and Sayings in the Dialect of South Worcestershire*. Oxford: J. Parker & Co., 1875.

Bonaparte, Prince Louis Lucien. *On the Dialects of Eleven Southern and South-Western Counties with a New Classification of English Dialects*. London: Trübner & Co. for the English Dialect Society, 1877.

Jackson, Georgina F. *Shropshire Word Book: A Glossary of Archaisms and Provincial Words Used in the County*. London: Trübner, 1879–1881.

Charnock, Richard Stephen. *A Glossary of the Essex Dialect.* London: Trübner & Co., 1880.

Poole, Charles Henry. *An Attempt Towards a Glossary of the Archaic and Provincial Words of the County of Stafford.* Stratford-upon-Avon: St. Gregory's Press, 1880.

Jago, F.W.P. *Glossary of the Cornish Dialect.* Truro: Netherton & Worth, 1882.

Barnes, William. *A Glossary of the Dorset Dialect.* Dorchester: M. & E. Case; London: Trübner & Co., 1886.

Long, W.H. *A Dictionary of the Isle of Wight Dialect.* London: Reeves & Turner, 1886.

Havergal, Francis T. *Herefordshire Words and Phrases, Colloquial and Archaic.* Walsall: Privately printed, 1887.

Lowsley, Barzillai. *A Glossary of Berkshire Words and Phrases.* London: Trübner & Co. for the English Dialect Society, 1888.

Mackay, Charles. *A Dictionary of Lowland Scotch.* Edinburgh: Privately printed, 1888.

Nicholson, John. *The Folk Speech of East Yorkshire.* London: Simpkin, Marshall & Co., 1889.

Morris, Marmaduke Charles Frederick. *Yorkshire Folk-Talk.* London: H. Frowde, 1892.

Sweetman, George. *A Glossary of Words Used by the Rural Population in the Parish and Neighbourhood of Wincanton, Somerset.* Wincanton: Sweetman, 1892.

Dartnell, George Edward. *A Glossary of the Essex Dialect.* London: Trübner & Co., 1893.

Dartnell, George Edward; and Edward Hungerford Goddard. *A Glossary of Words Used in the County of Wiltshire.* London: Henry Frowde for the English Dialect Society, 1893.

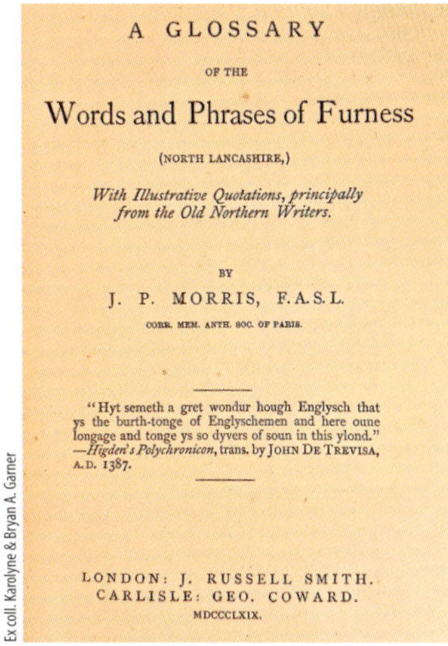
A GLOSSARY
OF THE
Words and Phrases of Furness
(NORTH LANCASHIRE,)
With Illustrative Quotations, principally from the Old Northern Writers.
BY
J. P. MORRIS, F.A.S.L.
CORR. MEM. ANTH. SOC. OF PARIS.
"Hyt semeth a gret wondur hough Englysch that ys the burth-tonge of Englyschemen and here oune longage and tonge ys so dyvers of soun in this ylond." —*Higden's Polychronicon*, trans. by JOHN DE TREVISA, A.D. 1387.
LONDON: J. RUSSELL SMITH.
CARLISLE: GEO. COWARD.
MDCCCLXIX.

Ex coll. Karolyne & Bryan A. Garner

Ex coll. Karolyne & Bryan A. Garner

A Glossary of Words
USED IN THE
COUNTY OF WILTSHIRE.
BY
GEORGE EDWARD DARTNELL
AND THE
REV. EDWARD HUNGERFORD GODDARD, M.A.
London:
PUBLISHED FOR THE ENGLISH DIALECT SOCIETY
BY HENRY FROWDE, OXFORD UNIVERSITY PRESS WAREHOUSE,
AMEN CORNER, LONDON, E.C.
1893.
[*All rights reserved.*]

Ex coll. Karolyne & Bryan A. Garner

Ex coll. Karolyne & Bryan A. Garner

The 1873 book that brought attention to James A.H. Murray.

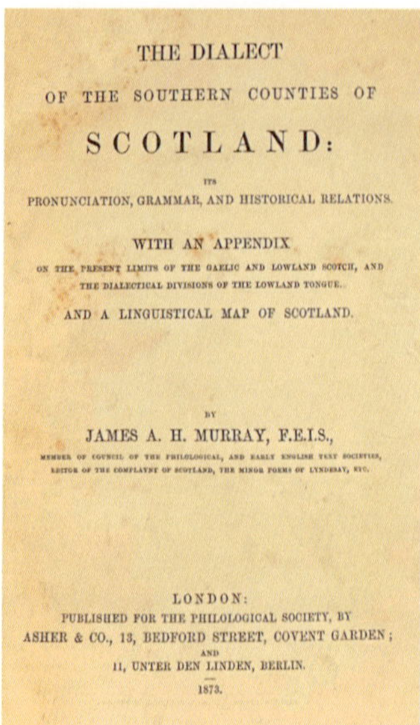

THE DIALECT

OF THE SOUTHERN COUNTIES OF

SCOTLAND:

ITS

PRONUNCIATION, GRAMMAR, AND HISTORICAL RELATIONS.

WITH AN APPENDIX

ON THE PRESENT LIMITS OF THE GAELIC AND LOWLAND SCOTCH, AND THE DIALECTICAL DIVISIONS OF THE LOWLAND TONGUE.

AND A LINGUISTICAL MAP OF SCOTLAND.

BY

JAMES A. H. MURRAY, F.E.I.S.,

MEMBER OF COUNCIL OF THE PHILOLOGICAL, AND EARLY ENGLISH TEXT SOCIETIES, EDITOR OF THE COMPLAYNT OF SCOTLAND, THE MINOR POEMS OF LYNDESAY, ETC.

LONDON:

PUBLISHED FOR THE PHILOLOGICAL SOCIETY, BY ASHER & CO., 13, BEDFORD STREET, COVENT GARDEN; AND 11, UNTER DEN LINDEN, BERLIN.

1873.

Ex coll. Karolyne & Bryan A. Garner

Montgomerie-Fleming, James B. *Desultory Notes on Jamieson's Scottish Dictionary*. 3d ed. Glasgow & Edinburgh: William Hodge & Co., 1899.

From Cawdrey through Webster and Worcester, most English lexicographers concerned themselves exclusively with mainstream language. Though they rarely said so in as many words, in practice that meant the English of London, Oxford, and Cambridge in Britain, and of educated people in the northeastern United States. Do they speak differently in rural Cumberland or in the poor neighborhoods of Savannah? Does a different word for a given thing prevail among sailors in Swansea or among farmers in North Carolina? No matter; most English dictionaries couldn't be bothered to record variants.

All that changed: an 18th-century trickle became a 19th-century flood, as collecting dialectal words and provincialisms into glossaries and dictionaries became all the rage. Listed above are the commercially and privately printed books. The list is therefore quite incomplete because it omits all the dozens of publications of the English Dialect Society, the English Philological Society, and learned journals such as *Notes and Queries*. In fact, as an 1873 publication of the Philological Society, James A.H. Murray compiled *The Dialect of the Southern Counties of Scotland*. That is partly how he made his reputation before being named, six years later, the chief editor of the *Oxford English Dictionary*.

Suffice it to say that all this dialect-hunting had become a craze among the expert and inexpert alike. If not circumscribed here by century, the category might start in 1787 with Francis Grose's *Provincial Glossary, with a Collection of Local Proverbs, and Popular Superstitions*. In fact, Samuel Pegge edited and reissued the book in 1839 as *A Glossary of Provincial and Local Words Used in England*. He had begun with a supplement to Grose in 1814 and then expanded that into a full revision.

Together, these publications were a great help to generalist lexicographers. They were consulted by the editors at the *Oxford English Dictionary*, the *Century Dictionary*, Funk & Wagnalls, and G. & C. Merriam Co. They amounted to regional crowdsourcing of the most valuable kind, and many of them remain useful sources of regional speech to this day.

113

Albert Marie Victor Barrère
Confidently Wrongheaded?

Barrère, Albert, and Charles G. Leland. *A Dictionary of Slang, Jargon & Cant, embracing English, American, and Anglo-Indian slang, pidgin English, tinkers' jargon and other irregular phraseology*. 2 vols. London: Ballantyne Press. Vol. 1, 1889; vol. 2, 1890.

Albert Marie Victor Barrère (1846?–1921) is unusual among English-language lexicographers in not being a native English speaker. Information about him is hard to come by. In his native France, he was an officier de la Legion d'Honneur and an officier de l'Institution Publique; in London, he was a French tutor in the 1890s. Beyond that, we know only what we can glean from his publications, including a pair of bilingual French and English dictionaries, one on military terms, one on slang. (See Coleman 2009a:35–52.)

Charles G. Leland.

His partner in this monolingual slang dictionary was Charles Godfrey Leland (1824–1903), a Philadelphia-born and Princeton-educated humorist and folklorist. Slang authority Julie Coleman succinctly recounts some of Leland's colorful life:

> He took part in the French Revolution in 1848 and, having sent eyewitness accounts back to America, became a journalist after his law practice failed. He was outspoken in his support for the abolition of slavery during the Civil War, and fought at the Battle of Gettysburg. He travelled widely in America as a prospector for oil, but inheriting his father's wealth allowed him to retire to England in 1870. [Coleman 2009a:41.]

The pair's *Dictionary of Slang, Jargon & Cant* was first privately printed in a deluxe limited edition in 1889–1890. The book's extensive front matter includes a list of authorities consulted, a historical introduction, and canting samples from the 15th to the 19th centuries.

Though neither author was British, their dictionary focused primarily on the English of England, with Scotland, Wales, and Ireland also well represented. So, too, were the versions of English spoken in

"Anything like a distinct history of the development of English slang has hitherto been impossible, owing to the ignorance of most of those who have put themselves forward as its analysts and lexicographers." ("A Brief History of Slang," 1:xxi.)

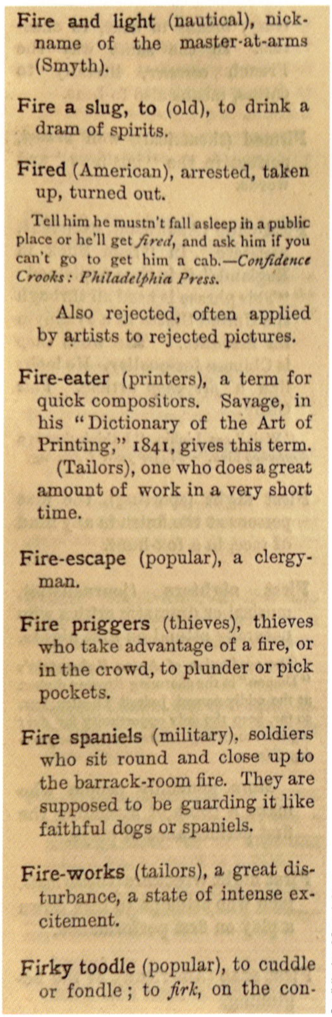

Fire and light (nautical), nickname of the master-at-arms (Smyth).

Fire a slug, to (old), to drink a dram of spirits.

Fired (American), arrested, taken up, turned out.

Tell him he mustn't fall asleep in a public place or he'll get *fired*, and ask him if you can't go to get him a cab.—*Confidence Crooks: Philadelphia Press.*

Also rejected, often applied by artists to rejected pictures.

Fire-eater (printers), a term for quick compositors. Savage, in his "Dictionary of the Art of Printing," 1841, gives this term. (Tailors), one who does a great amount of work in a very short time.

Fire-escape (popular), a clergyman.

Fire priggers (thieves), thieves who take advantage of a fire, or in the crowd, to plunder or pick pockets.

Fire spaniels (military), soldiers who sit round and close up to the barrack-room fire. They are supposed to be guarding it like faithful dogs or spaniels.

Fire-works (tailors), a great disturbance, a state of intense excitement.

Firky toodle (popular), to cuddle or fondle; to *firk*, on the con-

Ex coll. Karolyne & Bryan A. Garner

Australia and India, then both part of the British Empire. But the most notable source of international slang was America, which probably reflects Leland's influence. Hardly a page goes by without at least one Americanism, though the two were sometimes too quick to use the "American" label, since a nontrivial number of words so labeled were also in use in Britain. They also drew attention to the influence of Yiddish on English, a subject that would prove exceptionally rewarding for later slang lexicographers.

Almost every word in the dictionary is classified into one of a few dozen categories. About one in five entries is tagged with a geographical note ("Anglo-Indian," "American," "provincial"). Some of the labels refer to professions ("medical," "nautical," "military," "legal"), and others are tied to social class ("low," "common," "popular," "vulgarism").

As with most other slang dictionaries, much of the vocabulary is charming: *taradiddles* ("falsehoods"), *affygraphy* ("said of anything that fits nicely"), *flush in the fob* ("well supplied with money"), *mushroom-faker* ("umbrella-maker"), *muzzy* ("drunk, properly bewildered"), *the needful* ("money"), and *to vowel* ("acknowledge [a debt] with an I.O.U.") are all rewarding. We've all felt *Mondayish* ("disinclined for work") from time to time, though we aspire to be *up to dictionary* ("learned"). Other entries, though, are less endearing, especially those that let us see the late-Victorian demimonde. The references to child labor, prostitution, opium dens, and crime can be disturbing, and the racial and ethnic stereotypes that inform the definitions are sometimes hard to take.

Some slang terms in the book have survived to the present: *all get-out*, *hen party*, and some Cockney rhyming slang like *apples and pears* for "stairs" are still heard. Other words, though labeled slang in 1889, are still in use but part of the standard language: Barrère and Leland label *pub* as slang for *public-house*, but today it's perfectly acceptable in even the most formal contexts. In their day, *trampolin* was circus jargon, and *quiz* and *flunk* were heard only among students. *Wire tap* was still an informal Americanism meaning "to obtain surreptitious possession of the electric telegraph wire and extract the information with which it is charged."

Slang dictionaries are often raunchy, piling up dozens of synonyms for body parts and erotic proclivities. Not so Barrère and Leland. Much is undignified, but only a few entries can be called indecent, and they're usually hidden behind euphemisms. On the very few occasions when euphemisms aren't an option, the "licentious passages," as historian Edward Gibbon famously put it, "are left in the decent obscurity of a learned language." Latin restricts the naughty bits to the educated, who are presumably mature enough to handle them.

The privately printed original publication was followed by a lightly revised and substantially cheaper edition in 1897. A facsimile reprint of 1967 included a preface by the 20th century's greatest slang lexicographer, Eric Partridge, who said that Barrère and Leland "achieved a high place in the literature of Slang. Although they made several claims that might be difficult to substantiate, their book is neither arrogant nor wrong-headed." (Partridge 1967:iii.) Coleman, though, is less impressed, finding their *Dictionary* "confidently wrong-headed in many respects." (Coleman 2009a:42.) She faults them for sloppy citations, inconsistent usage labels, etymologies based only on guesswork, and plagiarized definitions from John Camden Hotten and Alfred Trumble.

"To a very great number of respectable and by no means uneducated persons, slang is simply a collective name for vulgar expressions, the most refined individual being the one who uses it least. To them it is all that which in speech is 'tabu,' or forbidden." (Preface, p. v.)

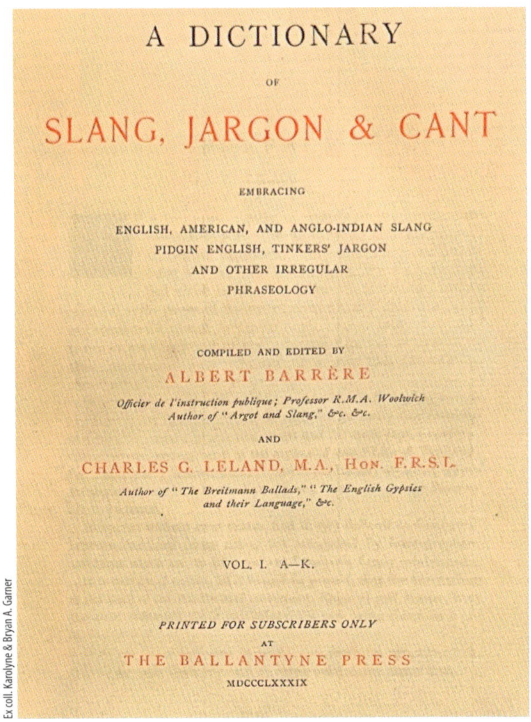
A DICTIONARY

OF

SLANG, JARGON & CANT

EMBRACING

ENGLISH, AMERICAN, AND ANGLO-INDIAN SLANG
PIDGIN ENGLISH, TINKERS' JARGON
AND OTHER IRREGULAR
PHRASEOLOGY

COMPILED AND EDITED BY

ALBERT BARRÈRE

Officier de l'instruction publique; Professor R.M.A. Woolwich
Author of "Argot and Slang," &c. &c.

AND

CHARLES G. LELAND, M.A., HON. F.R.S.L.

Author of "The Breitmann Ballads," "The English Gypsies and their Language," &c.

VOL. I. A—K.

PRINTED FOR SUBSCRIBERS ONLY

AT

THE BALLANTYNE PRESS

MDCCCLXXXIX

Ex coll. Karolyne & Bryan A. Garner

"Perhaps the best general definition at which one can arrive is that 'slang' is a conventional tongue with many dialects, which are as a rule unintelligible to outsiders. In one case at least it has been framed with the intention of its being intelligible only to the initiated—the vagabond and thievish fraternity." (Preface, p. vi.)

Ex coll. Karolyne & Bryan A. Garner

114

John Farmer & William Henley

Of Flimsies and Gingleboys

Farmer, John S. *Americanisms—Old & New: A Dictionary of Words, Phrases and Colloquialisms Peculiar to the United States, British America, the West Indies, &c., &c.* London: Thomas Poulter & Sons, 1889.

Farmer, John S., and W[illiam] E[rnest] Henley. *Slang and Its Analogues, Past and Present: a dictionary, historical and comparative, of the heterodox speech of all classes of society for more than three hundred years.* 7 vols. London: Privately printed for subscribers, 1890–1904.

"Of all spoken tongues the English language is, perhaps, alone destined to occupy a predominant place among the peoples of the earth." (Farmer, *Americanisms*, p. v.)

The 19th century's biggest slang dictionary was compiled by two Englishmen. The first, John Stephen Farmer (1854–1916), "believed in the occult, never had any money, and lived with a woman to whom he was not married." (Green 2015:274.) He's been accused of bigamy and writing pornography, though evidence is murky. In 1889, he published *Americanisms—Old & New*, a 550-page dictionary focusing on "the divergence . . . between the Queen's English and the English of the New World" (p. vi)—words like *dime*, *ding!*, and *Dixie*. His particular interest was words "employed by general and respectable usage in America in a way not sanctioned by the best standards of the English language," supplemented by "the racy, pungent vernacular of Western life." (P. vii.) Farmer then teamed up with William Ernest Henley (1849–1903), a journalist best known for "Invictus," a poem beloved by Winston Churchill, Nelson Mandela, and Timothy McVeigh. Henley lost part of his left leg as a child; years later, after he was befriended by Robert Louis Stevenson, he provided a model for Long John Silver in *Treasure Island*.

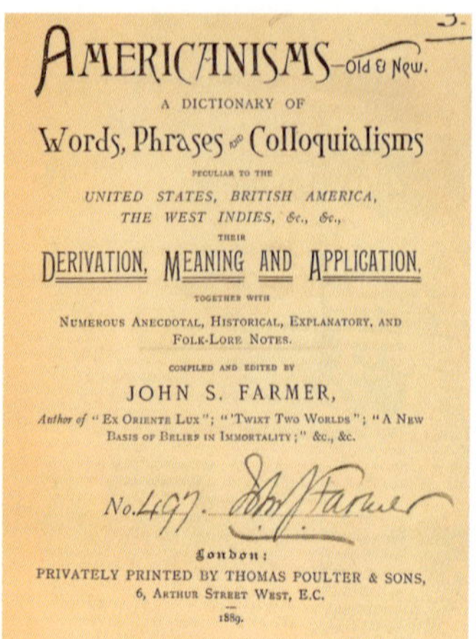

Ex coll. Karolyne & Bryan A. Garner

Farmer saw his work as a kind of complement to the in-progress *Oxford English Dictionary*. His first installment appeared just a few years after that of the *OED*, and he often corresponded with James Murray. He adopted Murray's method as his own: "I have adopted, though not in its entirety, what is commonly known as the 'historical method.'" (1:vii.) The dictionary comes with many of the markers of scholarly authority—parts of speech, documented etymologies, precise usage notes, illustrative quotations (though not always cited correctly; see Coleman 2004–10:3:61)—which had hardly ever been seen in slang lexicography. (Adams 2020a:80.) It is also unusual in its attention to American and Australian slang in addition to British.

The dictionary contains roughly 20,300 entries, and while Farmer boasted about having "upwards of 100,000" citations, Coleman thinks the true number is around 38,000. Farmer promised "a chapter on the comparative study of European slang, a bibliography, a list of authorities and references to periodical literature, and a complete list of all the foreign slang terms included" (Coleman 2009a:54), but he never delivered any of them.

Despite its shortcomings, though, *Slang and Its Analogues* remains the most extensive record of informal Victorian speech. The cross-references are especially valuable. The entry *rhino*, for instance, includes more than 150 terms for money in general—*dimmock*, *gingleboys*, *oof*, *spondulicks*—along with dozens more for specific denominations: a £5 note could be a *finnup* or a *flimsy*; 2*s.* 6*d.*, formally a *half-crown*, could be a *coach-wheel*, a *flatch*, or a *half-Oxford*.

Much of the book is more sexually explicit than we might expect in Queen Victoria's reign, with its more than 800 nouns for genitalia and 600 verbs meaning "To possess carnally" or "To enjoy, procure, or confer the sexual favour." The obscenity led to a legal battle: after producing volume 1, the printer refused to handle a work so filled with indecency. Farmer took him to court for breach of promise. Farmer lost, and was forced to find a new printer in Amsterdam. (Coleman 2009b:321; Green 2015:277–78.)

Slang and Its Analogues was first published in a deluxe limited edition, seven thick-paper quarto volumes, and only later reprinted for a general audience. Volume 1 was revised in two parts, in 1903 and 1909, but the rest was never revisited. It never sold particularly well, but it did have a long afterlife through its influence on other lexicographers. The traffic between Farmer and Murray ran both ways: the *OED* cites Farmer and Henley about 350 times. And the 20th century's greatest slang lexicographer, Eric Partridge, called *Slang and Its Analogues* "always courageous, often brilliant," and "one of the three or four most remarkable one-handed achievements in the whole record of dictionary making." (Partridge 1935:106.) That generous appraisal antedated Partridge's own slang dictionary by two years. In fact, his big *Dictionary of Slang and Unconventional English* (no. 116), was originally conceived as a revised and expanded version of Farmer and Henley.

Ex coll. Karolyne & Bryan A. Garner

The seven-volume *Slang and Its Analogues* (at bottom). Shortly after the set was issued, a one-volume abridgment appeared (at top, ca. 1905).

"It seems certain that, in another hundred years, no less than one thousand millions of people will, at the present rate of increase, be speaking the English language—a number far in excess of any other nationality. Rich in metaphor, full of vitality and creative vigor—as it has proved itself—with untold possibilities of adaptation to the needs and genius of the age, it already stands unique in many respects, and forms a medium of communication to the like of which no other spoken tongue can show an analogy." (Farmer, *Americanisms*, p. v.)

Ex coll. Karolyne & Bryan A. Garner

Ex coll. Karolyne & Bryan A. Garner

115

Ambrose Bierce
Diabolical Words

Bierce, Ambrose. *The Cynic's Word Book*. New York: Doubleday, Page & Co., 1906.

———. *The Devil's Dictionary*. Vol. 7 of Bierce's *Collected Works*. New York & Washington, D.C.: Neale Pub. Co., 1911.

Bierce (1842–1914?), the noted author and journalist, was a sardonic lexicographer in the tradition of Charles Pigott (no. 111) and Gustave Flaubert: his *Cynic's Word Book* grew, five years later, into *The Devil's Dictionary*, one of the wittiest, most irreverent compilations of quotably cynical definitions ever assembled. It has remained constantly in print since it first appeared more than a century ago.

Born in Ohio to evangelical parents, Bierce from a young age resented indoctrination and became an unbeliever. In 1859, he enlisted in the Union Army and fought in no fewer than 23 Civil War battles. Finally, in the last year of the war, he suffered wounds that brought his military career to an end—though he came to see all of life as a war.

He worked for the Treasury Department in Alabama for a year in 1866, resigning to join a mapping expedition through Indian Country. When the expedition reached San Francisco, he quit and began employment there with the U.S. Mint. Soon he began submitting fiction and journalism to San Francisco periodicals, and his writing career was launched. For the rest of his life, he supported himself primarily through writing. Apart from a three-year stint in London, he stayed in the Bay Area through 1899, when he moved permanently to Washington, D.C.—continuing his work as a journalist. From 1909 to 1912, he edited the 12-volume set of his own collected works, where *The Devil's Dictionary* first appeared. Then, in 1913, he traveled to Mexico to monitor Pancho Villa's revolution. His last letter having been sent in December of that year, he mysteriously disappeared.

The Devil's Dictionary was written over a period of 30 years: it began in 1881 as a series in a weekly newspaper, was published in part as *The Cynic's Word Book* in 1906, and then appeared in full form in 1911. He addressed the book to "enlightened souls who prefer dry wines to sweet, sense to sentiment, wit to humor and clean English to slang."

Ex coll. Karolyne & Bryan A. Garner

Although many of the wry entries consist of only one sentence, most are short paragraphs. They're to be savored:

- "ABDICATION, *n.* An act whereby a sovereign attests his sense of the high temperature of the throne." (P. 11.)
- "ACTUALLY, *adv.* Perhaps, possibly." (P. 18.)
- "BACKBITE, *v.t.* To speak of a man as you find him when he can't find you." (P. 31.)
- "COMFORT, *n.* A state of mind produced by contemplation of a neighbor's uneasiness." (P. 52.)
- "ENVELOPE, *n.* The coffin of a document; the scabbard of a bill; the husk of a remittance; the bed-gown of a love-letter." (P. 86.)
- "FRIENDLESS, *adj.* Having no favors to bestow. Destitute of fortune. Addicted to utterance of truth and common sense." (P. 109.)
- "IMPUNITY, *n.* Wealth." (P. 153.)
- "JEALOUS, *adj.* Unduly concerned about the preservation of that which can be lost only if not worth keeping." (P. 175.)
- "KILT, *n.* A costume sometimes worn by Scotchmen in America and Americans in Scotland." (P. 178.)
- "LAWFUL, *adj.* Compatible with the will of a judge having jurisdiction." (P. 186.)
- "MAUSOLEUM, *n.* The final and funniest folly of the rich." (P. 214.)
- "MONDAY, *n.* In Christian countries, the day after the baseball game." (P. 222.)
- "OCEAN, *n.* A body of water occupying about two-thirds of a world made for man—who has no gills." (P. 235.)
- "PRESIDENCY, *n.* The greased pig in the field game of American politics." (P. 266.)
- "REFERENDUM, *n.* A law for submission of proposed legislation to a popular vote to learn the nonsensus of public opinion." (P. 280.)
- "REVELATION, *n.* A famous book in which St. John the Divine concealed all that he knew. The revealing is done by the commentators, who know nothing." (P. 292.)
- "SELF-EVIDENT, *adj.* Evident to one's self and to nobody else." (P. 318.)
- "TELEPHONE, *n.* An invention of the devil which abrogates some of the advantages of making a disagreeable person keep his distance." (P. 341.)
- "WIT, *n.* The salt with which the American humorist spoils his intellectual cookery by leaving it out." (P. 367.)
- "YEAR, *n.* A period of three hundred and sixty-five disappointments." (P. 371.)

"Ambrose Bierce's 'What I Saw of Shiloh' and 'An Occurrence at Owl Creek Bridge' may be his greatest works, but *The Devil's Dictionary* is quintessential Bierce." (Schultz & Joshi 2000:ix.)

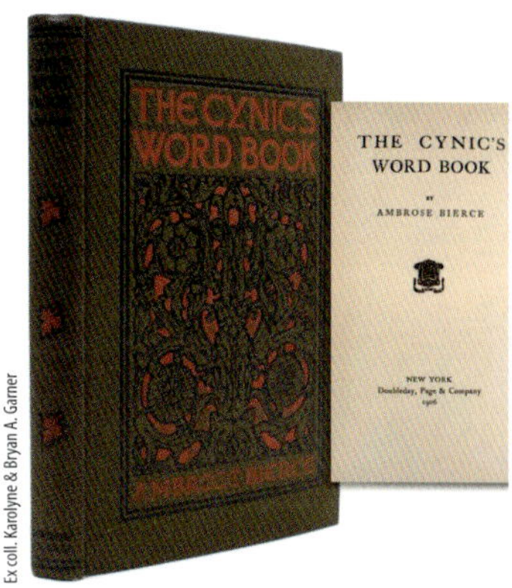

Ex coll. Karolyne & Bryan A. Garner

"At times Bierce includes poetry in the definitions, written by himself but typically attributed to fictitious authors with silly Dickensian names; the poetry allows Bierce to exemplify and expatiate on a word's customary usage (or to send it up) while crucifying the habits and the language of fusty Victorian crackpot poetasters." (Parini 2004 1:179.)

Photo by Press Portrait Bureau

Ex coll. Karolyne & Bryan A. Garner

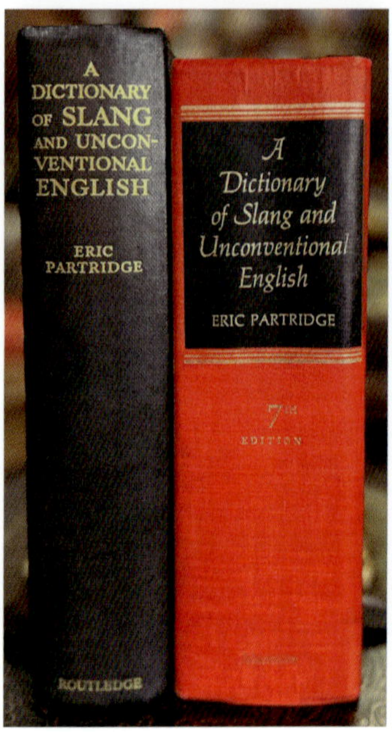

Ex coll. Karolyne & Bryan A. Garner

Two editions: the first (1937) and the seventh (1970).

116

Eric Partridge

A Slangy, Unconventional Man

Partridge, Eric. *A Dictionary of Slang and Unconventional English*. New York: Macmillan, 1937.

Although Eric Partridge (1894–1979) was a published translator as early as 1914 and an author as early as 1919—and had no fewer than 22 books or booklets appear under his name during the 1920s—it wasn't until the 1930s that his works in the realm of lexicography began appearing. First came *Songs and Slang of the British Soldier (1914–1918)* and *American Tramp and Underworld Slang* (both in 1930), followed by an edition of *Francis Grose's A Classical Dictionary of the Vulgar Tongue* (1931), *Slang Today and Yesterday* (1933), and the alphabetically arranged *Name This Child* (1936).

Then in 1937, Partridge's first big dictionary was issued: *A Dictionary of Slang and Unconventional English*. In the preface he explains: "This dictionary, at which I have worked harder than (I hope, but would not swear) I shall ever work again and which incorporates the results of a close observation of colloquial speech for many years, is designed to form a humble companion to the monumental *Oxford English Dictionary*." (P. ix.) He estimates the proportions of the various kinds of locutions included in the book being as follows:

Slang and Cant	44%
Colloquialisms	42%
Solecisms and Catachreses	6.5%
Catchphrases	5.5%
Nicknames	1.5%
Vulgarisms	0.5%

By *vulgarisms*, Partridge means "words and phrases that, in no way slangy, are avoided in polite society."

Speaking of which, many were appalled by his detached, clinical treatment of the "unspeakable" words in English. The book was therefore kept for many years on "restricted access" in many public libraries. Some places banned it. After all, the *F*-word has 2 substantial entries (noun and verb), plus 15 compounds. He printed them all with a modest asterisk (*f*ck*), but in the buttoned-up 1930s, readers must have been astounded to encounter compounds ending *able*, *beggar*, *finger*, *hole*, *ish*, *some*, *ster*, and *stress*. He asked the indulgence of his readers: "Should a lexicographer, if he includes *any* vulgarisms (in any sense of that term), omit the others? I have given them all." (P. x.) To make his exhaustiveness less objectionable, he treated "unpleasant terms . . . as briefly, as astringently, as aseptically as was consistent with clarity and adequacy." (*Id.*) He even tried to protect himself against readers' squeamishness by declaring that he shared it: "in a few instances, I had to force myself to overcome an instinctive repugnance." (*Id.*)

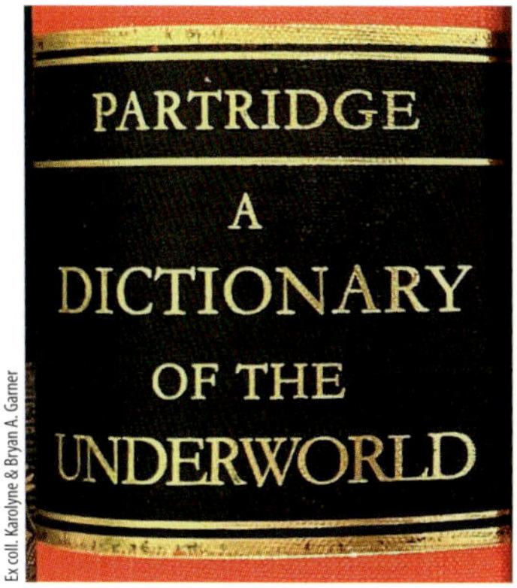

Ex coll. Karolyne & Bryan A. Garner

A related title first published in 1949.

What made definitions "aseptic"? Often the use of Latinisms. For example, *f-hole* is defined as "the *pudendum muliebre*." Those with classical learning were allowed to see the naughty terms; those without were presumed unable to handle them.

"As a detailed examination of these pages will show, I have added considerably from my own knowledge of language-byways and from my own reading, much of the latter having been undertaken with this specific end in view." (1937 preface, p. x.)

Partridge's main debts were to the *OED* and to Farmer and Henley's *Slang and Its Analogues*. Yet he estimated that his slang dictionary, even in its first edition, contained 35% more than the other two taken together. More and more new material was added with each successive edition: 2d (1938), 3d (1949), 4th (1951), 5th (1961), 6th (1967), and 7th (1970). Because of the fecundity of the *F*-word in various compounds—the rich variety of neologisms that arose between 1937 and 1970—Partridge recorded 26 more compounds in his 7th-edition Supplement (in the back matter). He never lost his nerve.

In the end, Partridge's lexicography became something of a period piece: because it wasn't grounded in fieldwork and could be somewhat unreliable (Partridge would fudge here and there), it gradually lost status among language scholars. But even his big slang dictionary remains in print, edited now by Tom Dalzell, a labor lawyer and business manager for the International Brothers of Electrical Workers.

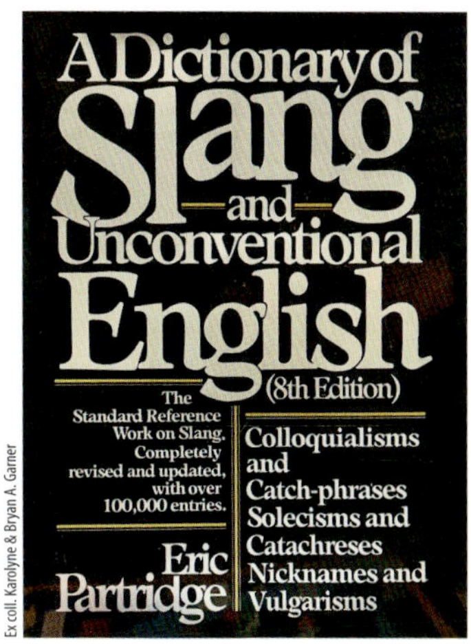

Ex coll. Karolyne & Bryan A. Garner

The eighth edition (1985).

Ex coll. Jack Lynch

117

Cab Calloway

Always Hep to the Jive

Calloway, Cab. *The New Cab Calloway's Hepsters Dictionary: Language of Jive*. Privately printed, 1944.

In the 1930s and '40s, Cabell "Cab" Calloway (1907–1994) led the most popular Black swing band in America. He was a regular at Harlem's legendary Cotton Club, one of the few places in America where largely white audiences could be exposed to Black music and Black speech.

As early as 1899, those "in the know" were described as *hep*. By the mid-1930s, those who were hep to swing music were called *hepcats* or *hepsters*. And many of these hepsters used a vocabulary of their own known as *jive*.

Saxophonist Ben Webster loved jive, and his enthusiasm rubbed off on his bandleader. Calloway began introducing the latest lingo into his stage patter and even his song lyrics, as in "Are You Hep to the Jive! (Yas, Yas)." He sometimes appeared in the character of "Professor Cab Calloway," facetiously lecturing mostly white audiences on how to speak "Harlemese." Audiences loved it.

Seeing a marketing opportunity, his manager, Irving Mills, encouraged Calloway to produce a little guide to jive. The result was *Cab Calloway's Cat-ologue: A "Hepster's" Dictionary* (1938), a tiny stapled pamphlet containing about 150 terms with short definitions. Calloway was selective in his coverage: terms relating to crime and drugs were excluded so as not to disturb audiences, the space instead being given over to terminology for fashion, food, and music. The booklet was a marketing gimmick, small and cheap enough to be given away like business cards. Mills and Calloway distributed copies to fans and especially to journalists, who often obliged by publishing newspaper articles about the latest and heppest slang. Although traditionalists clucked their tongues at the decline of the language, their complaints just translated into ever more record sales.

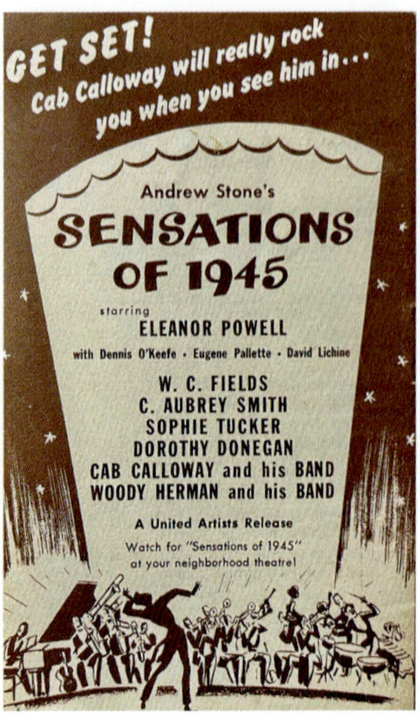

The 1944 edition of *Cab Calloway's Hepsters Dictionary* served as promotion for a new movie.

Some of Calloway's terms had a short lifespan—*icky*, "a stupid person, can't collar the jive"; *killer-diller*, "a great thrill"; and *mash me a fin*, "give me $5"—but some jive terms outlived the swing era to become enduring parts of the American vernacular: *chick*, "girl"; *groovy*, "fine"; *joint is jumping*, "the place is lively"; *kopasetic*, "absolutely okay"; *riff*, "hot lick, musical phrase"; *the man*, "the law"; and *yeah, man*, "an exclamation of assent"—all could be heard for decades, and some even today.

The *Hepsters Dictionary* is more jeu d'esprit than triumph of slang lexicography, and it is unmistakably gimmicky and commercial. Still, it holds an important place in the history of English dictionaries: it is, as far as anyone has been able to determine, the first published dictionary of any description composed by an African American.

JACK (N)—name for all male friends (see gate and pops).
JAM—(1) (N)—improvised swing music. Ex.—"*That's swell jam*". (2) (V)—to play such music. Ex.—"*That cat surely can jam*".
JEFF (N)—a pest, a bore, an icky.
JELLY (N)—anything free, on the house.
JITTER BUG (N)—a swing fan.
JIVE—(1) (N)—Harlemese speech.
JOINT IS JUMPING—the place is lively, the club is leaping with fun.
JUMPED IN PORT (V)—to arrive in town.

K

KICK (N)—a pocket. Ex.—"*I've got five bucks in my kick*".
KILL ME (V)—show me a good time, send me.
KILLER-DILLER (N)—a great thrill.
KNOCK (V)—give. Ex.—"*Knock me a kiss*".
KOPASETIC (ADJ)—absolutely okay, the tops.

L

LAMP (V)—to see, to look at.
LAND O'DARKNESS (N)—Harlem.

Ex coll. Jack Lynch

"To counter Benny Goodman's success with the youth market, Cab gave his fans their own means of communicating. Even if they were 'beat to their socks' (flat broke), they could still remain 'mellow' (fine) if their 'main queen' (sweetheart) 'had her boots on' (knew what it was all about). At the end of the day they 'nixed out their garments' (undressed) and 'copped a nod' (went to sleep). Like all slang, from the moment much of it was published, it was out of date ('capped'), but the little book provoked hours of harmless fun with readers who had seldom if ever heard Harlem street slang spoken in real life, and with journalists who protested that this was 'English as she never should be spoken.'" (Shipton 2013:127.)

FRAUGHTY ISSUE (N)—a very sad message, a deplorable state of affairs.
FREEBY (N)—no charge, gratis. Ex.—"*The meal was a freeby*".
FRISKING THE WHISKERS (V)—what the cats do when they are warming up for a swing session.
FROLIC PAD (N)—place of entertainment, like stage show, theatre, night club.
FROMPY (ADJ)—a frompy queen is a battle or faust.
FRONT (N)—suit of clothing.
FRUITING (V)—fickle, fooling around with no particular object.
FRY (V)—to go to get hair straightened.

G

GABRIELS (N)—trumpet players.
GAMMIN' (ADJ)—showing off, flirtatious.
GASSER (N, ADJ)—sensational. Ex.—"*When it comes to dancing, she's a gasser*".
GATE (N)—a male person (a salutation), abbr. for "*gate-mouth*".
GET IN THERE—(an exclamation) go to work, get busy, make it hot, give all you've got.
GIMME SOME SKIN (V)—shake hands.
GLIMS (N)—the eyes.
GOT YOUR BOOTS ON—you know what it is all about, you are a hep cat, you are wise.
GOT YOUR GLASSES ON—you are ritzy or snooty, you fail to recognize your friends, you are up-stage.

Ex coll. Jack Lynch

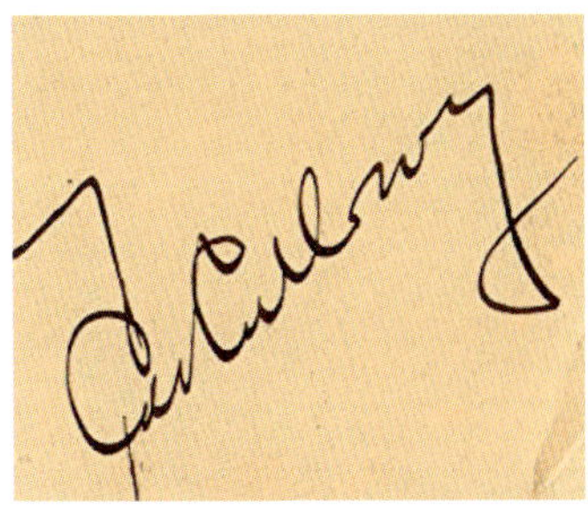

Clarence Major.

118

Clarence Major
The Will to Survive on Black Terms

Major, Clarence. *Dictionary of Afro-American Slang*. New York: International Pubs., 1970.

NOT ALL DIALECTS are regional. Some linguistic communities are defined not by geography but by shared experience.

The shared experience of African Americans has been unusually linguistically productive. In the days of the slave trade, speakers of many languages were brought into contact with one another. (Linguists still argue over the extent of the influence of African languages on American speech.) Even after slavery ended, Black American populations have had varying degrees of seclusion from the white mainstream, whether voluntary or enforced by Jim Crow. Distinct traditions and artistic cultures have all contributed to the language.

As early as the 18th century white writers were conscious of distinctive speech habits in Black communities. But attempts to capture this speech have usually been based on stereotype rather than observation, as when Daniel Defoe's *Col. Jacque* gives an enslaved man's speech in Virginia in the 1720s:

> *Negro.* Master, me speakee de true, they never give Merciè̀, they always Whippee, Lashee, Knockee down, all Cruel: *Negroe* be muchee better Man do muchee better Work, but they tell us no Mercee. [Defoe, *Col. Jacque*, 1723, p. 175.]

Most early representations of Black American speech are similarly crude.

In the early 20th century, though, linguists began to take African American speech—called, at various times, Black English, Ebonics, and African American Vernacular English (AAVE)—more seriously. But the discussion tended to focus on isolated features—phonology, verb aspect—and it appeared mostly in academic journal articles. No one had attempted a book-length dictionary in English focused on the African American vocabulary.

Ex coll. Jack Lynch

That changed with Clarence Major's *Dictionary of Afro-American Slang*, published in 1970. Major (b. 1936), poet, painter, and novelist, settled in New York City in the mid-1960s after a stint in the U.S. Air Force. He passed his days as a teacher in Harlem and his evenings as a writer. His publishing career began with a novel, *All Night Visitors* (1969), and a collection of poems, *Swallow the Lake* (1970), which won a National Council on the Arts Award. Soon afterward he published his *Dictionary of Afro-American Slang*.

As the title reveals, Major didn't attempt to survey the whole of AAVE, just "slang," that is, the features that are not part of Standard English. This poses a challenge that all slang lexicographers face: the shortage of surviving evidence. Lexicography has always depended on written sources, but complex politics dictate whose language gets written down and whose gets preserved. Major is not precise about his sources, but they include the spoken language. "I have gathered these words," he writes, "not only from a scattering of printed sources but from the reliability of my own ethnic experience." (P. 15.)

Black English was long conceived in terms of *lack*—it was an inferior form of Standard English, a failed attempt to speak "properly." Departures from Standard English were branded mistakes and treated as evidence of stupidity or laziness. The only book that the Library of Congress catalogues under the subject heading "African Americans—Languages—Dictionaries" before Major is titled *How They Talk: One Thousand Misused Words and Idiomatic Expressions*.

Major confronts these attitudes directly: "I assert that the speech habits of the most oppressed segment (which is the largest) of the black population in the United States do not spring solely from an inability to handle acceptable forms of spoken English." (P. 10.) In fact the distinctiveness of Black English is "a powerful medium of self-defense against a world demanding participation while at the same time laying a boobytrap-network of rejection and exploitation." (P. 9.) He sums it up in a powerful slogan: "Afro-American slang is created out of the will to survive on black terms." (P. 10.)

Not all of Major's words originated among Black speakers; some have very long histories, even predating the European settlement of North America. *Man*, for instance, can be traced back to early Old English, but for Major it is "a word brought into popular use by black males to counteract the degrading effects of being addressed by whites as 'boy'; black males address each other as one man to another."

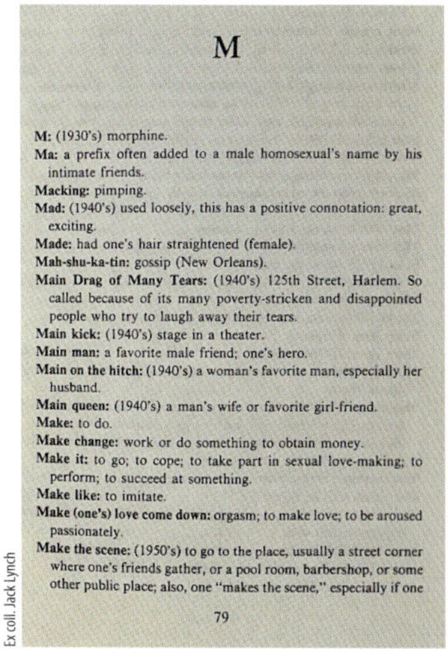
M

M: (1930's) morphine.
Ma: a prefix often added to a male homosexual's name by his intimate friends.
Macking: pimping.
Mad: (1940's) used loosely, this has a positive connotation: great, exciting.
Made: had one's hair straightened (female).
Mah-shu-ka-tin: gossip (New Orleans).
Main Drag of Many Tears: (1940's) 125th Street, Harlem. So called because of its many poverty-stricken and disappointed people who try to laugh away their tears.
Main kick: (1940's) stage in a theater.
Main man: a favorite male friend; one's hero.
Main on the hitch: (1940's) a woman's favorite man, especially her husband.
Main queen: (1940's) a man's wife or favorite girl-friend.
Make: to do.
Make change: work or do something to obtain money.
Make it: to go; to cope; to take part in sexual love-making; to perform; to succeed at something.
Make like: to imitate.
Make (one's) love come down: orgasm; to make love; to be aroused passionately.
Make the scene: (1950's) to go to the place, usually a street corner where one's friends gather, or a pool room, barbershop, or some other public place; also, one "makes the scene," especially if one

79

Ex coll. Jack Lynch

"It is a language unconsciously designed to pave a way toward positive self-images: though it may seem, in effect, monotonous and certainly no less than tragic, the sociocultural factors at the root of it are revolutionary. In essence, it is a natural attempt to counteract the classic and dreary weight of political and social oppression, and at a very basic level of human experience." (P. 10.)

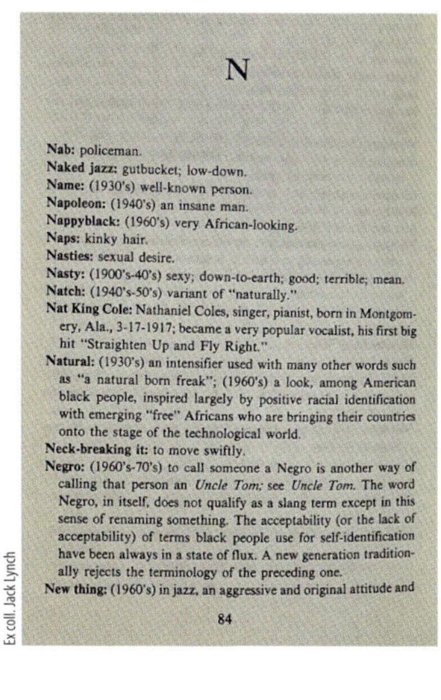
N

Nab: policeman.
Naked jazz: gutbucket; low-down.
Name: (1930's) well-known person.
Napoleon: (1940's) an insane man.
Nappyblack: (1960's) very African-looking.
Naps: kinky hair.
Nasties: sexual desire.
Nasty: (1900's-40's) sexy; down-to-earth; good; terrible; mean.
Natch: (1940's-50's) variant of "naturally."
Nat King Cole: Nathaniel Coles, singer, pianist, born in Montgomery, Ala., 3-17-1917; became a very popular vocalist, his first big hit "Straighten Up and Fly Right."
Natural: (1930's) an intensifier used with many other words such as "a natural born freak"; (1960's) a look, among American black people, inspired largely by positive racial identification with emerging "free" Africans who are bringing their countries onto the stage of the technological world.
Neck-breaking it: to move swiftly.
Negro: (1960's-70's) to call someone a Negro is another way of calling that person an *Uncle Tom;* see *Uncle Tom.* The word Negro, in itself, does not qualify as a slang term except in this sense of renaming something. The acceptability (or the lack of acceptability) of terms black people use for self-identification have been always in a state of flux. A new generation traditionally rejects the terminology of the preceding one.
New thing: (1960's) in jazz, an aggressive and original attitude and

84

Ex coll. Jack Lynch

"**Sambo:** any black American who accepts meekly his or her oppression; from 'Little Black Sambo,' a story with stereotypes that serve the purpose of false propaganda."

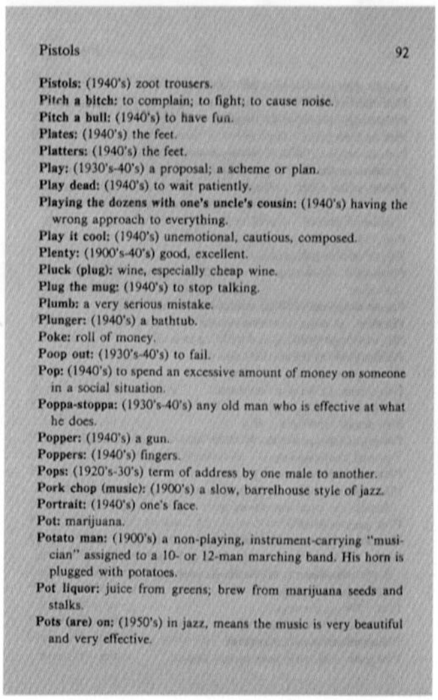

Pistols 92

Pistols: (1940's) zoot trousers.
Pitch a bitch: to complain; to fight; to cause noise.
Pitch a bull: (1940's) to have fun.
Plates: (1940's) the feet.
Platters: (1940's) the feet.
Play: (1930's-40's) a proposal; a scheme or plan.
Play dead: (1940's) to wait patiently.
Playing the dozens with one's uncle's cousin: (1940's) having the wrong approach to everything.
Play it cool: (1940's) unemotional, cautious, composed.
Plenty: (1900's-40's) good, excellent.
Pluck (plug): wine, especially cheap wine.
Plug the mug: (1940's) to stop talking.
Plumb: a very serious mistake.
Plunger: (1940's) a bathtub.
Poke: roll of money.
Poop out: (1930's-40's) to fail.
Pop: (1940's) to spend an excessive amount of money on someone in a social situation.
Poppa-stoppa: (1930's-40's) any old man who is effective at what he does.
Popper: (1940's) a gun.
Poppers: (1940's) fingers.
Pops: (1920's-30's) term of address by one male to another.
Pork chop (music): (1900's) a slow, barrelhouse style of jazz.
Portrait: (1940's) one's face.
Pot: marijuana.
Potato man: (1900's) a non-playing, instrument-carrying "musician" assigned to a 10- or 12-man marching band. His horn is plugged with potatoes.
Pot liquor: juice from greens; brew from marijuana seeds and stalks.
Pots (are) on: (1950's) in jazz, means the music is very beautiful and very effective.

Ex coll. Jack Lynch

"**Soul:** the sensitivity and emotional essence that derives from the blues; the heritage that is black; a natural process; black authenticity; feeling for one's roots, as demonstrated in black music and literature."

Some of Major's words are joyous: *hot dog!*, "a cry of excitement"; *solid sender*, "a very 'together' and satisfying person"; and *right on*, "cry of approval; affirmation of a revolutionary spirit." Because "the language of the black musician has had the greatest total effect on the informal language Americans speak" (pp. 12–13), jazz is the source of many words, as with *offbeat*, "a cymbal note hit by the drummer; odd; fantastic," and one of Black English's most enduring contributions to the standard language, *cool*, "loosely used, but generally means anything favorably regarded." Many of the terms are playful, as with *cute suit with the loop droop*, "a flashy, drape-like suit of clothes." Occasionally Major offers little prose poems where we might expect definitions, as with *eel-ya-dah*, "black existential verbal jazz sounds originating in bebop."

Not all the vocabulary is as cheery as *hot dog!* Major invokes "the horror of the disproportionate number of black men who have been subjected to imprisonment and died frequently at the hands of white 'law.'" (P. 12.) He doesn't shy away from "Prison slang, the jargon arising out of the drug scene, prostitute and pimp parlance, the gambling and numbers racket lingo," giving us entries like *horse*, "heroin"; *trick*, "a prostitute's customer or the transaction itself"; and *roust*, "to be harassed, especially by the police."

Pronunciations and etymologies are few, but historical, geographical, and usage information features in many entries. Most words come with dates of currency—*loot*, "(1930's–40's) money; cash"—and some come with indications of range—*pad of stiffs*, "a funeral parlor (Southern Negro college student use)."

Nearly a quarter-century after this edition, Major returned to the subject and produced *Juba to Jive: A Dictionary of African-American Slang* (1994), a much-expanded version. Still the focus is on slang. Only now is a large-scale scholarly dictionary of the distinctive features of broader African American usage—the *Oxford Dictionary of African American English* (no. 132), with Henry Louis Gates Jr. as editor in chief—underway.

119

Bruce Rodgers

An Unapologetic Look at LGBTQ Lingo

Rodgers, Bruce. *The Queens' Vernacular: A Gay Lexicon*. San Francisco: Straight Arrow Books, 1972.

Ex coll. Jack Lynch

BRUCE RODGERS (1942–2009) had no formal training in lexicography, but an "early fondness for philology" prompted him to imagine "a book recording the street poetry of queens, those lively stereotypes forming yet another subculture within the homosexual minority."

After completing high school in Wisconsin, junior college in California, and a bachelor's degree at the University of Southern Nevada in 1963, Rodgers worked as a teletype operator in several newsrooms. His passion, though, was the languages of subcultures, which led him to acquire some degree of proficiency "in Spanish, French, Judeo-Spanish, . . . Hebrew, . . . Japanese, Chinese, Russian, Italian, German, and Turkish."

By the late 1960s, he had settled on his plan to write a serious and learned dictionary of the language used by and about gays and lesbians. He was not the first to catalogue the language of the LGBTQ community, but he was the first to do so at book length and the first openly gay writer to do it. He insisted that his personal immersion in gay culture made him uniquely qualified for the task, which had until then been undertaken only by outsiders:

> Previously gay slang has been explored only in slight, dated glossaries or in booklets, not much more than glossaries themselves. I found that many entries were faulty simply because the authors, too far removed from the gays' community, didn't really know what they were hearing; they weren't using slang themselves and so were simply wrong.

The result was *The Queens' Vernacular*, issued late in 1972 by Straight Arrow Press, a San Francisco–based publisher that had recently made a splash with the magazine *Rolling Stone* and was taking on a number of projects related to the hippie counterculture. As

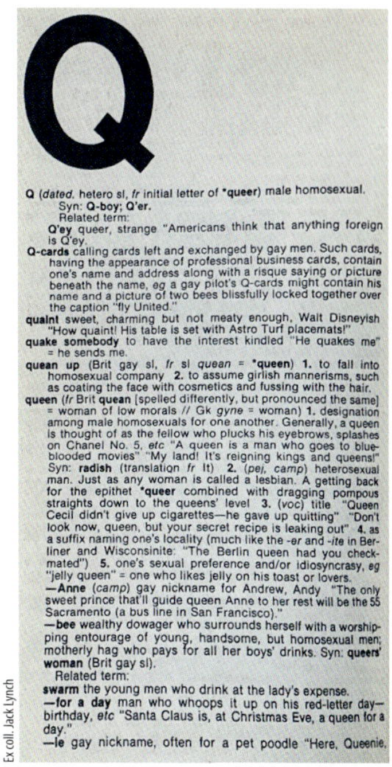

Q

Q (*dated.* hetero sl, *fr* initial letter of ***queer**) male homosexual.
Syn: **Q-boy; Q'er.**
Related term:
Q'ey queer, strange "Americans think that anything foreign is Q'ey."
Q-cards calling cards left and exchanged by gay men. Such cards, having the appearance of professional business cards, contain one's name and address along with a risque saying or picture beneath the name, *eg* a gay pilot's Q-cards might contain his name and a picture of two bees blissfully locked together over the caption "fly United."
quaint sweet, charming but not meaty enough, Walt Disneyish "How quaint! His table is set with Astro Turf placemats!"
quake somebody to have the interest kindled "He quakes me" = he sends me.
quean up (Brit gay sl, *fr* sl *quean* = ***queen**) **1.** to fall into homosexual company **2.** to assume girlish mannerisms, such as coating the face with cosmetics and fussing with the hair.
queen (*fr* Brit **quean** [spelled differently, but pronounced the same] = woman of low morals // Gk *gyne* = woman) **1.** designation among male homosexuals for one another. Generally, a queen is thought of as the fellow who plucks his eyebrows, splashes on Chanel No. 5, *etc* "A queen is a man who goes to blue-blooded movies" "My land! It's reigning kings and queens!" Syn: **radish** (translation *fr* It) **2.** (*pej, camp*) heterosexual man. Just as any woman is called a lesbian. A getting back for the epithet ***queer** combined with dragging pompous straights down to the queens' level **3.** (*voc*) title "Queen Cecil didn't give up cigarettes—he gave up quitting" "Don't look now, queen, but your secret recipe is leaking out" **4.** as a suffix naming one's locality (much like the *-er* and *-ite* in Berliner and Wisconsinite: "The Berlin queen had you checkmated") **5.** one's sexual preference and/or idiosyncrasy, *eg* "jelly queen" = one who likes jelly on his toast or lovers.
—Anne (*camp*) gay nickname for Andrew, Andy "The only sweet prince that'll guide queen Anne to her rest will be the 55 Sacramento (a bus line in San Francisco)."
—bee wealthy dowager who surrounds herself with a worshipping entourage of young, handsome, but homosexual men; motherly hag who pays for all her boys' drinks. Syn: **queers' woman** (Brit gay sl).
Related term:
swarm the young men who drink at the lady's expense.
—for a day man who whoops it up on his red-letter day—birthday, *etc* "Santa Claus is, at Christmas Eve, a queen for a day."
—ie gay nickname, often for a pet poodle "Here, Queenie,

Ex coll. Jack Lynch

a book intended for a popular audience rather than scholarly libraries, it was released as an inexpensive paperback (MSRP $3.50) with a bright lavender cover, the color associated with gay rights before the LGBTQ Pride Flag's rainbow edged it out.

"In essence, this is the book of my childhood. My early fondness for philology led me to conceive a book recording the street poetry of queens, those lively stereotypes forming yet another subculture within the homosexual minority." (Preface, p. 11.)

Rodgers links himself to a long tradition of cant lexicography by describing his book as "a dictionary of homophile cant." (P. 11.) The vocabulary ranges widely, covering both terms familiar today (*beard*, "a woman who dates homosexual men to help them socially"; *closet case*, "homosexual who denies his sexual longings") and long-forgotten ephemera (*missiletoes*, "attractive astronauts"). Entries come with grim reminders that being visibly gay in 1972 was risky business: some definitions describe the dangers of arrest (the *police* are supposed to be "crime-fighters paid to protect us from each other (muggers, rapists, etc.) and *not* from ourselves"), and others describe the risk of violence, such as *four doors*, "carload of young men intent upon finding and beating a gay boy." Slang, he understood, was shared among oppressed subcultures; it

> is social protest, used to deflate the hypocrisy of nice-sounding labels that mean nothing to the people who use them. Slang is also the expression of the underdog—it is always aimed against the establishment. Because the people who use slang words most frequently in their everyday speech are the economically oppressed—blacks, chicanos, hippies, ex-convicts, prostitutes—slang also records their desire to obtain what they do not have.

"Slang flourishes in the ghetto. Those who struggle to leave the ghetto shake off its language first and then decry its message. Slang is secretive, a form of protest and an expression of social recognition." (Preface, p. 11.)

Because much of his evidence was spoken rather than written, Rodgers was unable to date many words precisely, and his quotations are mostly invented rather than discovered in print. He was, however, careful to document as much as possible about every word's origin: a note like "*kwn* LV, mid '60s" indicates that he had evidence that a word was known in Las Vegas in the mid-1960s.

Rodgers disavowed any intention "to shock or anger," but he was not concerned with making the straight world comfortable. Sex acts are described in graphic detail and blunt language, and many of his entries could not have appeared in print before the landmark First Amendment cases of the 1960s. This bluntness was by design: earlier glossaries of gay language, he complained, "would even label some words as vulgarisms, 'best left undefined.'" Not for him. "Linguistically," he insisted, "the book is nonapologetic."

The publisher freely admitted that Rodgers was a lexicographic amateur—"This book is not 'scientific' or 'scholarly' in the academic sense; nor is it definitive or objective"—and Rodgers's lack of lexicographic experience sometimes led him astray. Though he promised global coverage and included a decent number of British, Irish, Australian, and South African examples, American usage dominated. Gay men are much better represented than lesbians, and bisexuals are close to invisible. The definitions are sometimes more witty than accurate, and some, like the very long one for *camp*, are personal essays rather than dictionary entries. Some lexicographic pros expressed reservations about the book. Robert Burchfield, then editor of the *Oxford English Dictionary*, gave the book a mostly sympathetic *New York Times* review, but complained that "the canons of etymology are treated with something approaching disdain." But it remains a pioneering work, and without Rodgers we would have lost one of our most thorough attempts to document the language of a ubiquitous but largely invisible subculture.

"The principal aim of this book is to make available a dictionary of homophile cant." (Preface, p. 11.)

Publishing a "gay dictionary" in 1972 was an act of courage. *The Queens' Vernacular* appeared just three years after the Stonewall uprising, when homosexuality was still listed in the *Diagnostic and Statistical Manual of Mental Disorders* as "sexual deviation." Hardly any public figures were out, and sex acts between same-sex partners were still felonies in 46 of the 50 states. Rodgers carried out his research because he believed that "Gay slang, like black slang, enriches our language immeasurably," and that "'Camp,' 'straight,' and 'vibrations' were once solely gay inventions that are today part of every hip vocabulary."

"It is the result of years of interviews with hundreds of informants whom Bruce Rodgers sought out in bars, steam baths, dance halls, public johns and on street corners. He did not have at his disposal a team of field workers or researchers or editors, nor did he have a foundation grant to underwrite his labors. He had only his own energy and uncommon zeal. This book is the impressive result." (Note from Douglas Mount, the publisher, p. 9.)

Rodgers died from complications of Parkinson's in August 2009. His papers, including materials for a never-published revised edition of *The Queen's Vernacular*, were acquired by the GLBT Historical Society in San Francisco.

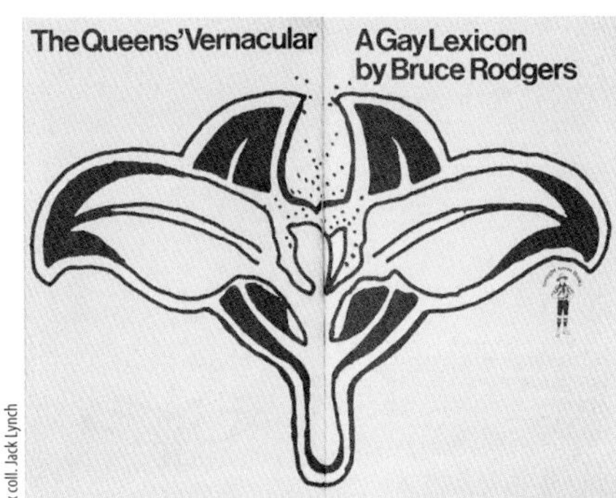

Ex coll. Jack Lynch

Photo by Francine Winham

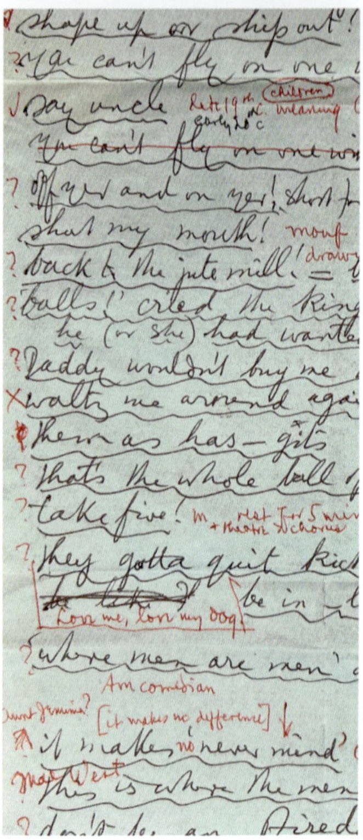

Ex coll. Karolyne & Bryan A. Garner

Detail from the list of queries that Partridge sent to Shipley on 7 July 1975. The red ink is Shipley's.

120

Two Coveys of Partridge

Thirty-three letters and postcards (1961–1977) exchanged between two lexicographers, Eric Partridge and Joseph T. Shipley. (Part of the Garner Collection.)

Two letters and two postcards (1974–1979) sent by Eric Partridge to the London publisher Philip Dossé. (Part of the Garner Collection.)

THE LEXICOGRAPHER ERIC PARTRIDGE's letters reside in various archives, from the University of San Francisco to the British Library to King's College, London, to the University of Birmingham. The Garner Collection possesses 40 autograph letters (beginning in 1929) and some 24 inscribed books (as early as 1927). Two sets of letters—to Shipley and to Dossé—are of special interest.

Eric Partridge (1894–1979) and Joseph T. Shipley (1893–1988) exchanged letters and postcards during the last 18 years of Partridge's life. Partridge praised Shipley throughout but, even though Shipley had written two dictionaries, seemed to regard him as an amateur—an exceedingly helpful one. Shipley was an "aficionado," as he wrote in his Christmas 1975 card. Much of the time, Partridge was working on his final book, *A Dictionary of Catchphrases* (1979), for which he was constantly seeking data from this American informant. The words in square brackets here are Shipley's:

7 July 1975

Dear Joseph,

An American pen friend—a Colonel of Marines, inevitably less familiar with c.pp. than you are—has sent me two bare lists of what he thinks may be eligible phrases. I've selected the genuine and the potential (my ignorance) c.pp. for your *very* brief comment, set forth, if you wish, in tabulated form:—

Phrases//Sense, if necessary//Date or Period, approx. //Milieu & if any, yr comment

& 'Unknown to me'

I list 'em in any order, or none, as they come:—

who struck (or hit) Billy Pat(t)erson?[?]
we have met the enemy—and they is us [Am. comedian]
shape up or ship out! [marine]
you can't fly one wing [come in on a wing & after WW song]
say uncle early 20c [late 19th children meaning ask for mercy/ me to let up (e.g. twisting arm behind back, etc.]
off yer and on yer! short for *off your fanny and on your feet!* [marine]
shut my mouth! [mouf negro/after having said too much or wrong thing]
back to the jute mill! = back to the salt mines!
balls! cried the king (or *queen*) *because he* (or *she*) *had wanted to* (or *two*)
Daddy wouldn't buy me a bow-wow
waltz me around again, Willie [Title & begins popular song early 20th c.]
them as has—gits
that's the whole ball of wax [that's the way the cookie crumbles / that's the way things are / too bad, but]
take five! [in rest for 5 minutes + theatre & chorus]
they gotta quit kicking my dog around [love me, love my dog]
be in like Flynn <? c.p. or a 'free' slang phrase>
where men are men and women are {glad of it; like it; are double-breasted} [Am. comedian]
it makes no never mind [Aunt Jemima? it makes no difference "it makes no never mind" children of 1930s white & negro]
This is where the mean are separated from the top [Mae West]
don't be an Airedale [Euphemism (bitch!)]
stewed, screwed and tattooed [Marine]
or *screwed, blewed* <? blued> *and tattooed*
(go) see the chaplain [M]
Sorry! This is a rather formidable list. I sha'n't feel in the least offended if you decline.

Yours ever,

Eric

In a missive later that year, Partridge (Ep) begins with the query: "What would 'Ep' do without 'Ship'? Otiose question. Otiose Answer: 'He'd come off rather badly.'" Then he posed more questions.

The letters to Philip Dossé, the London publisher who founded the literary magazine *Books and Bookman* (printed from 1959 to 1986),

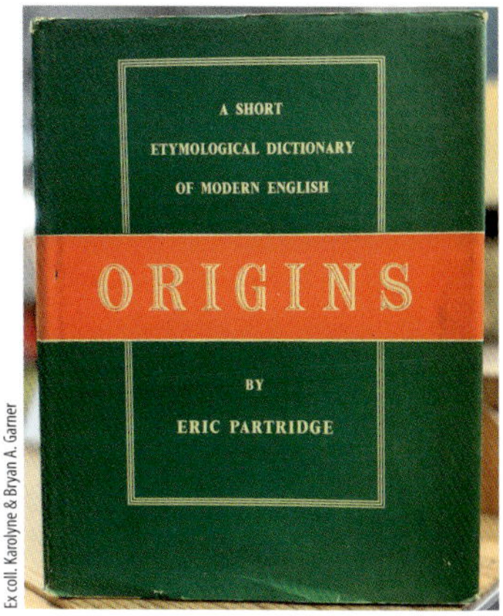

Ex coll. Karolyne & Bryan A. Garner

Partridge's book on etymology (1958).

"That I should early have acquired a taste for the origins and histories of words and phrases was probably inevitable, for even as a young child I possessed an uncomfortably inquisitive mind. That it should have taken me some thirty years to transcend the stage of the purest amateurism was perhaps equally inevitable, for both education and a strong inclination long kept me on a literary rather than a linguistic course." (Partridge 1963:85–86.)

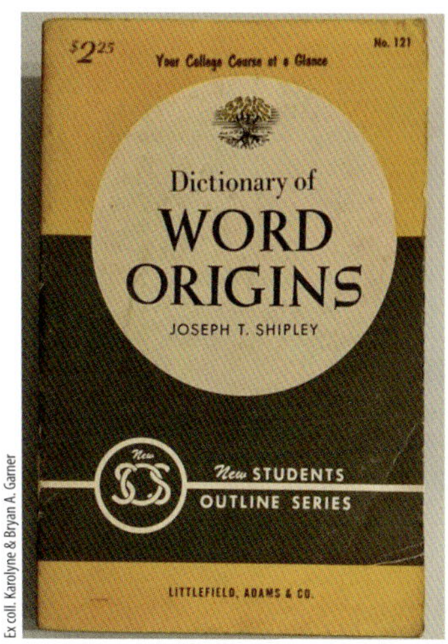

Ex coll. Karolyne & Bryan A. Garner

Shipley's book on etymology (1943).

are among the last that he wrote. The first substantial letter to Dossé came in September 1977, the month before Partridge's correspondence with Shipley came to an end. Dossé had apparently suggested putting Partridge's name forward for a knighthood or other honor, given his significant contributions to English letters. Charmingly, Partridge declined:

> I very much appreciate what you say about my work. But, truly, I don't *want* any honours. Some ten years ago, I declined one—& I remain of the same opinion, my attitude being that a scholar-writer should be prepared to stand or fall by his work. This doesn't imply any adverse criticism of those who accept honours; they may have the most praiseworthy reasons for doing so. And I'm profoundly grateful to you (& several others) for putting my name forward. Also, conversely, I 'feel a heel'—churlish—ungracious—for having, unwittingly, caused you embarrassment & unnecessary waste of time. Please forgive me.

"In short, every adventure of the mind is an adventure vehicle by words. Every adventure of the mind is an adventure *with* words; every such adventure is an adventure *among* words; and occasionally an adventure is an adventure *of* words. It is no exaggeration to say that, in every word of every language—every single word or phrase of every language, however primitive or rudimentary or fragmentarily recorded, and whether living or dead—we discover an enlightening, sometimes a rather frightening, vignette of history." (Partridge 1980:37.)

On the back of this letter, below Partridge's return address, appears this mysterious postscript: "I prefer to let the matter of that journalist be forgotten, *please*."

By 1979, Partridge's health had begun failing. He was living in a grand Tudor house in Moretonhampstead, Devon, called Holcombe Court. It is a poignant letter, especially when read with the knowledge that Partridge would live barely a month longer:

> Dear Mr. Dossé,
>
> It is rare that one encounters a sympathy so rare as yours, bless you!
>
> It's final. I'm bound to stay in this home for the rest of my working life—except that there's to be no more working life.
>
> I've made the necessary arrangements for the completion of my two main jobs: *A Dictionary of Slang* & [*A Dictionary of*] *Catch Phrases* by amicable & practicable treaty with publisher, a very knowledge [sic] friend & self.
>
> And I've entrusted the over-all direction & guidance of my livelihood to my excellent friend, my solicitor.
>
> So I've done what I can.
>
> Thank you again for your good wishes & concern.

"Near the end of a not too dull life, Albert Jay Nock proclaimed: 'As sheer casual reading-matter, I still find the English dictionary the most interesting book in the language': and that's as it should be, for what is more fundamental than, what so indispensable as, a dictionary?" (Partridge 1963:14.)

(No need, of course, to answer this scrappy letter.)
Yours with kindest regards,
with best wishes,
Eric Partridge

Partridge did live to see his *Dictionary of Catch Phrases* appear—it had first been published in 1977. He had issued a corrected version in 1978, and the book was reprinted about the time of his death. In fact, Partridge created the category: since his time, dictionaries of catchphrases (the term is now generally solidified) have appeared under the imprints of Oxford University Press, Cassell, Chambers, MacFarland, and Routledge.

But this innovation was only one of his *many* contributions to the world of dictionaries. These are delightfully explored in two books: his own *The Gentle Art of Lexicography as Pursued and Experienced by an Addict* (1963) and the posthumous anthology edited by David Crystal, *Eric Partridge in His Own Words* (1980). The latter includes worthy appreciations by Crystal, Anthony Burgess, and Randolph Quirk. As Crystal, who had never met Partridge personally, observed about preparing the volume: "I was quite unprepared for the enormous range and variety of his output. . . . For Partridge, language was a key to our understanding of civilization—its present social structure and its history." Partridge, he asserted, was "always informative, lucid, entertaining, and only occasionally repetitive. . . . The scope of his work was at once macrolinguistic, in its focus on universal themes, and microlinguistic, in its concentration on language detail." (Crystal 1980:11.)

"Why is it that most [people] are so incoherent, long-winded, rambling? Because they have not thought out what they wish to say, much less the order in which to say it, still less the way in which to say it. When they come to write about it, in a letter to a friend or in an essay at school, they have the time, both to plan their letter or their essay before they start and to work out the details as they go along. Even then the results are often rather dreadful, not because they could not do any better but because they have prevented themselves from doing better. They will not go to the trouble of thinking." (Partridge 1957 2:9.)

"Letter-writing can . . . be . . . an art. Too often it is a disgrace. But if you cannot achieve artistry—so few of us do—you can at least be natural. Indeed, naturalness is, here, more important than art. But to be natural is not the same thing as being uncouth. You don't go to church in clothes a tramp would spurn: to a friend, a relative, you write with some regard for his eyesight, his feelings, his intelligence. So, too, if you are writing to a friendly acquaintance." (Partridge 1957 1:160.)

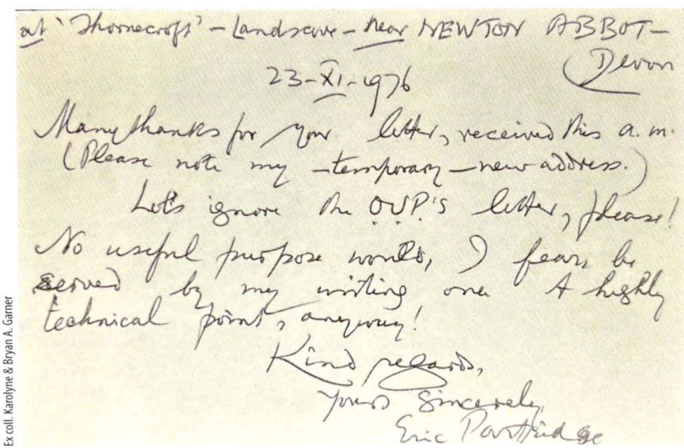
at 'Thornecroft' – Landscove – near NEWTON ABBOT – Devon
23-XI-1976
Many thanks for your letter, received this a.m.
(Please note my – temporary – new address.)
Let's ignore the OUP's letter, please!
No useful purpose would, I fear, be served by my writing one. A highly technical point, anyway!
Kind regards,
Yours sincerely,
Eric Partridge

Ex coll. Karolyne & Bryan A. Garner

An early postcard to Dossé.

121

Jargon File

The Birth of Cyberspeak

Steele, Guy L., Raphael Finkel, Donald Woods, and Mark Crispin. "Computer Slang." In *CoEvolution Quarterly* 29:26–35 (1981).

Raphael Finkel.

Ex coll. Jack Lynch

THE COORDINATED COOPERATION of far-flung volunteers—what we now call crowdsourcing—has been a part of lexicography for generations. The *Oxford English Dictionary*, for instance, has for a century and a half depended on volunteers who gather material from around the world and submit it to the editorial team in Oxford. But the 1970s gave us something new: a crowdsourced dictionary with no editor or publisher.

Computer enthusiasts have long constituted a subculture with their own ways of speaking, but no one thought to record their distinctive language until 1975. That's when Raphael Finkel (b. 1951), a doctoral student at Stanford, imagined a just-for-fun project to occupy his spare moments. With friends and colleagues he collected the lingo of the computer lab in a computer text file nicknamed "The Jargon File."

Soon they shared it with friends by transferring it over ARPANET, the progenitor of today's Internet, which at that time consisted of a few dozen computers at major research universities. Each time it went from one lab to another, it grew and mutated. The file—which, as far as we know, no one ever bothered to print out—bounced around computer networks for a decade, always growing and changing.

The Jargon File was intended as a lark, and no one in the 1970s thought it worth preserving. We therefore have no copies of its earliest forms. But in 1981, *CoEvolution Quarterly*, a spinoff from *The Whole Earth Catalog*, published brief selections. And in 1983, as computers began appearing in homes, a much-expanded version appeared as *The Hacker's Dictionary*, edited by Guy Steele and promising "A Guide to the World of Computer Wizards . . . HackSpeak and Body Language, Computer Lifestyles and more."

Some of the jargon remains opaque to nonspecialists—*PDL*, for instance, is "A LIFO queue (stack)"—but much of it is playful, as with *frobnicate* "To manipulate or adjust," *glork* "Term of mild surprise," and *gronk* "To clear the state of a wedged device and restart it." Some of these terms were "used to save typing," like *BCNU* ("be seeing you") and *BTW* ("by the way"), anticipating today's *LOL* and *c u l8r*. And a few terms from that era have remained in general use, including the Yiddish-derived *glitch* "A sudden interruption in electric service, sanity, or program function."

things, a crock. Of people, somewhere in between a turkey and a toad. 4. Jake Brown (FRG@SAIL). 5. FROGGY: *adj.* Similar to BAGBITING (q.v.), but milder. "This froggy program is taking forever to run!"

GLITCH [from the Yiddish "glitshen," to slide] 1. *n.* A sudden interruption in electric service, sanity, or program function. Sometimes recoverable. 2. *v.* (Stanford) To scroll a display screen.

GLORK 1. *interj.* Term of mild surprise, usually tinged with outrage, as when one attempts to save the results of two hours of editing and finds that the system has just crashed. 2. Used as a name for just about anything. See FOO. 3. *v.* Similar to GLITCH (q.v.), but usually used reflexively. "My program just glorked itself."

GRONK [popularized by the cartoon strip "B.C." by Johnny Hart, but the word apparently predates that] *v.* 1. To clear the state of a wedged device and restart it. More severe than "to frob" (q.v.). 2. To break. "The teletype scanner was gronked, so we took the system down." 3. GRONKED: *adj.* Of people, the condition of feeling very tired or sick. 4. GRONK OUT: *v.* To cease functioning. Of people, to go home and go to sleep. "I guess I'll gronk out now; see you all tomorrow."

GROVEL *v.* To work interminably and without apparent progress. Often used with "over." "The compiler grovelled over my code." Compare CRUNCH. Emphatic form: GROVEL OBSCENELY.

HACK *n.* 1. Originally a quick job that produces what is needed, but not well. 2. The result of that job. 3. NEAT HACK: A clever technique. Also, a brilliant practical joke, where neatness is correlated with cleverness, harmlessness, and surprise value. Example: the Caltech Rose Bowl card display switch circa 1961. 4. REAL HACK: A crock (occasionally affectionate). *v.* 5. With "together," to throw something together so it will work. 6. To bear emotionally or physically. "I can't hack this heat!" 7. To

Ex coll. Jack Lynch

The first published selections for the now-legendary Jargon File.

Ex coll. Jack Lynch

The Jargon File made its first appearance in this spinoff from *The Whole Earth Catalog*.

"All nouns can be verbed. E.g.: 'All nouns can be verbed', 'I'll mouse it up', 'Hang on while I clipboard it over', 'I'm grepping the files'. English as a whole is already heading in this direction . . . . Hackers are simply a bit ahead of the curve." (Anon., from the 2000 version of the Jargon File.)

122

American Regional English
DARE We Compile It?

A Dictionary of American Regional English. Frederic G. Cassidy & Joan Houston Hall eds. 5 vols. Cambridge: Belknap Press. Vol. 1, 1985; vol. 2, 1991; vol. 3, 1996; vol. 4, 2002; vol. 5, 2012; vol. 6, 2012.

Photo courtesy of AP Newsfeatures

Frederic G. Cassidy.

"Cassidy, DARE's chief editor, oversees a staff of sixteen. He became eighty-one in 1989 and is lively, articulate, and helpful as ever: 'I'm in a race with this dictionary, to see who finishes first.'" (Safire 1990:94.)

In the mid-19th century, the heyday for the study of British dialects (see no. 112), Victorian philologists began paying attention to English in its many varieties. The surge in interest culminated in one of the great lexicographic projects, Joseph Wright's *English Dialect Dictionary*, which began its work in 1889 and published its sixth and final volume in 1905.

Across the Atlantic, where people were eager for the same sort of comprehensive dictionary, the American Dialect Society was founded in 1889 to promote "the investigation of the English Dialects of America with regard to pronunciation, grammar, vocabulary, phraseology, and geographical distribution." (1:xi.) The society's members collected material for decades, publishing short reports in the society's journal, *Dialect Notes*. But no larger publication came of it. Seventeen years into the project, the editor, William Mead, lamented that the work was "fragmentary in the extreme" and amounted to only about 5% of what they would need to produce an American rival to the *English Dialect Dictionary*.

The work continued, producing useful journal articles but making no progress on a dictionary until Frederic G. Cassidy took over in 1962. Cassidy (1907–2000), a Jamaican-born linguist, was educated at Oberlin and the University of Michigan before becoming a professor of linguistics at Michigan. He and his team—Allen Walker Read and James B. McMillan, both of whom had worked with Mitford Mathews on *A Dictionary of Americanisms on Historical Principles* (see no. 101)—developed the policies and principles that would guide the project.

It's notoriously difficult to collect nonstandard varieties of English, especially varieties that are not captured in print. Johnson and Webster could collect their materials from their armchairs. Murray called on an army of volunteers for the *OED*, but because all their evidence was written, the work could be done in the comparative comfort of libraries. But regionalisms are another matter: they are rarely committed to print. Under Cassidy's leadership, therefore, from 1965 to 1970 the dozens of members of the *DARE* team, usually armed with tape recorders, conducted face-to-face interviews with more than 2,500 people spread out over more than a thousand communities. They supplemented the fieldwork with written evidence for other regionalisms.

"The history of the *Dictionary of American Regional English (DARE)* goes back almost a hundred years, to the founding in 1889 of its sponsoring body, the American Dialect Society." (1:xi.)

The focus is not on slang or vulgarisms but on everyday things like frying pans, dragonflies, children's games, sudden rainstorms, and noisy eaters. The volunteers brought with them a questionnaire of 1,847 questions—question N6, "An old car that has been fixed up to make it go fast or make a lot of noise"; question Y38n, "Mixed together, confused: 'The things in the drawer are all ______'"; question BB61b, "Any joking names for a cemetery?"—and put them to people of all ages, professions, races, religions, and ethnicities, recording everything that was reported to them. In the end, 504 workers, funded by more than 2,000 donors, collected 2.3 million pieces of information from 4,459 people. They then took this mountain of evidence and, with the aid of some nascent digital tools, synthesized the results.

Ex coll. Karolyne & Bryan A. Garner

This entry is typical of the dictionary, here without its supporting quotations:

> **cooter** n, also attrib Usu |ˈkutə(r)|; in coastal SC and GA, |ˈkutə| Pronc-spp *coota, cootuh* [Afr, akin to Bambara, Malinké *kuta* turtle; also Central Afr *nkudu*; cf *DA*] **chiefly S Atl, Gulf States, esp SC** Cf **alligator cooter, box cooter, coodle** n[1], **cow-dung cooter, hard-backed cooter**
>
> 1 A freshwater turtle of the genus *Chrysemys*, found chiefly in the eastern part of the US. chiefly S Atl, Gulf States, esp SC See Map Also called **slider** For other names of var spp see **hard-shell cooter, neat turtle, soft-shell cooter**

"To attempt a work of the scope of *DARE* is to give hostages to imperfection. The task of covering all the regional variation in American English is beyond human accomplishment. Compromise is inescapable. . . . Editors have spent days, months, and even years in tracking down individual items, correcting bibliographic references, finding original editions, establishing correct authorship, dates, pagination, the exact wording and spelling of entries—only to have the findings condensed into a few inconspicuous lines no different, in appearance, from the easy and obvious entries." (1:xxii.)

Precisely defined usage notes and regional descriptors indicate the register and the geographic spread of most terms. Extensive cross-references allow users to see a variety of alternatives to a given term: *corn pone*, for instance, is also *cornmeal pone*, *corn pone bread*, *corn pony*, *ashcake*, *corn bread*, *corn cake*, *corn dodger*, and *johnnycake*. Many entries are accompanied by stylized maps of the Continental United

States—distorted to give more area to the more populated states—with dots indicating the terms used in each region. On the few occasions when they suspected that their sources might have been pulling their legs—does anyone actually use *Mexican twala-twala* to refer to a bird that "flies backwards to see only where it's been"?—they prudently used a double dagger (‡) to flag "a word or sense of questionable genuineness." (1:clxvi.)

"In *DARE* the editors have sought to produce a work of useful scholarship, one also that will testify to the wondrous variety and creativeness of human language, and specifically of the English language as it is used regionally in the United States. To this task they have given many years, much thought, and much hope. May *DARE* prove a worthy monument to their labors." (1: xxii.)

They were clear, though, that it was not their job to clean up the racier parts of the language. "There has been no bowdlerizing or expurgation," they insisted, invoking "the story of the ladies who commended Dr. Johnson for omitting from his Dictionary all naughty words. 'What, my dears!' replied the Doctor, 'then you have been looking for them?' If the reader sets out to look for them, he will certainly find in *DARE* the normal vulgarities and crudenesses of everyday American speech." (Introduction, 1:xvii–xviii)

The first volume, covering *A–C*, appeared in 1985; *D–H* followed six years later, with another editor sharing the masthead: Joan Houston Hall (b. 1950). Cassidy and Hall worked together on *I–O*, published in 1996, but Cassidy did not live to see volume 4—Hall published *P–Sk* in 2002, *Sl–Z* in 2012, and a sixth volume devoted to "Contrastive Maps, Index to Entry Labels, Questionnaire, and Fieldwork Data" in 2012. A digital version of the entire thing was completed in 2013.

"The Jamaican-born Cassidy, who died on June 14, 2000, at 92 while still hard at work on the final volumes of his great dictionary, never snibbed anybody. Though an intensely purposeful scholar, he was a gentle soul whose love of the dialects and colorful metaphors of the American language was contagious. I have been an unabashed *shill* (slang origin in 'gambler's decoy,' now meaning 'pitchman') for the University of Wisconsin's DARE for nearly two decades because Fred's organized wonderment made me a believer." (Safire 2001:ix.)

The reviews were uniformly enthusiastic, with praise not only from linguists but also from historians, folklorists, even botanists. It got a shout-out from a forensic linguist who used its evidence to identify kidnappers from their ransom notes and track down the Unabomber on the basis of his manifesto. (Shuy 2001:2–3.) William Safire called *DARE* "the most exciting new linguistic project in the twentieth century" (Safire 2008:xxii); John Algeo praised it for "a popular appeal unmatched by any other academic wordbook in our time" (Algeo 1993:140); and Frank Abate praised it as "the greatest achievement in American lexicography in the past 50 years" (Abate 2012:245). Michael Adams spoke for many lexicographers when he called for "an ongoing project" that "could follow regional lexis generation by generation." (Adams 2013:178.) But it was not to be. Grant money ran out with the publication of the digital edition in 2013, and there is no ongoing research project to keep the dictionary up to date.

123

Kramarae & Treichler

Women's Intellectual, Emotional, Editorial, and Clerical Contributions

Kramarae, Cheris, and Paula Treichler, with the assistance of Ann Russo. *A Feminist Dictionary*. Boston: Pandora Press, 1985.

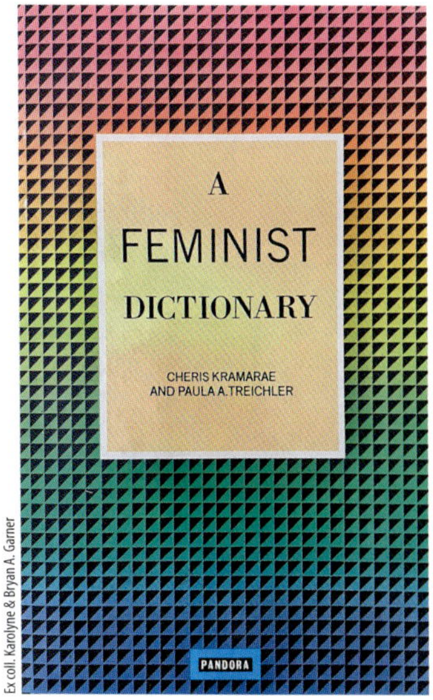

Ex coll. Karolyne & Bryan A. Garner

IF THE PUBLISHING BUSINESS has always been dominated by men, that's especially true in the reference field. In the early 1980s, two scholars set about redressing that imbalance: Cheris Kramarae (b. 1938), a professor of communications and women's studies, and Paula Treichler (b. 1943), a professor of medicine, communication, and women's studies. They traced a tradition of feminist lexicography back to Elizabeth Cady Stanton in the 19th century, culminating in several works in the 1970s such as Ruth Todasco's *Intelligent Woman's Guide to Dirty Words* (1973) and Midge Lennert and Norma Willson's *Woman's New World Dictionary* (1973). This was the tradition in which they very intentionally placed themselves.

"We chose for inclusion, out of the centuries of women's explanations of the world, those statements which have been especially important for the women's movement." (Preface, p. 16.)

If *A Feminist Dictionary* doesn't look much like other dictionaries, that's because it's an avowed polemic rather than a work of practical lexicography. One archivist who helped the authors described it as "sort of a cross between the *OED* and the Whole Earth Catalog!" (p. 14), which captures the spirit of the enterprise well. The large majority of the headwords are nouns, more characteristic of an encyclopedia than a dictionary. Kramarae and Treichler use the form of the dictionary to get readers to question the ideology behind ostensibly neutral and objective reference books, "constructed almost entirely by men with male readers and users in mind." (P. 7.) Readers are asked to acknowledge that "the systematic—even when inadvertent—exclusion of one sex replicates and preserves the linguistic and cultural rule of the other." (P. 3.)

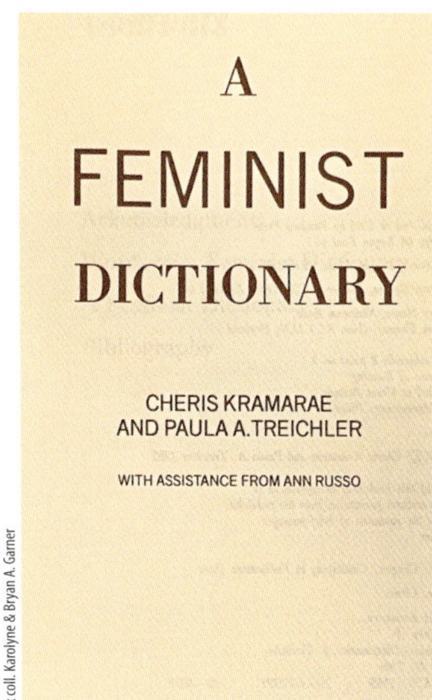

Ex coll. Karolyne & Bryan A. Garner

Many of the book's 2,500 entries are terms that we would expect in *A Feminist Dictionary*: *abortion*, *birth control*, *child support*, *chivalry*, *coeducation*, *divorce*, *housewife*, *lesbian*, *pornography*, *prostitution*,

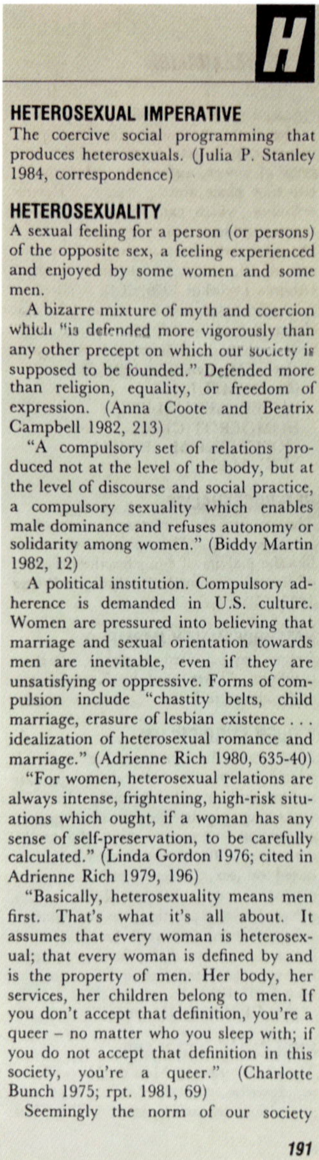

H

HETEROSEXUAL IMPERATIVE
The coercive social programming that produces heterosexuals. (Julia P. Stanley 1984, correspondence)

HETEROSEXUALITY
A sexual feeling for a person (or persons) of the opposite sex, a feeling experienced and enjoyed by some women and some men.
A bizarre mixture of myth and coercion which "is defended more vigorously than any other precept on which our society is supposed to be founded." Defended more than religion, equality, or freedom of expression. (Anna Coote and Beatrix Campbell 1982, 213)
"A compulsory set of relations produced not at the level of the body, but at the level of discourse and social practice, a compulsory sexuality which enables male dominance and refuses autonomy or solidarity among women." (Biddy Martin 1982, 12)
A political institution. Compulsory adherence is demanded in U.S. culture. Women are pressured into believing that marriage and sexual orientation towards men are inevitable, even if they are unsatisfying or oppressive. Forms of compulsion include "chastity belts, child marriage, erasure of lesbian existence . . . idealization of heterosexual romance and marriage." (Adrienne Rich 1980, 635-40)
"For women, heterosexual relations are always intense, frightening, high-risk situations which ought, if a woman has any sense of self-preservation, to be carefully calculated." (Linda Gordon 1976; cited in Adrienne Rich 1979, 196)
"Basically, heterosexuality means men first. That's what it's all about. It assumes that every woman is heterosexual; that every woman is defined by and is the property of men. Her body, her services, her children belong to men. If you don't accept that definition, you're a queer – no matter who you sleep with; if you do not accept that definition in this society, you're a queer." (Charlotte Bunch 1975; rpt. 1981, 69)
Seemingly the norm of our society

191

Ex coll. Karolyne & Bryan A. Garner

The copy in the Garner Collection was once the property of a middle school in Charlotte, North Carolina. The book, which teems with taboo words, bears no indicia of when or why it was withdrawn.

reproductive freedom, *suffragette*, *virginity*, and *wife*. Other entries, though, have no obvious connection to feminism beyond progressive politics: *ableism*, *Black*, *capitalism*, *ethnocentrism*. There are almost no pronunciations or etymologies, and the definitions are distinctly unconventional. Some pointedly redefine familiar terms, as when the authors gloss *B.C.* as "Before Consciousness" and *A.D.* as "After Defiance." Some are earnest but then-controversial suggestions for nonsexist usage, as with *chair*: "a label which is an obvious solution to the problem caused by *chairman*, a sex-specific word." Some are simply zingers, like *Eve*: "The brave one in the biblical story." And some are mini-essays inspired by the headword, as with *acknowledgments*:

> Before feminism, that portion of a book where authors acknowledged the ideas and intellectual contributions of males and the clerical and editorial assistance of females and where men thanked their wives for critically reading their manuscripts without asking for co-authorship. After feminism, the place where women authors often acknowledge the intellectual, emotional, editorial, and clerical contributions of women and sometimes of men.

One reviewer pointed out that the contributors display "wit and humor, and utter seriousness, throughout the book." (Nichols 1988:601.) On occasion, though, they drop the good humor and demand that we reckon with ugly facts. *Casanova*, for instance, is "an Italian (1725–98) named in traditional dictionaries as an 'amorous adventurer,' 'romantic' and 'libertine.' In writing about his sex life Casanova boasted of seducing children." As one hears on social media, that got dark fast.

Dictionaries compiled by men are always under implicit critique, but sometimes the criticism is front and center. The definition of *dictionary* itself reads:

> A dictionary is a word-book which collects somebody's words into somebody's book. Whose words are collected, and how they are collected, and who collects them all influence what kind of book a given dictionary turns out to be and, in turn, whose purpose it can best serve. Though thousands of dictionaries exist for many different purposes, men have edited or written virtually all of them.

And they're not afraid to name names. The culturally conservative *American Heritage Dictionary* (no. 104) notoriously defined *feminism* as "militant advocacy of equal rights and status for women." Kramarae and Treichler fired back, saying that it "contains many instances of sexist usage." (P. 45.)

A second edition appeared in 1992 as *Amazons, Bluestockings, and Crones: A Feminist Dictionary*. Although neither edition is of much practical use as dictionary, both capture the spirit of second-wave feminism at its height.

Ex coll. Karolyne & Bryan A. Garner

"This is a feminist dictionary, and a nonsexist dictionary, and a dictionary for women." (Preface, p. 14.)

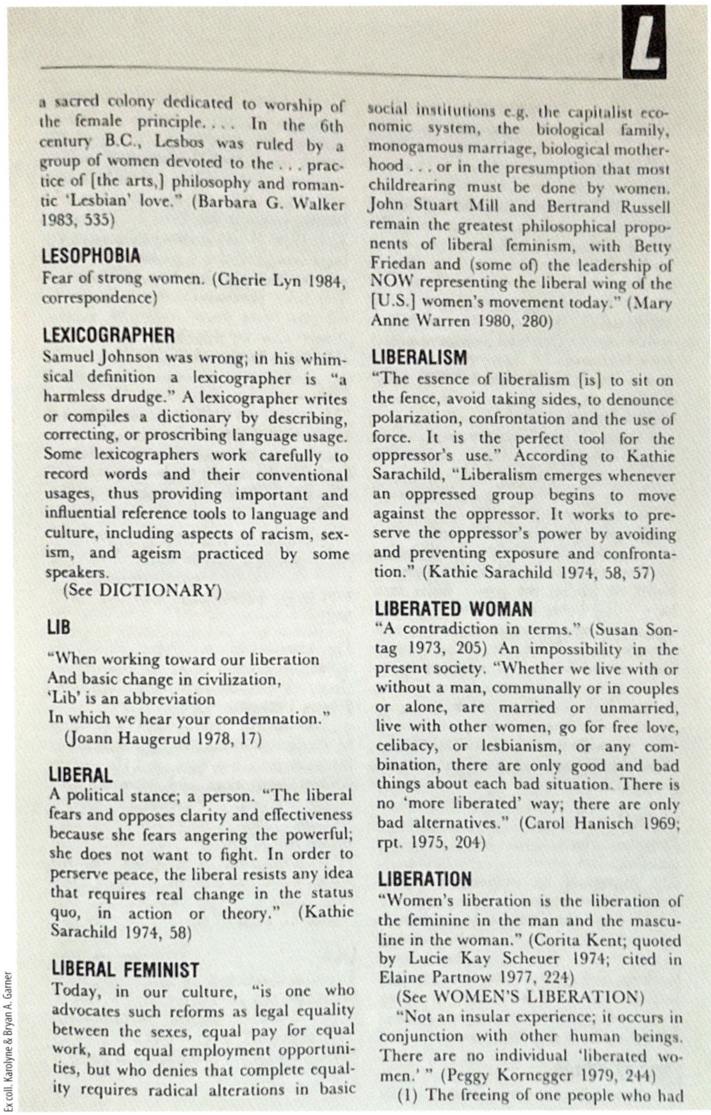

L

a sacred colony dedicated to worship of the female principle. . . . In the 6th century B.C., Lesbos was ruled by a group of women devoted to the . . . practice of [the arts,] philosophy and romantic 'Lesbian' love." (Barbara G. Walker 1983, 535)

LESOPHOBIA
Fear of strong women. (Cherie Lyn 1984, correspondence)

LEXICOGRAPHER
Samuel Johnson was wrong; in his whimsical definition a lexicographer is "a harmless drudge." A lexicographer writes or compiles a dictionary by describing, correcting, or proscribing language usage. Some lexicographers work carefully to record words and their conventional usages, thus providing important and influential reference tools to language and culture, including aspects of racism, sexism, and ageism practiced by some speakers.
(See DICTIONARY)

LIB
"When working toward our liberation
And basic change in civilization,
'Lib' is an abbreviation
In which we hear your condemnation."
(Joann Haugerud 1978, 17)

LIBERAL
A political stance; a person. "The liberal fears and opposes clarity and effectiveness because she fears angering the powerful; she does not want to fight. In order to perserve peace, the liberal resists any idea that requires real change in the status quo, in action or theory." (Kathie Sarachild 1974, 58)

LIBERAL FEMINIST
Today, in our culture, "is one who advocates such reforms as legal equality between the sexes, equal pay for equal work, and equal employment opportunities, but who denies that complete equality requires radical alterations in basic social institutions e.g. the capitalist economic system, the biological family, monogamous marriage, biological motherhood . . . or in the presumption that most childrearing must be done by women. John Stuart Mill and Bertrand Russell remain the greatest philosophical proponents of liberal feminism, with Betty Friedan and (some of) the leadership of NOW representing the liberal wing of the [U.S.] women's movement today." (Mary Anne Warren 1980, 280)

LIBERALISM
"The essence of liberalism [is] to sit on the fence, avoid taking sides, to denounce polarization, confrontation and the use of force. It is the perfect tool for the oppressor's use." According to Kathie Sarachild, "Liberalism emerges whenever an oppressed group begins to move against the oppressor. It works to preserve the oppressor's power by avoiding and preventing exposure and confrontation." (Kathie Sarachild 1974, 58, 57)

LIBERATED WOMAN
"A contradiction in terms." (Susan Sontag 1973, 205) An impossibility in the present society. "Whether we live with or without a man, communally or in couples or alone, are married or unmarried, live with other women, go for free love, celibacy, or lesbianism, or any combination, there are only good and bad things about each bad situation. There is no 'more liberated' way; there are only bad alternatives." (Carol Hanisch 1969; rpt. 1975, 204)

LIBERATION
"Women's liberation is the liberation of the feminine in the man and the masculine in the woman." (Corita Kent; quoted by Lucie Kay Scheuer 1974; cited in Elaine Partnow 1977, 224)
(See WOMEN'S LIBERATION)
"Not an insular experience; it occurs in conjunction with other human beings. There are no individual 'liberated women.'" (Peggy Kornegger 1979, 244)
(1) The freeing of one people who had

Ex coll. Karolyne & Bryan A. Garner

In their iconoclastic book, Kramarae and Treichler took issue with Samuel Johnson's definition of *lexicographer*.

124

Jonathan Lighter
An Unfinished Dictionary

***Random House Historical Dictionary of American Slang*.**
Jonathan E. Lighter ed. New York: Random House, 1994–97.

Ex coll. Karolyne & Bryan A. Garner

THE *RANDOM HOUSE HISTORICAL DICTIONARY of American Slang* is a frustrating reminder of what might have been.

Jonathan E. Lighter (b. 1949) made his first foray into slang lexicography while he was still an undergraduate: an article of more than 120 pages, "The Slang of the American Expeditionary Forces in Europe, 1917–1919." Jonathan Green calls it a "magisterial lexicon." (Green 2015:378.) Lighter then began work on a full-size slang dictionary, and a demonstration of his method—similar to the *OED*'s historical approach—covered the letter *A* and served as his doctoral dissertation at the University of Tennessee in 1980. He reached an agreement with Random House in 1984 to produce a definitive historical lexicon of slang in the United States.

The format recalls the *OED*. Usage notes are abundant, and under each sense are a series of quotations in chronological order, from the earliest known example to the 20th century. The noun *beef*, sense 4—"complaint; complaining; objection, protest, grounds for complaint"—comes with 13 quotations from 1899 to 1991; *blowhard*'s first sense, "an obnoxiously boastful or garrulous person; windbag," comes with quotations from 1823 to 1928. Some terms prove older or newer than many would guess: *flop sweat* is unattested before 1966, and *high-maintenance* as a description for a hard-to-please person was popularized by *When Harry Met Sally* in 1989. And since it's a historical dictionary, many terms are no longer in use: *peanut* for "a native of North Carolina or Georgia," used among Confederate soldiers, is supported by evidence from 1863 to 1937, but nothing more recent.

The first volume (*A–G*), which appeared in 1994, was hailed as "an extraordinary work . . . a delight to anyone interested in informal and colloquial English." (Spears 1995:196.) Volume 2 (*H–O*) arrived to great fanfare in 1997; scholars eagerly expected the final volume. But

"Public and professional interest in slang has never been greater than it is today. The purpose of this and succeeding volumes is, through the use of established historical methods, to shed fresh light on the slang element in American English and, by so doing, to better our understanding of American English as a whole." (Introduction, p. xi.)

then—nothing. The closure of Random House's language reference division left the dictionary without a home. (Adams 2020a:83; Green 2001.) In 2003 Oxford University Press announced an intention to bring the dictionary through the end of the alphabet, but two decades have passed and nothing has appeared.

Ex coll. Karolyne & Bryan A. Garner

"Verve is more central than vulgarity to the phenomenon of slang. The tolerance—in fact, the demand—of contemporary literature and journalism for a vigorous informal vocabulary, innocently trusted to be free of pretension and insincerity, leads us to expect that, in coming decades, more slang will achieve standard status more quickly than ever before." (Introduction, p. xxxvii.)

"Words must be sought where they are found. Our bibliography is a true list of sources rather than a listing of all 'works consulted.' If the reader discovers there a disproportionate number from working-class and military life, various forms of adventure and misadventure, malice and mischief, it is because these—rather than the novels of Henry James and Edith Wharton—are the kinds of sources that have yielded the earliest and most numerous examples of American slang." (Introduction, p. xxxvii.)

125

Urban Dictionary
Anthropologist of the Internet

Urban Dictionary. www.urbandictionary.com.

Ok boomer

An internet word for when old people (65+) always talk about how "lucky" are generation is and say something stupid about it. So people respond with "ok boomer"

Boomer- Back in my day, we didn't have all this fancy iPhones
Regular person- ok boomer

by Yeeyeeehaw November 29, 2019

DICTIONARY.COM WENT the respectable route, acquiring the rights to a serious dictionary and employing professional lexicographers to keep it current (no. 129). Urban Dictionary, founded four years later, took another path. Its founder, Aaron Peckham—still a first-year undergraduate when the project launched—started from scratch, and invited volunteer users to build their own collection of slang and nonstandard English.

The crowdsourced entries are often amusing and repay browsing: *eeriesistible*, "What adrenaline-junkies find haunted houses, creepy movies, and other fear-inducing objects/presentations"; *sharksploitation*, "a subgenre of exploitation film that involves sharks or shark attacks." And Urban Dictionary is sometimes the first, or only, reference work to note the existence of informal terms. The *New York Times* called it "the anthropologist of the Internet, taking the pulse of the web and capturing cultural moments in real time." (Wortham 2014.) But its definitions can be sloppy, imprecise, and idiosyncratic, as with *mullet*, "a travesty upon someones head which shoudl [sic] carry the death penalty." The entry for *one thousand* reads simply "One thousand is a big ass number."

With more than 12 million definitions—that's about 15 times as many as in the entire *Oxford English Dictionary*—no one has an estimate of how many of those terms have any existence "in the wild." Dictionaries have different policies on how long-lived and widespread a word must be to be included, but they admit only words that have real existence among users of the language. By contrast, many—most?—entries in Urban Dictionary seem to be words that someone *wishes* existed, or that are used only among a small circle of friends. The entry for *Martina*—"Martina is an incredible human being. She is an amazing friend and she will always help you when you need it"—captures what must have been a tender moment in a contributor's life (though, predictably, vituperative personal definitions far outnumber touching ones). Still, no lexicographer would admit a word on the basis of one person's whim.

Definitions were once subject to moderation by a team of volunteers, but a come-one-come-all policy now prevails. An openness to informal and even obscene terms without any vetting poses challenges. A few years ago, the leadership was disturbed to discover that "we've been inundated by hate speech and abusive content," and declared, "We will not allow Urban Dictionary to be a home for hate speech and abusive content." The struggle continues.

Ex coll. Karolyne & Bryan A. Garner

The founder, Aaron Peckham, has issued various print collections as well.

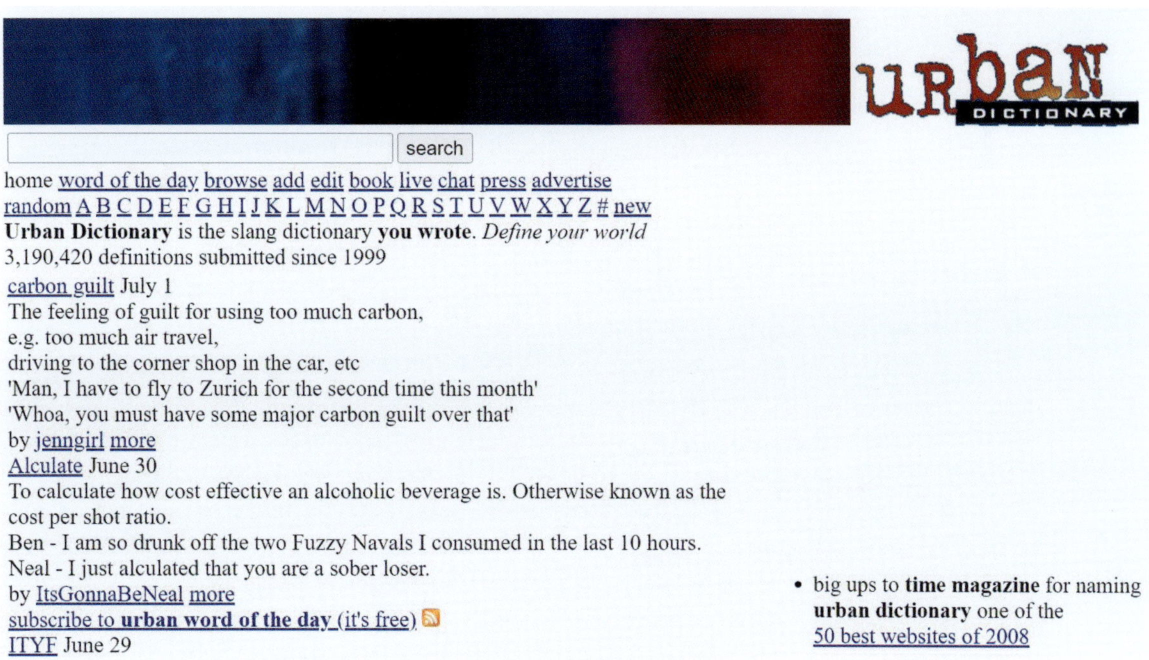

Urban Dictionary as it appeared in 2012.

126

Jonathon Green

Odd Job Man

Green, Jonathon. *Green's Dictionary of Slang*. 3 vols. Edinburgh: Chambers, 2010.

Photo courtesy of Little, Brown

"It is my job: lexicography, the making of dictionaries. Specifically dictionaries of slang. It is not a common job, though it is a valuable one, and I suspect that for most of those who use its products it is an almost invisible one." (Green 2014:1.)

English-language slang lexicography began at the very end of the 17th century, when an otherwise unknown "B.E." published *A New Dictionary of the Terms Ancient and Modern of the Canting Crew* (no. 109). Countless slang dictionaries have appeared since, but only a few are essential parts of the story of English dictionaries. The giant of slang lexicography in the 18th century was Francis Grose, whose *Classical Dictionary of the Vulgar Tongue* (1785, no. 110) expanded B.E.'s coverage from cant to other kinds of "vulgar" speech. In the 19th, it was John Stephen Farmer, who with William Ernest Henley published *Slang and Its Analogues* (no. 114). The 20th-century giant was Eric Partridge, whose eccentric *Dictionary of Slang and Unconventional English* (1937, no. 116) was reprinted for decades. And the undisputed master of slang in our day is Jonathon Green (b. 1948), whose magnum opus appeared in 2010.

Green's Dictionary of Slang contains 110,000 headwords supported by 415,000 quotations spread out over 6,200 pages in three volumes. It is the fullest scholarly treatment of slang available, spanning the Anglophone world over a thousand years. As in the *OED*, every entry is supported by documented quotations, with the earliest known citation of every sense.

The reviews, both scholarly and popular, were nearly uniformly ecstatic. The printed book earned the American Library Association's Dartmouth medal. Julie Coleman, a linguist specializing in slang, calls it "the best historical dictionary of English slang there is, ever has been or (in print at least) is ever likely to be." (Coleman 2012:193.)

The dictionary was 17 years in the making. What could possibly prompt someone to spend so many years chasing down citations?—what could motivate someone who had identified 1,359 words for *drunk* to find the 1,360th one? Green tells us. *Odd Job Man: Some*

Confessions of a Slang Lexicographer (2014) is his contribution to a genre that we might call the lexicographic memoir. Perhaps the oldest work in this category is Émile Littré's *Comment j'ai fait mon dictionnaire de la langue française* (1880), which has been joined by Eric Partridge's *Gentle Art of Lexicography as Pursued and Experienced by an Addict* (1963), David Crystal's *Just a Phrase I'm Going Through: My Life in Language* (2009), and John Simpson's *Word Detective: Searching for the Meaning of It All at the Oxford English Dictionary* (2016). Green gives us insight into the kinds of obsessions and passions one needs to devote years, even decades, to the language.

Ex coll. Karolyne & Bryan A. Garner

Green's Dictionary of Slang

Home Browse Search Bibliography About

drunk as a boiled owl *adj.*

also **drunk as a biled owl, ...an owl, a scrambled owl, ...two hoot owls, full as a boiled owl, look like a ..., lushy as..., tight as..., stewed as an owl, tight as...**

(*orig. US*) very drunk; intensified as *drunker than a boiled owl*; thus *boiled owl*, a drunk person; note one-off extrapolation in cit. 1900.

1770 | 1800 | 1850 | 1900 | 1950 | 1981

1770 Gent.'s Mag. 560: As drunk as an Owl.

1793 Sporting Mag. July II 243/1: *Comparisons of Drunkenness.* As drunk *as an owl.*

1815 'The Sailor's Frolic' in *A Garland of New Songs* 7: And when you come home you're drunk as an owl.

1820 'The Sailor's Frolic' in *Goldfinch Song Book* 19: [as cit. 1815].

1852 G.C. Mundy *Our Antipodes* III 61: Many a gudeman [...] without the guardianship of his thrifty dame would have returned drunk as an owl.

1862 'Artemus Ward' *Artemus Ward, His Book* 84: Obsarve how Iargo got Casheo drunk as a biled owl on corn whisky in order to karry out his sneekin desines.

1864 G.A. Sala *Quite Alone* III 99: She's a regular devil that woman, and four nights out of six she's as lushy as a boiled owl.

1869 W.M. Howell *Diggings and the Bush* 35: The others are drunk as owls.

1877 'A High Private' *Man who was not a Colonel* 9: He would get drunk as an owl.

1881 *Knoxville Dly Chron.* (TN) 11 Nov. 1/5: Ven I got home I don't can tell if I vas a saw-mill or a brass band I vas dvice so drunk as a boiled owl.

1882 *Fifeshire Jrnl* 2 Nov. 3/5: '[G]allivanting about the streets tight as a boiled owl'.

"What I do is sit alone in a room, a screen in front of me, a book more than likely to my left, held open by the weight of a discarded piece of chain. To my right, a wall full of more books that are not just books, but tools, and both extensions of and bastions for my existence. Some of them I have even made myself. With this screen and books and book-shaped tools I chase down words. And by placing these words in alphabetical order, by naming, defining and providing a word-based background for their existence and more words that illustrate examples of their use, I create another book that is designated to be a tool in its turn." (Green 2014:2.)

Ex coll. Karolyne & Bryan A. Garner

A 1986 advertisement.

XI. The Digital Age

Computers, as the name suggests, were built to compute, and that meant manipulating numbers. They were developed to produce artillery firing tables, and scientists and corporations quickly came to depend on their fast and accurate calculations. But not long after the first electronic digital computers were developed, people began to think of them not as number- but as symbol-manipulating machines. It became possible to imagine applications for these machines far from the battlefield, the laboratory, or the boardroom.

The first dictionary developed with the help of a computer was the 1966 Random House (no. 103). Since that time, computers have transformed research, composition, editing, and distribution of dictionaries. It has proved a symbiotic relationship: lexicographers today use big data every day, often every hour. Just as often, every computer user who uses a spelling or grammar checker depends on lexicographers. Many of the most impressive dictionaries of recent decades have never had existence as printed books; they exist only online. This chapter tells the story of this progression—though, by the time you read these lines, the computing environment will have evolved to make the words here written outdated.

Translating languages is just the beginning.
The revolutionary Craig M100.
We introduced the Craig M100 as an electronic language translator; an amazing hand-held interpreter that could translate as many as three languages simultaneously. But that was just the beginning. Because of advanced new technology the M100 opens the door to instant information on an incredible variety of subjects far beyond language translations. The key to this revolution is the amazing Ami Memory System, the heart of the Craig M100. This system is the latest in micro-memory technology, making it possible to store in one tiny capsule an amount of information that yesterday required a large computer.
CEREAL +MILK=225
Diet
FOOT= .30 METERS
Metric
LA RUE =RU
Phonetic
Today, there are language capsules in French, German, Spanish, Italian and Japanese, even a new phonetic language pronunciation capsule. Next will be fascinating new capsules featuring Memory Improvement, First Aid, a Tax Guide and word games.
The Craig M100, with the exclusive Ami Memory System is the recognized standard for hand-held computers. There are virtually unlimited possibilities for storage of knowledge.
You must see a demonstration of the Craig M100 to believe it. It's the first revolution you can hold in the palm of your hand.
CRAIG®
M100
HELLO = BONJOUR
SPACE
DIET GUIDE
TAX GUIDE
MEMORY IMPROVEMENT
SPELLING GUIDE
THESAURUS
THE Ami MEMORY SYSTEM.
"Putting the power of computers in the palm of your hand."
© Craig Corporation, 1979. In Canada ... Withers, Evans Ltd., Burnaby, B.C. V5G 3E3.

127

Storehouses in the Palm of Your Hand

LK-3000. Lexicon Corporation, 1978.

The Craig M100 Translator and Information Center. Craig Corporation, 1979.

Ex coll. Jack Lynch

IN MANY LANGUAGES, the earliest dictionaries are bilingual. Latin–English dictionaries, for instance, appeared centuries before Cawdrey's *Table Alphabeticall*. It's somehow fitting that the earliest handheld digital dictionaries were also intended as translators' assistants.

The mid-century interest in electronic dictionaries was driven by Cold War concerns about keeping up with Soviet and East German research. Since computational methods had proved indispensable in cracking enemy codes in the Second World War, and since electronic computers were developed beginning in the late 1940s, pioneers in machine translation imagined automating translation by treating it as a kind of decryption—treating the Russian journal text as a cipher, and using computers to turn it into English. Experts confidently declared that within five years, computers would be routinely producing serviceable, albeit inelegant, translations from many languages.

Ex coll. Jack Lynch

It was an intriguing idea, but through the 1950s and 1960s it delivered only embarrassing failures. This was largely because languages are *not* simply encoded versions of one another—no modern linguist would approach translation this way—but it was also because no computers at that time had the processing power to handle the tens of thousands of words necessary for the most rudimentary communication.

By the late 1970s, though, technology had reached the point at which it might be useful in some real-world translation tasks. First to market with a device for consumers was Lexicon Corporation, founded by electrical engineer Mike Levy. At the end of 1977, he applied for a patent for an "Electronic dictionary and language interpreter," and by the next year, he had reached a marketing and manufacturing agreement with the German company Nixdorf, selling

Ex coll. Karolyne & Bryan A. Garner

the LK-3000. The documentation described the new device as the dawn of a new digital age: "Whether you know it or not," the product literature declared, "you've just bought a true hand-held computer." A *computer!*—that fits in your *hand!*

A few months later Lexicon got some competition. Ron Gordon, then vice president for marketing at video-game company Atari, developed the "Ami LANGUAGE System." Gordon licensed his technology to Paul Heckel at Craig Electronics, which had made a splash eight years earlier with one of the first pocket calculators. His creation, the M100 Translator, boasted of being able "to look up and translate thousands of words, phrases, and even complete sentences in many languages." The instructions declared: "Now, in the palm of your hand, you can hold a storehouse of information—not only in your native language but in foreign languages as well. And you can easily translate back and forth between different languages at the touch of a button."

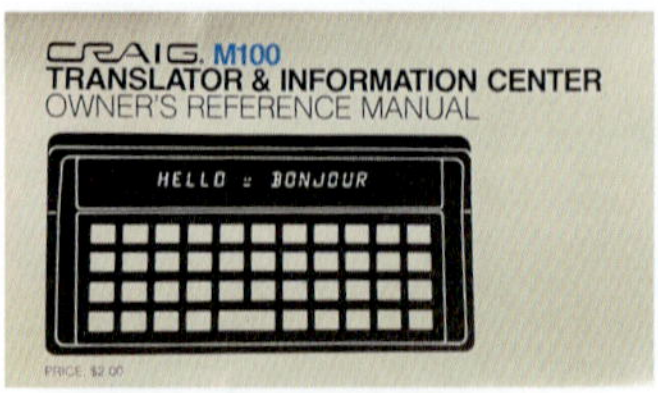

Ex coll. Jack Lynch

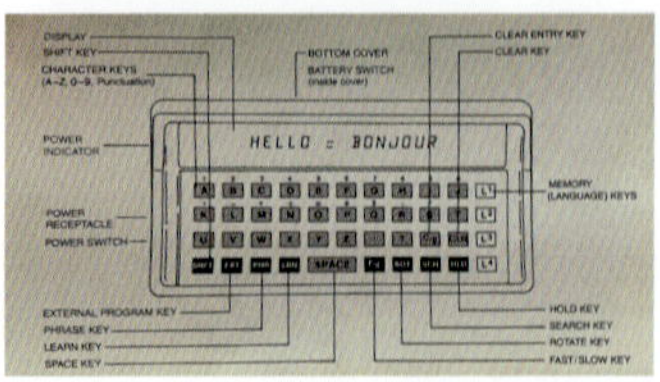

Ex coll. Jack Lynch

Both gizmos were around 7¾ × 3¾ × 1¾ inches and 12 ounces. Both had LED screens that displayed sixteen characters; "Longer entries circulate from right to left, much like a theater marquee." (Anon. 1979:4.) Both had keypads to enter either numbers or digits, depending on the modes they were in and the cartridges that were installed. Both had rechargeable batteries that lasted around four hours between charges, and both could work on 110 or 220 volts. Both relied on removable modules to contain the actual dictionaries, which were developed for languages including Arabic, Dutch, French, German, Italian, Japanese, Polish, Portuguese, and Spanish, along with "phonetic Greek"—the LED display couldn't handle any alphabet other than the Latin. "Switch modules," Lexicon's instructions advise, "and the LK-3000 becomes a completely different machine."

There were differences. The LK-3000 was just a keypad and a display with no microprocessor or memory—that was on the cartridges. That meant that, as technology advanced, new modules could offer increased power, staving off obsolescence. But it also meant that the cartridges were significantly more expensive than on the Craig, which had a processor and about 2K of memory built into the machine itself. (By way of comparison, today's entry-level iPhone model has more than 64 million times as much memory.) Only the LK-3000, though, could boast of being "the officially licensed hand-held translator for the 1980 Olympic Games in Moscow and Lake Placid." (Anon. 1979:4.)

Early users seem to have been impressed, but these devices were extremely limited as technology, and even more limited as dictionaries. Though the ads promised translators capable of handling "thousands of words," memory limitations meant that the vocabularies were limited to around 1,500 to 2,000 words in each language—fewer words than in even the smallest printed dictionaries. The Craig documentation instructed users not to get bogged down in "'helper' words that make the sentence flow smoothly but don't necessarily contribute to the ideas conveyed," and therefore recommended limiting all expressions to "the present tense singular. For example, say 'I buy book' instead of 'I am going to buy some books.'" Both also moved slowly: it took the Craig 10–13 seconds to translate a simple sentence, and the Lexicon 27 seconds—an eternity by modern digital standards. (Anon. 1980:127.) Users complained about the fragility of the Lexicon: the cartridge connector was wont to bend or even snap. And both were expensive: the Craig was released at $250 plus $25 for each capsule, the Lexicon at $225 plus $65 per cartridge. Both, in other words, cost more than a thousand of today's dollars.

Ex coll. Jack Lynch

Still, both were successful upon first appearance. Nixdorf sold 30,000 units in the first year, Craig 200,000 in three years. But as the novelty wore off, the limitations of the vocabulary became more and more obvious. It didn't help that both projects had been developed almost entirely by computer experts, not linguists or lexicographers, and the translations produced were often unusable. Ads continued to appear for a few years, with declining prices signaling increasing desperation to lure new buyers. But the market continued to dwindle. Although Lexicon tried to reassure consumers that "your LK-3000 will constantly become more versatile and never become obsolete," within a few years both devices were largely forgotten. It would take another few decades, and vastly more computing power, before pocket-sized digital translators were able to deliver on the promises of the 1950s.

Courtesy of Oxford University Press

1993 OUP publicity photo.

"With the electronic *OED* you can do everything you could do with the printed edition—only much faster." (User's manual.)

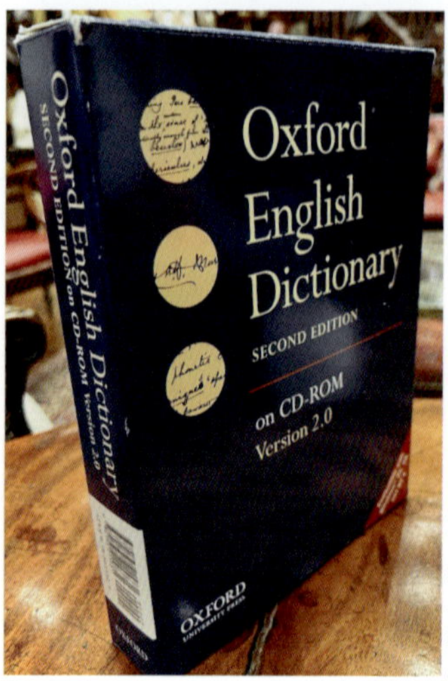

Ex coll. Karolyne & Bryan A. Garner

The box as purchased.

128

The *OED* on CD-ROM—or Was It VHS?

***The OED on CD-ROM*. Oxford: Oxford Univ. Press, 1992.**

The second edition of the *OED* was a major achievement, a worthy late-20th-century successor to the Victorian and Edwardian original. But the lexicographers had recently been working much as they had in Murray's day, using pen and ink and slips of paper. In the 1970s and 1980s, the inkpots and dipped pens began to give way to keyboards, silicon chips, and magnetic tape.

The *OED* was not the first dictionary to make significant use of computers; both the *Dictionary of Old English* and the *Dictionary of American Regional English* had been developed with digital assistance. As early as 1977, Oxford University Press appointed Joyce Hawkins the dictionary department's "Computer Liaison Officer." But no one had a clear idea of how, or even whether, computers would prove useful in lexicography.

As part of the project that created *OED2* (no. 106), Oxford University Press signed agreements with the International Computaprint Corporation, IBM United Kingdom Ltd., and the University of Waterloo in Ontario to help with digitizing the entire *OED*. This involved three primary tasks: converting the original *OED* and *Supplement* into electronic form; merging the separate files into one alphabetical sequence; and making additions (about 5,000 words) and corrections that had never been made to the original *Supplement* of 1933. The team considered using optical-character-recognition software, but the complexity of the *OED* text far exceeded the technology's capability in the 1980s. The entire thing, around 350,000,000 characters, had to be retyped.

It wasn't simply a keyboarding challenge. The dictionary was a structured text, and the electronic file had to represent its structure. Edmund Weiner, with the assistance of software engineers, developed a tagging system to differentiate headwords, definitions, quotations, etymologies, and so on. It was a necessary step both for the digital typesetting and for enabling electronic searches for specific kinds of information.

The team adapted a text editor, Mike Cowlishaw's LEXX, into a proprietary program called the "OED Integration, Publishing, and Updating System," and so produced the glorious compound acronym OEDIPUS-LEXX. The work was carried out on an IBM 4341 mainframe, and the database was regularly backed up on magnetic tape and stored off-site to guard against catastrophes.

At the time, the relationship between the electronic text and the print volume was unclear. One function of the digitizing project was to produce the kind of bound volumes that Sir James Murray would have been comfortable with. But already in the early 1980s, Richard Charkin, the *OED*'s head of reference, had an inkling of the digital future. He imagined that computers might someday be used not just to produce books, but *instead of* books. He realized that the time might come when the *OED* would not be a book at all, but a database.

Courtesy of Oxford University Press

1993 OUP publicity photos.

Courtesy of Oxford University Press.

No home computer at the time could handle files running to hundreds of megabytes. A floppy disk in 1983 could hold 180 kilobytes; it would take some 2,500 of them to contain the full text of the *OED*. Charkin suggested that it might be possible for computers equipped with modems to dial in to mainframes, allowing libraries and universities, for instance, to subscribe to online services. Some even imagined that instead of hard-copy publication every few decades, the *OED* might be kept perpetually up to date.

OUP never had the opportunity to implement this project, but as the 1980s drew to a close, the development of a new technology made it possible for people to have the entire *OED* in digital form at home: the CD-ROM debuted at the COMDEX (Computer Dealers' Exhibition) show in Tokyo in 1985. Now it would be possible to contain the entire text of the *OED*, more than 50 million words, on a removable disc. For the publisher, it meant a huge saving in materials and shipping costs—a set of books that weighed nearly 150 pounds and filled an entire bookcase was now a shiny half-ounce platter, 5 inches across. A consumer could buy the CD-ROM and a fairly high-powered computer for less than the twenty-volume *OED2*.

The *OED on CD-ROM* made distribution much easier, but even more important, the dictionary was searchable in new ways. When *OED2* was conceived, it was easy to take it for granted that people would search for a headword and read the associated entry, just as

"In order to maintain the security of this CD-ROM, the data has been encrypted and discs have been watermarked." (Customer-service note.)

they had done with printed dictionaries since time out of mind. But when users could search the entire text, not merely the headwords, it became possible to ask new questions. John Simpson, editor of *OED2*, sums it up:

> Since the dawn of dictionaries, access had only been through the word you looked up. If you wanted to know what *strategy* meant, you found your dictionary and turned to the letter *S*, struggled to find *st-*, etc., and then read the brief definition which (you hoped) enlightened you as to the meaning of the word. But supposing you suddenly developed wider interests. Supposing you were interested in finding all of the words in English that ended in *-ology*? You had to start on page 1 of the dictionary and read every entry until you reached *Z*. And there was quite a good chance that you would miss one or two as your eyes glazed over or the telephone interrupted your concentration. Once you'd spent an unconscionable amount of time discovering how many words in the *OED* ended in *-ology* (the dictionary currently knows of 1,011), you might then want to compare this with the number of words ending in *-ography* (508 this time). So then you would have to start all over again. [Simpson 2016:136–37.]

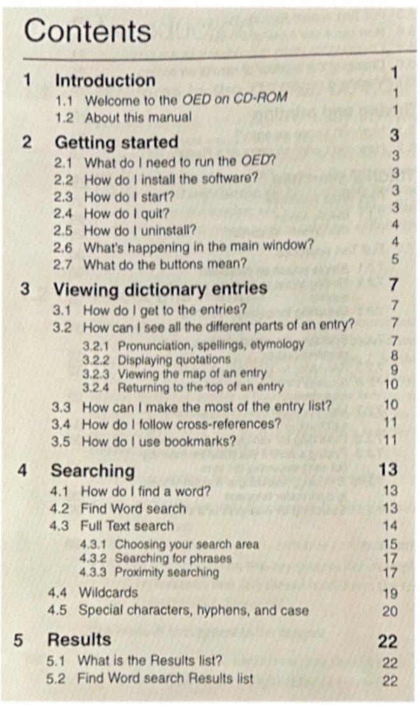
Contents

Everything was different with an electronic dictionary. A user might ask to see every quotation in the *OED* from *Paradise Lost*, or all the words that entered English from Arabic in the 14th century, and get an answer in an instant. The curious could trace the history of the Raj by counting the borrowings from Hindi, decade by decade, over the course of the 19th century. They could look for every word that first appeared in Chaucer's works, or every word with the combining form *-phobia*.

"Licensee agrees that it will not transfer or sell the CD-ROM to another party, unless all media and written materials provided are also conveyed and no copies of the CD-ROM are retained for the Licensee's use." (Customer license agreement.)

The search capabilities of the earliest editions of the *OED on CD-ROM* were limited, largely because it was hard to imagine the possibilities without the practical experience of doing searches. With each digital generation, the search functions have grown more sophisticated. Today's *OED* is only online (no. 131)—it is unlikely that there will ever be a 50-something-volume set when *OED3* is declared "complete" (whatever that means). Users can now answer questions in seconds that would once have taken decades of research. While many are content, even today, just to look up headwords, as they could do with the first *OED* fascicle in 1884, we continue to expand the possibilities for reimagining what a dictionary is and what it's for.

129

Dictionary.com

Not a Pinkwashing Hellscape

Dictionary.com.

"The Internet is approaching mass-market penetration much more quickly than earlier studies had projected," the *New York Times* reported in October 1995, "but it's not there yet." It's worth remembering what the digital world looked like at the time. Internet Explorer 1.0 had been released in August 1995. There were fewer than 25,000 sites on the entire World Wide Web, compared to more than a billion today. The Internet-using population was about 2% of the size of today's.

"*Dictionary.com* is . . . particularly popular. . . . The popularity, one might suspect, has a lot to do with the attractive domain name, which to many users (and search engines?) strongly suggests that this is *the* dictionary." (Lew 2011:241.)

It was daring to create an online-only dictionary in that environment, but that was the plan of Brian Kariger and Daniel Fierro of Lexico Publishing. They registered the domain name Dictionary.com in May 1995, along with Thesaurus.com and Reference.com, and began building the project in earnest in 1998. In its early days, it was more of a technology platform than a dictionary: all the lexicographic content belonged to other companies, for which Dictionary.com acted merely as a host. It hosted several old dictionaries that no longer had copyright protection, and in 1999 it signed a contract with Houghton Mifflin to put the *American Heritage Dictionary* online.

The company moved into the lexicographic big leagues in December 2004 with the acquisition of the *Random House Unabridged Dictionary*. Random House in 1966 had published an original dictionary, edited by Jess Stein and Laurence Urdang, with an expanded second edition in 1987 (see no. 103). Around the turn of the millennium, though, Random House, like many other American publishers, decided to get out of the reference game, closing its dictionary offices in 2002. But the research behind the *Random House Unabridged* did not go to waste. Dictionary.com licensed it—the right not merely to distribute it, but to use it as the basis of a dictionary that it could modify over time—and hired in-house lexicographers to update it.

Today the dictionary is available as a website and an app. It's accompanied by a thesaurus and a blog for logophiles. Together they boast of 70 million users every month and 5.5 billion searches each year, which places Dictionary.com among the 500 most used websites in America. Like many other Internet start-ups, Dictionary.com has had a constantly shifting series of owners and partners. In the 1990s, it was controlled by Lexico Publishing; Lexico was supposed to be acquired by Answers Corp. in 2007, but the deal fell through; in 2008, it was acquired by Ask.com. Today the company is owned by Rock Holdings as part of a portfolio including Rocket Mortgage LLC and Core Digital media. The lexicographic content is overseen by Grant Barrett, head of lexicography, and Kory Stamper, senior editor of lexicography, both experienced and distinguished lexicographers. The dictionary developed by Random House continues to be the core, though it continues to provide information from other dictionaries with whom it has contracts, including the *Collins English Dictionary* and *American Heritage*.

"For many students and teachers, online dictionaries are the references of choice. Dictionary.com (*www.dictionary.com*) is the 'granddaddy' of electronic resources." (Blachowicz et al. 2013:149.)

The online-only nature of the enterprise makes the company more nimble than many others, since its update schedules aren't tied to print schedules. Dictionaries often tout the addition of new words; a press release highlighting recent additions like *hellscape*, *rage farming*, *petfluencer*, *pinkwashing*, *queerbaiting*, and *Latinx* is a surefire way to attract free media attention, and even when much of the attention is negative ("decline of the English language!"), the no-such-thing-as-bad-publicity principle can still attract clicks.

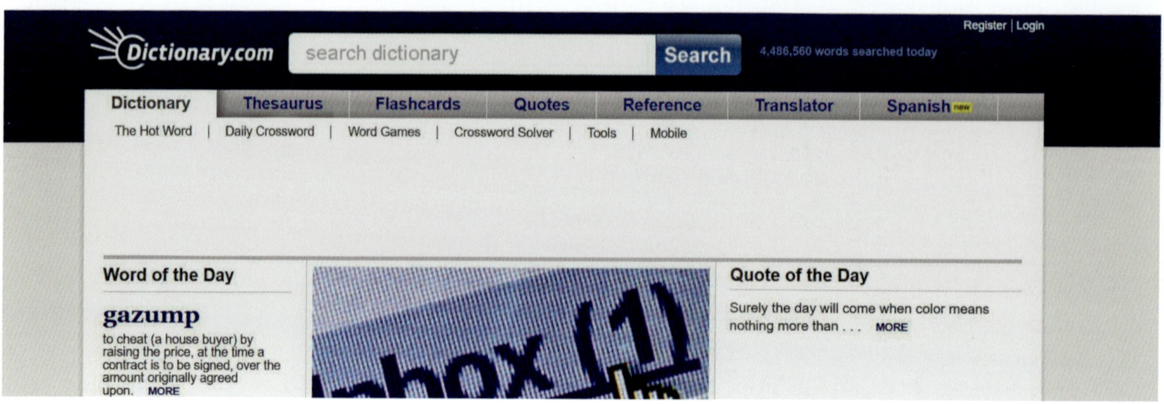

130

Wiktionary

Not Just for Cheugy Covidiots

***Wiktionary*. www.wiktionary.com.**

LIKE ITS MORE FAMOUS SISTER PROJECT, Wikipedia, Wiktionary is overseen—if that's the right word—by the Wikimedia Foundation. It's a wholly online polyglot dictionary, compiled entirely by volunteers, and includes materials in more than 150 languages.

The lack of any need to publish a print version lets the dictionary stay up to date: there are entries for *cheugy* "Uncool in a tryhard, out-of-touch way" and *covidiot* "A person who is foolishly reckless with respect to avoiding contracting or spreading COVID-19." But the dictionary avoids a problem common to dictionaries compiled by volunteers, and is not overstuffed with contributors' pet coinages. Compared to the other high-profile all-volunteer effort, Urban Dictionary, Wiktionary is positively scholarly.

Wiktionary doesn't strive to compete with the *OED*. It's not a historical dictionary, and while there are occasional quotations showing words in use, there is no attempt to identify a word's earliest written occurrence. Still, there are etymologies, pronunciations rendered in the International Phonetic Alphabet, carefully discriminated senses with well-crafted definitions, and sets of synonyms and antonyms. Hyperlinked translations are a distinctive feature: *sprawl*, to take one example, comes with three noun meanings and three more for the verb, and these senses come with translations into more than a dozen languages, including Bulgarian, Catalan, Maori, and Slovene.

The dictionary's polyglot character makes it possible to follow etymologies backward through history: *synthesizer* is linked to *synthesize*, which is linked to English *synthesis*, which is linked to Latin *synthesis* "mixture, compound," which is linked to Greek σύνθεσις "putting together, composition, combination," which is linked to συντίθημι "assemble, put together," which is linked to τίθημι "put, place, set," which is linked to the Proto-Indo-European *$*d^h\acute{e}d^heh_1ti$* "to be putting, placing," which leads us all the way back to the Proto-Indo-European root, *$*d^heh_1$-*. The dictionary is supplemented by a thesaurus, a rhyming dictionary, and collections of phrases.

Nepali [edit]

Etymology [edit]

Borrowed from Sanskrit शब्दकोश (*śabdakośa*).

Pronunciation [edit]

- IPA(key): [sʌb̚d̪ʌkos]
- Phonetic Devanagari: सब्दकोस्

Noun [edit]

शब्दकोश • (śabdakoś)

1. dictionary

References [edit]

- "शब्दकोश", in *नेपाली बृहत् शब्दकोश (Nepālī Bṛhat Śabdakoś) [Comprehensive Nepali Dictionary]*, Kathmandu: Nepal Academy, 2018
- Schmidt, Ruth L. (1993), "शब्दकोश", in *A Practical Dictionary of Modern Nepali*, Ratna Sagar

131

Digital Dictionaries

Waiting for Payday

***Merriam-Webster Online*. www.merriam-webster.com.**

***Merriam-Webster Unabridged*. unabridged.merriam -webster.com.**

***The Oxford English Dictionary*. John Simpson and Michael Proffitt eds. www.oed.com.**

"I might go back to the past for some things, if I could. There's a romantic aspect to writing out definitions late on a cold October evening, lit only by a bright desk-light, to the accompaniment of the shuffle of paper as your colleagues sort their index cards into order, ready to attack their next word. The smell of the loosely folded, freshly printed galley proofs returned to your desk from the printer and waiting to be corrected is something that editors won't experience again. That has all given way to greater accuracy, more and better evidence, and a sense that the dictionary is now accessible to so many more people. But those old ways should be remembered, because they were essential steps to the present, which will eventually be other editors' pasts." (Simpson 2016:338.)

Online dictionaries have many advantages over print books. The cost of paper, ink, and binding is nil. There's no need for small fonts or crowded layouts. Freed from the need to transport heavy volumes around the world (*Webster's Third* weighs more than 10 pounds, and *OED2* nearly 150), we save both shipping costs and carbon emissions. New entries can be added as soon as they're ready, not when an entire new edition goes to press, and embarrassing errors can be corrected as soon as they're discovered. Online dictionaries can be searched in ways that were unthinkable in the print age. Pronunciations can be audio clips rather than cryptic symbols. Hyperlinks make it easy to follow cross-references. Though prolonged reading on a screen can still be uncomfortable, dictionaries are usually read only in short bursts. And in the smartphone age, dozens of volumes can now fit in a pocket or purse.

Online dictionaries have just one disadvantage: no one wants to pay for them. And this one disadvantage is almost enough to outweigh all the benefits.

It didn't always seem that way. In the early days of the Internet, the *New York Times* could refer to the "increasingly lucrative market" for online reference books and express amazement that "electronic dictionaries are actually making money." (Kirkpatrick 2000.) But as long as someone is willing to make a bad dictionary—sloppily prepared, decades out of date—available for free, it will be hard to convince users to pay for something better. Many people are convinced that a dictionary is a dictionary, and as the saying goes, you can't compete with free.

Making dictionaries is unavoidably expensive. Heaven knows, few lexicographers get rich, but they do need to be paid for years, even decades. Johnson's quarrel with Lord Chesterfield (no. 34), Webster's mortgage on his house (no. 70), the never-ending battle over how long the *OED* would be (no. 96)— all show the challenges of maintaining a lexicographic project over a long period.

Courtesy of Oxford University Press

John Simpson joined the *OED* team in 1976 and was coeditor or chief editor from 1986 to 2013.

Publishers are therefore still struggling, hoping to figure out how to cover expenses, and maybe even make a profit, on dictionaries in the digital age. Should they be sold like books, one-time purchases? If so, do purchasers have any claim on updates or new editions? Or should they be sold as a subscription service? If so, are subscriptions priced for universities and libraries, or for individual subscribers? Few publishers can manage thousands of online subscription accounts, so that will take another substantial investment. Or is it possible to make it free to users, supported only by advertising? We don't yet have consensus on any of these questions.

The *OED* is the most sophisticated English dictionary, so it's appropriate that it also has the most sophisticated online presence. The main digitizing work was done for the *OED on CD-ROM* (no. 128). As early as 1990—before the development of the World Wide Web—there were discussions about an online presence. There was even an experimental web version developed in 1994. But the *OED Online* was officially unveiled to the world on 13 March 2000, in an event with Thomas Murray, the great-great-great-grandson of Sir James A.H. Murray, the first editor. (Gilliver 2016:563, 569.)

Courtesy of Oxford University Press

Michael Proffitt joined the *OED* team in 1989 and became chief editor in 2013.

The dictionary was called *OED3*, but at the time it was almost indistinguishable from *OED2* (1989—no. 106), which itself was mostly *OED1* (1888–1928—no. 96) combined with the *Supplement* (1972–1986—no. 105). Most of it, that is to say, had been written more than a century earlier. But English is always picking up new words and senses, and new evidence about older senses continues to turn up. And old definitions sometimes show their age. The first edition notoriously defined *canoe* as "a kind of boat in use among uncivilized nations," adding, for good measure, that "most savages use paddles instead of oars." It was time, at last, for the dictionary's first comprehensive revision—not merely supplements and occasional corrections but a top-to-bottom reconsideration, scrutinizing every etymology,

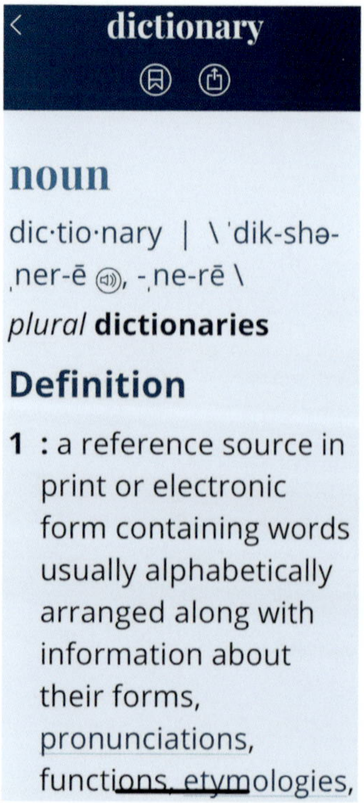

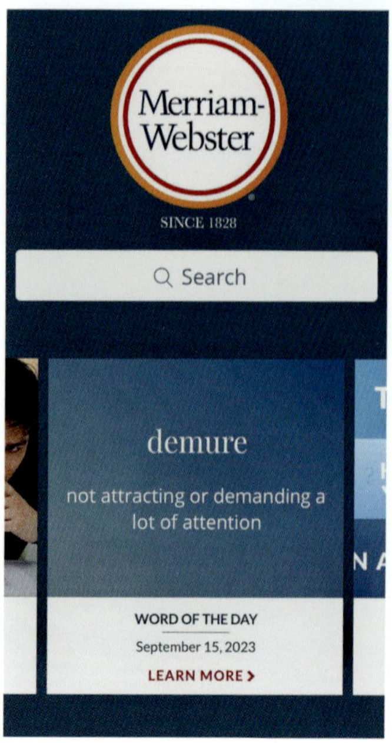

every usage note, every definition, every date, and every quotation. Although nothing in Murray's original vision has changed, the editors can now bring to bear 21st-century understandings and 21st-century digital tools.

The revision allows the editors to rectify some of the shortcomings of the original dictionary. The old reading program drew too much from literary sources and male authors, and it depended on serendipity rather than databases to find earliest citations. In the revision, more than half the earliest citations have been antedated, some by just a year or two, but some by decades.

The revision originally proceeded in alphabetical order, but they didn't start with *A*. Lexicographers are usually still finding their footing in the early part of a dictionary, so the *OED3* team decided to start their work with *M*, when their predecessors had a good idea of what they were doing. By the end of 2010, they had made it as far as *ryvita* before ranging widely through the alphabet, and they'll keep going until every entry has been revisited.

Over the years, the *OED* has made many minor and several major revisions to its interface. Much of the attention is devoted to enabling searches that couldn't be done on paper: it's now possible to say, for instance, that the *OED* records twice as many Yiddish borrowings in the 20th century as in the 19th, or that 57 food and drink terms come from Hindi. The online *OED* also features hyperlinks that make it possible to integrate related projects like the *Historical Thesaurus of the OED* (2009) and the *Dictionary of Old English* into the online *OED*.

The current *OED*, therefore, is a mélange of old and new material, with the new slowly taking over the old at the rate of a few thousand entries every year. Though discussions are still happening in Oxford, it's unlikely that there will be a print version of the third edition. If it comes to fruition, it will probably be about twice the size of the second.

The other big player in the online realm is Merriam-Webster, which entered the digital age with a CD-ROM in 1995: *Merriam-Webster's Collegiate Dictionary, Deluxe Electronic Edition*. Merriam-Webster acquired a web presence a year later with an online version of *Merriam-Webster's Collegiate Dictionary*, 11th edition. That same dictionary, regularly updated, is now available as a free website supported by advertising, a free app supported by advertising, or an inexpensive app without the advertising. There is also an online *Merriam-Webster Unabridged*, though this is a subscription service; it is based on the *Third New International* (1961—no. 102), also updated from time to time. Merriam-Webster devotes a great deal of energy to its web presence beyond the dictionary proper: there are blogs, an integrated thesaurus, short videos about usage, word-of-the-day features, and word games. The electronic presence allows users to be in touch with lexicographers, both to ask questions and to volunteer information that might be useful to the lexicographers. "Editorial correspondence is one of the duties of the Merriam-Webster lexicographer," writes Kory Stamper, though she acknowledges that it's not always an entirely welcome one. (Stamper 2017:217.)

All the major dictionary publishers now have some electronic presence. Some, including American Heritage, Collins, Cambridge University Press, and Oxford University Press, have made some of their dictionaries available through Mobile Systems' MSDict program, which runs as an app on iPhones and Android devices. Others, including Chambers and Merriam-Webster, have had custom software developed for them.

Publishers are still figuring out how to stay afloat in a period of significant disruption, and not all will manage it successfully. The article cited above that was enthusiastic about the "increasingly lucrative market" for online dictionaries singled out two success stories: *Encarta* and *American Heritage*. (Kirkpatrick 2000.) Neither has survived the transition to digital publication: *Encarta* discontinued its dictionary site in 2011, and though *American Heritage* remains available, it has not been updated since 2011 and has no plans for further publication.

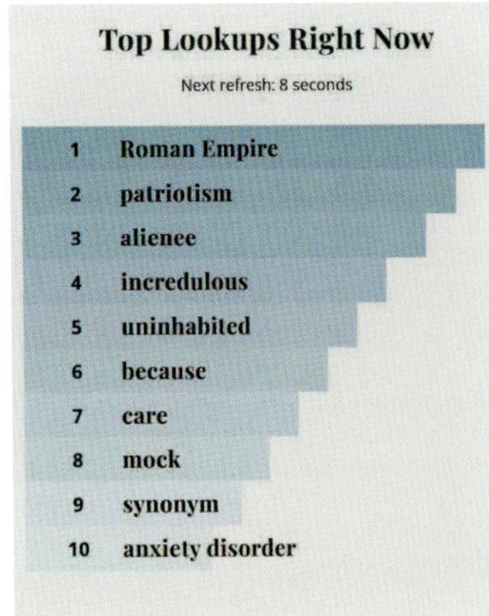

Merriam-Webster's "top lookups" feature is updated with real-time information every 30 seconds.

"Apart from the new visual aesthetic and the more sophisticated search functionality, the ongoing revision of the *OED* provides . . . frequency information [and] . . . a view of the previous version of an entry, important for anyone wanting to study the Dictionary's editorial history." (Crystal 2019:501.)

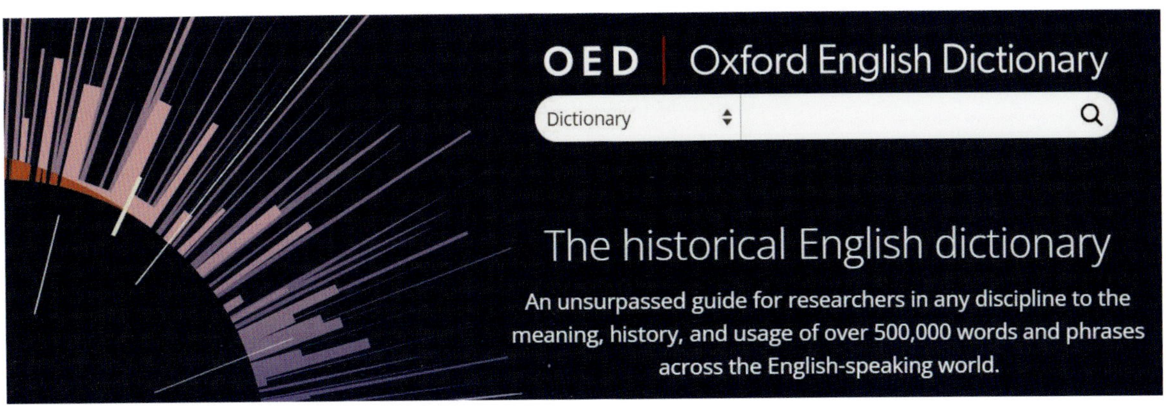

Courtesy of Harvard University Faculty of Arts and Sciences

Henry Louis Gates Jr.

"Every speaker of American English borrows heavily from words invented by African Americans, whether they know it or not." (Henry Louis Gates press release [2023].)

The Oxford Dictionary of African American English - First 100 Words

The Oxford Dictionary of African American English - First 100 Words

The *Oxford Dictionary of African American English (ODAAE)*, a joint project of **Oxford Languages (Oxford University Press)** and **Harvard University's Hutchins Center for African & African American Research**, is now well underway, and the first 100 entries have recently been completed. The project is spearheaded by Prof Henry Louis Gates, Jr., Editor-in-Chief, Director of the Center, and Alphonse Fletcher, University Professor at Harvard.

Read more about the project and its progress via the button below.

Find out more

132

Oxford Dictionary of African American English

Endlessly Inventive

***The Oxford Dictionary of African American English*. Henry Louis Gates Jr. ed. Oxford: Oxford Univ. Press, projected for 2025.**

STRANGE TO SAY, but as we write this in 2024, we *still* don't have a proper dictionary of African American English. Clarence Major was the first to give book-length treatment to the subject (no. 118), but his concern was strictly slang. African American English is much broader than that.

The gap will soon be filled. In July 2022 came the announcement of an in-progress *Oxford Dictionary of African American English*, to be prepared by a team of researchers split between Oxford University Press and Harvard's Hutchins Center for African and African American Research, overseen by Harvard's Henry Louis Gates Jr. (b. 1950).

Countless varieties of English are spoken in North America. Every ethnic group that has settled here has its own distinctive linguistic habits, and all deserve attention. But the varieties of the language associated with African Americans make particular claims on our attention. People of African descent have been in the territory that is now the United States since 1619. Those who were brought here by slave traders spoke a variety of mutually unintelligible West African languages—thereby creating the conditions for the development of a creole. They then experienced four centuries of a paradoxical combination of segregation from, and influence on, mainstream Anglophone culture, with disparagement and emulation of African American English in almost equal measure. Black English has been called improper and illiterate, but the language associated with African American communities—think of musical forms like blues, jazz, gospel, R&B, soul, funk, hip-hop—has had tremendous influence on the larger American Anglophone community. All these factors make

Black English especially illuminating to linguists. What's more, says Gates, there's a long history of African Americans' linguistic playfulness and invention:

> We are endlessly inventive with language, and we had to be. We had to develop what literary scholars call double-voiced discourse. We had to learn to speak the master's language, then you had to learn to speak *under* the masters so that you could have a coded way of speaking English that would allow you to voice your feelings without being killed, whipped or—worst-case scenario—without being lynched. [Garcia 2023:D2.]

"*Bussin* (adj. and participle): 1. Especially describing food: tasty, delicious. Also more generally: impressive, excellent. 2. Describing a party, event, etc.: busy, crowded, lively."

In Gates's words, Black speakers took the English language and "reinvented it, to make it reflect their sensibilities and to make it mirror their cultural selves."

The project will not be large: this isn't a dictionary of *all* English used by African Americans, but only the words that are distinct from those in the larger English-speaking community. It's expected to contain about a thousand words upon its first appearance. Yet the editors are casting a wide net in terms of geography, chronology, and register. Ten words were publicly released as a teaser of the project: *Aunt Hagar's children*, *bussin*, *cakewalk*, *chitterlings*, *grill*, *kitchen*, *old school*, *pat* (vb.), *Promised Land*, and *ring shout*.

"*Old school* (adj.): Characteristic of early hip-hop or rap music that emerged in New York City between the late 1970s to the mid 1980s, which often includes the use of couplets, funk and disco samples, and playful lyrics. Also used to describe the music and artists of that style and time period."

The lexicographic policies will be essentially those of the *OED*—fitting, since the project was originally conceived as an opportunity for Gates and his team to offer commentary on in-progress *OED* revisions. All words will need to be backed up by citations; all will come with etymologies and variant spellings and pronunciations.

Gates is no stranger to dictionaries. At the age of eight, he fell in love with wordbooks, convinced that his school's Webster's dictionary was "magical." More than six decades later, as the world was suffering the shared trauma of the COVID pandemic, he sought comfort in another dictionary. "I was sitting here in this kitchen, sheltering in, doing a Zoom. . . . I said: 'You know what? We could die at any time. I'm going to buy a first edition of the Samuel Johnson dictionary.'" And so he did. (Garcia 2023:D2.)

"*cakewalk* (n.): 1. A contest in which Black people would perform a stylized walk in pairs, typically judged by a plantation owner. The winner would receive some type of cake. 2. Something that is considered easily done, as in 'This job is a cakewalk.'"

The Oxford Dictionary of African American English is a reminder that lexicography remains a vital enterprise, and that there are still urgent tasks to do, more than half a millennium after the earliest printed dictionaries.

Ex coll. Karolyne & Bryan A. Garner

Afterword

WHAT IS THE FUTURE of dictionaries? As one publisher after another closes its reference division, do dictionaries have any future at all? Prognosticating is often unwise and notoriously unreliable, but we'll hazard a few predictions based on the recent past:

(1) As more and more apps, software programs, and websites embed digital dictionaries into their content, fewer and fewer print dictionaries will be kept up by publishers.

(2) Multivolume dictionaries are likely to become a thing of the past, as users find online dictionaries and apps more convenient than hauling from the shelves one volume at a time to look things up. Besides, the digital environment has made it possible to perform a once-arduous task in a single keystroke. For example: How many times is Shakespeare cited in the *OED* as the earliest known user of a word? Getting the answer now takes seconds; it once took years of labor.

(3) The high-quality single-volume print dictionary is here to stay, at least for a few more generations. A few years ago, people were forecasting the end of print books, but that simply hasn't come to pass. Many readers prefer reading physical books, and the same is true of dictionary users. The college-size one-volume dictionary continues to sell and looks as if it has a robust life ahead.

(4) In this way, dictionaries are fundamentally different from encyclopedias, which seem to be a defunct print category. Besides, encyclopedias go out of date much faster than dictionaries. Why? Encyclopedias deal with people who die, cities whose population numbers vary from year to year, and momentous events that must be recorded. Though new words are always being coined, most of the changes in meanings, etymologies, and pronunciations happen at a glacial pace. True, this year's slang won't appear in a dictionary printed last year, but that fact is likely to go unnoticed. A dictionary from 1950 remains useful in ways that an encyclopedia from 1950 does not.

(5) As the mania for "correctness" has subsided among English-speaking peoples, so has the passion for checking dictionaries. That means, too, that less is commercially at stake than was true in the 18th century through the 19th and into the 20th.

(6) Standardization in language is unlikely to decline. It once required memorization. Now, though, computers encourage it (perhaps enforce it!) automatically. Just as students are no longer required to learn multiplication

and division—your handheld device does it for you—so computers of one size or another tell us how to spell, and they flag much of our faulty grammar.

(7) Although artificial intelligence may contribute to lexicography, it will not be reliable as long as the problem of "AI hallucinating" isn't resolved. In any event, we're highly skeptical about whether AI could replace skillful lexicographers in any foreseeable future.

The fifth point is culturally interesting. Dictionaries at once reflected and shaped people's relationship with their language. That will remain so, but the fact that we no longer live in a dictionary-crazed society, much less a grammar-crazed one, means that we can look on our own past with a kind of bemused bewilderment. How did the population move from a state of frenzied interest to a state of widespread unconcern in such a relatively brief time? Nobody would have predicted that. Certainly not the lexicographic drudges of yesteryear, who would have considered this seismic cultural shift hardly harmless.

Ex coll. Karolyne & Bryan A. Garner

The Garner–Lynch Index

Most famous name in lexicography: Samuel Johnson (over Noah Webster by a factor of 4.8)
First English-language dictionary: John Rastell, 1523 [no. 1] or 1579 [no. 1], or Robert Cawdrey, 1604 [no. 7] (it depends)
First female English-language lexicographer: Ann Fisher, 1771 [no. 41]
First English dictionary published in North America: William Perry, 1788 [no. 46]
First written in North America: Samuel Johnson Jr., 1798 [no. 54]
First published in Ireland: unauthorized edition of Bullokar's *English Expositor*, 1726 [no. 11]
First published in Scotland: John Skene, 1597 [no. 4]
Earliest lexicographer in this volume for whom we have a likeness: Johannes Calderinus (d. 1348) [p. 2]
Average lifespan of the lexicographers in this book: 70.5 years
Longest-lived lexicographer: Hans Kurath (100) [no. 107]
Shortest-lived: Herbert Coleridge (30) [nos. 82 & 96]
Shortest-lived who actually finished a dictionary: Elisha Coles [no. 20] & John Quincy [no. 25] (both 40)
Lexicographer with most different dictionary titles: Eric Partridge (9) [nos. 116 & 120]
17th-century dictionary with the most entries: Elisha Coles, 1676 (25,000) [no. 20]
18th-century dictionary with the most entries: Nathan Bailey, 1736 & 1755 (60,000) [nos. 26 & 36]
19th-century dictionary with the most entries: *Funk & Wagnalls*, 1895 (304,000) [no. 91]
20th-century dictionary with the most entries: *Webster's Second New International*, 1934 (552,000) [no. 100]
21st-century dictionary with the most entries: *OED3* (600,000) [no. 131]
First dictionary to be called a *dictionary*: Sir Thomas Elyot, 1538 [no. 2]
First to include etymologies to any significant degree: Thomas Blount, 1656 [no. 16]
First to show stressed syllable: Nathan Bailey, 1730 [no. 26]
First to show how to pronounce the vowels in each word: James Buchanan, 1757 [no. 38]
First to deal with phrasal verbs to a significant degree: Samuel Johnson, 1755 [no. 35]
First to cite authorities to a significant degree: John Cowell, 1607 [no. 9]
First to include quotations: John Cowell, 1607 [no. 9]
First to include illustrative quotations for every word: Samuel Johnson, 1755 [no. 35]
First to list alternative spellings: John Cowell, 1607 [no. 9]
First to distinguish near-synonyms: John Cowell, 1607 [no. 9]
First to use numbered senses: Benjamin Martin, 1754 [no. 33]
First to mark archaisms and obsolete terms: John Bullokar, 1616 [no. 11]
First to clearly differentiate between *I* & *J* and *U* & *V*: Ann Fisher, 1773 [no. 41]
First to include an English grammar in front matter: Thomas Dyche & William Pardon, 1735 [no. 30]
First to feature thumbcuts: *Webster's International Dictionary*, 1890 [no. 89]
First to feature color pages: *Funk & Wagnalls*, 1895 [no. 91]
First to use computers in editing and production: *Random House*, 1966 [no. 103]
First lexicographer whose dictionary was officially banned: John Cowell, 1607 [no. 9]
First lexicographer subjected to unreasonable search and seizure by government agents: John Entick, 1762 [no. 40]
Lexicographer with the highest rate of alphabetization errors: Elisha Coles (11%) [no. 20]

Percentage of pre-1657 English-language lexicographers who were lawyers: 54%
Who were teachers: 23%
Who were clerics: 15%
Who were physicians: 7%
Who were goldsmiths: 7%
Number of publishing firms that pooled resources to publish Johnson's 1755 *Dictionary*: 5
Number of them still publishing dictionaries in 2024: 1 (Longman)
Word with the most senses in Johnson's *Dictionary*: *take* (113 transitive, 21 intransitive)
Named contributors to Johnson's *Dictionary*: 1
Named contributors to *American Heritage Dictionary* [no. 104], 5th ed.: 316
Contributors, mostly unnamed, to *OED1* [no. 84]: 2,000
Heaviest one-volume dictionary on record: *Century Dictionary* (20 lbs.) [see p. 289]
Heaviest multivolume dictionary on record: *OED2* (115 lbs.) [no. 106]
Amount of ink used in the complete print run of *OED2* [no. 106]: 6,243 lbs.
Number of books in the Library of Congress with *dictionary* in the title: 34,365
Number of books in the British Library with *dictionary* in the title: 49,197
Number of books with both *Webster* and *Dictionary* in the title in the Library of Congress: 1,374 [see no. 108]
Number of books with *Oxford* and *Dictionary* in the title in the British Library: 2,115
Longest time between publishing the first and last volumes of an English dictionary: 49 years (*Middle English Dictionary*) [no. 107]
Longest entry in *OED2*: *set*, v., with 430 senses
Longest entry in *OED3*: *run*, v., with 654 senses
Length of the entire entry for *run* in *OED3*: 140,000 words
Length of Dickens's *Tale of Two Cities*: 137,000 words
Total meanings included in *OED3*: 878,485
Total quotations included in *OED3*: 3,840,299
First dictionary published by an African American: Cab Calloway, *The Hepsters Dictionary*, 1938 [no. 117]
First English dictionary on CD-ROM: The *Oxford English Dictionary*, 1987 [no. 128]
First handheld electronic English dictionary: Lexicon LK-3000, 1978 [no. 127]
Percentage of American households that owned a dictionary in 1988: 89%
That owned one in 2015: 45%
That owned a foreign-language dictionary: 32%
That owned a crossword-puzzle dictionary: 20%
Percentage of people who look up words daily: 15%
Who do so at least once a week: 17%
Who do so at least once a month: 19%
Who have never in their lives looked up a definition: 5%
Monthly page views on Merriam-Webster.com [no. 131]: 100 million
Percentage of people who think it's a good idea to add new words to dictionaries periodically: 63%
Bestselling dictionary in the world: *Oxford Advanced Learner's Dictionary* (100 million learners since 1948)

(You're wondering about our sources for these facts and figures?
They're safely on file in the structure shown at right.)

Ex coll. Karolyne & Bryan A. Garner

The Scriptorium at Penrose, which houses part of the Garner Collection.

Ex coll. Karolyne & Bryan A. Garner

Some Folio-Size "Also-Rans" for This Volume

Although the word *dictionary* appears in their titles, they are more in the nature of encyclopedias: on top, Erasmus Middleton's *New Complete Dictionary of Arts and Sciences* (1778); underneath that, and to the right, in five volumes, *The Dictionary Historical and Critical of Mr. Peter Bayle* (2d ed. 1734–1738); to the left, in four tan volumes, Ephraim Chambers's *Cyclopædia: Or, an Universal Dictionary of Arts and Sciences* (top two vols. are 5th ed., 1741–1743; bottom two vols. are a 1753 supplement); and bottom left, in three volumes, Jeremy Collier's *Great Historical, Geographical, Genealogical, and Poetical Dictionary; Being a Curious Miscellany of Sacred and Profane History* (1st English ed. in 2 vols., 1701; plus a one-vol. supplement, 1705).

Some Little Curiosities: The Original Handheld Devices

In the foreground, beside the nickel, left to right: **(1)** *The Smallest English Dictionary in the World*. Glasgow: David Bryce & Son, 1893. With a metal clasp having a built-in magnifying glass. Text block 2 × 2.75 cm. **(2)** *The Little Webster Dictionary: 18000 Words*. New York: Tiny Book & Novelty Co., ca. 1930. Text block 3.5 × 4.5 cm. **(3)** Same enclosed in leather packet. **(4)** Charles Boardman, *An Improved Pocket Dictionary Containing all the Principal Words in the English Language*. Cazenovia: Henry, Hitchcock & Co., 1844. Text block 4.5 × 7.5 cm. **(5)** *English Language: The Little Linguist; Or, a Complete Guide to English Philology*. London: W.S. Johnson. Text block 4.5 × 7.5 cm. **(6)** Lyman Cobb, *The Reticule and Pocket Companion*. New York: Harper & Bros., 1841. Text block 5.5 × 8.5 cm.

Ex coll. Karolyne & Bryan A. Garner

Comments

Ex coll. Karolyne & Bryan A. Garner

Many of the books exhibited in this catalogue are on carts in the foreground here.

Seventeenth-Century English Lexicography and the First Line of *Macbeth*

John Considine
Professor Emeritus, Department of English
University of Alberta

"WHEN SHALL WE THREE MEET AGAINE?" Six words, and although the question they make up is a mysterious one when we hear or read them at the beginning of *Macbeth*, it is expressed in plain English. So should we expect to find those six words treated in a 17th-century English dictionary? We will look for them in vain in any of the six canonical English dictionaries published in the course of the century: Cawdrey (no. 7), Bullokar (no. 11), Cockeram (no. 13), Blount (no. 16), Phillips (no. 17), and Coles (no. 20). They all had other words to explain—other work to do.

There was, however, one 17th-century English dictionary that treated all six words, and of course it's in the Garner Collection: Stephen Skinner's *Etymologicon Linguæ Anglicanæ* of 1671 (no. 18). Skinner wasn't interested in explaining, for instance, how *when* is used, but he tells us that it is from "Anglo-Saxon" (we might say Old English) *hwænne*, and he compares German and Dutch forms with the English one before overreaching himself and deriving them all from Latin *quando*—a relative of theirs, to be sure, but not their mother. The mistake doesn't matter as much as Skinner's interest in the whole vocabulary of English. An abridged translation of his dictionary, Richard Hogarth's *Gazophylacium Anglicanum* of 1689, made some of its core content accessible to the Latinless reader.

Making a list of all the commonest words in English is a difficult task, and Skinner found the basis of his wordlist ready-made, in another etymologically oriented dictionary with English headwords. Nor is it in the canonical list. But it is in the Garner Collection, namely, John Minsheu's *Ductor in Linguas* of 1617 (no. 12). Minsheu was the very first lexicographer to attempt a full list of common English words for their own sake, rather than simply to help people translate English into another language. He recorded five of the six words with which we began, missing only the elusive modal verb *shall*.

Two questions follow. First, why did Skinner catch *shall*? Simple: because he studied William Somner's *Dictionarium Saxonico–Latino–Anglicum* of 1659, the first printed dictionary of Old English, which included the verb *sceal*, and he realized that he should document its modern English descendant, which Somner identifies.

Second, where did Minsheu get his list of English headwords for the *Ductor in Linguas*? Not quite so simple: but it was certainly based on the English–Spanish section of his Spanish dictionary of 1599, also in the Garner Collection (no. 6). And where did he get that list of English words? From John Rider's English–Latin *Bibliotheca Scholastica* of 1589 . . . and although it is, in fact, easy to say where Rider found his English headwords, we must not let dictionary genealogy distract us from the 17th century.

Apart from Skinner's *Etymologicon* (in Latin, and also as translated by Hogarth), only one other 17th-century dictionary can, as far as I know, be said to have registered all six of the words with which we began, in order to analyze them as English words. That was the "Alphabetical Dictionary" by William Lloyd, which formed part of John Wilkins's *Essay Towards a Real Character and a Philosophical Language*, published in 1668. Wilkins thought that it might be possible to devise an artificial ("philosophical") language to express all the concepts that natural languages like English could express, in a perfectly clear and orderly way. His work was an intellectual ancestor of Roget's *Thesaurus* (no. 76). Lloyd's "Alphabetical Dictionary" was a proof of Wilkins's concept. It showed that a set of more or less common English words could all have their meanings analyzed in such a way as to show that they fit into the framework of the philosophical language, so that *meet*, for example, could be explained as "Come together" and analyzed as "TA. VI. 7," or in other words, as belonging to the genus of transcendental relation of action, and to the sixth "difference" within that genus (which, as Wilkins explained elsewhere, referred to motion), and to the seventh "species" within that difference.

Skinner, like Minsheu before him, was using the dictionary to understand English words in relation to other words. Wilkins and Lloyd were using their dictionary to understand English words in relation to concepts. The canonical lexicographers mentioned at the beginning of this essay all served their readers well, but their work was less intellectually ambitious and less wide-ranging. A pioneering book about the history of English lexicography is called *The English Dictionary from Cawdrey to Johnson*, as if Cawdrey's *Table Alphabeticall* were where the English dictionary started. But the dictionaries of Minsheu and Skinner (and Somner) are not offshoots of Cawdrey's. Nor is that of Wilkins and Lloyd. Nor, indeed, are the seminal dictionaries of Cowell (no. 9) and Wilson (no. 10). A serious collection of early English dictionaries is bound, like the Garner Collection, to bear witness to the intelligence and diversity of the 17th-century lexicographers among whom Cawdrey stands among equals, perhaps, but not the first among equals.

Drudges, Drudgery, and Under-Drudges: Lexicography as Work

Lynda Mugglestone
Professor of the History of English
Pembroke College, Oxford University

"I WAS BRED A BOOKSELLER and have not forgotten my trade," Samuel Johnson is reputed to have said in reference to his own early history in books and bookmaking in his father's business in Lichfield. He would undoubtedly have appreciated this richly illustrated volume, and the material as well as the intellectual history it presents. He would, I suspect, have enjoyed, too, the juxtaposition between the elegant bindings that, as we can see, often accompanied dictionaries as finished products, and the reminders of the underlying drudgery by which they were made. Whether in the embossed leather of Edward Cocker's *English Dictionary* (no. 22) or the heft of the *OED*, the material text can easily be seen as a proxy for other enduing values that dictionaries contain.

Dictionaries, as this volume therefore usefully reminds us, always have this kind of double narrative, one by which we typically refer to the endpoint (Johnson's *Dictionary* of 1755, or say Blount's of 1656) but in which we must also remain alert to the often laborious means by which this point was reached. Johnson, for example, carefully explained both *dictionary* and *drudge* long before he got to *lexicographer*. If a dictionary was "a book containing the words of any language," *drudges*, as he made plain, were perhaps inevitably "employed in mean labor" and "servile occupation," toiling behind the scenes where the real work of dictionary-making takes place. A dictionary is a "Work of Labor rather than Genius," as the lexicographer and encyclopedist Ephraim Chambers had stressed in his *Considerations Offered to the Publick* (1728). Motifs of dictionary-making as work or labor proliferate in Johnson's account of what he does ("I have laboured with diligence," he writes; the "great labour" is that of interpretation; his "labour" was increased by the verbal structures of English). Johnson's working texts, of which 14 now remain extant, provide their own eloquent testimonies in this respect, visibly setting out the processes of collection, collation, and copying out—all done by hand—that lexicography of this kind required.

This semantic overlap—the dictionary-maker as drudge—alongside, as Johnson makes plain, the slow trudging of the alphabet from *A* to *Z*, provides its own ironic backdrop to the heroic narratives and adventures that, across the history of lexicography, have popularly framed the dictionary-maker's triumph. Garrick's celebratory poem (see p. 110) easily evoked a sense of Johnson's national (and international) stature once publication was complete. Johnson's own poem, headed "The Vanity of Human Wishes," written in 1749 during the *Dictionary*'s composition, tells a different story. Here, "toil, envy, want, [and] the garret" take center stage. His dictionary garret, still intact in Gough Square in London, was, as the preface to the *Dictionary* made plain, not a "bower" or place of quiet retirement. Instead, Johnson stressed, the good lexicographer must remain a "slave of science," subordinated to knowledge and where this might be located, in a process iterated over months and years until the end of the alphabet is reached.

Drudges might, in this, need other co-drudges or under-drudges. Here, too, the finished text can be deceptive. Title pages routinely invite us to focus on the dictionary-maker in isolation. Helpers and assistants are relegated to the small print or, like Johnson's six amanuenses, silenced altogether. Cawdrey (as no. 7 confirms) slips in a quick mention of his son. Ray (or Wray) in his *Collection of English Words Not Generally Used* (no. 19) confers similar anonymity on his early crowdsourcing among his friends. Johnson's amanuenses can, if in other texts, make their own role as the "laborious brethren" of the *Dictionary* plain; a private letter by William Macbean, written in 1785, still vividly evokes his sense of the shared endeavor and fellowship that the *Dictionary* required. For the first edition of the *OED* (pp. 263ff.), crowdsourcing was wider still, with readers across the world sharing the vital collection of data, though—playing the numbers game—only the most productive secured recognition in the prefaces that accompanied its serial publication. Dictionary-making for James Murray was likened to the collaborative building of a "cairn" in which each stone, however small, contributes to the structure that results. Whose work is presented, and how, is a further aspect of the narratives that can, in this respect, variously unfold. As for Johnson's amanuenses, there is often more to say.

Drudgery, then, remains a compelling invitation for us to think about the text behind the text, and the forms and skills that this requires, as well as the different communities of practice—from scribes, copyists, assistants, readers, to printers, compositors, typesetters (and, in later texts, those in charge of its digital architecture and data input)—who, in different ways, contribute to the text that readers consult and, at times, contest. Modern "drudges" might do different tasks; Johnson's quill has been replaced by a computer. But labor—and the intricate anatomization of language that lexicography requires—is a constant.

Ironies and Double-Crosses

Peter Sokolowski
Editor-at-Large, Merriam-Webster Inc.
Springfield, Mass.

At the end of his life, Noah Webster could look back on the body of work that had made his name famous. He would leave behind influential works of reference and educational publishing, a large family, and a stately home. But he also left behind grudges and resentments that did not end with his death, among them a grudge that crossed the professional with the personal. In his final weeks, Webster spoke of his son-in-law Chauncey Goodrich, a respected Yale professor, wishing that he would "never again have the power to alter my dictionary."

Webster couldn't see into the future, but he had a vivid recollection of the past, especially the specific histories of the publications that bore his name. His hopes for the big two-volume quarto dictionary that he had produced in 1828 (no. 62) weighed heavily on his mind. Quite apart from the many years of work that it represented, it had been hugely expensive to typeset and print. And at a price of $20 per copy, its prospects for commercial success had been limited. His publisher, Sherman Converse, desperate to recoup some of his investment, insisted on an affordable octavo abridgment as quickly as possible. Webster himself begged off, fatigued from years of work and by then over 70 years of age. But Converse couldn't delay. He had heard the name of a scholar with qualifications uniquely suited to the task of making a successful shorter version of a dictionary because this scholar had very recently done just that: a fresh abridgment of Samuel Johnson's *Dictionary* had been published in 1827 and was selling briskly. Its editor was Joseph Worcester.

Chauncey Goodrich was designated to act for Webster's interests, both as a representative of the family and as a capable scholar himself. Different reactions to Worcester can be perceived in the tone of letters that Webster and Goodrich sent the new hire; Webster wrote with resignation that he had had nothing to do with selecting him, "but under the circumstances, I have consented to it." Goodrich's enthusiastic note, on the other hand, sings his "highest satisfaction; for there is no man in the United States, as you know from conversation with me, who would be equally acceptable."

Together, Goodrich and Worcester then did something remarkable. Their job was to produce a smaller and more affordable dictionary, so, obviously, they shortened definitions. But because many of Webster's entries had long sermons, digressions, and editorializations embedded in them, it was possible to retain the best lexical parts of his entries—the parts for which he is justifiably famous to this day—and still cut many lines of text. Their edits made his dictionary a crisper and better one. Astonishingly, they managed not only to keep all of Webster's headwords in the process, but also to *add* many thousands of new words. This was no ordinary abridgment (see no. 63).

In fact, adding words was a condition of the contract between Converse and Webster. Among the provisions for the work was an unusual one that doesn't mention Worcester by name but makes clear that his recent labors and consequent expertise should be put to good use:

> Any words to be found in Todd's edition of Johnson's Dictionary [no. 52] which may have been omitted in the Dictionary of s[ai]d Webster may be inserted in the abridgment.

Although Webster may well have objected to this idea, he signed the contract.

Along the way, Goodrich and Worcester also smoothed over the most egregious of Webster's fetishistic and unconventional spellings, dropped many of his oddball and fanciful etymologies, and updated the system of showing pronunciations. It was clear that they agreed that the dictionary would be improved by removing the most idiosyncratic, opinionated, and unusual parts of the original. They took much of Webster out of *Webster's*.

Goodrich next proved to be a savvy businessman. He bought the copyright of the new octavo from Webster, who didn't like seeing his work altered. (See pp. 230–31.) Then, in order to protect the new abridgment, he prodded Webster to sign an injunction against any future publication of a version of the big dictionary that would compete with what was now, in law as well as in deed, Goodrich's property. Since the 1828 original had been sold as two large quarto volumes, there could no longer be any other octavo reduction derived from it. From Webster's point of view, it was good riddance; the octavo "must not be considered mine," he wrote. Still, his name was on it, and Lyman Cobb made the most of that fact (no. 64).

Goodrich's acquisition was good business. His abridgment went through five printings in twelve months and would earn him a whopping six thousand dollars per year. He even endowed his own chair at Yale with the proceeds. We can begin to understand why Webster, disappointed with his finances at the end of his life, came to resent Goodrich.

After Webster's death in 1843, Goodrich would again "have the power to alter" his dictionary. The Merriam brothers by now owned the rights to the big book and admired his work on the octavo (see no. 74). They recognized that it might hurt the future sales of the dictionary if some consistency in spelling and style were not established among the different dictionaries under Webster's name in the marketplace. They asked Goodrich to become the editor for their new printing—the first "Merriam" edition of Webster—of 1847. He made their updates but also sent along changes to the publisher of the octavo. Since the Merriams apparently didn't know that the copyright to the octavo was owned by Goodrich, they seem never to have known that he was double-dipping, taking a salary to update their dictionary and making the same updates to his own.

It's a story full of complicated double-crosses that had far-reaching consequences for dictionaries bearing the Webster name. In the end, Goodrich and Worcester removed the most amateurish parts of Webster's work—they murdered his darlings—and helped establish a line of reputable dictionaries. During Webster's lifetime, no one did more than these two men to preserve Webster's name for posterity. Worcester then set about producing the most threatening competition yet seen for the Webster brand, driving Goodrich to greater heights with Webster dictionaries. But these vibrant contributions to the dictionary market could be achieved only by squelching Webster's quirky and combative confidant, William C. Fowler (see no. 73), who wanted to restore Webster's darlings. It was only by defying Webster's wishes that Goodrich, with Worcester's help, immortalized Webster's name.

Whose American Dictionary?

Kory Stamper
Editor, Dictionary.com
Former Associate Editor, Merriam-Webster Inc.

The 19th-century Webster–Worcester Dictionary Wars (nos. 63 & 77) have been called many things by scholars. They were perhaps the longest-lasting and most public slap-fight over plagiarism's long history in lexicography. The Dictionary Wars were also the proving ground for the limits of linguistic innovation—notably Webster's etymological and orthographical schemes. But these touch on what we might consider to be the first campaign of the war, which ran from Noah Webster's first private letter of complaint to Joseph Worcester in 1831 to the latter's death in 1860 (nearly 20 years after the complainant had joined the Scriptorium Invisible). There is a second, less studied campaign of the Dictionary Wars: the later fight over what made an American dictionary truly *American*.

Webster would have loved it. He came of age during the American Revolutionary War, and his patriotism (and Yankee cussedness) burned bright from the get-go. He was so desperate to fight for his nascent nation that he left Yale and headed west to join American forces at the Battle of Saratoga. (Arriving late, he saw no action.) The first part of his reference suite for schoolchildren, *The American Spelling Book* (no. 53), was published in 1783—the same year that the Revolutionary War formally ended with the Treaty of Paris, signed between Great Britain and the new United States. Six years later, in an essay in his *Dissertations on the English Language*, Webster would write that "customs, habits, and *language*, as well as government should be national." (Webster 1789:179.) He insisted: "America should have her *own* distinct from all the world. Such is the policy of other nations, and such must be *our* policy, before the states can be either independent or respectable." (*Id.*)

Webster claimed that everything he did in his dictionaries was for the civic education of a new nation. His spelling conventions were undertaken *specifically* to distance the American language from British. He boasted in the preface to his 1806 *Compendious Dictionary* (no. 57) that "in fifty years from this time, the American-English will be spoken by more people, than all the other dialects of the language," thereby coining the name of the language he set about cataloguing. And his 1828 magnum opus can be best summarized as "Johnson, but make it American." This means, then, that any challenges to his work weren't just personal affronts, but national ones. Webster's initial irk at Worcester's prolific output (no. 63) was publicly couched as "an act of great injustice to a man who has rendered the country an invaluable service." Worcester, it must be noted, wasn't interested in being a patriot. He was primarily interested in writing dictionaries that weren't full of what Oliver Wendell Holmes later called "the American author's fancies." (Letter from Oliver Wendell Holmes, reprinted in an ad for Worcester's dictionaries, *Boston* [*Mass.*] *Evening Transcript*, 3 Nov. 1871, p. 3.)

Nor did the country at large seem interested in the question of which lexicographer was a true patriot. Worcester's dictionaries sold well; Webster's sold better after his successors quietly edited out his spelling innovations meant to liberate patriots from the tyranny of British English. The publisher of each lexicographer's works continued to chuck mud at the other while trumpeting any encomiums that a person of quality or power gave to its own latest dictionary. The public went on their merry way—that is, until after the American Civil War.

Like the war that shaped Webster the man, the war that shaped Webster the dictionary had repercussions for how Americans thought of their national and regional identities—and the language that best described those identities—long after the last shots were fired. The trouble for Webster's legacy began in 1863, when a pro-slavery newspaper in Nebraska printed a vignette about a young boy and his grandfather reviewing the Websterian definition for *Democrat*: "one who adheres to a government by the people, or who favors the extension of the right of suffrage to all men." The vignette ends with the grandfather's calling Webster "a blasted old Whig" who was "sort of favoring the n——," and telling his grandson that he'd get him a proper dictionary when he was next in town. (Untitled vignette, *Nebraska Advertiser* [Brownville, Neb.], 11 June 1863, p. 1.) The first shot had been fired. It continued in 1865, with a two-line report in a Buffalo newspaper noting that the previous year's new edition of Noah Webster's Big Book included an entry for the word *copperhead* that was defined as "a Northern sympathiser [sic] with Southern rebellion." (Untitled news note, *Buffalo Weekly Express*, 26 Dec. 1865, p. 1.) No such definition ever appeared in a dictionary published by the G. &. C. Merriam Co. Nonetheless, this aggression would not stand.

Webster's dictionary was, for the next decade or two, dissected word by word in Southern papers—and found wanting. The Merriams' new editor, Noah Porter, was a renowned abolitionist; the company was founded and run by Yankees; was there any doubt where their sympathies lay? Southern papers carried essays poring over the entries for *confederation*, *congress*, and *sovereignty*; one essay, reprinted in several papers, asked outright: "Why does Dr. Porter ignore the Constitution of the United States?" ("Falsifying Partisanship of Webster's Dictionary," *The McArthur* [*Ohio*] *Enquirer*, 3 Apr. 1872, p. 1.) Other papers called Webster's 1864 *Unabridged Dictionary* "the Mongrel Edition." All these essays noted anecdotally that sales of Worcester's dictionaries were on the rise.

And from the company that had taken on the legacy of the firebrand curmudgeon Noah Webster? Not a peep—publicly, at least. But the Merriams understood that it would be best to distance themselves from the furor over whose American their *American Dictionary of the English Language* covered. In 1890, the Merriams turned away from the past and looked toward the global future: *American* was dropped from the title of their Big Book, and *International* was substituted in its place.

Dictionaries on Exhibit and at the U.S. Supreme Court

Edward Finegan
Professor Emeritus of Linguistics and Law
University of Southern California

No ordinary catalogue of books at an exhibition, this! *Hardly Harmless Drudgery* is rich with pictorial illustrations of dictionary covers, title pages, and illustrative entries, alongside photographic and other representations of the lexicographers themselves. More than that, all the chapters offer fresh discussion of the writers and their dictionaries, at times proffering arguable, indeed provocative, proposals about what constitutes an English dictionary and even the identity of the earliest English dictionary.

Let me begin with a brief report. Shortly after the first anniversary of the attack on the United States Capitol on January 6, 2021, *The Joplin Globe*—a 125-year-old Missouri newspaper—ran two opinion pieces. In one, the paper's editor claimed that the events of January 6 constituted an "insurrection," citing definitions from a few general-purpose dictionaries. In an opposing piece, a local attorney cited only *Black's Law Dictionary* (no. 90), claiming implicitly that as a legal term, *insurrection* is solely a law dictionary's prerogative to define, and he did not judge the January 6 events to comport with *Black's* definition.

Beyond newspapers, *Black's* is often cited in legal matters, even to support opinions by justices of the U.S. Supreme Court. In one case, *Black's* was seemingly the primary authority for the outcome.[1] In dissent, Justice Ruth Bader Ginsburg argued that *Black's* should not be treated as "preclusively definitive."[2] But she was in the minority. Over the past five years (2018–2023), *Black's Law Dictionary* has been the single most frequently cited dictionary by the Court, whose members have relied on 10 of *Black's* 11 editions in about 90 cases during that period. One might imagine that Supreme Court justices would have little need to consult a legal dictionary in their work. In the preface to the most recent edition, chief editor Bryan A. Garner identifies

1 *Buckhannon Bd. & Care Home, Inc. v. W. Va. Dep't of Health & Human Res.*, 532 U.S. 598, 603, 121 S. Ct. 1835, 1839, 149 L. Ed. 2d 855 (2001).

2 *Id.* at 628–29, 121 S. Ct. at 1853 (Ginsburg, J., dissenting).

a range of the dictionary's anticipated users, from students to practicing lawyers to historians—but he makes no mention of judges.

Whereas throughout the 18th and 19th centuries dictionaries were not commonly cited by the Court, they found a welcome in 20th-century opinions, and that welcome has grown stronger in the first quarter of the present century. Over the past five years, Supreme Court opinions have cited dictionaries in about 140 cases—more than 40% of all those heard by the Court in that period. The justices also cite a variety of general-purpose dictionaries in their interpretations of contested meanings in disputes before them. Most of these are treated in chapters of *Hardly Harmless Drudgery*, among them the *Oxford English Dictionary* (no. 96), the *American Heritage Dictionary* (no. 104), *Webster's Third* (no. 102), and various *Random House* dictionaries (no. 103).

Given that the Court is often tasked with interpreting expressions in the U.S. Constitution and its amendments, as well as statutes written in the 18th and 19th centuries, it's not surprising that in addition to 20th- and 21st-century dictionaries, the justices have relied on several 18th- and 19th-century dictionaries, including Webster's *American Dictionary* (no. 62—cited in 6 cases) and Nathan Bailey's *Universal Etymological English Dictionary* (no. 26—cited in 7), and several editions of Samuel Johnson's *Dictionary* (no. 35—cited in 11).

In a well-known mid-20th-century Supreme Court case, no fewer than 34 dictionaries published in the 17th, 18th, and 19th centuries were cited by the distinguished jurist Felix Frankfurter in an appendix to a concurring opinion that centrally involved the meaning of *sacrilege* and *sacrilegious* as applied to *The Miracle*, a foreign-language film.[3] Most of the dictionaries cited by Justice Frankfurter find a chapter in *Hardly Harmless Drudgery* (including those by Cockeram [no. 13], Blount [no. 16], Phillips [no. 17], Cowell [no. 9], Kersey [no. 21], Cocker [no. 22], Bailey [no. 26], Coles [no. 20], Bullokar [no. 11], Defoe [no. 29], Martin [no. 33], Johnson [no. 35], Buchanan [no. 38], Kenrick [no. 43], Ash [no. 45], Barclay [no. 44], Entick [no. 40], Sheridan [no. 50], Richardson [no. 68], and Bouvier [no. 69]). In the opinion itself, Frankfurter invokes Webster's 1828 dictionary, several dictionaries published by Merriam, and a Funk & Wagnalls (no. 91), all of them likewise discussed in this book and on display at the exhibition.

Frankfurter also cites John Rastell's *Law Terms* (no. 1), as he calls an edition of 1708. In discussing Rastell, Bryan A. Garner and Jack Lynch suggest that instead of Robert Cawdrey's *Table Alphabeticall* (no. 7), universally regarded as the first English

3 *Joseph Burstyn, Inc. v. Wilson*, 343 U.S. 495, 72 S. Ct. 777, 96 L. Ed. 1098 (1952).

dictionary, this distinction might rightly belong to Rastell's *Exposiciones Terminorum Legum* of 1523, some 80 years earlier than Cawdrey.

For their frequent reliance on dictionaries, judges have been sharply criticized by some. Recall Judge Learned Hand's oft-quoted comment that "it is one of the surest indexes of a mature and developed jurisprudence not to make a fortress out of the dictionary; but to remember that statutes always have some purpose or object to accomplish, whose sympathetic and imaginative discovery is the surest guide to their meaning."[4] With the rise of textualism since the 1980s, Hand's view has been in retreat.

In recent decades, with dictionaries taking on radically different forms from the printed books that are historically familiar and chiefly illustrated throughout *Hardly Harmless Drudgery*, what lies ahead for courts and their use of dictionaries can hardly be guessed. And from the occasional move by a few judges to complement citation of dictionaries with reliance on bodies of historical texts called corpora, it remains to be seen how courts will use dictionaries. Will they turn to corpora for the kind of undigested linguistic data that skillful lexicographers have traditionally fashioned into dictionary entries?

Hardly Harmless Drudgery is an exciting and enriching read, an intellectually delectable feast for anyone who loves the beauty of dictionaries and the richness of their cultural content. And for those wanting to see the books themselves, the exhibition is an unmatched reward.

4 *Cabell v. Markham*, 148 F.2d 737, 739 (2d Cir. 1945), *aff'd*, 326 U.S. 404, 66 S. Ct. 193, 90 L. Ed. 165 (1945).

Celebrating This New Pictorial History

David E. Vancil
Retired Director, Department of Rare Books and Special Collections
Indiana State University

WHAT AN ACHIEVEMENT for both Bryan A. Garner and Jack Lynch—in bookmaking and in scholarship. *Hardly Harmless Drudgery* is a worthy companion volume to Garner's earlier Grolier Club exhibition catalogue titled *Taming the Tongue: In the Heyday of English Grammar (1711–1855)*. Both books highlight examples from Garner's massive library of books, manuscripts, and other germane materials. These heavily illustrated works reveal his lifelong fascination with wordbooks, particularly English grammars and, here, with books, manuscripts, and even gizmos illustrating the development and sometimes peculiarities of English-language dictionaries. Whereas *Taming the Tongue* has 100 entries, the newer work, *Hardly Harmless Drudgery*, has 32 more entries and around 200 additional pages. Though the two books share a similar design, the smaller font size here allows the authors to incorporate more information into these handsome pages.

The resulting work packs a wallop. The imagery and even the layout used to create the 132 catalogue entries invite its users to linger over the individual entries while creating an impetus to move forward. There's definitely a sense of curiosity created about what comes next. Yes, you can jump around as much as you want through the book, but because of the chronological element involving the arc of English lexicography, it makes much more sense to follow the lead of the authors and proceed item by item. You can revisit anything that you want to later; you'll certainly want to. As this book demonstrates so well, a great catalogue not only represents an exhibition but augments it.

Some items might not have been considered in a more conventional exhibit on this topic. For me, entry no. 4, John Skene's *De Verborum Significatione* (1597), a law dictionary, was unexpected. But this speaks to my ignorance, not to the choice to include it—and I like being surprised. Neither Sidney Landau's *Dictionaries* (2d ed. 2001) nor Jonathon Green's *Chasing the Sun* (1996) mentions Skene, for example. Nor is there a copy in the Warren N. and Suzanne B. Cordell Collection of Dictionaries. Landau's not including the Skene work is no surprise, since his book has only a short chapter on the history of dictionaries. But it's entirely feasible that it could have been mentioned by Green or held by the Cordell Collection.

Garner's private library houses many items that are extremely scarce or even unique, providing him with an opportunity to make assessments unavailable to anyone else. This presents an opportunity for a peruser of this book to learn all kinds of things. That in itself is exciting. But it's worth noting that aside from rarity of items, the field of law dictionaries in and of itself isn't well covered elsewhere. And it's a vast and poorly understood body of material. Luckily, Garner, himself a lawyer, is well versed in the history of his profession. In fact, I'm fairly certain that he is the leading expert. We are in his debt for sharing not only his holdings but his knowledge of their significance. Similarly, we are indebted to Professor Lynch for his expertise. Both Garner and Lynch are cogent and engaging writers: it's a pleasure to read their commentary.

Hardly Harmless Drudgery serves multiple constituencies, appealing both to the curious lover of books and to the scholar. We are fortunate that through Godine, the authors have made the book commercially accessible to everyone. It's a rare coffee-table book that marries beautiful photography with first-rate scholarship.

Bibliography

Aarsleff, Hans

1967 *The Study of Language in England, 1780–1860*. Princeton, N.J.: Princeton Univ Press.

Abate, Frank

2012 Review of *DARE*. *Dictionaries: Journal of the Dictionary Society of North America* 33:245–50.

Adams, Michael

1995 "Sanford Brown Meech at the *Middle English Dictionary*." *Dictionaries* 16:151–85.

2008 Review of *Middle English Dictionary: Plan and Bibliography*. *Dictionaries: Journal of the Dictionary Society of North America* 29:63–70.

2009a "The Period Dictionaries." In *The Oxford History of English Lexicography* (A.P. Cowie ed.). Vol. 1, pp. 326–52. Oxford: Clarendon Press.

2009b "Stephen Skinner's *Etymologicon* and Other English Etymological Dictionaries, 1650–1700." *Studia Etymologica Cracovensia* 14:123–353.

2010a *"Cunning Passages, Contrived Corridors": Unexpected Essays in the History of Lexicography* (Michael Adams ed.). Monza: Polimetrica.

2010b "Legacies of the *Early Modern English Dictionary*." In *Adventuring in Dictionaries: New Studies in the History of Lexicography* (John Considine ed.), pp. 269–308. Newcastle upon Tyne: Cambridge Scholars Pub.

2013 "The Lexical Ride of a Lifetime." *American Speech* 88[2]:168–95 (Summer).

2019 "Regional Varieties of English." In *The Cambridge World History of Lexicography* (John Considine ed.), pp. 109–29). Cambridge: Cambridge Univ. Press.

2020a "English Slang Dictionaries." In *The Cambridge Companion to English Dictionaries* (Sarah Ogilvie ed.), pp. 75–86. Cambridge: Cambridge Univ. Press.

2020b "The Making of American English Dictionaries." In *The Cambridge Companion to English Dictionaries* (Sarah Ogilvie ed.), pp. 157–69. Cambridge: Cambridge Univ. Press.

2020c "The Lexical Object: Richardson's *New Dictionary of the English Language (1836–1837)*." In *The Whole World in a Book: Dictionaries in the Nineteenth Century* (Sarah Ogilvie & Gabriella Safran eds.), pp. 34–53. Oxford: Oxford Univ. Press.

Aitken, A.J.

1987 "The Period Dictionaries." In *Studies in Lexicography* (Robert W. Burchfield ed.), pp. 94–116. Oxford: Clarendon Press.

1992 "Scottish Dictionaries." In *The Oxford Companion to the English Language* (Tom McArthur ed.), pp. 901–3. Oxford: Oxford Univ. Press.

Algeo, John

1993 "*DARE* in the Classroom." In *Language Variation in North American English: Research and Teaching* (A. Wayne Glowka & Donald M. Lance eds.), pp. 140–43. New York: Modern Language Association.

Allen, F. Sturges

1909 *Noah Webster's Place Among English Lexicographers*. Springfield: G. & C. Merriam Co. [Reprint.]

Allen, Harold B.

1977 *Linguistics and English Linguistics: A Goldentree Bibliography*. 2d ed. Arlington Heights, Ill.: AHM.

Allen, Robert

1986 "A Concise History of the *Concise Oxford Dictionary*." In *The History of Lexicography: Papers from the Dictionary Research Centre Seminar at Exeter, March 1986* (R.R.K. Hartmann ed.), pp. 1–11. Amsterdam: John Benjamins.

1999 "Lumping and Splitting." *English Today* 15[4]:61–63.

2009 "Dictionaries of Usage." In *The Oxford History of English Lexicography* (A.P. Cowie ed.). Vol. 2, pp. 339–60. Oxford: Clarendon Press.

Alston, R.C. *A Bibliography of the English Language from the Invention of Printing to the Year 1800*.

1965 Vol. 1: *English Grammars Written in English*. Leeds: E.J. Arnold & Son.

1967 Vol. 2: *Polyglot Dictionaries and Grammars: Treatises on English Written for Speakers of French, German, Dutch, Danish, Swedish, Portuguese, Italian, Hungarian, Persian, Bengali, and Russian*. Bradford: Printed for the author by Ernest Cummins.

1970 Vol. 3[1]: *Old English, Middle English, Early Modern English, Miscellaneous Works, Vocabulary*. Menston: Scolar Press.

1971 Vol. 3[2]: *Punctuation, Concordances, Works on Language in General, Origin of Language, Theory of Grammar*. Menston: Scolar Press.

1967 Vol. 4: *Spelling Books*. Bradford: Ernest Cummins. [Edition limited to 500 copies.]

1966 Vol. 5: *The English Dictionary*. Leeds: E.J. Arnold. [Edition limited to 500 copies.]

1969 Vol. 6: *Rhetoric, Style, Elocution, Prosody, Rhyme, Pronunciation, Spelling Reform*. Leeds: E.J. Arnold.

1967 Vol. 7: *Logic, Philosophy, Epistemology, Universal Language*. Bradford: Printed for the author by Ernest Cummins.

1966 Vol. 8: *Treatises on Short-hand.* Leeds: E.J. Arnold.

1971 Vol. 9: *Non-Standard English: English Dialects; Scottish Dialects; Cant and Vulgar English.* Leeds: Menston Press. Plus supplement of 1973.

1972 Vol. 10: *Place and Personal Names: Geographical Dictionaries, Glossaries, Gazetteers, London Street Names, etc.* Leeds: Menston Press.

1977 Vol. 11: *Place Names and Personal Names.* Ilkley: Grove Press.

1985 Vol. 12[1]: *The French Language Grammars, Miscellaneous Treatises, Dictionaries.* Otley, West Yorkshire: Smith Settle for the author.

1987 Vol. 12[2]: *The Italian, Spanish, Portuguese, and Romansh Languages; Grammars, Dictionaries, Miscellaneous Treatises.* Otley, West Yorkshire: Smith Settle for the author.

1973 *Supplement: Additions and Corrections, vols. 1–10. List of Libraries, Cumulative Index.* Leeds: Univ. of Leeds.

Andresen, Julie

1990 *Linguistics in America 1769–1924.* London: Routledge.

Anon.

1815 Review of Taylor, *English Synonyms Discriminated. Monthly Review* 78:313–17.

1816 Review of Taylor, *English Synonyms Discriminated*, and Crabb, *English Synonymes Explained. Critical Review* 4:581–92.

1860 "New Publications: Worcester's Dictionary." *Supplement to the New York Times*, 26 May 1860, p. 1. (Perhaps by William Swinton—according to M. Kripke as quoted in Sokolowski 2022:187.)

1957 "W. A. Craigie Dies; a Lexicographer." *New York Times*, 3 Sept., p. 28.

1979 "Lexicon's Translator Expanded to Include a Variety of Applications." *Intelligent Machines Journal*, 18 July, p. 4.

1980 "Take-Along Translators: Electronic Dictionaries." *Popular Mechanics*, Apr. 1980, p. 127.

1994 "Looking It Up: Dictionaries and Statutory Interpretation." *Harv. L. Rev.* Vol. 107, p. 1437.

Apresjan, Juri

2000 *Systematic Lexicography* (Kevin Windle trans.). Oxford: Oxford Univ. Press.

Aprill, Ellen P.

1998 "The Law of the Word: Dictionary Shopping in the Supreme Court." *Arizona St. L.J.* Vol. 30, p. 275.

Atkins, B.T. Sue; and Michael Rundell

2008 *The Oxford Guide to Practical Lexicography.* Oxford: Oxford Univ. Press.

Aubrey, John

1690 *Aubrey's Brief Lives* (ca. 1690) (Oliver Lawson Dick ed.). Ann Arbor: Univ. of Michigan Press, 1957.

Babbidge, Homer D. (ed.)

1967 *Noah Webster: On Being American, Selected Writings, 1783–1828.* New York: Frederick A. Praeger.

Bailey, Richard W.

1978 *Early Modern English: Additions and Antedatings to the Record of the English Vocabulary, 1475–1700.* Hildesheim & New York: Georg Olms.

1987 *Dictionaries of English: Prospects for the Record of Our Language.* Ann Arbor: Univ. of Michigan Press. Introduction by Clarence L. Barnhart.

2000a "'This Unique and Peerless Specimen': The Reputation of the *OED*." In *Lexicography and the OED: Pioneers in the Untrodden Forest* (Lynda Mugglestone ed.), pp. 207–27. Oxford: Oxford Univ. Press.

2000b "Appendix III. The *OED* and the Public." In *Lexicography and the OED: Pioneers in the Untrodden Forest* (Lynda Mugglestone ed.), pp. 253–84. Oxford: Oxford Univ. Press.

2009 "National and Regional Dictionaries of English." In *The Oxford History of English Lexicography* (A.P. Cowie ed.). Vol. 1, pp. 279–301. Oxford: Clarendon Press.

Bajer, Peter Paul

2012 *Scots in the Polish-Lithuanian Commonwealth, 16th to 18th Centuries.* Leiden: Brill.

Baker, J.H.

2003 "John Rastell and The Terms of the Law." In *Language and the Law: Proceedings of a Conference December 6–8, 2001, Tarlton Law Library, The University of Texas School of Law* (Marlyn Robinson ed.), pp. 15–30. Buffalo, N.Y.: William S. Hein & Co.

Baker, Sheridan

1972 "The Sociology of Dictionaries and the Sociology of Words." In *New Aspects of Lexicography: Literary Criticism, Intellectual History, and Social Change* (Howard Weinbrot ed.), pp. 138–51. Carbondale, Ill.: Southern Illinois Univ. Press.

Baldwin, Stanley

1928 *The Oxford English Dictionary, 1884–1928: An Address Delivered in Goldsmiths' Hall, 6 June 1928.* Oxford: Clarendon Press.

Barber, Charles

1976 *Early Modern English.* London: Andre Deutsch.

Barfield, Owen

1926 *History in English Words.* London: Methuen & Co. [2d ed. London: Faber & Faber, 1956.]

Barkas, Michael

2015 "English Lexicography Through the Ages: A Case Study Based on Four Dictionary Entries." Norderstedt, Germany: GRIN Pub.

Barns, Florence Elberta

1927 "Reading for the Historical Dictionary of American English." *The English Journal* 16[8]:624–32.

Baron, Dennis E.

1982 *Grammar and Good Taste: Reforming the American Language*. New Haven: Yale Univ. Press.

Bate, Walter Jackson

1975 *Storming the Main Gate: The Dictionary from Samuel Johnson*. New York: Harcourt Brace Jovanovich.

Bately, Janet

2009 "Bilingual and Multilingual Dictionaries of the Renaissance and Early Seventeenth Century." In *The Oxford History of English Lexicography* (A.P. Cowie ed.). Vol. 1, pp. 41–64. Oxford: Clarendon Press.

Bauer, Renate; and Ulrike Krischke (eds.)

2011 *More than Words: English Lexicography and Lexicology Past and Present: Essays Presented to Hans Sauer on the Occasion of His 65th Birthday—Part I*. Frankfurt: Peter Lang.

Beal, Joan C.

2009 "Pronouncing Dictionaries—I Eighteenth and Early Nineteenth Centuries." In *The Oxford History of English Lexicography* (A.P. Cowie ed.). Vol. 2, pp. 149–75. Oxford: Clarendon Press.

Becker, Christine

2005 "Edward J. Bloustein Dictionary Collection Bibliography." *Journal of the Rutgers Univ. Libraries* 61:48–75.

Béjoint, Henri

2001 *Modern Lexicography: An Introduction*. Oxford: Clarendon Press.

2010 *The Lexicography of English: From Origins to Present*. Oxford: Oxford Univ. Press.

Bell, Alan

2013 "Scholarly and Reference Publishing." In *A History of Oxford University Press* (William Roger Louis ed.). Vol. 3, pp. 325–88. Oxford: Oxford Univ. Press.

Berg, Donna Lee

1993 *A Guide to the Oxford English Dictionary*. Oxford: Oxford Univ. Press.

Blachowicz, Camille; Peter Fisher; Donna Ogle; and Susan Watts Taffe

2013 *Teaching Academic Vocabulary K–8*. New York: The Guilford Press.

Blades, Andrew; and Piers Pennington (eds.)

2020 *Poetry & the Dictionary*. Liverpool: Liverpool Univ. Press.

Bland, D.S.

1980 "Some Notes on the Evolution of the Legal Dictionary." *J. Leg. Hist.* Vol. 1, p. 75.

Bogholm, N.

1939 *English Speech from an Historical Point of View*. London: George Allen & Unwin.

Boswell, James

1791 *The Life of Samuel Johnson, LL.D.* (G.B. Hill ed., rev. by L.F. Powell). 6 vols. Oxford: Clarendon Press, 1934–64.

Boulton, James T. (ed.)

1971 *Samuel Johnson: The Critical Heritage*. London: Routledge & Kegan Paul.

Brack, O M, Jr.

1997 *Samuel Johnson in New Albion: A Descriptive Census of Rare and Useful Johnson Books and Manuscripts and Johnsoniana Now Located in California*. Introduction by Loren Rothschild. Tempe, Ariz.: Impression Makers.

Bradley, Henry

1895 *Historical Outlines of English Accidence* (with Richard Morris & Leon Kellner). London: Macmillan. [Also an 1899 edition.]

1915 *The Making of English*. London: Macmillan. [Also a revised edition with Simeon Potter, 1957. Another revised edition with Simeon Potter & Bergen Evans, 1967.]

1916 *Elementary Lessons in Historical English Grammar: Containing Accidence and Word-Formation* (with Richard Morris). London: Macmillan & Co.

1928 *The Collected Papers of Henry Bradley: With a Memoir* (Robert Bridges ed.). Oxford: Clarendon Press.

1940 *Correspondence of Robert Bridges and Henry Bradley, 1900–1923*. Oxford: Clarendon Press.

Brewer, Annie M.; and Marie Browne

1982 *Dictionaries, Encyclopedias, and Other World-Related Books*. 3d ed. Detroit: Gale Research Co.

Brewer, Charlotte

2000 "*OED* Sources." In *Lexicography and the OED: Pioneers in the Untrodden Forest* (Lynda Mugglestone ed.), pp. 40–58. Oxford: Oxford Univ. Press.

2007a "Pronouncing the 'P': Prescription or Description in 19th- and 20th-Century English Dictionaries?" *Historiographia Linguistica* 34[2/3]:72–112.

2007b *Treasure-House of the Language: The Living* OED. New Haven: Yale Univ. Press.

2009 "The *OED* Supplements." In *The Oxford History of English Lexicography* (A.P. Cowie ed.). Vol. 1, pp. 260–78. Oxford: Clarendon Press.

2019 "Standard Varieties of English from c. 1700." In *The Cambridge World History of Lexicography* (John Considine ed.), pp. 484–508. Cambridge: Cambridge Univ. Press.

Brewer, Charlotte; and Stephen Turton

2021 "Aggravated Mischief: Editing and Digitizing the Papers of Sir James Murray." *Dictionaries: Journal of the Dictionary Society of North America* 42[1]:259–80.

British Museum

1910 *List of Books Forming the Reference Library in the Reading Room of the British Museum*. 4th ed. 2 vols. London: Printed for the Trustees.

Brook, G.L.

1981 *Words in Everyday Life*. London: Palgrave Macmillan.

Bryson, William Hamilton

1975 *A Dictionary of Sigla and Abbreviations to and in Law Books Before 1607*. Charlottesville: Univ. of Va. Legal Studies.

Burchfield, Robert W.

1972 "Four-letter Words and the OED." *Times Literary Supplement* (13 Oct. 1972), p. 1233.

1975 "The Treatment of Controversial Vocabulary in the Oxford English Dictionary." *The Trademark Reporter* 65[4]:291–317.

1979 Preface to Samuel Johnson's *Dictionary of the English Language* (facsimile ed.).

1981 "Bookmen and Workbooks." *The Guardian*, 17 Dec. 1981, p. 12.

1984a "Dictionaries, New & Old." *Encounter* 63[3]: 10–22.

1984b "Robert Burchfield Replies [to Laurence Urdang]." *Encounter* 63[5]:73.

1985 "The Recording of English in Dictionaries and Grammars." In *The English Language*, pp. 77–104. Oxford: Oxford Univ. Press.

1987 "The *Supplement to the Oxford English Dictionary:* The End of the Alphabet." In *Dictionaries of English: Prospects for the Record of Our Language* (Richard W. Bailey ed.), pp. 11–21. Ann Arbor: Univ. of Michigan Press.

1991 *Unlocking the English Language*. New York: Hill & Wang.

Burkett, Eva Mae

1979 *American Dictionaries of the English Language Before 1861*. Metuchen, N.J.: Scarecrow Press.

Carlyle, Thomas

1831 Review of Taylor, *Historic Survey of German Poetry*. *Edinburgh Review* 19:151–80.

Chalmers, Alexander

1812–17 *The General Biographical Dictionary*. 24 vols. London: J. Nichols.

Chapman, R.W.; and Allen T. Hazen

1939 *Johnsonian Bibliography: A Supplement to Courtney*. Oxford: Oxford Univ. Press.

Christensen, Francis

1967 "A Case for *Webster's Third*." In *The Role of the Dictionary* (Philip B. Gove ed.), pp. 22–25. Indianapolis: Bobbs-Merrill Co.

Cincinnati Public Library, Department of Rare Books

1972 *A Catalog of Dictionaries*. Cincinnati: Public Library of Cincinnati.

Clark, John Taggart

1918 "Lexicological Evolution and Conceptual Progress." *University of California Publications in Modern Philology* 7[1]:175 20. Berkeley: Univ. of California Press.

Clifford, James L.

1979 *Dictionary Johnson: Samuel Johnson's Middle Years*. London: Heinemann.

Clingham, Greg (ed.)

1997 *The Cambridge Companion to Samuel Johnson*. Cambridge: Cambridge Univ. Press.

Cohen, Morris

2003 "English Legal Lexicography After Rastell." In *Language and the Law: Proceedings of a Conference December 6–8, 2001, Tarlton Law Library, The University of Texas School of Law* (Marlyn S. Robinson ed.), pp. 47–61. Buffalo, N.Y.: William S. Hein & Co.

Coleman, Julie

2004a *A History of Cant and Slang Dictionaries. Vol. 1: 1567–1784*. Oxford: Oxford Univ. Press.

2004b *A History of Cant and Slang Dictionaries. Vol. 2: 1785–1858*. Oxford: Oxford Univ. Press.

2009a *A History of Cant and Slang Dictionaries. Vol. 3: 1859–1936*. Oxford: Oxford Univ. Press.

2009b "Slang and Cant Dictionaries." In *The Oxford History of English Lexicography* (A.P. Cowie ed.). Vol. 2, pp. 314–36. Oxford: Oxford Univ. Press.

2010a *A History of Cant and Slang Dictionaries. Vol. 4: 1937–1984*. Oxford: Oxford Univ. Press.

2010b "Can You Adam and Eve It? Dictionaries of Rhyming Slang." In *Adventuring in Dictionaries: New Studies in the History of Lexicography* (John Considine ed.), pp. 187–96. Newcastle upon Tyne: Cambridge Scholars Pub.

2012 Review of Jonathon Green, *Green's Dictionary of Slang*. *English Language & Linguistics* 16:193–99.

Coleman, Julie; and Kay Christian

2000 *Lexicology, Semantics and Lexicography*. Amsterdam: John Benjamins Pub. Co.

Coleridge, Herbert
1860 "On the Exclusion of Certain Words from a Dictionary." *Transactions of the Philological Society* 7:37–44.

Collins, Beverley; and Inger M. Mees
2009 "Pronouncing Dictionaries—II Mid-Nineteenth Century to the Present Day." In *The Oxford History of English Lexicography* (A.P. Cowie ed.). Vol. 2, pp. 176–218. Oxford: Clarendon Press.

Collison, Robert L.
1966 *Encyclopaedias: Their History Through the Ages*. New York: Hafner Pub. Co.
1971 *Dictionaries of English and Foreign Languages: A Bibliographical Guide to Both General and Technical Dictionaries with Historical and Explanatory Notes and References*. 2d ed. New York: Hafner Pub. Co.

Congleton, J.E.; and Elizabeth Congleton
1984 *Johnson's Dictionary: Bibliographical Survey 1746–1984 with Excerpts for All Entries*. Terra Haute, Ind.: Dictionary Society of North America.

Congleton, J.E.; J. Edward Gates; and Donald Hobar
1979 *Papers on Lexicography in Honor of Warren N. Cordell*. Terre Haute, Ind.: Dictionary Society of North America.

Considine, John
2007 *Words and Dictionaries from the British Isles in Historical Perspective* (with Giovanni Iamartino). Newcastle upon Tyne: Cambridge Scholars Pub.
2008 *Dictionaries in Early Modern Europe: Lexicography and the Making of Heritage*. Cambridge: Cambridge Univ. Press.
2010a *Adventuring in Dictionaries: New Studies in the History of Lexicography* (John Considine ed.). Newcastle upon Tyne: Cambridge Scholars Pub.
2010b "Henry Cockeram: The Social World of a Seventeenth-Century Lexicographer." In *Adventuring in Dictionaries: New Studies in the History of Lexicography* (John Considine ed.), pp. 23–44. Newcastle upon Tyne: Cambridge Scholars Pub.
2010c *Webs of Words: New Studies in Historical Lexicology*. Newcastle upon Tyne: Cambridge Scholars Pub.
2010d *Current Projects in Historical Lexicography*. Newcastle upon Tyne: Cambridge Scholars Pub.
2012 *Ashgate Critical Essays on Early English Lexicographers: The Seventeenth Century*. London: Routledge.
2013 "English Guides to Etymology from Skeat to Durkin." *Studia Etymologica Cracoviensia* 18:9–40.
2014 *Academy Dictionaries 1600–1800*. Cambridge: Cambridge Univ. Press.
2015 "In Praise of Edward Phillips." *Studia Linguistica Iagellonicae Cracoviensis* 132:211–28.
2016 "Historical Dictionaries." In *The Oxford Handbook of Lexicography* (Philip Durkin ed.), pp. 163–75. Oxford: Oxford Univ. Press.
2017 *Small Dictionaries and Curiosity: Lexicography Fieldwork in Post-Medieval Europe*. Oxford: Oxford Univ. Press.
2019a *The Cambridge World History of Lexicography* (John Considine ed.). Cambridge: Cambridge Univ. Press.
2019b "Medieval Latin Christendom." In *The Cambridge World History of Lexicography* (John Considine ed.), pp. 267–89. Cambridge: Cambridge Univ. Press.
2019c "Medieval Latin Christendom." In *The Cambridge World History of Lexicography* (John Considine ed.), pp. 290–314. Cambridge: Cambridge Univ. Press.
2020a "A Dictionary Ecosystem: Four Centuries of English Lexicography." In *The Cambridge Companion to English Dictionaries* (Sarah Ogilvie ed.), pp. 89–100. Cambridge: Cambridge Univ. Press.
2020b "The Unfinished Business of Eighteenth-Century European Lexicography." In *The Whole World in a Book: Dictionaries in the Nineteenth Century* (Sarah Ogilvie & Gabriella Safran eds.), pp. 1–16. Oxford: Oxford Univ. Press.
2022 *Sixteenth-Century English Dictionaries*. Oxford: Oxford Univ. Press.

Considine, John; and Peter Gilliver
2022 "Derwent Coleridge's 'Rough Notes': A Newly Discovered Manuscript from the Formative Years of the *Oxford English Dictionary*." *Dictionaries: Journal of the Dictionary Society of N. Am.* 13[2]:1–54.

Cormier, Monique C.
2009 "Bilingual Dictionaries of the Late Seventeenth and Eighteenth Centuries." In *The Oxford History of English Lexicography* (A.P. Cowie ed.). Vol. 1, pp. 65–85. Oxford: Oxford Univ. Press.

Coulmas, Florian
2016 *Guardians of Language: Twenty Voices Through History*. Oxford: Oxford Univ. Press.

Courtney, William Prideaux; and David Nichol Smith
[1915] *A Bibliography of Samuel Johnson*. Oxford: Clarendon Press, 1968. [Reprint.]

Cowie, A[nthony] P[aul]
1999 *English Dictionaries for Foreign Learners: A History*. New York: Oxford Univ. Press.
2009a *The Oxford History of English Lexicography*. 2 vols. Oxford: Clarendon Press.
2009b "The Earliest Foreign Learners' Dictionaries." In *The Oxford History of English Lexicography* (A.P. Cowie ed.). Vol. 2, pp. 385–411. Oxford: Clarendon Press.

Cowley, John D.

1932 *A Bibliography of Abridgments, Digests, Dictionaries and Indexes of English Law to the Year 1800.* London: Quaritch.

Craigie, William A.

1926 "The Historical Dictionary of American English." *The English Journal* 15[1]:13–23.

1931 "Collecting for the Historical Dictionary of American English." *American Speech* 6[3]:173–79.

Crystal, David

1980 Foreword to Eric Partridge, *Eric Partridge in His Own Words* (David Crystal ed.). London: Andre Deutsch.

2004 *The Stories of English.* London: Allen & Lane.

2009 *Just a Phrase I'm Going Through: My Life in Language.* London: Routledge.

2010 *A Little Book of Language.* New Haven: Yale Univ. Press.

2011 *The Story of English in 100 Words.* New York: St. Martin's Press.

2012 *Evolving English: One Language, Many Voices.* London: British Library.

2013a "Old St Pancras Church, London NW1: John Walker and Pronunciation." In *Wordsmiths & Warriors: The English-Language Tourist's Guide to Britain* (with Hilary Crystal), pp. 279–85. Oxford: Oxford Univ. Press.

2013b "Lichfield and London: Johnson and His Dictionary." In *Wordsmiths & Warriors: The English-Language Tourist's Guide to Britain* (with Hilary Crystal), pp. 271–77. Oxford: Oxford Univ. Press.

2013c "York: Lindley Murray and English Grammar." In *Wordsmiths & Warriors: The English-Language Tourist's Guide to Britain* (with Hilary Crystal), pp. 287–91. Oxford: Oxford Univ. Press.

2013d "Oxford: James Murray and the *Oxford English Dictionary.*" In *Wordsmiths & Warriors: The English-Language Tourist's Guide to Britain* (with Hilary Crystal), pp. 333–39. Oxford: Oxford Univ. Press.

2013e "Joseph Wright and the English Dialects." In *Wordsmiths & Warriors: The English-Language Tourist's Guide to Britain* (with Hilary Crystal), pp. 355–59. Oxford: Oxford Univ. Press.

2013f "Hinton St George: Henry Fowler and English Usage." In *Wordsmiths & Warriors: The English-Language Tourist's Guide to Britain* (with Hilary Crystal), pp. 361–65. Oxford: Oxford Univ. Press.

2019 *The Cambridge Encyclopedia of the English Language.* 3d ed. Cambridge: Cambridge Univ. Press.

Dareau, Margaret; and Iseabail Macleod

2009 "Dictionaries of Scots." In *The Oxford History of English Lexicography* (A.P. Cowie ed.). Vol. 1, pp. 302–25. Oxford: Clarendon Press.

DeBenedictis, Don J.

1992 "Dictionary Trademark Wars." *ABA Journal,* Jan. 1992, p. 25 (Jan.).

DeMaria, Robert, Jr.

1986 *Johnson's Dictionary and the Language of Learning.* Chapel Hill: Univ. of North Carolina Press.

1997 "Johnson's *Dictionary.*" In *The Cambridge Companion to Samuel Johnson* (Greg Clingham ed.), pp. 85–101. Cambridge: Cambridge Univ. Press.

1998 "Johnson's *Dictionary* and Dictionary Johnson" (with Gwin J. Kolb). *The Yearbook of English Studies* (Andrew Gurr ed.) 28:19–43.

Devereux, E.J.

1999 *A Bibliography of John Rastell.* Montreal & Kingston: McGill-Queen's Univ. Press.

DeWispelare, Daniel

2012 "Spectacular Speech: Performing Language in the Late Eighteenth Century." *Journal of British Studies* 51:858–82.

Dictionary-War Pamphlets

1853 Worcester, Joseph E. *A Gross Literary Fraud Exposed: relating to the publication of Worcester's Dictionary in London.* Boston: Jenks, Hickling, and Swan.

1854a *A Summary Summing of the Charges, with their refutations, in attacks upon Noah Webster, LL.D., his dictionaries, or his publishers, made by Mr. Joseph Worcester, Mr. Sherman Converse, Messrs. Jenks, Hickling, and Swan.* Springfield: G. & C. Merriam Co.

1854b *A Gross Literary Fraud Exposed: Relating to the Publication of Worcester's Dictionary in London, as Webster's Dictionary.* Springfield: G. & C. Merriam Co.

1854c [Gould, Edward.] *A Reply to Messrs. G. and C. Merriam's Attack upon the Character of Dr. Worcester and His Dictionaries.* Boston: Jenks, Hickling & Swan.

1855 *Have We a National Standard of English Lexicography? Or some comparisons of the claims of Webster's dictionaries and Worcester's dictionaries.* Springfield: G. & C. Merriam Co.

1856a Andrews, I.W. *Webster's Dictionaries.* Springfield: G. & C. Merriam Co.

1856b Sargent, Epes. *The Critic Criticised: A reply to a review of Webster's system in the Democratic Review for March, 1856. From the Democratic Review for June, 1856.* Springfield: G. & C. Merriam Co.

1856c *Dictionaries in the Boston Mercantile Library and Boston Atheneum.* Springfield: G. & C. Merriam Co.

1859 Philorthos. [Poole, William Frederick.] *The Orthographical Hobgoblin*. Springfield: G. & C. Merriam Co.

1860 *"Equal Justice": The Two Dictionaries or the Reviewer Reviewed. A reply to a correspondent of the New York World.* Springfield: G. & C. Merriam Co.

1860b William D. Swan, *A Critic Criticized: And Worcester Vindicated. Consisting of a review of an article in the "Congregationalist" upon the comparative merits of Worcester's and Webster's quarto dictionaries*. Boston: Swan Brewer.

Dille, Catherine

2005 "Johnson's *Dictionary* in the Nineteenth Century: A Legacy in Transition." In *The Age of Johnson* (Paul J. Korshin & Jack Lynch eds.). Vol. 16, pp. 21–37. New York: AMS Press, Inc.

Dixon, Arthur W.

1967 "Dr. Johnson and Emily Post." In *The Role of the Dictionary* (Philip B. Gove ed.), pp. 19–21. Indianapolis: Bobbs-Merrill Co.

Dixon, R.M.W.

2018 *The Unmasking of English Dictionaries*. Cambridge: Cambridge Univ. Press.

Dolezal, Frederic Thomas

1985 *Forgotten but Important Lexicographers, John Wilkins and William Lloyd: A Modern Approach to Lexicography Before Johnson.* Tübingen: Max Niemeyer.

Dolezal, Frederic Thomas; and Don R. McCreary

1999 *Pedagogical Lexicography Today: A Critical Bibliography on Learners' Dictionaries with Special Emphasis on Language Learners and Dictionary Users.* Tübingen: Max Niemeyer.

Durkin, Philip

2011 "An Influential Voice in the Germanic Etymologies in the First Edition of the *OED*: Correspondence between Early Editors and Eduard Sievers." In *More than Words: English Lexicography and Lexicology Past and Present: Essays Presented to Hans Sauer on the Occasion of His 65th Birthday—Part I* (Renate Bauer & Ulrike Krischke eds.), pp. 23–38. Frankfurt: Peter Lang.

Dykema, Karl W.

1967 "Cultural Lag and Reviewers of Webster's III." In *The Role of the Dictionary* (Philip B. Gove ed.), pp. 43–50. Indianapolis: Bobbs-Merrill Co.

Elliot, W. Hume

1997 *The Life of Robert Hunter (1823–1897): Lexicographer, Missionary, Geologist, and Naturalist*. Loughton: Loughton & District Historical Society.

Ellis, Alexander

1869–89 *On Early English Pronunciation, with especial reference to Shakspere and Chaucer* (with William Salesbury & Johann Andreas Schmeller). 5 vols. London: Trübner & Co.

Emery, Donald W.

1973 *Variant Spellings in Modern American Dictionaries*. Rev. ed. Urbana, Ill.: NCTE.

Emrich, Richard S.

1962 "New Dictionary Cheap, Corrupt." *The Detroit News*, 10 Feb. 1962. [Reprinted in Sledd & Ebbitt 1962:127–29.]

Evans, Bergen

1967 "Let's Stop Maligning the Dictionary." In *The Role of the Dictionary* (Philip B. Gove ed.), pp. 40–42. Indianapolis: Bobbs-Merrill Co.

Farmer, John S.; and W.E. Henley

2003 *The Correspondence of John Stephen Farmer and W. E. Henley on Their Slang Dictionary, 1890–1904* (Damian Atkinson ed.). Lewiston: The Edwin Mellen Press.

Fern, Tracey

2015 *W Is for Webster: Noah Webster and His American Dictionary*. New York: Farrar, Straus & Giroux.

Ferris, Jeri

1988 *What Do You Mean? A Story About Noah Webster*. Minneapolis: Carolrhoda Books, Inc.

Finegan, Edward

1987 "On the Linguistic Forms of Prestige: Snobs and Slobs Using English." In *The Legacy of Language: A Tribute to Charlton Laird* (Phillip C. Boardman ed.), pp. 146–61. Reno: Univ. of Nevada Press.

2001 "Usage." In *Cambridge History of the English Language. Vol. 6: English in North America* (John Algeo ed.), pp. 358–421. Cambridge: Cambridge Univ. Press.

2003 "Linguistic Prescription: Familiar Practices and New Perspectives." *Annual Review of Applied Linguistics* 23:213–24.

2012 "Standardization: Prescriptive Tradition." In *Historical Linguistics of English: An International Handbook* (Alexander Bergs & Laurel Brinton eds.), pp. 967–80. Berlin: Walter de Gruyter.

2020a "Christian Nationalism in Noah Webster's Lexicography." In *The Whole World in a Book: Dictionaries in the Nineteenth Century* (Sarah Ogilvie & Gabriella Safran eds.), pp. 152–67. Oxford: Oxford Univ. Press.

2020b "Description and Prescription: The Roles of English Dictionaries." In *The Cambridge Companion to English Dictionaries* (Sarah Ogilvie ed.), pp. 45–57. Cambridge: Cambridge Univ. Press.

Finley, John H.

1917 Introduction, *Crabb's English Synonymes*. Pp. v–vii. New York: Grosset & Dunlap.

Fisher, John H.

1996 "The History of Received Pronunciation." In *The Emergence of Standard English*. Lexington: Univ. Press of Kentucky.

Flaherty, Martin C[harles]

1923 *How to Use the Dictionary*. New York: The Ronald Press Co.

Fleeman, J.D.

2000 *A Bibliography of the Works of Samuel Johnson: Treating His Published Works from the Beginnings to 1984*. 2 vols. Oxford: Oxford Univ. Press, 2000.

Fontenelle, Thierry (ed.)

2008 *Practical Lexicography: A Reader*. Oxford: Oxford Univ. Press.

Ford, Emily Ellsworth Fowler

1971 *Notes on the Life of Noah Webster* (Emily Ellsworth Ford Skeel ed.). 2 vols. New York: Burt Franklin.

Friend, Joseph Harold

1967 *The Development of American Lexicography 1798–1864*. The Hague: Mouton.

Fuertes-Olivera, Pedro A.

2021 *The Routledge Handbook of Lexicography*. London: Routledge.

Fuertes-Olivera, Pedro A.; and Henning Bergenholtz (eds.)

2011 *e-Lexicography: The Internet, Digital Initiatives and Lexicography*. London: Continuum International Pub. Group.

Fussell, Paul, Jr.

1951 "William Kenrick's 'Courtesy' Book." *PMLA* 66:538–40.

Gagnier, Regenia

2005 "Cultural Philanthropy, Gypsies and Interdisciplinary Scholars: Dream of a Common Language." *19: Interdisciplinary Studies in the Long Nineteenth Century* 1:1–24.

Garcia, Sandra E.

2023 "10 Words From the African American English Dictionary." *New York Times*, 25 May 2023, p. D2.

Garner, Bryan A.

1980 *Shakespeare's Latinate Diction*. Plan II Senior Thesis. Austin: Univ. of Texas.

1982a "Shakespeare's Latinate Neologisms." *Shakespeare Studies* 15:149–70. [Reprinted in *A Reader in the Language of Shakespearean Drama* (V. Salmon & E. Burness eds.), pp. 207–28. Amsterdam: John Benjamins Pub. Co., 1987.]

1982b "Meretricious Words, or The Quean's English." *Verbatim* 8[3]:1–5.

1983 "Latin-Saxon Hybrids in Shakespeare and the Bible." *Studies in the Humanities* 10[1]: 39–44. [Reprinted in *A Reader in the Language of Shakespearean Drama* (V. Salmon & E. Burness eds.), pp. 229–34. Amsterdam: John Benjamins Pub. Co., 1987.]

1984 "Learned Length and Thund'ring Sound: A Word-Lover's Panegyric." *Verbatim* 10[3]:1–3.

1985 "Latinate Past Participles as Metrical and Tonal Variants in Shakespeare." *Language and Style* 18:242–47.

1987 *A Dictionary of Modern Legal Usage*. Oxford & New York: Oxford Univ. Press.

1989 "*The Oxford Law Dictionary:* A Historical Dictionary for English-Speaking Jurisdictions." *Law Librarian* 20:55–63.

1990 "The Missing Common-Law Words." In *The State of the Language* (Christopher Ricks & Leonard Michaels eds.), pp. 235–45. Berkeley: Univ. of California Press.

1997 "Reconstructing Lindley Murray's Bibliophilic Legacy." *Bookman's Weekly* 99[2]:73–74.

1998 *A Dictionary of Modern American Usage*. Oxford: Oxford Univ. Press. 2d ed. 2003.

1999 *Black's Law Dictionary* (Bryan A. Garner ed.). 7th ed. St. Paul: West Group. 8th ed. 2004. 9th ed. 2009. 10th ed. 2014. 11th ed. 2019. 12th ed. 2024.

2002 "Lindley Murray." In *Invisible Giants: Fifty Americans Who Shaped the Nation but Missed the History Books* (Mark Carnes ed.), pp. 209–13. Oxford: Oxford Univ. Press.

2003a "Legal Lexicography: A View from the Front Lines." In *Language and the Law: Proceedings of a Conference December 6–8, 2001, Tarlton Law Library, The University of Texas School of Law* (Marlyn S. Robinson ed.), pp. 109–24. Buffalo, N.Y.: William S. Hein & Co.

2003b Introduction to Vincent J. Monteleone, *Criminal Slang: The Vernacular of the Underworld Lingo*. [Facsimile reprint of 1949 glossary.] Clark, N.J.: Lawbook Exchange.

2003c Introduction to John Rastell, *An Exposition of Certaine Difficult and Obscure Wordes, and Termes of the Lawes of This Realme*. [Facsimile reprint of 1579 dictionary.] Clark, N.J.: Lawbook Exchange.

2004 "Making Peace in the Language Wars." *Green Bag 2d* 7[3]:227–35.

2007 "Harmless Drudgery?" *Essays in Criticism* 57[1]:65–72. [Reprinted in Garner 2009a:627–32.]

2008 *Garner's Modern American Usage*. 3d ed. Oxford & New York: Oxford Univ. Press.

2009a *Garner on Language and Writing*. Chicago: American Bar Ass'n.

2009b "The Latest Illiteracy: The Ongoing Struggles of Garlic-Hangers." *Forum* 3:20–32.

2011 Foreword to William Marriott, *A New Law Dictionary*. [Facsimile reprint of 1798 dictionary.] Clark, N.J.: Lawbook Exchange.

2012a Foreword to Benjamin W. Pope, *Legal Definitions*. [Facsimile reprint of 1919 dictionary.] Clark, N.J.: Lawbook Exchange.

2012b "A Note on the Use of Dictionaries." In Antonin Scalia & Bryan A. Garner, *Reading Law: The Interpretation of Legal Texts*, pp. 415–24. St. Paul: Thomson Reuters.

2014 "A Lexicographic Look at Magna Carta." In *Magna Carta: Muse & Mentor* (Randy J. Holland ed.), pp. 85–102. St. Paul: Thomson Reuters in association with the Library of Congress.

2016 *Garner's Modern English Usage*. 4th ed. Oxford: Oxford Univ. Press.

2018 *Nino and Me: My Unusual Friendship with Justice Antonin Scalia*. New York: Threshold Editions.

2020a "The Scholar-Collector." *Essays in Criticism*. 70[4] (Oct.).

2020b "Sex and the Singular Pronoun." *National Review* 72[2]:33–36 (Feb. 10).

2020c "It Ain't a Word!" *National Review* 72[15]:42 (Aug. 24).

2021a *Taming the Tongue in the Heyday of English Grammar: 1711–1851*. New York: Grolier Club.

2021b "Literary Sleuthing." *National Review* 73[24]:50 (Dec. 27). [On Noah Webster's fabricated blurbs.]

2022a *Garner's Modern English Usage*. 5th ed. Oxford: Oxford Univ. Press.

2022b "The Storied *OED*." *National Review* 74[2]:42 (Feb. 7).

2022c "All Ize on Oxford." *National Review* 74[4]:42 (Mar. 7).

2022d "W Is for *Webster*, *Worcester*, *Woe*, and *Wrath*." *National Review* 74[6]:33–34 (Apr. 4).

2023a "Under an Orthographic Spell: Part I." *National Review* 75[2]:46 (Feb. 6).

2023b "Under an Orthographic Spell: Part II." *National Review* 75[4]:46 (Mar. 6).

2023c "Why Judges Use Dictionaries and Grammars." *National Review* 75[8]:46 (May 1).

2023d "Drudges of Some Description." *National Review* 75[12]:46 (June 26).

2023e "Look *That* Up in Your Funk & Wagnalls!" *National Review* 75[18]:50 (Oct. 2).

Geritz, Albert J.; and Amos Lee Laine

1983 *John Rastell*. Boston: Twayne Pubs.

Gilliver, Peter

2010 "'Not Altogether Treated as I Should Treat It Now': James Murray's Early Editorial Decisions for the *New English Dictionary*." In *Adventuring in Dictionaries: New Studies in the History of Lexicography* (John Considine ed.), pp. 212–37. Newcastle upon Tyne: Cambridge Scholars Pub.

2011 "Harvesting England's Ancient Treasure: Dialect Lexicography and the Philological Society's First Plans for a National Dictionary." *Dictionaries* 32:82–92.

2016 *The Making of the Oxford English Dictionary*. Oxford: Oxford Univ. Press.

Gilliver, Peter; Jeremy Marshall; and Edmund Weiner

2006 *The Ring of Words: Tolkien and the Oxford English Dictionary*. Oxford: Oxford Univ. Press.

Glowka, A. Wayne; and Donald M. Lance (eds).

1993 *Language Variation in North American English: Research and Teaching*. New York: Modern Language Association.

Gneuss, Helmut

1996 *English Language Scholarship: A Survey and Bibliography from the Beginnings to the End of the Nineteenth Century*. Binghamton, N.Y.: Medieval & Renaissance Texts & Studies.

Görlach, Manfred

1999 *English in Nineteenth-Century England: An Introduction*. Cambridge: Cambridge Univ. Press.

Gotti, Maurizio

1999 *The Language of Thieves and Vagabonds: 17th and 18th Century Canting Lexicography in England*. Tübingen: Max Niemeyer.

Gove, Philip B.

1961 "Letter to the Editor." *Life Magazine*, 17 Nov. 1961, p. 13. [Reprinted in Sledd & Ebbitt 1962:91–92.]

1967a *The Role of the Dictionary*. Indianapolis: Bobbs-Merrill Co.

1967b "Introduction: The Dictionary's Function." In *The Role of the Dictionary* (Philip B. Gove ed.), pp. 5–8. Indianapolis: Bobbs-Merrill Co.

1967c "Usage in the Dictionary." In *The Role of the Dictionary* (Philip B. Gove ed.), pp. 51–57. Indianapolis: Bobbs-Merrill Co.

1970 Introduction to facsimile reprint of *A Compendious Dictionary of the English Language* (1806) (by Noah Webster), pp. vii–ix. New York: Bounty Books, a division of Crown Pubs., Inc.

1972 "English Dictionaries of the Future." In *New Aspects of Lexicography: Literary Criticism, Intellectual History, and Social Change* (Howard Weinbrot ed.), pp. 152–68. Carbondale, Ill.: Southern Illinois Univ. Press.

Graband, Gerhard

2012 "The Early Modern English Tradition of 'Hard Words' and the *Vindex Anglicus* (1644)." John Considine, trans. In *Ashgate Critical Essays on Early English Lexicographers: The Seventeenth Century* (John Considine ed.), 3:23–39.

Graham, Howard Jay

1954 "The Rastells and the Printed English Law Book of the Renaissance." *Law Library Journal* 47:6.

Granfield, Marcella A.

1965 *Meet Dr. Webster*. New York: Vantage Press.

Granger, Sylviane; and Magali Paquot (eds.)

2012 *Electronic Lexicography*. Oxford: Oxford Univ. Press.

Gray, Jack (ed.)

1943 *Words, Words, Words About Dictionaries*. San Francisco: Chandler Pub. Co.

Green, Jonathon

1996 *Chasing the Sun: Dictionary Makers and the Dictionaries They Made*. New York: Henry Holt.

2001 "Language: A Light(er) Extinguished." *Critical Quarterly* 43:104–8.

2014 *Odd Job Man: Some Confessions of a Slang Lexicographer*. London: Jonathan Cape.

2015 *The Vulgar Tongue: Green's History of Slang*. New York: Oxford Univ. Press.

Grossman, George

2003 "Early American Legal Lexicographers." In *Language and the Law: Proceedings of a Conference December 6–8, 2001, Tarlton Law Library, The University of Texas School of Law* (Marlyn S. Robinson ed.), pp. 63–91. Buffalo, N.Y.: William S. Hein & Co.

Gunn, Daniel P.

2000 "The Lexicographer's Task: Language, Reason, and Idealism in Johnson's *Dictionary* Preface." In *The Age of Johnson* (Paul J. Korshin & Jack Lynch eds.). Vol. 11, pp. 105–24. New York: AMS Press, Inc.

Guralnik, David B.

1953 "The Beginnings of English Dictionaries" (1953), in *Harbrace Guide to Dictionaries* (Kenneth G. Wilson et al. eds.), pp. 3–6. New York: Harcourt Brace & World, 1963.

1971 "The Lexicographer as Social Chronicler." In *The Legacy of Language: A Tribute to Charlton Laird* (Phillip C. Boardman ed.), pp. 53–68. Reno & Las Vegas: Univ. of Nevada Press.

Gurr, Andrew (ed.)

1998 *The Yearbook of English Studies: Eighteenth-Century Lexis and Lexicography*. Vol. 28. London: W.S. Maney & Son Ltd. for the Modern Humanities Research Association.

Hall, Robert A., Jr.

1967 "Telling the Truth." In *The Role of the Dictionary* (Philip B. Gove ed.), pp. 26–27. Indianapolis: Bobbs-Merrill Co.

Hansen, David A.

1972 "Redefinitions of *Style*, 1600–1800." In *New Aspects of Lexicography: Literary Criticism, Intellectual History, and Social Change* (Howard Weinbrot ed.), pp. 95–116. Carbondale, Ill.: Southern Illinois Univ. Press.

Harington, John

1653 *A Briefe View of the State of the Church of England as It Stood in Q. Elizabeths and King James His Reigne, to the Yeere 1608*. London: Printed for Jos. Kirton.

Harris, Roy; and Christopher Hutton

2013 *Definition in Theory and Practice: Language, Lexicography and the Law*. London: Bloomsbury.

Hartmann, R.R.K.

1979 *Dictionaries and Their Users*. Exeter: Univ. of Exeter.

1987 *History of Lexicography* (R.R.K. Hartmann ed.). London: John Benjamins Pub. Co.

2001 *Teaching and Researching Lexicography*. Harlow, England: Pearson Education Ltd.

2003a *Lexicography: Reference Works Across Time, Space, and Languages*. London: Taylor & Francis.

2003b *Lexicography: Critical Concepts*. London: Routledge.

Hartmann, R.R.K.; and Gregory James

1998 *Dictionary of Lexicography*. London: Routledge.

Hawkins, Sir John

2009 *The Life of Samuel Johnson, LL.D.* (O M Brack Jr. ed.). Athens: Univ. of Georgia Press.

Hayakawa, Isamu

2014 *A Comprehensive Catalog of Webster's Dictionaries, 1806–2000*. Tokyo: Texnai.

Hayashi, Tetsuro

1978 *The Theory of English Lexicography 1530–1791*. Studies in the History of Linguistics 18. Amsterdam: John Benjamins B.V.

Hickey, Raymond

2010 *Eighteenth-Century English: Ideology and Change*. Cambridge: Cambridge Univ. Press.

Hicks, Frederick C.

1921 *Men and Books Famous in the Law*. Rochester, N.Y.: Lawyers Co-operative Pub. Co.

Higgins, Matthew

2007 *Joseph Emerson Worcester: A Distinguished and Gracious New England Lexicographer*. Concord, N.H.: Duncross Books.

Hitchings, Henry

2005 *Defining the World: The Extraordinary Story of Dr Johnson's Dictionary*. New York: Farrar, Straus & Giroux.

2008 *The Secret Life of Words: How English Became English*. New York: Farrar, Straus & Giroux.

Hoare, Michael Rand

2009 "Scientific and Technical Dictionaries." In *The Oxford History of English Lexicography* (A.P. Cowie ed.). Vol. 2, pp. 47–93. Oxford: Oxford Univ. Press.

Hoare, Michael Rand; and Vivian Salmon

2000 "The Vocabulary of Science in the *OED*." In *Lexicography and the OED: Pioneers in the Untrodden Forest* (Lynda Mugglestone ed.), pp. 156–71. Oxford: Oxford Univ. Press.

Hogrefe, Pearl

1967 *The Life and Times of Sir Thomas Elyot: Englishman.* Ames, Iowa: Iowa State Univ. Press.

Holdsworth, William

1972 *A History of English Law.* 17 vols. [1903–1966.] London: Methuen & Co.

Householder, Fred W.; and Sol Saporta (eds.)

1967 *Problems in Lexicography.* Bloomington, Ind.: Indiana Univ. Press.

Howard, Donald R.

1972 "Lexicography and the Silence of the Past." In *New Aspects of Lexicography: Literary Criticism, Intellectual History, and Social Change* (Howard Weinbrot ed.), pp. 3–16. Carbondale, Ill.: Southern Illinois Univ. Press.

Hudson, Nicholas

1998 "Johnson's *Dictionary* and the Politics of 'Standard English.'" *The Yearbook of English Studies* (Andrew Gurr ed.) 28:77–93.

Hulbert, J[ames] R.

1955 *Dictionaries British and American.* New York: Philosophical Library.

Hüllen, Werner

1994 *The World in a List of Words* (Werner Hüllen ed.). Tübingen: Max Niemeyer.

1999 *English Dictionaries, 800–1700: The Topical Tradition.* Oxford: Clarendon Press.

2009a *Network and Knowledge in Roget's Thesaurus.* Oxford: Oxford Univ. Press.

2009b "Dictionaries of Synonyms and Thesauri." In *The Oxford History of English Lexicography* (A.P. Cowie ed.). Vol. 2, pp. 25–46. Oxford: Clarendon Press.

Hume, David

1741 *Essays, Moral and Political.* Edinburgh: A. Kincaid.

Hunt, Leigh

1962 *Political and Occasional Essays* (Lawrence Huston Houtchens and Carolyn Washburn Houtchens eds.). New York: Columbia Univ. Press.

Hunter, Robert

1895 "English Lexicography." In *Lloyd's Encyclopædic Dictionary.* Vol. 7, pp. 641–43. London: Edward Lloyd Ltd.

Iamartino, Giovanni

2010 "Words by Women, Words on Women in Samuel Johnson's *Dictionary of the English Language.*" In *Adventuring in Dictionaries: New Studies in the History of Lexicography* (John Considine ed.), pp. 94–125. Newcastle upon Tyne: Cambridge Scholars Pub.

2020 "European Cross-Currents in English Lexicography." In *The Cambridge Companion to English Dictionaries* (Sarah Ogilvie ed.), pp. 58–74. Cambridge: Cambridge Univ. Press.

Ikeda, Makoto

1999 *Competing Grammars: Noah Webster's Vain Efforts to Defeat Lindley Murray.* Tokyo: Shinozaki Shorin.

Ilson, Robert

1986 *Lexicography: An Emerging International Profession.* London: Manchester Univ. Press.

Jackson, Howard

2002 *Lexicography: An Introduction.* London: Routledge.

2015 *The Bloomsbury Companion to Lexicography* (Howard Jackson ed.). London: Bloomsbury Academic.

2022 *An Introduction to English Lexicology: Words, Meaning, and Vocabulary* (with Etienne Zé Amvela). London: Bloomsbury Academic.

James, Gregory (ed.)

1989 *Lexicographers and Their Works.* Exeter Linguistic Studies. Vol. 14. Exeter: Univ. of Exeter Press.

Ježek, Elisabetta

2016 *The Lexicon: An Introduction.* Oxford: Oxford Univ. Press.

Johnson, Samuel

2005 *Johnson on the English Language* (Gwin J. Kolb & Robert DeMaria Jr. eds.). New Haven & London: Yale Univ. Press.

Kaminski, Thomas

1981 "Johnson and Oldys as Bibliographers: An Introduction to the Harleian Catalogue." *Philological Quarterly* 60:439–53.

Kendall, Joshua

2010 *The Forgotten Founding Father: Noah Webster's Obsession and the Creation of an American Culture.* New York: G.P. Putnam's Sons.

Kennedy, Arthur G.

1927 *A Bibliography of Writings on the English Language from the Beginning of Printing to the End of 1922.* Cambridge, Mass.: Harvard Univ. Press.

1935 *Current English: A Study of the Present-Day Usages and Tendencies, Including Pronunciation, Spelling, Grammatical Practice, Word-Coining, and the Shifting of Meanings.* New York: Ginn & Co. [Reprint, Westport, Conn.: Greenwood Press, 1970.]

Kerling, Johan

1979 *Chaucer in Early English Dictionaries: The Old-Word Tradition in English Lexicography down to 1721 and Speght's Chaucer Glossaries.* Leiden: Leiden Univ. Press.

King, Ethel M.

1962 *The Rainbow in the Sky: Concerning Noah Webster and His Dictionary.* Brooklyn: Theo. Gaus's Sons.

Kirkpatrick, David D.

2000 "Dictionary Publishers Going Digital: A Low Margin Business Sees Profits on the Web Dictionary Publishers, Looking for Big Profits, Step Up Efforts to Go Digital." *New York Times*, 21 Aug., p. C1.

Koda, Paul S.

1974 *A Descriptive Catalogue of the Warren N. Cordell Collection of Dictionaries*. PhD dissertation, Indiana Univ., Bloomington.

Kogan, Herman

1958 *The Great EB: The Story of the Encyclopædia Britannica*. Chicago: Univ. of Chicago Press.

Kolb, Gwin J.; and Ruth A. Kolb

1972 "The Selection and Use of the Illustrative Quotations in Dr. Johnson's *Dictionary*." In *New Aspects of Lexicography: Literary Criticism, Intellectual History, and Social Change* (Howard Weinbrot ed.), pp. 61–72. Carbondale, Ill.: Southern Illinois Univ. Press.

Krapp, George Philip

[1925] *The English Language in America*. 2 vols. [Repr., New York: Frederick Ungar Pub. Co., 1960.]

Kraske, Robert

1975 *The Story of the Dictionary*. New York: Harcourt Brace Jovanovich.

Kuster, Elisabeth

2014 *Lexicography on the Internet*. Munich: GRIN Verlag.

Laird, Charlton

1970 *Language in America*. New York: World Pub. Co.

Lancashire, Ian

2010 "Why Did Tudor England Have No Monolingual English Dictionary?" In *Webs of Words: New Studies in Historical Lexicology* (John Considine ed.), pp. 8–23. Newcastle upon Tyne: Cambridge Scholars Pub.

2012 Ashgate Critical Essays on Early English Lexicographers (Ian Lancashire gen. ed.). Vol. 1, *Old English* (Christine Franzen ed.); vol. 2, *Middle English* (Christine Franzen ed.); vol. 3, *The Sixteenth Century* (Roderick McConchie ed.); vol. 4, *The Seventeenth Century* (John Considine ed.); vol. 5, *The Eighteenth Century* (Anne C. McDermott ed.). Burlington, Vt.: Ashgate, 2012.

Landau, Sidney I.

2002 *Dictionaries: The Art and the Craft of Lexicography*. 2d ed. Cambridge: Cambridge Univ. Press.

2009a "Major American Dictionaries." In *The Oxford History of English Lexicography* (A.P. Cowie ed.). Vol. 1, pp. 182–229. Oxford: Oxford Univ. Press.

2009b "The American Collegiate Dictionaries." In *The Oxford History of English Lexicography* (A.P. Cowie ed.). Vol. 2, pp. 361–84. Oxford: Oxford Univ. Press.

Leavitt, Robert Keith

1947 *Noah's Ark, New England Yankees, and the Endless Quest: A Short History of the Original Webster Dictionaries*. Springfield: G. & C. Merriam Co.

Leff, Arthur Allan

1985 "The Leff Dictionary of Law: A Fragment (A–Chiltern Hundreds)." *Yale L.J.* Vol. 94, p. 1855.

Leidecker, Kurt F.

1946 *Yankee Teacher: The Life of William Torrey Harris*. New York: Philosophical Library.

Lepore, Jill

2006 "Noah's Mark: Webster and the Original Dictionary Wars." *New Yorker*, 6 Nov., pp. 78–87.

Lew, Robert

2011 "Online Dictionaries of English." In *e-Lexicography: The Internet, Digital Initiatives and Lexicography* (Pedro A. Fuertes-Olivera & Henning Bergenholtz eds.), pp. 230–50. London: Continuum International Pub. Group.

Lewis, Robert E.

2007 "History of the *Middle English Dictionary* Project." In *Middle English Dictionary Plan and Bibliography*, 2d ed., 1–7. Ann Arbor: Univ. of Michigan Press, 2007.

Liberman, Anatoly

2009 "English Etymological Dictionaries." In *The Oxford History of English Lexicography* (A.P. Cowie ed.). Vol. 2, pp. 269–89. Oxford: Clarendon Press.

2010 "The Growth of the English Etymological Dictionary." In *Adventuring in Dictionaries: New Studies in the History of Lexicography* (John Considine ed.), pp. 164–86. Newcastle upon Tyne: Cambridge Scholars Pub.

Littlejohn, David

1971 *Dr. Johnson and Noah Webster: Two Men and Their Dictionaries*. Illustrated with a matched pair of original leaves from *A Dictionary of the English Language by Samuel Johnson, A.M. (1755) and An American Dictionary of the English Language by Noah Webster, LL.D. (1828)*. San Francisco: Book Club of California.

Lloyd, Donald J.; and Harry R. Warfel

1956 "The Development of the American Dictionary" (1956), in *Harbrace Guide to Dictionaries* (Kenneth G. Wilson et al. eds.), pp. 7–12. New York: Harcourt Brace & World, 1963.

Lodwig, Richard R.; and Eugene F. Barrett

1981 *Words, Words, Words: Vocabularies and Dictionaries*. 2d ed. Montclair, N.J.: Boynton/Cook. The first edition is called *The Dictionary and the Language* (1967), published in New York by Hayden Book Co.

Louw, J.P.

1985 *Lexicography and Translation*. Cape Town: Bible Society of South Africa, 1985.

Luna, Paul

2005 "The Typographic Design of Johnson's *Dictionary*." In *Anniversary Essays on Johnson's "Dictionary"* (Jack Lynch & Anne McDermott eds.), pp. 175–97. Cambridge: Cambridge Univ. Press, 2005.

Lynch, Jack

2002 *Samuel Johnson's Dictionary: Selections from the 1755 Work That Defined the English Language*. Jack Lynch ed. Delray Beach, Fla.: Levenger Press.

2004 *Samuel Johnson's Insults*. New York: Levenger Press.

2005 *Anniversary Essays on Johnson's "Dictionary."* With Anne McDermott. Cambridge: Cambridge Univ. Press.

2008 *The English Language: A User's Guide*. Newburyport, Mass.: Focus Pubs./R. Pullins Co.

2009 *The Lexicographer's Dilemma: The Evolution of "Proper" English from Shakespeare to* South Park. New York: Walker & Co.

2011a "Modes of Definition in Johnson's Dictionary." *Harvard Library Bulletin* 20[3–4]:73–88.

2011b "Studies of Johnson's Dictionary, 1955–2009: A Bibliography." *Harvard Library Bulletin* 20[3–4]:89–133.

2016 *You Could Look It Up*. New York: Bloomsbury.

2017 See Shapiro 2017.

2020 "Samuel Johnson and the 'First English Dictionary.'" In *The Cambridge Companion to English Dictionaries* (Sarah Ogilvie ed.), pp. 142–53. Cambridge: Cambridge Univ. Press.

2022 *The Oxford Handbook of Samuel Johnson* (Jack Lynch ed.). Oxford: Oxford Univ. Press.

Lynch, James J.

1967 "Lost Causes in English Usage." In *The Role of the Dictionary* (Philip B. Gove ed.), pp. 28–30. Indianapolis: Bobbs-Merrill Co.

Mac Aodha, Máirtín

2014 *Legal Lexicography: A Comparative Perspective*. Farnham, Surrey: Ashgate.

MacMahon, M.K.C.

1985 "James Murray and the Phonetic Notation in the *New English Dictionary*." *Transactions of the Philological Society* 83[1]:72–112.

Malone, Kemp

1937 Review of *A Dictionary of American English on Historical Principles*, vol. 1. *The American Journal of Philology* 58[3]:374–76.

Marckwardt, Albert H.

1967 "Dictionaries and the English Language." In *The Role of the Dictionary* (Philip B. Gove ed.), pp. 31–39. Indianapolis: Bobbs-Merrill Co.

Marello, Carla

2009 "Bilingual Dictionaries of the Nineteenth and Twentieth Centuries." In *The Oxford History of English Lexicography* (A.P. Cowie ed.). Vol. 1, pp. 86–104. Oxford: Oxford Univ. Press.

Marke, Julius J.

1953 *A Catalogue of the Law Collection at New York University*. New York: Law Center of New York University.

1965 *Vignettes of Legal History*. South Hackensack, N.J.: Fred B. Rothman & Co.

Marsden, William

2012 *A Catalogue of Dictionaries, Vocabularies, Grammars, and Alphabets (Cambridge Library Collection—Linguistics)*. Cambridge: Cambridge Univ. Press.

Martin, Peter

2019 *The Dictionary Wars: The American Fight over the English Language*. Princeton, N.J.: Princeton Univ. Press.

Mathews, Mitford M.

1931 *The Beginnings of American English*. Chicago: Univ. of Chicago Press.

1933 *A Survey of English Dictionaries*. London: Oxford Univ. Press. [Reprint, New York: Russell & Russell, 1966.]

McArthur, Tom

1986 *Worlds of Reference: Lexicography, Learning, and Language from the Clay Tablet to the Computer*. Cambridge: Cambridge Univ. Press.

1992 *The Oxford Companion to the English Language*. Oxford: Oxford Univ. Press. 2d ed. (with Jacqueline Lam-McArthur & Lise Fontaine). Oxford: Oxford Univ. Press, 2018.

1998a *Living Words: Language, Lexicography, and the Knowledge Revolution*. Exeter: Univ. of Exeter Press.

1998b *The English Languages*. Cambridge: Cambridge Univ. Press.

2002 *The Oxford Guide to World English*. Oxford: Oxford Univ. Press.

McCarthy, William

1997 "The Celebrated Academy at Palgrave: A Documentary History of Anna Letitia Barbauld's School." *The Age of Johnson: A Scholarly Annual* 8:279–392.

2008 *Anna Letitia Barbauld: Voice of the Enlightenment*. Baltimore: Johns Hopkins Univ. Press.

McConchie, Roderick W.

1997 *Lexicography and Physicke: The Record of Sixteenth-Century English Medical Terminology*. Oxford: Clarendon Press.

2018 "The Use of 'Mechanical Reasoning': John Quincy and His *Physico-Medicum* (1719)." In *Historical Dictionaries in Their Paratextual Context* (Roderick W. McConchie & Jukka Tyrkkö eds.). Berlin: De Gruyter.

2020 "Cawdrey, Coote, and 'Hard Usual English Wordes.'" In *The Cambridge Companion to English Dictionaries* (Sarah Ogilvie ed.), pp. 103–13. Cambridge: Cambridge Univ. Press.

McConchie, Roderick W.; and Jukka Tyrkkö (eds.)

2018 *Historical Dictionaries in Their Paratextual Context*. Berlin: De Gruyter.

McDermott, Anne

1998 "Johnson's *Dictionary* and the Canon: Authors and Authority." *The Yearbook of English Studies* (Andrew Gurr ed.) 28:44–65.

2005 "The Compilation Methods of Johnson's *Dictionary*." In *The Age of Johnson* (Paul J. Korshin & Jack Lynch eds.). Vol. 16, pp. 1–20. New York: AMS Press, Inc.

McIntosh, Carey

1998 "Eighteenth-Century English Dictionaries and the Enlightenment." *The Yearbook of English Studies* (Andrew Gurr ed.) 28:3-18.

McMahon, April

2012 "Restructuring Renaissance English." In *The Oxford History of English* (Lynda Mugglestone ed., updated ed.), pp. 180–218. Oxford: Oxford Univ. Press.

Mellinkoff, David

1983 "The Myth of Precision and the Law Dictionary." *UCLA L. Rev.* Vol. 31, p. 422.

Mencken, H.L.

1919 *The American Language*. New York: A.A. Knopf.

1936 *The American Language*. 4th ed. New York: A.A. Knopf.

1945 *The American Language: Supplement One*. New York: A.A. Knopf.

1948 *The American Language: Supplement Two*. New York: A.A. Knopf.

1963 *The American Language*. One-volume abridgment. Raven I. McDavid ed. New York: Knopf.

Merriam, George S. (ed.)

1893 *Noah Porter: A Memorial by Friends*. London: Sampson, Low, Marston & Co.

Micklethwait, David

2000 *Noah Webster and the American Dictionary*. Jefferson, N.C.: McFarland.

Miles, Edwin A.

1991 "William Allen and the Webster-Worcester Dictionary Wars." *Dictionaries: Journal of the Dictionary Society of N. Am.* 13:1–15.

Miller, D. Gary

2014 *English Lexicogenesis*. Oxford: Oxford Univ. Press.

Mitchell, Linda C.

2001 *Grammar Wars: Language as Cultural Battlefield in Seventeenth and Eighteenth Century England*. Aldershot, U.K.: Ashgate.

2010 "Dictionaries as Behavior Guides in Seventeenth- and Eighteenth-Century England." In *Adventuring in Dictionaries: New Studies in the History of Lexicography* (John Considine ed.), pp. 82–93. Newcastle upon Tyne: Cambridge Scholars Pub.

Mitchell, William S.

1955 *Catalogue of the Heslop Collection of Dictionaries in the Library of King's College Newcastle upon Tyne*. Newcastle upon Tyne: King's College.

Miyoshi, Kusujiro

2010 "Cawdrey's *Table Alphabeticall* (1604) Reconsidered: Its Driving Force for Early English Lexicography." In *Adventuring in Dictionaries: New Studies in the History of Lexicography* (John Considine ed.), pp. 14–22. Newcastle upon Tyne: Cambridge Scholars Pub.

Momma, Haruko

2013 *From Philology to English Studies: Language and Culture in the Nineteenth Century*. Cambridge: Cambridge Univ. Press.

Monaghan, Charles

1997 "Lindley Murray Rediscovered." *Book Source Monthly* 13[8]:21–26 (Nov.).

1998 *The Murrays of Murray Hill*. Brooklyn: Urban Univ. Press.

Monaghan, E. Jennifer

1983 *A Common Heritage: Noah Webster's Blue-Back Speller*. Hamden, Conn.: Archon Books.

Moon, Rosamund

1987 "Monosemous Words and the Dictionary." In *The Dictionary and the Language Learner: Papers from the EURALEX Seminar at the University of Leeds, 1–3 April 1985* (Anthony Cowie ed.), pp. 173–82. Tübingen: Max Niemeyer Verlag.

Morgan, John S.

1975 *Noah Webster*. New York: Mason/Charter.

Morton, Herbert C.

1994 *The Story of Webster's Third: Philip Gove's Controversial Dictionary and Its Critics*. Cambridge: Cambridge Univ. Press.

Moss, Richard J.

1984 *Noah Webster*. Boston: Twayne Pubs.

Mugglestone, Lynda

2000 *Lexicography and the OED: Pioneers in the Untrodden Forest* (Lynda Mugglestone ed.) Oxford: Oxford Univ. Press.

2003 *Talking Proper: The Rise of Accent as Social Symbol.* 2d ed. Oxford: Oxford Univ. Press.

2005 *Lost for Words: The Hidden History of the Oxford English Dictionary.* New Haven: Yale Univ. Press.

2006 *The Oxford History of English.* Oxford: Oxford Univ. Press.

2007 "Decent Reticence: Coarseness, Contraception, and the First Edition of the *OED.*" *Dictionaries* 28:1–22.

2009 "*The Oxford English Dictionary.*" In *The Oxford History of English Lexicography* (A.P. Cowie ed.). Vol. 1, pp. 230–59. Oxford: Oxford Univ. Press.

2011 *Dictionaries: A Very Short Introduction.* Oxford: Oxford Univ. Press.

2015 *Samuel Johnson & the Journey into Words.* Oxford: Oxford Univ. Press.

2016 "Description and Prescription in Dictionaries." In *The Oxford Handbook of Lexicography* (Philip Durkin ed.), pp. 546–60. Oxford: Oxford Univ. Press.

Muir, Percy Horace.

1947 *Book Collecting as a Hobby.* New York: Knopf.

Murray, James A.H.

1878 "English Language." In *Encyclopædia Britannica* (Thomas Spencer Baynes ed.). Vol. 8, pp. 390–402. Edinburgh: Adam & Charles Black.

1879a *An Appeal to the English-Speaking and English-Reading Public to Read Books and Make Extracts for the Philological Society's New English Dictionary* [2d ed.]. Oxford: Clarendon Press.

1879b "Eighth Annual Address of the President to the Philological Society, Delivered at the Anniversary Meeting, Friday, 16th of May, 1879." *Transactions of the Philological Society* 17:561–624.

1884 "Thirteenth Address of the President, to the Philological Society, Delivered at the Anniversary Meeting, Friday, 16th May, 1884." *Transactions of the Philological Society* 19:501–642.

1891a "Content: Contents." *Notes and Queries*, 7th series, 12:267 (Oct.).

1891b "'Content,' 'Contents.'" *The Academy* 1020:456–57 (Nov. 21).

1892 "Report on the Progress of the Philological Society's New English Dictionary." *Transactions of the Philological Society*, 22:268–78.

1896 "The Late James Dixon, F.R.C.S." *Notes and Queries*, 8th series, 9:101–2.

1897 "'Harvestry': 'Harveyized.'" *Notes and Queries*, 8th series, 11:487.

1900 *The Evolution of English Lexicography.* Oxford: Clarendon Press.

1957 *Sir James A.H. Murray: A Self Portrait, with a Commemorative Poem by Sir Owen Seaman, Bart.* Gloucester: John Bellows.

Murray, K.M. Elisabeth

1977 *Caught in the Web of Words: James Murray and the Oxford English Dictionary.* New Haven: Yale Univ. Press.

Nagashima, Daisuke

1996 "How Johnson Read Hale's *Origination* for His *Dictionary*: A Linguistic View." In *The Age of Johnson* (Paul J. Korshin & Jack Lynch eds.). Vol. 7, pp. 247–97. New York: AMS Press, Inc.

1998 "Johnson's Revisions of His Etymologies." *The Yearbook of English Studies* (Andrew Gurr ed.) 28:94–105.

1999 "The Biblical Quotations in Johnson's *Dictionary.*" In *The Age of Johnson* (Paul J. Korshin & Jack Lynch eds.). Vol. 10, pp. 89–126. New York: AMS Press, Inc.

Nelson, Clifford C.

1995 *Noah Webster: A Familiar Essay.* West Hartford, Conn.: Noah Webster House, Inc.

Nesi, Hilary

2009 "Dictionaries in Electronic Form." In *The Oxford History of English Lexicography* (A.P. Cowie ed.). Vol. 2, pp. 458–78. Oxford: Clarendon Press.

Nichols, Patricia

1988 Review of Cheris Kramarae and Paula A. Treichler, *Grammar and Gender*, and Dennis Baron, *Grammar and Gender. Signs* 13:600–3.

Noyes, Gertrude E.

1951 "The Beginnings of the Study of Synonyms in England." *PMLA* 66:951–70.

Ogilvie, Sarah

2013 *Words of the World: A Global History of the* Oxford English Dictionary. Cambridge: Cambridge Univ. Press.

2020a *The Cambridge Companion to English Dictionaries.* Cambridge: Cambridge Univ. Press.

2020b "The Oxford English Dictionary." In *The Cambridge Companion to English Dictionaries* (Sarah Ogilvie ed.), pp. 170–80. Cambridge: Cambridge Univ. Press.

2020c "A Nineteenth-Century Garment Throughout: Description, Collaboration, and Thorough Coverage in the *Oxford English Dictionary (1884–1928).*" In *The Whole World in a Book: Dictionaries in the Nineteenth Century* (Sarah Ogilvie & Gabriella Safran eds.), pp. 54–72. Oxford: Oxford Univ. Press.

Ogilvie, Sarah; and Gabriella Safran (eds.)

2020 *The Whole World in a Book: Dictionaries in the Nineteenth Century.* Oxford: Oxford Univ. Press.

2023 *The Dictionary People: The Unsung Heroes Who Created the Oxford English Dictionary.* New York: Knopf.

O'Neill, Robert Keating

1988 *English-Language Dictionaries, 1604–1900: The Catalog of the Warren N. and Suzanne B. Cordell Collection.* New York: Greenwood Press.

Osselton, N.E.

1958 *Branded Words in English Dictionaries Before Johnson.* Groningen: Wolters.

1995 *Chosen Words: Past and Present Problems for Dictionary Makers.* Exeter: Univ. of Exeter Press.

2000 "Murray and His European Counterparts." In *Lexicography and the OED* (Lynda Mugglestone ed.), pp. 59–76. Oxford: Oxford Univ. Press.

2009 "The Early Development of the English Monolingual Dictionary (Seventeenth and Eighteenth Centuries)." In *The Oxford History of English Lexicography* (A.P. Cowie ed.). Vol. 1, pp. 131–54. Oxford: Oxford Univ. Press.

Ostler, Rosemarie

2015 *Founding Grammars.* New York: St. Martin's Press.

Parini, Jay (ed.)

2004 *The Oxford Encyclopedia of American Literature.* 4 vols. Oxford: Oxford Univ. Press.

Partridge, Eric

1935 *Slang To-day and Yesterday: With a Short Historical Sketch and Vocabularies of English, American and Australian Slang.* London: Routledge.

1953 *The "Shaggy Dog" Story: Its Origin, Development and Nature (with a Few Seemly Examples).* London: Faber & Faber.

1957 *English: A Course for Human Beings.* Books I & II (originally published 1949). London: Macdonald & Co.

1963 *The Gentle Art of Lexicography as Pursued and Experienced by an Addict.* London: Andre Deutsch.

1967 Preface to Barrère and Leland, *A Dictionary of Slang, Jargon & Cant.* Detroit: Gale Research Company.

1980 *Eric Partridge in His Own Words* (David Crystal ed.). London: Andre Deutsch.

Pearce, Chris

2004 "Johnson's Proud Folio: The Material and Rhetorical Contexts of Johnson's Preface to the Dictionary." In *The Age of Johnson* (Paul J. Korshin & Jack Lynch eds.). Vol. 15, pp. 1–35. New York: AMS Press, Inc.

Penhallurick, Robert

2009 "Dialect Dictionaries." In *The Oxford History of English Lexicography* (A.P. Cowie ed.). Vol. 2, pp. 290–313. Oxford: Clarendon Press.

Peters, R.A.

1966 Introduction to *A Table Alphabeticall of Hard Usual English Words (1604): The First English Dictionary.* [Facsimile reproduction.] Delmar, N.Y.: Scholars' Facsimiles & Reprints.

Pickering, Mary Orne

1887 *Life of John Pickering.* Boston: Privately printed.

Pinnavaia, Laura

2010 "The Lost and Found in Richardson's *A New Dictionary of the English Language* (1836–1837/1855): An Insight into the State of the Vocabulary." In *Adventuring in Dictionaries: New Studies in the History of Lexicography* (John Considine ed.), pp. 197–211. Newcastle upon Tyne: Cambridge Scholars Pub.

Plimpton, George Arthur

1933 "Grammatical Manuscripts and Early Printed Grammars in the Plimpton Library." *Transactions and Proceedings of the American Philological Association* 64:150–78.

Pollard, A.W.; and G.R. Redgrave

1986 *A Short Title Catalogue of Books Printed in England, Scotland, & Ireland and of English Books Printed Abroad, 1475–1640* (W.A. Jackson, F.S. Ferguson & Katharine F. Pantzer eds.). 2d ed. London: Bibliographical Society.

Pouillon, Véronique

2018 "Eighteenth-Century Pronouncing Dictionaries: Reflecting Usage or Setting Their Own Standard?" In *Standardising English: Norms and Margins in the History of the English Language*, pp. 102–26. Cambridge: Cambridge Univ. Press.

Proudfit, Isabel

1942 *Noah Webster: Father of the Dictionary.* New York: J. Messner.

Pyles, Thomas

1952 "Noah Webster, Man and Symbol." In *Weigh the Word* (Charles B. Jennings et al. eds.), pp. 167–72. New York: Harper & Bros., 1957.

Radford, George

1920 "Johnson's Dictionary." In *Johnson Club Papers by Various Hands*, pp. 103–21. London: T. Fisher Unwin.

Randolph, A. Raymond

1994 "Dictionaries, Plain Meaning, and Context in Statutory Interpretation." *Harv. J.L. & Pub. Pol'y.* Vol. 17, p. 71.

Read, Allen Walker

1966 "The Spread of German Linguistic Learning in New England During the Lifetime of Noah Webster." *American Speech* 41[3]:163–81.

Reddick, Allen Hilliard

1996 *The Making of Johnson's Dictionary, 1746–1773.* Rev. ed. Cambridge: Cambridge Univ. Press.

1998 "Johnson's *Dictionary of the English Language* and Its Texts: Quotation, Context, Anti-Thematics." *The Yearbook of English Studies* (Andrew Gurr ed.) 28:66–76.

2005 *Samuel Johnson's Unpublished Revisions to the* Dictionary of the English Language: *A Facsimile Edition.* Cambridge: Cambridge Univ. Press.

2009 "Johnson and Richardson." In *The Oxford History of English Lexicography* (A.P. Cowie ed.). Vol. 1, pp. 155–81. Oxford: Oxford Univ. Press.

2020 "Recording the Most Proper and Significant Words." In *The Cambridge Companion to English Dictionaries* (Sarah Ogilvie ed.), pp. 129–41. Cambridge: Cambridge Univ. Press.

Reed, John Allen

1967 "A New Big Dictionary: Its Virtues and Faults." In *The Role of the Dictionary* (Philip B. Gove ed.), pp. 61–63. Indianapolis: Bobbs-Merrill Co.

Reed, Joseph W., Jr.

1962 "Noah Webster's Debt to Samuel Johnson." *American Speech* 27: 95–105.

Rennie, Susan

2012 *Jamieson's Dictionary of Scots: The Story of the First Historical Dictionary of the Scots Language*. Oxford: Oxford Univ. Press.

2020 "The First Scottish 'National' Dictionary: John Jamieson's *Etymological Dictionary of the Scottish Language* (1808/1825)." In *The Whole World in a Book: Dictionaries in the Nineteenth Century* (Sarah Ogilvie & Gabriella Safran eds.), pp. 110–30. Oxford: Oxford Univ. Press.

Robertson, Michael

2022 "New Solutions for Words in Thomas Speght's Chaucer Glossaries." *Dictionaries: Journal of the Dictionary Society of N. Am.* 13[2]:55–93.

Robinson, Fred

2010 "Noah Webster as Etymologist." *Bulletin of the Modern Language Society*. 111[2]:167–74.

Robinson, Marlyn (ed.)

2003 *Language and the Law: Proceedings of a Conference December 6–8, 2001, Tarlton Law Library, The University of Texas School of Law*. Buffalo, N.Y.: William S. Hein & Co.

Rollins, Richard M.

1980 *The Long Journey of Noah Webster*. Philadelphia: Univ. of Pennsylvania Press.

Ross, A.S.C.

1934 "*A New English Dictionary on Historical Principles*: Introduction, Supplement and Bibliography." *Neuphilologische Mitteilungen* 35[2]:128–32.

Rothschild, Loren

1984 *Samuel Johnson (1709–1784): An Appreciation*. Los Angeles: The Samuel Johnson Society of Southern California.

1986 *Two Letters from Samuel Johnson to Sir Robert Chambers: September 14, 1773 & October 4, 1783*. Pacific Palisades, Cal.: Rasselas Press.

1988 *Samuel Johnson: Author for All Seasons*. An Exhibition of Manuscripts & Books from the Library of Loren & Frances Rothschild held at the Doheny Memorial Library, University of Southern California, Fall 1988. Pacific Palisades & Los Angeles: Rasselas Press & USC Fine Arts Press.

2016 *Moses Thomas's Proposals for the First American Edition of a Complete Johnson's Dictionary*. With Robert Allen. Ojai, Cal.: Classic Letterpress.

2019 *Prospectus Comprising the Preface to Volume 1 and Some Sample Entries for the Publication in Two Volumes Quarto of A Descriptive Catalogue of the Loren & Frances Rothschild Library of Eighteenth-Century British Authors*. Ojai, Cal.: Classic Letterpress.

Russell, Lindsay Rose

2021 *Women and Dictionary-Making: Gender, Genre, and English-Language Lexicography*. Cambridge: Cambridge Univ. Press.

Rynd, Aaron J.

1991 "Dictionaries and the Interpretation of Words: A Summary of Difficulties." *Alberta L. Rev.* Vol. 29, p. 712.

Safire, William

1990 *Language Maven Strikes Again*. New York: Doubleday.

2001 *Let a Simile Be Your Umbrella*. New York: Crown Pubs.

2008 *Safire's Political Dictionary*. Updated ed. Oxford: Oxford Univ. Press.

Sauer, Hans

2009 "Glosses, Glossaries, and Dictionaries in the Medieval Period." In *The Oxford History of English Lexicography* (A.P. Cowie ed.). Vol. 1, pp. 17–40. Oxford: Clarendon Press.

Schäfer, Jürgen

1980 *Documentation in the "OED": Shakespeare and Nashe as Test Cases*. Oxford: Clarendon Press.

1989 *Early Modern English Lexicography*. 2 vols. Oxford: Clarendon Press.

Schaub, Edward L. (ed.)

1936 *William Torrey Harris, 1835–1935: A collection of essays, including papers and addresses presented in commemoration of Dr. Harris' centennial at the St. Louis meeting of the western division of the American Philosophical Society*. Chicago: Open Court Pub. Co.

Schulman, Arthur

2008 *Websterisms: A Collection of Words and Definitions Set Forth by the Founding Father of American English*. Introductory essay by Jill Lepore. New York: Free Press.

Schultz, David E.; and S.T. Joshi (eds.)

2000 Introduction to Ambrose Bierce, *The Unabridged Devil's Dictionary* (David E. Schultz & S.T. Joshi eds.). Athens: Univ. of Georgia Press.

Scudder, Horace E.

1890 *Noah Webster*. Boston: Houghton, Mifflin & Co.

Serjeantson, Mary S.

1935 *A History of Foreign Words in English*. London: Kegan, Paul, Trench, Trübner & Co.

Shapiro, Rebecca

2017 *Fixing Babel: An Historical Anthology of Applied English Lexicography*. Lewisburg, Pa.: Bucknell Univ. Press. Foreword by Jack Lynch.

2020 "Seventeenth- and Eighteenth-Century English Lexicography." In *The Cambridge Companion to English Dictionaries* (Sarah Ogilvie ed.), pp. 114–26. Cambridge: Cambridge Univ. Press.

Shea, Ammon

2008 *Reading the OED: One Man, One Year, 21,730 Pages*. New York: Penguin Group.

Sheard, J.A.

1954 *The Words We Use*. London: Andre Deutsch.

Sheldon, Esther K.

1946 "Pronouncing Systems in Eighteenth-Century Dictionaries." *Language* 22:27–41.

Shenker, Israel

1979 *Harmless Drudges: Wizards of Language—Ancient, Medieval and Modern*. Bronxville, N.Y.: Barnhart Books.

Sheridan, Thomas

1762 *Course of Lectures on Elocution*. London.

Shipton, Alyn

2013 *Hi-de-ho: The Life of Cab Calloway*. Oxford: Oxford Univ. Press.

Shoemaker, Ervin C.

1936 *Noah Webster: Pioneer of Learning*. New York: Columbia Univ. Press. [Reprint, New York: AMS Press, 1960.]

Shuy, Roger W.

2001 "DARE's Role in Linguistic Profiling." *DARE Newsletter*. 4(3):1, 2–3 (Summer).

Simpson, A.W.B.

1984 *Biographical Dictionary of the Common Law*. London: Butterworth.

Simpson, David

1986 *The Politics of American English, 1776–1850*. New York: Oxford Univ. Press.

Simpson, John

1989 "Nathaniel Bailey and the Search for a Lexicographical Style." In *Lexicographers and Their Work* (Gregory James ed.), pp. 181–91. Exeter: Univ. of Exeter.

2007 Introduction to *The First English Dictionary 1604: Robert Cawdrey's* A Table Alphabeticall. Pp. 7–29. Oxford: Bodleian Library.

2016 *The Word Detective: Searching for the Meaning of It All in the Oxford English Dictionary*. New York: Basic Books.

Singh, Brijraj

2009 "Revisiting *Purley*: John Horne Tooke's Logocentrism." In *The Age of Johnson* (Jack Lynch ed.). Vol. 19, pp. 187–212. New York: AMS Press, Inc.

Skeat, W.W.

1887 "The President's Address for 1886." In *Transactions of the Philological Society (1885–1887)*. Vol. 2, pp. 343-74. London: Trübner & Co.

Skeel, Emily Ellsworth

1912 *Notes on the Life of Noah Webster*. 2 vols. New York: Privately printed.

1958 *A Bibliography of the Writings of Noah Webster*. (Edwin H. Carpenter Jr. ed.). New York: N.Y. Public Library.

Skinner, David

2014 *The Story of Ain't: America, Its Language, and the Most Controversial Dictionary Ever Published*. New York: Harper Perennial.

Slater, R.J.

1967 "Noah Webster, Founding Father of American Scholarship and Education." In *Noah Webster's First Edition of an American Dictionary of the English Language*, pp. 11–27. San Francisco: Foundation for American Christian Education.

Sledd, James H.

1962 "Reply to Mr. McDonald." In *Dictionaries and* That *Dictionary: A Casebook on the Aims of Lexicographers and the Targets of Reviewers* (James H. Sledd & Wilma R. Ebbitt eds.), pp. 268–72. Glenview, Ill.: Scott, Foresman & Co.

1972 "Dollars and Dictionaries: The Limits of Commercial Lexicography." In *New Aspects of Lexicography: Literary Criticism, Intellectual History, and Social Change* (Howard Weinbrot ed.), pp. 119–37. Carbondale, Ill.: Southern Illinois Univ. Press.

Sledd, James H.; and Wilma R. Ebbitt

1962 *Dictionaries and* That *Dictionary: A Casebook on the Aims of Lexicographers and the Targets of Reviewers*. Glenview, Ill.: Scott, Foresman & Co.

Sledd, James H.; and Thomas P. Harrison

1967 *Studies in Honor of DeWitt T. Starnes*. Austin, Tex.: Univ. of Texas Press/Harry Ransom Center.

Sledd, James H.; and Gwin J. Kolb

1955 *Dr. Johnson's Dictionary: Essays in the Biography of a Book*. Chicago: Univ. of Chicago Press.

Snyder, K. Alan

1990 *Defining Noah Webster: Mind and Morals in the Early Republic*. Lanham: Univ. Press of America.

Sokolowski, Peter

2020 "The Invention of the Modern Dictionary: *Webster's Unabridged* of 1864." In *The Whole World in a Book: Dictionaries in the Nineteenth Century* (Sarah Ogilvie & Gabriella Safran eds.), pp. 168–89. Oxford: Oxford Univ. Press.

Solan, Lawrence M.

1993 "When Judges Use the Dictionary." *American Speech* 68:50.

2003 "Finding Ordinary Meaning in the Dictionary." In *Language and the Law: Proceedings of a Conference December 6–8, 2001, Tarlton Law Library, The University of Texas School of Law* (Marlyn S. Robinson ed.), pp. 255–78. Buffalo, N.Y.: William S. Hein & Co.

Sorensen, Janet

2017 *Strange Vernaculars: How Eighteenth-Century Slang, Cant, Provincial Languages, and Nautical Jargon Became English*. Princeton: Princeton Univ. Press.

Spears, Richard A.

1995 Review of J. E. Lighter, *Random House Historical Dictionary of American Slang*. *Dictionaries* 16:186–203.

Stamper, Kory

2017 *Word by Word: The Secret Life of Dictionaries*. New York: Pantheon Books.

2020 "How a Word Gets into an English Dictionary." In *The Cambridge Companion to English Dictionaries* (Sarah Ogilvie ed.), pp. 7–17. Cambridge: Cambridge Univ. Press.

Starnes, DeWitt T[almage]

1949 "Thomas Cooper's *Thesaurus*: A Chapter in Renaissance Lexicography." *University of Texas Studies in English* 28:15–48.

1954 *Renaissance Dictionaries: English-Latin and Latin-English*. Austin: Univ. of Texas Press.

1963 *Robert Estienne's Influence on Lexicography*. Austin: Univ. of Texas Press.

Starnes, DeWitt T[almage]; and Gertrude E. Noyes

1946 *The English Dictionary from Cawdrey to Johnson, 1604–1755*. Chapel Hill: Univ. of North Carolina Press.

Starnes, DeWitt T[almage]; and Ernest William Talbert

1955 *Classical Myth and Legend in Renaissance Dictionaries*. Chapel Hill: Univ. of North Carolina Press.

Stavans, Ilan

2005 *Dictionary Days: A Defining Passion*. St. Paul: Graywolf Press.

Steadman, John M.

1972 "Renaissance Dictionaries and Manuals as Instruments of Literary Scholarship: The Problem of Evidence." In *New Aspects of Lexicography: Literary Criticism, Intellectual History, and Social Change* (Howard Weinbrot ed.), pp. 17–35. Carbondale, Ill.: Southern Illinois Univ. Press.

Steger, Stewart Archer

1913 *American Dictionaries: A Dissertation*. Danville, Va.: By the author. [Reprinted by Pranava Books.]

Stein, Gabriele

1985 *The English Dictionary Before Cawdrey*. Berlin: De Gruyter.

2014 *Sir Thomas Elyot as Lexicographer*. Oxford: Oxford Univ. Press.

2017 *Word Studies in the Renaissance*. Oxford: Oxford Univ. Press.

Stephens, Alexander

1813 *Memoirs of John Horne Tooke*. 2 vols. London: J. Johnson.

Stewart, Stanley

1972 "Thomas Wilson's *Christian Dictionary* and the 'Idea' of Marvell's 'Garden.'" In *New Aspects of Lexicography: Literary Criticism, Intellectual History, and Social Change* (Howard Weinbrot ed.), pp. 36–60. Carbondale, Ill.: Southern Illinois Univ. Press.

Surrency, Erwin C.

1990 *A History of American Law Publishing*. New York: Oceana Pubs.

Svensén, Bo

2009 *A Handbook of Lexicography: The Theory and Practice of Dictionary-Making*. Cambridge: Cambridge Univ. Press.

Sweet, Henry

1900 *The Practical Study of Languages: A Guide for Teachers and Learners*. New York: Henry Holt & Co.

1913 *Collected Papers of Henry Sweet*. H.C. Wyld ed. Oxford: Clarendon Press.

Tankard, Paul

2022 "Journalism." In *The Oxford Handbook of Samuel Johnson* (Jack Lynch ed.), pp. 103–19. Oxford: Oxford Univ. Press.

Taussig, Anthony

2003 "William Rastell and the Development of the Law Book for Students and Practitioners." In *Language and Law: Proceedings of a Conference December 6–8, 2001, Tarlton Law Library, The University of Texas School of Law* (Marlyn S. Robinson ed.), pp. 31–44. Buffalo, N.Y.: William S. Hein & Co.

Teall, Edward N.

1940 *Putting Words to Work: A Lively Guide to Correct and Vigorous English*. New York: D. Appleton-Century Co.

Thorp, Margaret Farrand

1956 *Neilson of Smith*. New York: Oxford Univ. Press.

Thumma, Samuel A.; and Jeffrey L. Kirchmeier

1999 "The Lexicon Has Become a Fortress: The United States Supreme Court's Use of Dictionaries." *Buffalo L. Rev.* 47:227–302.

Tieken-Boon van Ostade, Ingrid

2017 *Prescription and Tradition in Language: Establishing Standards Across Time and Space* (with Carol Percy). Bristol: Multilingual Matters.

2009 *Current Issues in Late Modern English* (Ingrid Tieken-Boon van Ostade & Wim Van der Wurff eds.). Berlin: Peter Lang.

Timpson, George F.

1957 "Interlude." In *Sir James A.H. Murray: A Self-Portrait* (George F. Timpson ed.). Eastgate & Gloucester: John Bellows Ltd.

Tonelli, Giorgio

1971 *A Short-Title List of Subject Dictionaries of the Sixteenth, Seventeenth, and Eighteenth Centuries.* London: Warburg Institute, Univ. of London.

Tooke, John Horne

1813 *Memoirs of John Horne Tooke* (Alexander Stephens ed.). 2. vols. London: J. Johnson & Co.

Tucker, Gilbert Milligan

1895 *Our Common Speech; six papers on topics connected with the proper use of the English language, the changes which that tongue is undergoing on both sides of the sea, and the labors of lexicographers to explain the meaning of the words of which it is composed.* New York: Mead & Co.

Turton, Stephen

2020 "The Confessional Sciences: Scientific Lexicography and Sexology in the *Oxford English Dictionary.*" *Language & History* 63[3]:214–32.

Twyman, Michael

1993 "The Bold Idea: The Use of Bold-Looking Types in the Nineteenth Century." *Journal of the Printing Historical Society* 22:107–43.

Tyson, A. Mervin

1967 "Exciting New Volume." In *The Role of the Dictionary* (Philip B. Gove ed.), pp. 15–18. Indianapolis: Bobbs-Merrill Co.

Unger, Harlow Giles

1998 *The Life and Times of Noah Webster: An American Patriot.* New York: John Wiley & Sons.

Urdang, Laurence

1984 "To Plagiarise, to Purloin, or to Borrow: A Reply to R.W. Burchfield." *Encounter* 63[5]:71–73.

Vancil, David E.

1993 *Catalog of Dictionaries, Word Books, and Philological Texts, 1440–1900: Inventory of the Cordell Collection, Indiana State University.* Westport, Conn.: Greenwood Press.

1994 *Incunable Dictionaries: A Checklist and Publishing History.* Terre Haute, Ind.: Friends of the Cunningham Memorial Library.

2001 *Supplement to Catalog of Dictionaries, Word Books, and Philological Texts, 1440–1900: Inventory of the Cordell Collection, Indiana State University.* Terre Haute, Ind.: Indiana State University: By the author.

Van Sterkenburg, Piet (ed.)

2003 *A Practical Guide to Lexicography.* Amsterdam & Philadelphia: John Benjamins Pub. Co.

Vizetelly, Frank H. [Francis Horace]

1915 *The Development of the Dictionary of the English Language with special reference to the Funk & Wagnalls New Standard Dictionary.* New York: Funk & Wagnalls.

1923 *How to Use the Dictionary.* New York: Ronald Press.

Vonnegut, Kurt, Jr.

1967 "The Latest Word." In *The Role of the Dictionary* (Philip B. Gove ed.), pp. 58–60. Indianapolis: Bobbs-Merrill Co.

Walsh, S. Padraig

1968 *Anglo-American General Encyclopedias: A Historical Bibliography 1703–1967.* New York: Bowker.

Warburton, William

1747 *The Works of Shakespeare.* 8 vols. London: J. and P. Knapton.

Warfel, Harry R.

1936 *Noah Webster: Schoolmaster to America.* New York: Macmillan Co.

1951 Introduction in reprint of Noah Webster, *Dissertations on the English Language.* Gainesville, Fla.: Scholars' Facsimiles & Reprints.

1953 *Letters of Noah Webster* (Harry R. Warfel ed.). New York: Library Pubs.

1956 See Lloyd & Warfel.

Way, Albert (ed.)

1843–65 *Promptorium Parvulorum sive Clericorum, Lexicon Anglo-Latinum Princeps* [ca. 1490]. 3 vols. [vol. 1, 1843; vol. 2, 1853; vol. 3, 1865]. London: Sumptibus Societatis Camdenensis.

Webster, Noah

1789 *Dissertations on the English Language.* Boston: Isaiah Thomas.

1790 *A Collection of Essays and Fugitiv Writings: On Moral, Historical, Political Subjects.* Boston: For the author.

1831 *To the Friends of American Literature* [broadside].

1839 *Observations on Language.* New Haven: S. Babcock.

1989 *The Autobiographies of Noah Webster* (Richard M. Rollins ed.). Columbia: Univ. of South Carolina Press.

Weinbrot, Howard D.

1972a *New Aspects of Lexicography: Literary Criticism, Intellectual History, and Social Change*. Howard Weinbrot ed. Carbondale, Ill.: Southern Illinois Univ. Press.

1972b "Samuel Johnson's *Plan* and Preface to the *Dictionary*: The Growth of a Lexicographer's Mind." In *New Aspects of Lexicography: Literary Criticism, Intellectual History, and Social Change* (Howard Weinbrot ed.), pp. 73–94. Carbondale, Ill.: Southern Illinois Univ. Press.

Weiner, Edmund [S.C.]

2000 "Medieval Multilingualism and the Revision of the *OED*." In *Multilingualism in Later Medieval Britain* (D.A. Trotter ed.), pp. 169–74. Woodbridge: D.S. Brewer.

2009 "The Electronic *OED*: The Computerization of a Historical Dictionary." In *The Oxford History of English Lexicography* (A.P. Cowie ed.). Vol. 1, pp. 378–409. Oxford: Clarendon Press.

Weis, James L.

1988 "Jurisprudence by Webster's: The Role of the Dictionary in Legal Thought." *Mercer L. Rev.* Vol. 39, p. 961.

Wells, Ronald A.

1973 *Dictionaries and the Authoritarian Tradition: A Study in English Usage and Lexicography*. The Hague: Mouton.

West, Michael

2000 *Transcendental Wordplay: America's Romantic Punsters and the Search for the Language of Nature*. Athens, Ohio: Ohio Univ. Press.

Wheatley, Henry B.

1854 "Chronological Notices of the Dictionaries of the English Language." *Transactions of the Philological Society*. 1865:218–93.

Whisner, Mary

2000 "Bouvier, Black's, and Tinkerbell." *Law Libr. J.* Vol. 92, p. 99.

2003 "Dictionaries Make Strange Bedfellows." In *Language and the Law: Proceedings of a Conference December 6–8, 2001, Tarlton Law Library, The University of Texas School of Law* (Marlyn S. Robinson ed.), pp. 93–108. Buffalo, N.Y.: William S. Hein & Co.

Widener, Michael

2003 "The Jamail Rastell Dictionary and Its Hidden Surprises." In *Language and the Law: Proceedings of a Conference December 6–8, 2001, Tarlton Law Library, The University of Texas School of Law* (Marlyn S. Robinson ed.), pp. 3–13. Buffalo, N.Y.: William S. Hein & Co.

Williams, R[alph] O[lmstead]

1890 *Our Dictionaries and Other Language Topics*. New York: Henry Holt & Co.

Willinsky, John

1994 *Empire of Words: The Reign of the OED*. Princeton, N.J.: Princeton Univ. Press.

2001 *After Literacy: Essays*. New York: Peter Lang.

Wilson, Frances.

2021 *Burning Man: The Trials of D.H. Lawrence*. New York: Farrar, Straus & Giroux.

Wilson, Kenneth G.; R.H. Hendrickson; and Peter Alan Taylor

1963 *Harbrace Guide to Dictionaries*. New York: Harcourt, Brace & World Inc.

Wimsatt, W.K., Jr.

1948 *Philosophic Words: A Study of Style and Meaning in the* Rambler *and* Dictionary *of Samuel Johnson*. New Haven: Yale Univ. Press.

Winchester, Simon

1998 *The Professor and the Madman*. New York: HarperCollins.

2003 *The Meaning of Everything: The Story of the Oxford English Dictionary*. Oxford: Oxford Univ. Press.

Worcester, Joseph Emerson

1860 "History of English Lexicography." In *A Dictionary of the English Language*, pp. liii–lviii. Boston: Hickling, Swan & Brewer.

World Publishing Company

1947 *An Interim Statement by the World Publishing Company on the Right to Use the Name of Noah Webster in the Title of Dictionaries*. Cleveland: World Pub. Co.

Wortham, Jenna

2014 "A Lexicon of Instant Argot." *New York Times*, 4 Jan. 2014, p. B1.

Wright, Elizabeth Mary

1932 *The Life of Joseph Wright*. 2 vols. London: Oxford Univ. Press.

Zaunmüller, Wolfram

1958 *Bibliographisches Handbuch der Sprachwörterbücher*. New York & London: Hafner Pub. Co.

Zgusta, Ladislav

2006 *Lexicography Then and Now* (Frederic S.F. Dolezal & Thomas B.I. Creamer eds.). Lexicographica Series Maior 129. Tübingen: Niemeyer.

Zimmer, Anne Y.

1978 *Jonathan Boucher: Loyalist in Exile*. Detroit: Wayne State Univ. Press.

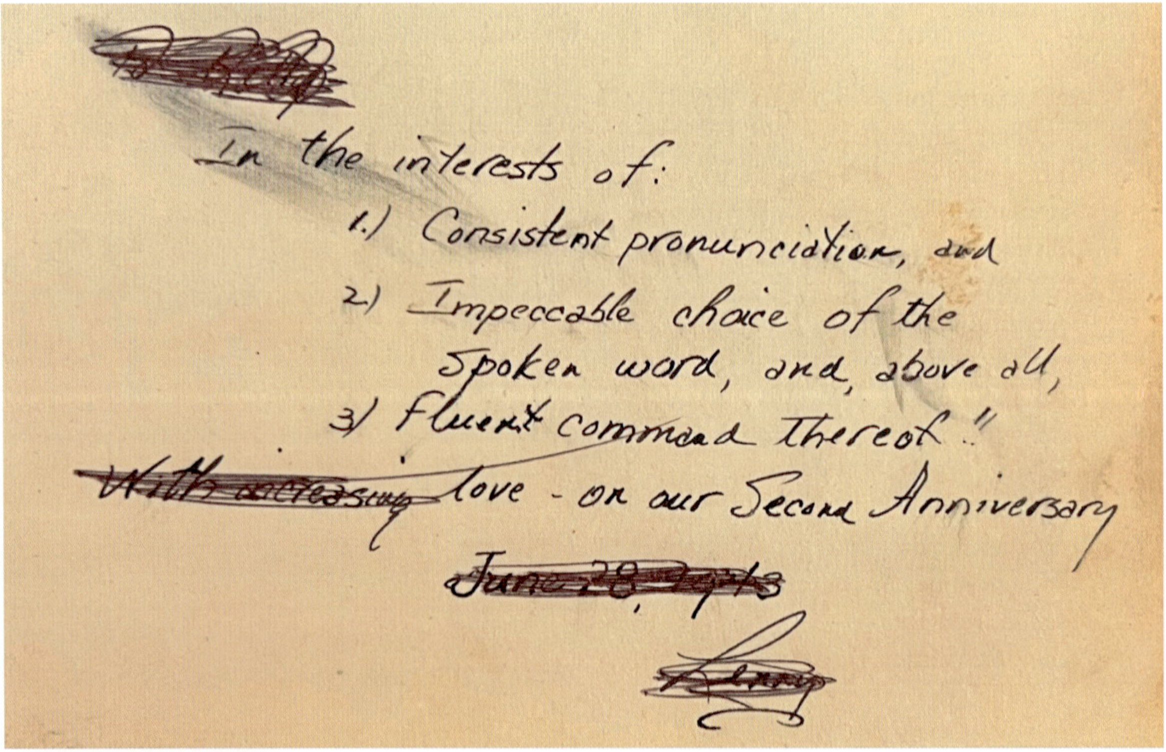

To Kelly

In the interests of:

1.) Consistent pronunciation, and

2.) Impeccable choice of the spoken word, and, above all,

3.) Fluent command thereof!!

With increasing love - on our Second Anniversary

June 28, 1943

Lenny

Ex coll. Karolyne & Bryan A. Garner

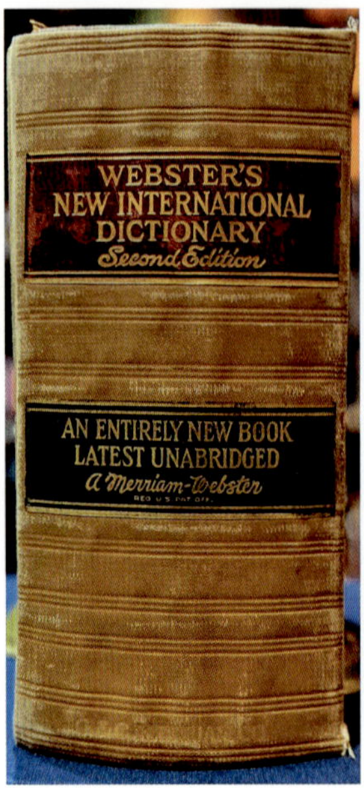

Ex coll. Karolyne & Bryan A. Garner

Can the gift of a dictionary be a symptom of marital difficulties? With this 1943 inscription, Lenny gave his wife Kelly a second-anniversary gift: a copy of *Webster's Second New International Dictionary* (no. 100). With "increasing love," he exhorted her to achieve (1) consistent pronunciation, (2) impeccable choice of the spoken word, and (3) fluent command thereof. (Note the two exclamation marks.) Although their identities are unknown other than their first names, the cross-outs suggest, rather eloquently, an unhappy end to the union.

Acknowledgments

SAMUEL JOHNSON ENDED THE PREFACE to his great *Dictionary* (no. 35) on a peculiarly lugubrious note: his "*English Dictionary* was written with little assistance of the learned, and without any patronage of the great; not in the soft obscurities of retirement, or under the shelter of academick bowers, but amidst inconvenience and distraction, in sickness and in sorrow."

We've been considerably more fortunate in preparing our book, having received plentiful assistance from the learned. It's a pleasure to acknowledge it here. This book wouldn't exist without the help of many generous friends. For answering queries and generally supporting the project we thank Timothy Benbow, Charlotte Brewer, Mildred Budny, John Considine, Harlan Crow, James Cummins, Robert DeMaria Jr., Edward Finegan, Sam Fore, Karolyne H.C. Garner, Henry Louis Gates Jr., Peter Gilliver, John Gormley, Greg Ivy, Ryan Kemrite, Cheris Kramarae, Maria Lin, Jeremy Markovits, Russell L. Martin III, Stephen Massey, David Micklethwait, Lynda Mugglestone, Andrew Nadell, John Overholt, Sir Christopher Ricks, Loren Rothschild, Rob Rulon-Miller, John Simpson, Peter Sokolowski, Kory Stamper, Timothy Stewart-Winter, David E. Vancil, Edmund S.C. Weiner, Daniel Wechsler, and John Windle.

We owe a debt of gratitude to many institutions as well, including Oxford University Press; Merriam-Webster, Inc.; Rulon-Miller Books of St. Paul, Minnesota; the Bodleian Library at Oxford University; the New York Public Library; the Donald and Mary Hyde Collection in the Houghton Library at Harvard University; Harvard Law Library; the Tarlton Law Library at the University of Texas; and the Underwood Law Library at the Southern Methodist University Dedman School of Law.

This book was prompted by an exhibition at the Grolier Club in New York City, and we're grateful to our fellow Grolierites—Gretchen Adkins, Shira Buchsbaum, Bruce Crawford, Mary Crawford, Ann Donahue, Eric Holzenberg, Chris Loker, Michael Ryan, Jennifer Sheehan, and Mark Tomasko—for giving us the opportunity to indulge our lexicographic obsessions.

It has been a pleasure to work with David Allender, Caroline Brink, and Virginia Downes at Godine. Ryden Anderson and Tiger Jackson of LawProse Inc. in Dallas worked miracles in turning our messy drafts into a beautiful book.

B.A.G. & J.L.

Index